COPYRIGHT
FOR THE EIGHTIES

CONTEMPORARY LEGAL EDUCATION SERIES

Copyright
for the Eighties

CASES AND MATERIALS

ALAN LATMAN

Professor of Law
New York University

ROBERT A. GORMAN

Professor of Law
University of Pennsylvania

MICHIE
BOBBS-MERRILL
Law Publishers
CHARLOTTESVILLE, VIRGINIA

To
Carol
and
Caryl

Foreword

This casebook was first fixed in a tangible medium of expression after the new copyright law was passed. Its component materials nevertheless predate 1976 to a significant degree because the new statute directly and indirectly enacts or incorporates so much that preceded it. Accordingly, the authors emphasize the problems and background that gave rise to particular provisions of the new statute. We do so to facilitate understanding and discussion of the provisions. We think this is necessary for students who know not the 1909 statute.

We are also convinced of the need to set forth pertinent legislative history of the 1976 Act at appropriate places in the casebook. The glimpses into this comprehensive and purposeful history are most frequently furnished by the reports of the 96th Congress, H.R. Rep. No. 94-1476 (1976) ("the House Report"), S. Rep. No. 94-373 (1975) ("the Senate Report"), and H.R. Rep. No. 94-1733 (1976) ("the Conference Report"). Copyright law has always been fascinating to many students because of its philosophical aspects. Exposure to the substantial amounts of legislative materials in this book should add other challenging dimensions, particularly a better understanding of the socioeconomic aspects of the subject, and an appreciation of the legislative process in action with its clash of interest groups being manifested in the shifting intricacies of draftsmanship.

The materials have been assembled and produced in recognition of the increasing number of courses focusing on copyright alone, as opposed to surveys including patents, trademarks and unfair competition, as well. They permit assignments of approximately fifteen pages per class for a three-credit course and, one hopes, convenient selection for a two-credit course.

As so often happens, the genesis of this project was informal class materials. Two students at New York University School of Law, Marc Jacobson (now of the New York and California Bars) and Susan Manca (now of the New York Bar), suggested converting the materials into a more formal casebook and assisted in the early stages. Helpful contributions were later made by Audrey Schultz of the New York Bar, Thomas R. Herwitz, University of Pennsylvania Law School 1981, and Daniel Goldschmidt and Terence Fagan, New York University School of Law 1981. Our sincere appreciation is expressed to these former law students and to Margaret Catapano Diaz, Shirley Gray, Francene O'Connor and Kathleen McClendon for their expert logistical and secretarial assistance. We also acknowledge gratefully the research grant furnished to Professor Latman by the Law Center Foundation of New York University in connection with this project. The authors are particularly grateful to the Bureau of National Affairs, Inc. of Washington, D.C., publishers of Professor Latman's *The Copyright Law: Howell's Copyright Law Revised and the 1976 Act.** Many of the notes found in these pages have been adapted from material in that book with the kind permission of the publisher. Finally, we thank sincerely Deans Norman Redlich and James O. Freedman for their singular and unstinting encouragement to the editors to devote the time and energy necessary to bring this casebook to the academic community.

The student using this book can supplement his or her learning with other works from a rich and diverse literature. Professor Nimmer's monumental treatise is consulted by all lawyers and judges faced with a copyright problem. The one-volume book by Professor Latman mentioned above has long been

* Copyright © 1942, 1948, 1952, 1962, 1979 The Bureau of National Affairs, Inc.

considered a standard. Specific topics are explored in depth in periodical literature expanded through the efforts of the American Society of Composers, Authors and Publishers in its Nathan Burkan Memorial Competition. A bimonthly journal devoted exclusively to copyright is published by The Copyright Society of the U.S.A., which has also co-sponsored with New York University Law School a unique compendium and analytical index for use with the 1976 Act called the Kaminstein Legislative History Project. Even more current material is offered by the weekly BNA Patent, Trademark & Copyright Journal and the monthly CCH Copyright Law Reports.

All of this material, as well as the present work, emanates from a broad-based instinct to spread knowledge about a fascinating and challenging subject. The spiritual forbears of this effort have been many, but two must be mentioned here. The path was initially blazed by the legendary Walter Derenberg who inspired generations of students from all over the world. We valued his leadership and his friendship. Each of us also had the extraordinary good fortune to begin learning about this subject from that brilliant scholar and masterful instructor, Benjamin Kaplan, recently retired as a Justice of the Massachusetts Supreme Judicial Court and happily rejoining us in our common love — the teaching of copyright.

AL
RAG

March 1981

Summary Table of Contents

Table of Contents

Table of Cases

Principal cases are those with page references in italics.

Anno Octavo

Annæ Reginæ.

An Act for the Encouragement of Learning, by Vesting the Copies of Printed Books in the Authors or
Purchasers of such Copies, during the Times therein
mentioned.

 hereas Printers, Booksellers, and other
Persons have of late frequently taken
the Liberty of Printing, Reprinting,
and Publishing, or causing to be Printed, Reprinted, and Published Books,
and other Writings, without the Consent of the Authors or Proprietors of
such Books and Writings, to their
very great Detriment, and too often
to the Ruin of them and their Families : For Preventing therefore such
Practices for the future, and for the
Encouragement of Learned Men to Compose and Write useful Books ; May it please Your Majesty, that it may be Enacted, and be it Enacted by the Queens most Excellent Majesty,
by and with the Advice and Consent of the Lords Spiritual and
Temporal, and Commons in this present Parliament Assembled,
and by the Authority of the same, That from and after the
Tenth Day of April, One thousand seven hundred and ten, the
Author of any Book or Books already Printed, who hath not
Transferred to any other the Copy or Copies of such Book or
Books, Share or Shares thereof, or the Bookseller or Booksellers, Printer or Printers, or other Person or Persons, who
hath or have Purchased or Acquired the Copy or Copies of any
Book or Books, in order to Print or Reprint the same, shall
have the sole Right and Liberty of Printing such Book and
Books for the Term of One and twenty Years, to Commence
from the said Tenth Day of April, and no longer ; and that
the Author of any Book or Books already Composed and not
Printed and Published, or that shall hereafter be Composed, and
his Assignee, or Assigns, shall have the sole Liberty of Printing
and Reprinting such Book and Books for the Term of Four-

6   Ttt 2   teen

(Statute of Anne, 8 Anne C. 19 (1710).

Chapter 1

THE CONCEPT OF COPYRIGHT

A. HISTORICAL PERSPECTIVE

1. ENGLAND AND THE STATUTE OF ANNE

Our whole law relating to literary and artistic property is essentially an inheritance from England. It seems that from the time "whereof the memory of man runneth not to the contrary," the author's right to his or her manuscript was recognized on principles of natural justice, being the product of intellectual labor and as much the author's own property as the substance on which it was written. Blackstone, 2 COMMENTARIES 405, associates it with the Law of Occupancy, which involves personal labor and results in "property," something peculiarly one's own (as implied by the Latin root "proprius"). But ages before Blackstone, an Irish king had enunciated the same principle in settling the question of property rights in a manuscript: "To every cow her calf."

When printing from type was invented and works could be reproduced in quantities for circulation, however, it seems that the author was without protection as soon as the work got into print.

In 1556, the Stationers' Company, made up of the leading publishers of London, was established by royal decree for the primary purpose of checking the spread of the Protestant Reformation by concentrating the whole printing business in the hands of the members of that company. Printing was subject to the orders of the Star Chamber so that the Government and the Church could exercise effective censorship and prevent seditious or heretical works from getting into print. HALLAM, 1 CONSTITUTIONAL HISTORY 238. It was essentially a means of controlling the press and in no sense afforded protection to authors.

Under this decree all published works had to be entered in the register of the Stationers' Company and in the name of some member of that company. By virtue of this entry and supported by the Star Chamber, the stationer successfully claimed the sole right to print and publish the work for himself, his heirs, and assigns forever. In the course of time, and especially after the last of the old Licensing Acts expired in 1694, the ban against unlicensed printing was lifted and independent printers began to spring up and invade the sacred domain of the Stationers' Company. As a result, the company applied to Parliament for a law to protect its alleged rights in perpetuity against these pirates. As the event turned out, the stationers got much less than they had reckoned on, for Parliament, instead of recognizing their perpetual rights, proceeded to pass a law limiting the exclusive right of publication to a paltry term of years. DRONE, LAW OF PROPERTY IN INTELLECTUAL PRODUCTIONS 69 (1879).

This was the celebrated Statute of Anne (8 Anne c. 19, 1710), the first statute of all time specifically to recognize the rights of authors and the foundation of all subsequent legislation on the subject of copyright both here and abroad. *See* RANSOM, THE FIRST COPYRIGHT STATUTE (1956). Because of its historical importance in relation to the study of our own copyright laws, it is well to note some of its provisions.

Title

An Act for the Encouragement of Learning, by Vesting the Copies of Printed Books in the Authors or Purchasers of such Copies, during the Times therein mentioned.

Preamble

Whereas Printers, Booksellers and other Persons have of late frequently taken the Liberty of Printing, Reprinting, and Publishing . . . Books and other Writings without the Consent of the Authors or Proprietors . . . to their very great Detriment, and too often to the Ruin of them and their Families:

For Preventing therefore such Practices for the future, and for the Encouragement of Learned Men to Compose and write useful Books; May it please your Majesty that it may be Enacted . . . .

Key Provisions

1. exclusive right of author of new work to print book for 14 years
2. renewal period of 14 years if author living
3. registration requirement
   a. register title at Stationers' Hall
   b. deposit nine copies at official libraries
4. ". . . if any other Bookseller, Printer, or other Person whatsoever, . . . shall Print, Reprint or Import . . . any such Book or Books without the Consent of the Proprietor . . . then such Offender or Offenders shall forfeit such Book or Books to the Proprietor or Proprietors of the Copy thereof, who shall forthwith Damask and make Waste Paper of them; and further, that every such Offender or Offenders shall forfeit one Penny for every Sheet which shall be found in his, her, or their Custody."

Interesting Sidelights

1. "Provided, That nothing in this Act contained do extend, or shall be construed to extend, to Prohibit the Importation, Vending, or Selling of any Books in Greek, Latin, or any other Foreign Language Printed beyond the Seas; Any thing in this Act contained to the contrary notwithstanding."

2. It was further provided that if any printer or bookseller shall sell any book "at such a Price or Rate as shall be Conceived by any Person or Persons to be High and Unreasonable;" then such person may "make Complaint thereof to the Lord Archbishop of Canterbury for the time being; the Lord Chancellor, or Lord Keeper of the Great Seal of Great Britain for the time being; the Lord Bishop of London for the time being; [or other judges or Government or academic officials] who . . . shall and have hereby full Power and Authority from time to time, to Send for, Summon, or Call before him or them such Bookseller or Booksellers, Printer or Printers, and to Examine and Enquire of the reason of the Dearness and Inhauncement of the Price or Value of such Book or Books by him or them so Sold or Exposed to Sale; and if upon such Enquiry and Examination it shall be found, that the Price of such Book or Books is Inhaunced, or any wise too High or Unreasonable, Then and in such case the said [official shall] have hereby full Power and Authority to Reform and Redress the same, and to Limit and Settle the Price of every such Printed Book and Books, from time to time, according to the best of their Judgments, and as to them shall seem Just and Reasonable; . . . ."

In such case the offending bookseller or printer had to pay costs and give public notice of the new, limited price. Any bookseller or printer selling in excess of such price

"shall Forfeit the Sum of Five Pounds for every such Book so by him, her, or
them Sold or Exposed to Sale, One Moiety thereof to the Queens most Excellent Majesty, Her Heirs and Successors, and the other Moiety to any Person
or Persons that shall Sue for the Same, to be Recovered, with Costs of Suit, in
any of Her Majesties Courts of Record at Westminister, by Action of Debt, Bill,
Plaint or Information, in which no Wager of Law, Essoign, Privilege or Protection, or more than one Imparlance shall be allowed."

So far as existing works were concerned, the statute provided that the "authors
or their assigns" should have the sole right of publication for 21 years, but it will
be noted that for new works the right was to run for 14 years, and the author,
if living at the expiration of such term, was granted the privilege of renewal for
14 more years. Suitable penalties were provided for violation of the Act, but
conditioned always upon entry of the title of the work in the Register books of
the Stationers' Hall as evidence of ownership and deposit of copies of the work
itself in certain designated libraries of the Kingdom. Somewhat later, as a further
security to the general public so that "none may offend through ignorance of the
copyright," the provision for notice of such entry was required to appear on
every copy of the published work.

While the statute seemed plain enough, the stationers nevertheless still
contended that their perpetual rights were not taken away but that the purpose
of the Act was merely to enable them to obtain speedier relief against piracy, this
being the only thing they had sought from Parliament in the first place. For more
than half a century the lower courts sustained them in this view by granting many
injunctions, even after the expiration of the term fixed by the statute. But in the
famous case of *Donaldson v. Becket,* 4 Burrows 2303, 98 Eng. Rep. 257 (1774),
the judicial branch of the House of Lords ruled against them by the narrow
margin of six to five, holding that the author or his assigns had, under the
common law, sole rights in perpetuity only so long as the work remained
unpublished, but that upon publication the duration of the right could only be
for the terms fixed by the statute. This decision overruled a case decided only
five years earlier by King's Bench, *Millar v. Taylor,* 4 Burrows 2302, 98 Eng. Rep.
201 (1769). (The possible impact of this time sequence on the meaning of our
constitutional clause authorizing copyright is explored in a fascinating and
prophetic article, Whicher, *The Ghost of* Donaldson v. Becket, 9 BULL. COPY-
RIGHT SOC'Y 102, 124-41 (1961).)

The Statute of Anne expressly sanctioned the importation of books in foreign
languages without the recognition of any rights on the part of the foreign
authors; but it said nothing about importation of books in English printed or
reprinted abroad. Such a contingency seemed out of the question, as the printing
business had not as yet become an outstanding institution in the Colonies. But
later on, had Benjamin Franklin chosen to enlarge his printing plant, it is conceivable that books rather than tea might well have become the bone of contention leading to the Revolution.

The Statute of Anne has long been treated as a startling result of the
parliamentary process. Perhaps the most significant shift in English law was its
recognition of the rights of authors, and not merely those of printers and
booksellers. Equally dramatic, but less frequently noted, is its reflection of con-
sumerism, eighteenth century style. Thus, one finds the inclusion of a provision
for judicial rate-making in the very first Anglo-American copyright law,
triggered by the copyright proprietor's sales of books at "High and
Unreasonable" prices.

Although this pro-consumer approach in England was repealed in 1739, supposedly as ineffective (see Ransom, The First Copyright Statute 107 n.13 (1956)), it was followed in the last quarter of the eighteenth century by several colonial statutes in America. Indeed the statutes of New York, Connecticut and Georgia provided for a remedy not only for unreasonably high prices, but for insufficient editions as well. (These remarkable provisions might be viewed as early examples of a "compulsory license." *See* p. 396 *infra*.) For other provisions of the colonial statutes, *see* Crawford, *Pre-Constitutional Copyright Statutes*, 23 Bull. Copyright Soc'y 11 (1975).

2. THE COLONIES AND THE CONSTITUTION

After the close of the Revolution, all of the Colonies except Delaware passed laws to afford a measure of protection to authors, pursuant to a recommendation of the Continental Congress, 24 Journals, Continental Congress 326 (1783), and the entreaties of one Noah Webster. But these laws were limited in their operation to the boundaries of each state. Hence, if the author of one state wished to secure protection for his work throughout the other states, he was obliged to comply with a multitude of laws. See *Hudson & Goodwin v. Patten*, 1 Root 133 (Conn. 1789), for a clash of interests between the assignees of copyright in different states. The same situation prevailed at that time in Europe, but on this side of the Atlantic, where all spoke the same language and read the same books, a uniform national law soon became imperative.

The framers of the Constitution, therefore, embodied in that immortal instrument a simple and direct clause empowering Congress "to promote the progress of science and useful arts, by securing for limited times to authors and inventors the exclusive right to their respective writings and discoveries." U.S. Const., Art. I, Sec. 8, Cl. 8. *See* Fenning, *The Origin of the Patent and Copyright Clause of the Constitution*, 17 Geo. L.J. 109 (1929). It should be noted that this clause does not use the terms "copyrights" and "patents," but nevertheless covers both forms of property. The selection of the "writings" of "authors" terminology for copyrights was made by the committee on detail or style and the clause was adopted by the Constitutional Convention without debate.

Some contemporaneous light on the clause is often sought from the succinct, if not enigmatic, comment of Madison in The Federalist, No. 43 at 279 (Mod. Lib. ed. 1941):

> The utility of this power will scarcely be questioned. The copyright of authors has been solemnly adjudged, in Great Britain, to be a right of common law. The right to useful inventions seems with equal reason to belong to the inventors. The public good fully coincides in both cases with the claims of individuals. The States cannot separately make effectual provision for either of the cases, and most of them have anticipated the decision of this point, by laws passed at the instance of Congress.

3. THE FIRST UNITED STATES COPYRIGHT STATUTE

There is no committee report on the first federal Copyright Act of May 31, 1790, 1 Stat. 124, and the Act itself must be looked to for enlightenment as to its purpose and policy. Rather than follow the lead of France, which granted copyright protection to all authors throughout the world without the need of complying with formalities of any kind, Congress fell back upon the system of formalities and restrictions inaugurated by the old Statute of Anne, which had been enacted purely as a municipal measure to replace the Licensing Acts and, incidentally, curb the pretentious claims to perpetual copyright on the part of the members of the Stationers' Company.

The Act of 1790 assured protection to the author or his assigns of any "book, map or chart" for 14 years upon:

(1) recording the title, prior to publication, in the register book of the clerk's office of the district court where the author or proprietor resided;
(2) publishing a copy of the record so made in one or more newspapers for four weeks; and
(3) depositing a copy of the work itself in the office of the Secretary of State within six months after publication.

The privilege of renewal of the copyright for 14 more years was granted to the author or his assigns on condition of again entering the title and publishing the record. The renewal term, as in the Statute of Anne, was dependent on the survival of the author throughout the first term. By subsequent Act, 2 Stat. 171 (1802), the notice of entry, including the date thereof, was required to be inserted in every copy of the published work. Suitable penalties were provided in the case of infringement.

There was also a provision against the unauthorized use of an author's manuscript, thus recognizing the old common law right before publication, without requiring the proprietor to observe any formality. With respect to published works, however, Congress seemed extremely solicitous to safeguard the public in general from offending against the Act and incurring the penalties through ignorance of the copyright claim. It is not so clear, however, why it was deemed necessary to shift the burden from those who might want to use the work to those who created it, but presumably it was because copyright is in the nature of a monopoly and, therefore, "odious in the eye of the law." Likewise, the courts at the beginning construed the Act very strictly and hence the author was obliged to proceed with the utmost caution along the tortuous copyright route lest any slip prove his undoing.

In the first copyright case that came before the Supreme Court, *Wheaton v. Peters,* 33 U.S. (8 Pet.) 591 (1834), the same legal question was presented as in the English case of *Donaldson v. Becket.* The Supreme Court reached the same conclusion as had the House of Lords in construing the Statute of Anne, namely, that whatever exclusive rights the author might have in his manuscript at common law before publication, upon publication these were gone forever unless he had complied strictly with all the requirements of the Copyright Act. The survival of state law rights in certain published works was upheld almost a century and a half later by the Supreme Court, in a 5-to-4 decision; without even citing *Wheaton v. Peters,* the Court introduced a limitation of the preemptive effect of the federal statute. *Goldstein v. California,* 412 U.S. 546, 178 USPQ 129 (1973).

4. STATUTORY REVISION

Step by step after the 1790 statute, new subjects were added, and the scope and term of protection enlarged. In 1802 prints were added (2 Stat. 171); in 1831, musical compositions (4 Stat. 436), but not the right of public performance (this right came for the first time in 1897, Rev. Stat. § 4966). At the same time (1831), the first term was extended to 28 years with the privilege of renewal for 14 years solely to the author or his widow and children. In 1856, dramatic compositions, with the right of public performance thereof, were added (11 Stat. 138); in 1865, photographs (13 Stat. 540); in 1870, paintings, drawings, sculpture, and models or designs for works of the fine arts. This Act of 1870 (16 Stat. 212, Rev. Stat. § 4948-71) facilitated the whole process by centralizing the copyright business in the Library of Congress, then located in the Capitol Building.

It was about this time that the general movement for international copyright began to gather momentum and there was much agitation for it in this country as well as abroad. The result in the United States was the so-called International Copyright Act of 1891 (26 Stat. 1106), by the terms of which the copyright privilege was for the first time made available to foreigners — but only on the hard condition of their complying with the age-old requirements of entry of title, notice, and deposit, as well as that of American manufacture of "any book, photograph, chromo or lithograph." Thus it was essentially a national rather than an international measure, maintaining a good part of the century-old pattern of "encouraging learning" by granting incentives to *American* authors, while permitting pirating of most foreign works. There may have been some cultural, if not ethical, justification for allowing freebooters to offer inexpensive foreign reprints at a time when it could be said that no one "in the four quarters of the globe . . . reads an American book." (Statement of Sidney Smith in 1820, quoted in *United Dictionary Co. v. Merriam Co.,* 208 U.S. 260, 264 (1908).) But toward the end of the nineteenth century it seemed to many, especially those abroad, that more than a token international protection was needed.

The result was the Berne Convention, which established an International Copyright Union in 1886, making a distinct contribution to universal law. Under this Convention, as subsequently amended, protection was made automatic throughout all the countries acceding to it on behalf of the authors and artists of every country in the world, whether inside or outside of the Union, and without the need of complying with any formalities whatever, the sole condition being publication of the work in any Union country not later than the date of publication elsewhere. The protection of unpublished works under the Convention was and still is limited to citizens or residents of a Union country. Beginning with a membership of only 10 countries, it has now increased to over 65, embracing all the leading countries of the world except the United States, Russia, China, and a number of Latin-American countries. Periodic revisions of the Convention have taken place at Paris (1896), Berlin (1908), Rome (1928), Brussels (1948), Stockholm (1967), and Paris (1971).

In place of a comprehensive revision of United States laws to enable this country to qualify for the International Copyright Union, there followed still more piecemeal domestic legislation, so that by the beginning of the twentieth century there existed a variety of miscellaneous copyright acts difficult of interpretation and full of traps for the unwary author. In 1903, the then recently appointed first Register of Copyrights, Mr. Thorvald Solberg, who was ever an outstanding champion of copyright law reform, made a special report on the whole subject of domestic legislation and recommended one consolidated act. This came to fruition in the Copyright Act of March 4, 1909, 35 Stat. 1075-88, U.S.C. Title 17, which, with some minor amendments, was the law in force for the next 68 years. Its provisions in certain areas will remain at least indirectly effective for many more. For a review of these early developments, see Solberg, *Copyright Law Reform,* 35 YALE L.J. 61 (1925).

5. THE 1909 ACT

An Appeal from the President

Our copyright laws urgently need revision. They are imperfect in definition, confused and inconsistent in expression; they omit provision for many articles which, under modern reproductive processes, are entitled to protection; they impose hardships upon the copyright proprietor which are not essential to the fair protection of the public; they are difficult for the courts to interpret and impossible for the Copyright Office to administer with satisfaction to the public. Attempts to improve them by amendment have been frequent, no less than twelve acts for the purpose having been passed since the Revised Statutes. To perfect them by further amendment seems impracticable. A complete revision of them is essential.

Theodore Roosevelt, December 1905 message to Congress.

The Copyright Act of 1909 was the outcome of several years of painstaking labor and extensive discussion on the part of every interest involved, including eminent members of the bar. Care was taken to use in the text, as far as possible, words and phrases that had already received judicial construction. In its final form, however, the Act was very largely a compromise measure, being a composite of several tentative bills and proposals embodying different points of view and interests. Changes appear to have often been made in one place without the necessary corresponding changes in other places. This process resulted in a lack of clarity and coherence in certain sections that has caused no little perplexity in the practical administration of the Act, not to speak of disturbance in the mind of the interested public.

Moreover, the subsequent development of the motion picture, the phonograph, radio, television, and other techniques of aural and visual recording, together with changes in business methods and practices, created new factors to be considered. While the courts found the terms of the Act fairly adaptable to meet the situation, there was a lack of uniformity in their application to particular cases. However, some notable improvements over the old law were achieved in 1909, among which may be mentioned:

(1) making the subject matter of copyright include "all the writings of an author" (this also caused problems);

(2) exempting books of foreign origin in foreign languages from the need of being reprinted in the United States (this being the greatest advance from the international standpoint);

(3) in the case of published works, making copyright date from publication with the notice, instead of from the date of filing the title, which often took place long before the work was ready for publication;

(4) making statutory copyright available for unpublished works designed for exhibition, performance, or oral delivery;

(5) extending the renewal term of protection by 14 years, to bring the possible maximum term of protection up to 56 years;

(6) making the certificate of registration prima facie evidence of the facts recorded in relation to any work.

Nevertheless, this substantial progress fell far short of meeting the fundamental requisites of the Berne Convention, because the formalities of notice, deposit, and registration were retained, as well as the requirement of American manufacture of books and periodicals in the English language even though of foreign origin.

6. THE UNIVERSAL COPYRIGHT CONVENTION

Most of the attempted comprehensive revisions of our law after 1909 were motivated by an interest in United States membership in the Berne Union. *See* Goldman, *The History of U.S.A. Copyright Law Revision From 1901 to 1954,* 2 Studies on Copyright 1106 (Arthur Fisher Mem. ed. 1963). The last unsuccessful attempt was the so-called "Shotwell Committee" bill of 1940. When activity was resumed after World War II, a new approach toward international copyright was taken. It was apparently recognized that comprehensive revision of the United States law to conform with the Berne Convention was then as unlikely as modification of the Convention to permit United States adherence. The formation of the United Nations and the establishment of UNESCO offered a new international organ through which some compromise might be reached. In 1952 success was achieved with the signing of the Universal Copyright Convention.

This multilateral treaty, which did not alter the obligations of the Berne Convention as among its adherents, offered a new route for international protection. Works by a national of a member nation, as well as works first published within its borders, were protected in every other member nation. Domestic formalities were excused if all published copies of the work bore a prescribed notice, or if the work remained unpublished. A member could add other requirements with respect to works written by its own nationals or first published within its territory, no discrimination against protected foreigners, of course, being permitted.

The United States in 1954 was one of the first nations to ratify this Convention, amending its domestic law slightly more than necessary to comply with its treaty obligations. Public Law 743, 83d Cong., 68 Stat. 1030 (1954). The Convention actually became effective in 1955 and there have been more than 70 ratifications and accessions to date.

7. THE 1976 ACT

Notwithstanding the 1954 amendments, the American system under the 1909 law was in direct contrast to that existing in most foreign countries; the latter have largely dispensed with formalities as a prerequisite to protection, as a result of which everything published therein is automatically protected against unauthorized copying. In the United States, however, in only a small percentage of the total number of literary, informational, musical, and artistic works published has the creator or his assigns been sufficiently interested to seek and perfect by registration the privileges of a statutory monopoly. The percentage varies with different classes of works, and music has constituted the largest class of all.

Despite the lingering argument by some that the American system had on the whole proved eminently suited to American needs, it had long been accepted that an intensive and objective examination of our law, with a view to its general revision, was overdue. *See, e.g.,* Note, *Revision of the Copyright Law,* 51 Harv. L. Rev. 906 (1938).

A comprehensive project along these lines was authorized by Congress in 1955. Under this authorization, the Copyright Office prepared a number of legal and factual studies of the major substantive problems inherent in any revision of the law. Distribution of these studies gave rise to the healthy interchange of ideas, comments, and suggestions necessary for the development of an improved law. (In addition, they serve as valuable research tools irrespective of their original purpose and have accordingly been published in an Arthur Fisher Memorial

Edition in honor of the Register of Copyrights who launched the project.) In July 1961, Register Kaminstein submitted to Congress a detailed report of his tentative recommendations for revision with a view to the introduction, after further public comment, of a new proposed law. *Report of the Register of Copyrights on the General Revision of the U.S. Copyright Law, Report to House Committee on the Judiciary*, 87th Cong., 1st Sess. (1961) (hereinafter cited as *Register's Report of 1961*). (A 1965 *Supplementary Report* and 1975 *Draft Second Supplementary Report* were later issued by the Register).

During the next three years, a tentative draft and resulting comments led to the development and introduction in 1964 of H.R. 11947 and S. 3008, 88th Cong., 2d Sess. In 1965 and 1966 unusually extensive hearings followed, culminating in H.R. Rep. No. 83, 90th Cong., 1st Sess. (1967). In 1967, the House, but not the Senate, passed a revision bill, H.R. 2512, 90th Cong., 1st Sess. After a delay occasioned by political and technological issues, such as cable television and educational and library uses, the Senate passed S. 1361, 93d Cong., in 1974, and the substantially similar S. 22, 94th Cong., in February 1976. An important piece of legislative history is embodied in S. Rep. No. 94-473, 94th Cong., 1st Sess. (1975), which preceded such passage.

Another set of extensive hearings produced a House-passed version of S. 22 supported by another comprehensive Judiciary Committee report, H.R. Rep. No. 94-1476, 94th Cong., 2d Sess. (1976), which recapitulated significant segments of the tortuous legislative history. The differences between the chambers were resolved in a conference report, H.R. Rep. No. 94-1733, 94th Cong., 2d Sess. (1976), accepted by both houses, and the President approved Public Law 94-553, 90 Stat. 2541, on October 19, 1976.

The new law marks a significant philosophical departure from the centuries-old traditions reflected in the Statute of Anne, the first U.S. statute in 1790, and the 1909 statute. At the same time, much of the substance of the 1909 Act will remain with us, either directly or indirectly, well into the twenty-first century, if not indefinitely.

The key provisions of the new law include the following:

(1) A single federal system of protection for all "original works of authorship," published or unpublished, from the moment they are fixed in a tangible medium of expression. (Pertinent state law is expressly preempted.)

(2) A single term of protection generally measured by the life of the author(s) plus 50 years after his or her death, with a term based on publication (or creation, in the case of unpublished works) reserved only for special situations, such as works made for hire.

(3) A provision for an inalienable option in individual authors generally permitting termination of any transfer after 35 years, but with the transferee still permitted to exploit derivative works produced under the transfer before it was terminated.

(4) A provision for notice on visually perceptible copies distributed to the public, with some flexibility as to the form and position of the notice, curative provisions for notice deficiencies, and incentives for use of a proper notice, as well as for prompt registration.

(5) Recognition of a fair use limitation on exclusive rights (with an indication of the criteria for its applicability) as well as other limitations in favor of nonprofit, library, educational, and public broadcasting uses.

(6) Imposition of copyright liability on cable television systems and jukeboxes which use copyrighted material, but subject to compulsory license provisions and other limitations.

(7) Establishment of a Copyright Royalty Tribunal to review or establish rates under compulsory licenses and to provide for certain distributions to proprietors under such licenses.

(8) Protection of unpublished works regardless of the nationality of the author, as well as contraction and scheduled deletion of the requirement of domestic manufacture of books.

(9) Provisions implementing divisibility of copyright ownership.

During the long progress of the revision effort, three significant matters were resolved by separate legislative action. First, beginning on September 19, 1962, terms of renewal copyrights which would otherwise have expired were extended so as to bring these copyrights under the protection of the new Act. Second, in 1971 and 1974, limited federal copyright protection was extended to recorded performances insofar as duplication of recordings was concerned, but not as to independently recorded imitation of sound or as to the performance of the recordings. Third, a National Commission on New Technological Uses of Copyrighted Works (CONTU) was established to study new technology, such as computers and reprography, for recommendation to Congress of detailed provisions to replace the stopgap provisions in the 1976 Act governing these fast-moving areas. In this connection, the frustrating history of decades of attempts to revise the 1909 Act seems to have convinced Congress to provide machinery for the amendment of the 1976 Act before it had even become effective. Several amendments were recommended by CONTU in its Final Report of July 31, 1978 and were adopted by Congress on December 12, 1980. Pub. L. 96-517. See p. 130 infra.

B. AN OVERVIEW AND THE CONSTITUTION

REPORT OF THE REGISTER OF COPYRIGHTS ON THE GENERAL REVISION OF THE U.S. COPYRIGHT LAW 3-6 (1961)

B. The Nature of Copyright

1. In General

In essence, copyright is the right of an author to control the reproduction of his intellectual creation. As long as he keeps his work in his sole possession, the author's absolute control is a physical fact. When he discloses the work to others, however, he makes it possible for them to reproduce it. Copyright is a legal device to give him the right to control its reproduction after it has been disclosed.

Copyright does not preclude others from using the ideas or information revealed by the author's work. It pertains to the literary, musical, graphic, or artistic form in which the author expresses intellectual concepts. It enables him to prevent others from reproducing his individual expression without his consent. But anyone is free to create his own expression of the same concepts, or to make practical use of them, as long as he does not copy the author's form of expression.

2. Copyright as Property

Copyright is generally regarded as a form of property, but it is property of a unique kind. It is intangible and incorporeal. The thing to which the property right attaches — the author's intellectual work — is incapable of possession except as it is embodied in a tangible article such as a manuscript, book, record, or film. The tangible articles containing the work may be in the possession of many persons other than the copyright owner, and they may use the work for their own enjoyment, but copyright restrains them from reproducing the work without the owner's consent.

Justice Holmes, in his famous concurring opinion in *White-Smith Music Publishing Co. v. Apollo Co.* (209 U.S. 1 (1908)), gave a classic definition of the special characteristics of copyright as property:

> The notion of property starts, I suppose, from confirmed possession of a tangible object and consists in the right to exclude other[s] from interference with the more or less free doing with it as one wills. But in copyright property has reached a more abstract expression. The right to exclude is not directed to an object in possession or owned, but is now in vacuo, so to speak. It restrains the spontaneity of men where, but for it, there would be nothing of any kind to hinder their doing as they saw fit. It is a prohibition of conduct remote from the persons or tangibles of the party having the right. It may be infringed a thousand miles from the owner and without his ever becoming aware of the wrong.

3. Copyright as a Personal Right

a. GENERALLY

Some commentators, particularly in European countries, have characterized copyright as a personal right of the author, or as a combination of personal and property rights. It is true that an author's intellectual creation has the stamp of his personality and is identified with him. But insofar as his rights can be assigned to other persons and survive after his death, they are a unique kind of personal rights.

b. MORAL RIGHTS

On the theory of personal right, some countries have included in their copyright laws special provisions for "moral rights" of authors. These provisions are intended to protect the author against certain acts injurious to his personal identity or reputation. They give the author the following rights:

- To have his name appear on copies of his work;
- To prevent the attribution to him of another person's work;
- To prevent the reproduction of his work in a distorted or degrading form.

These moral rights are regarded as not assignable, but the author may sometimes agree to waive them in particular cases. In some countries the moral rights survive the author's death and may be enforced by his heirs or representatives.

In the United States the moral rights of authors have never been treated as aspects of copyright. But authors have been given much the same protection of personal rights under general principles of the common law such as those relating to implied contracts, unfair competition, misrepresentation, and defamation.

. . . .

4. Copyright as a Monopoly

Copyright has sometimes been said to be a monopoly. This is true in the sense that the copyright owner is given exclusive control over the market for his work. And if his control were unlimited, it could become an undue restraint on the dissemination of the work.

On the other hand, any one work will ordinarily be competing in the market with many others. And copyright, by preventing mere duplication, tends to encourage the independent creation of competitive works. The real danger of monopoly might arise when many works of the same kind are pooled and controlled together.

C. The Purposes of Copyright

1. Constitutional Basis of the Copyright Law

. . . As reflected in the Constitution, the ultimate purpose of copyright legislation is to foster the growth of learning and culture for the public welfare, and the grant of exclusive rights to authors for a limited time is a means to that end. A fuller statement of these principles was contained in the legislative report (H. Rep. No. 2222, 60th Cong., 2d Sess.) on the Copyright Act of 1909:

> The enactment of copyright legislation by Congress under the terms of the Constitution is not based upon any natural right that the author has in his writings, for the Supreme Court has held that such rights as he has are purely statutory rights, but upon the ground that the welfare of the public will be served and progress of science and useful arts will be promoted by securing to authors for limited periods the exclusive rights to their writings. The Constitution does not establish copyrights, but provides that Congress shall have the power to grant such rights if it thinks best. Not primarily for the benefit of the author, but primarily for the benefit of the public, such rights are given. Not that any particular class of citizens, however worthy, may benefit, but because the policy is believed to be for the benefit of the great body of people, in that it will stimulate writing and invention to give some bonus to authors and inventors.
>
> In enacting a copyright law Congress must consider . . . two questions: First, how much will the legislation stimulate the producer and so benefit the public, and, second, how much will the monopoly granted be detrimental to the public? The granting of such exclusive rights, under the proper terms and conditions, confers a benefit upon the public that outweighs the evils of the temporary monopoly.

2. The Rights of Authors and the Public Interest

a. IN GENERAL

Although the primary purpose of the copyright law is to foster the creation and dissemination of intellectual works for the public welfare, it also has an important secondary purpose: To give authors the reward due them for their contribution to society.

These two purposes are closely related. Many authors could not devote themselves to creative work without the prospect of remuneration. By giving authors a means of securing the economic reward afforded by the market, copyright stimulates their creation and dissemination of intellectual works. Similarly, copyright protection enables publishers and other distributors to invest their resources in bringing those works to the public.

b. LIMITATIONS ON AUTHOR'S RIGHTS

Within reasonable limits, the interests of authors coincide with those of the public. Both will usually benefit from the widest possible dissemination of the author's works. But it is often cumbersome for would-be users to seek out the copyright owner and get his permission. There are many situations in which copyright restrictions would inhibit dissemination, with little or no benefit to the author. And the interests of authors must yield to the public welfare where they conflict.

Accordingly, the U.S. copyright law has imposed certain limitations and conditions on copyright protection:

- The rights of the copyright owner do not extend to certain uses of the work. (See ch. III of this report.)
- The term of copyright is limited, as required by the Constitution. (See ch. V.)
- A notice of copyright in published works has been required. (See ch. VI.) The large mass of published material for which the authors do not wish copyright is thus left free of restrictions.
- The registration of copyrights and the recordation of transfers of ownership have been required. (See chs. VII and VIII.) The public is thus given the means of determining the status and ownership of copyright claims.

c. THE AUTHOR'S REWARD

While some limitations and conditions on copyright are essential in the public interest, they should not be so burdensome and strict as to deprive authors of their just reward. Authors wishing copyright protection should be able to secure it readily and simply. And their rights should be broad enough to give them a fair share of the revenue to be derived from the market for their works.

CHAFEE, REFLECTIONS ON THE LAW OF COPYRIGHT, 45 Columbia Law Review 503, 506-11 (1945)

We should start by reminding ourselves that copyright is a monopoly. Like other monopolies, it is open to many objections; it burdens both competitors and the public. Unlike most other monopolies, the law permits and even encourages it because of its peculiar great advantages. Still, remembering that it is a monopoly, we must be sure that the burdens do not outweigh the benefits. So it becomes desirable for us to examine who is benefited and how much and at whose expense.

The primary purpose of copyright is, of course, to benefit the author.

. . . [I]ntellectual property is, after all, the only absolute possession in the world. . . . The man who brings out of nothingness some child of his thought has rights therein which cannot belong to any other sort of property. . . .

As Macaulay said in his first speech on the bill which led to the English Act of 1842: [9]

It is desirable that we should have a supply of good books: we cannot have such a supply unless men of letters are liberally remunerated; and the least objectionable way of remunerating them is by means of copyright.

We do not expect that much of the literature and art which we desire can be produced by men who possess independent means or who derive their living from other occupations and make literature a by-product of their leisure hours.

---

[9] Macaulay, Copyright (1841 speech in House of Commons), in 8 Works (Trevelyan ed. 1879) 195, 197.

Support by the government or by patrons on which authors used to depend, is today no good substitute for royalties. So we resort to a monopoly, in spite of the plain disadvantage which Macaulay forcibly points out: [10]

> The principle of copyright is this. It is a tax on readers for the purpose of giving a bounty to writers. The tax is an exceedingly bad one; it is a tax on one of the most innocent and most salutary of human pleasures. . . .

Here, as in the case of patents, the Constitution takes the unusual course of expressly sanctioning a gain by private persons. Authors, musicians, painters are among the greatest benefactors of the race. So we incline to protect them. Yet the very effect of protecting them is to make the enjoyment of their creations more costly and hence to limit the possibility of that enjoyment especially by persons of slender purses. Moreover, a monopoly, here as always, makes it possible for the wares to be kept off the market altogether. Therefore, we must be sure that a particular provision of the Copyright Act really helps the author — that it does not impose a burden on the public substantially greater than the benefit it gives to the author.

If we were dealing with only authors and readers, this adjustment of conflicting interests would be fairly simple. But the problem is greatly complicated by the intervention of two other groups who may also be heavily benefited by copyright.

There is the author's surviving family. It often happens that the author does not receive the full benefit of a copyright because he dies before it expires. The benefit and the monopoly may then pass to his widow and children, or to more remote relatives. So far as the widow and minor children go, we all recognize this result as eminently desirable. It goes against the conscience of society that destitution should seize on the family of a man who has made possible great public good. Furthermore, the wish to provide for one's widow and children is one of the strongest incentives to work for all human beings. Erskine, after his maiden argument at the bar, was asked how he had the courage to stand up so boldly before Lord Mansfield, and answered: "I could feel my little children tugging at my gown." [11] The biographies of authors show that they are more subject than most men to indolence. It is pleasanter to satisfy their active minds with conversation and observation and random reflections than to sit for many lonely hours at a table and push a pen. They must somehow be blasted out of this agreeable aimlessness, and one of the best ways is the hope of providing a competence for their children. Consequently, the prolongation of the benefit beyond the author's life so that it reaches his immediate family is amply justified. On the other hand, the surviving family are less capable of controlling the monopoly than the author. We can trust the mind which created the new work to decide whether it should be published and in what form because it was his mind which gave it birth. There is no assurance whatever that the ability to make such decisions wisely will pass to his widow or his offspring. And even the benefit becomes dubious when it is conferred on the author's remote relatives; then the tax on the public is less justifiable.

Still another possible beneficiary of copyright has to be considered. Often neither the author nor his family owns the copyright. It belongs to the publisher. (I use the word to include other marketing agencies such as motion-picture companies.) Historically, it was not authors who got the Statute of Anne, but publishers — the London booksellers of those days. A publisher may own the

---

[10] *Id.* at 201.
[11] 6 Campbell, Lives of the Lord Chancellors (1848), c. CLXXVII.

copyright free and clear, and take all the gross income; or he may pay royalties, and take most of the gross income. Either way, he usually gets more from a copyrighted book than when he is subject to open competition. Therefore, much of the tax which the Copyright Act imposes on readers goes directly to publishers.

Then is not the talk of helping authors just a pretense? A vigorous attack of this sort has been widely made on the patent system. Most patents are not owned by the inventors, but by manufacturers, who are often very big corporations. Consequently, it is said that we are betraying the purpose of the Constitution, which was to secure to "Inventors the exclusive Right to their . . . Discoveries." Big business is hiding behind the inventor's skirts. This reasoning seems to me unsound. After the inventor makes his invention *work,* an immense expenditure of money is usually necessary to make it *sell.* The inventor is rarely in a position to finance this great development expense himself. . . . Consequently, the inventor is indirectly benefited by the assignability of his patent.

Similar reasoning applies to copyrights. Although the development expense is not so huge for a book as for a machine or a process, it does cost a good deal to print a book and to attract buyers. Even if an author could afford to publish his own book, he would not do the job well. And if the publishers did not get the benefit of the copyright monopoly, it would be hard for an author to find a publisher to bring out the book. Once the book was launched and became a success, any authorized competitor would eagerly jump into the market because his advertising would be low. He could reap where he had not sown. Both authors and readers would be helpless without publishers. As the poet Wither quaintly said of the good publisher: [12]

> He is the caterer that gathers together provision to satisfy the curious appetite of the soule. . . .

One reason, therefore, for protecting the copyright in the hands of the publisher is to give an indirect benefit to authors by enabling them to get royalties or to sell the manuscript outright for a higher price. A second reason is, that it is only equitable that the publisher should obtain a return on his investment. No doubt the return to a publisher from a particular book which becomes a bestseller may be far above the customary six per cent. But we mustn't concentrate our gaze on this one book. Publishing is close to gambling. Many of the same publisher's books never pay back his original outlay. Only an occasional killing makes it possible for us to read a number of less popular but perhaps more valuable books. If we look at the rate of return on *all* books published by any firm, it does not seem excessive. Few publishers become millionaires. Thus copyright is necessary to make good publishers possible. . . .

These general considerations will be made clearer by later concrete examples, but for the moment I will summarize my ideal of proper protection for copyright. The burden which the monopoly imposes on readers and competing publishers should be roughly limited to what will produce the following benefits: (a) for the author, to supply a direct or indirect pecuniary return as an incentive to creation and to confer upon him control over the marketing of his creation; (b) for the surviving family, to give a pecuniary return which will save them from destitution and impel the author to create, without allowing the family to abuse

---

[12] Wither, The Scholler's Purgatory (1624), quoted in Birrell, Seven Lectures on the Law and History of Copyright in Books (1899) 84.

a prolonged monopoly; (c) for the publisher, to give a continued pecuniary return which will indirectly benefit the author and yield to the publisher an equitable return on his investment, but which will not prevent the public from getting easy access to the creation after the author's death.

———————

A bold article written in 1970 questioned some of these basic tenets of Macauley, as developed and well articulated by Chafee. *See* Breyer, *The Uneasy Case for Copyright: A Study of Copyright in Books, Photocopies, and Computer Programs*, 84 HARV. L. REV. 281 (1970). Professor Breyer (now judge on the United States Court of Appeals for the First Circuit) argues that "copyright is not the only way to resolve the conflict between revenues high enough to secure adequate production and prices low enough not to interfere with widespread dissemination." *Id.* at 282. After examining some data and patterns in book publishing and speculating on alternatives to copyright, he concludes that "the case for copyright rests not on proven need, but rather upon uncertainty as to what would happen if protection were removed." *Id.* at 322.

Professor Breyer's article was greeted with the enthusiasm usually accorded heresy. A rebuttal addressing itself to Breyer's various alternatives concludes that copyright provides "a relatively efficient, and, most importantly time-proven system for ensuring both that authors find it intellectually and financially profitable to write and that the American publishing industry is capable of producing a broad spectrum of book titles, and not merely a few commercially popular books." Tyerman, *The Economic Rationale for Copyright Protection for Published Books: A Reply to Professor Breyer*, 19 BULL. COPYRIGHT SOC'Y 99, 103 (1971), also published in 18 U.C.L.A. L. REV. 1100 (1971). The coda to this debate is found in Breyer, *Copyright: A Rejoinder*, 20 U.C.L.A. L. REV. 75 (1972).

———————

UNITED STATES CONSTITUTION

Article I, Section 8

The Congress shall have power . . . To promote the Progress of Science and useful Arts, by securing for limited Times to Authors and Inventors the exclusive Right to their respective Writings and Discoveries.

Mazer v. Stein, 347 U.S. 201 (1954).

"The copyright law, like the patent statutes, makes reward to the owner a secondary consideration." *United States v. Paramount Pictures*, 334 U.S. 131, 158. However, it is "intended definitely to grant valuable enforceable rights to authors, publishers, etc., without burdensome requirements; 'to afford greater encouragement to the production of literary [or artistic] works of lasting benefit to the world.' " *Washingtonian Pub. Co. v. Pearson*, 306 U.S. 30.

The economic philosophy behind the clause empowering Congress to grant patents and copyrights is the conviction that encouragement of individual effort by personal gain is the best way to advance public welfare through the talents of authors and inventors in "Science and useful Arts." Sacrificial days devoted to such creative activities deserve rewards commensurate with the services rendered.

Goldstein v. California, 412 U.S. 546 (1973).

The [constitutional] clause thus describes both the objective which Congress may seek and the means to achieve it. The objective is to promote the progress of science and the arts. As employed, the terms "to promote" are synonymous with the words "to stimulate," "to encourage," or "to induce." To accomplish its purpose, Congress may grant to authors the exclusive right to the fruits of their respective works. An author who possesses an unlimited copyright may preclude others from copying his creation for commercial purposes without permission. In other words, to encourage people to devote themselves to intellectual and artistic creation, Congress may guarantee to authors and inventors a reward in the form of control over the sale or commercial use of copies of their works.

The Court noted that the terms in the copyright clause of the Constitution "have not been construed in their narrow literal sense but, rather, with the reach necessary to reflect the broad scope of constitutional principles." The Court interpreted "writings" to "include any physical rendering of the fruits of creative intellectual or aesthetic labor." In so doing, it relied on more than a century of precedents.

BURROW-GILES LITHOGRAPHIC CO. v. SARONY

111 U.S. 53 (1884)

Mr. Justice Miller delivered the opinion of the court.

This is a writ of error to the Circuit Court for the Southern District of New York.

Plaintiff is a lithographer and defendant a photographer, with large business in those lines in the city of New York.

The suit was commenced by an action at law in which Sarony was plaintiff and the lithographic company was defendant, the plaintiff charging the defendant with violating his copyright in regard to a photograph, the title of which is "Oscar Wilde No. 18." A jury being waived, the court made a finding of facts on which a judgment in favor of the plaintiff was rendered for the sum of $600 for the plates and 85,000 copies sold and exposed to sale, and $10 for copies found in his possession, as penalties under section 4965 of the Revised Statutes.

Among the findings of fact made by the court the following presents the principal question raised by the assignment of errors in the case:

"3. That the plaintiff about the month of January, 1882, under an agreement with Oscar Wilde, became and was the author, inventor, designer, and proprietor of the photograph in suit, the title of which is 'Oscar Wilde No. 18,' being the number used to designate this particular photograph and of the negative thereof; that the same is a useful, new, harmonious, characteristic, and graceful picture, and that said plaintiff made the same at his place of business in said city of New York, and within the United States, entirely from his own original mental conception, to which he gave visible form by posing the said Oscar Wilde in front of the camera, selecting and arranging the costume, draperies, and other various accessories in said photograph, arranging the subject so as to present graceful outlines, arranging and disposing the light and shade, suggesting and evoking the desired expression, and from such disposition, arrangement, or representation, made entirely by the plaintiff, he produced the picture in suit,

Exhibit A, April 14th, 1882, and that the terms 'author,' 'inventor,' and 'designer,' as used in the art of photography and in the complaint, mean the person who so produced the photograph."

Other findings leave no doubt that plaintiff had taken all the steps required by the act of Congress to obtain copyright of this photograph; and section 4952 names photographs among other things for which the author, inventor, or designer may obtain copyright, which is to secure him the sole privilege of reprinting, publishing, copying and vending the same. That defendant is liable under that section and section 4965 there can be no question, if those sections are valid as they relate to photographs.

Accordingly, the two assignments of error in this court by plaintiff in error, are:

1. That the court below decided that Congress had and has the constitutional right to protect photographs and negatives thereof by copyright.

The second assignment related to the sufficiency of the words "Copyright, 1882, by N. Sarony," in the photographs, as a notice of the copyright of Napoleon Sarony under the act of Congress on that subject.

. . . .

The constitutional question is not free from difficulty.

The eighth section of the first article of the Constitution is the great repository of the powers of Congress, and by the eighth clause of that section Congress is authorized:

"To promote the progress of science and useful arts, by securing, for limited times to authors and inventors, the exclusive right to their respective writings and discoveries."

The argument here is, that a photograph is not a writing nor the production of an author. Under the acts of Congress designed to give effect to this section, the persons who are to be benefited are divided into two classes, authors and inventors. The monopoly which is granted to the former is called a copyright, that given to the latter, letters patent, or, in the familiar language of the present day, *patent right.*

We have, then, copyright and patent right, and it is the first of these under which plaintiff asserts a claim for relief.

It is insisted in argument, that a photograph being a reproduction on paper of the exact features of some natural object or of some person, is not a writing of which the producer is the author.

Section 4952 of the Revised Statutes places photographs in the same class as things which may be copyrighted with "books, maps, charts, dramatic or musical compositions, engravings, cuts, prints, paintings, drawings, statues, statuary, and models or designs intended to be perfected as works of the fine arts." "According to the practice of legislation in England and America," says Judge Bouvier, 2 LAW DICTIONARY, 363, "the copyright is confined to the exclusive right secured to the author or proprietor of a writing or drawing which may be multiplied by the arts of printing in any of its branches."

The first Congress of the United States, sitting immediately after the formation of the Constitution, enacted that the "author or authors of any map, chart, book or books, being a citizen or resident of the United States, shall have the sole right and liberty of printing, reprinting, publishing and vending the same for the period of fourteen years from the recording of the title thereof in the clerk's office, as afterwards directed." 1 Stat. 124, 1.

This statute not only makes maps and charts subjects of copyright, but mentions them before books in the order of designation. The second section of an act to amend this act, approved April 29, 1802, 2 Stat. 171, enacts that from the first day of January thereafter, he who shall invent and design, engrave, etch or work, or from his own works shall cause to be designed and engraved, etched or worked, any historical or other print or prints shall have the same exclusive right for the term of fourteen years from recording the title thereof as prescribed by law.

By the first section of the act of February 3d, 1831, 4 Stat. 436, entitled an act to amend the several acts respecting copyright, musical compositions and cuts, in connection with prints and engravings, are added, and the period of protection is extended to twenty-eight years. The caption or title of this act uses the word copyright for the first time in the legislation of Congress.

The construction placed upon the Constitution by the first act of 1790, and the act of 1802, by the men who were contemporary with its formation, many of whom were members of the convention which framed it, is of itself entitled to very great weight, and when it is remembered that the rights thus established have not been disputed during a period of nearly a century, it is almost conclusive.

Unless, therefore, photographs can be distinguished in the classification on this point from the maps, charts, designs, engravings, etchings, cuts, and other prints, it is difficult to see why Congress cannot make them the subject of copyright as well as the others.

These statutes certainly answer the objection that books only, or writing in the limited sense of a book and its author, are within the constitutional provision. Both these words are susceptible of a more enlarged definition than this. An author in that sense is "he to whom anything owes its origin; originator; maker; one who completes a work of science or literature." Worcester. So, also, no one would now claim that the word writing in this clause of the Constitution, though the only word used as to subjects in regard to which authors are to be secured, is limited to the actual script of the author, and excludes books and all other printed matter. By writings in that clause is meant the literary productions of those authors, and Congress very properly has declared these to include all forms of writing, printing, engraving, etching, & c., by which the ideas in the mind of the author are given visible expression. The only reason why photographs were not included in the extended list in the act of 1802 is probably that they did not exist, as photography as an art was then unknown, and the scientific principle on which it rests, and the chemicals and machinery by which it is operated, have all been discovered long since that statute was enacted.

Nor is it to be supposed that the framers of the Constitution did not understand the nature of copyright and the objects to which it was commonly applied, for copyright, as the exclusive right of a man to the production of his own genius or intellect, existed in England at that time. . . .

We entertain no doubt that the Constitution is broad enough to cover an act authorizing copyright of photographs, so far as they are representatives of original intellectual conceptions of the author.

But it is said that an engraving, a painting, a print, does embody the intellectual conception of its author, in which there is novelty, invention, originality, and therefore comes within the purpose of the Constitution in securing its exclusive use or sale to its author, while the photograph is the mere mechanical reproduction of the physical features or outlines of some object animate or inanimate, and involves no originality of thought or any novelty in the intellectual operation connected with its visible reproduction in shape of a picture. That while the effect of light on the prepared plate may have been a discovery in the production of these pictures, and patents could properly be obtained for the combination of the chemicals, for their application to the paper or other surface, for all the machinery by which the light reflected from the object was thrown on the prepared plate, and for all the improvements in this machinery, and in the materials, the remainder of the process is merely mechanical, with no place for novelty, invention or originality. It is simply the manual operation, by the use of these instruments and preparations, of transferring to the plate the visible representation of some existing object, the accuracy of this representation being its highest merit.

This may be true in regard to the ordinary production of a photograph, and, further, that in such case a copyright is no protection. On the question as thus stated we decide nothing.

In regard, however, to the kindred subject of patents for invention, they cannot by law be issued to the inventor until the novelty, the utility, and the actual discovery or invention by the claimant have been established by proof before the Commissioner of Patents; and when he has secured such a patent, and undertakes to obtain redress for a violation of his right in a court of law, the question of invention, of novelty, of originality, is always open to examination. Our copyright system has no such provision for previous examination by a proper tribunal as to the originality of the book, map, or other matter offered for copyright. A deposit of two copies of the article or work with the Librarian of Congress, with the name of the author and its title page, is all that is necessary to secure a copyright. It is, therefore, much more important that when the supposed author sues for a violation of his copyright, the existence of those facts of originality, of intellectual production, of thought, and conception on the part of the author should be proved, than in the case of a patent right.

In the case before us we think this has been done.

The third finding of facts says, in regard to the photograph in question, that it is a "useful, new, harmonious, characteristic, and graceful picture, and that plaintiff made the same . . . entirely from his own original mental conception, to which he gave visible form by posing the said Oscar Wilde in front of the camera, selecting and arranging the costume, draperies, and other various accessories in said photograph, arranging the subject so as to present graceful outlines, arranging and disposing the light and shade, suggesting and evoking the desired expression, and from such disposition, arrangement, or representation, made entirely by plaintiff, he produced the picture in suit."

These findings, we think, show this photograph to be an original work of art, the product of plaintiff's intellectual invention, of which plaintiff is the author, and of a class of inventions for which the Constitution intended that Congress should secure to him the exclusive right to use, publish and sell, as it has done by section 4952 of the Revised Statutes.

. . . .

The judgment of the Circuit Court is accordingly affirmed.

BLEISTEIN v. DONALDSON LITHOGRAPHING CO.

188 U.S. 239 (1903)

HOLMES, J. . . . The alleged infringements consisted in the copying in reduced form of three chromolithographs prepared by employes of the plaintiffs for advertisements of a circus owned by one Wallace. Each of the three contained a portrait of Wallace in the corner and lettering bearing some slight relation to the scheme of decoration, indicating the subject of the design and the fact that the reality was to be seen at the circus. One of the designs was of an ordinary ballet, one of a number of men and women, described as the Stirk family, performing on bicycles, and one of groups of men and women whitened to represent statues. The Circuit Court directed a verdict for the defendant on the ground that the chromolithographs were not within the protection of the copyright law, and this ruling was sustained by the Circuit Court of Appeals. *Courier Lithographing Co. v. Donaldson Lithographing Co.,* 104 Fed. Rep. 993.

. . . .

We shall do no more than mention the suggestion that painting and engraving unless for a mechanical end are not among the useful arts, the progress of which Congress is empowered by the Constitution to promote. The Constitution does not limit the useful to that which satisfies immediate bodily needs. *Burrow-Giles Lithographic Co. v. Sarony,* 111 U.S. 53. It is obvious also that the plaintiffs' case is not affected by the fact, if it be one, that the pictures represent actual groups — visible things. They seem from the testimony to have been composed from hints or description, not from sight of a performance. But even if they had been drawn from the life, that fact would not deprive them of protection. The opposite proposition would mean that a portrait by Velasquez or Whistler was common property because others might try their hand on the same face. Others are free to copy the original. They are not free to copy the copy. *Blunt v. Patten,* 2 Paine, 397, 400. See *Kelly v. Morris,* L. R. 1 Eq. 697; *Morris v. Wright,* L. R. 5 Ch. 279. The copy is the personal reaction of an individual upon nature. Personality always contains something unique. It expresses its singularity even in handwriting, and a very modest grade of art has in it something irreducible, which is one man's alone. That something he may copyright unless there is a restriction in the words of the act.

If there is a restriction it is not to be found in the limited pretensions of these particular works. The least pretentious picture has more originality in it than directories and the like, which may be copyrighted. Drone, Copyright, 153. See *Henderson v. Tomkins,* 60 Fed. Rep. 758, 765. The amount of training required for humbler efforts than those before us is well indicated by Ruskin. "If any young person, after being taught what is, in polite circles, called 'drawing,' will try to copy the commonest piece of real *work,* — suppose a lithograph on the title page of a new opera air, or a woodcut in the cheapest illustrated newspaper of the day — they will find themselves entirely beaten." Elements of Drawing, 1st ed. 3. There is no reason to doubt that these prints in their *ensemble* and in all their details, in their design and particular combinations of figures, lines and colors, are the original work of the plaintiffs' designer. If it be necessary, there is express testimony to that effect. It would be pressing the defendant's right to the verge, if not beyond, to leave the question of originality to the jury upon the evidence in this case, as was done in *Hegeman v. Springer,* 110 Fed. Rep. 374.

We assume that the construction of Rev. Stat. § 4952, allowing a copyright to the "author, inventor, designer, or proprietor . . . of any engraving, cut, print . . . [or] chromo" is affected by the act of 1874, c. 301, § 3, 18 Stat. 78, 79. That section provides that "in the construction of this act the words 'engraving,' 'cut' and 'print' shall be applied only to pictorial illustrations or works connected with the fine arts." We see no reason for taking the words "connected with the fine arts" as qualifying anything except the word "works," but it would not change our decision if we should assume further that they also qualified "pictorial illustrations," as the defendant contends.

These chromolithographs are "pictorial illustrations." The word "illustrations" does not mean that they must illustrate the text of a book, and that the etchings of Rembrandt or Steinla's engraving of the Madonna di San Sisto could not be protected today if any man were able to produce them. Again, the act however construed, does not mean that ordinary posters are not good enough to be considered within its scope. The antithesis to "illustrations or works connected with the fine arts" is not works of little merit or of humble degree, or illustrations addressed to the less educated classes; it is "prints or labels designed to be used for any other articles of manufacture." Certainly works are not the less connected with the fine arts because their pictorial quality attracts the crowd and therefore gives them a real use — if use means to increase trade and to help to make money. A picture is none the less a picture and none the less a subject of copyright that it is used for an advertisement. And if pictures may be used to advertise soap, or the theatre, or monthly magazines, as they are, they may be used to advertise a circus. Of course, the ballet is as legitimate a subject for illustration as any other. A rule cannot be laid down that would excommunicate the paintings of Degas.

Finally, the special adaptation of these pictures to the advertisement of the Wallace shows does not prevent a copyright. That may be a circumstance for the jury to consider in determining the extent of Mr. Wallace's rights, but it is not a bar. Moreover, on the evidence, such prints are used by less pretentious exhibitions when those for whom they were prepared have given them up.

It would be a dangerous undertaking for persons trained only to the law to constitute themselves final judges of the worth of pictorial illustrations, outside of the narrowest and most obvious limits. At the one extreme some works of genius would be sure to miss appreciation. Their very novelty would make them repulsive until the public had learned the new language in which their author spoke. It may be more than doubted, for instance, whether the etchings of Goya or the paintings of Manet would have been sure of protection when seen for the first time. At the other end, copyright would be denied to pictures which appealed to a public less educated than the judge. Yet if they command the interest of any public, they have a commercial value — it would be bold to say that they have not an aesthetic and educational value — and the taste of any public is not to be treated with contempt. It is an ultimate fact for the moment, whatever may be our hopes for a change. That these pictures had their worth and their success is sufficiently shown by the desire to reproduce them without regard to the plaintiffs' rights. See *Henderson v. Tomkins,* 60 Fed. Rep. 758, 765. We are of opinion that there was evidence that the plaintiffs have rights entitled to the protection of the law.

The judgment of the Circuit Court of Appeals is reversed; the judgment of the Circuit Court is also reversed and the cause remanded to that court with directions to set aside the verdict and grant a new trial.

MR. JUSTICE HARLAN, with whom concurred MR. JUSTICE MCKENNA, dissenting.

Judges Lurton, Day and Severens, of the Circuit Court of Appeals, concurred in affirming the judgment of the District Court. Their views were thus expressed in an opinion delivered by Judge Lurton: "What we hold is this: That if a chromo, lithograph, or other print, engraving, or picture has no other use than that of a mere advertisement, and no value aside from this function, it would not be promotive of the useful arts, within the meaning of the constitutional provision, to protect the 'author' in the exclusive use thereof, and the copyright statute should not be construed as including such a publication, if any other construction is admissible. If a mere label simply designating or describing an article to which it is attached, and which has no value separated from the article, does not come within the constitutional clause upon the subject of copyright, it must follow that a pictorial illustration designed and useful only as an advertisement, and having no intrinsic value other than its function as an advertisement, must be equally without the obvious meaning of the Constitution. It must have some connection with the fine arts to give it intrinsic value, and that it shall have is the meaning which we attach to the act of June 18, 1874, amending the provisions of the copyright law. We are unable to discover anything useful or meritorious in the design copyrighted by the plaintiffs in error other than as an advertisement of acts to be done or exhibited to the public in Wallace's show. No evidence, aside from the deductions which are to be drawn from the prints themselves, was offered to show that these designs had any original artistic qualities. The jury could not reasonably have found merit or value aside from the purely business object of advertising a show, and the instruction to find for the defendant was not error. Many other points have been urged as justifying the result reached in the court below. We find it unnecessary to express any opinion upon them, in

view of the conclusion already announced. The judgment must be affirmed."
Courier Lithographing Co. v. Donaldson Lithographing Co., 104 Fed. Rep. 993, 996.

I entirely concur in these views, and therefore dissent from the opinion and judgment of this court. The clause of the Constitution giving Congress power to promote the progress of science and useful arts, by securing for limited terms to authors and inventors the exclusive right to their respective works and discoveries, does not, as I think, embrace a mere advertisement of a circus.

Mr. Justice McKenna authorizes me to say that he also dissents.

QUESTIONS

Consider the following issues in connection with the copyright clause of the United States Constitution:

1. Is the constitutional power one to: (a) promote progress, (b) secure rights, or (c) promote progress by securing rights?

2. Why, in establishing a new federal government, did the founding fathers repose this power in the central government, rather than in the separate states? More generally, why give this power to *any* government unit? More specifically, would state copyright control be effectual, and would it be constitutional after the adoption of the copyright clause?

3. Does the copyright monopoly promote "the Progress of Science" or does it promote "the useful Arts"? *How* does such an exclusive right promote one or the other? Can a specific copyright be struck down because it does *not* promote science or the useful arts? Who would so decide? Is a comic strip constitutionally subject to copyright protection? A design for a flag? A pornographic work? An unpublished work kept in a desk drawer? Does the purpose of promoting progress make for broader or narrower protection in particular cases?

4. Could Congress extend the period of copyright protection to 1,000 years? Ninety-nine years? Life of the author plus fifty years? Why is the "property" interest in works of literature, music and art limited in time, when the "property" interest in real and personal property is typically of indefinite duration? Could a *state* grant perpetual copyright protection?

5. Does the reference in the copyright clause to "Authors" have substantive import regarding the nature and amount of work necessary to secure valid copyright protection? Can Congress give such protection to one who copies the work of another? To one who, although not copying, "originates" a work exactly identical to one already written? Or is there a requirement, such as in the patent law, that the work in order to secure copyright protection must be "novel"? If an "Author" is necessary, can Congress extend copyright protection to music, photographs and sculpture?

6. Can Congress constitutionally provide that under certain circumstances, all persons are free, without the prior consent of the copyright owner, to make copies of a copyrighted work upon the payment of a statutorily specified royalty?

7. Is the definition of "Writings" to be limited to the conventional understanding, or to the understanding in 1789? In either case, may Congress constitutionally grant copyright protection of a map, a painting, a photograph, a motion picture, a choreographed dance, a puppet, a sculpture, a Frank Lloyd Wright building? Can a work which is reduced to form only in a phonograph record or a tape be given copyright protection? A computer program? A completely unrecorded work, such as a conversation or an improvised "live" performance? If a work is treated as a "non-writing," may the states grant copyright protection?

STRUCTURE AND OPERATIONS OF THE COPYRIGHT OFFICE

The Copyright Office, a division of the Library of Congress, has for almost a century been charged with the registration of claims to copyright and with related duties. The deposit of copies of works in conjunction with such registration has been used to enrich the holdings of the library. *See, e.g.,* §§ 13, 14, and 213 of the 1909 Copyright Act (repealed). *Compare* §§ 407 and 408 of the 1976 Act. While registration has important procedural, and even substantive ramifications, see Chapter 5 *infra,* it must be emphasized that the Copyright Office does not *grant* copyrights; copyright subsists in a work as soon as that work is "created," i.e., "fixed in a copy or phonorecord for the first time." Sections 101, 302. (Even under the 1909 Act, copyright attached to a work when it was publicly disseminated with an appropriate notice; registration could follow later. Section 10 of the 1909 Act.) But compare § 304 (a) of the 1976 Act regarding copyright renewal registrations, Chapter 3 *infra.* Copyright is to be distinguished in this respect from the functions of the Patent and Trademark Office, in the Department of Commerce, which issues patents (the effectiveness of which dates only from the date of issuance, the claim of "patent pending" to the contrary notwithstanding). *See* 35 U.S.C. § 131. *Compare* § 7(a) of the Lanham Trademark Act, 15 U.S.C. § 1057(a) (registration of trademarks).

When an application for copyright registration is filed, however, the function of the Examining Division, though modest, is not altogether nonexistent. It has commonly been assumed that the Register of Copyrights has the power to decline to register a work, a power of some significance since registration — while not a condition of copyright itself — has long been a condition to suing for infringement. *See* § 13 of the 1909 Act. *Cf.* § 411 (a) of the 1976 Act. Registration has been denied for works deemed by the Register to lack sufficient originality, see *Bailie v. Fisher,* p. 137 *infra;* or to be solely utilitarian in design, see *Esquire, Inc. v. Ringer,* p. 150 *infra;* or to be covered by an existing design patent, see 37 CFR § 202.10(b); or to be obscene, see 41 Op. Att'y Gen. 73 (1958), 121 USPQ 329. *(But see Mitchell Bros. Film Group v. Cinema Adult Theatre,* p. 177 *infra.)*

The power to deny registration has been controversial and has been exercised sparingly; the Register, in fact, adheres to a policy which, in cases of doubt, dictates registration. (This policy was, for example, employed beginning in 1964 to explain the Register's willingness to register computer programs.) When registration was denied, and a copyright claimant wished to sue for infringement, his or her recourse under the 1909 Act was to institute a mandamus action against the Register, see *Vacheron & Constantin Le Coultre Watches, Inc. v. Benrus Watch Co.,* 260 F.2d 637 (2d Cir. 1958). Under the 1976 Act, the applicant may sue for infringement and provide notice thereof to the Register, who is empowered to intervene with respect to the issue of registrability. Section 411(a).

Recordation of assignments, mortgages and other transactions involving copyright has long complemented the basic examining and registration function of the office. This sphere of activities will undoubtedly be increased under the 1976 Act. The Act also imposes on the office the duty to implement or monitor, by way of regulations (found in 37 CFR) or report to Congress, a wide variety of substantive provisions, ranging from termination of transfers and distribution of phonorecords to use of copyrighted material through library photocopying or public broadcasting.

As part of regulations issued in 1977 in compliance with the Freedom of Information Act, the functions of the various operating divisions and offices of the Copyright Office were described as follows:

(1) The Acquisitions and Processing Division which receives incoming materials, dispatches outgoing materials, establishes controls over fiscal accounts and controls over the collections of the Library of Congress through implementation of deposit requirements of the copyright statute.

(2) The Examining Division which examines all applications and material presented to the Copyright Office for registration of original and renewal copyright claims and which determines whether the material deposited constitutes copyrightable subject matter and whether the other legal and formal requirements of Title 17 have been met.

(3) The Planning and Technical Office which has immediate responsibility for studies and recommendations concerned with automation of copyright procedures and related organizational studies and for implementation of approved automation applications in the Copyright Office.

(4) The Cataloging Division which prepares the bibliographic description of all copyrighted works registered or received in the Copyright Office, produces catalog cards for such works, and prepares the Catalog of Copyright Entries.

(5) The Information and Reference Division which provides a national copyright information service through the public information office, educates staff and the public on the copyright law, issues and distributes information materials, responds to reference requests regarding copyright matters, prepares search reports based upon copyright records, certifies copies of legal documents concerned with copyright, and maintains liaison with the United States Customs Service, the Department of Treasury, and the United States Postal Service.

(6) The Licensing Division which implements the sections of Pub. L. 94-553 dealing with secondary transmissions of radio and television programs, compulsory licenses for making and distributing phonorecords of nondramatic musical works, public performances through coin-operated phonorecord players, and use of published nondramatic musical, pictorial, graphic, and sculptural works in connection with noncommercial broadcasting.

(7) The Records Management Division develops, services, stores, and preserves the official records and catalogs of the Copyright Office, including applications for registration, biographic and other historical records, and materials deposited for copyright registration that are not selected by the Library of Congress for addition to its collections.

A Copyright Office Announcement describes a recent reorganization of the Office's management structure. The following flowchart accompanying the Announcement illustrates the new lines of authority within the Office.

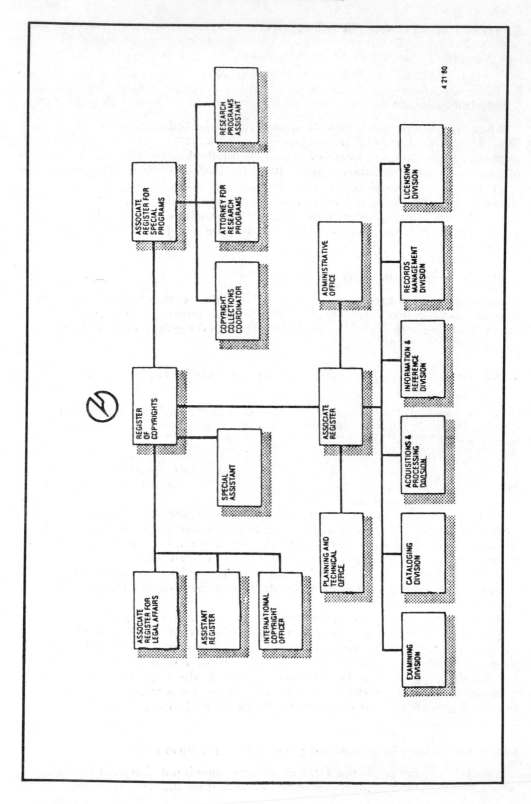

C. DISTINCTIONS: PATENTS

PATENT STATUTE

35 U.S.C. §§ 100-03, 171, 271

§ 100. Definitions

When used in this title unless the context otherwise indicates —

(a) The term "invention" means invention or discovery.

(b) The term "process" means process, art or method, and includes a new use of a known process, machine, manufacture, composition of matter, or material.

(c) The terms "United States" and "this country" mean the United States of America, its territories and possessions.

(d) The word "patentee" includes not only the patentee to whom the patent was issued but also the successors in title to the patentee. July 19, 1952, c. 950, § 1, 66 Stat. 797.

§ 101. Inventions patentable

Whoever invents or discovers any new and useful process, machine, manufacture, or composition of matter, or any new and useful improvement thereof, may obtain a patent therefor, subject to the conditions and requirements of this title. July 19, 1952, c. 950, § 1, 66 Stat. 797.

§ 102. Conditions for patentability; novelty and loss of right to patent

A person shall be entitled to a patent unless —

(a) the invention was known or used by others in this country, or patented or described in a printed publication in this or a foreign country, before the invention thereof by the applicant for patent, or

(b) the invention was patented or described in a printed publication in this or a foreign country or in public use or on sale in this country, more than one year prior to the date of the application for patent in the United States, or

(c) he has abandoned the invention, or

(d) the invention was first patented or caused to be patented by the applicant or his legal representatives or assigns in a foreign country prior to the date of the application for patent in this country on an application filed more than twelve months before the filing of the application in the United States, or

(e) the invention was described in a patent granted on an application for patent by another filed in the United States before the invention thereof by the applicant for patent, or

(f) he did not himself invent the subject matter sought to be patented, or

(g) before the applicant's invention thereof the invention was made in this country by another who had not abandoned, suppressed, or concealed it. In determining priority of invention there shall be considered not only the respective dates of conception and reduction to practice of the invention, but also the reasonable diligence of one who was first to conceive and last to reduce to practice, from a time prior to conception by the other. July 19, 1952, c. 950, § 1, 66 Stat. 797.

§ 103. Conditions for patentability; non-obvious subject matter

A patent may not be obtained though the invention is not identically disclosed or described as set forth in section 102 of this title, if the differences between the subject matter sought to be patented and the prior art are such that the subject matter as a whole would have been obvious at the time the invention was made to a person having ordinary skill in the art to which said subject matter pertains. Patentability shall not be negatived by the manner in which the invention was made. July 19, 1952, c. 950, § 1, 66 Stat. 798.

§ 171. Patents for designs

Whoever invents any new, original and ornamental design for an article of manufacture may obtain a patent therefor, subject to the conditions and requirements of this title.

The provisions of this title relating to patents for inventions shall apply to patents for designs, except as otherwise provided. July 19, 1952, c. 950, § 1, 66 Stat. 805.

§ 271. Infringement of patent

(a) Except as otherwise provided in this title, whoever without authority makes, uses or sells any patented invention, within the United States during the term of the patent therefor, infringes the patent.

(b) Whoever actively induces infringement of a patent shall be liable as an infringer.

(c) Whoever sells a component of a patented machine, manufacture, combination or composition, or a material or apparatus for use in practicing a patented process, constituting a material part of the invention, knowing the same to be especially made or especially adapted for use in an infringement of such patent, and not a staple article or commodity of commerce suitable for substantial noninfringing use, shall be liable as a contributory infringer.

(d) No patent owner otherwise entitled to relief for infringement or contributory infringement of a patent shall be denied relief or deemed guilty of misuse or illegal extension of the patent right by reason of his having done one or more of the following: (1) derived revenue from acts which if performed by another without his consent would constitute contributory infringement of the patent; (2) licensed or authorized another to perform acts which if performed without his consent would constitute contributory infringement of the patent; (3) sought to enforce his patent rights against infringement or contributory infringement. July 19, 1952, c. 950, § 1, 66 Stat. 811.

ALFRED BELL & CO. v. CATALDA FINE ARTS, INC.

191 F.2d 99 (2d Cir. 1951)

[Plaintiff sought protection for certain reproductions of public domain paintings by the old masters. These were produced by plaintiff through a tedious and exacting form of engraving known as the "mezzotint method." Among its detailed findings, the district court stated: "The work of the engraver upon the plate requires the individual conception, judgment and execution by the engraver on the depth and shape of the depressions in the plate to be made by the scraping process in order to produce in this other medium the engraver's concept of the effect of the oil painting. No two engravers can produce identical interpretations of the same oil painting."]

FRANK, CIRCUIT JUDGE.

1. Congressional power to authorize both patents and copyrights is contained in Article 1, § 8 of the Constitution. In passing on the validity of patents, the

Supreme Court recurrently insists that this constitutional provision governs. On this basis, pointing to the Supreme Court's consequent requirement that, to be valid, a patent must disclose a high degree of uniqueness, ingenuity and inventiveness, the defendants assert that the same requirement constitutionally governs copyrights. As several sections of the Copyright Act — e.g., those authorizing copyrights of "reproductions of works of art," maps, and compilations — plainly dispense with any such high standard, defendants are, in effect, attacking the constitutionality of those sections. But the very language of the Constitution differentiates (a) "authors" and their "writings" from (b) "inventors" and their "discoveries." Those who penned the Constitution,[2] of course, knew the difference. The pre-revolutionary English statutes had made the distinction.[3] In 1783, the Continental Congress had passed a resolution recommending that the several states enact legislation to "secure" to authors the "copyright" of their books. Twelve of the thirteen states (in 1783-1786) enacted such statutes. Those of Connecticut and North Carolina covered books, pamphlets, maps, and charts.

Moreover, in 1790, in the year after the adoption of the Constitution, the first Congress enacted two statutes, separately dealing with patents and copyrights. The patent statute, enacted April 10, 1790, 1 Stat. 109, provided that patents should issue only if the Secretary of State, Secretary of War and the Attorney General, or any two of them "shall deem the invention or discovery sufficiently useful and important"; the applicant for a patent was obliged to file a specification "so particular" as "to distinguish the invention or discovery from other things before known and used . . ."; the patent was to constitute *prima facie* evidence that the patentee was "the first and true inventor or . . . discoverer . . . of the thing so specified." The Copyright Act, enacted May 31, 1790, 1 Stat. 124, covered "maps, charts, and books". A printed copy of the title of any map, chart or book was to be recorded in the Clerk's office of the District Court, and a copy of the map, chart or book was to be delivered to the Secretary of State within six months after publication. Twelve years later, Congress in 1802, 2 Stat. 171, added, to matters that might be copyrighted, engravings, etchings and prints.

---

[2] Many of them were themselves authors.

[3] The Act of Anne 8, c. 10, was entitled "An Act for the encouraging of learning, by vesting of the copies of printed books in the authors or purchasers of such copies, during the times therein mentioned."

The previous history shows the source of the word "copyright." See 1 Laddas, The International Protection of Literary and Artistic Property (1938) 15:

"In England, the royal grants of privilege to print certain books were not copyrights. They were not granted to encourage learning or for the benefit of authors; they were commercial monopolies, licenses to tradesman to follow their calling. As gradually monopolies became unpopular, the printers sought to base their claims on other grounds, and called the 'right of copy' not a monopoly, but a property right. The Stationers Company had a register in which its members entered the titles of the works they were privileged to print. A custom developed by which members refrained from printing the books which stood on the register in the name of another. Thus members respected each other's 'copy,' as it was called, and there grew up a trade recognition of 'the right of copy' or copyright. This right was subsequently embodied in a by-law of the Stationers Company. The entry in the register was regarded as a record of the rights of the individual named, and it was assumed that possession of a manuscript carried with it the right to print copies." See also Sheavyn, The Literary Profession in the Elizabethan Age (1909) 52-53, 64-65, 70-71, 76-80.

Thus legislators peculiarly familiar with the purpose of the Constitutional grant, by statute, imposed far less exacting standards in the case of copyrights. They authorized the copyrighting of a mere map which, patently, calls for no considerable uniqueness. They exacted far more from an inventor. And, while they demanded that an official should be satisfied as to the character of an invention before a patent issued, they made no such demand in respect of a copyright. In 1884, in *Burrow-Giles Lithographic Co. v. Sarony,* 111 U.S. 53, 57 the Supreme Court, adverting to these facts said: "The construction placed upon the constitution by the first act of 1790 and the act of 1802, by the men who were contemporary with its formation, many of whom were members of the convention which framed it, is of itself entitled to very great weight, and when it is remembered that the rights thus established have not been disputed during a period of nearly a century, it is almost conclusive." Accordingly, the Constitution, as so interpreted, recognizes that the standards for patents and copyrights are basically different.

The defendants' contention apparently results from the ambiguity of the word "original." It may mean startling, novel or unusual, a marked departure from the past. Obviously this is not what is meant when one speaks of "the original package," or the "original bill," or (in connection with the "best evidence" rule) an "original" document; none of those things is highly unusual in creativeness. "Original" in reference to a copyrighted work means that the particular work "owes its origin" to the "author." No large measure of novelty is necessary. Said the Supreme Court in *Baker v. Selden,* 101 U.S. 99, 102-103: "The copyright of the book, if not pirated from other works, would be valid without regard to the novelty, or want of novelty, of its subject-matter. The novelty of the art or thing described or explained has nothing to do with the validity of the copyright. To give to the author of the book an exclusive property in the art described therein, when no examination of its novelty has ever been officially made, would be a surprise and a fraud upon the public. That is the province of letters-patent, not of copyright. The claim to an invention or discovery of an art or manufacture must be subjected to the examination of the Patent Office before an exclusive right therein can be obtained; and it can only be secured by a patent from the government. The difference between the two things, letters-patent and copyright, may be illustrated by reference to the subjects just enumerated. Take the case of medicines. Certain mixtures are found to be of great value in the healing art. If the discoverer writes and publishes a book on the subject (as regular physicians generally do), he gains no exclusive right to the manufacture and sale of the medicine; he gives that to the public. If he desires to acquire such exclusive right, he must obtain a patent for the mixture as a new art, manufacture, or composition of matter. He may copyright his book, if he pleases; but that only secures to him the exclusive right of printing and publishing his book. So of all other inventions or discoveries."

In *Bleistein v. Donaldson Lithographing Co.,* 183 U.S. 239, 250, 252, the Supreme Court cited with approval *Henderson v. Tompkins,* C.C., 60 F. 758, where it was said, 60 F. at page 764: "There is a *very broad distinction between what is implied in the word 'author,' found in the constitution, and the word 'inventor.' The latter carries an implication which excludes the results of only ordinary skill, while nothing of this is necessarily involved in the former.* Indeed, the statutes themselves make broad distinctions on this point. So much as relates to copyrights . . . is expressed, so far as this particular is concerned, by the mere words, 'author, inventor, designer or proprietor,' with such aid as may be derived from the words 'written, composed or made,' . . . . But a *multitude of books rest safely under copyright, which show only ordinary skill and diligence in their preparation.* Compilations are noticeable examples of this fact. With reference to this subject, the courts have not undertaken to assume the functions of critics, or to measure carefully the degree of originality, or literary skill or training involved."

It is clear, then, that nothing in the Constitution commands that copyrighted matter be strikingly unique or novel. Accordingly, we were not ignoring the Constitution when we stated that a "copy of something in the public domain" will support a copyright if it is a "distinguishable variation"; or when we rejected the contention that "like a patent, a copyrighted work must be not only original, but new", adding, "That is not . . . the law as is obvious in the case of maps or compendia, where later works will necessarily be anticipated." All that is needed to satisfy both the Constitution and the statute is that the "author" contributed something more than a "merely trivial" variation, something recognizably "his own." Originality in this context "means little more than a prohibition of actual copying."[13] No matter how poor artistically the "author's" addition, it is enough if it be his own. *Bleistein v. Donaldson Lithographing Co.,* 188 U.S. 239, 47 L.Ed. 460.

On that account, we have often distinguished between the limited protection accorded a copyright owner and the extensive protection granted a patent owner. So we have held that "independent reproduction of a copyrighted . . . work is not infringement", whereas it is *vis a vis* a patent. Correlative with the greater immunity of a patentee is the doctrine of anticipation which does not apply to copyrights: The alleged inventor is chargeable with full knowledge of all the prior art, although in fact he may be utterly ignorant of it. The "author" is entitled to a copyright if he independently contrived a work completely identical with what went before; similarly, although he obtains a valid copyright, he has no right to prevent another from publishing a work identical with his, if not copied from his. A patentee, unlike a copyrightee, must not merely produce something "original"; he must also be "the first inventor or discoverer." "Hence it is possible to have a plurality of valid copyrights directed to closely identical or even identical works. Moreover, none of them, if independently arrived at without copying, will constitute an infringement of the copyright of the others."[16]

---

[13] Hoague-Sprague Corp. v. Frank C. Meyer, Inc., D.C.N.Y., 31 F.2d 583, 586. See also as to photographs Judge Learned Hand in Jewelers Circular Publishing Co. v. Keystone Pub. Co., D.C.N.Y., 274 F. 932, 934.

The English doctrine is the same. See Copinger, The Law of Copyrights (7th ed. 1936) 40-44: "Neither original thought nor original research is essential"; he quotes the English courts to the effect that the statute "does not require that the expression must be in an original or novel form, but that the work must not be copied from another work — that it should originate from the author," but only that "though it may be neither novel or ingenious, [it] is the claimant's original work in that it originates from him, and is not copied."

[16] *Id.* See Lawrence v. Dana, 15 Fed.Cas. 26, 60 No. 8,136: "Persons making, using or vending to others to be used, the patented article are guilty of infringing the letters-patent, even though they may have subsequently invented the same thing without any knowledge of the existence of the letters-patent; but the recomposition of the same book without copying, though not likely to occur, would not be an infringement." See also Fred Fisher, Inc. v. Dillingham, D.C.N.Y., 298 F. 145, 147.

The English doctrine is the same. See Copinger, The Law of Copyrights (7th ed. 1936) 2: "It is not infrequently urged as an objection to granting copyright protection for a long

2. We consider untenable defendants' suggestion that plaintiff's mezzotints could not validly be copyrighted because they are reproductions of works in the public domain. Not only does the Act include "Reproductions of a work of art", but — while prohibiting a copyright of "the original text of any work . . . in the public domain" — it explicitly provides for the copyrighting of "translations, or other versions of works in the public domain". The mezzotints were such "versions." They "originated" with those who made them, and — on the trial judge's findings well supported by the evidence — amply met the standards imposed by the Constitution and the statute.[22] There is evidence that they were not intended to, and did not, imitate the paintings they reproduced. But even if their substantial departures from the paintings were inadvertent, the copyrights would be valid.[23] A copyist's bad eyesight or defective musculature, or a shock caused by a clap of thunder, may yield sufficiently distinguishable variations. Having hit upon such a variation unintentionally, the "author" may adopt it as his and copyright it.[25]

---

term, that the effect is to create a monopoly, but at least, it is not a monopoly of knowledge. The grant of a patent does prevent full use being made of knowledge, but the reader of a book is not by the copyright laws prevented from making full use of any information he may acquire from his reading. He is only prohibited from disseminating that information or knowledge by multiplying copies of the book or of material portions of it: or, possibly, by reading the book aloud in public. Copyright is, in fact, only a negative right to prevent the appropriation of the labours of an author by another. If it could be shown that two precisely similar works were in fact produced wholly independently of one another, the author of the work that was published first would have no right to restrain the publication by the other author of that author's independent and original work. A patentee, on the other hand, has the right to prevent another from using his invention if it in fact infringes the former's patent, notwithstanding that the latter's invention was the subject of independent investigation on his part."

[22] See Copinger, The Law of Copyrights (7th ed. 1936) 46: "Again, an engraver is almost invariably a copyist, but although his work may infringe copyright in the original painting if made without the consent of the owner of the copyright therein, his work may still be original in the sense that he has employed skill and judgment in its production. He produces the resemblance he is desirous of obtaining by means very different from those employed by the painter or draughtsman from whom he copies; means which require great labour and talent. The engraver produces his effects by the management of light and shade, or, as the term of his art expresses it, the *chiarooscuro*. The due degrees of light and shade are produced by different lines and dots; he who is the engraver must decide on the choice of the different lines or dots for himself, and on his choice depends the success of his print."

[23] See Kallen, Art and Freedom (1942) 977 to the effect that "the beauty of the human singing voice, as the western convention of music hears it, depends upon a physiological dysfunction of the vocal cords. . . ."

Plutarch tells this story: A painter, enraged because he could not depict the foam that filled a horse's mouth from champing at the bit, threw a sponge at his painting; the sponge splashed against the wall — and achieved the desired result.

[25] Consider inadvertent errors in a translation. Compare cases holding that a patentable invention may stem from an accidental discovery. See, e. g., Radiator Specialty Co. v. Buhot, 3 Cir., 39 F.2d 373, 376; Nichols v. Minnesota Mining & Mfg. Co., 4 Cir., 109 F.2d 162, 165; New Wrinkle v. Fritz, D.C.W.D.N.Y., 45 F.Supp. 108, 117; Byerley v. Sun Co., 3 Cir., 184 F. 455, 456-457.

Many great scientific discoveries have resulted from accidents, e.g., the galvanic circuit and the x-ray.

QUESTIONS

1. How is the "progress of science and the useful arts" advanced by sustaining copyright in a work that is the same, although unknowingly and independently created, as an earlier work? How is it advanced by a knowing adaptation of an earlier work, such as an engraving of an old master, or a translation of a great novel?

2. If the plaintiff's engraving in the *Catalda* case had been based not on an old master but on a copyrighted painting, should it be eligible for copyright? Is it eligible for copyright under the 1976 Copyright Act?

3. Do you agree that a stroke of the pen resulting from "bad eyesight or defective musculature" is copyrightable? Can you distinguish from such a situation the results of "a shock caused by a clap of thunder"? How would dropping globs of paint from a ladder be treated by the *Catalda* court?

4. When Judge Frank quotes from an earlier opinion which notes that "originality in this context means little more than a prohibition of actual copying," what does he mean by "little more"?

5. Three standards (at least) might be applied to determine eligibility for copyright: (a) *Originality,* in the sense of independent origination or non-copying; (b) *Creativity,* in the sense of some modest level of imagination or "escape from the commonplace"; or (c) *Novelty and Invention,* in the sense (like a patent) of a "leap" beyond the "prior art" which would represent a major development in that art (and one which would not be obvious to a person skilled in that art). What are the arguments for and against the application of one or more of these standards? Which standard would Judge Frank apply on the basis of the *Catalda* case?

6. In *Runge v. Lee,* 441 F.2d 579 (9th Cir. 1971), $80,000 in damages plus $12,000 in attorney's fees were awarded to plaintiff for infringement of the copyright in a book entitled *Face Lifting by Exercise* (in addition to substantial damages for unfair competition). When the Supreme Court denied certiorari, 404 U.S. 887 (1971), Mr. Justice Douglas dissented, writing an opinion suggesting that the standards for copyrightability should not be more lenient than they are for patentability. *See* Nimmer, *Comment on the Douglas Dissent in* Lee v. Runge, 19 Bull. Copyright Soc'y 68 (1971). Justice Douglas' suggestion was based on the common constitutional foundation and underlying interests with respect to copyrights and patents. Compare his subsequent views in *Kewanee Oil Corp. v. Bicron Corp.,* 416 U.S. 470, 489 n.4 (1974) at p. 596 *infra.* How would the standards of "novelty," which Justice Douglas thus appears to embrace, be applied to literary or musical works? Could a choreographic rendition (in a stage dance accompanied by music) of the Faust story ever conceivably be held uncopyrightable, as Justice Douglas suggested in his dissent? Who would make that decision — a functionary in the Copyright Office, the Register of Copyright, a federal judge or judges?

7. How would any standard of originality, or creativity, or novelty, be applied to maps and informational charts, which were covered in the first Copyright Act in 1790 (drafted by many of those who had also drafted the Copyright Clause of the Constitution)?

SAKRAIDA v. AG PRO, INC.

425 U.S. 273 (1976)

MR. JUSTICE BRENNAN delivered the opinion of the Court.

Respondent Ag Pro, Inc., filed this action against petitioner Sakraida on October 8, 1968, in the District Court for the Western District of Texas for infringement of United States Letters Patent 3,223,070, entitled "Dairy Establishment," covering a water flush system to remove cow manure from the floor of a dairy barn. The patent was issued December 14, 1965, to Gribble and Bennett, who later assigned it to respondent.

The District Court's initial grant of summary judgment for petitioner was reversed by the Court of Appeals for the Fifth Circuit. 437 F.2d 99 (1971). After a trial on remand, the District Court again entered a judgment for petitioner. The District Court held that the patent "does not constitute invention, is not patentable, and is not a valid patent, it being a combination patent, all of the elements of which are old in the dairy business, long prior to 1963, and the combination of them as described in the said patent being neither new nor meeting the test of non-obviousness." The Court of Appeals again reversed and held the patent valid. 474 F.2d 167 (1973). On rehearing, the court remanded "with directions to enter a judgment holding the patent valid, subject, however, to . . . consideration of a motion under Rule 60(b)(2), F.R. Civ.P., to be filed in the District Court by the [petitioner] Sakraida on the issue of patent validity based on newly discovered evidence." 481 F.2d 668, 669 (1973). The District Court granted the motion and ordered a new trial. The Court of Appeals again reversed, holding that the grant of the motion was error, because "the record on the motion establishes that [petitioner] failed to exercise due diligence to discover the new evidence prior to entry of the former judgment." 512 F.2d 141, 142 (1975). The Court of Appeals further held that "[o]ur prior determination of patent validity is reaffirmed." Id., at 144. We granted certiorari. 423 U.S. 891 (1975). We hold that the Court of Appeals erred in holding the patent valid and also in reaffirming its determination of patent validity. We therefore reverse and direct the reinstatement of the District Court's judgment for petitioner, and thus we have no occasion to decide whether the Court of Appeals properly found that petitioner had not established a case for a new trial under Rule 60(b)(2).

Systems using flowing water to clean animal wastes from barn floors have been familiar on dairy farms since ancient times.[1] The District Court found, and

---

[1] Among the labors of Hercules is the following:

Heracles now set out to perform his fifth Labour, and this time his task was to cleanse the stables of Augeas in a single day. Augeas was a rich king of Elis, who had three thousand cattle. At night the cattle always stood in a great court surrounded with walls, close to the king's palace, and as it was quite ten years since the servants had cleaned it out, there was enough refuse in the court to build up a high mountain. Heracles went to Augeas and asked if he would give him the tenth part of his flocks if he thoroughly cleansed his stables in a single day. The king looked upon this as such an absolutely impossible feat that he would not have minded promising his kingdom as a reward for it, so he laughed and said, "Set to work, we shall not quarrel about the wages," and he further promised distinctly to give Heracles what he asked, and this he did in the presence of Phyleus, his eldest son, who happened to be there. The next morning Heracles set to work, but even his strong arms would have failed to accomplish the task if they had not been aided by his mother-wit. He compelled a mightly torrent to work for him, but you would hardly guess how he did it. First he opened great gates on two opposite sides of the court, and then he went to the stream, and when he had blocked up its regular course with great stones, he conducted it to the court that required to be cleansed, so that the water streamed in at one end and streamed out at the other, carrying away all the dirt with it. Before evening the stream had done its work and was restored to its usual course.

C. Witt, Classic Mythology 119-120 (1883).

respondent concedes, that none of the 13 elements of the Dairy Establishment combination is new,[2] and many of those elements, including storage of the water in tanks or pools, appear in at least six prior patented systems.[3] The prior art involved spot delivery of water from tanks or pools to the barn floor by means of high pressure hoses or pipes. That system required supplemental hand labor, using tractor blades, shovels, and brooms, and cleaning by these methods took several hours. The only claimed inventive feature of the Dairy Establishment combination of old elements is the provision for abrupt release of the water from the tanks or pools directly onto the barn floor, which causes the flow of a sheet of water that washes all animal waste into drains within minutes and requires no supplemental hand labor. As an expert witness for respondent testified concerning the effect of Dairy Establishment's combination: "[W]ater at the bottom has more friction than this water on the top and it keeps moving ahead and as this water keeps moving ahead we get a rolling action of this water which produced the cleaning action. . . . you do not get this in a hose. . . . [U]nless that

---

[2] The District Court found as follows respecting Claims 1 and 3, the only claims involved in the case:

1. I find that the "dairy establishment" as described in United States Letters Patent 3,233,070 is composed of 13 separate items, as follows:
(a) ". . . a smooth, evenly contoured, paved surface forming a floor providing a walking surface. . . ."
(b) ". . . drain means for draining wash water from such floor opening to the top of the floor."
(c) ". . . said smooth, evenly contoured surface which forms such floor sloping toward said drain. . . ."
(d) ". . . multiple rest areas with individual stalls for each cow and with each of said stalls having a bottom which is also a smooth pavement. . . ."
(e) ". . . . which is disposed at an elevation above the paved surface forming the floor. . . ."
(f) ". . . said stalls being dimensioned so that a cow can comfortably stand or lie in the stall, but offal from the cow falls outside the stall bottom and onto the floor providing the walking surface in the barn. . . ."
(g) ". . . said barn further including defined feeding areas having feeding troughs. . . ."
(h) ". . . a cow-holding area."
(i) ". . . a milking area."
(j) ". . . a transfer area all bottomed with the walking surface forming said floor in the barn. . . ."
(k) ". . . and floor washing means for washing the floor providing the walking surface in the barn where said floor bottom, said feeding, holding, milking and transfer areas operable to send wash water flowing over the floor with such water washing any cow offal thereon into the said drain means, said floor washing means including means located over a region of said floor which is uphill from said drain means constructed to collect water as a pool above said floor and operable after such collection of water as a pool to dispense the water as a sheet of water over said floor."
(l) A tank on a mounting so that it can be tilted, and the water poured out to cascade on the floor to form a sheet.
(m) A floor-washing means comprising a dam for damming or collecting water as a pool directly on the floor, which such dam abruptly openable to send water cascading as a sheet over the floor towards the drain.
2. I further find that each of the items above-described were not new, but had been used in the dairy business prior to the time the application for the said Gribble patent, made the subject of this action, had been filed in the Patent Office of the United States on November 5, 1963.

[3] The District Court found:

water is continuously directed toward the cleaning area the cleaning action almost ceases instantaneously. . . ." [4]

The District Court found that "[n]either the tank which holds the water, nor the means of releasing the water quickly is new, but embrace[s] tanks and doors which have long been known," and further that "their use in this connection is one that is obvious, and the patent in that respect is lacking in novelty. The patent does not meet the non-obvious requirements of the law." The District Court therefore held that Dairy Establishment "may be relevant to commercial success, but not to invention," because the combination "was reasonably obvious to one with ordinary skill in the art." Moreover, even if the combination filled a "long-felt want and . . . has enjoyed commercial success, those matters, without invention, will not make patentability." Finally, the District Court concluded: "[T]o those skilled in the art, the use of the old elements in combination was not an invention by the obvious-nonobvious standard. Even though the dairy barn in question attains the posture of a successful venture, more than that is needed for invention." [5] The Court of Appeals disagreed with the District Court's conclusion on the crucial issue of obviousness.

It has long been clear that the Constitution requires that there be some "invention" to be entitled to patent protection. *Dann v. Johnston,* 425 U.S. 219. As we explained in *Hotchkiss v. Greenwood,* 11 How. 248, 267 (1851): "[U]nless more ingenuity and skill . . . were required . . . than were possessed by an ordinary mechanic acquainted with the business, there was an absence of that decree [sic] of skill and ingenuity which constitute essential elements of every invention. In other words, the improvement is the work of the skillful mechanic, not that of the inventor." This standard was enacted in 1952 by Congress in 35 U.S.C. § 103 "as a codification of judicial precedents . . . with congressional directions that inquiries into the obviousness of the subject matter sought to be patented are a prerequisite to patentability." *Graham v. John Deere Co.,* 383 U.S. 1, 17 (1966). Section 103 provides:

[M]any of the items going to make up Plaintiff's claim for a patent were disclosed in prior patents, known respectively as the McCornack patent, the Holz patent, the Ingraham patent, the Kreutzer patent, the Bogert patent, and the Luks patent; and that the statements of the Examiner's opinions refusing to issue a patent are true as to all items there stated to be covered in prior patents or publications.

[4] This witness further testified that:
[W]ater has energy and it can be used in many different ways. In a hose the energy is used by impact, under pressure, external force that is applied to this pressure — to this water, whereas the water that comes down as a sheet or wall of water has built in energy because of its elevation and as this water is released it does the same thing water does in a flooded stream. As this water — I will try to make this clear, and I hope I can, on the surface of this pavement there are these piles of manure droppings. This pavement is smooth and this water moves down over this manure. The water at the bottom has more friction than this water on the top and it keeps moving ahead and as this water keeps moving ahead we get a rolling action of this water which produced the cleaning action. That is the key to this method of cleaning. You do not get this in a hose. You do not get it in a gutter as has been used in the past. I might just mention a little bit about the hose. This squirting water on a floor — probably have done it on our own sidewalks or walkways, and I just mention that, that unless that water is continuously directed towards the cleaning area the cleaning action almost ceases instantaneously. Now the movie that was shown earlier very dramatically illustrated that point. The cleaning action — as soon as the hoses moved to one side the cleaning action ceased here and that is why this hose was moved back and forth, to drive this stuff on down to where we want it.

[5] The court also concluded that "while the combination of old elements may have performed a useful function, it added nothing to the nature and quality of dairy barns theretofore used."

A patent may not be obtained though the invention is not identically disclosed or described as set forth in section 102 of this title, if the differences
between the subject matter sought to be patented and the prior art are such
that the subject matter as a whole would have been obvious at the time the
invention was made to a person having ordinary skill in the art to which said
subject matter pertains. Patentability shall not be negatived by the manner in
which the invention was made.

The ultimate test of patent validity is one of law, *Great A. & P. Tea Co. v.
Supermarket Corp.*, 340 U.S. 147, 155 (1950), but resolution of the obviousness
issue necessarily entails several basic factual inquiries, *Graham v. John Deere Co.*,
supra, 383 U.S. at 17.

Under § 103, the scope and content of the prior art are to be determined;
differences between the prior art and the claims at issue are to be ascertained;
and the level of ordinary skill in the pertinent art resolved.

Ibid.

The Court of Appeals concluded that "the facts presented at trial clearly do
not support [the District Court's] finding of obviousness under the
three-pronged *Graham* test . . . ." 474 F.2d, at 172. We disagree and hold that the
Court of Appeals erroneously set aside the District Court's findings.

The scope of the prior art was shown by prior patents, prior art publications,
affidavits of people having knowledge of prior flush systems analogous to
respondent's, and the testimony of a dairy operator with 22 years of experience
who described flush systems he had seen on visits to dairy farms throughout the
country. Our independent examination of that evidence persuades us of its
sufficiency to support the District Court's finding "as a fact that each and all of
the component parts of this patent . . . were old and well-known throughout the
dairy industry long prior to the date of the filing of the application for the
Gribble patent. . . . What Mr. Gribble referred to . . . as the essence of the patent,
to-wit, the manure flush system, was old, various means for flushing manure from
dairy barns having been used long before the filing of the application. . . ." [6]
Indeed, respondent admitted at trial "that the patent is made up of a combination
of old elements" and "that all elements are individually old. . . ." Accordingly, the
District Court properly followed our admonition in *Great A. & P. Tea Co. v.
Supermarket Corp., supra,* 340 U.S., at 152, 71 S.Ct., at 130, 95 L.3d., at 167:
"Courts should scrutinize combination patent claims with a care proportioned to
the difficulty and improbability of finding invention in an assembly of old
elements. . . . A patent for a combination which only unites old elements with no
change in their respective functions . . . obviously withdraws what already is
known into the field of its monopoly and diminishes the resources available to
skillful men. . . ."

---

[6] The court stated:
   I therefore find as a fact that each and all of the component parts of this patent as
listed under the applicant's claims set out in said patent, were old and well-known
throughout the dairy industry long prior to the date of the filing of the application for
the Gribble patent. I further find that what Mr. Gribble referred to in this deposition
as the essence of the patent, to-wit the manure flush system, was old, various means for
flushing manure from dairy barns having been used long before the filing of the
application for the Gribble patent, the general idea in that connection being a hard
surfaced sloping floor onto which the cows' offal was dropped, and some system of
introducing water in sufficient quantities and force onto said floor to wash the offal
therefrom, with a ditch or drain to carry the offal so washed away from the barn, either
into a manure container or otherwise.

The Court of Appeals recognized that the patent combined old elements for applying water to a conventional sloped floor in a dairy barn equipped with drains at the bottom of the slope and that the purpose of the storage tank — to accumulate a large volume of water capable of being released in a cascade or surge — was equally conventional. 474 F.2d, at 169. It concluded, however, that the element lacking in the prior art was any evidence of an arrangement of the old elements to effect the abrupt release of a flow of water to wash animal wastes from the floor of a dairy barn. *Ibid.* Therefore, "although the [respondent's] flush system does not embrace a complicated technical improvement, it does achieve a synergistic result through a novel combination." *Id.,* at 173.

We cannot agree that the combination of these old elements to produce an abrupt release of water directly on the barn floor from storage tanks or pools can properly be characterized as synergistic, that is, "result[ing] in an effect greater than the sum of the several effects taken separately." *Anderson's-Black Rock v. Pavement Co.,* 396 U.S. 57, 61 (1969). Rather, this patent simply arranges old elements with each performing the same function it had been known to perform, although perhaps producing a more striking result than in previous combinations. Such combinations are not patentable under standards appropriate for a combination patent. *Great A. & P. Tea Co. v. Supermarket Corp., supra; Anderson's-Black Rock v. Pavement Co., supra.* Under those authorities this assembly of old elements that delivers water directly rather than through pipes or hoses to the barn floor falls under the head of "the work of the skillful mechanic, not that of the inventor." *Hotchkiss v. Greenwood,* 11 How., at 267, 13 L.Ed., at 691. Exploitation of the principle of gravity adds nothing to the sum of useful knowledge where there is no change in the respective functions of the elements of the combination; this particular use of the assembly of old elements would be obvious to any person skilled in the art of mechanical application. See *Dann v. Johnston,* 425 U.S., at 229.

Though doubtless a matter of great convenience, producing a desired result in a cheaper and faster way, and enjoying commercial success, Dairy Establishment "did not produce a 'new or different function' . . . within the test of validity of combination patents." *Anderson's-Black Rock v. Pavement Co., supra,* 396 U.S., at 60. These desirable benefits "without invention will not make patentability." *Great A. & P. Tea Co. v. Supermarket Corp.,* 340 U.S., at 153. See *Dann v. Johnston,* 425 U.S., at 229, n. 4.

Reversed.

QUESTIONS

1. Would an anthology of public-domain poetry be eligible for copyright (apart from any newly written editorial commentary) if the *Sakraida* test were applied, or if the *Catalda* test were applied? Which test is the more appropriate one, and why?

2. The district court findings in footnote 2 afford a glimpse into the exotic art of patent claims-drafting, whereby the applicant seeks the broadest protection consistent with the need to narrow the claim to avoid prior art. Note also the dogged consistency of the Court of Appeals for the Fifth Circuit in upholding the validity of the patent.

TAYLOR INSTRUMENT COS. v. FAWLEY-BROST CO.

139 F.2d 98, 59 USPQ 384 (7th Cir. 1943)

MAJOR, CIRCUIT JUDGE. Plaintiff brought this action to recover damages for and to enjoin alleged copyright and trade mark infringement and alleged unfair competition in connection with the manufacture and sale of charts used in recording machinery. Defendant denied the charges and counterclaimed for certain relief, including a declaratory judgment that such charts were not copyrightable. The court below decided all issues in favor of the plaintiff and entered an interlocutory judgment from which defendant appeals.

Plaintiff is a manufacturer and vendor of a recording thermometer which is a combination of numerous elements, including a clock which shows the time, a thermometer which measures and indicates the temperature, and a writing machine which draws upon the chart a graphical record disclosing the hourly temperature. The chart is circular in form and about ten inches in diameter. It has arc lines extending from the center outwardly by which the time is indicated, and lines extending in a circle around the chart by which the temperature is indicated. The writing machine feature includes a pen or stylus which, co-acting with other elements of the machine, produces a traced line which indicates the temperature at different times during any desired period. The chart upon which this record is made is commonly known in the trade as such, although it appears more accurate to describe it as a paper dial.

Plaintiff prints its copyright notice upon charts manufactured by it, in conformity with copyright certificates issued by the United States Register of Copyrights. Plaintiff relies upon eighteen of such copyright certificates out of several hundred which it has procured. Plaintiff also prints upon its charts its registered trade mark "Taylor" and a number, which indicates the type of machine with which the chart is to be used.

Charts manufactured and sold by the defendant are admittedly copied from plaintiff's charts insofar as the circular and arc lines are concerned. Defendant omits, however, plaintiff's trade mark and copyright notice. Defendant prints on its charts in boldface type, "Fawley-Brost Co., Chicago." It also prints upon the chart a number for the purpose of indicating the type of machine, whether manufactured by plaintiff or others, for which the chart is designed. This means that defendant's number corresponds with plaintiff's number where the charts are manufactured for the same type of plaintiff's machine. Some of defendant's charts also bear the letter "T," which indicates that they are designed for use on a machine manufactured and sold by the plaintiff.

The statement thus made appears sufficient for a consideration of defendant's contention that plaintiff's copyrights are invalid and of no effect. (Other facts will be subsequently stated relative to the charge of trade mark infringement and unfair competition.) Plaintiff, as might be expected, relies heavily upon the findings and conclusion of the trial court. It may be said, so we think, that there is little, if any, dispute concerning the facts of the case. The dispute is largely dependent upon the conclusion to be drawn from such facts.

Art. 1, Sec. 8, Clause 8 of the Constitution of the United States empowers Congress "To promote the Progress of Science and useful Arts, by securing for limited Times to Authors and Inventors the exclusive Right to their respective Writings and Discoveries." In the exercise of the power thus conferred, Congress has legislated with reference to copyrights (Title 17, U.S.C. 1, et seq.), thereby furnishing protection to "Authors" in their "Writings," and has legislated with reference to patents (Title 35, U.S.C. 31, et seq.), thereby furnishing protection to "Inventors" in their "discoveries." Thus it appears that Congress has provided two separate and distinct fields of protection, the copyright and the patent. In the former (Sec. 4), it has placed "all the writings of an Author," and in the latter (Sec. 31), inventions and discoveries of "any new and useful art, machine, manufacture . . . or any new and useful improvement thereof. . . ." While it may be difficult to determine in which field protection must be sought, it is plain, so we think, that it must be in one or the other; it cannot be found in both. In other words, there is no overlapping territory, even though the line of separation may in some instances be difficult of exact ascertainment.

Defendant bottoms its contention that the charts in suit are not the proper subject of copyright, largely upon the oft cited and much quoted case of *Baker v. Selden,* 101 U.S. 99, and cases which have followed that decision. There, the distinction between copyright and patent protection is stated thus (page 105):

> The description of the art in a book, though entitled to the benefit of copyright, lays no foundation for an exclusive claim to the art itself. The object of the one is explanation; the object of the other is use. The former may be secured by copyright. The latter can only be secured, if it can be secured at all, by letters patent.

The reason assigned by the court for such distinction is (page 102):

> To give to the author of the book an exclusive property in the art described therein, when no examination of its novelty has ever been officially made, would be a surprise and a fraud upon the public. That is the province of letters patent, not of copyright. The claim to an invention or discovery of an art or manufacture must be subjected to the examination of the Patent Office before an exclusive right therein can be obtained; and it can only be secured by a patent from the government.

In *Brief English Systems, Inc. v. Owen, et al.,* 48 F.2d 555, 556 [9 USPQ 20, 21], the court stated; ". . . it may be said that the way to obtain the exclusive property right to an art, as distinguished from a description of the art, is by letters patent and not by copyright." This same distinction has been recognized in *Arnstein v. Edward B. Marks Music Corp.,* 82 F.2d 275 [28 USPQ 426], *Amberg File & Index Co. v. Shea Smith & Co.,* 82 F. 314 (7th Circuit), and in *Dymow v. Bolton, et al.,* 11 F.2d 690, 691. In the latter case, the court said: "Just as a patent affords protection only to the means of reducing an inventive idea to practice, so the copyright law protects the means of expressing an idea. . . ."

. . . None of the cases relied upon by the plaintiff announces a contrary rule. None of them, so far as we are able to ascertain, has sustained a copyright upon an object which did not teach or convey information.

This brings us to a consideration of whether plaintiff's copyrighted chart is an object of explanation or an object of use. If the former, it is subject to copyright protection; if the latter, it is not entitled to such protection, but the same must be obtained, if at all, by letters patent. The character of the chart is aptly stated in a letter written by plaintiff's counsel to defendant's counsel shortly prior to the commencement of the instant suit. It states, "The chart in question is, in effect, a replaceable dial which cooperates with the pointer or index of the instrument, to indicate a temperature reading. The fact that this pointer carries an inked stylus to make a record of this indicated temperature, does not change the replaceable dial into a blank book."

The proof, as well as an examination of plaintiff's recording thermometer, including its chart, leaves no room for doubt but that the latter is a mechanical element of the instrument of which it is an integral part. The chart is as indispensable to the operation of a recording thermometer as are any of the other elements. They are interdependent. As was stated by plaintiff's president: "I would say that you must have the pen and you must have the chart and the two together will determine the temperature."

Notwithstanding plaintiff's rather feeble argument to the contrary, the chart neither teaches nor explains the use of the art. It is an essential element of the machine; it is the art itself. It is our judgment that plaintiff's charts are not the proper subject of copyright and that the recognition of an exclusive property right therein would be, in the words of the Supreme Court in the *Baker case*, "a surprise and a fraud upon the public."

Defendant introduced some twenty-five patents, the subject matter of which was recording thermometers which displayed representations of charts. All of such patents have expired and it seems reasonable to think that plaintiff's chart is extremely old in the art. Plaintiff, however, seeks to justify its copyright protection by pointing out that none of these patents would give the defendant measurements necessary for printing the charts alleged to infringe. This argument, if true, ignores the fact that it now seeks protection in the copyright field for an art long protected in the field of patents, and where undoubtedly it still belongs. The absurdity of plaintiff's position appears from the fact that each new model of machine, whether manufactured by plaintiff or others, requires a chart with different measurements. As a result, these different measurements afford the excuse for obtaining another copyright. Thus is produced the intolerable situation that plaintiff may extend indefinitely the fifty-six years of protection afforded by the copyright laws. In fact, the protection thus afforded would be without end.

What we have just said is perhaps unnecessary to a decision of the question under consideration. It is, however, a graphic illustration of the wrong which can be, and which we think in the instant case has been, perpetrated by allowing plaintiff copyright protection upon a mechanical device which clearly belongs exclusively in the patent field. Judge Chitty, in *Davis v. Comitti*, 52 L.T. Rep. (N.S.) 539, 540, used this pertinent language:

> It would be strange if the inventor, who, by means of a patent could obtain a monopoly for his invention for the term of fourteen years, was enabled to obtain a distinct right of copyright for a period of at least forty-two years for the letterpress on the dial, or some other essential part of his invention, and thus, after the expiration of the period for which his patent was granted, be in a position to restrain the serviceable user of some letterpress which formed an essential part of his invention. In my opinion the statutes do not lead to any such anomaly. . . .

The fact, if such it be, that plaintiff's chart has long since lost its patentable status does not impair the conclusion that it has no place in the copyright field. In fact, it strengthens such conclusion, even though it leaves plaintiff unprotected.

. . . .

It follows that the judgment appealed from must be and is hereby reversed and remanded, with directions to dismiss plaintiff's complaint. This is without prejudice to the right of the court to allow to defendant its costs of suit, including as part thereof a reasonable attorney fee, as provided by Sec. 4., [sic] Title 17, U.S.C.A.

QUESTIONS

1. Why is "explanation" necessary for copyright protection? Is an "explanatory" component necessary in a painting, sculpture or choreographic work in order to be eligible for copyright protection?

2. The court states that there is "no overlapping territory" between patent and copyright. Is that so, and if so, why? Would a request for (or grant of) patent protection automatically exclude copyright protection? Why could not copyright be extended to the charts and only patent to the machine?

3. Is the kind of blank form involved in this case, whose use is the recording of information, eligible for copyright under the Constitution as a "Writing"? Does it contain adequate "Authorship"?

4. Would the decision in this case dictate the ineligibility for copyright of a detailed scoring sheet for baseball which would permit the user to reflect such information as balls and strikes for each batter, the kind of pitches thrown, the direction in which the ball was hit, and the "closeness" of the plays at the bases?

D. DISTINCTIONS: TRADEMARKS

TRADE-MARK CASES

100 U.S. 82 (1879)

MR. JUSTICE MILLER delivered the opinion of the court.

The three cases whose titles stand at the head of this opinion are criminal prosecutions for violations of what is known as the trade-mark legislation of Congress. The first two are indictments in the southern district of New York, and the last is an information in the southern district of Ohio. In all of them the judges of the circuit courts in which they are pending have certified to a difference of opinion on what is substantially the same question; namely, are the acts of Congress on the subject of trade-marks founded on any rightful authority in the Constitution of the United States?

The entire legislation of Congress in regard to trade-marks is of very recent origin. It is first seen in sects. 77 to 84, inclusive, of the act of July 8, 1870, entitled "An Act to revise, consolidate, and amend the statutes relating to patents and copyrights." 16 Stat. 198. The part of this act relating to trade-marks is embodied in chap. 2, tit. 60, sects. 4937 to 4947, of the Revised Statutes.

It is sufficient at present to say that they provide for the registration in the Patent Office of any device in the nature of a trade-mark to which any person has by usage established an exclusive right, or which the person so registering intends to appropriate by that act to his exclusive use; and they make the wrongful use of a trade-mark, so registered, by any other person, without the owner's permission, a cause of action in a civil suit for damages. Six years later we have the act of Aug. 14, 1876 (19 Stat. 141), punishing by fine and imprisonment the fraudulent use, sale, and counterfeiting of trade-marks registered in pursuance of the statutes of the United States, on which the informations and indictments are founded in the cases before us.

The right to adopt and use a symbol or a device to distinguish the goods or property made or sold by the person whose mark it is, to the exclusion of use by all other persons, has been long recognized by the common law and the chancery courts of England and of this country, and by the statutes of some of the States.

It is a property right for the violation of which damages may be recovered in an action at law, and the continued violation of it will be enjoined by a court of equity, with compensation for past infringement. This exclusive right was not created by the act of Congress, and does not now depend upon it for its enforcement. The whole system of trade-mark property and the civil remedies for its protection existed long anterior to that act, and have remained in full force since its passage.

These propositions are so well understood as to require neither the citation of authorities nor an elaborate argument to prove them.

As the property in trade-marks and the right to their exclusive use rest on the laws of the States, and, like the great body of the rights of person and of property, depend on them for security and protection, the power of Congress to legislate on the subject, to establish the conditions on which these rights shall be enjoyed and exercised, the period of their duration, and the legal remedies for their enforcement, if such power exist at all, must be found in the Constitution of the United States, which is the source of all the powers that Congress can lawfully exercise.

In the argument of these cases this seems to be conceded, and the advocates for the validity of the acts of Congress on this subject point to two clauses of the Constitution, in one or in both of which, as they assert, sufficient warrant may be found for this legislation.

The first of these is the eighth clause of sect. 8 of the first article. That section, manifestly intended to be an enumeration of the powers expressly granted to Congress, and closing with the declaration of a rule for the ascertainment of such powers as are necessary by way of implication to carry into efficient operation those expressly given, authorizes Congress, by the clause referred to, "to promote the progress of science and useful arts, by securing for limited times, to authors and inventors, the exclusive right to their respective writings and discoveries."

As the first and only attempt by Congress to regulate the *right of trade-marks* is to be found in the act of July 8, 1870, to which we have referred, entitled "An Act to revise, consolidate, and amend the statutes relating to *patents and copyrights,*" terms which have long since become technical, as referring, the one to inventions and the other to the writings of authors, it is a reasonable inference that this part of the statute also was, in the opinion of Congress, an exercise of the power found in that clause of the Constitution. It may also be safely assumed that until a critical examination of the subject in the courts became necessary, it was mainly if not wholly to this clause that the advocates of the law looked for its support.

Any attempt, however, to identify the essential characteristics of a trade-mark with inventions and discoveries in the arts and sciences, or with the writings of authors, will show that the effort is surrounded with insurmountable difficulties.

The ordinary trade-mark has no necessary relation to invention or discovery. The trade-mark recognized by the common law is generally the growth of a considerable period of use, rather than a sudden invention. It is often the result of accident rather than design, and when under the act of Congress it is sought to establish it by registration, neither originality, invention, discovery, science, nor art is any way essential to the right conferred by that act. If we should endeavor to classify it under the head of writings of authors, the objections are equally strong. In this, as in regard to inventions, originality is required. And while the word *writings* may be liberally construed, as it has been, to include original designs for engravings, prints, &c., it is only such as are *original,* and are founded in the creative powers of the mind. The writings which are to be protected are *the fruits of intellectual labor,* embodied in the form of books, prints, engravings, and the like. The trade-mark may be, and generally is, the adoption of something already in existence as the distinctive symbol of the party using it. At common law the exclusive right to it grows out of its *use,* and not its mere adoption. By the act of Congress this exclusive right attaches upon registration. But in neither case does it depend upon novelty, invention, discovery, or any work of the brain. It requires no fancy or imagination, no genius, no laborious thought. It is simply founded on priority of appropriation. We look in vain in the statute for any other qualification or condition. If the symbol, however plain, simple, old, or well-known, has been first appropriated by the claimant as his distinctive trade-mark, he may by registration secure the right to its exclusive use. While such legislation may be a judicious aid to the common law on the subject of trade-marks, and may be within the competency of legislatures whose general powers embrace that class of subjects, we are unable to see any such power in the constitutional provision concerning authors and inventors, and their writings and discoveries.

The other clause of the Constitution supposed to confer the requisite authority on Congress is the third of the same section, which, read in connection with the granting clause, is as follows: "The Congress shall have power to regulate commerce with foreign nations, and among the several States, and with the Indian tribes."

The argument is that the use of a trade-mark — that which alone gives it any value — is to identify a particular class or quality of goods as the manufacture, produce, or property of the person who puts them in the general market for sale; that the sale of the article so distinguished is commerce; that the trade-mark is, therefore, a useful and valuable aid or instrument of commerce, and its regulation by virtue of the clause belongs to Congress, and that the act in question is a lawful exercise of this power.

Every species of property which is the subject of commerce, or which is used or even essential in commerce, is not brought by this clause within the control of Congress. The barrels and casks, the bottles and boxes in which alone certain articles of commerce are kept for safety and by which their contents are transferred from the seller to the buyer, do not thereby become subjects of congressional legislation more than other property. *Nathan v. Louisiana,* 8 How. 73.

[The Court found that the statutes in question were not limited to interstate transactions and were accordingly invalid. The Court expressly left undecided the question "whether the trade-mark bears such a relation to commerce in general terms as to bring it within congressional control, when used or applied to classes of commerce which fall within that control. . .".]

QUESTIONS

1. Are there weaknesses in the Court's distinction of trademark and patent? Are there any additional weaknesses in its distinction of trademark and copyright?

2. Does this case hold that trademarks are *per se* not copyrightable?

3. Can the title of a book or song be protected by copyright?

4. Why couldn't the trademarks in question have been subject to congressional regulation under the commerce clause? Does the procedural setting of the case affect the answer? If Congress enacted a copyright law pursuant to the commerce clause, what additional restrictions on its power would be imposed? What restrictions would be lifted?

TRADEMARKS AND THE LANHAM ACT

Trademarks are symbols used in such a way that they perform an identification function. Thus, a word, name, logo or design may signify to the public some kind of association between a product or service and a particular source. It is essentially such identifying use that develops the trademark.

Common law recognition of trademarks is thus based on twin objectives — to protect against misappropriation the trademark owner's goodwill embodied in a mark and to protect the public from being confused. This property interest and consumer-protection objective are akin to many other state interests. The federal perfection of such common law protection found in the Lanham Act, while important, is not equivalent to federal law of copyrights and patents which respectively create rights.

LANHAM ACT

15 U.S.C. §§ 1051, 1052, 1114, 1125, 1127

Sec. 1 (15 U.S.C. § 1051). Requirements for registering trademarks on the principal register

The owner of a trademark used in commerce may register his trademark under this Act on the principal register hereby established:

(a) By filing in the Patent Office —

(1) a written application, in such form as may be prescribed by the Commissioner, verified by the applicant, or by a member of the firm or an officer of the corporation or association applying, specifying applicant's domicile and citizenship, the date of applicant's first use of the mark, the date of applicant's first use of the mark in commerce, the goods in connection with which the mark is used and the mode or manner in which the mark is used in connection with such goods, and including a statement to the effect that the person making the verification believes himself, or the firm, corporation, or association in whose behalf he makes the verification, to be the owner of the mark sought to be registered, that the mark is in use in commerce, and that no other person, firm, corporation, or association, to the best of his knowledge and belief, has the right to use such mark in commerce either in the identical form thereof or in such near resemblance thereto as to be likely, when applied to the goods of such other person, to cause confusion, or to cause mistake, or to deceive: Provided, That in the case of every application claiming concurrent use the applicant shall state exceptions to his claim of exclusive use, in which he shall specify, to the extent of his knowledge, any concurrent use by others, the goods in connection with which and the areas in which each concurrent use exists, the periods of each use, and the goods and area for which the applicant desires registration;

(2) a drawing of the mark; and

(3) such number of specimens or facsimiles of the mark as actually used as may be required by the Commissioner.

. . . .

Sec. 2 (15 U.S.C. § 1052). Trademarks registrable on the principal register

No trademark by which the goods of the applicant may be distinguished from the goods of others shall be refused registration on the principal register on account of its nature unless it —

(a) consists of or comprises immoral, deceptive, or scandalous matter; or matter which may disparage or falsely suggest a connection with persons, living or dead, institutions, beliefs, or national symbols, or bring them into contempt, or disrepute;

(b) consists of or comprises the flag or coat of arms or other insignia of the United States, or of any State or municipality, or of any foreign nation, or any simulation thereof;

(c) consists of or comprises a name, portrait, or signature identifying a particular living individual except by his written consent, or the name, signature, or portrait of a deceased President of the United States during the life of his widow, if any, except by the written consent of the widow;

(d) consists of or comprises a mark which so resembles a mark registered in the Patent Office or a mark or trade name previously used in the United States by another and not abandoned, as to be likely, when applied to the goods of the applicant, to cause confusion, or to cause mistake, or to deceive; . . . [subject to a proviso which specifies the circumstances under which the same mark may be registered concurrently by different persons].

(e) consists of a mark which, (1) when applied to the goods of the applicant is merely descriptive or deceptively misdescriptive of them, or (2) when applied to the goods of the applicant is primarily geographically descriptive or deceptively misdescriptive of them, except as indications of regional origin may be registrable under section 4 hereof, or (3) is primarily merely a surname;

(f) except as expressly excluded in paragraphs (a), (b), (c), and (d) of this section, nothing herein shall prevent the registration of a mark used by the applicant which has become distinctive of the applicant's goods in commerce. The Commissioner may accept as prima facie evidence that the mark has become distinctive, as applied to the applicant's goods in commerce, proof of substantially exclusive and continuous use thereof as a mark by the applicant in commerce for the 5 years next preceding the date of the filing of the application for its registration (Amended Oct. 9, 1962, 76 Stat. 769).

Sec. 32(1) (15 U.S.C. § 1114(1)). Remedies — Infringement

Any person who shall, without the consent of the registrant —

(a) use in commerce any reproduction, counterfeit, copy, or colorable imitation of a registered mark in connection with the sale, offering for sale, distribution, or advertising of any goods or services on or in connection with which such use is likely to cause confusion, or to cause mistake, or to deceive; or

(b) reproduce, counterfeit, copy or colorably imitate a registered mark and apply such reproduction, counterfeit, copy, or colorable imitation to labels, signs, prints, packages, wrappers, receptacles or advertisements intended to be used in commerce upon or in connection with the sale, offering for sale, distribution, or advertising of goods or services on or in connection with which such use is likely to cause confusion, or to cause mistake, or to deceive;

shall be liable in a civil action by the registrant for the remedies hereinafter provided. Under subsection (b) hereof, the registrant shall not be entitled to recover profits or damages unless the acts have been committed with knowledge that such imitation is intended to be used to cause confusion, or to cause mistake, or to deceive (Amended Oct. 9, 1962, 76 Stat. 769).

Sec. 43 (15 U.S.C. § 1125). False designations of origin and false descriptions forbidden

(a) Any person who shall affix, apply, or annex, or use in connection with any goods or services, or any container or containers for goods, a false designation of origin, or any false description or representation, including words or other symbols tending falsely to describe or represent the same, and shall cause such goods or services to enter into commerce, and any person who shall with knowledge of the falsity of such designation of origin or description or representation cause or procure the same to be transported or used in commerce or deliver the same to any carrier to be transported or used, shall be liable to a civil action by any person doing business in the locality falsely indicated as that of origin or in the region in which said locality is situated, or by any person who believes that he is or is likely to be damaged by the use of any such false description or representation.

Sec. 45 (15 U.S.C. § 1127). Construction and definitions

In the construction of this Act, unless the contrary is plainly apparent from the context:

. . . .

Commerce. The word "commerce" means all commerce which may lawfully be regulated by Congress.

. . . .

Trademark. The term "trademark" includes any word, name, symbol, or device or any combination thereof adopted and used by a manufacturer or merchant to identify his goods and distinguish them from those manufactured or sold by others.

Service mark. The term "service mark" means a mark used in the sale or advertising of services to identify the services of one person and distinguish them from the services of others. Titles, character names and other distinctive features of radio or television programs may be registered as service marks notwithstanding that they, or the programs, may advertise the goods of the sponsor.

Certification mark. The term "certification mark" means a mark used upon or in connection with the products or services of one or more persons other than the owner of the mark to certify regional or other origin, material, mode of manufacture, quality, accuracy or other characteristics of such goods or services or that the work or labor on the goods or services was performed by members of a union or other organization.

Collective mark. The term "collective mark" means a trademark or service mark used by the members of a cooperative, an association or other collective group or organization and includes marks used to indicate membership in a union, an association or other organization.

Mark. The term "mark" includes any trademark, service mark, collective mark, or certification mark entitled to registration under this Act whether registered or not.

Use in commerce. For the purposes of this Act a mark shall be deemed to be used in commerce (a) on goods when it is placed in any manner on the goods or their containers or the displays associated therewith or on the tags or labels affixed thereto and the goods are sold or transported in commerce and (b) on services when it is used or displayed in the sale or advertising of services and the services are rendered in commerce, or the services are rendered in more than one State or in this and a foreign country and the person rendering the services is engaged in commerce in connection therewith.

Abandonment of mark. A mark shall be deemed to be "abandoned" —
(a) when its use has been discontinued with intent not to resume. Intent not to resume may be inferred from circumstances. Non-use for two consecutive years shall be prima facie abandonment.
(b) when any course of conduct of the registrant, including acts of omission as well as commission, causes the mark to lose its significance as an indication of origin.

Colorable imitation. The term "colorable imitation" includes any mark which so resembles a registered mark as to be likely to cause confusion or mistake or to deceive.

. . . .

QUESTIONS

1. Could an author secure a trademark for a character name in a popular story or series of stories (e.g., James Bond or Sam Spade)? Could an author secure a trademark for a character apart from the name, e.g., the physical appearance of a character or the personality traits of a character? What would be the scope of protection afforded by trademark for such a name or character?

2. Could a copyright be secured for such a name or character? (Consider both the Constitution and the Copyright Act.) What would be the scope of copyright protection?

3. It is generally thought that the title of a book is not registrable as a trademark under the Lanham Act because of the somewhat metaphysical notion that:

> Man is a creative animal. By the labor of his hands he creates things and by the labor of his mind he creates thoughts which are woven together into the form of essays, reports, speeches, court opinions, stories and the like. Man is a verbal animal and each new thing brings into being before long a new name — hammer, wheel, wagon, automobile, airplane. . . . Each [book] is a new thing, unique, which has to have a name. . . . [H]owever arbitrary, novel or nondescriptive _of contents_ the name of a book — its title — may be, it nevertheless _describes_ the book.

In re Cooper, 254 F.2d 611, 615 (C.C.P.A.), _cert. denied,_ 358 U.S. 840 (1958). Is this objection applicable to the title of a _series_ of books or of a magazine? Should the non-registrability of ordinary book titles leave authors and publishers helpless against the use of their title on another book?

TITLES IN THE LAW OF UNFAIR COMPETITION

The law of unfair competition protects the title of a copyrightable work against potentially confusing usage by another, much as it does with respect to other designations of goods, services, persons, or organizations. Under this branch of the law, the test is whether the public will assume some connection between the works designated by the same or confusingly similar titles. A problem is created, however, by the fact that copyrighted works enter the public domain from which they may be utilized by anyone. In the ordinary case, when a work has fallen into the public domain, the title goes with it and may be freely used. _Clemens v. Belford,_ 14 F. 728 (N.D. Ill. 1883); _Chamberlain v. Columbia Pictures Corp.,_ 186 F.2d 923, 89 USPQ 7 (9th Cir. 1951). In _G. & C. Merriam Co. v. Ogilvie,_ 159 F. 638 (1st Cir. 1908), the defendant was held entitled to use the title

"Webster's Dictionary," but was required to print in large type on the title page of the public domain reprint a statement clearly differentiating it from earlier copyrighted editions by the plaintiff, whose name had been associated with the famous dictionary from the beginning.

The public-confusion test in the context of titles relating to the public domain is illustrated by a pair of cases involving, respectively, "Alice in Wonderland" and "Wyatt Earp." When two motion pictures using the former title were released at about the same time, the producer of the more costly and widely advertised picture was denied a preliminary injunction because the title had not become riveted in the public mind to plaintiff's picture (as distinct from the Lewis Carroll story). *Walt Disney Productions, Inc. v. Souvaine Selective Pictures, Inc.,* 98 F. Supp. 774, 90 USPQ 138 (S.D.N.Y.), *aff'd,* 192 F.2d 856, 91 USPQ 313 (2d Cir. 1951). On the other hand, the obscure historical basis for a U.S. marshal in the early West named "Wyatt Earp" did not permit a manufacturer to use the name, which was likely to be connected by the public with the television series responsible for injecting this little-known U.S. marshal into the public's consciousness. *Wyatt Earp Enterprises, Inc. v. Sackman, Inc.,* 157 F. Supp. 621, 116 USPQ 122 (S.D.N.Y. 1958).

The problems become even more complicated when a title is used to designate a *series* of works, one or more of which is in the public domain. Reprinting the public domain work under its title (but perhaps with a disclaimer) is permissible under the cases discussed above. But what of an adaptation or other derivative work? The right to produce such works is part of an author's rights under copyright which, by definition, is no longer subsisting; the value of having a public domain is to facilitate public exercise of those rights which have expired. On the other hand, a new version of a mystery novel or a cartoon character by someone unconnected with the original creator is likely to confuse the public. These questions arise with respect not only to titles but to character names. *See* Waldheim, *Characters — May They Be Kidnapped?,* 12 BULL. COPYRIGHT SOC'Y 210 (1965).

The law of unfair competition is constantly changing. Thus, even with respect to the use of titles, we find courts tending to be less concerned with actual competition between the media involved than with the unfairness of the use. *Compare Atlas Mfg. Co. v. Street & Smith,* 204 F. 398 (8th Cir. 1913), *with Golenpaul v. Rosett,* 174 Misc. 114, 18 N.Y.S.2d 889, 45 USPQ 45 (N.Y. Sup. Ct. 1940), and *Children's Television Workshop v. Sesame Nursery Centers, Inc.,* 171 USPQ 105 (N.Y. Sup. Ct. 1970), *aff'd,* 319 N.Y.S.2d 589 (1st Dep't 1971). These developments may account for a conservative attitude on the part of large users of literary and musical material who may pay substantial amounts for titles. *See* Tannenbaum, *Uses of Titles for Copyright and Public Domain Works,* 6 BULL. COPYRIGHT SOC'Y 64 (1958).

It also appears that titles or names may in some cases qualify for registration as trademarks, especially as applied to periodicals or a series of cartoons or other works, but without thereby extending the term of copyright in the work itself. So also an arbitrary designation applied to a set or series of books may constitute a valid trademark, such as "Dr. Eliot's five-foot shelf of books." *Collier v. Jones,* 66 Misc. 97, 120 N.Y.S. 991 (N.Y. Sup. Ct. 1910). But if the title is merely the name of one of the books in the series, it is regarded as "merely descriptive" and therefore not subject to trademark protection. *In re Page Co.,* 47 App. D.C. 195 (D.C. Cir. 1917); *In re Cooper,* 254 F.2d 611, 117 USPQ 396 (C.C.P.A.), *cert. denied,* 358 U.S. 840, 119 USPQ 501 (1958).

The preemption provisions of § 301 of the 1976 Act (see Chapter 8 *infra* at p. 605) would not seem likely to bar state actions for deceptive use of titles. Such use has traditionally been deemed not to violate rights equivalent to copyright. Moreover, "deceptive trade practices such as passing off and false representation" were long among the noncontroversial examples of non-preempted rights in § 301(b)(3) until all examples were deleted on the House floor. Finally, registration of a trademark under the Lanham Act, 15 U.S.C. § 1501 *et seq.,* or assertion of a claim for false representation under § 43(a) of that statute will avoid preemption under this provision of the 1976 Act because it is inapplicable to other *federal* remedies. § 301(d) of 1976 Act. Thus, unfair competition remedies for misappropriation of titles should easily survive the new copyright law.

A change in title does not authorize or require a second registration in the Copyright Office. However, a "supplementary registration" (Form CA) may be made to reflect a change in title. The change may also be made in a formal manner by submitting a separate signed document, giving the old and new title as well as the registration number and copyright data, and having this information recorded in the assignment records.

QUESTIONS

1. A motion picture called "Best Man Wins" was based upon the Mark Twain short story "The Celebrated Jumping Frog of Calaveras County," which was in the public domain. The film was advertised as "A Story Only Mark Twain Could Tell," "Mark Twain's Favorite Story," etc. If Mark Twain did not author (or otherwise endorse) the screenplay of the motion picture, and if that motion picture was "corny" and inferior to Twain's "Jumping Frog" story, would Mark Twain's literary executor have a cause of action for trademark infringement or unfair competition in the form of "passing off" ? *See Chamberlain v. Columbia Pictures Corp.,* 186 F.2d 923 (9th Cir. 1951).

2. Had a film company used the title, "The Celebrated Jumping Frog of Calaveras County," on a motion picture depicting a completely different story, having no incidents in common with the Twain story, would that have constituted infringement of copyright? Would it have constituted trademark infringement?

3. The famous children's book author Dr. Seuss created a number of cartoons for Liberty Magazine in 1932. The copyrights were owned by Liberty. More than thirty years later, Liberty authorized Don Poynter to make three-dimensional dolls based on these cartoons. Dr. Seuss, finding these dolls to be "tasteless, unattractive and of an inferior quality," sought to enjoin the use of his name and to recover damages therefor. Should he succeed with respect to the following hang-tag?

See Geisel v. Poynter Products, Inc., 283 F. Supp. 261 (S.D.N.Y. 1968).

Does the following tag call for a different answer (*see* 295 F. Supp. 331 (S.D.N.Y. 1968))?

FREDERICK WARNE & CO. v. BOOK SALES, INC.

481 F. Supp. 1191 (S.D.N.Y. 1979)

SOFAER, DISTRICT JUDGE.

Frederick Warne & Co., Inc. ("Warne"), brings this trademark infringement action against Book Sales, Inc. ("BSI") under Sections 32(1) and 43(a) of the Lanham Act, 15 U.S.C. § 1114(1) and § 1125(a) respectively, as well as under the New York Anti-Dilution Statute, General Business Law § 368-d. The case is before the court on cross motions for summary judgment filed pursuant to Rule 56 of the Federal Rules of Civil Procedure.

Plaintiff Warne publishes the well-known series of children's books written and illustrated by Beatrix Potter, and sold under the trademark "The Original Peter Rabbit Books." Warne was, in fact, Miss Potter's original publisher, printing the first volume of her series, *The Tale of Peter Rabbit,* in 1902. Since then, millions of children have been delighted — and some, no doubt, terrified — by the adventures of the naughty rabbit. Subsequent volumes brought to life the antics of Squirrel Nutkin, the mischief of the Two Bad Mice, the mysterious ways of Mrs. Tiggy-Winkle, and tales of Miss Potter's many other endearing characters.

For years, Warne and Miss Potter enjoyed the profits generated by their extraordinarily popular series. Substantial sales continue today. But because seven of the books, in issue here, are no longer — or never were — covered by copyright protection in the United States, several new editions of Miss Potter's works have recently appeared on the market to compete with the Warne's editions. Warne concedes that the seven works are in the public domain. Nevertheless, Warne claims exclusive rights in the cover illustrations, and character marks derived from those illustrations, which were originally created by Miss Potter for Warne's editions of the seven books, and which do not appear within the text of the books themselves.[1] In addition, it claims exclusive trademark rights in an illustration appearing within *The Tale of Peter Rabbit,*

---

[1] Seven of the trademarks involved in this litigation are derived from the cover illustrations of the following works by Miss Potter:

referred to as the "sitting rabbit." Three of the covers have been registered under the Lanham Act as book trademarks — the "running rabbit," the "dancing squirrel," and the "reading mouse." Protection for the unregistered marks is claimed on the basis of Section 43(a) of the Act, which permits claimants to prove validity without the benefit of the presumption of validity that registration confers.

Warne has creatively exploited public affection for Miss Potter's characters by using, and licensing the use of, the eight illustrations on a variety of commercial products.[2] Thanks to its marketing efforts, Warne claims, the characters portrayed in the eight illustrations, "particularly the 'running rabbit' have attained a place in the public esteem comparable to Mickey Mouse, Peter Pan, and Raggedy Ann and Andy." (Aff. of Richard Billington, ¶ 16.) The notion that a British cony, however endearing, could gain as important a place in American hearts as Mickey Mouse seems dubious. Both are rodents, it is true, and thus equally entitled to our affections. But Mickey has had the benefit of competing for the American heart and dollar through moving pictures, an insurmountable advantage. Luckily for plaintiff, though, its burden is far less than its papers suggest.

The controversy here concerns defendant's use of the illustrations in which plaintiff claims trademark protection. Since October 1977, defendant has marketed a book entitled "Peter Rabbit and Other Stories" ("the BSI Peter Rabbit book"). It combines the seven Potter stories now in the public domain into a single, large and colorful volume. In its book defendant photographically reproduced the drawings of Miss Potter that appeared in early Warne editions and juxtaposed these illustrations with text from the books in a sequence corresponding to those of the original works. Defendant went beyond reproducing the works as originally published, however. It also produced redrawings of the cover illustrations from the seven Warne books and a redrawing of the "sitting rabbit" illustration. It placed the cover reproductions at the beginning and end of the stories for which they were originally designed. In addition, it used

---

The Tale of Peter Rabbit
The Tale of Two Bad Mice
The Tale of Mrs. Tiggy-Winkle
The Tale of Mr. Jeremy Fisher
The Tale of Squirrel Nutkin
The Tale of Benjamin Bunny
The Tailor of Gloucester

[2] The seven cover illustrations have been used on the individual books for which they were created as well as on packaging for sets of Miss Potter's books. In addition, Warne has extensively used the cover illustration for the *Tale of Peter Rabbit,* referred to as the "running rabbit," on a variety of products, including the dust covers for several of Miss Potter's works. The "sitting rabbit" mark has been used on a number of original Warne publications, including "Peter Rabbit's Natural Food Cookbook", "The History of the Tale of Peter Rabbit", "Beatrix Potter Coloring Book", and Warne's "Complete Catalogue" of 1977. Finally, since 1972 Warne has licensed the right to use the marks to manufacturers of toys, clothing and a host of other commercial products. This licensing program has proved lucrative; Warne presently claims to earn $250,000 in royalties per year, representing sales of licensed products of approximately $5,000,000 a year.

photographic reproductions from each of the original Warne covers as "corner ornaments" on most of the pages of each of the seven stories; the *Tale of Peter Rabbit,* for example, has a picture of the "running rabbit" on the lower right-hand corner of every page. Finally, BSI initially used a reproduction of the "sitting rabbit" design on the cover of its book. This design, it should be recalled, appeared within Miss Potter's original books, but has been used by Warne since 1972 as the principal symbol of its licensing enterprise. After publishing its editions with the "sitting rabbit" cover, and after plaintiff instituted this action, BSI switched to a "standing rabbit" design of its own creation.

Warne contends that BSI's use of all eight illustrations constitutes trademark infringement. It seeks injunctive relief as well as damages and an accounting.

Both plaintiff and defendant have moved for summary judgment. When these motions were made, representations by the parties suggested that no disputed facts existed that would require a trial. In particular, defendant seemed willing to concede the validity of plaintiff's claim to trademark protection, in order to test its argument that when copyright protection ended the books could be copied in their entirety. But, after briefs were submitted and argument held, it became clear that defendant is unwilling to concede that the illustrations in issue have acquired trademark significance, identifying Warne's publishing enterprise and not merely the Beatrix Potter works it publishes.

As the Second Circuit has admonished, "[d]isputes between parties as to trade-mark validity and infringement can rarely be determined satisfactorily on a motion for summary judgment." *Marcus Breier Sons v. Marvlo Fabrics,* 173 F.2d 29 (2d Cir. 1949). Given the difficulty, indeed novelty, of the issues presented, full development of the facts at trial will be particularly important to a proper resolution of this case. That the parties have filed cross motions for summary judgment, arguing simultaneously that there is no genuine issue of material fact, has no bearing on this determination. *Rains v. Cascade Industries,* 402 F.2d 241, 245 (3d Cir. 1968). Consequently, and for the reasons that follow, summary judgment must be denied to both parties.

I. Plaintiff's Claim to Trademark Protection

To succeed in this action, plaintiff must first establish that it has valid trademark rights in the eight character illustrations as used on its books and other products. Section 45 of the Lanham Act defines a trademark as any "word, name, symbol, or device . . . adopted and used by a manufacturer or merchant to identify his goods and distinguish them from those manufactured or sold by others." 15 U.S.C. § 1127. Although the illustrations here are *capable* of distinguishing Warne's books from those of others, it cannot be said that they are so arbitrary, unique, and non-descriptive as to constitute "technical trademarks," which are presumed valid as soon as they are affixed to the goods and the goods are sold. *Blisscraft of Hollywood v. United Plastics Co.,* 294 F.2d 694 (2d Cir. 1961). Accordingly, plaintiff has the burden of establishing that these illustrations have acquired secondary meaning, defined as "[t]he power of a name or other configuration to symbolize a particular business, product or company." *Dallas Cowboys Cheerleaders, Inc. v. Pussycat Cinema, Ltd.,* 604 F.2d 200, 203, n. 5 (2d Cir. 1979), *quoting Ideal Toy Corp. v. Kenner Products Division of General Mills Fun Group, Inc.,* 443 F. Supp. 291, 305 n. 14 (S.D.N.Y. 1977).

In the instant case, it would not be enough that the illustrations in question have come to signify Beatrix Potter as author of the books; plaintiff must show that they have come to represent its goodwill and reputation as *publisher* of those books. Whether or not the illustrations have acquired that kind of secondary meaning is a question of fact, *Speed Products Co. v. Tinnerman Products, Inc.*, 222 F.2d 61 (2d Cir. 1955); *Turner v. HMH Publishing Co.*, 380 F.2d 224 (5th Cir.), *cert. denied*, 389 U.S. 1006 (1967); *see generally* McCarthy, *Trademarks and Unfair Competition* § 5:10, which may be proven by either direct or circumstantial evidence. As to those marks registered under the Lanham Act, the registration constitutes prima facie evidence of trademark validity. *See* Section 33(a), 15 U.S.C. § 1115(a); *see generally* McCarthy, *supra*, § 11:16, § 15:12.

In addition, plaintiff must establish that defendant's use of the eight illustrations is trademark infringement. Under Section 32(1) of the Act, a cause of action for infringement of a registered mark exists where a person uses the mark "in connection with the sale . . . or advertising of any goods . . . [where] such use is likely to cause confusion, or to cause mistake, or to deceive." 15 U.S.C. § 1114(1). With respect to the unregistered illustrations, plaintiff may succeed under Section 43(a), a broadly worded provision which creates a federal cause of action for false designation of origin or false representation of goods or services. *Boston Professional Hockey Association, Inc. v. Dallas Cap & Emblem Manufacturing, Inc.*, 510 F.2d 1004, 1010 (5th Cir.), *cert. denied*, 423 U.S. 868 (1975); *Joshua Meier Co. v. Albany Novelty Manufacturing Co.*, 236 F.2d 144, 147 (2d Cir. 1956). As a general rule, the same facts which support an action for trademark infringement — facts indicating likelihood of confusion — will support an action for unfair competition under Section 43(a). *Dallas Cap, supra*, 510 F.2d at 1010; *see American Footwear Corp. v. General Footwear Co., Ltd.*, 609 F.2d 655, 665 (2d Cir. 1979). Likelihood of confusion is a factual inquiry, depending on a host of factors, no one of which is controlling. *E.g., Mushroom Makers, Inc. v. R. G. Barry Corporation*, 580 F.2d 44 (2d Cir. 1978), *cert. denied*, 439 U.S. 1116 (1979).

Contrary to what the parties suggested in their motion papers, and even though some of plaintiff's illustrations have been registered under the Lanham Act, defendant is unwilling to concede that any of the illustrations in issue are valid trademarks. Nor is defendant prepared to admit that there would be a likelihood of confusion arising from its use of those illustrations and marks in connection with its own Peter Rabbit publication. Because the present record does not permit a finding that the necessary elements of trademark infringement — secondary meaning and likelihood of confusion — exist, the plaintiff's motion for summary judgment must be denied. *See, e. g. Syntex Laboratories, Inc. v. Norwich Pharmacal Co.*, 315 F. Supp. 45 (S.D.N.Y. 1970) (granting plaintiff's motion for preliminary injunction but denying plaintiff's motion for summary judgment), *aff'd*, 437 F.2d 556 (2d Cir. 1971) (affirming injunctive relief); *National Color Laboratories, Inc. v. Philip's Foto Co.*, 273 F. Supp. 1002 (S.D.N.Y. 1967); *see generally* McCarthy, *supra*, § 32:36.

II. Defendant's Claim to Publish Freely

Defendant contends that the disputed questions of fact requiring denial of plaintiff's motion need not be reached to find in defendant's favor. Defendant argues that its use of the illustrations and marks is legally protected because they are part of copyrightable works now in the public domain. This argument is not persuasive. The fact that a copyrightable character or design has fallen into the public domain should not preclude protection under the trademark laws so long as it is shown to have acquired independent trademark significance, identifying in some way the source or sponsorship of the goods. *See Wyatt Earp Enterprises v. Sackman, Inc.,* 157 F. Supp. 621 (S.D.N.Y. 1958). Because the nature of the property right conferred by copyright is significantly different from that of trademark, trademark protection should be able to co-exist, and possibly to overlap, with copyright protection without posing preemption difficulties. As the Fifth Circuit persuasively reasoned in *Boston Professional Hockey Association, Inc. v. Dallas Cap & Emblem Manufacturing, Inc.,* 510 F.2d 1004, 1014 (5th Cir.), *cert. denied,* 423 U.S. 868 (1975):

> A trademark is a property right which is acquired by use. *Trade-Mark Cases,* C origin
> 100 U.S. 82 (1879). It differs substantially from a copyright, in both its legal
> genesis and its scope of federal protection. The legal cornerstone for the
> protection of copyrights is Article I, section 8, clause 8 of the Constitution. In
> the case of a copyright, an individual creates a unique design and, because the
> Constitutional fathers saw fit to encourage creativity, he can secure a copyright
> for his creation for a [limited period of time]. After the expiration of the
> copyright, his creation becomes part of the public domain. In the case of a
> trademark, however, the process is reversed. An individual selects a word or
> design that might otherwise be in the public domain to represent his business
> or product. If that word or design comes to symbolize his product or business
> in the public mind, the individual acquires a property right in the mark. The
> acquisition of such a right through use represents the passage of a word or
> design out of the public domain into the protective ambits of trademark law.
> Under the provisions of the Lanham Act, the owner of a mark acquires a
> protectable [sic] property interest in his mark through registration and use.

Dual protection under copyright and trademark laws is particularly appropriate for graphic representations of characters. A character deemed an artistic creation deserving copyright protection, *see Walt Disney Productions v. Air Pirates,* 581 F.2d 751 (9th Cir. 1978), *cert. denied,* 439 U.S. 1132 (1979), may also serve to identify the creator, thus meriting protection under theories of trademark or unfair competition, *see Edgar Rice Burroughs, Inc. v. Manns Theaters,* 195 U.S.P.Q. 159 (C.D. Cal. 1976); *Patten v. Superior Talking Pictures,* 8 F. Supp. 196 (S.D.N.Y. 1934); *see generally* Waldheim, *Characters — May They Be Kidnapped?* 55 T.M.R. 1022 (1965). Indeed, because of their special value in distinguishing goods and services, names and pictorial representations of characters are often registered as trademarks under the Lanham Act. 5 U.S.C. §§ 1052 & 1053; *See* Brylawski, *Protection of Characters — Sam Spade Revisited,* 22 Bull. Soc. Cr. 77 (1974); Adams, *Superman, Mickey Mouse and Gerentology,* 64 T.M.R. 183 (1974).[3]

Plaintiff correctly admits that, under *G. Ricordi v. Haendler,* 194 F.2d 914 (2d Cir. 1952) (L. Hand, J.), defendant is entitled to reproduce the contents of the seven public domain works as they were originally published. But as Judge Hand also acknowledged in *G. Ricordi,* the reproduction of a public domain work may result in unfair competition if the party goes beyond mere copying. The defendant in *G. Ricordi* had made an exact photographic reproduction of the book in question. Here, defendant assembled a new book consisting of multiple stories, and embellished the cover and interior with plaintiff's character illustrations in a way in which those illustrations were never used in the public domain books.

---

[3] Some commentators have suggested that trademark and unfair competition theories might serve to protect a character beyond the term of copyright applicable to the underlying work. This provocative question need not be reached, since plaintiff does not seek to establish exclusive trademark rights in the characters themselves but only to protect its limited right to use specific illustrations of those characters.

If any of these illustrations, including the "sitting rabbit" design, has come to identify Warne publications, defendant's use of it may lead the public to believe that defendant's different, and allegedly inferior, publication has been published by or is somehow associated with plaintiff. This kind of danger of misrepresentation as to the source of copied public domain material may establish a claim for unfair competition. *See Desclee & Cie, S. A. v. Nemmers,* 190 F. Supp. 381, 390 (E.D. Wis. 1961).

Defendant argues, however, that it has the right to copy the covers as well as the contents of the original books. Relying on *Triangle Publications, Inc. v. Knight-Ridder Newspapers, Inc.,* 445 F. Supp. 875 (S.D. Fla. 1978), and *Nimmer on Copyright,* defendant contends that a book cover should be deemed a copyrightable component of the copyrighted book. Once copyright protection ends, it contends, the entire book should be free to copy.

In principle, defendant seems correct. Covers of books as well as their contents may be entitled to copyright protection. But defendant exaggerates the significance of its logic. None of the authorities it relies upon suggests that trademark and copyright protection are mutually exclusive or that the fate of a book cover is necessarily wedded to the fate of the underlying work. Professor Nimmer suggests only that, where a cover is sufficiently original to merit copyright protection, the copyright applicable to the underlying work should *extend* to the cover. Thus, for example, a separate copyright registration should be unnecessary for the cover of a periodical. M. Nimmer, 1 *Nimmer on Copyright* § 2.04[D], at 2-50. In *Triangle Publications,* the purpose of finding copyrightability of a cover was similarly limited. There, plaintiff sought to enjoin defendant from copying the cover of its magazine for use in an advertisement designed to distinguish defendant's magazine from the plaintiff's. The court held that the cover fell within the purview of the copyright laws and that the "fair use" exception of copyright protection, now codified in 17 U.S.C. § 107, should therefore apply to permit defendant's comparative advertising use.

Furthermore, the rule urged by defendant — that copyrightable book covers may not obtain trademark or unfair competition protection — would permit incongruous results: a book cover lacking sufficient originality to warrant copyright protection could be protected for a potentially unlimited duration under the trademark laws, while covers revealing great artistry or ingenuity would be limited to the duration of the copyright. The better rule would protect all book covers according to the same standards that govern traditional trade dress or packaging cases. *See Sub-Contractors Register, Inc. v. McGovern's Contractors & Builders Manual, Inc.,* 69 F. Supp. 507, 511 (S.D.N.Y. 1946), *citing with approval, E. P. Dutton & Co. v. Cupples,* 117 App. Div. 172, 102 N.Y.S. 309 (1st Dept. 1907). Thus, the proper factual inquiry in this case is not whether the cover illustrations were once copyrightable and have fallen into the public domain, but whether they have acquired secondary meaning, identifying Warne as the publisher or sponsor of goods bearing those illustrations, and if so, whether defendant's use of these illustrations in "packaging" or "dressing" its editions is likely to cause confusion. Summary judgment is an inappropriate vehicle for determining these questions.

Defendant's "fair use" defense based on Section 33(b)(4) of the Lanham Act, 15 U.S.C. § 1115(b)(4), is also unpersuasive.[4] First, as defendant admits, whether a party is making "fair use" of another's trademark is generally a question of fact, precluding summary judgment. *See Laura Secord Candy Shops Ltd.*

---

[4] Section 33(b)(4) provides a defense to a charge of infringement if the use is "otherwise than as a trade or service mark . . . of a term or device which is descriptive of

v. Barton's Candy Corp., 368 F. Supp. 851 (N.D. Ill. 1973). <u>Second, it is not at</u> <u>all clear that fair use analysis is applicable to the facts at bar</u>. The fair use doctrine is typically invoked in comparative advertising cases where use of another's mark is necessary to describe truthfully a characteristic of the defendant's product. *See Societe Comptoir De L'Industrie Cotonniere Establissements Boussac v. Alexander's Department Stores, Inc.,* 299 F.2d 33 (2d Cir. 1962); *Herbert Products, Inc. v. S & H Industries, Inc.,* 200 U.S.P.Q. 247 (E.D.N.Y. 1977). Certainly, it cannot be said that defendant is using the illustrations for comparative advertising as that concept is generally understood. Nor is it clear that defendant's use of these illustrations is necessary to the full and effective exploitation of the public domain works. Defendant twice changed the cover of its Peter Rabbit book, suggesting that the "sitting rabbit" — which has been abandoned — was never necessary for its cover. With respect to the seven original cover illustrations, <u>the fact that other publishers have reproduced Miss</u> <u>Potter's stories without copying the covers suggests they may not be crucial to the</u> <u>successful exploitation of the works</u>. And, contrary to what defendant contends, the cover illustrations are not analogous to titles of public domain works, which, Professor Nimmer suggests, may be essential to effective distribution of the works. 1 *Nimmer on Copyright* § 2.16. <u>A title is generally the primary identifier</u> <u>of a literary work</u>; <u>the cover illustrations are not.</u> Of course, as noted at the outset, if the illustrations merely identify Miss Potter and her works, plaintiff will have no claim to trademark protection. <u>If, however, plaintiff can establish a</u> <u>specialized secondary meaning — that the illustrations represent Warne's</u> <u>goodwill and reputation as the source of children's books and other products —</u> <u>it will have a protectible trademark interest, except to the extent that the covers</u> <u>contain material necessary to identify the book itself.</u> Resolution of these questions must await trial.

The foregoing should not be construed to suggest that plaintiff will have an easy task at trial. Because the claimed marks are derived from or are similar in appearance to the illustrations in the text of the books, they may well prove to be "weak" marks. <u>As a general rule, weak or descriptive marks are accorded less</u> <u>protection than inherently distinctive marks.</u> *See generally* McCarthy, *supra,* § 11.24. Plaintiff must, however, be given an opportunity to meet this relatively greater burden by producing evidence of consumer recognition and likelihood of confusion with respect to each of the marks in dispute.[5]

---

and used fairly and in good faith only to describe to users the goods or services of such party, or their geographic origin." 15 U.S.C. § 1115(b)(4).

[5] As noted at the outset, plaintiff contends that defendant's use of its cover illustrations violates the New York anti-dilution statute. General Business Law § 368-d. Although it may be that a cause of action for dilution of a trademark is governed by somewhat more lenient standards than those provided by the Lanham Act, *see* Montellito v. Nina of California, Inc., 335 F. Supp. 1288, 1296 (S.D.N.Y. 1972), *citing* Renofab Process Corp. v. Renotex Corp., 158 N.Y.S.2d 70, 77 (N.Y. Sup. 1956), plaintiff is not entitled to summary judgment on this theory. The dilution doctrine embodied in Section 368-d presupposes the existence of a strong, well-recognized mark, which would merit protection even in the absence of likelihood of confusion. *See* McCarthy, *supra,* § 24:13. Plaintiff has yet to establish it has valid trademark rights in the character illustrations in question. Moreover, the applicability of Section 368-d to similar, competitive products like the books here in issue is doubtful. *See* Ives Laboratories, Inc. v. Darby Drug Co., Inc., 455 F. Supp. 939 (E.D.N.Y. 1978); *see generally* McCarthy, *supra,* §§ 24:13, 24:15.

The motions for summary judgment are denied. The parties will complete discovery within ninety days of this order, at which time the case will be set down for trial.

So ordered.

E. DISTINCTIONS: CHATTELS

CHAMBERLAIN v. FELDMAN
300 N.Y. 135, 89 N.E.2d 863 (1949)

DESMOND, JUDGE. In 1876, Samuel L. Clemens, under his pen name of "Mark Twain", wrote a story entitled "A Murder, A Mystery and A Marriage", and in the same year offered the manuscript to William Dean Howells, editor of the Atlantic Monthly, for publication. There followed, during the same year, some correspondence between Twain and Howells, in which was discussed an unusual project which the author had in mind: he proposed that a number of other famous writers of the period (such as Bret Harte and Howells himself) be enlisted, each to write his own final chapter for the work, so that for the mystery set up in the first few chapters, each author would compose a solution, in addition to, or in competition with Twain's own denouement. In other words, as planned by Twain, there was to be a common plot for the story, with a number of different endings. For one reason or another, including the reluctance of famous writers to dance to a rival's music, Twain's pet scheme came to nothing. Twenty years later, an entry in Twain's diary dated March 18, 1897, records a rather vague hope of the author to "make a skeleton novelette plot and write all the stories myself" or use it as the basis for a prize story competition. Whether that entry referred to "A Murder, A Mystery and A Marriage" we do not know, but there is undisputed proof, credited by both courts below, that when Mark Twain died in 1910, the manuscript of "A Murder, A Mystery and A Marriage" was not found among his effects and had never been published anywhere, by anyone.

In 1945, defendant Feldman bought the original manuscript (holographic and signed) at an auction sale, in New York City, of the rare books and manuscripts that had been in the possession, during his life, of Dr. James Brentano Clemens (no kin of Mark Twain) and had passed by inheritance to Dr. Clemens' wife. How Dr. Clemens came to have the writing is unknown. Mr. Feldman sought permission from plaintiffs, who are the present owners of all literary property formerly belonging to Mark Twain and not otherwise disposed of, to publish the work, but permission was refused. Defendant Feldman went ahead with the publication, however, and this suit was brought to enjoin him from reproducing or publishing the story, in any way. The complaint prays also for a direction to defendant to cancel a purported statutory copyright entered by defendant in the office of the Federal Register of Copyrights. It is not claimed that this statutory copyrighting, or attempt at such, was with the permission of plaintiffs, or any of them.

The trial court was of the opinion that "it must be presumed that its transfer [by Twain] was legal and that all rights in connection with it have passed to defendant, the ultimate purchaser." The trial court therefore made a finding that Twain during his lifetime had transferred and conveyed the manuscript, and that such transfer and conveyance "was made without any reservation of his [Twain's] right to publish or reproduce the same." Under the rule of *Pushman v. New York Graphic Soc.*, 287 N.Y. 302, 39 N.E.2d 249, and many older authorities, such an unrestricted transfer of this fictional manuscript (if it ever occurred) would probably have carried with it, and amounted to, a transfer of the common-law copyright and right to reproduce. On the trial therefore, the complaint was dismissed on the merits.

On appeal, however, the Appellate Division reversed the findings below, and made new fact findings of its own. It concluded that "it is impossible to spell out from the known conduct of the author that there was a voluntary transfer of the manuscript to anyone which carried with it the privilege of publication." 274 App. Div. 515, 518, 84 N.Y.S.2d 713, 715. In other words, the Appellate Division, noting that there was no direct evidence of any unrestricted transfer during the author's lifetime, found no basis for presuming or inferring such a grant by Twain, much less for presuming or inferring that such a transfer, or a series of transfers, all unrestricted, had carried the paper into the ownership and possession of Dr. James Brentano Clemens. Putting its views into a formal decision, the Appellate Division made new findings of fact to the effect that during Twain's lifetime the manuscript had been rejected, for publication, by the *Atlantic Monthly* and William Dean Howells, and that Twain "finally regarded the manuscript as unsuitable and never intended it for publication." The finding just quoted, with others made by the Appellate Division, amounts to a determination of fact that neither the author nor his successors in interest ever granted to anyone the literary property in "A Murder, A Mystery and A Marriage". The Appellate Division therefore directed judgment for plaintiffs, which judgment perpetually restrained defendant from publishing, producing or reproducing the story.

Under familiar rules, Civil Practice Act, § 605; *Pocket Books, Inc. v. Meyers,* 292 N.Y. 58, 54 N.E.2d 6, we are, because of the reversal and the making of new findings by the Appellate Division, required to determine whether the weight of evidence lies with one or the other set of findings. From the proofs briefly referred to herein, and other convincing items in the record, we conclude that the great weight of evidence is that Mark Twain never parted with the publication rights to this novelette or plot, and that neither defendant nor anyone else ever acquired them. (In coming to that conclusion we do not rely, since the Appellate Division made no finding in this connection, on any of the indications that this material was only a plot or outline and never really finished).

With the facts in that posture, little problem remains. The common-law copyright, or right of first publication, is a right different from that of ownership of the physical paper; the first of those rights does not necessarily pass with the second; and "the separate common law copyright or control of the right to reproduce belongs to the artist or author until disposed of by him and will be protected by the courts" see *Pushman v. New York Graphic Soc.,* 287 N.Y. 302, 307, 39 N.E.2d 249, 250 *supra,* and cases cited thereat; see similarly, as to statutory copyright, U.S. Code, tit. 17, § 27, 17 U. S. C. A. § 27. Since it has here been found to be the fact that, however the manuscript left the possession of the author, he never intended that it be published, it follows that defendant could not have bought the publication rights.

A recent commentary on this case, 62 Harv. L. Rev. 1406-1407, suggests that it may be contrary to sound policy to keep meritorious literary achievement out of the public domain for so long a time as is here involved. Without expressing any views of our own as to the advisability of permitting literary flowers so to blush unseen, we state our agreement with the last sentence of that Law Review article, in which it is pointed out that any such change of public policy must be the doing of the Legislature.

The judgment should be affirmed, with costs.

Loughran, Ch. J., and Lewis, Conway, Dye, Fuld and Bromley, JJ., concur.

Judgment affirmed.

QUESTIONS

1. The court speaks of a presumption that, under state law, copyright is transferred along with a transfer of the physical object. To what sources does a common law court turn to create such a presumption? Does it reflect the likely intention of the parties? Does it reflect a broader social policy?

2. Would the result in *Chamberlain v. Feldman* have been different if the manuscript had been discovered among Mr. Howells' papers in the *Atlantic Monthly* office?

3. Under common law copyright, it was generally understood that the author of a letter retained the copyright while the physical object was the property of the recipient. Is that consistent with the presumption noted in Question 1 *supra?*

4. Does the recipient of a letter have a duty to preserve it, in order that the writer might exercise the right of reproduction?

5. Consult § 202 of the 1976 Act (which became generally effective on January 1, 1978). How would *Chamberlain v. Feldman* be decided today, assuming that all of the incidents took place after January 1, 1978? How would it be decided today, assuming that all of the incidents took place before January 1, 1978 but that the lawsuit was brought thereafter?

6. If, in your historical researches, you were to unearth a letter written by Miles Standish to Priscilla Alden, would you feel free to publish it without concern for copyright infringement? If not, how would you go about securing legal immunity for your publication? Is § 202 of the Copyright Act in the public interest?

7. Under § 202 of the 1976 Act, transfer of the object does not "of itself" transfer the copyright. Transfer of the copyright does not transfer the object "in the absence of an agreement." What is the difference, if any, between "of itself" and "in the absence of an agreement"? That is, can there ever be circumstances when, even in the absence of an agreement, the transfer of ownership in the physical object would be deemed also to transfer ownership of the copyright? Could, for example, the purchaser of a canvas prove that, although nothing was said about copyright at the time of the transfer of the canvas, the right to reproduce the painting was also conveyed, because that was the unwritten understanding pursuant to a trade custom among local art dealers? (Would such a custom, in any event, become part of "an agreement" between buyer and seller, or does that phrase contemplate a writing?)

Section 202 must be read in conjunction with § 109 which provides that rights of copyright do not limit the right of the owner of a particular lawfully made copy or phonorecord to sell or otherwise dispose of such chattel. The House Report explains this provision as follows:

HOUSE REPORT

H.R. Rep. No. 94-1476, 94th Cong., 2d Sess. 79 (1976)

Section 109(a) restates and confirms the principle that, where the copyright owner has transferred ownership of a particular copy or phonorecord of a work, the person to whom the copy or phonorecord is transferred is entitled to dispose of it by sale, rental, or any other means. Under this principle, which has been established by the court decisions and section 27 of the present law, the copyright owner's exclusive right of public distribution would have no effect upon anyone who owns "a particular copy or phonorecord lawfully made under this title" and who wishes to transfer it to someone else or to destroy it.

Thus, for example, the outright sale of an authorized copy of a book frees it from any copyright control over its resale price or other conditions of its future disposition. A library that has acquired ownership of a copy is entitled to lend it under any conditions it chooses to impose. This does not mean that conditions on future disposition of copies or phonorecords, imposed by a contract between their buyer and seller, would be unenforceable between the parties as a breach of contract, but it does mean that they could not be enforced by an action for infringement of copyright. Under section 202 however, the owner of the physical copy or phonorecord cannot reproduce or perform the copyrighted work publicly without the copyright owner's consent.

To come within the scope of section 109(a), a copy or phonorecord must have been "lawfully made under this title," though not necessarily with the copyright owner's authorization. For example, any resale of an illegally "pirated" phonorecord would be an infringement, but the disposition of a phonorecord legally made under the compulsory licensing provisions of section 115 would not.

Chapter 2

COPYRIGHTABLE SUBJECT MATTER

A. IN GENERAL

§ 102. Subject matter of copyright: In general *

(a) Copyright protection subsists, in accordance with this title, in original works of authorship fixed in any tangible medium of expression, now known or later developed, from which they can be perceived, reproduced, or otherwise communicated, either directly or with the aid of a machine or device. Works of authorship include the following categories:

    (1) literary works;
    (2) musical works, including any accompanying words;
    (3) dramatic works, including any accompanying music;
    (4) pantomimes and choreographic works;
    (5) pictorial, graphic, and sculptural works;
    (6) motion pictures and other audiovisual works; and
    (7) sound recordings.

HOUSE REPORT

H.R. Rep. No. 94-1476, 94th Cong., 2d Sess. 51-53 (1976)

"Original works of authorship"

The two fundamental criteria of copyright protection — originality and fixation in tangible form — are restated in the first sentence of this cornerstone provision. The phrase "original works of authorship," which is purposely left undefined, is intended to incorporate without change the standard of originality established by the courts under the present copyright statute. This standard does not include requirements of novelty, ingenuity, or esthetic merit, and there is no intention to enlarge the standard of copyright protection to require them.

In using the phrase "original works of authorship," rather than "all the writings of an author" now in section 4 of the statute, the committee's purpose is to avoid exhausting the constitutional power of Congress to legislate in this field, and to eliminate the uncertainties arising from the latter phrase. Since the present statutory language is substantially the same as the empowering language of the Constitution, a recurring question has been whether the statutory and the constitutional provisions are coextensive. If so, the courts would be faced with the alternative of holding copyrightable something that Congress clearly did not intend to protect, or of holding constitutionally incapable of copyright something that Congress might one day want to protect. To avoid these equally undesirable results, the courts have indicated that "all the writings of an author" under the present statute is narrower in scope than the "writings" of "authors" referred to in the Constitution. The bill avoids this dilemma by using a different phrase — "original works of authorship" — in characterizing the general subject matter of statutory copyright protection.

---

* Material in this format, unless otherwise indicated, will comprise sections of the 1976 Act, Pub. L. 94-553, 94th Cong., Title 17, U.S.C.

The history of copyright law has been one of gradual expansion in the types of works accorded protection, and the subject matter affected by this expansion has fallen into two general categories. In the first, scientific discoveries and technological developments have made possible new forms of creative expression that never existed before. In some of these cases the new expressive forms — electronic music, film-strips, and computer programs, for example — could be regarded as an extension of copyrightable subject matter Congress had already intended to protect, and were thus considered copyrightable from the outset without the need of new legislation. In other cases, such as photographs, sound recordings, and motion pictures, statutory enactment was deemed necessary to give them full recognition as copyrightable works.

Authors are continually finding new ways of expressing themselves, but it is impossible to foresee the forms that these new expressive methods will take. The bill does not intend either to freeze the scope of copyrightable technology or to allow unlimited expansion into areas completely outside the present congressional intent. Section 102 implies neither that that subject matter is unlimited nor that new forms of expression within that general area of subject matter would necessarily be unprotected.

The historic expansion of copyright has also applied to forms of expression which, although in existence for generations or centuries, have only gradually come to be recognized as creative and worthy of protection. The first copyright statute in this country, enacted in 1790, designated only "maps, charts, and books"; major forms of expression such as music, drama, and works of art achieved specific statutory recognition only in later enactments. Although the coverage of the present statute is very broad, and would be broadened further by the explicit recognition of all forms of choreography, there are unquestionably other areas of existing subject matter that this bill does not propose to protect but that future Congresses may want to.

Fixation in tangible form

As a basic condition of copyright protection, the bill perpetuates the existing requirement that a work be fixed in a "tangible medium of expression," and adds that this medium may be one "now known or later developed," and that the fixation is sufficient if the work "can be perceived, reproduced, or otherwise communicated, either directly or with the aid of a machine or device." This broad language is intended to avoid the artificial and largely unjustifiable distinctions, derived from cases such as *White-Smith Publishing Co. v. Apollo Co.*, 209 U.S. 1 (1908), under which statutory copyrightability in certain cases has been made to depend upon the form or medium in which the work is fixed. Under the bill it makes no difference what the form, manner, or medium of fixation may be — whether it is in words, numbers, notes, sounds, pictures, or any other graphic or symbolic indicia, whether embodied in a physical object in written, printed, photographic, sculptural, punched, magnetic, or any other stable form, and whether it is capable of perception directly or by means of any machine or device "now known or later developed."

Under the bill, the concept of fixation is important since it not only determines whether the provisions of the statute apply to a work, but it also represents the dividing line between common law and statutory protection. As will be noted in more detail in connection with section 301, an unfixed work of authorship, such as an improvisation or an unrecorded choreographic work, performance, or broadcast, would continue to be subject to protection under State common law or statute, but would not be eligible for Federal statutory protection under section 102.

The bill seeks to resolve, through the definition of "fixation" in section 101, the status of live broadcasts — sports, news coverage, live performances of music, etc. — that are reaching the public in unfixed form but that are simultaneously being recorded. When a football game is being covered by four television cameras, with a director guiding the activities of the four cameramen and choosing which of their electronic images are sent out to the public and in what order, there is little doubt that what the cameramen and the director are doing constitutes "authorship." The further question to be considered is whether there has been a fixation. If the images and sounds to be broadcast are first recorded (on a video tape, film, etc.) and then transmitted, the recorded work would be considered a "motion picture" subject to statutory protection against unauthorized reproduction or retransmission of the broadcast. If the program content is transmitted live to the public while being recorded at the same time, the case would be treated the same; the copyright owner would not be forced to rely on common law rather than statutory rights in proceeding against an infringing user of the live broadcast.

Thus, assuming it is copyrightable — as a "motion picture" or "sound recording," for example — the content of a live transmission should be accorded statutory protection if it is being recorded simultaneously with its transmission. On the other hand, the definition of "fixation" would exclude from the concept purely evanescent or transient reproductions such as those projected briefly on a screen, shown electronically on a television or other cathode ray tube, or captured momentarily in the "memory" of a computer.

Under the first sentence of the definition of "fixed" in section 101, a work would be considered "fixed in a tangible medium of expression" if there has been an authorized embodiment in a copy or phonorecord and if that embodiment "is sufficiently permanent or stable" to permit the work "to be perceived, reproduced, or otherwise communicated for a period of more than transitory duration." The second sentence makes clear that, in the case of "a work consisting of sounds, images, or both, that are being transmitted," the work is regarded as "fixed" if a fixation is being made at the same time as the transmission.

Under this definition "copies" and "phonorecords" together will comprise all of the material objects in which copyrightable works are capable of being fixed. The definitions of these terms in section 101, together with their usage in section 102 and throughout the bill, reflect a fundamental distinction between the "original work" which is the product of "authorship" and the multitude of material objects in which it can be embodied. Thus, in the sense of the bill, a "book" is not a work of authorship, but is a particular kind of "copy." Instead, the author may write a "literary work," which in turn can be embodied in a wide range of "copies" and "phonorecords," including books, periodicals, computer punch cards, microfilm, tape recordings, and so forth. It is possible to have an "original work of authorship" without having a "copy" or "phonorecord" embodying it, and it is also possible to have a "copy" or "phonorecord" embodying something that does not qualify as an "original work of authorship." The two essential elements — original work and tangible object — must merge through fixation in order to produce subject matter copyrightable under the statute.

QUESTIONS

1. Is a live performance of music in a coffee house, simultaneously being tape recorded by the performer, within the coverage of the federal Copyright Act?

2. Is a lecture in a law school classroom protected under the federal Act? What if it is being tape recorded without the consent of the instructor? What if students are taking copious (but not verbatim) written notes?

3. Study the definitions of "copy" and "phonorecord" and "fixed" in § 101. What is the difference between a copy and a phonorecord? Can a copyrightable work be embodied in a material object other than these two formats?

B. KAPLAN, AN UNHURRIED VIEW OF COPYRIGHT 45-46 (1967)

Are there compositions which though original are too small to qualify for copyright or to figure as the subjects of actionable infringement? Some of Holmes's language suggests that any emanation of personality, however slight, any uncopied collocation, however slim, should be protected, and his abnegation of judicial responsibility for passing on the merit of intellectual productions points in the same direction.[25] So also does the appearance in the statute of so mean a category as "prints or labels used for articles of merchandise" [26] — though we must always beware of a false development of copyright law by a process of treating extreme applications as being normal, thus inviting applications even more extreme.[27] There are, on the other hand, definite indications of some rule *de minimis*.

Some have thought it inherent in the very notion of "personality," of spontaneity, that a copyright claimant must exceed the utterly stilted or trite, must satisfy some threshold requirement of "creativity." [28] And though Judge Frank pushed hard in the *Alfred Bell* case to show the theoretical protectibility of any original production, he still admitted that a variation, say, on a public domain work must be more than "trivial" to support copyright.[29] Judge Hand wrote to similar effect in the *National Comics* case.[30] Courts are disinclined to permit copyright to attach to short word sequences or to find plagiarism in the copying of such sequences; this lies close to the slogan that "titles" are not protected through copyright.[31] More generally it has been said that only substantial takings are actionable: Judge Hand would apply this to the appropriation of a separate scene or part of the dialogue of a play, and thought the same question of substantiality

---

[25] *See* Bleistein v. Donaldson Lithographing Co., 188 U.S. 239 (1903). . . .

[26] 17 U.S.C. § 5(k).

[27] *Cf.* Lord Robertson's remarks, dissenting in Walter v. Lane, [1900] A.C. 539, 561.

[28] *See* Register of Copyrights, Copyright Law Revision: Report on the General Revision of the U.S. Copyright Law, printed for the use of the House Comm. on the Judiciary, 87th Cong., 1st Sess., at 9 (Comm. Print 1961). *But see* Supplementary Report, COPYRIGHT LAW REVISION, PT. 6, at 3 (Comm. Print 1965) (89th Cong., 1st Sess.), where an express requirement of "creativity" is abandoned.

[29] Alfred Bell & Co., Ltd. v. Catalda Fine Arts, Inc., 191 F.2d 99, 103 (2d Cir. 1951).

[30] National Comics Pub., Inc. v. Fawcett Pub., Inc., 191 F.2d 594, 600 (2d Cir. 1951).

[31] *Cf.* Regulations of the Copyright Office, 37 C.F.R., ch. II, § 202.1(a) (1959). *See also* Nimmer, Copyright § 34 (1965). *But cf.* Heim v. Universal Pictures Co., Inc., 154 F.2d 480, 487 n.8 (2d Cir. 1946); Life Music, Inc. v. Wonderland Music Co., 241 F. Supp. 653, 656 (S.D.N.Y. 1965).

arose in adjudging infringement of any work.[32] We can, I think, conclude that to make the copyright turnstile revolve, the author should have to deposit more than a penny in the box, and some like measure ought to apply to infringement. Surely there is danger in trying to fence off small quanta of words or other collocations; these pass quickly into the idiom; to allow them copyright, particularly if aided by a doctrine of "unconscious" plagiarism, could set up untoward barriers to expression.

QUESTIONS

Are the following works copyrightable under the Copyright Act of 1976?

(a) A design of a cross (with arms of equal length) inside a circle.

(b) The rearrangement of the three color bars upon a flag.

(c) A slogan "Things Go Better with Glurp" (Glurp being a carbonated beverage).

(d) A drawing of the University Law School (to be used for display in the law building or in an advertising brochure for applicants).

(e) A snapshot of the Law School on a cloudy day.

(f) The Zapruder films of the assassination of President Kennedy.

(g) A Picasso "re-treatment" of a Velasquez painting of the members of the royal family in Spain.

(h) A three-dimensional replica, as statues, of the Velasquez painting.

(i) A black-and-white photocopy of the Velasquez painting.

(j) A printing of a long-lost play by Shakespeare (printed and performed in Shakespeare's time but only recently discovered after years of search and analysis by Professor Falstaff of the University's English Department).

(k) A translation of a Moliere play.

(l) A telephone book, derived by original gathering and collection of names, addresses and telephone numbers.

(m) A chart containing, in headings and columns, information about Latin American countries (e.g., capital, population, principal products, square miles), gathered from one encyclopedia.

(n) A map, derived from original exploration (or derived from collating several public domain maps of different age and size).

(o) An article in *Time* magazine about a current news event, derived from original investigation (or derived from other published news reports).

HOUSE REPORT

H.R. Rep. No. 94-1476, 94th Cong., 2d Sess. 53-56 (1976)

Categories of copyrightable works

The second sentence of section 102 lists seven broad categories which the concept of "works of authorship" is said to "include." The use of the word "include," as defined in section 101, makes clear that the listing is "illustrative and not limitative," and that the seven categories do not necessarily exhaust the scope of "original works of authorship" that the bill is intended to protect. Rather, the list sets out the general area of copyrightable subject matter, but with sufficient flexibility to free the courts from rigid or outmoded concepts of the scope of particular categories. The items are also overlapping in the sense that a work falling within one class may encompass works coming within some or all of the

---

[32] Nichols v. Universal Pictures Corp., 45 F.2d 119, 121 (2d Cir. 1930), *cert. denied,* 282 U.S. 902 (1931).

other categories. In the aggregate, the list covers all classes of works now specified in section 5 of title 17; in addition, it specifically enumerates "pantomimes and choreographic works".

Of the seven items listed, four are defined in section 101. The three undefined categories — "musical works," "dramatic works," and "pantomimes and choreographic works" — have fairly settled meanings. There is no need, for example, to specify the copyrightability of electronic or concrete music in the statute since the form of a work would no longer be of any importance, nor is it necessary to specify that "choreographic works" do not include social dance steps and simple routines.

The four items defined in section 101 are "literary works," "pictorial, graphic, and sculptural works," "motion pictures and audiovisual works", and "sound recordings." In each of these cases, definitions are needed not only because the meaning of the term itself is unsettled but also because the distinction between "work" and "material object" requires clarification. The term "literary works" does not connote any criterion of literary merit or qualitative value: it includes catalogs, directories, and similar factual, reference, or instructional works and compilations of data. It also includes computer data bases, and computer programs to the extent that they incorporate authorship in the programmer's expression of original ideas, as distinguished from the ideas themselves.

. . . .

Enactment of Public Law 92-140 in 1971 marked the first recognition in American copyright law of sound recordings as copyrightable works. As defined in section 101, copyrightable "sound recordings" are original works of authorship comprising an aggregate of musical, spoken, or other sounds that have been fixed in tangible form. The copyrightable work comprises the aggregation of sounds and not the tangible medium of fixation. Thus, "sound recordings" as copyrightable subject matter are distinguished from "phonorecords," the latter being physical objects in which sounds are fixed. They are also distinguished from any copyrighted literary, dramatic, or musical works that may be reproduced on a "phonorecord."

As a class of subject matter, sound recordings are clearly within the scope of the "writings of an author" capable of protection under the Constitution, and the extension of limited statutory protection to them was too long delayed. Aside from cases in which sounds are fixed by some purely mechanical means without originality of any kind, the copyright protection that would prevent the reproduction and distribution of unauthorized phonorecords of sound recordings is clearly justified.

The copyrightable elements in a sound recording will usually, though not always, involve "authorship" both on the part of the performers whose performance is captured and on the part of the record producer responsible for setting up the recording session, capturing and electronically processing the sounds, and compiling and editing them to make the final sound recording. There may, however, be cases where the record producer's contribution is so minimal that the performance is the only copyrightable element in the work, and there may be cases (for example, recordings of bird calls, sounds of racing cars, et cetera) where only the record producer's contribution is copyrightable.

Sound tracks of motion pictures, long a nebulous area in American copyright law, are specifically included in the definition of "motion pictures," and excluded in the definition of "sound recordings." To be a "motion picture," as defined, requires three elements: (1) a series of images, (2) the capability of showing the images in certain successive order, and (3) an impression of motion when the images are thus shown. Coupled with the basic requirements of original authorship and fixation in tangible form, this definition encompasses a wide range of cinematographic works embodied in films, tapes, video disks, and other media. However, it would not include: (1) unauthorized fixation of live performances or telecasts, (2) live telecasts that are not fixed simultaneously with their transmission, or (3) filmstrips and slide sets which, although consisting of a series of images intended to be shown in succession, are not capable of conveying an impression of motion.

On the other hand, the bill equates audiovisual materials such as filmstrips, slide sets, and sets of transparencies with "motion pictures" rather than with "pictorial, graphic, and sculptural works." Their sequential showing is closer to a "performance" than to a "display," and the definition of "audiovisual works," which applies also to "motion pictures," embraces works consisting of a series of related images that are by their nature, intended for showing by means of projectors or other devices.

QUESTION

Are the categories in § 102(a) discrete or overlapping? Watch for the substantive significance of these categories as you proceed through your study of the statute.

B. DERIVATIVE WORKS AND COMPILATIONS

§ 103. Subject matter of copyright: Compilations and derivative works

(a) The subject matter of copyright as specified by section 102 includes compilations and derivative works, but protection for a work employing preexisting material in which copyright subsists does not extend to any part of the work in which such material has been used unlawfully.

(b) The copyright in a compilation or derivative work extends only to the material contributed by the author of such work, as distinguished from the preexisting material employed in the work, and does not imply any exclusive right in the preexisting material. The copyright in such work is independent of, and does not affect or enlarge the scope, duration, ownership, or subsistence of, any copyright protection in the preexisting material.

HOUSE REPORT

H.R. Rep. No. 94-1476, 94th Cong., 2d Sess. 57-58 (1976)

Section 103 complements section 102: A compilation or derivative work is copyrightable if it represents an "original work of authorship" and falls within one or more of the categories listed in section 102. Read together, the two sections make plain that the criteria of copyrightable subject matter stated in section 102 apply with full force to works that are entirely original and to those containing preexisting material. Section 103(b) is also intended to define, more sharply and clearly than does section 7 of the present law, the important interrelationship and correlation between protection of preexisting and of "new" material in a particular work. The most important point here is one that is commonly misunderstood today: copyright in a "new version" covers only the material added by the later author, and has no effect one way or the other on the copyright or public domain status of the preexisting material.

Between them the terms "compilations" and "derivative works" which are defined in section 101, comprehend every copyrightable work that employs preexisting material or data of any kind. There is necessarily some overlapping between the two, but they basically represent different concepts. A "compilation" results from a process of selecting, bringing together, organizing, and arranging previously existing material of all kinds, regardless of whether the individual items in the material have been or ever could have been subject to copyright. A "derivative work," on the other hand, requires a process of recasting, transforming, or adapting "one or more preexisting works"; the "preexisting work" must come within the general subject matter of copyright set forth in section 102, regardless of whether it is or was ever copyrighted.

The second part of the sentence that makes up section 103(a) deals with the status of a compilation or derivative work unlawfully employing preexisting copyrighted material. In providing that protection does not extend to "any part of the work in which such material has been used unlawfully," the bill prevents an infringer from benefiting, through copyright protection, from committing an unlawful act, but preserves protection for those parts of the work that do not employ the preexisting work. Thus, an unauthorized translation of a novel could not be copyrighted at all, but the owner of copyright in an anthology of poetry could sue someone who infringed the whole anthology, even though the infringer proves that publication of one of the poems was unauthorized. Under this provision, copyright could be obtained as long as the use of the preexisting work was not "unlawful," even though the consent of the copyright owner had not been obtained. For instance, the unauthorized reproduction of a work might be "lawful" under the doctrine of fair use or an applicable foreign law, and if so the work incorporating it could be copyrighted.

KUDDLE TOY, INC. v. PUSSYCAT-TOY, INC.

183 USPQ 642 (E.D.N.Y. 1974)

[In the course of considering the copyrightability of a stuffed teddy bear, Judge Dooling was faced with the broad dicta in *Alfred Bell & Co. v. Catalda Fine Arts, Inc.,* p. 30 *supra.* Before finding that the bear in question had "[n]o touch of fresh authorship," he analyzed the *Bell* dicta as follows:]

Against this background Judge Frank's later opinion in *Alfred Bell & Co. v. Catalda Fine Arts, Inc., supra,* 191 F.2d 99, 90 USPQ 153, falls into place. Plaintiff had obtained copyrights on mezzotint engravings of eight paintings of the late 18th and early 19th centuries which were in the public domain. The laborious and highly skilled process of preparing mezzotint engravings is described in the proceeding below (74 F. Supp. 973, 75 USPQ 66); the very idea of the mezzotint is to reproduce as precisely as the craftsman can manage the impression of the original public-domain paintings. The Court below noted (74 F. Supp. at 975, 75 USPQ at 67-68) that, since the engraver had to use an individual engraving conception and exercise judgment, no two engravers could produce identical interpretations of the same oil painting and a color-photographically exact reproduction of the painting could not be produced by the method in question. What the Court considered that it had to decide in *Bell v. Catalda* was really whether such difficult and elevated copying was itself sufficiently an exercise of authorship — an originality in copying — to be independently the subject of a copyright. Such engravings might fall under Section 5(h) as "Reproductions of a work of art," and certainly they were within the idea of so much of Section 7 as treated as "new works subject to copyright" "versions of works in the public domain . . . ." Section 7 continued, ". . . but the publication of any such new works shall not . . . be construed to imply an exclusive right to such use of the original works . . . ." The Court in *Bell v. Catalda* concluded, as had the Court below, that the mezzotint craftsmen were the authors of what it was that they brought to the art of making excellently veracious copies, and so much they could copyright. It was just that that defendant purloined, using the plaintiff's plates, which carried plaintiff's notice of copyright. Defendant photographed the plates with continuous tone negatives, used color filters, etc., to prepare printing plates, and, simply, printed plaintiff's mezzotint etchings by the familiar color printing process. Nothing of mistaken or inadequate copying of old oil paintings was involved in *Bell v. Catalda*. The more nearly the mezzotints approached perfection of copying, the more brilliantly "original" within their own special art of copying they were: the "authorship" lay in the very art of the copying, and it was that artfulness of copying that the case protected, not any interest of any kind in the eight underlying oil paintings or in the mezzotints of them as copyrightable variants of the paintings and thus, as new works of art copyrightable as colored works of art. The mezzotint was a transformation of the original oil painting into a different medium of artistic presentation and of that transformation only the copyright owner was the author. The paintings remained wholly in the public domain completely accessible to other craftsmen who could produce other mezzotint engravings or color prints of the original paintings. The only thing protected was what was original with the plaintiffs, the mezzotint engravings as such.

When *Bell v. Catalda* is subdued to its facts, it is seen that it has nothing to do with limited "originality"; every line of the mezzotint was "original" with the engravers. It has nothing to do with imperfect or variant copying; it was a copy and the plaintiffs were the authors of an independently copyrightable copy where copying itself required new and genuine "authorship." It was not a tracing of an old map. It was not a copy of an old text, with advertent or inadvertent blunders. And *Bell v. Catalda* had nothing to do with modesty of originality or meanness of conception. It had to do only with whether an honest copy made in a new medium by a laborious process could be protected against color reprinting. The Court held that it was protected.

QUESTION

Why should a reproduction of a public domain work be eligible for copyright? Consider, on the one hand, a color postcard embodying a Picasso painting, and on the other hand, a newly typeset edition of a play by Shakespeare.

L. BATLIN & SON v. SNYDER

536 F.2d 486 (2d Cir. 1976)

Before KAUFMAN, CHIEF JUDGE, and FEINBERG, MANSFIELD, MULLIGAN, OAKES, TIMBERS, GURFEIN, VAN GRAAFEILAND, and MESKILL, CIRCUIT JUDGES.

OAKES, CIRCUIT JUDGE:

Appellants Jeffrey Snyder and Etna Products Co., Inc., his licensee, appeal from a preliminary injunction granted L. Batlin & Son, Inc. (Batlin), compelling appellants to cancel a recordation of a copyright with the United States Customs Service and restraining them from enforcing that copyright. The district court held, 394 F. Supp. 1389 (S.D.N.Y. 1975), as it had previously in *Etna Products Co. v. E. Mishan & Sons,* 75 Civ. 428 (S.D.N.Y. Feb. 13, 1975), that there was "little probability" that appellants' copyright "will be found valid in the trial on the merits" on the basis that any variations between appellants' copyrighted plastic bank and a cast iron bank in the public domain were merely "trivial," and hence appellants' bank insufficiently "original" to support a copyright. 394 F. Supp. at 1390, *citing Alfred Bell & Co. v. Catalda Fine Arts, Inc.,* 191 F.2d 99 (2d Cir. 1951). We agree with the district court and therefore affirm the judgment granting the preliminary injunction.

Uncle Sam mechanical banks have been on the American scene at least since June 8, 1886, when Design Patent No. 16,723, issued on a toy savings bank of its type. The basic delightful design has long since been in the public domain. The banks are well documented in collectors' books and known to the average person interested in Americana. A description of the bank is that Uncle Sam, dressed in his usual stove pipe hat, blue full dress coat, starred vest and red and white striped trousers, and leaning on his umbrella, stands on a four- or five-inch wide base, on which sits his carpetbag. A coin may be placed in Uncle Sam's extended hand. When a lever is pressed, the arm lowers, and the coin falls into the bag, while Uncle Sam's whiskers move up and down. The base has an embossed American eagle on it with the words "Uncle Sam" on streamers above it, as well as the word "Bank" on each side. Such a bank is listed in a number of collectors' books, the most recent of which may be F. H. Griffith, Mechanical Banks (1972 ed.) where it was listed as No. 280, and is said to be not particularly rare.

Appellant Jeffrey Snyder doing business as "J.S.N.Y." obtained a registration of copyright on a plastic "Uncle Sam bank" in Class G ("Works of Art") as "sculpture" on January 23, 1975. According to Snyder's affidavit, in January, 1974, he had seen a cast metal antique Uncle Sam bank with an overall height of the figure and base of 11 inches.[1] In April, 1974, he flew to Hong Kong to arrange for the design and eventual manufacture of replicas of the bank as Bicentennial items, taking the cast metal Uncle Sam bank with him. His Hong Kong buying agent selected a firm, "Unitoy," to make the plastic "prototype" because of its price and the quality of its work. Snyder wanted his bank to be made of plastic and to be shorter than the cast metal sample "in order to fit into the required price range and quality and quantity of material to be used." The figure of Uncle Sam was thus shortened from 11 to nine inches, and the base shortened and narrowed. It was also decided, Snyder averred, to change the shape of the carpetbag and to include the umbrella in a one-piece mold for the Uncle Sam figure, "so as not to have a problem with a loose umbrella or a separate molding process." The Unitoy representative made his sketches while looking at the cast metal bank. After a "clay model" was made, a plastic "prototype" was approved by Snyder and his order placed in May, 1974. The plastic bank carried the legend "© Copyright J.S.N.Y." and was assertedly first "published" on October 15, 1974, before being filed with the Register of Copyrights in January, 1975.

Appellee Batlin is also in the novelty business and as early as August 9, 1974, ordered 30 cartons of cast iron Uncle Sam mechanical banks from Taiwan where

---

[1] No cast iron *antique* bank was introduced in evidence below. A cast metal *replica* bank was, and the court below, the parties, the witnesses, and this court have treated the case as if the appellants' plastic bank were to be compared to the cast metal replica.

its president had seen the bank made. When he became aware of the existence of a plastic bank, which he considered "an almost identical copy" of the cast iron bank, Batlin's trading company in Hong Kong procured a manufacturer and the president of Batlin ordered plastic copies also. Beginning in April, 1975, Batlin was notified by the United States Customs Service that the plastic banks it was receiving were covered by appellants' copyright. In addition the Customs Service was also refusing entry to cast iron banks previously ordered, according to the Batlin affidavit. Thus Batlin instituted suit for a judgment declaring appellants' copyright void and for damages for unfair competition and restraint of trade. The sole question on this appeal is whether Judge Metzner abused his discretion in granting Batlin a preliminary injunction. We find that he did not.

This court has examined both the appellants' plastic Uncle Sam bank made under Snyder's copyright and the uncopyrighted model cast iron mechanical bank which is itself a reproduction of the original public domain Uncle Sam bank. Appellant Snyder claims differences not only of size but also in a number of other very minute details: the carpetbag shape of the plastic bank is smooth, the iron bank rough; the metal bank bag is fatter at its base; the eagle on the front of the platform in the metal bank is holding arrows in his talons while in the plastic bank he clutches leaves, this change concededly having been made, however, because "the arrows did not reproduce well in plastic on a smaller size." The shape of Uncle Sam's face is supposedly different, as is the shape and texture of the hats, according to the Snyder affidavit. In the metal version the umbrella is hanging loose while in the plastic item it is included in the single mold. The texture of the clothing, the hairline, shape of the bow tie and of the shirt collar and left arm as well as the flag carrying the name on the base of the statue are all claimed to be different, along with the shape and texture of the eagles on the side. Many of these differences are not perceptible to the casual observer. Appellants make no claim for any difference based on the plastic mold lines in the Uncle Sam figure which are perceptible.

Our examination of the banks results in the same conclusion as that of Judge Metzner in *Etna Products,* the earlier case enjoining Snyder's copyright, that the Snyder bank is "extremely similar to the cast iron bank, save in size and material" with the only other differences, such as the shape of the satchel and the leaves in the eagle's talons being "by all appearances, minor." Similarities include, more importantly, the appearance and number of stripes on the trousers; buttons on the coat, and stars on the vest and hat, the attire and pose of Uncle Sam, the decor on his base and bag, the overall color scheme, the method of carpetbag opening, to name but a few. [The court below saw the banks and heard] conflicting testimony from opposing expert witnesses as to the substantiality or triviality of the variations and as to the skill necessary to make the plastic model. . . . The substance of appellee's expert's testimony on which the district judge evidently relied was that the variations found in appellants' plastic bank were merely "trivial" and that it was a reproduction of the metal bank made as simply as possible for the purposes of manufacture. In other words, there were no elements of difference that amounted to significant alteration or that had any purpose other than the functional one of making a more suitable (and probably less expensive) figure in the plastic medium.

. . . It has been the law of this circuit for at least 30 years that in order to obtain a copyright upon a reproduction of a work of art under 17 U.S.C. § 5(h) [2] that

---

[2] While appellant Snyder's copyright was obtained for a "Work of Art," it may be treated as one obtained for "reproductions of a work of art," Soptra Fabrics Corp. v.

the work "contain some substantial, not merely trivial originality ...." *Chamberlin v. Uris Sales Corp., supra,* 150 F.2d at 513.

Originality is, however, distinguished from novelty; there must be independent creation, but it need not be invention in the sense of striking uniqueness, ingeniousness, or novelty, since the Constitution differentiates "authors" and their "writings" from "inventors" and their "discoveries." *Alfred Bell & Co. v. Catalda Fine Arts, Inc., supra,* 191 F.2d at 100; *Runge v. Lee,* 441 F.2d 579, 581 (9th Cir.), *cert. denied,* 404 U.S. 887 (1971). Originality means that the work owes its creation to the author and this in turn means that the work must not consist of actual copying. *Alfred Bell & Co. v. Catalda Fine Arts, Inc., supra,* 191 F.2d at 102-03; *Sheldon v. Metro-Goldwyn Pictures Corp.,* 81 F.2d 49, 54 (2d Cir. 1936), *aff'd,* 309 U.S. 390 (1940). [3]

The test of originality is concededly one with a low threshold in that "[a]ll that is needed . . . is that the 'author' contributed something more than a 'merely trivial' variation, something recognizably 'his own.'" *Alfred Bell & Co. v. Catalda Fine Arts, Inc.,* 191 F.2d at 103. But as this court said many years ago, "[w]hile a copy of something in the public domain will not, if it be merely a copy, support a copyright, a distinguishable variation will...." *Gerlach-Barklow Co. v. Morris & Bendien, Inc.,* 23 F.2d 159, 161 (2d Cir. 1927).

Necessarily, none of these underlying principles is different in the case of "[r]eproductions of a work of art," 17 U.S.C. § 5(h), from the case of "[w]orks of art...," 17 U.S.C. § 5(g). . . .

. . . .

According to Professor Nimmer, moreover, "the mere reproduction of a work of art in a different medium should not constitute the required originality for the reason that no one can claim to have independently evolved any particular medium." [THE LAW OF COPYRIGHT at 94 (1975).] *See Millworth Converting Corp. v. Slifka,* 276 F.2d 443, 444-45 (2d Cir. 1960). *Cf. Gardenia Flowers, Inc. v. Joseph Markovitz, Inc.,* 280 F. Supp. 776, 781 (S.D.N.Y. 1968). Professor Nimmer refers to *Doran v. Sunset House Distributing Corp.,* 197 F. Supp. 940 (S.D. Cal. 1961), *aff'd,* 304 F.2d 251 (9th Cir. 1962), as suggesting "the ludicrous result that the first person to execute a public domain work of art in a different medium thereafter obtains a monopoly on such work in such medium, at least as to those persons aware of the first such effort." 1 M. NIMMER, *supra,* § 20.2, at 94. We do not follow the *Doran* case. We do follow the school of cases in this circuit and elsewhere supporting the proposition that to support a copyright there must be at least some substantial variation, not merely a trivial variation such as might occur in the translation to a different medium.

Nor can the requirement of originality be satisfied simply by the demonstration of "physical skill" or "special training" which, to be sure, Judge Metzner found was required for the production of the plastic molds that furnished the basis for appellants' plastic bank. A considerably *higher* degree of skill is required, true artistic skill, to make the reproduction copyrightable. Thus in

---

Stafford Knitting Mills, Inc., 490 F.2d 1092, 1094 (2d Cir. 1974), since errors in classification do not invalidate or impair copyright protection under this express language of 17 U.S.C. § 5.

[3] The only case that appears to be an exception to this rule is the "Hand of God" case. Alva Studios, Inc. v. Winninger, 177 F. Supp. 265 (S.D.N.Y. 1959) (exact scale artistic reproduction of highly complicated statue made with great precision was "original" as requiring "great skill and originality"). This case is discussed in the text *infra*.

Alfred Bell & Co. v. Catalda Fine Arts, Inc., supra, 191 F.2d at 104-05 n.22, Judge Frank pointed out that the mezzotint engraver's art there concerned required "great labour and talent" to effectuate the "management of light and shade . . . produced by different lines and . . .," means "very different from those employed by the painter or draughtsman from whom he copies. . . ." *See also Millworth Converting Corp. v. Slifka, supra* (fabric designer required one month of work to give three-dimensional color effect to flat surface). Here on the basis of appellants' own expert's testimony it took the Unitoy representative "[a]bout a day and a half, two days work" to produce the plastic mold sculpture from the metal Uncle Sam bank. If there be a point in the copyright law pertaining to reproductions at which sheer artistic skill and effort can act as a substitute for the requirement of substantial variation, it was not reached here.

Appellants rely heavily upon *Alva Studios, Inc. v. Winninger,* [177 F. Supp. 265 (S.D.N.Y. 1959)] the "Hand of God" case, where the court held that "great skill and originality [were required] to produce a scale reduction of a great work with exactitude." 177 F. Supp. at 267. There, the original sculpture was, "one of the most intricate pieces of sculpture ever created" with "[i]nnumerable planes, lines and geometric patterns . . . interdependent in [a] multi-dimensional work." *Id.* Originality was found by the district court to consist primarily in the fact that "[i]t takes 'an extremely skilled sculptor' many hours working directly in front of the original" to effectuate a scale reduction. *Id.* at 266. The court, indeed, found the exact replica to be so original, distinct, and creative as to constitute a work of art in itself. The complexity and exactitude there involved distinguishes that case amply from the one at bar. As appellants themselves have pointed out, there are a number of trivial differences or deviations from the original public domain cast iron bank in their plastic reproduction. Thus concededly the plastic version is not, and was scarcely meticulously produced to be, an exactly faithful reproduction. Nor is the creativity in the underlying work of art of the same order of magnitude as in the case of the "Hand of God." Rodin's sculpture is, furthermore, so unique and rare, and adequate public access to it such a problem that a significant public benefit accrues from its precise, artistic reproduction. No such benefit can be imagined to accrue here from the "knock-off" reproduction of the cast iron Uncle Sam bank. Thus appellants' plastic bank is neither in the category of exactitude required by *Alva Studios* nor in a category of substantial originality; it falls within what has been suggested by the amicus curiae is a copyright no-man's land.

Absent a genuine difference between the underlying work of art and the copy of it for which protection is sought, the public interest in promoting progress in the arts — indeed, the constitutional demand, *Chamberlin v. Uris Sales Corp., supra* — could hardly be served. To extend copyrightability to minuscule variations would simply put a weapon for harassment in the hands of mischievous copiers intent on appropriating and monopolizing public domain work. Even in *Mazer v. Stein, supra,* which held that the statutory terms "works of art" and "reproduction of works of art" (terms which are clearly broader than the earlier term "works of the fine arts") permit copyright of quite ordinary mass-produced items, the Court expressly held that the objects to be copyrightable, "must be original, that is, the author's tangible expression of his ideas." 347 U.S. at 214. No such originality, no such expression, no such ideas here appear.

To be sure, the test of "originality" may leave a lot to be desired, although it is the only one we have, in that as one scholar has said, the originality requirement does not perform the function of excluding commonplace matters in the public domain from copyright status very effectively. *See* Comment, *Copyright*

Protection for Mass Produced Commercial Products: A Review of the Developments Following Mazer v. Stein, 38 U. Chi. L. Rev. 807 (1971). In any event, however, the articles should be judged on their own merits, *id.* at 823, and on these merits appellants' claim must fail. Here as elsewhere in the copyright law there are lines that must be drawn even though reasonable men may differ where.

Judgment affirmed.

MESKILL, CIRCUIT JUDGE (dissenting) (with whom TIMBERS and VAN GRAAFEILAND, CIRCUIT JUDGES, concur):

I respectfully dissent.

In the instant case the author has contributed substantially more than a merely trivial variation. "Any 'distinguishable variation' of a prior work will constitute sufficient originality to support a copyright if such variation is the product of the author's independent efforts, and is more than merely trivial." 1 Nimmer on Copyright § 10.1 at 34.2. In accord with the purposes of the copyright law to promote progress by encouraging individual effort through copyright protection, we should require only minimal variations to find copyrightability. The independent sculpting of the mold for the plastic bank and the aggregated differences in size and conformation of the figurine should satisfy this standard.

The plastic bank in question admittedly is based on a work now in the public domain. This does not render it uncopyrightable since "[i]t is hornbook [law] that a new and original plan or combination of existing materials in the public domain is sufficiently original to come within the copyright protection. . . ." *Alva Studios, Inc. v. Winninger,* 177 F. Supp. 265, 267 (S.D.N.Y. 1959). The courts have repeatedly emphasized that only a modest level of originality is necessary to be eligible for a copyright. . . . *Dan Kasoff, Inc. v. Novelty Jewelry Co., Inc.,* 309 F.2d 745, 746 (2 Cir. 1962), where this Court required only a "faint trace of originality" to support a copyright.

Looking first to copyright cases involving sculptures, in *Puddu v. Buonamici Statuary, Inc.,* 450 F.2d 401, 402 (2 Cir. 1971), this Court found that where plaintiff's employee had sculpted statuettes from scratch, even though there was a "strong family resemblance between the copyrighted and the uncopyrighted models, the differences suffice to satisfy the modest requirement of originality. . . . Originality sufficient for copyright protection exists if the 'author' has introduced any element of novelty as contrasted with the material previously known to him." . . .

The fabric cases likewise have found designs copyrightable with only a "very modest grade of originality." *Peter Pan Fabrics, Inc. v. Dan River Mills, Inc.,* 295 F. Supp. 1366, 1368 (S.D.N.Y. 1969). In the latter case, the embellishment and expansion of purchased designs before being rolled onto fabric constituted the "slight addition" sufficient to quality as originality. Finally, there are also cases where *no* changes were required because the process of reproduction itself required great skill.

. . . .

Turning to the case at bar, Judge Metzner made a factual finding that the plastic bank embodied only trivial variations from the bank in the public domain. . . . I make no claim that the process of sculpting involved here is as complex as in *Alva Studios* (scaled version of Rodin sculpture) or in *Alfred Bell* (mezzotint engravings of art classics). However, those cases depended solely on difficulty of process to establish originality, since there was no attempt to alter or improve upon the underlying work.

The most obvious differences between the two exhibits in this case are size and medium. While these factors alone may not be sufficient to render a work copyrightable, they surely may be considered along with the other variations. On the other hand, the author's reasons for making changes should be irrelevant to a determination of whether the differences are trivial. As noted in *Alfred Bell, supra,* 191 F.2d at 105, even an inadvertent variation can form the basis of a valid copyright. After the fact speculation as to whether Snyder made changes for aesthetic or functional reasons should not be the basis of decision.

The primary variations between the two banks involve height; medium; anatomical proportions of the Uncle Sam figure, including shape and expression of face; design of the clothing (hat, tie, shirt, collar, trousers); detail around the eagle figure on the platform; placement of the umbrella; and the shape and texture of the satchel. Granting Snyder a copyright protecting these variations would ensure only that no one could copy his particular version of the bank now in the public domain, i. e., protection from someone using Snyder's figurine to slavishly copy and make a mold. In *Alva Studios, supra,* 177 F. Supp. at 267, where the author produced no distinctive variations of his own in reproducing the Rodin sculpture, the court still found that the reproduction was copyrightable and that infringement was possible; although mere resemblance would not justify a finding of infringement where the principal elements of a design were taken from the public domain, evidence of actual copying would support such a finding.

This approach seems quite in accord with the purpose of the copyright statute — to promote progress by encouraging individual effort through copyright protection. The relatively low standard of originality required for copyrightability is derived from this purpose. The objective is to progress first and, if necessary, litigate the question of infringement later. In the meantime, the public culture benefits from progress; the issue of who is entitled to the profits should not induce rigidity and slowness in industries and fields naturally subject to great flux.

Accordingly, I would reverse the district court decision.

QUESTIONS

1. In the field of art reproductions, presumably the aesthetic and educational value of the work derives from its being as exact a reproduction as possible. Is it therefore proper — either under the Constitution or the statute — for the court to deny copyright to such a reproduction unless there is a substantial variation from the original?

2. Would a photograph of the public domain cast iron bank be a proper subject of copyright? If so, then why is not Snyder's rendition in plastic? Do you understand Professor Nimmer's point endorsed by the court on p. 76?

3. Is there a constitutional or philosophical justification for the court's suggestion that "sheer effort" or "great labour" in making a reproduction may substitute for artistic variation? Is not the distinguishing of the *Alva* case patently baseless?

4. Is there a constitutional or philosophical justification for the court's suggestion that copyright may be used to protect reproductions when the underlying work is "unique and rare" and not readily accessible to the public? Does copyright make works more or less accessible to the public?

5. Had the Snyder plastic bank been granted copyright, would that effectively remove the cast iron original from the public domain so that others would be forbidden to copy it?

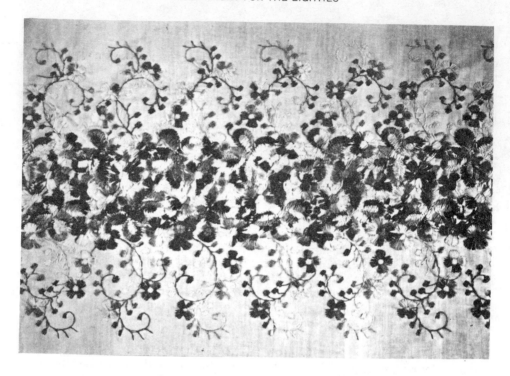

Copyrighting Fabric Designs

MILLWORTH CONVERTING CORP. v. SLIFKA

276 F.2d 443 (2d Cir. 1960)

FRIENDLY, CIRCUIT JUDGE.

As in *Peter Pan Fabrics, Inc. v. Martin Weiner Corp.*, 2 Cir., 274 F.2d 487, these appeals from orders granting temporary injunctions bring before us questions arising from the use of copyright to protect fabric designs.

. . . .

In contrast with Peter Pan, the design that plaintiff's fabric reproduced was not original with it. Plaintiff had seen the design embroidered on a dress which its stylist bought. The embroidery was what is known in the trade as "Schiffli," this referring to a machine making embroidery of quality. Plaintiff's stylist had the embroidered design photographed and then worked with its fabric printer for some months to develop an arrangement of varying colors that would give on a flat surface something of the three-dimensional effect of embroidery. Plaintiff copyrighted a fabric reproduction so made in the summer of 1959, and offered the fabrics for sale to dress manufacturers shortly thereafter. No question is raised as to plaintiff's compliance with 17 U.S.C. § 10 concerning the copyright notice, see *Peter Pan v. Martin Weiner Corp., supra.*

At the end of 1959, defendants began to market among dress manufacturers fabrics which plaintiff claims to infringe its copyrights. One of plaintiff's salesmen testified that a salesman of defendants, to whom he had complained of defendants' copying, admitted they had purchased a dress containing plaintiff's copyrighted design. Defendants offered no evidence to rebut the inference from this.

. . . .

Defendants do not dispute that the "Schiffli" embroidered design was a "work of art," 17 U.S.C. § 5(h), *Mazer v. Stein,* 1954, 347 U.S. 201. Their principal argument both in the District Court and here was that, despite this, plaintiff's copyright was invalid since, in contrast with Peter Pan, the embroidered design was in the public domain and, as defendants alleged, plaintiff's reproduction contained no element of originality. We think Judge Dawson correctly held defendants' attack on the validity of the copyrights to be foreclosed by the principle enunciated in *Alfred Bell & Co. v. Catalda Fine Arts, Inc.,* 2 Cir., 1951, 191 F.2d 99. . . . Here plaintiff offered substantial evidence that its creation of a three-dimensional effect, giving something of the impression of embroidery on a flat fabric, required effort and skill. Although others may have done the same with respect to other "Schifflis," plaintiff's contribution to its reproduction of this design sufficed to meet the modest requirement made of a copyright proprietor "that his work contains some substantial, not merely trivial, originality." *Chamberlin v. Uris Sales Corp.,* 2 Cir., 1945, 150 F.2d 512, 513.

Plaintiff's case fails not on validity but on infringement. Here also the opinion in *Alfred Bell & Co. v. Catalda Fine Arts, supra,* went to the heart of the problem in pointing out, 191 F.2d at page 105, that, while "defendants' arguments about the public domain" had proved irrelevant on the issue of validity, they could be relevant "in their bearing on the issue of infringement, i.e., whether the defendants copied the mezzotints," Judge Frank made his precise thought plain by reference to the "Dishonored Lady" case, *Sheldon v. Metro-Goldwyn-Mayer Pictures Corp.,* 2 Cir., 81 F.2d 49, 54, *certiorari denied,* 1936, 298 U.S. 669. There the basic story, of the ill-fated Madeleine Smith, had long been in the public domain. However, plaintiffs had taken from this "but the merest skeleton," and the requirement of originality was amply satisfied. Nevertheless as Judge Learned Hand explained, the "public demesne" remained important on the issue of infringement since defendants are "entitled to use, not only all that had gone before, but even the plaintiffs' contribution itself, if they drew from it only the more general patterns; that is, if they kept clear of its 'expression.'"

We think that is what defendants' fabric did. The claimed originality and the distinctive feature of plaintiff's reproduction is the three-dimensional look; this is what defendants' fabric lacks. Additionally, the butterfly patterns in plaintiff's fabrics do not appear in defendants'; the well defined bands of color in plaintiff's cloth are not duplicated; and the sharp outline of plaintiff's patterns contrasts with the somewhat diffuse nature of the patterns and coloring in defendants' fabrics. We need not determine whether if the basic design had been original with plaintiff, defendants' fabric might not be sufficiently imitative to infringe under the test laid down by Judge Hand in Peter Pan. For here, in contrast, the basic design was in the public domain and plaintiff was entitled to relief only if defendants copied its "expression," as the defendant in *Alfred Bell v. Catalda Fine Arts, supra,* was found to have done. See Judge Smith's full opinion in the District Court, D.C.S.D.N.Y. 1947, 74 F. Supp. 973, 977. *See also Gross v. Seligman,* 2 Cir., 1914, 212 F. 930. *Cf. Eggers v. Sun Sales Corp.,* 2 Cir., 1920, 263 F. 373. This defendants did not succeed in doing, whatever their intent.

We recognize that the District Judge found the contrary and that, in reviewing his order, we are bound by Fed. R. Civ. Proc. 52, 28 U.S.C. However, the record contains almost no evidence on the issue of infringement other than the fabrics themselves. In such a case, as has been said with respect to trademark infringement, "we are in as good a position as the trial judge to determine" the issue. *Eastern Wine Corp. v. Winslow Warren, Ltd.,* 2 Cir., 137 F.2d 955, 960,

82 COPYRIGHT FOR THE EIGHTIES

certiorari denied, 1943, 320 U.S. 758. *See Orvis v. Higgins,* 2 Cir., 180 F.2d 537, 539, *certiorari denied,* 1950, 340 U.S. 810. Moreover, the District Judge's citation of the Peter Pan decision on the issue of infringement at least suggests that he may have used a test that was not wholly applicable where the "work of art" was in the public domain and thus only plaintiff's "expression" was protected.

The orders granting temporary injunctions are therefore reversed.

ROTH GREETING CARDS v. UNITED CARD CO.

429 F.2d 1106 (9th Cir. 1970)

HAMLEY, CIRCUIT JUDGE:

Roth Greeting Cards (Roth) and United Card Company (United), both corporations, are engaged in the greeting card business. Roth brought this suit against United to recover damages and obtain injunctive relief for copyright infringement of seven studio greeting cards. After a trial to the court without a jury, judgment was entered for defendant. Plaintiff appeals.

Roth's claim involves the production and distribution by United of seven greeting cards which bear a remarkable resemblance to seven of Roth's cards on which copyrights had been granted. Roth employed a writer to develop the textual material for its cards. When Roth's president determined that a textual idea was acceptable, he would integrate that text into a rough layout of a greeting card with his suggested design for the art work. He would then call in the company artist who would make a comprehensive layout of the card. If the card was approved, the artist would do a finished layout and the card would go into production.

During the period just prior to the alleged infringements, United did not have any writers on its payroll. Most of its greeting cards came into fruition primarily through the activities of United's president, Mr. Koenig, and its vice-president, Edward Letwenko.

The source of the art and text of the cards of United, here in question, is unclear. Letwenko was unable to recall the origin of the ideas for most of United's cards. He speculated that the gags used may have come from plant personnel, persons in bars, friends at a party, Koenig, or someone else. He contended that the art work was his own. But he also stated that he visited greeting card stores and gift shows in order to observe what was going on in the greeting card business. Letwenko admitted that he may have seen the Roth cards during these visits or that the Roth cards may have been in his office prior to the time that he did his art work on the United cards.

. . . .

Turning to the merits, the trial court found that the art work in plaintiff's greeting cards was copyrightable, but not infringed by defendant. The trial court also found that, although copied by defendant, the wording or textual matter of each of the plaintiff's cards in question consist of common and ordinary English words and phrases which are not original with Roth and were in the public domain prior to first use by plaintiff.

Arguing that the trial court erred in ruling against it on merits, Roth agrees that the textual material involved in their greeting cards may have been in the public domain, but argues that this alone did not end the inquiry into the copyrightability of the entire card. Roth argues that "[I]t is the arrangement of the words, their combination and plan, together with the appropriate art work. . . ." which is original, the creation of Roth, and entitled to copyright protection.

In order to be copyrightable, the work must be the original work of the copyright claimant or of his predecessor in interest. M. NIMMER, COPYRIGHT (hereafter NIMMER), § 10 at 32 (1970). But the originality necessary to support a copyright merely calls for independent creation, not novelty. *Alfred Bell & Co., Ltd. v. Catalda Fine Arts, Inc.,* 191 F.2d 99, 102 (2d Cir. 1951). *Cf. Baker v. Selden,* 101 U.S. 99 (1879).

United argues, and we agree, that there was substantial evidence to support the district court's finding that the textual matter of each card, considered apart from its arrangement on the cards and its association with artistic representations, was not original to Roth and therefore not copyrightable.[3] However, proper analysis of the problem requires that all elements of each card, including text, arrangement of text, art work, and association between art work and text, be considered as a whole.

Considering all of these elements together, the Roth cards are, in our opinion, both original and copyrightable. In reaching this conclusion we recognize that copyright protection is not available for ideas, but only for the tangible expression of ideas. *Mazer v. Stein,* 347 U.S. 201, 217 (1954). We conclude that each of Roth's cards, considered as a whole, represents a tangible expression of an idea and that such expression was, in totality, created by Roth. *See Dorsey v. Old Surety Life Ins. Co.,* 98 F.2d 872, 873 (10th Cir. 1938).

This brings us to the question of infringement. Greeting cards are protected under 17 U.S.C. § 5(a) or (k) as a book, *Jackson v. Quickslip Co., Inc.,* 110 F.2d 731 (2d Cir. 1940), or as a print, 37 C.F.R. § 202.14. They are the embodiment of humor, praise, regret or some other message in a pictorial and literary arrangement. As proper subjects of copyright, they are susceptible to infringement in violation of the Act. *Detective Comics, Inc. v. Bruns Publications, Inc.,* 111 F.2d 432 (2d Cir. 1940).

To constitute an infringement under the Act there must be substantial similarity between the infringing work and the work copyrighted; and that similarity must have been caused by the defendant's having copied the copyright holder's creation. The protection is thus against copying — not against any possible infringement caused when an independently created work coincidentally duplicates copyrighted material. *Sheldon v. Metro-Goldwyn Pictures Corp.,* 81 F.2d 49, 54 (2d Cir. 1936).

It appears to us that in total concept and feel the cards of United are the same as the copyrighted cards of Roth. With the possible exception of one United card (exhibit 6), the characters depicted in the art work, the mood they portrayed, the combination of art work conveying a particular mood with a particular message, and the arrangement of the words on the greeting card are substantially the same as in Roth's cards. In several instances the lettering is also very similar.

It is true, as the trial court found, that each of United's cards employed art work somewhat different from that used in the corresponding Roth cards. However, "[T]he test of infringement is whether the work is recognizable by an ordinary observer as having been taken from the copyrighted source." *White-Smith Music Pub. Co. v. Apollo Company,* 209 U.S. 1, 17 (1907) [sic], *Bradbury v. Columbia Broadcasting System, Inc.,* 287 F.2d 478, 485 (9th Cir. 1961).

---

[3] Thus, if United had copied only the textual materials, which were not independently copyrightable, United might have been able to do so with impunity. Jackson v. Quickslip Co., 110 F.2d 731 (2d Cir. 1940).

The remarkable similarity between the Roth and United cards in issue (with the possible exception of exhibits 5 and 6) is apparent to even a casual observer. For example, one Roth card (exhibit 9) has, on its front, a colored drawing of a cute moppet suppressing a smile and, on the inside, the words "i wuv you." With the exception of minor variations in color and style, defendant's card (exhibit 10) is identical. Likewise, Roth's card entitled "I miss you already," depicts a forlorn boy sitting on a curb weeping, with an inside message reading "... and You Haven't even Left ..." (exhibit 7), is closely paralleled by United's card with the same caption, showing a forlorn and weeping man, and with the identical inside message (exhibit 8).

The question remains whether United did in fact copy the Roth cards. Since direct evidence of copying is rarely available, copying may be established by proof of access and substantial similarity. NIMMER § 141.2 at 613. Although in some circumstances the mere proof of access and substantial similarity will not demand that the trier automatically find copying, the absence of any countervailing evidence of creation independent of the copyrighted source may well render clearly erroneous a finding that there was not copying.

In the present case there was clear and uncontradicted testimony establishing United's access to the Roth cards. United brought Roth cards to its offices. It sent its employees out to gift shows and retail stores where the Roth cards were on display to observe "what the competition was doing." In addition, there was testimony almost compelling the inference that it was United's practice to look at the cards produced by other companies and make similar cards for sale under the United label. These circumstances, together with the marked similarity between the cards on which this suit was brought, with the possible exception of one card, convince us that each of United's cards in question, considered as combined compositions of art and text, were in fact copied from the Roth cards. It follows that there was infringement. See Detective Comics, Inc. v. Bruns Publications, Inc., 111 F.2d 432 (2d Cir. 1940).

The judgment is therefore reversed and the cause is remanded for further proceedings consistent with this opinion.

KILKENNY, CIRCUIT JUDGE (dissenting).

The majority agrees with a specific finding of the lower court that the words on the cards are not the subject of copyright. By strong implication, it likewise accepts the finding of the trial court that the art work on the cards, although subject to copyright, was not infringed. Thus far, I agree.

I cannot, however, follow the logic of the majority in holding that the uncopyrightable words and the imitated, but not copied art work, constitutes such total composition as to be subject to protection under the copyright laws. The majority concludes that in the overall arrangement of the text, the art work and the association of the art work to the text, the cards were copyrightable and the copyright infringed. This conclusion, as I view it, results in the whole becoming substantially greater than the sum total of its parts. With this conclusion, of course, I cannot agree.

The majority relies principally on Detective Comics, Inc. v. Bruns Publications, Inc., 111 F.2d 432 (2d Cir. 1940). This case, as I read it, does not even intimate that the whole can exceed the sum total of its parts. It involved an imitation of the "Superman" image by a rival company. In finding infringement, the "Superman" court emphasized that "So far as the pictorial representations and verbal descriptions of 'Superman' are not a mere delineation of a benevolent Hercules, but embody an arrangement of incidents and literary expressions original with the author, they are proper subjects of copyright and susceptible of infringement because of the monopoly afforded by the Act." P. 433 (Emphasis added.) Moreover, the "Superman" case involved the creation of a character, a written dialogue and description which were clearly protected by copyright law in much the same way that a dialogue and description found in a novel is protected. The district court in the "Superman" case found that both the art work and the text materials were copyrightable and that each was infringed. In the case before us, the findings of the trial judge are in direct opposition to appellant's contentions. The language of the district court in "Superman" is worthy of note: "Short of 'Chinese copies' of the plaintiff's 'Superman' strip, the defendant could hardly have gone further than it has done." P. 400. The challenged cards before us, I submit, in no way resemble "Chinese copies" of appellant's material. Other cases cited by the majority are no more in point than *Detective Comics.*

Aside from the above, I call attention to the fact that a number of experts appeared in the lower court and testified that the phrases on the cards were in common use and that Roth's writer often obtained his ideas from others. In these circumstances, we should not set aside the findings of the lower court. *Williams v. Kaag Manufacturers, Inc.,* 338 F.2d 949 (9th Cir. 1964). Beyond that, ordinary phraseology within the public domain is not copyrightable. *Dorsey v. Old Surety Life Insurance Co.,* 98 F.2d 872 (10th Cir. 1938); *American Code Co. v. Bensinger,* 282 F. 829 (2d Cir. 1922).

Feeling, as I do, that the copyright act is a grant of limited monopoly to the authors of creative literature and art, I do not think that we should extend a 56-year monopoly in a situation where neither infringement of text, nor infringement of art work can be found. On these facts, we should adhere to our historic philosophy requiring freedom of competition. I would affirm.

QUESTIONS

1. Under what category of copyrightable work in § 102(a) do the Roth greeting cards fit?

2. It is not too early to consider the kind of copyright notice that should be placed on derivative and composite works. Consult §§ 401-404. What notice should be placed on greeting cards such as those involved in this case? (If the statute departs from the usually applicable form of notice, what is the explanation?) Where should the notice be placed?

3. Does the notice you have just placed on the plaintiff's greeting cards provide the reader with an accurate statement of what can and cannot be copied? Suppose a greeting card consists of no more than a reproduction of an old master accompanied by a trite phrase. (a) Would the card be copyrightable? (b) What would the notice be? (c) What elements of the card could be copied by a purchaser?

4. Is the reasoning and result of the *Roth* case compatible with the *Batlin* decision?

COMPILATIONS OF FACTS

In requiring that a work, in order to be eligible for copyright, must be "an original work of authorship" (§ 102(a)), the 1976 Act — as was also true of the 1909 Act — fits only uncomfortably around works which constitute little more than the compilation of facts. The names in a telephone directory, for example, are in the public domain and are not the subject of copyright; the same is true of the addresses and presumably also the telephone numbers; although the sequencing of noncopyrightable works may be the subject of copyright (witness an anthology of public domain poetry or the collection of cases in a book for law students), surely the alphabetical sequencing of names, addresses and telephone numbers does not reflect the kind of originality warranting copyright protection. Yet most telephone directories have a copyright notice on every page, are routinely accepted for registration in the Copyright Office, and are protected by the courts in copyright litigation. What is the original work of authorship?

Maps raise similar problems for the law of copyright. In their nature, they do not invite or permit artistic license; the most desirable map, from the point of view of social utility, is that which most accurately tracks nature. Where are the original elements of authorship? (The reader should be mindful of the fact that maps, along with only books and charts, were subject to protection under the first Copyright Act, enacted in 1790 by many of the same men who framed the Constitution and its copyright clause.)

Two leading circuit court opinions have articulated strikingly different views about the protectability of maps. In _Amsterdam v. Triangle Publications, Inc._, 189 F.2d 104 (3d Cir. 1951), the plaintiff had published and copyrighted in 1932 a map of Delaware County, Pennsylvania. In preparing the map, the plaintiff made no actual surveys of roads, county lines, rivers and the like; with minor exceptions, he secured all of his information from studying already existing maps in his possession or in the possession of local governmental authorities, a task consuming considerable time and effort. The total information reflected on his map had never before been published on any one map. The defendant, publisher of the Philadelphia Inquirer, reproduced the plaintiff's map without his consent in connection with an historical article about Delaware County. The district court dismissed the complaint for infringement, and the court of appeals affirmed. The court, stating that a map, to be copyrightable, must result from some original work, held that such was lacking: the plaintiff engaged in only the most negligible surveying work, and did no more than look at other maps and determine what information he would depict and such matters as emphasis, coloring scheme and symbols; the location of geographic boundaries and information in government maps are in the public domain and not copyrightable; "the presentation of information available to everybody, such as is found on maps, is protected only when the publisher of the map in question obtains originally some of that information by the sweat of his own brow. Almost anybody could combine the information from several maps onto one map, but not everybody can go out and get that information originally and then transcribe it into a map."

A similar issue was raised in _United States v. Hamilton_, 583 F.2d 448 (9th Cir. 1978), and although the case arose from a criminal prosecution for wilful infringement, the court disagreed with _Amsterdam,_ and found both copyrightability and infringement. The court framed the issue before it as "whether the mapmaker's selection, arrangement, and presentation of terrain features which were already either in the public domain or subject [to its own earlier copyright] . . . may be considered as part of the efforts and skill which constitute a cartographer's authorship." The court concluded that "[t]he so-called direct observation rule of _Amsterdam_ is squarely before us here, and we decline to follow it." The court surmised that _Amsterdam_ may have been based on a fear that granting copyright to the plaintiff there would have precluded others from having recourse to the same public domain maps and making their own synthesis as he had done; but it stated that this fear of sheltering the public domain maps through the plaintiff's copyright was of course unfounded. The court believed that analysis of copyrightability in map cases should be no different from other cases, and that a cartographer's "creative compilation or synthesis" should be eligible for copyright. It stated that originality may be found in making a new combination or arrangement of the commonplace (citing, among other cases, one involving a telephone directory), and that the cartographer's "art" (as distinguished from the mere selection of colors, symbols or keys) involves significant elements of "selection, design, and synthesis" (with a citation to *Burrow-Giles Lithographic Co. v. Sarony*). The court affirmed the finding of fact that there was originality both in the direct observation of many geographic features by the mapmaker from whom the defendant had copied, and in the compilation and synthesis from earlier maps.

Which is the sounder approach, that in *Amsterdam* or that in *Hamilton*? Which approach will more likely "promote the progress of science and the useful arts"? What is the justification for the "sweat of the brow" theory? Can one rationally distinguish between copyrightable synthesis of earlier maps and uncopyrightable selection of colors, symbols and keys? Were the references in *Hamilton* to the telephone directory cases or to *Burrow-Giles* helpful?

There are numerous other areas in which the courts have had to adapt the principles of "originality" and "authorship" to fact compilations. One, for example, is that of horse racing data developed through direct observation and compiled in elaborate and detailed charts published for the delectation of the aficionados, and promptly "distilled" in somewhat different format in a competing publication. If the defendant takes only the data and changes the form of presentation, has it taken from the plaintiff a copyrightable element of its copyrighted chart? (Compare the person who takes the information in a copyrighted telephone directory and devises and publishes his own directory, with listings not in alphabetical order of telephone owner but rather by sequences of street addresses or telephone numbers. See *Leon v. Pacific Telephone Co.*, 91 F.2d 484 (9th Cir. 1937).)

The battle of the horse racing charts has been litigated in *Triangle Publications, Inc. v. New England Newspaper Publishing Co.*, 46 F. Supp. 198 (D. Mass. 1942); and *Triangle Publications, Inc. v. Sports Eye, Inc.*, 415 F. Supp. 682 (E.D. Pa. 1976).

The *New England Newspaper* case involved a claim of copyright infringement and unfair competition asserted by the publishers of a horse racing daily against the publishers of a newspaper which carried in its sport pages information about race horses. The plaintiffs, at an expense of more than a half million dollars annually, stationed at every licensed race track in North America teams of representatives who observed and recorded detailed information about each day's races; the plaintiff's daily paper carried "race result charts" for the previous day's races (with facts such as the track where the race was run, its condition and distance, the horses racing and their jockeys and post position, the position of the horses at six stages of the race, the time of the race, and "several staccato sentences commenting in race track parlance on the showing of the horses in that race"). Plaintiff's paper also set forth "past performance tables" for every horse scheduled to run the next day (showing when and where that horse previously raced, the condition of the track, the jockey, the horse's position at six stages of the race, the names of the best performers in that race, and a one- or two-word summation of the horse's form that day). From 1939 to 1941, the defendants published information about the past performances of race horses; on what the court found to be "an excessive number of occasions," defendants secured their information (such as dates, locations, and jockeys at recent races, the condition of the track, the performance of the horse) from "race result charts" in the plaintiffs' publications.

The court found that the plaintiffs' individual race result charts were not as a whole copyrightable "compilations" under the 1909 Act since "the arrangement includes only about a hundred items with reference to a single event that takes less than two minutes to observe and record, and the majority of those items could be collected without labor, skill or judgment by any spectator. To constitute a copyrightable compilation, a compendium must ordinarily result from the labor of assembling, connecting and categorizing disparate facts which in nature occurred in isolation." With no relevant definition in the 1909 Act, was this judicial definition sound? Although the parts of the charts which were copied from the race track program or from public bulletin boards were held by the court not to be copyrightable (principally because copied themselves), the court concluded that "there may be a separate copyright on those parts of a single chart which could not be observed and recorded by one person but which require the combined skill, judgment and effort of several highly trained persons working in unison." The court therefore found that there could be copyright upon those parts of the plaintiffs' charts showing the positions of and distances between the horses at various stages of the race, and the staccato sentences or narrative comments in the chart. Moreover, the court found that the arrangement in the plaintiffs' daily paper of the various race result charts and past performance tables was a copyrightable compilation, as were the plaintiffs' monthly indexes to the race result charts.

The court then concluded that the defendants had infringed when they initially (in 1939 and 1940) "read the symbols, mathematical notations and cryptic expressions in plaintiffs' race result charts and then stated the same information in equivalent words"; and when they later (in 1941) incorporated the same symbols and notations, after editing out certain facts, in charts of their own. There was no infringement, however, when the defendants referred to the plaintiffs' monthly indexes to locate information about particular horses from defendants' own race result charts. The court also held that there was no liability under the Massachusetts law of unfair competition, since the defendants were not deceiving the public as to the source of the information in its charts. An injunction issued, barring not only copying of copyrightable information from the plaintiffs' race result charts but also use of the plaintiffs' indexes to get clues to the defendants' own materials (since such use would so clearly provide a temptation to further infringements).

In the *Sports Eye* case, the same plaintiff brought an action alleging, once again, copyright infringement and unfair competition, this time for copying of its past performance tables (rather than its race result charts). The raw data for the plaintiff's past performance tables (which contained detailed information regarding the previous ten races for each horse in each race at each track) were drawn from its race result charts, now compiled and maintained with the use of data processing equipment. The defendant's publication, titled "Fast Performances," was a chart containing one vertical column for each race to be run at a particular track, bearing the name of a particular horse or horses in that race which corresponded to each of thirty-two categories in the left-hand column (such as "beaten within one length of winner last race" and "fastest comparative speed in recent races"). The court found that the defendant obtained the information for its Fast Performances charts from the plaintiff's Past Performances charts; indeed, the copying and calculation were done for the defendant by a former employee of the plaintiff. The court, noting that "while the form or mode of expressing an idea (or in this case data) may be copyrighted, the data or ideas may not be," concluded that although defendant "made use of the plaintiff's copyrighted materials," there was no infringement because there was no "substantial similarity" between the two kinds of charts. Rejecting the claim that the defendant's charts were merely a "translation" of the plaintiff's, the court concluded: "Plaintiff does not attempt to make any comparisons or judgments about the horses entered in a given race beyond that available in the raw data; defendant's publication is in essence a comparison of the horses in any one race. Both in visual and factual apprehension . . . the two papers differ substantially." The court also concluded that no state unfair competition claim would lie for copying which was permitted under the federal copyright law. It concluded: "Since there is no place or show window in federal court, the request for a preliminary injunction must be denied."

Which is the better ground for decision in *Sports Eye* — that what the defendant copied from the plaintiff's charts was not copyrightable, or that the defendant modified the copied material to such a degree that there was no infringement? (This difference in analysis would matter, for example, if the defendant transplanted the plaintiff's factual data onto substantially similar charts. Should that be an infringement, as the *New England* court had held?)

The *New England* court found that the defendants infringed when they took bits of information from plaintiffs' race result charts and incorporated them in narrative sentence form (e.g., the horse Sheknows "may be the right one here. Finished third behind Paul Lee and Rafter in recent sprint outing at Tropical Park, December 27, in slop."). The court stated that "copying need not be in ipsissima verba" and that a dictionary of synonyms "is not a licensed sanctuary for literary pirates"; it cited for support a case in which an unauthorized motion picture of Ben Hur was held to infringe the novel. Evaluate the court's analysis.

C. FACTS AND IDEAS AS DISTINGUISHED FROM THEIR EXPRESSION

BAKER v. SELDEN

101 U.S. 99 (1879)

Mr. Justice Bradley delivered the opinion of the court.

Charles Selden, the testator of the complainant in this case, in the year 1859 took the requisite steps for obtaining the copyright of a book, entitled "Selden's Condensed Ledger, or Bookkeeping Simplified," the object of which was to exhibit and explain a peculiar system of book-keeping. In 1860 and 1861, he took the copyright of several other books, containing additions to and improvements upon the said system. The bill of complaint was filed against the defendant, Baker, for an alleged infringement of these copyrights. The latter, in his answer, denied that Selden was the author or designer of the books, and denied the infringement charged, and contends on the argument that the matter alleged to be infringed is not a lawful subject of copyright.

The parties went into proofs, and the various books of the complainant, as well as those sold and used by the defendant, were exhibited before the examiner, and witnesses were examined on both sides. A decree was rendered for the complainant, and the defendant appealed.

The book or series of books of which the complainant claims the copyright consists of an introductory essay explaining the system of book-keeping referred to, to which are annexed certain forms or blanks, consisting of ruled lines, and headings, illustrating the system and showing how it is to be used and carried out in practice. This system effects the same results as book-keeping by double entry; but, by a peculiar arrangement of columns and headings, presents the entire operation, of a day, a week, or a month, on a single page, or on two pages facing each other, in an account-book. The defendant uses a similar plan so far as results are concerned; but makes a different arrangement of the columns, and uses different headings. If the complainant's testator had the exclusive right to the use of the system explained in his book, it would be difficult to contend that the defendant does not infringe it, notwithstanding the difference in his form of arrangement; but if it be assumed that the system is open to public use, it seems to be equally difficult to contend that the books made and sold by the defendant are a violation of the copyright of the complainant's book considered merely as a book explanatory of the system. Where the truths of a science or the methods of an art are the common property of the whole world, any author has the right to express the one, or explain and use the other, in his own way. As an author, Selden explained the system in a particular way. It may be conceded that Baker makes and uses account-books arranged on substantially the same system; but the proof fails to show that he has violated the copyright of Selden's book, regarding the latter merely as an explanatory work; or that he has infringed Selden's right in any way, unless the latter became entitled to an exclusive right in the system.

The evidence of the complainant is principally directed to the object of showing that Baker uses the same system as that which is explained and illustrated in Selden's books. It becomes important, therefore, to determine whether, in obtaining the copyright of his books, he secured the exclusive right to the use of the system or method of book-keeping which the said books are intended to illustrate and explain. It is contended that he has secured such exclusive right, because no one can use the system without using substantially the same ruled lines and headings which he has appended to his books in illustration of it. In other words, it is contended that the ruled lines and headings, given to illustrate the system, are a part of the book, and, as such, are secured by the copyright; and that no one can make or use similar ruled lines and headings, or ruled lines and headings made and arranged on substantially the same system, without violating the copyright. And this is really the question to be decided in this case. Stated in another form, the question is, whether the exclusive property in a system of book-keeping can be claimed, under the law of copyright, by means of a book in which that system is explained? The complainant's bill, and the case made under it, are based on the hypothesis that it can be.

It cannot be pretended, and indeed it is not seriously urged, that the ruled lines of the complainant's account-book can be claimed under any special class of objects, other than books, named in the law of copyright existing in 1859. The law then in force was that of 1831, and specified only books, maps, charts, musical compositions, prints, and engravings. An account-book, consisting of ruled lines and blank columns, cannot be called by any of these names unless by that of a book.

There is no doubt that a work on the subject of book-keeping, though only explanatory of well-known systems, may be the subject of a copyright; but, then, it is claimed only as a book. Such a book may be explanatory either of old systems, or of an entirely new system; and, considered as a book, as the work of an author, conveying information on the subject of book-keeping, and containing detailed explanations of the art, it may be a very valuable acquisition to the practical knowledge of the community. But there is a clear distinction between the book, as such, and the art which it is intended to illustrate. The mere statement of the proposition is so evident, that it requires hardly any argument to support it. The same distinction may be predicated of every other art as well as that of book-keeping. A treatise on the composition and use of medicines, be they old or new; on the construction and use of ploughs, or watches, or churns; or on the mixture and application of colors for painting or dyeing; or on the mode of drawing lines to produce the effect of perspective, — would be the subject of copyright; but no one would contend that the copyright of the treatise would give the exclusive right to the art or manufacture described therein. The copyright of the book, if not pirated from other works, would be valid without regard to the novelty, or want of novelty, of its subject-matter. The novelty of the art or thing described or explained has nothing to do with the validity of the copyright. To give to the author of the book an exclusive property in the art described therein, when no examination of its novelty has ever been officially made, would be a surprise and a fraud upon the public. That is the province of letters-patent, not of copyright. The claim to an invention or discovery of an art or manufacture must be subjected to the examination of the Patent Office before an exclusive right therein can be obtained; and it can only be secured by a patent from the government.

The difference between the two things, letters-patent and copyright, may be illustrated by reference to the subjects just enumerated. Take the case of medicines. Certain mixtures are found to be of great value in the healing art. If the discoverer writes and publishes a book on the subject (as regular physicians generally do), he gains no exclusive right to the manufacture and sale of the medicine; he gives that to the public. If he desires to acquire such exclusive right, he must obtain a patent for the mixture as a new art, manufacture, or composition of matter. He may copyright his book, if he pleases; but that only secures to him the exclusive right of printing and publishing his book. So of all other inventions or discoveries.

The copyright of a book on perspective, no matter how many drawings and illustrations it may contain, gives no exclusive right to the modes of drawing described, though they may never have been known or used before. By publishing the book, without getting a patent for the art, the latter is given to the public. The fact that the art described in the book by illustrations of lines and figures which are reproduced in practice in the application of the art, makes no difference. Those illustrations are the mere language employed by the author to convey his ideas more clearly. Had he used words of description instead of diagrams which he employs to explain them, so as to prevent an engineer from

slightest doubt that others, applying the art to practical use, might lawfully draw the lines and diagrams which were in the author's mind, and which he thus described by words in his book.

The copyright of a work on mathematical science cannot give to the author an exclusive right to the methods of operation which he propounds, or to the diagrams which he employs to explain them, so as to prevent an engineer from using them whenever occasion requires. The very object of publishing a book on science or the useful arts is to communicate to the world the useful knowledge which it contains. But this object would be frustrated if the knowledge could not be used without incurring the guilt of piracy of the book. And where the art it teaches cannot be used without employing the methods and diagrams used to illustrate the book, or such as are similar to them, such methods and diagrams are to be considered as necessary incidents to the art, and given therewith to the public; not given for the purpose of publication in other works explanatory of the art, but for the purpose of practical application.

Of course, these observations are not intended to apply to ornamental designs, or pictorial illustrations addressed to the taste. Of these it may be said, that their form is their essence, and their object, the production of pleasure in their contemplation. This is their final end. They are as much the product of genius and the result of composition, as are the lines of the poet or the historian's periods. On the other hand, the teachings of science and the rules and methods of useful art have their final end in application and use; and this application and use are what the public derive from the publication of a book which teaches them. But as embodied and taught in a literary composition or book, their essence consists only in their statement. This alone is what is secured by the copyright. The use by another of the same methods of statement, whether in words or illustrations, in a book published for teaching the art, would undoubtedly be an infringement of the copyright.

Recurring to the case before us, we observe that Charles Selden, by his books, explained and described a peculiar system of book-keeping, and illustrated his method by means of ruled lines and blank columns, with proper headings on a page, or on successive pages. Now, whilst no one has a right to print or publish his book, or any material part thereof, as a book intended to convey instruction in the art, any person may practice and use the art itself which he has described and illustrated therein. The use of the art is a totally different thing from a publication of the book explaining it. The copyright of a book on book-keeping cannot secure the exclusive right to make, sell, and use account-books prepared upon the plan set forth in such book. Whether the art might or might not have been patented, is a question which is not before us. It was not patented, and is open and free to the use of the public. And, of course, in using the art, the ruled lines and headings of accounts must necessarily be used as incident to it.

The plausibility of the claim put forward by the complainant in this case arises from a confusion of ideas produced by the peculiar nature of the art described in the books which have been made the subject of copyright. In describing the art, the illustrations and diagrams employed happen to correspond more closely than usual with the actual work performed by the operator who uses the art. Those illustrations and diagrams consist of ruled lines and headings of accounts; and it is similar ruled lines and headings of accounts which, in the application of the art, the book-keeper makes with his pen, or the stationer with his press; whilst in most other cases the diagrams and illustrations can only be represented in concrete forms of wood, metal, stone, or some other physical embodiment. But the principle is the same in all. The description of the art in a book, though entitled to the benefit of copyright, lays no foundation for an exclusive claim to the art itself. The object of the one is explanation; the object of the other is use. The former may be secured by copyright. The latter can only be secured, if it can be secured at all, by letters-patent. . . .

. . . .

The conclusion to which we have come is, that blank account-books are not the subject of copyright; and that the mere copyright of Selden's book did not confer upon him the exclusive right to make and use account-books, ruled and arranged as designated by him and described and illustrated in said book.

The decree of the Circuit Court must be reversed, and the cause remanded with instructions to dismiss the complainant's bill; and it is.

So ordered.

QUESTIONS

1. What is the precise holding of this case: that the accounting forms were copyrightable (and copyrighted) but that such copyright was not infringed? Or that the accounting forms were not eligible for copyright?   *no infringement*

2. Could the Court simply have ruled for the defendant on the ground that his form did not substantially copy the plaintiff's? Would not such an approach avoid the question whether copyright extended to the accounting system described in the plaintiff's book?

3. Professor Nimmer has argued that had the defendant's forms been identical copies of the plaintiff's there should have been a finding of infringement. *See* 1 NIMMER ON COPYRIGHT § 2.18(C)(2). Do you agree?

4. What would be the proper analysis of the case if the defendant had been an accountant and had photocopied (assuming that was possible at the time the case arose) the plaintiff's forms? What if the defendant, instead, was in the printing business, and had printed thousands of copies of the forms, which he then sold in a retail store to accountants (along with ledger pads, electronic calculators, accounting magazines, and the like)?

5. If the defendant had written a book describing, in his own words, plaintiff's accounting system, would that be an infringement of copyright? If, in that book, the defendant had included exact copies of the plaintiff's forms in an appendix for the purpose of illustrating the system described in the book, would that be an infringement? If the former question is answered no, does that not compel the same answer to the latter question?

6. Do you agree with the Court's statement that a book on perspective gives no exclusive rights to the illustrations therein? Why doesn't such a book fall on the side of the line characterized by "ornamental designs, or pictorial illustrations addressed to the taste"?

---

§ 102. Subject matter of copyright: In general

. . . .

(b) In no case does copyright protection for an original work of authorship extend to any idea, procedure, process, system, method of operation, concept, principle, or discovery, regardless of the form in which it is described, explained, illustrated, or embodied in such work.

HOUSE REPORT

H.R. Rep. No. 94-1476, 94th Cong., 2d Sess. 56-57 (1976)

Copyright does not preclude others from using the ideas or information revealed by the author's work. It pertains to the literary, musical, graphic, or artistic form in which the author expressed intellectual concepts. Section 102 (b) makes clear that copyright protection does not extend to any idea, procedure, process, system, method of operation, concept, principle, or discovery, regardless of the form in which it is described, explained, illustrated, or embodied in such work.

Some concern has been expressed lest copyright in computer programs should extend protection to the methodology or processes adopted by the programmer, rather than merely to the "writing" expressing his ideas. Section 102 (b) is intended, among other things, to make clear that the expression adopted by the programmer is the copyrightable element in a computer program, and that the actual processes or methods embodied in the program are not within the scope of the copyright law.

Section 102 (b) in no way enlarges or contracts the scope of copyright protection under the present law. Its purpose is to restate, in the context of the new single Federal system of copyright, that the basic dichotomy between expression and idea remains unchanged.

CONTINENTAL CASUALTY CO. v. BEARDSLEY

253 F.2d 702 (2d Cir.), *cert. denied,* 358 U.S. 816 (1958)

HINCKS, CIRCUIT JUDGE.

These are cross-appeals arising out of a suit brought by Continental Casualty Company (Continental) which sought a declaratory judgment that defendants' copyrights were invalid together with an injunction, an accounting, and counsel fees. Continental also demanded damages for unfair competition and violation of the antitrust laws. The defendant, Beardsley, counterclaimed alleging infringement by Continental of his valid copyrights and that Continental was liable for unfair competition. The District Court held that the material in question was not properly copyrightable; that, even if it were, the copyright had been lost; and, further, that there was no infringement. The District Court granted the declaratory relief sought by Continental and an injunction. It rejected the unfair competition claims of both parties and Continental's antitrust claim and its request for an accounting and counsel fees. Each party has appealed from every adverse ruling below. In addition, Beardsley contends that in any event the injunction is too broad.

Copyrightability

This controversy had its inception in the late 1930's. Defendant Beardsley was an insurance broker (also a member of the bar) who allegedly developed a blanket bond to cover replacement of lost securities which would operate *in futuro.* In September 1939, he published his "plan" in a six-page pamphlet. The entire pamphlet carried a copyright notice and Continental admits that the introductory three pages of narrative are validly copyrighted. As to these three pages, however, there is no claim of infringement. Continental contended below, and the court agreed, that the remaining three pages of forms to carry out the "plan" were not copyrightable. The forms included a proposed bond, an affidavit of loss and indemnity agreement, and drafts of an instruction letter and board resolutions. Beardsley had also devised various insurance instruments, some but not all of which he had copyrighted.

We find nothing which, as a matter of law, prevents the copyrighting of forms and insurance instruments such as those now before us. Article I, Section 8, Cl. 8 of the United States Constitution grants Congress power to "promote the Progress of Science and useful Arts, by securing for limited Times to Authors and Inventors the exclusive Right to their respective Writings and Discoveries." Congress in 17 U.S.C.A. § 4 has provided that "The works for which copyright may be secured under this title shall include all the works * of an author." See also *Brightley v. Littleton,* C.C.E.D.Pa., 37 F. 103.

Notwithstanding this general authority in support of the copyrightability of forms, Continental relies upon *Baker v. Selden,* 101 U.S. 99. In that case Selden had written a book explaining a simplified system of bookkeeping. This system used the so-called "T accounts," familiar to any student of accounting or bookkeeping, which had the usual headings. The court held that though the explanation of the system was copyrightable, the system itself — as evidenced by the account forms — was not copyrightable. A distinction was drawn between "explanation" and "use," the court stating that material relating to "use" could be protected, if at all, only by patent. *Mazer v. Stein,* 347 U.S. 201, does not weaken *Selden* in any way. Mazer was concerned with electric lamp bases which had been copyrighted as works of art. The court held that the fact that these bases were also put to practical use did not destroy their copyrightability.

In *Baker v. Selden,* supra, the subject matter was such that the explanation of the system could be treated as separable from account books prepared and arranged for the practice of the system. But not so here. For inseparably included in Beardsley's bonds and affidavits, which constitute the means for the practice of his Plan, is language explanatory of the Plan. Consequently, the holding of *Baker v. Selden* in not applicable here. See also *Taylor Instrument Companies v. Fawley-Brost Co.,* 7 Cir., 139 F.2d 98, certiorari denied 321 U.S. 785, chart for recording temperatures; *Aldrich v. Remington-Rand,* D.C.N.D. Texas, 52 F.Supp. 732, sheets for keeping tax records; *Page v. Wisden,* 20 L.T.R. (n. s.) 435, cricket scoring sheet. And since the Constitution and Copyright Act read directly upon all the forms here involved, we hold them to be copyrightable.

This resolution of the question of copyrightability raises several very serious questions as to the scope of the protection granted which we now come to consider.

---

* Section 4 of the 1909 Act actually provided: "The works for which copyright may be secured under this title shall include all the *writings* of an author." [Emphasis added.] *See* p. 65 *supra.* — Eds.

Infringement

We agree completely with the conclusion of the trial court. . . .

. . . .

There have been several cases dealing with the copyrighting of insurance and similar forms. Significantly, they uniformly are decided by holdings of non-infringement and leave undecided the copyrightability point.[3] These cases have set a stiff standard for proof of infringement.

In *Dorsey v. Old Surety Life Ins. Co.*, 10 Cir., 98 F.2d 872, 874, 119 A.L.R. 1250, the court found non-infringement declaring, "To constitute infringement in such cases a showing of appropriation in the exact form or substantially so of the copyrighted material should be required."

In *Crume v. Pacific Mut. Life Ins. Co.*, 7 Cir., 140 F.2d 182, certiorari denied 322 U.S. 755, the court found non-infringement of plaintiff's pamphlet describing a method for reorganizing insurance companies. As in all of these cases, the court was keenly aware that to prohibit similarity of language would have the effect of giving the copyright owner a monopoly on his idea — which the cases uniformly deny to copyright owners. Thus, the court stated, 140 F.2d at pages 184-185:

> . . . In the instant situation there is no room for the skill of the mechanic or artisan in utilizing the plan or the method disclosed. Its use, to which the public is entitled, can be effected solely by the employment of words descriptive thereof. In our view, where the use can be effected only in such manner, there can be no infringement even though the plan or method be copied. We realize that such a view leaves little, if any, protection to the copyright owners; in fact, it comes near to invalidating the copyright. This situation, however, results from the fact that the practical use of the art explained by the copyright and lodged in the public domain can be attained solely by the employment of language which gives expression to that which is disclosed.

Further,

> We also observe that such comparison [of the documents] adds strength to the view heretofore expressed that defendant's rightful use of the art disclosed could only be accomplished by the employment of words which describe plaintiff's method. To hold that an idea, plan, method or art described in a copyright is open to the public but that it can be used only by the employment of different words and phrases which mean the same thing, borders on the preposterous. It is to exalt the accomplishment of a result by indirect means which could not be done directly. It places a premium upon evasion and makes this the test of infringement. Notwithstanding some authorities which support a theory permitting such a result, we think it is wrong and disapprove it.

. . . .

These cases indicate that in the fields of insurance and commerce the use of specific language in forms and documents may be so essential to accomplish a desired result and so integrated with the use of a legal or commercial conception that the proper standard of infringement is one which will protect as far as possible the copyrighted language and yet allow free use of the thought beneath the language. The evidence here shows that Continental in so far as it has used

---

[3] We have had to decide the copyright question here because one portion of the judgment appealed from enjoined Beardsley from claiming a copyright on any of his forms.

the language of Beardsley's forms has done so only as incidental to its use of the underlying idea. *Chautauqua School of Nursing v. National School of Nursing,* 2 Cir., 238 F. 151. In so doing it has not infringed.

Publication

[The court affirmed the alternative holding that a distribution without a copyright notice, unlimited as to persons and purpose, amounted to a "publication" forfeiting copyright.]

Conclusion

Judge Palmieri, on the ground of noncopyrightability of all forms, granted an injunction which forbade Beardsley from asserting the claim that any of his forms were copyrighted. Judge Palmieri further supported this injunction as to the forms appearing in the Beardsley pamphlet by a finding that the copyright as to those forms had been forfeited.

Our disposition of this case requires that the injunction be modified. Since we affirm Judge Palmieri's determination of forfeiture of copyright on the forms in the Beardsley pamphlet, the injunction as to those forms was proper. But since we held that in general insurance forms are copyrightable, the injunction should be modified so as to extend no further than to the forms included in the forfeiture as determined by Judge Palmieri.

Modified and affirmed.

DONALD v. ZACK MEYER'S T.V. SALES & SERVICE

426 F.2d 1027 (5th Cir. 1970), *cert. denied,* 400 U.S. 997 (1971)

GOLDBERG, CIRCUIT JUDGE.

In this infringement suit a maker of business forms seeks copyright protection for a common legal form. The characters in this drama are O.W. Donald, the copyright claimant; Moore Business Forms, Inc., the alleged infringer; and Zack Meyer's T. V. Sales and Service, the innocent bystander. Act I of this play ended when the trial court found for Donald. We rewrite the script and reverse.

In 1961 Donald registered with the copyright office the following paragraph:

Agreement

For value received, the undersigned jointly and severally promise to pay to the Dealer, or order, the unpaid balance shown on this invoice according to the agreed terms. Title to said Chattel, described hereon by model, make and serial number, is hereby retained, or transferred to Dealer until Customer has paid in cash all amounts owing said Dealer. Customer shall not misuse, secrete, sell, encumber, remove or otherwise dispose of or lose possession of said Chattel. There is no outstanding lien, mortgage, or other encumbrance against said Chattel. Should Customer fail to pay its indebtedness when due, or breach this contract, the entire unpaid balance shall at once become due and payable, and Dealer may without notice or demand, by process of law, or otherwise, take possession of said Chattel wherever located and retain all monies paid thereon for use of said Chattel. This Agreement may be assigned.

This language, known as the "Agreement," was printed at the bottom of standard invoice forms which Donald printed and sold to television dealers and repairmen. Moore began using this language on its forms when one of its customers ordered a set of invoices and specifically requested that this language be included on the forms. The customer apparently had clipped the requested language from a form prepared by Donald. Subsequently, when Zack Meyer ordered invoice forms from Moore, Moore copied the language that its previous customer had requested.

Upon discovering Zack Meyer's forms, Donald brought suit against Moore and Zack Meyer, claiming that their use of the language contained in the "Agreement" infringed Donald's copyright. The trial court, while expressing doubt concerning the originality of the "Agreement," found that Donald had a valid copyright on the language used by Moore and that Moore had infringed Donald's copyright by printing and selling the offending forms. The court enjoined Moore from any future infringement and assessed the costs of suit against Moore as required by 17 U.S.C.A. § 116. Finding that Zack Meyer had nothing whatever to do with the selection of language in the forms supplied by Moore, the court held that Zack Meyer was not liable for any copyright infringement and had been unnecessarily joined as a party defendant by Donald. Zack Meyer's counsel fees were divided equally between Moore and Donald.

Moore has appealed from the decision of the trial court, claiming that Donald's copyright is invalid for lack of originality. We agree.

It is too plain to be denied that the "Agreement" is nothing more than an ordinary conditional sales contract or chattel mortgage agreement, an instrument familiar to even the most inexperienced legal practitioner. It is the type of contract which has been published in numerous form books, many of which are themselves copyrighted. See, e. g., Am. Jur. Legal Forms and Stayton Texas Forms.

Plaintiff, a non-lawyer who stated that he studied law for approximately one year, has denied that he used these prior works in preparing the "Agreement." However, considering the technical difficulties involved in drafting such a form, plaintiff's limited legal education, and his obvious access to and knowledge of these forms from his uncompleted legal studies, we have no doubt that plaintiff either consciously or unconsciously availed himself of these prior works while drafting the "Agreement." Moreover, the striking similarity in arrangement, order, and wording between plaintiff's "Agreement" and the standard forms is sufficient to compel a finding that plaintiff used these earlier works. *Orgel v. Clark Boardman Co.,* 2 Cir. 1962, 301 F.2d 119, cert. denied, 371 U.S. 817; *Arnstein v. Porter,* 2 Cir. 1946, 154 F.2d 464.

Neither the existence of these earlier forms nor Donald's use of them, however, necessarily renders his paragraph ineligible for copyright protection. It is settled law that to obtain a valid copyright, as distinguished from a patent, the applicant need not show that the material in question is unique or novel; it need only be original. *Gelles-Widmer Co. v. Milton Bradley Co.,* 7 Cir. 1963, 313 F.2d 143, cert. denied, 373 U.S. 913; *Alfred Bell & Co. v. Catalda Fine Arts,* 2 Cir. 1951, 191 F.2d 99. Thus a work may be protected by copyright even though it is based on a prior copyrighted work or something already in the public domain if the author, through his skill and effort, has contributed a distinguishable variation from the older works. *Gelles-Widmer Co. v. Milton Bradley Co., supra; Millworth Converting Corp. v. Slifka,* 2 Cir. 1960, 276 F.2d 443; *Alfred Bell & Co. v. Catalda Fine Arts, supra.* In such a case, of course, only those parts which are new are protected by the new copyright. *Dorsey v. Old Surety Life Ins. Co.,* 10 Cir. 1938, 98 F.2d 872.

In determining the amount of originality required it is frequently stated that the standards are minimal and that in copyright law "originality means little more than a prohibition against copying." *Gelles-Widmer Co. v. Milton Bradley Co., supra. Day-Brite Lighting, Inc. v. Sta-Brite Fluorescent Manufacturing Co.,* 5 Cir. 1962, 308 F.2d 377; *Alfred Bell & Co. v. Catalda Fine Arts, supra.* Nevertheless, something more than merely refraining from outright copying is required before a new variation on an old work has sufficient originality to be copyrightable. The author must add "some substantial, not merely trivial, originality." *Chamberlin v. Uris Sales Corp.,* 2 Cir. 1945, 150 F.2d 512, 513. The variation must be meaningful and must result from original creative work on the author's part. *Amsterdam v. Triangle Publications, Inc.,* 3 Cir. 1951, 189 F.2d 104; *Andrews v. Guenther Publishing Co.,* S.D.N.Y.1932, 60 F.2d 555; *Jeweler's Circular Publishing Co. v. Keystone Publishing Co.,* 2 Cir. 1922, 281 F. 83, cert. denied, 259 U.S. 581; *McIntyre v. Double-A Music Corp.,* S.D.Cal.1959, 179 F.Supp. 160; *Alva Studios, Inc. v. Winninger,* S.D.N.Y.1959, 177 F.Supp. 265; *Smith v. George E. Muehlebach Brewing Co.,* W.D.Mo.1956, 140 F.Supp. 729. As the court said in *Smith,*

> "Originality" in the above context means that the material added to what is in the public domain, must have aspects of "novelty" and be something more than a trivial addition or variation. Cf. *Chamberlin v. Uris Sales Corporation,* 2 Cir., 150 F.2d 512. If what is added does not itself give some value to a public domain composition, or serve some purpose other than to merely emphasize what is present and subsisting in the public domain, it is not entitled to copyright.... 140 F.Supp. at 731.

In the case before us we search in vain for the requisite originality in plaintiff's "Agreement." The "Agreement" contains nothing of substance which resulted from Donald's creative work. The order and arrangement of the subject matter in the "Agreement" are identical with several forms suggested in prior works. See e. g., 11 Am. Jur. Legal Forms, § 1447 (1958). The word arrangement used, while not identical, is at most only a paraphrase of various portions of earlier forms, and in copyright law paraphrasing is equivalent to outright copying. *Nutt v. National Institute Incorporated for the Improvement of Memory,* 2 Cir. 1929, 31 F.2d 236; *Davis v. E. I. DuPont de Nemours & Co.,* S.D.N.Y.1965, 240 F.Supp. 612. The plaintiff did no original legal research which resulted in a significant addition to the standard conditional sales contract or chattel mortgage forms; he merely made trivial word changes by combining various forms and servilely imitating the already stereotyped language found therein. In fact it may be fairly assumed that such variations in language as did occur in plaintiff's "Agreement" were deliberately insignificant, for he plainly wanted a valid conditional sales contract or chattel mortgage, and validity was an attribute which the earlier forms had been proved through use to have.

In *Amsterdam v. Triangle Publications, Inc., supra,* the Third Circuit faced a claim to copyright protection in a similar situation. The plaintiff in that case had used several existing maps but little independent original research of his own to prepare a map upon which he claimed a copyright. In denying his map copyright protection from a claimed infringement, the court, adopting the language of the trial court, said:

> To make his map, the plaintiff had to determine only what information he was going to use from other maps, the emphasis to be given to that information and the coloring scheme and symbols he was going to use. When he finished, his map by comparison was a new map that contained some information that was not on any one of his base maps but was collectively on all of these maps.

Is this exercise of judgment and discretion by the plaintiff the type of original work that is intended to be protected by the Copyright Act? I think not.

. . . .

. . . The presentation of ideas in the form of books, movies, music and other similar creative work is protected by the Copyright Act. However, the presentation of information available to everybody, such as is found on maps, is protected only when the publisher of the map in question obtains originally some of that information by the sweat of his own brow. Almost anybody could combine the information from several maps onto one map, but not everybody can go out and get that information originally and then transcribe it into a map.

The plaintiff's reputation as a qualified map maker cannot make copyrightable maps for him. He, or his agents, must first do some original work, get more than an infinitesimal amount of original information. With no reflection whatsoever upon the plaintiff's ability as a map maker or upon other maps published and copyrighted by the plaintiff, it seems to me that the plaintiff's map entitled "Map of Delaware County, Pa." is, for lack or (sic) original work, not subject to copyright. 189 F.2d at 106.

In the case before us Donald has contributed nothing more than the map maker in *Amsterdam*. While the "Agreement" is not identical to any single existing form, the substance of each sentence can be found in an earlier form. Thus, like the map in *Amsterdam,* Donald's form is nothing more than a mosaic of the existing forms, with no original piece added. The Copyright Act was not designed to protect such negligible efforts. We reward creativity and originality with a copyright but we do not accord copyright protection to a mere copycat. As one noted authority has observed, "to make the copyright turnstile revolve, the author should have to deposit more than a penny in the box." B. Kaplan, An Unhurried View of Copyright 46 (1966). In our case not even the proverbial penny has been placed in the box. Indeed the box is virtually empty. We hold, therefore, that Donald's copyright is invalid for lack of originality. Having concluded that Donald's "Agreement" was not subject to copyright, we think it goes without saying that Moore's use of the form language was not an infringement.

The only remaining questions concern the assessment of costs and attorneys' fees. The trial court assessed the costs of suit against the losing party, Moore, as required by 17 U.S.C.A. § 116. Since we have reversed the trial court's determination on the merits, Donald, the losing party, must pay the costs as required by statute. An award of attorneys' fees is discretionary under § 116, and the trial court exercised this discretion by directing that Donald and Moore pay their own counsel fees. We see no reason to disturb this determination. The counsel fees incurred by Zack Meyer were divided by the trial court equally between Donald and Moore. We think, however, that the entire amount of this expense must be assessed against Donald. Moore has already been put to the expense of defending an infringement suit against an invalid copyright claim. It was Donald who unnecessarily joined Zack Meyer as a party defendant, and it is Donald who should bear the expense for this error.

Reversed.

QUESTIONS

1. Is there support in theory for the court's requirement that a work, to be copyrightable, must be "novel" and "creative"? In the *Jeweler's Circular* case, cited by the court, it was held that a photograph of an uncopyrightable trademark could be copyrighted. In the *Alva* case, cited by the court, it was held

that an exact duplicate (except for being smaller) of a public domain Rodin sculpture could be copyrighted. The *Catalda* case, of course, also cited by the court, upheld the copyrightability of a mezzotint engraving of an old master painting. How can the court justify a different outcome in the *Zack Meyer* case?

2. Is an anthology of public domain poetry copyrightable under § 103? Are greeting cards which combine simplistic illustrations with brief and trite phrases copyrightable? Why not chattel mortgage forms?

3. Is not the key to understanding the decision in *Zack Meyer* — and the distinction of the cases mentioned in the above problems — simply that this was not a case of a painting, drawing, sculpture or poetry, but a case of lawyers' prose, a subject on which courts will hardly be inhibited by the kind of strictures articulated by Justice Holmes in the *Bleistein* case? Ought not the court have heeded those strictures?

4. Reconsider the court's reliance on the *Amsterdam* case, involving map collation, after noting the *Hamilton* case, at p. 86 *supra*.

5. In holding that the plaintiff in *Zack Meyer* had not contributed sufficient authorship to his forms, the court stated that "in copyright law paraphrasing is equivalent to outright copying." It cited, for support, two cases which articulated this view in concluding that the defendant's modest modifications or paraphrasings of the plaintiff's copyrighted work cannot avoid infringement. Is that a persuasive maxim when the issue is the extent of authorship necessary to secure a copyright?

6. Both the *Zack Meyer* case and the *Beardsley* case permitted copying of the plaintiffs' forms; in the former case, by holding no copyright, and in the latter case, by holding no infringement. Which is the sounder approach?

7. Since lawyers, in drafting commercial forms, are necessarily confined by the holdings of earlier cases construing and implementing language in earlier forms, are there any circumstances in which any legal form would be copyrightable under the reasoning of the court in *Zack Meyer?*

8. What exactly is protected by the copyright on a formbook containing a collection of litigation forms or commercial forms? Would it infringe such a copyright for a lawyer to copy and use a form from such a book, in servicing a client? Would it infringe for a commercial printer to print and sell thousands of copies of such a form? Would it infringe to copy all of the forms for incorporation in a competing formbook (assuming, for example, the later publisher changes the sequence in which the forms appear in his book)?

9. As a law student, how would you evaluate the court's conclusion that the plaintiff in *Zack Meyer* could not properly be treated as the author of his chattel mortgage form, since it could be assumed that he, after his first year of law school, was familiar with the standard forms of chattel mortgage? (Surely an ill-founded exercise in judicial notice, wouldn't you say?)

MORRISSEY v. PROCTER & GAMBLE CO.

379 F.2d 675 (1st Cir. 1967)

ALDRICH, CHIEF JUDGE.

This is an appeal from a summary judgment for the defendant. The plaintiff, Morrissey, is the copyright owner of a set of rules for a sales promotional contest of the "sweepstakes" type involving the social security numbers of the participants. Plaintiff alleges that the defendant, Procter & Gamble Company, infringed, by copying, almost precisely, Rule 1. In its motion for summary judgment, based upon affidavits and depositions, defendant denies that plaintiff's

Rule 1 is copyrightable material, and denies access. The district court held for the defendant on both grounds.

[The court found an issue of fact as to access precluding summary judgment.]

The second aspect of the case raises a more difficult question. Before discussing it we recite plaintiff's Rule 1, and defendant's Rule 1, the italicizing in the latter being ours to note the defendant's variations or changes.

1. Entrants should print name, address and social security number on a boxtop, or a plain paper. Entries must be accompanied by . . . boxtop or by plain paper on which the name . . . is copied from any source. Official rules are explained on . . . packages or leaflets obtained from dealer. If you do not have a social security number you may use the name and number of any member of your immediate family living with you. Only the person named on the entry will be deemed an entrant and may qualify for prize.

Use the correct social security number belonging to the person named on entry . . . wrong number will be disqualified.

(Plaintiff's Rule)

1. Entrants should print name, address and Social Security number on a Tide boxtop, or *on* [a] plain paper. Entries must be accompanied by Tide boxtop *(any size)* or by plain paper on which the name 'Tide' is copied from any source. Official rules are *available* on Tide Sweepstakes packages, or *on* leaflets *at* Tide dealers, *or you can send a stamped, self-addressed envelope to:* Tide "Shopping Fling" Sweepstakes, P.O. Box 4459, Chicago 77, Illinois.

If you do not have a Social Security number, you may use the name and number of any member of your immediate family living with you. Only the person named on the entry will be deemed an entrant and may qualify for a prize.

Use the correct Social Security number, belonging to the person named on *the* entry — wrong numbers will be disqualified.

(Defendant's Rule)

The district court, following an earlier decision, *Gaye v. Gillis,* D.Mass.,1958, 167 F.Supp. 416, took the position that since the substance of the contest was not copyrightable, which is unquestionably correct, *Baker v. Selden,* 1879, 101 U.S. 99; *Affiliated Enterprises v. Gruber,* 1 Cir., 1936, 86 F.2d 958; *Chamberlin v. Uris Sales Corp.,* 2 Cir., 1945, 150 F.2d 512, and the substance was relatively simple, it must follow that plaintiff's rule sprung directly from the substance and "contains no original creative authorship." 262 F.Supp. at 738. This does not follow. Copyright attaches to form of expression, and defendant's own proof, introduced to deluge the court on the issue of access, itself established that there was more than one way of expressing even this simple substance. Nor, in view of the almost precise similarity of the two rules, could defendant successfully invoke the principle of a stringent standard for showing infringement which some courts apply when the subject matter involved admits of little variation in form of expression. E. g., *Dorsey v. Old Surety Life Ins. Co.,* 10 Cir., 1938, 98 F.2d 872, 874, 119 A.L.R. 1250 ("a showing of appropriation in the exact form or substantially so."); *Continental Casualty Co. v. Beardsley,* 2 Cir., 1958, 253 F.2d 702, 705, cert. denied, 358 U.S. 816 ("a stiff standard for proof of infringement.").

Nonetheless, we must hold for the defendant. When the uncopyrightable subject matter is very narrow, so that "the topic necessarily requires," *Sampson & Murdock Co. v. Seaver-Radford Co.,* 1 Cir., 1905, 140 F. 539, 541; cf. Kaplan, An Unhurried View of Copyright, 64-65 (1967), if not only one form of expression, at best only a limited number, to permit copyrighting would mean that a party or parties, by copyrighting a mere handful of forms, could exhaust all possibilities of future use of the substance. In such circumstances it does not seem accurate to say that any particular form of expression comes from the subject matter. However, it is necessary to say that the subject matter would be appropriated by permitting the copyrighting of its expression. We cannot recognize copyright as a game of chess in which the public can be checkmated. Cf. *Baker v. Selden,* supra.

Upon examination the matters embraced in Rule 1 are so straightforward and simple that we find this limiting principle to be applicable. Furthermore, its operation need not await an attempt to copyright all possible forms. It cannot be only the last form of expression which is to be condemned, as completing defendant's exclusion from the substance. Rather, in these circumstances, we hold that copyright does not extend to the subject matter at all, and plaintiff cannot complain even if his particular expression was deliberately adopted.

Affirmed.

QUESTION

Harcourt, Brace and World, Inc. publishes a large number of educational tests, including the Stanford Achievement Test (SAT), taken by school children throughout the United States. The test questions are contained in booklets, and are of the multiple-choice type. The student makes a mark on an accompanying answer sheet which corresponds to the letter or number alongside one of the several possible answers in the test booklet. The completed answer sheets are then viewed by an optical scanning machine which automatically scores the responses. The format of the answer sheets is designed to meet the requirements of the optical scanning machine (e.g., the IBM 805 or the Digitek), which determine the size and shape of the answer sheet and of the spaces in which the student records his response, as well as the maximum number of answer spaces per sheet and the distance between the spaces. Within these confines, Harcourt fashions the balance of the content of the answer sheet. It decides where the student's name, school, teacher and like information are to be recorded; which of the possible response spaces shall be used and which left blank, and how the numbers of the questions and answer choices shall be placed; and what titles shall be placed on the sheets to correspond to title headings in the examination booklet. Harcourt secured a copyright on both its examination booklet and its answer forms. When the City of Buffalo invited bids for the printing and sale of 100,000 SAT answer sheets for use in conjunction with the IBM 805, a bid of $9,000 was submitted by Harcourt and a bid of $2,500 was submitted by Graphic Controls Corp., a printer of business forms. The form proffered by Graphic, although containing two original items (including the student's ethnic grouping), was based substantially on a copy of Harcourt's form, which was supplied by the Buffalo Board of Education; the Graphic from utilized the same placement of response positions, numbers for questions and letters or numbers for responses, name of the examination, instructions for use of the answer sheet with the test booklet, and certain other details. Graphic made no use of Harcourt's test booklets as distinguished from its answer sheets.

Harcourt has brought an action against Graphic for copyright infringement, and both parties have moved for summary judgment. The issues are whether Harcourt's answer sheets are proper subjects of copyright and whether Graphic has infringed. You are the judge. Rule on the motion, with reasons. *See Harcourt, Brace & World, Inc. v. Graphic Controls Corp.,* 329 F. Supp. 517 (S.D.N.Y. 1971).

A. A. HOEHLING v. UNIVERSAL CITY STUDIOS, INC.

618 F.2d 972 (2d Cir. 1980)

KAUFMAN, CHIEF JUDGE: A grant of copyright in a published work secures for its author a limited monopoly over the expression it contains. The copyright provides a financial incentive to those who would add to the corpus of existing knowledge by creating original works. Nevertheless, the protection afforded the copyright holder has never extended to history, be it documented fact or explanatory hypothesis. The rationale for this doctrine is that the cause of knowledge is best served when history is the common property of all, and each generation remains free to draw upon the discoveries and insights of the past. Accordingly, the scope of copyright in historical accounts is narrow indeed, embracing no more than the author's original expression of particular facts and theories already in the public domain. As the case before us illustrates, absent wholesale usurpation of another's expression, claims of copyright infringement where works of history are at issue are rarely successful.

I

This litigation arises from three separate accounts of the triumphant introduction, last voyage, and tragic destruction of the Hindenburg, the colossal dirigible constructed in Germany during Hitler's reign. The zeppelin, the last and most sophisticated in a fleet of luxury airships, which punctually floated its wealthy passengers from the Third Reich to the United States, exploded into flames and disintegrated in 35 seconds as it hovered above the Lakehurst, New Jersey Naval Air Station at 7:25 p.m. on May 6, 1937. Thirty-six passengers and crew were killed but, fortunately, 52 persons survived. Official investigations conducted by both American and German authorities could ascertain no definitive cause of the disaster, but both suggested the plausibility of static electricity or St. Elmo's Fire, which could have ignited the highly explosive hydrogen that filled the airship. Throughout, the investigators refused to rule out the possibility of sabotage.

The destruction of the Hindenburg marked the concluding chapter in the chronicle of airship passenger service, for after the tragedy at Lakehurst, the Nazi regime permanently grounded the Graf Zeppelin I and discontinued its plan to construct an even larger dirigible, the Graf Zeppelin II.

The final pages of the airship's story marked the beginning of a series of journalistic, historical, and literary accounts devoted to the Hindenburg and its fate. Indeed, weeks of testimony by a plethora of witnesses before the official investigative panels provided fertile source material for would-be authors. Moreover, both the American and German Commissions issued official reports, detailing all that was then known of the tragedy. A number of newspaper and magazine articles had been written about the Hindenburg in 1936, its first year of trans-Atlantic service, and they, of course, multipled many fold after the crash. In addition, two passengers — Margaret Mather and Gertrud Adelt — published separate and detailed accounts of the voyage. C.E. Rosendahl, commander of the Lakehurst Naval Air Station and a pioneer in airship travel himself, wrote a book titled *What About the Airship?*, in which he endorsed the theory that the Hindenburg was the victim of sabotage. In 1957, Nelson Gidding, who would return to the subject of the Hindenburg some 20 years later, wrote an unpublished "treatment" for a motion picture based on the deliberate destruction of the airship. In that year as well, John Toland published *Ships in the Sky* which, in its seventeenth chapter, chronicled the last flight of the

Hindenburg. In 1962, Dale Titler released *Wings of Mystery,* in which he too devoted a chapter to the Hindenburg.[1]

Appellant A.A. Hoehling published *Who Destroyed the Hindenburg?,* a full-length book based on his exhaustive research in 1962. Mr. Hoehling studied the investigative reports, consulted previously published articles and books, and conducted interviews with survivors of the crash as well as others who possessed information about the Hindenburg. His book is presented as a factual account, written in an objective, reportorial style.

The first half recounts the final crossing of the Hindenburg, from Sunday, May 2, when it left Frankfurt, to Thursday, May 6, when it exploded at Lakehurst. Hoehling describes the airship, its role as an instrument of propaganda in Nazi Germany, its passengers and crew, the danger of hydrogen, and the ominous threats received by German officials, warning that the Hindenburg would be destroyed. The second portion, headed *The Quest,* sets forth the progress of the official investigations, followed by an account of Hoehling's own research. In the final chapter, spanning eleven pages, Hoehling suggests that all proffered explanations of the explosion, save deliberate destruction, are unconvincing. He concludes that the most likely saboteur is one Eric Spehl, a "rigger" on the Hindenburg crew who was killed at Lakehurst.

According to Hoehling, Spehl had motive, expertise, and opportunity to plant an explosive device, constructed of dry-cell batteries and a flashbulb, in "Gas Cell 4," the location of the initial explosion. An amateur photographer with access to flashbulbs, Spehl could have destroyed the Hindenburg to please his ladyfriend, a suspected communist dedicated to exploding the myth of Nazi invincibility.

Ten years later appellee Michael MacDonald Mooney published his book, *The Hindenburg.* Mooney's endeavor might be characterized as more literary than historical in its attempt to weave a number of symbolic themes through the actual events surrounding the tragedy. His dominant theme contrasts the natural beauty of the month of May, when the disaster occurred, with the cold, deliberate progress of "technology." The May theme is expressed not simply by the season, but also by the character of Spehl, portrayed as a sensitive artisan with needle and thread. The Hindenburg, in contrast, is the symbol of technology, as are its German creators and the Reich itself. The destruction is depicted as the ultimate triumph of nature over technology, as Spehl plants the bomb that ignites the hydrogen. Developing this theme from the outset, Mooney begins with an extended review of man's efforts to defy nature through flight, focusing on the evolution of the zeppelin. This story culminates in the construction of the Hindenburg, and the Nazis' claims of its indestructibility. Mooney then traces the fateful voyage, advising the reader almost immediately of Spehl's scheme. The book concludes with the airship's explosion.

Mooney acknowledges, in this case, that he consulted Hoehling's book, and that he relied on it for some details. He asserts that he first discovered the "Spehl-as-saboteur" theory when he read Titler's *Wings of Mystery.* Indeed, Titler concludes that Spehl was the saboteur, for essentially the reasons stated by Hoehling. Mooney also claims to have studied the complete National Archives and New York Times files concerning the Hindenburg, as well as all previously published material. Moreover, he traveled to Germany, visited Spehl's birthplace, and conducted a number of interviews with survivors.

After Mooney prepared an outline of his anticipated book, his publisher succeeded in negotiations to sell the motion picture rights to appellee Universal

---

[1] Titler's account was published after the release of appellant's book. In an affidavit in this litigation, Titler states that he copied Hoehling's theory of sabotage. Hoehling, however, has never instituted a copyright action against Titler.

City Studios.[2] Universal then commissioned a screen story by writers Levinson and Link, best known for their television series, *Columbo*, in which a somewhat disheveled, but wise detective unravels artfully conceived murder mysteries. In their screen story, Levinson and Link created a Columbo-like character who endeavored to identify the saboteur on board the Hindenburg. Director Robert Wise, however, was not satisfied with this version, and called upon Nelson Gidding to write a final screenplay. Gidding, it will be recalled, had engaged in preliminary work on a film about the Hindenburg almost twenty years earlier.

The Gidding screenplay follows what is known in the motion picture industry as a "Grand Hotel" formula, developing a number of fictional characters and subplots involving them. This formula has become standard fare in so-called "disaster" movies, which have enjoyed a certain popularity in recent years. In the film, which was released in late 1975, a rigger named "Boerth," who has an anti-Nazi ladyfriend, plans to destroy the airship in an effort to embarrass the Reich. Nazi officials, vaguely aware of sabotage threats, station a Luftwaffe intelligence officer on the zeppelin, loosely resembling a Colonel Erdmann who was aboard the Hindenburg. This character is portrayed as a likable fellow who soon discovers that Boerth is the saboteur. Boerth, however, convinces him that the Hindenburg should be destroyed and the two join forces, planning the explosion for several hours after the landing at Lakehurst, when no people would be on board. In Gidding's version, the airship is delayed by a storm, frantic efforts to defuse the bomb fail, and the Hindenburg is destroyed. The film's subplots involve other possible suspects, including a fictional countess who has had her estate expropriated by the Reich, two fictional confidence men wanted by New York City police, and an advertising executive rushing to close a business deal in America.

Upon learning of Universal's plans to release the film, Hoehling instituted this action against Universal for copyright infringement and common law unfair competition in the district court for the District of Columbia in October 1975. Judge Smith declined to issue an order restraining release of the film in December, and it was distributed throughout the nation.

In January 1976, Hoehling sought to amend his complaint to include Mooney as a defendant. The district court, however, decided that it lacked personal jurisdiction over Mooney. In June 1976, Hoehling again attempted to amend his complaint, this time to add Mooney's publishers as defendants. Judge Smith denied this motion as well, but granted Hoehling's request to transfer the litigation to the Southern District of New York, 28 U.S.C. § 1404(a), where Mooney himself was successfully included as a party. Judge Metzner, with the assistance of Magistrate Sinclair, supervised extensive discovery through most of 1978. After the completion of discovery, both Mooney and Universal moved for summary judgment, Fed. R. Civ. P. 56, which was granted on August 1, 1979.

---

[2] Mooney, his publishers, and Universal entered into an agreement under which (1) Universal acquired the film rights to Mooney's book, (2) Universal agreed to promote sales of the book, and (3) Mooney would receive a percentage fee, tied to sales of his book. Hoehling claims that because of this arrangement, Universal is vicariously liable if Mooney's book, but not the motion picture, is held to infringe his copyright. In view of our disposition of the appeal, however, we need not address this issue.

II

It is undisputed that Hoehling has a valid copyright in his book. To prove infringement, however, he must demonstrate that defendants "copied" his work and that they "improperly appropriated" his "expression." *See Arnstein v. Porter,* 154 F.2d 464, 468 (2d Cir. 1946). Ordinarily, wrongful appropriation is shown by proving a "substantial similarity" of *copyrightable* expression. *See Nichols v. Universal Pictures Corp.,* 45 F.2d 119, 121 (2d Cir. 1930), *cert. denied,* 282 U.S. 902 (1931). Because substantial similarity is customarily an extremely close question of fact, *see Arnstein, supra,* 154 F.2d at 468, summary judgment has traditionally been frowned upon in copyright litigation. *Id.* at 474. Nevertheless, while *Arnstein*'s influence in other areas of the law has been diminished, *see SEC v. Research Automation Corp.,* 585 F.2d 31 (2d Cir. 1978); 6 *Moore's Federal Practice* ¶ 56.17[14] (2d ed. 1976), a series of copyright cases in the Southern District of New York have granted defendants summary judgment when all alleged similarity related to *non*-copyrightable elements of the plaintiff's work, *see, e.g., Alexander v. Haley,* 460 F. Supp. 40 (S.D.N.Y. 1978); *Musto v. Meyer,* 434 F. Supp. 32 (S.D.N.Y. 1977); *Gardner v. Nizer,* 391 F. Supp. 940 (S.D.N.Y. 1975); *Fuld v. National Broadcasting Co.,* 390 F. Supp. 877 (S.D.N.Y. 1975). These cases signal an important development in the law of copyright, permitting courts to put "a swift end to meritless litigation" and to avoid lengthy and costly trials. *Quinn v. Syracuse Model Neighborhood Corp.,* No. 79-7561, slip op. at 835 (2d Cir. Jan. 8, 1980); *accord, Donnelly v. Guion,* 467 F.2d 290, 293 (2d Cir. 1972); *American Manufacturers Mutual Insurance Co. v. American Broadcasting-Paramount Theatres, Inc.,* 388 F.2d 272, 278 (2d Cir. 1967). Drawing on these cases, Judge Metzner assumed both copying and substantial similarity, but concluded that all similarities pertained to various categories of non-copyrightable material. Accordingly, he granted appellees' motion for summary judgment. We affirm the judgment of the district court.

A

Hoehling's principal claim is that both Mooney and Universal copied the essential plot of his book — *i.e.,* Eric Spehl, influenced by his girlfriend, sabotaged the Hindenburg by placing a crude bomb in Gas Cell 4. In their briefs, and at oral argument, appellees have labored to convince us that their plots are not substantially similar to Hoehling's. While Hoehling's Spehl destroys the airship to please his communist girlfriend, Mooney's character is motivated by an aversion to the technological age. Universal's Boerth, on the other hand, is a fervent anti-fascist who enlists the support of a Luftwaffe colonel who, in turn, unsuccessfully attempts to defuse the bomb at the eleventh hour.

Although this argument has potential merit when presented to a fact finder adjudicating the issue of substantial similarity, it is largely irrelevant to a motion for summary judgment where the issue of substantial similarity has been eliminated by the judge's affirmative assumption. Under Rule 56(c), summary judgment is appropriate only when "there is no genuine issue as to any material fact." *Accord, Heyman v. Commerce & Industry Insurance Co.,* 524 F.2d 1317 (2d Cir. 1975). Perhaps recognizing this, appellees further argue that Hoehling's plot is an "idea," and ideas are not copyrightable as a matter of law. *See Sheldon v. Metro-Goldwyn Pictures Corp.,* 81 F.2d 49, 54 (2d Cir.), *cert. denied,* 298 U.S. 669 (1936).

Hoehling, however, correctly rejoins that while ideas themselves are not subject to copyright, his "expression" of *his* idea is copyrightable. *Id.* at 54. He relies on Learned Hand's opinion in *Sheldon, supra,* at 50, holding that *Letty Lynton* infringed *Dishonored Lady* by copying its story of a woman who poisons her lover, and Augustus Hand's analysis in *Detective Comics, Inc. v. Bruns Publications, Inc.,* 111 F.2d 432 (2d Cir. 1940), concluding that the exploits of "Wonderman" infringed the copyright held by the creators of "Superman," the original indestructible man. Moreover, Hoehling asserts that, in both these cases, the line between "ideas" and "expression" is drawn, in the first instance, by the fact finder.

Sheldon and *Detective Comics,* however, dealt with works of fiction,[4] where the distinction between an idea and its expression is especially elusive. But, where, as here, the idea at issue is an interpretation of an historical event, our cases hold that such interpretations are not copyrightable as a matter of law. In *Rosemont Enterprises, Inc. v. Random House, Inc.,* 366 F.2d 303 (2d Cir. 1966), *cert. denied,* 385 U.S. 1009 (1967), we held that the defendant's biography of Howard Hughes did not infringe an earlier biography of the reclusive alleged billionaire. Although the plots of the two works were necessarily similar, there could be no infringement because of the "public benefit in encouraging the development of historical and biographical works and their public distribution." *Id.* at 307; *accord, Oxford Book Co. v. College Entrance Book Co.,* 98 F.2d 688 (2d Cir. 1938). To avoid a chilling effect on authors who contemplate tackling an historical issue or event, broad latitude must be granted to subsequent authors who make use of historical subject matter, including theories or plots. Learned Hand counseled in *Myers v. Mail & Express Co.,* 36 C.O. Bull. 478, 479 (S.D.N.Y. 1919), "[t]here cannot be any such thing as copyright in the order of presentation of the facts, nor, indeed, in their selection." [5]

In the instant case, the hypothesis that Eric Spehl destroyed the Hindenburg is based entirely on the interpretation of historical facts, including Spehl's life, his girlfriend's anti-Nazi connections, the explosion's origin in Gas Cell 4, Spehl's duty station, discovery of a dry-cell battery among the wreckage, and rumors about Spehl's involvement dating from a 1938 Gestapo investigation. Such an historical interpretation, whether or not it originated with Mr. Hoehling, is not protected by his copyright and can be freely used by subsequent authors.

---

[4] In *Sheldon,* both works were loosely based on an actual murder committed by a young Scottish girl. Judge Hand, however, clearly dealt only with the fictional plots conceived by the respective authors. *See* Sheldon v. Metro-Goldwyn Pictures Corp., 81 F.2d 49, 54 (2d Cir.), *cert. denied,* 298 U.S. 669 (1936).

[5] This circuit has permitted extensive reliance on prior works of history. *See, e.g.,* Gardner v. Nizer, 391 F. Supp. 940 (S.D.N.Y. 1975) (the story of the Rosenberg trial not copyrightable); Fuld v. National Broadcasting Co., 390 F. Supp. 877 (S.D.N.Y. 1975) ("Bugsy" Siegel's life story not copyrightable); Greenbie v. Noble, 151 F. Supp. 45 (S.D.N.Y. 1957) (the life of Anna Carroll, a member of Lincoln's cabinet, not copyrightable). The commentators are in accord with this view. *See, e.g.,* 1 Nimmer on Copyright § 2.11[A] (1979); Chafee, Reflections on the Law of Copyright: I, 45 Colum. L. Rev. 503, 511 (1945).

B

The same reasoning governs Hoehling's claim that a number of specific facts, ascertained through his personal research, were copied by appellees.[6] The cases in this circuit, however, make clear that factual information is in the public domain. *See, e.g., Rosemont Enterprises, Inc., supra,* 366 F.2d at 309; *Oxford Book Co., supra,* 98 F.2d at 691. Each appellee had the right to "avail himself of the facts contained" in Hoehling's book and to "use such information, whether correct or incorrect, in his own literary work." *Greenbie v. Noble,* 151 F. Supp. 45, 67 (S.D.N.Y. 1957). Accordingly, there is little consolation in relying on cases in other circuits holding that the fruits of original research are copyrightable. *See, e.g., Toksvig v. Bruce Publications Corp.,* 181 F.2d 664, 667 (7th Cir. 1950); *Miller v. Universal City Studios, Inc.,* 460 F. Supp. 984 (S.D. Fla. 1978). Indeed, this circuit has clearly repudiated *Toksvig* and its progeny. In *Rosemont Enterprises, Inc., supra,* 366 F.2d at 310, we refused to "subscribe to the view that an author is absolutely precluded from saving time and effort by referring to and relying upon prior published material . . . . It is just such wasted effort that the proscription against the copyright of ideas and facts . . . are designed to prevent." *Accord,* 1 *Nimmer on Copyright* § 2.11 (1979).

C

The remainder of Hoehling's claimed similarities relate to random duplications of phrases and sequences of events. For example, all three works contain a scene in a German beer hall, in which the airship's crew engages in revelry prior to the voyage. Other claimed similarities concern common German greetings of the period, such as "Heil Hitler," or songs, such as the German national anthem. These elements, however, are merely *scenes a faire,* that is, "incidents, characters or settings which are as a practical matter indispensable, or at least standard, in the treatment of a given topic." *Alexander, supra,* 460 F. Supp. at 45; *accord, Bevan v. Columbia Broadcasting System, Inc.,* 329 F. Supp. 601, 607 (S.D.N.Y. 1971). Because it is virtually impossible to write about a particular historical era or fictional theme without employing certain "stock" or standard literary devices, we have held that *scenes a faire* are not copyrightable as a matter of law. *See Reyher v. Children's Television Workshop,* 533 F.2d 87, 91 (2d Cir.), *cert. denied,* 429 U.S. 980 (1976).

---

[6] In detailed comparisons of his book with Mooney's work and Universal's motion picture, Hoehling isolates 266 and 75 alleged instances of copying, respectively. Judge Metzner correctly pointed out that many of these allegations are patently frivolous. The vast majority of the remainder deals with alleged copying of historical facts. It would serve no purpose to review Hoehling's specific allegations in detail in this opinion. The following ten examples, however, are illustrative: (1) Eric Spehl's age and birthplace; (2) Crew members had smuggled monkeys on board the Graf Zeppelin; (3) Germany's ambassador to the United States dismissed threats of sabotage; (4) A warning letter had been received from a Mrs. Rauch; (5) The Hindenburg's captain was constructing a new home in Zeppelinheim; (6) Eric Spehl was a photographer; (7) The airship flew over Boston; (8) The Hindenburg was "tail heavy" before landing; (9) A member of the ground crew had etched his name in the zeppelin's hull; and (10) The navigator set the Hindenburg's course by reference to various North Atlantic islands.

D

All of Hoehling's allegations of copying, therefore, encompass material that is non-copyrightable as a matter of law, rendering summary judgment entirely appropriate. We are aware, however, that in distinguishing between themes, facts, and *scenes a faire* on the one hand, and copyrightable expression on the other, courts may lose sight of the forest for the trees. By factoring out similarities based on non-copyrightable elements, a court runs the risk of overlooking wholesale usurpation of a prior author's expression. A verbatim reproduction of another work, of course, even in the realm of nonfiction, is actionable as copyright infringement. *See Wainwright Securities, Inc. v. Wall Street Transcript Corp.*, 558 F.2d 91 (2d Cir. 1977), *cert. denied*, 434 U.S. 1014 (1978). Thus, in granting or reviewing a grant of summary judgment for defendants, courts should assure themselves that the works before them are not virtually identical. In this case, it is clear that all three authors relate the story of the Hindenburg differently.

In works devoted to historical subjects, it is our view that a second author may make significant use of prior work, so long as he does not bodily appropriate the expression of another. *Rosemont Enterprises, Inc., supra*, 366 F.2d at 310. This principle is justified by the fundamental policy undergirding the copyright laws — the encouragement of contributions to recorded knowledge. The "financial reward guaranteed to the copyright holder is but an incident of this general objective, rather than an end in itself." *Berlin v. E.C. Publications, Inc.*, 329 F.2d 541, 543-44 (2d Cir.), *cert. denied*, 379 U.S. 822 (1964). Knowledge is expanded as well, by granting new authors of historical works a relatively free hand to build upon the work of their predecessors.[7]

III

Finally, we affirm Judge Metzner's rejection of Hoehling's claims based on the common law of "unfair competition." Where, as here, historical facts, themes, and research have been deliberately exempted from the scope of copyright protection to vindicate the overriding goal of encouraging contributions to recorded knowledge, the states are pre-empted from removing such material from the public domain. *See, e.g., Sears, Roebuck & Co. v. Stiffel Co.*, 376 U.S. 225 (1964); *Compco Corp. v. Day-Brite Lighting, Inc.*, 376 U.S. 234 (1964). "To forbid copying" in this case, "would interfere with the federal policy . . . of allowing free access to copy whatever the federal patent and copyright laws leave in the public domain." *Id.* at 237.

The judgment of the district court is affirmed.

D. COMPUTERS

1. INTRODUCTION*

From the Renaissance through the Industrial Revolution to the present,

---

[7] We note that publication of Mooney's book and release of the motion picture revived long dormant interest in the Hindenburg. As a result, Hoehling's book, which had been out of print for some time, was actually re-released after the film was featured in theaters across the country.

* See Final Report of Commission on New Technological Uses of Copyrighted Works (1978); Gottschalk v. Benson, 409 U.S. 63 (1972); Synercom Technology, Inc. v. University Computing Co., 462 F. Supp. 1003 (N.D. Tex. 1978).

technological developments have consistently extended society's power to control natural phenomena and to shape its own destiny. The rapid developments in communications and information technology of the past three decades have immeasurably expanded and extended the power of human communication.

One of the most important contributions to the communication and information revolution has been the digital computer. Animated by elements of human creative genius, these machines are opening new avenues for recording, storing and transmitting human thought. New means of communication transcend words fixed on paper or images on film and permit authors to communicate creatively, adaptively and dynamically with their audience.

A digital computer operates on data expressed in digits, solving a problem by doing arithmetic as a person would do it by head and hand. The speed of the computer is awesome, but the digits are based on combinations of ones and zeros representing on and off positions of switches. Some of the digits are stored as components of the computer. Others are introduced into the computer in a form which it is designed to recognize. The computer operates then upon both new and previously stored data.

Most digital computers have five functional components: (1) input; (2) storage of the input by memory; (3) a control unit which receives data from memory and gives instructions for the arithmetic; (4) an arithmetic which carries out the control's commands; and (5) an output capability.

The computer program in a general sense instructs the computer regarding the things it is to do. In the industry, the physical machinery is referred to as hardware and the instructional material as software.

The first commercial computers, built shortly after World War II, were based largely on vacuum tubes and were so expensive that only the government or the largest corporations could even consider owning them. In order to function, the typical early computer required an environment in which temperature and humidity were carefully monitored. It was controlled by programs created by its manufacturer and users exclusively for that particular computer.

Subsequent generations of computers have been characterized by dramatic reductions in the size, energy requirements and price for a given amount of computational power. These generations are measured by the changes in the electronic circuitry of the computer. The four generations now generally acknowledged have been based upon vacuum tubes, transistors, printed circuits and integrated circuits, respectively.

In the course of this development the Copyright Office was faced with the question of the registrability of computer programs. In 1964 the Office determined to make registration of such works under its "rule of doubt," but required deposit of a human-readable form of the program (e.g., a printout) if the program had been published in only machine-readable form. *See*, e.g., Circular 61 (June 1977).

Although there were no judicial decisions under the 1909 Act validating the Copyright Office practice of registering claims to copyright in computer programs, the more controversial question during the 1960s seemed to be the issue of infringement by computer, i.e., "the impact of [copyright] on the use of copyrighted materials in computers and other forms of information storage and retrieval systems." H.R. Rep. No. 94-1476 at 48. The congressional response to the problem was twofold. First, Congress established a National Commission on New Technological Uses of Copyrighted Works ("CONTU") to study computers and copyright as well as photocopying and to make specific recommendations to

Congress. Pub. L. No. 93-573, 93d Cong., 2d Sess. (1974). Second, a stop-gap provision (presumably pending the CONTU report) was inserted as § 117 of the revision bill that eventually became the 1976 Act. This section carried forward the law in effect on December 31, 1977, as to rights with respect to computer usage of copyrighted works. The Act quite clearly provided for protection under § 102 not only for computer programs but computerized data bases as well.

The National Commission, consisting of distinguished individuals selected, pursuant to congressional directive, from authors and other copyright owners; copyright users; and "the public," and assisted by an expert staff, produced a Final Report on July 31, 1978. A surprising consensus developed to consider copyright liability as potentially attaching to the unauthorized storage of a work in a computer memory. An equally surprising controversy arose as to whether computer programs should remain copyrightable. The majority was of the view that they should; Commissioners Hersey and Karpatkin disagreed; and Commissioner Nimmer filed a statement concurring with the majority. The following materials through p. 130 are excerpts from the FINAL REPORT OF THE NATIONAL COMMISSION ON NEW TECHNOLOGICAL USES OF COPYRIGHTED WORKS.

2. COMPUTER PROGRAMS

Computer programs are a form of writing virtually unknown twenty-five years ago. They consist of sets of instructions which, when properly drafted, are used in an almost limitless number of ways to release human beings from such diverse mundane tasks as preparing payrolls, monitoring aircraft instruments, taking data readings, making calculations for research, setting type, operating assembly lines, and taking inventory. Computer programs are prepared by the careful fixation of words, phrases, numbers, and other symbols in various media. The instructions that make up a program may be read, understood, and followed by a human being. For both economic and humanitarian reasons, it is undesirable for people to carry out manually the process described in painstaking detail in a computer program. Machines, lacking human attributes, cannot object to carrying out repetitious, boring, and tedious tasks. Because machines can and do perform these tasks, people are free to do those other things which they alone can do or in which they find a more rewarding expenditure of their efforts.

Great changes have occurred in the construction of computers, as well as in the media in which programs are recorded. Periodic progress has seen the development, utilization, and, in some cases, passage into obsolescence of bulky plug boards, punched paper cards and tape, magnetic tapes and disks, and semiconductor chips. It should be emphasized that these developments reflect differences only in the media in which programs are stored and not in the nature of the programs themselves.

The evolution of these media is similar to that of devices for playing recorded music. Circuit boards may be compared to music boxes, and punched paper to piano rolls, while magnetic disks and tapes store music and programs in precisely the same manner. Both recorded music and computer programs are sets of information in a form which, when passed over a magnetized head, cause minute currents to flow in such a way that desired physical work is accomplished.

The need for protecting the form of expression chosen by the author of a computer program has grown proportionally with two related concurrent trends. Computers have become less cumbersome and expensive, so that individuals can and do own computers in their homes and offices with more power than the first commercial computers, while at the same time, programs have become less and less frequently written to comply with the requirements imposed by a single-purpose machine.

Just as there was little need to protect the ridged brass wheel in a nineteenth-century music box, so too was there little reason to protect the wired circuit or plug boards of early computers. The cost of making the wheel was inseparable from the cost of producing the ridged final product. The cost of copying a reel of magnetic tape, whether it contains a Chopin étude or a computer program, is small. Thus, the following proposition seems sound: if the cost of duplicating information is small, then it is simple for a less than scrupulous person to duplicate it. This means that legal as well as physical protection for the information is a necessary incentive if such information is to be created and disseminated.

. . . .

As the number of computers has increased dramatically, so has the number of programs with which they may be used. While the first computers were designed and programmed to perform one or a few specific tasks, an ever increasing proportion of all computers are general-purpose machines which perform diverse tasks, depending in part upon the programs with which they are used. Early programs were designed by machine manufacturers to be used in conjunction with one model or even one individual computer. Today, many programs are designed to operate on any number of machines from one or more manufacturers. In addition, and perhaps even more importantly, there is a growing proportion of programs created by persons who do not make machines. These people may be users or they may be — and increasingly are — programmers or small firms who market their wares for use by individual machine owners who are not in a position to write their own programs. Just as Victrola once made most of the first record players and records, so too did early machine manufacturers write most of the first programs. Victrola's successor, RCA, still produces sound recordings (but, interestingly enough, not phonographs), but so do hundreds of other firms. If present computer industry trends continue, it is all but certain that programs written by nonmachine manufacturers will gain an increasing share of the market, not only because writing programs and building machines are two very different skills that need not necessarily occur simultaneously, but also because program writing requires little capital investment.

The cost of developing computer programs is far greater than the cost of their duplication. Consequently, computer programs, as the previous discussion illustrates, are likely to be disseminated only if:

1. the creator may recover all of its costs plus a fair profit on the first sale of the work, thus leaving it unconcerned about the later publication of the work; or

2. the creator may spread its costs over multiple copies of the work with some form of protection against unauthorized duplication of the work; or

3. the creator's costs are borne by another, as, for example, when the government or a foundation offers prizes or awards; or

4. the creator is indifferent to cost and donates the work to the public.

The consequence of the first possibility would be that the price of virtually any program would be so high that there would necessarily be a drastic reduction in the number of programs marketed. In this country, possibilities three and four occur, but rarely outside of academic and government-sponsored research. Computer programs are the product of great intellectual effort and their utility is unquestionable. The Commission is, therefore, satisfied that some form of protection is necessary to encourage the creation and broad distribution of computer programs in a competitive market.

The Commission's conclusion is that the continued availability of copyright protection for computer programs is desirable. This availability is in keeping with nearly two centuries' development of American copyright doctrine, during which the universe of works protectible by statutory copyright has expanded along with the imagination, communications media, and technical capabilities of society. Copyright, therefore, protects the program so long as it remains fixed in a tangible medium of expression but does not protect the electro-mechanical functioning of a machine. The way copyright affects games and game-playing is closely analogous: one may not adopt and republish or redistribute copyrighted game rules, but the copyright owner has no power to prevent others from playing the game.[100]

Thus, one is always free to make a machine perform any conceivable process (in the absence of a patent), but one is not free to take another's program. This general rule is subject to exceptions which restrict the power of copyright owners. These exceptions might be thought of as the "insufficient intellectual labor" exception and the "idea-expression identity" exception. Although they lead to similar results, they are really slightly different.

Apparent works of authorship may not qualify for copyright if they are not "the fruits of intellectual labor."[101] This reasoning has barred copyright for blank forms for recording data[102] and for instructions of the rankest obviousness and simplicity, such as "apply hook to wall."[103] This exception would mean that a "program" consisting of a very few obvious steps could not be a subject of copyright.

The "idea-expression identity" exception provides that copyrighted language may be copied without infringing when there is but a limited number of ways to express a given idea. This rule is the logical extension of the fundamental principle that copyright cannot protect ideas.[104] In the computer context this means that when specific instructions, even though previously copyrighted, are the only and essential means of accomplishing a given task, their later use by another will not amount to an infringement. In discussing an insurance company's use of a lawyer's copyrighted forms, a federal court of appeals stated in *Continental Casualty Co. v. Beardsley:*

> [T]he use of specific language . . . may be so essential to accomplish a desired result and so integrated with the use of a ´ . . . conception that the proper standard of infringement is one which will protect as far as possible the copyrighted language and yet allow the free use of the thought beneath the language. *The evidence here shows that [the company] insofar as it has used the language of [the lawyer's] forms has done so only as incidental to its use of the underlying idea. . . . In so doing it has not infringed* [emphasis added].[105]

---

[100] 1 Nimmer on Copyright, § 37.83 (1976).

[101] Trade-Mark Cases, 100 U.S. 82 (1879).

[102] Brown Instrument Co. v. Warner, 161 F.2d 910 (D.C. Cir. 1947).

[103] E. H. Tate Co. v. Jiffy Enterprises, Inc., 16 F.R.D. 371 (E.D. Pa. 1954).

[104] See 2 Nimmer on Copyright, § 166 (1976) and 17 U.S.C. § 102(b).

[105] 253 F.2d 702, 706 (2d Cir. 1958); see also, Harcourt, Brace & World, Inc. v. Graphic Controls Corp., 329 F.Supp. 517 (S.D.N.Y. 1971).

The emphasized language from the *Beardsley* decision indicates that copyright protection for programs does not threaten to block the use of ideas or program language previously developed by others when that use is necessary to achieve a certain result. When other language *is* available, programmers are free to read copyrighted programs and use the ideas embodied in them in preparing their own works.[106] This practice, of course, is impossible under a patent system, where the process itself is protected, and difficult under trade secrecy, where the text of a program is designed not to be revealed.

Programs are a relatively new type of writing, and how copyright protects them is not universally understood. Because programs are used in conjunction with machines, there has not been universal agreement concerning the propriety of copyright protection. Programs should no more be considered machine parts than videotapes should be considered parts of projectors or phonorecords parts of sound reproduction equipment. All three types of works are *capable* of communicating with humans to a far greater extent than the coined code words discussed by Judge Hand in *Reiss v. National Quotation Bureau.* In all three instances, the medium in which copyrighted material is stored is moved past a sensing device at a set speed, causing electric current to flow, and ultimately resulting in the movement of machine parts to print words, display pictures, or create sounds. All of these events may occur through the use of machines without placing copyrighted works in them. A typist may create a printed document that is indistinguishable from computer output; a television system may produce pictures without the use of a fixed work; and instruments may be used to create the sounds which are found on phonorecords. All that copyright protection for programs, videotapes, and phonorecords means is that users may not take the works of others to operate their machines. In each instance, one is always free to make the machine do the same thing as it would if it had the copyrighted work placed in it, but only by one's own creative effort rather than by piracy.

. . . .

It is difficult, either as a matter of legal interpretation or technological determination, to draw the line between the copyrightable element of style and expression in a computer program and the process which underlies it. Some examples [of] how copies of programs may be made may help to explain the nature of this problem and to place it in its proper perspective.

---

[106] The availability of alternative noninfringing language is the rule rather than the exception. The following colloquy to that effect took place at the tenth Commission meeting (Transcript, CONTU Meeting No. 10, pp. 44-45):

Commissioner Miller: How many different ways are there to produce a program . . .?
Dan McCracken [vice-president of the Association for Computing Machinery]: An infinite number in principle, and in practice dozens, hundreds.
Miller: So it is comparable to the theoretically infinite number of ways of writing *Hamlet?*
McCracken: I believe so. It is not really true that there is a very restrictive way to write a program [which might make it] not copyrightable. I don't believe that at all.
Miller: When you say "infinite," I assume that along that scale there are increases and decreases in the efficiency with which the machine will operate?
McCracken: Perhaps.
Miller: In all of the programs that we have been talking about this morning, with particular reference to . . . compiler programs, does it continue to be true that there are an infinite number of ways of writing particular programs to do particular jobs?
McCracken: Yes. . . . There are hundreds of [different] compiler [programs for] going from FORTRAN to some machines. . . .

A computer program may be misappropriated in a variety of ways. In the first and most straightforward instance, the program listing or the programmer's original coding sheets might be photocopied, which would clearly be an infringement. The unarguably copyrightable writing has been taken. But, what if the program, rather than being recorded on paper, is recorded on magnetic tape or disk? If the tape is used without authorization to produce a printed, human-readable version of the program, again an infringement has occurred. Should the result be different if the tape is copied? That copy may still be used to prepare a printed version at will. There is a one-to-one correspondence between the printed characters on paper and the magnetized areas of the tape. The tape is simply a version of the program from which a human-readable copy may be produced with the aid of a machine or device.

When a program is copied into the memory of a computer, it still exists in a form from which a human-readable version may be produced. That is, the copy in the computer's memory may be duplicated, just as a version listed on paper or coded on magnetic tape may be. Only when the program is inserted — instruction by instruction — into the processing element of the computer and electrical impulses are sent through the circuitry of the processor to initiate work is the ability to copy lost. This is true at least under the present state of technology. If it should prove possible to tap off these impulses then, perhaps, the process would be all that was appropriated, and no infringement of the copyright would occur.

The movement of electrons through the wires and components of a computer is precisely that process over which copyright has no control. Thus, copyright leads to the result that anyone is free to make a computer carry out any unpatented process, but not to misappropriate another's writing to do so.

Drawing the line between the copyrightable form of a program and the uncopyrightable process which it implements is simple in the first instance described above. But the many ways in which programs are now used and the new applications which advancing technology will supply may make drawing the line of demarcation more and more difficult. To attempt to establish such a line in this report written in 1978 would be futile. Most infringements, at least in the immediate future, are likely to involve simply copying. In the event that future technology permits programs to be stated orally for direct input to a computer through auditory sensing devices or permits future infringers to use an author's program without copying, difficult questions will arise. Should a line need to be drawn to exclude certain manifestations of programs from copyright, that line should be drawn on a case-by-case basis by the institution designed to make fine distinctions — the federal judiciary.

Copyright and Other Methods Compared

The purpose of copyright is to grant authors a limited property right in the form of expression of their ideas. The other methods used to protect property interests in computer programs have different conceptual bases and, not surprisingly, work in different ways. An appreciation of those differences has contributed to the Commission's recommendation that copyright protection not be withdrawn from programs. Patents are designed to give inventors a short-term, powerful monopoly in devices, processes, compositions of matter, and designs which embody their ideas. The doctrine of trade secrecy is intended to protect proprietors who use a "formula, pattern, device or compilation of information" in their business "which gives [them] an opportunity to obtain an advantage over competitors who do not know or use it." Unfair competition is a legal theory which, among other things, proscribes misrepresentation about the nature and origin of products in commerce. Each of these forms of protection may inhibit the dissemination of information and restrict competition to a greater extent than copyright.

In certain circumstances, proprietors may find patent protection more attractive than copyright, since it gives them the right not only to license and control the use of their patented devices or processes but also to prevent the use of such devices or processes when they are independently developed by third parties. Such rights last for seventeen years. The acquisition of a patent, however, is time consuming and expensive, primarily because a patentee's rights are great and the legal hurdles an applicant must overcome are high. A work must be useful, novel, and nonobvious to those familiar with the state of the art in which the patent is sought. The applicant must prove these conditions to the satisfaction of the Patent and Trademark Office or, failing that, to the Court of Customs and Patent Appeals or the Supreme Court.

Even if patents prove available in the United States, only the very few programs which survive the rigorous application and appeals procedure could be patented. Once such protection attached, of course, all others would be barred from using the patented process, even if independently developed.

Trade secrecy is a doctrine known in every American jurisdiction. As a creature of state statute or common law it differs somewhat from state to state. The premise on which trade secrecry is based is this: if a business maintains confidentiality concerning either the way in which it does something or some information that it has, then courts should protect the business against the misappropriation of that secret. Although many proprietors feel secure when using trade secrecy, there are several problems they must face with respect to its use in protecting programs. Because secrecy is paramount, it is inappropriate for protecting works that contain the secret and are designed to be widely distributed. Although this matters little in the case of unique programs prepared for large commercial customers, it substantially precludes the use of trade secrecy with respect to programs sold in multiple copies over the counter to small businesses, schools, consumers, and hobbyists. Protection is lost when the secret is disclosed, without regard to the circumstances surrounding the disclosure. The lack of uniform national law in this area may also be perceived by proprietors as reducing the utility of this method of protection.

From the user's standpoint, there are additional drawbacks. Users must cover the seller's expenses associated with maintaining a secure system through increased prices. Their freedom to do business in an unencumbered way is reduced, since they may need to enter into elaborate nondisclosure contracts with employees and third parties who have access to the secrets and to limit that access to a very small number of people. Since secrets are by definition known to only a few people, there is necessarily a reduced flow of information in the marketplace, which hinders the ability of potential buyers to make comparisons and hence leads to higher prices.

Experts in the computer industry state that a further problem with respect to trade secrecy is that there is much human effort wasted when people do for themselves that which others have already done but are keeping secret. This was emphasized in the reports to the Commission prepared by the Public Interest Economics Center and the New York University economists.

The availability of copyright for computer programs does not, of course, affect the availability of trade secrecy protection. Under the Act of 1976 only those state rights that are equivalent to the exclusive rights granted therein (generally, common law copyright) are preempted. Any decline in use of trade secrecy might be based not upon preemption but on the rapid increase in the number of widely distributed programs in which trade secret protection could not be successfully asserted.

The common law doctrine of unfair competition of the misappropriation variety is based upon the principle that one may not appropriate a competitor's skill, expenditure, and labor. It prohibits false advertising and the "passing off" of another's work as one's own. While there is a small body of federal unfair competition law, it is largely a state doctrine with the same lack of national uniformity that besets trade secrecy. Although unfair competition may provide relief ancillary to copyright in certain situations, its scope is not as broad, and it seems unlikely that it alone could provide sufficient protection against the misappropriation of programs. For example, the unauthorized copying of any work for any purpose could be a copyright infringement without amounting to unfair competition.

The answers to such economic questions as the effect of protection on the market and the opportunity it creates for an uncompetitive rate of return tend to show that, of the various potential modes of protection, copyright has the smallest negative impact.

3. THE INPUT ISSUE [INFRINGEMENT BY COMPUTER]

The issue whether copyright liability should attach at the input or output stage of use in conjunction with a computer — i.e., at the time a work is placed in machine-readable form in a computer memory unit or when access is sought to the work existing in computer memory — has been the primary source of disagreement regarding copyright protection for works in computer-readable form. This issue provided the major impetus for the introduction of section 117 into the copyright revision bill.[163] It appears, nevertheless, that the provisions of the new copyright law offer appropriate and sufficient guidance to determine what acts create copyright liability in this area. The protection afforded by section 106 of the new law seemingly would prohibit the unauthorized storage of a work within a computer memory, which would be merely one form of reproduction, one of the exclusive rights granted by copyright.[164]

---

[163] 17 U.S.C. § 117 provides as follows: "Notwithstanding the provisions of sections 106 through 116 and 118, this title does not afford to the owner of copyright in a work any greater or lesser rights with respect to the use of the work in conjunction with automatic systems capable of storing, processing, retrieving, or transferring information, or in conjunction with any similar device, machine, or process, than those afforded to works under the law, whether title 17 or the common law or statutes of a State, in effect on December 31, 1977, as held applicable and construed by a court in an action brought under this title."

This section was first introduced in the copyright revision bill in 1969 (see 91st Cong., 1st Sess., December 10, 1969, S. 543 [Committee Print]), at which time the impact of the computer, and particularly the "input-output" question, was causing great concern on the part of copyright proprietors. Section 117 was agreed upon by interested parties as a means of permitting passage of the revision bill without committing Congress to a position on the computer-related issue until more study could be undertaken.

[164] It may be that the use of the term *input* to describe the act to which copyright liability attaches has been misleading. A more accurate description of the process by which a work may be stored in a computer memory would indicate that a reproduction is created within the computer memory to make the work accessible by means of the computer.

Considering the act of storing a computerized data base in the memory of a computer as an exclusive right of the copyright proprietor appears consistent both with accepted copyright principles and with considerations of fair treatment for potentially affected parties. Making a copy of an entire work would normally, subject to some possible exception for fair use, be considered exclusively within the domain of the copyright proprietor. One would have to assume, however, that fair use would apply rarely to the reproduction in their entirety of such compendious works as data bases.[165] If a copy of the work is to be stored in a computer and subsequently made accessible to others, its creation would have to be properly authorized by the copyright proprietor. That only one copy is being made, or even that the owner of the computer system intends to exact no fee for providing access to the work, would no more insulate the copies from liability for copyright infringement than would similar circumstances insulate a public library which made unauthorized duplications of entire copyrighted works for its basic lending functions.[166]

Under normal circumstances, the transfer by sale or lease of a copyrighted work in computer-readable form, such as a data base, would be a meaningless transaction unless implicit in the transfer was the authorization to place or reproduce a copy in the memory unit of the transferee's computer. Any limitations on the use to be made of the copy would be a matter to be negotiated between private parties, guided by applicable public policy considerations.[167] The proprietor of a work in computer-readable form would, under any foreseeable circumstances, be able to control by contract the future disposition of machine-readable copies of his proprietary work. The proprietor of copyright in such a work would always have a valid cause of action, arising either under copyright or contract, if a reproduction of the work were entered into a computer without the proprietor's authorization, or if a transferee authorized a third party to enter a copy into the memory unit of a computer in violation of the terms of a valid agreement with the proprietor. That copyright would not provide the sole right and remedy for unauthorized use of a protected work neither is it unique to the protection of proprietary interests in computer-readable works nor is it a situation to be considered undesirable.[168]

---

[165] See 17 U.S.C. § 107 for statutory criteria governing fair use.

[166] The example of a copyrighted work placed in a computer memory solely to facilitate an individual's scholarly research has been cited as a possible fair use. The Commission agrees that such a use, restricted to individual research, should be considered fair. To prevent abuse of fair use principles, any copy created in a machine memory should be erased after completion of the particular research project for which it was made.

[167] Outright sale by a copyright proprietor of a copy of a protected work, rather than a lease under which the proprietor retains ownership of a copy which the lessee may use in accord with negotiated terms and conditions, normally results in a complete loss of control over the copy which has been sold. This reflects the unwillingness of courts to enforce restrictions on the alienation of property once a complete transfer of ownership interest in any item of property has been accomplished.

[168] Remedies for breach of contract, if the right being protected is not equivalent to copyright, would not be preempted under the provisions of section 301 of the new law, and would accordingly be available to one who, on the strength of a copyright interest, granted permission to another to make certain uses of the copyrighted work only to have the terms of the authorization violated. There continues to be some scope for state enforcement of proprietary rights in intellectual property under the new copyright law.

Accordingly, the Commission believes that the application of principles already embodied in the language of the new copyright law achieves the desired substantive legal protection for copyrighted works which exist in machine-readable form. The introduction of a work into a computer memory would, consistent with the new law, be a reproduction of the work, one of the exclusive rights of the copyright proprietor. The unauthorized transfer of an existing machine-readable embodiment of a work could subject the violators to remedies for breach of contract. Principles of fair use would be applicable in limited instances to excuse an unauthorized input of a work into computer memory. Exemplifying such fair uses could be the creation of a copy in a computer memory to prepare a concordance of a work or to perform a syntactical analysis of a work, which but for the use of a computer would require a prohibitive amount of human time and effort. To satisfy the criteria of fair use, any copies created for such research purposes should be destroyed upon completion of the research project for which they were created. Should the individual or institution carrying on this research desire to retain the copy for archival purposes or future use, it should be required to obtain permission to do so from the copyright proprietor.

4. COPYRIGHTABILITY OF DATA BASES

. . . .

Similar also to a telephone directory, copyright in a dynamic data base protects no individual datum, but only the systematized form in which the data are presented. The use of one item retrieved from such a work — be it an address, a chemical formula, or a citation to an article — would not under reasonable circumstances merit the attention of the copyright proprietor. Nor would it conceivably constitute infringement of copyright. The retrieval and reduplication of any substantial portion of a data base, whether or not the individual data are in the public domain, would likely constitute a duplication of the copyrighted element of a data base and would be an infringement. In any event, the issue of how much is enough to constitute a copyright violation would likely entail analysis on a case-by-case basis with considerations of fair use bearing on whether the unauthorized copying of a limited portion of a data base would be held noninfringing. Fair use should have very limited force when an unauthorized copy of a data base is made for primarily commercial use. Only if information of a substantial amount were extracted and duplicated for redistribution would serious problems exist, raising concerns about the enforcement of proprietary rights.

It appears that adequate legal protection for proprietary rights in extracts from data bases exists under traditional copyright principles as expressed in the new law, supplemented by still-available relief under common-law principles of unfair competition. The unauthorized taking of substantial segments of a copyrighted data base should be considered infringing, consistent with the case law developed from infringement of copyright in various forms of directories.[171] In

---

See House Report, *supra* note 1, pp. 130-33. That state law rather than federal would be involved presents few real problems. The existence of parallel but not equal rights under state and federal law reflects advantages as well as disadvantages inherent in a federal policy, and generally both claims could be joined in the same federal cause of action under principles of pendent jurisdiction.

[171] See Leon v. Pacific Tel. & Tel. Co., 91 F.2d 484 (9th Cir. 1937); Jeweler's Circular Pub. Co. v. Keystone Pub. Co., 281 F. 83 (2d Cir. 1922), *cert. denied,* 259 U.S. 581 (1922), *aff'g* 274 F. 932 (S.D.N.Y. 1921); New York Times Co. v. Roxbury Data Interface, Inc., 434 F.Supp. 217, 194 U.S.P.Q. 371 (D.N.J. 1977).

addition, common-law principles of misappropriation which, according to the legislative reports accompanying the new law, are not preempted with regard to computer data bases are available to enforce proprietary rights in these works.

5. COMPUTER-AUTHORED WORKS

On the basis of its investigations and society's experience with the computer, the Commission believes that there is no reasonable basis for considering that a computer in any way contributes authorship to a work produced through its use. The computer, like a camera or a typewriter, is an inert instrument, capable of functioning only when activated either directly or indirectly by a human. When so activated it is capable of doing only what it is directed to do in the way it is directed to perform.

Computers may be employed in a variety of ways in creating works that may be protected by copyright. Works of graphic art may consist of designs, lines, intensities of color, and the like selected and organized with the assistance of a computer in any way contributes authorship to a work produced through its use. frames in an animation sequence, thus reducing the amount of time and effort otherwise needed to prepare an animated work.

In the case of computer music, a program may be designed to select a series of notes and arrange them into a musical composition, employing various tonal qualities and rhythmic patterns. The computer may also be used to simulate musical instruments and perform the music so composed.

In other instances, a computer may be used to manipulate statistical information to produce an analysis of that information. The resulting work may bear little similarity to the original form or arrangement of the work being analyzed, as in the case of an economic forecast produced by the manipulation of raw economic data. A computer may, on the other hand, be employed to extract and reproduce portions of a work. In every case, the work produced will result from the contents of the data base, the instructions indirectly provided in the program, and the direct discretionary intervention of a human involved in the process.

To be entitled to copyright, a work must be an original work of authorship. It must be a writing within the meaning of that term as used in the Copyright Clause of the Constitution. The Supreme Court has interpreted this requirement to include "any physical rendering of the fruits of creative intellectual or aesthetic labor." The history of the development of the concept of originality shows that only a modicum of effort is required. In *Alfred Bell & Co. Ltd. v. Catalda Fine Arts, Inc.,* a federal court of appeals, speaking through Judge Frank, observed:

> All that is needed to satisfy both the Constitution and the statute is that the "author" contributed something more than a "merely trivial" variation, something recognizably "his own." ... No matter how poor artistically the "author's" addition, it is enough if it be his own.

Thus, it may be seen that although the quantum of originality needed to support a claim of authorship in a work is small, it must nevertheless be present. If a work created through application of computer technology meets this minimal test of originality, it is copyrightable. The eligibility of any work for protection by copyright depends not upon the device or devices used in its creation, but rather upon the presence of at least minimal human creative effort at the time the work is produced.

Computers are enormously complex and powerful instruments which vastly extend human powers to calculate, select, rearrange, display, design, and do other things involved in the creation of works. However, it is a human power they extend. The computer may be analogized to or equated with, for example, a camera, and the computer affects the copyright status of a resultant work no more than the employment of a still or motion-picture camera, a tape recorder, or a typewriter. Hence, it seems clear that the copyright problems with respect to the authorship of new works produced with the assistance of a computer are not unlike those posed by the creation of more traditional works.

The Commission is unanimous in its belief that computer programs are entitled to legal protection. But the unanimity has not extended to the precise form that protection should take. The law as it exists today with respect to the protection of computer programs is not totally clear. What is clear is that today there are different and often conflicting methods used by proprietors to attempt to protect their products. These include patent and copyright — exclusively federal statutory methods; trade secret law — derived from statutory and judicial state law; and unfair competition — based on elements of common law and federal statute.

To provide reasonable protection for proprietors without unduly burdening users of programs and the general public, the following statements concerning program copyright ought to be true:

1. Copyright should proscribe the unauthorized copying of these works.

2. Copyright should in no way inhibit the rightful use of these works.

3. Copyright should not block the development and dissemination of these works.

4. Copyright should not grant anyone more economic power than is necessary to achieve the incentive to create.

Relatively few changes in the Copyright Act of 1976 are required to attain these objectives, and the promulgation of regulations by the Copyright Office will ease the burden of compliance for both copyright owners and users.

6. RECOMMENDATIONS FOR STATUTORY CHANGE

To make the law clear regarding both proprietors' and users' rights, the Commission suggests that the following changes to the Copyright Act of 1976 be made:

1. That section 117 as enacted be repealed.

2. That section 101 be amended to add the following definition:

A "computer program" is a set of statements or instructions to be used directly or indirectly in a computer in order to bring about a certain result.

3. That a new section 117 be enacted as follows:

§ 117: Limitations on exclusive rights: computer programs

Notwithstanding the provisions of § 106, it is not an infringement for the rightful possessor of a copy of a computer program to make or authorize the making of another copy or adaptation of that computer program *provided:*

(1) that such a new copy or adaptation is created as an essential step in the utilization of the computer program in conjunction with a machine and that it is used in no other manner, or

(2) that such new copy or adaptation is for archival purposes only and that all archival copies are destroyed in the event that continued possession of the computer program should cease to be rightful.

Any exact copies prepared in accordance with the provisions of this section may be leased, sold, or otherwise transferred, along with the copy from which such copies were prepared, only as part of the lease, sale, or other transfer of all rights in the program. Adaptations so prepared may be transferred only with the authorization of the copyright owner.

The 1976 Act, without change, makes it clear that the placement of any copyrighted work into a computer is the preparation of a copy and, therefore, a potential infringement of copyright. Section 117, designed to subject computer uses of copyrighted works to treatment under the old law, vitiates that proscription, at least insofar as machine-readable versions are not *copies* under the 1909 Act. Therefore, to prevent any question concerning the impropriety of program piracy and to assure that all works of authorship are treated comparably under the new law, section 117 should be repealed.

Because the placement of a work into a computer is the preparation of a copy, the law should provide that persons in rightful possession of copies of programs be able to use them freely without fear of exposure to copyright liability. Obviously, creators, lessors, licensors, and vendors of copies of programs intend that they be used by their customers, so that rightful users would but rarely need a legal shield against potential copyright problems. It is easy to imagine, however, a situation in which the copyright owner might desire, for good reason or none at all, to force a lawful owner or possessor of a copy to stop using a particular program. One who rightfully possesses a copy of a program, therefore, should be provided with a legal right to copy it to that extent which will permit its use by that possessor. This would include the right to load it into a computer and to prepare archival copies of it to guard against destruction or damage by mechanical or electrical failure. But this permission would not extend to other copies of the program. Thus, one could not, for example, make archival copies of a program and later sell some while retaining some for use. The sale of a copy of a program by a rightful possessor to another must be of all rights in the program, thus creating a new rightful possessor and destroying that status as regards the seller. This is in accord with the intent of that portion of the law which provides that owners of authorized copies of a copyrighted work may sell those copies without leave of the copyright proprietor.

Because of lack of complete standardization among programming languages and hardware in the computer industry, one who rightfully acquires a copy of a program frequently cannot use it without adapting it to that limited extent which will allow its use in the possessor's computer. The copyright law, which grants to copyright proprietors the exclusive right to prepare translations, transformations, and adaptations of their work, should no more prevent such use than it should prevent rightful possessors from loading programs into their computers. Thus, a right to make those changes necessary to enable the use for which it was both sold and purchased should be provided. The conversion of a program from one higher-level language to another to facilitate use would fall within this right, as would the right to add features to the program that were not present at the time of rightful acquisition. . . .

7. CONCURRING OPINION OF COMMISSIONER NIMMER *

I concur in the Commission's opinion and in its recommendations regarding software. I do, however, share in a number of the doubts and concerns expressed

---

* Commissioners Nimmer and Hersey filed separate opinions limited to the issue of copyrightability for computer programs.

in Commissioner Hersey's thoughtful dissenting opinion. What is most troubling about the Commission's recommendation of open-ended copyright protection for all computer software is its failure to articulate any rationale which would not equally justify copyright protection for the tangible expression of any and all original ideas (whether or not computer technology, business, or otherwise). If "literary works" are to be so broadly construed, the Copyright Act becomes a general misappropriation law, applicable as well in what has traditionally been regarded as the patent arena, and, indeed, also in other areas to which neither copyright nor patent law has previously extended. This poses a serious constitutional issue in that it is arguable that such an approach stretches the meaning of "authors" and "writings" as used in the Copyright Clause of the Constitution beyond the breaking point. Apart from the constitutional issue, it raises policy questions, the full implications of which remain murky at best. Still, at this time, knowing what we now know about the nature of the computer industry, its needs, and its potential for great contributions to the public welfare, I am prepared, on balance, to support the Commission's conclusions and recommendations.

At the same time I should like to suggest a possible line of demarcation which would distinguish between protectible and nonprotectible software in a manner more consistent with limiting such protection to the conventional copyright arena. This suggestion is made not because I recommend its immediate implementation, but rather because it may prove useful in the years to come if the Commission's recommendation for protection of all software should prove unduly restrictive. In such circumstances it may prove desirable to limit copyright protection for software to those computer programs which produce works which themselves qualify for copyright protection. A program designed for use with a data base, for example, would clearly be copyrightable since the resulting selection and arrangement of items from such data base would itself be copyrightable as a compilation. Thus, a program designed for use in conjunction with a legal information retrieval system would be copyrightable since the resulting enumeration of cases on a given topic could claim copyright. A program designed for a computer game would be copyrightable because the output would itself constitute an audiovisual work. (For this purpose the fact that such audiovisual work is not fixed in a tangible medium of expression, and for that reason is ineligible for copyright protection should not invalidate the copyright in the computer program as long as the program itself is fixed in a tangible medium of expression.) On the other hand, programs which control the heating and air-conditioning in a building, or which determine the flow of fuel in an engine, or which control traffic signals would not be eligible for copyright because their operations do not result in copyrightable works. The fact that such a program might also provide for a printout of written instructions (which would be copyrightable) would only render protectible that particular aspect of such a program.

The distinction here suggested appears to me to be consistent with the recognized copyrightability of sound recordings. It sometimes has been argued that while printed instructions tell *how* to do work, computer programs actually *do* the work. But this is also true of sound recordings, which in a sense constitute a machine (the phonorecord) communicating with another machine (the record player). A sound recording contained in a phonorecord does not tell a record player *how* to make sounds which constitute a Cole Porter melody. Rather, it activates the record player in such manner as actually to create such a melody. But Commissioner Hersey has made another and most important distinction. "The direct product of a sound recording, when it is put in a record player, is the sound of music — the writing of the author in its audible form." The point is that the operation of the sound recording produces a musical work which itself is copyrightable. That is sufficient to render the sound recording itself copyrightable quite apart from the separate copyright in the musical work. This principle is directly analogical to the distinction suggested above with respect to computer programs.

8. DISSENTING OPINION OF COMMISSIONER HERSEY

This dissent from the Commission Report on computer programs takes the view that copyright is an inappropriate, as well as unnecessary, way of protecting the usable forms of computer programs.

It main argument, briefly summarized, is this:

In the early stages of its development, the basic ideas and methods to be contained in a computer program are set down in written forms, and these will presumably be copyrightable with no change in the 1976 Act. But the program itself, in its mature and usable form, is a machine control element, a mechanical device, which on Constitutional grounds and for reasons of social policy ought not to be copyrighted.

The view here is that the investment of creative effort in the devising of computer programs does warrant certain modes of protection for the resulting devices, but that these modes already exist, or are about to be brought into being, under other laws besides copyright; that the need for copyright protection of the machine phase of computer programs, quite apart from whether it is fitting, has not been demonstrated to this Commission; and that the social and economic effects of permitting copyright to stand alongside these other forms of protection would be, on balance, negative.

The heart of the argument lies in what flows from the distinction raised above, between the written and mechanical forms of computer programs: Admitting these devices to copyright would mark the first time copyright had ever covered a means of communication, not with the human mind and senses, but with machines.

Are Mature Programs "Writings"?

Programs are profoundly different from the various forms of "works of authorship" secured under the Constitution by copyright. Works of authorship have always been intended to be circulated to human beings and to be used by them — to be read, heard, or seen, for either pleasurable or practical ends. Computer programs, in their mature phase, are addressed to machines.

All computer programs go through various stages of development. In the stages of the planning and preparation of software, its creators set down their ideas in written forms, which quite obviously do communicate to human beings and may be protected by copyright with no change in the present law.

But the program itself, in its mature and usable form, is a machine control element, a mechanical device, having no purpose beyond being engaged in a computer to perform mechanical work.

The stages of development of a program usually are: a definition, in eye-legible form, of the program's task or function; a description; a listing of the program's steps and/or their expression in flow charts; the translation of these steps into a "source code," often written in a high-level programming language such as FORTRAN or COBOL; the transformation of this source code within the computer, through intervention of a so-called compiler or assembler program, into an "object code." This last is most often physically embodied, in the present state of technology, in punched cards, magnetic disks, magnetic tape, or silicon chips — its mechanical phase.

Every program comes to fruition in its mechanical phase. Every program has but one purpose and use — one object: to control the electrical impulses of a computer in such a particular way as to carry out a prescribed task or operation. In its machine-control form it does not describe or give directions for mechanical work. When activated it does the work.

An argument commonly made in support of the copyrightability of computer programs is that they are just like ordinary printed (and obviously copyrightable) lists of instructions for mechanical work. The Computer Report calls programs . . . "a form of writing [which] consists of sets of instructions." But this metaphor does not hold up beyond a certain point. Descriptions and printed instructions tell human beings how to use materials or machinery to produce desired results. In the case of computer programs, *the instructions themselves eventually become an essential part of the machinery that produces the results.* They may become (in chip or hardwire form) a permanent part of the actual machinery; or they may become interchangeable parts, or tools, insertable and removable from the machine. In whatever material form, the machine-control phase of the program, when activated, enters into the computer's mechanical process. This is a device capable of commanding a series of impulses which open and close the electronic gates of the computer in such order as to produce the desired result.

Printed instructions tell how to do; programs are able to do. The language used to describe and discuss computer programs commonly expresses this latter, active, functional capability, not the preparatory "writing" phases. For example, this Commission's report on New Works . . . uses the following verbs to characterize the doings of various programs in computers: "select," "arrange," "simulate," "play," "manipulate," "extract," "reproduce," and so on. It is not said that the programs "describe" or "give instructions for" the functions of the computer. They control them. This is the mechanical fact.

The Commission report on Computer Programs suggests that musical recordings also do work, analogous to what we have been describing. "Both recorded music and computer programs are sets of information in a form which, when passed over a magnetized head, cause minute currents to flow in such a way that desired physical work gets done." . . .

But these are radically different orders of work. And the difference touches on the very essence of copyright.

We take it as a basic principle that copyright should subsist in any original work of authorship that is fixed in any way (including books, records, film, piano rolls, video tapes, etc.) which communicate the work's means of expression.

But a program, once it enters a computer and is activated there, does not communicate information of its own, intelligible to a human being. It utters work. Work is its only utterance and its only purpose. So far as the mode of expression of the original writing is concerned, the matter ends there; it has indeed become irrelevant even before that point. The mature program is purely and simply a mechanical substitute for human labor.

The functions of computer programs are fundamentally and absolutely different in nature from those of sound recordings, motion pictures, or videotapes. Recordings, films, and videotape produce for the human ear and/or eye the sounds and images that were fed into them and so are simply media for transmitting the means of expression of the writings of their authors. The direct product of a sound recording, when it is put in a record player, is the sound of music — the writing of the author in its audible form. Of film, it is a combination of picture and sound — the writing of the author in its visible and audible forms. Of videotape, the same. But the direct product of a computer program is a series of electronic impulses which operate a computer; the "writing" of the author is spent in the labor of the machine. The first three communicate with human beings. The computer program communicates, if at all, only with a machine.

And the nature of the machine that plays the sound recording is fundamentally and absolutely different from that of the machine that uses software. The record player has as its sole purpose the performance of the writing of the author in its audible form. The computer may in some instances serve as a storage and transmission medium for writings (but different writings from those of the computer programmer — i.e., data bases) in their original and entire text, in which cases these writings can be adequately secured at both ends of the transaction by the present copyright law; but in the overwhelming majority of cases its purposes are precisely to use programs to transform, to manipulate, to select, to edit, to search and find, to compile, to control and operate computers and a vast array of other machines and systems — with a result that the preparatory writings of the computer programmer are nowhere to be found in recognizable form, because the program has been fabricated as a machine control element that does these sorts of work. It is obvious that the means of expression of the preparatory writing — that which copyright is supposed to protect — is not to be found in the computer program's mechanical phase.

An appropriate analogy to computer programs, in their capacity to do work when passed over a magnetized head, would be such mechanical devices as the code-magnetized cards which open and close locks or give access to automated bank tellers. These are not copyrightable.

But a more telling analogy, since it speaks to the supposed instructional nature of programs, is afforded by that relatively primitive mechanical device, the cam. A cam, like a mature computer program, is the objectification of a series of instructions: "Up, down, up, down . . .," or, "In, out, in, out . . . ." A cam may be the mechanical fixation of rather intricate and elegant instructions. A cam controlling a drill may embody such instructions as, "Advance rapidly while the hole is shallow, pause and retract for a short distance to clear chips, advance more slowly as the hole goes deeper, stop at a precise point to control the depth of the hole, retract clear of the hole, dwell without motion while the work piece is ejected and another loaded; repeat procedure." (Computer programs can and do embody precisely similar instructions.) But although such a cam was originally conceptualized, described, and written out as this series of instructions for desired work and is, in its mature form, the material embodiment of the instructions, capable of executing them one by one, no one would say (as the Commission now says of another form of "instructions," the mature computer program) that it is a literary work and should be copyrighted.

To support the proposition that programs are works of authorship the Report says . . . that "the instructions that make up a program can be read, understood, and followed by a human being," and . . . that programs "are *capable* [emphasis theirs] of communicating with humans. . . ." Programmers can and sometimes do read each other's copyrightable *preparatory* writings, the early phases of software, but the implication of these statements is that programs in their machine form also communicate with human "readers" — an implication that is necessarily hedged by the careful choices of the verbs "could be" and "are *capable* of"; for if a skilled programmer can "read" a program in its mature, machine-readable form, it is only in the sense that a skilled home-appliance technician can "read" the equally mechanical printed circuits of a television receiver.

It is clear that the machine control phase of a computer program is not designed to be read by anyone; it is designed to do electronic work that substitutes for the very much greater human labor that would be required to get the desired mechanical result. In the revealing words of the Report . . . programs "are used in an almost limitless number of ways to release human beings from . . . diverse mundane tasks . . . ."

The Commission Report thus recommends affording copyright protection to a labor-saving mechanical device.

Is Copyright Protection Needed?

We can agree with a memorandum of the Commission's Software Subcommittee that computer programs "are the result of intellectual endeavors involving at least as much human creativity as the preparation of telephone books or tables of compound interest" — or, we might add (thinking of the mechanical phases of programs), as the design of high-pressure valves for interplanetary rockets or of special parts for racing cars for the Indianapolis 500. The investment in these endeavors, often dazzling in their intricacy and power, does indeed warrant legal protection of the resulting devices.

But is copyright a necessary form of protection? According to the evidence placed before the Commission it is not.

In all the months of its hearings and inquiries, this Commission has not been given a single explicit case of a computer "rip-off" that was not amenable to correction by laws other than copyright. Interestingly, this exactly parallels the experience of the World Intellectual Property Organization (WIPO) in its search for a model form of protection for computer programs. . . . Alistair J. Hirst, attending the WIPO discussions as representative of the International Confederation of Societies of Authors and Composers, noted in an article of June, 1978,[148]

> At no stage in the meetings of the Group was any convincing case ever made out for the proposition that computer software did actually *need* any additional legal protection; the most the representatives of the computer industry could say was that they "would *like* some further form of legal protection." No documented instances of piracy were adduced; and there was no serious suggestion that technological progress in the software field had been inhibited by any shortcomings there might be in the legal protection presently available.

CONTU has had precisely the same lack of evidence on this score. A book recently published,[149] describing a large number of computer crimes committed in this country, cites no single piracy or other misappropriation that would have fallen under copyright law. A study of 168 computer crimes by the Stanford Research Institute,[150] made available to the Commission, also failed to turn up any single such case.

---

[148] CISAC document no. CJL/78/45.266, p. 2.

[149] T. Whiteside. Computer Capers: Tales of Electronic Thievery, Embezzlement and Fraud (1978).

[150] D. Parker. Computer Abuse, Stanford Research Institute (1973).

It appears that the existing network of technological, contractual, non-disclosure, trade-secret, common-law misappropriation, and (in a few instances) patent forms of protection, possibly to be joined soon by Senator Abraham Ribicoff's Computer System Protection Act [151] — to say nothing of laws on fraud, larceny, breaking and entering, and so on — will be wholly adequate, as they apparently have been up to now, to the needs of developers.

We will discuss below . . . the ways the various forms of protection will likely affect the issue of access versus secrecy.

Legislative Intent and the Constitutional Barrier

"It was clearly the Congress' intent," the Report says . . . "to include computer programs within the scope of copyrightable subject matter in the Act of 1976." This intent was by no means clear. It is true that in several places in the legislative reports there are passing references to computer programs which seem to assume their copyrightability under the 1909 Act and, by extension, the 1976 Act. Prior to these reports, the only authority for considering them potentially copyrightable was the Register of Copyright's letter of May 19, 1964 — itself hedged with doubt whether programs were within the category of "writings of an author" in the Constitutional sense. . . . And even these legislative reports contain cautionary language on computer programs, to the effect that they would be copyrightable only "to the extent that they incorporate authorship in the programmer's expression of original ideas, as distinguished from the ideas themselves." [152] Section 117 of the new copyright law provided for a moratorium precisely awaiting the conclusions of this Commission, and it indicates beyond a doubt that Congress has not reached the point of clear intention at least with respect to the use of copyrighted works.

The legislative history of the new law can give little comfort to any who would suggest that a thoughtful legislative judgment had been made about the propriety of copyright protection for computer programs. Where the Commission Report finds the legislative history disconcerting, it simply avers, on its own authority, that the House Report "should be regarded as incorrect and should not be followed." . . .

Even if the legislative intent were unmistakable, there would remain the distinct possibility of a Constitutional barrier to the copyrighting of computer programs. It is an underlying principle of copyright law, expressed in Section 102(b) of the 1976 Act, that copyright does not extend to "any idea, procedure, process, system, method of operation . . . regardless of the form in which it is described, explained . . . or embodied in such work." This section of the statute is intended to recognize the distinction between works conveying descriptions of processes and works which are themselves the embodiment of a system or process. In *Baker v. Selden* (101 U.S. 99 (1879)), the Supreme Court found that, as a matter of Constitutional law, the latter are not protected by copyright.

That decision has been consistently applied to deny copyright to utilitarian works — not those, like phonorecords, which contain expression made perceptible by the use of a machine, but rather those which exist solely to assist

---

[151] S. 1766, 95th Cong., 1st Sess. (1977).

[152] H.R. Rep. No. 94-1476, 94th Cong., 2d Sess. at 54.

a machine to perform its mechanical function. Professor Nimmer, while criticizing some interpretations of the *Baker v. Selden* decision, recognized that it properly bars copyright protection for a work embodying a method of operation when duplicated of necessity in the course of its use.[153] This dissent urges the view (to which Commissioner Nimmer's Concurrence..., seems to lend further weight) that computer programs are exactly the type of work barred from copyright by these considerations.

In December 1980 a law was enacted implementing the CONTU recommendations set forth at pp. 122-23 *supra*. Pub. L. 96-517, § 10. The law deletes the original, stop-gap version of Section 117, thus making fully applicable all other provisions of the 1976 Act; it also substitutes a new Section 117 which allows owners of a computer program to duplicate their own copy of that program (or even adapt it) under certain circumstances. If such duplication was essential to using the program with a machine or done for archival purposes only, there would be no infringement. The duplicate copies could not be used or sold apart from the original, however. The amendment also added to the end of § 101 a definition of "computer program" as a "set of statements or instructions to be used directly or indirectly in a computer in order to bring about a certain result."

QUESTIONS

1. If a copyrighted business form were stolen from the owner of copyright, and photocopied for actual use in effecting a business transaction, would this copying be an infringement? Under § 117 as amended pursuant to CONTU's recommendation, would it infringe to reproduce a computer program for direct use in a computer when that program had been stolen? If there is a difference in your answer to these two questions, is that justifiable?

2. Are there sound economic reasons which underlie Professor Nimmer's distinction between programs used to produce copyrightable works and programs not so used?

3. Articulate the relevance of such cases as *Baker v. Selden, Beardsley, Morrissey* and *Harcourt, Brace* to the issue of copyright protection for computer programs.

9. EMERGING CASE LAW

DATA CASH SYSTEMS, INC. v. J S & A GROUP, INC.

203 U.S.P.Q. 735 (N.D. Ill. 1979)

FLAUM, DISTRICT JUDGE:
This action for copyright infringement and unfair competition is brought by the creator of a computer program [1] against the corporations and the officers of these corporations which are allegedly reproducing, importing, distributing,

---

[153] 1 Nimmer on Copyright, § 37.2 (1976).

[1] In the industry computer programs are collectively known as computer software, as distinguished from computer hardware, *i.e.,* the physical equipment itself. 21 Cath. L. Rev. 181 n.2 (1971); Synercom Technology, Inc. v. University Computing Co., 462 F. Supp. 1003, 1005 (N.D. Tex. 1978).

selling, marketing and advertising copies of plaintiff's computer program. Plaintiff has filed a motion for a preliminary injunction and defendants JS&A Group, Inc. ("JS&A"), Joseph Sugarman ("Sugarman"), and Mary Stanke ("Stanke") have filed a motion for summary judgment. For the reasons set forth below, the motion of defendants JS&A, Sugarman and Stanke for summary judgment is granted on Count I of the First Amended Complaint for Infringement of Copyright and for Unfair Competition (the "First Amended Complaint") and is denied on Count II of the First Amended Complaint and the motion of plaintiff for a preliminary injunction is denied.

Before discussing the facts in this case, it is necessary to set forth what exactly a computer program is. A computer program has been defined generally as a set of precise instructions that tells the computer how to solve a problem. C. J. Sippl & C. P. Sippl, Computer Dictionary 333 (2d ed. 1974); *Synercom Technology, Inc. v. University Computing Co.*, 462 F. Supp. 1003, 1005 (N.D. Tex. 1978). Normally, a computer program consists of several phases which may be summarized as follows. The first phase is the development of a flow chart which is a schematic representation of the program's logic. It sets forth the logical steps involved in solving a given problem. The second phase is the development of a "source program" which is a translation of the flow chart into computer programming language, such as FORTRAN or COBOL. Source programs may be punched on decks of cards or imprinted on discs, tapes or drums. The third phase is the development of an "assembly program" which is a translation of the programming language into machine language, *i.e.*, mechanically readable computer language. Unlike source programs, which are readable by trained programmers, assembly programs are virtually unintelligible except by the computer itself. Finally, the fourth phase is the development of an "object program" which is a conversion of the machine language into a device commanding a series of electrical impulses. Object programs, which enter into the mechanical process itself, cannot be read without the aid of special equipment and cannot be understood by even the most highly trained programmers. J. Brown & R. Workman, How a Computer System Works 149-175 (1976); Keplinger, Computer Intellectual Property Claims: Computer Software & Data Base Protection, 1977 Wash. L.Q. 461, 464; M. Pope & P. Pope, Protection of Proprietary Interests in Computer Software, 30 Ala. L. Rev. 527, 530-31 (1979).

Thus, at some point in its development, a computer program is embodied in material form and becomes a mechanical device which is engaged in the computer to be an essential part of the mechanical process. At different times, then, a given program is both "source" and "object". The "source program" is a writing while the "object program" is a mechanical tool or machine part.

In this case plaintiff retained an independent consultant, D. B. Goodrich and Associates, to design and develop a computer program for a computerized chess game, CompuChess, which was to be manufactured and sold by plaintiff. From September 1976 to April 1977 D. B. Goodrich and Associates designed and developed the basic instructions which told the computer how to play chess at six different levels of difficulty. This process involved the four phases in the development of a computer program discussed above. The instructions were translated into programming language, the source program, which then was translated into machine language, the assembly program. This assembly program was then used to create the object program, the Read Only Memory (the "ROM"). This ROM was then installed in the computer as part of its circuitry.

Thus, CompuChess is a hand-held computer which uses keyboard and data display devices to input and output information. The human player enters his move on the keyboard device by pressing certain keys and the computer relays its move on the data display device by displaying certain letters and numbers.

In late 1977 plaintiff began to market the CompuChess. No copyright notice appeared anywhere on the ROM, the CompuChess itself, its packaging, or its accompanying literature. The copyright notice did appear, however, on the source program and all copies thereof.[2] In November of 1978 the source program was filed with the Register of Copyrights and on November 28, 1978 a Certificate of Copyright Registration was issued to plaintiff.

In late 1978 defendants JS&A, Sugarman and Stanke began marketing the JS&A Chess Computer. The ROM in the JS&A Chess Computer is identical to the ROM in plaintiff's CompuChess.[3] In early 1979 plaintiff filed this action for copyright infringement and unfair competition.

Where, as here, the pleadings, depositions, answers to interrogatories and affidavits show that there is no genuine issue as to any material fact, then summary judgment should go to the party entitled to judgment as a matter of law. However, motions for summary judgment in copyright infringement and unfair competition cases have been generally frowned upon. 6 Moore's Federal Practice ¶¶ 56.17[14] and 56.17[71] (2d ed. 1976). Nevertheless, such motions may be granted for the defendant in a copyright infringement action if, after assuming copying, the court finds that any similarity between the works is insubstantial or that undisputed facts raise a complete defense as a matter of law. 3 Nimmer on Copyright § 12.10 (1979); *Musto v. Meyer,* 434 F. Supp. 32, 36 (S.D.N.Y. 1977).

Since the ROM in the JS&A Chess Computer is identical to the ROM in plaintiff's CompuChess, the court can assume that there was direct copying of plaintiff's ROM. However, the undisputed facts show that defendants JS&A, Sugarman and Stanke have a complete defense as a matter of law with respect to plaintiff's claim of copyright infringement.

Count I of the First Amended Complaint, the count alleging copyright infringement by defendants JS&A, Sugarman and Stanke, is brought under the Copyright Act of 1976, 17 U.S.C. § 101 *et seq.* (App. 1976) (the "1976 Act"). Although this action should be brought under the 1976 Act, the 1976 Act itself does not apply.[4] Section 117 of the 1976 Act states:

---

[2] Each and every copy of the source program had printed on it the words "Copyrighted by D. B. Goodrich & Associates" and the date when it was printed out. On November 2, 1978, D. B. Goodrich & Associates, Inc. assigned its copyright to plaintiff.

[3] Although defendants JS&A, Sugarman and Stanke do not know how the ROM was manufactured by defendant Novag Industries, Inc., defendants JS&A, Sugarman and Stanke and plaintiff have stipulated that the chess computer program of the JS&A Chess Computer is identical to the chess computer program of plaintiff's CompuChess.

[4] Even if the 1976 Act did apply, copying of the ROM would not be actionable. Under the 1976 Act "copies" are defined as

material objects, other than phonorecords, in which a work is fixed by any method now known or later developed, and from which the work can be perceived, reproduced, or otherwise communicated, either directly or with the aid of a machine or device. The term "copies" includes the material object, other than a phonorecord, in which the work is first fixed. 17 U.S.C. § 101 (App. 1976).

this title [title 17] does not afford to the owner of copyright in a work any greater or lesser rights with respect to the use of the work in conjunction with automatic systems capable of storing, processing, retrieving, or transferring information, or in conjunction with any similar device, machine or process, than those afforded to works under the law, whether title 17 or the common law or statutes of a State, in effect on December 31, 1977, as held applicable and construed by a court in an action brought under this title.

The legislative history for section 117 explains that this section was enacted because the problems in the area of computer uses of copyrighted works are not sufficiently developed for a definitive legislative solution.[5] Thus, the purpose of section 117 is to preserve the *status quo*. It is not intended to cut off any rights that existed on December 31, 1977 or to create new rights that might be denied under the predecessor to the 1976 Act, the Copyright Act of 1909, 17 U.S.C. § 1 (1976) (the "1909 Act"), or under common law principles applicable on December 31, 1977. H.R. Rep. No. 94-1476, 94th Cong., 2d Sess. 116, *reprinted in* [1976] U.S. Code Cong. & Admin. News, pp. 5659, 5731.

Therefore, a court, in deciding the scope of exclusive rights in the computer area, first must determine the applicable law, whether state statutory or common law or the 1909 Act. After determining which law is applicable, the court's decision must depend upon its interpretation of what that law was on December

---

While the new definition of copy encompasses works which may be perceived "with the aid of a machine or device," the court believes that the 1976 Act applies to computer programs in their flow chart, source and assembly phases but not in their object phase, *i.e.*, the ROM, for the following reasons:

(1) Proposed Regulation § 201.20, which sets forth the suggested methods of affixing and positioning the copyright notice on various types of works in order to satisfy the requirement in section 401(c) of the 1976 Act, 17 U.S.C. § 401(c) (App. 1976), that the copyright notice "be affixed to the copies in such manner and location as to give reasonable notice of the claim of copyright," states:

(g) Works Reproduced in Machine-Readable Copies. For works reproduced in machine-readable copies (such as magnetic tapes or disks, punched cards, or the like) from which the work cannot ordinarily be visually perceived except with the aid of a machine or device, the following constitute examples of acceptable methods of affixation and position of the notice:

(1) A notice embodied in the copies in machine-readable form in such a manner that on visually perceptible printouts it appears either with or near the title, or at the end of the work;

(2) A notice that is displayed at the user's terminal at sign on;

(3) A notice that is continuously on terminal display;

(4) A permanently legible notice reproduced on a gummed or other label securely affixed to the copies or to a box, reel, cartridge, cassette, or other container used as a permanent receptacle for the copies.

Copyright L. Rep. (CCH) ¶ 14,001 (footnote omitted).

(2) In its object phase, the computer program is a mechanical device which is engaged in the computer to become an essential part of the mechanical process. Keplinger, Computer Intellectual Property Claims: Computer Software & Data Base Protection, 1977 Wash. L.Q. 461, 464. Mechanical devices which cannot qualify as pictorial, graphic or sculptural works are not writings and may not obtain copyright protection. 1 Nimmer on Copyright § 2.18[F] (1979).

[5] The National Commission on New Technological Uses of Copyrighted Works was established to recommend, *inter alia*, definitive copyright provisions to deal with these problems. Act of Dec. 31, 1974, Pub. L. No. 93-573 §§ 201-208, 88 Stat. 1873-1875.

31, 1977. H.R. Rep. No. 94-1476, 94th Cong., 2d Sess. 116, *reprinted in* [1976] U.S. Code Cong. & Admin. News, p. 5731. If, as of the date of the alleged act of infringement, the computer program allegedly infringed had been neither published nor registered in the copyright office, then the common law copyright rule should be applied. Otherwise, the law under the 1909 Act should be applied. 1 Nimmer on Copyright § 2.08[D], at 2-106 (1979).

Prior to the complete revision of the 1909 Act, the American law of copyright had been the subject of a dichotomy between federal and state law. Unpublished works were automatically protected by state law, referred to somewhat inaccurately as common law copyright.[6] Such protection began at the moment of creation and terminated upon publication when common law copyright was lost. Thereafter, protection was available, if at all, only through federal, or as it is generally known, statutory copyright. 1 Nimmer on Copyright § 2.02, at 2-16 (1979).

The parties have assumed that the ROM is a "copy" of the computer program created by plaintiff within the meaning of both the common law and the 1909 Act.[7] The court does not agree. Both at common law and under the 1909 Act, a "copy" must be in a form which others can see and read.

At common law the author's property in his unpublished work included the right to publish, or to refrain from publishing, at his option, and the right of restraining others from publishing without his consent. The original manuscript and the incorporeal right of first publication were the private and exclusive property of the author. He had the sole right of first printing and publishing it for sale. Thus, the unauthorized publication of an author's work was a violation of the author's common law right to the "copy". H. Ball, The Law of Copyright and Literary Property § 4 (1944).

At common law the noun "copy" signified a tangible object that was a reproduction of the original work. Although any mode of reproduction, whether by printing, writing, photography, or by some other method not yet invented, constituted a copying, to be a "copy" there must have been an appeal to the eye. Thus, the term "copy" has been defined as that which comes so near to the original as to give to every person seeing it the idea created by the original. 18 Am. Jur. Copyright & Literary Property § 94 (1965) (quoting *Boosey v. Whight,* [1900] 1 Ch. 122).

That the ROM at common law does not constitute a copy of plaintiff's computer program is supported by the cases which hold that a completed building is not a copy of the architectural plans upon which the building is based. *E.g., Nucor Corp. v. Tennessee Forging Steel Service, Inc.,* 476 F.2d 386, 391 n. 8 (8th Cir. 1973); *Smith v. Paul,* 174 Cal. App. 2d 744, 345 P.2d 546, 553 (1959). An architectural plan is a technical writing which is capable of being copied only by similar technical writings, *i.e.,* by other plans. A building is the result of plans not

---

[6] Although the term "common-law copyright" is not technically and strictly accurate, it is useful and suggestive. More accurate is the term "common-law right of first publication." 18 Am. Jur. Copyright & Literary Property § 2 (1965).

[7] Since the parties have assumed that the ROM is a "copy" of plaintiff's computer program, they have perceived the issue here to be whether the sale of the CompuChess, which contains the ROM, was a publication of the computer program. Since the court concludes that the ROM is not a "copy" of the computer program, it need not reach this issue.

a "copy" of them. *Nucor Corp. v. Tennessee Forging Steel Service, Inc.*, 476 F.2d at 391 n. 8 (quoting Katz, Copyright Protection of Architectural Plans, Drawings & Designs, 19 L. & Contemp. Prob. 224, 236 (1954)). It follows that at common law a copy of a computer program is another computer program in its flow chart or source phase because these are comparable technical writings. While the ROM is the mechanical embodiment of the source program, it is not a "copy" of it.

This same conclusion is reached under the 1909 Act. The 1909 Act and its predecessors gave authors the exclusive right, *inter alia,* to copy the copyrighted work. 17 U.S.C. § 1(a) (1976). In *White-Smith Music Publishing Co. v. Apollo Co.,* 209 U.S. 1 (1908), the Supreme Court held that a piano roll [8] was not a "copy" of the musical composition recorded thereon and therefore, that the defendant, in making an unauthorized piano roll of plaintiff's musical composition, had not infringed plaintiff's "right to copy". After quoting the definition of copy set forth in *Boosey v. Whight,* the Supreme Court defined a copy of a musical composition as "a written or printed record of it in intelligible notation". 209 U.S. at 17. In reaching this result the Court stated:

> It may be true that in a broad sense a mechanical instrument which reproduces a tune copies it; but this is a strained and artificial meaning. When the combination of musical sounds is reproduced to the ear it is the original tune as conceived by the author which is heard. These musical tones are not a copy which appeals to the eye. In no sense can musical sounds which reach us through the sense of hearing be said to be copies as that term is generally understood, and as we believe it was intended to be understood in the statutes under consideration.

209 U.S. at 17. Noting that the perforated rolls were parts of a machine which, when duly applied and properly operated in connection with the mechanism to which they were adopted, produced musical tones in harmonious combination, the Supreme Court concluded that they were not "copies" within the meaning of the copyright act then in existence.

Congress in the 1909 Act implicitly adopted the *White-Smith* definition of "copy". 1 Nimmer on Copyright § 2.03[B], at 2-29 (1979). Thus, since the ROM is not in a form which one can "see and read" with the naked eye, it is not a "copy" within the meaning of the 1909 Act. In its object phase, the ROM, the computer program is a mechanical tool or a machine part but it is not a "copy" of the source program.[9]

Dicta in *Synercom Technology, Inc. v. University Computing Co.,* 462 F. Supp. 1003 (N.D. Tex. 1978), supports this conclusion. There suit was brought for copyright infringement of instruction manuals and input formats used with a computer program designed to solve engineering problems incident to the analysis of building structures.[10] The plaintiff argued that the sequencing and ordering of data was the expression of an idea, not the idea. After rejecting this argument, the court observed that

---

[8] A piano roll is a perforated roll of music used in connection with player pianos.

[9] A structure is not a copy of the architectural plans upon which the structure is based under the 1909 Act, as at common law. *E.g.,* DeSilva Construction Corp. v. Herrald, 213 F. Supp. 184, 196 (M.D. Fla. 1962). Thus, the conclusion that the ROM is not a "copy" of the source program under the 1909 Act could be supported on that ground also.

[10] In using a computer program, it is necessary to have a format for input so that the input of data and the instruction to the computer are compatible with its program. Synercom Technology, Inc. v. University Computing Co., 462 F. Supp. at 1005.

the formulation of the problem [to be solved] in sufficient detail and with sufficient precision to enable it to be converted into an unambiguous set of computer instructions requires substantial imagination, creativity, independent thought, and exercise of discretion, and the resulting program can in no way be said to be merely a copy or version of the problem statement. The program and the statement are so different, both in physical characteristics and in intended purpose, that they are really two different expressions of the same idea, rather than two different versions of the same expression.

462 F. Supp. at 1013 n. 5.

Even assuming that the ROM in plaintiff's CompuChess was copied by defendants JS&A, Sugarman and Stanke, the ROM is not a "copy" of plaintiff's computer program and therefore the copying is not actionable. Since a complete defense as a matter of law with respect to plaintiff's claim of copyright infringement exists, the motion of defendants JS&A, Sugarman and Stanke for summary judgment is granted on Count I of the First Amended Complaint.

. . . .

It is so ordered.

The *Data Cash* case was affirmed on appeal, 628 F.2d 1038 (7th Cir. 1980). The court of appeals held that the distribution of ROMs in 1977 without a copyright notice forfeited copyright in the program, and stated: "Since we find the forfeiture issue dispositive, we do not reach the merits of the district court's decision."

Upon analysis, the appellate court *did* reach the merits of the district court's decision — at least indirectly — and disagreed with it. The lower court presumably held that a ROM was not a "copy" for infringement purposes under the 1909 Act. In other words, defendant's ROM does not infringe plaintiff's exclusive right to "copy" under § 1(a) of that Act. By way of dicta, the court stated that the result would be the same under the 1976 Act, relying in part on its inference from proposed Copyright Office regulations, that a ROM is not a "copy" for notice purposes, i.e., no copyright notice need be affixed to the ROM. *See* footnotes 4 and 7 *supra*. The appellate court clearly disagreed with this latter inference, expressly holding that a ROM *is* a copy requiring a notice.

The court of appeals agreed that the 1909 Act was applicable to the 1977 distribution despite plaintiff's argument that no one was shown to have unloaded the ROM and viewed the program at that time. Indeed, plaintiff argued that it failed to include a notice because it did not know it was possible so to read the program. The 1977 distribution was nevertheless held a publication forfeiting copyright because of the absence of a notice.

QUESTIONS

1. The court equates the common law right of first "publication" to the right to make the first "copy," and finds that the defendant had made no unauthorized copy. Is this limitation of common law copyright sensible? For example, if an individual happened upon an unpublished manuscript of a play or song or poem, and merely performed it publicly for the first time, without making or selling copies, ought that not be considered a violation of the author's right of first publication? What if that unauthorized individual made and sold

phonograph records of the unpublished play or song or poem; although not eye-readable, why should that not be deemed an infringement of common law copyright? Is there any justification for the court's conclusion that common law copyright may be infringed only by eye-readable copies?

2. The court also concludes that an unauthorized person building a work of architecture from unpublished plans does not infringe because he is making no "copy." Is this the proper explanation for finding no infringement in these cases? Isn't a better reason found in the policy reflected in § 102(b) of the federal act, and if so how does that policy relate to the defendant's use of the ROM from the plaintiff's CompuChess?

E. PICTORIAL, GRAPHIC AND SCULPTURAL WORKS

Bailie v. Fisher, 258 F.2d 425 (D.C. Cir. 1958). "The appellants devised a cardboard star with a circular center bearing the photograph of an entertainer, upon which is superimposed a transparent phonograph record from which the voice of the pictured person may be heard. The cardboard has two flaps which, when folded back, enable it to stand for display." They tried to register this for copyright as a "work of art" under the 1909 Act, seeking protection not for the photograph or the recording but for the actual shaping of the "self-supporting star-shaped photograph bearing phonograph record." The Register of Copyrights refused registration, and this action was brought against him for a declaration that the picture-record device was a copyrightable work of art and for an order requiring registration. Summary judgment for the Register was affirmed on appeal. The court of appeals concluded that the Register has the discretion, subject to judicial review, to refuse to accept for registration works which are not copyrightable under the act, and also that the Register was correct in determining that appellants' work was not a "work of art" within the 1909 Act. The court defined a work of art as one which "appears to be within the historical and ordinary conception of the term art," and concluded that "a cardboard star which stands because of folded flaps does not fall within that conception."

Kitchens of Sara Lee, Inc. v. Nifty Foods Corp., 266 F.2d 541 (2d Cir. 1957). Both plaintiff and defendant bake and sell to the public frozen bakery products. On the plaintiff's cardboard covering over the aluminum foil pans in which it sells its chocolate cake, cream cheese cake and pound cake are realistic color drawings of those cakes, as a part of the Sara Lee label.

According to the court, "visual inspection plus the testimony and exhibits more than justify the district court's conclusion that the [defendant's] drawings or pictures of the chocolate cake, cheese cake and pound cake were copied from plaintiff's labels." The plaintiff had copyrighted its labels under the 1909 Act, which permitted registration of "prints and labels published in connection with the sale or advertisement of articles of merchandise." The court, acknowledging that a commercial label to be copyrightable must contain "an appreciable amount of original text or pictorial material," concluded that the Sara Lee drawings, despite their prosaic subject matter and their accurate depiction, were copyrightable. "Plaintiff's artists and lithographers have achieved most realistic pictures of cakes which resemble all well-baked cakes of similar type including those baked by fondly remembered grandmothers. A fanciful, imaginary or unique representation of such standard commodities might well not serve its desired purpose to attract the American appetite .... [D]espite the force of arguments questioning the copyrightability of pictures of these homely and domestic articles of food, such obvious copying as here occurred is not be to encouraged. Plaintiff has put time, some creative thought and money into its pictorial representations of its cakes and for the copying it is entitled to damages.... The pictures of the cakes used by plaintiff on its labels although possibly not achieving the quality of a Leonardo 'Still Life' nevertheless have sufficient commercial artistry to entitle them to protection against obvious copying." The court concluded, however, that the plaintiff could not use copyright to prevent the copying of such uncopyrightable features of the label as the circular, rectangular or octagonal shape, or the ingredients or serving directions. The court also reversed the conclusion of the trial court that the defendant had engaged in unfair competition under New York law; the lower court had erred in finding that customers would be confused by the defendants' cake labels into believing that its products were in fact baked by Sara Lee.

QUESTIONS

1. Does the court's decision in the *Bailie* case violate the principles articulated by Justice Holmes in *Bleistein*, p. 22 *supra?* Is it compatible with the court's decision in *Sara Lee?* Does the *Sara Lee* decision represent the present view of the Court of Appeals for the Second Circuit, in light of the *en banc* decision of that court in *L. Batlin & Son v. Snyder,* at p. 73 *supra?*

2. One reason for attacking the plaintiff's case in *Sara Lee* is that the cake drawings are commonplace depictions of commonplace objects; this was rejected by the court. Could not the defendant use the same claim to show that it had not copied the plaintiff's drawings? How *could* the plaintiff prove copying in *Sara Lee,* absent direct admissions by the defendant's artists?

3. Could the defendant argue that even if it did copy from the Sara Lee drawings, the copying should be allowed as *de minimis?* Could the defendant argue that even if it did copy, it was copying only the "idea" embodied in the plaintiff's cake drawings rather than the "expression"? Compare the *Morrissey* and *Kalpakian* cases, at pp. 102 and 343, regarding the limited number of ways in which the contest or bee-pin "idea" can be "expressed."

4. Note the emphasis placed by the *Sara Lee* court upon the time, thought and money invested by the plaintiff in designing and executing its cake labels. Is that what copyright protects? Although the court chided the defendants (and found them liable) for their copying, copying something which is not the subject of copyright is ordinarily to be applauded, as part of our competitive economic system, and the fact that the plaintiff invested time, thought and money is not sufficient reason to bar that copying. Did not the court, however, come close to endorsing such an anti-competitive theory as the basis for its holding?

DRAFT, SECOND SUPPLEMENTARY REPORT OF THE REGISTER OF COPYRIGHTS ON THE GENERAL REVISION OF THE U.S. COPYRIGHT LAW, CHAPTER VII, 4-13 (1975)

Legislative History of Section 113 and Title II

Until 1954 it had been widely assumed that the only statutory protection for the designs of utilitarian articles was that available under the design patent law, which dated back to 1842. That patents have proved inadequate as a practical form of protection for designs is something on which most people will agree. The main arguments usually advanced against the patent law as a means of protecting designs are:

1) *Inappropriateness.* Patentable designs must be more than "original" (created independently without copying); they must also be "novel" (new in the absolute sense of never having existed before anywhere) and "non-obvious" (the product of a creative act going beyond mere talent or artistry). A patented design that meets these extraordinarily high standards gets more than rights against copying; a design patent consists of a complete monopoly over the use of the design in any manner.

2) *Judicial hostility.* Because the standards of protection are so high and the scope of protection is so broad, the mortality rate of those design patents that have been tested in the courts has been extremely high.

3) *Cost.* Obtaining a design patent is expensive, in some cases prohibitively so. Nearly all applicants are required to retain an attorney, and the substantial costs of filing and pursuing an application through the searching process often operate as a deterrent, especially since the chances of issuance are problematical. An applicant with several new designs has no way of knowing which will be popular, but in most cases cannot afford to apply for design patents on all of them.

4) *Delay.* The patent examining process consists of searching the "prior art" to determine novelty in an absolute sense. Whatever realistically may be the effectiveness of prior-art searching in the case of designs, the process is inevitably a slow one. In the design patent area, the Patent and Trademark Office now has a backlog of about 7 months, and the average time lag between filing and issuance for a design patent is about 21 months. It must be emphasized that protection under a patent starts only upon issuance, so that a design may be vulnerable to copying during the time a patent application is pending.

Beginning around 1914, the growth and economic impact of design piracy, and the nearly total failure of the patent law as a method to combat it, led to a variety of alternative efforts to protect original designs. The attempts to stop design piracy by industry self-regulation through the NRA Codes, and later through the formation of "originators' guilds" combined with a form of boycott, were quite effective for a time during the 1930's, but were eventually struck down by the courts. Judicial actions aimed at getting the courts to declare design piracy illegal on any one of a number of theories — Federal copyright, State common law copyright, Federal and State trademarks, unfair competition (including claims of "passing off" and "misappropriation"), fraud and breach of confidence, implied contract, etc. — were almost entirely unsuccessful.

During this period there were constant and frequently intense efforts to obtain Congressional enactment of separate design legislation. Between 1914 and 1957 nearly 50 design protection bills were introduced, and a number of hearings were held. Some of the bills were closer to copyright than patent; some leaned the other way; most of them took the form of special protection based on copyright principles but considerably more limited in scope and duration than traditional copyright. Several of the bills came close to enactment, but none made it all the way through both Houses.

In 1952, a successful program for the general revision of the patent laws resulted in comprehensive new patent legislation in which the design patent provisions were deliberately left untouched. The basic reason for leaving the design provisions alone was an agreement among the sponsors of the legislation that the patent law was not the place to deal with design protection. It was understood that, as soon as the general patent bill had been enacted into law, the Coordinating Committee of the National Council of Patent Law Associations would turn to the development of separate design legislation based on a registration system similar to copyright.

This effort started several years before the current program for general revision of the copyright law got underway in 1955, and for some time the two legislative efforts proceeded independently of each other. However, in addition to spearheading the general revision effort during its first decade, the Copyright Office was actively and intimately involved with the NCPLA Coordinating Committee and the Patent Office in the development and drafting of the design bill, and with the compromises that produced what is now Title II of the 1975 copyright bill. It was originally contemplated, with considerable optimism, that the design bill would be enacted before the legislative phase of the general revision bill had even begun.

[Eds. — As it turned out, the Senate passed the Design Bill as Title II of the bill which ultimately became the Copyright Act of 1976. S. 22, 94th Cong., 2d Sess. (Feb. 1976). Title II, however, was stricken in its entirety by the House Judiciary Committee and was not restored by the conference committee after the bill passed the full House.]

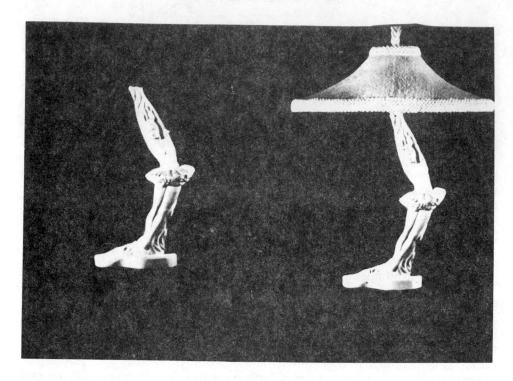

Statue and Lamp

A radical change in the legal status of original designs in the United States occurred on March 8, 1954. On that date the United States Supreme Court, by a 7 to 2 majority in *Mazer v. Stein,* 347 U.S. 201, upheld the copyrightability of "works of art" that had been incorporated as the designs of useful articles. The Court strongly endorsed a Copyright Office Regulation accepting as copyrightable "works of artistic craftsmanship, in so far as their form but not their mechanical or utilitarian aspects are concerned, such as artistic jewelry, enamels, glassware, and tapestries, as well as all works belonging to the fine arts, such as paintings, drawings and sculpture. . . .

The *Mazer* case involved identical copies of lamp bases in the form of statuettes representing human figures. The figurines had been registered for copyright as "works of art." The majority of the Court, with Justices Douglas and Black dissenting, held that works of art are copyrightable as the "writings of an author," that original works of art do not cease to be copyrightable, as works of art, when they are embodied in useful articles, and that for this purpose the following factors make no difference whatever:

1) the potential availability of design patent protection for the same subject matter; on this point Justice Reed said:

> We . . . hold that the patentability of the statuettes, fitted as lamps or unfitted, does not bar copyright as works of art. Neither the Copyright Statute nor any other says that because a thing is patentable it may not be copyrighted. We should not so hold.
>
> . . . The dichotomy of protection for the aesthetic is not beauty and utility but art for the copyright and the invention of original and ornamental

design for design patents. We find nothing in the copyright statute to support the argument that the intended use or use in industry of an article eligible for copyright bars or invalidates its registration. We do not read such a limitation into the copyright law.

2) the intention of the artist as to commercial application and mass production of the design.

3) the aesthetic value of the design, or its total lack thereof; the majority opinion on this point states:

> The successive acts, the legislative history of the 1909 Act and the practice of the Copyright Office unite to show that "works of art" and "reproductions of works of art" are terms that were intended by Congress to include the authority to copyright these statuettes. Individual perception of the beautiful is too varied a power to permit a narrow or rigid concept of art. . . . They must be original, that is, the author's tangible expression of his ideas. . . . Such expression, whether meticulously delineating the model or mental image or conveying the meaning by modernistic form or color, is copyrightable.

4) the fact that the design, in its useful embodiment, was mass-produced and merchandised commercially on a nation-wide scale. . . .

The revolutionary impact of the *Mazer* decision upon design protection took some time to sink in. Its reach clearly went beyond lamp base designs, but did it go so far as to cover all original industrial designs (machinery, automobiles, refrigerators, etc.)? The Copyright Office decided that, for purposes of registration, the following lines should be drawn in its regulations, which are still in effect:

§ 202.10. Works of art (Class G)

(a) *General.* This class includes published or unpublished works of artistic craftsmanship, insofar as their form but not their mechanical or utilitarian aspects are concerned, such as artistic jewelry, enamels, glassware, and tapestries, as well as works belonging to the fine arts, such as paintings, drawings and sculpture.

(b) In order to be acceptable as a work of art, the work must embody some creative authorship in its delineation or form. The registrability of a work of art is not affected by the intention of the author as to the use of the work, the number of copies reproduced, or the fact that it appears on a textile material or textile product. The potential availability of protection under the design patent law will not affect the registrability of a work of art, but a copyright claim in a patented design or in the drawings or photographs in a patent application will not be registered after the patent has been issued.

(c) If the sole intrinsic function of an article is its utility, the fact that the article is unique and attractively shaped will not qualify it as a work of art. However, if the shape of a utilitarian article incorporates features, such as artistic sculpture, carving, or pictorial representation, which can be identified separately and are capable of existing independently as a work of art, such features will be eligible for registration.

This meant that virtually all original two-dimensional designs for useful articles (textile fabrics, wallpaper, floor tiles, painted or printed decorations, etc.), were subject to copyright registration. The same was true of those three-dimensional designs that can be conceptually separated and are capable of existing independently of the utilitarian aspects of the article embodying them (lamp bases, carvings on furniture, costume jewelry, decorator items, etc.). This interpretation has been accepted in a number of court decisions and has not been successfully challenged. During fiscal year 1975 the Patent and Trademark Office issued 3,631 design patents, and the Copyright Office made 9,617 registrations covering designs for useful articles. Although it has substantially expanded the scope of designs subject to copyright registration as "works of art," the *Mazer* case, as interpreted by the courts and the Copyright Office, leaves unprotected a large body of creative work: three-dimensional designs of utilitarian articles as such, as distinguished from three-dimensional ornamentation or embellishment incorporated in them.

In its origin in the early 1950's, the design bill was intended as the main alternative to design patents for all original designs of useful articles. After the impact of the *Mazer* decision and its interpretation had been absorbed, the interaction between the proposed design legislation and the present or proposed copyright law had to be carefully reexamined. Extended discussions and debates produced a compromise, now embodied in section 113 of Title I and sec. 227 of Title II.

§ 113. Scope of exclusive rights in pictorial, graphic, and sculptural works

(a) Subject to the provisions of subsections (b) and (c) of this section, the exclusive right to reproduce a copyrighted pictorial, graphic, or sculptural work in copies under section 106 includes the right to reproduce the work in or on any kind of article, whether useful or otherwise.

(b) This title does not afford, to the owner of copyright in a work that portrays a useful article as such, any greater or lesser rights with respect to the making, distribution, or display of the useful article so portrayed than those afforded to such works under the law, whether title 17 or the common law or statutes of a State, in effect on December 31, 1977, as held applicable and construed by a court in an action brought under this title.

(c) In the case of a work lawfully reproduced in useful articles that have been offered for sale or other distribution to the public, copyright does not include any right to prevent the making, distribution, or display of pictures or photographs of such articles in connection with advertisements or commentaries related to the distribution or display of such articles, or in connection with news reports.

HOUSE REPORT

H.R. Rep. No. 94-1476, 94th Cong., 2d Sess. 105 (1976)

Section 113 deals with the extent of copyright protection in "works of applied art." The section takes as its starting point the Supreme Court's decision in *Mazer v. Stein,* 347 U.S. 201 (1954), and the first sentence of subsection (a) restates the basic principle established by that decision. The rule of *Mazer,* as affirmed by the bill, is that copyright in a pictorial, graphic or sculptural work will not be affected if the work is employed as the design of a useful article, and will afford protection to the copyright owner against the unauthorized reproduction of his work in useful as well as nonuseful articles. The terms "pictorial, graphic, and sculptural works" and "useful article" are defined in section 101, and these definitions are discussed above in connection with section 102.

The broad language of section 106(1) and of subsection (a) of section 113 raises questions as to the extent of copyright protection for a pictorial, graphic, or sculptural work that portrays, depicts, or represents an image of a useful article in such a way that the utilitarian nature of the article can be seen. To take the example usually cited, would copyright in a drawing or model of an automobile give the artist the exclusive right to make automobiles of the same design?

The 1961 Report of the Register of Copyrights stated, on the basis of judicial precedent, that "copyright in a pictorial, graphic, or sculptural work, portraying a useful article as such, does not extend to the manufacture of the useful article itself," and recommended specifically that "the distinctions drawn in this area by existing court decisions" not be altered by the statute. The Register's Supplementary Report, at page 48, cited a number of these decisions, and explained the insuperable difficulty of finding "any statutory formulation that would express the distinction satisfactorily." Section 113(b) reflects the Register's conclusion that "the real need is to make clear that there is no intention to change the present law with respect to the scope of protection in a work portraying a useful article as such."

SUMMARY OF PROPOSED DESIGN LEGISLATION

Despite the fact that the design provisions of the copyright bill were deleted, these provisions are instructive for a number of reasons. First, they provide the general format for continuing efforts to enact design legislation in this country. Moreover, they remind us of the various forms of specialized design statutes abroad. These provisions are summarized as follows:

1. *Standard for Protection* — A design can be protected if it is the original creation of its author. An original design is one which *has not been copied* from someone else's work or from a design in the public domain. The protected design need not meet any test of novelty, unobviousness, or inventiveness. But the design cannot be staple or commonplace or close to it, nor can it be dictated by the function of the article embodying it.

2. *Scope of Protection* — The original designer is *protected only against the unauthorized copying* of the substance of his protected design. If the author of a similar design can prove that he created it independently, rather than through copying, no infringement has taken place.

3. *Duration of Protection* — Five years, with an optional second five-year term.

4. *Commencement of Protection* — Protection begins upon the public exhibition, sale or offering of an actual existing article embodying the design. This is called "making public" the design.

5. *Registration* — A claim to protection must be registered in a Government office within six months after the design is made known.* An Administrator is to be designated by the President. (In approving S. 1361, 93d Cong., the Senate Judiciary Committee expressed the view that the Office of the Administrator should be located in the Patent Office.) There is no requirement of a search or comparison with earlier designs, but a proper party is given the opportunity to petition the Administrator for cancellation of registration of a design not subject to protection.

---

* There is the possibility of suing an infringer even if registration is denied.

6. *Notice or Marking* — Protection is not forever forfeited if the prescribed form of notice is omitted, though omission may sharply limit the design owner's legal remedies against infringers. The requirements as to form and position of notice are very flexible.

7. *Infringement* — The design owner may generally recover from anyone who without his authority, purposefully makes or imports articles embodying a copy of the protected design and cannot recover from sellers, assemblers, processors or innocent parties generally.

8. *Remedies* —

(a) Injunction;

(b) Damages, which the court in its discretion can increase to $1.00 per copy, or $5,000, whichever is greater;

(c) Possible forfeiture or destruction of all infringing articles, plates, molds, etc.;

(d) Recovery of costs and possibly attorneys fees.

9. *Interrelation with Design Patent and Copyright* —

(a) The new design protection does not affect the availability of design patents to those design inventions which qualify. Protection under the new law would, however, terminate as soon as a design patent is issued.

(b) Basically, the bill neither expands nor contracts the scope of copyright coverage or protection. Copyrighted works which are subsequently utilized as designs for useful articles are specifically made eligible for protection under the bill. Thus, although a copyright proprietor utilizing his artistic work in this manner is not required to rely solely upon the design law for protecting his work as embodied in useful articles, he is afforded the opportunity to seek that type of protection. Where the proprietor of copyright in a work later embodied in a useful article *obtains registration* of the resulting design under the bill, he cannot thereafter claim copyright protection in useful applications of his work.

APPLICATION OF YARDLEY

493 F.2d 1389 (C.C.P.A. 1974)

LANE, JUDGE.

This appeal is from the decision of the Patent Office Board of Appeals affirming the examiner's rejections of the claim in appellant's application [1] for an ornamental design for a watch. There are two rejections: (1) a rejection based on obviousness under 35 U.S.C. § 103, and (2) a rejection based on estoppel in view of prior copyright registrations. We *reverse*.

The Claimed Design

Appellant's design comprises a novelty watch face with a caricatured figure thereon. Extended arms and hands serve as the hour and minute hands of the watch. The drawing in the application is reproduced below.

---

[1] Design patent application serial No. 21,125 filed January 28, 1970. The record indicates that The Novelty Watch Company, Inc. is the assignee of the entire interest in the application.

The sole claim in the application is in the conventional form and it reads as follows:

The ornamental design for a watch as shown and described.

The Rejections

The first rejection is for obviousness under 35 U.S.C. § 103 in view of the single reference Breger, design patent D-82,245 issued October 14, 1930.

The prior art Breger design patent discloses a watch dial including hour numerals and a caricatured figure thereon. It states that the arms and hands of the figure are carried by the hour hand and the minute hand of the watch. The Breger design is reproduced below.

The examiner's rejection under 35 U.S.C. § 103 was affirmed by the board.

The second rejection is based on estoppel in view of appellant's prior copyright registrations. This rejection first appeared in the Examiner's Answer. The following passage therefrom explains the examiner's position:

Appellant has made of record as attachments to his Brief, copies of newspaper articles dealing with the subject matter of this application. Inspection of the photographs therein reveal[s] that a copyright has been claimed on the subject matter disclosed. Further investigation has revealed the fact that three copyright registrations have in fact been secured on this subject matter, namely BB 37381, GP 67931 and GP 67932. In view thereof, and in view of the decision *In re Blood* (1928 CD 60; [57 App.D.C. 351] 23 F.2d 772), the claim must be rejected on the principle that while the subject matter might be eligible for protection under either copyright or design patent, the obtaining of protection under one constitutes an election of protection, and there is an estoppel to seek the other. The *Blood* case followed the decision of *De Jonge & Co. v. Breuker & Kessler Co.* [3 Cir.] (182 F. 150) which held in an apparent first impression case that the owner could not have protection under both the copyright and design patent acts. Cases dealing with the similar conflict which followed *Blood* are *Jones Bros. Co. v. J. W. Underkoffler et al.* [D.C., 16 F.Supp. 729] (31 USPQ 197) and *Taylor Instrument Cos. v. Fawley-Brost Co.* [7 Cir., 139 F.2d 98] (59 USPQ 384). The Supreme Court in *Mazer v. Stein* (347 U.S. 201; 100 USPQ 325) referred to the cases dealing with this conflict in a footnote to their denial of a ruling on the question, since they felt the issue was not before them. Accordingly, the claim is rejected on the principle of election of protection and estoppel to seek another.

The newspaper photographs referred to in the Examiner's Answer are reproduced below:

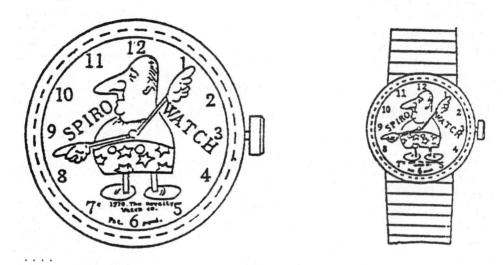

. . . .

The Rejection Based on 35 U.S.C § 103

... The basic consideration in determining the patentability of designs over prior art is similarity of appearance. See *In re Phillips,* 315 F.2d 943, 50 CCPA 1223 (1963). We find no similarity of appearance between appellant's design and the Breger design other than that both relate to watch faces. We reverse the rejection based on 35 U.S.C. § 103.

The Rejection Based on Estoppel in View of Prior Copyright Registrations

The second ground of rejection, advanced in the Examiner's Answer and affirmed by the board, is that three copyright registrations have been secured on the subject matter of appellant's design, and that both copyright and design patent protection cannot be obtained for the same subject matter. The precise nature of the three copyright registrations is not shown in the record before us, but appellant does not deny that both copyright protection and design patent protection have been sought on the subject matter involved.

. . . .

Turning now to the legal merits of the instant rejection based on estoppel in view of the prior copyright registrations, the rejection must be reversed.

We analyze the issue by asking two questions:

(1) Is there an area of overlap wherein a certain type of subject matter is both "statutory subject matter" under the copyright statute (meaning a type of subject matter which, by definition, may be copyrighted if the other statutory conditions and requirements are met) *and* "statutory subject matter" under the design patent statute (meaning a type of subject matter which, by definition, may be patented as a design if the other statutory conditions and requirements are met)?

(2) If the answer to question (1) is in the affirmative, and if a particular creation is of that type of subject matter which is within the area of overlap, may the "author-inventor" secure both a copyright and a design patent?

We answer both questions in the affirmative for the following reasons.

Under the power granted to the Congress in Art. I, § 8, cl. 8 of the Constitution, the Congress has enacted the copyright statute as Title 17, United States Code, and the patent statute as Title 35, United States Code. In the two statutes, the Congress has created an area of overlap with regard to at least one type of subject matter.

Thus, the Congress has provided that subject matter of the type involved in the instant appeal is "statutory subject matter" under the copyright statute and "statutory subject matter" under the design patent statute. The statutory language clearly shows the intent of Congress.

. . . .

The existence of an area of overlap was accepted by the examiner and the board. Nevertheless, both held that an author-inventor *must* elect between securing a copyright *or* securing a design patent. We disagree.

We believe that the "election of protection" doctrine is in direct conflict with the clear intent of Congress manifested in the two statutory provisions quoted above. The Congress has provided that subject matter of the type involved in this appeal is "statutory subject matter" under the copyright statute and is "statutory subject matter" under the design patent statute, but the Congress has *not* provided that an author-inventor must elect between securing a copyright or securing a design patent. Therefore, we conclude that it would be contrary to the intent of Congress to hold that an author-inventor *must* elect between the two available modes of securing exclusive rights.

. . . .

Finally, we come to the board's additional ground for affirmance of the rejection — that "[t]he framers of the Constitution presumably recognized the difference between the endeavors of authors and inventors, because they used the word 'respective' in reference to their 'writings and discoveries.'"

We agree with the board's view that the framers of the Constitution recognized a distinction between "authors" and "inventors" and "writings" and "discoveries." But, we do not think that the constitutional provision requires an election. The Congress, through its legislation under the authority of the Constitution, has interpreted the Constitution as authorizing an area of overlap where a certain type of creation may be the subject matter of a copyright and the subject matter of a design patent. We see nothing in that legislation which is contradictory and repugnant to the intent of the framers of the Constitution. Congress has not required an author-inventor to elect between the two modes which it has provided for securing exclusive rights on the type of subject matter here involved.

If anything, the concurrent availability of both modes of securing exclusive rights aids in achieving the stated purpose of the constitutional provision.

In summary, the rejection based on obviousness under 35 U.S.C. § 103 and the rejection based on estoppel in view of the prior copyright registrations are reversed.

Reversed.

QUESTIONS

1. The interaction of patent principles and pre-1978 copyright law raises another problem not mentioned by the Court of Customs and Patent Appeals in the *Yardley* case. An important feature of the patent law is the requirement of public disclosure of the invention so that the public may "design around" the invention and practice the disclosed art upon expiration of the patent. An equally central feature of copyright law until the 1976 statute was the concept that the act of "publication" (as defined, or perhaps ill-defined, in a potpourri of judicial decisions, see p. 265 *infra*) divested common law copyright in a work and led to either statutory copyright upon compliance with formalities or no copyright at all.

Does not the disclosure of an invention, effected through the issuance of the patent, constitute a "publication" divesting common law copyright? For a negative answer *see Zachary v. Western Publishing Co.*, 196 U.S.P.Q. 690 (Cal. Ct. App. 1977).

2. *Yardley* deals with patentability following the securing of a copyright. Assume a design patent had in fact been granted to the manufacturer of the lamp base in *Mazer v. Stein*. Should the Copyright Office thereafter consider an application for registration of a claim to copyright? *See* 37 CFR § 202.10(b), p. 143 *supra*.

3. What other classes of works would invite protection against copying by design patent and/or copyright? What are the benefits and detriments of securing one form of protection rather than the other? Consider these issues in the context of, for example, a design of a dress (as distinguished from a pictorial design on a fabric which might be used in the making of the dress).

4. The requirements of "novelty" and "nonobviousness" apply just as much to a design patent as they do to a mechanical or process patent. Do you think that courts can as readily apply these concepts to designs? If they can, then why have they not been incorporated in the standards for copyright protection as well?

5. Once the Mickey Mouse watch was marketed, can the depiction of any other cartoon or real-life character — using the hands of the watch to carry the arms and hands of the character — ever satisfy the requirement of "novelty" or "nonobviousness"? Should a design patent have been granted (had it been sought) on the statuette/lamp-base in *Mazer v. Stein?* If it had been granted, would that have prevented the patenting of a lamp base (or a candy jar) in the shape of a dancer posed in exotic garb?

ESQUIRE, INC. v. RINGER

591 F.2d 796 (D.C. Cir. 1978)

BAZELON, CIRCUIT JUDGE: This case presents the question whether the overall shape of certain outdoor lighting fixtures is eligible for copyright as a "work of art." The Register of Copyrights determined that the overall shape or configuration of such articles is not copyrightable. The district court disagreed, and issued a writ of mandamus directing the Register to enter the claim to copyright. *Esquire, Inc. v. Ringer,* 414 F.Supp. 939 (D.D.C. 1976). For the reasons expressed below, we reverse.

I

Although the issues involved are fairly complex, the facts may be briefly stated. Appellee, Esquire, Inc. (Esquire) submitted three applications to the Copyright Office for registration of what it described as "artistic design[s] for lighting fixture[s]." Photographs accompanying the applications showed stationary outdoor luminaries or floodlights, of contemporary design, with rounded or elliptically-shaped housings. The applications asserted that the designs were eligible for copyright protection as "works of art." 17 U.S.C. § 5(g).

The Register of Copyrights (Register) refused to register Esquire's claims to copyright. The principal reason given was that Copyright Office regulations, specifically 37 C.F.R. § 202.10(c) (1976), preclude registration of the design of a utilitarian article, such as lighting fixtures, "when all of the design elements . . . are directly related to the useful functions of the article. . . ." The fixtures, according to the Register's analysis, did not contain "elements, either alone or in combination, which are capable of independent existence as a copyrightable pictorial, graphic, or sculptural work apart from the utilitarian aspect." Esquire twice requested reconsideration of its copyright applications, and was twice refused.

Esquire then filed suit in the district court, seeking a writ of mandamus directing the Register to issue a certificate of copyright for its lighting fixture designs. This time, Esquire met with success. The court, per Judge Gesell, concluded that registration was compelled by *Mazer v. Stein,* 347 U.S. 201 (1954), where the Supreme Court upheld the copyright of statuettes intended to be mass-produced for use as table lamp bases. The district court reasoned that to uphold the issuance of the copyrights in *Mazer,* but deny Esquire's applications, would amount to affording certain copyright privileges to traditional works of art, but not to abstract, modern art forms. The court went on to find that "[t]he forms of the articles here in dispute are clearly art" and concluded that they were "entitled to the same recognition afforded more traditional sculpture." 414 F. Supp. at 941. The court also suggested that registration of Esquire's designs was compelled by prior "interpretative precedent." *Id.* This appeal followed.

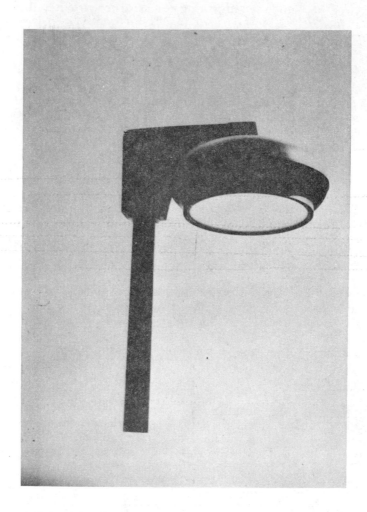

The heart of the controversy in this case involves, in the district court's words, an "elusive semantic dispute" over the applicable regulation, 37 C.F.R. § 202.10(c). We have divided our analysis of this dispute into two parts: Part II considers whether the Register adopted a permissible interpretation of the regulation; Part III, whether the regulation, as interpreted, was properly applied to the facts presented by Esquire's application.

II

A

Section 5(g) of the Copyright Act of 1909, 17 U.S.C. § 5(g), indicates that "[w]orks of art; models or designs for works of art" are eligible for copyright.[8]

---

[8] The Copyright Act of 1976, 17 U.S.C. §§ 101-810 (1976) does not apply to this case. Section 103 of the Act, 90 Stat. 2599, indicates that "[t]his Act does not provide copyright protection for any work that goes into the public domain before January 1, 1978."

The terse language of the statute is more fully elaborated in regulations drafted by the Register pursuant to Congressional authorization. The provision at issue, 37 C.F.R. § 202.10(c), provides as follows:

> (c) If the sole intrinsic function of an article is its utility, the fact that the article is unique and attractively shaped will not qualify it as a work of art. However, if the shape of a utilitarian article incorporates features, such as artistic sculpture, carving, or pictorial representation, which can be identified separately and are capable of existing independently as a work of art, such features will be eligible for registration.

The parties have advanced conflicting interpretations of § 202.10(c). The Register interprets § 202.10(c) to bar copyright registration of the overall shape or configuration of a utilitarian article, no matter how aesthetically pleasing that shape or configuration may be. As support for this interpretation, the Register notes that the regulation limits copyright protection to features of a utilitarian article that "can be identified separately and are capable of existing independently as a work of art." The Register argues that this reading is required to enforce the congressional policy against copyrighting industrial designs, and that it is supported by the continued practice of the Copyright Office and by legislative history.

Esquire on the other hand, interprets § 202.10(c) to allow copyright registration for the overall shape or design of utilitarian articles, as long as the shape or design satisfies the requirements appurtenant to works of art — originality and creativity.[10] Esquire stresses that the first sentence of § 202.10(c) reads in its entirety, "If the *sole* intrinsic function of an article is its utility, the fact that the article is unique and attractively shaped will not qualify it as a work of art." Esquire maintains that it designed its lighting fixtures with the intent of creating "works of modernistic form sculpture," and therefore that their *sole* intrinsic function is not utility. Esquire also contends that the language of § 202.10(c) referring to "features . . . which can be identified separately and are capable of existing independently as a work of art" is not inconsistent with its interpretation. In effect, Esquire asserts that the *shape* of the lighting fixtures is the "feature" that makes them eligible for copyright as a work of art. Esquire argues that its reading of § 202.10(c) is required by the decisions of the Supreme Court in *Mazer v. Stein*, 347 U.S. 201 (1954) and *Bleistein v. Donaldson Lithographing Co.*, 188 U.S. 239 (1903).

B

We conclude that the Register has adopted a reasonable and well-supported interpretation of § 202.10(c).

The Register's interpretation of § 202.10(c) derives from the principle that industrial designs are not eligible for copyright. Congress has repeatedly rejected proposed legislation that would make copyright protection available for consumer or industrial products. Most recently, Congress deleted a proposed section

---

[10] "[T]he courts have uniformly inferred the [originality] requirement from the fact that copyright protection may only be claimed by 'authors,' or their successors in interest." 1 M. Nimmer, Copyright § 10 at 32 (1976). The requirement of creativity with respect to works of art is embodied in 37 C.F.R. § 202.10(b), *supra* n.9: "In order to be acceptable as a work of art, the work must embody some creative authorship in its delineation or form."

from the Copyright Act of 1976 that would have "create[d] a new limited form of copyright protection for 'original' designs which are clearly a part of a useful article, regardless of whether such designs could stand by themselves, separate from the article itself." In rejecting proposed Title II, Congress noted the administration's concern that to make such designs eligible for copyright would be to create a "new monopoly" having obvious and significant anticompetitive effects.[15] The issues raised by Title II were left for further consideration in "more complete hearings" to follow the enactment of the 1976 Act.

In the Register's view, registration of the overall shape or configuration of utilitarian articles would lead to widespread copyright protection for industrial designs. The Register reasons that aesthetic considerations enter into the design of most useful objects. Thus, if overall shape or configuration can qualify as a "work of art," the whole realm of consumer products — garments, toasters, refrigerators, furniture, bathtubs, automobiles, etc. — and industrial products designed to have aesthetic appeal — subway cars, computers, photocopying machines, typewriters, adding machines, etc. — must also qualify as works of art."

Considerable weight is to be given to an agency's interpretation of its regulations. "[T]he ultimate criterion is the administrative interpretation, which becomes of controlling weight unless it is plainly erroneous or inconsistent with the regulation." *Bowles v. Seminole Rock & Sand Co.*, 325 U.S. 410, 414 (1945); *accord, Udall v. Tallman*, 380 U.S. 1, 16-18 (1965); *Stein v. Mazer*, 204 F.2d 472, 477 (4th Cir. 1953), *aff'd*, 347 U.S. 201 (1954). This is particularly so if an administrative interpretation relates to a matter within the field of administrative expertise and has been consistently followed for a significant period of time. *Southern Mutual Help Ass'n v. Califano*, 574 F.2d 518, 526 (D.C. Cir. 1977). The Register's interpretation of § 202.10(c) reflects both administrative expertise and consistent application.

. . . .

The Register's interpretion of § 202.10(c) finds further support in the legislative history of the recently-enacted 1976 Copyright Act. Although not applicable to the case before us, the new Act was designed in part to codify and clarify many of the regulations promulgated under the 1909 Act, including those governing

---

[15] The Register's brief illustrates the problems involved in allowing copyright of the shape of utilitarian articles.

There are several economic considerations that Congress must weigh before deciding whether, for utilitarian articles, shape alone, no matter how aesthetically pleasing, is enough to warrant copyright protection. First, in the case of some utilitarian objects, like scissors or paper clips, shape is mandated by function. If one manufacturer were given the copyright to the design of such an article, it could completely prevent others from producing the same article. Second, consumer preference sometimes demands uniformity of shape for certain utilitarian articles, like stoves for instance. People simply expect and desire certain everyday useful articles to look the same particular way. Thus, to give one manufacturer the monopoly on such a shape would also be anticompetive [sic]. Third, insofar as geometric shapes are concerned, there are only a limited amount of basic shapes, such as circles, squares, rectangles and ellipses. These shapes are obviously in the public domain and accordingly it would be unfair to grant a monopoly on the use of any particular such shape, no matter how aesthetically well it was integrated into a utilitarian article.

Brief for Appellant at 13-19. *See also* Note, Protection for the Artistic Aspects of Articles of Utility, 72 Harv. L. Rev. 1520, 1532 (1959).

"works of art." [23] Thus, the 1976 Act and its legislative history can be taken as an expression of congressional understanding of the scope of protection for utilitarian articles under the old regulations. "Subsequent legislation which declares the intent of an earlier law is not, of course, conclusive. . . . But the later law is entitled to weight when it comes to the problem of construction." *Federal Housing Administration v. The Darlington, Inc.*, 358 U.S. 84, 90 (1958).

The House Report indicates that the section of the 1976 Act governing "pictorial, graphic and sculptural works" was intended "to draw as clear a line as possible between copyrightable works of applied art and uncopyrighted works of industrial design." The Report illustrates the distinction in the following terms:

> although the shape of an industrial product may be aesthetically satisfying and valuable, the Committee's intention is not to offer it copyright protection under the bill. Unless the shape of an automobile, airplane, ladies' dress, food processor, television set, or any other industrial product contains some element that, physically or conceptually, can be identified as separable from the utilitarian aspects of that article, the design would not be copyrighted under the bill. The test of separability and independence from "the utilitarian aspects of the article" does not depend upon the nature of the design — that is, *even if the appearance of an article is determined by esthetic (as opposed to functional) considerations, only elements, if any, which can be identified separately from the useful article as such are copyrightable*. And, even if the three dimensional design contains some such element (for example, a carving on the back of a chair or a floral relief design on silver flatware), *copyright protection would extend only to that element, and would not cover the over-all configuration of the utilitarian article as such*.

H. Rep. No. 1476, 94th Cong., 2d Sess. 55 (1976) (emphasis added).

This excerpt is not entirely free from ambiguity. Esquire could arguably draw some support from the statement that a protectable element of a utilitarian article must be separable "physically *or conceptually*" from the utilitarian aspects of the design. But any possible ambiguity raised by this isolated reference disappears when the excerpt is considered in its entirety. The underscored

---

[23] The former classification "works of art" has been reformulated as "pictorial, graphic, and sculptural works" under the new Act. 17 U.S.C. § 102(a)(5) (1976). Section 101 of the Act advises that works encompassed within this category

> include two-dimensional and three-dimensional works of fine, graphic, and applied art, photographs, prints and art reproductions, maps, globes, charts, technical drawings, diagrams, and models. Such works shall include *works of artistic craftsmanship insofar as their form but not their mechanical or utilitarian aspects are concerned;* the design of a useful article . . . shall be considered a pictorial, graphic, or sculptural work only if, and only to the extent that, *such design incorporates pictorial, graphic or sculptural features that can be identified separately from, and are capable of existing independently of, the utilitarian aspects of the article.*

17 U.S.C. § 101 (1976). The two italicized passages are drawn from 37 C.F.R. §§ 202.10(a) and (c), respectively. Section 202.10(a) was expressly endorsed by the Supreme Court in *Mazer v. Stein*, 347 U.S. 201 (1954). The Committee on the Judiciary incorporated its language into "the definition of 'pictorial, graphic, and sculptural works' in an effort to make clearer the distinction between works of applied art protectable under the bill and industrial designs not subject to copyright protection." H.R. Rep. No. 1476, *supra* n.13, at 54. The second italicized passage "is an adoption of [§ 202.10(c)], added to the Copyright Office Regulations in the mid-1950's in an effort to implement the Supreme Court's decision in the Mazer case." *Id.* at 54-55.

passages indicate unequivocally that the overall design or configuration of a utilitarian object, even if it is determined by aesthetic as well as functional considerations, is not eligible for copyright. Thus the legislative history, taken as congressional understanding of existing law, reinforces the Register's position.

The legislative history of the 1976 Act also supports the Register's practice of ascribing little weight to the phrase "sole intrinsic function." As noted above, Esquire contends that as long as the overall shape of a utilitarian article embodies *dual* intrinsic functions — aesthetic and utilitarian — that shape may qualify for registration. But the new Act includes a definition of "useful article," referred to by the House Report as "an adaptation" of the language of § 202.10(c), H.R. Rep. No. 1476, *supra* n. 13, at 54, which provides:

> A "useful article" is an article having *an* intrinsic utilitarian function that is not merely to portray the appearance of the article or to convey information.

17 U.S.C. § 101 (1976) (emphasis added). In deleting the modifier "sole" from the language taken from § 202.10(c), the draftsmen of the 1976 Act must have concluded that the definition of "useful article" would be more precise without this term. Moreover, Congress may have concluded that literal application of the phrase "sole intrinsic function" would create an unworkable standard. For as one commentator has observed, "[t]here are no two-dimensional works and few three-dimensional objects whose design is absolutely dictated by utilitarian considerations." [25]

C

The district court basically ignored the foregoing considerations. Instead, it advanced two reasons for rejecting the Register's interpretation of § 202.10(c) as a matter of law. It concluded, first, that the Register's construction was inconsistent with the Supreme Court's decision in *Mazer v. Stein,* 347 U.S. 201 (1954). Second, it found that the Register's interpretation amounted to impermissible discrimination against abstract modern art. We respectfully disagree on both counts.

We are unable to join in the district court's broad reading of *Mazer v. Stein, supra.* The principal issue in *Mazer* was whether objects that are concededly "works of art" can be copyrighted if incorporated into mass-produced utilitarian articles. The Register had issued copyright certificates for the statuettes of Balinese dancing figures created with the intent to reproduce and sell them as bases for table lamps. The Court noted that the "long-continued construction of the statutes" by the Copyright Office permitted registration of the statuettes as "works of art." 347 U.S. at 213. It then concluded that there was "nothing in the copyright statute to support the argument that the intended use or use in industry of *an article eligible for copyright* bars or invalidates its registration." *Id.* at 218 (emphasis added).

The issue here — whether the overall shape of a utilitarian object is "an article eligible for copyright" — was not addressed in *Mazer.* In fact, under the Register's interpretation of § 202.10(c), the dancing figures considered in *Mazer* would clearly be copyrightable. The statuettes were undeniably capable of existing as a work of art independent of the utilitarian article into which they were incorporated. And they were clearly a "feature" segregable from the overall

---

[25] Comment, Copyright Protection for Mass-Produced, Commercial Products: A Review of the Developments Following Mazer v. Stein, 38 U. CHI. L. REV. 807, 812 (1971).

shape of the table lamps. There is thus no inconsistency between the copyright upheld in *Mazer* and the Register's interpretation of § 202.10(c) here.

The district court's second conclusion is somewhat more problematical. The court found, in effect, that the Register's interpretation of § 202.10(c) amounted to impermissible discrimination against designs that "emphasize line and shape rather than the realistic or the ornate. . . ." 414 F.Supp. at 941.

We agree with the district court that the Copyright Act does not enshrine a particular conception of what constitutes "art." *Id.* As Justice Holmes noted in *Bleistein v. Donaldson Lithographing Co.*, 188 U.S. 239, 251 (1903), "[i]t would be a dangerous undertaking for persons trained only to the law to constitute themselves final judges of the worth of pictorial illustrations. . . ." Neither the Constitution nor the Copyright Act authorizes the Copyright Office or the federal judiciary to serve as arbiters of national taste. These officials have no particular competence to assess the merits of one genre of art relative to another. And to allow them to assume such authority would be to risk stultifying the creativity and originality the copyright laws were expressly designed to encourage. *Id.* at 251-52; *accord, Mazer v. Stein, supra* at 214.

But in our view the present case does not offend the nondiscrimination principle recognized in *Bleistein*. *Bleistein* was concerned only with conscious bias against one form of art — in that case the popular art reflected in circus posters. Esquire's complaint, in effect, is that the Register's interpretation of § 202.10(c) places an inadvertent burden on a particular form of art, namely modern abstract sculpture. We may concede, for present purposes, that an interpretation of § 202.10(c) that bars copyright for the overall design or configuration of a utilitarian object will have a disproportionate impact on designs that exhibit the characteristics of abstract sculpture. But we can see no justification, at least in the circumstances of this case, for extending the nondiscrimination principle of *Bleistein* to include action having an unintentional, disproportionate impact on one style of artistic expression. Such an extension of the nondiscrimination principle would undermine other plainly legitimate goals of copyright law — in this case the congressional directive that copyright protection should not be afforded to industrial designs.

. . . .

III

Given that the Register adopted an appropriate interpretation of § 202.10(c), the question remains whether the regulation was properly applied to the materials presented by Esquire's copyright claims. In general, the Copyright Act "establishes a wide range of selection within which discretion must be exercised by the Register in determining what he has no power to accept." *Bouve v. Twentieth Century-Fox Film Corp., supra* at 53; *accord,* Op. Att'y Gen., 183 U.S.P.Q. 624, 628 (1974); 30 Op. Att'y Gen. 422, 424 (1915). Here, the application of the regulation to the facts presented by Esquire's copyright applications unquestionably involved the exercise of administrative discretion.

. . . The denial of registration in these circumstances did not amount to an abuse of discretion.

For the aforesaid reasons, the decision of the district court is

Reversed.

LEVENTHAL, CIRCUIT JUDGE, concurs. . . .

QUESTIONS

1. Suppose copyright protection is sought for an abstract shape embodied in plaster and entitled "Repose." Would embodiment of this shape in a bed or other piece of furniture disqualify the design as the kind of "overall shape or configuration of a utilitarian article" excluded from protection in *Esquire* or would it still be protectible under the holding in *Mazer v. Stein?*

2. What is an "intrinsic" function? Is there a difference between "the sole intrinsic function" of an article as set forth in 37 CFR § 202.10(c), and "*an* intrinsic function" as set forth in the definition of a "useful article" in § 101 of the 1976 Act?

3. Do you agree with the court's view that *Bleistein* prohibits only "conscious bias against one form of art," permitting "unintentional" discrimination?

4. Suppose Esquire pictures its lighting fixtures in a copyrighted catalog. Can a competitor use this catalog to produce copies of the fixtures? Can the competitor then photograph his or her fixtures and produce a catalog? Does the *Data Cash* case have anything to do with this question? Does *Baker v. Selden? See Kashins v. Lightmakers, Inc.,* 155 F. Supp. 202 (S.D.N.Y. 1956).

The *Esquire* court quoted from a particularly detailed discussion in the House Report (at pp. 54-55) regarding Section 102 and the protection of applied art. The full discussion follows:

... [T]he definition of "pictorial, graphic, and sculptural works" carries with it no implied criterion of artistic taste, aesthetic value, or intrinsic quality. The term is intended to comprise not only "works of art" in the traditional sense but also works of graphic art and illustration, art reproductions, plans and drawings, photographs and reproductions of them, maps, charts, globes, and other cartographic works, works of these kinds intended for use in advertising and commerce, and works of "applied art." There is no intention whatever to narrow the scope of the subject matter now characterized in section 5(k) as "prints or labels used for articles of merchandise." However, since this terminology suggests the material object in which a work is embodied rather than the work itself, the bill does not mention this category separately.

In accordance with the Supreme Court's decision in *Mazer v. Stein,* 347 U.S. 201 (1954), works of "applied art" encompass all original pictorial, graphic, and sculptural works that are intended to be or have been embodied in useful articles, regardless of factors such as mass production, commercial exploitation, and the potential availability of design patent protection. The scope of exclusive rights in these works is given special treatment in section 113, to be discussed below.

The Committee has added language to the definition of "pictorial, graphic, and sculptural works" in an effort to make clearer the distinction between works of applied art protectable under the bill and industrial designs not subject to copyright protection. The declaration that "pictorial, graphic, and sculptural works" include "works of artistic craftsmanship insofar as their form but not their mechanical or utilitarian aspects are concerned" is classic language: it is drawn from Copyright Office regulations promulgated in the 1940's and expressly endorsed by the Supreme Court in the *Mazer* case.

The second part of the amendment states that "the design of a useful article ... shall be considered a pictorial, graphic, or sculptural work only if, and only to the extent that, such design incorporates pictorial, graphic, or sculptural features that can be identified separately from, and are capable of existing independently of, the utilitarian aspects of the article." A "useful article" is defined as "an article having an intrinsic utilitarian function that is not merely to portray the appearance of the article or to convey information." This part of the amendment is an adaptation of language added to the Copyright Office Regulations in the mid-1950's in an effort to implement the Supreme Court's decision in the *Mazer* case.

In adopting this amendatory language, the Committee is seeking to draw as clear a line as possible between copyrightable works of applied art and uncopyrighted works of industrial design. A two-dimensional painting, drawing, or graphic work is still capable of being identified as such when it is printed on or applied to utilitarian articles such as textile fabrics, wallpaper, containers, and the like. The same is true when a statue or carving is used to embellish an industrial product or, as in the *Mazer* case, is incorporated into a product without losing its ability to exist independently as a work of art. On the other hand, although the shape of an industrial product may be aesthetically satisfying and valuable, the Committee's intention is not to offer it copyright protection under the bill. Unless the shape of an automobile, airplane, ladies' dress, food processor, television set, or any other industrial product contains some element that, physically or conceptually, can be identified as separable from the utilitarian aspects of that article, the design would not be copyrighted under the bill. The test of separability and independence from "the utilitarian aspects of the article" does not depend upon the nature of the design — that is, even if the appearance of an article is determined by aesthetic (as opposed to functional) considerations, only elements, if any, which can be identified separately from the useful article as such are copyrightable. And, even if the three-dimensional design contains some such element (for example, a carving on the back of a chair or a floral relief design on silver flatware), copyright protection would extend only to that element, and would not cover the over-all configuration of the utilitarian article as such.

A special situation is presented by architectural works. An architect's plans and drawings would, of course, be protected by copyright, but the extent to which that protection would extend to the structure depicted would depend on the circumstances. Purely non-functional or monumental structures would be subject to full copyright protection under the bill, and the same would be true of artistic sculpture or decorative ornamentation or embellishment added to a structure. On the other hand, where the only elements of shape in an architectural design are conceptually inseparable from the utilitarian aspects of the structure, copyright protection for the design would not be available.

The Committee has considered, but chosen to defer, the possibility of protecting the design of typefaces. A "typeface" can be defined as a set of letters, numbers, or other symbolic characters, whose forms are related by repeating design elements consistently applied in a notational system and are intended to be embodied in articles whose intrinsic utilitarian function is for use in composing text or other cognizable combinations of characters. The Committee does not regard the design of typeface, as thus defined, to be a copyrightable "pictorial, graphic, or sculptural work" within the meaning of this bill and the application of the dividing line in section 101.

DRAFT, SECOND SUPPLEMENTARY REPORT OF THE REGISTER OF COPYRIGHTS ON THE GENERAL REVISION OF THE U.S. COPYRIGHT LAW, Chapter VII, 15-21 (1975): "The Typeface Issue"

In a letter to Chairman Kastenmeier of the House Judiciary Subcommittee dated June 6, 1975, the Register of Copyrights stated that the question of protection for designs of typefaces had become a major point of concern for the Copyright Office. The letter went on as follows:

...To the best of my recollection, no issue of protection for typeface designs as works of art under the copyright law was raised during the early part of the revision program, including the period during which the bill was under consideration by your Subcommittee. I first became aware of typeface design as a major domestic copyright issue in the early 1970's when the widespread introduction of photo-mechanical processes for reproducing the printed word promised to alter the typographic industry radically.

In the Copyright Office, my predecessor, Mr. Kaminstein gave serious consideration to industry arguments that we should register claims to copyright in typeface designs as works of art. We had, and still have, a regulation [37 C.F.R. 202.1 (a)] that has been interpreted to prohibit copyright registration for typeface designs, and the Copyright Office was urged either to change the regulation or to interpret it differently. Following Mr. Kaminstein's retirement the issue was reserved, but has been raised again during the past two years, both in the Copyright Office and in the courts.

Meanwhile, the technological developments in this field were being felt throughout the world, and resulted in a movement to obtain better international protection for typeface designers. The United States participated in the development of, but did not sign, the Vienna Typeface Convention of 1973, which would obligate members to protect original typeface designs for a minimum of 15 years under one or another form of law, specifically including copyright protection.

Shortly after I became Register of Copyrights, I was once more presented with the petition and arguments of domestic proponents of copyright protection for typeface designs, some of whom had been active in formulating the international treaty. However, I was also made aware of considerable opposition to any change in the Copyright Office Regulations to permit registration of typeface designs. To provide an opportunity for both sides to present their arguments openly, I held a public hearing on November 6, 1974, the first rulemaking hearing ever held by the Copyright Office, and received testimony on the issues implicit in any change in the regulations affecting typeface designs.... We specifically requested comment on five points. Written comments were received through January 15, 1975.

In my closing statement at the conclusion of a highly informative all-day hearing, I had to say that I felt I was "between a rock and a hard place." A strong case was made by each side. Proponents of a change in the regulation sought to demonstrate the significance of artistry in designing typefaces — a "beautiful group of letters," and the differences between the typefaces of different designers. Opponents of any change raised the issues as to the scope of my regulatory authority, and the practical ramifications of an administrative change in this case.

Among others, Irwin Karp, Counsel for the Authors' League, insisted that protection for typeface designs should be dealt with solely as a legislative matter.... At the Office's hearing I asked proponents and opponents to reflect on the design bill as a possible solution to the question of protection for typefaces.

From the written comments, two primary issues emerged. First, the term of protection in the design bill is considered by many to be too short for typeface designs; enactment in its present form would not enable us to join the Vienna Typeface Convention. Some doubt was also expressed as to whether typeface designs are within the subject matter of the design bill, since the bill protects "ornamental designs of useful articles" and the various physical embodiments of typeface designs might not come within the bill's definition of "useful articles."

Under the circumstances, I believe it would be highly appropriate for you to schedule time at your hearings to receive testimony from both sides on the question of protection for typeface designs under either title I or title II of your bill.

The hearing, which was held on July 17, 1975, produced a sharp controversy. Proponents of typeface design protection argued that new photocomposition techniques have made unauthorized copying of typefaces an urgent problem, that original designs for fonts of type are the "writings of an author" in both the constitutional and the statutory sense, that no case law in any field rules out their copyrightability, that registration for typeface designs would impose no burden on authors and reprinters, and that both Titles I and II of the revision bill should be amended to make clear that typeface designs can be considered "original" and that fonts of type are "useful articles." They also recommended that the term of protection under the design bill be extended to 15 years, to conform with international standards.

Opponents argued that neither Title I nor Title II of the bill as drafted protects typeface designs; they oppose any amendment of Title I to bring typeface designs within the scope of traditional copyright protection, and they stated that Title II would be inappropriate without "very extensive amendment including mandatory licensing at reasonable rates." They argued that the issue is not one of "typeface piracy," but of creating exclusive rights for a few big manufacturers, who would use them to enforce tying arrangements between their machines and fonts. Concern was expressed by a representative of magazine publishers lest recognition of exclusive rights might lead to suits to enjoin publication of printed matter. Representatives of typographers and the American Institute of Graphic Arts expressed concern about the danger of excessive protection that would foreclose the use of certain typefaces.

In a letter dated July 28, 1975 to Chairman Kastenmeier, supplementing his testimony on July 17, Michael Parker, Director of Typographical Development for the Mergenthaler Linotype Company, stated:

As stated at the hearings, Mergenthaler has no objection to compulsory licensing of protected typeface designs at a reasonable fee. Additionally, it does not seek unfettered protection for original typeface designs. It seeks only to protect original typeface designs:

1. from unauthorized use to make means for composing text, and
2. from such unauthorized means being used to compose a page of text.

We make no claim to the composed page, and would have no objection to expressly stating that text composed from an unauthorized means is not an infringement of the protected typeface design. These limitations and disclaimers provide a complete answer to the objections of the International Typographers' Association, and Mr. Wasserstrom, Counsel for Hearst Corporation.

A recent letter to the Register of Copyrights from Mergenthaler's attorney states:

. . . The sole question that should be considered by the Copyright Office is whether original typeface designs are copyrightable subject matter under the present Copyright Law. If there is any doubt, this doubt must be resolved in favor of registration in accordance with established Copyright Office practice. . . .

It is courteously urged that the Copyright Office reach an early determination whether it will or will not register the claim of copyright in original typeface designs under current law. The decision should not be deferred pending the "political winds" which might blow from Congress.

The Copyright Office has had pending for more than a year an application by Eltra Corporation, parent of Mergenthaler Linotype Company, to register its claim of copyright in an original typeface design entitled ORION. Prompt action on this application is urged. In this regard, it is the desire of

Mergenthaler to have a judicial determination, if necessary, on whether it is entitled to register the claim of copyright in ORION in order to clarify the status of the current law insofar as original typeface designs in view of the limitations in Section 113 of Title I, H.R. 2223.

It appeared for a while that a form of protection for typeface with additional limitations might be forthcoming under Title II. The deletion by the House Committee of Title II in its entirety remitted the proponents of protection to the courts, where a mandamus action to compel Copyright Office registration had been pending. This proved no more successful when a denial of relief, initially based solely on Copyright Office practice and congressional inaction, was affirmed on the broader ground that typeface was not a "work of art" under the 1909 Act. *Eltra Corp. v. Ringer,* 579 F.2d 294 (4th Cir. 1978).

F. CHARACTERS

Nichols v. Universal Pictures Corp., 45 F.2d 119, 121 (2d Cir. 1930) (L. Hand, J.): "[W]e do not doubt that two plays may correspond in plot closely enough for infringement. How far that correspondence must go is another matter. Nor need we hold that the same may not be true as to the characters, quite independently of the 'plot' proper, though, as far as we know, such a case has never arisen. If Twelfth Night were copyrighted, it is quite possible that a second comer might so closely imitate Sir Toby Belch or Malvolio as to infringe, but it would not be enough that for one of his characters he cast a riotous knight who kept wassail to the discomfort of the household, or a vain and foppish steward who became amorous of his mistress. These would be no more than Shakespeare's 'ideas' in the play, as little capable of monopoly as Einstein's Doctrine of Relativity, or Darwin's theory of the Origin of Species. It follows that the less developed the characters, the less they can be copyrighted; that is the penalty an author must bear for marking them too indistinctly."

WARNER BROTHERS, INC. v. COLUMBIA BROADCASTING SYSTEM, INC.

216 F.2d 945 (9th Cir. 1954), *cert. denied,* 348 U.S. 971 (1955)

STEPHENS, CIRCUIT JUDGE.

Dashiell Hammett composed a mystery-detective story entitled "The Maltese Falcon" which was published serially, and each installment was copyrighted by the publisher. Subsequently, Alfred A. Knopf, Inc., entered into a contract with the author to publish the work in book form, Knopf published the book and, in accord with the terms of the contract, copyrighted it.

In 1930, after publication in book form and after publication of all installments of the first serial thereof, Knopf and Hammett, designated as "Owners", for a consideration of $8,500.00, granted certain defined rights in and to The Maltese Falcon (called "writings" in the agreement) to Warner Bros., as "Purchaser".

... Coincidentally, Knopf executed an instrument to Warner called "Assignment of Copyright" for a nominal consideration. The text of the "assignment" shows on its face that it is not an assignment of the copyright but that it is a grant to Warner of specified rights to the use of the writings in The

Maltese Falcon. Both the contract between Hammett-Knopf and Warner, and the "assignment" from Knopf, purport to grant to Warner certain defined and detailed exclusive rights to the use of The Maltese Falcon "writings" in moving pictures, radio, and television. . . .

It is claimed by Warner that it acquired the exclusive right to the use of the writing, The Maltese Falcon, including the individual characters and their names, together with the title, "The Maltese Falcon", in motion pictures, radio, and television. The use of the title is not in issue, since the grant to Warner specifically includes it.

It is the position of Hammett and the other defendants, all of whom claim some interest under him, that the rights acquired by Warner are those specifically mentioned in the conveying or granting instruments, and that the exclusive right to the use of the characters and/or their names [was] not mentioned as being granted; that the instruments, properly construed, do not convey any exclusive right to the use of characters with or without names, hence Hammett could use them in other stories. However, if, by reason of the silence in the instruments as to such claimed rights, the instruments should be held to be ambiguous on this point, the custom and practice demonstrate that such rights are not customarily parted with by authors, but that characters which are depicted in one detective story together with their names are customarily retained and used in the intricacies of subsequent but different tales.

Hammett did so use the characters with their names and did contract with others for such use. In 1946 he used The Maltese Falcon characters including Sam Spade, the detective and the leading character in the Falcon, by name, and granted to third parties the sole and exclusive right, except their use in the Falcon, to use that character by name (later orally enlarged to include other characters of the Falcon) in radio, television, and motion pictures. Under such claimed rights, radio broadcasts of "Adventures of Sam Spade", including "The Kandy Tooth", were broadcast in weekly half-hour episodes from 1946 to 1950.

Warner claims infringement of copyright and "unfair use and competition" by such re-use and, as well, for infringement of parts of the story and the whole of the writing inclusive of characters and their names. Hammett and the other defendants deny infringement or unfair use and competition on any count, and Hammett requests the court to declare his rights in the premises. Knopf is a nominal party asking and claiming nothing, and is made a plaintiff under the right granted Warner in the Hammett-Knopf-Warner contract.

The trial court denied relief to Warner, declared Hammett's rights, and assessed costs against Warner, who appeals.

The instruments under which Warner claims were prepared by Warner Bros. Corporation which is a large, experienced moving picture producer. It would seem proper, therefore, to construe the instruments under the assumption that the claimant knew what it wanted and that in defining the items in the instruments which it desired and intended to take, it included all of the items it was contracting to take. We are of the opinion that since the use of characters and character names are nowhere specifically mentioned in the agreements, but that other items, including the title, "The Maltese Falcon", and their use are specifically mentioned as being granted, that the character rights with the names cannot be held to be within the grants, and that under the doctrine of *ejusdem generis,* general language cannot be held to include them. As was said in *Phillip v. Jerome H. Remick & Co.,* S.D., N.Y., Op. No. 9,999, 1936, "Such doubt as there is should be resolved in favor of the composer. The clearest language is necessary to divest the author of the fruits of his labor. Such language is lacking here." See, also, *Tobani v. Carl Fischer, Inc.,* 1942, 263 App.Div. 503, 507, 33 N.Y.S.2d 294, 299, affirmed 1942, 289 N.Y. 727, 46 N.E.2d 347.

The conclusion that these rights are not within the granting instruments is strongly buttressed by the fact that historically and presently detective fiction writers have and do carry the leading characters with their names and individualisms from one story into succeeding stories. This was the practice of Edgar Allen Poe, Sir Arthur Conan Doyle, and others; and in the last two decades of S. S. Van Dine, Earle Stanley Gardner, and others. The reader's interest thereby snowballs as new "capers" of the familiar characters are related in succeeding tales. If the intention of the contracting parties had been to avoid this practice which was a very valuable one to the author, it is hardly reasonable that it would be left to a general clause following specific grants. Another buttressing fact is that Hammett wrote and caused to be published in 1932, long after the Falcon agreements, three stories in which some of the leading characters of the Falcon were featured, and no objection was voiced by Warner. It is also of some note that the evidence shows that Columbia, long subsequent to the conveying instruments, dickered with Warner for the use of the Falcon on its "Suspense" radio program and, failing in its efforts, substituted "The Kandy Tooth" which uses the Falcon characters under license of Hammett. Warner made no claim against Columbia at or reasonably soon afterward. The conclusion we have come to, as to the intention of the parties, would seem to be in harmony with the fact that the purchase price paid by Warner was $8,500.00, which would seem inadequate compensation for the complete surrender of the characters made famous by the popular reception of the book, The Maltese Falcon; and that the intention of the parties, inclusive of the "Assignment", was not that Hammett should be deprived of using the Falcon characters in subsequently written stories, and that the contract, properly construed, does not deprive Hammett of their use.

Up to this point we have discussed the points at issue by construing the contract and by seeking the intention of the parties to it, and we have concluded that the parties never intended by their contract to buy and sell the future use of the personalities in the writing.

It will now be profitable to consider whether it was ever intended by the copyright statute that characters with their names should be under its protection. The practice of writers to compose sequels to stories is old, and the copyright statute, though amended several times, has never specifically mentioned the point. It does not appear that it has ever been adjudicated, although it is mentioned in *Nichols v. Universal Pictures Corp.,* 2 Cir., 1930, 45 F.2d 119. If Congress had intended that the sale of the right to publish a copyrighted story would foreclose the author's use of its characters in subsequent works for the life of the copyright, it would seem Congress would have made specific provision therefor. Authors work for the love of their art no more than other professional people work in other lines of work for the love of it. There is the financial motive as well. The characters of an author's imagination and the art of his descriptive talent, like a painter's or like a person with his penmanship, are always limited and always fall into limited patterns.[5] The restriction argued for is unreasonable, and would effect the very opposite of the statute's purpose which is to encourage the production of the arts.

---

[5] "He must be a poor creature that does not often repeat himself. Imagine the author of the excellent piece of advice, 'Know thyself', never alluding to that sentiment again during the course of a protracted existence! Why, the truths a man carries about with him are his tools; and do you think a carpenter is bound to use the same plane but once to

It is our conception of the area covered by the copyright statute that when a study of the two writings is made and it is plain from the study that one of them is not in fact the creation of the putative author, but instead has been copied in substantial part exactly or in transparent re-phrasing to produce essentially the story of the other writing, it infringes.

It is conceivable that the character really constitutes the story being told, but if the character is only the chessman in the game of telling the story he is not within the area of the protection afforded by the copyright. The subject is given consideration in the *Nichols* case, *supra,* 45 F.2d at page 121 of the citation. At page 122 of 45 F.2d of the same case the court remarks that the line between infringement and non-infringement is indefinite and may seem arbitrary when drawn; nevertheless it must be drawn. *Nichols v. Universal Pictures Corp.,* 2 Cir., 1930, 45 F.2d 119. See *Warner Bros. Pictures v. Majestic Pictures Corp.,* 2 Cir., 70 F.2d 310, 311.

We conclude that even if the owners assigned their complete rights in the copyright to the *Falcon,* such assignment did not prevent the author from using the characters used therein, in other stories. The characters were vehicles for the story told, and the vehicles did not go with the sale of the story.

We turn to the consideration of general infringement. It is agreed that a story entitled "The Kandy Tooth" is the closest to *The Maltese Falcon,* and from a practical standpoint if the Tooth does not infringe the Falcon, there has been no infringement.

We have set out in notes 7 and 8 at the end of this opinion, short summations of the two works. There is a sameness in the tricks of spinning out the yarn so as to sustain the reader's suspense as to hinted mystery, and there is a similarity in the two stories in that there is a long complicated search for a lost article of fabulous value. The searches are filled with complications, fatalities, and moral delinquencies by characters in name, description, and action of some similarities. The script of the Tooth was not composed by Hammett and, except for a few expressions, is not written in the Hammett literary style.

We see no clear error in the trial court's holding that the similarities of the two stories do not go to the degree of constituting practically the same story. There is no textual copying; the mystery of the Tooth and the suspense to the reader would not be dulled through his having read the Falcon. In a phrase, they are different stories though of the same general nature.

Unfair Use and Competition

Warner claims the radio broadcasts, "The Adventures of Sam Spade" and the "Suspense" broadcast of "The Kandy Tooth", and others, wherein the characters of the Falcon were used by name and their pecularities, constituted unfair use and competition. The trial court found against such contention and we think the conclusion does not constitute clear error.

It is patent that the characters of The Maltese Falcon could not fairly be used in such a manner as to cause the Falcon to be materially lessened in its commercial worth by degrading or cheapening them so that the public would not be

smooth a knotty board with, or to hang up his hammer after it has driven its first nail? I shall never repeat a conversation, but an idea, often. I shall use the same types when I like, but not commonly the same stereotypes. A thought is often original, though you have uttered it a hundred times. It has come to you over a new route, by a new and express train of associations." The Autocrat of the Breakfast Table, by O. W. Holmes, M.D., p. 9, reprint of original edition.

interested in their capers. They could not be used in such a manner as to deceive the public or to "palm off" to the public the idea that they were really witnessing The Maltese Falcon when they viewed showings of the other stories. We think there was no reversible error in the court's conclusions on these points.

WINCOR, BOOK REVIEW OF KAPLAN, AN UNHURRIED VIEW OF COPYRIGHT, 76 Yale Law Journal 1473, 1478-83 (1967)*

How far should the bounds of protection extend? *An Unhurried View of Copyright* sets out many of the standards used in measuring traditional copyrights. Professor Kaplan relies on existing case law, which is a reasonable road for a lawyer to travel. But it is not the way life is lived in the communications industries.

There a dynamic world is making ground rules for current contracts and future laws. If the genius of the common law is its ability to catch up with the market place, it had better look twice at the communications field. As suggested earlier, "copyright" is the wrong word — wrong chiefly in being incomplete — for describing the exotic new plants that grow in this surrealist garden.

Consider the following passage, introduced less in the hope of affording readers innocent amusement than of bringing out a point:

> Florienbad was burning. The world's espionage capital, on the outskirts of Bucharest, was half destroyed. Among the ruins strolled tall, indifferent Secret Agent Leverett Lowell (Harvard, '42) wearing as always his Black Belt, Fifth Degree for Kiaijutsu (Zen combat by Screaming), puffing casually on a consciousness-expanding cigarette and followed by Alec, his lame ocelot who had figured so gallantly in the Tower of London Demolition Case. Lowell was flanked, as always, by two of his luscious Eurasian girl bodyguards.
>
> A small man disguised as a passerby stood by a burning building, watching the flames with satisfaction. Lowell recognized him as Q 50, a medium-ranking agent of the dreaded ACL, Arson Consultants, Ltd. Q 50's eyes glistened as he turned from the conflagration and addressed Lowell.
>
> "That's one for the insurance company, mate," observed Q 50.
>
> "Touché," Lowell replied indifferently.

That deeply affecting passage, by this reviewer, appears in Vol. IV, *Television Quarterly*, Fall, 1965. Its want of literary excellence makes it thoroughly part of a tradition in copyright cases.

Leverett Lowell and his bizarre entourage may actually constitute property. Taken together, they are a sort of compound of elements that the public values. Taken separately, each element may have value in its own right, even in a different setting. As things actually happen, especially in television, one of the girl bodyguards, with or without the lame ocelot, may be extracted from a series about Leverett Lowell and star in her own series without Lowell next season.

Television is the most voracious consumer of literary property on a repeating basis. It serves, accordingly, as the ideal subject for the study of new theories, new forms of legal life, new property concepts. Snobbishness has no place in such studies. Judge Learned Hand's concern was not confined to *Twelfth Night*.

In television the Leverett Lowell extract might be the subject of protracted negotiation and sale. Probably but not inevitably the character would in fact have been more fully developed in successive episodes without appreciable enrichment. Be that as it may, Lowell and his entourage might be dealt with as a commodity.

---

* Reprinted by permission of The Yale Law Journal Company and Fred B. Rothman & Company.

They might originate in a spy novel, or a film, or a series "presentation" designed specifically for television. Typically an independent production company acquires an option, sometimes on the text of Leverett Lowell stories, sometimes merely on the character himself and his attendant props. The most elaborate negotiations accompany such acquisitions. Does one remember to secure rights to Mrs. Hudson besides Holmes and Watson? How much does the original owner receive per new program episode if the series is one hour, how much if the series is half-hour? To what extent does he share in proceeds from a sound track album, or Leverett Lowell figurines, or theatrical exhibition of two program segments stuck together as a feature film? Does he share "spin-off" proceeds when one of the minor characters goes into a different series? All of it sounds fantastic, but it happens.

The J. R. R. Tolkien mythology affords even more vivid illustration of the kinds of intangibles which may be sold in the market place of incorporeal property these days. This author creates a fictitious world filled with imaginary people, imaginary races, imaginary eras, languages, curses, treasures — all of it, each element in the compound, at least partly original and potentially valuable on its own. H. P. Lovecraft did the same thing, and a devoted readership kept buying his macabre fancies.

Television thrives on this sort of traffic. *Honey West* was telecast weekly as a spin-off from *Burke's Law.* For each spin-off that gets on, there are hundreds that occupy serious men and women in tortured negotiation for months at a time, but never appear. The spin-off concept is crucial. It means the transplant of one or more fictitious elements into new settings. It describes extraction in business terms, and it comes up in nearly all contracts for the acquisition of television rights. There is no use pretending it will all go away if we ignore it.

Professor Kaplan and others who decry excessive protection may have a plausible rebuttal to the argument that real life has outrun their law. They may suggest that purchasers in this field merely buy quit-claims to avoid lawsuits. Sometimes that will be true; television moves quickly, and there is no time for test cases. Some of the fictitious elements that command royalties probably are nothing but ideas with names, and belong in the public domain. Certainly a slight shift in presentation, a change of name, a different occupation or nationality is sufficient to avoid legal trouble in many instances of copying. Still, there is more to it. Once in a long time we find fictitious elements such as characters that are both original and valuable, even under a different name, even snipped off and planted in a new garden. The point is that conceptually protection for elements such as these is all quite possible.

If trade custom means anything, the broadcasting industry has created standards that the common law must consider. Industry-wide collective bargaining agreements between management and the Writers Guild of America contain royalty provisions for the use of characters. Some day they may encompass additional elements, at least in general language.

Nevertheless trade custom is not everything, and Professor Kaplan is entitled to legal analysis in support of our new heresies.

In supplying it, one comes back to the question of names again. Fictitious characters are not "copyrights." Neither are fictitious eras, languages or battles. If Shakespeare were under copyright today, another's piracy of Falstaff might be a crucial factor in determining copyright infringement of particular plays, but Sir John is no copyright. He is something else, something without a name.

And yet not entirely without a name. The right name is "literary service mark protected against dilution." It lacks grace, but perhaps we shall coin something better after examining what lies behind it.

The trademark, sibling concept to the service mark, began as a liability and became an asset. In this happy course it ran parallel to the copyright. One originated as a device for policing measures and standards in the medieval guilds. The other began (in England, at any rate) as a device to record heretical authors and publishers. Then the trademark became a sales badge identifying the source of products, and the copyright turned into an economic res, a legal claim to rights in a work of art.

The two doctrines have different rules. Trademark is of uncertain duration; its geography is not fixed, and there are sometimes restrictions on its transfer so as to avoid deceiving the public. It depends largely on facts postulated at a given moment. Such and such a name is well known in Hawaii this year as a device for identifying pineapples, but not in Bonn, where it was famous a decade ago as a name for bicycles. Copyright is quite different. The owner has the security of fixed time periods, and his protection is national, often international, in scope. Trademark is the more flexible, copyright the more certain. The trouble with copyright is that it leaves off too soon, and fails to protect characters and related imaginings by Lovecraft and Tolkien.

Here trademark is a useful supplement — or service mark to be more exact about it, since the author's creations identify his services. These services are literary, hence the term "literary service mark." Dilution in turn is a German doctrine, adopted by several states including New York and Massachusetts, that protects marks against "whittling away" by use on disparate products, even where there is no likelihood of public confusion. In this doctrine the medieval mark ripens fully into an asset without any of the old hurdles in the way of protection. Rolls-Royce shoes, theoretically, would be enjoined under the dilution doctrine. With this concept we round out the translation of that awkward phrase for Sir John Falstaff: "literary service mark protected against dilution." Today that is what Falstaff would be in law.

. . . .

An Unhurried View of Copyright is a way of looking at things in terms of franchises and grants from the sovereign. It has on its side American copyright history, with its concern for the public interest in free or cheap communications and its unconcern for authors. At least it has American history on its side as far as it goes.

Against this Kaplanesque view is a different way of looking at things, more as writers and publishers and producers do. A good statement of this second view is what G. K. Chesterton wrote in *Charles Dickens* (Methuen, 1906) at p. 81:

> Ordinary men would understand you if you referred currently to Sherlock Holmes. Sir Arthur Conan Doyle would no doubt be justified in rearing his head to the stars, remembering that Sherlock Holmes is the only really familiar figure in modern fiction. But let him droop that head again with a gentle sadness, remembering that if Sherlock Holmes is the only familiar figure in modern fiction, Sherlock Holmes is also the only familiar figure in the Sherlock Holmes Tales. Not many people could say offhand what was the name of the owner of Silver Blaze, or whether Mrs. Watson was dark or fair. But if Dickens had written the Sherlock Holmes stories, every character in them would have been equally arresting and memorable. A Sherlock Holmes would have cooked the dinner for Sherlock Holmes; a Sherlock Holmes would have driven his cab. If Dickens brought in a man merely to carry a letter, he had time for a touch or two, and made him a giant.

The touch that creates giants, there perhaps is the point Professor Kaplan forgets. It appears only occasionally, and not even the most avid protectionist wants to dignify stock characters and mere ideas with property attributes. By all means enlarge the public domain with unworthy artifice, but recognize too that there are magicians among us.

King Features Syndicates v. Fleischer, 299 F.2d 533 (2d Cir. 1924). The plaintiff was engaged in the creation and syndication to daily newspapers of a copyrighted comic strip known as "Barney Google and Spark Plug." "Spark Plug" (sometimes referred to as "Sparky") was, in the court's language, "a new grotesque and comic race horse." The defendant manufactured and sold a toy which was an exact reproduction of "Sparky." The district court denied a preliminary injunction, but the court of appeals reversed. The court concluded that, even though the defendant had not plagiarized all of the comic strip or all of its principal characters, it had infringed by copying "Sparky": "We do not think it avoids the infringement of the copyright to take the substance or idea, and produce it through a different medium, . . . Differences which relate merely to size and material are not important." [The court's language was surely broader than it had to be?] "The concept of beauty expressed in the materials of statuary or drawing, is the thing which is copyrighted. That is what the infringer copies. The Copyright Act was intended to prohibit the taking of this conception. The Copyright Act protects the conception of humor which a cartoonist may produce, as well as the conception of genius which an artist or sculptor may use. . . . The artist's concept of humor . . . cannot be copied, by manufacturing a toy or doll as the [defendant] did, without taking the copyrightable form of that concept, and without at the same time taking the commercial value — the fruits of the cartoonist's genius which consisted in his capacity to entertain and amuse."

Detective Comics, Inc. v. Bruns Publishing, Inc., 111 F.2d 432 (2d Cir. 1940). Plaintiff owned the copyright in the comic book "Action Comics," which portrayed "Superman," while the defendants published and distributed a "Wonderman" comic book. The court affirmed the conclusion of the district court that the defendants had infringed plaintiff's copyright by copying the pictures in "Action Comics." Both Superman and Wonderman are men "of miraculous strength and speed"; their "attributes and antics . . . are closely similar"; each sheds his ordinary clothing to stand "revealed in full panoply in a skin-tight acrobatic costume," the only real difference being that Superman's is blue and Wonderman's is red; each can crush a gun in his powerful hands and can deflect bullets without injury; Superman is shown leaping over buildings while Wonderman leaps from roof to roof, and each is described as being the strongest man in the world and an enemy of evil and injustice. The court rejected the defendant's argument that Superman's attributes were general and unoriginal, with prototypes among heroes of literature and mythology. "[I]f the author of 'Superman' has portrayed a comic Hercules, yet if his production involves more than the presentation of a general type he may copyright it and say of it 'A poor thing but mine own.' Perhaps the periodicals of the complainant are foolish rather than comic, but they embody an original arrangement of incidents and a pictorial and literary form which preclude the contention that Bruns was not copying the antics of 'Superman' portrayed in 'Action Comics.' We think it plain that the defendants have used more than general types and ideas

and have appropriated the pictorial and literary details embodied in the complainant's copyrights." Although plaintiff is not entitled to a monopoly "of the
mere character of a 'Superman' who is a blessing to mankind," it may invoke
copyright protection to the extent its work embodies "an arrangement of incidents and literary expressions original with the author." The court's injunction
forbade, among other things, printing or distributing any cartoon or book
"portraying any of the feats of strength or powers performed by 'Superman' or
closely imitating his costume or appearance in any feat whatever."

QUESTIONS

1. If the "Spark Plug" case had arisen under the 1976 Act, what would the
analysis and result be? What is the appropriate subject matter category under
§ 102? If the comic strip or its components might fit under different subsections,
is there any legal relevance to which subsection applies? What is the appropriate
act of infringement under § 106?

2. In the period preceding the decision of the Supreme Court in *Mazer v.
Stein,* p. 142 *supra,* what alternative measures were available to the creator of a
cartoon character to protect himself against the unauthorized marketing of dolls
or other three-dimensional objects based on that character?

3. Why do you believe the court in the "Spark Plug" case articulated such a
labored and over-broad rationale for its decision? Was any difficulty presented
by the cases holding that copyright of a drawing or photograph of a useful object
did not prevent the unauthorized manufacture of the three-dimensional object?
How would you distinguish those cases?

4. Does not the injunction in the "Wonderman" case overreach the breadth of
the court's analysis and of the defendant's infringement? Has the court properly
limited itself to protecting the plaintiff's "expression" rather than its "idea"?

5. If the defendant in the "Wonderman" case were subsequently to publish a
prose book, without pictures, depicting Wonderman engaging in the same heroic
feats as it had done in its comic books, would it be in contempt of court? Should
it be?

WALT DISNEY PRODUCTIONS v. AIR PIRATES

581 F.2d 751 (9th Cir. 1978)

CUMMINGS, CIRCUIT JUDGE.

This case involves the admitted copying of plaintiff Walt Disney Productions'
("Disney") cartoon characters in defendants' adult "counter-culture" comic
books. The present defendants are three individuals and two business entities
operated by them. The complaint alleges that they infringed Disney copyrights,
a Disney trademark and engaged in unfair competition, trade disparagement
and interference with Disney's business. Disney sought injunctive relief, destruction of infringing materials, damages, costs and attorney's fees.

The district court awarded Disney a temporary restraining order and subsequently granted its motion for a preliminary injunction, simultaneously issuing
an opinion reported in 345 F.Supp. 108 (N.D.Cal.1972). As Judge Wollenberg
noted in his opinion, the basic facts are undisputed. He found as follows (at
109-110):

Plaintiff holds valid copyrights on the various works noted in the first seven
causes of action. The works protected by the copyrights comprise a series of

cartoon drawings ranging from a single page to "book length". The cartoons depict the antics of characters created by plaintiff, with "balloons" over each of the characters' heads containing dialog. Cartoons are drawn to form a narrative.

According to plaintiff, defendants infringed Disney copyrights by copying the graphic depiction of over 17 characters.[5] Two of the characters are represented as insects, and the others as animals endowed with human qualities. Each character has a recognizable image.

The individual defendants have participated in preparing and publishing two magazines of cartoons entitled "Air Pirates Funnies." The characters in defendants' magazines bear a marked similarity to those of plaintiff. The names given to defendants' characters are the same names used in plaintiff's copyrighted work. However, the themes of defendants' publications differ markedly from those of Disney. While Disney sought only to foster "an image of innocent delightfulness," defendants supposedly sought to convey an allegorical message of significance. Put politely by one commentator, the "Air Pirates" was "an 'underground' comic book which had placed several well-known Disney cartoon characters in incongruous settings where they engaged in activities clearly antithetical to the accepted Mickey Mouse world of scrubbed faces, bright smiles and happy endings." It centered around "a rather bawdy depiction of the Disney characters as active members of a free thinking, promiscuous, drug ingesting counterculture." Note, *Parody, Copyrights and the First Amendment*, 10 U.S.F.L.Rev. 564, 571, 582 (1976).

In awarding Disney a preliminary injunction, the district court held that Disney's graphic depictions were protectable under Section 3 of the then Copyright Act as component parts of Disney's copyrighted work. Next, the defense of fair use was rejected because defendants had copied the substance of the Disney products. Finally, after balancing the competing interests of free speech and press versus "encouraging creation by protecting expression" of ideas as reflected in the Copyright Clause of the Constitution, the district court held that the First Amendment did not bar the issuance of a preliminary injunction (at 115-116).

Three years after granting the preliminary injunction, the district court granted summary judgment for plaintiff because the issues were "purely legal and ripe for decision" (R. 512). In its unreported summary judgment order, the court followed the rationale of its preliminary injunction opinion, adding that defendants' parody of Disney's copyrighted work without the consent of Disney "may not be achieved through outright copying of the original work" (R. 514). The court considered it immaterial that in some instances defendants used the challenged cartoon figures in different plots than Disney's or portrayed them with altered personalities, stating that "The test is whether the figures drawn by Defendants are substantial copies of the work of Plaintiff" (R. 515). The court concluded that defendants' challenged publications constituted trade[mark] infringements (concerning the Disney "Silly Symphony" trademark) and violated Disney's valid copyrights and that defendants were guilty of "unfair competition in the form of trade disparagement" (R. 515). In addition to granting Disney a permanent injunction, the court ordered defendants to deliver all infringing

---

[5] Subsequently Toby Tortoise, Max Hare and other cartoon characters were added in Count 11 (R. 466-467, 486; plaintiff's Br. 3). At least 21 characters are now involved (R. 486) including such well known favorites as Mickey and Minnie Mouse, Donald Duck, the Big Bad Wolf, the Three Little Pigs, and Goofy.

materials to Disney's counsel. Costs were awarded to Disney, and the amount of damages and reasonable attorney's fees to be paid to Disney was submitted to a magistrate for preliminary assessment. Only the question of defendants' liability is before us. We affirm as to copyright violation and reverse and remand as to the remainder.

I. Copyright Infringement

The issue that has attracted the most attention from the parties in this case is whether defendants' copies of the images of Disney's characters are infringements of Disney's copyright. . . .

A. Copyrightability

In some instances Disney's copyrights cover a book and others an entire strip of several cartoon panels. The fact that its characters are not the separate subject of a copyright does not preclude their protection, however, because Section 3 of the then Copyright Act provided that Disney's copyrights included protection for "all the copyrightable component parts of the work copyrighted."

The essence of defendants' argument is that characters are never copyrightable and therefore cannot in any way constitute a copyrightable component part. That argument flies in the face of a series of cases dating back to 1914 that have held comic strip characters protectable under the old Copyright Act. See *Detective Comics, Inc. v. Bruns Publications Inc.*, 111 F.2d 432 (2d Cir. 1940); *Fleischer Studios v. Freundlich*, 73 F.2d 276 (2d Cir. 1934), certiorari denied, 294 U.S. 717; *King Features Syndicate v. Fleischer*, 299 F. 533 (2d Cir. 1924); *Detective Comics, Inc. v. Fox Publications Inc.*, 46 F. Supp. 872 (S.D.N.Y.1942); *Hill v. Whalen & Martell, Inc.*, 220 F. 359 (S.D.N.Y.1914); 1 *Nimmer on Copyright* § 30.

It is true that this Court's opinion in *Warner Brothers Pictures v. Columbia Broadcasting System*, 216 F.2d 945 (9th Cir. 1954), certiorari denied, 348 U.S. 971, lends some support to the position that characters ordinarily are not copyrightable. . . . Judge Stephens' opinion considered "whether it was ever intended by the copyright statute that characters with their names should be under its protection.[10] In that context he concluded that such a restriction on Hammett's future use of a character was unreasonable, at least when the characters were merely vehicles for the story and did not "really constitute" the story being told. Judge Stephens' reasons for that conclusion provide an important indication of the applicability of that conclusion to comic book characters as opposed to literary characters. In reasoning that characters "are always limited and always fall into limited patterns," Judge Stephens recognized that it is difficult to delineate distinctively a literary character. Cf. *Nichols v. Universal Pictures Corp.*, 45 F.2d 119 (2d Cir. 1930), certiorari denied, 282 U.S. 902. When the author can add a visual image, however, the difficulty is reduced. See generally 1 *Nimmer on Copyright* § 30. Put another way, while many literary characters may embody little more than an unprotected idea (see *Sid & Marty Krofft Television v.*

---

[10] Judge Wollenberg's opinion viewed this language as an alternate holding rather than dicta, rekindling an old dispute about the status of the language. See 1 Nimmer on Copyright § 30 n. 587. For the reasons that follow, either characterization of the language would not affect the result in this case.

McDonald's Corp., 562 F.2d 1157 (9th Cir. 1977)), a comic book character, which has physical as well as conceptual qualities, is more likely to contain some unique elements of expression. Because comic book characters therefore are distinguishable from literary characters, the *Warner Brothers* language does not preclude protection of Disney's characters.[11]

B. *Infringement and Fair Use*

Defendants do not contend that their admitted copying was not substantial enough to constitute an infringement, and it is plain that copying a comic book character's graphic image constitutes copying to an extent sufficient to justify a finding of infringement. See 2 *Nimmer on Copyright* § 143.12; see generally *Sid & Marty Krofft Television v. McDonald's Corp.,* 562 F.2d 1157 (9th Cir. 1977); *Henry Holt & Co. Inc. v. Liggett & Myers Tobacco Co.,* 23 F.Supp. 302 (E.D.Pa.1938). Defendants instead claim that this infringement should be excused through the application of the fair use defense, since it purportedly is a parody of Disney's cartoons. [The court rejected this defense for reasons set forth at p. 480 *infra.*]

QUESTIONS

1. The 1976 Act contains no counterpart to § 3 of the 1909 Act which expressly provided that copyright protects "all the copyrightable component parts of the work copyrighted. . . ." Would this omission change the result in *Air Pirates* if that case were to arise under the 1976 Act?

2. To what extent are literary characters which are "delineate[d] distinctively" by way of physical attributes, personality traits and mode of dress, such as "Sherlock Holmes," "Charlie Chan" or "Tarzan," subject to copyright protection? *See* Brylawski, *Protection of Characters — Sam Spade Revisited,* 22 BULL. COPYRIGHT SOC'Y 77, 84 (1975).

3. Is a chair in the shape of Mickey Mouse, manufactured by Disney, copyrightable? Does this situation differ from that presented by the abstract shape entitled "Repose" mentioned above? *See* p. 158 *supra.* On what basis? Do you now understand what led the drafters of the 1976 Act to throw up their hands, thereby producing § 113(b)? Note in this connection the following observation:

"For some reason which is not entirely clear, cartoons, whether still or animated, are the most advantageous form in which to embody anything designed for copyright." Umbreit, *A Consideration of Copyright,* 87 U. PA. L. REV. 932, 936 (1939).

---

[11] Because this conclusion is sufficient to justify protection of the characters, we need not endorse the district court's conclusion that Disney's characters fell within the *Warner Brothers* exception for characters who "really constitute" the story. The district judge did not state which Disney stories were the basis of the protection for any character, nor did it state which characters were so protected. Apart from failing to recognize that this exception seems to be limited to a "story devoid of plot" (1 Nimmer on Copyright § 30), the district court's conclusion may have been based on the incorrect assumption that Disney's characters could be protected if together they constitute a whole story. Obviously the larger the group of characters that is selected, the easier it is to say that they "constitute" the entire story, particularly when only a general abstraction and not a particular story is analyzed.

Sid & Marty Krofft Television Productions, Inc. v. McDonald's Corp., 562 F.2d 1157 (9th Cir. 1977). Plaintiffs are creators of a popular children's television series, "H.R. Pufnstuf" which included "several fanciful costumed characters . . . who lived in a fantasyland . . . inhabited by moving trees and talking books." Plaintiffs were originally contacted by an advertising agency attempting to obtain defendant's account with an advertising campaign based on plaintiff's characters. By letter, the agency had confirmed that it was going forward with the proposed campaign based on plaintiff's characters and acknowledged the need to pay plaintiffs for preparing artistic designs and engineering plans. Shortly thereafter plaintiffs were told that the proposed campaign had been cancelled. In fact, the agency was proceeding with a campaign based on "McDonaldland" characters designed and executed by former employees of plaintiffs.

After television commercials based on these characters were broadcast, plaintiffs filed suit alleging that the campaign infringed the copyright in the television series and articles of Pufnstuf merchandise as well. In finding liability for copyright infringement the court made the following comments on the details of similarity:

> A dissection of the two works reveals their similarities. The "Living Island" locale of Pufnstuf and "McDonaldland" are both imaginary worlds inhabited by anthropomorphic plants and animals and other fanciful creatures. The dominant topographical features of the locales are the same: trees, caves, a pond, a road, and a castle. Both works feature a forest with talking trees that have human faces and characteristics.
>
> The characters are also similar. Both lands are governed by mayors who have disproportionately large round heads dominated by long wide mouths. They are assisted by "Keystone cop" characters. Both lands feature strikingly similar crazy scientists and a multi-armed evil creature.
>
> It seems clear that such similarities go beyond merely that of the idea into the area of expression. The use of the basic idea of the works does not inevitably result in such similarities. Certainly a jury . . . could find such similarities of expression substantial.

The Court also noted that "[t]he characters each have developed personalities and particular ways of interacting with each other and their environment. The physical setting also has several unique features."

G. GOVERNMENT WORKS AND OTHER PUBLIC POLICY ISSUES

§ 105. Subject matter of copyright: United States Government works

Copyright protection under this title is not available for any work of the United States Government, but the United States Government is not precluded from receiving and holding copyrights transferred to it by assignment, bequest, or otherwise.

HOUSE REPORT

H.R. Rep. No. 94-1476, 94th Cong., 2d Sess. 58-60 (1976)

Scope of the prohibition

The basic premise of section 105 of the bill is the same as that of section 8 of the present law — that works produced for the U.S. Government by its officers and employees should not be subject to copyright. The provision applies the principle equally to unpublished and published works.

The general prohibition against copyright in section 105 applies to "any work of the United States Government," which is defined in section 101 as "a work prepared by an officer or employee of the United States Government as part of that person's official duties." Under this definition a Government official or employee would not be prevented from securing copyright in a work written at that person's own volition and outside his or her duties, even though the subject matter involves the Government work or professional field of the official or employee. Although the wording of the definition of "work of the United States Government" differs somewhat from that of the definition of "work made for hire," the concepts are intended to be construed in the same way.

A more difficult and far-reaching problem is whether the definition should be broadened to prohibit copyright in works prepared under U.S. Government contract or grant. As the bill is written, the Government agency concerned could determine in each case whether to allow an independent contractor or grantee to secure copyright in works prepared in whole or in part with the use of Government funds. The argument that has been made against allowing copyright in this situation is that the public should not be required to pay a "double subsidy," and that it is inconsistent to prohibit copyright in works by Government employees while permitting private copyrights in a growing body of works created by persons who are paid with Government funds. Those arguing in favor of potential copyright protection have stressed the importance of copyright as an incentive to creation and dissemination in this situation and the basically different policy considerations applicable to works written by Government employees and those applicable to works prepared by private organizations with the use of Federal funds.

The bill deliberately avoids making any sort of outright, unqualified prohibition against copyright in works prepared under Government contract or grant. There may well be cases where it would be in the public interest to deny copyright in the writings generated by Government research contracts and the like; it can be assumed that, where a Government agency commissions a work for its own use merely as an alternative to having one of its own employees prepare the work, the right to secure a private copyright would be withheld. However, there are almost certainly many other cases where the denial of copyright protection would be unfair or would hamper the production and publication of important works. Where, under the particular circumstances, Congress or the agency involved finds that the need to have a work freely available outweighs the need of the private author to secure copyright, the problem can be dealt with by specific legislation, agency regulations, or contractual restrictions.

The prohibition on copyright protection for United States Government works is not intended to have any effect on protection of these works abroad. Works of the governments of most other countries are copyrighted. There are no valid policy reasons for denying such protection to United States Government works in foreign countries, or for precluding the Government from making licenses for the use of its works abroad.

The effect of section 105 is intended to place all works of the United States Government, published or unpublished, in the public domain. This means that the individual Government official or employee who wrote the work could not secure copyright in it or restrain its dissemination by the Government or anyone else, but it also means that, as far as the copyright law is concerned, the Government could not restrain the employee or official from disseminating the work if he or she chooses to do so. The use of the term "work of the United States Government" does not mean that a work falling within the definition of that term is the property of the U.S. Government.

. . . .

Works of the United States Postal Service

The intent of section 105 is to restrict the prohibition against Government copyright to works written by employees of the United States Government within the scope of their official duties. In accordance with the objectives of the Postal Reorganization Act of 1970, this section does not apply to works created by employees of the United States Postal Service. In addition to enforcing the criminal statutes proscribing the forgery or counterfeiting of postage stamps, the Postal Service could, if it chooses, use the copyright law to prevent the reproduction of postage stamp designs for private or commercial non-postal services (for example, in philatelic publications and catalogs, in general advertising, in art reproductions, in textile designs, and so forth). However, any copyright claimed by the Postal Service in its works, including postage stamp designs, would be subject to the same conditions, formalities, and time limits as other copyrightable works.

QUESTIONS

1. Examine the official reports of the United States Supreme Court and the volumes in the *Federal Second* series. What parts of these volumes, if any, are eligible for copyright?

2. Are state statutes and court decisions eligible for federal copyright? What about statutes based on model laws created and copyrighted by private organizations with a view toward legislative adoption? See *Building Officials & Code Admin. v. Code Technology, Inc.,* 628 F.2d 730 (1st Cir. 1980).

3. Is the *Scott Stamp Catalogue* — which reproduces all United States stamps and lists such accompanying information as perforations, watermarks and value new and used — an infringement of copyright? Can United States stamps be freely reproduced as part of a fabric design for curtains or clothing?

4. The Administrative Office of the United States Courts entered into a contract with a public television station to "produce for the Judicial Conference of the United States five films about the Supreme Court entitled 'Equal Justice Under the Law.'" The station was to copyright the films and thereafter assign the copyright to the Government. The films have been produced starring professional actors in the role of Supreme Court Justices and depicting the background of five major cases in Supreme Court history. They have been exhibited on public television through the Public Broadcasting Service. Copyright has been registered for each film in the name of the station. A journalist has commenced an action for declaratory and injunctive relief (with the Director of the Administrative Office, the Register of Copyrights, the producing television station, PBS and one of its exhibiting stations as named defendants) seeking a determination that the copyrights are invalid. What ruling should the court make? See *Schnapper v. Foley,* 471 F. Supp. 426 (D.D.C. 1979).

5. Messrs. Goodman and Scherr served for two years in the United States Army and were stationed at Fort Dix. Their military occupation classification was "illustrator," and they were assigned to prepare visual training aids. During their

leisure hours, they worked on a small clay table model of an infantryman; the deputy post commander saw their work, which impressed him, and he asked if they would construct a larger, life-size statue which would serve as a symbol of Fort Dix. When they agreed, they were relieved of their regular duties as illustrators and for the next nine months they devoted substantially all of their duty hours and some (allegedly nearly 2,000 hours) of their leisure time to redesigning and constructing the statue, which was to be called "The Ultimate Weapon." Substantially all of the expenses of the project — the physical facilities, equipment, materials and additional labor — were borne by the Army, totalling some $12,000. The statue, set on a twelve-foot base, is itself twelve feet high, and depicts a charging infantryman in full battle dress, with rifle thrust forward, with a field pack on his back, and with a bayonet, sheath, a shovel, canteen, hand grenades, and other implements attached to a cartridge belt supported by suspenders. Approximately five years after the statue was unveiled, and Goodman and Scherr had completed their tour of duty in the Army, it came to their attention that the Universal Match Corporation was manufacturing and selling matchbooks which bore a picture of "The Ultimate Weapon." They have brought an action against Universal, seeking an injunction and damages. Universal has moved for summary judgment, asserting that the statue it concededly copied was in the public domain. What arguments can be made on behalf of the plaintiffs? How should the court rule? See *Scherr v. Universal Match Corp.*, 417 F.2d 497 (2d Cir. 1969), *cert. denied*, 397 U.S. 936 (1970).

6. Hyman Rickover was Vice Admiral in the Navy Department as Assistant Chief of the Bureau of Ships for Nuclear Propulsion. During his tenure in that position, Admiral Rickover prepared a number of speeches on a wide range of subjects, such as "Nuclear Power and the Navy," "Engineering and Scientific Education," "The Education of Our Talented Children," "Nuclear Power — Challenge to Industry," "Energy Resources and Our Future," "Revolution at Sea," and "European Secondary Schools." These speeches were delivered at such places as chambers of commerce, the Minnesota State Medical Association, the Detroit Engineering Society, the Nuclear Power Training School, and the Columbia University Forum. In all instances, the locations were near places where Rickover had duties of supervision and inspection, so that no transportation costs were borne by him; he made the speeches in free or off-duty hours. The final drafts of the speeches were typed by his Navy secretary on his office typewriter, and copies were made with Navy photocopy machines on the paper stock used for press releases by the Department of Defense. (Assume that all copies bore a copyright notice in the name of Admiral Rickover.) An educational publishing company has compiled many of the Rickover speeches and is about to publish them in hard-cover form. Rickover has brought an action to enjoin this publication, but the publishing company has asserted that his speeches are in the public domain. Should the injunction be granted? See *Public Affairs Associates v. Rickover*, 177 F. Supp. 601 (D.D.C. 1959), *rev'd and remanded*, 284 F.2d 262 (D.C. Cir. 1960), *vacated for further proceedings*, 369 U.S. 111 (1962), *on remand*, 268 F. Supp. 444 (D.D.C. 1967).

MITCHELL BROTHERS FILM GROUP v. CINEMA ADULT THEATER

604 F.2d 852 (5th Cir. 1979)

GODBOLD, CIRCUIT JUDGE:

This is a copyright infringement suit, arising under the now-superseded Copyright Act of 1909. But it is more than the usual commercial contest between copyright holder and alleged infringer. The infringers asserted as an affirmative defense that the copyrighted material — a movie — was obscene, and that, therefore, under the equitable rubric of "unclean hands" plaintiffs were barred from relief. After viewing the film the court found it obscene, adopted the unclean hands rationale, and denied relief to the copyright owners. Review of this holding requires us to consider the constitutional limits upon the power granted to Congress to issue copyrights, the manner in which Congress has chosen to exercise that power, and the applicability of the unclean hands doctrine.

Plaintiffs-appellants owned a properly registered copyright on a motion picture titled "Behind the Green Door," issued under the 1909 Act, 17 U.S.C. § 34 (1970) (repealed). Two groups of defendants, each group consisting of a theater and several individuals, obtained copies of the movie without plaintiffs' permission and infringed the copyright by exhibiting the film at the theaters.

. . . .

We hold that the district court erred in permitting the assertion of obscenity as an affirmative defense to the claim of infringement, and, accordingly, reverse without reaching the question whether the film is obscene.

I. The Statutory Language

The statutory provision that controls in this case reads:

The works for which copyright may be secured under this title shall include all the writings of an author.

17 U.S.C. § 4 (1970) (repealed). Motion pictures are unquestionably "writings" under the Copyright Act.

The district court did not base its decision on standards found within the Act, which it described as "silent as to works which are subject to registration and copyright." The Act is not "silent." Rather, the statutory language "all the writings of an author" is facially all-inclusive, within itself admitting of no exceptions. There is not even a hint in the language of § 4 that the obscene nature of a work renders it any less a copyrightable "writing." There is no other statutory language from which it can be inferred that Congress intended that obscene materials could not be copyrighted.[3]

Moreover, there is good reason not to read an implied exception for obscenity into the copyright statutes. The history of content-based restrictions on copyrights, trademarks, and patents suggests that the absence of such limitations in the Copyright Act of 1909 is the result of an intentional policy choice and not simply an omission. See generally 74 Colum. L. Rev. 1351, 1354 n.27 (1974). From the first copyright act in 1790, Congress has seldom added restrictions on copyright based on the subject matter of the work, and in each instance has later

---

[3] See 1 M. Nimmer, On Copyright § 2.17, at 2-193 (1978); Chafee, Coming into Equity with Clean Hands, 47 Mich. L. Rev. 1065, 1068 (1947); Schneider, Authority of the Register of Copyrights to Deny Registration of a Claim to Copyright on the Ground of Obscenity, 51 Chi.-Kent L. Rev. 691, 692-93 (1975); Note, Immorality, Obscenity and the Law of Copyright, 6 S. Dakota L. Rev. 109, 111 (1961); 74 Colum. L. Rev. 1351, 1354 (1974); 46 Fordham L. Rev. 1037, 1038 (1978).

removed the content restriction. These congressional additions and subsequent deletions, though certainly not conclusive, suggest that Congress has been hostile to content-based restrictions on copyrightability. In contrast Congress has placed explicit content-related restrictions in the current statutes governing the related areas of trademarks and patents. The Lanham Act prohibits registration of any trademark that "[c]onsists of or comprises immoral, deceptive, or scandalous matter," 15 U.S.C. § 1052(a), and inventions must be shown to be "useful" before a patent is issued. See 35 U.S.C. § 101.

The legislative history of the 1976 Act reveals that Congress intends to continue the policy of the 1909 Act of avoiding content restrictions on copyrightability. In recommending passage of the 1976 Act, the House Judiciary Committee stated:

> The phrase "original works of authorship," [§ 102] which is purposely left undefined, is intended to incorporate without change the standard of originality established by the courts under the present copyright statute. This standard does not include requirements of novelty, ingenuity, or esthetic merit, and there is no intention to enlarge the standard of copyright protection to require them.

H. R. Rep. No. 1476, 94th Cong., 2d Sess. 51, *reprinted in* [1976] U.S. Code Cong. & Admin. News pp. 5659, 5664 (emphasis added).

It appears to us that Congress has concluded that the constitutional purpose of its copyright power, "[t]o promote the Progress of Science and useful Arts," U.S. Const. art. 1, § 8, cl. 8, is best served by allowing all creative works (in a copyrightable format) to be accorded copyright protection regardless of subject matter or content, trusting to the public taste to reward creators of useful works and to deny creators of useless works any reward.

. . . [The Ninth Circuit recently rejected the defense of fraudulent content in copyright infringement actions, saying]:

> There is nothing in the Copyright Act to suggest that the courts are to pass upon the truth or falsity, the soundness or unsoundness, of the views embodied in a copyrighted work. The gravity and immensity of the problems, theological, philosophical, economic and scientific, that would confront a court if this view were adopted are staggering to contemplate. It is surely not a task lightly to be assumed, and we decline the invitation to assume it.

Belcher v. Tarbox, 486 F.2d 1087, 1088 (CA9, 1973).

In our view, the absence of content restrictions on copyrightability indicates that Congress has decided that the constitutional goal of encouraging creativity would not be best served if an author had to concern himself not only with the marketability of his work but also with the judgment of government officials regarding the worth of the work.

Further, if Congress were receptive to subject matter restrictions on copyright, there are many reasons why it would be unlikely to choose obscenity as one of those restrictions. Obscenity law is a concept not adapted for use as a means for ascertaining whether creative works may be copyrighted. Obscenity as a constitutional doctrine has developed as an effort to create a tolerable compromise between First Amendment considerations and police power. It is an awkward, barely acceptable concept that continues to dog our judicial system and society at large. The purpose underlying the constitutional grant of power to Congress to protect writings is the promotion of original writings, an invitation to creativity. This is an expansive purpose with no stated limitations of taste or governmental acceptability. Such restraints, if imposed, would be antithetical to promotion of creativity. The pursuit of creativity requires freedom to explore into the gray areas, to the cutting edge, and even beyond. Obscenity, on the other hand, is a limiting doctrine constricting the scope of acceptability of the written word.[7]

> Denial of [copyright] Registration could work to discourage the development of the Arts. At least one commentator has argued that denial of registration will increase the circulation of material to the public, by removing the right to sue for unauthorized publication and dissemination of copied material. [Cite omitted.] This view, however, ignores the potentially discouraging effect a stated policy of denial on the ground of obscenity would have on authors, publishers and promoters of works inhabiting the hazy border between obscenity and protected speech.

Schneider, *supra* note 3, at 719.

Society's view of what is moral and immoral continually changes. To give one example, in *Martinetti v. Maguire,* 16 Fed. Cas. p. 920 (No. 9173) (C.C. Cal. 1867), the play "The Black Crook," because it featured women clad in flesh-colored tights, was held to be "grossly indecent, and calculated to corrupt the morals of the people" and hence uncopyrightable.

. . . .

Denying copyright protection to works adjudged obscene by the standards of one era would frequently result in lack of copyright protection (and thus lack of financial incentive to create) for works that later generations might consider to be not only non-obscene but even of great literary merit. *See* Phillips, *Copyright in Obscene Works: Some British and American Problems,* 6 Anglo-Am. L. Rev. 138, 168-69 (1977). Many works that are today held in high regard have been adjudged obscene in previous eras. English courts of the nineteenth century found the works of Byron, Southey and Shelley to be immoral. *See U.S. v. One Book Entitled Ulysses,* 72 F.2d 705, 708 (CA2, 1934). American courts have found these books, among others, obscene: Edmund Wilson, *Memories of Hecate County, see People v. Doubleday & Co.,* 297 N.Y. 687, 77 N.E.2d 6 (1947), *aff'd per curiam by an equally divided court,* 335 U.S. 848, 69 S. Ct. 79, 93 L.Ed. 398 (1948); Henry Miller, *Tropic of Cancer* and *Tropic of Capricorn, see Besig v. U. S.,* 208 F.2d 142 (CA9, 1953); Erskine Caldwell, *God's Little Acre, see Attorney General v. Book Named "God's Little Acre,"* 326 Mass. 281, 93 N.E.2d 819 (1950); Lillian Smith, *Strange Fruit, see Commonwealth v. Isenstadt,* 318 Mass. 543, 62 N.E.2d 840 (1945); D. H. Lawrence, *Lady Chatterly's Lover, see Commonwealth v. Delacey,* 271 Mass. 327, 171 N.E. 455 (1930); Theodore Dreiser, *An American Tragedy, see Commonwealth v. Friede,* 271 Mass. 318, 171 N.E. 472 (1930). *See generally* Lewis, *Literature, Obscenity and Law* (1976); Alpert, *Judicial Censorship of Obscene Material,* 52 Harv. L. Rev. 40 (1938).

Further, Congress in not enacting an obscenity exception to copyrightability avoids substantial practical difficulties and delicate First Amendment issues. Since what is obscene in one local community may be non-obscene protected speech in another, *see Miller v. California,* 413 U.S. 15 (1973), and the copyright

---

[7] One commentator has suggested that the inconsistent purposes of the obscenity doctrine and the copyright power might render any use of the copyright power for the purpose of suppressing obscenity an unconstitutional misuse of the copyright power. "[P]olicies which discourage creation and publication fail to pursue the constitutional justification for the grant of power to Congress to enact Copyright legislation: to promote the progress of science and the useful arts." Schneider, *supra* note 3, at 720.

statute does not in other respects vary in its applicability from locality to locality, Congress in enacting an obscenity exception would create the dilemma of choosing between using community standards that would (arguably unconstitutionally) fragment the uniform national standards of the copyright system and venturing into the uncharted waters of a national obscenity standard.[11] *See* Phillips, *Copyright in Obscene Works: Some British and American Problems,* 6 Anglo-Am. L. Rev. 138, 170-71 (1977); Schneider, *supra* note 3, at 715; Comment, *Constitutional Protection of Obscene Material Against Censorship as Correlated with Copyright Protection of Obscene Material Against Infringement,* 31 S. Cal. L. Rev. 301, 306 (1958); 46 Fordham L. Rev. 1037, 1043-47 (1978). We can only conclude that we must read the facially all-inclusive 1909 copyright statute as containing no explicit or implicit bar to the copyrighting of obscene materials, and as therefore providing for the copyright of all creative works, obscene or non-obscene, that otherwise meet the requirements of the Copyright Act.[12]

II. Constitutionality of the Copyright Statute

The conclusion that the 1909 Act was all-inclusive [13] and did not provide an exception for obscenity does not end our inquiry, however. We must consider whether the statute, in allowing copyright of obscene material, was constitutional and whether despite congressional intent the courts should take it upon themselves to permit the defense of obscenity in copyright infringement cases. We first turn to the question of constitutionality.

---

[11] Congress in formulating such a standard would encounter substantial difficulty. It might well be unconstitutional for Congress to allow a New York writer who is seeking copyright on a work he plans to distribute only in New York, where it is not obscene, to be denied that copyright because, judged by a national standard, the book is obscene. If, as the Supreme Court held in Miller v. California, 413 U.S. 15, 32 (1973), "It is neither realistic nor constitutionally sound to read the First Amendment as requiring that the people of Maine or Mississippi accept public depiction of conduct found tolerable in Las Vegas, or New York City, then it may conversely be argued that the First Amendment does not permit the people of New York or Las Vegas be barred from freely obtaining works acceptable to them simply because those works would be intolerable to the people of Maine or Mississippi. For, as Justice Frankfurter said in holding that a state cannot restrict its adult population's reading material to that suitable for children, the government cannot "burn the house to roast the pig." That is, the means chosen must be reasonably restricted to the evil dealt with. *See* Butler v. Michigan, 352 U.S. 380, 383 (1957).

[12] Of course, Congress does not approve of obscenity and has enacted several measures aimed at reducing the distribution of obscene materials. *See, e.g.,* 18 U.S.C. § 1461 (crime to mail obscene materials); 18 U.S.C. § 1462 (crime to ship obscene materials interstate by common carrier); 18 U.S.C. § 1465 (crime to ship obscene materials interstate for purposes of sale or distribution). However, the existence of such statutes does not indicate that Congress intends obscene material to be uncopyrightable. Rendering obscene material uncopyrightable would add little to the existing arsenal of weapons against pornography and would have many undesirable consequences, as discussed in the text.

[13] The 1976 Act substitutes the equally-inclusive phrase "original works of authorship" for the phrase "all the writings of an author" in the 1909 Act. *See* 17 U.S.C. § 102 (1976, App.).

The Copyright and Patent Clause of the Constitution provides that "The Congress shall have Power . . . To promote the Progress of Science and useful Arts, by securing for limited Times to Authors and Inventors the exclusive Right to their respective Writings and Discoveries . . . ." U.S. Const. art. I, § 8, cl. 8. The district court construed this clause to limit the congressional power to grant copyrights solely to works that promote the sciences and useful arts. If one carries the district court's reasoning to its necessary conclusion, Congress acted unconstitutionally in enacting an all-inclusive statute that allows copyrighting of non-useful works (such as, arguably, obscenity) as well as useful works. Several lower courts and commentators have agreed with this construction of the Copyright and Patent Clause.[16] Other commentators disagree, however, and argue that Congress has power to grant copyrights even for individual works that cannot be shown to promote the useful arts so long as Congress in its exercise of its copyright power generally promotes the constitutional goal.[17] In our view the district court's reading of the Copyright and Patent Clause is unduly restrictive of Congress' power and is inconsistent with the Supreme Court's broad view of the congressional powers granted by this Clause. As one commentator has pointed out,

> The words of the copyright clause of the constitution do not require that *writings* shall promote science or useful arts: they require that *Congress* shall promote those ends. It could well be argued that by passing general laws to protect all works, Congress better fulfills its designated ends than it would by denying protection to all books the contents of which were open to real or imagined objection.

Phillips, *op. cit. supra* note 15, at 165-66 (emphasis original).

The courts will not find that Congress has exceeded its power so long as the means adopted by Congress for achieving a constitutional end are "appropriate" and "plainly adapted" to achieving that end. *McCulloch v. Maryland,* 17 U.S. (4 Wheat.) 316, 421 (1819). It is by the lenient standard of *McCulloch* that we must judge whether Congress has exceeded its constitutional powers in enacting an all-inclusive copyright statute.

Judging by this standard, it is obvious that although Congress could require that each copyrighted work be shown to promote the useful arts (as it has with patents), it need not do so. As discussed in the previous section, Congress could reasonably conclude that the best way to promote creativity is not to impose any governmental restrictions on the subject matter of copyrightable works. By making this choice Congress removes the chilling effect of governmental judgments on potential authors and avoids the strong possibility that governmental officials (including judges) will err in separating the useful from the non-useful.

---

[16] See Barnes v. Miner, 122 F. 480, 489-90 (C.C.S.D.N.Y. 1903); Martinetti v. Maguire, 16 Fed. Cas. p. 920 (No. 9173) (C.C.Cal. 1867); Bullard v. Esper, 72 F.Supp. 548 (N.D.Tex. 1947); Dane v. M. & H. Co., 136 U.S.P.Q. 426, 429 (N.Y.Sup.Ct. 1963); 1 M. Nimmer, On Copyright § 1.03[B] (1978); Rogers, *supra* note 15; Note, Obscenity and Copyright, 6 S.DakotaL.Rev. at 111-12 (1961); Comment, Copyright Protection of Obscene Material Against Censorship as Correlated with Copyright Protection of Obscene Material Against Infringement, 31 S.Cal.L.Rev. 301, 306 (1958); 6 St. Mary's L.J. 274, 278 (1974); *cf.* Argos Films, S.A. v. Barry International Properties Inc., 77 Civ. 1062 (S.D.N.Y., July 7, 1977) (constricting Copyright Act to not allow copyright of obscenity apparently adopted to avoid constitutional difficulties).

[17] *See* Phillips, *op. cit. supra,* at 165-66; Schneider, *supra* note 3, at 698 n.36; 74 Colum.L.Rev. 1351, 1353 (1974).

Moreover, unlike patents, the grant of a copyright to a non-useful work impedes the progress of the sciences and the useful arts only very slightly, if at all, for the possessor of a copyright does not have any right to block further dissemination or use of the ideas contained in his works.[20] *See Baker v. Selden,* 101 U.S. 99 (1879).

The all-inclusive nature of the 1909 Act reflects the policy judgment that encouraging the production of wheat also requires the protection of a good deal of chaff. We cannot say this judgment was so unreasonable as to exceed congressional power. We conclude that the protection of all writings, without regard to their content, is a constitutionally permissible means of promoting science and the useful arts.

III. Judicially-Created Defenses to Infringement Actions Involving Immoral or Obscene Works

Some courts have denied legal redress in infringement suits to holders of copyrights on immoral or obscene works by applying judicially-created doctrines. Two of these doctrines are largely vestiges of a bygone era and need be addressed only briefly. The theory that judges should act as conservators of the public morality was succinctly summarized by the court in *Shook v. Daly,* 49 How. Prac. 366, 368 (N.Y. Sup. Ct. 1895): "The rights of the writer are secondary to the rights of the public to be protected from what is subversive of good morals." Application of this theory by the English courts in the nineteenth century led to the suppression of works because they were inconsistent with Biblical teachings or because they were seditious. *See* 46 Fordham L. Rev. 1037, 1038-39 (1978); Schneider, *supra* note 3, at 694-96. Although this theory has been relied on as recently as 1963, *see Dane v. M. & H. Co.,* 136 U.S.P.Q. 426, 429 (N.Y. Sup. Ct. 1963) (common law copyright protection denied striptease because it did not "elevate, cultivate, inform, or improve the moral or intellectual natures of the audience"), it is evident to us that it is inappropriate for a court, in the absence of some guidance or authorization from the legislature, to interpose its moral views between an author and his willing audience.

A second judicially-created doctrine, the theory that a person can have no property in obscene works, merely expresses by means of a legal fiction the underlying judicial moral conclusion that the work is not worthy of protection. The doctrine has not been adopted in this country, *see* Schneider, *supra* note 3, at 696-97, and should not be. *Cf. Board of Trade v. Christie Grain & Stock Co.,* 198 U.S. 236, 251 (1905): "If, then, the plaintiffs' collection of information is otherwise entitled to protection, it does not cease to be so, even if it is information concerning illegal acts. The statistics of crime are property to the same extent as any other statistics, even if collected by a criminal who furnishes some of the data."

The third judicially created doctrine, that of unclean hands, has seldom been relied upon by courts that have denied copyright to obscene or immoral works. For the most part, only English courts have relied on this theory. *See generally* Chafee, *supra* note 3, at 1065-70. Of the various American cases allowing obscen-

---

[20] This is not true in the patent area, where an inventor has the right to prevent others from using his discovery. Thus Congress and the courts have been careful to require that each patented invention advance the useful arts in some way. *See generally* Brenner v. Manson, 383 U.S. 519 (1966); Alfred Bell & Co. v. Catalda Fine Arts, Inc., 191 F.2d 99 (CA2, 1951).

ity as a defense to a copyright infringement action, few even mention the doctrine of unclean hands. *See Bullard v. Esper,* 72 F.Supp. 548, 549 (N.D. Tex. 1947) (semble); *Richardson v. Miller,* 20 Fed. Cas. 722 (No. 11,791) (C.C.D. Mass. 1877). Nevertheless, since the district court permitted obscenity to be asserted as a defense through the medium of the unclean hands rubric, the concept of unclean hands requires more extended discussion.

Assuming for the moment that the equitable doctrine of unclean hands has any field of application in this case, it should not be used as a conduit for asserting obscenity as a limit upon copyright protection. Creating a defense of obscenity — in the name of unclean hands or through any other vehicle — adds a defense not authorized by Congress that may, as discussed above, actually frustrate the congressional purpose underlying an all-inclusive copyright statute. It will discourage creativity by freighting it with a requirement of judicial approval. Requiring authors of controversial, unpopular, or new material to go through judicial proceedings to validate the content of their writings is antithetical to the aim of copyrights. If the copyright holder cannot obtain financial protection for his work because of actual or possible judicial objections to the subject matter, the pro-creativity purpose of the copyright laws will be undercut.

The Supreme Court and this court have held that equitable doctrines should not be applied where their application will defeat the purpose of a statute.

Furthermore, the need for an additional check on obscenity is not apparent. Most if not all states have statutes regulating the dissemination of obscene materials, and there is an array of federal statutes dealing with this subject, as well. *See* note 16 *supra.* As Professor Chafee concluded, the difficulty inherent in formulating a workable obscenity defense to copyright is sufficient reason not to allow such a defense unless the other criminal and civil statutes dealing with the obscenity problem are shown to be plainly ineffective:

> Sometimes the legislature has expressly entrusted questions of obscenity to the courts, as in criminal statutes, and then judges have to do the best they can, but the results have been quite erratic. This should be a warning against rushing into new obscenity jobs which no legislature has told them to undertake.
>
> The penalties for obscenity are defined by statute. Why should the courts add a new penalty out of their own heads by denying protection to a registered copyright which complies with every provision of the copyright act? . . . I think that the added penalty is justifiable only if there is a serious need for extra pressure to induce obedience to the criminal law. In the obscenity situation, this need is not obvious.

Chafee, *supra* note 3, at 1068-69.

The effectiveness of controlling obscenity by denying copyright protection is open to question. The district court thought that on the whole the long-term discouragement of the creation of obscene works would outweigh the short-term increase in the dissemination of obscene works caused by the refusal of an injunction. This theory, reached without empirical evidence or expert opinion, is at least doubtful. Many commentators disagree and are of the view that denial of injunctions against infringers of obscene materials will only increase the distribution of such works. The existence of this difference of view, which we need not resolve, makes clear that the question of how to deal with the relationship between copyrights and obscenity is not best suited for case-by-case judicial resolution but is instead most appropriately resolved by legislatures. Congress has not chosen to refuse copyrights on obscene materials, and we should be cautious in overriding the legislative judgment on this issue.

Finally, permitting obscenity as a defense would introduce an unmanageable array of issues into routine copyright infringement actions. It was for this reason that the Ninth Circuit rejected the defense of fraudulent content in copyright infringement cases. *See Belcher v. Tarbox,* 486 F.2d 1087, 1088 (CA9, 1973), *accord* 2 M. Nimmer, *On Copyright* § 2.17, at 2-194. *Cf. Coca-Cola Co. v. Howard Johnson Co.,* 386 F. Supp. 330, 337 (N.D. Ga. 1974) (James C. Hill, District Judge) (rejecting violation of antitrust law as defense in trademark infringement suit because it would convert courts into "a battleground for extensive antitrust litigation whenever a trademark holder seeks any, totally unrelated, equitable relief").

Now, we turn to examine our momentary assumption that the unclean hands doctrine can be invoked at all in this case. For reasons that we have set out, obscenity is not an appropriate defense in an infringement action, whether piggybacked on the unclean hands rubric or introduced in some other manner. But even if obscenity were not objectionable as a defense, the unclean hands doctrine could not properly be used as the vehicle for that defense.

The maxim of unclean hands is not applied where plaintiff's misconduct is not directly related to the merits of the controversy between the parties, but only where the wrongful acts "in some measure affect the equitable relations between the parties in respect of something brought before the court for adjudication." *Keystone Driller Co. v. General Excavator Co.,* 290 U.S. 240, 245 (1933). The alleged wrongdoing of the plaintiff does not bar relief unless the defendant can show that he has personally been injured by the plaintiff's conduct. *Lawler v. Gillam,* 569 F.2d 1283, 1294 (CA4, 1978). The doctrine of unclean hands "does not purport to search out or deal with the general moral attributes or standing of a litigant." *NLRB v. Fickett-Brown Mfg. Co.,* 140 F.2d 883, 884 (CA5, 1944). Here it is clear that plaintiffs' alleged wrongful conduct has not changed the equitable relationship between plaintiffs and defendants and has not injured the defendants in any way.

. . . .

Reversed and remanded.

Chapter 3

DURATION AND RENEWAL

A. DURATION

CHAFEE, REFLECTIONS ON THE LAW OF COPYRIGHT, 45 Columbia Law Review 719-21, 725-27, 729-30 (1945)

a. *A long or a short monopoly?* Recall that our primary purpose is to benefit the author.* One's first impression is, that the longer the monopoly, the better for him. How far this is from being true was pointed out by Macaulay in 1841: [1]

> ... the evil effects of the monopoly are proportioned to the length of its duration. But the good effects for the sake of which we bear with the evil effects are by no means proportioned to the length of its duration. A monopoly of sixty years produces twice as much evil as a monopoly of thirty years, and thrice as much evil as a monopoly of twenty years. But it is by no means the fact that a posthumous monopoly of sixty years gives to an author thrice as much pleasure and thrice as strong a motive as a posthumous monopoly of twenty years. On the contrary, the difference is so small as to be hardly perceptible. We all know how faintly we are affected by the prospect of very distant advantages, even when they are advantages which we may reasonably hope that we shall ourselves enjoy. But an advantage that is to be enjoyed more than half a century after we are dead, by somebody, we know not by whom, perhaps by somebody unborn, by somebody utterly unconnected with us, is really no motive at all to action.... Considered as a boon to [authors, long posthumous duration of the copyright monopoly] is a mere nullity; but, considered as an impost on the public, it is no nullity, but a very serious and pernicious reality. I will take an example. Dr. Johnson died fifty-six years ago. If the law [prolonged the copyright for sixty years after the author's death], somebody would now have the monopoly of Dr. Johnson's works. Who that somebody would be it is impossible to say; but we may venture to guess. I guess, then, that it would have been some bookseller, who was the assign of another bookseller, who was the grandson of a third bookseller, who had bought the copyright from Black Frank, the Doctor's servant and residuary legatee, in 1785 or 1786. Now, would the knowledge that this copyright would exist in 1841 have been a source of gratification to Johnson? Would it have stimulated his exertions? Would it have once drawn him out of his bed before noon? Would it have once cheered him under a fit of the spleen? Would it have induced him to give us one more allegory, one more life of a poet, one more imitation of Juvenal? I firmly believe not. I firmly believe that a hundred years ago, when he was writing our debates for the Gentleman's Magazine, he would very much rather have had twopence to buy a plate of shin of beef at a cook's shop underground. Considered as a reward to him, the difference between a twenty years' term and a sixty years' term of posthumous copyright would have been nothing or next to nothing. But is the difference nothing to us? I can buy Rasselas for sixpence; I might have had to give five shillings for it. I can buy the Dictionary, the entire genuine Dictionary, for two guineas, perhaps for less; I might have had to give five or six guineas for it. Do I grudge this to a man like Dr. Johnson? Not at all. Show me that the prospect of this boon roused him to any vigorous effort, or sustained his spirits under depressing

---

* *But see* Mazer v. Stein, p. 16 *supra.* — Eds.

[1] 8 Macaulay, Works (Trevelyan ed. 1879) 199-201 (hereafter cited as Works).

circumstances, and I am quite willing to pay the price of such an object, heavy as that price is. But what I do complain of is that my circumstances are to be worse, and Johnson's none the better; that I am to give five pounds for what to him was not worth a farthing.

Johnson was a childless widower, and it may be supposed that an author with a widow and progeny would care more about a prolonged monopoly. Yet Macaulay tells us [2] that in the middle of the eighteenth century when the common law copyright on Milton's Works was supposed to be perpetual, Milton's grand-daughter had to be relieved from abject poverty by a benefit performance of *Comus* at the very time that the publisher who owned Milton's Works was enjoining a pirate in Chancery. Milton had sold his perpetual rights to the booksellers for cash down, and whatever happened after that was of no use to him or his family.

Plainly the kind of pecuniary bargain which the author makes with his publisher is a vital fact in determining whether a long monopoly is of value to the author or not. If the author makes a royalty agreement for the life of the copyright, then he and his family will gain, the longer it is. But if the author sells his rights for a lump sum, the only value to him from length depends on whether it enhances the price which the publisher pays. Given the speculative nature of publishing, the price is not likely to be affected by the difference between fifty-six years, let us say, and life plus fifty years. How much more would any publisher pay for the right to monopolize after fifty-six years a book brought out in 1945? As Birrell says,[3] "The money market takes short views." A businessman remarked to J. M. Maguire that for him "fifteen years was eternity." [4] The publisher must have always shaped his lump-sum offer according to his expectation of sales within the first few years of the copyright. That is when he makes his killing. This is probably truer today then ever, because of the rapid waning of most books and songs. Where are the Hit Parades of yesteryear? Leave out classics and lawbooks — how many books published before 1940 did lawyers read during 1944? Good publishing accounting writes off all books within three years after publication as no longer an asset. Rudy Vallee keeps *The Maine Stein Song* alive and the current motion picture *To The Victor* is drawn from a dog-story of 1898, but such resurrections are too problematical to raise the lump-sum price for a new book or song. Royalties, however, reflect the ups-and-downs of sales.

In view of this great practical importance of the difference between an outright sale and a royalty contract, a copyright statute ought to pay some attention to the distinction. The 1909 Act does not. It is one of the merits of the Shotwell Bill that it does.[5]

Therefore, the last part of a long copyright does no good to the author who sells all his rights at once. It really taxes the readers for the benefit of the

---

[2] *Id.* at 203.

[3] Birrell, Seven Lectures on the Law and History of Copyright in Books (1899) 25. The whole passage, 23-26, is excellent.

[4] Maguire, Capitalization of Periodical Payments by Gift (1920) 34 Harv. L. Rev. 20, 40.

[5] Shotwell Bill, § 13(4), 86 Cong. Rec. 63, 67 (1940); see *infra* pp. 724-725.

publisher. He gets a windfall for which he paid practically nothing. A long term is desirable only if the author and his family are sure to get the benefit of the latter years. The law can accomplish this in various ways. It can require a royalty contract, at least for the latter years; or it can make rights in those years revert to the author and limit the effect of an outright sale to the early part of the copyright. The Act of 1909 attempts to use the second method, how successfully we shall now ask.

. . . .

   c. *Should all the incidents of the author's monopoly pass to his surviving family?* Insofar as copyright yields pecuniary benefits to the author, these should pass to his family on his death. Copyright, however, involves several non-pecuniary rights which are much more useful in the hands of the author than in the hands of those who did not create the work.

   The author has the power to keep a copyrighted work off the market entirely. It is right for him to decide whether what he has created shall be published or not. Thus when Southey in his flaming youth entrusted the manuscript of a revolutionary poem on Wat Tyler to a bookseller, who after years of inaction proposed to publish it when Southey had become a sedate poet laureate, it was harsh on him to lose his injunction on the ground that a revolutionary author did not come into equity with clean hands.[11] Yet the veto power of the copyright owner loses most of its desirability on the author's death and may become a nuisance when it passes to his descendants.

   . . . Yet the 1909 Act gives a posthumous veto power to the surviving relatives, perhaps for decades. They have the same control of his unpublished works under the common law of literary property. The letters of James McNeill Whistler are lost to the world because his crabbed niece would not allow his chosen biographers to print them.[14] Suppose that the manuscript of a new poem by Poe should be discovered tomorrow. His descendants could keep it hidden if they so desired, and according to judicial *dicta* [15] they could do so forever. The British statute avoids this dog-in-the-manger situation. It gives copyright for life plus fifty years; but after the author has been dead twenty-five years, anybody can publish his work on paying a 10 per cent royalty to the copyright owner. This not only prevents the family from burying the book, but also keeps a single publisher from controlling it exclusively and charging high prices. And even during the first twenty-five years, if the copyright-owner has let a book go out of print or refused to allow the public performance of a play,

---

   [11] Southey v. Sherwood, 2 Mer. 435, 35 Eng. Rep. 1006 (1817).

   [14] Phillip v. Pennell, [1907] 2 Ch. 577; 1 Pennell, Life of James McNeill Whistler (1908) xxiv.

   [15] Bobbs-Merrill Co. v. Straus, 147 Fed. 15, 18 (C. C. A. 2d. 1906); Crowe v. Aiken, 2 Biss. 208, 212 (C. C. N. D. Ill. 1870). *But see* Lord Mansfield in Millar v. Taylor, 4 Burr. 2303, 2397, 98 Eng. Rep. 251, (1769); Eyre v. Higbee, 35 Barb. 502, 512 (N. Y. 1861) (letters of George Washington). . . .

   Ownership of the manuscript itself. A perpetual veto power is surely possessed by the surviving relative or the book-collector who owns the physical paper and ink, as distinct from the literary property in the author's expression. This veto is even more dangerous to the cause of literature, because ownership of the manuscript carries no right to publish. Baker v. Libbie, 210 Mass. 599, 97 N. E. 109 (1912), 60 U. of Pa. L. Rev. 662, 15 Law Notes 233. Hence this owner is under no pecuniary inducement to disclose his treasure to the world. Thus either the surviving family or the physical owner can block publication, even though the other desires it and the author's creation would enrich American culture.

   The British Act, § 11 (2), has a useful provision that the author's bequest of the

a compulsory license may be ordered on terms fixed by the Judicial Committee of the Privy Council.[16]

. . . (In) order to protect the public from the evil of garbled editions of the books of a dead author, a distinguished novelist and essayist desires to prolong copyright far beyond the English period of 50 years after death, and even make it perpetual. In *The House of Macmillan*, Charles Morgan writes:

> That the public interest is, in fact, served by throwing a great writer's work to the wolves and depriving his representatives of control of it is a delusion. . . . The only plausible argument for the present system rests upon the notion that, if an author's heirs are deprived of copyright, his books will be more easily and cheaply available to the public, and this notion is false. . . .
>
> . . . [B]y depriving an author's work of copyright within a few decades of his death . . . there is nothing to prevent its being garbled or bowdlerized, nothing to induce any publisher with a long view to nurse a work of art or scholarship during the periods when it is out of fashion, and, since reduction of the price of a book depends much more upon one publisher's assurance of a steady market than upon a sacrifice of the author's royalty, there is a tendency to raise prices against the public rather than to lower them. . . . Apart from any financial consideration, it is to the public advantage that works of literature should be protected from those whose habit is to mutilate or misapply them, and that the author's representative and one publisher should have power and interest to do so.[23]

Morgan's attitude is the opposite of Macaulay's. Macaulay wants a short copyright period because he is afraid that the owner after an author's death will be a dog in the manger. Morgan wants a long period because he is sure that the surviving owner will be a watch dog. I think that it is just a matter of chance what kind of a dog you get. If all publishers were as fond of "a steady, long-term and consistent enterprise" as the founders of the House of Macmillan, perhaps we could safely entrust to them the supervision of an author's works forever. Unfortunately, many publishers are disposed to sleep on their rights when the author is no longer able to write letters demanding a new edition. Thus Henry James is one of the greatest of American novelists and constantly the object of attention; and yet the owners of his remaining copyrights have shown little interest in making his books accessible to the public in cheap editions or indeed any editions at all. His publishers are probably too busy with authors of a later vintage. Who believes that a perpetual copyright would spur them into activity? The best prospect for popular reprints of Henry James lies in the fact that everything he wrote will soon be in the public domain.

Furthermore, much of what any dead author wrote loses interest with time, so that a considerable amount of selection becomes very desirable to the public. Yet the authorized publisher can stop a rival from issuing selections just as easily as he can suppress garbled editions. He is in no position to decide impartially

---

manuscript of an unpublished work presumptively passes the copyright with the manuscript.

[16] Copyright Act, 1911, 1 & 2 Geo. V, c. 46, §§ 3, 4. This device of compulsory licenses originated in the early seventies with Sir Thomas Henry Farrer, a distinguished civil servant. See Supplement I, 2 Dict. Nat. Biog. 201. Birrell, *op. cit. supra* note 3, at 207, calls it "This preposterous scheme . . . knocked on the head by Mr. Herbert Spencer. . . ." But it became law twelve years after Birrell wrote.

[23] Morgan, The House of Macmillan (1944) 174-177.

whether a proposed partial reprint of *his* author is mangling or wise weeding. Some Frenchman has suggested entrusting the supervision of new editions of the classics to a state official or an academy of scholars, but our country is not so well equipped as France with titular arbiters of literary taste.

Therefore, I conclude that the copyright period after an author's death should be roughly limited by the lives of his children, subject perhaps to compulsory licensing in order to prevent them from keeping his books off the market. The evil of garbled editions is not sufficiently serious to justify the imposition of a possible tax on readers for the benefit of his remote descendants and a monopolizing publisher. Simpler remedies for this evil are the production of adequate new editions by good publishers, and the alertness of book-reviewers and scholars, who ought to denounce vigorously any publisher of a mangled edition.

HOUSE REPORT: § 302

H.R. Rep. No. 94-1476, 94th Cong., 2d Sess. 133-36 (1976)

The debate over how long a copyright should last is as old as the oldest copyright statute and will doubtless continue as long as there is a copyright law. With certain exceptions, there appears to be strong support for the principle, as embodied in the bill, of a copyright term consisting of the life of the author and 50 years after his death. In particular, the authors and their representatives stressed that the adoption of a life-plus-50 term was by far their most important legislative goal in copyright law revision. The Register of Copyrights now regards a life-plus-50 term as the foundation of the entire bill.

Under the present law statutory copyright protection begins on the date of publication (or on the date of registration in unpublished form) and continues for 28 years from that date; it may be renewed for a second 28 years, making a total potential term of 56 years in all cases.[1] The principal elements of this system — a definite number of years, computed from either publication or registration, with a renewal feature — have been a part of the U.S. copyright law since the first statute in 1790. The arguments for changing this system to one based on the life of the author can be summarized as follows:

1. The present 56-year term is not long enough to insure an author and his dependents the fair economic benefits from his works. Life expectancy has increased substantially, and more and more authors are seeing their works fall into the public domain during their lifetimes, forcing later works to compete with their own early works in which copyright has expired.

2. The tremendous growth in communications media has substantially lengthened the commercial life of a great many works. A short term is particularly discriminatory against serious works of music, literature, and art, whose value may not be recognized until after many years.

3. Although limitations on the term of copyright are obviously necessary, too short a term harms the author without giving any substantial benefit to the public. The public frequently pays the same for works in the public domain as it does for copyrighted works, and the only result is a commercial windfall to

---

[1] Under Public Laws 87-668, 89-142, 90-141, 90-416, 91-147, 91-555, 92-170, 92-566, and 93-573, copyrights that were subsisting in their renewal term on September 19, 1962, and that were scheduled to expire before Dec. 31, 1976, have been extended to that later date, in anticipation that general revision legislation extending their terms still further will be enacted by then.

certain users at the author's expense. In some cases the lack of copyright protection actually restrains dissemination of the work, since publishers and other users cannot risk investing in the work unless assured of exclusive rights.

4. A system based on the life of the author would go a long way toward clearing up the confusion and uncertainty involved in the vague concept of "publication," and would provide a much simpler, clearer method for computing the term. The death of the author is a definite, determinable event, and it would be the only date that a potential user would have to worry about. All of a particular author's works, including successive revisions of them, would fall into the public domain at the same time, thus avoiding the present problems of determining a multitude of publication dates and of distinguishing "old" and "new" matter in later editions. The bill answers the problems of determining when relatively obscure authors died, by establishing a registry of death dates and a system of presumptions.

5. One of the worst features of the present copyright law is the provision for renewal of copyright. A substantial burden and expense, this unclear and highly technical requirement results in incalculable amounts of unproductive work. In a number of cases it is the cause of inadvertent and unjust loss of copyright. Under a life-plus-50 system the renewal device would be inappropriate and unnecessary.

6. Under the preemption provisions of section 301 and the single Federal system they would establish, authors will be giving up perpetual, unlimited exclusive common law rights in their unpublished works, including works that have been widely disseminated by means other than publication. A statutory term of life-plus-50 years is no more than a fair recompense for the loss of these perpetual rights.

7. A very large majority of the world's countries have adopted a copyright term of the life of the author and 50 years after the author's death. Since American authors are frequently protected longer in foreign countries than in the United States, the disparity in the duration of copyright has provoked considerable resentment and some proposals for retaliatory legislation. Copyrighted works move across national borders faster and more easily than virtually any other economic commodity, and with the techniques now in common use this movement has in many cases become instantaneous and effortless. The need to conform the duration of U.S. copyright to that prevalent throughout the rest of the world is increasingly pressing in order to provide certainty and simplicity in international business dealings. Even more important, a change in the basis of our copyright term would place the United States in the forefront of the international copyright community. Without this change, the possibility of future United States adherence to the Berne Copyright Union would evaporate, but with it would come a great and immediate improvement in our copyright relations. All of these benefits would accrue directly to American and foreign authors alike.

The need for a longer total term of copyright has been conclusively demonstrated. It is true that a major reason for the striking statistical increase in life expectancy since 1909 is the reduction in infant mortality, but this does not mean that the increase can be discounted. Although not nearly as great as the total increase in life expectancy, there has been a marked increase in longevity, and with medical discoveries and health programs for the elderly this trend shows every indication of continuing. If life expectancy in 1909, which was in the neighborhood of 56 years, offered a rough guide to the length of copyright protection, then life expectancy in the 1970's which is well over 70 years, should offer a similar guide; the Register's 1961 Report included statistics indicating that something between 70 and 76 years was then the average equivalent of life-plus-50 years. A copyright should extend beyond the author's lifetime, and judged by this standard the present term of 56 years is too short.

The arguments as to the benefits of uniformity with foreign laws, and the advantages of international comity that would result from adoption of a life-plus-50 term, are also highly significant. The system has worked well in other countries, and on the whole it would appear to make computation of terms considerably simpler and easier. The registry of death dates and the system of presumptions established in section 302 would solve most of the problems in determining when an individual author died.

No country in the world has provisions on the duration of copyright like ours. Virtually every other copyright law in the world bases the term of protection for works by natural persons on the life of the author, and a substantial majority of these accord protection for 50 years after the author's death. This term is required for adherence to the Berne Convention. It is worth noting that the 1965 revision of the copyright law of the Federal Republic of Germany adopted a term of life plus 70 years.

A point that has concerned some educational groups arose from the possibility that, since a large majority (now about 85 percent) of all copyrighted works are not renewed, a life-plus-50 year term would tie up a substantial body of material that is probably of no commercial interest but that would be more readily available for scholarly use if free of copyright restrictions. A statistical study of renewal registrations made by the Copyright Office in 1966 supports the generalization that most material which is considered to be of continuing or potential commercial value is renewed. Of the remainder, a certain proportion is of practically no value to anyone, but there are a large number of unrenewed works that have scholarly value to historians, archivists, and specialists in a variety of fields. This consideration lay behind the proposals for retaining the renewal device or for limiting the term for unpublished or unregistered works.

It is true that today's ephemera represent tomorrow's social history, and that works of scholarly value, which are now falling into the public domain after 29 [sic] years, would be protected much longer under the bill. Balanced against this are the burdens and expenses of renewals, the near impossibility of distinguishing between types of works in fixing a statutory term, and the extremely strong case in favor of a life-plus-50 system. Moreover, it is important to realize that the bill would not restrain scholars from using any work as source material or from making "fair use" of it; the restrictions would extend only to the unauthorized reproduction or distribution of copies of the work, its public performance, or some other use that would actually infringe the copyright owner's exclusive rights. The advantages of a basic term of copyright enduring for the life of the author and for 50 years after the author's death outweigh any possible disadvantages.

TRANSITIONAL AND SUPPLEMENTARY PROVISIONS

In addition to the substantive provisions of a new copyright law which Congress enacted on October 19, 1976, it also enacted a number of "transitional and supplementary provisions" to clarify when the various sections of the 1976 Act would become effective. For example, Transitional and Supplementary [T&S] § 102 provides: "This Act becomes effective on January 1, 1978, except as otherwise expressly provided by this Act . . . . The provisions of sections 118 [licenses in connection with noncommercial broadcasting], 304(b) [extension of subsisting copyrights in their renewal term], and chapter 8 of title 17 [the Copyright Royalty Tribunal] . . . take effect upon enactment of this Act."

T & S § 103 provides, in pertinent part: "This Act does not provide copyright protection for any work that goes into the public domain before January 1, 1978."

QUESTIONS

1. Is the sentence quoted from Transitional and Supplementary § 103 constitutionally required? Consider Priv. L. No. 92-60, 92d Cong., 1st Sess., 85 Stat. 857 (1971), which "granted" copyright to the trustees under the will of Mary Baker Eddy in the work "Science and Health with Key to Scriptures," in all editions "heretofore published, or hereafter published . . . for a term of seventy-five years from the effective date of this Act or from the date of first publication, *whichever is later.*" (Emphasis added.)

2. What impact does T & S § 103 have on the necessity of studying the 1909 Act?

§ 302. Duration of copyright: Works created on or after January 1, 1978

(a) IN GENERAL — Copyright in a work created on or after January 1, 1978, subsists from its creation and, except as provided by the following subsections, endures for a term consisting of the life of the author and fifty years after the author's death.

(b) JOINT WORKS — In the case of a joint work prepared by two or more authors who did not work for hire, the copyright endures for a term consisting of the life of the last surviving author and fifty years after such last surviving author's death.

(c) ANONYMOUS WORKS, PSEUDONYMOUS WORKS, AND WORKS MADE FOR HIRE — In the case of an anonymous work, a pseudonymous work, or a work made for hire, the copyright endures for a term of seventy-five years from the year of its first publication, or a term of one hundred years from the year of its creation, whichever expires first. If, before the end of such term, the identity of one or more of the authors of an anonymous or pseudonymous work is revealed in the records of a registration made for that work under subsection (a) or (d) of section 408, or in the records provided by this subsection, the copyright in the work endures for the term specified by subsection (a) or (b), based on the life of the author or authors whose identity has been revealed. Any person having an interest in the copyright in an anonymous or pseudonymous work may at any time record, in records to be maintained by the Copyright Office for that purpose, a statement identifying one or more authors of the work; the statement shall also identify the person filing it, the nature of that person's interest, the source of the information recorded, and the particular work affected, and shall comply in form and content with requirements that the Register of Copyrights shall prescribe by regulation.

(d) RECORDS RELATING TO DEATH OF AUTHORS — Any person having an interest in a copyright may at any time record in the Copyright Office a statement of the date of death of the author of the copyrighted work, or a statement that the author is still living on a particular date. The statement shall identify the person filing it, the nature of that person's interest, and the source of the information recorded, and shall comply in form and content with requirements that the

Register of Copyrights shall prescribe by regulation. The Register shall maintain current records of information relating to the death of authors of copyrighted works, based on such recorded statements and, to the extent the Register considers practicable, on data contained in any of the records of the Copyright Office or in other reference sources.

(e) PRESUMPTION AS TO AUTHOR'S DEATH — After a period of seventy-five years from the year of first publication of a work, or a period of one hundred years from the year of its creation, whichever expires first, any person who obtains from the Copyright Office a certified report that the records provided by subsection (d) disclose nothing to indicate that the author of the work is living, or died less than fifty years before, is entitled to the benefit of a presumption that the author has been dead for at least fifty years. Reliance in good faith upon this presumption shall be a complete defense to any action for infringement under this title.

HOUSE REPORT

H.R. Rep. No. 94-1476, 94th Cong., 2d Sess. 136-38 (1976)

Basic copyright term

Under subsection (a) of section 302, a work "created" on or after the effective date of the revised statute would be protected by statutory copyright "from its creation" and, with exceptions to be noted below, "endures for a term consisting of the life of the author and 50 years after the author's death."

Under this provision, as a general rule, the life-plus-50 term would apply equally to unpublished works, to works published during the author's lifetime, and to works published posthumously.

The definition of "created" in section 101, which will be discussed in more detail in connection with section 302 (c) below, makes clear that "creation" for this purpose means the first time the work is fixed in a copy or phonorecord; up to that point the work is not "created," and is subject to common law protection, even though it may exist in someone's mind and may have been communicated to others in unfixed form.

Joint works

Since by definition a "joint work" has two or more authors, a statute basing the term of copyright on the life of the author must provide a special method of computing the term of "joint works." Under the system in effect in many foreign countries, the term of copyright is measured from the death of the last survivor of a group of joint authors, no matter how many there are. The bill adopts this system as the simplest and fairest of the alternatives for dealing with the problem.

Anonymous works, pseudonymous works, and works made for hire

Computing the term from the author's death also requires special provisions to deal with cases where the authorship is not revealed or where the "author" is not an individual. Section 302(c) therefore provides a special term for anonymous works, pseudonymous works, and works made for hire: 75 years from publication or 100 years from creation, whichever is shorter. The definitions in section 101 make the status of anonymous and pseudonymous works depend on what is revealed on the copies or phonorecords of a work; a work is "anonymous" if "no natural person is identified as author," and is "pseudonymous" if "the author is identified under a fictitious name."

Section 302(c) provides that the 75- and 100-year terms for an anonymous or pseudonymous work can be converted to the ordinary life-plus-50 term if "the identity of one or more authors . . . is revealed" in special records maintained for this purpose in the Copyright Office. The term in such cases would be "based on the life of the author or authors whose identity has been revealed." Instead of forcing a user to search through countless Copyright Office records to determine if an author's identity has been revealed, the bill sets up a special registry for the purpose, with requirements concerning the filing of identifying statements that parallel those of the following subsection (d) with respect to statements of the date of an author's death.

The alternative terms established in section 302(c) — 75 years from publication or 100 years from creation, whichever expires first — are necessary to set a time limit on protection of unpublished material. For example, copyright in a work created in 1978 and published in 1988 would expire in 2063 (75 years from publication). A question arises as to when the copyright should expire if the work is never published. Both the Constitution and the underlying purposes of the bill require the establishment of an alternative term for unpublished works and the only practicable basis for this alternative is "creation." Under the bill a work created in 1980 but not published until after 2005 (or never published) would fall into the public domain in 2080 (100 years after creation).

The definition in section 101 provides that "creation" takes place when a work "is fixed in a copy or phonorecord for the first time." Although the concept of "creation" is inherently lacking in precision, its adoption in the bill would, for example, enable a scholar to use an unpublished manuscript written anonymously, pseudonymously, or for hire, if he determines on the basis of internal or external evidence that the manuscript is at least 100 years old. In the case of works written over a period of time or in successive revised versions, the definition provides that the portion of the work "that has been fixed at any particular time constitutes the work as of that time," and that, "where the work has been prepared in different versions, each version constitutes a separate work." Thus, a scholar or other user, in attempting to determine whether a particular work is in the public domain, needs to look no further than the particular version he wishes to use.

Although "publication" would no longer play the central role assigned to it under the present law, the concept would still have substantial significance under provisions throughout the bill, including those on Federal preemption and duration. Under the definition in section 101, a work is "published" if one or more copies or phonorecords embodying it are distributed to the public — that is, generally to persons under no explicit or implicit restrictions with respect to disclosure of its contents — without regard to the manner in which the copies or phonorecords changed hands. The definition clears up the question of whether the sale of phonorecords constitutes publication, and it also makes plain that any form of dissemination in which a material object does not change hands — performances or displays on television, for example — is not a publication no matter how many people are exposed to the work. On the other hand, the definition also makes clear that, when copies or phonorecords are offered to a group of wholesalers, broadcasters, motion picture theaters, etc., publication takes place if the purpose is "further distribution, public performance, or public display."

Although the periods of 75 or 100 years for anonymous and pseudonymous works and works made for hire seem to be longer than the equivalent term provided by foreign laws and the Berne Conventions, this difference is more apparent than real. In general, the terms in these special cases approximate, on the average, the term of the life of the author plus 50 years established for other works. The 100-year maximum term for unpublished works, although much more limited than the perpetual term now available under common law in the United States and under statute in some foreign countries, is sufficient to guard against unjustified invasions of privacy and to fulfill our obligations under the Universal Copyright Convention.

Records and presumption as to author's death

Subsections (d) and (e) of section 302 together furnish an answer to the practical problems of how to discover the death dates of obscure or unknown authors. Subsection (d) provides a procedure for recording statements that an author died, or that he was still living, on a particular date, and also requires the Register of Copyrights to maintain obituary records on a current basis. Under subsection (e) anyone who, after a specified period, obtains certification from the Copyright Office that its records show nothing to indicate that the author is living or died less than 50 years before, is entitled to rely upon a presumption that the author has been dead for more than 50 years. The period specified in subsection (e) — 75 years from publication or 100 years from creation — is purposely uniform with the special term provided in subsection (c).

QUESTIONS

1. Would it be feasible to have different periods of copyright protection for different classes of works (e.g., artistic designs of useful articles, news photographs, compilations of public domain data)? A number of foreign nations so provide. Why has Congress chosen not to do so?

2. What are the benefits and detriments of having the copyrights in all of an author's works terminate at the same time? What are the reasons for having the copyright of some works measured by the author's life and the copyright of other works measured from the creation or publication of those works?

3. Will the "limited times" feature of the law of copyright be substantially frustrated by collaborations between an author and much younger joint authors?

4. Under the 1909 Copyright Act, as originally enacted, copyright could never subsist for more than fifty-six years from the date of publication of a work. What public interest is served by extending copyright in anonymous works or in works made for hire to seventy-five years from the date of publication?

§ 303. Duration of copyright: Works created but not published or copyrighted before January 1, 1978

Copyright in a work created before January 1, 1978, but not theretofore in the public domain or copyrighted, subsists from January 1, 1978, and endures for the term provided by section 302. In no case, however, shall the term of copyright in such a work expire before December 31, 2002; and, if the work is published on or before December 31, 2002, the term of copyright shall not expire before December 31, 2027.

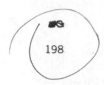

HOUSE REPORT

H.R. Rep. No. 94-1476, 94th Cong., 2d Sess. 138-39 (1976)

Theoretically, at least, the legal impact of section 303 would be far reaching. Under it, every "original work of authorship" fixed in tangible form that is in existence would be given statutory copyright protection as long as the work is not in the public domain in this country. The vast majority of these works consist of private material that no one is interested in protecting or infringing, but section 303 would still have practical effects for a prodigious body of material already in existence.

Looked at another way, however, section 303 would have a genuinely restrictive effect. Its basic purpose is to substitute statutory for common law copyright for everything now protected at common law, and to substitute reasonable time limits for the perpetual protection now available. In general, the substituted time limits are those applicable to works created after the effective date of the law; for example, an unpublished work written in 1945 whose author dies in 1980 would be protected under the statute from the effective date through 2030 (50 years after the author's death).

A special problem under this provision is what to do with works whose ordinary statutory terms will have expired or will be nearing expiration on the effective date. The committee believes that a provision taking away subsisting common law rights and substituting statutory rights for a reasonable period is fully in harmony with the constitutional requirements of due process, but it is necessary to fix a "reasonable period" for this purpose. Section 303 provides that under no circumstances would copyright protection expire before December 31, 2002, and also attempts to encourage publication by providing 25 years more protection (through 2027) if the work were published before the end of 2002.

§ 304. Duration of copyright: Subsisting copyrights

1st term 2.

(a) COPYRIGHTS IN THEIR FIRST TERM ON JANUARY 1, 1978. — Any copyright, the first term of which is subsisting on January 1, 1978, shall endure for twenty-eight years from the date it was originally secured: *Provided,* That in the case of any posthumous work or of any periodical, cyclopedic, or other composite work upon which the copyright was originally secured by the proprietor thereof, or of any work copyrighted by a corporate body (otherwise than as assignee or licensee of the individual author) or by an employer for whom such work is made for hire, the proprietor of such copyright shall be entitled to a renewal and extension of the copyright in such work for the further term of forty-seven years when application for such renewal and extension shall have been made to the Copyright Office and duly registered therein within one year prior to the expiration of the original term of copyright: *And provided further,* That in the case of any other copyrighted work, including a contribution by an individual author to a periodical or to a cyclopedic or other composite work, the author of such work, if still living, or the widow, widower, or children of the author, if the author be not living, or if such author, widow, widower, or children be not living, then the author's executors, or in the absence of a will, his or her next of kin shall be entitled to a renewal and extension of the copyright in such work for a further term of forty-seven years when application for such renewal and extension shall have been made to the Copyright Office and duly registered therein within one year prior to the expiration of the original term of copyright: *And provided further,* That in default of the registration of such application for renewal and extension, the copyright in any work shall terminate at the expiration of twenty-eight years from the date copyright was originally secured.

(b) COPYRIGHTS IN THEIR RENEWAL TERM OR REGISTERED FOR RENEWAL BEFORE JANUARY 1, 1978. — The duration of any copyright, the renewal term of which is subsisting at any time between December 31, 1976, and December 31, 1977, inclusive, or for which renewal registration is made between December 31, 1976, and December 31, 1977, inclusive, is extended to endure for a term of seventy-five years from the date copyright was originally secured.

HOUSE REPORT

H.R. Rep. No. 94-1476, 94th Cong., 2d Sess. 139-40 (1976)

The arguments in favor of lengthening the duration of copyright apply to subsisting as well as future copyrights. The bill's basic approach is to increase the present 56-year term to 75 years in the case of copyrights subsisting in both their first and their renewal terms.

Copyrights in their first term

Subsection (a) of section 304 reenacts and preserves the renewal provision, now in section 24 of the statute, for all of the works presently in their first 28-year term. A great many of the present expectancies in these cases are the subject of existing contracts, and it would be unfair and immensely confusing to cut off or alter these interests. Renewal registration will be required during the 28th year of the copyright but the length of the renewal term will be increased from 28 to 47 years.

Although the bill preserves the language of the present renewal provision without any change in substance, the Committee intends that the reference to a "posthumous work" in this section has the meaning given to it in *Bartok v. Boosey & Hawkes, Inc.*, 523 F.2d 941 (2d Cir. 1975) — one as to which no copyright assignment or other contract for exploitation of the work has occurred during an author's lifetime, rather than one which is simply first published after the author's death.

Copyrights in their renewal term

Renewed copyrights that are subsisting in their second term at any time during the period between December 31, 1976, and December 31, 1977, inclusive, would be extended under section 304(b) to run for a total of 75 years. This provision would add another 19 years to the duration of any renewed copyright whose second term started during the 28 years immediately preceding the effective date of the act (January 1, 1978). In addition, it would extend by varying lesser amounts the duration of renewal copyrights already extended under Public Laws 87-668, 89-142, 90-416, 91-147, 91-555, 92-170, 92-566, and 93-573, all of which would otherwise expire on December 31, 1976. The subsection would also extend the duration of renewal copyrights whose second 28-year term is scheduled to expire during 1977. In none of these cases, however, would the total terms of copyright for the work be longer than 75 years.

§ 305. Duration of copyright: Terminal date

All terms of copyright provided by sections 302 through 304 run to the end of the calendar year in which they would otherwise expire.

HOUSE REPORT

H.R. Rep. No. 94-1476, 94th Cong., 2d Sess. 142-43 (1976)

Under section 305, which has its counterpart in the laws of most foreign countries, the term of copyright protection for a work extends through December 31 of the year in which the term would otherwise have expired. This will make the duration of copyright much easier to compute, since it will be enough to determine the year, rather than the exact date, of the event from which the term is based.

Section 305 applies only to "terms of copyright provided by sections 302 through 304," which are the sections dealing with duration of copyright. It therefore has no effect on the other time periods specified in the bill; and, since they do not involve "terms of copyright," the periods provided in section 304(c) with respect to termination of grants are not affected by section 305.

The terminal date section would change the duration of subsisting copyrights under section 304 by extending the total terms of protection under subsections (a) and (b) to the end of the 75th year from the date copyright was secured. A copyright subsisting in its first term on the effective date of the act would run through December 31 of the 28th year and would then expire unless renewed. Since all copyright terms under the bill expire on December 31, and since section 304 (a) requires that renewal be made "within one year prior to the expiration of the original term of copyright," the period for renewal registration in all cases will run from December 31 through December 31.

QUESTIONS

1. Do you agree with the House Committee that "the arguments in favor of lengthening the term of copyright apply to subsisting as well as future copyrights"?

2. What obstacles were there to Congress simply declaring that *all* works — whether or not already covered by a subsisting copyright — should be protected by federal copyright until fifty years after the death of the author?

3. Assuming that works were first published and copyrighted in the following years, when did or will copyright terminate? 1900, 1910, 1977, 1978. What further facts, if any, would you have to know to answer this question? (Assume that the 1900 work is covered by the 1909 Act.)

4. Suppose a work was first published on September 1, 1960. Would a renewal application filed on September 2, 1987 be timely? How about one filed on September 2, 1988?

B. RENEWAL

RINGER, RENEWAL OF COPYRIGHT, in STUDIES ON COPYRIGHT (Fisher mem. ed. 1960) (Study No. 31)

... In structure, § 24 [of the 1909 Act] falls into four parts:

1) The main body of the section provides that copyright shall endure for 28 years "from the date of first publication."

2) The first proviso provides that, in the following cases, the copyright proprietor is entitled to a second term of 28 years if renewal registration is made within the 28th year of the first term:

a) "Any posthumous work"

b) "Any periodical, cyclopedic, or other composite work upon which the copyright was originally secured by the proprietor thereof"

c) "Any work copyrighted by a corporate body (otherwise than as assignee or licensee of the individual author)"

d) "Any work copyrighted . . . by an employer for whom such work is made for hire."

3) The second proviso provides that, in all other cases, the following are entitled to the renewal: "the author . . . if still living, or the widow, widower, or children of the author, if the author be not living, or if such author, widow, widower, or children be not living, then the author's executors, or in the absence of a will, his next of kin. . . ."

4) The last proviso provides that, unless renewal registration has been made, copyright terminates at the end of the first 28-year term.

The Nature and Theoretical Basis of Renewal Copyright

The renewal copyright established in the Act of 1831 and elaborated in the Act of 1909 is a unique form of property whose nature and theoretical basis are still unclear. The courts and the commentators have repeatedly characterized a renewal as a "new estate" or a "new grant" rather than a mere continuation or extension. Renewals are said to be separate from and independent of the original copyright, to be "free and clear of any rights, interests, or licenses attached to the copyright for the initial term," and to have "absolutely all of the attributes of a new work copyrighted at the time the renewal is effected." The right of renewal is considered a personal right given directly to certain named beneficiaries; it "does not follow the author's estate but . . . is derived directly from the statute."

These generalizations, though mostly true, have suffered from too much uncritical repetition. To get at what renewals really are, one must look closely at what Congress wanted to do, what it said in the statute, and what the courts have said the statute means.

The legislative history shows that, in retaining the reversionary aspect of renewals, Congress was trying to accomplish two things:

1) If the author were still living, Congress wanted to give him an opportunity to benefit from the success of his work and to renegotiate disadvantageous bargains. It has often been said that the renewal provision was based on "the familiar imprudence of authors in commercial matters." While superficially logical, there is nothing in the legislative history to support this supposition. There is more evidence of a Congressional recognition that author-publisher contracts must frequently be made at a time when the value of the work is unknown or conjectural and the author (regardless of his business ability) is necessarily in a poor bargaining position.[128]

2) If the author were dead, Congress wanted to insure that his "dependent relatives"[129] would receive the benefits of the renewal, regardless of any agreements the author had entered into.

To attain these results Congress had to depart from ordinary concepts of property in two important respects:

---

[128] See H.R. Rep. No. 2222, 60th Cong., 2d Sess. 15 (1909); Comment, 33 N.Y.U.L. Rev. 1027, 1029 n.20 (1958); 6 U. Det. L.J. 79, 83-84 (1943). . . .

[129] S. Rep. No. 6187, 59th Cong., 2d Sess. 8 (Pt. I, 1907).

1) *Reversion.* The statute had to break the continuity of title at the end of the first term and provide for a reversion of ownership to the author, if living.

2) *Statutory designation of beneficiaries.* To make sure that the renewal benefits went to "those naturally dependent upon the deceased author's bounty," something more than a reversion to the author's "executors, administrators, or heirs" had to be provided. If the renewal reverted to the author's estate, it was entirely possible that legatees and creditors might gain the benefits at the expense of the author's family and dependents. Apparently in a deliberate effort to avoid this result, Congress set up a schedule of successive classes of persons who were entitled to take the renewal as "a new personal grant of a right."

These features made renewals so unusual that, immediately after the 1909 Act came into effect, there was uncertainty whether this could really be what Congress intended. Within a few years, however, it had been firmly established that a proprietor or assignee, as such, had no right in a renewal copyright, that the right was a personal one, and that a renewal is not "really and truly an extension to the author, his assigns, executors, and administrators, but a new grant to the author or others enumerated."

Acceptance of these basic principles still left open some important questions:

1) *Is a future copyright assignable?* Assuming that assignment of the first term does not carry with it the renewal copyright, can the author or any other statutory beneficiary make a valid separate assignment of his potential renewal copyright before he has secured it? This turned out to be a very close question, which the Supreme Court finally settled in favor of alienability.[135]

2) *Whom does the executor represent?* The executor is different from the author's widow, children, and next of kin, since he obviously cannot take the renewal for his own personal benefit. Does he take it as representative of (1) the author, (2) the corpus of the author's estate, or (3) the legatees? The cases have now established that the executor represents neither the author[136] nor the author's estate,[137] but that he takes the renewal as personal representative or trustee of the author's legatees; since the renewal does not become part of the author's estate, an assignment by the author of his renewal rights would be invalidated at the author's death, and the executor would take the renewal for the benefit of the author's legatees rather than his assignees. The decisions, culminating in a recent 5-4 holding by the Supreme Court, thus indicate a most unusual role for the executor.

3) *Does a proprietor take a "new estate"?* With respect to the five types of works that a proprietor can renew in his own right — works made for hire, composite works, etc. — does the proprietor take a "new estate" free and clear of any pre-existing contractual obligations, including his own? Or is a renewal simply a continuation or extension of term in these cases? This basic question has never been litigated, and seems to have been overlooked by the commentators. . . .

---

[135] Fred Fisher Music Co. v. M. Witmark & Sons, 318 U.S. 643 (1943).

[136] Fox Film Corp. v. Knowles, 261 U.S. 326 (1923).

[137] Miller Music Corp. v. Charles N. Daniels, Inc., 158 F. Supp. 188 (1957), *aff'd mem.,* 265 F.2d 925 (1959), *aff'd,* 362 U.S. 373, 125 U.S.P.Q. 147 (1960).

Rights of Statutory Renewal Beneficiaries

It is now well-established that, even though the author can assign away his own renewal expectancy, he cannot cut off, defeat, or diminish the independent statutory renewal rights of his widow and children or next of kin. And, as we have seen, the Supreme Court has now settled that executors take the renewal for the direct benefit of the author's legatees, without regard to any assignment of renewal rights the author may have made before he died. At one time there was some feeling that, if the author parted absolutely with all of his rights in a work, both he and his family would be estopped from claiming rights under the renewal term, but this theory is now completely discredited. It is clear that the rights of the author's assignees are dependent on his survival and fail if he dies before the renewal year.

At the same time it is settled that the widow, children, and next of kin can also assign their own rights in the renewal expectancy, no matter how contingent or fragmentary. They can join the author in his assignment or execute an independent transfer, although in either case a separate consideration for each assignor would probably be needed for validity.

Rights of Assignees and Licensees Under a Binding Transfer

The renewal assignee stands in the shoes of his assignor, and takes the renewal only if the assignor is the beneficiary entitled under the statute....

QUESTIONS

1. Author writes a novel in 1975, and in 1976 he assigns "all of my copyright interest" to Publisher for $10,000. Publisher prints and distributes the book and secures copyright in its own name, in 1976. In the year 2004, both Author and Publisher apply for renewal of the copyright. Whose claim should prevail?

2. Assume instead that Author had in 1976 conveyed "both the initial and renewal terms of copyright" to Publisher, which published and copyrighted the work that year. If Author is alive throughout the year 2004, who is entitled to the enjoyment of the renewal term (upon timely application)? If Author dies before the year 2004, leaving a widow and child, who is entitled to the enjoyment of the renewal term? See _De Sylva v. Ballentine,_ 351 U.S. 570 (1956).

3. If, after 1978, an author (who has retained copyright throughout the initial term) dies before the twenty-eighth year of the initial term, leaving a widow and three children who survive into the twenty-eighth year, who owns the renewal term and in what shares? Does the widow lose her share in the renewal term if, before the final year of the initial term, she remarries? (Consult the definition of "widow" in § 101, and consider whether it would apply to cases in which the author's death preceded the effective date of the Act.)

4. Is it sound policy to empower an author, after he has during the initial term assigned inter vivos and for value his interest in the renewal term, to override that grant (in the event there is no widow or child surviving him) by making a gift of the renewal term in his will? See _Miller Music Corp. v. Charles N. Daniels, Inc.,_ 362 U.S. 373 (1960).

5. If an assignee of the renewal term wishes to assure that its rights will not be cut off by the author's death before the twenty-eighth year of the initial term, can it effectively do this by taking assignments of the renewal term not only from the author but also from the author's wife and children?

6. By virtue of the renewal format under the 1909 Act, a great many copyrights terminated a mere twenty-eight years after publication. Indeed, it was probably a contemplated benefit in the public interest thus to shorten the copyright term. Has Congress, then, provided adequate justification for extending copyright protection for almost all works created after January 1, 1978 to the life of the author plus fifty years?

VENUS MUSIC CORP. v. MILLS MUSIC, INC.

261 F.2d 577 (2d Cir. 1958)

I.R. KAUFMAN, DISTRICT JUDGE. This action concerns the ownership of the renewal right in the copyright on a popular song entitled "Mary Lou." Both plaintiff and defendant claim renewal rights through Abe Lyman, one of three co-authors. Defendant's claim arises under an unrecorded assignment from Lyman in 1936, plaintiff's under a 1942 assignment, duly recorded. After a trial without a jury the court below entered judgment for defendant, finding that the 1936 assignment to defendant included Lyman's renewal right and that plaintiff may not claim priority under the recording statute. Plaintiff appeals from this judgment.

"Mary Lou" was composed in 1926 by Abe Lyman, George Waggner and J. Russel Robinson and assigned by them to Henry Watterson, Inc. which thereafter registered it for copyright on April 17, 1926.

In 1931 Watterson assigned its rights, including the renewal rights, to defendant, and this assignment was duly recorded. However, there is no contention that Lyman conveyed his renewal right to Watterson in 1926, nor that Watterson was able to convey it to defendant in 1931. Thus the renewal right was still owned by Lyman when, in 1936, he executed an unrecorded bill of sale conveying all of his right, title and interest in "Mary Lou" to defendant, its executors, administrators and assigns "forever" in exchange for $200 consideration. In 1947 Lyman and his wife executed an instrument, recorded in the copyright office, conveying to defendant their rights to the renewal copyrights on "Mary Lou" and five other songs. Defendant paid $500 advance royalties on this agreement.

In the meantime, Lyman had executed in 1942 an assignment to plaintiff's predecessor in interest, Fred Fisher Music Co., Inc., conveying his right to the renewal copyright to "Mary Lou" and other songs, in return for One Dollar consideration and a promise to pay royalties. Plaintiff claims that Lyman confirmed this assignment to Fisher by an instrument executed on July 9, 1953. However, Lyman later wrote Fisher denying any knowledge of this 1953 assignment.

Relying on this court's decisions in *Rossiter v. Vogel,* 2 Cir., 1943, 134 F.2d 908, and *Edward B. Marks Music Corp. v. Charles K. Harris Music Publishing Co.,* 2 Cir., 1958, 255 F.2d 518, certiorari denied 1958, 79 S.Ct. 51, plaintiff argues that we must find "as a matter of law" that Lyman's 1936 assignment to the defendant did not include the renewal right. We do not believe that *Rossiter* and *Marks* compel such a holding. Both cases make it clear that general words of assignment can include renewal rights if the parties had so intended. Whether the evidence discloses such an intent is to be determined by the trier of the facts. *Rossiter* was an appeal from an order granting plaintiff's motion for summary judgment. Plaintiff there relied on two assignments, one in 1910 employing general words of assignment, the other in 1926 specifically including renewal rights. In reversing the lower court's ruling, this court held that the evidence and circumstances did not support a finding that the 1910 agreement was intended to transfer renewal rights,[1] and that, at the very least, an issue of fact was presented. In *Marks* this court sustained the district court's determination that intent to convey renewal rights had not been proven. In neither case did this court hold that a trial court may not infer from the surrounding circumstances an intention to convey renewal rights by general words of assignment.

Further, in both *Rossiter* and *Marks* the assignor still held his original copyright as well as his renewal right at the time of making the conveyance in question. In the instant case, Lyman had conveyed away his copyright to Watterson in 1926, and defendant owned the copyright at the time of the 1936 assignment. It is clear, therefore, that the 1936 assignment could not possibly have been intended to convey the original copyright which had already been assigned. Under these circumstances, we cannot say that the trial court's finding that the renewal right was what was being bargained for and assigned in 1936 is "clearly erroneous." While the fact that defendant discontinued royalty payments to Lyman between 1936 and 1947 may constitute some evidence to rebut this finding, we do not believe that it is controlling here.[2]

[The court held for the defendant on the basis of the recording provisions of the 1909 Act; see p. 249 *infra*.]

QUESTIONS

1. Given the strong policy of author protection which underlay the renewal format, should not assignments of the renewal term be ineffective unless knowing, clear and explicit?

2. Is the promise to pay royalties sufficiently "valuable" to avoid an author's argument that a grant of renewal rights — an expectancy or future interest — based on such consideration is unconscionable? Consider in connection with the provisions for recordation of assignments (pp. 248-49 *infra*) whether such promise would constitute "value" to allow plaintiff to prevail as a *bona fide* purchaser.

EPOCH PRODUCING CORP. v. KILLIAM SHOWS, INC.

522 F.2d 737 (2d Cir. 1975)

MANSFIELD, CIRCUIT JUDGE:

The central issue presented by this appeal is the validity of a renewal copyright in D. W. Griffith's famous film classic The Birth of a Nation ("The Birth"), which was a pioneer in the field of full-length feature motion pictures. The renewal was issued in 1942 by the Copyright Office to Epoch Producing Corporation ("Epoch"). . . .

---

[1] "A complete transfer was obviously not intended here, for then there would have been no occasion for the supplemental agreement of 1926." 134 F.2d at page 911.

[2] Nor does Lyman's 1947 assignment to defendant necessarily prove that Lyman believed that he had not conveyed his renewal rights to defendant before that date. Mrs. Lyman, who joined in that conveyance, still had her survivor's interest (17 U.S.C.A. § 24) in the renewal rights. It is fair to infer that the 1947 assignment was intended to confirm Lyman's previous assignment and to convey Mrs. Lyman's previously unconveyed interest.

. . . Killiam answered, contending that under the law governing copyright renewal, 17 U.S.C. § 24, Epoch had no legal right to the renewal and that the motion picture passed into the public domain at the expiration of the original 28-year copyright term for lack of a valid renewal application.

A jury trial resulted in special verdicts upholding the validity of the renewal. . . . We hold that since the evidence introduced at trial permitted but one reasonable conclusion, namely, that Epoch had failed to sustain its burden of establishing the validity of its renewal copyright, it was error not to have directed a verdict in favor of Killiam on Epoch's claim.

On June 22, 1942, Epoch applied to the Copyright Office for a renewal copyright in The Birth, describing itself as both the "author," original claimant, and "the proprietor of copyright in a work made for hire." The term "author" is defined in the Copyright Act to include, "an employer in the case of works made for hire," 17 U.S.C. § 26. D. W. Griffith was listed as the director of the film and, along with Frank E. Woods, as author of the scenario. Thus Griffith was represented to be the employee who made the work for hire and Epoch as the "author," or his employer. A renewal certificate was issued by the Copyright Office in the name of Epoch as "the proprietor in a work made for hire." No other person or entity has ever applied for or received a renewal copyright in the film.[3]

In support of its characterization of the film as a "work made for hire," Epoch introduced into evidence at trial several agreements involving the proposed production of a film based on Thomas Dixon's novel. The earliest of these agreements, dated December 20, 1913, which was before The Birth was made or first publicly exhibited, was between Dixon and Majestic Motion Picture Company. It granted to Majestic the "sole and exclusive right" to produce, license and exhibit a motion picture based upon Dixon's novel "The Clansman" and upon a dramatic version of the novel written by Dixon. The film was to be completed by July 1, 1914. Majestic was apparently unable to meet its obligations under this contract as a later agreement was entered into by Majestic and Dixon, dated June 9, 1914, extending the date for completion of the film to October 1, 1914, and changing the financial arrangements between the parties. There is no evidence, however, that Majestic participated in the making of The Birth or that it hired Griffith or anyone else to do so.

Epoch was not formed until February 6, 1915, which was after The Birth had been made. Its Certificate of Incorporation was filed in New York State on February 8, 1915, the date of the first public exhibition of The Birth in Los Angeles. Majestic had until this time apparently been unable to fulfill its obligations to Dixon. Epoch assumed those obligations in an agreement dated June 14, 1915. Dixon released Majestic from its obligations, which were increased from $75,000 to $110,000, and accepted Epoch in its place. The two corporations, Majestic and Epoch, appear to have been closely related, since Harry E. Aitken was president of both. Their familiarity to D. W. Griffith is confirmed by Albert H. T. Banzhaf's status as treasurer of both Epoch and [David W. Griffith Corporation ("DWG Corp."), a company controlled by Griffith]. However, there is no evidence of any employer-employee relationship between Majestic or Epoch, on the one hand, and D. W. Griffith, on the other. There is no contract

---

[3] Although the 28-year renewal period was to expire in 1971, Congress has enacted special legislation periodically for the past 13 years which has had the effect of extending renewal copyrights, under the most recent enactment, through December 31, 1976. See, e. g., Pub. L. 93-573, Title I, § 104, 88 Stat. 1873 (1974).

of employment, record of salary payments, or proof that Majestic or Epoch supervised or controlled Griffith in the making of the picture.

The acquisition of initial statutory term and renewal copyrights in the United States is governed exclusively by the Copyright Act of 1909, 35 Stat. 1075 (1909), amended and enacted into law as Title 17, United States Code. Under that statute the term of protection provided for a copyrightable work is divided into two separate time periods, each 28 years in length. The right to obtain the initial 28-year term is vested in "[t]he author or proprietor of any work made the subject of copyright by [Title 17]." 17 U.S.C. § 9. As one would expect, the person claiming this initial term must either himself be the author of the copyrightable work (i. e., either the individual creator or the employer in the case of works made for hire, 17 U.S.C. § 26) or he must have succeeded to the rights of the author through an assignment or other device. 1 M. Nimmer, Copyright § 60, at 233 (1974).

The right to the renewal term copyright is not so simply defined. The renewal term is not merely an extension of the initial-term copyright vesting in the current owner of the original term. Rather, it has been described as a "new grant," e. g., G. Ricordi & Co. v. Paramount Pictures, Inc., 189 F.2d 469, 471 (2d Cir.), cert. denied, 342 U.S. 849 (1951); see Fred Fisher Music Co. v. M. Witmark & Sons, 318 U.S. 643 (1942), which is "a separate interest distinct from the original copyright," Edward B. Marks Music Corp. v. Charles K. Harris Music Pub. Co., Inc., 255 F.2d 513, 521 (2d Cir.), cert. denied, 358 U.S. 831 (1958).

. . . Bearing in mind these basic principles and that the burden was on Epoch to make a prima facie showing of validity of its renewal copyright, see Houghton Mifflin Co. v. Stackpole Sons, Inc., 113 F.2d 627 (2d Cir. 1940); 2 M. Nimmer, Copyright § 141.1 (1974), we turn to an evaluation of the proof and theories put forth by Epoch.

Grounds Asserted by Epoch or by Amici Curiae for Upholding Validity of Renewal Copyright in "The Birth of a Nation"

1. The Theory that Epoch and/or Majestic Was an Employer of Griffith for Hire

Epoch advances several theories upon which it argues that the jury could have upheld the validity of its renewal copyright. The first of these is the ground upon which it sought and obtained the Certificate of Renewal from the Copyright Office in 1942, i. e., that the work had originally been copyrighted by it in 1915 as "an employer for whom such work [was] made for hire," thus making it the "author" within the Copyright Act's definition, 17 U.S.C. § 26. In support of this theory it points (a) to the three agreements between Dixon, Majestic and Epoch, entered into on December 20, 1913, June 9, 1914, and June 14, 1915, respectively, (b) to the two copyright assignments from DWG Corp. to Epoch, dated April 17, 1915, and (c) to the Certificate of Renewal issued in 1942 by the Copyright Office to Epoch as "the proprietor of copyright in a work made for hire," which was uncontested by Griffith during his lifetime or by his next of kin since his death.

On the basis of these documents it contends that an inference may be drawn that Majestic and/or Epoch hired D. W. Griffith to produce The Birth and that Griffith recognized Epoch's primary right to the copyright in the film. We disagree.

In our view this evidence is clearly insufficient to permit any jury reasonably to draw the inference urged by Epoch. An inference will be upheld only if application of common experience and logic to the underlying evidence will support it. See, *e. g., Bruce Lincoln-Mercury, Inc. v. Universal C. I. T. Credit Corp.,* 325 F.2d 2, 22 (3d Cir. 1963); *United States v. Patterson,* 219 F.2d 659, 661-62 (2d Cir. 1955). Here, even giving Epoch the benefit of every doubt, no such process is possible. To permit a finding that Griffith was employed for hire by Majestic or Epoch on the basis of the evidence relied upon by Epoch would be to substitute mere speculation for reason and experience. At most the evidence shows that Dixon assigned to Majestic the right to produce a motion picture based on his novel, that Majestic was to finance the production, and that Majestic may have financed Griffith's production of the film. Even this last step toward the inference sought by Epoch stretches the reasoning process to the breaking point, since there is no showing that Majestic and/or Epoch actually supervised or paid any money for the making of the motion picture. Of importance to us, however, is the fact that the evidence sheds absolutely no light on the critical issue, which is what relationship, if any, existed between Griffith, on the one hand, and Majestic or Epoch, on the other. The evidence relied upon by Epoch does not, for instance, indicate whether Majestic and/or Epoch simply supplied capital for the production of the picture, whether they commissioned Griffith independently to produce the film, whether they "hired" Griffith as employee to do the work and, most important, whether they could have exercised the requisite power to control or supervise Griffith's work, which is the hallmark of "an employment for hire" relationship. . . .

The contention that Griffith may have been an employee for hire of Epoch is further belied by the fact that Epoch did not come into existence until February 8, 1915, which was after The Birth had been produced by Griffith. Indeed, February 8, 1915, was the very day on which the film was first publicly exhibited at Clune's Auditorium. These undisputed facts directly contradict Epoch's representations in its application for renewal copyright in 1942 that it was the "author" (i. e., employer for whom the work was made for hire) of the film.

Any contention that DWG Corp., the only other possibility, was the employer of Griffith must be discarded for similar reasons. Evidence produced at trial by defendant Killiam, and uncontradicted by plaintiff, conclusively proved that DWG Corp. was essentially an inactive shell corporation in 1914 and 1915, the years during which the film was created. Its financial records for those years, including its federal income tax returns, show no expenditures for the production of any motion pictures. It engaged in no business at all in 1914 and obtained some slight income in 1915, mostly from motion picture rentals. Under these circumstances it could not have been an employer for whom the film was made for hire.

2. The Theory that Epoch's Certificate of Copyright Renewal Registration Creates a Presumption of Validity

Having failed to point to evidence on the record from which a jury could reasonably conclude that The Birth was made by D. W. Griffith in the employment of another party, Epoch argues, pursuant to 17 U.S.C. § 209, that the Certificate of Copyright Renewal that it obtained in 1942 was prima facie proof of the facts stated therein and of the validity of the renewal copyright. Further, it contends that the passage of time without challenge to the renewal adds significant support to its validity. Both of these contentions must be rejected.

Title 17 U.S.C. § 209 does create a presumption of validity with respect to a certificate of initial copyright registration, stating that it "shall be admitted in any court as prima facie evidence of the facts stated therein." It is clear from the construction of § 209, however, that the presumption was meant to attach only to *original* certificates. All of § 209 is concerned with the contents of the original certificate of registration, the information that must be supplied by the original claimant and various other mechanics of the original registration procedure. No reference at all is made to the requirements of renewal applications and certificates. In this context the reference to "[s]aid certificate" in regard to the presumption can only refer to the *original* registration certificate.

Additionally, the minimal verification of the information supplied in connection with an application for an original copyright certificate is wholly absent in the case of a renewal application. The Copyright Office directs in its regulations that the application for original registration accurately reflect "the facts existing at the time of first publication." 37 C.F.R. § 202.3(b)(3). No such admonition is applied to applications for renewal copyright. Indeed, the Copyright Office will accept and register more than one claim to the renewal copyright in a particular work, even if the claims are in obvious conflict. B. Ringer, *Renewal of Copyright, in Report of the Register of Copyrights on the Revision of the U. S. Copyright Law, Study No. 31,* at 107, 184 (1960) (hereinafter cited as "Ringer"). The Office will point out the conflict to the later applicant and request confirmation of the later claim, but does not view its function as making "judicial determinations of substantive renewal rights" and will register the conflicting claim of a determined applicant. *Id.* This drastic diversity in the treatment of original and renewal applications confirms our interpretation of § 209. Congress surely did not intend that such great weight attach to renewal certificates issued to all claimants regardless of questions concerning validity.

Finally, even assuming that some presumption of validity might attach to Epoch's renewal certificate, at least where 27 years passed without challenge, that presumption would certainly be dissipated, as in the case of the § 209 presumption, see, e. g., *Lauratex Textile Corp. v. Citation Fabrics Corp.*, 322 F.Supp. 554, 555 (S.D.N.Y.1971); *United Merchants and Manufacturers, Inc. v. Sarne Co., Inc.*, 278 F.Supp. 162, 164 (S.D.N.Y.1967), by proof that material statements in the certificate were false. As outlined above, the documentary evidence introduced at trial showed that Epoch could not have been the author of the film, even though this status was claimed in the renewal application and there is no proof that Majestic or DWG Corp. employed Griffith to make the motion picture for hire. Indeed, none of the evidence supports the assertion made in the renewal certificate that the film was made for hire, and much of it (including the documentary records regarding the original copyright) points to a contrary conclusion. In these circumstances, any evidentiary weight that the renewal certificate might otherwise have had is offset and the burden of proving the validity of its renewal is shifted back to Epoch, *Gardenia Flowers, Inc. v. Joseph Markovits, Inc.*, 280 F.Supp. 776, 780-81 (S.D.N.Y. 1968). Epoch has failed to sustain that burden.

3. The Theory that the 1915 Assignments Conveyed the Renewal Rights

Epoch's alternative ground upon which a jury might have upheld its renewal is based on the assignment of the original term copyright from DWG Corp. in 1915. . . . [T]he copyright in both the published and unpublished versions of the film was originally secured by DWG Corp. and then assigned to Dixon and Epoch in instruments dated April 17, 1915. Relying mainly upon broad language found in each assignment, which purports to transfer to Epoch all of the rights in the copyright enjoyed by the assignor, DWG Corp., Epoch now argues that these assignments can be fairly construed to have conveyed to it the right to both the original term copyright and the renewal copyright in The Birth. We disagree.

The construction of the assignments urged by Epoch is not one that a jury could fairly adopt, given the record in this case. While Epoch is correct that both assignments contain broad general language purporting to convey to Epoch all of the DWG Corp.'s interest in the film, that language is necessarily limited in its application by the specific description in each assignment of the interest conveyed, see Corbin, Contracts §§ 547, 549 (1960). In both assignments the interest is clearly identified as the first 28-year term only. The assignment of the unpublished work specifically describes the copyright as one "for the term of twenty-eight years." The assignment of the published work conveyed "the copyright acquired by [DWG Corp.] by public presentation of the motion picture photoplay"; a clear reference to the initial 28-year term, since the renewal term is separate from the initial term and not acquired through publication with notice, see Fred Fisher Music Co. v. M. Witmark & Sons, supra.

Moreover, there is no specific reference in either assignment to the renewal term. This deficiency has generally been held as a matter of law, absent contrary evidence, to preclude a holding that a transfer of renewal rights was intended. "[A] general transfer by an author of the original copyright without mention of renewal rights conveys no interest in the renewal rights without proof of a contrary intention." Edward B. Marks Music Corp. v. Charles K. Harris Music Pub. Co., supra, 255 F.2d at 521; see, e. g., G. Ricordi & Co. v. Paramount Pictures, Inc., supra, 189 F.2d at 471. Epoch points to no evidence of a different intention in the present case.

While Epoch correctly observes that the assignment here is from a corporation and not from an individual author, we do not think that difference is critical here, where the corporation was controlled by the author. The policy behind the rule of construction restricting an assignment to the original term unless it refers to renewal rights is to protect authors from inadvertent transfers of renewal rights. That policy, it is true, might not govern a transfer from a corporation unrelated to the author, see Rohauer v. Friedman, 306 F.2d 933, 935-36 (9th Cir. 1962). Here, however, DWG Corp. was in effect the author's alter ego. Epoch adduced no proof that DWG Corp. had any independent right (i. e., as purchaser for value or as employer for hire) to obtain the film copyrights.

. . . The transfer from the DWG Corp. is analogous to a transfer from the individual author and the assignments should be construed in accordance with the rule of Marks Music Corp. Since there is no other proof of an intention to transfer renewal rights, the assignments must be limited in their effect to the original term [of] copyright.

. . . .

In sum there was insufficient evidence introduced at trial from which the jury could reasonably find Epoch's renewal copyright valid under any of the theories advanced below and on this appeal. As Epoch was unable to produce even a prima facie case supporting the validity of its renewal copyright at trial, we hold that the district court should have granted Killiam's motion for a directed verdict. . . .

QUESTIONS

1. Why did Congress decide that the right to secure renewal copyright in works made for hire should be given to the then current owner of the initial term rather than to the "true" author or creator of the work or the person who was the employer at the time the work was first created?

2. In what circumstances does the 1976 Copyright Act continue to give special treatment to works made for hire, and why?

3. What does the *Epoch* case teach us as to whether our concern with renewals will end on January 1, 2006, i.e., twenty-eight years from the effective date of the 1976 Act?

4. We will see later that in the 1976 Act the wrong name in a copyright notice in no case affects the validity of the copyright. *See* § 406(a), and pp. 296-97 *infra*. What can we anticipate when a renewal application is filed by the wrong person as found in *Epoch?*

BARTOK v. BOOSEY & HAWKES, INC.

523 F.2d 941 (2d Cir. 1975)

OAKES, CIRCUIT JUDGE:

This appeal presents the question whether a musical composition the rights to which are assigned by the composer and which is performed during his lifetime is nevertheless "posthumous" within the meaning of the copyright renewal provision, § 24 of the Copyright Act, 17 U.S.C. § 24, because it has not been published or, more precisely, printed (and therefore not copyrighted) until after his death. Appellant, Peter Bartok, a son of composer Bela Bartok, is appealing the decision of Judge Richard Owen of the United States District Court for the Southern District of New York holding that Bartok's *Concerto for Orchestra,* one of the contemporary composer's most popular compositions, is a posthumous work. According to the renewal provision of the very loosely drawn 17 U.S.C. § 24, a proprietor of *inter alia* a copyrighted "posthumous work" is entitled to renew the copyright, whereas the author or certain of the author's surviving kin is entitled to the renewal of most other works. Here both Boosey & Hawkes, Inc. (Boosey), the music publisher and proprietor of the initial copyright of *Concerto for Orchestra,* and Peter Bartok are claiming the right to renew the copyright. Boosey argues that it is the proprietor of a posthumous work; Peter Bartok argues that the work is not posthumous. The trustee for Bela Bartok's estate, Benjamin Suchoff, argues as does Boosey that the work is posthumous.[2] Judge Owen's holding confers that right on Boosey. We must reverse.

Concerto for Orchestra was composed by Bartok between August 15 and October 8, 1943, after a visit by the conductor Serge Koussevitzky to Bartok's hospital room. Bartok was suffering from leukemia, which was to take his life in September, 1945. The *Concerto for Orchestra* was first performed by the Boston Symphony, Koussevitzky conducting, on December 1 and 2, 1944, in Symphony Hall, Boston. The *Concerto* was again performed in Boston on December 29 and 30, 1944, and at Carnegie Hall in New York on January 10 and 13, 1945, and broadcast over radio.

After completing the *Concerto,* Bartok assigned his rights in the work to Boosey pursuant to their 1939 publishing contract. Boosey was to prepare the

---

[2] Under a 1949 agreement signed by appellant Peter Bartok, the composer's widow and the estate, Boosey will pay royalties during the renewal period to the estate which, pursuant to the provisions of Bela Bartok's will, pays the proceeds to Mrs. Bartok for her lifetime and then to her sons after her death. Should appellant prevail the royalties presumably will be paid in equal shares to Mrs. Bartok and her two sons. The proprietor, Boosey, has been wholly scrupulous in protecting the Bartok family's rights in any case.

orchestra parts and print the full score within six months. The printing was to be done in England, but wartime conditions delayed completion, as did some rewriting by Bartok after the premiere. Thus Bartok was still receiving and correcting printer's proofs as late as June, 1945, three months before his death. Printing of the manuscript was not completed and therefore not copyrighted by Boosey until March 20, 1946, six months *after* Bartok's death.

The first 28 year copyright term held by Boosey, defined by 17 U.S.C. § 24, expired in March, 1974. Both Boosey and Peter Bartok filed renewal applications. The Register of Copyrights permitted the filing of both renewals, expressly declining to adjudicate between them.

Judge Owen felt "constrained to conclude" that *Concerto for Orchestra* is a "posthumous work" for purposes of § 24, finding that it was "published" and copyrighted after Bartok's death. Judge Owen relied on the definition of "posthumous" used by the Register of Copyrights and examples in musical history. He concluded, however, that were he to look solely to congressional intent he would hold the work not posthumous. *Bartok v. Boosey & Hawkes, Inc.,* 382 F. Supp. 880, 883 (S.D.N.Y.1974). We find that we must give controlling weight to the legislative purpose in this case of first impression, and thus reverse. . . .

As the Supreme Court said in *Fred Fisher Music Co. v. Witmark & Sons,* 318 U.S. 643, 653-54 (1943), the "basic consideration of policy underlying the renewal provision" was the right of "the author to sell his 'copyright' without losing his renewal interest."

A "posthumous work" is one of the three exceptions to the renewal statute. The only definition of "posthumous" which fulfills the legislative purpose of protecting authors and their families is that in the narrow situation — not present here — where a contract for copyright was never executed by the author during his life. *See* 2 M. Nimmer, *supra,* § 114.1, at 464; Kupferman, *Renewal of Copyright,* 44 Colum. L. Rev. 712 (1944). In that case the estate can make its own contract and thereby protect itself. For example, had the work here been found among Bartok's effects, his widow and children could and presumably would have made their own arrangements to have it published. In that case the logical basis for excepting the widow and children from statutory protection is that, as original proprietors, they would have no need of it. *See* Kupferman, *supra,* 44 Colum. L. Rev. at 715.

In this case, however, where the copyright contract was executed before the author's death, the family has no means of protection other than the statutory renewal right;[4] this is equally true whether the work is available in print or not. Yet the district court's definition of "posthumous" would create a legislative discrimination between families in these two equally unprotected situations. Where, as here, death occurs after copyright sale, but before publication, one commentator agrees that "no one has suggested any possible reason why the rights of the statutory beneficiaries should be defeated in such an instance." Bricker, *Renewal and Extension of Copyright,* 29 S. Cal. L. Rev. 23, 38-39 (1955). *See* Kupferman, *supra,* 44 Colum. L. Rev. at 715.

As Nimmer points out, the legislative purpose of protecting authors and their families derives not so much from a paternalistic view toward authors as a class as from the economic reality that

---

[4] *But see* note 2 *supra.* For purposes of this case it has to be assumed that the publisher would have only its own interests in mind on renewal.

the form of property designated copyright, unlike real property and other forms of personal property, is by its very nature incapable of accurate monetary evaluation prior to its exploitation.

2 M. Nimmer, *supra* § 113, at 462. This purpose is equally salient for all families where the copyright sale is during the author's lifetime. In short, where the legislative purpose of the statute is to extend protection to an author and his family, it makes better sense to read the "posthumous work" exception as a withholding of unnecessary protection where the family can protect itself, rather than as an illogical discrimination between families who are in equal need of protection.

Given this legislative purpose we do not feel compelled to define the term "posthumous," as did Judge Owen, by correlating it to one particular definition of the word "publish," a term which itself has a variety of definitions in the Copyright Act depending upon the context. Judge Owen used the definition of "posthumous work" as a work "published after the death of its author." . . . In this case Bartok had completed the *Concerto*, had heard it performed, had executed a contract for its copyright, and had corrected published proofs, all before his death. While the tangible copies had not been distributed to the public before Bartok's death, orchestra parts had been distributed at least to members of the Boston Symphony and the general public had heard the *Concerto* both in concert and on the radio. The work, as they heard it, was substantially as Bartok intended it to be heard, and the proofs contained his revisions. This is not the case where a composer never released a work for public dissemination, although he may have performed it occasionally,[7] so that when the work is distributed after the composer's death, the public never knows whether he intended substan-

---

[7] The district court analogized the *Concerto* to Frederic Chopin's *Rondo in C Major for Two Pianos, Opus 73*. Judge Owen, himself a composer, relates that the *Rondo* was published as a "posthumous" work six years after Chopin's death even though it had been previously performed by the composer approximately 20 years earlier. From these facts the court concluded that the term "posthumous" had been internationally defined in terms of publication for at least 120 years, as Chopin died in 1849. 382 F.Supp. at 884.

True, both the Chopin work and the Bartok work had been performed in their respective authors' lifetimes. The Chopin *Rondo* was composed 21 years prior to Chopin's death and was played by him soon afterward, but the manuscript was thereafter laid aside by Chopin for reasons not known. It was not given to any publisher. *No arrangement for publication of the work was made by Chopin in his life,* and the manuscript and associated copyright of the *Rondo* remained Chopin's property until his death. The manuscript was later found among those of numerous other published works by a friend named Julian Fontana, who arranged the publication of these works in cooperation with Chopin's family in 1855, six years after the composer's death.

As for the emphasis in note 2 of the dissent upon the practice of numbering compositions according to the date of publication, we do not consider this system, artificially devised by publishers themselves, to be objective or relevant in determining the intended policy of § 24 of the Copyright Act. Nor do we believe that a publisher's designation of "op. posth." can be relied upon as the last word in the characterization of a composition. Paradoxically, Bartok's *Concerto for Orchestra* itself, which the dissent would make "posthumous," was *not* designated as an "op. posth." by its publisher.

Finally, the dissent's reference to the 21-year delay in the publication of Chopin's *Variations for the Piano on a German Air* could very well be a prime example of the danger of Copyright Act abuse by a publisher purposely delaying publication to secure renewal rights to which an author's family would otherwise be entitled.

tial revisions.[8] We need not pass on the question when publication has occurred; we simply point out that defining a "posthumous work" as one that is not published until after the author's death carries with it the implicit problem what is publication as well as the implicit danger that an unscrupulous publisher could purposely delay publication in order to obtain renewal rights.

Judge Owen also relied on the form provided by the Register of Copyrights (Circular 1B) which defines "posthumous" as a "work first published and copyrighted after the death of the author." And yet the Copyright Office has no authority to give opinions or define legal terms [9] and its interpretation on an issue never before decided [10] should not be given controlling weight. *See DeSylva v. Ballentine,* 351 U.S. 570, 577-78 (1956).

. . . .

Finally, the rationale for the exemption for posthumous works, if defined as works the right to copyright which has passed by will or intestacy, is more analogous to the rationale for the other exceptions in § 24. Where such a "passing" has occurred, it may be many years before the work is performed, distributed and copyrighted originally; therefore the renewal right may vest beyond the life of the author's children; there may be many heirs difficult to locate. In a periodical or cyclopedic work, presumably the rationale of the renewal term is to avoid the inconvenience of needing many contributors to join in order to renew the entire work, although contributors can renew individual contributions, raising the question whether the proprietor in the event of such an individual renewal has a right to renew such works, a question in grave doubt. *See* B. Ringer and P. Gitlin, Copyrights 60-61 (1965); 2 M. Nimmer, *supra* § 114.2. Commentators agree that the provision for renewal rights for a "corporate body (otherwise than as assignee or licensee of the individual author)" is practically meaningless, *see* Ringer & Gitlin, *supra* at 59 n. 42, except as a statement that corporate assignees of a copyright, as in this case, are *not* entitled

---

[8] Judge Owen himself states that Peter Bartok argues "not illogically" that the work here in question does not conform even to the dictionary definition of "posthumous," in the light of its public performance prior to the composer's death.

[9] *See* 37 C.F.R. § 201.2(a)(1) which provides in relevant part:

The Copyright Office, however, does not undertake the making of comparisons of copyright deposits to determine similarity between works, nor does it give legal opinions or advice on such matters as:

(i) The validity or status of any copyright other than the facts shown in the records of the Office;

(ii) The rights of persons, whether in connection with cases of alleged copyright infringement, contracts between authors and publishers or other matters of a similar nature;

(iii) The scope and extent of protection of works in foreign countries or interpretation of foreign copyright laws or court opinions;

(iv) The sufficiency, extent or scope of compliance with the copyright law.

In addition the Circular 1B states:

The Copyright Office is primarily an office of record: a place where claims to copyright are registered when the claimant has complied with the requirements of the copyright laws. However, the regulations of the Copyright Office (Code of Federal Regulations, Title 37, Ch. II) prohibit us from giving legal advice or opinions.

[10] As this is a case of first impression, it is unlikely, when preparing the form, that the Register of Copyrights considered the situation where a work has been widely performed and a contract to copyright has been executed by a composer during his lifetime, with the intent that the copyright should be completed during his lifetime. Publication here probably would have occurred in Bartok's lifetime had London not been extensively bombed and mail delivery extensively delayed.

to renew the copyright.[11] 2 M. Nimmer, *supra* § 114.3, at 469. As for employers' renewal rights, if those who have paid employees to create a work were not able to renew the copyright, it would be less profitable, for example, to make films, and it would be difficult in the case where many employees create a work, such as a Disney cartoon, to determine who the author or authors are. The "posthumous work" exclusion appears to us consistent with the other exclusions from § 24 as we have read that section.

Most of the arguments made in the dissent are answered in the course of the foregoing opinion. The dissent's quarrel with our "philosophy" is evidently a quarrel with the House Committee report on the 1909 Act quoted in our opinion [omitted] (and in 2 M. Nimmer, *supra* App. I, at 967-77) and with the underlying rationale of the renewal concept as set forth in 2 M. Nimmer, *supra* § 113, at 462, also quoted above. The suggestion made that somehow this decision will result in voiding copyright renewals made by assignees at the expense of the author's family is based on the overly broad and gratuitous assertion in a district court opinion, *Von Tilzer v. Jerry Vogel Music Co.*, 53 F. Supp. 191, 196 (S.D.N.Y. 1942), *aff'd sub nom. Gumm v. Gerry Vogel Music Co.*, 158 F.2d 516 (2d Cir. 1946); the actual source of the assertion is the inapposite context of *Tobani v. Carl Fischer, Inc.*, 98 F.2d 57, 60 (2d Cir.), *cert. denied*, 305 U.S. 650 (1938), which denied to those who fail to renew a copyright the right to sue for the conveyance of void copyright renewal registrations of others. . . . To avoid any possibility of invalidation of renewal copyrights previously made by proprietors in the limited class of those in Boosey's position here upon reliance on the Copyright Office's Circular No. 15, the effect of this decision shall be prospective only. That is, our decision will apply only to future and pending renewals, as well as to the parties here, and will not operate to void the legal title to renewal copyrights held by those proprietors in Boosey's class. Instead, the author's "widow, widower, or children, if the author be not living, or if such author, widow, widower, or children be not living, then the author's executors, or in the absence of a will, his next of kin" shall be deemed to be the equitable owners of the renewal rights and have their remedy against the legal proprietors for the rights to which they are entitled under our decision here.[12]

For the above reasons the judgment is reversed.

---

[11] A mere licensee may not claim an original term copyright, much less its renewal, 1 M. Nimmer, *supra* §§ 61, 114.3, 468 n. 55, so that the exclusion with respect to a licensee in this very ambiguous statute appears meaningless.

[12] The dissent refers throughout to "widows" and pictures the "distraught widow" negotiating with the publisher for the sale and assignment of renewal rights. Most authors or composers, we should suppose, like other testators, rely on others to act on their family's behalf; Congress, when it contemplated exercise of renewal rights by an author's family in the case of an assignment in which the author does not live to the end of the original term, evidently was not concerned about any undue disadvantage of a "distraught widow." We do not think it was so concerned in its definition of what is a posthumous work. Similarly, the argument that the decision reduces the value of what the composer has to sell when he is most in need is belied by the way Congress deals with renewal rights where the author does not live out the original term. Nimmer agrees with us that the construction we give the statute "would better seem to protect the interests of those for whom the author wishes to provide upon his death." 2 M. Nimmer, *supra* § 114.1, at 464.

VAN GRAAFEILAND, CIRCUIT JUDGE (dissenting):

As one whose musical accomplishments go barely beyond a mastery of "Chopsticks", I take up the cudgels for appellees with some diffidence. However, since I believe that this case is being wrongly decided, I must respectfully express my dissent.

To place the opinion of my brothers in proper perspective, one should bear in mind that the contest herein is not between the penurious family of a deceased composer and an "unscrupulous" publisher; it is between a son and his mother. Bela Bartok, as a loving and thoughtful husband, executed a will in which he left the royalties from all copyrights and renewal copyrights in trust for his widow with the remainder, upon her death, to his son Peter, the appellant herein. Apparently, appellant is unwilling to wait for his remainder to accrue.

He asks this Court to declare that appellee publisher has no right to renew the copyright of his father's works and to continue to pay all royalties following such renewal to his mother. Instead, he claims the right of renewal with his mother and brother, with the result that Bela Bartok's widow, to whom the composer left all the royalties during her lifetime, will end up getting only one-third of them, the remaining two-thirds going to appellant and his brother. I believe that the injustice to Mr. Bartok's widow which results from the majority's frustration of Mr. Bartok's wishes is neither required nor justified by the Copyright Law.

. . . .

Judge Owen found that the word "posthumous" as used in the field of music for over a century has a specific meaning, *i. e.*, "published after the death of its author". My colleagues do not hold this finding to be erroneous, as indeed they could not. My limited facilities for research completely substantiate it and indicate further that the same finding could be made in the field of literature. The following references are illustrative:

Dunstan, A Cyclopaedic Dictionary of Music (1973):

Published after the composer's death.

[The judge referred to more than a dozen definitions from dictionaries and other sources.]

The Century Dictionary and Encyclopedia (1895):

> . . . appearing or existing after the death or cessation of that to which its origin is due; especially of books published after the death of the author: as to posthumous works.[2]

Having established the existence of a commonly accepted and well established meaning for the term "posthumous works", Judge Owen then applied an equally accepted and established rule of statutory interpretation, viz., "The popular or

---

[2] The abbreviated phrase "Op. posth." (posthumous work) which appears on many published compositions is well known to every student of music. Equally well known is the fact that opus numbers for many classical compositions were assigned by the publishers according to the dates of the publication, many of which were after the death of the composer. For example, compositions 66 through 74 of Chopin were all published and numbered posthumously. Bidou, Chopin 264 (1927).

Whatever may be the situation regarding Chopin's *Rondo* discussed in n. 7 of the majority opinion, the fact remains that some of Chopin's posthumous works were in the hands of publishers prior to his death. Bidou points out that Chopin's "Variations for the Piano on a German Air", published by Haslinger in 1851, two years after Chopin's death, had been in Haslinger's possession since 1830. In any event, the classification of a work as posthumous was determined in each instance by the date of publication.

accepted import of words furnishes the general rule for the interpretation of statutes."

. . . .

My brothers, nonetheless, rely heavily on certain congressional dialogue which they quote at some length.

. . . .

In short, I agree with the commentator in 29 S.Cal.L.Rev. 23, 39, *supra,* who said, ". . . there is nothing in the statute, Committee Report or any judicial opinion which would indicate that the term posthumous works was intended to have anything but its ordinary and usual meaning."

Finally, and most significantly, the United States Copyright Office itself has adopted and used the same definition as the above cited authorities.

. . . .

One wonders, also, how many widows like Mrs. Bartok, will be deprived of the full benefit of their husband's testate bounty because this Court is now changing the long-standing rules of the Copyright Office upon which the will was predicated.

My brothers are creating a definition of "posthumous works" which appears nowhere in the legislation or the legislative history; which is completely at odds with long-standing and accepted usage; which is contrary to the definition accepted by the Copyright Office and most authorities in the copyright field; and which is not unanimously recommended by those who seek change.[7] This is not the proper role of the judiciary.

I have no quarrel with my brothers' good intentions but question the philosophy which underlies them. I am not convinced, for example, that the distraught widow of an author or composer is more capable than he to negotiate with a publisher for the sale and assignment of renewal rights. Giving full recognition to the increased worldliness of what was once described as the "weaker sex", it can hardly be seriously contended that a widow is in as good a position to evaluate the merits of a musical composition as was her husband who composed it. Neither does she have as complete and accurate knowledge of the music publishing field.[8]

Of course, a widow can wait for twenty-eight years before assigning her right to renew. But will she? She, like her deceased husband, must put groceries on the table today. Insofar as the composer is concerned, the decision of my brothers reduces the value of what he has to sell at the time when he probably is most in need.[9]

---

[7] Nimmer suggests, for example, that "posthumous works" shall include only those which have received no public dissemination during the author's life. 2 Nimmer, The Law of Copyright § 114.1 at 464-5 (1975).

[8] Mr. Bartok's contract with his publisher provided for the following royalties:

15% of the selling price of all copies;
15% to 20% from the hire or purchase of orchestral material;
50% to 66$^2/_3$% of performing right fees;
70% to 80% of performing right fees from stage performances;
66$^2/_3$% of royalties and fees from mechanical adaptations;
50% of royalties and fees from reproduction in movies and television.
No one has expressed any dissatisfaction with this monetary arrangement.

[9] If promotion of artistic production *as a whole* is the overriding purpose of copyright, regulation of copyright transfers in the author's interest should be concerned predominantly with revenues that can be realized for the author relatively soon after

I see no compelling reasons why the resolution of these differences cannot await the considered judgment of the Congress which has been working on a revision of the 1909 Copyright Act for a number of years. Justice would then be accorded to Mrs. Bartok, and her husband's wishes would be fulfilled.

. . . .

I believe Judge Owen's decision was correct, and I would affirm.

QUESTIONS

1. Articulate the reasons why Congress awarded the renewal copyright in posthumous works to the then owner of copyright rather than to the author's widow, children, legatees or survivors. Given what appears to have been the prevailing understanding of the meaning of "posthumous" (as substantiated in the dissenting opinion), i.e., works first published after the death of the author, would that not be the kind of situation in which the widow's claim to the renewal term (as protection against an unremunerative transfer) is the most compelling, rather than the least?

2. The court in *Bartok* states that the widow and children do not need the protection afforded by the renewal term when it is they (rather than the author during his life) who convey copyright after the death of the author. Can this be so (or any more so than when the author himself conveys copyright, which does not divest him of the renewal), given all of the usual concerns for unremunerative transfers of works having speculative value?

3. Which of the following events prior to the death of the author does the court hold to be sufficient to deprive a work of posthumous status? The conveyance of a license to print it. The transfer of copyright. The printing and marking (by the author) of page proofs. Public performance.

4. If, in his will, an author transfers copyright in a work which remained unprinted, undistributed and otherwise unexploited at the time of his death, does the court treat this as a posthumous work? Or does the court hold that a work is posthumous only if the widow and children transfer the copyright after the death of the author?

5. Is this case explainable as anything other than an attempt to construe the statute in a manner which will help the widows and children of authors, who generally need more help than do copyright assignees? (Is it not ironic that the decision resulted in the diminution of protection for Mrs. Bartok in comparison to her interest had the judgment been for the assignee Boosey & Hawkes?)

---

creation, since the prospect of receiving a reward in the distant future will probably have negligible effect on an author's production. Little concern should be paid to revenues that will accrue only to the author's heirs.

Curtis, Protecting Authors in Copyright Transfers: Revision Bill § 203 and the Alternatives 194 (ASCAP Copyright Law Symposium, Number twenty-one, 1971).

ROHAUER v. KILLIAM SHOWS, INC.

551 F.2d 484 (2d Cir. 1977)

FRIENDLY, CIRCUIT JUDGE:

This well briefed and argued appeal raises a question of copyright law of first impression. The question is of considerable importance despite the small amount of money here at stake. The issue is this: When the author of a copyrighted story has assigned the motion picture rights and consented to the assignee's securing a copyright on motion picture versions, with the terms of the assignment demonstrating an intention that the rights of the purchaser shall extend through a renewal of the copyright on the story, does a purchaser which has made a film and obtained a derivative copyright and renewal copyright thereon infringe the copyright on the story if it authorizes the performance of the copyrighted film after the author has died and the copyright on the story has been renewed by a statutory successor under 17 U.S.C. § 24, who has made a new assignment of motion picture and television rights? As has been so often true in cases arising under the Copyright Act of 1909, neither an affirmative nor a negative answer is completely satisfactory. A court must grope to ascertain what would have been the thought of the 1909 Congress on an issue about which it almost certainly never thought at all. *See Twentieth Century Music Corp. v. Aiken,* 422 U.S. 151, 156 (1975). In returning an affirmative answer to the question posed, Judge Bauman recognized that the negative would not be illogical, *see* 379 F. Supp. at 727. While we recognize that an affirmative answer likewise is by no means illogical, we believe a negative answer is more in keeping with the letter and purposes of the statute as best we can discern them.

There is no dispute about the facts. Sometime before May 15, 1925, Edith Maude Hull (Mrs. Hull), a British subject, wrote a novel entitled "The Sons of the Sheik." The novel was published in the United States about that time by Small, Maynard & Co., Inc., which obtained a United States copyright, assigned by it to Mrs. Hull in November 1925. By an instrument dated December 7, 1925, Mrs. Hull, as Seller, for a consideration of $21,000, granted, sold and assigned to Joseph H. Moskowitz, as Purchaser, all the motion picture rights to the story for the entire world, "together with the sole and exclusive right to make motion picture versions thereof," to secure copyright on the films, and to "vend, exhibit, exploit and otherwise dispose of the same." The Seller agreed "to renew or procure the renewal of the copyrights" in the story prior to their expiration and thereupon to assign to the Purchaser the motion picture rights for the renewal term.[2]

Pursuant to this agreement, a highly successful silent motion picture entitled "The Son of the Sheik," starring Rudolph Valentino, was produced and released for exhibition in the United States in 1926. On August 24, 1926, the picture was registered in the Copyright Office by and in the name of Feature Productions, Inc., an assignee of Moskowitz. This copyright was renewed on March 18, 1954, in the name of Artcinema Associates, Inc., the then proprietor of the copyright;

---

[2] The appellants concede that because of Mrs. Hull's death before the accrual of the right to a renewal of the United States copyright in the novel, they could not obtain specific enforcement of this agreement in respect of such copyright; they rely on the clause as demonstrating an intention of the parties, which appellees do not dispute, that the Purchaser should be entitled to the motion picture rights both for the original and for any renewal term.

the renewal copyright was sold in 1961 to Gregstan Enterprises, Inc., a corporation headed by Paul Killiam, and was assigned by Gregstan to the defendant Killiam Shows, Inc. (hereafter Killiam) in 1968.

Mrs. Hull died in 1943. On May 22, 1952, the United States copyright in the novel was renewed in the name of her daughter, Cecil Winstanley Hull (Miss Hull), a party plaintiff herein, the author's sole surviving child. On May 6, 1965, Miss Hull assigned to plaintiff Rohauer all of her "right, title and interest (if any) in and to the motion picture and television rights of every kind and character throughout the world and in all languages" to "Sons of the Sheik." Rohauer paid 446 pounds 10 shillings (then the equivalent of $1250) for this assignment.

On July 13, 1971, the motion picture was shown on television station WNET, owned by defendant Educational Broadcasting Corporation (hereafter Broadcasting) and operating on Channel 13 in the New York metropolitan area. The videotape required for this exhibition was made by Broadcasting from a print of the film made available to it by Killiam. No license had been obtained from plaintiffs Rohauer or Miss Hull, although Rohauer's attorney had informed an officer of Killiam in 1966 of his assignment from Miss Hull and had advised that any showing of the picture would constitute an infringement. Similar notice was given by Rohauer's counsel to Broadcasting the day before the first television showing. After this action was commenced the film was shown twice more on Channel 13.

The plaintiffs claimed and the District Court held, 379 F. Supp. 723 (S.D.N.Y. 1974), that upon the expiration of the original term of the copyright in the novel and Miss Hull's succession to the renewal term, all rights of defendants and their predecessors to authorize the exhibition of the motion picture terminated. Defendants-appellants contend that while after the expiration of the original term of the copyright in the novel and the daughter's succession, no new motion picture versions could lawfully be made on the basis of the 1925 grant from Mrs. Hull, their predecessors and they were entitled to renew the copyright on a film already made and copyrighted and to authorize its exhibition.

I

. . . .

Turning to the precedents, we do not find that any of the Supreme Court decisions discussed at length in the briefs, primarily *Fox Film Corporation v. Knowles*, 261 U.S. 326 (1923), *Fred Fisher Music Co. v. M. Witmark & Sons*, 318 U.S. 643 (1943), *De Sylva v. Ballentine*, 351 U.S. 570 (1956), and *Miller Music Corp. v. Charles N. Daniels, Inc.*, 362 U.S. 373 (1960), has any real bearing on the issue here before us, either in holding or in opinion. All these cases were concerned with the relative rights of persons claiming full assignment or ownership of the renewal term of an underlying copyright. None involved the question here presented of effecting a proper reconciliation between the grant of derivative copyright in § 7 and the final proviso of § 24 with respect to renewals of underlying copyrights.

Appellees contend that even if this be so, the question here at issue has been settled in their favor by lower court decisions, notably *Fitch v. Shubert*, 20 F.Supp. 314 (S.D.N.Y. 1937); *G. Ricordi & Co. v. Paramount Pictures, Inc.*, 189 F.2d 469 (2 Cir.), *cert. denied*, 342 U.S. 849 (1951); and *Sunset Securities Company v. Coward McCann, Inc.*, 297 P.2d 137 (Dist. Ct. of Appeal 2d Dist. 1956), *vacated*, 47 Cal. 2d 907, 306 P.2d 777 (1957). Apart from the fact that none of these cases except *Ricordi* would bind us as a precedent, we do not find that any of them decided the question here at issue.

. . . .

Ricordi was a suit by G. Ricordi & Co. for a declaratory judgment against Paramount Pictures, Inc. The case involved the story, play and opera entitled "Madame Butterfly." The novel was written in 1897 by John Luther Long, published that year in Century Magazine and copyrighted by the Century Company. In 1900 David Belasco wrote a play with the consent of the copyright owner which, however, was not copyrighted until 1917. In 1901 Long and Belasco entered into a contract with Ricordi giving it the exclusive right to make a libretto for an opera of Belasco's dramatic version of Madame Butterfly. In 1904 Ricordi copyrighted the famous opera composed by Puccini and subsequently secured an assignment from Puccini's son of the renewal copyright therein. In 1925 Long obtained a renewal of the copyright on his novel and in 1932, subsequent to Long's death, his administrator granted the motion picture rights therein to Paramount. In the same year, with the Belasco play still in its first copyright term, Paramount obtained from the trustee of Belasco's will an assignment of the motion picture rights to the play; no renewal of the copyright in the play was ever effected. Ricordi sought a declaration that it was entitled to make a motion picture of the opera free from any interference by Paramount. This court, speaking through Judge Swan for a particularly distinguished bench including Judge Learned Hand and Judge Frank, held that Ricordi was not entitled to so broad a declaration. Ricordi's renewal copyright in the opera extended only to so much of the opera as was "a new work." Hence it was not entitled to make general use of the novel for a motion picture version of its opera but was restricted for that purpose to what was copyrightable as new matter in its operatic version.

Ricordi is not determinative here, however, for a fundamental reason: the original 1901 agreement between Long, Belasco, and Ricordi did not purport to run beyond the original term of Long's copyright on the novel. Ricordi neither sought nor obtained operatic rights in the renewal term of the novel in the 1901 agreement, or in any other negotiation.[8] To conclude that the renewal term of a copyright is a new estate free from previous licenses is one thing when, as in *Ricordi,* the parties have never bargained for renewal rights, and another when, as in the case of Mrs. Hull and Joseph Moskowitz, the assignment agreement explicitly included rights to the derivative work during the renewal term.

We find even less helpful to the plaintiffs the decisions previously cited in the California case of *Sunset Securities Company v. Coward McCann, Inc.* For whatever it may be worth, the opinion of the District Court of Appeal is favorable to the defendants and the reversal by the California Supreme Court was on the grounds of contract rather than of copyright law.

The short of the matter is that we have been cited to no case holding that the inability of an author to carry out his promise to effect a renewal of a copyright because of his death prior to the date for obtaining renewal terminates *as a matter of copyright law* the right of a holder of a derivative copyright to continue to publish a derivative work copyrighted before the author's death on which the copyright was thereafter renewed. It is equally true that we have been cited no case upholding such a right.

---

[8] As the *Ricordi* court noted, the 1901 agreement "made no allusion to renewal of copyright." 189 F.2d at 471. It did not even contain more oblique language granting operatic rights "for all time." Though Belasco's play fell into the public domain in 1945 at the end of its first term, Long did renew the copyright on his novel, and Ricordi conceded it had never sought a new license for operatic rights from Long for the renewal term.

... [W]e do not believe, despite language in the cases to the effect that the proprietor of a derivative copyright is "protected" only as to the "new matter" conceived by him and that a statutory successor obtains a "new estate" in the underlying copyright, that the vesting of renewed copyright in the underlying work in a statutory successor deprives the proprietor of the derivative copyright of a right, stemming from the § 7 "consent" of the original proprietor of the underlying work, to use so much of the underlying copyrighted work as already has been embodied in the copyrighted derivative work, as a matter of copyright law. That view is only a slight extension of this court's decision in *Edmonds v. Stern*, 248 F. 897 (2 Cir. 1918). There the purchaser of a song, having copyrighted it with the consent of the composer, prepared an operetta and copyrighted an orchestral medley based on the operetta which utilized, among other things, the notes of the song. Later the purchaser assigned the copyright in the song back to the composer. The court held, as an alternate ground of decision, that the reassignment would not deprive the proprietor of the copyright of the score of the right to sell copies of the medley since, as Judge Hough said, 248 F. at 898,

> The two things [the song and the orchestral score] were legally separate, and independent of each other; it makes no difference that such separate and independent existence might to a certain extent have grown out of plaintiff's consent to the incorporation of his melody in the orchestration. When that consent was given, a right of property sprang into existence, not at all affected by the conveyance of any other right.[9]

So here when the purchaser from Mrs. Hull embodied her story in a motion picture which was copyrighted under § 7, the vesting of the renewal right of the story in her daughter did not affect the property right in the copyrighted derivative work.

The District Court and appellees rely also on the views of the leading text writer, Professor Nimmer, and of commentators to the effect that in circumstances such as those here presented performance of the derivative copyrighted film after the expiration of the original term of the underlying copyright and renewal by a statutory successor constitutes an infringement. . . . [A]ppellants cite an article by Professor Donald Engel, 12 Bulletin of the Copyright Society 83, 119-20 & n. 126 (1964), which concludes:

> The cases indicate that the proprietor of the copyright in an authorized new work who no longer has authorization to use the underlying work may continue to use the new work in substantially identical form but may not create a new version of the new work which also constitutes a new version of the underlying work.

and says of *Ricordi*, correctly in our judgment:

> the "Madame Butterfly" case did not hold that the proprietor of the copyright in the new work was precluded from making copies of or permitting public performances of the opera, but merely held that he could not make *general* use of the protected underlying material for the creation of a motion picture, itself a new work based upon the underlying copyright which he no longer had authorization to use.

---

[9] It is true that in stating the facts the court noted that the orchestral arrangement "of course, contained no words." We think that in saying this, the court was simply following the usual and proper judicial practice of deciding only an easier case that is before it rather than a harder one that is not. To our minds the court's reasoning would cover the sale of a text and score of the operetta as well as of the purely orchestral medley.

. . . .

To such extent as it may be permissible to consider policy considerations, the equities lie preponderantly in favor of the proprietor of the derivative copyright. In contrast to the situation where an assignee or licensee has done nothing more than print, publicize and distribute a copyrighted story or novel, a person who with the consent of the author has created an opera or a motion picture film will often have made contributions both literary, musical and economic as great as or greater than the original author. As pointed out in the Bricker article, *supra,* 29 S. Cal. L. Rev. at 33, the purchaser of derivative rights has no truly effective way to protect himself against the eventuality of the author's death before the renewal period since there is no way of telling who will be the surviving widow, children or next of kin or the executor until that date arrives. To be sure, this problem exists in equal degree with respect to assignments or licenses of underlying copyright, but in such cases there is not the countervailing consideration that large and independently copyrightable contributions will have been made by the transferee. As against this, the author can always protect his heirs by imposing a contractual limit upon the assignment. It is true that this might not be practicable from a business standpoint in cases where the assignment was made shortly before the expiration of the initial term, but those are the very cases where the inequity of terminating the transferee's rights with respect to so much of the underlying work as is embodied in the derivative work is the greatest.

We find recognition of these policy considerations in §§ 203(b)(1) and 304(c)(6)(A) of the recently enacted copyright revision bill, 90 Stat. 2541 (1976). In connection with a new plan whereby copyright in any work created on or after January 1, 1978 or created before that date but not then yet published or copyrighted shall, with certain exceptions, run for the life of the author plus 50 years, with any grant of a transfer or license subject to a right of termination between the 35th and 40th year of the grant; and the renewal term of any existing copyright is extended for another 19 years subject to a right of termination of any transfer or license at the end of the 28th year of the renewal term over a like period of five years, Congress expressly provided:

> A derivative work prepared under authority of the grant before its termination may continue to be utilized under the terms of the grant after its termination, but this privilege does not extend to the preparation after the termination of other derivative works based upon the copyrighted work covered by the terminated grant.

§§ 203(b)(1), 304(c)(6)(A). While it is true that this proviso was part of a package which extended the temporal rights of authors (but also of their assignees) and that the proviso thus does not deal with the precise situation here presented, we nevertheless regard it as evidence of a belief on the part of Congress of the need for special protection for derivative works.[11] We agree, of course, that provisions of the new Act cannot be read as varying clear provisions of the 1909 Act in cases to which the new Act does not apply. However, the present situation fits rather well under Judge Lumbard's language in *Goodis v. United Artists Television, Inc.,* 425 F.2d 397, 403 (2 Cir. 1970):

---

[11] *See* S. Rep. No. 473, 94th Cong., 1st Sess. 111 (1975):

An important limitation on the rights of a copyright owner under a terminated grant is specified in section 203(b)(1). This clause provides that, notwithstanding a termination, a derivative work prepared earlier may "continue to be utilized" under the condi-

Our decision today is that the result which the proposed legislation would compel is not precluded in any way by the decisions rendered under the present Copyright Act. As discussed earlier, the "problem" with which the proposed legislation deals is one which exists because of judicial dicta rendered in cases not apposite to the factual situation before us in this case.

For these reasons we hold that the licensing by Killiam of exhibition of the film already copyrighted and its exhibition by Broadcasting did not violate the renewal copyright.[12]

. . . .

The judgment is reversed with instructions to dismiss the complaint.

QUESTIONS

1. Is not the question whether the renewal term is a "new estate," free and clear of earlier transfers, to be determined by construction of the statute and its underlying policy, rather than by a construction of the contractual intention of the author? If, that is, the statute is designed, in the instant case, to protect Miss Hull as the author's daughter, who did not join in the attempted assignment of the renewal term, how can that protection be ousted by the author's contractual dealings in her lifetime?

2. At a number of points in its opinion, the court suggests that the derivative work (here the motion picture) takes on an existence which is separate and independent from that of the underlying work. If that is so, does it not follow that the derivative work can continue to be used during the renewal term of the underlying work even when there has been no attempt by the author in the initial term to convey the renewal?

3. Assume that the author of a novel, during the initial term of copyright, conveys to A the right to base a drama thereon, to B the right to make a musical, to C the right to make a motion picture, to D the right to make a television program or serial, and to E the right to make a choreographic work. Assume too that these grants are stated to embrace the renewal term of the copyright on the underlying novel. Would it not follow from the court's opinion that all of these

---

tions of the terminated grant; the clause adds, however, that this privilege is not broad enough to permit the preparation of other derivative works. In other words, a film made from a play could continue to be licensed for performance after the motion picture contract had been terminated, but any remake rights covered by the contract would be cut off.

See also Second Supplementary Report of the Register of Copyrights on the General Revision of the U.S. Copyright Law: 1975 Revision Bill, October—December 1975, ch. XI, p. 10:

Section 203 is a compromise that attempts to balance the interests of individual authors and their transferees in a fairer way than the present renewal provision.

[12] Plaintiffs-appellees contend that even assuming the general correctness of our conclusion, there would be an infringement here since the print licensed by Killiam was used by Broadcasting to create a new videotape for television transmission; plaintiffs contend that this amounts to a "new version" of the original film. Since it was stipulated that such a videotape was necessary for television transmission, we see no reason to consider this tape to be a new version of the film. As appellees admit, only a few new subtitles were used in the videotape; the newly incorporated music alone, which was certainly not within plaintiffs' copyright, is not sufficient to make it a new work.

works can continue to be exploited even after the renewal term has been properly claimed by the author's widow and children? Was it likely Congress' intention to permit the renewal rights of the author's survivors to be thus diluted?

4. The court states that its holding will not entitle a person who has been granted merely a right to print the underlying work (during both its initial and renewal terms of copyright) to continue to do so in the event the author dies and the renewal term becomes vested in his widow and children. What statutory language, logic or economic policy warrants such a distinction? Will the court's statement be controlling if the author conveys, for the initial and renewal terms, the right also to make annotations and minor editorial revisions of the underlying work?

5. While it is true that the author of a derivative work may make many significant contributions in its preparation and marketing, does not the court's decision give too little attention to the statutory concern for the widow and children during the renewal term of the underlying work? Might not there be a better accommodation of the pertinent interests by permitting the continued marketing of the derivative work while requiring that there be payment of a reasonable royalty to the widow and children once the renewal term in the underlying work commences?

6. Does the decision of the court suggest any answer to the question whether the owner of renewal copyright (Miss Hull) in the underlying work ("The Sons of the Sheik") may license another person (Rohauer) to prepare a completely new motion picture (presumably with sound and in color) based on that underlying work?

7. The court suggests that Killiam, the owner of copyright in the Valentino motion picture, is not entitled during the renewal term of "The Sons of the Sheik" to make a new motion picture or any other new version of the underlying novel. Do you agree with the court's conclusion at footnote 12 that the translation of the Valentino motion picture to videotape, the addition of new printed dialogue, and the incorporation of music, do not constitute a "new version"?

RUSSELL v. PRICE

612 F.2d 1123 (9th Cir. 1979)

GOODWIN, CIRCUIT JUDGE:

Defendants distributed copies of the film "Pygmalion", the copyright for which had expired. They were sued by the owners of the renewal copyright in the George Bernard Shaw play upon which the film was based. Defendants appeal the resulting judgment for damages and attorney fees.

Plaintiffs cross appeal, claiming that the court erred in not awarding them statutory "in lieu" damages. We affirm.

In 1913 Shaw registered a copyright on his stage play "Pygmalion". The renewal copyright on the play, obtained in 1941 and originally scheduled to expire in 1969, was extended by Congressional action to the year 1988. Shaw died in 1950 and the plaintiffs, except for Janus Films, are current proprietors of the copyright. Janus Films is a licensee.

In 1938 a derivative version of the play, a motion picture also entitled "Pygmalion", was produced under a license from Shaw; neither the terms nor the licensee's identity appear in the record. The film was produced by Gabriel Pascal, copyrighted by Loew's, and distributed by Metro-Goldwyn-Mayer ("MGM"). For undisclosed reasons, the film's copyright was allowed to expire in 1966. When and if the original film rights agreement expired is also not disclosed.

In 1971 the play's copyright proprietors licensed Janus Films to be the exclusive distributor of the film "Pygmalion". Shortly after discovering in 1972 that Budget Films was renting out copies of the 1938 film, Janus brought an action against Budget in a California state court, alleging state causes of action — in particular, unfair competition. That case ended in Budget's favor upon a determination that the action was essentially one for copyright infringement over which the state court lacked jurisdiction. The English copyright proprietors then executed a power of attorney in favor of their licensee Janus, and Janus promptly brought this action in federal district court in May 1975.

. . . .

II. Infringement

Defendants' main contention on the primary issue in this litigation is simply stated: Because the film copyright on "Pygmalion" has expired, that film is in the public domain, and, consequently, prints of that film [9] may be used freely by anyone. Thus, they argue that their renting out of the film does not infringe the statutory copyright on Shaw's play.

Defendants rely almost entirely on the recent opinion of Judge Friendly in *Rohauer v. Killiam Shows, Inc.,* 551 F.2d 484 (2d Cir.), *cert. denied,* 431 U.S. 949 (1977). However, in so relying, they ignore or fail to appreciate the significant differences between that case and this one.[10]

In *Rohauer* the author of a novel which was statutorily copyrighted in 1925 assigned exclusive movie rights to one Moskowitz, specifically promising in the contract to reassign to him or his successor in interest all film rights for the novel's copyright renewal term. A successful silent film was made under that assignment and separately copyrighted in 1926 by an assignee of Moskowitz. Unfortunately, the novel's author died prior to the end of the novel's first copyright term. The author's daughter, as statutory beneficiary of the right to renew, inherited the renewal term free from the film license granted by her mother.[11] The daughter then granted exclusive movie and television rights for the renewal term to Rohauer. Killiam Shows, Inc., successor in interest to the 1926 film's renewal copyright, allowed the film to be shown on educational television without Rohauer's or the daughter's authorization, whereupon the latter two brought a copyright infringement action against Killiam.

---

[9] Defendants admit that any new motion picture or other derivative work produced without the permission of the proprietors of the copyright on Shaw's play would infringe that underlying copyright.

[10] We express no opinion about the merits of Rohauer v. Killiam Shows, Inc., 551 F.2d 484 (2d Cir.), *cert. denied,* 431 U.S. 949 (1977), which has been the subject of adverse critical commentary. *See* 1 Nimmer on Copyright § 3.07[A] at 3-25 — 3-32 (1979); Comment, Derivative Copyright and the 1909 Act — New Clarity or Confusion?, 44 Brooklyn L.Rev. 905 (1978).

[11] The optional renewal term under the Copyright Act of 1909, 17 U.S.C. § 24 (1976), was considered to be a "new estate", so that the proprietor of the renewal term copyright could exploit it free of any rights, interests or licenses assigned or made during the copyright's initial term. *See, e.g.,* G. Ricordi & Co. v. Paramount Pictures, Inc., 189 F.2d 469, 471 (2d Cir.), *cert. denied,* 342 U.S. 849 (1951); Miller Music Corp. v. Daniels, Inc., 362 U.S. 373 (1960).

The Second Circuit held on those facts that the derivative film's independent copyright entitled the defendant to continue showing the film without infringing rights under the renewal copyright in the underlying novel. Defendants here understand by this that a derivative copyright covers more than the new matter which the producer of the derivative work added to the underlying work. Thus, they say that when the derivative copyright expires the whole product enters the public domain free of the monopoly protection of any subsisting copyright in the underlying work. The court's opinion in *Rohauer,* however, makes it clear that this is simply not the case.

First, the *Rohauer* court placed heavy emphasis on the nongratuitous intent of the nonsurviving author to convey film rights in the novel's renewal term, a promise which had been bargained for in the initial assignment.[12] The defendants here have never bargained with Shaw or his successors for anything, nor do they enjoy any relationship with anyone who had so bargained.

A second important difference between the favored party in *Rohauer* and the defendants here is that the defendant Killiam there was the proprietor of the still valid copyright in the film. By virtue of that copyright, Killiam was held to have sufficient rights in the matter derived from the novel to continue showing it as part of the film.[13] A prominent rationale in that case for awarding those limited rights in favor of the owner of the derivative copyright is the protection and encouragement of the "large and independently copyrightable" "literary, musical and economic" contributions of the "person who with the consent of the author has created an opera or a motion picture film" from a copyrighted novel. 551 F.2d at 493. However, whatever place sympathy for the position of creators of derivative works might properly have under the 1909 Copyright Act,[14] the

---

[12] It is on this basis that the court in Rohauer v. Killiam Shows, Inc., *supra* note 10, distinguished *Ricordi, supra* note 11, and Fitch v. Shubert, 20 F.Supp. 314 (S.D.N.Y. 1937). *Rohauer,* 551 F.2d at 490-91. The court noted, for example, that the "fundamental reason" *Ricordi's* holding, that the renewal copyright in the derivative work extended only to the new matter in that version, was not determinative in *Rohauer* was that in the former the assignment agreement

> did not purport to run beyond the original term of [the] copyright on the novel . . . . To conclude that the renewal term of a copyright is a new estate free from previous licenses is one thing when, as in *Ricordi,* the parties have never bargained for renewal rights, and another when, as in the [*Rohauer*] case . . ., the assignment agreement explicitly included rights to the derivative work during the renewal term.

551 F.2d at 491.

[13] We note that the so-called "new property rights" theory which Rohauer v. Killiam Shows, Inc., *supra* note 10, seems partially to adopt, had been consistently rejected in earlier decisions as well as by the nation's foremost authority on copyright law. G. Ricordi & Co. v. Paramount Pictures, Inc., *supra* note 11; Fitch v. Shubert, *supra* note 12; Gilliam v. American Broadcasting Cos., Inc., *supra* note 6; 1 Nimmer on Copyright § 3.07[A] at 3.23-24 (1979). *See also* Comment, *supra* note 10, at 921-26. Professor Nimmer states the theory as follows:

> [O]nce a derivative work is created pursuant to a valid license to use the underlying material, a new property right springs into existence with respect to the entire derivative work, so that even if the license is thereafter terminated the proprietor of the derivative work may nevertheless continue to use the material from the underlying work as contained in the derivative work.

§ 3.07[A] at 3.23 (footnotes omitted).

[14] This case arose under the Copyright Act of Mar. 4, 1909, codified at 17 U.S.C. §§ 1-216 (1976). Thus, all references are to that version of the copyright statute unless otherwise noted.

defendants here can take advantage of none, having contributed nothing to the production of the film "Pygmalion".

Nor is it apparent under *Rohauer* that such sympathy should have any place at all when the independent copyright on the derivative work has been allowed to expire. For then there is no longer a conflict between two copyrights, each apparently granting "their proprietors overlapping 'exclusive' rights to use whatever underlying material . . . had been incorporated into the derivative film." Comment, *Derivative Copyright and the 1909 Act — New Clarity or Confusion?*, 44 Brooklyn L.Rev. 905, 912 (1978) (footnote omitted). Thus, the persons who might have had standing to raise the *Rohauer* claim here could, consistently with that case, be held to have forfeited it by their failure to renew the derivative copyright. Defendants here could never have laid claim to the right recognized in *Rohauer*, and we perceive no reason to award it to them at the expense of the holders of the renewal copyright which still covers the Shaw play.

Thus, we reaffirm, without finding it necessary to repeat the rationale, the well-established doctrine that a derivative copyright protects [15] only the new material contained in the derivative work, not the matter derived from the underlying work. 1 *Nimmer on Copyright* § 3.04 (1979). Thus, although the derivative work may enter the public domain, the matter contained therein which derives from a work still covered by statutory copyright is not dedicated to the public. *G. Ricordi & Co. v. Paramount Pictures, Inc.*, 189 F.2d 469 (2d Cir.), *cert. denied*, 342 U.S. 849 (1951); *Filmvideo Releasing Corp. v. Hastings*, 426 F.Supp. 690 (S.D.N.Y.1976); *Grove Press, Inc. v. Greenleaf Publishing Co.*, 247 F.Supp. 518 (E.D.N.Y. 1965); 1 *Nimmer on Copyright* § 3.07[C] at 334 (1979). The established doctrine prevents unauthorized copying or other infringing [16] use of the underlying work or any part of that work contained in the derivative product so long as the underlying work itself remains copyrighted. Therefore, since exhibition of the film "Pygmalion" necessarily involves exhibition of parts of Shaw's play, which is still copyrighted, plaintiffs here may prevent defendants from renting the film for exhibition without their authorization.

In 1976 the 1909 Act was revised in its entirety, superseded by the Copyright Act of Oct. 19, 1976, now codified at 17 U.S.C. §§ 101-810 (Supp. 1977), which became wholly effective as of Jan. 1, 1978. In contrast to the earlier act, the 1976 Copyright Act expressly allows use of derivative works "under the terms of the grant" upon termination of the license under which they were produced. 17 U.S.C. § 203(b)(1) (Supp. 1977). Although inapplicable to the case before him, Judge Friendly took this to be "evidence for a belief on the part of Congress of the need for special protection for derivative works." Rohauer v. Killiam Shows, Inc., 551 F.2d at 494.

[15] It is not at all apparent that the Second Circuit would allow its holding in Rohauer v. Killiam Shows, Inc., to extend the limited monopoly permitted by the underlying copyright despite the fear expressed in the student comment, *supra* note 10, at 921. The protection advanced in that case was no doubt limited to the derivative copyright owner's continued use of the derivative work, and not the right to prevent others from using the underlying work once that work falls into the public domain.

[16] A copyright proprietor has an exclusive monopoly over *all* uses of the protected work, including the right to copy, print, vend, publish, make other versions of, perform or exhibit the work. 17 U.S.C. § 1. Thus, we find Judge Friendly's attempt to limit G. Ricordi & Co. v. Paramount Pictures, Inc., *supra* note 11, to its specific facts unconvincing.

Defendants seek finally to avoid this result by citing *Classic Film Museum, Inc. v. Warner Bros., Inc.,* 597 F.2d 13 (1st Cir. 1979), *aff'g* 453 F.Supp. 852 (D.Me.1978). That decision concerned "the legal effect of an expired statutory copyright on work derived from an underlying work in which there exists a common-law copyright". 597 F.2d at 13. Although defendants would have us ignore the major difference between an underlying common-law copyright and an underlying statutory copyright (the former extending in perpetuity,[17] the latter restricted in length) that difference is the linchpin of the court's holding in *Classic Film* that a person could exhibit the motion picture "A Star is Born", on which the film copyright had expired, without infringing the common-law copyright in the unpublished screenplay and musical score from which the film was derived. The court found the *Ricordi* doctrine inapplicable for the following reason:

> [A]ny protection offered by the *Ricordi* doctrine was limited to the fixed life of the underlying copyright (28 years plus the renewal period). The *Ricordi* doctrine is not equally applicable where there is an underlying common-law copyright which might extend indefinitely. Such unending protection of the derivative work would allow the *Ricordi* exception to swallow the rule of limited monopoly found in the constitution and copyright statutes.

597 F.2d at 14. The underlying statutory copyright in the instant case will expire in 1988. After that time Budget may freely distribute its copies of the 1938 film. The result we reach here does not conflict with the limited monopoly policy rooted in the Copyrights Clause of the constitution and advanced in the congressional acts.

For the foregoing reasons, we conclude that defendants' activities here infringed the subsisting copyright in Shaw's play and were properly enjoined.

. . . .

Affirmed.

QUESTIONS

1. The court distinguished the "A Star is Born" case because the underlying screenplay and story there had been covered by a common law copyright, whereas the underlying play "Pygmalion" was covered by statutory copyright. This was, indeed, the same distinction relied upon by the "A Star is Born" court as a means of distinguishing earlier precedents protecting underlying copyrights when derivative copyrights were no longer protected. Of course, in that case the court was deciding the matter under the 1909 Act (when common law copyrights still flourished). Is the distinction a sensible one and one which is consistent with § 2 of the 1909 Act? (Or was it simply a convenient way of distinguishing adverse

---

Rohauer v. Killiam Shows, Inc., 551 F.2d at 493. The 1909 Act made no distinction between a copyright owner's right to authorize copying or exhibition of the work as it appears in an existing derivative work and the right to authorize creation of a new derivative work. Nor did the court in a case involving essentially the same question as that which confronts us. Filmvideo Releasing Corp. v. Hastings, 426 F.Supp. 690 (S.D.N.Y.1976).

[17] A common-law copyright, which exists from the time the original work is created, was lost only upon the proprietor's publication of the matter protected. 1 Nimmer on Copyright § 2.02 at 2.16 (1979). Common-law copyright is no longer recognized under the new Act, 17 U.S.C. § 301 (1978), although one existing prior to January 1, 1978 may continue to receive lengthy protection. 17 U.S.C. §§ 303, 302 (1978). *See, e. g., Classic Film Museum, Inc. v. Warner Bros., Inc.,* 453 F.Supp. at 856 n. 4.

precedent?) How is this distinction affected by the fact that the screenplay "common law" copyright was, by virtue of § 301 of the 1976 Act, absorbed into the statute on January 1, 1978?

2. In the "A Star is Born" case the plaintiff was making the rather unappealing argument that the text of the movie dialogue should remain in common law copyright even though the motion picture itself had fallen into the public domain. While that argument is difficult to abide when the underlying screenplay and the "derivative" script are so similar, would it have more force concerning the "text" of a musical comedy and the music in the production?

3. Which of the "Pygmalion" court's attempts to distinguish *Rohauer v. Killiam Shows, Inc.* do you find the most convincing?

Chapter 4

OWNERSHIP

A. INITIAL OWNERSHIP

1. INDIVISIBILITY

The 1976 Act contains "the first explicit statutory recognition of the principle of divisibility of copyright in our law." H.R. Rep. No. 94-1476 at 123. Repudiation of the concept of indivisibility rooted in prior law was long an important objective of authors and other groups.

The indivisibility concept mandated a single owner or proprietor of copyright at any one time; all others having an interest under the copyright were deemed licensees. The ramifications of indivisibility reached such questions as notice, ownership, recordation of transfers, standing to sue, and taxes. See generally Kaminstein, *Divisibility of Copyright,* 1 STUDIES ON COPYRIGHT 623 (Arthur Fisher Mem. Ed. 1963). Thus, it was early held that the intent, express or necessarily implied by the circumstances, to transfer the entire copyright was necessary for a grantee to be a "proprietor" and that a "mere licensee" could not secure copyright. See *Public Ledger Co. v. New York Times Co.,* 275 F. 562 (S.D.N.Y. 1921), *aff'd,* 279 F. 747 (2d Cir.), *cert. denied,* 258 U.S. 627 (1922). The inconveniences, if not injustices, of such an approach were many. *See* Henn, *Magazine Rights — A Division of Indivisible Copyright,* 40 CORN. L.Q. 411 (1955). For example, an oral "assignment" of a statutory copyright was invalid while oral licenses were not. *Id.* at 439.

The indivisibility doctrine made it advisable for contributing authors and periodicals to structure their arrangement so that a complete transfer or "assignment" to the magazine was effected. A single notice in the name of the magazine would thus secure copyright. *Cf. Kaplan v. Fox Film Corp.,* 19 F. Supp. 780 (S.D.N.Y. 1937). The author would sometimes seek reconveyance of the copyright in his or her contribution. See *Geisel v. Poynter Products, Inc.,* 295 F. Supp. 331, 337-42 (S.D.N.Y. 1968).

The courts had whittled away at the doctrine, perhaps most notably in *Goodis v. United Artists Television, Inc.,* 425 F.2d 397, 165 USPQ 3 (2d Cir. 1970), where the court held that a notice naming a periodical publisher as copyright proprietor protected copyright in a story in which the publisher clearly had only a limited license. This was the logical outgrowth of holdings that under certain circumstances one authorized to secure copyright in his own name may nevertheless hold such copyright in trust for another. See *Manning v. Miller Music Corp.,* 174 F. Supp. 192, 121 USPQ 600 (S.D.N.Y. 1959). *Cf. April Productions, Inc. v. G. Schirmer, Inc.,* 308 N.Y. 366, 105 USPQ 286 (Ct. App. 1955). For example, if it was agreed that a publisher would "attend to the copyrighting" for an author, the author would be the equitable owner of the copyright held by the publisher. *Bisel v. Ladner,* 1 F.2d 436 (3d Cir. 1924). Similarly, where one of three joint owners takes out copyright in his or her own name, he or she is a constructive trustee for the others to the extent of the latter's interest. *Maurel v. Smith,* 271 F. 211 (2d Cir. 1921).

In any event, the 1976 Act expressly contemplates a divisible copyright by providing: " 'Copyright owner', with respect to any one of the exclusive rights comprised in a copyright, refers to the owner of that particular right." § 101. This definition underlies § 201(d)(2) which provides that "[a]ny of the exclusive

231

rights comprised in a copyright, including any subdivision of any of the rights specified by section 106 [the provision enumerating protected rights], may be transferred . . . and owned separately." In line with the definition quoted immediately above, this subsection then provides that "[t]he owner of any particular exclusive right is entitled, to the extent of that right, to all of the protection and remedies accorded to the copyright owner by this title."

The committee reports indicate that this provision may be taken literally. The House report states:

> It is thus clear, for example, that a local broadcasting station holding an exclusive license to transmit a particular work within a particular geographic area and for a particular period of time, could sue, in its own name as copyright owner, someone who infringed that particular exclusive right.

H.R. Rep. No. 94-1476, *supra* at 123. *Cf.* S. Rep. No. 94-473, *supra* at 107.

2. JOINT WORKS: RIGHTS OF CO-OWNERS

Section 201(a) restates the established proposition that "the authors of a joint work are co-owners of copyright in the work." A "joint work" is defined in § 101 as "a work prepared by two or more authors with the intention that their contributions be merged into inseparable or interdependent parts of a unitary whole." A touchstone of collaborative intent follows traditional notions. Thus, in *Maurel v. Smith,* 271 F. 211 (2d Cir. 1921), joint ownership of copyright in an operetta arose through the collaboration of the composer and writers of the scenario, lyrics, and libretto in producing a unitary work.

The new Act's definition emphasizes the authors' intent at the time the writing is done and presumably attempts to contract, at least to some extent, the considerable dilution of the collaborative intent requirement for joint works found in some cases within the Second Circuit. For example, where the complementary efforts were performed at different times by authors unacquainted with each other, their product was held a joint work because they had a common design. *See Edward B. Marks Music Corp. v. Jerry Vogel Music Co., Inc.,* 47 F. Supp. 490, 55 USPQ 288 (S.D. N.Y. 1942). *Cf. Shapiro, Bernstein & Co., Inc. v. Jerry Vogel Music Co., Inc.,* 161 F.2d 406, 71 USPQ 286 (2d Cir. 1946), *cert. denied,* 331 U.S. 820, 73 USPQ 550 (1947) ("Melancholy Baby" held to be a joint work though lyrics were substituted for those written earlier in personal collaboration with composer). It had even been held that an assignee's decision to add words to a melody composed years earlier was sufficient to produce joint ownership. *Shapiro, Bernstein & Co., Inc. v. Jerry Vogel Music Co., Inc.,* 221 F.2d 569, 105 USPQ 178, *modified on rehearing,* 223 F.2d 252, 105 USPQ 460 (2d Cir. 1955) ("Twelfth Street Rag"). *But cf. Szekely v. Eagle Lion Films, Inc.,* 242 F.2d 266, 113 USPQ 98 (2d Cir.), *cert. denied,* 354 U.S. 922, 113 USPQ 549 (1957) (contractual provision requiring author's consent to revision precluded joint work where reviser was engaged without such consent). The new Act clearly intends to reject this expanded concept of "joint works" in the "Twelfth Street Rag" case by its emphasis on the intent of the *authors* at the time their respective contributions were made. *See* S. Rep. No. 94-473, 94th Cong., 1st Sess. 103 (1975); H.R. Rep. No. 94-1476, 94th Cong., 2d Sess. 120 (1976).

The expansion of the concept of joint works within the Second Circuit was probably motivated by a desire to avoid characterization of the works as "composite," with attendant renewal ownership by the proprietor rather than the author. A third alternative is to consider the contributions separable and owned separately by their respective authors. *See Harris v. Coca Cola Co.,* 73 F.2d 370, 23

USPQ 182 (5th Cir. 1934). The result of expansion of joint works was a confusing and potentially unfair array of renewal interests, particularly where derivative works were involved. For example, would the author of a play necessarily be deemed coauthor of a motion picture later using his dramatic material? Although an affirmative answer might well be beyond even the extreme holding in the "Twelfth Street Rag" case, such an approach was expressly rejected in the congressional explanation of joint works. S. Rep. No. 94-473, *supra* at 104; H.R. Rep. No. 94-1476, *supra* at 120.

A joint owner may generally use or license the use of the work without the consent of his or her coowners, but must account to them for their share of profits derived from such license of a third party. *Jerry Vogel Music Co., Inc. v. Miller Music, Inc.,* 272 App. Div. 571, 74 N.Y.S.2d 425, 75 USPQ 205 (1st Dep's 1947), *aff'd,* 299 N.Y. 782, 82 USPQ 458 (1949), and possibly even for his or her own use. *See Crosney v. Edward Small Productions, Inc.,* 52 F. Supp. 559, 59 USPQ 193 (S.D.N.Y. 1942). *But cf. Carter v. Bailey,* 64 Me. 458 (Sup. Ct. 1876). This applies not only to ownership of joint works but also to coownership in other situations, e.g., where rights of a single owner are transferred to several who own an undivided interest.

3. WORKS MADE FOR HIRE

§ 201. Ownership of copyright

. . . .

(b) *Works Made For Hire* — In the case of a work made for hire, the employer or other person for whom the work was prepared is considered the author for purposes of this title, and, unless the parties have expressly agreed otherwise in a written instrument signed by them, owns all of the rights comprised in the copyright.

HOUSE REPORT

H.R. Rep. No. 94-1476, 94th Cong., 2d Sess. 121 (1976)

Section 201(b) of the bill adopts one of the basic principles of the present law: that in the case of works made for hire the employer is considered the author of the work, and is regarded as the initial owner of copyright unless there has been an agreement otherwise. The subsection also requires that any agreement under which the employee is to own rights be in writing and signed by the parties.

The work-made-for-hire provisions of this bill represent a carefully balanced compromise, and as such they do not incorporate the amendments proposed by screenwriters and composers for motion pictures. Their proposal was for the recognition of something similar to the "shop right" doctrine of patent law: with some exceptions, the employer would acquire the right to use the employee's work to the extent needed for purposes of his regular business, but the employee would retain all other rights as long as he or she refrained from the authorizing of competing uses. However, while this change might theoretically improve the bargaining position of screenwriters and others as a group, the practical benefits that individual authors would receive are highly conjectural. The presumption that initial ownership rights vest in the employer for hire is well established in American copyright law, and to exchange that for the uncertainties of the shop right doctrine would not only be of dubious value to employers and employees alike, but might also reopen a number of other issues.

The status of works prepared on special order or commission was a major issue in the development of the definition of "works made for hire" in section 101, which has undergone extensive revision during the legislative process. The basic problem is how to draw a statutory line between those works written on special order or commission that should be considered as "works made for hire," and those that should not. The definition now provided by the bill represents a compromise which, in effect, spells out those specific categories of commissioned works that can be considered "works made for hire" under certain circumstances.

Of these, one of the most important categories is that of "instructional texts." This term is given its own definition in the bill: "a literary, pictorial, or graphic work prepared for publication with the purpose of use in systematic instructional activities." The concept is intended to include what might be loosely called "textbook material," whether or not in book form or prepared in the form of text matter. The basic characteristic of "instructional texts" is the purpose of their preparation for "use in systematic instructional activities," and they are to be distinguished from works prepared for use by a general readership.

BRATTLEBORO PUBLISHING CO. v. WINMILL PUBLISHING CORP.

369 F.2d 565 (2d Cir. 1966)

KAUFMAN, CIRCUIT JUDGE: Appellant publishes a daily newspaper known as the "Brattleboro Daily Reformer" (hereafter Reformer), which is circulated in the environs of Brattleboro, Vermont. Appellee publishes a weekly pamphlet or direct-mail circular known as the "Brattleboro Town Crier" (hereafter Town Crier), and distributes it without charge in the same area. The Reformer contends that through use of a photo off-set printing process, the Town Crier reproduced four advertisements in substantially the same form as had appeared in the Reformer. All the advertisements were published in the Town Crier at the request of the advertisers.

Appellant brought the present action pursuant to 28 U.S.C. § 1338, claiming that the Town Crier had infringed its copyrights in the four advertisements in violation of 17 U.S.C. § 101, and had also engaged in unfair competition and unfair trade practices. Reformer asked the district court to permanently enjoin the Town Crier from any future infringements, and to order it to pay damages and to account for all profits that had resulted from the alleged infringements.

The case was tried before Judge Gibson in the District Court for the District of Vermont. After making certain findings of fact, he concluded that the advertisements could not be copyrighted by the Reformer, and therefore no infringement of any of its copyrights had occurred. He also found that the Town Crier had not been guilty of unfair competition or unfair trade practices, and, accordingly, ordered the suit dismissed. 250 F. Supp. 215 (D. Vt. 1966).

In light of the conclusions we reach, it is not necessary to determine the copyrightability of any of the advertisements in question, and we therefore proceed directly to the grounds for our disposition. Section 26 of the Copyright Act, 17 U.S.C. § 26, provides that the "author" of a work "shall include an employer in the case of works made for hire." Moreover, Professor Nimmer, in his treatise on copyright law, states that there is a presumption in the absence of an express contractual reservation to the contrary, that the copyright shall be in the person at whose instance and expense the work is done. NIMMER ON COPYRIGHT 238 (1964). This so-called "works for hire" doctrine was recognized earlier by the Supreme Court in *Bleistein v. Donaldson Lithographing Co.*, 188 U.S.

239, 248 (1903), and was later codified in the Copyright Act. In *Bleistein*, the Court held that the copyright to certain advertisements created by an employee during the course of his employment, belonged to his employer. While the "works for hire" doctrine has been invoked most frequently in instances involving music publishers, see, e. g., *Tobani v. Carl Fischer, Inc.*, 98 F.2d 57 (2d Cir. 1938), *cert. denied*, 305 U.S. 650 (1938); *Von Tilzer v. Jerry Vogel Music Co.*, 53 F. Supp. 191 (S.D.N.Y. 1943), *aff'd sub nom.*, *Gumm v. Jerry Vogel Music Co.*, 158 F.2d 516 (2d Cir. 1946), it is applicable whenever an employee's work is produced at the instance and expense of his employer. In such circumstances, the employer has been presumed to have the copyright. See, e.g., *Sawyer v. Crowell Publishing Co.*, 46 F.Supp. 471 (S.D.N.Y. 1942), *aff'd*, 142 F.2d 497 (2d Cir.), *cert. denied*, 323 U.S. 735 (1944) (map created by a government employee).

We see no sound reason why these same principles are not applicable when the parties bear the relationship of employer and independent contractor. "Whether the copyright resides in the person thus commissioning the work or in the independent contractor creating the work will always turn on the intention of the parties where that intent can be ascertained." NIMMER, *supra*, at 244. Where that intent cannot be determined, the presumption of copyright ownership runs in favor of the employer. *Ibid.* For example, in *Yardley v. Houghton Mifflin Co.*, 108 F.2d 28 (2d Cir.), *cert. denied*, 309 U.S. 686 (1940), a painter was commissioned to create a mural for the walls of a public school. We held:

> If he is solicited by a patron to execute a commission for pay, the presumption should be indulged that the patron desires to control the publication of copies and that the artist consents that he may, unless by the terms of the contract, express or implicit, the artist has reserved a copyright to himself. *Id.* at 31.

A similar result was reached with respect to pictures taken by a professional photographer, *Lumiere v. Robertson-Cole Distributing Co.*, 280 F. 550 (2d Cir.), *cert. denied*, 259 U.S. 583 (1922), and commercial illustrations designed by an artist for an advertising catalog, *Lin-Brook Builders Hardware v. Gertler*, 352 F.2d 298 (9th Cir. 1965).

In the present case, appellant admits that 95-98% of the advertisements placed by local merchants and published in the Reformer were created in whole or in part by the paper's staff. The price paid by the advertisers to the Reformer for publishing their advertisements included, in effect, a charge for the paper's preparation of the form, words, and illustrations of the advertisements. In these circumstances, absent an agreement to the contrary, the advertisements could not be copyrighted by the Reformer.[3] See *Inter-City Press, Inc. v. Siegfried*, 172 F. Supp. 37 (W.D. Mo. 1958).

Moreover, it is clear that the services of Reformer's advertising department were offered as an inducement to the local businessmen to use appellant's paper

---

[3] It is wholly irrelevant that the Reformer may have complied with the notice requirements, provided in 17 U.S.C. § 20, necessary to protect all copyrightable material contained in the newspaper. It is clear that such notice would only protect those materials which appellant could properly copyright. In this connection, it is interesting that in *Yardley v. Houghton Mifflin Co.*, *supra*, the mural in question contained an inscription that the painter had the copyright. We stated, however, that "His subsequent unilateral act in placing on the painting the copyright notice would be ineffective to modify his contract of employment." 108 F.2d at 31. This is equally true in the present case.

as a medium of exposing their wares to the public. It is of interest that Reformer's soliciting agents failed to inform any local merchant, whose advertising business was actively sought, that the paper would have exclusive copyright control over his advertisement, and that the advertiser (in all instances a small merchant) would be barred for years to come from reproducing it anywhere without the Reformer's consent. It seems likely that the local businessmen, who often cooperated in designing the advertisements, were naive with respect to the complex provisions of the copyright law, and assumed, because of this naivete, that the price they paid the Reformer for publishing their advertisements entitled them to have the same advertisements published elsewhere. It would be unfair in these circumstances to place the burden on the advertiser; it is far more equitable to require the Reformer to provide by express agreement with the advertisers that it shall own any copyright to the advertisements. Cf., *Welles v. Columbia Broadcasting System, Inc.*, 308 F.2d 810 (9th Cir. 1962).

We also agree with Judge Gibson's holding that the Town Crier was not guilty of unfair competition or unfair trade practices.

Affirmed.

Concurrence

LUMBARD, CHIEF JUDGE (concurring): I concur in the holding that in the absence of agreement between newspaper publisher and advertiser the advertiser is entitled to the copyright in the advertisement. While I do not believe that this result can be based on the presumption invoked by the Court, that one who commissions a work owns the copyright in it, because the advertisers here did not pay any extra sum for the design and composition of the advertisements, see *Altman v. New Haven Union Co.*, 254 F. 113, 118 (D. Conn. 1918), I feel that the parties' probable intent requires this result.

bases decision on parties' intent

It is the newspaper publisher who copyrights the material in each issue of the newspaper by a single notice somewhere in the issue. See 17 U.S.C. § 3. On the other hand, the great majority of local advertisers, such as those who paid for the advertisements here at issue, have little or no knowledge of copyright law. It is altogether likely that some or all of them were not even aware that such advertisements might be the subject of copyright. It seems equally likely that they would suppose that after the newspaper had prepared and run their advertisements they could use them again. It would not seem likely to occur to such advertisers that the prices they paid might not cover the cost of preparing the advertisements; nor do they have any way of knowing the economics of the situation.

Under these circumstances, it would be an inequitable interpretation of the copyright law to place the burden of inquiry upon advertisers to whom the need for such inquiry would not suggest itself. It is far more practical and equitable to place upon the newspaper publisher the burden of securing the consent of the advertiser that the copyright should be the property of the publisher, if the publisher feels that he should be protected by copyright against the competition of cheap reproduction by others of advertisements his staff has created.

QUESTIONS

1. After studying the materials on copyright notice, consider whether the masthead notice in the Reformer would have protected the copyright held by the various advertisers in the advertisements printed in that newspaper.

2. Who is the "author" of these advertisements? In the unlikely event that renewal of copyright were to be sought for advertisements first published before

1978, who would be entitled to claim the renewal? *See* Beckett, *The Copyright Act of 1976: When Is It Effective?* 24 BULL. COPYRIGHT SOC'Y 393, 396-99 (1977).

3. What would be the duration of copyright protection for advertisements such as those in the above case which are created and published after 1978? (Would the answer be the same for portrait-photographs which are commissioned by the sitter?)

Ronell   *Berlin*

PICTURE MUSIC, INC. v. BOURNE, INC.

457 F.2d 1213 (2d Cir. 1972)

HAYS, CIRCUIT JUDGE: This is an appeal from a judgment of the United States District Court for the Southern District of New York, which held that appellant had no copyright interest in the song "Who's Afraid of the Big Bad Wolf," and that appellant had infringed appellee's copyright in the song. The opinion of the district court is reported at 314 F. Supp. 640 (S.D.N.Y. 1970), and the facts are set out more fully there.

In May, 1933, Walt Disney Productions, Inc. released an animated cartoon film entitled "The Three Little Pigs." The film contained a musical score, portions of which agents of Disney and Irving Berlin, Inc., appellee's predecessor in interest, believed could be adapted as a popular song. With Disney's approval Berlin asked Ann Ronell, appellant's predecessor in interest, to assist in the adaptation; she did so, rearranging the musical themes in collaboration with an employee of Berlin, and arranging the existing lyrics and adding new ones of her own. The trial court found that the new song was revised somewhat by another employee of Berlin and approved by Disney. In exchange for an agreement to pay certain royalties, Disney assigned all its rights in the new song to Berlin, 314 F. Supp. at 643. Disney later agreed that either one-third or one-fourth of its royalties should be paid to Miss Ronell for her services.

In 1960, the twenty-eighth year of the copyright, when the right to apply for a renewal accrued, 17 U.S.C. § 24 (1970), Miss Ronell for the first time asserted a one-half ownership interest in the copyright as a joint author, and obtained registration in her name, while Bourne, Berlin's assignee, registered as "proprietor."[3] In the present action, appellant, as Miss Ronell's assignee, seeks an adjudication that since 1960 it owned one-half interest in the copyright of the song, together with an accounting of one-half the profits from that date. Appellee has counterclaimed for infringement, alleging as a basis for its claim a new edition of the song published by appellant in 1961. The trial court rejected appellant's claim of ownership and sustained appellee's claim of infringement.

Bourne offered alternative theories in support of its claim to total ownership of the song: (1) that Miss Ronell's contribution was not substantial enough to constitute authorship, and (2) that her contribution was "done for hire," see 314 F. Supp. at 644, and that the "proprietor" was thus entitled to the renewal copyright under Section 24 of the Copyright Act, 17 U.S.C. § 24 (1970). In finding for the appellee, 314 F. Supp. at 647, the trial court appears to have relied principally on the first theory, though it also suggests a theory of assignment in its finding that the conduct of the parties shows that Miss Ronell

---

[3] It is apparently customary for the Register of Copyrights to allow conflicting claimants to register, without making any determination as to the validity of their claims. See Ringer, Renewal of Copyright, in 1 The Copyright Society of the U.S.A., Studies on Copyright 537 (1963).

intended to convey all rights to the work in return for royalties and credits. *Id.* at 652-653. Though the trial court discussed the work for hire doctrine, *id.* at 650-651, it did not explicitly rule on that issue.

We affirm the judgment, but do so on the ground that the findings of the trial court establish the conclusion that Miss Ronell's contribution was work done for hire within the meaning of that term as it is used in the statute. In view of this result we need not reach the issue of whether Miss Ronell's efforts were sufficient to make her an author, or whether she assigned her rights.

As this Court said in *Shapiro, Bernstein & Co. v. Bryan,* 123 F.2d 697, 700 (2d Cir. 1941), "when the employer has become the proprietor of the original copyright because it was made by an employee 'for hire,' the right of renewal goes with it, unlike an assignment." The rationale of this doctrine, which is embodied in Section 24, has been said to be "that the motivating factor in producing the work was the employer who induced the creation . . . ." Note, *Renewal of Copyright — Section 23 of the Copyright Act of 1909 [now Section 24],* 44 COLUM. L. REV. 712, 716 (1944). See also *Brattleboro Publishing Co. v. Winmill Publishing Corp.,* 369 F.2d 565, 567 (2d Cir. 1966) ("there is a presumption . . . that the copyright shall be in the person at whose instance and expense the work is done."). In the present case appellant itself says in its brief that "arrangements were made through [Berlin] for a copy of the entire musical score of the film cartoon to be forwarded by Disney with the express intention of having Ronell create a popular song inspired by the cartoon."

The purpose of the statute is not to be frustrated by conceptualistic formulations of the employment relationship. In *Brattleboro Publishing Co., supra,* this Court held that advertisements designed and printed by a newspaper, obviously at the "instance" of the advertiser, were done for hire. The Court expressly applied the statutory work for hire doctrine to the case of an independent contractor, 369 F.2d at 568, relying in part on *Yardley v. Houghton Mifflin Co.,* 108 F.2d 28 (2d Cir. 1939), *cert. denied,* 309 U.S. 686 (1940), where it was held that one who commissions an artist to paint a mural owns all rights to its reproduction. See also *Dielman v. White,* 102 F. 892 (C.C.D. Mass. 1900), which reached the same result, although the court expressly noted that the "subject of the design [was] largely [the designer's] choice." *Id.* at 892. See *Lin-Brook Builders Hardware v. Gertler,* 352 F.2d 298 (9th Cir. 1965).

Appellant argues that we have held that "an essential element of the employer-employee relationship, [is] the right of the employer 'to direct and supervise the manner in which the writer performs his work,'" *Donaldson Publishing Co., supra,* 375 F.2d, at 643, quoting NIMMER, COPYRIGHT § 62.31 (1964) [now § 62.2 (1971)], and that that "right" is not found in the present case. However, the trial court found that employees of Berlin did in fact make some revisions in Miss Ronell's work. Moreover since Disney had control of the original song on which Miss Ronell's work was based, Disney (and Berlin, with Disney's permission), at all times had the right to "direct and supervise" Miss Ronell's work.

The Court in *Donaldson, supra,* 375 F.2d at 643, listed as among the factors that show that there was no employment for hire, the absence of a fixed salary and the author's "freedom to engage in profitable outside activities without sharing the proceeds with" the alleged employer. *Id.* The absence of a fixed salary, however, is never conclusive, see *Brattleboro Publishing Co., supra;* NIMMER, COPYRIGHT § 62.2 (1971), nor is the freedom to do other work, especially in an independent contractor situation, *Brattleboro Publishing Co., supra. Donaldson* was quite different from the present case since it involved an

[margin note: was work done for hire]

[margin note: where er was motivating factor]

[margin note: agency law / right to control is essential to find relationship]

[margin note: absence of fixed salary is not conclusive]

author who was the dominant person in the corporation alleged to be his employer. In such a situation it could not be said that his work was done at the "instance" of the corporation.

In short, the "motivating factors" in the composition of the new song, "Who's Afraid of the Big Bad Wolf," were Disney and Berlin. They controlled the original song, they took the initiative in engaging Miss Ronell to adapt it, and they had the power to accept, reject, or modify her work. She in turn accepted payment for it without protest, except as to the amount, for 27 years. That she acted in the capacity of an independent contractor does not preclude a finding that the song was done for hire. We so find, and therefore the right to renew the copyright in the song in 1960 accrued exclusively to appellee, the "proprietor."

Affirmed.

OAKES, CIRCUIT JUDGE (concurring); I concur in the result.

---

§ 101. Definitions

As used in this title, the following terms and their variant forms mean the following:

A "work made for hire" is —

(1) a work prepared by an employee within the scope of his or her employment; or

(2) a work specially ordered or commissioned for use as a contribution to a collective work, as a part of a motion picture or other audiovisual work, as a translation, as a supplementary work, as a compilation, as an instructional text, as a test, as answer material for a test, or as an atlas, if the parties expressly agree in a written instrument signed by them that the work shall be considered a work made for hire. For the purpose of the foregoing sentence, a "supplementary work" is a work prepared for publication as a secondary adjunct to a work by another author for the purpose of introducing, concluding, illustrating, explaining, revising, commenting upon, or assisting in the use of the other works, such as forewords, afterwords, pictorial illustrations, maps, charts, tables, editorial notes, musical arrangements, answer material for tests, bibliographies, appendixes, and indexes, and an "instructional text" is a literary, pictorial, or graphic work prepared for publication with the purpose of use in systematic instructional activities.

QUESTIONS

1. If all of the facts in this case had arisen under the 1976 Act, what would be the analysis and result? If the result would be different, is there good reason for Congress to have made such a change? (Consider the same two questions with regard to the *Brattleboro* case.)

2. Does the court in *Picture Music* properly state the holding of the *Brattleboro* case?

B. TRANSFERS AND THEIR RECORDATION AND TERMINATION

§ 201. Ownership of Copyright

. . . .

(d) TRANSFER OF OWNERSHIP. —

(1) The ownership of a copyright may be transferred in whole or in part by any means of conveyance or by operation of law, and may be bequeathed by will or pass as personal property by the applicable laws of intestate succession.

(2) Any of the exclusive rights comprised in a copyright, including any subdivision of any of the rights specified by section 106, may be transferred as provided by clause (1) and owned separately. The owner of any particular exclusive right is entitled, to the extent of that right, to all of the protection and remedies accorded to the copyright owner by this title.

(e) INVOLUNTARY TRANSFER. — When an individual author's ownership of a copyright, or of any of the exclusive rights under a copyright, has not previously been transferred voluntary by the individual author, no action by any governmental body or other official or organization purporting to seize, expropriate, transfer, or exercise rights of ownership with respect to the copyright, or any of the exclusive rights under a copyright, shall be given effect under this title.*

§ 204. Execution of transfers of copyright ownership

(a) A transfer of copyright ownership, other than by operation of law, is not valid unless an instrument of conveyance, or a note or memorandum of the transfer, is in writing and signed by the owner of the rights conveyed or such owner's duly authorized agent.

(b) A certificate of acknowledgement is not required for the validity of a transfer, but is prima facie evidence of the execution of the transfer if—

(1) in the case of a transfer executed in the United States, the certificate is issued by a person authorized to administer oaths within the United States; or

(2) in the case of a transfer executed in a foreign country, the certificate is issued by a diplomatic or consular officer of the United States, or by a person authorized to administer oaths whose authority is proved by a certificate of such an officer.

HOUSE REPORT

H.R. Rep. No. 94-1476, 94th Cong., 2d Sess. 123-24 (1976)

Transfer of ownership

The principle of unlimited alienability of copyright is stated in clause (1) of section 201 (d). Under that provision the ownership of a copyright, or of any part of it, may be transferred by any means of conveyance or by operation of law, and is to be treated as personal property upon the death of the owner. The term "transfer of copyright ownership" is defined in section 101 to cover any "conveyance, alienation, or hypothecation," including assignments, mortgages, and exclusive licenses, but not including nonexclusive licenses. Representatives of motion picture producers have argued that foreclosures of copyright mortgages should not be left to varying State laws, and that the statute should establish a Federal foreclosure system. However, the benefits of such a system would be of

---

* As originally enacted.

very limited application, and would not justify the complicated statutory and procedural requirements that would have to be established.

Clause (2) of subsection (d) contains the first explicit statutory recognition of the principle of divisibility of copyright in our law. This provision, which has long been sought by authors and their representatives, and which has attracted wide support from other groups, means that any of the exclusive rights that go to make up a copyright, including those enumerated in section 106 and any subdivision of them, can be transferred and owned separately. The definition of "transfer of copyright ownership" in section 101 makes clear that the principle of divisibility applies whether or not the transfer is "limited in time or place of effect," and another definition in the same section provides that the term "copyright owner," with respect to any one exclusive right, refers to the owner of that particular right. The last sentence of section 201(d)(2) adds that the owner, with respect to the particular exclusive right he or she owns, is entitled "to all of the protection and remedies accorded to the copyright owner by this title." It is thus clear, for example, that a local broadcasting station holding an exclusive license to transmit a particular work within a particular geographic area and for a particular period of time, could sue, in its own name as copyright owner, someone who infringed that particular exclusive right. . . .

The purpose of [subsection (e)] is to reaffirm the basic principle that the United States copyright of an individual author shall be secured to that author, and cannot be taken away by any involuntary transfer. It is the intent of the subsection that the author be entitled, despite any purported expropriation or involuntary transfer, to continue exercising all rights under the United States statute, and that the governmental body or organization may not enforce or exercise any rights under this title in that situation.

It may sometimes be difficult to ascertain whether a transfer of copyright is voluntary or is coerced by covert pressure. But subsection (e) would protect foreign authors against laws and decrees purporting to divest them of their rights under the United States copyright statute, and would protect authors within the foreign country who choose to resist such covert pressures.

Traditional legal actions that may involve transfer of ownership, such as bankruptcy proceedings and mortgage foreclosures, are not within the scope of this subsection; the authors in such cases have voluntarily consented to these legal processes by their overt actions— for example, by filing in bankruptcy or by hypothecating a copyright.

When the bankruptcy act was comprehensively revised in 1978, this last comment of the House Committee was enacted into law. Section 313 of Pub. L. No. 95-598 adds to the end of Section 201(e) the language "except as provided under Title 11."

BARTSCH v. METRO-GOLDWYN-MAYER, INC.

391 F.2d 150 (2d Cir. 1968)

FRIENDLY, CIRCUIT JUDGE: This appeal from a judgment of the District Court for the Southern District of New York raises the question whether, on the facts here appearing, an assignee of motion picture rights to a musical play is entitled to authorize the telecasting of its copyrighted film. Although the issue seems

considerably closer to us than it did to Judge Bryan, we affirm the judgment
dismissing the complaint of the copyright owner.

In January 1930, the authors, composers, and publishers of and owners of
certain other interests in a German musical play "Wie Einst im Mai," which had
been produced in this country as "Maytime" with a changed libretto and score,
assigned to Hans Bartsch

> the motion picture rights and all our right, title and interest in and in con-
> nection with such motion picture rights of the said operetta or musical play,
> throughout the world, together with the sole and exclusive rights to use, adapt,
> translate, add to and change the said operetta or musical play and the title
> thereof in the making of motion picture photoplays, and to project, transmit
> and otherwise reproduce the said work or any adaptation or version thereof,
> visually or audibly by the art of cinematography or any process analogous
> thereto, and to copyright, vend, license and exhibit such motion picture
> photoplays throughout the world; together with the further sole and exclusive
> rights by mechanical and/or electrical means to record, reproduce and
> transmit sound, including spoken words, dialogue, songs and music, and to
> change such dialogue, if extracted from said works, and to interpolate or use
> other dialogue, songs and music in or in connection with or as part of said
> motion picture photoplays, and the exhibition, reproduction and transmission
> thereof, and to make, use, license, import and vend any and all records or
> other devices required or desired for any such purposes.

In May of that year Bartsch assigned to Warner Bros. Pictures, Inc.

> the motion picture rights throughout the world, in and to a certain musical
> play entitled "WIE EINST IM MAI," libretto and lyrics by Rudolf Schanzer and
> Rudolph Bernauer, music by Walter Kollo and Willy Bredschneider, for the
> full period of all copyrights and any renewed and extended terms thereof,
> together with the sole and exclusive right to use, adapt, translate, add to,
> subtract from, interpolate in and change said musical play, and the title thereof
> (subject so far as the right to use said title is concerned to Paragraph 7 hereof),
> in the making of motion picture photoplays and to project, transmit and
> otherwise reproduce the said musical play or any adaptation or version thereof
> visually or audibly by the art of cinematography or any process analogous
> thereto, and to copyright, vend, license and exhibit such motion picture
> photoplays throughout the world, together with the further sole and exclusive
> right by mechanical and/or electrical means to record, reproduce and transmit
> sound, including spoken words, dialogue, songs and music, and to change such
> dialogue, if extracted from said musical play, and at its own expense and
> responsibility to interpolate and use other dialogue, songs and music in or in
> connection with or as part of said motion picture photoplays, and the
> exhibition, reproduction and transmission thereof, and to make, use, license,
> import, vend and copyright any and all records or other devices made or
> required or desired for any such purposes.

By another clause Bartsch reserved the right to exercise for himself the rights
generally granted to Warner Brothers insofar as these concerned German language motion pictures in certain countries and subject to specified restrictions:

> but it is expressly understood and agreed that nothing herein contained shall
> in any way limit or restrict the absolute right of Purchaser to produce, release,
> distribute and/or exhibit the photoplay or photoplays produced hereunder
> based in whole or in part on "Wie Einst im Mai" and/or "Maytime," in all
> countries of the world, including the territory mentioned in this paragraph, at
> any time, and regardless of the right herein reserved to the Owner.

A further clause recited

> The rights which the Purchaser obtains from the Owner in "Wie Einst im Mai" and/or "Maytime" are specifically limited to those granted herein. All other rights now in existence or which may hereafter come into existence shall always be reserved to the Owner and for his sole benefit, but nothing herein contained shall in any way limit or restrict the rights which Purchaser has acquired or shall hereafter acquire from any other person, firm or corporation in and to "Wie Einst im Mai" and/or "Maytime."

Warner Brothers transferred its rights to defendant Metro-Goldwyn-Mayer, Inc. early in 1935, which made, distributed and exhibited a highly successful motion picture "Maytime." The co-authors of the German libretto, one in 1935 and the other in 1938, transferred all their copyright interests and renewal rights to Bartsch, whose rights in turn have devolved to the plaintiff, his widow. The controversy stems from MGM's licensing its motion picture for television, beginning in 1958.

Although the district judge upheld MGM's contention that the 1930 assignment from Bartsch to Warner Brothers included the right to permit telecasting of the motion picture to be made from the musical play, he thought there was "a further reason why plaintiff cannot prevail in this action," namely, that Bartsch had granted all that he had. This does not do justice to plaintiff's argument. Her position is that in 1930 Bartsch not only did not but could not grant the right to televise the motion picture since, under the similar language of the assignment to him, it was not his to grant; her claim of infringement is based not on the 1930 assignment to Bartsch of the motion picture rights but on the authors' later assignments of the full copyright.

The district court, appearing to consider that defendant's rights turned on the authorization "to project, transmit and otherwise reproduce the said musical play or any adaptation or version thereof visually and audibly by the art of cinematography *or any process analogous thereto,*" concluded that television came within the phrase we have italicized. We have grave doubt on that score. We freely grant that "analogous" is a broader word than "similar," and also that the first step in a telecast of a film, namely, the projection of the motion picture to an electronic pickup, is "analogous" to throwing the picture on a theatre screen. But to characterize the to us nigh miraculous processes whereby these images actuate airwaves so as to cause electronic changes in sets in millions of homes which are then "unscrambled" or "descanned" and thus produce pictures on television screens along with the simultaneous electronic transmission of sound — as "analogous" to cinematography pushes the analogy beyond the breaking point. This is particularly so since the district court's construction would seem to lead to the conclusion that the assignment would entitle the assignee to "project, transmit and otherwise reproduce" the musical play by a live telecast — a right which pretty clearly was not granted and indeed has not been claimed.

As we read the instruments, defendant's rights do not turn on the language we have been discussing but rather on the broad grant, in the assignments to and from Bartsch, of "the motion picture rights throughout the world," which were spelled out to include the right "to copyright, vend, license and exhibit such motion picture photoplays throughout the world." The "to project, transmit and otherwise reproduce" language appears rather to have been directed at how the musical play was to be made into a photoplay. This may well have seemed a more vexing problem in 1930, due to uncertainties as to the best method for linking visual and audible reproduction, cf. *Paramount Publix Corp. v. American Tri-Ergon Corp.,* 294 U.S. 464 (1935), and whether a grant of motion picture rights to a play or novel included the right to sound reproduction, see *L. C. Page & Co. v. Fox Film Corp.*, 83 F.2d 196 (2 Cir. 1936), than today. Being unclear whether sound reproduction would require alterations in previous methods of converting a play into a photoplay, Warner Brothers sought and obtained a considerable degree of freedom in that regard. On this view the clause whose meaning has been so hotly debated is irrelevant to the point here at issue, and decision turns rather on whether a broad assignment of the right "to copyright, vend, license and exhibit such motion picture photoplays throughout the world" includes the right to "license" a broadcaster to "exhibit" the copyrighted motion picture by a telecast without a further grant by the copyright owner.

A threshold issue — which the pre-*Erie L. C. Page* decision was not required to take into account — is whether this question should be determined under state or federal law. The seventeenth paragraph of Bartsch's assignment says, somewhat unhelpfully, that "Each and every term of this agreement shall be construed in accordance with the laws of the United States of America *and* of the State of New York." [Emphasis supplied.] We hold that New York law governs. The development of a "federal common law" of contracts is justified only when required by a distinctive national policy and, as we found in *T.B. Harms v. Eliscu,* 339 F.2d 823, 828 (2 Cir. 1964), citing many cases, "the general interest that copyrights, like all other forms of property, should be enjoyed by their true owner is not enough to meet this . . . test." Contrast *Murphy v. Colonial Savings and Loan Ass'n,* 388 F.2d 609 (2 Cir. 1967), and *Ivy Broadcasting Company, Inc. v. American Telephone & Telegraph Co.,* 391 F.2d 486 (2 Cir. 1968), with *McFaddin Express, Inc. v. Adley Corp.,* 363 F.2d 546 (2 Cir.), *cert. denied,* 385 U.S. 900 (1966). The fact that plaintiff is seeking a remedy granted by Congress to copyright owners removes any problem of federal jurisdiction but does not mean that federal principles must govern the disposition of every aspect of her claim. Cf. *DeSylva v. Ballentine,* 351 U.S. 570 (1956).

Unfortunately, when we turn to state law, we find that it offers little assistance. Two other situations must be distinguished. This is not a case like *Manners v. Morosco,* 252 U.S. 317 (1920), cited with approval, *Underhill v. Schenck,* 238 N.Y. 7, 143 N.E. 773, 33 A.L.R. 303 (1924), in which an all encompassing grant found in one provision must be limited by the context created by other terms of the agreement indicating that the use of the copyrighted material in only one medium was contemplated. The words of Bartsch's assignment, as we have shown, were well designed to give the assignee the broadest rights with respect to *its* copyrighted property, to wit, the photoplay. "Exhibit" means to "display" or to "show" by any method, and nothing in the rest of the grant sufficiently reveals a contrary intention.[1] Nor is this case like *Kirke La Shelle Co. v. Paul Armstrong Co.,* 263 N.Y. 79, 188 N.E. 163 (1938), in which the new medium was completely unknown at the time when the contract was written. Rather, the trial court correctly found that, "During 1930 the future possibilities of television were recognized by knowledgeable people in the entertainment and motion picture industries," though surely not in the scope it has attained. While *Kirke La Shelle* teaches that New York will not charge a grantor with the duty of expressly saving television rights when he could not know of the invention's

---

[1] The plaintiff points to paragraph 13 of the agreement, reproduced in the text, as indicating an intention to exclude television rights. The provision limits the rights of the assignee to those "specifically . . . granted herein," and saves to Bartsch "all other rights now in existence or which may hereafter come into existence." We cannot read this as standing for more than the truism that whatever Bartsch had not granted, he had retained.

existence, we have found no case holding that an experienced businessman like Bartsch is not bound by the natural implications of the language he accepted when he had reason to know of the new medium's potential.[2]

Plaintiff, naturally enough, would not frame the issue in precisely this way. Instead, she argues that even in 1930 Warner Brothers often attempted to obtain an express grant of television rights and that its failure to succeed in Bartsch's case should persuade us that, despite the broad language, only established forms of exhibition were contemplated. She buttresses this argument by producing a number of 1930 assignments to Warner Brothers, some of which specifically granted the right to televise motion pictures and others of which granted full television rights, and by adducing testimony of the Warner Brothers lawyer who had approved the assignment from Bartsch that on many occasions Warner Brothers attempted to secure an express grant of such rights but did not always succeed.

However, this is not enough to show that the Bartsch assignments were a case of that sort. For all that appears Warner Brothers may have decided that, in dealing with Bartsch, it would be better tactics to rely on general words that were sufficiently broad rather than seek an express inclusion and perhaps end up with the opposite, or may have used a form regular in the industry without thinking very precisely about television, or — perhaps most likely — may simply have parroted the language in the grant from Bartsch's assignors to him on the theory it would thus be getting all he had, whatever that might be. Indeed, it is really the assignment to Bartsch rather than the one from him that must control. While plaintiff suggests that Warner Brothers may have furnished Bartsch the forms to be used with his assignors, this is sheer speculation. There is no showing that the form was unique to Warner Brothers; indeed the contrary appears.

With Bartsch dead, his grantors apparently so, and the Warner Brothers lawyer understandably having no recollection of the negotiation, any effort to reconstruct what the parties actually intended nearly forty years ago is doomed to failure. In the end, decision must turn, as Professor Nimmer has suggested, THE LAW OF COPYRIGHT § 125.3 (1964), on a choice between two basic approaches more than on an attempt to distill decisive meaning out of language that very likely had none. As between an approach that "a license of rights in a given medium (e. g., 'motion picture rights') includes only such uses as fall within the unambiguous core meaning of the term (e. g., exhibition of motion picture film in motion picture theaters) and exclude any uses which lie within the ambiguous penumbra (e. g., exhibition of motion picture film on television)" and another whereby "the licensee may properly pursue any uses which may reasonably be said to fall within the medium as described in the license," he prefers the latter. So do we. But see WARNER, RADIO AND TELEVISION RIGHTS § 52 (1953). If the words are broad enough to cover the new use, it seems fairer that the burden of framing and negotiating an exception should fall on the grantor; if Bartsch or his assignors had desired to limit "exhibition" of the motion picture to the conventional method where light is carried from a projector to a screen directly beheld by the viewer, they could have said so. A further reason favoring the broader view in a case like this is that it provides a single person who can

---

[2] In Ettore v. Philco Television Broadcasting Corp., 229 F.2d 481, *cert. denied,* 351 U.S. 926 (1956), the Third Circuit, applying Pennsylvania law, held that a 1935 contract granting moving picture rights did not permit the grantee to televise the film. However, unlike Bartsch, the grantor, Ettore, was not an experienced businessman but a prize fighter, and the Court relied heavily on his lack of sophistication in determining whether it was fair to charge him with knowledge of the new medium. *Id.* at 491, n. 14.

make the copyrighted work available to the public over the penumbral medium, whereas the narrower one involves the risk that a deadlock between the grantor and the grantee might prevent the work's being shown over the new medium at all. Quite apart from the probable impracticality, the assignments are broad enough even on plaintiff's view to prevent the copyright owners from licensing anyone else to make a photoplay for telecasting. The risk that some May might find the nation's television screens bereft of the annual display of "Maytime," interlarded with the usual liberal diet of commercials, is not one a court can take lightly.

Affirmed.

QUESTIONS

1. Note the presumption by the court, near the end of its opinion, that a grant of rights to exploit a work should be construed in a reasonably all-embracing manner. In § 202 of the Copyright Act, in a not dissimilar setting, Congress adopted a different presumption with regard to transfers of a material object which are to be treated as not transferring the copyright as well, even though that might limit the reproduction and exploitation of the work and generate conflicts between the owners of the two different rights. Does this suggest that the court's presumption in *Bartsch* is unsound?

2. Suppose an author grants "the exclusive, complete and entire motion picture rights" in a novel, licensing not only the production and theatrical exhibition of a "photoplay" based on the novel, but also "the right to broadcast and transmit any photoplay produced hereunder by the process of television. . .". Does this grant cover a television *series* of photoplays? *See Goodis v. United Artists Television,* 425 F.2d 397 (2d Cir. 1970).

3. Prior to 1975, television broadcasting was nonexistent in the Republic of South Africa. As a substitute form of entertainment, film libraries made films available on a rental basis for home viewing. Plaintiff, an operator of such a business, entered into an exclusive license for South Africa with defendant, a United States film distributor. The license expressly included "non-theatrical distribution." Plaintiff paid more than $50,000 to secure a modification expressly providing for "video-cassette rights." He thereafter argued that this payment was made as a result of fraud and duress, offering as evidence thereof the fact that video-cassette rights were granted in his original agreement. How convincing is this argument? *See Waldbaum v. Worldvision Enterprises, Inc.,* 203 USPQ 926 (S.D.N.Y. 1978).

4. Does a grant of "all book rights" include paperback books? Translations? Microform? *Cf. Dolch v. Garrard Publishing Co.,* 289 F. Supp. 687 (S.D.N.Y. 1968).

5. Does the requirement in § 204 that transfers of copyright are to be in writing and signed by the grantor affect the result in *Bartsch* or any of the situations described in questions 2, 3 and 4 above?

§ 201. Ownership of Copyright

. . . .

(c) CONTRIBUTIONS TO COLLECTIVE WORKS. — Copyright in each separate contribution to a collective work is distinct from copyright in the collective work as a whole, and vests initially in the author of the contribution. In the absence of an express transfer of the copyright or of any rights under it, the owner of copyright in the collective work is presumed to have acquired only the privilege of reproducing and distributing the contribution as part of that particular collective work, any revision of that collective work, and any later collective work in the same series.

HOUSE REPORT

H.R. Rep. No. 94-1476, 94th Cong., 2d Sess. 122-23 (1976)

Contributions to collective works

Subsection (c) of section 201 deals with the troublesome problem of ownership of copyright in contributions to collective works, and the relationship between copyright ownership in a contribution and in the collective work in which it appears. The first sentence establishes the basic principle that copyright in the individual contribution and copyright in the collective work as a whole are separate and distinct, and that the author of the contribution is, as in every other case, the first owner of copyright in it. Under the definitions in section 101, a "collective work" is a species of "compilation" and, by its nature, must involve the selection, assembly, and arrangement of "a number of contributions." Examples of "collective works" would ordinarily include periodical issues, anthologies, symposia, and collections of the discrete writings of the same authors, but not cases, such as a composition consisting of words and music, a work published with illustrations or front matter, or three one-act plays, where relatively few separate elements have been brought together. Unlike the contents of other types of "compilations," each of the contributions incorporated in a "collective work" must itself constitute a "separate and independent" work, therefore ruling out compilations of information or other uncopyrightable material and works published with editorial revisions or annotations. Moreover, as noted above, there is a basic distinction between a "joint work," where the separate elements merge into a unified whole, and a "collective work," where they remain unintegrated and disparate.

The bill does nothing to change the rights of the owner of copyright in a collective work under the present law. These exclusive rights extend to the elements of compilation and editing that went into the collective work as a whole, as well as the contributions that were written for hire by employees of the owner of the collective work, and those copyrighted contributions that have been transferred in writing to the owner by their authors. However, one of the most significant aims of the bill is to clarify and improve the present confused and frequently unfair legal situation with respect to rights in contributions.

The second sentence of section 201 (c), in conjunction with the provisions of section 404 dealing with copyright notice, will preserve the author's copyright in a contribution even if the contribution does not bear a separate notice in the author's name, and without requiring any unqualified transfer of rights to the owner of the collective work. This is coupled with a presumption that, unless there has been an express transfer of more, the owner of the collective work acquires "only the privilege of reproducing and distributing the contribution as part of that particular collective work, any revision of that collective work, and any later collective work in the same series."

The basic presumption of section 201(c) is fully consistent with present law and practice,* and represents a fair balancing of equities. At the same time, the last

---

* The "basic presumption" of a grant of limited, rather than all rights, by a periodical contributor, when nothing is said, does not appear "fully consistent" with 1909 law interpretations. *See,* e.g., Best Medium Publishing Co. v. National Insider, Inc., 385 F.2d 384 (7th Cir. 1967), *cert. denied,* 390 U.S. 955 (1968). — Eds. note.

clause of the subsection, under which the privilege of republishing the contribution under certain limited circumstances would be presumed, is an essential counterpart of the basic presumption. Under the language of this clause a publishing company could reprint a contribution from one issue in a later issue of its magazine, and could reprint an article from a 1980 edition of an encyclopedia in a 1990 revision of it; the publisher could not revise the contribution itself or include it in a new anthology or an entirely different magazine or other collective work.

RECORDATION OF TRANSFERS AND OTHER DOCUMENTS

"The recording and priority provisions of section 205 [of the 1976 Act] are intended to clear up a number of uncertainties arising from sections 30 and 31 of the present [1909] law and to make them more effective and practical in operation." S. Rep. No. 94-473, *supra* at 112; H.R. Rep. No. 94-1476, *supra* at 128.

A key purpose of recording provisions is, of course, to protect a purchaser or mortgagee against the possibility of a conflicting preexisting grant. Accordingly, the 1909 law provisions (§§ 29-31) were similar in purpose to real estate recording statutes and might have been even more necessary in view of the intangible nature of copyrightable property. The 1976 Act provides that recordation of instruments received in the Copyright Office before January 1, 1978, shall be made in accordance with the 1909 law (Trans. & Suppl. Sec. 109 (90 Stat. 2600)) and it is intended that such recordation would satisfy the provisions of the 1976 Act prescribing recordation as a prerequisite for certain purposes. S. Rep. No. 94-473, *supra* at 161; H.R. Rep. No. 94-1476, *supra* at 181-182. Accordingly, it may be worthwhile to glance briefly at the formal requirements for recordation under the 1909 law. Section 30 provided:

> Every assignment of copyright shall be recorded in the copyright office within three calendar months after its execution in the United States or within six calendar months after its execution without the limits of the United States, in default of which it shall be void as against any subsequent purchaser or mortgagee for a valuable consideration, without notice, whose assignment has been duly recorded.

Failure to record an assignment in the Copyright Office did not invalidate the instrument as between the parties thereto, nor was it available as a defense to an infringer. *New Fiction Publishing Co. v. Star Co.,* 220 F. 994 (S.D.N.Y. 1915). But it must have been recorded before the assignee was entitled under Section 32 to substitute its name for that of the assignor in the copyright notice; otherwise, the copyright was held to be abandoned. *Group Publishers, Inc. v. Winchell,* 86 F. Supp. 573, 83 USPQ 461 (S.D.N.Y. 1949).

The general rule in regard to the actual time of recording was that when the document is lodged in proper form and accompanied by the statutory fee, the recordation exists as of the date of its receipt. *Thompson v. American Law Book Co.,* 119 F. 217 (C.C.S.D. N.Y. 1902).

The number of documents presented to the Office for recordation vastly increased in the latter years under the 1909 Act and they included not only assignments but also mortgages, see *In re Leslie-Judge Co.,* 272 F. 886 (2d Cir. 1921), licenses and contracts covering specific rights embraced in copyright, and even authenticated copies of wills or extracts therefrom. *Witwer v. Harold Lloyd Corp.,* 46 F.2d 792, 795 (S.D. Cal. 1930), *rev'd on other grounds,* 65 F.2d 1 (9th Cir.), *cert. denied,* 296 U.S. 669 (1933); *Commissioner of Internal Revenue v. Wodehouse,* 337 U.S. 369, 401, 81 USPQ 482, 495 (1949) (dissenting opinion).

Whether the recording of these miscellaneous documents operated as constructive notice, as with assignments and mortgages proper, may be open to question, but it would at least have had the effect of giving actual notice to any party making inquiry at the Copyright Office. *See Photo-Drama Motion Picture Co. v. Social Uplift Film Corp.,* 213 F. 374 (S.D.N.Y. 1913), *aff'd,* 220 F. 448 (2d Cir. 1915) (grant of dramatic rights in novel found subject to recordation provision).

The recordation system established by the 1976 Act expressly provides that, in addition to transfers of copyright ownership, any signed document pertaining to a copyright may be recorded (§ 205(a)). Its operation as constructive notice is also expressly provided, subject to two conditions: (1) specific identification of the work and (2) registration of a claim to copyright in the work (§ 205(c)).

Such recordation of a transfer affords the transferee priority over any subsequent transfer later so recorded. The first transferee is also granted a one-month grace period (two months, if the transfer was executed abroad) in which he or she will in any event prevail. Even without observing these time limits, the first transferee may prevail if the subsequent transferee had notice of the earlier transfer or otherwise was not in good faith or had not taken his or her transfer "for valuable consideration or on the basis of a binding promise to pay royalties." (§ 205(e).)

The last requirement undoubtedly changes the result under the 1909 law. See *Rossiter v. Vogel,* 134 F.2d 908, 57 USPQ 161 (2d Cir. 1943) (reliance on other contexts for holding that promise to pay royalties not "valuable consideration" within meaning of Section 30). *Accord, Venus Music Corp. v. Mills Music Inc.,* 261 F.2d 577, 119 USPQ 360 (2d Cir. 1958) (nominal consideration of one dollar also insufficient). *But cf. Rose v. Bourne, Inc.,* 176 F. Supp. 605, 123 USPQ 29 (S.D.N.Y. 1959), *aff'd,* 279 F.2d 79, 125 USPQ 509 (2d Cir.), *cert. denied,* 364 U.S. 880, 127 USPQ 555 (1960) (promise to pay royalties adequate consideration to support assignment as between author and publisher).

The 1976 Act also tackles the difficult problem of priority between conflicting transfers and nonexclusive licenses. It will be recalled that such licenses, being excluded from the definition of a "transfer of copyright ownership," need not even be in writing much less recorded. (Of course, they *may* be recorded.) But whether or not recorded, written, signed nonexclusive licenses prevail over conflicting transfers if the license was taken either before the transfer or in good faith before recordation of the transfer and without notice of it. § 205(f).

An important innovation of the 1976 Act is the establishment of recordation as a prerequisite to an infringement suit. Section 205(d) provides:

> No person claiming by virtue of a transfer to be the owner of copyright or of any exclusive right under a copyright is entitled to institute an infringement action under this title until the instrument of transfer under which such person claims has been recorded in the Copyright Office, but suit may be instituted after such recordation on a cause of action that arose before recordation.

An immediate question arises as to whether "the instrument of transfer under which such person claims" should be read to cover the entire chain of title or only the immediate link in the chain on which plaintiff relies. The latter would seem the only practicable solution where prior links may be unknown or unavailable (or indeed oral); yet the defendant may be prevented from effectively testing the chain of title under such an interpretation. In any event, proprietors must develop new procedures for recording many, if not all, transfers which would not have been previously recorded. This will undoubtedly lead to a "short form" assignment, but care should be taken to make sure that this is "the instrument under which" the plaintiff took title, i.e., the actual grant of rights must have taken place under the recorded instrument.

HOUSE REPORT

H.R. Rep. No. 94-1476, 94th Cong., 2d Sess. 124-28 (1976)

The problem in general

The provisions of section 203 are based on the premise that the reversionary provisions of the present section on copyright renewal (17 U.S.C. sec. 24) should be eliminated, and that the proposed law should substitute for them a provision safeguarding authors against unremunerative transfers. A provision of this sort is needed because of the unequal bargaining position of authors, resulting in part from the impossibility of determining a work's value until it has been exploited. Section 203 reflects a practical compromise that will further the objectives of the copyright law while recognizing the problems and legitimate needs of all interests involved.

Scope of the provision

Instead of being automatic, as is theoretically the case under the present renewal provision, the termination of a transfer or license under section 203 would require the serving of an advance notice within specified time limits and under specified conditions. However, although affirmative action is needed to effect a termination, the right to take this action cannot be waived in advance or contracted away. Under section 203(a) the right of termination would apply only to transfers and licenses executed after the effective date of the new statute, and would have no retroactive effect.

The right of termination would be confined to inter vivos transfers or licenses executed by the author, and would not apply to transfers by the author's successors in interest or to the author's own bequests. The scope of the right would extend not only to any "transfer of copyright ownership," as defined in section 101, but also to nonexclusive licenses. The right of termination would not apply to "works made for hire," which is one of the principal reasons the definition of that term assumed importance in the development of the bill.

Who can terminate a grant

Two issues emerged from the disputes over section 203 as to the persons empowered to terminate a grant: (1) the specific classes of beneficiaries in the case of joint works; and (2) whether anything less than unanimous consent of all those entitled to terminate should be required to make a termination effective. The bill to some extent reflects a compromise on these points, including a recognition of the dangers of one or more beneficiaries being induced to "hold out" and of unknown children or grandchildren being discovered later. The provision can be summarized as follows:

1. In the case of a work of joint authorship, where the grant was signed by two or more of the authors, majority action by those who signed the grant, or by their interests, would be required to terminate it.

2. There are three different situations in which the shares of joint authors, or of a dead author's widow or widower, children, and grandchildren, must be divided under the statute: (1) The right to effect a termination; (2) the ownership of the terminated rights; and (3) the right to make further grants of reverted rights. The respective shares of the authors, and of a dead author's widow or widower, children, and grandchildren, would be divided in exactly the same way in each of these situations. The terms "widow," "widower," and "children" are defined in section 101 in an effort to avoid problems and uncertainties that have arisen under the present renewal section.

3. The principle of per stirpes representation would also be applied in exactly the same way in all three situations. Take for example, a case where a dead author left a widow, two living children, and three grandchildren by a third child who is dead. The widow will own half of the reverted interests, the two children will each own $16^2/_3$ percent, and the three grandchildren will each own a share of roughly $5^1/_2$ percent. But who can exercise the right of termination? Obviously, since she owns 50 percent, the widow is an essential party, but suppose neither of the two surviving children is willing to join her in the termination; is it enough that she gets one of the children of the dead child to join, or can the dead child's interest be exercised only by the action of a majority of his children? Consistent with the per stirpes principle, the interest of a dead child can be exercised only as a unit by majority action of his surviving children. Thus, even though the widow and one grandchild would own $55^1/_2$ percent of the reverted copyright, they would have to be joined by another child or grandchild in order to effect a termination or a further transfer of reverted rights. This principle also applies where, for example, two joint authors executed a grant and one of them is dead; in order to effect a termination, the living author must be joined by a per stirpes majority of the dead author's beneficiaries. The notice of termination may be signed by the specified owners of termination interests or by "their duly authorized agents," which would include the legally appointed guardians or committees of persons incompetent to sign because of age or mental disability.

When a grant can be terminated

Section 203 draws a distinction between the date when a termination becomes effective and the earlier date when the advance notice of termination is served. With respect to the ultimate effective date, section 203(a)(3) provides, as a general rule, that a grant may be terminated during the 5 years following the expiration of a period of 35 years from the execution of the grant. As an exception to this basic 35-year rule, the bill also provides that "if the grant covers the right of publication of the work, the period begins at the end of 35 years from the date of publication of the work under the grant or at the end of 40 years from the date of execution of the grant, whichever term ends earlier." This alternative method of computation is intended to cover cases where years elapse between the signing of a publication contract and the eventual publication of the work.

The effective date of termination, which must be stated in the advance notice, is required to fall within the 5 years following the end of the applicable 35- or 40-year period, but the advance notice itself must be served earlier. Under section 203(a)(4)(A), the notice must be served "not less than two or more than ten years" before the effective date stated in it.

As an example of how these time-limit requirements would operate in practice, we suggest two typical contract situations:

Case 1: Contract for theatrical production signed on September 2, 1987. Termination of grant can be made to take effect between September 2, 2022 (35 years from execution) and September 1, 2027 (end of 5 year termination period). Assuming that the author decides to terminate on September 1, 2022 (the earliest possible date) the advance notice must be filed between September 1, 2012 and September 1, 2020.

Case 2: Contract for book publication executed on April 10, 1980; book finally published on August 23, 1987. Since contract covers the right of publication, the 5-year termination period would begin on April 10, 2020 (40 years from execution) rather than April 10, 2015 (35 years from execution) or August 23, 2022 (35 years from publication). Assuming that the author decides to make the termination effective on January 1, 2024, the advance notice would have to be served between January 1, 2014, and January 1, 2022.

Effect of termination

Section 203(b) makes clear that, unless effectively terminated within the applicable 5-year period, all rights covered by an existing grant will continue unchanged, and that rights under other Federal, State, or foreign laws are unaffected. However, assuming that a copyright transfer or license is terminated under section 203, who are bound by the termination and how are they affected?

Under the bill, termination means that ownership of the rights covered by the terminated grant reverts to everyone who owns termination interests on the date the notice of termination was served, whether they joined in signing the notice or not. In other words, if a person could have signed the notice, that person is bound by the action of the majority who did; the termination of the grant will be effective as to that person, and a proportionate share of the reverted rights automatically vests in that person. Ownership is divided proportionately on the same per stirpes basis as that provided for the right to effect termination under section 203(a) and, since the reverted rights vest on the date notice is served, the heirs of a dead beneficiary would inherit his or her share.

Under clause (3) of subsection (b), majority action is required to make a further grant of reverted rights. A problem here, of course, is that years may have passed between the time the reverted rights vested and the time the new owners want to make a further transfer; people may have died and children may have been born in the interim. To deal with this problem, the bill looks back to the date of vesting; out of the group in whom rights vested on that date, it requires the further transfer or license to be signed by "the same number and proportion of the owners" (though not necessarily the same individuals) as were then required to terminate the grant under subsection (a). If some of those in whom the rights originally vested have died, their "legal representatives, legatees, or heirs at law" may represent them for this purpose and, as in the case of the termination itself, any one of the minority who does not join in the further grant is nevertheless bound by it.

An important limitation on the rights of a copyright owner under a terminated grant is specified in section 203(b)(1). This clause provides that, notwithstanding a termination, a derivative work prepared earlier may "continue to be utilized" under the conditions of the terminated grant; the clause adds, however, that this privilege is not broad enough to permit the preparation of other derivative works. In other words, a film made from a play could continue to be licensed for performance after the motion picture contract had been terminated but any remake rights covered by the contract would be cut off. For this purpose, a motion picture would be considered as a "derivative work" with respect to every "preexisting work" incorporated in it, whether the preexisting work was created independently or was prepared expressly for the motion picture.

Section 203 would not prevent the parties to a transfer or license from voluntarily agreeing at any time to terminate an existing grant and negotiating a new one, thereby causing another 35-year period to start running. However, the bill seeks to avoid the situation that has arisen under the present renewal provision, in which third parties have bought up contingent future interests as a form of speculation. Section 203(b)(4) would make a further grant of rights that revert under a terminated grant valid "only if it is made after the effective date of the termination." An exception, in the nature of a right of "first refusal," would permit the original grantee or a successor of such grantee to negotiate a new agreement with the persons effecting the termination at any time after the notice of termination has been served.

Nothing contained in this section or elsewhere in this legislation is intended to extend the duration of any license, transfer or assignment made for a period of less than thirty-five ,years. If, for example, an agreement provides an earlier termination date or lesser duration, or if it allows the author the right of cancelling or terminating the agreement under certain circumstances, the duration is governed by the agreement. Likewise, nothing in this section or legislation is intended to change the existing state of the law of contracts concerning the circumstances in which an author may cancel or terminate a license, transfer, or assignment.

Section 203(b)(6) provides that, unless and until termination is effected under this section, the grant, "if it does not provide otherwise," continues for the term of copyright. This section means that, if the agreement does not contain provisions specifying its term or duration, and the author has not terminated the agreement under this section, the agreement continues for the term of the copyright, subject to any right of termination under circumstances which may be specified therein. If, however, an agreement does contain provisions governing its duration — for example, a term of fifty years — and the author has not exercised his or her right of termination under the statute, the agreement will continue according to its terms — in this example, for only fifty years. The quoted language is not to be construed as requiring agreements to reserve the right of termination.

SUMMARY OF TERMINATION PROVISIONS UNDER § 203

1. Grants covered

(a) transfers *or* licenses of *any* rights under copyright — exclusive or non-exclusive

(b) executed *on or after* January 1, 1978

(c) by an author

(d) as to *any* work — i.e., created before or after January 1, 1978 and whether, on that date, work was subject to common law (§ 303), statutory first term (§ 304(a)), renewal (§ 304(b)), life-plus-fifty (§ 302(a)) or alternative fixed term (§ 302(c)) protection

(e) except as to:

(i) works made for hire

(ii) dispositions by will

2. *Persons who may exercise right*

(a) the author or a majority of the authors who made grant

(b) if an author is dead, his or her right may be exercised by (or if he or she was one of joint authors, his or her interest may be "voted" by) majority action of the owners of more than one-half of author's termination interest, such interest being owned as follows:

> (i) by surviving spouse (if no children or grandchildren)
>
> (ii) by children and surviving children of deceased child (if no surviving spouse) or
>
> (iii) shared, one-half by widow and one-half by children and deceased child's children (per stirpes and by majority action)

3. *Effective date of termination*

(a) designated time during 36th through 40th year after grant or

(b) if grant covers right of publication, designated time during five-year period beginning on the earlier of the following dates:

> (i) 35 years after publication
>
> (ii) 40 years after grant

(c) Upon 2-10 years notice

4. *Manner of terminating*

(a) written and signed notice by required persons to "grantee or grantee's successor in title"

(b) specification of effective date, within above limits

(c) form, content and manner of service in accordance with Copyright Office regulation

(d) recordation in Copyright Office before effective date

(e) termination right may not be waived or contracted away in advance

(f) interests under termination vest on service of notice

5. *Effect of termination*

reversion to author, authors or others owning author's termination interest (including those who did not join in signing termination notice) in proportionate shares

6. *Exceptions to termination*

(a) utilization of derivative work made under grant prior to termination (but no right to make a new derivative work)

(b) rights outside federal copyright statute

7. *Further grants of terminated rights*

(a) must be made by same number and proportion of owners required for termination, then binds all

(b) must be made after termination, except, as to original grantee or successor in title, agreement may be made after service of notice of termination

HOUSE REPORT: § 304

H.R. Rep. No. 94-1476, 94th Cong., 2d Sess. 140-42 (1976)

. . . .

Termination of grants covering extended term

An issue underlying the 19-year extension of renewal terms under both subsections (a) and (b) of section 304 is whether, in a case where their rights have already been transferred, the author or the dependents of the author should be given a chance to benefit from the extended term. The arguments for granting rights of termination are even more persuasive under section 304 than they are under section 203; the extended term represents a completely new property right, and there are strong reasons for giving the author, who is the fundamental beneficiary of copyright under the Constitution, an opportunity to share in it.

Subsection (c) of section 304 is a close but not exact counterpart of section 203. In the case of either a first-term or renewal copyright already subsisting when the new statute becomes effective, any grant of rights covering the renewal copyright in the work, executed before the effective date, may be terminated under conditions and limitations similar to those provided in section 203. Except for transfers and licenses covering renewal copyrights already extended under Public Laws 87-668, 89-142, 90-141, 90-416, 91-147, 91-555, 92-170, 92-566, and 93-573, which would become subject to termination immediately upon the coming into effect of the revised law, the 5-year period during which termination could be made effective would start 56 years after copyright was originally secured.

The bill distinguishes between the persons who can terminate a grant under section 203 and those entitled to terminate a grant covering an extended term under section 304. Instead of being limited to transfers and licenses executed by the author, the right of termination under section 304(c) also extends to grants executed by those beneficiaries of the author who can claim renewal under the present law: his or her widow or widower, children, executors, or next of kin.

There is good reason for this difference. Under section 203, an author's widow or widower and children are given rights of termination if the author is dead, but these rights apply only to grants by the author, and any effort by a widow, widower, or child to transfer contingent future interests under a termination would be ineffective. In contrast, under the present renewal provisions, any statutory beneficiary of the author can make a valid transfer or license of future renewal rights, which is completely binding if the author is dead and the person who executed the grant turns out to be the proper renewal claimant. Because of this, a great many contingent transfers of future renewal rights have been obtained from widows, widowers, children, and next of kin, and a substantial number of these will be binding. After the present 28-year renewal period has ended, a statutory beneficiary who has signed a disadvantageous grant of this sort should have the opportunity to reclaim the extended term.

As explained above in connection with section 203, the bill adopts the principle that, where a transfer or license by the author is involved, termination may be effected by a per stirpes majority of those entitled to terminate, and this principle also applies to the ownership of rights under a termination and to the making of further grants of reverted rights. In general, this principle has also been adopted with respect to the termination of rights under an extended renewal copyright in section 304, but with several differences made necessary by the differences between the legal status of transfers and licenses made after the effective date of the new law (governed by section 203) and that of grants of renewal rights made earlier and governed by section 304(c). The following are the most important distinctions between the termination rights under the two sections:

1. Joint authorship. — Under section 304, a grant of renewal rights executed by joint authors during the first term of copyright would be effective only as to those who were living at the time of renewal; where any of them are dead, their statutory beneficiaries are entitled to claim the renewal independently as a new estate. It would therefore be inappropriate to impose a requirement of majority action with respect to transfers executed by two or more joint authors.

2. Grants not executed by author. — Section 304(c) adopts the majority principle underlying the amendments of section 203 with respect to the termination rights of a dead author's widow or widower and children. There is much less reason, as a matter of policy, to apply this principle in the case of transfers and licenses of renewal rights executed under the present law by the author's widow, widower, children, executors, or next of kin, and the practical arguments against doing so are conclusive. It is not clear how the shares of a class of renewal beneficiaries are to be divided under the existing law, and greater difficulties would be presented if any attempt were made to apply the majority principle to further beneficiaries in cases where one or more of the renewal beneficiaries are dead. Therefore, where the grant was executed by a person or persons other than the author, termination can be effected only by the unanimous action of the survivors of those who executed it.

3. Further grants. — The reason against adopting a principle of majority action with respect to the right to terminate grants by joint authors and grants not executed by the author apply equally with respect to the right to make further grants under section 304(c). The requirement for majority action in clause (6)(c) is therefore confined to cases where the rights under a grant by the author have reverted to his or her widow or widower, or children, or both. Where the extended term reverts to joint authors or to a class of renewal beneficiaries who have joined in executing a grant, their rights would be governed by the general rules of tenancy in common; each coowner would have an independent right to sell his share, or to use or license the work subject to an accounting.

Nothing contained in this section or elsewhere in this legislation is intended to extend the duration of any license, transfer, or assignment made for a period of less than fifty-six years. If, for example, an agreement provides an earlier termination date or lesser duration, or if it allows the author the right of cancelling or terminating the agreement under certain circumstances, the duration is governed by the agreement. Likewise, nothing in this section or legislation is intended to change the existing state of the law of contracts concerning the circumstances in which an author may terminate a license, transfer or assignment.

Section 304(c)(6)(E) provides that, unless and until termination is effected under this section, the grant, "if it does not provide otherwise," continues for the term of copyright. This section means that, if the agreement does not contain provisions specifying its term or duration, and the author has not terminated the agreement under this section, the agreement continues for the term of the copyright, subject to any right of termination under circumstances which may be specified therein. If, however, an agreement does contain provisions governing its duration — for example, a term of sixty years — and the author has not exercised his or her right of termination under the statute, the agreement will continue according to its terms — in this example, for only sixty years. The quoted language is not to be construed as requiring agreements to reserve the right of termination.

SUMMARY OF TERMINATION PROVISIONS UNDER § 304(c)

1. *Grants covered*

   (a) transfers *or* licenses of *renewal* rights — exclusive or nonexclusive
   (b) executed *before* January 1, 1978
   (c) by a person designated by the second proviso of § 304(a)
   (d) where statutory copyright — first or renewal term — is subsisting on January 1, 1978 (common law copyrights are not covered)
   (e) except as to
      (i) works made for hire
      (ii) dispositions by will

2. *Persons who may exercise right*

   (a) as to grants by author(s):
      (i) the author(s) to extent of such author(s)' interest
      (ii) if an author is dead, by owners of more than one-half of author's termination interest, such interest being owned as follows:

      (A) By surviving spouse (if no children or grandchildren)
      (B) By children and surviving children of dead child (if no surviving spouse) or
      (C) shared, one-half by widow and one-half by children and deceased's child's children (per stirpes and by majority action)
   (b) as to grants by others — *all* surviving grantors

3. *Effective date of termination*

   (a) Designated time during five-year period beginning on *later* of following dates:
      (i) end of 56th year of copyright *or*
      (ii) January 1, 1978
   (b) Upon 2-10 years notice

4. *Manner of terminating*

   (a) written and signed notice by required persons or agents to grantee or grantee's "successor in title"
   (b) specification of effective date, within above limits
   (c) form, content and manner of service in accordance with Copyright Office regulations (These have now been issued. 37 CFR § 201.10.)
   (d) recordation in Copyright Office before effective date
   (e) termination right may not be waived or contracted away in advance
   (f) interests under termination vest on service of notice

5. *Effect of a termination*

   (a) of grant by author
      (i) reversion to that author or, if dead, those owning author's termination interest (including those who did not join in signing termination notice) in proportionate shares

(b) of grant by others — reversion to all entitled to terminate

(c) in either case, future rights to revert vest upon proper service of notice of termination

6. *Exceptions to termination*

(a) utilization of derivative work prepared under grant prior to termination (no right to make another derivative work)

(b) rights outside federal copyright statute

7. *Further grants of terminated rights*

(a) each owner is tenant in common except that a further grant by owners of particular dead author's rights must by same number and proportion of his beneficiaries as required to terminate, but then binds them all, including non-signers, as to such rights

(b) must be made after termination, except that, as to original grantee or successor in title, agreement may be after *notice* of termination

COMPARISON OF TERMINATION PROVISIONS

The key distinctions between termination rights under § 304(c) and § 203 may be summarized as follows:

1. *Grants Covered*

§ 304(c)	*§ 203*
(a) before Jan. 1., 1978	(a) on or after Jan. 1, 1978
(b) by author or other person designated by second proviso of § 304(a)	(b) by author
(c) of renewal right in statutory copyright	(c) of any right under any copyright

2. *Persons Who May Exercise*

Author or majority interest of his statutory beneficiaries (per stirpes) to the extent of that author's share or in case of grant by others, *all* surviving grantors	Author or majority of granting authors or majority of their respective beneficiaries, voting as a unit for each author and per stirpes

3. *Beginning of Five-Year Termination Period*

End of 56 years of copyright or January 1, 1978, whichever is later	End of 35 years from grant, or if covering publication right, either 35 years from publication or 40 years from grant whichever is earlier

4. *Further Grants*

Generally tenants in common with right to deal separately, except where dead author's rights are shared, then majority action (per stirpes) as to that author's share	Requires same number and proportion as required for termination

TRANSFERS, RENEWALS AND TERMINATIONS

1. Work is created, published and copyrighted in 1960. In 1960, Author (hereinafter *A*) assigns the initial and renewal terms to *B*. If *A* lives until 1987, the assignment to *B* is effective and *A* will take the renewal on behalf of *B*. If *A* dies before 1987, leaving Widow (hereinafter *W*), *W* is entitled to claim the renewal, and *B* will have no rights in the renewal term. (These results flow from § 304(a), as embellished (in its earlier form as § 24 of the 1909 Act) by *Fred Fisher Music Co. v. M. Witmark & Sons,* 318 U.S. 643 (1943).

However, the additional nineteen years added to the renewal term by the 1976 Act can be recaptured by the giving of timely notice to *B*. If when notice is given, *A* is alive, then it is *A* who is entitled to give the notice. If when notice is given, *A* is dead and *W* is alive, then it is *W* who is entitled to give the notice. The right to give this notice and recapture the added nineteen years of the renewal term cannot be waived or assigned in advance by either *A* or *W*. (These results flow from § 304(c).)

2. Work is created (and therefore automatically copyrighted) by *A* in 1980. *A* transfers inter vivos his copyright (which will last for his life plus fifty years) to *B* the same year. That transfer may be terminated effective thirty-five to forty years thereafter (i.e., beginning in 2015) by timely notice. If, when notice of termination is given, *A* is alive, then it is *A* who is entitled to give the notice and claim the "reversion." If, when notice is given, *A* is dead and *W* is alive, then it is *W* who is entitled to give the notice and claim the "reversion." Neither *A* nor *W* can waive or assign in advance that power to terminate. (These results flow from § 203(a).)

3. As in case 2 work is created by *A* in 1980, but *A* transfers his copyright to *B* by a will upon his death in 1980, rather than inter vivos. The transfer may *not* be terminated and the copyright may *not* be recaptured by *W*, at any date in the future. (*See* § 203(a).) Is there any sense to the different outcomes in case 2 and case 3?

4. Work is created, published and copyrighted in 1960 by *A*. In 1980, *A* assigns the initial and renewal terms to *B*.

If *A* lives into 1987, the assignment to *B* of the renewal term will be effective: under *Fisher v. Witmark,* *A* will apply for the renewal but *B* will really own it. *A* will not be able to recapture the added nineteen years of the renewal term pursuant to § 304(c), since that section governs only transfers executed prior to January 1, 1978, and this transfer was made by *A* in 1980. Therefore, *B* will be entitled to ownership of the renewal term throughout its duration, 1988 through 2035.

However, § 203 *will* govern, since the transfer by *A* to *B* was executed after January 1, 1978. Therefore, *A* may "recapture" the copyright thirty-five years after the 1980 transfer, or in 2015, even though at that time there are still twenty years remaining in *B*'s renewal term. And, if *A* dies between 1987 when he renewed and 2015, then his widow *W* can exercise the termination right under

§ 203. In short, although *W* cannot oust *B* of his right to claim the renewal under these facts, she can shorten the renewal term enjoyed by *B*, simply by a timely termination.

5. As in case 4, the work is created, published and copyrighted by *A* in 1960, and the initial and renewal terms are assigned by *A* to *B* in 1980. However, *A* dies before 1987. By § 304(a), the assignment of the renewal term is ineffective, and *W* will be entitled to secure the renewal term, to the exclusion of *B*.

6. Finally, as in the above two cases, the work is created, published and copyrighted by *A* in 1960. *A* dies in 1980, and by will transfers the initial and renewal terms to *B*. *W* will not be able to terminate that transfer in 2015, pursuant to § 203, because the transfer by *A* was not inter vivos. But do not anguish for *W* just yet. Although *A* can, in 1980, assign the remaining eight years of the initial term — either inter vivos or by will — his death before 1987 makes *W* the proper claimant of the renewal term, to the exclusion of *B*.

QUESTIONS

1. Author secures copyright in his novel in 1950, and in 1970 he executes a will in which he purports to devise the initial and renewal terms of the copyright to Princeton University. In 1978 he applies for and secures a renewal of the copyright. Author dies in 1980, leaving three daughters. In the year 2006 (fifty-six years from the date of the initial copyright, and twenty-eight years from the beginning of the renewal term) the daughters seek to join together to terminate the transfer of the renewal term in order to enjoy the remaining nineteen years of that term. May they do so under the 1976 Copyright Act? If not, why not?

2. Author creates a work in 1979, and transfers his copyright to Publisher by a will upon his death in 1980. At his death, Author leaves a widow, a son and a daughter. In the year 2015, thirty-five years from the date of the transfer of the copyright to Publisher, Author's widow, son and daughter are still living and wish to terminate the transfer in order to enjoy the remaining fifteen years of the copyright term. May they do so under the 1976 Copyright Act? If not, why not?

3. Section 203(a)(5) explicitly seeks to assure that the termination right will not be bargained away by the author and his family at the same time (or later) as they transfer their interest in the copyright itself. As attorney for the transferee of the copyright, is there a contract provision you can draft which would permit you, in effect, to prolong the transfer for more than thirty-five years? For example, would it be effective to provide that the grant shall terminate in thirty years and that the author (and any spouse and children making the initial grant) shall be obligated to re-transfer the copyright for an additional thirty years at a stipulated price? (Even assuming some such provision to comply technically with the statute, would you as counsel conclude that this so frustrates the spirit of § 203(a)(5) that it would be improper for you to insert this in the contract of transfer?)

4. Suppose a grant is made in 1978 by an author who later decides to terminate at the earliest possible moment. To exercise his thirty-five-year termination right in 2013, he may give notice ten years earlier, in 2003. Although § 203 provides (as does § 304(c)) that the future right to be terminated "vest" upon the service of such notice, we still have the renewal provision to reckon with, since 2003 is only the twenty-fifth year of the first-term copyright. If the author dies shortly after serving notice of termination and his widow renews two years later, what is the effect of the author's termination notice? The clash of these two

provisions with the same reversionary objective is pointed out in Dreben, *Section 203 and a Call for a Hurried Review,* in *The Copyright Act of 1976: Dealing with the New Realities,* 229, 232-33 (N.J.L.J.-Copyright Soc'y 1977).

5. Is a termination right available in the following situations: (a) Work is created, published and copyrighted in 1975. In 1980, *both* the author and his wife assign original and renewal copyrights to B. A dies in 1985 and W renews in 2003. (b) A produces a manuscript in 1976 pursuant to a 1974 agreement. The work is published in 1978.

Chapter 5

FORMALITIES

A. PUBLICATION AND NOTICE BEFORE THE 1976 ACT

The pivot of the 1909 law was the concept of "publication." This event was generally the dividing line between common law protection on the one hand and either statutory or no protection on the other. Thus, the traditional litany was that publication with the prescribed copyright notice secured statutory copyright, while publication without such notice placed a work in the public domain. As a corollary, the term of copyright was measured from "the date of first publication" according to § 24 of the statute, and other ramifications of publication pervaded the statute. See, e.g., § 1(a) (exclusive right to "publish"), § 8 (Government "publications"), § 9(c) (nationality of the author at time of "publication").

Because of the potentially crucial impact of publication on the existence or unavailability of protection, the courts imparted a considerable gloss to the term. Accordingly, "publication" in copyright matters has meant different things in different contexts. Its significance in dividing federal and state protection was diluted even under the 1909 law by a statutory option to register certain classes of works in unpublished form (§ 12), and by the judicial recognition of areas of state protection for published works. See Goldstein v. California, 412 U.S. 546, 178 USPQ 129 (1973).

In any event, the adoption of a single federal statutory copyright from creation, instead of a dual system with publication as its line of bifurcation, has been considered to "accomplish a fundamental and significant change" in copyright law. S. Rep. No. 94-473, 94th Cong., 1st Sess. 112 (1975); H.R. Rep. No. 94-1476, 94th Cong., 2d Sess. 129 (1976). This by no means should suggest that publication is not important under the 1976 Act. Its pervasive impact will be examined in a number of contexts. For example, its role in determining duration for anonymous and pseudonymous works and works made for hire has already been noted.

But the significance of publication under the 1909 law also remains with us, both directly and indirectly. Its indirect significance is its precedential value in filling the interstices of the 1976 Act definition. Its direct significance is based on the underlying principle that the new law "does not provide copyright protection for any work that goes into the public domain before January 1, 1978." Trans. & Suppl. Sec. 103 (90 Stat. 2599). Thus, it seems inescapable that a court reviewing an alleged infringement committed in 1980, with respect to a work arguably first "published" in 1970, will examine the statutory conditions of protection in 1970 to determine whether or not the work was in the public domain on January 1, 1978. See Nimmer, *Preface — The Old Copyright Act as a Part of the New Act,* 22 N.Y.L.S. L. Rev. 471 (1977). Among these will be the question whether "publication" has taken place at all and, if so, whether publication occurred with or without a notice proper under the 1909 Act. Of course, as the principles of the 1976 Act become judicially absorbed, one may foresee possible application of some of its philosophy to 1909 Act situations, even as, ironically, some 1909 Act cases were decided before January 1, 1978, with a glance at the impending 1976 Act. See, e.g., *Rohauer v. Killiam Shows, Inc.,* 551 F.2d 484, 192

USPQ 545 (2d Cir.), *cert. denied,* 431 U.S. 949, 194 USPQ 304 (1977); *Goodis v. v. United Artists Television, Inc.,* 425 F.2d 397, 403, 165 USPQ 3, 7 (2d Cir. 1970).

In any event, one would be foolhardy to approach the problem of a 1970 publication without a knowledge of the pertinent provisions and judicial construction of the 1909 Act.

The starting point of this study is § 10 of the 1909 Act which provides: "Any person entitled thereto by this title may secure copyright for his work by publication thereof with the notice of copyright required by this title...." (Emphasis added.) Publication, as the traditional requirement for statutory protection in this country, results from the legendary bargain between the public and the author reflected in a statutory system of copyright as construed by *Donaldson v. Becket,* 4 Burrows 2303, 98 Eng. Rep. 257 (1774). In order to induce the author to disclose his work to the public notwithstanding the resulting loss of his common law protection, the statute substitutes new rights, albeit limited in time.

It is for this reason that for many works publication was not only the appropriate requisite for statutory protection but, as noted above, also the point from which the term of protection has been computed (§ 24). What is perhaps less expected is that the concept of "publication" as utilized in § 10 developed into a rather technical construct; it is not always coterminous with the general notion of "making public," nor even with the act which divests the author of common law rights.

1. "DIVESTITIVE" VERSUS "INVESTITIVE" PUBLICATION

It had long been assumed that the point at which the disclosure of a work becomes sufficiently extensive and unrestricted to cause forfeiture of common law rights should be precisely the instant at which, assuming proper observance of the notice requirement, statutory protection might be secured. There is undeniably abstract justice in such a result. But courts are faced with specific cases, many of which present the possibility of an unintentional and irrevocable forfeiture of all rights in a work. For example, an author innocently distributes a number of copies of his work without the proper notice. If this distribution is considered a "publication," common law rights are extinguished and the author can forever have forfeited his right to secure statutory copyright. *Wheaton v. Peters,* 33 U.S. (8 Pet.) 591 (1834). Apparently because of the harshness of this result, a judicial trend, acknowledged relatively late in the day, demanded a more convincing showing of extensive and unrestricted distribution for loss of copyright than would be required of an author who has affixed a notice to copies of his work and seeks to invoke Section 10. *See American Visuals Corp. v. Holland,* 239 F.2d 740, 743, 111 USPQ 288, 290 (2d Cir. 1956). On the other hand, the perpetual rights enjoyed under the common law led a few courts to the view that commercial exploitation of a work should terminate common law protection, even if such exploitation does not amount to "publication" under Section 10. *See Shapiro, Bernstein & Co., Inc. v. Miracle Record Co.,* 91 F. Supp. 473, 475, 85 USPQ 39, 40, 86 USPQ 193 (N.D. Ill. 1950). But see *Rosette v. Rainbo Record Mfg. Corp.,* 354 F. Supp. 1183, 177 USPQ 631 (S.D. N.Y. 1973), *aff'd per curiam,* 546 F.2d 461, 192 USPQ 673 (2d Cir. 1976). Thus, in a number of different contexts to be examined below, attention should be paid to the possibility of divergent definitions of "publication."

2. DEFINITION OF "PUBLICATION"

The 1909 Act did not expressly define "publication." This omission was apparently based on the assumption that a general definition of this concept was too difficult. *Hearings on S. 6330 and H.R. 19853 Before Committee on Patents,* 59th Cong., 1st Sess. 71 (June 1906). In § 26, however, we are told that in the case of a work "of which copies are reproduced for sale or distribution," "the 'date of publication' shall . . . be held to be the earliest date when copies of the first authorized edition were placed on sale, sold or publicly distributed by the proprietor of the copyright or under his authority." As noted by the court in *Cardinal Film Co. v. Beck,* 248 F. 368 (S.D.N.Y. 1918), the section was evidently intended to fix the date from which the term of copyright should begin to run for such a work, rather than to provide a general definition of what should constitute publication in all cases. The importance of the actual date of publication arose because, in the case of every work copyrighted in the first instance by publication with notice, the first term of 28 years began to run from that date; hence any error on the part of the applicant could have had serious consequences, especially in connection with applications for renewals of copyright, which had to be made "within one year prior to the expiration of the original term of copyright." (This problem is avoided in the 1976 Act by the calendar-year ending of all terms, including those with renewals.)

3. LIMITED PUBLICATION

It should be apparent that disclosure or communication of a work to another person does not always amount to "publication" under the copyright law. Restricted communication of the contents of a work is not a publication of the work. *See Stanley v. Columbia Broadcasting System, Inc.,* 35 Cal. 2d 653, 221 P.2d 73, 86 USPQ 520 (Cal. Sup. Ct. 1950). Distribution with limitation by the proprietor of the persons to whom the work is communicated and of the purpose of the disclosure was long known as "limited," "restricted," or "private" publication, but is, more accurately, no publication at all. *See White v. Kimmell,* 193 F.2d 774, 92 USPQ 400 (9th Cir.), *cert. denied,* 343 U.S. 957, 93 USPQ 535 (1952).

The absence of any effort to limit distribution or use of copies of speeches by a public official can result in a finding of publication with divestitive effect. In *Public Affairs Associates, Inc. v. Rickover,* 284 F.2d 262, 127 USPQ 231 (D.C. Cir. 1960), *judgment vacated,* 369 U.S. 111, 132 USPQ 535 (1962), *on remand,* 268 F. Supp. 444, 153 USPQ 598 (D.D.C. 1967), Mr. Justice Reed (sitting by designation) stated:

> Certainly when all of Admiral Rickover's acts of distribution are considered together — performance, distribution to the press, the copies sent to individuals at the recipient's request and those sent unsolicited, the copies sent in batches of 50 for distribution by the sponsors of speeches — it is difficult to avoid the conclusion that these acts, in their totality, constitute publication of the speeches and their dedication to the public domain.

284 F.2d at 271, 127 USPQ at 238.

The court remanded for further hearing, but its judgment was vacated by the Supreme Court for a more adequate record.

The *Rickover* case was distinguished in *King v. Mister Maestro, Inc.,* 224 F. Supp. 101, 140 USPQ 366 (S.D.N.Y. 1963), in which distribution in a press kit of "advance copies" of Rev. Martin Luther King Jr.'s famous "I Had a Dream" speech was held to be a limited publication because the copies were not offered to the public.

It is noteworthy that despite the stricter approach of the court of appeals in *Rickover*, that court nevertheless had recognized that limited distribution is easier to find in the case where divestiture, rather than securing copyright, is in issue. Thus, the significance of "divestitive" versus "investitive" publication cannot be overlooked in this area. For example, it has been held that distribution of no less than two thousand copies of sheet music for "plugging" purposes did not divest copyright. *Hirshon v. United Artists Corp.*, 243 F.2d 640, 113 USPQ 110 (D.C. Cir. 1957) (§ 12 copyright preserved). On the other hand, unsupervised distribution of approximately 200 copies of a book at a convention of persons potentially interested in using it was held to be a "publication" of the book within the meaning of § 10. *American Visuals Corp. v. Holland*, 239 F.2d 740, 111 USPQ 288 (2d Cir. 1956). Cf. *Atlantic Monthly Co. v. Post Publishing Co.*, 27 F.2d 556 (D. Mass. 1928) (sale of proof copy of magazine to publisher's treasurer held investitive publication "insofar as the statutory formalities are concerned").

4. PUBLICATION AND PERFORMANCE

It has generally been accepted that the public performance of a spoken drama does not constitute publication. This rule was established under the pre-1909 law. *Ferris v. Frohman*, 223 U.S. 424 (1912). It has been observed that the *Ferris* rule was based on outmoded concepts developed before statutory performing rights were available for plays, particularly if not printed. Yet, it survived the provision for such rights and reexamination of the question "whether the oral presentation alone would or would not be a publication under the Copyright Act" was found unnecessary by the Court of Appeals for the District of Columbia in the *Rickover* case, *supra*, 284 F.2d at 271, 127 USPQ at 238. And thus the oral delivery of the Martin Luther King speech before 200,000 people over radio and television did not amount to a divestitive publication. *King v. Mister Maestro, Inc.*, 224 F. Supp. 101, 107, 140 USPQ 366, 371.

The *Ferris* rule has been applied by analogy to the exhibition of a motion picture, *DeMille v. Casey*, 12 Misc. 78, 201 N.Y.S. 20 (N.Y. Sup. Ct. 1923); the public performance of a musical composition, whether for profit or not, *McCarthy v. White*, 259 F. 364 (S.D.N.Y. 1919); and the oral delivery of a lecture or address, *Nutt v. National Institute, Inc.*, 31 F.2d 236 (2d Cir. 1929), all irrespective of the methods employed, including radio broadcasting. *Uproar Co. v. National Broadcasting Co.*, 81 F.2d 373, 28 USPQ 250 (1st Cir. 1936). Cf. *Metropolitan Opera Ass'n v. Wagner-Nichols Recorder Corp.*,199 Misc. 787, 101 N.Y.S.2d 483, 87 USPQ 173 (Sup. Ct. 1950), aff'd, 279 App. Div. 632, 107 N.Y.S.2d 795 (1st Dept. 1951) (performance of opera). Performances on television could have presented new questions, in view of techniques for not only "live" performances and network transmissions but kinescopes and later tapes for rebroadcasting and prerecording purposes, but despite many uncertainties, no significant judicial test occurred.

5. PUBLICATION AND THE DISTRIBUTION OF PHONOGRAPH RECORDS

The interrelation of publication and phonograph records has a particularly relevant history. Familiarity with such history is necessary in order to understand a number of distinctions which are continually made in the 1976 Act (e.g., "copy" and "phonorecord").

The history begins under the pre-1909 law, when the Supreme Court held that a perforated "pianola" music roll was not a "copy" of a musical composition and therefore did not infringe the copyright in the composition. *White-Smith Music Publishing Co. v. Apollo Co.,* 209 U.S. 1 (1908). While Congress directly remedied this situation in 1909 by establishing control in § 1(e) over mechanical reproduction of music, it did so without equating mechanical reproduction with "copy."

Accordingly, for many years, it was generally accepted in a number of contexts that a recording is not a "copy" of the work recorded. A current of judicial thought in the 1950s began suggesting that the sale of phonograph records *should* be considered divestitive publication. The keynote was sounded by Judge Igoe who stated, by way of dicta, in *Shapiro, Bernstein & Co. v. Miracle Record Co.,* 91 F. Supp. 473, 475, 85 USPQ 39, 40, 86 USPQ 193 (N.D. Ill. 1950):

> It seems to me that production and sale of a phonograph record is fully as much a publication as production and sale of sheet music.

Despite practical problems raised by this approach, and the furor created in many copyright circles, it would have managed to avoid perpetual common law protection for fully exploited works. Nevertheless, the tide of history began quieting these ripples in 1955 with the decision under New York law that the sale of records does not forfeit the performer's common law right in his recorded performance. *Capitol Records, Inc. v. Mercury Records Corp.,* 221 F.2d 657, 105 USPQ 163 (2d Cir. 1955). The most detailed treatment of the problem was in *Rosette v. Rainbo Mfg. Corp.,* 354 F. Supp. 1183, 177 USPQ 631 (S.D.N.Y. 1973), *aff'd per curiam,* 546 F.2d 461, 192 USPQ 673 (2d Cir. 1976).

The next pre-1976 chapter in this saga is the Sound Recording Amendment of 1971. In addition to providing the first federal protection covering the recorded *performance,* the amendment also addressed itself to the separate question of remedies for infringement of copyright in the *underlying music* recorded without authority. In equating remedies for such infringement by recording to other types of infringement, § 101(e) of the 1909 law was amended to provide that discs, tapes, etc., "shall be considered *copies* of the copyrighted musical works which they serve to reproduce mechanically *for the purposes of this section 101 and sections 106 and 109* [restrictions on importation of unauthorized copies]. . . ." (Emphasis added.) This, of course, did not make recordings "copies" for purposes of Copyright Office deposit or presumably for purposes of determining whether their distribution constitutes "publication."

The final link in the chain of confusion is the fact that *as to the recorded performance,* i.e., the "sound recording," the record *is* a copy of the "work." We will return to this particular subject when we consider the relationship under the 1976 Act between records, called "phonorecords," and the musical or other compositions recorded thereon.

6. PUBLICATION OF DERIVATIVE WORKS

Considerable uncertainty has been created as to the effect of publication of a derivative work on the status of the underlying work on which it is based. Compare *Rushton v. Vitale,* 218 F.2d 434, 104 USPQ 158 (2d Cir. 1955), with *Leigh v. Gerber,* 86 F. Supp. 320, 82 USPQ 271 (S.D.N.Y. 1949). This question has been most troublesome in connection with notice requirements. Presumably the answer in this context depends on whether the derivative work should be considered a "copy" of the underlying work within the meaning of the notice provisions.

BURKE v. NATIONAL BROADCASTING CO.

598 F.2d 688 (1st Cir. 1979)

CAMPBELL, CIRCUIT JUDGE. Dr. Burke, an amateur photographer, brought this action alleging that the National Broadcasting Company (NBC) broadcast parts of a movie filmed by him in violation of his alleged common law copyright therein. The parties agreed that there were no issues of fact bearing on the question of liability and filed cross-motions for summary judgment on that issue. The district court held that Dr. Burke had forfeited his common law copyright by allowing a general publication of his film to occur; from that judgment, Dr. Burke appeals.

The evidence on liability, which the parties indicated at appellate argument was all the evidence they wished to submit, consisted of only affidavits by Burke and NBC and a series of letters. These and the admissions in the complaint and answer show that the movie in issue was shot by Dr. Burke while on a safari on the Serengeti Plain of East Africa (now Tanzania) in March 1972. It captured on film a highly unusual and dramatic encounter: a lioness attacks and kills a zebra foal and then, contrary to accepted belief about zebra behavior, the zebra mare returns and attacks the lioness. Only a month after this film was shot, *Natural History* magazine published an article stating that zebras do not protect their young against lions; in response, Dr. Burke wrote to the magazine and the author, telling them what he had witnessed and enclosing a photograph.

Dr. Burke's letter and photograph were published in the August/September 1972 issue of *Natural History* and were read by a Professor Bernhard Grzimek of the University of Giessen in Frankfurt, Germany. In September 1973 Grzimek wrote to Burke saying,

> I hope that you have no objection that we print a German translation of your letter in our journal DAS TIER (THE ANIMAL). We also would like to get a copy of your pictures and, in case you have done several, of the other ones too.
>
> I personally would like to use the film which was done of this incident in my lectures at the university and in a television programme. Is this film still available? Was it done in colour? Would it be possible to get a copy of it on my expenses?

Grzimek was a co-editor of Das Tier and the host of an educational program about animals broadcast on German public (non-commercial) television, and was known to Dr. Burke as such by reputation. Dr. Burke sent Grzimek the following reply, in relevant part:

> It is for me a great honour that you wish to translate my letter "Incident in the Serengeti" into "das Tier." Naturally, I give you permission.
>
> The pictures and the film will be returned to me shortly, and as soon as I receive them I shall send them to you.
>
> The interesting film and the pictures are in colour. The film was taken with Super 8mm film and 18 frames per second, therefore I am not quite certain if the film is feasible for television-broadcasting. This I will leave to the technicians.

Burke did send his film and pictures to Grzimek who, as far as the record shows, made a 16mm copy of the movie, used the copy in his lectures and on public television in Germany, and returned to Burke the 8mm original. Dr. Burke stated in his affidavit that he "never gave anyone else permission to use [the] film for any purpose."

The events leading to the alleged copyright infringement began three years later, in November 1976, when Survival Anglia Limited (SAL), a British company specializing in nature films, wrote to Grzimek asking about the footage he had of a zebra attacking a lioness. Grzimek forwarded the film with a cover letter in which he said, "In the text must be mentioned that this shot was taken by an American visitor, [Dr. Burke]." The Executive Director of SAL thanked Grzimek for the film and wrote,

> We will make sure that a credit is given to Dr. Burke and will return a complete dupe master to you.
>
> Can you please let me know what we should do about paying Dr. Burke?

In response, Grzimek wrote that he had paid Burke for some still photographs but not for the movie film, and that he "had the impression that [Dr. Burke] was quite happy that his film was used in television. If you want to contact him, his address is . . . ."

SAL proceeded to use 33 feet of Burke's film in its production, "The Parenthood Game," without contacting Burke. NBC thereafter brought "The Parenthood Game" and broadcast it in this country between 8 and 9 p.m. on January 27, 1977. Only on February 14, 1977, did someone from SAL write to Burke telling him that his film had been used and saying,

> We have a letter from Prof. Grzimek telling us you are happy for your film to be used, but not mentioning any reimbursement.
>
> Could you please let me know what payment is due to you, and I will process this.

In reply, Dr. Burke denied that Grzimek had permission to release the film, asserted that he retained the copyright in the film, and requested reimbursement according to SAL's usual rates. To date, he has received nothing.

This action against NBC is based on a claim of common law copyright, Dr. Burke never having obtained a statutory copyright on his film. Because we find the case close, and because we are in disagreement with the judgment below, we shall first review at some length the relevant legal principles.

At common law the creator of a literary or artistic work has the right to copy and profit from it, and can distribute or show it to a limited class of persons for a limited purpose without losing that right. The right continues until the creator allows a "general" publication of his work to occur; the work then passes into the public domain and, unless the creator has obtained a statutory copyright, anyone can copy, distribute or sell it for his own benefit. *Caliga v. Inter Ocean Newspaper Co.,* 215 U.S. 182, 188 (1909); *American Tobacco Co. v. Werckmeister,* 207 U.S. 284, 299 (1907).[2]

The common law recognizes three ways of exposing a work to the public: exhibition or performance, limited publication, and general publication. Of these, only general publication results in loss of the common law copyright by the creator.

Mere performance or exhibition of a work results, at common law, in no publication at all. *Ferris v. Frohman,* 223 U.S. 424, 435 (1912); *American Tobacco,* 207 U.S. at 300.[3] Under this principle, a film is not "published" if it

---

[2] Under the Copyright Act of 1976, 17 U.S.C. §§ 101-810, common law copyright is abolished. The Act does not affect rights with respect to causes of action that arose before January 1, 1978, however. 17 U.S.C. §§ 301(a), (b)(2).

[3] The doctrine that performance is not publication has been criticized because it allows an artist to profit from his work indefinitely, contrary to the policies of the copyright

merely is shown but the general public is not permitted to own — as opposed to borrow — tangible copies of it. *E.g., Patterson v. Century Productions, Inc.,* 93 F.2d 489 (2d. Cir. 1937), *cert. denied,* 303 U.S. 655 (1938); *DeMille Co. v. Casey,* 121 Misc. 78, 201 N.Y. Supp. 20 (Sup. Ct. 1923); *see* M. Nimmer, *Nimmer on Copyright* § 4.08[A], at 4-41-44 (1978) [hereafter *Nimmer on Copyright*]. Publication may be found if the circumstances suggest that the public was free to copy a work on exhibit, but a prohibition against copying can be "tacitly understood" or implied. *American Tobacco,* 207 U.S. at 300.

A general publication occurs when a work is made available to members of the public at large without regard to who they are or what they propose to do with it. *See Public Affairs Associates, Inc. v. Rickover,* 284 F.2d 262, 270-71 (D.C. Cir. 1960), *vacated on other grounds,* 369 U.S. 111 (1962); *American Jewelers' Mercantile Agency, Ltd. v. Jewelers' Weekly Publishing Co.,* 155 N.Y. 241, 49 N.E. 872 (1898); *Nimmer on Copyright* § 4.04, at 4-18-22. A general publication is such dissemination of the work itself among the public as justifies the belief that it has been dedicated to the public and rendered common property. *American Tobacco,* 207 U.S. at 300-01; *Patterson,* 93 F.2d at 492; *King v. Mister Maestro, Inc.,* 224 F. Supp. 101, 106 (S.D.N.Y. 1963). It is said that courts have hesitated to find general publication if to do so would divest the common law right to profit from one's own work. *See Hirshon v. United Artists Corp.,* 243 F.2d 640, 644-45 (D.C. Cir. 1957); *American Visuals Corp. v. Holland,* 239 F.2d 740, 744 (2d Cir. 1956) (Frank, J.).

A general publication can be found where only one copy of the work passes to a member of the general public, as general publication depends on the author making the work available to those interested, and not on the number of people who actually express an interest. *American Jewelers',* 49 N.E. at 875; *Nimmer on Copyright* § 4.13[A], at 4-67. Thus "[t]he common-law right is lost by the general publication or unrestricted sale of a single copy." *Bobbs-Merrill Co. v. Straus,* 147 F. 15, 19 (2d Cir. 1906), *aff'd,* 210 U.S. 339 (1908). Thereafter, a copyright can be preserved only by timely compliance with the copyright statute. In at least two cases involving a dispute over whether a statutory copyright existed, the sale of a single copy of a written work has been held to constitute publication such as to require compliance with or invoke the protection of the copyright statute. *Gottsburger v. Aldine Book Publishing Co.,* 33 F. 381 (D. Mass. 1887); *Atlantic Monthly Co. v. Post Publishing Co.,* 27 F.2d 556 (D. Mass. 1928).

A "limited publication," by contrast, occurs when tangible copies of the work are distributed, but to a limited class of persons and for a limited purpose. One frequently quoted formulation of this concept is that a limited publication

communicates the contents of a [work] to a definitely selected group and for a limited purpose, . . . without the right of diffusion, reproduction, distribution or sale . . . . [T]he circulation must be *restricted both as to persons and purpose,* or it cannot be called a private or limited publication.

White v. Kimmell, 193 F.2d 744, 746-47 (9th Cir. 1952) (emphasis added). While the distribution must be so restricted, however, the restrictions can be implied as well as express. *Werckmeister v. American Lithograph Co.,* 134 F. 321, 324 (2d Cir. 1904).

---

statute, which limit the life of a statutory copyright. *E.g.,* B. Kaplan, *An Unhurried View of Copyright* 85 (1967). Under the Copyright Act of 1976, distribution of copies of films for television broadcast is publication, but broadcasting in itself is not. *See* 17 U.S.C. § 101; M. Nimmer, 1 *Nimmer on Copyright* § 4.11[B], at 4-55 (1978).

distinction depends on author's actions

The distinction between "general" and "limited" publication is one of degree, and depends less on the creator's intentions than on his actions. *See Rickover,* 284 F.2d at 270; *National Comics Publications, Inc. v. Fawcett Publications, Inc.,* 191 F.2d 594, 598 (2d Cir. 1951); *King,* 224 F. Supp. at 103. In cases where general publication has been found, the creator had made his work available in a manner that suggested that any interested person could have a copy. *See Nimmer on Copyright* § 4.04, at 4-20-21. Thus in *Rickover, supra,* copies of Admiral Rickover's speeches had been given to the press, sent to individuals both on request and without solicitation, and sent in batches of 50 to sponsors for distribution. 284 F.2d at 271. In short, "Anyone was welcome to a copy." *Id.* General publication was also found in *White v. Kimmell, supra,* 193 F.2d 744: the author of a manuscript had distributed copies to friends, acquaintances and strangers, telling many to pass them on and authorizing some to make additional copies, provided they did not distribute the manuscript "in published form." 193 F.2d at 745-47. The recipients were not members of any group or association, and the author set no limitations on the number of copies to be made or on the persons to receive them — "a mere request" apparently sufficed to obtain one. 193 F.2d at 747. In *American Visuals, supra,* 239 F.2d 740, the plaintiff had placed copies of his brochures on a table in a hotel where an insurance industry convention was being held, and had given additional copies to an insurance association for distribution to its member companies. The court found that, while the plaintiff had a limited purpose in distributing the work, no limitation was placed on the persons who could obtain copies, either from the hotel table or from the insurance association's member companies. *Id.* at 744.

Mere limited publication has been found where the range and purpose of distribution did not suggest that the general public was free to obtain and use the work. Thus in *Patterson, supra,* 93 F.2d 489, the court found no general publication despite the fact that copies of the film in issue were circulated widely; the copies were sent only to non-profit groups to be shown for non-commercial purposes, with no authorization to copy them further and, apparently, with the understanding that they would be returned. In *King, supra,* 224 F. Supp. 101, the district court held that the Rev. Martin Luther King's speech, "I Have a Dream," was not in the public domain. "Advance copies" of the text were given to the press, and excerpts were later broadcast on national television and used in movie house newsreels. Although countless people heard and saw the speech given, the oral delivery was mere performance, not publication. *Id.* at 106-07. Publication occurred when the text was given to the press, but was "limited" rather than "general" — tangible copies were given only to a specific group to assist it in covering the event, and were never offered to the public at large. *Id.* at 107.[4] In *Allen v. Walt Disney Productions, Ltd.,* 41 F. Supp. 134 (S.D.N.Y. 1941), the composer of a song — "Old Eli March" — had loaned manuscripts thereof to various musicians, and had sent a copy to two different music companies. No copies had been sold, however, and the composition was not printed until 1936 — almost thirty years after it was written. The court found that no general publication occurred until 1936, noting that there was "no general offer or dedication to the public." *Id.* at 136. Similarly, in *McCarthy & Fischer, Inc. v. White,* 259 F. 364 (S.D.N.Y. 1919) (A. Hand, J.), a composer had given a copy

---

[4] The result in *King* has been questioned on the ground that the distribution of the speech to the press was for ultimate dissemination to the general public. Nimmer on Copyright § 4.13[A], at 4-66 n.11.

of his song to a singer for performance, but had not dedicated it to the public: "It was not . . . a [general] publication to give the song to a limited number of artists to sing . . . . There [was] no evidence or probability that any of the copies were sold, or that they were given out for any purpose but a limited use by a few vaudeville artists." *Id.* at 365.

The parties in the present case have called our attention to no decision that fits precisely the circumstances surrounding Dr. Burke's release of his film to Dr. Grzimek. In light of the principles and precedents just reviewed, however, we conclude that the district court erred in finding that a general publication occurred.

The district court thought that, when Dr. Burke voluntarily sent the film to Germany knowing that it would be copied and used on German television, "he did not expressly or impliedly restrict it either as to persons or purposes." In the court's view, Burke's letter of September 1973 "placed no restrictions on the persons who could view the film, nor . . . upon the purposes for which it could be shown."

As performance in itself is not publication, the fact that Dr. Burke knew the film would be copied by Dr. Grzimek and used in his lecture or on television, was not determinative. Publication did not occur merely because the film was shown to the general public. *See Patterson, supra,* 93 F.2d 489. The decisive issue was whether Burke's release of the film itself to Dr. Grzimek was, under the circumstances, a general publication. We find that it was not.

Dr. Burke sent the film to Dr. Grzimek in response to a request to have a copy to use personally in lectures and on a television program. Dr. Grzimek made a copy, apparently for his own use, but this was the extent of the copying and distribution authorized at that time. As Dr. Burke knew, Dr. Grzimek was a professor and hosted an educational program on non-commercial television. Allowing the film to be used for the purposes requested was not a blanket authorization to use it for any purpose, much less to release it to a commercial producer. True, Dr. Burke did not state explicitly in his letter that Dr. Grzimek could not distribute copies of the film to others, or use it for other purposes, but we think such limitations are reasonably to be implied: Dr. Grzimek made a specific request to use the film for a specific purpose, and Dr. Burke's affirmative response cannot be thought to have authorized any further use or other purpose.

This is not a case like *Rickover, supra,* 284 F.2d 262, *White v. Kimmell, supra,* 193 F.2d 744, or *American Visuals, supra,* 239 F.2d 740, where the owners distributed copies of their work in a way that made them available to the general public. That Dr. Burke was "honored" by Dr. Grzimek's request and readily agreed to it seems a function of Dr. Grzimek's stature as a naturalist, and is consistent with believing Dr. Grzimek would use the film only for his own stated purposes. Burke states in his affidavit that he never made the film available to anyone else — there is thus no evidence of a practice of releasing copies on demand. Nor is this a case in which the recipient was directly or impliedly invited to put the film to any use he wished. Dr. Grzimek had no reason to suppose that he was free to distribute copies of the film at will, or to license its commercial use. We find that only a "limited" publication occurred, and that Dr. Burke's common law copyright was not lost.

The judgment below is reversed. As there remain no disputed facts on the question of liability, the case is remanded so that appellant's cross-motion for summary judgment may be granted. 6 J. Moore, *Federal Practice* ¶ 56.13 at

56-348-49 (2d ed. 1976). The case is also remanded for disposition on the issue of damages.

So ordered.

QUESTIONS

1. What was the policy that underlay the divestiture of perpetual common law copyright once a work was "published"? Is that policy not frustrated when it is held that the delivery of a speech before 200,000 people (plus all of the news media) is not divestitive? Would your analysis be the same with regard to a Broadway play which runs for three years before capacity audiences but which is not yet marketed in book form?

2. Even assuming that "performance" does not constitute a divestitive publication, can the same be said, in the context of the *King* case, for the distribution of the speech to the press corps (without notice of copyright) with obvious knowledge (if not intention) as to the press's purpose?

3. Why does the exhibition of a painting, or of a motion picture, not divest common law copyright? Would the sale of a painting divest common law copyright?

4. Had it been held that Dr. Burke had consented to a general publication of his motion picture, what would the consequences have been? Had Dr. Burke believed that there would be a general publication of his motion picture, what steps should he have taken? If a federal district judge could not accurately decide whether there was a general or a limited publication, how could Dr. Burke be expected to do so?

5. Are the cases cited by the court in *Burke,* particularly the *King* and *Rickover* cases, consistent?

6. Is divestitive publication (at the time of the 1909 Act) to be determined by state law (whose?) or by federal law? See *Capitol Records, Inc. v. Mercury Records Corp.,* 221 F.2d 657 (2d Cir. 1955).

7. Would copyright in the King speech be infringed if today a person makes the following uses? (a) Sells phonograph records of the speech as actually delivered by Dr. King in 1963? (b) Sells phonograph records of another person delivering the text of the speech? (c) Distributes the text of the speech at a civil rights rally? (d) Delivers the speech at a civil rights rally? (e) Quotes very lengthy excerpts from the speech in a magazine article tracing the civil rights struggle of the 1960s?

LETTER EDGED IN BLACK PRESS, INC.
v. PUBLIC BUILDING COMMISSION

320 F. Supp. 1303 (N.D. Ill. 1970)

NAPOLI, DISTRICT JUDGE.

Plaintiff seeks a declaratory judgment invalidating defendant's copyright to the Pablo Picasso sculpture entitled "The Chicago Picasso." The defendant is the Public Building Commission of Chicago (Commission) and the plaintiff is a publisher who desires to market a copy of the sculpture. Pursuant to Rule 56 of the Federal Rules of Civil Procedure both parties have moved for summary judgment. Succinctly, plaintiff maintains that defendant's copyright is invalid because the sculpture is in the public domain. Defendant asserts that the Chicago Picasso has never been in the public domain.

Statement of Facts

In 1963 certain of the Civic Center architects, representing the Commission, approached Picasso with a request to design a monumental sculpture for the plaza in front of the proposed Chicago Civic Center. By May, 1965, Picasso completed the maquette (model) of the sculpture. William E. Hartmann, the architect, who had been the chief liaison with Picasso, then had the maquette brought to the basement of the Art Institute of Chicago, without public notice. The design of the maquette was subjected to an engineering analysis to determine the feasibility of constructing the monumental sculpture and three Chicago charitable foundations undertook to finance the actual construction by contributing $300,000 toward the total cost of $351,959.17. An aluminum model of the design with some slight revisions was prepared as a guide to the construction of the sculpture, and Picasso approved a picture of this model on August 9, 1966.

The Commission, through its board, had been given a private viewing of the maquette. Subsequently, the Commission passed a resolution authorizing the payment of $100,000 to Picasso. This sum was intended as the purchase price for the entire right, title and interest in and to the maquette constituting Picasso's design for the monumental sculpture including the copyright, and copyright renewals. Hartmann proffered the $100,000 check to Picasso and asked the artist to sign a document referred to as the "Formal Acknowledgment and Receipt." Picasso refused to accept the money or to sign the document. He stated that he wanted to make a gift of his work. In accordance with Picasso's wish, counsel for the Commission and William Hartmann prepared the following "Deed of Gift" which Picasso signed on August 21, 1966:

> The monumental sculpture portrayed by the maquette pictured above has been expressly created by me, Pablo Picasso, for installation on the plaza of the Civic Center in the City of Chicago, State of Illinois, United States of America. This sculpture was undertaken by me for the Public Building Commission of Chicago at the request of William E. Hartmann, acting on behalf of the Chicago Civic Center architects. I hereby give this work and the right to reproduce it to the Public Building Commission, and I give the maquette to the Art Institute of Chicago, desiring that these gifts shall, through them, belong to the people of Chicago.

In the fall of 1966 the Commission, the public relations department of the City of Chicago, the Art Institute of Chicago and the U. S. Steel Corporation, the latter being the prime contractor for the construction of the sculpture, began a campaign to publicize the Chicago Picasso. The campaign was directed by Hartmann, with help from Al Weisman, head of the public relations department of the advertising firm of Foote, Cone and Belding.

As part of the campaign at least two press showings were conducted. The first was held on September 20, 1966, when the maquette was placed on public exhibition at the Art Institute. No copyright notice was affixed to the maquette. The following notice was, however, posted in the Art Institute:

> The rights of reproduction are the property of the Public Building Commission of Chicago. © 1966. All Rights Reserved.

Press photographers attended the showing at the invitation of the Commission and the Art Institute and later published pictures of the maquette and aluminum model in Chicago newspapers and in magazines of national and international circulation. In addition the Commission supplied photographs of the maquette and the uncopyrighted architect's aluminum model to members of the public who requested them for publication. The second showing took place in December of 1966 when the U. S. Steel Corporation, with the knowledge of the Commission, had completed a twelve-foot six-inch wooden model of the sculpture and invited the press to photograph the model. There was no copyright notice on the model and the pictures were published without copyright notice. U. S. Steel also hired a professional photographer to take pictures of the model and these pictures were used in the publicity drive.

The drive was seemingly successful for pictures of the Picasso design appeared in Business Week Magazine on May 6, 1967, and in Holiday Magazine in March, 1967. Fortune Magazine published three pages of color photographs about the Chicago Picasso including pictures of the U. S. Steel wooden model. The Chicago Sun Times, Midwest magazine published a cover story on the sculpture with a drawing of the maquette on the cover of the magazine. And a picture of the maquette was printed in U. S. Steel News, a house organ with a circulation of over 300,000. None of the photographs or drawings that were published in the above named publications bore any copyright notice whatever.

From June, 1967, through August 13, 1967, the maquette was displayed at the Tate Gallery in London, England. In conjunction with the exhibit at the Tate, a catalog was published wherein a picture of the maquette appeared. Neither on the maquette itself nor on the photograph in the catalog did copyright notice appear. The Commission had knowledge of these facts for on July 6, 1967, Hartmann had sent to the Chairman of the Commission the catalog which was placed in the Commission files.

On August 15, 1967, the monumental sculpture, "The Chicago Picasso" was dedicated in ceremonies on the Civil Center Plaza. The sculpture bore the following copyright:

At the dedication, Mr. Hartmann, co-chairman of the event and master of ceremonies said:

Pablo Picasso . . . as you know gave the creation of the sculpture to the people of Chicago and his maquette to the Art Institute of Chicago.

The Chairman of the Public Building Commission, in his speech of dedication to the approximately 50,000 persons assembled for the ceremony said:

It's an occasion we've all been anticipating — the dedication of this great gift to our city by the world-renowned artist, Pablo Picasso.

. . . I dedicate this gift in the name of Chicago and wish it an abiding and happy stay in the City's heart.

In conjunction with the dedication a commemorative souvenir booklet of the Chicago Picasso dedication ceremonies was prepared by the Commission. The booklet which contained drawings and photographs of the maquette and the aluminum model were [sic] distributed to 96 distinguished men and women from all areas of Chicago life and to honored guests. Neither the booklet itself, nor any of the photographs shown therein, bore any copyright notice. Also, on the day of the dedication the United States Steel public relations office sent out a press release together with a photo of the monumental sculpture. The photograph bore no copyright notice.

Subsequent to the dedication, the Art Institute published its Annual Report which contained an uncopyrighted picture of the maquette. This publication had a circulation of 40,000 copies, including museums and libraries. The Art Institute also continued selling a photograph of the maquette on a postcard. Between October 1966 and October 1967, 800 copies of this postcard were sold. In 1967, however, the Commission asked the Art Institute to stop selling the postcard and the Art Institute complied with this request.

In October 1967, the Commission caused to be engraved in the granite base of the sculpture the following legend:

CHICAGO PICASSO
THE CREATION OF THE SCULPTURE WAS GIVEN TO THE PEOPLE OF CHICAGO BY THE ARTIST PABLO PICASSO
THE ERECTION OF THE SCULPTURE WAS MADE POSSIBLE THROUGH THE GENEROSITY OF WOODS CHARITABLE FUND, INC. CHAUNCEY AND MARION DEERING McCORMICK FOUNDATION FIELD FOUNDATION OF ILLINOIS DEDICATED AUGUST 15, 1967 RICHARD J. DALEY, MAYOR.

In November, 1967, the Commission stated its policy that no individuals shall be restricted from "full personal enjoyment of the sculpture, including the right to take photographs and make paintings, etchings and models of the same for personal, non-commercial purposes." The Commission has also had a policy of granting licenses to copy the sculpture for commercial purposes. The Commission requires payment of a nominal fee and a royalty on copies sold. Several such licenses have been granted.

Finally, on January 12, 1968, the Public Building Commission filed its application with the Register of Copyrights asking a copyright in the monumental sculpture entitled "The Chicago Picasso." In due course a certificate of copyright registration was issued to defendant.

Statement of Applicable Law

Defendant submits that the attaching of notice to the monumental sculpture on August 4, 1967, and the later registration of the copyright were acts sufficient to obtain a statutory copyright under 17 U.S.C. § 10 and 17 U.S.C. § 11. This attempt to establish a statutory copyright must fail, however, if the Chicago Picasso was in the public domain prior to August 4, 1967. Such a conclusion is inescapable given the statutory admonition of 17 U.S.C. § 8 that "[n]o copyright shall subsist in the original text of any work which is in the public domain . . .".

To determine how a work comes to be in the public domain it is necessary to explore the basis of the copyright protection. The common law copyright arises upon the creation of any work of art, be it a first sketch or the finished product. This common law right protects against unauthorized copying, publishing, vending, performing, and recording. The common law copyright is terminated by publication of the work by the proprietor of the copyright. Upon termination of the common law copyright, the work falls into the public domain if statutory protection is not obtained by the giving of the requisite notice.

In some of the early English decisions there was debate as to whether publication did indeed divest its owner of common law protection.[8] Arguing that divestment should not occur upon publication, because of the seeming

---

[8] Millar v. Taylor, 4 Burr. 2303, 98 Eng. Rep. 201 (1769 KB); *contra*, Donaldson v. Becket, 4 Burr. 2408 (1774).

irrationality of such a rule, Lord Mansfield observed: "'The copy is made common, because the law does not protect it: and the law can not protect it because it is made common.'"

In the United States, however, it has been clear, from the date the question first reached the Supreme Court, that the common law copyright is terminated upon the first publication.[10] And as Judge Learned Hand noted in *National Comics Publications v. Fawcett Publications,* citing *Donaldson v. Becket,* "It is of course true that the publication of a copyrightable 'work' puts the 'work' into the public domain except so far as it may be protected by copyright. That has been unquestioned law since 1774."

One justification for the doctrine, that publication *ipso facto* divests an author of common law copyright protection, can be found in the copyright clause of the United States Constitution. Protection is granted, but only "for limited times." The inclusion of this caveat in the Constitution makes manifest the right of society to ultimately claim free access to materials which may prove essential to the growth of the society. The copyright clause, however, does not impinge on the right of privacy of a creator. An author who refrains from publication and uses his work for his own pleasure may enjoy the common law copyright protection in perpetuity. Once a work is published, however, the Constitution dictates that the time for which the statutory copyright protection is accorded starts to run. An author is not allowed to publish a work and then after a period of time has elapsed choose to invoke statutory copyright protection. If the statutory protection is not acquired at the time of publication by appropriate notice, the work is lost to the public domain. Any other rule would permit avoidance of the "limited times" provision of the Constitution.

An exception to this rule is that a limited publication does not divest the holder of his common law protection. A good definition of limited publication can be found in *White v. Kimmell* wherein the court found that limited publication is a publication "which communicates the contents of a manuscript to a definitely selected group and for a limited purpose, without the right of diffusion, reproduction, distribution or sale." For example, if an artist shows a painting to a selected group of his friends, for the limited purpose of obtaining their criticism, the publication will be said to be limited and thus not divestive of the artist's common law copyright.

Applying these general principles of copyright law to the facts of the case at bar the court is persuaded that the copyright to the work of art known as the "Chicago Picasso" is invalid. General publication occurred without the requisite notice. Accordingly, the common law protection was lost upon publication and the work was thrust into the public domain.

While this suit could have been resolved on any one of several distinct theories[*] the court has decided to base its opinion on the proposition that the Chicago Picasso was placed into the public domain prior to the attachment of copyright notice on the monumental sculpture. Accordingly, only cursory reference will be paid to the other issues presented in this action. Even limiting the opinion in this fashion, however, multiple and rather sophisticated arguments of the defendant must be met in order to sustain the court's opinion.

---

[10] Wheaton v. Peters, 33 U.S. 591 (1934).

[*] The court has found it unnecessary to deal with the following issues: 1) Whether a monumental sculpture of the type at issue can be copyrighted. See Carns v. Keefe Bros.,

Defendant's Claim That the
Models Did Not Need
Copyright Notice

The defendant's basic contention is that the work of art is the properly copyrighted monumental sculpture not the models. In support of this thesis defendant correctly points out that what was always envisioned by the Civic Center architects and Picasso was a monumental sculpture for the Civic Center Plaza. There can only be one copyright in one work of art it is asserted, and that work allegedly is the sculpture in the Civic Center Plaza; not the various models used in its development. It is therefore concluded that copyright notice on the models was unnecessary before publication of the monumental sculpture.

The court takes a different view of the facts. When Picasso signed the deed of gift on August 21, 1966, there existed but a single copyright. Picasso had a common law copyright in the maquette. He gave the maquette itself to the Art Institute and the right to reproduce it to the defendant. The monumental sculpture did not exist at this point in time and accordingly there could be no copyright in the monumental sculpture, either common law or statutory. It is settled that a copyright can exist only in a perceptible, tangible work. It cannot exist in a vision. When Picasso made his deed of gift the monumental sculpture was undeniably but a vision and thus not subject to copyright protection.

The maquette, however, was an original, tangible work of art which would have qualified for statutory copyright protection under 17 U.S.C. § 5 (g).[19] The court finds that when the maquette was published without statutory notice Picasso's work was forever lost to the public domain. When the monumental sculpture was finally completed it could not be copyrighted for it was a mere copy, albeit on a grand scale, of the maquette, a work already in the public domain.

Defendant's Claim That Display of the Maquette
Did Not Constitute General Publication

Three arguments have been submitted to the effect that display of the maquette did not constitute general publication. First, defendant urges that display of the maquette at the Art Institute was a "limited" publication and thus did not place the Chicago Picasso in the public domain. In support of this position the defendant's prime authority is *American Tobacco Co. v. Werckmeister*. In the American Tobacco case an English artist painted a picture depicting a company of gentlemen with filled glasses, singing in chorus. The artist transferred the copyright in the picture to the Berlin Photographic

---

242 F. 745 (D.C. Mont. 1917); 2) Whether the sculpture was dedicated to the public and thus incapable of being copyrighted; 3) Whether a valid copyright can be maintained where the public is totally free to make copies, albeit for non-commercial use; and 4) Whether uncopyrighted copies of the sculpture published after the dedication caused the sculpture to be placed in the public domain.

[19] *Classification of works for registration*

The application for registration shall specify to which of the following classes the work in which copyright is claimed belongs: . . . (g) Works of art; models or designs for works of art.

Company, which company made copies of the painting bearing appropriate copyright notice. Immediately subsequent to transferring the copyright the artist, who retained ownership of the painting, placed the picture on exhibit at the Royal Academy. The picture as it hung in the gallery bore no notice of copyright. Several years later the Berlin Photographic Company brought an action claiming that the American Tobacco Company had infringed upon its copyright to the painting. As one of its defenses the American Tobacco Company argued that because the painting had been displayed in a public gallery without copyright notice it had been lost to the public domain and accordingly, the copyright was invalid. The court rejected this argument finding that the display in the gallery amounted to a limited publication and thus did not operate to divest the holder of the copyright of its rights. The basis for this decision was the finding that absolutely no copies were permitted to be made by anyone viewing the picture at the gallery. In fact, it was noted that guards were stationed in the gallery to rigidly enforce the rule of the Royal Academy that no copying take place. The court properly decided that the rational basis for the notice requirement would not be transgressed by showing a picture bearing no notice where that picture could not be copied. In closing dicta the Court in American Tobacco noted: "We do not mean to say that the public exhibition of a painting or statue, where all might see and freely copy it, might not amount to publication within the statute, regardless of the artist's purpose or notice of reservation of rights which he takes no measure to protect."

It is this court's finding that the case at bar more closely resembles the situation postulated in the aforementioned dicta than it does the actual facts of the American Tobacco case. In the case at bar there were no restrictions on copying and no guards preventing copying. Rather every citizen was free to copy the maquette for his own pleasure and camera permits were available to members of the public.[22] At its first public display the press was freely allowed to photograph the maquette and publish these photographs in major newspapers and magazines. Further, officials at this first public showing of the maquette made uncopyrighted pictures of the maquette available upon request. Were this activity classified as limited publication, there would no longer be any meaningful distinction between limited and general publication. The activity in question does not comport with any definition of limited publication. Rather, the display of the maquette constituted general publication.

Defendant's second assertion is that the display of the maquette was inconsequential since an unpublished work, model thereof, or copy thereof does not require a copyright notice. The court has no quarrel with this statement of law. The problem with this argument, however, is that it begs the question of whether or not there was general publication. Since there was general publication of the maquette, notice was required.

Finally, defendant argues that the Art Institute did not hold the copyright to the maquette and therefore could not have placed notice on the maquette. The answer to this assertion is that the Commission, the alleged holder of the copyright, was required to insure that proper notice was placed on the maquette. The Commission was able to place improper notice at the showing, i. e., notice in the room, but it did not comply with the statutory requirement that notice be placed on the work itself in order to be effective.

---

[22] The Art Institute camera regulations do, however, require that permission be obtained in order to use photographic copies of works of art commercially.

Defendant's Claim That Uncopyrighted Pictures Could Be Used in the Publicity Campaign

The defendant's major defense to the use of uncopyrighted pictures of the models in the publicity drive is what appears to be an inverse application of the doctrine of "fair use". Generally it can be stated that certain acts of copying are defensible as "fair use". The doctrine of fair use, however, was meant to be used and has only been used, as a defense in infringement actions. The defendant can not cite a single authority to support its unique claim that the doctrine can be asserted to excuse a failure to put copyright notice on copies of a work of art intended for distribution to the press. The court after diligent research has also failed to find any support for the defendant's position. It seems appropriate to ask why defendant's desire for wide and favorable distribution of copies of the maquette and the other models could not have been fulfilled by distribution of pictures which had copyright notice printed on them?

Defendant has an additional defense to the uncopyrighted printing of pictures of the maquette, the wooden model, and the aluminum model. It is contended that the copies of the work of art that appeared in various newspapers and magazines without notice did not amount to divesting publication because these pictures were protected under the copyright secured by the media in their own publication. It is settled law that if a work is published in the press, without a separate notice in the name of the holder of the copyright of the work in question, that work has been published without valid notice. Defendant contends that the above statement of law has been overruled by *Goodis v. United Artists Television Inc.*[29] and that the *Goodis* case supports its position that the press copyright protects the interests of the work's owner. The issue in the *Goodis* case was "whether a magazine publisher who acquires only the right to serialize a novel before it is published in book form has such an interest in the work that notice of copyright in the publisher's name will protect the copyright of the author of the novel." The court in finding that the publisher's copyright did protect the author, based its opinion on the fact that the magazine had purchased a property interest in the novel, i. e., the right of first publication. Thus, the court found that the publisher's notice was sufficient since the magazine had obtained proprietorship of a portion of the copyright to the novel. The basic issue that the *Goodis* court decided was whether the doctrine of indivisibility of copyright was applicable to the situation presented in that case.

The case at bar is distinguishable from the *Goodis* decision for in the instant case the newspapers and magazines that published the pictures of the work of art did not have as the *Goodis* court said, "such an interest in the work that notice of copyright in the publisher's name will protect the copyright . . . ." The publishers in the case at bar had no interest whatever in the pictures of the work that they published. Accordingly, the court finds that the copyrights of the publishers in their own publications do not serve to rescue the defendant's copyright in this case.

Defendant's Claim That Publication of Pictures of the Models Constituted Infringement

The last major defense that the defendant advances in an attempt to excuse the uncopyrighted publication of the work of art is that the publications constituted unauthorized infringement, and therefore they did not place the work in

---

[29] Goodis v. United Artists Television, Inc., 425 F.2d 397 (2nd Cir. 1970).

the public domain. In a letter to Hartmann, before the deed of gift was signed, which letter the defendant characterizes as "instruction to architects", the following directions were set out:

> In order for the PUBLIC BUILDING COMMISSION to preserve all rights in and to this work of art, it is essential that every publication of the work, whether of the maquette, photographs of the maquette, or the ultimate monumental sculpture, bear the following notice:
>
> © 1966 Public Building Commission of Chicago All Rights Reserved.
>
> The notice must appear legibly on an exposed surface of the sculpture. Since notice is the essence of protection, we suggest consultation between us before publication of the work in any form.
>
> Would you, or someone at your office, see that the photographs, drawings, and all other reproductions of this work of art are marked with the foregoing copyright notice.

Also, in its contract with the builder of the sculpture the defendant included provision requiring that notice be placed on the sculpture and on all reproductions and drawings of the design.

Given these instructions the defendant argues that many of the instances of publication were actually acts of infringement because they were unauthorized and accordingly did not defeat defendant's copyright. The court has found no evidence for the period before notice was attached to the monumental sculpture on August 4, 1967, that the Commission intended to have its orders carried out. Rather, the great bulk of the evidence before the Court, shows that the Commission itself disregarded its own instructions. That instead of objecting to uncopyrighted publications, the Commission passively and in some cases actively engaged in the distribution of uncopyrighted pictures promoting the Chicago Picasso. The court on the facts before it could not find that any of the publications here in question constituted unauthorized infringing publications. Accordingly, this last defense submitted by the defendant must be rejected.

An analysis of the legal issues presented in this action compels the conclusion that the copyright to the Chicago Picasso is invalid due to the fact that the sculpture has entered the public domain. This decision comports with a strict adherence to copyright law and is also in consonance with the policy of enriching society which underlies our copyright system. The broadest and most uninhibited reproduction and copying of a provocative piece of public sculpture can only have the end result of benefiting society.

For all of the foregoing reasons this court hereby enters summary judgment in favor of the plaintiff and against the defendant.

QUESTIONS

1. Note all the embodiments of the Chicago Picasso identified by the court. Try to determine which ones laid the foundation for a finding of divestitive publication. Is there any reason peculiar to this case, that can explain the court's appetite for finding a way to reach its result?

2. Do you agree with the penultimate paragraph of the opinion?

J. A. RICHARDS, INC. v. NEW YORK POST, INC.

23 F. Supp. 619 (S.D.N.Y. 1938)

PATTERSON, DISTRICT JUDGE.

The suit is for infringement of copyright. The defendant moves to dismiss the second and third counts as showing on their face that the plaintiff has not a valid copyright on the pamphlets involved in those counts.

The first count is for infringement of the plaintiff's cyclopedia. No question is raised as to the sufficiency of that count. The second count is for infringement of an advertising pamphlet put out by the plaintiff. It is alleged that the plaintiff created a pamphlet consisting of extracts from the cyclopedia and of writings descriptive of it, a copy of the pamphlet being annexed, that it secured copyright by publication of the pamphlet with notice of copyright, that copies with notice of copyright were deposited with the Register of Copyrights, and that the defendant has infringed. The pamphlet annexed has 28 pages. It has no title on the cover or elsewhere. The copyright notice is on the rear cover, "Copyright 1933, J. A. Richards, Inc."

The third count charges infringement of a later pamphlet descriptive of the cyclopedia. It contains appropriate allegations as to securing of copyright and infringement, and a copy of the pamphlet is annexed. This pamphlet has 52 pages. There is a title on the front cover, "Richards Cyclopedia". The notice of copyright is on the rear cover, "Copyright 1934, J. A. Richards, Inc."

The defendant's point is that the bill itself discloses that the copyright on the two pamphlets is void, for failure to comply with the Copyright Act. Section 19 of the Act, 17 U.S.C.A. § 19, provides:

The notice of copyright shall be applied, in the case of a book or other printed publication, upon its title page or the page immediately following, or if a periodical either upon the title page or upon the first page of text of each separate number or under the title heading, or if a musical work either upon its title page or the first page of music. One notice of copyright in each volume or in each number of a newspaper or periodical published shall suffice.

By explicit provision of the statute the place for copyright notice in the case of a book or printed pamphlet is on the title page or the page immediately following. It follows that a notice on any other page, no matter how prominent, is ineffective. *United Thrift Plan, Inc. v. National Thrift Plan, Inc.,* D.C.N.Y., 34 F.2d 300; *Bessett v. Germain,* D.C.Mass., 18 F. Supp. 249. See also *Freeman v. The Trade Register,* C.C.Wash., 173 F. 419. The plaintiff's two pamphlets did not carry copyright notice in the place designated by law. With the later pamphlets this is evident at a glance, the title "Richards Cyclopedia" appearing on the front cover and the notice on the back cover, many pages intervening. With the earlier pamphlet the case is not so plain, because the pamphlet has no title page. As section 19 shows, Congress in enacting the Copyright Act contemplated that each book or publication, to be protected, should have a title and should contain a page devoted, in part at least, to the title. See *Freeman v. The Trade Register,* supra. I will not say that a copyright notice on the front cover or on the page following, a title page being absent, would not suffice. In any event, a notice on the back cover will not do.

Section 20 of the Act, 17 U.S.C.A. § 20, does not save the plaintiff. That section cures omission of copyright notice on particular copies where the omis-

[handwritten margin note: cure of accident or mistake]

sion is due to accident or mistake; it has no application where copyright notice on all copies is substantially defective, as was the case here. *Goes Lithographing Co. v. Apt Lithographic Co.,* D.C.N.Y., 14 F.Supp. 620.

The plaintiff is right in urging that substantial compliance with the Copyright Act is all that is required. But when the Act requires that copyright notice be applied at a particular place in a work (the title page or page next following), the courts may not dispense with the requirement and say that a notice appearing somewhere else is enough. The motion to dismiss the second and third causes of action as insufficient on their face will be granted.

[handwritten margin note: does not meet substantial compliance]

AMERICAN GREETINGS CORP. v. KLEINFAB CORP.

400 F. Supp. 228 (S.D.N.Y. 1975)

Owen, District Judge.

Plaintiff, American Greetings Corporation, claiming that defendant, Kleinfab Corporation, a fabric converter, in two of its fabric designs has infringed copyrights owned by plaintiff in the design of a gift wrap, a greeting card in an illustrated book, seeks a preliminary injunction enjoining further infringement by Kleinfab. Defendant while neither admitting nor denying the claim that its fabric designs were copied from plaintiff's creations, asserts that the plaintiff is not entitled to an injunction for the following reasons: 1) the alleged infringing works are not substantially similar to plaintiff's copyrighted materials, 2) plaintiff has forfeited its copyrights by publication without the notice required by 17 U.S.C. § 10 or by publication with a defective notice, 3) plaintiff is guilty of laches in seeking injunctive relief and 4) plaintiff will suffer no irreparable injury should preliminary relief be denied. I find none of them persuasive.

. . . .

Defendant's second argument is that even if its fabrics are substantially similar to plaintiff's gift wrap, book illustration and greeting card, nevertheless plaintiff's publication of the relevant portions thereof with defective copyright notices has stripped plaintiff of its right to protection from infringement.[2] With respect to defendant's alleged infringement by fabric #905, defendant has demonstrated that the picture of plaintiff's "Holly Hobbie Blue Girl" has been used on plastic shopping bags, packages of soap, jars of bath oil, jars of body lotion and cosmetic sets without any copyright notice whatsoever. Plaintiff concedes that copyright notice was inadvertently omitted from at least 500,000 copies of the Blue Girl, but point out that approximately twenty-two million copies were printed overall. Thus plaintiff argues that since the omissions amount to only about 1% of total Holly Hobbie production, were totally by accident or mistake, and in no way responsible for misleading defendant or for defendant's copying, plaintiff is entitled to invoke 17 U.S.C. § 21 to retain copyright protection. That section provides:

> Where the copyright proprietor has sought to comply with the provisions of this title with respect to notice, the omission by accident or mistake of the prescribed notice from a particular copy or copies shall not invalidate the copyright or prevent recovery for infringement against any person who, after actual notice of the copyright, begins an undertaking to infringe it, but shall prevent the recovery of damages against an innocent infringer who has been misled by the omission of the notice. . . .

---

[2] There is no dispute that plaintiff originally obtained copyright certificates for its gift wrap, birthday book and greeting card. (Exhibits 1, 4 and 7). Such certificates are *prima*

Assuming plaintiff's version of the facts is true, a close question, which I might have been inclined to resolve in plaintiff's favor, is presented as to the applicability of 17 U.S.C. § 21. See, e.g. *United Merchants and Manuf. Inc. v. Sarne Co.*, 278 F. Supp. 162 (S.D.N.Y. 1967); *Kramer Jewelry Creations, Inc. v. Capri Jewelry Inc.*, 143 F. Supp. 120 (S.D.N.Y. 1956). However, had infringement of the Hollie Hobbie Blue Girl been the only basis on which to enjoin fabric design #905, I would agree with defendant that before the applicability of 17 U.S.C. § 21 could be determined, it should be allowed to explore at a hearing 1) the extent to which omissions of the copyright notice of the Blue Girl did occur, 2) how they came into existence, 3) why they occurred on several different types of products and 4) why copies with omissions have been contained on products sold right up to the date of the hearing of this injunction.

[handwritten margin note: factors considered as to mis?/take & accident]

However, since I find that defendant's fabric design #905 without question infringed the illustration of the girl in oval mirror contained in plaintiff's copyrighted book "It's Nice to Have Birthdays" and since there is no showing that the latter illustration was ever distributed with a defective copyright notice, there is no need to hold an evidentiary hearing. Defendant has introduced into evidence porcelain boxes which contain the oval mirror illustration under the inscription "Put on a Happy Face" on the top cover. In the illustration appears the inscription "© WWA" and affixed to the underside of the dish is either the inscription "© World Wide Arts Inc." or "© WWA Inc." beneath which is the year 1973 in Roman numerals. Defendant argues that the presence of two different inscriptions on the same work is confusing and defeats copyright protection. However, the copyright law specifically provides that in the case of an art design it is proper to affix a monogram on the face of the design preceded by the symbol © as long as the symbol © followed by the proprietor's full name appears elsewhere on the article. 17 U.S.C. § 19 provides:

> In the case, however, of copies of works specified in subsections (f) to (k), inclusive, of section 5 of this title, [which includes works of art] the notice may consist of the letter C enclosed with a circle, thus ©, accompanied by the initials, monogram, mark, or symbol of the copyright proprietor: *Provided,* That on some accessible portion of such copies or of the margin, back, permanent base, or pedestal, or of the substance on which such copies shall be mounted, his name shall appear. . . .

Defendant also claims that since plaintiff American Greeting Corp. and not WWA Inc. or World Wide Arts Inc. is the true copyright owner, the illustration of the girl in the oval mirror using the inscription of the latter corporations is ineffective because the true copyright proprietor is not named in the notice. However, as defendant concedes, where a corporate subsidiary of a copyright proprietor has the same officers, directors and shareholders as its parent, a copyright notice in its name is proper. *National Comics Publications, Inc. v. Fawcett Publications, Inc.*, 191 F.2d 594, 602 (2d Cir. 1951); *B & B Auto Supply, Inc. v. Plesser*, 205 F. Supp. 36 (S.D.N.Y. 1962).[3] The affidavit of Paul Ozan,

---

facie proof of the validity of the copyright to which they refer, 17 U.S.C. § 209: *Herbert Rosenthal Jewelry Corp.* v. *Grossbardt*, 428 F.2d 551 (2d Cir. 1970). The issue here is whether plaintiff forfeited copyright protection by failure to protect its copyright when it affixed improper copyright notice to copies of its artwork.

[3] There is in addition some authority to the effect that if two copyright notices appear on the same items, one correct and one incorrect, and no confusion would result, no forfeiture of copyright protection will ensue. See authorities cited in 1 Nimmer on Copyright § 91 (1975).

plaintiff's Assistant Secretary, satisfies me that WWA Inc.[4] and World Wide Arts Inc. are or have been subsidiaries of American Greeting Corp. with identical officers, directors and shareholders. Defendant, demanding the opportunity to test these facts, was offered the chance of examining Mr. Ozan at the hearing but did not avail itself of the opportunity (Transcript of hearing August 18, 1975, pp. 78-9). Thus, I have no hesitancy at this time in accepting the validity of the use of WWA Inc. or World Wide Arts Inc. in place of American Greetings, Inc. on plaintiff's copyright notices.

Finally, defendant argues that since the year "1973" appears on the porcelain container depicting the girl in the oval mirror, plaintiff must forfeit copyright protection since the illustration of the girl was published in a 1967 book. Forfeiture, defendant argues, must result because post-dating a book copyright is an impermissible attempt to extend the period of statutory protection beyond that prescribed in the copyright law. Defendant's argument, however, ignores the fact that the oval mirror illustration appears with the inscription "Put on a Happy Face" which never appeared in the original book. With this addition plaintiff has created a derivative work containing additional matter making the later work distinguishable from the underlying work alone. 17 U.S.C. § 7.[6] Such work is independently copyrightable as a new and separate creation and no inscription concerning or reference to the underlying copyrighted work need be made. See 1 Nimmer on Copyright § 85.2 (1975):

> Another question unresolved by the statutory language [of 17 U.S.C. § 7] relates to the publication of a derivative work. If such a work incorporates material copyrighted by prior publication or by a prior registration as an unpublished work, should the notice for the derivative work contain the year of such prior publication or registration? The judicial decisions are clear that the notice contained on the derivative work need only contain the year of the first publication (or prior registration) of the derivative work *per se* and need not contain the earlier year of first publication or registration of any previously copyrighted material contained therein. . . . (footnotes omitted).

Nom Music, Inc. v. Kaslin, 343 F.2d 198 (2d Cir. 1965); *National Comics Publications, Inc. v. Fawcett Publications, Inc.,* 191 F.2d 594, 598 (2d Cir. 1951) approving the opinion of the District Court on this point, 93 F. Supp. 349 (S.D.N.Y. 1950).

Accordingly I do not conclude that the plaintiff's copyright of the illustration of the girl in the oval mirror infringed by fabric #905 has been forfeited through defective notice.

---

[4] WWA Inc. is the full name of the successor corporation to World Wide Arts Inc. and not an abbreviation.

[6] 17 U.S.C. § 7 provides:

Compilations or abridgments, adaptations, arrangements, dramatizations, translations or other versions of works in the public domain or of copyrighted works when produced with the consent of the proprietor of the copyright in such works, or works republished with new matter, shall be regarded as new works subject to copyright under the provisions of this title; but the publication of any such new works shall not affect the force or validity of any subsisting copyright upon the matter employed or any part thereof, or be construed to imply an exclusive right to such use of the original works, or to secure or extend copyright in such original works.

With respect to fabric #846, defendant's arguments claiming forfeiture by reasons of defective notice are even weaker. At best, defendant's attack could invalidate the copyrights to the illustrations of perhaps four of the eleven panels of the gift wrap copied on the fabric, even if all the objections were sustained. Thus, even if defendants were correct, fabric #846 still copied several panels to which there is no claim of copyright invalidity. And most importantly, defendant's fabric #846 copies the overall arrangement of the panels on plaintiff's gift wrap. Thus even if somehow plaintiff lost the copyright to all of the individual panels, defendant is not thereby permitted to infringe on plaintiff's copyrighted design arranging the panels in a distinct artistic pattern. . . .

B. 1976 ACT SOLUTIONS AS TO PUBLICATION AND NOTICE

1. THE STATUTORY DEFINITIONS

Section 101 defines publication as:

the distribution of copies or phonorecords of a work to the public by sale or other transfer of ownership, or by rental, lease, or lending. The offering to distribute copies or phonorecords to a group of persons for purposes of further distribution, public performance, or public display, constitutes publication. A public performance or display of a work does not itself constitute publication.

Against the background reviewed above, this definition is noteworthy in a number of respects:

• It purports to *be* a definition, i.e., to state what publication *is*, not what is "included" (cf. definition of "pictorial, graphic, and sculptural works") or what it is rebuttably presumed to be (cf. works made for hire, discussed at p. 233 *supra*). This is not to say that it resolves all definitional questions; indeed new ones may be created. For example, while the statute uses "copies" and "phonorecords" in the plural, the committee reports state that under this definition "a work is 'published' if *one or more* copies or phonorecords embodying it are distributed to the public." (Emphasis added.) S. Rep. No. 94-473 at 121; H.R. Rep. No. 94-1476 at 138. But Chairman Kastenmeier of the House subcommittee stated on the House Floor that "in the case of a work of art, such as a painting or statue, that exists in only one copy . . . [i]t is not the committee's intention that such a work should be regarded as 'published' when the single existing copy is sold or offered for sale in the traditional way — for example, through an art dealer, gallery, or auction house." 122 Cong. Rec. H10875 (Sept. 22, 1976).

• The definition is further muddied by the second sentence dealing with the offering to distribute for purposes of further distribution or public performance or display. This may simply be an example of an act which "constitutes" publication or an attempt to resolve specific uncertainties formerly surrounding motion picture and videotape distribution and exhibition.

• The line of authority holding that performance is *not* publication is accepted and codified.

• The possibility that some kind of exhibition may be publication has now been removed by the provision that public "display," as well as public performance of a work, "does not of itself constitute publication."

• The public distribution of recordings *does* constitute publication of the recorded work (as well as the sound recording), contrary to the 1909 law assumptions accepted in *Rosette v. Rainbo Record Mfg. Corp.*, 354 F. Supp. 1183, 177 USPQ 631 (S.D.N.Y. 1973), *aff'd per curiam*, 546 F.2d 461, 192 USPQ 673 (2d Cir. 1976). However, almost seventy years after *White-Smith Music Publishing Co. v. Apollo Co.*, 209 U.S. 1 (1908), Congress still declined to equate recordings with copies. Thus, in this definition and throughout the statute, one notes the refrain "copies or phonorecords." And, as will be noted below, there is no requirement for use of a © copyright notice on phonorecords pertaining to the underlying recorded work. (There *is* a requirement for a © notice pertaining to the recorded *performance* under § 402.)

2. THE CONTEXTS OF PUBLICATION

When one hears the overstatement that the 1976 Act "does away with" publication, one should consider at least the following contexts in which the concept of publication is significant:

• § 104 — *national origin:* Unpublished works are protected irrespective of the nationality of the author, while with respect to *published* works such nationality at the time of first publication is relevant.

• § 108 — *library photocopying:* Archival reproduction of *unpublished* works is permitted under subsection (b), while other privileges restricted to *published* works are provided in subsection (c).

• § 110(9) — *performance rights exemptions:* Certain privileged performances for handicapped persons are permitted with respect to certain works *published* at least 10 years earlier.

• § 118 and § 504(c)(2)(ii) — *public broadcasting compulsory license:* This is applicable only with respect to *published* nondramatic musical and pictorial, graphic, and sculptural works. Certain limitations on remedies for infringement with respect to *published* nondramatic literary works are found in § 504(c)(2)(ii).

• § 302(c) and (e) — *duration:* Duration of protection for anonymous and pseudonymous works and works made for hire, and presumptions regarding the date of an author's death, are measured from *publication* or creation under the formula already discussed.

• § 303 — *unpublished works:* As noted above, the thrust of this section is to provide for the duration of protection for *unpublished* material protected by the common law or state statutory law. Moreover, *publication* can extend such duration for 25 years.

• § 407 *et seq.* — *deposit and registration:* Deposit for Library of Congress purposes is mandatory for *published* works. § 407. Whether or not a work is *published* will also have ramifications for the details of Copyright Office registration and the remedies for infringement. *See* § 408(b) and § 412.

• § 601(b)(7) — *manufacturing clause:* Relief from the provisions of this clause is granted individual authors under certain limitations linked to the question of *publication*.

Over and above the foregoing, publication is most integrally connected under the 1976 Act (as it was under the 1909 Act) with the question of notice covered by Chapter 4 of Act.

QUESTIONS

Which of the following acts amount to "publication" under the 1976 Copyright Act:

1. A professor distributes outlines and questions to his students.

2. A computer programmer leases to banks a program, encoded on magnetic tape, for processing savings account deposits and withdrawals. The lease contains restrictions as to use.

3. A comic book publisher sends its books to a nationwide distributor for further distribution.

4. A comic book publisher sends its books to three regional distributors for further distribution.

5. An artist produces five signed prints from a master and offers them to an association of nonprofit museums and schools for distribution to appropriate association members.

6. An author, or her agent, offers copies of a manuscript to five publishers for their consideration.

7. A manufacturing company makes public distribution of stereo records or audio-cassettes of a song.

8. Any of the acts found in the Picasso case.

---

§ 401. Notice of copyright: Visually perceptible copies

(a) GENERAL REQUIREMENT. — Whenever a work protected under this title is published in the United States or elsewhere by authority of the copyright owner, a notice of copyright as provided by this section shall be placed on all publicly distributed copies from which the work can be visually perceived, either directly or with the aid of a machine or device.

(b) FORM OF NOTICE. — The notice appearing on the copies shall consist of the following three elements:

(1) the symbol © (the letter C in a circle), or the word "Copyright", or the abbreviation "Copr."; and

(2) the year of first publication of the work; in the case of compilations or derivative works incorporating previously published material, the year date of first publication of the compilation or derivative work is sufficient. The year date may be omitted where a pictorial, graphic, or sculptural work, with accompanying text matter, if any, is reproduced in or on greeting cards, postcards, stationery, jewelry, dolls, toys, or any useful articles; and

(3) the name of the owner of copyright in the work, or an abbreviation by which the name can be recognized, or a generally known alternative designation of the owner.

(c) POSITION OF NOTICE. — The notice shall be affixed to the copies in such manner and location as to give reasonable notice of the claim of copyright. The Register of Copyrights shall prescribe by regulation, as examples, specific methods of affixation and positions of the notice on various types of works that will satisfy this requirement, but these specifications shall not be considered exhaustive.

HOUSE REPORT

H.R. Rep. No. 94-1476, 94th Cong., 2d Sess. 143-44 (1976)

A requirement that the public be given formal notice of every work in which copyright is claimed was a part of the first U.S. copyright statute enacted in 1790, and since 1802 our copyright laws have always provided that the published copies of copyrighted works must bear a specified notice as a condition of protection. Under the present law the copyright notice serves four principal functions:

(1) It has the effect of placing in the public domain a substantial body of published material that no one is interested in copyrighting;
(2) It informs the public as to whether a particular work is copyrighted;
(3) It identifies the copyright owner; and
(4) It shows the date of publication.

Ranged against these values of a notice requirement are its burdens and unfairness to copyright owners. One of the strongest arguments for revision of the present statute has been the need to avoid the arbitrary and unjust forfeitures now resulting from unintentional or relatively unimportant omissions or errors in the copyright notice. It has been contended that the disadvantages of the notice requirement outweigh its values and that it should therefore be eliminated or substantially liberalized.

The fundamental principle underlying the notice provisions of the bill is that the copyright notice has real values which should be preserved, and that this should be done by inducing use of notice without causing outright forfeiture for errors or omissions. Subject to certain safeguards for innocent infringers, protection would not be lost by the complete omission of copyright notice from large numbers of copies or from a whole edition, if registration for the work is made before or within 5 years after publication. Errors in the name or date in the notice could be corrected without forfeiture of copyright.

Sections 401 and 402 set out the basic notice requirements of the bill, the former dealing with "copies from which the work can be visually perceived," and the latter covering "phonorecords" of a "sound recording." The notice requirements established by these parallel provisions apply only when copies or phonorecords of the work are "publicly distributed." No copyright notice would be required in connection with the public display of a copy by any means, including projectors, television, or cathode ray tubes connected with information storage and retrieval systems, or in connection with the public performance of a work by means of copies or phonorecords, whether in the presence of an audience or through television, radio, computer transmission, or any other process.

It should be noted that, under the definition of "publication" in section 101, there would no longer be any basis for holding, as a few court decisions have done in the past, that the public display of a work of art under some conditions (e.g., without restriction against its reproduction) would constitute publication of the work. And, as indicated above, the public display of a work of art would not require that a copyright notice be placed on the copy displayed.

Subsections (a) of both section 401 and section 402 require that a notice be used whenever the work "is published in the United States or elsewhere by authority of the copyright owner." The phrase "or elsewhere," which does not appear in the present law, makes the notice requirements applicable to copies or phonorecords distributed to the public anywhere in the world, regardless of where and when the work was first published. The values of notice are fully applicable to foreign editions of works copyrighted in the United States, especially with the increased flow of intellectual materials across national boundaries, and the gains in the use of notice on editions published abroad under the Universal Copyright Convention should not be wiped out. The consequences of omissions or mistakes with respect to the notice are far less serious under the bill than under the present law, and section 405(a) makes doubly clear that a copyright owner may guard himself against errors or omissions by others if he makes use of the prescribed notice an express condition of his publishing licenses.

Subsection (b) of section 401, which sets out the form of notice to appear on visually-perceptible copies, retains the basic elements of the notice under the present law: the word "Copyright", the abbreviation "Copr.", or the symbol "©"; the year of first publication; and the name of the copyright owner. The year of publication, which is still significant in computing the term and determining the status of a work, is required for all categories of copyrightable works. Clause (2) of subsection (b) makes clear that, in the case of a derivative work or compilation, it is not necessary to list the dates of publication of all preexisting material incorporated in the work; however, as noted below in connection with section 409, the application for registration covering a compilation or derivative work must identify "any preexisting work or works that it is based on or incorporates." Clause (3) establishes that a recognizable abbreviation or a generally known alternative designation may be used instead of the full name of the copyright owner.

By providing simply that the notice "shall be affixed to the copies in such manner and location 'as to give reasonable notice of the claim of copyright," subsection (c) follows the flexible approach of the Universal Copyright Convention. The further provision empowering the Register of Copyrights to set forth in regulations a list of examples of "specific methods of affixation and positions of the notice on various types of works that will satisfy this requirement" will offer substantial guidance and avoid a good deal of uncertainty. A notice placed or affixed in accordance with the regulations would clearly meet the requirements but, since the Register's specifications are not to "be considered exhaustive," a notice placed or affixed in some other way might also comply with the law if it were found to "give reasonable notice" of the copyright claim.

---

§ 402. Notice of copyright: Phonorecords of sound recordings

(a) GENERAL REQUIREMENT. — Whenever a sound recording protected under this title is published in the United States or elsewhere by authority of the copyright owner, a notice of copyright as provided by this section shall be placed on all publicly distributed phonorecords of the sound recording.

(b) FORM OF NOTICE. — The notice appearing on the phonorecords shall consist of the following three elements:

(1) the symbol ℗ (the letter P in a circle); and

(2) the year of first publication of the sound recording; and

(3) the name of the owner of copyright in the sound recording, or an abbreviation by which the name can be recognized, or a generally known alternative designation of the owner; if the producer of the sound recording is named on the phonorecord labels or containers, and if no other name appears in conjunction with the notice, the producer's name shall be considered a part of the notice.

(c) POSITION OF NOTICE. — The notice shall be placed on the surface of the phonorecord, or on the phonorecord label or container, in such manner and location as to give reasonable notice of the claim of copyright.

HOUSE REPORT

H.R. Rep. No. 94-1476, 94th Cong., 2d Sess. 145 (1976)

A special notice requirement, applicable only to the subject matter of sound recordings, is established by section 402. Since the bill protects sound recordings as separate works, independent of protection for any literary or musical works embodied in them, there would be a likelihood of confusion if the same notice requirements applied to sound recordings and to the works they incorporate. Like the present law, therefore, section 402 thus sets forth requirements for a notice to appear on the "phonorecords" of "sound recordings" that are different from the notice requirements established by section 401 for the "copies" of all other types of copyrightable works. Since "phonorecords" are not "copies," there is no need to place a section 401 notice on "phonorecords" to protect the literary or musical works embodied in the records.

In general, the form of the notice specified by section 402(b) consists of the symbol "℗"; the year of first publication of the sound recording; and the name of the copyright owner or an admissible variant. Where the record producer's name appears on the record label, album, sleeve, jacket, or other container, it will be considered a part of the notice if no other name appears in conjunction with it. Under subsection (c), the notice for a copyrighted sound recording may be affixed to the surface, label, or container of the phonorecord "in such manner and location as to give reasonable notice of the claim of copyright."

There are at least three reasons for prescribing use of the symbol "℗" rather than "©" in the notice to appear on phonorecords of sound recordings. Aside from the need to avoid confusion between claims to copyright in the sound recording and in the musical or literary work embodied in it, there is also a necessity for distinguishing between copyright claims in the sound recording and in the printed text or art work appearing on the record label, album cover, liner notes, et cetera. The symbol "℗" has also been adopted as the international symbol for the protection of sound recordings by the "Phonograms Convention" (the Convention for the Protection of Producers of Phonograms Against Unauthorized Duplication of Their Phonograms, done at Geneva October 29, 1971), to which the United States is a party.

---

§ 404. Notice of copyright: Contributions to collective works

(a) A separate contribution to a collective work may bear its own notice of copyright, as provided by sections 401 through 403. However, a single notice applicable to the collective work as a whole is sufficient to satisfy the requirements of sections 401 through 403 with respect to the separate contributions it contains (not including advertisements inserted on behalf of persons other than the owner of copyright in the collective work), regardless of the ownership of copyright in the contributions and whether or not they have been previously published.

(b) Where the person named in a single notice applicable to a collective work as a whole is not the owner of copyright in a separate contribution that does not bear its own notice, the case is governed by the provisions of section 406(a).

QUESTIONS

1. What is the purpose of requiring copyright notice on publicly distributed copies and phonorecords? What is the purpose of noting the copyright owner and the date?

2. If the purpose of copyright notice on an eye-readable copy of a literary work or a musical composition is to alert the user to claims of copyright in those works, why is the same not true when the literary work or musical composition is captured on a phonorecord?

3. Examine the Register's proposed regulations (Appendix D) setting forth non-exhaustive examples of the location and methods of affixing copyright notice. Consider whether the statute and regulations have not fallen unhappily between two stools — too rigid to protect the inexpert author but too flexible to alert the inexpert user?

4. Your client has had her short story accepted for publication by *Cosmopolitan Magazine;* it will be published early next year. What copyright notice should be affixed, and where? (What significant information will the notice give the reader, and what will be omitted?)

5. The year after the article is published in *Cosmopolitan,* your client wishes to reprint it, as written, in a paperback edition. Must she secure the consent of the Magazine? When reprinted, what notice should the story bear? (What is the consequence of the notice bearing the date 1976? What is the consequence of the notice bearing the date 1986?)

6. If the story mentioned above is reprinted not alone, but with an unpublished short story written by your client in 1968, what should the copyright notice be?

7. If the *Cosmopolitan* story contained a number of drawings specifically prepared by your client, and she wishes to sell reproductions of those drawings in 1986, what notice should they bear?

8. In 1980 your client conveys the right to *D* to dramatize the short story; *D* produces his play in 1982, and markets copies in 1985. What copyright notice should these copies bear?

9. *A,* an author, grants book rights to *B,* a publisher, which in turn grants paperback rights to *C.* Whose name should appear in the notice on the paperback edition?

10. You represent Pineapple Records, Inc., a manufacturer of phonograph records and tapes. A song composed by Alan Robert in 1978 is recorded by your client in 1979. The recording is released in 1980. (a) What copyright notice should be affixed and where? (b) Would your answer be any different if there were original artwork on the labels and jacket and textual notes on the jacket? (c) Sheet music embodying this song is distributed in 1981. What copyright notice should be affixed? Is this answer affected by the identity or lack of identity of the material embodied on the recording and on the sheet music? (d) Would "A. Robert" be a sufficient element of the copyright notice? "A. R."? "Pineapple Records"? "Pineapple"?

11. The 1976 Act is universally described as representing a liberalization of notice requirements. (But note that the year date is required more often than under the prior law. Compare §§ 401, 402 with 1909 Act § 19.) However, the following resolution was presented in August 1980 to the Section of Patent, Trademark and Copyright Law of the American Bar Association:

RESOLVED, that the Section of Patent, Trademark and Copyright Law approves in principle legislation providing for the elimination of all copyright notice requirements under the Copyright law of the United States.

How would you vote on this resolution?

---

§ 403. Notice of copyright: Publications incorporating United States Government works

Whenever a work is published in copies or phonorecords consisting preponderantly of one or more works of the United States Government, the notice of copyright provided by sections 401 or 402 shall also include a statement identifying, either affirmatively or negatively, those portions of the copies or phonorecords embodying any work or works protected under this title.

HOUSE REPORT

H.R. Rep. No. 94-1476, 94th Cong., 2d Sess. 145-46 (1976)

Section 403 is aimed at a publishing practice that, while technically justified under the present law, has been the object of considerable criticism. In cases where a Government work is published or republished commercially, it has frequently been the practice to add some "new matter" in the form of an introduction, editing, illustrations, etc., and to include a general copyright notice in the name of the commercial publisher. This in no way suggests to the public that the bulk of the work is uncopyrightable and therefore free for use.

To make the notice meaningful rather than misleading, section 403 requires that, when the copies or phonorecords consist "preponderantly of one or more works of the United States Government," the copyright notice (if any) [should] identify those parts of the work in which copyright is claimed. A failure to meet this requirement would be treated as an omission of the notice, subject to the provisions of section 405.

QUESTIONS

1. What should be the correct copyright notice in West's (unofficial) Supreme Court Reporter? Is this the notice presently being printed? What is the sanction for improper notice in such cases?

2. Should there not be a requirement, parallel to that in § 403, that all works consisting preponderantly of any kind of public domain material reflect this fact in the copyright notice? (What does "preponderantly" mean, 50.1 percent?) Why might Congress have neglected to require such disclosure in the notice? (Consider what the applicant for copyright registration must set forth under § 409.)

---

§ 405. Notice of copyright: Omission of notice

(a) EFFECT OF OMISSION ON COPYRIGHT. — The omission of the copyright notice prescribed by sections 401 through 403 from copies or phonorecords publicly distributed by authority of the copyright owner does not invalidate the copyright in a work if —

(1) the notice has been omitted from no more than a relatively small number of copies or phonorecords distributed to the public;

(2) registration for the work has been made before or is made within five years after the publication without notice, and a reasonable effort is made to add notice to all copies or phonorecords that are distributed to the public in the United States after the omission has been discovered; or

(3) the notice has been omitted in violation of an express requirement in writing that, as a condition of the copyright owner's authorization of the public distribution of copies or phonorecords, they bear the prescribed notice.

(b) EFFECT OF OMISSION ON INNOCENT INFRINGERS. — Any person who innocently infringes a copyright, in reliance upon an authorized copy or phonorecord from which the copyright notice has been omitted, incurs no liability for actual or statutory damages under section 504 for any infringing acts committed before receiving actual notice that registration for the work has been made under section 408, if such person proves that he or she was misled by the omission of notice. In a suit for infringement in such a case the court may allow or disallow recovery of any of the infringer's profits attributable to the infringement, and may enjoin the continuation of the infringing undertaking or may require, as a condition of permitting the continuation of the infringing undertaking, that the infringer pay the copyright owner a reasonable license fee in an amount and on terms fixed by the court.

(c) REMOVAL OF NOTICE. — Protection under this title is not affected by the removal, destruction, or obliteration of the notice, without the authorization of the copyright owner, from any publicly distributed copies or phonorecords.

HOUSE REPORT

H.R. Rep. No. 94-1476, 94th Cong., 2d Sess. 146-49 (1976)

Effect of omission on copyright protection

The provisions of section 405(a) make clear that the notice requirements of sections 401, 402, and 403 are not absolute and that, unlike the law now in effect, the outright omission of a copyright notice does not automatically forfeit protection and throw the work into the public domain. This not only represents a major change in the theoretical framework of American copyright law, but it also seems certain to have immediate practical consequences in a great many individual cases. Under the proposed law a work published without any copyright notice will still be subject to statutory protection for at least 5 years, whether the omission was partial or total, unintentional or deliberate.

Under the general scheme of the bill, statutory copyright protection is secured automatically when a work is created, and is not lost when the work is published, even if the copyright notice is omitted entirely. Subsection (a) of section 405 provides that omission of notice, whether intentional or unintentional, does not invalidate the copyright if either of two conditions is met:

(1) if "no more than a relatively small number" of copies or phonorecords have been publicly distributed without notice; or

(2) if registration for the work has already been made, or is made within 5 years after the publication without notice, and a reasonable effort is made to add notice to copies or phonorecords publicly distributed in the United States after the omission is discovered.

. . . .

The basic notice requirements set forth in sections 401(a) and 402(a) are limited to cases where a work is published "by authority of the copyright owner" and, in prescribing the effect of omission of notice, section 405(a) refers only to omission "from copies or phonorecords publicly distributed by authority of the copyright owner." The intention behind this language is that, where the copyright owner authorized publication of the work, the notice requirements would not be met if copies or phonorecords are publicly distributed without a notice, even if he expected a notice to be used. However, if the copyright owner authorized publication only on the express condition that all copies or phonorecords bear a prescribed notice, the provisions of section 401 or 402 and of section 405 would not apply since the publication itself would not be authorized. This principle is stated directly in section 405(a) (3).

Effect of omission on innocent infringers

In addition to the possibility that copyright protection will be forfeited under section 405(a) (2) if the notice is omitted, a second major inducement to use of the notice is found in subsection (b) of section 405. That provision, which limits the rights of a copyright owner against innocent infringers under certain circumstances, would be applicable whether the notice has been omitted from a large number or from a "relatively small number" of copies. The general postulates underlying the provision are that a person acting in good faith and with no reason to think otherwise should ordinarily be able to assume that a work is in the public domain if there is no notice on an authorized copy or phonorecord and that, if he relies on this assumption, he should be shielded from unreasonable liability.

Under section 405(b) an innocent infringer who acts "in reliance upon an authorized copy or phonorecord from which the copyright notice has been omitted", and who proves that he was misled by the omission, is shielded from liability for actual or statutory damages with respect to "any infringing acts committed before receiving actual notice" of registration. Thus, where the infringement is completed before actual notice has been served — as would be the usual case with respect to relatively minor infringements by teachers, librarians, journalists, and the like — liability, if any, would be limited to the profits the infringer realized from the act of infringement. On the other hand, where the infringing enterprise is one running over a period of time, the copyright owner would be able to seek an injunction against continuation of the infringement, and to obtain full monetary recovery for all infringing acts committed after he had served notice of registration. Persons who undertake major enterprises of this sort should check the Copyright Office registration records before starting, even where copies have been published without notice.

. . . .

Removal of notice by others

Subsection (c) of section 405 involves the situation arising when, following an authorized publication with notice, someone further down the chain of commerce removes, destroys, or obliterates the notice. The courts dealing with this problem under the present law, especially in connection with copyright notices on the selvage of textile fabrics, have generally upheld the validity of a notice that was securely attached to the copies when they left the control of the copyright owner, even though removal of the notice at some later stage was likely. This conclusion is incorporated in subsection (c).

QUESTIONS

1. Consider § 405(a)(3) and whether the same result — no invalidation of copyright — ought not to follow when the public distribution of copies is in violation of an express *oral* directive conditioning publication on the placement of proper notice. Would not such a result follow, even without § 405(a)(3), from a natural reading of § 401(a)?

2. The innocent infringer is said to be protected in copying from a work without copyright notice because he will ordinarily and reasonably assume that such a work is in the public domain. Is this true when, under the 1976 Copyright Act, copyright attaches as soon as a work is fixed in a tangible medium of expression (and not when it is published with notice)? Would you advise a client to search copyright office records in every case before using a work published without notice? Would you advise the client *not* to search? *See Quinto v. Legal Times of Washington,* 511 F. Supp. 579 (D.D.C. 1981).

3. A client deliberately wishes to omit a copyright notice. Is this permissible in the face of the provision in § 401(a) that a notice "shall be placed" on copies and in § 405 requiring reasonable steps to add notice after an omission "has been discovered"?

4. Suppose copies of a work are distributed solely in Europe. Must a copyright notice be used? Must any other steps be taken?

5. If the purpose of the copyright notice is to alert users to the claims of the copyright owner, why does § 405(c) treat as adequate the placement of notice on the selvage of a dress fabric with knowledge that the notice will inevitably be shorn at a later stage of the manufacturing process?

------

§ 406. Notice of copyright: Error in name or date

(a) ERROR IN NAME. — Where the person named in the copyright notice on copies or phonorecords publicly distributed by authority of the copyright owner is not the owner of copyright, the validity and ownership of the copyright are not affected. In such a case, however, any person who innocently begins an undertaking that infringes the copyright has a complete defense to any action for such infringement if such person proves that he or she was misled by the notice and began the undertaking in good faith under a purported transfer or license from the person named therein, unless before the undertaking was begun —

(1) registration for the work had been made in the name of the owner of copyright; or

(2) a document executed by the person named in the notice and showing the ownership of the copyright had been recorded.

The person named in the notice is liable to account to the copyright owner for all receipts from transfers or licenses purportedly made under the copyright by the person named in the notice.

(b) ERROR IN DATE. — When the year date in the notice on copies or phonorecords distributed by authority of the copyright owner is earlier than the year in which publication first occurred, any period computed from the year of first publication under section 302 is to be computed from the year in the notice. Where the year date is more than one year later than the year in which publication first occured, the work is considered to have been published without any notice and is governed by the provisions of section 405.

(c) OMISSION OF NAME OR DATE. — Where copies or phonorecords publicly distributed by authority of the copyright owner contain no name or no date that could reasonably be considered a part of the notice, the work is considered to have been published without any notice and is governed by the provisions of section 405.

HOUSE REPORT

H. R. Rep. No. 94-1476, 94th Cong., 2d Sess. 149-50 (1976)

. . . .

The situation dealt with in section 406 (a) presupposes a contractual relation between the copyright owner and the person named in the notice. The copies or phonorecords bearing the defective notice have been "distributed by authority of the copyright owner" and, unless the publication can be considered unauthorized because of breach of an express condition in the contract or other reasons, the owner must be presumed to have acquiesced in the use of the wrong name. If the person named in the notice grants a license for use of the work in good faith or under a misapprehension, that person should not be liable as a copyright infringer, but the last sentence of section 406 (a) would make the person named in the notice liable to account to the copyright owner for "all receipts, from transfers or licenses purportedly made under the copyright" by that person.

. . . .

Omission of name or date

Section 406 (c) provides that, if the copies or phonorecords "contain no name or no date that could reasonably be considered a part of the notice," the result is the same as if the notice had been omitted entirely, and section 405 controls. Unlike the present law, the bill contains no provision requiring the elements of the copyright notice to "accompany" each other, and under section 406 (c) a name or date that could reasonably be read with the other elements may satisfy the requirements even if somewhat separated from them. Direct contiguity or juxtaposition of the elements is no longer necessary; but if the elements are too widely separated for their relation to be apparent, or if uncertainty is created by the presence of other names or dates, the case would have to be treated as if the name or date, and hence the notice itself had been omitted altogether.

QUESTIONS

1. Suppose a copyright notice names a stranger as owner. Is copyright invalidated? Is the situation treated as a publication without notice?
2. Recall the publication of your client's short story in *Cosmopolitan Magazine* (see Question 4 on p. 292 *supra*). Assume that the only copyright notice in *Cosmopolitan* when your client's story was printed was the "masthead notice" in the name of *Cosmopolitan*. Assume, too, that a motion picture producer buys the motion picture rights to the story from *Cosmopolitan* for $20,000; that one month later, he hires a scriptwriter; that two months later, he hires stars; that five months later, he begins production; and that the movie, when released, quickly nets $5 million. When your client learns of this, what are her rights (if any) against *Cosmopolitan* and the producer?

When Author brings an action against Magazine for the unauthorized (indeed fraudulent) transfer of copyright to Movie Producer, will Author's recovery be limited to $20,000? If the last sentence of § 406(a) sets forth a limitation on recovery rather than a "floor," why should that be so? Is the House Report a reliable source when it states that the apparent limitation in § 406(a) does not apply to willful and knowing transfers by Magazine?

What steps would you recommend that your client have taken at the outset to avoid this problem? What steps should the producer have taken?

3. Assume that the *Cosmopolitan* issue in which your client's story appears lacks *any* copyright notice, either on the masthead or on the story itself. Are there any steps your client can take to prevent copyright from being forfeited? Is a motion picture producer who sees the story free to base a script on it?

4. Your client conveys to *XYZ* Press the exclusive right to print her story, worldwide, for twenty years. Will any adverse consequences follow if *XYZ* Press places its name in the copyright notice?

5. To what extent will the philosophy (or even the provisions) of the 1976 Act likely creep into the approach of a court called upon in 1988, after ten years of operating under the 1976 Act, to determine whether a work first published in 1968 was in the "public domain before January 1, 1978"?

C. REGISTRATION AND DEPOSIT

1. DEPOSIT FOR LIBRARY OF CONGRESS

The § 407 deposit, which "shall" be made by "the owner of copyright or of the exclusive right of publication" within three months after publication with notice in the United States, is to consist of "two complete copies of the best edition" or, if the work is a sound recording, two complete phonorecords of the best edition, together with all accompanying printed material.

The term "best edition" is defined in § 101 as "the edition, published in the United States at any time before the date of deposit, that the Library of Congress determines to be most suitable for its purposes." This definition presumably avoids the uncertainties surrounding the statutory phrase "the best edition . . . then published" found in § 13 of the 1909 law. *See*, e.g., *Twentieth Century-Fox Film Corp. v. Bouvé*, 33 F. Supp. 462, 45 USPQ 411 (D.D.C. 1940), *aff'd*, 122 F.2d 51, 50 USPQ 338 (D.C. Cir. 1941); *King Features Syndicate, Inc. v. Bouvé*, 48 USPQ 237 (D.D.C. 1940). (Both *Bouvé,* cases involved questions of proper deposit format of material to be syndicated in newspapers.) The Library has issued a policy statement on what constitutes such a "best edition," and this is now referred to in the implementing Copyright Office regulations. *See* 43 Fed. Reg. 766 (Jan. 4, 1978); 37 C.F.R. § 202.19 (1978).

The three-month provision may be contrasted with the 1909 law requirement that the work be deposited "promptly." The 1909 Act did not define the term "promptly," nor did it provide that any failure to make prompt deposit should in itself invalidate the copyright which had already been secured by publication with notice. Invalidation could result upon failure to make the deposit of copies after actual notice and demand by the Register of Copyrights as provided in § 14.

In *Washingtonian Publishing Co., Inc. v. Pearson,* 306 U.S. 30, 40 USPQ 190 (1939), the Supreme Court had held that once a copyright has been secured by publication with proper notice, the right to bring suit was not impaired by tardy deposit (14 months had elapsed in this case) whether the infringement occurred before or after the deposit is actually made. The *Washingtonian* doctrine became so extended that the word "promptly" came to be read in an Alice-in-Wonderland sense. Registration could apparently be made at any time during the first term of copyright, since a 27-year delay has been excused. *Shapiro, Bernstein & Co. v. Jerry Vogel Music Co., Inc.,* 161 F.2d 406, 71 USPQ 286 (2d Cir. 1946), *cert. denied,* 331 U.S. 820, 73 USPQ 550 (1947). *Cf. Silvers v. Russell,* 113 F. Supp. 119, 98 USPQ 376 (S.D. Cal. 1953) (13 years); *Ziegelheim v. Flohr,* 119 F. Supp. 324, 100 USPQ 189 (E.D.N.Y. 1954) (9 years).

The material for use or disposition of the Library of Congress under § 407(b) of the 1976 Act is to be deposited in the Copyright Office. And it is the Register of Copyrights who is given authority to issue regulations exempting categories of material from the deposit requirements of this section, reducing the required copies or phonorecords to one, or, in the case of certain pictorial, graphic, or sculptural works, providing for exemptions or alternative forms of deposit. § 407(c). Machine-readable computer programs and data bases, three-dimensional sculptural works, textiles and other fabrics and packaging material, and advertisements are among those exempt from Library deposit under the initial regulations issued by the Register, and motion pictures, multimedia kits, and small editions of pictorial and graphic works are permitted single-copy deposit. 37 C.F.R. § 202.19(c) and (d)(2) (1978). The Register is also to issue regulations governing the acquisition of copies or phonorecords of certain unpublished radio and television programs, including conditions under which the Librarian of Congress may, without liability, tape these programs off the air. § 407(e). (The Librarian may also tape news broadcasts, under certain conditions, as part of his or her duties to preserve programs under the American Television and Radio Archives Act, embodied in Trans. & Suppl. Sec. 113 (90 Stat. 2601).)

2. COPYRIGHT REGISTRATION

a. Procedure

If the Library deposit under § 407 is accompanied by a prescribed application for registration and fee, it may be used to satisfy the deposit requirements of registration. It should be noted that the registration provision permits a deposit of one copy or phonorecord, rather than two, in the case of unpublished works, works published abroad, and contributions to a collective work (where a copy of the collective work is required). Because of the statutory language, the Copyright Office will no longer make registration if the application and fee do not "accompany" the deposit. 37 C.F.R. § 202.20(e)(1977).

Registration under § 408 contrasts with the Library deposit provision under § 407 in the following respects: (1) it may be made by not only the owner of copyright but also the owner of any exclusive right thereunder rather than by the owner of the exclusive right of publication; (2) it applies to unpublished as well as published works; (3) it includes works published abroad; (4) it may be made "at any time" during the subsistence of copyright; (5) it can be a condition of preserving copyright *if (but only if)* notice is omitted. Note also that § 408 applies to domestic and foreign works equally. *Cf.* § 215 of the 1909 law.

Considerable flexibility is accorded the Register with respect to administrative classification, aggregation of related works, and alternative forms of deposit. § 408(c)(1). The new classifications are:

Class TX—Nondramatic Literary Works;
Class PA—Works of the Performing Arts;
Class VA—Works of the Visual Arts;
Class SR—Sound Recordings;
Class RE—Renewal Registration.

496A
FORM TX

UNITED STATES COPYRIGHT OFFICE

The TX form looks like this:

REGISTRATION NUMBER
TX   TXU

EFFECTIVE DATE OF REGISTRATION

. . . .
Month   Day   Year

DO NOT WRITE ABOVE THIS LINE. IF YOU NEED MORE SPACE, USE CONTINUATION SHEET (FORM TX/CON)

(1) Title

TITLE OF THIS WORK:

PREVIOUS OR ALTERNATIVE TITLES:

If a periodical or serial give: Vol...... No...... Issue Date.................................

PUBLICATION AS A CONTRIBUTION: (If this work was published as a contribution to a periodical, serial, or collection, give information about the collective work in which the contribution appeared.)

Title of Collective Work:.................................... Vol...... No...... Date................. Pages.............

(2) Author(s)

IMPORTANT: Under the law, the "author" of a "work made for hire" is generally the employer, not the employee (see instructions). If any part of this work was "made for hire" check "Yes" in the space provided, give the employer (or other person for whom the work was prepared) as "Author" of that part, and leave the space for dates blank.

1

NAME OF AUTHOR:

Was this author's contribution to the work a "work made for hire"?   Yes...... No......

DATES OF BIRTH AND DEATH:
Born.......... Died ....
(Year)   (Year)

AUTHOR'S NATIONALITY OR DOMICILE:
Citizen of .... } or { Domiciled in ....
(Name of Country)   (Name of Country)

AUTHOR OF: (Briefly describe nature of this author's contribution)

WAS THIS AUTHOR'S CONTRIBUTION TO THE WORK:
Anonymous?   Yes...... No......
Pseudonymous? Yes...... No......
If the answer to either of these questions is "Yes," see detailed instructions attached.

2

NAME OF AUTHOR:

Was this author's contribution to the work a "work made for hire"?   Yes...... No......

DATES OF BIRTH AND DEATH:
Born.......... Died ....
(Year)   (Year)

AUTHOR'S NATIONALITY OR DOMICILE:
Citizen of .... } or { Domiciled in ....
(Name of Country)   (Name of Country)

AUTHOR OF: (Briefly describe nature of this author's contribution)

WAS THIS AUTHOR'S CONTRIBUTION TO THE WORK:
Anonymous?   Yes...... No......
Pseudonymous? Yes...... No......
If the answer to either of these questions is "Yes," see detailed instructions attached.

3

NAME OF AUTHOR:

Was this author's contribution to the work a "work made for hire"?   Yes...... No......

DATES OF BIRTH AND DEATH:
Born.......... Died ....
(Year)   (Year)

AUTHOR'S NATIONALITY OR DOMICILE:
Citizen of .... } or { Domiciled in ....
(Name of Country)   (Name of Country)

AUTHOR OF: (Briefly describe nature of this author's contribution)

WAS THIS AUTHOR'S CONTRIBUTION TO THE WORK:
Anonymous?   Yes...... No......
Pseudonymous? Yes...... No......
If the answer to either of these questions is "Yes," see detailed instructions attached.

(3) Creation and Publication

YEAR IN WHICH CREATION OF THIS WORK WAS COMPLETED:

Year..........
(This information must be given in all cases.)

DATE AND NATION OF FIRST PUBLICATION:

Date.....................
(Month)   (Day)   (Year)
Nation.....................
(Name of Country)
(Complete this block ONLY if this work has been published.)

(4) Claimant(s)

NAME(S) AND ADDRESS(ES) OF COPYRIGHT CLAIMANT(S):

TRANSFER: (If the copyright claimant(s) named here in space 4 are different from the author(s) named in space 2, give a brief statement of how the claimant(s) obtained ownership of the copyright.)

• Complete all applicable spaces (numbers 5-11) on the reverse side of this page
• Follow detailed instructions attached   • Sign the form at line 10

DO NOT WRITE HERE
Page 1 of .... pages

496B

EXAMINED BY:	APPLICATION RECEIVED:	
CHECKED BY:		
CORRESPONDENCE: ☐ Yes	DEPOSIT RECEIVED:	FOR COPYRIGHT OFFICE USE ONLY
DEPOSIT ACCOUNT FUNDS USED: ☐	REMITTANCE NUMBER AND DATE:	

DO NOT WRITE ABOVE THIS LINE. IF YOU NEED ADDITIONAL SPACE, USE CONTINUATION SHEET (FORM TX/CON)

PREVIOUS REGISTRATION:

- Has registration for this work, or for an earlier version of this work, already been made in the Copyright Office? Yes . . . . No . . . .
- If your answer is "Yes," why is another registration being sought? (Check appropriate box)
  - ☐ This is the first published edition of a work previously registered in unpublished form.
  - ☐ This is the first application submitted by this author as copyright claimant.
  - ☐ This is a changed version of the work, as shown by line 6 of this application.
- If your answer is "Yes," give: Previous Registration Number . . . . Year of Registration . . . .

⑤ Previous Registration

COMPILATION OR DERIVATIVE WORK: (See instructions)

PREEXISTING MATERIAL: (Identify any preexisting work or works that this work is based on or incorporates.)

{ . . . .

MATERIAL ADDED TO THIS WORK: (Give a brief, general statement of the material that has been added to this work and in which copyright is claimed.)

{ . . . .

⑥ Compilation or Derivative Work

MANUFACTURERS AND LOCATIONS: (If this is a published work consisting preponderantly of nondramatic literary material in English, the law may require that the copies be manufactured in the United States or Canada for full protection. If so, the names of the manufacturers who performed certain processes, and the places where these processes were performed *must* be given. See instructions for details.)

NAMES OF MANUFACTURERS   PLACES OF MANUFACTURE

⑦ Manufacturing

REPRODUCTION FOR USE OF BLIND OR PHYSICALLY-HANDICAPPED PERSONS: (See instructions)

- Signature of this form at space 10, and a check in one of the boxes here in space 8, constitutes a non-exclusive grant of permission to the Library of Congress to reproduce and distribute solely for the blind and physically handicapped and under the conditions and limitations prescribed by the regulations of the Copyright Office: (1) copies of the work identified in space 1 of this application in Braille (or similar tactile symbols): or (2) phonorecords embodying a fixation of a reading of that work: or (3) both.

  a ☐ Copies and phonorecords   b ☐ Copies Only   c ☐ Phonorecords Only

⑧ License For Handicapped

DEPOSIT ACCOUNT: (If the registration fee is to be charged to a Deposit Account established in the Copyright Office, give name and number of Account.)

Name: . . . .
Account Number: . . . .

CORRESPONDENCE: (Give name and address to which correspondence about this application should be sent.)
Name: . . . .
Address: . . . . (Apt.)
. . . .
(City)   (State)   (ZIP)

⑨ Fee and Correspondence

CERTIFICATION: ✱ I, the undersigned, hereby certify that I am the: (Check one)
☐ author ☐ other copyright claimant ☐ owner of exclusive right(s) ☐ authorized agent of: . . . .
(Name of author or other copyright claimant, or owner of exclusive right(s))
of the work identified in this application and that the statements made by me in this application are correct to the best of my knowledge.

Handwritten signature: (X) . . . .

Typed or printed name. . . . . Date . . . .

⑩ Certification (Application must be signed)

. . . .
(Name)

. . . .
(Number, Street and Apartment Number)

. . . .
(City)   (State)   (ZIP code)

MAIL CERTIFICATE TO

(Certificate will be mailed in window envelope)

⑪ Address For Return of Certificate

✱ 17 U.S.C. § 506(e): Any person who knowingly makes a false representation of a material fact in the application for copyright registration provided for by section 409, or in any written statement filed in connection with the application, shall be fined not more than $2,500.

✩ U.S. GOVERNMENT PRINTING OFFICE: 1980: 311-425/3

Jan. 1980—500,000

Under § 408(c)(1) "the Register could, where appropriate, permit deposit of phonorecords rather than notated copies of musical compositions, allow or require deposit of print-outs of computer programs under certain circumstances, or permit deposit of one volume of an encyclopedia for purposes of registration of a single contribution." H.R. Rep. No. 94-1476, 94th Cong., 2d Sess. 153 (1976). The Register has issued regulations permitting such deposit of phonorecords and printouts under certain circumstances. 37 C.F.R. § 202.20(c)(1) and (c)(2)(vii) (1978).

Authors of contributions to periodicals are specifically authorized to group their works published within a 12-month period under a single application for registration provided that the works each bear a separate notice naming the same owner. § 408(c)(2). Form GR/CP has now been prescribed for this purpose. See also § 408(c)(1). A similar option is given such authors to renew pursuant to § 304(a) under somewhat parallel conditions. § 408(c)(3). These provisions are of considerable economic significance to authors of poems, cartoons, and other relatively short works. An additional form (CA) has been introduced to cover "supplementary registrations."

The application for registration will clearly contain more information than it traditionally has. The statute specifies that it will include various items of information potentially required for computation of duration, e.g., dates of death, year of creation, and year of publication if any, as well as the basis of ownership for persons other than authors and a brief, general statement of preexisting and added material used in any derivative work or compilation. § 409. The difficulties attendant upon the introduction of the new forms resulted in unprecedented delays within the Copyright Office during the early months of operation under the 1976 Act.

b. Register's Authority and Effect of Registration

The 1976 Act expressly provides that the Register may refuse registration upon his or her determination that a claim is invalid. § 410(b). For a discussion of implied authority to that effect under the 1909 law, see Berger, *Authority of the Register of Copyrights to Reject Applications for Registration,* 2 STUDIES ON COPYRIGHT 813 (Arthur Fisher mem. ed. 1963).

Actual registration, rather than merely application for registration, was required as a prerequisite for an infringement action under the 1909 law. *See Vacheron & Constantin-Le Coultre Watches, Inc. v. Benrus Watch Co., Inc.,* 260 F.2d 637, 119 USPQ 189 (2d Cir. 1958); *Imperial Toy Corp. v. Ben Cooper, Inc.,* 185 USPQ 453 (C.D. Cal. 1975). This result is legislatively reversed by § 411(a), which permits an infringement suit even where registration has been refused, provided that the deposit, application, and fee are in proper form *and* notice is given to the Register who is given the right to intervene. A specialized timetable and procedure are set forth in the new law for the owner of a broadcast program tape made simultaneously with its transmission. *See* § 411(b).

The statute refines the "prima facie effect" provisions of the 1909 Act which accorded such effect to the "facts stated" in the certificate. As to the application of this 1909 provision amounting to a presumption of validity, compare *Wihtol v. Wells,* 231 F.2d 550, 553, 109 USPQ 200 (7th Cir. 1956), and *Epoch Producing Corp. v. Killiam Shows, Inc.,* 522 F.2d 737, 745, 187 USPQ 270, 276 (2d Cir. 1975), *cert. denied,* 424 U.S. 955, 189 USPQ 256 (1976), with *Krafft v. Cohen,* 117 F.2d 578, 48 USPQ 401 (3d Cir. 1941) (certificate did not necessarily establish that work when first published bore correct copyright notice). Section 410(c) of the 1976 Act provides:

In any judicial proceedings the certificate of a registration made before or within five years after first publication of the work shall constitute prima facie evidence of the validity of the copyright and of the facts stated in the certificate. The evidentiary weight to be accorded the certificate of a registration made thereafter shall be within the discretion of the court.

The discussion of registration thus far reveals the following incentives: (1) preservation of copyright if notice has been omitted (§ 405(a)(2)); (2) protection of actual owner where the wrong owner is named in the notice (§ 406(a)(1)); (3) early registration will insure prima facie proof of validity (§ 410(c)); and (4) generally a prerequisite to suit under § 411. The statute also conditions the potential remedies of statutory damages and attorneys' fees on registration before infringement but provides a three-month grace period in the case of published works, i.e., these remedies are potentially available even as to infringements before registration if the latter is made within three months after first publication. § 412. Cf. § 205(c) and (e) (one-month grace period), and see also § 601(d) (manufacturing clause).

QUESTIONS

1. Making reference to other sections of the Act, what are the reasons for requiring that each of the items listed in § 409 be included in the application for copyright registration?

2. Under what circumstances may phonorecords rather than notated copies be deposited, with respect to musical compositions? With respect to sound recordings? Consult 37 C.F.R. § 202.20(c)(1) and (c)(2)(viii).

3. How do the deposit provisions (see pp. 298-302 supra) take into account the presence of confidential information contained in a writing — which is automatically (and without the necessary acquiescence of the owner) brought under the statute? Is the approach of the statute in this regard fair to the owner, and to the public?

4. Artist recently completed a painting tentatively titled "When Autumn Is Here," which he has kept in his studio, along with other paintings and sculptures of his. Several months ago, a burglar broke into Artist's studio and stole several of his works, including "When Autumn Is Here." Artist has just learned that ownership of the painting is now being claimed by the Grand Gallery, which is also marketing full-size color reproductions. Artist consults you, wishing to know whether he has any legal rights against the Gallery and, if so, whether he may enforce them in an infringement action in the federal court. What answer would you give?

5. What are the policy considerations for and against the provision in § 411(a) permitting suit for infringement without actual registration?

Chapter 6

INTERNATIONAL DIMENSION OF COPYRIGHT

A. INTERNATIONAL CONVENTIONS

1. UNIVERSAL COPYRIGHT CONVENTION

As indicated earlier, the United States adhered to the Universal Copyright Convention in 1954. The ramifications of this historical development bear significantly upon notice, the manufacturing clause, and eligibility as a proprietor of copyright. *See generally* BOGSCH, THE UNIVERSAL COPYRIGHT CONVENTION (1964); UNIVERSAL COPYRIGHT CONVENTION ANALYZED (Kupferman & Foner ed. 1955).

The essential feature of the Convention is nondiscrimination or national treatment: A member nation must accord works protected by the UCC the same protection as it grants to domestic works. Art. II. Eligible for national treatment are works authored by a national of a UCC nation or first published there.

National treatment by the United States in and of itself would have been of no value to most foreign nationals over and above the advantages already enjoyed under bilateral treaties. National treatment for foreigners would have still included the same requirements of registration and domestic manufacture as are imposed upon United States authors. Accordingly, the UCC excuses compliance with all domestic formalities with respect to unpublished works and to published works which bear the prescribed notice. Such notice consists of "the symbol © accompanied by the name of the copyright proprietor and the year of first publication placed in such manner and location as to give reasonable notice of claim of copyright." Art. III, para. 1.

In implementing the Convention, Congress took advantage of the restrictive option provided in paragraph 2 of Article III: Formalities were *not* excused in the case of works first published in the United States (even if authored by a UCC national) and of works by United States nationals or residents (even if first published in a UCC country). 17 U.S.C. § 9(c) of 1909 law. Thus, § 9(c) of the Act specifically exempted from compliance with the manufacturing requirements works (1) authored by a UCC national (other than a United States citizen or resident) and published abroad or (2) first published in a UCC country (other than the United States) and not authored by a United States citizen or resident.

For the purpose of the Convention "publication" is defined as "the reproduction in tangible form and the general distribution to the public of copies of a work from which it can be read or otherwise visually perceived." Art. VI.

Several substantive obligations were imposed on member nations over and above their obligation to afford national treatment. Each signatory must provide a minimum term of protection: duration must generally be at least 25 years after publication, prior registration, or the death of the author. Art. IV, para. 2. In addition, a limited compulsory license scheme may be introduced under Article V with respect to the right of translation. This was supplemented in the Paris Revision of 1971 by a broader translation license (Art. V *ter*), as well as by a new compulsory license to publish protected works for instructional purposes (Art. V *quater*) available under certain conditions to "developing countries" (Art. V *bis*).

The 1971 revisions of the UCC were an outgrowth of a movement, crystallized in Stockholm in 1967, whereby a number of developing countries sought to reduce their treaty obligations, particularly under the Berne Convention, to be discussed below. Along with broader translation and instructional use privileges in the UCC, the developing nations were given more latitude in withdrawing from Berne by the potential suspension of a clause found in Article XVII of the UCC designed to safeguard Berne Convention obligations. At the same time, the basic obligation under Article I of the UCC to provide "adequate and effective protection" for authors and other copyright proprietors was fleshed out to "include the basic rights ensuring the author's economic interests, including the exclusive right to authorize reproduction by any means, public performance and broadcasting." Art. IV *bis*.

2. BERNE CONVENTION

This Convention originated in 1886 and has been revised six times. It extends copyright protection not only to authors of member countries but also to authors of nonmember countries (e.g., the United States) on the sole condition of publishing their works for the first time in a member country. This includes "simultaneous" publication elsewhere, which under the current revision of the Convention means within 30 days. Art. III(4). Thus, the "backdoor" to protection is open to an American author or publisher who effects such publication in any one of the countries adhering to this Convention; he or she thereby becomes assimilated to the status of a national of the country where the publication took place, and enjoys in other member countries all the rights accorded by the Convention. It is to be noted that the Convention as amended in Brussels in 1948 defines "published works" for these purposes as works of which copies have been issued to the public and made available in sufficient quantities to meet the demand. Art. III(3).

Instead of adhering to Berne (a goal of many unsuccessful copyright law revision efforts during the 1920s and 1930s), the United States, several years after the Brussels revision, was to embark upon a new road that led to the formulation and ratification of the Universal Copyright Convention. Our 1976 domestic revision overcomes a number of obstacles to our joining Berne, but the requirement of Article V(2) of the Paris revision that enjoyment of rights "shall not be subject to any formality" would seem to require further revisions in United States law. *See* Note, *Abandon Restrictions, All Ye Who Enter!: The New United States Copyright Law and the Berne Convention*, 9 N.Y.U.J. INT'L L. & POL. 455 (1977).

3. INTER-AMERICAN RELATIONS

Prior to the consummation of the Universal Copyright Convention, the Pan-American Conventions were the nearest the United States came to reciprocity in the international copyright field. The first of these was the Mexico City Convention, 35 Stat. 1934 (1902). This multilateral treaty was soon followed by the Buenos Aires Convention, 38 Stat. 1785 (1911), ratified to date by 17 American countries, including the United States. Since El Salvador is the only Mexico City Convention adherent which has not also ratified the Buenos Aires Convention, the former treaty governs our relations with that country only. After a revision of the Buenos Aires Convention in Havana in 1928, ratified by only five countries, a more thorough-going revision was effected in Washington in 1946 but was never ratified by the United States.

The key provision of the Buenos Aires Convention is found in Article 3:

The acknowledgement of a copyright obtained in one State, in conformity with its laws, shall produce its effects of full right in all the other States without the necessity of complying with any other formality, provided always there shall appear in the work a statement that indicates the reservation of the property right.

It is the law in force in the country of first publication in the Americas that determines what formalities, if any, must be complied with in the first instance. But upon such compliance the intention seems clearly to be that the work shall be automatically protected in all the other countries party to this Convention, without the need of complying with any additional requirements in such countries, provided the work bears notice of reservation of the property right. The words "Copyright Reserved," "All Rights Reserved," or the equivalent in any other language would seem sufficient to meet the requirement. Although a notice under the Universal Copyright Convention is arguably a notice of "the reservation of the property right," many conservative proprietors include both a UCC notice and "All Rights Reserved."

There was one important right under the 1909 Act, however, which this Convention does not expressly cover, namely, the right of mechanical musical reproduction by means of phonograph records, etc. In the case of *Todamerica Musica, Ltda. v. Radio Corp. of America,* 171 F.2d 369, 79 USPQ 364 (2d Cir. 1948), the court observed that § 1(e) of the 1909 law denied this right unless substantially similar protection was accorded to citizens of the United States, and that the existence of the necessary reciprocal conditions must be signalized by a presidential proclamation. *Accord: Portuondo v. Columbia Phonograph Co.,* 81 F. Supp. 355, 36 USPQ 104 (S.D.N.Y. 1937).

The impact of the UCC on the inter-American copyright relations of the United States and the contracted scope of the Pan-American Conventions are surveyed in Rinaldo, *The Scope of Copyright Protection in the United States Under Existing Inter-American Relations,* 22 BULL. COPYRIGHT SOC'Y 417 (1975).

B. MANUFACTURING CLAUSE

1. HISTORY AND GENERAL APPLICABILITY

Our statutory copyright scheme has long contained a unique provision emanating from international copyright relations and greatly complicating them — the so-called "manufacturing clause." In the 1909 Act this requirement is not a "clause" at all, but rather a set of no less than nine sections — §§ 16, 17, 18, 22, 23, 106, 107, 108, and 109. This set of provisions has linked full enjoyment of United States copyright protection to the "manufacture" of copies of certain works in this country and has prohibited general importation of copies not so produced.

The "clause" was exacted by the printing industry as the price of qualifying foreign nationals for copyright protection initially in 1891. Its coverage has been gradually contracted and its requirements relaxed. A most significant modification was introduced pursuant to the Universal Copyright Convention in 1955 (to be discussed *infra.*)

Consideration of the 1976 statute afforded a further opportunity for Congress to reevaluate the merits of retaining the clause. A basic decision was finally made to delete it, but to defer the effective date of such deletion until July 1, 1982. (The Register has been asked to submit to Congress well before that date a study of the likely economic impact of deletion.) From January 1, 1978, until June 30,

1982, the provision will operate, but with substantially narrowed scope and effect.

It is not clear which statute will govern questions arising after January 1, 1978, concerning copies of works "manufactured" before. The manufacturing requirements of Section 16 of the 1909 law purport to cover "all copies accorded protection under this title," thus suggesting that failure to comply can place a work in the public domain. Although this interpretation has been generally expressed, see, e.g., H.R. Rep. No. 94-1476, there are authorities suggesting that the effect of noncompliance is less drastic. See, e.g., *Bentley v. Tibbals,* 223 Fed. 247 (2d Cir. 1915); *Meccano, Ltd. v. Wagner,* 234 F. 912 (S.D. Ohio 1916), *modified on other grounds,* 246 F. 603 (6th Cir. 1917); 28 Op. Att'y Gen. 150, 155 (1910). But cf. *Grove Press, Inc. v. Greenleaf Publishing Co.,* 247 F. Supp. 518, 147 USPQ 99 (E.D.N.Y. 1965) (failure to identify portions not complying with manufacturing clause excused infringement); *Hoffenberg v. Kaminstein,* 396 F.2d 684, 157 USPQ 358 (D.C. Cir.), *cert. denied,* 393 U.S. 913, 159 USPQ 799 (1968).

If a work is in the public domain on January 1, 1978, for this reason (or any other), it is not protected under the new Act. Trans. & Suppl. Sec. 103 (90 Stat. 2599). On the other hand, if failure to comply with manufacturing requirements results in something less than forfeiture (e.g., unclean hands for the proprietor in an infringement action or exposure of particular copies wrongfully imported to public copying), pre-1978 works will survive into the new era and the legislative attitude toward the manufacturing clause in the 1976 Act may well dominate interpretation of the details. In any event, the 1909 Act should be consulted. For the student's purposes, it will be sufficient here to summarize the pertinent provisions of the 1976 Act, and offer a glimpse into the problems raised under the prior law.

(1) Section 601 of the 1976 Act applies only to (a) "copies of a [copyrighted] work consisting preponderantly of nondramatic literary material" (b) "in the English language" (c) by one or more American nationals (unless domiciled outside the United States continuously for at least a year immediately preceding importation) or domiciliaries.

(2) This limited scope is further modified by exceptions in favor of braille works, and governmental, scholarly, educational, religious, or personal use. Moreover, testing the market is possible through an exemption of 2,000 copies of each work which may be printed abroad and imported. § 601(b)(2) and (6). (Works covered by the predecessor section in the 1909 law providing for 5-year ad interim copyrights automatically enjoy full-term protection under the 1976 Act. Trans. & Suppl. Sec. 107 (90 Stat. 2600).)

(3) An exemption of great potential breadth was introduced which permits *individual* authors to arrange for first publication and manufacture abroad. § 601(b)(7).

(4) If the manufacturing provision applies, only the portions consisting of nondramatic literary material must comply, i.e., be "manufactured" in either the United States *or Canada.* Importation of noncomplying copies is prohibited, subject to the exceptions already noted.

(5) The troublesome question of what constitutes "manufacture" may perhaps be best summarized by the following quotation from the House report:

Under subsection (c) [of § 601] the manufacturing requirement is confined to the following processes: (1) Typesetting and platemaking "where the copies are printed directly from type that has been set, or directly from plates made from such type"; (2) the making of plates, "where the making of plates by a lithographic or photoengraving process is a final or intermediate step preceding the printing of the copies"; and (3) in all cases, the "printing or other final process of producing multiple copies and any binding of the copies." Under the subsection there would be nothing to prevent the importation of reproduction proofs, however they were prepared, as long as the plates from which the copies are printed are made here and are not themselves imported. Similarly, the importation of computer tapes from which plates can be prepared here would be permitted. However, regardless of the process involved, the actual duplication of multiple copies, together with any binding, are required to be done in the United States or Canada.

(6) A key means of implementing the manufacturing clause has been administrative enforcement of the prohibition of importation. What happens if copies are imported in violation of this prohibition? Section 601(d) expressly provides that such acts do not invalidate copyright or affect the owner's rights generally; but they may afford a defense to one who infringes by reproducing and distributing copies (themselves complying with the provision) before registration for an authorized edition complying with the provision. (The application for registration under § 409 will have to indicate compliance, as would a complaint for infringement. § 601(e).)

Does this defense apply to the copying of illustrations (which do not have to be domestically manufactured) contained in a book subject to the clause but manufactured abroad? The answer is clearly in the affirmative if, but only if, copyright in the illustrations is owned by the owner of copyright in the text. However, many other questions concerning the scope of this defense remain (e.g., will registration of an authorized edition negate the defense if the copying is from a noncomplying copy?).

OLYMPIA PRESS v. LANCER BOOKS, INC.

267 F. Supp. 920 (S.D.N.Y. 1967)

RYAN, DISTRICT JUDGE.

This action charges an alleged infringement by defendants of American copyrights issued to plaintiff on Volumes 2, 3, 4 and 5 of the English-language translation of "Juliette" by Wainhouse.

It comes before us on plaintiff's motion for a preliminary injunction restraining defendants from marketing any copy of their one-volume book entitled "Juliette" or from otherwise infringing plaintiff's copyrights. We have concluded that for the reasons hereafter stated plaintiff should be denied the relief now sought.[1]

Both defendants, New York corporations with their offices and principal place of business in New York City, are in the paperback "adult reader" business.

Plaintiff, THE OLYMPIA PRESS, is a French limited liability company, of which one Maurice Girodias is the managing director. For some years, at least since 1953, OLYMPIA has been publishing in Paris English-language translations of works of French authorship. Among the writings so published by OLYMPIA has been "The Bedroom Philosophers", "Justine", "120 Days of Sodom", "The Story of Juliette", and some books described by Girodias as "little literary jokes", which "the American public knows as the English-language dirty books".

---

[1] We do not have before us for decision whether these "adult" writings may be lawfully imported into or marketed in the United States.

We are concerned here only with the English-language translation of "Juliette" printed in paperback books in Paris by OLYMPIA, a French work attributed to the notorious and unfortunate Donatien-Aldonse-Francois, Marquis De Sade. The English-language translation of this noisome writing was made under arrangement of OLYMPIA with one Austryn Wainhouse, an American citizen, who took the fanciful pen name — Pieralessandro Casavini. The book "Juliette" so translated was marketed by OLYMPIA in Paris as one of its "Travelers Companion Series"; planned to consist of five volumes, it was subsequently expanded by OLYMPIA to seven volumes. Wainhouse was the translator of the first five volumes and one John Crombie was the translator of Volumes six and seven. Volumes 1, 6 and 7 are not involved in this action.

It is undisputed that the French version of "The Story of Juliette" has long been in the public domain. The one-volume publication of the defendants — described as the "De Sade First American Publication of his greatest novel Juliette" — is stated on the cover to be a "revised and edited abridgement of Pieralessandro Casavini's translation of Juliette by the Marquis de Sade" and on the title page to be "abridged but unexpurgated from the original five volume work especially for the adult reader". The Wainhouse English-language translation was a "new work" subject to United States copyright, even though the original work written in French was in the public domain (17 U.S.C. Section 7). For the present motion only, we find that plaintiff has made a substantial showing that defendants' American one-volume publication is in principal part a verbatim and slavish copy which infringes the Wainhouse English-language translation. The defendants question the validity of the four copyrights in suit, asserting in fact and in law that plaintiff was not and cannot legally claim to be the "author" under the copyright law of the English-language translation which admittedly was the work of Wainhouse. They charge the plaintiff with fraudulent concealment and misstatements to the Copyright Office in order to procure the copyrights. While the certificates of registration are admissible as prima facie evidence of validity (17 U.S.C. Sec. 209), we find upon the present record that defendants have raised a substantial question as to the validity of plaintiff's copyrights which dictates that the temporary injunctive relief sought by plaintiff be denied.

The applications for all four copyright registrations were filed in the Copyright Office on May 27, 1966. It was not until plaintiff discovered defendants' publication prior to August, 1965, that he inquired of the Copyright Office what steps he should take to obtain copyright certificates in order to bring an action for infringement; the four certificates in suit were issued to plaintiff in July, 1966.

We first examine the four Certificates of Registration of a Claim to Copyright issued by the United States Register of Copyrights. The statements of plaintiff filed on these registrations disclose the following:

Registration No. A.F. 24390 — *covering Volume II* — "The Story of Juliette" — lists as author "The Olympia Press" of French citizenship, address 7, rue Saint-Séverin, Paris 5 France; date of publication, July 30, 1959; place of publication, France; new matter in this version — English Translation.

Registration No. A.F. 24391 — *covering Volume III* — again sets forth the identical statements as made with respect to Volume II, except that the date of publication is stated as April 30, 1960.

Registration No. A.F. 24393 — *covering Volume IV* — is identical to Volumes II and III, except that the date of publication is given as June 30, 1960.

Registration No. A.F. 24392 — covering Volume V — is identical to the other three volumes except that the date of publication is given as April 30, 1961.

None of the four applications disclose that the actual English language translation sought to be registered was the work of Austryn Wainhouse; his name does not appear at all on the applications. On the application forms are instructions concerning copyrights of English language books manufactured abroad and works by United States citizens, alerting an applicant to the peculiar status of such works and to the necessity of disclosing such pertinent information in order to determine their eligibility for copyright protection. That plaintiff did not supply this information was, as we shall demonstrate, no innocent omission but a deliberate one because of its awareness of the provisions of the Act.

This brings us to the pertinent statute — the Manufacturing Clause of the Copyright Act, 17 U.S.C. § 16, which requires that English language works, in order to receive copyright protection, must be typeset, printed and bound within the United States. There is no question but that plaintiff's works were not so done. The only exception to this clause which need detain us is that which permits copyright on a foreign book in the English language imported into the United States within five years after first publication in a foreign state if ad interim copyright in said work has been obtained pursuant to Section 22 of the Act prior to the importation in the United States of any copy. Plaintiff did not obtain ad interim copyright under Section 22.

The Act under Section 9(c) exempts from the Manufacturing Clause alien authors whose country is a signatory to the Universal Copyright Convention or whose work was first published in such country, but significantly excepts from this exception "works of an author who is a citizen of, or domiciled in the United States of America regardless of place of first publication...." France is a signatory to the Universal Copyright Convention; the works in suit were first published there; the question is who was their author. On the assumption that Wainhouse, the translator, is the author of the works, defendants conclude that the exception to the Manufacturing Clause does not apply to them, and that they cannot be copyrighted. On the assumption that plaintiff and not Wainhouse is the "author" of the work, plaintiff argues that the works do come within the exception, relying for its position that it is the author of the works on the language of Section 26, 17 U.S.C., which includes within the definition of author "an employer in the case of works made for hire"; that is, that the translator Wainhouse was an employee of plaintiff rather than an independent writer.

This is the crux of the case. Plaintiff in his later arguments has attempted to minimize the importance of Wainhouse's citizenship and his status as employee or independent contractor by relying on the argument and the cases which have to do with plaintiff's rights as owner of the copyrighted works — which defendants do not dispute — as contrasted with its right initially to secure the copyright. That there is no connection between the legal right to secure a copyright and the property in the material copyrighted is clear from the statute. Section 27 specifically distinguishes between the two. The cases cited by plaintiff in this connection to the effect that whether one is an employee or an independent contractor is not determinative of ownership, are not relevant. The question is of paramount importance in determining, however, who is the person entitled to secure the copyright especially under the statutes in question, and we turn, therefore, to consider the evidence which plaintiff has adduced in support of its position that Wainhouse was a mere employee for hire — and not an independent writer qualifying as the author of the works in question. Obviously, if plaintiff cannot on this motion show sufficient likelihood of succeeding in establishing its right to secure the copyrights and their validity, it may not secure the injunction.

On his deposition, plaintiff's president, Girodias, admitted that he knew Wainhouse to be an American, although he did not know whether he was a citizen or not. It is clear that he knew him to be a resident of France for many years, married to a French woman, so he probably did not consider him an American domiciliary, but an American citizen. Their association — an apparently warm friendship — appears to have lasted over many years.

The plaintiff has stated in answer to defendants' interrogatory that there was no written agreement entered into between plaintiff and Wainhouse relating to the translation by Wainhouse for "The Story of Juliette". Wainhouse, in an affidavit given by him to defendants, sworn to before the American Consul at Nice, on January 20, 1967, agrees with this admission of plaintiff, stating that when "requesting a contract of the customary sort between publisher and translator, Girodias assured me that no contract need be established between us for the pure and simple reason that 'contracts are always made to be broken.'" His affidavit also recites that he is an American citizen, that he graduated from Harvard in 1948 (English and Comparative Literature, A.B., Magna cum laude, Phi Beta Kappa); was an instructor of English in a Pennsylvania college for one year, a graduate student in a mid-west college during the following year, went to France in 1950 to pursue research toward a thesis and has resided abroad ever since, save only for occasional trips (three since 1958) to the United States. In support of his position that he was not a hired writer but an independent author, he relates that he began his translations of Sade in 1952, at which time he had completed an essay of his own on Sade, had translated into French "La Phylosophie dans le Boudoir"; that it was this completed text that he presented to Maurice Girodias at the time of their first meeting in March, 1953, and that it was this text, unaltered and "integral", that plaintiff published in May, 1953, under the title of "The Bedroom Philosophers", for which Girodias paid him by check seventy five thousand francs ($200.00 approximately). Wainhouse further states that he worked on his translations in cafes, at his home and at the homes of his parents in Vienna and Washington, but "never at any time on the premises of the Olympia press." He is positive in his statement that in the majority of the instances he proposed that a translation be made and the work published, that no editing whatsoever was done upon any of his translations and that Girodias exerted absolutely no control over their style and content; and that he, Wainhouse, selected and used his own pseudonym for purely personal reasons. He swears that, concerning payment, it was from the first and last agreed that payment in full was to be made upon submission of the finished text; royalty considerations, at Girodias' repeated insistence, being deferred again and again.

Plaintiff, in its insufficient supporting affidavit, says that it engaged Wainhouse and commissioned the work for hire in return for a set fee of 300,000 francs per volume. This equivocal language, coupled with the vague reference to an oral agreement, the terms of which are not set forth, certainly do not support the naked conclusion that Wainhouse was an employee for hire. Quite to the contrary, the correspondence from Wainhouse to Girodias, beginning early in 1957, speaks of how much Wainhouse was "to charge" plaintiff, of the difficulty of obtaining a lump sum payment from plaintiff in the past and of Wainhouse's need to receive periodic payments from plaintiff in order to be paid at all — the amount of which Wainhouse set (not Girodias) and called a "salary" — and of his demands for royalties. It appears from these also that Wainhouse chose the titles of the works, wrote the blurbs for the Juliette books, that he procured the typing at his own expense and that, prior to his hiring, he had completed the translation of Volume I of the Juliette series, suggested manuscripts for translation to Girodias and submitted unsolicited translations for Girodias to try to have published for him.

The tenor of these letters bespeaks much more two independent men working together — one as author, the other as publisher — rather than employer and hired hand. See *Donaldson Pub. Co. v. Bregman, Vocco & Conn, Inc.,* C.A.2, 375 F.2d 639, 3/24/67, #30367. What followed evidences a recognition by plaintiff of the difficulty, if not the impossibility, of having the works copyrighted if the above facts were disclosed to the Copyright Office. In the first place, the long delay in applying for copyright protection by one engaged in the publishing business indicates a realization that copyright would not lie. By contrast with respect to the last two volumes, also translated by an American citizen, plaintiff did not delay for, by letter of Girodias to the Register of Copyright dated August 24, 1965, he filed two ad interim copyright applications for the English version of Volumes VI and VII, stating that these volumes had been translated by John Crombie, an American citizen. Girodias' letter also informed the Register that:

> The first five volumes as published by our company (which company is registered in France) have been translated into the English language by Pieralessandro Casavini who is not a citizen of the U.S.A. and we therefore consider that these five volumes are protected by the UCC.

The letter continued that plaintiff had bought the translations of Crombie for a set fee "and it seems therefore that our company should be granted the privilege of authorship on these two volumes." No claim was then made by plaintiff of any right to copyright "under the privilege of authorship" in the five volumes translated by Wainhouse, by reason of payment to Wainhouse of a "set fee". It is apparent also that plaintiff's reference to Wainhouse under the pen name "Pieralessandro Casavini" was done with the purpose of lending the support of a foreign name to plaintiff's statement that the author of the translation of the first five volumes (Wainhouse) was not an American citizen.

It is evident from a letter from the Register of Copyrights, dated October 8, 1965, addressed to plaintiff, that plaintiff was fully advised of the provisions applicable to an English language book manufactured and published outside the United States and authored by a United States citizen or domiciliary for it called attention to the importance of "the status of authorship" as follows:

> If Mr. Crombie was employed for the purpose of translating these works, the citizenship of the author would be that of the employer. In this event, full term (28 years) copyright would be possible under the provisions of the Universal Copyright Convention, application being made on Form A-B Foreign.
> On the other hand, if Mr. Crombie was not employed for the purpose of translating these works, but the completed translations being bought later, Mr. Crombie would appear to be the author and ad interim registration appropriate.

The reply of Girodias, claiming registration by the company because Crombie had "been employed for that work against payment of a fee" and his very vague reference to the publication of the first five volumes without any mention of authorship or dates, reveals plaintiff's full understanding of the copyright requirements and of what he could not disclose regarding those five volumes if he was to obtain a copyright. Still Girodias' restrained disclosure of the details of Crombie's employment did not satisfy the Register and, in a long, informative letter, the latter requested further clarification of this crucial detail, giving its reasons for its importance. With all the pitfalls of the problem pointed out to Girodias by the Register (even going so far as to instruct him on judicial application and interpretation of the statute, and the statement that it was its policy to leave it up to the applicant rather than to the Copyright Office to determine whether a work "was made for hire" in a particular case, and, because of its crucial importance, suggesting that Girodias might want to explore this difficult and important problem further) it did not take Girodias too long to proceed with the claim that the author of Volumes 2 through 4 was not Casavini, or Wainhouse, but OLYMPIA, and that this was so because of the special terms of Wainhouse's employment by OLYMPIA, omitting all reference to the role played by Wainhouse or even to his existence!

Even plaintiff's attempt to explain its sudden spurt of activity in securing the four copyrights after such a passage of time, falls far short of the facts. The explanation given that it was negotiating with an American publishing company for the publication of various works and knew that its rights to "Juliette" was one of its most important assets, is belied by its refusal or inability to produce any evidence in this respect, and by the fact that any such negotiations apparently began and were dissolved long before the procurement of the copyrights.

Because we conclude that there is serious question as to the validity of the copyrights in suit, an injunction will not lie and it is unnecessary to discuss the defenses of laches and absence of irreparable harm.

Motion denied; so ordered.

QUESTIONS

1. How could Olympia have arranged things to avoid the copyright pitfall it encountered?

2. Suppose a *bona fide* employment for hire relationship is established but its sole purpose is to insure the "correct" national origin for a work. Is this motive relevant for the purposes of our copyright statute?

3. Foreign countries which recognize at least presumptive ownership rights in employers do not necessarily elevate employers to the status of "authors." What is the basis for importing into the Universal Copyright Convention, and our obligations thereunder, the concept that employers are authors? Is this another example of national egocentricity or simply a domestic law filling in interstices of international obligations?

C. PROTECTION OF ALIEN AUTHORS: HISTORY AND THE 1976 ACT

The Register's Report recommended in 1961 that all foreign and domestic works be protected on the same basis, without regard to the nationality of the author (subject to restriction by presidential proclamation). *Report of the Register of Copyrights on the General Revision of the U.S. Copyright Law, Report to House Committee on the Judiciary,* 87th Cong., 1st Sess. 119 (1961). But this proposal never saw the light of legislative day; at least as to published works, the 1976 Act carries forward, though in liberalized form, the policy laid down in the Act of 1891, 26 Stat. 1106, and followed in the 1909 Act. Under this policy, the United States demands a quid pro quo for the extension of the copyright privilege to the nationals of any foreign state or nation who are not domiciled here.

Absent treaty obligations most foreign countries likewise condition copyright for nondomiciliary aliens on the existence of protection for their own nationals in the alien's country. E.g., United Kingdom Copyright Act, 1956, 4 & 5 Eliz. 2, c. 74, Sec. 32(3). Even France finally reserved the right to retaliate against nonprotection of its works. Decree of July 8, 1964.

The basic rule, both in the United States and abroad, is "national" rather than strictly "reciprocal" treatment; copyright is granted to an alien on the same terms as apply to a citizen and not on the terms of protection available in the alien's country.

In its coverage of all unpublished material (much of which had been protected by the common law), the 1976 Act adopts the common law rule of protection for unpublished works irrespective of the nationality or domicile of the author. § 104(a). With respect to published works, however, protection is available under § 104(b) only if at least one of the following four conditions is satisfied:

(1) one or more of the authors is, at the time of first publication, a national or domiciliary of:

(a) the United States, or

(b) a country with'which we have a copyright treaty, including the Universal Copyright Convention (or is the sovereign authority of such a country), or

(c) no country, i.e., a stateless person. Cf. *Houghton-Mifflin Co. v. Stackpole Sons, Inc.*, 104 F.2d 306, 42 USPQ 96 (2d Cir.), *cert. denied*, 308 U.S. 597, 43 USPQ 521 (1939)(stateless persons protected under general grant of § 9 of 1909 law, since only citizens of foreign states must meet the specified nationality requirements);

(2) the work is first published in the United States or in a Universal Copyright Convention country;

(3) the work is first published by the United Nations (or any of its specialized agencies) or the Organization of American States; or

(4) the work comes within the scope of a presidential proclamation finding that the author's country accords nondiscriminatory or national treatment to works of United States authorship or first publication. (Preexisting proclamations remain in force until further presidential action. Trans. & Suppl. Sec. 104 (90 Stat. 2599).)

In addition to its provision as to unpublished works, § 104 liberalizes the requirements of § 9 of the 1909 law by adding first publication in the United States as a basis for protection (§ 104(b)(2)) and also simplifies the presidential proclamation provision in § 9 (which had covered countries according Americans reciprocal, rather than national, treatment and countries that were members of a convention "open" to the United States).

General proclamations have been issued in favor of more than 30 countries and their possessions. All have been on the basis of actual national or reciprocal treatment (rather than membership in an "open" convention). For the extension of mechanical music rights under § 1(e) of the 1909 law, special proclamations were necessary, except where the original general proclamation expressly covered these rights. 29 Op. Att'y Gen. 64 (1911).

The President's power to issue proclamations in this area includes the granting of extensions to foreigners who are found to be prevented from complying with United States formalities because of the disruption or suspension of facilities essential for compliance. This power, added in 1941, 55 Stat. 732, has been exercised on a number of occasions as a result of World War II. E.g., 25 Fed. Reg. 5373 (June 15, 1960) (Austria).

In determining the identity of an "author" for nationality requirements, one must not neglect the special provisions of both the 1909 law and the 1976 law which make an employer for hire an "author." Needless to say, any such relationship must be bona fide, even though motivated by nationality requirements, and not a sham attempt to create an employment relationship retroactively. *See Olympia Press v. Lancer Books, Inc.,* 267 F. Supp. 920, 153 USPQ 349 (S.D.N.Y. 1967).

Domicile within the meaning of this section is no different from the ordinary usage of this legal term. To acquire domicile, there must be (1) residence with (2) intention to remain in the United States, which may be inferred from various circumstances such as declarations, marriage to an American, payment of taxes, voting, establishment of a home, etc. *See G. Ricordi & Co. v. Columbia Graphophone Co.,* 258 F. 72 (S.D.N.Y. 1919).

Of course, aside from these specific provisions, another basis of protection is any treaty supplementing Title 17 of the United States Code as the copyright "law of the land."

QUESTION

France is a member of the Universal Copyright Convention. China (the People's Republic of China) has recently entered into a bilateral agreement with the United States which includes mutual obligations with respect to copyright (earlier bilateral agreements with predecessor Chinese regimes posed intriguing problems of international law). Egypt is one of the countries with which the United States has no copyright relations. Against this background, would a work by a Chinese author, first published in Egypt, be protected in the United States? What about a work by an Egyptian author first published in China, in France, or in the United States? Suppose the Egyptian is a free-lance writer living in Paris or is employed by a French company which gives dramatic presentations in Cairo?

RIGHTS, LIMITATIONS AND REMEDIES

A. THE RIGHT TO REPRODUCE THE WORK IN COPIES AND PHONORECORDS UNDER § 106(1) — THE RIGHT TO COPY

§ 106. Exclusive rights in copyrighted works

Subject to sections 107 through 118, the owner of copyright under this title has the exclusive rights to do and to authorize any of the following:

(1) to reproduce the copyrighted work in copies or phonorecords;

(2) to prepare derivative works based upon the copyrighted work;

(3) to distribute copies or phonorecords of the copyrighted work to the public by sale or other transfer of ownership, or by rental, lease, or lending;

(4) in the case of literary, musical, dramatic, and choreographic works, pantomimes, and motion pictures and other audiovisual works, to perform the copyrighted work publicly; and

(5) in the case of literary, musical, dramatic, and choreographic works, pantomimes, and pictorial, graphic, or sculptural works, including the individual images of a motion picture or other audiovisual work, to display the copyrighted work publicly.

HOUSE REPORT

H.R. Rep. No. 94-1476, 94th Cong., 2d Sess. 61-62 (1976)

General scope of copyright

The five fundamental rights that the bill gives to copyright owners — the exclusive rights of reproduction, adaptation, publication, performance, and display — are stated generally in section 106. These exclusive rights, which comprise the so-called "bundle of rights" that is a copyright, are cumulative and may overlap in some cases. Each of the five enumerated rights may be subdivided indefinitely and, as discussed below in connection with section 201, each subdivision of an exclusive right may be owned and enforced separately.

The approach of the bill is to set forth the copyright owner's exclusive rights in broad terms in section 106, and then to provide various limitations, qualifications, or exemptions in the 12 sections that follow. Thus, everything in section 106 is made "subject to sections 107 through 118," and must be read in conjunction with those provisions.

The exclusive rights accorded to a copyright owner under section 106 are "to do and to authorize" any of the activities specified in the five numbered clauses. Use of the phrase "to authorize" is intended to avoid any questions as to the liability of contributory infringers. For example, a person who lawfully acquires an authorized copy of a motion picture would be an infringer if he or she engages in the business of renting it to others for purposes of unauthorized public performance.

317

Rights of reproduction, adaptation, and publication

The first three clauses of section 106, which cover all rights under a copyright except those of performance and display, extend to every kind of copyrighted work. The exclusive rights encompassed by these clauses, though closely related, are independent; they can generally be characterized as rights of copying, recording, adaptation, and publishing. A single act of infringement may violate all of these rights at once, as where a publisher reproduces, adapts, and sells copies of a person's copyrighted work as part of a publishing venture. Infringement takes place when any one of the rights is violated: where, for example, a printer reproduces copies without selling them or a retailer sells copies without having anything to do with their reproduction. The references to "copies or phonorecords," although in the plural, are intended here and throughout the bill to include the singular (1 U.S.C. § 1).

Reproduction. — Read together with the relevant definitions in section 101, the right "to reproduce the copyrighted work in copies or phonorecords" means the right to produce a material object in which the work is duplicated, transcribed, imitated, or simulated in a fixed form from which it can be "perceived, reproduced, or otherwise communicated, either directly or with the aid of a machine or device." As under the present law, a copyrighted work would be infringed by reproducing it in whole or in any substantial part, and by duplicating it exactly or by imitation or simulation. Wide departures or variations from the copyrighted works would still be an infringement as long as the author's "expression" rather than merely the author's "ideas" are taken. An exception to this general principle, applicable to the reproduction of copyrighted sound recordings, is specified in section 114.

"Reproduction" under clause (1) of section 106 is to be distinguished from "display" under clause (5). For a work to be "reproduced," its fixation in tangible form must be "sufficiently permanent or stable to permit it to be perceived, reproduced, or otherwise communicated for a period of more than transitory duration." Thus, the showing of images on a screen or tube would not be a violation of clause (1), although it might come within the scope of clause (5).

ARNSTEIN v. PORTER

154 F.2d 464 (2d Cir. 1946), *cert. denied*, 330 U.S. 851 (1947)

Before L. HAND, CLARK and FRANK, CIRCUIT JUDGES.

Plaintiff, a citizen and resident of New York, brought this suit, charging infringement by defendant, a citizen and resident of New York, of plaintiff's copyrights to several musical compositions, infringement of his rights to other uncopyrighted musical compositions, and wrongful use of the titles of others. Plaintiff, when filing his complaint, demanded a jury trial. Plaintiff took the deposition of defendant, and defendant, the deposition of plaintiff. Defendant then moved for an order striking out plaintiff's jury demand, and for summary judgment. Attached to defendant's motion papers were the depositions, phonograph records of piano renditions of the plaintiff's compositions and defendant's alleged infringing compositions, and the court records of five previous copyright infringement suits brought by plaintiff in the court below against other persons, in which judgments had been entered, after trials, against plaintiff. Defendant also moved for dismissal of the action on the ground of "vexatiousness."

Plaintiff alleged that defendant's "Begin the Beguine" is a plagiarism from plaintiff's "The Lord Is My Shepherd" and "A Mother's Prayer." Plaintiff testified, on deposition, that "The Lord Is My Shepherd" had been published and about 2,000 copies sold, that "A Mother's Prayer" had been published, over a million copies having been sold. In his depositions, he gave no direct evidence that defendant saw or heard these compositions. He also alleged that defendant's "My Heart Belongs to Daddy" had been plagiarized from plaintiff's "A Mother's Prayer."

Plaintiff also alleged that defendant's "I Love You" is a plagiarism from plaintiff's composition "La Priere," stating in his deposition that the latter composition had been sold. He gave no direct proof that defendant knew of this composition.

He also alleged that defendant's song "Night and Day" is a plagiarism of plaintiff's song "I Love You Madly," which he testified had not been published but had once been publicly performed over the radio, copies having been sent to divers radio stations but none to defendant; a copy of this song, plaintiff testified, had been stolen from his room. He also alleged that "I Love You Madly" was in part plagiarized from "La Priere." He further alleged that defendant's "You'd Be So Nice To Come Home To" is plagiarized from plaintiff's "Sadness Overwhelms My Soul." He testified that this song had never been published or publicly performed but that copies had been sent to a movie producer and to several publishers. He also alleged that defendant's "Don't Fence Me In" is a plagiarism of plaintiff's song "A Modern Messiah" which has not been published or publicly performed; in his deposition he said that about a hundred copies had been sent to divers radio stations and band leaders but that he sent no copy to defendant. Plaintiff said that defendant "had stooges right along to follow me, watch me, and live in the same apartment with me," and that plaintiff's room had been ransacked on several occasions. Asked how he knew that defendant had anything to do with any of these "burglaries," plaintiff said, "I don't know that he had [anything] to do with it, but I only know that he could have." He also said ". . . many of my compositions had been published. No one had to break in to steal them. They were sung publicly."

Defendant in his deposition categorically denied that he had ever seen or heard any of plaintiff's compositions or had had any acquaintance with any persons said to have stolen any of them.

The prayer of plaintiff's original complaint asked "at least one million dollars out of the millions the defendant has earned and is earning out of all the plagiarism." In his amended complaint the prayer is "for judgment against the defendant in the sum of $1,000,000 as damages sustained by the plagiarism of all the compositions named in the complaint." Plaintiff, not a lawyer, appeared pro se below and on this appeal.

FRANK, CIRCUIT JUDGE.

1. Plaintiff with his complaint filed a jury demand which defendant moved to strike out. Defendant urges that the relief prayed in the complaint renders a jury trial inappropriate. We do not agree. Plaintiff did not ask for an injunction but solely for damages. Such a suit is an action at "law." That it is founded solely on a statute does not deprive either party of a right to a trial by jury; an action for treble damages under the Sherman Act is likewise purely statutory, but it is triable at "law" and by a jury as of right.

2. The principal question on this appeal is whether the lower court, under Rule 56, properly deprived plaintiff of a trial of his copyright infringement action. The answer depends on whether "there is the slightest doubt about the facts." *Doehler Metal Furniture Co. v. United States,* 149 F. 2d 130, 135 (C.C.A.

2); *Sartor v. Arkansas Natural Gas Corp.,* 321 U.S. 620; *Arenas v. United States,* 322 U. S. 419, 434; *Associated Press v. United States,* 326 U. S. 1, 6-7 . . . . In applying that standard here, it is important to avoid confusing two separate elements essential to a plaintiff's case in such a suit: (a) that defendant copied from plaintiff's copyrighted work and (b) that the copying (assuming it to be proved) went so far as to constitute improper appropriation.

As to the first — copying — the evidence may consist (a) of defendant's admission that he copied or (b) of circumstantial evidence — usually evidence of access — from which the trier of the facts may reasonably infer copying. Of course, if there are no similarities, no amount of evidence of access will suffice to prove copying. If there is evidence of access and similarities exist, then the trier of the facts must determine whether the similarities are sufficient to prove copying. On this issue, analysis ("dissection") is relevant, and the testimony of experts may be received to aid the trier of the facts. If evidence of access is absent, the similarities must be so striking as to preclude the possibility that plaintiff and defendant independently arrived at the same result.

If copying is established, then only does there arise the second issue, that of illicit copying (unlawful appropriation). On that issue (as noted more in detail below) the test is the response of the ordinary lay hearer; accordingly, on that issue, "dissection" and expert testimony are irrelevant.

In some cases, the similarities between the plaintiff's and defendant's work are so extensive and striking as, without more, both to justify an inference of copying and to prove improper appropriation. But such double-purpose evidence is not required; that is, if copying is otherwise shown, proof of improper appropriation need not consist of similarities which, standing alone, would support an inference of copying.

Each of these two issues — copying and improper appropriation — is an issue of fact. If there is a trial, the conclusions on those issues of the trier of the facts — of the judge if he sat without a jury, or of the jury if there was a jury trial — binds this court on appeal, provided the evidence supports those findings, regardless of whether we would ourselves have reached the same conclusions. But a case could occur in which the similarities are so striking that we would reverse a finding of no access, despite weak evidence of access (or no evidence thereof other than the similarities); and similarly as to a finding of no illicit appropriation.

3. We turn first to the issue of copying. After listening to the compositions as played in the phonograph recordings submitted by defendant, we find similarities; but we hold that unquestionably, standing alone, they do not compel the conclusion, or permit the inference, that defendant copied. The similarities, however, are sufficient so that, if there is enough evidence of access to permit the case to go to the jury, the jury may properly infer that the similarities did not result from coincidence.

Summary judgment was, then, proper if indubitably defendant did not have access to plaintiff's compositions. Plainly that presents an issue of fact. On that issue, the district judge, who heard no oral testimony, had before him the depositions of plaintiff and defendant. The judge characterized plaintiff's story as "fantastic"; and, in the light of the references in his opinion to defendant's deposition, the judge obviously accepted defendant's denial of access and copying. Although part of plaintiff's testimony on deposition (as to "stooges" and the like) does seem "fantastic," yet plaintiff's credibility, even as to those improbabilities, should be left to the jury. If evidence "is of a kind that greatly taxes the credulity of the judge, he can say so, or, if he totally disbelieves it, he may announce that fact, leaving the jury free to believe it or not." If, said Winslow J., "evidence is always to be disbelieved because the story told seems remarkable or impossible, then a party whose rights depend on the proof of some facts out of the usual course of events will always be denied justice simply because his story is improbable." We should not overlook the shrewd proverbial admonition that sometimes truth is stranger than fiction.

But even if we were to disregard the improbable aspects of plaintiff's story, there remains parts by no means "fantastic." On the record now before us, more than a million copies of one of his compositions were sold; copies of others were sold in smaller quantities or distributed to radio stations or band leaders or publishers, or the pieces were publicly performed. If, after hearing both parties testify, the jury disbelieves defendant's denials, it can, from such facts, reasonably infer access. It follows that, as credibility is unavoidably involved, a genuine issue of material fact presents itself. With credibility a vital factor, plaintiff is entitled to a trial where the jury can observe the witnesses while testifying. Plaintiff must not be deprived of the invaluable privilege of cross-examining the defendant — the "crucial test of credibility" — in the presence of the jury. Plaintiff, or a lawyer on his behalf, on such examination may elicit damaging admissions from defendant; more important, plaintiff may persuade the jury, observing defendant's manner when testifying, that defendant is unworthy of belief.

. . . .

With all that in mind, we cannot now say — as we think we must say to sustain a summary judgment — that at the close of a trial the judge could properly direct a verdict.

. . . .

We do not believe that, in a case in which the decision must turn on the reliability of witnesses, the Supreme Court, by authorizing summary judgments, intended to permit a "trial by affidavits," if either party objects. That procedure which, so the historians tell us, began to be outmoded at common law in the 16th century, would, if now revived, often favor unduly the party with the more ingenious and better paid lawyer. Grave injustice might easily result.

. . . .

4. Assuming that adequate proof is made of copying, that is not enough; for there can be "permissible copying," copying which is not illicit. Whether (if he copied) defendant unlawfully appropriated presents, too, an issue of fact. The proper criterion on that issue is not an analytic or other comparison of the respective musical compositions as they appear on paper or in the judgment of trained musicians.[19] The plaintiff's legally protected interest is not, as such, his reputation as a musician but his interest in the potential financial returns from his compositions which derive from the lay public's approbation of his efforts. The question, therefore, is whether defendant took from plaintiff's works so much of what is pleasing to the ears of lay listeners, who comprise the audience for whom such popular music is composed, that defendant wrongfully appropriated something which belongs to the plaintiff.

Surely, then, we have an issue of fact which a jury is peculiarly fitted to

---

[19] Where plaintiff relies on similarities to prove copying (as distinguished from improper appropriation) paper comparisons and the opinions of experts may aid the court.

determine.[22] Indeed, even if there were to be a trial before a judge, it would be desirable (although not necessary) for him to summon an advisory jury on this question.

We should not be taken as saying that a plagiarism case can never arise in which absence of similarities is so patent that a summary judgment for defendant would be correct. Thus, suppose that Ravel's "Bolero" or Shostakovitch's "Fifth Symphony" were alleged to infringe "When Irish Eyes Are Smiling."[23] But this is not such a case. For, after listening to the playing of the respective compositions, we are, at this time, unable to conclude that the likenesses are so trifling that, on the issue of misappropriation, a trial judge could legitimately direct a verdict for defendant.

At the trial, plaintiff may play, or cause to be played, the pieces in such manner that they may seem to a jury to be inexcusably alike, in terms of the way in which lay listeners of such music would be likely to react. The plaintiff may call witnesses whose testimony may aid the jury in reaching its conclusion as to the responses of such audiences. Expert testimony of musicians may also be received, but it will in no way be controlling on the issue of illicit copying, and should be utilized only to assist in determining the reactions of lay auditors. The impression made on the refined ears of musical experts or their views as to the musical excellence of plaintiff's or defendant's works are utterly immaterial on the issue of misappropriation; for the views of such persons are caviar to the general — and plaintiff's and defendant's compositions are not caviar.

. . . .

8. Defendant [moved] in the court below not only for summary judgment but also for dismissal of plaintiff's action as "vexatious." For in aid of that latter motion, defendant asked the judge to take judicial notice of five previous copyright infringement actions, including . . . one . . . brought by the plaintiff in the same court against other persons, in which plaintiff had advanced some legal arguments like those he advances here, and in which he had been defeated. The judge in his opinion referred to but one of those suits, *Arnstein v. American Soc. of Composers,* and purported not to pass on the motion to dismiss for vexatiousness. But in his order for final judgemet he specifically referred to the "records" of the court in the five cases, naming them, as constituting in part the basis of the judgment.

Defendant, in his brief in this court, says, "This is perhaps the most significant" argument in "this case," and presses us to hold that affirmance of the dismissal should be based thereon. Coupled with this request is an implied suggestion that, with respect to the summary judgment, we should not so concern ourselves with fear of creating a "bad" precedent for the future that we reach an unjust decision in this particular case. With that suggestion we are in thorough accord. We decide against summary judgment here because we consider it improper in this case. Our decision to that effect will have precedential significance only to the extent that, in any future case, summary judgment is sought when the facts are not beyond the range of actual dispute.

But, in the spirit of that suggestion, we regard it as entirely improper to give any weight to other actions lost by plaintiff. Although, as stated above, the judge in his opinion, except as to one of the previous actions, did not say that he rested his decision on those other suits, the language of his final judgment order

---

[22] It would, accordingly, be proper to exclude tone-deaf persons from the jury, cf. Chatterton v. Cave, 3 A.C. 483, 499-501, 502-504.

[23] In such a case, the complete absence of similarity would negate both copying and improper appropriation.

indicates that he was probably affected by them. If so, he erred. Absent the factors which make up res judicata (not present here), each case must stand on its own bottom, subject, of course, to the doctrine of stare decisis. Succumbing to the temptation to consider other defeats suffered by a party may lead a court astray; see, e. g., *Southern Pacific Co. v. Bogert,* 250 U.S. 483, 489 note 1. When a particular suit is vexatious, sometimes at its conclusion the court can give some redress to the victorious party. Perhaps the legislature can and should meet this problem more effectively. But we surely must not do so, as defendant here would have us do, by prejudicing the merits of the case before us.

Modified in part; otherwise reversed and remanded.

CLARK, CIRCUIT JUDGE (dissenting). While the procedure followed below seems to me generally simple and appropriate, the defendant did make one fatal tactical error. In an endeavor to assist us, he caused to be prepared records of all the musical pieces here involved, and presented these transcriptions through the medium of the affidavit of his pianist. Though he himself did not stress these records and properly met plaintiff's claims as to the written music with his own analysis, yet the tinny tintinnabulations of the music thus canned resounded through the United States Courthouse to the exclusion of all else, including the real issues in the case. Of course, sound is important in a case of this kind, but it is not so important as to falsify what the eye reports and the mind teaches. Otherwise plagiarism would be suggested by the mere drumming of repetitious sound from our usual popular music, as it issues from a piano, orchestra, or hurdygurdy — particularly when ears may be dulled by long usage, possibly artistic repugnance or boredom, or mere distance which causes all sounds to merge. And the judicial eardrum may be peculiarly insensitive after long years of listening to the "beat, beat, beat" (I find myself plagiarizing from defendant and thus in danger of my brothers' doom) of sound upon it, though perhaps no more so than the ordinary citizen juror — even if tone deafness is made a disqualification for jury service, as advocated.

Pointing to the adscititious fortuity inherent in the stated standard is, it seems to me, the fact that after repeated hearings of the records, I could not find therein what my brothers found. The only thing definitely mentioned seemed to be the repetitive use of the note e^2 in certain places by both plaintiff and defendant, surely too simple and ordinary a device of composition to be significant. In our former musical plagiarism cases we have, naturally, relied on what seemed the total sound effect; but we have also analyzed the music enough to make sure of an intelligible and intellectual decision. Thus in *Arnstein v. Edward B. Marks Music Corp.,* 2 Cir., 82 F. 2d 275, 277, Judge L. Hand made quite an extended comparison of the songs, concluding, inter alia: ". . . the seven notes available do not admit of so many agreeable permutations that we need be amazed at the reappearance of old themes, even though the identity extended through a sequence of twelve notes." See also the discussion in *Marks v. Leo Feist, Inc.,* 2 Cir., 290 F. 959, and *Darrell v. Joe Morris Music Co.,* 2 Cir., 113 F.2d 80, where the use of six similar *bars* and of an eight-note sequence frequently repeated were respectively held not to constitute infringement, and *Wilkie v. Santly Bros.,* 2 Cir., 91 F.2d 978, affirming D.C.S.D.N.Y., 13 F. Supp. 136, certiorari denied *Santly Bros. v. Wilkie,* 302 U.S. 735, where use of eight *bars* with other similarities amounting to over three-quarters of the significant parts was held infringement.[1]

---

[1] In accord is Shafter, Musical Copyright, 2d Ed.1939, c. 6, particularly p. 205, where the author speaks of "the 'comparative method,' worked out by Judge Learned Hand with

It is true that in *Arnstein v. Broadcast Music, Inc.,* 2 Cir., 137 F.2d 410, 412, we considered "dissection" or "technical analysis" not the proper approach to support a finding of plagiarism, and said that it must be "more ingenuous, more like that of a spectator, who would rely upon the complex of his impressions." But in its context that seems to me clearly sound and in accord with what I have in mind. Thus one may look to the total impression to repulse the charge of plagiarism where a minute "dissection" might dredge up some points of similarity. Hence one cannot use a purely theoretical disquisition to supply a total resemblance which does not otherwise exist. Certainly, however, that does not suggest or compel the converse — that one must keep his brain in torpor for fear that otherwise it would make clear differences which do exist. Music is a matter of the intellect as well as the emotions; that is why eminent musical scholars insist upon the employment of the intellectual faculties for a just appreciation of music.[2]

---

great success," and "his successful method of analysis," citing Hein v. Harris, C.C.S.D.N.Y., 175 F. 875, affirmed 2 Cir., 183 F. 107, and Haas v. Leo Feist, Inc., D.C.S.D.N.Y., 234 F. 105; and p. 194, where he approves of Judge Yankwich's course in attaching an exhibit of analysis to his opinion in Hirsch v. Paramount Pictures, Inc., D.C.S.D.Cal., 17 F. Supp. 816 — "this sensible procedure," "a splendid model for future copyright decisions." I find nowhere any suggestion of two steps in adjudication of this issue, one of finding copying which may be approached with musical intelligence and assistance of experts, and another that of illicit copying which must be approached with complete ignorance; nor do I see how rationally there can be any such difference, even if a jury — the now chosen instrument of musical detection — could be expected to separate those issues and the evidence accordingly. If there is actual copying, it is actionable, and there are no degrees; what we are dealing with is the claim of similarities sufficient to justify the inference of copying. This is a single deduction to be made intelligently, not two with the dominating one to be made blindly.

[2] Thus Stewart Macpherson, Professor of Harmony and Composition in the Royal Academy of Music, says in his standard text, Form in Music, Rev.Ed.1930, 1, 2: "Music appeals to us in a threefold way, which may be described under the headings of (i) Physical Sensation; (ii) Emotion, or feeling; (iii) Intellect (i.e. critical judgment, based upon certain reasoning powers within us). The first of these agencies, that of physical sensation, is without doubt the lowest of the three, and is one we share with the rest of the animal creation, upon whom — as we all know — certain sounds seem to have a distinct and immediate effect — often that of pain. . . . [The second] lies on a much higher plane than mere physical sensation. It is more subjective, and is the response of something in our own consciousness to some (often indescribable) quality in the music to which we are listening. . . . But, in judging of the emotional effect of a work, the factor of association has to be taken into account, and it is a truism to say that we are often tempted to estimate a poem or a musical work quite out of all proportion to its real value as a work of art, simply because it is associated, perhaps, in our thoughts with certain events or crises in our own lives, or is the expression — probably the very imperfect expression — of some sentiment with which we are in sympathy and accord.

"Here then, in order that we may the better arrive at a just and critical appreciation of that to which we may be directing our attention, comes the necessity for the employment of the intellectual faculties of our nature. 'To judge a composition simply from the manner in which it works upon our feelings, is no better than judging a picture or a poem merely from our sympathy with its subject.' Sir Henry Hadow, Studies in Modern Music, Vol. II. We here are called upon to exercise our judgment, to decide upon such questions as style, symmetry, and balance of design — to say, in fact, whether the composer has put his thoughts into the most convincing shape, into that form which will best convey their meaning."

Consequently I do not think we should abolish the use of the intellect here even if we could. When, however, we start with an examination of the written and printed material supplied by the plaintiff in his complaint and exhibits, we find at once that he does not and cannot claim extensive copying, measure by measure, of his compositions. He therefore has resorted to a comparative analysis — the "dissection" found unpersuasive in the earlier cases — to support his claim of plagiarism of small detached portions here and there, the musical fillers between the better known parts of the melody. And plaintiff's compositions, as pointed out in the cases cited above, are of the simple and trite character where small repetitive sequences are not hard to discover. It is as though we found Shakespeare a plagiarist on the basis of his use of articles, pronouns, prepositions, and adjectives also used by others. The surprising thing, however, is to note the small amount of even this type of reproduction which plaintiff by dint of extreme dissection has been able to find.

Though it is most instructive, it will serve no good purpose for me to restate here this showing as to each of the pieces in issue. As an example of the rest, we may take plaintiff's first cause of action. This involves his "A Modern Messiah" with defendant's "Don't Fence Me In." The first is written in 6/8 time, the second in common or 4/4 time; and there is only one place where there is a common sequence of as many as five consecutive notes, and these without the same values. Thus it goes. The usual claim seems to be rested upon a sequence of three, of four, or of five — never more than five — identical notes, usually of different rhythmical values. Nowhere is there anything approaching the twelve-note sequence of the *Marks* case, supra. Interesting is the fact that the closest tonal resemblance is to be found between a piece by defendant written back in 1930 and an uncopyrighted waltz by plaintiff (rejected here by my brothers because it is uncopyrighted) which was never published, but, according to his statement, was publicly performed as early as 1923, 1924, and 1925.

In the light of these utmost claims of the plaintiff, I do not see a legal basis for the claim of plagiarism. So far as I have been able to discover, no earlier case approaches the holding that a simple and trite sequence of this type, even if copying may seem indicated, constitutes proof either of access or of plagiarism. In addition to the cases already cited, see the fine statements of Bright, J., in *Arnstein v. Broadcast Music, Inc.,* D.C.S.D.N.Y., 46 F. Supp. 379, 381, affirmed 2 Cir., 137 F. 2d 410, supra, and of Yankwich, J., in *Carew v. R. K. O. Radio Pictures,* D.C.S.D.Cal., 43 F. Supp. 199. That being so, the procedure whereby the demonstration is made does not seem to me overimportant. A court is a court whether sitting at motion or day calendar; and when an issue of law is decisively framed, it is its judicial duty to pass judgment. Hence on the precedents I should feel dismissal required on the face of the complaint and exhibits.

. . . .

Since the legal issue seems thus clear to me, I am loath to believe that my colleagues will uphold a final judgment of plagiarism on a record such as this. The present holding is therefore one of those procedural mountains which develop where it is thought that justice must be temporarily sacrificed, lest a mistaken precedent be set at large. The conclusion that the precedent would be mistaken appears to rest on two premises: a belief in the efficacy of the jury to settle issues of plagiarism, and a dislike of the rule established by the Supreme Court as to summary judgments. Now, as to the first, I am not one to condemn jury trials (cf. *Keller v. Brooklyn Bus Corp.,* 2 Cir., 128 F. 2d 510, 517; Frank, If Men Were Angels, 1942, 80-101; Frank, Law and the Modern Mind, 1930, 170-185, 302-309, 344-348), since I think it has a place among other quite finite methods of fact-finding. But I should not have thought it pre-eminently fitted to decide questions of musical values, certainly not so much so that an advisory jury should be brought in if no other is available. And I should myself hesitate to utter so clear an invitation to exploitation of slight musical analogies by clever musical tricks in the hope of getting juries hereafter in this circuit to divide the wealth of Tin Pan Alley. This holding seems to me an invitation to the strike suit par excellence. . . .

The second premise — dislike of the summary-judgment rule — I find difficult to appraise or understand. . . .

In fact, however, cases, texts, and articles without dissent accept and approve the summary judgment as an integral and useful part of the procedural system envisaged by the rules. . . . Plagiarism suits are not excepted from F. R. 56; and often that seems the most useful and direct procedure, since the cases so overwhelmingly turn ultimately and at long length upon an examination and a comparison of the challenged and the challenging compositions. Cf. *MacDonald v. Du Maurier,* 2 Cir., 144 F. 2d 696, 701-703. Here I think we ought to assume the responsibility of decision now. If, however, we are going to the other extreme of having all decisions of musical plagiarism made by ear, the more unsophisticated and musically naive the better, then it seems to me we are reversing our own precedents to substitute chaos, judicial as well as musical.

[On remand, after jury trial, judgment was entered for the defendant. *See* 158 F.2d 795 (2d Cir. 1946), *cert. denied,* 330 U.S. 851 (1947).]

QUESTIONS

1. Given the limited tonal range that a popular song composer uses, the confinements of conventional harmony, and the frequency with which we observe that many pop songs sound alike, how likely is it that a defendant will ever be able to prevail on a motion for summary judgment after the *Arnstein* decision? Is not that decision an invitation to litigate frivolous claims, which are almost certain to reach a jury or to force an unfair settlement? (At any time on the dockets of the federal courts in New York City and Los Angeles, one is likely to find a few song-infringement suits, typically brought by the affronted aspiring songwriter pro se.)

2. Would it not be sensible to have some judicially recognized "rule of thumb" regarding the number of consecutive notes of an earlier copyrighted song that may be duplicated (consciously or not) without fear of liability for infringement? (Judge Clark appears to opt for twelve notes, more or less. Is that too many?) Would it be feasible to formulate such a rule? Would it have to take into account whether the notes were in the accompaniment or in the melody? In the verse (introduction) or chorus (main melody section)? In the main theme or in the "bridge"?

3. To what extent do you agree with the position taken by Judge Clark in footnote 1? For example, what do you think of the assertion that Judge Frank's two-step analysis is unsound and that there is only one question on the infringement issue, i.e., whether the defendant actually copied, and that a finding of copying leads automatically to a judgment of infringement? Would such a rule lead in too many cases to a judicial (or jury) reluctance to find liability, lest the defendant be burdened with overwhelming damages? (Perhaps Judge Clark for this reason concluded that Porter had not copied, as a matter of law.)

4. Could the concern expressed in the preceding question be addressed by "parsing" damages or profits, comparing the amount of the song copied from the

plaintiff's with the amount originated by the defendant (or copied from other sources)? Similarly, how should damages or profits be determined when the plaintiff took an Italian folk melody, modified the rhythm slightly, and added words to generate a popular copyrighted song, and the defendant without authority sold sheet music of that song? *Cf. Italian Book Co. v. Rossi,* 27 F.2d 1014 (S.D.N.Y. 1928).

5. Is it relevant in determining infringement that the plaintiff's song ceased to be popular five years ago? Is it relevant that the plaintiff's work is an operatic aria and the defendant's is a jukebox hit with little or no overlapping audience?

6. What should be the role of experts in musical, artistic or literary infringement cases? On what issues can they make the greatest contribution? On what issues should the fact-finder rely primarily on personal observation or on intuition?

A. SHAFTER, MUSICAL COPYRIGHT 194-200, 202-04, 208-10, 214-15 (2d ed. 1939)*

Elements of Music

Music, in many respects, is a science,[10] even though the essence of music is an art and indefinable. Judge Holmes' definition of it as a "rational collocation of sounds, apart from concepts," is the classic judicial description, and it covers the subject thoroughly. As a science, music has its attributes and components — melody, harmony, rhythm, tone, pitch, and so forth. Our moderns dispense, at times, with the second and third elements, and the result, according to liberal critics who are usually absent from the ordeals, is still "music."

To draw an obvious comparison, language has several hundred thousand words composed of any of the twenty-six letters comprising the alphabet; music has only thirteen tones, thus:

Continuing the comparison, one may say that figures are the musical syllables; phrases the musical words, which are combined into musical sentences and paragraphs as in language and literature. It is a generally accepted theory that music and the spoken language originated in the same source; and probably music came first. Most of the attributes of music and literature are similar, but the great difference lies in the scope of the two forms of expression, literature being far superior in this respect. The limit of musical expression, as has already been mentioned, lies in the thirteen tones, their octaves, and their variations. An ordinary singer's voice rarely ranges beyond an octave; instruments range from three to five, and even the staff notation on music paper will limit the range of the repetitious musical tones varying only in pitch. Harmonic and orchestral treatment, which cannot be had in literary productions, constitute the limit of musical variation, unless we include the new electrical devices which produce notes never before heard. And it must be remembered that some notes, both high and low, are beyond the possibilities of the human ear. The lowest bass reed on a great organ has too few vibrations per second to make itself heard; it can

*Reprinted with permission from Musical Copyright (2d ed. 1939), published by Callaghan & Co., Wilmette, IL 60091.

[10] Bach v. Longman, 1 Chit. 26 (1777). See also discussion of Judge Morley in Dunbar v. Spratt-Snyder Co., 208 Iowa 490 (1929).

be detected only as a sort of weight in the air, a vibration of the atmosphere itself, which gives the hearer a feeling of relief when it ceases.

Physical Limits to Creative Ability. The average composer who indulges in songs has a limited number of tones at his disposal. The combinations and permutations of the thirteen tones give the amazing total of 6,227,020,800 combinations, of which only a small fraction may be used ordinarily. Popular songs, particularly, lie within a very small radius. In a confined space, similarity of tone construction is inevitable. Practically every original idea the composer can think of has appeared somewhere before; it is a matter of probabilities, and every day the number of new possibilities grows less.

If composers could adopt a system of numbering notes, as the telephone company has done in the case of its exchanges — since it was running out of new names and combinations — there might be a wider opportunity for originality. A new quarter-tone scale, spoken of enthusiastically by some, offers some hope. But such things, at present, are out of the question. Only the elements of music offer new possibilities — harmony and rhythm, or their absence. If originality were determined by the absence of certain accepted standards, rather than by their inclusion, many modern composers would be considered great original geniuses.

Olin Downes, one of our foremost music critics, sums up this situation excellently in an article in which he states: "When a scale of twelve semi-tones [*] has been used for a few centuries, there inevitably develop certain thematic coincidences, possibly as far apart in meaning and origin as the phrase of the slow movement of Beethoven's C minor piano concerto, is apart from the opening phrase of 'Salut, demeure' of the 'Faust' of Gounod. Those two phrases are identical in contour and in rhythmic arrangement. Obviously they never had anything to do with each other.... Instances of this sort are innumerable. Lawsuits have been based upon them...."

Since it is generally agreed that the original fund of melodic ideas has been exhausted, serious composers, and others, have turned to the two other important elements of music — harmony and rhythm. In the use and treatment of these there is a certain originality to be attained; but even that is necessarily limited by obvious physical limitations.

Of the *three essential elements* — rhythm, harmony, and melody — the first two are usually emphasized, whereas the third is taken as a matter of course; and when it is impossible to invent new melodic ideas, the composer may display his skill in the means he uses to develop what theme he has. Brahms' "Variations on a Theme of Haydn" is a classic example. Beethoven's Fifth Symphony is a marvelous structure on a commonplace theme. It may be said that the true talent of a composer is shown in these elements, rather than in the mere invention of a new combination of notes — which may be an ingenious combination of old strains. Melody is the paramount consideration in folk songs; but in orchestral works and complex instrumental pieces the other two elements are of supreme importance. Any symphonic works which depend largely upon melody for their effect — like Schubert's "Unfinished Symphony" — are exceptions.

The omission of one of the elements will not render a work unmusical. Peter Cornelius' "Ein Ton" ("One Tone") is composed entirely of G in the bass, and achieves its effects by harmonic methods. Among primitive peoples and dance devotees the predominant interest in music lies in the rhythm; for the aborigine,

---

[*] Thirteen, including the final completing note.

the tom-tom suffices; for the modern jazz maniac, nothing less than a writhing orchestra, under the direction of a writhing, dress-suited leader, playing at its fastest and with special emphasis on the drum and cymbal, is satisfactory. On the other hand, plain chants have melody, but no measured time. From an artistic as well as aural sense, an entirely new composition may be evoked by either the alteration or omission of any of these essential elements. But in regard to infringement, and its detection, a different opinion governs. Again the clash between artistic and legal concepts arises. The importance of these elements in an infringement suit will now occupy our attention.

A. Rhythm

Rhythm is the sole natural element of music, the one medium of expression known from prehistoric times. It constitutes the instinctive undercurrent of action and thought. In music especially is rhythm fundamental. Rhythm means time, the beats per bar; everything that can be checked by the metronome. Rhythm includes as a part of its essential make-up accent, time, pace, metre; when it is distorted we have the effect which so grated on Shakespeare's musical ear:

"How sour sweet music is, when time is broke and no proportion kept."

Yet this "breaking of time" is the basis for an entirely new school of composers, chief among whom are Stravinsky and his imitators. They have done away with the regular metre described as "the systematic grouping of notes with regard to duration."

For our purposes, a difference in rhythm may mask an infringement. For example, much has been made of the fact that Brahms took the melody of the Westminster Chimes as the theme for his famous horn motif in his First Symphony. A comparison of the notes, as illustrated, will reveal the copy.

Westminster Chimes

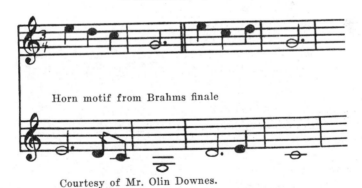

Horn motif from Brahms finale

Courtesy of Mr. Olin Downes.

Olin Downes says that what Brahms changed is *not the notes, but their rhythm.*[11] In the case of a copyrighted composition this change might be the colorable variation mentioned; but in the instance of music in the common domain, the copy is permissible. What is important in this respect is the fact that one may copy a melody by changing the rhythm — and still be infringing.

---

[11] N. Y. Times, November 30, 1930. But see Mr. Downes' further conclusion as to the origin of this famous motif in N. Y. Times, April 19, 1931.

Time and accent, as elements of rhythm, have been used to diguise plagiarized melodies. Time — which gives musical works their tempo, such as 4/4 or 3/4 or 6/8 — aids in establishing a central rhythmic metre. Some of the classic works have been "jazzed up" so that their composers would never recognize them. The rate of performance ipso facto determines the general nature of the piece. Presumably, that majestic work of Chopin's, popularly known as the "Funeral March," could be transformed into a "hot" dance melody with jungle rhythm, if the arranger were skillful and resourceful enough to accomplish that miracle. Similarly, if a piece of jazz music were played very slowly, it would lose all its meaning and effect and be revealed for what it really is — discord, sound and fury. Time, in many cases, is a disguise, and a most necessary adjunct to the use of the piece.

Accent is an element of time and rhythm, since by accenting certain notes at regular intervals, one may set the rhythm. A fox-trot rhythm has a double accent; in swing-time music the accent falls on the wrong or offbeats, which gives the breathless and exhilarating effect; while in marches the accent is on the first beat.

In waltzes a beat is accented and lengthened to indicate the glide. A foxtrot may be metamorphosed into a waltz by changing the tempo and accent, and the melody itself will become unrecognizable. This is a very common form of copying. Famous songs, arias and dances have thus been made from the ordinary ascending and descending scale. This manner of utilizing common materials is legitimate.

From the legal standpoint, what part does change in rhythm play in infringement? Judge Manton, in a case involving "The Wedding Dance Waltz," conceded that, because of a paucity of original compositions within the confines of the scales, "different results may be obtained by varying the accent and tempo." His opinion was based on an expert's report which stated that no one who played the "Wedding Dance Waltz" and "Swanee River Moon" in the manner written would confuse one with the other, even though the tone successions were similar, because the rhythm and accent were different:

Wedding Dance Waltz

Swanee River Moon

Unfortunately, the suit was dismissed on the grounds that the melody harkened back to an earlier work, and only six out of four hundred and fifty bars had been taken.[12]

The question of originality in rhythm remains as clouded as before, although, musically, Judge Manton is correct in his intimation. Unquestionably, one may take an old work in the common domain, change the rhythm and obtain copy-

---

[12] Marks v. Leo Feist, Inc., 290 Fed. 959, aff'd 8 F. (2d) 460 (1923-1925).

"Slight variations in the use of rhythm or harmony — of accent and tempo — may achieve originality." Justice Yankwich in Hirsch v. Paramount Pictures, Inc. [17 F. Supp. 816 (1937)].

right. Infringement always looms, however, when the original work is protected by copyright. Courts, in order to strip songs down to their essentials, may dispense with rhythm and accent, giving notes equal value, and leaving for their consideration only the melodies, which are transposed to the same key and mode. In such cases, where it appears the infringer has cleverly disguised the original composition, the charge of pilfering will be upheld.[13] In seeking to establish the derivation of one chorus from another, Judge Hand said: "If the choruses be transposed into the same key and played in the same time, their similarities become at once apparent." [14]

B. Melody

This musical element, which forms the basis of most infringement suits, is a "succession of notes musically effective." [15] Melodies, analyzed in the impersonal light of science,[16] will be found to consist of certain intervals or short phrases brought together in different combinations, so as to form a great variety of tunes, just as words are used to form a sentence. A "taking" melody is usually composed of familiar phrases or clichés. The name is appropriate, because these phrases are usually taken from any number of previous successes. It is almost impossible for a composer to resist appropriating certain "natural" phrases which have won popular favor and, by deft combination or changes in rhythm, present them as his own. The number of successful resurrections is almost infinite. From the graveyard of old and forgotten music have come hundreds of unforgettable hits. Chopin, fortunately unaware of the crime, furnished the themes for "I'm Always Chasing Rainbows" and "When the Honeymoon Is Over." A modern composition, achieving tremendous success both as an organ number and as a popular song, was taken from Beethoven's "Moonlight Sonata." Even Sullivan, a truly original composer, is said to have copied his music for the song "Come, Friends, Who Plow the Sea" in the "Pirates of Penzance" from the opening of the "Anvil Chorus" in "Il Trovatore." This tune has been adopted for the famous "Hail, Hail, the Gang's All Here."

Whenever a composer takes a theme that has been used before, and takes it innocently, he merely uses the strains that, as we mentioned, are floating about in his mind; the result of the numberless songs he has heard — "the flotsam and jetsam which may have drifted in from the great sea of melody beyond the bar." How these ghosts are brought to life is one of the interesting phenomena of nature.

Another reason why melody is usually the basis of infringement, is the undeniable fact that that part of a song makes it a commercial success or failure. . . .

C. Harmony

Harmony and melody, inextricably interwoven as they are, may together form the basis of an infringement suit. That harmony, independently considered, is a most vital and potent element in music is undeniable. It is largely concerned

---

[13] Hein v. Harris, 175 Fed. 875, aff'd 183 Fed. 107 (1910).

[14] Haas v. Leo Feist, Inc., 234 Fed. 105 (1916).

[15] Grove's "Dictionary of Music and Musicians," vol. 3, p. 371.

[16] G. H. Clutson "Musical Clichés and Copyright," London Musical Times, June 6, 1914, and August 1, 1914. See also S. Spaeth "Common Sense in Music."

with the formation of chords and their progression as accompaniment to a melody (including also the use of counter melodies or counterpoint). While harmony depends upon melody, it is a complete art and science in itself; orchestration depends upon it; conservatories give courses in harmony and counterpoint. Sometimes harmony, which is not stressed in our popular songs, is the main feature, as in oriental melodies (Chinese, Japanese and Hindu). Especially is this true in such songs as the "Japanese Sandman," where more than half of the melody in the chorus is limited to two or three notes. Without the variations of harmony, the tune would become monotonous. It was Virgil who said that genius is one part inspiration and three parts perspiration, and in music it may be said that melody is the inspiration; harmony the perspiration.

Harmony may be employed to disguise melody, just as rhythm is used. Harmonic changes are assuredly far superior to rhythmic changes for the purpose of masking copies. They are more adroit; they have greater camouflaging power, and represent effective means by which a "familiar phrase" may be turned into something distinctly novel. But, for purposes of detection of musical infringements, the two are placed in the same category. Harmonic ingenuity will also be disregarded when the taking of a melody is concerned. Thus, it was harmony that changed "Tosca" in minor to "Avalon" in major — a copy which did not turn out as happily as expected; the imitation was discovered.[22]

Tosca

Avalon

But the concession that, in an infringement suit, harmonization may be entitled to protection due to its originality, is a notable advance in musical copyright progress coming within recent years. The famous "Dardanella" case, in 1924, arose as a result of harmonic accompaniment; that rolling undercurrent which formed a background — and a satisfying one — for the meagre melody. The "ostinato" in the accompaniment gave the effect of beating tom-toms in the distance, yet it had a simple melodic character of its own. It was written in two measures, consisting of eight notes played over and over with no change except the variation of a musical fifth in the scale to accommodate itself harmonically to the changes in the melody:

Dardanella

----
[22] N. Y. Times, January 29, 1921, p 9.

Jerome Kern's "Kalua," which was alleged to infringe the accompaniment, had likewise a rolling ostinato based upon the same fundamental tones and designed to give the impression of the rolling of the surf on the palm-fringed shores of a south sea isle:

Kalua

Although there was no similarity between the melodies, and although the ostinato was traced back to earlier sources, this harmonic figure, as employed in "Dardanella," was held original with the composer, and "Kalua" was declared an infringement. It was held that the continuous persistency of the phrase "materially qualifies, if it does not dominate, the melody."[23]

A repeated bass accompaniment is in many cases the dominant feature of a composition, as witness the "rumba" accompaniment in the popular "Peanut Vendor," or the striking phrase heard throughout Ravel's "Bolero."

. . . .

Quality: When judicial precedent speaks of "substantial" and "material" parts of compositions which must be appropriated before an infringement results, that does not by any means imply the copying of a large part of the work. It is quality that counts — not quantity. Every part of a work should be protected. But we have been unable to determine how much of a melody constitutes infringement. Among many people, musicians as well as laymen, four bars constitute the arbitrary minimum — a ridiculous standard; for this would place almost every popular song, no matter how original, under suspicion, simply because there are so few effective openings for these works. The average popular song is based upon a prescribed formula. It has three parts in the chorus: the opening strain, which usually runs for eight bars and is repeated for another eight; a "middle" tune of eight bars, and a concluding eight, which repeats the first strain with little variation. The opening strain is composed of two phrases, each of four bars, which are not only similar or identical to each other, but are repeated in the first part and in the concluding eight bars. Thus, what began supposedly as four bars may turn out to be eight, twelve, or sixteen. Therefore, if we are going to count bars and base our decision upon that, the entire method is falsified at the very outset.

The amount taken is not the question at issue, provided a musical idea is sufficiently expressed. An infringement is present whether seventeen bars out of thirty-two are taken or whether an eight-note accompaniment or a striking phrase are appropriated. Obviously, then, quality and not quantity is the deciding factor.[29] Quantity should be used, if at all, to determine only the extent of damages involved, and not the fact of infringement.[30]

_____

[23] Fred Fisher, Inc. v. Dillingham, 298 Fed. 145 (1924).

[29] But see Marks v. Leo Feist, Inc., supra, note 12, where six out of four hundred fifty bars were held not a "substantial" infringement. But again, four out of these six same bars were found to be identical to those in an earlier work.

[30] M. Witmark & Sons v. Pastime Amusement Co., 298 Fed. 470, aff'd 2 F. (2d) 1020 (1924).

BRIGHT TUNES MUSIC CORP. v. HARRISONGS MUSIC, LTD.

420 F. Supp. 177 (S.D.N.Y. 1976)

OWEN, DISTRICT JUDGE.

This is an action in which it is claimed that a successful song, My Sweet Lord, listing George Harrison as the composer, is plagiarized from an earlier successful song, He's So Fine, composed by Ronald Mack, recorded by a singing group called the "Chiffons," the copyright of which is owned by plaintiff, Bright Tunes Music Corp.

He's So Fine, recorded in 1962, is a catchy tune consisting essentially of four repetitions of a very short basic musical phrase, "sol-mi-re," (hereinafter motif A),[1] altered as necessary to fit the words, followed by four repetitions of another short basic musical phrase, "sol-la-do-la-do," (hereinafter motif B).[2] While neither motif is novel, the four repetitions of A, followed by four repetitions of B, is a highly unique pattern.[3] In addition, in the second use of the motif B series, there is a grace note inserted making the phrase go "sol-la-do-la-re-do."[4]

My Sweet Lord, recorded first in 1970, also uses the same motif A (modified to suit the words) four times, followed by motif B, repeated three times, not four. In place of He's So Fine's fourth repetition of motif B, My Sweet Lord has a transitional passage of musical attractiveness of the same approximate length, with the identical grace note in the identical second repetition.[5] The harmonies of both songs are identical.[6]

---

[1]

[2]

[3] All the experts agreed on this.
[4]

[5] This grace note, as will be seen *infra,* has a substantial significance in assessing the claims of the parties hereto.

[6] Expert witnesses for the defendants asserted crucial differences in the two songs. These claimed differences essentially stem, however, from the fact that different words and number of syllables were involved. This necessitated modest alterations in the repetitions or the places of beginning of a phrase, which, however, has nothing to do whatsoever with the essential musical kernel that is involved.

George Harrison, a former member of The Beatles, was aware of He's So Fine. In the United States, it was No. 1 on the billboard charts for five weeks; in England, Harrison's home country, it was No. 12 on the charts on June 1, 1963, a date upon which one of the Beatle songs was, in fact, in first position. For seven weeks in 1963, He's So Fine was one of the top hits in England.

According to Harrison, the circumstances of the composition of My Sweet Lord were as follows. Harrison and his group, which include[d] an American gospel singer named Billy Preston,[7] were in Copenhagen, Denmark, on a singing engagement. There was a press conference involving the group going on backstage. Harrison slipped away from the press conference and went to a room upstairs and began "vamping" some guitar chords, fitting on to the chords he was playing the words, "Hallelujah" and "Hare Krishna" in various ways.[8] During the course of this vamping, he was alternating between what musicians call a Minor II chord and a Major V chord.

At some point, germinating started and he went down to meet with others of the group, asking them to listen, which they did, and everyone began to join in, taking first "Hallelujah" and then "Hare Krishna" and putting them into four part harmony. Harrison obviously started using the "Hallelujah," etc., as repeated sounds, and from there developed the lyrics, to wit, "My Sweet Lord," "Dear, Dear Lord," etc. In any event, from this very free-flowing exchange of ideas, with Harrison playing his two chords and everybody singing "Hallelujah" and "Hare Krishna," there began to emerge the My Sweet Lord text idea, which Harrison sought to develop a little bit further during the following week as he was playing it on his guitar. Thus developed motif A and its words interspersed with "Hallelujah" and "Hare Krishna."

Approximately one week after the idea first began to germinate, the entire group flew back to London because they had earlier booked time to go to a recording studio with Billy Preston to make an album. In the studio, Preston was the principal musician. Harrison did not play in the session. He had given Preston his basic motif A with the idea that it be turned into a song, and was back and forth from the studio to the engineer's recording booth, supervising the recording "takes." Under circumstances that Harrison was utterly unable to recall, while everybody was working toward a finished song, in the recording studio, somehow or other the essential three notes of motif A reached polished form.

Q. [By the Court]: . . . you feel that those three notes . . . the motif A in the record, those three notes developed somewhere in that recording session?

Mr. Harrison: I'd say those three there were finalized as beginning there.

. . . .

Q. [By the Court]: Is it possible that Billy Preston hit on those [notes comprising motif A]?

Mr. Harrison: Yes, but it's possible also that I hit on that, too, as far back as the dressing room, just scat singing.

---

[7] Preston recorded the first Harrison copyrighted recording of My Sweet Lord, of which more *infra*, and from his musical background was necessarily equally aware of He's So Fine.

[8] These words ended up being a "responsive" interjection between the eventually copyrighted words of My Sweet Lord. In He's So Fine the Chiffons used the sound "dulang" in the same places to fill in and give rhythmic impetus to what would otherwise be somewhat dead spots in the music.

Similarly, it appears that motif B emerged in some fashion at the recording session as did motif A. This is also true of the unique grace note in the second repetition of motif B.

Q. [By the Court]: All I am trying to get at, Mr Harrison, is if you have a recollection when that [grace] note popped into existence as it ends up in the Billy Preston recording.

. . . .

Mr. Harrison: . . . [Billy Preston] might have put that there on every take, but it just might have been on one take, or he might have varied it on different takes at different places.

The Billy Preston recording, listing George Harrison as the composer, was thereafter issued by Apple Records. The music was then reduced to paper by someone who prepared a "lead sheet" containing the melody, the words and the harmony for the United States copyright application.[9]

Seeking the wellsprings of musical conposition — why a composer chooses the succession of notes and the harmonies he does — whether it be George Harrison or Richard Wagner — is a fascinating inquiry. It is apparent from the extensive colloquy between the Court and Harrison covering forty pages in the transcript that neither Harrison nor Preston were conscious of the fact that they were utilizing the He's So Fine theme.[10] However, they in fact were, for it is perfectly obvious to the listener that in musical terms, the two songs are virtually identical except for one phrase. There is motif A used four times, followed by motif B, four times in one case, and three times in the other, with the same grace note in the second repetition of motif B.[11]

---

[9] It is of interest, but not of legal significance, in my opinion, that when Harrison later recorded the song himself, he chose to omit the little grace note, not only in his musical recording but in the printed sheet music that was issued following that particular recording. The genesis of the song remains the same, however modestly Harrison may have later altered it. Harrison, it should be noted, regards his song as that which he sings at the particular moment he is singing it and not something that is written on a piece of paper.

[10] Preston may well have been the "composer" of motif B and the telltale grace note appearing in the second use of the motif during the recording session, for Harrison testified:

The Court: To be as careful as I can now in summing this up, you can't really say that you or Billy Preston or somebody else didn't somewhere along the line suggest these; all you know is that when Billy Preston sang them that way at the recording session, you felt they were a successful way to sing this, and you kept it?
The Witness: Yes, I mean at that time we chose what is a good performance.
The Court: And you felt it was a worthy piece of music?
The Witness: Yes . . . .

[11] Even Harrison's own expert witness, Harold Bartow, long in the field, acknowledged that although the two motifs were in the public domain, their use here was so unusual that he, in all his experience, had never come across this unique sequential use of these materials. He testified:

The Court: And I think you agree with me in this, that we are talking about a basic three-note structure that composers can vary in modest ways, but we are still talking about the same heart, the same essence?
The Witness: Yes.
The Court: So you say that you have not seen anywhere four A's followed by three B's or four?

What happened? I conclude that the composer,[12] in seeking musical materials to clothe his thoughts, was working with various possibilities. As he tried this possibility and that, there came to the surface of his mind a particular combination that pleased him as being one he felt would be appealing to a prospective listener; in other words, that this combination of sounds would work. Why? Because his subconscious knew it already had worked in a song his conscious mind did not remember. Having arrived at this pleasing combination of sounds, the recording was made, the lead sheet prepared for copyright and the song became an enormous success. Did Harrison deliberately use the music of He's So Fine? I do not believe he did so deliberately. Nevertheless, it is clear that My Sweet Lord is the very same song as He's So Fine with different words, and Harrison had access to He's So Fine. This is, under the law, infringement of copyright, and is no less so even though subconsciously accomplished. *Sheldon v. Metro-Goldwyn Pictures Corp.,* 81 F.2d 49, 54 (2d Cir. 1936); *Northern Music Corp. v. Pacemaker Music Co., Inc.,* 147 U.S.P.Q. 358, 359 (S.D.N.Y. 1965).

Given the foregoing, I find for the plaintiff on the issue of plagiarism, and set the action down for trial on November 8, 1976 on the issue of damages and other relief as to which the plaintiff may be entitled. The foregoing constitutes the Court's findings of fact and conclusions of law.

So ordered.

QUESTIONS

1. It is uniformly held that copyright is infringed when one intentionally makes copies of a copyrighted work, even though the person copying does not know (and has no reason to know) of the copyright. For example, if a book publisher publishes a manuscript which has been represented to be an original work but is in fact a copy of a copyrighted work, the book publisher infringes. *De Acosta v. Brown,* 146 F.2d 408 (2d Cir. 1944). Is this a sound rule? What are the arguments for and against this rule?

2. Even assuming the above rule to be sound and widely endorsed, is not the case for infringement much more difficult when the defendant does not intend to reproduce any work by another and is unaware that he is copying at all? Why should liability be imposed in such a case?

3. How do you think the court should have ruled had defendant Harrison copied only motif A or motif B?

4. What if Harrison, idly sitting at the piano, purposely played the notes of motifs A and B *backwards* and, finding the resulting tune to be pleasant, added lyrics, and published and performed the new song. Is this an infringement?

The Witness: Or four A's followed by four B's.

The uniqueness is even greater when one considers the identical grace note in the identical place in each song.

[12] I treat Harrison as the composer, although it appears that Billy Preston may have been the composer as to part. (*See* fn. 10 *supra*). Even were Preston the composer as to part, this is immaterial. Peter Pan Fabrics, Inc. v. Dan River Mills, Inc., 295 F. Supp. 1366, 1369 (S.D.N.Y.), *aff'd,* 415 F.2d 1007 (2d Cir. 1969).

NOVELTY TEXTILE MILLS, INC. v. JOAN FABRICS CORP.

558 F.2d 1090 (2d Cir. 1977)

GURFEIN, CIRCUIT JUDGE:

This is an appeal from an order of the District Court for the Southern District of New York (Werker, D.J.) denying plaintiff's motion for a preliminary injunction against the continued use by defendant of a fabric design which it allegedly copied from plaintiff's fabric design. The complaint charges copyright infringement under 17 U.S.C. §§ 101, 112 and 116 and seeks a permanent injunction, impoundment and destruction of the allegedly infringing copies, and damages. Jurisdiction is based on 28 U.S.C. § 1338(a).

I

The basic facts as found by the court below are not in dispute. Plaintiff Novelty Textile Mills, Inc. ("Novelty") and defendant Joan Fabrics Corporation ("Joan") both manufacture upholstery fabrics which they sell in competition with each other to furniture manufacturers. Novelty created Style 253 during the latter part of 1975 and copyrighted it. It was first displayed to the trade in January, 1976. The fabric sold well and was delivered to furniture manufacturers in commercial quantities beginning in March, 1976. Several manufacturers exhibited display models of their furniture, upholstered with Style 253 fabric, at a regional furniture trade market held in April, 1976 at High Point, North Carolina. At that time both the sales and design personnel of defendant Joan viewed plaintiff's Style 253 and learned that there was a substantial demand for this type of design, known as "bias" or "argyle" plaid, among its customers.

Joan's management thereafter determined that it too should offer a collection of bias plaid upholstery fabrics. Its designers were instructed to make such a collection and were told "to avoid any infringement of fabrics manufactured by others." Subsequently five bias plaid designs were made by its designers and used in the manufacture of Joan's fabrics.

After the introduction of these Joan fabric designs, the sales of Novelty's Style 253 declined precipitously. The president of Novelty testified that its continuing loss in sales amounted to approximately $11,000 per week. He attributed this loss to the introduction of the Joan designs.

Within two months Novelty instituted this lawsuit and moved for a preliminary injunction. The District Court after an evidentiary hearing, as noted, denied the motion. This appeal followed.

II

In order to prove infringement a plaintiff must show ownership of a valid copyright and copying by the defendant. *See 2 M. Nimmer, Nimmer on Copyright* § 141 at 611 (1976) (*"Nimmer"*). Novelty's ownership and the validity of its copyright are not disputed for the purpose of this motion.[1] This leaves the

---

[1] The Copyright Office certificate of registration is prima facie evidence of the facts stated therein. 17 U.S.C. § 209. This has generally been held to mean prima facie proof of ownership and validity. *See 2 M. Nimmer, Nimmer on Copyright* § 141.1 at 611 (1976). In the absence of evidence to the contrary, therefore, the District Court was correct in its conclusion that such ownership and validity here must be presumed.

issue of whether Joan copied Novelty's design. Since direct evidence of copying is rarely, if ever, available, a plaintiff may prove copying by showing access and "substantial similarity" of the two works. *See, e.g., Arnstein v. Porter,* 154 F.2d 464, 468 (2d Cir. 1946); *Whitney v. Ross Jungnickel, Inc.,* 179 F. Supp. 751, 753 (S.D.N.Y. 1960), *2 Nimmer, supra,* § 141.2 at 613. Here Joan not only admits access, but also the actual viewing by its designers of Novelty's Style 253 before its own designs were produced.[2]

The District Court found, however, that there was no substantial similarity because certain differences in the works "would be apparent to a furniture manufacturer, or for that matter to a consumer seriously contemplating purchase of a couch covered with one or another of the fabrics."

"Substantial similarity" is to be determined by the "ordinary observer" test.[3] Judge Learned Hand in defining this test stated there is substantial similarity where "the ordinary observer, unless he set out to detect the disparities, would be disposed to overlook them, and regard their aesthetic appeal as the same." *Peter Pan Fabrics, Inc. v. Martin Weiner Corp.,* 274 F.2d 487, 489 (2d Cir. 1960). More recently this court formulated the test as "whether an average lay observer would recognize the alleged copy as having been appropriated from the copyrighted work." *Ideal Toy Corp. v. Fab-Lu Ltd.,* 360 F.2d 1021, 1022 (2d Cir. 1966). And, of course, by definition "[t]he copying need not be of every detail so long as the copy is substantially similar to the copyrighted work." *Comptone Co. v. Rayex Corp.,* 251 F.2d 487, 488 (2d Cir. 1958); *United Merchants &*

---

[2] We note that while access and substantial similarity are *sine qua non* to a finding of copying, such evidence does not *require* the trier of fact to find copying. The defendant may introduce evidence of independent creation which would rebut the plaintiff's prima facie case. However, "the absence of any countervailing evidence of creation independent of the copyrighted source may well render clearly erroneous a finding that there was not copying." Roth Greeting Cards v. United Card Co., 429 F.2d 1106, 1110 (9th Cir. 1970). And even with such evidence from the defendant, there may be such substantial similarity that "no explanation other than copying is reasonably possible." *2 Nimmer, supra* note 1, § 141.2 at 613-14. *See* Arrow Novelty Co. v. Enco National Corp., 393 F. Supp. 157, 160 (S.D.N.Y. 1974).

[3] Appellee Joan argues that besides the "ordinary observer" test there is another test for infringement in fabric design situations such as this one. This test requires a "comparison between the particular expression of the accused work and the particular expression of the copyrighted design." And "the extent to which an 'expression' is protected by copyrights depends upon the range of previous expressions of the same idea or theme which may be found in the public domain, and thus, are free for all to use." Appellee's Brief at 6-7. Joan is mistaken.

The existence of a prior work (whether in the public domain or not) is significant only if (1) the plaintiff copied from that work; or (2) the defendant copied from that work. Neither is claimed here by Joan.

As to the plaintiff's design it is clear that "a work is original and may command copyright protection even if it is completely identical with a prior work provided it was not copied from such prior work but is rather a product of the independent efforts of its author." *1 Nimmer, supra,* § 10.1 at 34. *See* Sheldon v. Metro-Goldwyn Pictures Corp., 81 F.2d 49, 54 (2d Cir. 1936), *aff'd,* 309 U.S. 390 (1940). Here there is no claim that Novelty's design was not created independently, and, as we noted, there is a presumption of validity, *see* note 1, *supra,* and therefore "originality."

As to the defendant's work, "the common practice of defendants at trial in pointing out a similar work created in antiquity, or at least prior to the defendant's creation is of no assistance unless the trier of fact believes that the defendant copied from such works." *1 Nimmer, supra,* § 101.6 at 381-82. Here Joan claims that its own designers independently created the designs, not that they were copied from a public domain work.

Manufacturers, Inc. v. K. Gimbel Accessories, Inc., 294 F. Supp. 151, 154 (S.D.N.Y. 1968).[4]

We have viewed the fabrics presented in the District Court. While it is true that "[t]he test for infringement of a copyright is of necessity vague", *Peter Pan Fabrics, Inc. v. Martin Weiner Corp., supra,* 274 F.2d at 489, it is clear to us that Joan's Fleetwood Spice is "substantially similar" to Novelty's Cane 253 and, in fact, to our "lay" eyes, is almost identical.[5] And "[a]s we have before us the same record, and as no part of the decision below turned on credibility, we are in as good a position to determine the question as is the district court." *Concord Fabrics, Inc. v. Marcus Bros. Textile Corp.,* 409 F.2d 1315, 1317 (2d Cir. 1969). We conclude that plaintiff has established a prima facie case of infringement as to Fleetwood Spice.

Plaintiff has also alleged that other Joan Fabrics infringe Style 253. The District Court, after determining that the two above fabrics (which were thought to present plaintiff's best case) were not substantially similar, did not make individual findings with regard to these other fabrics. In light of our determination, we remand for consideration of whether these other fabrics are also substantially similar to Style 253.[6]

In short, prior works in the public domain do not require a different test here for "substantial similarity", nor do they reduce the protection from copying afforded Novelty's design by its copyright.

[4] The key to the "ordinary observer" test is therefore the similarities rather than the differences. Only a slavish copy would have no differences and "[n]o one disputes that the copyright extends beyond a photographic reproduction of the design." Peter Pan Fabrics, Inc. v. Martin Weiner Corp., *supra,* 274 F.2d at 489. *Cf.* Concord Fabrics, Inc. v. Marcus Bros. Textile Corp., 409 F.2d 1315, 1316 (2d Cir. 1969) ("nature of [the] differences only tends to emphasize the extent to which the defendant has deliberately copied from the plaintiff").

[5] As the District Court found, both fabrics use brown and camel or beige on a light-colored background to form a plaid design consisting of intersecting diamonds with an interior dimension of approximately four inches. And in each fabric, one series of diamonds is formed by a stripe which is somewhat broader than the other. When the Joan Fleetwood Spice fabric is placed over a portion of the Novelty fabric, the design, dimensions and colors match-up and the appearance is of one fabric.

[6] Appellant has alleged that if Fleetwood Spice infringes Style 253, then at least some of Joan's other fabrics also infringe because they are simply expressions of the Fleetwood design in different colors. Indeed, testimony offered by Joan appears to concede that differences in the appearance of some of the Joan fabrics result essentially from variations in color and texture of yarn, rather than differences in a black and white rendering of the design. However, some of the color variations create such different effects that the ordinary observer might not consider them similar.

There thus arises the issue of whether a fabric infringes a copyrighted design when it employs the black and white outline of a design that is copied from a copyrighted design but expresses that outline in colors so different from those used in the fabric of the copyrighted design that no substantial similarity results. While recognizing that there may be color combinations, beyond the simple use of primary or calico colors, which may themselves be the subject of copyright as a work of art, it is the writer's view that, once a copyrighted design is found to have been copied, mere changes in the color scheme on the copied design would ordinarily not protect the defendant from a claim of infringement. Indeed, no such claim has been made on this appeal, nor has the question been briefed. Moreover, we have found no precedent or commentary on the question.

However, since we are not unanimous on this point nor on the appropriateness of deciding it on this record, we suggest that the District Court take proof of precisely what

The question remains whether Novelty is entitled to a preliminary injunction with respect to Fleetwood Spice or other Joan fabrics which the District Court on remand may find to be substantially similar to Style 253. In *Houghton Mifflin Co. v. Stackpole Sons, Inc.,* 104 F.2d 306, 307 (2d Cir.), *cert. denied,* 308 U.S. 597 (1939), this court stated that "it is settled in copyright cases that, if the plaintiff makes a prima facie showing of his right, a preliminary injunction should issue." *See also Rushton v. Vitale,* 218 F.2d 434, 436 (2d Cir. 1955). Much later in another fabric design case we stated that "[a]n injunction pending the outcome of trial . . . should issue if plaintiff can show a reasonable probability of prevailing on the merits." *Concord Fabrics, Inc. v. Marcus Bros. Textile Corp., supra,* 409 F.2d at 1317. And recently Chief Judge (then Judge) Kaufman in *Robert Stigwood Group Ltd. v. Sperber,* 457 F.2d 50, 55 (2d Cir. 1972), reaffirmed the statement made in *American Metropolitan Enterprises of New York, Inc. v. Warner Bros. Records, Inc.,* 389 F.2d 903, 905 (2d Cir. 1968), that:

> [a] copyright holder in the ordinary case may be presumed to suffer irreparable harm when his right to the exclusive use of the copyrighted material is invaded.

Here there is not even a need for a presumption of harm because the undisputed evidence shows that after the introduction of Joan's fabrics into the market, Novelty's sales declined by $11,000 a week. Consequently, we think that more than a sufficient showing has been made to require the issuance of a preliminary injunction.

For the foregoing reasons, we reverse the order of the District Court and remand for the issuance of an injunction with respect to Fleetwood Spice and a determination of whether the other Joan fabrics alleged to infringe Style 253 are "substantially similar," and therefore, on the facts of this case, should also be preliminarily enjoined.

Reversed and remanded with instructions.

MANSFIELD, CIRCUIT JUDGE (Concurring and Dissenting):

I concur in Judge Gurfein's carefully reasoned opinion, except for its remand of a portion of the case to the district court to determine whether color is an ingredient of the copyright and to dispose of the balance of the infringement claims. In my view the color scheme should be treated as one of the elements of the copyrighted design and, since we are in as good a position as the district court to resolve the infringement issue, we should hold that Novelty's Style 253 is not infringed by any of the alleged infringing fabrics produced by Joan other than its "Fleetwood Spice" and "Sand."

    . . . .

In short, what Novelty copyrighted was its plaid design in a brown, beige and white color combination. In this well-plowed field of Argyle and bias plaids, it obviously did not gain protection against the manufacture of all similar textile plaids, even though some might be produced by persons who had access to its copyrighted design. In my view it gained copyright protection for the overall effect or impression created by the particular combination of lines, space, juxtaposition, shading *and color scheme.* Whether another manufacturer could avoid infringement by changing the color scheme would depend in a particular case on how important the color scheme was in the overall effect or impression

---

was granted registration as a work of art to determine whether color was an ingredient of the copyright granted. The District Court will, in the first instance, have to determine the legal implications that flow from the facts found with respect to the fabrics subject to the remand.

of the design. Obviously if the design consisted merely of a simple red square or circle with dots, a change by the copier from red to green would be of great importance. On the other hand, if the design were an intricate or unusual one, as the court noted in *Soptra* [*Fabrics Corp. v. Stafford Knitting Mills, Inc.,* 490 F.2d 1092 (2d Cir. 1974)], a mere change in color would be insufficient to avoid infringement.

Since I believe the applicable principles are clear and that nothing would be gained by further prolongation of this case, I would rule now that, except for the "Fleetwood Spice" and "Sand" designs, there was no infringement of Novelty's 253 and to that extent affirm the decision of the district court.

QUESTIONS

1. Is the court holding that, regardless of color, the plaintiff's copyright on its plaid pattern protects against another's copying of that pattern? Would this be a sound conclusion? Is there anything "original" (for purposes of copyrightability) in the plaintiff's plaid pattern as such? (The size of the pattern? The exact extent of overlap of the adjacent patterns?) Could not the defendant readily demonstrate that the plaintiff has copied, if only unconsciously, its pattern from earlier plaid patterns in the public domain? (If so, would *Harrisongs* dictate a finding that the plaintiff's pattern was not copyrightable?)

2. Even if the court is holding only that the defendant's brown-and-beige plaid infringes the plaintiff's brown-and-beige plaid, is *that* a sound conclusion? That is, is the court correct in holding that the *color* of the plaid pattern is a copyrightable element of the total fabric design? Would this be true, for example, for the colors selected for various states or nations on a copyrighted map?

PETER PAN FABRICS CORP. v. MARTIN WEINER CORP.

274 F.2d 487 (2d. Cir 1960)

[A copyrighted design, "Byzantium" (see illustration), was imprinted upon bolts of cloth sold to garment manufacturers who later cut them into dresses. In doing so, the manufacturers cut or sewed the cloth so that copyright notices printed into the border or "selvage" of the cloth were no longer visible. The litigation was important in the area of copyrightability (accepting the extension of *Mazer v. Stein* to textile prints) and copyright notice (routine removal of the notice by customers of copyright owners did not forfeit copyright). But the words of Judge Learned Hand on the issue of substantial similarity have often been quoted:]

The test for infringement of a copyright is of necessity vague. In the case of verbal "works" it is well settled that although the "proprietor's" monopoly extends beyond an exact reproduction of the words, there can be no copyright in the "ideas" disclosed but only in their "expression." Obviously, no principle can be stated as to when an imitator has gone beyond copying the "idea," and has borrowed its "expression." Decisions must therefore inevitably be *ad hoc.* In the case of designs, which are addressed to the aesthetic sensibilities of an observer, the test is, if possible, even more intangible. No one disputes that the copyright extends beyond a photographic reproduction of the design, but one cannot say how far an imitator must depart from an undeviating reproduction to escape infringement. In deciding that question one should consider the uses for which

Plaintiff's
Design

Defendant's
Design

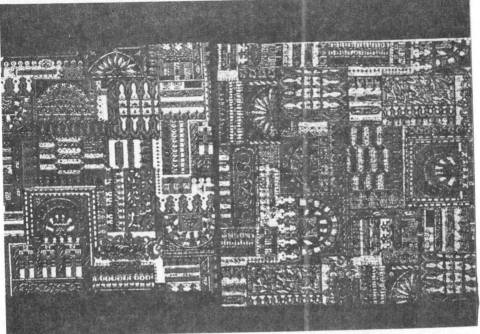

the design is intended, especially the scrutiny that observers will give to it as used. In the case at bar we must try to estimate how far its overall appearance will determine its aesthetic appeal when the cloth is made into a garment. Both designs have the same general color, and the arches, scrolls, rows of symbols, etc. on one resemble those on the other though they are not identical. Moreover, the patterns in which these figures are distributed to make up the design as a whole are not identical. However, the ordinary observer, unless he set out to detect the disparities, would be disposed to overlook them, and regard their aesthetic appeal as the same. That is enough; and indeed, it is all that can be said, unless protection against infringement is to be denied because of variants irrelevant to the purpose for which the design is intended.

HERBERT ROSENTHAL JEWELRY CORP. v. KALPAKIAN

446 F.2d 738 (9th Cir. 1971)

BROWNING, CIRCUIT JUDGE:

Plaintiff and defendants are engaged in the design, manufacture, and sale of fine jewelry.

Plaintiff charged defendants with infringing plaintiff's copyright registration of a pin in the shape of a bee formed of gold encrusted with jewels. A consent decree was entered, reciting that the parties had agreed to a settlement of the action and entry of the decree. It provided that plaintiff's copyright of the jeweled bee was "good and valid in law," that defendants had manufactured a jeweled bee "alleged to be similar," and that defendants were enjoined from infringing plaintiff's copyright and from manufacturing or selling copies of the plaintiff's jeweled bee pin.

Later plaintiff filed a motion for an order holding defendants in contempt of the consent decree. The district court, after an evidentiary hearing, found that while defendants had manufactured and sold a line of jeweled bee pins, they designed their pins themselves after a study of bees in nature and in published works and did not copy plaintiff's copyrighted bee. The court further found that defendant's jeweled bees were "not substantially similar" to plaintiff's bees, except that both "do look like bees." The court concluded that defendants had neither infringed plaintiff's copyright nor violated the consent decree, and entered a judgment order denying plaintiff's motion. We affirm.

. . . .

Plaintiff contends that its copyright registration of a jeweled bee entitles it to protection from the manufacture and sale by others of any object that to the ordinary observer is substantially similar in appearance. The breadth of this claim is evident. For example, while a photograph of the copyrighted bee pin attached to the complaint depicts a bee with nineteen small white jewels on its back, plaintiff argues that its copyright is infringed by defendants' entire line of a score or more jeweled bees in three sizes decorated with from nine to thirty jewels of various sizes, kinds, and colors.

Although plaintiff's counsel asserted that the originality of plaintiff's bee pin lay in a particular arrangement of jewels on the top of the pin, the elements of this arrangement were never identified. Defendants' witnesses testified that the "arrangement" was simply a function of the size and form of the bee pin and the size of the jewels used. Plaintiff's counsel, repeatedly pressed by the district judge, was unable to suggest how jewels might be placed on the back of a pin in the shape of a bee without infringing plaintiff's copyright. He eventually conceded, "not being a jeweler, I can't conceive of how he might rearrange the design so it is dissimilar."

If plaintiff's understanding of its rights were correct, its copyright would effectively prevent others from engaging in the business of manufacturing and selling jeweled bees. We think plaintiff confuses the balance Congress struck between protection and competition under the Patent Act and the Copyright Act. . . .

Obviously a copyright must not be treated as equivalent to a patent lest long continuing private monopolies be conferred over areas of gainful activity without first satisfying the substantive and procedural prerequisites to the grant of such privileges.

Because copyright bars only copying, perhaps this case could be disposed of on the district court's finding that defendants did not copy plaintiff's bee pin. It is true that defendants had access to the plaintiff's pin and that there is an obvious similarity between plaintiff's pin and those of defendants. These two facts constitute strong circumstantial evidence of copying. But they are not conclusive. *Overman v. Loesser,* 205 F.2d 521, 523 (9th Cir. 1953); Nimmer on Copyright §§ 139.4, 141.2, and there was substantial evidence to support the trial court's finding that defendants' pin was in fact an independent creation. Defendants testified to independent creation from identified sources other than plaintiff's pin. The evidence established defendants' standing as designers of fine jewelry and reflected that on earlier occasions they had designed jeweled pins in the form of living creatures other than bees, including spiders, dragonflies, and other insects, birds, turtles, and frogs. Any inference of copying based upon similar appearance lost much of its strength because both pins were lifelike representations of a natural creature. Moreover, there were differences between defendants' and plaintiff's bees — notably in the veining of the wings.

Although this evidence would support a finding that defendants' bees were their own work rather than copied from plaintiff's, this resolution of the problem is not entirely satisfactory, particularly in view of the principle that copying need not be conscious, but "may be the result of subconscious memory derived from hearing, seeing or reading the copyrighted work at some time in the past." Howell's Copyright Law 129 (4th ed. 1962). *See Sheldon v. Metro-Goldwyn Pictures Corp.,* 81 F.2d 49, 54 (2d Cir. 1936); *Harold Lloyd Corp. v. Witwer,* 65 F.2d 1, 16 (9th Cir. 1933). It seems unrealistic to suppose that defendants could have closed their minds to plaintiff's highly successful jeweled bee pin as they designed their own.

A finding that defendants "copied" plaintiff's pin in this sense, however, would not necessarily justify judgment against them. A copyright, we have seen, bars use of the particular "expression" of an idea in a copyrighted work but does not bar use of the "idea" itself. Others are free to utilize the "idea" so long as they do not plagiarize its "expression." As the court said in *Trifari, Krussman & Fishel, Inc. v. B. Steinberg-Kaslo Co.,* 144 F.Supp. 577, 580 (S.D.N.Y. 1956), where the copyrighted work was a jeweled pin representing a hansom cab, "though an alleged infringer gets the idea of a hansom cab pin from a copyrighted article there can be no infringement unless the article itself has been copied. The idea of a hansom cab cannot be copyrighted. Nevertheless plaintiff's expression of that idea, as embodied in its pin, can be copyrighted." Or as Judge Hand put it in *Sheldon v. Metro-Goldwyn Pictures Corp., supra,* 81 F.2d at 54, "defendants were entitled to use, not only all that had gone before, but even the plaintiff's contribution itself, if they drew from it only the more general patterns; that is, if they kept clear of its 'expression.'" *See also Millworth Converting Corp. v. Slifka,* 276 F.2d 443, 445 (2d Cir. 1960).

The critical distinction between "idea" and "expression" is difficult to draw. As Judge Hand candidly wrote, "Obviously, no principle can be stated as to when an imitator has gone beyond copying the 'idea,' and has borrowed its 'expression.'" *Peter Pan Fabrics, Inc. v. Martin Weiner Corp.,* 274 F.2d 487, 489 (2d Cir. 1960). At least in close cases, one may suspect, the classification the court selects may simply state the result reached rather than the reason for it. In our view, the difference is really one of degree as Judge Hand suggested in his striking "abstraction" formulation in *Nichols v. Universal Pictures Corp.,* 45 F.2d 119, 121 (2d Cir. 1930). The guiding consideration in drawing the line is the preservation of the balance between competition and protection reflected in the patent and copyright laws.

What is basically at stake is the extent of the copyright owner's monopoly — from how large an area of activity did Congress intend to allow the copyright owner to exclude others? We think the production of jeweled bee pins is a larger private preserve than Congress intended to be set aside in the public market without a patent. A jeweled bee pin is therefore an "idea" that defendants were free to copy. Plaintiff seems to agree, for it disavows any claim that defendants cannot manufacture and sell jeweled bee pins and concedes that only plaintiff's particular design or "expression" of the jeweled bee pin "idea" is protected under its copyright. The difficulty, as we have noted, is that on this record the "idea" and its "expression" appear to be indistinguishable. There is no greater similarity between the pins of plaintiff and defendants than is inevitable from the use of jewel-encrusted bee forms in both.

When the "idea" and its "expression" are thus inseparable, copying the "expression" will not be barred, since protecting the "expression" in such circumstances would confer a monopoly of the "idea" upon the copyright owner free of the conditions and limitations imposed by the patent law. *Baker v. Selden,* 101 U.S. 99, 103 (1879); *Morrissey v. Procter & Gamble Co.,* 379 F.2d 675, 678-679 (1st Cir. 1967); *Crume v. Pacific Mut. Life Ins. Co.,* 140 F.2d 182, 184 (7th Cir. 1944). *See also Continental Cas. Co. v. Beardsley,* 253 F.2d 702, 705-706 (2d Cir. 1958).

Affirmed.

QUESTIONS

1. Did the judgment for the defendant rest on a conclusion that it had not infringed, or on a conclusion that the plaintiff's pin was not the subject of copyright? (Are any clues provided by the court's reference to such cases as *Baker v. Selden* and *Morrissey v. Procter & Gamble?*)

2. Could the plaintiff have secured a design patent on its bee pin? If so, would that have protected it against defendant's copying (to the extent it did copy)?

AUTHORS INFRINGING COPYRIGHTS IN THEIR OWN WORKS

In *Gross v. Seligman,* 212 F. 930 (2d Cir. 1914), a photographer posed a nude young woman for a photograph entitled "Grace of Youth." He then sold all rights in the photograph to plaintiff. Two years later he posed the same young woman for another photograph entitled "Cherry Ripe." Apart from a minor variation of background (and, the court noted, slight changes in the contours of the woman's figure resulting from the passage of two years), the sole difference between the two photographs was that the first showed her face in repose and the second had the woman smiling with a cherry stem between her teeth.

The court stressed that where the photographer, as well as the model, pose, light and shade were the same in both photographs, there is a very strong indication that the second photograph was merely a copy of the first. The exercise of artistic talent, the sine qua non of the first photograph's copyrightability, was used in the second photograph to create, not a new independently copyrightable photograph, but a copy of the first photograph. Accordingly, infringement was found. By contrast, the court stated that another artist would be free to photograph the same young woman and create his own work, even though striking similarities might exist between this new photograph and the old, but that the original artist in this case had not created a new photograph, but copied the original.

More recently, in *Franklin Mint Corp. v. National Wildlife Art Exchange,* 575 F.2d 62 (3d Cir. 1978), a court was again faced with the situation whereby, in a later work, an artist had allegedly infringed the copyright that he no longer owned in one of his earlier works. This time the ruling was in favor of the artist, as the court resorted to the idea-expression distinction in finding that no infringement had occurred.

A nationally recognized wildlife artist was commissioned to paint a water color of cardinals for subsequent commercial exploitation by plaintiff National Wildlife Art Exchange. Using slides, photographs, sketches and two stuffed cardinals as source material, the artist completed "Cardinals on Apple Blossom" and, as previously agreed, sold it, along with all its attendant rights, to plaintiff. Three years later, as part of a series of birdlife water colors done for defendant Franklin Mint, the artist painted "The Cardinal," using some of the same source materials he had used to create "Cardinals on Apple Blossom." In addition, however, in painting "The Cardinal" he used new slides, photographs and sketches that had not been available to him earlier. The court held that an artist is free to use the same source material he has already used in creating a painting to create a different painting depicting the same subject matter.

In ruling for defendant, the court cited readily apparent dissimilarities between the two paintings in the area of color, body attitude and positioning of birds, linear effect, background, and composition. This "pattern of differences" was held sufficient to establish that the second painting represented "diversity of expression rather than only an echo."

Can these seemingly conflicting resolutions of similar problems be explained on the basis of the relative similarities and differences in the pair of works in each case? Can the complete identity of the source materials in *Gross* be contrasted with the lesser degree of overlap in *Franklin* to explain the different judgments? Or does the explanation for the opposite results reached in these two cases lie in the differences between the media of photography and water color painting? The *Franklin* court talked around this in a paragraph discussing the effect of the artist's style on the protectability of a copyright in an artistic work. (The *Gross* case is cited in a footnote to the discussion's conclusion.) The discussion concludes that a painting or drawing of photograph-like clarity and accuracy will be less protectable than a more abstract or impressionistic work where the expression is more personal and distinctive. This conclusion is confirmed by a moment's reflection on the characteristics and capabilities of the complementary art forms of photography and painting. A photograph is inevitably a more precise record of its subject than is a painting. Thus, it is far more difficult for a photographer to avoid "copying" an earlier work of his when shooting the identical subject in a similar setting than it is for a painter to do so when painting the identical subject in a similar setting. But should re-posing of models and taking of a *new* photograph ever be considered "copying" or "reproduction" in the copyright infringement sense? *Cf. Dallas Cowboy Cheerleaders, Inc. v. Scoreboard Posters, Inc.,* 600 F.2d 1184 (5th Cir. 1979).

Both courts skirted an issue raised by cases of this kind: Does a lawsuit against an artist for infringement of a copyright in a work he has created possibly inhibit him from continuing to operate in his own style? In *Gross* the court ignored the possibility, and in *Franklin* the court merely noted that "an artist is free to consult the same source for another original painting."

NICHOLS v. UNIVERSAL PICTURES CORP.

45 F.2d 119 (2d Cir. 1930)

L. HAND, CIRCUIT JUDGE.

The plaintiff is the author of a play, "Abie's Irish Rose," which it may be assumed was properly copyrighted under section five, subdivision (d), of the Copyright Act, 17 USCA § 5(d). The defendant produced publicly a motion picture play, "The Cohens and The Kellys," which the plaintiff alleges was taken from it. As we think the defendant's play too unlike the plaintiff's to be an infringement, we may assume, arguendo, that in some details the defendant used the plaintiff's play, as will subsequently appear, though we do not so decide. It therefore becomes necessary to give an outline of the two plays.

"Abie's Irish Rose" presents a Jewish family living in prosperous circumstances in New York. The father, a widower, is in business as a merchant, in which his son and only child helps him. The boy has philandered with young women, who to his father's great disgust have always been Gentiles, for he is obsessed with a passion that his daughter-in-law shall be an orthodox Jewess. When the play opens the son, who has been courting a young Irish Catholic girl, has already married her secretly before a Protestant minister, and is concerned to soften the blow for his father, by securing a favorable impression of his bride, while concealing her faith and race. To accomplish this he introduces her to his father at his home as a Jewess, and lets it appear that he is interested in her, though he conceals the marriage. The girl somewhat reluctantly falls in with the plan; the father takes the bait, becomes infatuated with the girl, concludes that they must marry, and assumes that of course they will, if he so decides. He calls in a rabbi, and prepares for the wedding according to the Jewish rite.

Meanwhile the girl's father, also a widower, who lives in California, and is as intense in his own religious antagonism as the Jew, has been called to New York, supposing that his daughter is to marry an Irishman and a Catholic. Accompanied by a priest, he arrives at the house at the moment when the marriage is being celebrated, but too late to prevent it, and the two fathers, each infuriated by the proposed union of his child to a heretic, fall into unseemly and grotesque antics. The priest and the rabbi become friendly, exchange trite sentiments about religion, and agree that the match is good. Apparently out of abundant caution, the priest celebrates the marriage for a third time, while the girl's father is inveigled away. The second act closes with each father, still outraged, seeking to find some way by which the union, thus trebly insured, may be dissolved.

The last act takes place about a year later, the young couple having meanwhile been abjured by each father, and left to their own resources. They have had twins, a boy and a girl, but their fathers know no more than that a child has been born. At Christmas, each, led by his craving to see his grandchild, goes separately to the young folks' home, where they encounter each other, each laden with gifts, one for a boy, the other for a girl. After some slapstick comedy, depending upon the insistence of each that he is right about the sex of the grandchild, they become reconciled when they learn the truth, and that each child is to bear the given name of a grandparent. The curtain falls as the fathers are exchanging amenities, and the Jew giving evidence of an abatement in the strictness of his orthodoxy.

"The Cohens and The Kellys" presents two families, Jewish and Irish, living side by side in the poorer quarters of New York in a state of perpetual enmity. The wives in both cases are still living, and share in the mutual animosity, as do two small sons, and even the respective dogs. The Jews have a daughter, the Irish a son; the Jewish father is in the clothing business; the Irishman is a policeman. The children are in love with each other, and secretly marry, apparently after the play opens. The Jew, being in great financial straits, learns from a lawyer that he has fallen heir to a large fortune from a great-aunt, and moves into a great house, fitted luxuriously. Here he and his family live in vulgar ostentation, and here the Irish boy seeks out his Jewish bride, and is chased away by the angry father. The Jew then abuses the Irishman over the telephone, and both become hysterically excited. The extremity of his feelings makes the Jew sick, so that he must go to Florida for a rest, just before which the daughter discloses her marriage to her mother.

On his return the Jew finds that his daughter has borne a child; at first he suspects the lawyer, but eventually learns the truth and is overcome with anger at such a low alliance. Meanwhile, the Irish family who have been forbidden to see the grandchild, go to the Jew's house, and after a violent scene between the two fathers in which the Jew disowns his daughter, who decides to go back with her husband, the Irishman takes her back with her baby to his own poor lodgings. The lawyer, who had hoped to marry the Jew's daughter, seeing his plan foiled, tells the Jew that his fortune really belongs to the Irishman, who was also related to the dead woman, but offers to conceal his knowledge, if the Jew will share the loot. This the Jew repudiates, and, leaving the astonished lawyer, walks through the rain to his enemy's house to surrender the property. He arrives in great dejection, tells the truth, and abjectly turns to leave. A reconciliation ensues, the Irishman agreeing to share with him equally. The Jew shows some interest in his grandchild, though this is at most a minor motive in the reconciliation, and the curtain falls while the two are in their cups, the Jew insisting that in the firm name for the business, which they are to carry on jointly, his name shall stand first.

It is of course essential to any protection of literary property, whether at common-law or under the statute, that the right cannot be limited literally to the text, else a plagiarist would escape by immaterial variations. That has never been the law, but, as soon as literal appropriation ceases to be the test, the whole matter is necessarily at large, so that, as was recently well said by a distinguished judge, the decisions cannot help much in a new case. *Fendler v. Morosco,* 253 N. Y. 281, 292, 171 N. E. 56. When plays are concerned, the plagiarist may excise a separate scene [*Daly v. Webster,* 56 F. 483 (C. C. A. 2); *Chappell v. Fields,* 210 F. 864 (C. C. A. 2); *Chatterton v. Cave,* L. R. 3 App. Cas. 483]; or he may appropriate part of the dialogue (*Warne v. Seebohm,* L. R. 39 Ch. D. 73). Then the question is whether the part so taken is "substantial," and therefore not a "fair use" of the copyrighted work; it is the same question as arises in the case of any other copyrighted work. *Marks v. Feist,* 290 F. 959 (C. C. A. 2); *Emerson v. Davies,* Fed. Cas. No. 4436, 3 Story, 768, 795-797. But when the plagiarist does not take out a block in situ, but an abstract of the whole, decision is more troublesome. Upon any work, and especially upon a play, a great number of patterns of increasing generality will fit equally well, as more and more of the incident is left out. The last may perhaps be no more than the most general statement of what the play is about, and at times might consist only of its title; but there is a point in this series of abstractions where they are no longer protected, since otherwise the playwright could prevent the use of his "ideas," to which, apart from their expression, his property is never extended. *Holmes v. Hurst,* 174 U. S. 82, 86; *Guthrie v. Curlett,* 36 F. (2d) 694 (C. C. A. 2). Nobody has ever been able to fix that boundary, and nobody ever can. In some cases the question has been treated as though it were analogous to lifting a portion out of the copyrighted work (*Rees v. Melville,* MacGillivray's Copyright Cases [1911-1916], 168); but the analogy is not a good one, because, though the skeleton is a part of the body, it pervades and supports the whole. In such cases we are rather concerned with the line between expression and what is expressed. As respects plays, the controversy chiefly centers upon the characters and sequence of incident, these being the substance.

We did not in *Dymow v. Bolton,* 11 F. (2d) 690, hold that a plagiarist was never liable for stealing a plot; that would have been flatly against out rulings in *Dam v. Kirk La Shelle Co.,* 175 F. 902, 41 L. R. A. (N. S.) 1002, 20 Ann. Cas. 1173, and *Stodart v. Mutual Film Co.,* 249 F. 513, affirming my decision in (D. C.) 249 F. 507; neither of which we meant to overrule. We found the plot of the second play was too different to infringe, because the most detailed pattern, common to both, eliminated so much from each that its content went into the public domain; and for this reason we said, "this mere subsection of a plot was not susceptible of copyright." But we do not doubt that two plays may correspond in plot closely enough for infringement. How far that correspondence must go is another matter. Nor need we hold that the same may not be true as to the characters, quite independently of the "plot" proper, though, as far as we know, such a case has never arisen. If Twelfth Night were copyrighted, it is quite possible that a second comer might so closely imitate Sir Toby Belch or Malvolio as to infringe, but it would not be enough that for one of his characters he cast a riotous knight who kept wassail to the discomfort of the household, or a vain and foppish steward who became amorous of his mistress. These would be no more than Shakespeare's "ideas" in the play, as little capable of monopoly as Einstein's Doctrine of Relativity, or Darwin's theory of the Origin of Species. It follows that the less developed the characters, the less they can be copyrighted; that is the penalty an author must bear for marking them too indistinctly.

In the two plays at bar we think both as to incident and character, the defendant took no more — assuming that it took anything at all — than the law allowed. The stories are quite different. One is of a religious zealot who insists upon his child's marrying no one outside his faith; opposed by another who is in this respect just like him, and is his foil. Their difference in race is merely an obbligato to the main theme, religion. They sink their differences through grandparental pride and affection. In the other, zealotry is wholly absent; religion does not even appear. It is true that the parents are hostile to each other in part because they differ in race; but the marriage of their son to a Jew does not apparently offend the Irish family at all, and it exacerbates the existing animosity of the Jew, principally because he has become rich, when he learns it. They are reconciled through the honesty of the Jew and the generosity of the Irishman; the grandchild has nothing whatever to do with it. The only matter common to the two is a quarrel between a Jewish and an Irish father, the marriage of their children, the birth of grandchildren and a reconciliation.

If the defendant took so much from the plaintiff, it may well have been because her amazing success seemed to prove that this was a subject of enduring popularity. Even so, granting that the plaintiff's play was wholly original, and assuming that novelty is not essential to a copyright, there is no monopoly in such a background. Though the plaintiff discovered the vein, she could not keep it to herself; so defined, the theme was too generalized an abstraction from what she wrote. It was only a part of her "ideas."

Nor does she fare better as to her characters. It is indeed scarcely credible that she should not have been aware of those stock figures, the low comedy Jew and Irishman. The defendant has not taken from her more than their prototypes have contained for many decades. If so, obviously so to generalize her copyright, would allow her to cover what was not original with her. But we need not hold this as matter of fact, much as we might be justified. Even though we take it that she devised her figures out of her brain de novo, still the defendant was within its rights.

There are but four characters common to both plays, the lovers and the fathers. The lovers are so faintly indicated as to be no more than stage properties. They are loving and fertile; that is really all that can be said of them, and anyone else is quite within his rights if he puts loving and fertile lovers in a play of his own, wherever he gets the cue. The plaintiff's Jew is quite unlike the defendant's. His obsession is his religion, on which depends such racial animosity as he has. He is affectionate, warm and patriarchal. None of these fit the defendant's Jew, who shows affection for his daughter only once, and who has none but the most superficial interest in his grandchild. He is tricky, ostentatious and vulgar, only by misfortune redeemed into honesty. Both are grotesque, extravagant and quarrelsome; both are fond of display; but these common qualities make up only a small part of their simple pictures, no more than any one might lift if he chose. The Irish fathers are even more unlike; the plaintiff's a mere symbol for religious fanaticism and patriarchal pride, scarcely a character at all. Neither quality appears in the defendant's, for while he goes to get his grandchild, it is rather out of a truculent determination not to be forbidden, than from pride in his progeny. For the rest he is only a grotesque hobbledehoy, used for low comedy of the most conventional sort, which any one might borrow, if he chanced not to know the exemplar.

The defendant argues that the case is controlled by my decision in *Fisher v. Dillingham* (D. C.) 298 F. 145. Neither my brothers nor I wish to throw doubt upon the doctrine of that case, but it is not applicable here. We assume that the plaintiff's play is altogether original, even to an extent that in fact it is hard to believe. We assume further that, so far as it has been anticipated by earlier plays of which she knew nothing, that fact is immaterial. Still, as we have already said, her copyright did not cover everything that might be drawn from her play; its content went to some extent into the public domain. We have to decide how much, and while we are as aware as any one that the line, wherever it is drawn, will seem arbitrary, that is no excuse for not drawing it; it is a question such as courts must answer in nearly all cases. Whatever may be the difficulties a priori, we have no question on which side of the line this case falls. A comedy based upon conflicts between Irish and Jews, into which the marriage of their children enters, is no more susceptible of copyright than the outline of Romeo and Juliet.

The plaintiff has prepared an elaborate analysis of the two plays, showing a "quadrangle" of the common characters, in which each is represented by the emotions which he discovers. She presents the resulting parallelism as proof of infringement, but the adjectives employed are so general as to be quite useless. Take for example the attribute of "love" ascribed to both Jews. The plaintiff has depicted her father as deeply attached to his son, who is his hope and joy; not so, the defendant, whose father's conduct is throughout not actuated by any affection for his daughter, and who is merely once overcome for the moment by her distress when he has violently dismissed her lover. "Anger" covers emotions aroused by quite different occasions in each case; so do "anxiety," "despondency" and "disgust." It is unnecessary to go through the catalogue for emotions are too much colored by their causes to be a test when used so broadly. This is not the proper approach to a solution; it must be more ingenuous, more like that of a spectator, who would rely upon the complex of his impressions of each character.

We cannot approve the length of the record, which was due chiefly to the use of expert witnesses. Argument is argument whether in the box or at the bar, and its proper place is the last. The testimony of an expert upon such issues, especially his cross-examination, greatly extends the trial and contributes nothing which cannot be better heard after the evidence is all submitted. It ought not to be allowed at all; and while its admission is not a ground for reversal, it cumbers the case and tends to confusion, for the more the court is led into the intricacies of dramatic craftsmanship, the less likely it is to stand upon the firmer, if more naive, ground of its considered impressions upon its own perusal. We hope that in this class of cases such evidence may in the future be entirely excluded, and the case confined to the actual issues; that is, whether the copyrighted work was original, and whether the defendant copied it, so far as the supposed infringement is identical.

The defendant, "the prevailing party," was entitled to a reasonable attorney's fee (section 40 of the Copyright Act [17 USCA § 40]).

Decree affirmed.

QUESTIONS

1. The plaintiff had obviously discovered a vein of extremely appealing popular drama — first-generation ethnic combatants reconciled, in the "melting pot" that was early twentieth century America, by the love of the younger generation. Defendant was apparently seeking to "horn in" on that eminently successful (and remunerative) theme. Reasoning from first principles, should that be permitted?

2. In these cases of literary plagiarism, to what extent and for what purposes might a defendant rely upon dramatic works which preceded that of the plaintiff?

3. What are the elements of a cause of action for copyright infringement, and on which of these elements was the plaintiff's case fatally weak?

4. When Judge Hand discusses the literal copying of dialogue, he states that takings which are "insubstantial" are allowable. Is "substantiality" to be determined by a quantitative test alone?

SHELDON v. METRO-GOLDWYN PICTURES CORP.

81 F.2d 49 (2d Cir. 1936)

L. HAND, CIRCUIT JUDGE.

The suit is to enjoin the performance of the picture play, "Letty Lynton," as an infringement of the plaintiffs' copyrighted play, "Dishonored Lady." The plaintiffs' title is conceded, so too the validity of the copyright; the only issue is infringement. The defendants say that they did not use the play in any way to produce the picture; the plaintiffs discredit this denial because of the negotiations between the parties for the purchase of rights in the play, and because the similarities between the two are too specific and detailed to have resulted from chance. The judge thought that, so far as the defendants had used the play, they had taken only what the law allowed, that is, those general themes, motives, or ideas in which there could be no copyright. Therefore he dismissed the bill.

An understanding of the issue involves some description of what was in the public demesne, as well as of the play and the picture. In 1857 a Scotch girl, named Madeleine Smith, living in Glasgow, was brought to trial upon an indictment in three counts; two for attempts to poison her lover, a third for poisoning him. The jury acquitted her on the first count, and brought in a verdict of "Not Proven" on the second and third. The circumstances of the prosecution aroused much interest at the time not only in Scotland but in England; so much indeed that it became a cause célèbre, and that as late as 1927 the whole proceedings were published in book form. An outline of the story so published, which became the original of the play here in suit, is as follows: The Smiths were a respectable middle-class family, able to send their daughter to a "young ladies' boarding school"; they supposed her protected not only from any waywardness of her own, but from the wiles of seducers. In both they were mistaken, for when at the age of twenty-one she met a young Jerseyman of French blood, Emile L'Angelier, ten years older, and already the hero of many amorous adventures, she quickly succumbed and poured out her feelings in letters of the utmost ardor

and indiscretion, and at times of a candor beyond the standards then, and even
yet, permissible for well-nurtured young women. They wrote each other as
though already married, he assuming to dictate her conduct and even her
feelings; both expected to marry, she on any terms, he with the approval of her
family. Nevertheless she soon tired of him and engaged herself to a man some
twenty years older who was a better match, but for whom she had no more than
a friendly complaisance. L'Angelier was not, however, to be fobbed off so easily;
he threatened to expose her to her father by showing her letters. She at first tried
to dissuade him by appeals to their tender memories, but finding this useless and
thinking herself otherwise undone, she affected a return of her former passion
and invited him to visit her again. Whether he did, was the turning point of the
trial; the evidence, though it really left the issue in no doubt, was too indirect to
satisfy the jury, perhaps in part because of her advocate's argument that to kill
him only insured the discovery of her letters. It was shown that she had several
times bought or tried to buy poison, — prussic acid and arsenic, — and that twice
before his death L'Angelier became violently ill, the second time on the day after
her purchase. He died of arsenical poison, which the prosecution charged that
she had given him in a cup of chocolate. At her trial, Madeleine being
incompetent as a witness, her advocate proved an alibi by the testimony of her
younger sister that early on the night of the murder as laid in the indictment, she
had gone to bed with Madeleine, who had slept with her throughout the night.
As to one of the attempts her betrothed swore that she had been with him at the
theatre.

This was the story which the plaintiffs used to build their play. As will appear
they took from it but the merest skeleton, the acquittal of a wanton young
woman, who to extricate herself from an amour that stood in the way of a
respectable marriage, poisoned her lover. The incidents, the characters, the mise
en scène, the sequence of events, were all changed; nobody disputes that the
plaintiffs were entitled to their copyright. All that they took from the story they
might probably have taken, had it even been copyrighted. Their heroine is
named Madeleine Cary; she lives in New York, brought up in affluence, if not
in luxury; she is intelligent, voluptuous, ardent and corrupt; but, though she has
had a succession of amours, she is capable of genuine affection. Her lover and
victim is an Argentinian, named Moreno, who makes his living as a dancer in
night-clubs. Madeleine has met him once in Europe before the play opens, has
danced with him, has excited his concupiscence; he presses presents upon her.
The play opens in his rooms, he and his dancing partner who is also his mistress,
are together; Madeleine on the telephone recalls herself to him and says she
wishes to visit him, though it is already past midnight. He disposes of his mistress
by a device which does not deceive her and receives Madeleine; at once he falls
to wooing her, luring her among other devices by singing a Gaucho song. He
finds her facile and the curtain falls in season.

The second act is in her home, and introduces her father, a bibulous dotard,
who has shot his wife's lover in the long past; Laurence Brennan, a self-made
man in the fifties, untutored, self-reliant and reliable, who has had with
Madeleine a relation, half paternal, half-amorous since she grew up; and Denis
Farnborough, a young British labor peer, a mannekin to delight the heart of well
ordered young women. Madeleine loves him; he loves Madeleine; she will give
him no chance to declare himself, remembering her mottled past and his supposedly immaculate standards. She confides to Brennan, who makes clear to her
the imbecility of her self-denial; she accepts this enlightenment and engages

herself to her high-minded paragon after confessing vaguely her evil life and being assured that to post-war generations all such lapses are peccadillo.

In the next act Moreno, who has got wind of the engagement, comes to her house. Disposing of Farnborough, who chances to be there, she admits Moreno, acknowledges that she is to marry Farnborough, and asks him to accept the situation as the normal outcome of their intrigue. He refuses to be cast off, high words pass, he threatens to expose their relations, she raves at him, until finally he knocks her down and commands her to go to his apartment that morning as before. After he leaves full of swagger, her eye lights on a bottle of strychnine which her father uses as a drug; her fingers slowly close upon it; the audience understands that she will kill Moreno. Farnborough is at the telephone; this apparently stiffens her resolve, showing her the heights she may reach by its execution.

The scene then shifts again to Moreno's apartment; his mistress must again be put out, most unwillingly for she is aware of the situation; Madeleine comes in; she pretends once more to feel warmly, she must wheedle him for he is out of sorts after the quarrel. Meanwhile she prepares to poison him by putting the strychnine in coffee, which she asks him to make ready. But in the course of these preparations during which he sings her again his Gaucho song, what with their proximity, and this and that, her animal ardors are once more aroused and drag her, unwillingly and protesting, from her purpose. The play must therefore wait for an hour or more until, relieved of her passion, she appears from his bedroom and while breakfasting puts the strychnine in his coffee. He soon discovers what has happened and tries to telephone for help. He does succeed in getting a few words through, but she tears away the wire and fills his dying ears with her hatred and disgust. She then carefully wipes away all traces of her finger prints and manages to get away while the door is being pounded in by those who have come at his call.

The next act is again at her home on the following evening. Things are going well with her and Farnborough and her father, when a district attorney comes in, a familiar of the household, now in stern mood; Moreno's mistress and a waiter have incriminated Madeleine, and a cross has been found in Moreno's pocket, which he superstitiously took off her neck the night before. The district attorney cross-questions her, during which Farnborough several times fatuously intervenes; she is driven from point to point almost to an avowal when as a desperate plunge she says she spent the night with Brennan. Brennan is brought to the house and, catching the situation after a moment's delay, bears her out. This puts off the district attorney until seeing strychnine brought to relieve the father, his suspicions spring up again and he arrests Madeleine. The rest of the play is of no consequence here, except that it appears in the last scene that at the trial where she is acquitted, her father on the witness stand accounts for the absence of the bottle of strychnine which had been used to poison Moreno.

At about the time that this play was being written an English woman named Lowndes wrote a book called Letty Lynton, also founded on the story of Madeleine Smith. Letty Lynton lives in England; she is eighteen years old, beautiful, well-reared and intelligent, but wayward. She has had a more or less equivocal love affair with a young Scot, named McLean, who worked in her father's chemical factory, but has discarded him, apparently before their love-making had gone very far. Then she chances upon a young Swede — half English — named Ekebon, and their acquaintance quickly becomes a standardized amour, kept secret from her parents, especially her mother, who is an uncompromising moralist, and somewhat estranged from Letty anyway. She and her lover use an old barn as their place of assignation; it had been fitted up as a play house for Letty when she was a child. Like Madeleine Smith she had written her lover a series of indiscreet letters which he has kept, for though he is on pleasure bent Ekebon has a frugal mind, and means to marry his sweetheart and set himself up for life. They are betrothed and he keeps pressing her to declare it to her parents, which she means never to do. While he is away in Sweden Letty meets an unmarried peer considerably older than she, poor, but intelligent and charming; he falls in love with her and she accepts him, more because it is a good match than for any other reason, though she likes him well enough, and will make him suppose that she loves him.

Thereupon Ekebon reappears, learns of Letty's new betrothal, and threatens to disclose his own to her father, backing up his story with her letters. She must at once disown her peer and resume her engagement with him. His motive, like L'Angelier's, is ambition rather than love, though conquest is a flattery and Letty a charming morsel. His threats naturally throw Letty into dismay; she has come to loathe him and at any cost must get free, but she has no one to turn to. In her plight she thinks of her old suitor, McLean, and goes to the factory only to find him gone. He has taught her how to get access to poisons in his office and has told of their effect on human beings. At first she thinks of jumping out the window, and when she winces at that, of poisoning herself; that would be easier. So she selects arsenic which is less painful and goes away with it; it is only when she gets home that she thinks of poisoning Ekebon. Her mind is soon made up, however, and she makes an appointment with him at the barn; she has told her father, she writes, and Ekebon is to see him on Monday, but meanwhile on Sunday they will meet secretly once more. She has prepared to go on a week-end party and conceals her car near the barn. He comes; she welcomes him with a pretence of her former ardors, and tries to get back her letters. Unsuccessful in this she persuades him to drink a cup of chocolate into which she puts the arsenic. After carefully washing the pans and cups, she leaves with him, dropping him from her car near his home; he being still unaffected. On her way to her party she pretends to have broken down and by asking the help of a passing cyclist establishes an alibi. Ekebon dies at his home attended by his mistress; the letters are discovered and Letty is brought before the coroner's inquest and acquitted chiefly through the alibi, for things look very bad for her until the cyclist appears.

The defendants, who are engaged in producing speaking films on a very large scale in Hollywood, California, had seen the play and wished to get the rights. They found, however, an obstacle in an association of motion picture producers presided over by Mr. Will Hays, who thought the play obscene; not being able to overcome his objections, they returned the copy of the manuscript which they had had. That was in the spring of 1930, but in the autumn they induced the plaintiffs to get up a scenario, which they hoped might pass moral muster. Although this did not suit them after the plaintiffs prepared it, they must still have thought in the spring of 1931 that they could satisfy Mr. Hays, for they then procured an offer from the plaintiffs to sell their rights for $30,000. These negotiations also proved abortive because the play continued to be objectionable, and eventually they cried off on the bargain. Mrs. Lowndes' novel was suggested to Thalberg, one of the vice-presidents of the Metro-Goldwyn Company, in July, 1931, and again in the following November, and he bought the rights to it in December. At once he assigned the preparation of a play to Stromberg, who had read the novel in January, and thought it would make a suitable play for an actress named Crawford, just then not employed. Stromberg chose Meehan,

Tuchock and Brown to help him, the first two with the scenario, the third with the dramatic production. All these four were examined by deposition; all denied that they had used the play in any way whatever; all agreed that they had based the picture on the story of Madeleine Smith and on the novel, "Letty Lynton." All had seen the play, and Tuchock had read the manuscript, as had Thalberg, but Stromberg, Meehan and Brown swore that they had not; Stromberg's denial being however worthless, for he had originally sworn the contrary in an affidavit. They all say that work began late in November or early in December, 1931, and the picture was finished by the end of March. To meet these denials, the plaintiffs appeal to the substantial identity between passages in the picture and those parts of the play which are original with them.

The picture opens in Montevideo where Letty Lynton is recovering from her fondness for Emile Renaul. She is rich, luxurious and fatherless, her father having been killed by his mistress's husband; her mother is seared, hard, selfish, unmotherly; and Letty has left home to escape her, wandering about in search of excitement. Apparently for the good part of a year she has been carrying on a love affair with Renaul; twice before she has tried to shake loose, has gone once to Rio where she lit another flame, but each time she has weakened and been drawn back. Though not fully declared as an amour, there can be no real question as to the character of her attachment. She at length determines really to break loose, but once again her senses are too much for her and it is indicated, if not declared, that she spends the night with Renaul. Though he is left a vague figure only indistinctly associated with South America somewhere or other, the part was cast for an actor with a marked foreign accent, and it is plain that he was meant to be understood, in origin anyway, as South American, like Moreno in the play. He is violent, possessive and sensual; his power over Letty lies in his strong animal attractions. However, she escapes in the morning while he is asleep, whether from his bed or not is perhaps uncertain; and with a wax figure in the form of a loyal maid — Letty in the novel had one — boards a steamer for New York. On board she meets Darrow, a young American, the son of a rich rubber manufacturer, who is coming back from a trip to Africa. They fall in love upon the faintest provocation and become betrothed before the ship docks, three weeks after she left Montevideo. At the pier she finds Renaul who has flown up to reclaim her. She must in some way keep her two suitors apart, and she manages to dismiss Darrow and then to escape Renaul by asking him to pay her customs duties, which he does. Arrived home her mother gives her a cold welcome and refuses to concern herself with the girl's betrothal. Renaul is announced; he has read of the betrothal in the papers and is furious. He tries again to stir her sensuality by the familiar gambit, but this time he fails; she slaps his face and declares that she hates him. He commands her to come to his apartment that evening; she begs him to part with her and let her have her life; he insists on renewing their affair. She threatens to call the police; he rejoins that if so her letters will be published, and then he leaves. Desperate, she chances on a bottle of strychnine, which we are to suppose is an accoutrement of every affluent household, and seizes it; the implication is of intended suicide, not murder. Then she calls Darrow, tells him that she will not leave with him that night for his parents' place in the Adirondacks as they had planned; she renews to him the pledge of her love, without him she cannot live, an intimation to the audience of her purpose to kill herself.

That evening she goes to Renaul's apartment in a hotel armed with her strychnine bottle, for use on the spot; she finds him cooling champagne, but in bad temper. His caresses which he bestows plentifully enough, again stir her disgust not her passions, but he does not believe it and assumes that she will spend the night with him. Finding that he will not return the letters, she believes herself lost and empties the strychnine into a wine glass. Again he embraces her; she vilifies him; he knocks her down; she vilifies him again. Ignorant of the poison he grasps her glass, and she, perceiving it, lets him drink. He woos her again, this time with more apparent success, for she is terrified; he sings a Gaucho song to her, the same one that has been heard at Montevideo. The poison begins to work and, at length supposing that she has meant to murder him, he reaches for the telephone; she forestalls him, but she does not tear out the wire. As he slowly dies, she stands over him and vituperates him. A waiter enters; she steps behind a curtain; he leaves thinking Renaul drunk; she comes out, wipes off all traces of her fingerprints and goes out, leaving however her rubbers which Renaul had taken from her when she entered.

Next she and Darrow are found at his parents' in the Adirondacks; while there a detective appears, arrests Letty and takes her to New York; she is charged with the murder of Renaul; Darrow goes back to New York with her. The finish is at the district attorney's office; Letty and Darrow, Letty's mother, the wax serving maid are all there. The letters appear incriminating to an elderly rather benevolent district attorney; also the customs slip and the rubbers. Letty begins to break down; she admits that she went to Renaul's room, not to kill him but to get him to release her. Darrow sees that that story will not pass, and volunteers that she came to his room at a hotel and spent the night with him. Letty confirms this and her mother, till then silent, backs up their story; she had traced them to the hotel and saw the lights go out, having ineffectually tried to dissuade them. The maid still further confirms them and the district attorney, not sorry to be discomfited, though unbelieving, discharges Letty.

We are to remember that it makes no difference how far the play was anticipated by works in the public demesne which the plaintiffs did not use. The defendants appear not to recognize this, for they have filled the record with earlier instances of the same dramatic incidents and devices, as though, like a patent, a copyrighted work must be not only original, but new. That is not however the law as is obvious in the case of maps or compendia, where later works will necessarily be anticipated. At times, in discussing how much of the substance of a play the copyright protects, courts have indeed used language which seems to give countenance to the notion that, if a plot were old, it could not be copyrighted. *London v. Biograph Co.* (C.C.A.) 231 F. 696; *Eichel v. Marcin* (D.C.) 241 F. 404. But we understand by this no more than that in its broader outline a plot is never copyrightable, for it is plain beyond peradventure that anticipation as such cannot invalidate a copyright. Borrowed the work must indeed not be, for a plagiarist is not himself pro tanto an "author"; but if by some magic a man who had never known it were to compose anew Keats's Ode on a Grecian Urn, he would be an "author," and, if he copyrighted it, others might not copy that poem, though they might of course copy Keats's. *Bleistein v. Donaldson Lithographing Co.,* 188 U.S. 239, 249; *Gerlach-Barklow Co. v. Morris & Bendien, Inc.,* 23 F.(2d) 159, 161 (C.C.A.2); Weil, Copyright Law, p. 234. But though a copyright is for this reason less vulnerable than a patent, the owner's protection is more limited, for just as he is no less an "author" because others have preceded him, so another who follows him, is not a tort-feasor unless he pirates his work. *Jewelers' Circular Publishing Co. v. Keystone Co.,* 281 F. 83, 92, 26 A.L.R. 571 (C.C.A.2); *General Drafting Co. v. Andrews,* 37 F.(2d) 54, 56 (C.C.A.2); *Williams v. Smythe* (C.C.) 110 F. 961; *American, etc., Directory Co. v. Gehring Pub. Co.* (D.C.) 4 F.(2d) 415; *New Jersey, etc., Co. v. Barton Business*

Service (D.C.) 57 F.(2d) 353. If the copyrighted work is therefore original, the public demesne is important only on the issue of infringement; that is, so far as it may break the force of the inference to be drawn from likenesses between the work and the putative piracy. If the defendant has had access to other material which would have served him as well, his disclaimer becomes more plausible.

In the case at bar there are then two questions: First, whether the defendants actually used the play; second, if so, whether theirs was a "fair use." The judge did not make any finding upon the first question, as we said at the outset, because he thought the defendants were in any case justified; in this following our decision in *Nichols v. Universal Pictures Corporation,* 45 F.(2d) 119. The plaintiffs challenge that opinion because we said that "copying" might at times be a "fair use"; but it is convenient to define such a use by saying that others may "copy" the "theme," or "ideas," or the like, of a work, though not its "expression." At any rate so long as it is clear what is meant, no harm is done. In the case at bar the distinction is not so important as usual, because so much of the play was borrowed from the story of Madeleine Smith, and the plaintiffs' originality is necessarily limited to the variants they introduced. Nevertheless, it is still true that their whole contribution may not be protected; for the defendants were entitled to use, not only all that had gone before, but even the plaintiffs' contribution itself, if they drew from it only the more general patterns; that is, if they kept clear of its "expression." We must therefore state in detail those similarities which seem to us to pass the limits of "fair use." Finally, in concluding as we do that the defendants used the play pro tanto, we need not charge their witnesses with perjury. With so many sources before them they might quite honestly forget what they took; nobody knows the origin of his inventions; memory and fancy merge even in adults. Yet unconscious plagiarism is actionable quite as much as deliberate. *Buck v. Jewell-La Salle Realty Co.,* 283 U. S. 191, 198; *Harold Lloyd Corporation v. Witwer,* 65 F.(2d) 1, 16 (C.C.A.9); *Fred Fisher, Inc. v. Dillingham* (D.C.) 298 F. 145.

The defendants took for their mise en scène the same city and the same social class; and they chose a South American villain. The heroines had indeed to be wanton, but Letty Lynton "tracked" Madeleine Cary more closely than that. She is overcome by passion in the first part of the picture and yields after announcing that she hates Renaul and has made up her mind to leave him. This is the same weakness as in the murder scene of the play, though transposed. Each heroine's waywardness is suggested as an inherited disposition; each has had an errant parent involved in scandal; one killed, the other becoming an outcast. Each is redeemed by a higher love. Madeleine Cary must not be misread; it is true that her lust overcomes her at the critical moment, but it does not extinguish her love for Farnborough; her body, not her soul, consents to her lapse. Moreover, her later avowal, which she knew would finally lose her her lover, is meant to show the basic rectitude of her nature. Though it does not need Darrow to cure Letty of her wanton ways, she too is redeemed by a nobler love. Neither Madeleine Smith, nor the Letty of the novel, were at all like that; they wished to shake off a clandestine intrigue to set themselves up in the world; their love as distinct from their lust, was pallid. So much for the similarity in character.

Coming to the parallelism of incident, the threat scene is carried out with almost exactly the same sequence of event and actuation; it has no prototype in either story or novel. Neither Ekebon nor L'Angelier went to his fatal interview to break up the new betrothal; he was beguiled by the pretence of a renewed affection. Moreno and Renaul each goes to his sweetheart's home to detach her from her new love; when he is there, she appeals to his better side, unsuccessfully; she abuses him, he returns the abuse and commands her to come to his rooms; she pretends to agree, expecting to finish with him one way or another. True, the assault is deferred in the picture from this scene to the next, but it is the same dramatic trick. Again, the poison in each case is found at home, and the girl talks with her betrothed just after the villain has left and again pledges him her faith. Surely the sequence of these details is pro tanto the very web of the authors' dramatic expression; and copying them is not "fair use."

The death scene follows the play even more closely; the girl goes to the villain's room as he directs; from the outset he is plainly to be poisoned while they are together. (The defendants deny that this is apparent in the picture, but we cannot agree. It would have been an impossible denouement on the screen for the heroine, just plighted to the hero, to kill herself in desperation, because the villain has successfully enmeshed her in their mutual past; yet the poison is surely to be used on some one.) Moreno and Renaul each tries to arouse the girl by the memory of their former love, using among other aphrodisiacs the Gaucho song; each dies while she is there, incidentally of strychnine not arsenic. In extremis each makes for the telephone and is thwarted by the girl; as he dies, she pours upon him her rage and loathing. When he is dead, she follows the same ritual to eradicate all traces of her presence, but forgets tell-tale bits of property. Again these details in the same sequence embody more than the "ideas" of the play; they are its very raiment.

Finally in both play and picture in place of a trial, as in the story and the novel, there is substituted an examination by a district attorney; and this examination is again in parallel almost step by step. A parent is present; so is the lover; the girl yields progressively as the evidence accumulates; in the picture, the customs slip, the rubbers and the letters; in the play, the cross and the witnesses, brought in to confront her. She is at the breaking point when she is saved by substantially the same most unexpected alibi; a man declares that she has spent the night with him. That alibi there introduced is the turning point in each drama and alone prevents its ending in accordance with the classic canon of tragedy; i. e., fate as an inevitable consequence of past conduct, itself not evil enough to quench pity. It is the essence of the authors' expression, the very voice with which they speak.

We have often decided that a play may be pirated without using the dialogue. *Daly v. Palmer,* Fed.Cas. No. 3,552, 6 Blatch, 256; *Daly v. Webster,* 56 F. 483, 486, 487; *Dam v. Kirke La Shelle Co.,* 175 F. 902, 907, 41 L.R.A.(N.S.) 1002, 20 Ann. Cas. 1173; *Chappell & Co. v. Fields,* 210 F. 864. *Dymow v. Bolton,* 11 F.(2d) 690; and *Nichols v. Universal Pictures Corporation,* supra, 45 F.(2d) 119, do not suggest otherwise. Were it not so, there could be no piracy of a pantomime, where there cannot be any dialogue; yet nobody would deny to pantomime the name of drama. Speech is only a small part of a dramatist's means of expression; he draws on all the arts and compounds his play from words and gestures and scenery and costume and from the very looks of the actors themselves. Again and again a play may lapse into pantomime at its most poignant and significant moments; a nod, a movement of the hand, a pause, may tell the audience more than words could tell. To be sure, not all this is always copyrighted, though there is no reason why it may not be, for those decisions do not forbid which hold that mere scenic tricks will not be protected. *Serrana v. Jefferson,* (C.C.) 33 F. 347; *Barnes v. Miner* (C.C.) 122 F. 480; *Bloom et al. v. Nixon* (C.C.) 125 F. 977. The play is the sequence of the confluents of all these means, bound together in an inseparable unity; it may often be most effectively pirated by leaving out the speech, for which a substitute can be found, which keeps the whole dramatic meaning. That as it appears to us is exactly what the defendants have done here;

the dramatic significance of the scenes we have recited is the same, almost to the letter. True, much of the picture owes nothing to the play; some of it is plainly drawn from the novel; but that is entirely immaterial; it is enough that substantial parts were lifted; no plagiarist can excuse the wrong by showing how much of his work he did not pirate. We cannot avoid the conviction that, if the picture was not an infringement of the play, there can be none short of taking the dialogue.

The decree will be reversed and an injunction will go against the picture together with a decree for damages and an accounting. The plaintiffs will be awarded an attorney's fee in this court and in the court below, both to be fixed by the District Court upon the final decree.

Decree reversed.

QUESTIONS

1. Was there any issue as to "access" in this case? Why or why not?

2. Was the court holding that the Letty of the defendant's motion picture so closely tracked the Madeleine Cary of the plaintiff's play as to infringe the copyright in the character?

3. How many of the dramatic devices utilized by the plaintiff in the crucial scenes from her play were in fact original with her and eligible for copyright? Were not some of those incidents taken from the historically factual story, e.g., the incriminating letters and the poisoning? Were not some of those incidents "stock" dramatic devices, e.g., recrimination of the villain, wiping away fingerprints, leaving behind telltale evidence? How could defendants' copying of these elements (assuming they did copy) constitute infringement? Does Judge Hand closely analyze these matters or simply state his conclusion, scene-by-scene?

4. How likely is it that defendants were being honest in the claims that they did not copy from the plaintiff's play? How likely is it that this affected the decision in the case?

5. Since not all of the defendants' motion picture was taken from the plaintiff's play, and a substantial part of its success was no doubt attributable to other elements (e.g., the public domain story itself, the cinematic contributions of the MGM studio, Joan Crawford as the star), what should the remedy be? Should MGM be enjoined from further exhibition? Should plaintiff be awarded damages measured by her lost opportunity to sell her play to Hollywood? If so, what is to be made of the fact that her play was apparently unsalable under the obscenity standards of the period? Should MGM disgorge its profits from the exhibition of the infringing film? How are "profits" to be calculated and, more obviously, should MGM be permitted to reduce the award by the profits attributable to the non-infringing components mentioned above?

NIMMER, INROADS ON COPYRIGHT PROTECTION, Fourth Copyright Law Symposium 3, 11, 18-19 (1952)*

Now in considering the above decisions it is important to bear in mind that no matter how commonplace and unoriginal these embellishments may be, the court is assuming that they did not occur to the defendants independently — by hypothesis the court is saying that the defendants did copy the embellishment from the plaintiff. Furthermore, it is well to recall that neither the Copyright Act

---

nor any court requires that material be profound, clever, or in any way unusual in order to command copyright protection. If the material is the product of the copyrighter's independent efforts it is entitled to protection regardless of how hackneyed or insignificant it may be.[37] Therefore, the only reason for denying the above embellishments protection is the fact that they are not sufficiently substantial. Surely one might reasonably construe these embellishments to be "component parts" within the meaning of the Act. What, then, are the policy considerations which contrary to a literal reading of the statute deny the original writer a right to damages? It can hardly be the fear of the unscrupulous complainant who brings a baseless action since the courts here assume that in fact there has been copying. Is it, then, a fear that the progress of the arts will be stultified if writers are not allowed to copy such embellishments? It cannot be denied that in some measure the protection of embellishments would retard freedom of creative efforts (albeit creation based on copying). But this is not particularly true of embellishments — it is an inherent and calculated risk basic to the very theory of copyright. Perhaps the basic issue to be faced is whether the secondary writer is in a relatively more unfavorable position when prevented from copying embellishments than when prevented from copying a "substantial" part of an original work. He would, it may be argued, be more severely restricted since not only would he have to avoid copying a given series of incidents,[39] he would incur liability by copying any one of these incidents. But balancing this greater restriction is the fact that the individual embellishment is worth less than the series of incidents, and if he copies it, it will command a proportionately smaller damages award.

. . . .

It is not the intention of this paper to suggest that ideas as such should be protected [60] but in drawing a line in the never-never-land between bare ideas and completed works, there does seem to be no reason based on statutory command or sound social policy (assuming the policy underlying the Copyright Act itself is accepted) why that line should not be extended farther in the direction of protecting infringed writers than has heretofore been the practice. *Golding v. R.K.O.* [61] presents a recent case where the plaintiff was granted a recovery although the defendant had copied merely the "dramatic core" or central dramatic situation,[62] the remainder of the two works being entirely

---

[37] Sheldon v. Metro-Goldwyn Pictures Corp., 81 F.2d 49 (2d Cir. 1936).

[39] The courts have long recognized that a *series* of incidents are entitled to copyright protection, *e.g.,* Dymow v. Bolton, 11 F. 2d 690, 692 (2d Cir. 1926) and Frankel v. Irwin, 34 F.2d 142, 143 (S.D.N.Y. 1918). More recently in Universal Pictures Co. v. Harold Lloyd Corp., 162 F. 2d 354 (9th Cir. 1947) a single motion picture sequence, which embodied 57 consecutive scenes was granted protection.

[60] It is interesting to note, however, that in the copyright case White-Smith Music Publishing Co. v. Apollo Co., 209 U.S. 1 (1907) at a time when the principle that ideas are not copyrightable was just being formulated, Justice Holmes stated in a concurring opinion at page 19 ". . . one would expect that, if it was to be protected at all . . . [it] would be protected according to what was its essence. One would expect the protection to be coextensive not only with the invention, which, though free to all, only one had the ability to achieve, but with the possibility of reproducing the result which gives to the invention its meaning and worth."

[61] 208 P. 2d 1 (1949).

[62] The dramatic core of both works involves a passenger aboard a ship who knows the ship captain to be a murderer. The captain, sure of his authority, informs his accuser that he is free to try to convince any one on board of the truth of his suspicions. The passenger tells the first mate, and others, but they refuse to believe him at first. Finally, however, the captain, aware that he is suspected, attempts another murder and loses his mind.

dissimilar. The force of this case as a precedent is highly questionable, however, in view of the following facts: 1. it is a state court decision; 2. the case involves a common law copyright to which the right of "fair use" (insubstantial appropriation) traditionally does not attach,[63] and 3. the California Supreme Court has granted a rehearing in the case.[64]

It is a general precept of tort law that if a property right is invaded the property owner is entitled to at least nominal damages even if no actual damage is proven.[65] Why, then, should the owner of literary property because he cannot show "substantial" appropriation be denied *any* recovery even if he can show actual appropriation of a very real product of his literary labors? It may indeed be argued that the entire concept of private property is contrary to greatest possible social welfare, but unless that thesis is accepted *in toto,* there does not seem to be any social necessity for singling out the property of the writer. Under existing law federal courts will protect a central dramatic situation plus embellishments but will grant protection to neither alone. Learned Hand in *Sheldon v. Metro-Goldwyn Pictures Corp.*[66] stated:

It is enough that substantial parts were lifted; no plagiarist can excuse the wrong by showing how much of his work he did not pirate.

It is suggested that in dealing with both embellishments and central dramatic situations, the courts would move in a salutary direction by deleting the word "substantial" from the above passage.

PROBLEM: "THE BLACKBOARD JUNGLE"

The author of a play called "Shadows in the City" alleges that the copyright in his play was infringed by the novel "The Blackboard Jungle." The play had been performed in New York City several years before "The Blackboard Jungle" was written. There had been three or four days of previews to which students, including students at Cooper Union, had been invited. The author of "The Blackboard Jungle" was a student at Cooper Union at that time. He testified that he never saw the play performed.

Synopses of the plots of the works follow. Has copyright infringement been established? *See Burnett v. Lambino,* 204 F. Supp. 327 (S.D.N.Y. 1962).

"Shadows in the City"

"Shadows" is a melodrama based on the violence and insensititivity of slum-reared high school students and deals with the disaster which a deranged student brings upon himself and other students. A teacher, who is unable to prevent the tragedy, is a prominent character, but the protagonists are the students.

Other than this common core, the two stories are quite different — one involving passengers on a pleasure cruise with the captain an imposter (actually an actor and understudy to the person who accuses him) and the other story occurs on a freighter with completely different embellishments.

[63] Golding v. R.K.O., 193 P.2d 153 (Cal. Dist. Ct. App. 1948).

[64] Rehearing granted July 28, 1949.

[65] Pollock, Torts 277 (14th ed. 1939).

[66] 81 F. 2d 49, 56 (2d Cir. 1936).

In the first scene, the trial begins of Tony Pessolano, a teen-age boy, for the murder of one of his classmates, Steven Ames. After a succession of defiant witnesses, all students, testify, one James Kirkland asks for permission to conduct Tony's defense. Kirkland was the teacher of all of the students who have appeared, and of Ames as well. After declaring that something more than a personal motive was the cause of the murder, Kirkland asks the audience to go back with him to a metropolitan vocational high school. It is there that the remainder of the play's action takes place.

Kirkland, a recently discharged wounded war veteran, begins at the school as an English teacher. He talks with several teachers, among them Lorimer, an earnest young man who speaks in passing of the difficulty of dealing with disciplinary problems in the school, and Walsh, a bantering but cynical man. Walsh advises Kirkland that the school is populated with the most stupid and incorrigible students in the high school system, and that physical punishment is the best means of insuring discipline. Kirkland then meets several of his students-to-be: Tony, a disciplinary problem and the leader of the class; McLemore, a brutish boy who wants Tony's sister, Rita, as his girl; Rita, an attractive seventeen year old who loves Ames; and Ames, an intelligent boy who is filled with bitterness which he fortifies by reading Housman. In Kirkland's class, these students and their fellows are unresponsive and unruly.

Kirkland recognizes Ames' intelligence. When he attempts after class to discover the reason for Ames' embitterment, he is rebuffed and is told by the boy that his father is a criminal and his mother a madam.

Kirkland's attempt to teach the class is, throughout the play, frustrated by its unresponsiveness and by Tony's trouble-making. This eventually leads to a fight between Tony and a provoked Kirkland. Tony complains to the principal that Kirkland struck him. Kirkland decides to leave of his own accord, in despair at having had to resort to physical force.

The major story in the play is that of Rita's infatuation with the unhappy Ames. Early in the second act, Rita tells Kirkland that she loves Ames and asks for his help, but he refuses. Rita is also concerned about Tony's possession of a gun belonging to their older brother, Joe, who has been sentenced to prison. Afraid that Tony will injure or kill someone with the gun, Rita entreats Ames to help her get it from Tony. Ames is bitter and sarcastic and quotes Housman to Rita. Rebuffed, she begins to cry; Ames attempts to soothe her. They are interrupted by McLemore, with whom Rita exits.

In the final act, Walsh expresses his rage at Tony for complaining to the principal that Kirkland had struck him, and encourages other students to strike Tony under Walsh's approving eye. Walsh is himself about to assault Tony when Lorimer enters to say that Kirkland is leaving but could be induced to remain by an expression from the students that they wanted him to stay. When Kirkland enters, they voice such sentiments, but Kirkland is immediately told by Ames that the students were coerced. Kirkland is hurt and leaves. Walsh attacks Tony only to be interrupted by the sound of a siren signalling an air raid drill.

When the room empties, Rita and Ames have their last meeting. She protests her love, but Ames is at first immovable. He complains of his father who deserted his mother, leaving her to bear him in a world of misery. Later, however, he softens, and they talk wildly about running away to marry. He indicates that he wishes to die. He pretends to become passionate towards her, though his real motive is to obtain the gun so that he can kill them both. At that point, Tony enters and Ames goads him into shooting him. He dies laughing. Kirkland closes the play saying Tony and thousands like him are "a product of our social system."

"The Blackboard Jungle"

The protagonist in "The Blackboard Jungle" is Richard Dadier, a young man who was graduated from college after his discharge from the Navy. The major theme of the book is his struggle, as a beginning teacher of English in a vocational high school, to communicate with his students and to avoid becoming a resigned or embittered failure. The novel traces Dadier through a detailed series of frustrations with his students, a transitory classroom success, and, at the end of the book, to a limited victory over the defiance and resentment of his students, and the feeling that he can be useful in his job by "reaching" a few students. A related theme is the effect of the job and the hazards incident to it on his relationship with his wife, Anne, with whom he is deeply in love.

Each of two other beginning teachers is the focus of a subplot of considerable scope. Lois Hammond is a highly attractive young woman who makes repeated attempts to seduce Dadier, which he rebuffs. Joshua Edwards is weak but idealistic; his idealism persists even after he and Dadier are badly beaten by some students one evening. However, when Edwards attempts to communicate to the students his enthusiasm for jazz by bringing to school his prized record collection, they smash it and soon after this event he leaves the school.

Dadier's students are, at the outset and throughout most of the book, unresponsive if not defiant. Among them are Gregory Miller, a Negro, the leader of the class and obviously equipped with greater intelligence than his fellows; Arthur West, a vicious thug; and Santini, a mentally retarded boy. During Dadier's first meeting with his class, he is threatened, West is openly insulting, and Miller defies him with constant remarks. After his first class, Dadier hypocritically attempts to enlist Miller on his side by flattering him in order to get Miller to cooperate with him and thereby set an example to his classmates.

As the plot unfolds, Dadier prevents Lois Hammond from being raped by a student, whom he forcibly subdues. The students, when they learn that the would-be rapist is to be prosecuted, resent and mistrust Dadier. His own class is deliberately obtuse as a gesture of rebellion. Dadier is told of the class' attitude by Miller, who now much resents Dadier's attempt to use him to keep order in the classroom.

Dadier's problems with his students multiply after he and Edwards are beaten by them in a vivid episode: in a class, he attempts to provoke them to write imaginative compositions by acting out the topic he assigns, but is deeply disappointed to find that they merely attempt literal descriptions of his actions in nearly illiterate prose; his attempt to arouse their interest in diction totally fails when Miller encourages one student to speak with his usual obscene vocabulary; Arthur West, who remains vicious, threatening and incorrigible throughout the novel, falsely reports to Mr. Small, the pompous school principal, that Dadier is a bigot, and Dadier must furiously explain that the report is a perversion of the true context of his words.

Dadier fights despair at his failure to communicate with his students. He refuses, however, to surrender to the cynicism of Solly Klein, a veteran teacher with whom he occasionally debates whether and what the students can be taught. Klein constantly tells him that the students cannot and will not learn and that the function of the teacher in a vocational high school is to occupy the students and keep them off the streets, while protecting himself physically as best as he can. Most of the other teachers with whom Dadier discusses his difficulties agree with Klein. Some, such as Captain Schaefer, a minor character who is the physical education teacher, go further and state bluntly that physical force is the only solution.

Dadier finally begins to have rare instances of success: he is deputized to direct the school's Christmas play, and Miller and a group of other boys volunteer to sing. They are cooperative and Dadier and Miller are able to speak frankly to each other at rehearsals, although Miller remains unruly in class. Also, Dadier finally feels that he has "reached" his class when he reads them a story which they excitedly realize is an allegory from which they can learn a message.

However, Dadier is unable to see his successful Christmas play and is unable to capitalize on his success at communicating to the class. His wife Anne has a miscarriage, partially brought on by worry over a series of anonymous letters sent by Arthur West which tell her that Dadier and Lois Hammond are having an affair. This is not true. Dadier is forced to miss a week of school. Upon his return after the Christmas holidays are over, he finds that he must begin again to try to "reach" his students and he is almost totally discouraged. Yet, at the climactic moment of the book, when he is attacked in the classroom and knifed by West, the students, led by Miller, intervene to protect him. The students also understand — again led by Miller — that Dadier must report the incident. The books ends after this incident, with Dadier convinced that his role as a teacher is to try to stimulate his students with the hope of inculcating in just a few of them a genuine desire to learn.

B. THE RIGHT OF PUBLIC DISPLAY UNDER § 106(5)

§ 106. Exclusive rights in copyrighted works

Subject to sections 107 through 118, the owner of copyright under this title has the exclusive rights to do and to authorize any of the following:

. . . .

(5) in the case of literary, musical, dramatic, and choreographic works, pantomimes, and pictorial, graphic, or sculptural works, including the individual images of a motion picture or other audiovisual work, to display the copyrighted work publicly.

§ 101. Definitions

As used in this title, the following terms and their variant forms mean the following:

. . . .

To "display" a work means to show a copy of it, either directly or by means of a film, slide, television image, or any other device or process or, in the case of a motion picture or other audiovisual work, to show individual images nonsequentially.

. . . .

To "perform or display a work 'publicly' means" —

(1) to perform or display it at a place open to the public or at any place where a substantial number of persons outside of a normal circle of a family and its social acquaintances is gathered; or

(2) to transmit or otherwise communicate a performance or display of the work to a place specified by clause (1) or to the public, by means of any device

or process, whether the members of the public capable of receiving the performance or display receive it in the same place or in separate places and at the same time or at different times.

§ 109. Limitations on exclusive rights: Effect of transfer of particular copy or phonorecord

. . . .

(b) Notwithstanding the provisions of section 106(5), the owner of a particular copy lawfully made under this title, or any person authorized by such owner, is entitled, without the authority of the copyright owner, to display that copy publicly, either directly or by the projection of no more than one image at a time, to viewers present at the place where the copy is located.

(c) The privileges prescribed by subsections (a) and (b) do not, unless authorized by the copyright owner, extend to any person who has acquired possession of the copy or phonorecord from the copyright owner, by rental, lease, loan, or otherwise, without acquiring ownership of it.

NOTE

"Clause (5) of section 106 represents the first explicit statutory recognition in United States copyright law of an exclusive right to show a copyrighted work, or an image of it, to the public. The existence or extent of this right under the present [1909] statute is uncertain and subject to challenge." S. Rep. No. 94-473, at 59; H.R. Rep. No. 94-1476, at 63. A particularly troubling issue was whether the showing of a pictorial work on a television broadcast was an infringing "copy" under the 1909 act; the evanescence of the image helped convince at least one court that it was not, *Mura v. Columbia Broadcasting System,* 245 F. Supp. 587 (S.D.N.Y. 1965).

The newly created right of display is limited, in common with the performing right in § 106(4), to *public* presentation, and it applies only to specified types of works. (The student should consult the definition of "publicly" in § 101.) It will be noted that sound recordings are not afforded a statutory right of public display, and that audiovisual works are covered only to the extent of nonsequential presentation of individual images; sequential presentation would amount to a "performance." Moreover, the right to display published pictorial, graphic and sculptural works by public broadcasters on television is covered by a compulsory license granted in § 118. Finally, the right of public display is limited by the provisions of § 109(b), discussed in the passages from the House Report immediately below.

HOUSE REPORT

H.R. Rep. No. 94-1476, 94th Cong., 2d Sess. 79-80 (1976)

Effect of display of copy

Subsection (b) of section 109 deals with the scope of the copyright owner's exclusive right to control the public display of a particular "copy" of a work (including the original or prototype copy in which the work was first fixed). Assuming, for example, that a painter has sold the only copy of an original work of art without restrictions, would it be possible for him to restrain the new owner from displaying it publicly in galleries, shop windows, on a projector, or on television?

Section 109(b) adopts the general principle that the lawful owner of a copy of a work should be able to put his copy on public display without the consent of the copyright owner. As in cases arising under section 109(a), this does not mean that contractual restrictions on display between a buyer and seller would be unenforceable as a matter of contract law.

The exclusive right of public display granted by section 106(5) would not apply where the owner of a copy wishes to show it directly to the public, as in a gallery or display case, or indirectly, as through an opaque projector. Where the copy itself is intended for projection, as in the case of a photographic slide, negative, or transparency, the public projection of a single image would be permitted as long as the views are "present at the place where the copy is located."

On the other hand, section 109(b) takes account of the potentialities of the new communications media, notably television, cable and optical transmission devices, and information storage and retrieval devices, for replacing printed copies with visual images. First of all, the public display of an image of a copyrighted work would not be exempted from copyright control if the copy from which the image was derived were outside the presence of the viewers. In other words, the display of a visual image of a copyrighted work would be an infringement if the image were transmitted by any method (by closed or open circuit television, for example, or by a computer system) from one place to members of the public located elsewhere.

Moreover, the exemption would extend only to public displays that are made "either directly or by the projection of no more than one image at a time." Thus, even where the copy and the viewers are located at the same place, the simultaneous projection of multiple images of the work would not be exempted. For example, where each person in a lecture hall is supplied with a separate viewing apparatus, the copyright owner's permission would generally be required in order to project an image of a work on each individual screen at the same time.

The committee's intention is to preserve the traditional privilege of the owner of a copy to display it directly, but to place reasonable restrictions on the ability to display it indirectly in such a way that the copyright owner's market for reproduction and distribution of copies would be affected. Unless it constitutes a fair use under section 107, or unless one of the special provisions of section 110 or 111 is applicable, projection of more than one image at a time, or transmission of an image to the public over television or other communication channels, would be an infringement for the same reasons that reproduction in copies would be. The concept of "the place where the copy is located" is generally intended to refer to a situation in which the viewers are present in the same physical surroundings as the copy, even though they cannot see the copy directly.

C. RIGHT TO PREPARE DERIVATIVE WORKS UNDER § 106(2)

§ 106. Exclusive rights in copyrighted works

Subject to sections 107 through 118, the owner of copyright under this title has the exclusive rights to do and to authorize any of the following:

. . . .

(2) to prepare derivative works based upon the copyrighted work: . . . .

HOUSE REPORT

H.R. Rep. No. 94-1476, 94th Cong., 2d Sess. 62 (1976)

Preparation of derivative works. — The exclusive right to prepare derivative works, specified separately in clause (2) of section 106, overlaps the exclusive right of reproduction to some extent. It is broader than that right, however, in the sense that reproduction requires fixation in copies or phonorecords, whereas the preparation of a derivative work, such as a ballet, pantomime, or improvised performance, may be an infringement even though nothing is ever fixed in tangible form.

To be an infringement the "derivative work" must be "based upon the copyrighted work," and the definition in section 101 refers to "a translation, musical arrangement, dramatization, fictionalization, motion picture version, sound recording, art reproduction, abridgment, condensation, or any other form in which a work may be recast, transformed, or adapted." Thus, to constitute a violation of section 106(2), the infringing work must incorporate a portion of the copyrighted work in some form; for example, a detailed commentary on a work or a programmatic musical composition inspired by a novel would not normally constitute infringements under this clause.

CHAFEE, REFLECTIONS ON COPYRIGHT LAW, 45 Columbia Law Review 503, 511 (1945)

The protection given the copyright-owner should not stifle independent creation by others. Nobody else should *market* the author's book, but we refuse to say nobody else should *use* it. The world goes ahead because each of us builds on the work of our predecessors. "A dwarf standing on the shoulders of a giant can see farther than the giant himself." Progress would be stifled if the author had a complete monopoly of everything in his book for fifty-six years or any other long period. Some use of its contents must be permitted in connection with the independent creation of other authors. The very policy which leads the law to encourage his creativeness also justifies it in facilitating the creativeness of others.

In the late eighteenth century, this ideal of the encouragement of independent creation was pushed so far as to allow translations and abridgments without the author's consent, on the ground that the new man had put in a great deal of his own work. Thus Lord Apsley, backed by Blackstone, gave immunity to an abridgment of Hawksworth's *Voyages,* calling it "a new and meritorious work," less expensive and more convenient to handle than the original; he said it could be read in a quarter of the time with all the substance preserved in language as good as Hawksworth's or better and in a more agreeable and useful manner.[16] This sort of reasoning made Dr. Johnson's blood boil. During the *Tour to the Hebrides,*[17] Boswell mentioned Lord Monboddo's opinion, that if a man could get a work by heart, he might print it, as by such an act "the mind is exercised."

---

[16] Anon., Loffit 775, 98 Eng. Rep. 913 (Ch. 1774). See also Dodsley v. Kennersley, Amb. 403, 27 Eng. Rep. 270 (Ch. 1761), refusing to enjoin abridgment of Johnson's *Rasselas;* this case may have influenced the Doctor's opinion of the iniquity of unauthorized abridgments.

[17] Boswell's Journal of a Tour to the Hebrides with Samuel Johnson (ed. Pottle & Bennett, 1936) 49 (Aug. 20, 1773).

JOHNSON: "No, sir, a man's repeating it no more makes it his property than a man may sell a cow which he drives home."

I said printing an abridgment of a work was allowed, which was only cutting the horns and tail off the cow.

JOHNSON: "No, sir, 'tis making the cow have a calf."

Certainly this "exercise of the mind" test will not hold water. The author should not lose a large portion of his market so easily. Fortunately, our copyright law has abandoned its early tolerance of unauthorized abridgments and translations. They are ways for the author to reach the public and properly belong to him, as the 1909 Act expressly recognizes.[18]

Even when there is access, the precise boundaries of this defensive ideal of independent creation are hard to fix. Everybody agrees that the ideas in the copyrighted book are not protected. Another physicist can read Einstein's book and write about relativity. But he must not tell about it in Einstein's words. Should protection be limited to the precise words? If so, a translation, which uses entirely different words, would not infringe. Yet, if we protect more than precise words, where shall we stop? The line is sometimes drawn between an idea and its expression. This does not solve the problem, because "expression" has too wide a range. To some extent, the expression of an abstract idea should be free for use by others. No doubt, the line does lie somewhere between the author's idea and the precise form in which he wrote it down. I like to say that the protection covers the "pattern" of the work. This is not a solution, but I find it helpful as an imaginative description of what should not be imitated. For example, the idea of an Irish-Jewish marriage in a play may be borrowed.[24] With this theme, some resemblance in characters and situations is inevitable, but the line of infringement may not yet be crossed. On the other hand, the pattern of the play — the sequence of events and the development of the interplay of the characters — must not be followed scene by scene. Such a correspondence of pattern would be an infringement although every word of the spoken dialogue was changed.

Even the first user of a plot or a human situation should not have a monopoly of it. The public should have the opportunity to see what other artists will do with the same plot or situation, after the fashion set by the Greek tragedians. Yet we want to encourage originality and not slavishness. There comes a point where the use of material is so close as not to give the public anything really new. At that point, the ideal of encouraging independent creation ceases to operate.

QUESTIONS

Are the following uses of a copyrighted work an infringement? If so, under what subsection of the 1976 Act?

(a) *X* secures a copy of the copyrighted motion picture film of the

---

[18] 35 Stat. 1075 (1909), 17 U. S. C. § (b) (1940): "the exclusive right . . . To translate . . ., or make any other version thereof, if it be a literary work. . . ." This last clause seems to comprise abridgments. The law before 1909 took the view condemned by Dr. Johnson. See 2 Ladas, § 368(5). The British law as to abridgments is also probably changed by the Act of 1911 . . . .

[24] L. Hand, J. in Nichols v. Universal Pictures Corp., 45 F.(2d) 119 (C. C. A. 2d, 1930). For other interesting cases, see Woolsey, J. in Lewys v. O'Neill, 49 F.(2d) 603 (S. D. N. Y. 1931); Wilbur, J. in Harold Lloyd Corp. v. Witwer, 65 F.(2d) 1 (C. C. A. 9th, 1933) (dissenting opinion by McCormick, J.); Patterson, J. in Bein v. Warner Bros. Pictures, Inc., 105 F.(2d) 969 (C. C. A. 2d, 1939).

assassination of President Kennedy, taken at the scene by Abraham Zapruder, and makes a direct copy of the film.

(b) *X*, a few feet away from Mr. Zapruder at the time of the assassination, films exactly the same sequence of events with his own motion picture camera.

(c) *X* re-poses Oscar Wilde to match the Sarony photograph and takes his own still photograph, this one in color. (Assume for the purpose of the example that Wilde is alive and that the Sarony photograph is still in copyright.)

(d) *X*, seeing an attractive copyrighted photograph of the Golden Gate Bridge at sunset, positions himself at the same location and time and takes his own still photograph.

(e) *X*, seeing a large color photograph of a Campbell's Tomato Soup can in an avant garde photographic exhibition, takes his own such photograph.

(f) An artist paints a cubistic version of the (copyrighted) Sarony photograph of Oscar Wilde.

(g) The defendant in the *Catalda* case makes an engraving directly from the old master.

(h) The defendant in the *Catalda* case reproduces the plaintiff's mezzotint engraving, but leaves out the deviations from the old master caused by the plaintiff's muscular tremor and poor eyesight.

(i) A sculptor makes a three-dimensional version of a copyrighted painting.

(j) A scholar makes a French translation of a copyrighted English-language novel.

(k) A novelist sees a copyrighted silent motion picture and writes a novel recounting all of the incidents in the film (and, obviously, supplying original dialogue).

(l) A journalist writing for a competing news weekly takes a news story from *Time* magazine and rewrites it for publication in his own words.

(m) A publisher photocopies the telephone directory after verifying the accuracy of each item.

(n) Without verifying the accuracy of each item in the telephone book, a publisher prints that information in a book which is organized in one section by street addresses in alphabetical order and numerical sequence, and in another section by telephone numbers in numerical sequence.

GILLIAM v. AMERICAN BROADCASTING COMPANIES, INC.

538 F.2d 14 (2d Cir. 1976)

LUMBARD, CIRCUIT JUDGE:

Plaintiffs, a group of British writers and performers known as "Monty Python," [1] appeal from a denial by Judge Lasker in the Southern District of a preliminary injunction to restrain the American Broadcasting Company (ABC) from broadcasting edited versions of three separate programs originally written and performed by Monty Python for broadcast by the British Broadcasting Corporation (BBC). We agree with Judge Lasker that the appellants have demonstrated that the excising done for ABC impairs the integrity of the original work. We further find that the countervailing injuries that Judge Lasker found might have accrued to ABC as a result of an injunction at a prior date no longer exist. We therefore direct the issuance of a preliminary injunction by the district court.

---

[1] Appellant Gilliam is an American citizen residing in England.

Since its formation in 1969, the Monty Python group has gained popularity primarily through its thirty-minute television programs created for BBC as part of a comedy series entitled "Monty Python's Flying Circus." In accordance with an agreement between Monty Python and BBC, the group writes and delivers to BBC scripts for use in the television series. This scriptwriters' agreement recites in great detail the procedure to be followed when any alterations are to be made in the script prior to recording of the program.[2] The essence of this section of the agreement is that, while BBC retains final authority to make changes, appellants or their representatives exercise optimum control over the scripts consistent with BBC's authority and only minor changes may be made without prior consultation with the writers. Nothing in the scriptwriters' agreement entitles BBC to alter a program once it has been recorded. The agreement further provides that, subject to the terms therein, the group retains all rights in the script.

Under the agreement, BBC may license the transmission of recordings of the television programs in any overseas territory. The series has been broadcast in this country primarily on non-commercial public broadcasting television stations, although several of the programs have been broadcast on commercial stations in Texas and Nevada. In each instance, the thirty-minute programs have been broadcast as originally recorded and broadcast in England in their entirety and without commercial interruption.

In October 1973, Time-Life Films acquired the right to distribute in the United States certain BBC television programs, including the Monty Python series. Time-Life was permitted to edit the programs only "for insertion of commercials, applicable censorship or governmental . . . rules and regulations, and National Association of Broadcasters and time segment requirements." No similar clause was included in the scriptwriters' agreement between appellants and BBC. Prior to this time, ABC had sought to acquire the right to broadcast excerpts from various Monty Python programs in the spring of 1975, but the group rejected the proposal for such a disjointed format. Thereafter, in July 1975, ABC agreed with Time-Life to broadcast two ninety-minute specials each comprising three thirty-minute Monty Python programs that had not previously been shown in this country.

---

[2] The Agreement provides:
   V. When script alterations are necessary it is the intention of the BBC to make every effort to inform and to reach agreement with the Writer. Whenever practicable any necessary alterations (other than minor alterations) shall be made by the Writer. Nevertheless the BBC shall at all times have the right to make (a) minor alterations and (b) such other alterations as in its opinion are necessary in order to avoid involving the BBC in legal action or bringing the BBC into disrepute. Any decision under (b) shall be made at a level not below that of Head of Department. It is however agreed that after a script has been accepted by the BBC alterations will not be made by the BBC under (b) above unless (i) the Writer, if available when the BBC requires the alterations to be made, has been asked to agree to them but is not willing to do so and (ii) the Writer has had, if he so requests and if the BBC agrees that times permits if rehearsals and recording are to proceed as planned, an opportunity to be represented by the Writers' Guild of Great Britain (or if he is not a member of the Guild by his agent) at a meeting with the BBC to be held within at most 48 hours of the request (excluding weekends). If in such circumstances there is no agreement about the alterations then the final decision shall rest with the BBC. Apart from the right to make alterations under (a) and (b) above the BBC shall not without the consent of the Writer or his agent (which consent shall not be unreasonably withheld) make any structural alterations as opposed to minor alterations to the script, provided that such consent shall not be necessary in any case where the Writer is for any reason not immediately available for consultation at the time which in the BBC's opinion is the deadline from the production point of view for such alterations to be made if rehearsals and recording are to proceed as planned.

Correspondence between representatives of BBC and Monty Python reveals that these parties assumed that ABC would broadcast each of the Monty Python programs "in its entirety." On September 5, 1975, however, the group's British representative inquired of BBC how ABC planned to show the programs in their entirety if approximately 24 minutes of each 90 minute program were to be devoted to commercials. BBC replied on September 12, "we can only reassure you that ABC have decided to run the programmes 'back to back,' and that there is a firm undertaking not to segment them."

ABC broadcast the first of the specials on October 3, 1975. Appellants did not see a tape of the program until late November and were allegedly "appalled" at the discontinuity and "mutilation" that had resulted from the editing done by Time-Life for ABC. Twenty-four minutes of the original 90 minutes of recording had been omitted. Some of the editing had been done in order to make time for commercials; other material had been edited, according to ABC, because the original programs contained offensive or obscene matter.

In early December, Monty Python learned that ABC planned to broadcast the second special on December 26, 1975. The parties began negotiations concerning editing of that program and a delay of the broadcast until Monty Python could view it. These negotiations were futile, however, and on December 15 the group filed this action to enjoin the broadcast and for damages. Following an evidentiary hearing, Judge Lasker found that "the plaintiffs have established an impairment of the integrity of their work" which "caused the film or program . . . to lose its iconoclastic verve." According to Judge Lasker, "the damage that has been caused to the plaintiffs is irreparable by its nature." Nevertheless, the judge denied the motion for the preliminary injunction on the grounds that it was unclear who owned the copyright in the programs produced by BBC from the scripts written by Monty Python; that there was a question of whether Time-Life and BBC were indispensable parties to the litigation; that ABC would suffer significant financial loss if it were enjoined a week before the scheduled broadcast; and that Monty Python had displayed a "somewhat disturbing casualness" in their pursuance of the matter.

Judge Lasker granted Monty Python's request for more limited relief by requiring ABC to broadcast a disclaimer during the December 26 special to the effect that the group dissociated itself from the program because of the editing. A panel of this court, however, granted a stay of that order until this appeal could be heard and permitted ABC to broadcast, at the beginning of the special, only the legend that the program had been edited by ABC. We heard argument on April 13 and, at that time, enjoined ABC from any further broadcast of edited Monty Python programs pending the decision of the court.

I

In determining the availability of injunctive relief at this early stage of the proceedings, Judge Lasker properly considered the harm that would inure to the plaintiffs if the injunction were denied, the harm that defendant would suffer if the injunction were granted, and the likelihood that plaintiffs would ultimately succeed on the merits. See *Hamilton Watch Co. v. Benrus Watch Co.*, 206 F.2d 738 (2d Cir. 1953). We direct the issuance of a preliminary injunction because we find that all these factors weigh in favor of appellants.

There is nothing clearly erroneous in Judge Lasker's conclusion that any injury suffered by appellants as a result of the broadcast of edited versions of their programs was irreparable by its nature. ABC presented the appellants with their first opportunity for broadcast to a nationwide network audience in this country. If ABC adversely misrepresented the quality of Monty Python's work, it is likely that many members of the audience, many of whom, by defendant's admission, were previously unfamiliar with appellants, would not become loyal followers of Monty Python productions. The subsequent injury to appellants' theatrical reputation would imperil their ability to attract the large audience necessary to the success of their venture. Such an injury to professional reputation cannot be measured in monetary terms or recompensed by other relief. See *Coca-Cola Co. v. Gemini Rising, Inc.,* 346 F.Supp.1183, 1189 (E.D.N.Y.1972); *Estee Lauder, Inc. v. Watsky,* 323 F.Supp. 1064, 1067 (S.D.N.Y.1970).

In contrast to the harm that Monty Python would suffer by a denial of the preliminary injunction, Judge Lasker found that ABC's relationship with its affiliates would be impaired by a grant of an injunction within a week of the scheduled December 26 broadcast. The court also found that ABC and its affiliates had advertised the program and had included it in listings of forthcoming television programs that were distributed to the public. Thus a last minute cancellation of the December 26 program, Judge Lasker concluded, would injure defendant financially and in its reputation with the public and its advertisers.

However valid these considerations may have been when the issue before the court was whether a preliminary injunction should immediately precede the broadcast, any injury to ABC is presently more speculative. No rebroadcast of the edited specials has been scheduled and no advertising costs have been incurred for the immediate future. Thus there is no danger that the defendant's relations with affiliates or the public will suffer irreparably if subsequent broadcasts of the programs are enjoined pending a disposition of the issues.

We then reach the question whether there is a likelihood that appellants will succeed on the merits. In concluding that there is a likelihood of infringement here, we rely especially on the fact that the editing was substantial, i.e., approximately 27 per cent of the original program was omitted, and the editing contravened contractual provisions that limited the right to edit Monty Python material. It should be emphasized that our discussion of these matters refers only to such facts as have been developed upon the hearing for a preliminary injunction. Modified or contrary findings may become appropriate after a plenary trial.

Judge Lasker denied the preliminary injunction in part because he was unsure of the ownership of the copyright in the recorded program. Appellants first contend that the question of ownership is irrelevant because the recorded program was merely a derivative work taken from the script in which they hold the uncontested copyright. Thus, even if BBC owned the copyright in the recorded program, its use of that work would be limited by the license granted to BBC by Monty Python for use of the underlying script. We agree.

Section 7 of the Copyright Law, 17 U.S.C. § 7, provides in part that "adaptations, arrangements, dramatizations ... or other versions of ... copyrighted works when produced with the consent of the proprietor of the copyright in such works ... shall be regarded as new works subject to copyright ...." Manifestly, the recorded program falls into this category as a dramatization of the script,[3]

---

[3] ABC has not argued that the principles of section 7 do not apply because Monty Python's copyright in its unpublished script is a common law copyright rather than a statutory copyright, which can exist only after publication. In any event, we find that the same principles discussed below with respect to derivative works adapted from material

and thus the program was itself entitled to copyright protection. However, section 7 limits the copyright protection of the derivative work, as works adapted from previously existing scripts have become known, to the novel additions made to the underlying work, *Reyher v. Children's Television Workshop*, 533 F.2d 87 (2d Cir. 1976), and the derivative work does not affect the "force or validity" of the copyright in the matter from which it is derived. See *Grove Press, Inc. v. Greenleaf Publishing Co.*, 247 F.Supp. 518 (S.D.N.Y.1965). Thus, any ownership by BBC of the copyright in the recorded program would not affect the scope or ownership of the copyright in the underlying script.

Since the copyright in the underlying script survives intact despite the incorporation of that work into a derivative work, one who uses the script, even with the permission of the proprietor of the derivative work, may infringe the underlying copyright. See *Davis v. E. I. DuPont deNemours & Co.*, 240 F. Supp. 612 (S.D.N.Y. 1965) (defendants held to have infringed when they obtained permission to use a screenplay in preparing a television script but did not obtain permission of the author of the play upon which the screenplay was based).

If the proprietor of the derivative work is licensed by the proprietor of the copyright in the underlying work to vend or distribute the derivative work to third parties, those parties will, of course, suffer no liability for their use of the underlying work consistent with the license to the proprietor of the derivative work. Obviously, it was just this type of arrangement that was contemplated in this instance. The scriptwriters' agreement between Monty Python and BBC specifically permitted the latter to license the transmission of the recordings made by BBC to distributors such as Time-Life for broadcast in overseas territories.

One who obtains permission to use a copyrighted script in the production of a derivative work, however, may not exceed the specific purpose for which permission was granted. Most of the decisions that have reached this conclusion have dealt with the improper extension of the underlying work into media or time, i.e., duration of the license, not covered by the grant of permission to the derivative work proprietor.[4] See *Bartsch v. Metro-Goldwyn-Mayer, Inc.*, 391

---

in which there is a statutory copyright also apply to material in which there is a common law copyright. See RCA Mfg. Co. v. Whiteman, 114 F.2d 86, 88 (2d Cir.), *cert. denied*, 311 U.S. 712 (1940); 17 U.S.C. § 2.

The law is apparently unsettled with respect to whether a broadcast of a recorded program constitutes publication of that program and the underlying script so as to divest the proprietor of the script of his common law copyright. See 1 M. Nimmer, Copyright §§ 56.3, 57. Arguably, once the scriptwriter obtains the economic benefit of the recording and the broadcast, he has obtained all that his common law copyright was intended to secure for him: thus it would not be unfair to find that publication of the derivative work divested the script of its common law protection. On the other hand, several types of performances from scripts have been held not to constitute divestive publication, *see, e.g.*, Uproar Co. v. NBC, 81 F.2d 373 (1st Cir. 1936), and it is unclear whether a broadcast of the recording in itself constitutes publication. See M. Nimmer, supra, § 56.3. Since ABC has not objected to Monty Python's assertion of common law copyright in an unpublished script, we need not entertain the question on this appeal from denial of a preliminary injunction. We leave initial determination of this perplexing question to the district court in its determination of all the issues on the merits. This disposition is especially proper in view of the fact that, apart from the copyright claims, there will be a trial of the unfair competition claim.

[4] Thus, a leading commentator on the subject concludes:

If the copyright owner of an underlying work limits his consent for its use in a derivative work to a given medium (e. g. opera), the copyright owner of the derivative

F.2d 150 (2d Cir.), cert. denied, 393 U.S. 826 (1968); *G. Ricordi & Co. v. Paramount Pictures Inc.,* 189 F.2d 469 (2d Cir.), cert. denied, 342 U.S. 849 (1951). Cf. *Rice v. American Program Bureau,* 446 F.2d 685 (2d Cir. 1971). Appellants herein do not claim that the broadcast by ABC violated media or time restrictions contained in the license of the script to BBC. Rather, they claim that revisions in the script, and ultimately in the program, could be made only after consultation with Monty Python, and that ABC's broadcast of a program edited after recording and without consultation with Monty Python exceeded the scope of any license that BBC was entitled to grant.

The rationale for finding infringement when a licensee exceeds time or media restrictions on his license — the need to allow the proprietor of the underlying copyright to control the method in which his work is presented to the public — applies equally to the situation in which a licensee makes an unauthorized use of the underlying work by publishing it in a truncated version. Whether intended to allow greater economic exploitation of the work, as in the media and time cases, or to ensure that the copyright proprietor retains a veto power over revisions desired for the derivative work, the ability of the copyright holder to control his work remains paramount in our copyright law. We find, therefore, that unauthorized editing of the underlying work, if proven, would constitute an infringement of the copyright in that work similar to any other use of a work that exceeded the license granted by the proprietor of the copyright.

If the broadcast of an edited version of the Monty Python program infringed the group's copyright in the script, ABC may obtain no solace from the fact that editing was permitted in the agreements between BBC and Time-Life or Time-Life and ABC. BBC was not entitled to make unilateral changes in the script and was not specifically empowered to alter the recordings once made; Monty Python, moreover, had reserved to itself any rights not granted to BBC. Since a grantor may not convey greater rights than it owns, BBC's permission to allow Time-Life, and hence ABC, to edit appears to have been a nullity. See *Hampton v. Paramount Pictures Corp.,* 279 F.2d 100 (9th Cir.), cert. denied, 364 U.S. 882 (1970); *Ilyin v. Avon Publications,* 144 F.Supp. 368, 372 (S.D.N.Y.1956).

ABC answers appellants' infringement argument with a series of contentions, none of which seems meritorious at this stage of the litigation. The network asserts that Monty Python's British representative, Jill Foster, knew that ABC planned to exclude much of the original BBC program in the October 3 broadcast. ABC thus contends that by not previously objecting to this procedure, Monty Python ratified BBC's authority to license others to edit the underlying script.

Although the case of *Ilyin v. Avon Publications, Inc.,* 144 F.Supp. 368, 373 (S.D.N.Y.1956), may be broadly read for the proposition that a holder of a derivative copyright may obtain rights in the underlying work through ratification, the conduct necessary to that conclusion has yet to be demonstrated in this case. It is undisputed that appellants did not have actual notice of the cuts in the October 3 broadcast until late November. Even if they are chargeable with the knowledge of their British representative, it is not clear that she had prior notice of the cuts or ratified the omissions, nor did Judge Lasker make any finding on

---

work may not exploit such derivative work in a different medium (e. g. motion pictures) to the extent the derivative work incorporates protectible material from the underlying work.

1 M. Nimmer, Copyright § 45.3.

the question. While Foster, on September 5, did question how ABC was to broadcast the entire program if it was going to interpose 24 minutes of commercials, she received assurances from BBC that the programs would not be "segmented." The fact that she knew precisely the length of material that would have to be omitted to allow for commercials does not prove that she ratified the deletions. This is especially true in light of previous assurances that the program would contain the original shows in their entirety. On the present record, it cannot be said that there was any ratification of BBC's grant of editing rights. ABC, of course, is entitled to attempt to prove otherwise during the trial on the merits.

ABC next argues that under the "joint work" theory adopted in *Shapiro, Bernstein & Co. v. Jerry Vogel Music, Inc.,* 221 F.2d 569 (2d Cir. 1955), the script produced by Monty Python and the program recorded by BBC are symbiotic elements of a single production. Therefore, according to ABC, each contributor possesses an undivided ownership of all copyrightable elements in the final work and BBC could thus have licensed use of the script, including editing, written by appellants.

The joint work theory as extended in *Shapiro* has been criticized as inequitable unless "at the time of creation by the first author, the second author's contribution [is envisaged] as an integrated part of a single work," and the first author intends that the final product be a joint work. See 1 M. Nimmer, Copyright §§ 67-73. Furthermore, this court appears to have receded from a broad application of the joint work doctrine where the contract which leads to collaboration between authors indicates that one will retain a superior interest. See *Szekely v. Eagle Lion Films, Inc.,* 242 F.2d 266 (2d Cir.), cert. denied, 354 U.S. 922 (1957). In the present case, the screenwriters' agreement between Monty Python and BBC provides that the group is to retain all rights in the script not granted in the agreement and that at some future point the group may license the scripts for use on television to parties other than BBC. These provisions suggest that the parties did not consider themselves joint authors of a single work. This matter is subject to further exploration at the trial, but in the present state of the record, it presents no bar to issuance of a preliminary injunction.

Aside from the question of who owns the relevant copyrights, ABC asserts that the contracts between appellants and BBC permit editing of the programs for commercial television in the United States. ABC argues that the scriptwriters' agreement allows appellants the right to participate in revisions of the script only *prior* to the recording of the programs, and thus infers that BBC had unrestricted authority to revise after that point. This argument, however, proves too much. A reading of the contract seems to indicate that Monty Python obtained control over editing the script only to ensure control over the program recorded from that script. Since the scriptwriters' agreement explicitly retains for the group all rights not granted by the contract, omission of any terms concerning alterations in the program after recording must be read as reserving to appellants exclusive authority for such revisions.

Finally, ABC contends that appellants must have expected that deletions would be made in the recordings to conform them for use on commercial television in the United States. ABC argues that licensing in the United States implicitly grants a license to insert commercials in a program and to remove offensive or obscene material prior to broadcast. According to the network, appellants should have anticipated that most of the excised material contained scatological references inappropriate for American television and that these scenes would be replaced with commercials, which presumably are more palatable to the American public.

The proof adduced up to this point, however, provides no basis for finding any implied consent to edit. Prior to the ABC broadcasts, Monty Python programs had been broadcast on a regular basis by both commercial and public television stations in this country without interruption or deletion. Indeed, there is no evidence of any prior broadcast of edited Monty Python material in the United States. These facts, combined with the persistent requests for assurances by the group and its representatives that the programs would be shown intact belie the argument that the group knew or should have known that deletions and commercial interruptions were inevitable.

Several of the deletions made for ABC, such as elimination of the words "hell" and "damn," seem inexplicable given today's standard television fare.[8] If, however, ABC honestly determined that the programs were obscene in substantial part, it could have decided not to broadcast the specials at all, or it could have attempted to reconcile its differences with appellants. The network could not, however, free from a claim of infringement, broadcast in a substantially altered form a program incorporating the script over which the group had retained control.

Our resolution of these technical arguments serves to reinforce our initial inclination that the copyright law should be used to recognize the important role of the artist in our society and the need to encourage production and dissemination of artistic works by providing adequate legal protection for one who submits his work to the public. See *Mazer v. Stein,* 347 U.S. 201 (1954). We therefore conclude that there is a substantial likelihood that, after a full trial, appellants will succeed in proving infringement of their copyright by ABC's broadcast of edited versions of Monty Python programs. In reaching this conclusion, however, we need not accept appellants' assertion that any editing whatsoever would constitute infringement. Courts have recognized that licensees are entitled to some small degree of latitude in arranging the licensed work for presentation to the public in a manner consistent with the licensee's style or standards.[9] See *Stratchborneo v. Arc Music Corp.,* 357 F.Supp. 1393, 1405 (S.D.N.Y. 1973); *Preminger v. Columbia Pictures Corp.,* 49 Misc.2d 383, 267 N.Y.S.2d 594 (Sup.Ct.), aff'd 25 App.Div.2d 830, 269 N.Y.S.2d 913 (1st Dept.), aff'd 18 N.Y.2d 659, 273 N.Y.S.2d 80, 219 N.E.2d 431 (1966). That privilege, however, does not extend to the degree of editing that occurred here especially in light of contractual provisions that limited the right to edit Monty Python material.

II

It also seems likely that appellants will succeed on the theory that, regardless of the right ABC had to broadcast an edited program, the cuts made constituted an actionable mutilation of Monty Python's work. This cause of action, which seeks redress for deformation of an artist's work, finds its roots in the continental concept of droit moral, or moral right, which may generally be summarized as including the right of the artist to have his work attributed to him in the form in which he created it. See 1 M. Nimmer, supra, at § 110.1.

---

[8] We also note that broadcast of the Monty Python specials was scheduled by ABC for an 11:30 p. m. to 1:00 a. m. time slot.

[9] Indeed, the scriptwriters' agreement permitted BBC to make "minor" changes without consulting Monty Python. See note 2, supra.

American copyright law, as presently written, does not recognize moral rights or provide a cause of action for their violation, since the law seeks to vindicate the economic, rather than the personal, rights of authors. Nevertheless, the economic incentive for artistic and intellectual creation that serves as the foundation for American copyright law, *Goldstein v. California,* 412 U.S. 546 (1973); *Mazer v. Stein,* 347 U.S. 201 (1954), cannot be reconciled with the inability of artists to obtain relief for mutilation or misrepresentation of their work to the public on which the artists are financially dependent. Thus courts have long granted relief for misrepresentation of an artist's work by relying on theories outside the statutory law of copyright, such as contract law, *Granz v. Harris,* 198 F.2d 585 (2d Cir. 1952) (substantial cutting of original work constitutes misrepresentation), or the tort of unfair competition, *Prouty v. National Broadcasting Co.,* 26 F.Supp. 265 (D.Mass.1939). See Strauss, The Moral Right of the Author 128-138, in Studies on Copyright (1963). Although such decisions are clothed in terms of proprietary right in one's creation, they also properly vindicate the author's personal right to prevent the presentation of his work to the public in a distorted form. See *Gardella v. Log Cabin Products Co.,* 89 F.2d 891, 895-96 (2d Cir. 1937); Roeder, The Doctrine of Moral Right, 53 Harv.L.Rev. 554, 568 (1940).

Here, the appellants claim that the editing done for ABC mutilated the original work and that consequently the broadcast of those programs as the creation of Monty Python violated the Lanham Act § 43(a), 15 U.S.C. § 1125(a).[10] This statute, the federal counterpart to state unfair competition laws, has been invoked to prevent misrepresentations that may injure plaintiff's business or personal reputation, even where no registered trademark is concerned. See *Mortellito v. Nina of California,* 335 F.Supp. 1238, 1294 (S.D.N.Y.1972). It is sufficient to violate the Act that a representation of a product, although technically true, creates a false impression of the product's origin. See *Rich v. RCA Corp.,* 390 F.Supp. 530 (S.D.N.Y.1975) (recent picture of plaintiff on cover of album containing songs recorded in distant past held to be a false representation that the songs were new); *Geisel v. Poynter Products, Inc.,* 283 F.Supp. 261, 267 (S.D.N.Y.1968).

These cases cannot be distinguished from the situation in which a television network broadcasts a program properly designated as having been written and performed by a group, but which has been edited, without the writer's consent, into a form that departs substantially from the original work. "To deform his work is to present him to the public as the creator of a work not his own, and thus makes him subject to criticism for work he has not done." Roeder, supra, at 569. In such a case, it is the writer or performer, rather than the network, who suffers the consequences of the mutilation, for the public will have only the final product by which to evaluate the work.[11] Thus, an allegation that a defendant has presented to the public a "garbled," *Granz v. Harris,* supra (Frank, J., concurring), distorted version of plaintiff's work seeks to redress the very rights

---

[10] That statute provides in part:

Any person who shall affix, apply, or annex, or use in connection with any goods or services, . . . a false designation of origin, or any false description or representation . . . and shall cause such goods or services to enter into commerce . . . shall be liable to a civil action by any person . . . who believes that he is or is likely to be damaged by the use of any such false description or representation.

[11] This result is not changed by the fact that the network, as here, takes public responsibility for editing. See *Rich v. RCA Corp.,* supra.

sought to be protected by the Lanham Act, 15 U.S.C. § 1125(a), and should be recognized as stating a cause of action under that statute. See *Autry v. Republic Productions, Inc.,* 213 F.2d 667 (9th Cir. 1954); *Jaeger v. American Intn'l Pictures, Inc.,* 330 F.Supp. 274 (S.D.N.Y.1971), which suggest the violation of such a right if mutilation could be proven.

During the hearing on the preliminary injunction, Judge Lasker viewed the edited version of the Monty Python program broadcast on December 26 and the original, unedited version. After hearing argument of this appeal, this panel also viewed and compared the two versions. We find that the truncated version at times omitted the climax of the skits to which appellants' rare brand of humor was leading and at other times deleted essential elements in the schematic development of a story line.[12] We therefore agree with Judge Lasker's conclusion that the edited version broadcast by ABC impaired the integrity of appellants' work and represented to the public as the product of appellants what was actually a mere caricature of their talents. We believe that a valid cause of action for such distortion exists and that therefore a preliminary injunction may issue to prevent repetition of the broadcast prior to final determination of the issues.[13]

[The court rejected ABC's claim that appellants were guilty of laches: "[W]e find no undue delay in the group's failure to institute this action until they were sufficiently advised regarding the facts necessary to support the action." It also held that the failure to name BBC and Time-Life as defendants was no bar to an injunction; they were not indispensable parties, since Monty Python rested its claim on its own copyright (not derived from the BBC's) and since it may secure complete relief by way of an injunction and damages against ABC alone.]

For these reasons we direct that the district court issue the preliminary injunction sought by the appellants.

Gurfein, Circuit Judge (concurring):

I concur in my brother Lumbard's scholarly opinion, but I wish to comment on the application of Section 43(a) of Lanham Act, 15 U.S.C. § 1125(a).

I believe that this is the first case in which a federal appellate court has held that there may be a violation of Section 43(a) of the Lanham Act with respect to a common-law copyright. The Lanham Act is a trademark statute, not a copyright statute. Nevertheless, we must recognize that the language of Section 43(a)

---

[12] A single example will illustrate the extent of distortion engendered by the editing. In one skit, an upper class English family is engaged in a discussion of the tonal quality of certain words as "woody" or "tinny." The father soon begins to suggest certain words with sexual connotations as either "woody" or "tinny," whereupon the mother fetches a bucket of water and pours it over his head. The skit continues from this point. The ABC edit eliminates this middle sequence so that the father is comfortably dressed at one moment and, in the next moment, is shown in a soaked condition without any explanation for the change in his appearance.

[13] Judge Gurfein's concurring opinion suggests that since the gravamen of a complaint under the Lanham Act is that the origin of goods has been falsely described, a legend disclaiming Monty Python's approval of the edited version would preclude violation of that Act. We are doubtful that a few words could erase the indelible impression that is made by a television broadcast, especially since the viewer has no means of comparing the truncated version with the complete work in order to determine for himself the talents of plaintiffs. Furthermore, a disclaimer such as the one originally suggested by Judge Lasker in the exigencies of an impending broadcast last December would go unnoticed by viewers who tuned into the broadcast a few minutes after it began.

We therefore conclude that Judge Gurfein's proposal that the district court could find some form of disclaimer would be sufficient might not provide appropriate relief.

is broad. It speaks of the affixation or use of false designations of origin or false descriptions or representations, but proscribes such use "in connection with any goods or services." It is easy enough to incorporate trade names as well as trademarks into Section 43(a) and the statute specifically applies to common law trademarks, as well as registered trademarks. Lanham Act § 45, 15 U.S.C. § 1127.

In the present case, we are holding that the deletion of portions of the recorded tape constitutes a breach of contract, as well as an infringement of a common-law copyright of the original work. There is literally no need to discuss whether plaintiffs also have a claim for relief under the Lanham Act or for unfair competition under New York law. I agree with Judge Lumbard, however, that it may be an exercise of judicial economy to express our view on the Lanham Act claim, and I do not dissent therefrom. I simply wish to leave it open for the District Court to fashion the remedy.

The Copyright Act provides no recognition of the so-called *droit moral,* or moral right of authors. Nor are such rights recognized in the field of copyright law in the United States. See 1 *Nimmer on Copyright,* § 110.2 (1975 ed.). If a distortion or truncation in connection with a use constitutes an infringement of copyright, there is no need for an additional cause of action beyond copyright infringement. *Id.* at § 110.3. An obligation to mention the name of the author carriers the implied duty, however, as a matter of contract, not to make such changes in the work as would render the credit line a false attribution of authorship, *Granz v. Harris,* 198 F.2d 585 (2d Cir. 1952).

So far as the Lanham Act is concerned, it is not a substitute for *droit moral* which authors in Europe enjoy. If the licensee may, by contract, distort the recorded work, the Lanham Act does not come into play. If the licensee has no such right by contract, there will be a violation in breach of contract. The Lanham Act can hardly apply literally when the credit line correctly states the work to be that of the plaintiffs which, indeed it is, so far as it goes. The vice complained of is that the truncated version is not what the plaintiffs wrote. But the Lanham Act does not deal with artistic integrity. It only goes to misdescription of origin and the like. See *Societe Comptoir De L'Industrie Cotonniere Etablissements Boussac v. Alexander's Dept. Stores, Inc.,* 299 F.2d 33, 36 (2d Cir. 1962).

The misdescription of origin can be dealt with, as Judge Lasker did below, by devising an appropriate legend to indicate that the plaintiffs had not approved the editing of the ABC version.[1] With such a legend, there is no conceivable violation of the Lanham Act. If plaintiffs complain that their artistic integrity is still compromised by the distorted version, their claim does not lie under the Lanham Act, which does not protect the copyrighted work itself but protects only against the misdescription or mislabelling.

So long as it is made clear that the ABC version is not approved by the Monty Python group, there is no misdescription of origin. So far as the content of the broadcast itself is concerned, that is not within the proscription of the Lanham Act when there is no misdescription of the authorship.

I add this brief explanation because I do not believe that the Lanham Act claim necessarily requires the drastic remedy of permanent injunction. That form of ultimate relief must be found in some other fountainhead of equity jurisprudence.

---

[1] I do not imply that the appropriate legend be shown only at the beginning of the broadcast. That is a matter for the District Court.

QUESTIONS

1. What copyright was considered infringed in the "Monty Python" case? Under the court's analysis, is the BBC an infringer?

2. What contractual provision was violated? Was the existence of a contractual restriction crucial to the result?

3. Does this opinion recognize "moral right" as part of copyright? Is not any unauthorized editing on the part of ABC — whether that editing makes Monty Python look better or worse — today an infringing derivative work under § 106(2)?

4. Does the plaintiff gain anything when the court articulates an alternative theory of liability, *i.e.*, that editing which makes Monty Python look worse (is that indeed an element of the court's Lanham Act theory?) is a violation of the Lanham Act? Would the court have granted recovery under the Lanham Act if the Monty Python script had not been properly copyrighted and was in the public domain?

5. Why wasn't a disclaimer sufficient relief, as Judge Gurfein suggested? What are the disadvantages of disclaimers from the point of view of a plaintiff or a defendant?

PROPOSED FEDERAL MORAL RIGHTS BILL

96TH CONGRESS
1ST SESSION

H. R. 288

To amend the copyright law to secure the rights of authors of pictorial, graphic, or sculptural works to prevent the distortion, mutilation, or other alteration of such works, and for other purposes.

IN THE HOUSE OF REPRESENTATIVES

JANUARY 15, 1979

Mr. DRINAN introduced the following bill; which was referred to the Committee on the Judiciary

---

A BILL

To amend the copyright law to secure the rights of authors of pictorial, graphic, or sculptural works to prevent the distortion, mutilation, or other alteration of such works, and for other purposes.

1   *Be it enacted by the Senate and House of Representa-*

2   *tives of the United States of America in Congress assembled,*

3   SECTION 1. This Act may be cited as the "Visual Artists

4   Moral Rights Amendment of 1979".

5   SEC. 2. Section 113 of Public Law 94–553 (90 Stat.

6   2541) is amended by adding at the end thereof the follow-

7   ing new subsection:

8   "(d) Independently of the author's copyright in a pic-

9   torial, graphic, or sculptural work, the author or the author's

I—O

2

1 legal representative shall have the right, during the life of

2 the author and fifty years after the author's death, to claim

3 authorship of such work and to object to any distortion,

4 mutilation, or other alteration thereof, and to enforce any

5 other limitation recorded in the Copyright Office that would

6 prevent prejudice to the author's honor or reputation.".

O

QUESTIONS

1. Is it constitutional for Congress to deal with the issue of moral rights as part of legislation dealing with copyright?

2. Is the cause of action granted here any more than one for defamation? If it is not, then what protection beyond defamation is to be accorded under the phrase "prejudice to the author's honor or reputation"? Regardless of whether the statute is merely creating a federal cause of action for artistic defamation, what is the constitutional source of power for Congress so to declare?

3. Does this bill conflict unduly with the policies underlying the first amendment and the doctrine of fair use?

4. Is it constitutional to limit the protection under this bill to the author of a pictorial work, to the exclusion of authors of literary works, musical works, choreographic works, motion pictures, etc.?

5. Is there any justification, other than statutory symmetry, for Congress to declare that the moral right is to survive for the life of the author plus fifty years? (Presumably, as to works in their first or second term of statutory copyright on January 1, 1978, the moral right will in almost all instances outlive the period of conventional copyright.)

6. What, under the Drinan bill, would be the effect of the author's "claiming" authorship or "objecting" to any distortion? Presumably, some remedies are contemplated. All of those catalogued in Chapter 5 of the 1976 Act?

7. Would an unauthorized derivative work based on a copyrighted work be an "alteration" forbidden by the Drinan bill? If so, would the cause of action given to the "owner of copyright" under the 1976 Act and the cause of action given to the "author" under this bill result in double liability?

CALIFORNIA CIVIL CODE

§ 987. Preservation of works of art

(a) Legislative findings and declaration

(a) The Legislature hereby finds and declares that the physical alteration or destruction of fine art, which is an expression of the artist's personality, is detrimental to the artist's reputation, and artists therefore have an interest in protecting their works of fine art against such alteration or destruction; and that there is also a public interest in preserving the integrity of cultural and artistic creations.

(b) Definitions

(b) As used in this section:

(1) "Artist" means the individual or individuals who create a work of fine art.

(2) "Fine art" means an original painting, sculpture, or drawing of recognized quality, but shall not include work prepared under contract for commercial use by its purchaser.

(3) "Person" means an individual, partnership, corporation, association or other group, however organized.

(4) "Frame" means to prepare, or cause to be prepared, a work of fine art for display in a manner customarily considered to be appropriate for a work of fine art in the particular medium.

(5) "Restore" means to return, or cause to be returned, a deteriorated or damaged work of fine art as nearly as is feasible to its original state or condition, in accordance with prevailing standards.

(6) "Conserve" means to preserve, or cause to be preserved, a work of fine art by retarding or preventing deterioration or damage through appropriate treatment in accordance with prevailing standards in order to maintain the structural integrity to the fullest extent possible in an unchanging state.

(c) Mutilation, alteration or destruction of a work

(c) (1) No person, except an artist who owns and possesses a work of fine art which the artist has created, shall intentially commit, or authorize the intentional commission of, any physical defacement, mutilation, alteration, or destruction of a work of fine art.

(2) In addition to the prohibitions contained in paragraph (1), no person who frames, conserves, or restores a work of fine art shall commit, or authorize the commission of, any physical defacement, mutilation, alteration, or destruction of a work of fine art by any act constituting gross negligence. For purposes of this section, the term "gross negligence" shall mean the exercise of so slight a degree of care as to justify the belief that there was an indifference to the particular work of fine art.

(d) Authorship

(d) The artist shall retain at all times the right to claim authorship, or, for just and valid reason, to disclaim authorship of his or her work of fine art.

(e) Remedies

(e) To effectuate the rights created by this section, the artist may commence an action to recover or obtain any of the following:

(1) Injunctive relief.

(2) Actual damages.

(3) Punitive damages. In the event that punitive damages are awarded, the court shall, in its discretion, select an organization or organizations engaged in charitable or educational activities involving the fine arts in California to receive such damages.

(4) Reasonable attorneys' and expert witness fees.

(5) Any other relief which the court deems proper.

(f) Determination of recognized quality

(f) In determining whether a work of fine art is of recognized quality, the trier of fact shall rely on the opinions of artists, art dealers, collectors of fine art, curators of art museums, and other persons involved with the creation or marketing of fine art.

(g) Rights and duties

(g) The rights and duties created under this section:

(1) Shall, with respect to the artist, or if any artist is deceased, his heir, legatee, or personal representative, exist until the 50th anniversary of the death of such artist.

(2) Shall exist in addition to any other rights and duties which may now or in the future be applicable.

(3) Except as provided in paragraph (1) of subdivision (h), may not be waived except by an instrument in writing expressly so providing which is signed by the artist.

(h) Removal from building: waiver

(h) (1) If a work of fine art cannot be removed from a building without substantial physical defacement, mutilation, alteration, or destruction of such work, the rights and duties created under this section, unless expressly reserved by an instrument in writing signed by the owner of such building and properly recorded, shall be deemed waived. Such instrument, if properly recorded, shall be binding on subsequent owners of such building.

(2) If the owner of a building wishes to remove a work of fine art which is a part of such building but which can be removed from the building without substantial harm to such fine art, the rights and duties created under this section shall apply unless the owner has diligently attempted without success to notify the artist, or, if the artist is deceased, his heir, legatee, or personal representative, in writing of his intended action affecting the work of fine art, or unless he did provide notice and that person failed within 90 days either to remove the work or to pay for its removal. If such work is removed at the expense of the artist, his heir, legatee, or personal representative, title to such fine art shall pass to that person.

(3) Nothing in this subdivision shall affect the rights of authorship created in subdivision (d) of this section.

(i) Limitation of actions

(i) No action may be maintained to enforce any liability under this section unless brought within three years of the act complained of or one year after discovery of such act whichever is longer.

(j) Operative date

(j) This section shall become operative on January 1, 1980, and shall apply to claims based on proscribed acts occurring on or after that date to works of fine art whenever created.

(k) Severability

(k) If any provision of this section or the application thereof to any person or circumstance is held invalid for any reason, such invalidity shall not affect any other provisions or applications of this section which can be effected without the invalid provision or application, and to this end the provisions of this section are severable. [1979 ch 409 § 1.]

QUESTIONS

1. Is this a "moral rights" law? If so, why isn't this time-honored phrase used?

2. Does this statute impinge on the rights of Congress to regulate rights in works of fine art? Recognizing that this question anticipates the problem of federal preemption, see Chapter 8 *infra,* does the supposed need for an amendment such as the Drinan bill, *supra,* and its language help furnish an answer?

3. How is a trier of fact to implement subsection (f) requiring it to "rely" on certain expert opinions?

D. THE RIGHT TO DISTRIBUTE UNDER § 106(3)

HOUSE REPORT

H.R. Rep. No. 94-1476, 94th Cong., 2d Sess. 62 (1976)

Public distribution. — Clause (3) of section 106 establishes the exclusive right of publication: The right "to distribute copies or phonorecords of the copyrighted work to the public by sale or other transfer of ownership, or by rental, lease, or lending." Under this provision the copyright owner would have the right to control the first public distribution of an authorized copy or phonorecord of his work, whether by sale, gift, loan, or some rental or lease arrangement. Likewise, any unauthorized public distribution of copies or phonorecords that were unlawfully made would be an infringement. As section 109 makes clear, however, the copyright owner's rights under section 106(3) cease with respect to a particular copy or phonorecord once he has parted with ownership of it.

FAWCETT PUBLICATIONS, INC. v. ELLIOT PUBLISHING CO.

46 F. Supp. 717 (S.D.N.Y. 1942)

CLANCY, DISTRICT JUDGE. This is a motion for summary judgment made by the plaintiff, the action being for an alleged infringement of a copyright. We note that the plaintiff states there is also involved a claim for unfair competition, but we find no such claim in the pleadings.

The plaintiff is engaged in the magazine publishing business as is the defendant. The plaintiff, on or about April 18, 1941, being then the author and proprietor of a publication known as "Wow Comics, No. 2 Summer Edition," copyrighted it and was, therefore, entitled to the exclusive right to print, reprint, publish, copy and vend it. Subsequent to this publication's issuance the defendant purchased secondhand copies of it and of another copyrighted publication of the plaintiff, which he makes the subject of the second cause of action, and bound them together with other comic publications not owned or copyrighted by the plaintiff within one copyrighted cover of its own with the words "Double Comics" thereon.

Section 1 of Title 17, U.S.C.A. grants to the copyright owner the exclusive right "to print, reprint, publish, copy, and vend the copyrighted work . . . ." The alleged infringement as set forth in the complaint is that the defendant published and placed upon the market said "Double Comics" containing the complete issue of plaintiff's publication, without its consent or approval, so that as thus limited, it must be determined whether the defendant violated the plaintiff's admitted exclusive right to publish and secondly to vend. The decision appears to be uniform that the purpose and effect of the copyright statute is to secure to the owner thereof the exclusive right to multiply copies. *Bobbs-Merrill Co. v. Straus,* 210 U. S. 339; *Jeweler's Circular Pub. Co. v. Keystone Pub. Co.,* 281 F. 83 (C.C.A. 2d), Cert. Den'd. 259 U. S. 581. It is conceded here that the defendant has not multiplied copies but merely resold the plaintiff's under a different cover. The exclusive right to vend is limited. It is confined to the first sale of any one copy and exerts no restriction on the future sale of that copy. *Bureau of National Literature v. Sells,* 211 F. 379; *Strauss v. American Publishers Ass'n.,* 231 U. S. 222; *Bentley v. Tibbals,* 223 F. 247 (C.C.A. 2d). The defendant is not charged with copying, reprinting or rearranging the copyrighted material of the plaintiff or any of its component parts nor has it removed the plaintiff's copyright notice.

The motion is denied.

[on reargument]

Because of a dearth of authority we have heard reargument in this case. We are not convinced that the copyright of a book or periodical includes the cover. We can think of no convincing reason why it should, or should be intended to do so since the law itself requires the presence of the notice on the title page or the one next to it and since the cover ordinarily has no literary copyrightable matter and, when an individual design is embodied in it, its relation to the copyrighted literary content is remote and its authorship and ownership do not prima facie appear as in the case of the book's contents. We will, therefore, adhere to our earlier decision.

The plaintiff is in serious difficulty by adopting the form appended to the Federal Rules of Civil Procedure. It is unfortunate, but we think the heading of the form employed by him is misleading. Nevertheless, we cannot accede to the theory that he has pleaded an action for unfair competition. *Washburn v. Moorman,* S. D. Cal., November 9, 1938. Inasmuch as there is little doubt that he has a valid action for unfair competition and in view of his insistence that it is pleaded in the complaint before me, I will accept that insistence as an application for permission to amend his complaint to incorporate a cause of action for unfair competition and grant such an application and permit him to serve an amended complaint.

NATIONAL GEOGRAPHIC SOCIETY v. CLASSIFIED GEOGRAPHIC, INC.

27 F. Supp. 655 (D. Mass. 1939)

BREWSTER, DISTRICT JUDGE. This is an action brought for injunctive and other relief against a corporate defendant and three individuals controlling said corporation.

The action is brought under the copyright and trade-mark statutes and also is based on allegations of unfair competition.

The facts are not in dispute. They are fairly and fully stated in plaintiff's brief and are abundantly supported by evidence.

1. The National Geographic Society is a scientific and educational institution, not organized for profit, which was originally incorporated under the laws of the District of Columbia in 1888. Its object is to gather and diffuse geographic knowledge. Since 1889, one of its chief vehicles for diffusing geographic knowledge has been, and still is, The National Geographic Magazine, which is published monthly by plaintiff.

2. In its work of gathering and diffusing geographic knowledge, plaintiff has conducted and sponsored numerous research expeditions, the work of which is described in its magazine. In carrying out this work and publishing The National Geographic Magazine, plaintiff has expended many millions of dollars. All of the component parts of The National Geographic Magazine are covered by copyrights under the Federal Copyright Law.

3. Over a long period of years plaintiff has compiled, adapted, arranged and published in book form material that has appeared in its Magazine. The National Geographic Magazine, and those publications, adaptations, and arrangements in book form, in turn, have been copyrighted under the provisions of Section 6 of that Copyright Law and offered for sale to the public. Among such compilations of the plaintiff are, "The Book of Birds," "Our Insect Friends and Foes and Spiders," "The Book of Fishes," "The Book of Dogs," "Horses of the World," and "Cattle of the World."

. . . .

5. In addition, the plaintiff conducts a School Service Department, which provides teachers and scholars with weekly bulletins and also it is prepared to furnish information to teachers and others on matters of the geographic nature. Much of the material for this service is compiled, abridged, or arranged from articles which have appeared or are about to appear in the Magazine.

. . . .

7. The defendant, Classified Geographic, Inc., is a corporation organized and existing under the laws of the Commonwealth of Massachusetts. Its chief business is the adaptation, arrangement, and compilation of material which has appeared in The National Geographic Magazine, the publication of that material as adapted, arranged, and compiled in book or pamphlet form and the sale of such books and pamphets to the general public. Defendant, Classified Geographic, Inc., does not reprint any of said material but obtains all of such material from copies of The National Geographic Magazine, which it has purchased in various markets and which it treats as second-hand property. Defendant, Classified Geographic, Inc., classifies the articles in these various magazines under topical subjects, tears the magazine apart, segregates the particular articles desired, then brings the articles under each one of the particular topics together for publication in book form, binds them in a substantial backing and finally

offers them for sale as an original compilation of articles from The National Geographic Magazine. Likewise, it takes from the magazines which it has purchased individual articles on various topics and publishes them in a pasteboard binding and offers them for sale in such changed form.

. . . .

9. Defendant, Classified Geographic, Inc., has adapted, arranged, compiled, published, and offered for sale copyrighted material taken from plaintiff's magazine, The National Geographic Magazine, in book form under the subjects of "Birds," "Fish," and "Domestic Animals and Insects," large portions of which copyrighted material also had been adapted, arranged, compiled, published, and offered for sale by plaintiff in its volumes hereinbefore referred to. As to a large portion of the material contained in all of the volumes of articles from The National Geographic Magazine published by the corporate defendant, there is no notice to the public in those volumes that the material has been copyrighted by the plaintiff although, in fact, all of it has been so copyrighted.

. . . .

Plaintiff seeks relief on three grounds: (1) infringement of plaintiff's copyright, (2) violation of plaintiff's trade-mark, and (3) unfair competition.

The defendant contends, on the other hand, that as owner of second-hand copies of The National Geographic Magazine, lawfully acquired, it does not impinge on any exclusive right of plaintiff by breaking down, rearranging, binding, and selling the copyrighted material. With equal confidence they claim that these operations do not constitute acts of unfair competition.

The Copyright Act of 1909 gives to any person entitled thereto the exclusive right "to publish" and "vend" the copyrighted work (17 U.S.C.A. 1). Section 3 of the Act further provided as follows:

> *Protection of component parts of work copyrighted; composite works or periodicals.* The copyright provided by this title shall protect all the copyrightable component parts of the work copyrighted, and all matter therein in which copyright is already subsisting, but without extending the duration or scope of such copyright. The copyright upon composite works or periodicals shall give to the proprietor thereof all the rights in respect thereto which he would have if each part were individually copyrighted under this title.

I am of the opinion that the arrangement of the defendant's material with the prefatory matter was intended to be, and was, a new publication of copyrighted material which invaded plaintiff's exclusive right to publish not only the magazine but also the books published by it in which it had compiled articles taken from the magazines. *United States v. Williams,* 3 F. 484.

> In its ordinary acceptation, the word "publication" means "the act of publishing a thing or making it public; offering to public notice; or rendering it accessible to public scrutiny." In copyright law it is "the act of making public a book; that is, offering or communicating it to the public by sale or distribution of copies." *D'Ole v. Kansas City Star Co.,* 94 F. 840, 842.

This is precisely what the defendant corporation has been doing with material taken from copyrighted magazines. I do not think the definition can be limited to the first publications only, when considered in the light of other provisions of the copyright law, hereafter noted.

The Act gives to the plaintiff the exclusive right to compile, adapt, or arrange its copyrighted work, to grant that privilege to others and, by necessary implication, it has the right to refuse its consent to any compilation, adaptation, or arrangement by others of the copyrighted work. This follows from the provisions of section 5 (a) which permits the copyrighting of books and other compilations; and also from the provisions of section 6, which reads as follows:

SEC. 6. *Copyright on compilations of works in public domain or of copyrighted works; subsisting copyrights not affected.* Compilations or abridgements, adaptations, arrangements, dramatizations, translations, or other versions of works in the public domain, or of copyrighted works when produced with the consent of the proprietor of the copyright in such works, or works republished with new matter, shall be regarded as new works subject to copyright under the provisions of this title: but the publication of any such new works shall not affect the force or validity of any subsisting copyright upon the matter employed or any part thereof, or be construed to imply an exclusive right to such use of the original works, or to secure or extend copyright in such original works.

It cannot be successfully denied that the use made of the material taken from the second-hand copies of the magazine amounted to a "compilation" or an "adaptation" or an "arrangement" of copyrighted works, within the usual and ordinary meaning of those words. It is established by the evidence that plaintiff not only refused to give its consent to this use, but notified the defendant in writing that it would regard such use as an infringement of its rights.

Sec. 41 of the Act provides as follows:

SEC. 41. *Copyright distinct from property in object copyrighted; effect of sale of object, and of assignment of copyright.* The copyright is distinct from the property in the material object copyrighted, and the sale or conveyance, by gift or otherwise, of the material object shall not of itself constitute a transfer of the copyright: nor shall the assignment of the copyright constitute a transfer of the title to the material object; but nothing in this title shall be deemed to forbid, prevent, or restrict the transfer of any copy of a copyrighted work the possession of which has been lawfully obtained.

It is clear that the Act distinguishes between the ownership of copyright and ownership of the material copyrighted by providing that the sale of the object shall not of itself constitute a transfer of the copyright, but the section recognizes the right of a lawful owner to transfer a copy of the copyrighted work.

Defendants argue that as an incident to the ownership of the magazines the owner may make a recompilation, or re-arrangement, of the material and publish it in the form of a book or pamphlet so long as he does not copy or reprint any part of the articles used.

The defendant's attorney concedes that he has been unable to find any case exactly in point. Decisions supporting the proposition that an owner of a copyrighted publication may resell it in its original form are clearly not in point. The right of an owner to restore a second-hand book to its original condition, so far as cover and binding are concerned, is established. *Doan v. American Book Co.,* 105 F. 772; *Bureau of National Literature v. Sells et al.,* 211 F. 379; *Ginn & Co. v. Apollo Pub. Co.,* 215 F. 772.

But such restoration may lay the dealer open to the charge of unfair competition if he sells the book without distinctive notice to the public that the book is a renovated work. *Ginn & Co. v. Apollo Pub. Co., supra; Doan v. American Book Co., supra.*

The right, however, to renovate and resell copyrighted works does not extend to printing, or replacing, pages lost or mutilated. *Ginn & Co. v. Apollo Pub. Co., supra.*

The case nearest in point is *Kipling v. G. P. Putnam's Sons,* 120 F. 631, where it appeared that unbound volumes were bound and resold. The court held there was no infringement of the copyright, but it is to be noted that these unbound volumes were purchased from the copyright proprietor, or his licensee, and it is difficult to escape the conclusion that the compilation was with the consent of the proprietor. In the case at bar, there was no such consent.

My conclusion, therefore, is that the compiling of the articles from plaintiff's magazines in book, or pamphlet form, and the sale of them, infringes plaintiff's exclusive right, secured by its copyright.

QUESTIONS

1. Had the defendant sold the back issues, or even individual articles from those issues, singly, would it have infringed plaintiff's copyright? Ought it not to follow, therefore, that there was no infringement in this case? Is any significant interest of the plaintiff impaired in the latter case that is not in the former?

2. Was the court's reference to § 6 of the 1909 Copyright Act, which became § 7 of that law and is parallel to § 103 of the 1976 Act, in any way pertinent to the question whether the defendant had infringed the plaintiff's copyright?

3. The defendant in *National Geographic* seems to have contributed more to its finished product than the defendant in the "Double Comics" case. Which way should this fact cut?

4. Of what significance would alleged inferiority of defendant's work be in *National Geographic?* Does the "Double Comics" opinion throw any light on this?

5. Plaintiff's dish towels contain copyrighted designs of strawberries on two panels. One panel on each towel contains a copyright notice in plaintiff's name. Defendant purchases the towels at retail, cuts each in half, combines each half with a matching solid-colored panel without design, and uses each combination as the cover of a handbag which it then markets. Does this constitute copyright infringement? Does sale of the panel *without* the copyright notice constitute fraudulent removal of notice in violation of § 506(d)? Does sale of the panel *with* the copyright notice violate any other right of plaintiff? *Cf. Scarves by Vera, Inc. v. American Handbag, Inc.,* 188 F. Supp. 255 (S.D.N.Y. 1960).

6. Suppose a bookstore receives from a publisher copyrighted prints picturing the mansion which is the setting of a novel. The bookstore is to distribute the print only as a premium with the purchase of copies of the novel; but instead it sells the prints. Does the publisher have a claim for copyright infringement, or for anything else? *Cf. Burke & Van Heusen, Inc. v. Arrow Drug, Inc.,* 233 F. Supp. 881 (E.D. Pa. 1964).

7. A motion picture theater, given a license to exhibit a picture starting on a Sunday, jumps the gun and begins exhibiting it on the preceding Friday evening. Is there copyright infringement? *Cf. Inge v. Twentieth Century Fox Film Corp.,* 143 F. Supp. 294 (S.D.N.Y. 1956).

Platt & Munk Co. v. Republic Graphics, Inc., 315 F.2d 847 (2d Cir. 1963). The plaintiff is a publisher and distributor of educational toys; it entered into a contract with the defendant to manufacture a number of items (a map puzzle, the "Blackboard Library," and the "I Can Print" toy) in which plaintiff owned copyright. When the defendant attempted to make delivery of the manufactured items, the plaintiff refused to accept, contending that they were improperly and poorly manufactured in breach of contract. When Republic asserted its intention to protect itself through a summary sale (i.e., without prior judicial proceedings) of the merchandise, as permitted by the New York Personal Property Law and Lien Law, Platt & Munk brought an action for damages for contract breach and for an injunction against the sale as an infringement of copyright. Plaintiff relied on § 1(a) of the 1909 Act, granting the exclusive right to "vend" the copyrighted work; defendant relied on § 27, which provided, in part, that "nothing in this title shall be deemed to forbid, prevent, or restrict the transfer of any copy of a copyrighted work the possession of which has been lawfully obtained." Although the court acknowledged that § 27 had been commonly understood to adopt the "first sale" doctrine — i.e., that the copyright owner retained the exclusive right to vend until it had itself made or authorized a first voluntary sale for a price — it was not prepared to read this principle so broadly as to render copyrighted goods totally immune "from the ordinary obligations of commercial life, such as judicial sales on execution or foreclosure . . . ." In these latter cases, it might be rationalized that the copyright owner has received from his creditor some value for which the copyrighted article is now demanded, so that one can find an "involuntary sale" by the copyright owner, or presumed consent, or estoppel.

The court considered, and rejected, the defendant's argument that it had title to the manufactured goods and therefore that Platt & Munk's exclusive right to vend never attached. "If the raw materials that went into the goods had been supplied by Platt & Munk instead of Republic, title would have been in the former rather than the latter . . . . Yet it would seem exceedingly odd that copyright protection should turn on which party has furnished the physical stuff to which the copyrighted conception is affixed — with the protection lost if the author does not assume a role for which others are usually better suited." The court agreed, however, with the defendant that its right to sell the goods might arise from a contractual default by Platt & Munk, as provided by state law, were it not for the fact that the state law granted the right of resale to the unpaid seller without any prior judicial determination that Platt & Munk was in default or that Republic had a valid lien on the goods. "Where the copyright owner makes a good faith claim that its failure to pay for the goods was justified, the manufacturer ought not be allowed to resort to the normal remedy of self-help with the result of impairing the rights granted by the federal copyright law; to that extent state contract or lien law must yield to the federally created right."

The court invited Republic to file a compulsory counterclaim for the purchase price, and directed the trial court to determine promptly thereafter whether Platt & Munk was justified in refusing to accept the goods; if it was not, then the temporary injunction granted below was to be lifted, permitting Republic to sell, unless within fifteen days thereafter Platt & Munk paid the full price with interest.

QUESTION

The court in *Platt & Munk* fashioned a compromise between the interests of the copyright owner and the unpaid contractor: the contractor retains his lien but must (unlike the manufacturers of most classes of chattels, who enjoy summary remedies) judicially establish its right thereto before enforcing it by resale. Would the result likely be the same under § 109 of the 1976 Act? (Consider in particular the court's discussion regarding which party was the owner of the "physical stuff" of which the "copyrighted" goods were made.)

BURDEN OF PROOF IN § 106(3) CASES

The student is advised to reread § 109 and the House Report discussion reproduced at p. 63 *supra.*

In most infringement cases, there is no issue as to whether defendant is committing his or her accused acts with or without plaintiff's authority. Under § 109 permission to sell or distribute may not be necessary in the case of copies made under plaintiff's authority, but sale of copies not "lawfully made" can infringe under § 106(2). A copy may be lawfully made under authorization by the statute or the copyright owner. Who has the burden of proof on the latter issue? Must the plaintiff prove the copy being sold by defendant is unauthorized or must defendant show that the copy was authorized? This can be important in the case of motion picture prints since neither party may know the complete geneology of the print.

In *American International Pictures, Inc. v. Foreman,* 400 F. Supp. 928, 188 USPQ 249 (S.D. Ala. 1975), *rev'd,* 198 USPQ 580 (5th Cir. 1978), an effort by eight motion picture companies against a 16-mm. film dealer initially failed because of the court's determination that plaintiffs had the burden of proving that defendant did *not* have lawful possession of the prints in question. The burden of proof was crucial because of the inability of both sides to trace the lineage of the prints. The court made "the nonoccurrence of a 'first sale' part and parcel of the plaintiff's case," finding that such a requirement was consistent with the purpose of the copyright laws to balance the reward of creative effort against the promotion of broad public availability for the results of such efforts.

This approach was pushed to the extreme in the criminal context by the Court of Appeals for the Ninth Circuit in *United States v. Wise,* 550 F.2d 1180, 194 USPQ 59 (9th Cir. 1977). The court held that the government partially failed to sustain its burden of showing nonoccurrence of a first sale because of (1) a contractual provision contemplating the sale of prints of one film to a television licensee and (2) the furnishing of a print of another film to a movie star in "a transaction strongly resembling a sale with restrictions on the use of print." *Accord, United States v. Atherton,* 561 F.2d 747, 195 USPQ 615 (9th Cir. 1977). Cf. *United States v. Bily,* 406 F. Supp. 726, 188 USPQ 344 (E.D. Pa. 1975) (probable cause not shown for search warrant because of failure of government to show that defendant had either manufactured the films or had not lawfully obtained them).

The House Report accompanying the 1976 Act went to some lengths to criticize this allocation of burden of proof as reflected in the *Foreman* case, announcing that "[i]t is the intent of the Committee, therefore, that in an action to determine whether a defendant is entitled to the privilege established by section 109(a) and (b), the burden of proving whether a particular copy was lawfully made or acquired should rest on the defendant." H.R. Rep. No. 94-1496, *supra* at 81.

On appeal of *Foreman,* the Court of Appeals for the Fifth Circuit found that § 109(c) of the 1976 Act and the House report criticism of the district court opinion "obviated" this question under the new Act. In reversing the 1909 Act decision, the appellate court spoke of the burden on defendant to show authority flowing from the owner and then found:

> Whether the occurrence of a first sale is an affirmative defense on which the defendant bears the burden of proof or is an element of the plaintiffs' case, the plaintiffs here came forward with evidence — the copyright certificates

and a course of conduct consistent with retaining all the rights therein granted — that no first sale had occurred.

576 F.2d 661 (5th Cir. 1978).

The court noted that the rules in criminal cases might have to be different because of due process requirements.

QUESTIONS

1. How does the plaintiff's introduction into evidence of its certificate of copyright tend to prove that no "first sale" was made?

2. What weight should properly be given the passages from the House Committee Report in construing § 109(c) of the 1976 Act?

PUBLIC LENDING RIGHT AND DROIT DE SUITE

Should the first-sale doctrine be modified by the creation of a statutory right of the copyright owner to receive a royalty each time a copy of his or her work (lawfully made and lawfully obtained) is resold or lent? Consider the following passages from Chapter II, p. 24 of the Draft Second Supplementary Report of the Register of Copyrights (Oct.-Dec. 1975):

> In his testimony before the House Subcommittee on June 5, 1975, Professor Rondo Cameron, appearing as an ordinary citizen as well as a teacher, research scholar, and author, urged that the bill provide for the payment of royalties for the commercial resale, through large, organized markets, of "used or 'second hand' books, especially textbooks." . . . The proposal that royalties be imposed on the large-scale commercial resale of used copies of textbooks and other works received no support; it runs counter to the traditional "first-sale" doctrine of copyright law embodied in section 109(a), which has attracted no opposition. In fairness, however, it should be noted that, purely as a legal concept, the idea is not unthinkable. Other countries are beginning to experiment with analogous systems, such as the "public lending right," involving library lending, and the "droit de suite," involving an artist's participation in the proceeds of later sales of a work of art. There is little doubt that, as technology continues to erode authors' ability to control various uses of their works, additional points at which control can be exercised will be sought.

Would you favor such a public lending right? If not, why? If so, try your hand at drafting statutory language. Consider, too, the recently enacted "droit de suite" statute in California:

CALIFORNIA CIVIL CODE

§ 986. Work of fine art; sale; payment of percentage to artist or deposit for Arts Council; failure to pay; action for damages; exemptions

(a) Whenever a work of fine art is sold and the seller resides in California or the sale takes place in California, the seller or his agent shall pay to the artist of such work of fine art or to such artist's agent 5 percent of the amount of such sale. The right of the artist to receive an amount equal to 5 percent of the amount of such sale is not transferable and may be waived only by a contract in writing providing for an amount in excess of 5 percent of the amount of such sale.

(1) When a work of art is sold at an auction or by a gallery, dealer, broker, museum, or other person acting as the agent for the seller the agent shall withhold 5 percent of the amount of the sale, locate the artist and pay the artist.

(2) If the seller or agent is unable to locate and pay the artist within 90 days, an amount equal to 5 percent of the amount of the sale shall be transferred to the Arts Council.

(3) If a seller or his agent fails to pay an artist the amount equal to 5 percent of the sale of a work of fine art by the artist or fails to transfer such amount to the Arts Council, the artist may bring an action for damages within three years after the date of sale or one year after the discovery of the sale, whichever is longer.

(4) Moneys received by the council pursuant to this section shall be deposited in an account in the Special Deposit Fund in the State Treasury.

(5) The Arts Council shall attempt to locate any artist for whom money is received pursuant to this section. If the council is unable to locate the artist and the artist does not file a written claim for the money received by the council within seven years of the date of sale of the work of fine art, the right of the artist terminates and such money shall be transferred to the operating fund of the council as reimbursement to fund programs of the council.

(6) Any amounts of money held by any seller or agent for the payment of artists pursuant to this section shall be exempt from attachment or execution of judgment by the creditors of such seller or agent.

(b) Subdivision (a) shall not apply to any of the following:

(1) To the initial sale of a work of fine art where legal title to such work at the time of such initial sale is vested in the artist thereof.

(2) To the resale of a work of fine art for a gross sales price of less than one thousand dollars ($1,000).

(3) To a resale after the death of such artist.

(4) To the resale of the work of fine art for a gross sales price less than the purchase price paid by the seller.

(5) To a transfer of a work of fine art which is exchanged for one or more works of fine art or for a combination of cash, other property, and one or more works of fine art where the fair market value of the property exchanged is less than one thousand dollars ($1,000).

(c) For purposes of this section, the following terms have the following meanings:

(1) "Artist" means the person who creates a work of fine art.

(2) "Fine art" means an original painting, sculpture, or drawing.

(d) The section shall become operative on January 1, 1977, and shall apply to works of fine art created before and after its operative date.

(e) If any provision of this section or the application thereof to any person or circumstances is held invalid for any reason, such invalidity shall not affect any other provisions or applications of this section which can be effected, without the invalid provision or application, and to this end the provisions of this section are severable. (Added by Stats. 1976, c. 1228, p. 5542, § 1.)

QUESTIONS

1. Could Congress enact a similar statute pursuant to the copyright clause of the Constitution?

2. Can it be reasonably argued that the California statute is in conflict with the federal Copyright Act, so that it is preempted under the supremacy clause of the Constitution? *See Morseburg v. Balyon,* 621 F.2d 972 (9th Cir.), *cert. denied,* 101 S. Ct. 399 (1980).

3. Might not California have better promoted its interests and those of its citizens by providing that the five percent resale right is to apply in all cases in which the artist is domiciled (or resident) in California? If so, why did it not do so? Does California violate the due process clause of the Constitution when it imposes a tax of this kind on one of its own residents (or indeed on even a nonresident seller, when the sale itself is in California) for the benefit of a nonresident artist?

4. How should a court determine whether a sale of a work of fine art "takes place" in California? If the owner of a work of art, living in New York, offers by mail to sell it to a person living in California, and the offeree sends a letter of acceptance from California, does the California statute apply?

E. PHONORECORDS AND SOUND RECORDINGS

1. COMPULSORY LICENSE TO MAKE PHONORECORDS OF NON-DRAMATIC MUSICAL COMPOSITIONS UNDER § 115

The concept of a compulsory license was introduced into our copyright law in 1909. The Supreme Court had already decided in *White-Smith Music Publishing Co. v. Apollo Co.,* 209 U.S. 1 (1908), that piano rolls (and by analogy phonograph records and the like) did not embody a system of notation that could be read and hence were not "copies" of the musical composition within the meaning of the law, but constituted merely parts of devices for mechanically performing the music. The exclusive right of the copyright owner to public performance already existed under the Act of 1897, and this undoubtedly included such *performance* by mechanical instruments. It was the right to *make* such devices that was lacking, and so Congress undertook to grant such right, but without intending to extend the right of copyright to the mechanical devices themselves. H.R. Rep. No. 2222, 60th Cong., 2d Sess. 9 (1909).

Because of what seemed at the time a well-grounded fear of monopolistic control of music for recording purposes, *id.,* Congress saw fit to qualify the right of mechanical control by providing in subsection (e) of § 1 that if the copyright proprietor himself used or sanctioned the use of his composition in this way, any other person was free to do so upon paying a royalty of two cents for each part (each roll or record) manufactured. A corresponding infringement provision was inserted in § 101(e). Mechanics were provided for the filing of notices by the compulsory licensor (notice of use) and licensee (notice of intention to use) and for payment.

These verbose and internally inconsistent provisions left many questions unanswered. However, the remarkable adjustment of the music industry to this unique provision resulted in its retention in 1976, but with changes designed to balance anew the competing interests and to answer some of these questions. See generally Rosenlund, *Compulsory Licensing of Musical Compositions for Phonorecords Under the Copyright Act of 1976,* 30 HASTINGS L.J. 683 (1979).

HOUSE REPORT

H.R. Rep. No. 94-1476, 94th Cong., 2d Sess. 107-11 (1976)

The provisions of sections 1(e) and 101(e) of the present law, establishing a system of compulsory licensing for the making and distribution of phonorecords of copyrighted music, are retained with a number of modifications in section 115 of the bill. Under these provisions, which represented a compromise of the most controversial issue of the 1909 act, a musical composition that has been reproduced in phonorecords with the permission of the copyright owner may generally be reproduced in phonorecords by another person, if that person notifies the copyright owner and pays a specified royalty.

The fundamental question of whether to retain the compulsory license or to do away with it altogether was a major issue during earlier stages of the program for general revision of the copyright law. At the hearings it was apparent that the argument on this point had shifted, and the real issue was not whether to retain the compulsory license but how much the royalty rate under it should be. The arguments for and against retention of the compulsory license are outlined at pages 66-67 of this Committee's 1967 report (H. Rept. No. 83, 90th Cong., 1st Sess.). The Committee's conclusion on this point remains the same as in 1967: "that a compulsory licensing system is still warranted as a condition for the rights of reproducing and distributing phonorecords of copyrighted music," but "that the present system is unfair and unnecessarily burdensome on copyright owners, and that the present statutory rate is too low."

Availability and scope of compulsory license

Subsection (a) of section 115 deals with three doubtful questions under the present law: (1) the nature of the original recording that will make the work available to others for recording under a compulsory license; (2) the nature of the sound recording that can be made under a compulsory license; and (3) the extent to which someone acting under a compulsory license can depart from the work as written or recorded without violating the copyright owner's right to make an "arrangement" or other derivative work. The first two of these questions are answered in clause (1) of section 115(a), and the third is the subject of clause (2).

The present law, though not altogether clear, apparently bases compulsory licensing on the making or licensing of the first recording, even if no authorized records are distributed to the public. The first sentence of section 115(a)(1) would change the basis for compulsory licensing to authorized public distribution of phonorecords (including disks and audio tapes but not the sound tracks or other sound records accompanying a motion picture or other audiovisual work). Under the clause, a compulsory license would be available to anyone as soon as "phonorecords of a nondramatic musical work have been distributed to the public in the United States under the authority of the copyright owner."

The second sentence of clause (1), which has been the subject of some debate, provides that "a person may obtain a compulsory license only if his or her primary purpose in making phonorecords is to distribute them to the public for private use." This provision was criticized as being discriminatory against background music systems, since it would prevent a background music producer from making recordings without the express consent of the copyright owner; it was argued that this could put the producer at a great competitive disadvantage with performing rights societies, allow discrimination, and destroy or prevent entry of businesses. The committee concluded, however, that the purpose of the compulsory license does not extend to manufacturers of phonorecords that are intended primarily for commercial use, including not only broadcasters and jukebox operators but also background music services.

The final sentence of clause (1) provides that a person may not obtain a compulsory license for use of the work in the duplication of a sound recording made by another, unless the sound recording being duplicated was itself fixed lawfully and the making of phonorecords duplicated from it was authorized by the owner of copyright in the sound recording (or, if the recording was fixed before February 15, 1972, by the voluntary or compulsory licensee of the music used in the recording). The basic intent of this sentence is to make clear that a person is not entitled to a compulsory license of copyrighted musical works for the purpose of making an unauthorized duplication of a musical sound recording originally developed and produced by another. It is the view of the Committee that such was the original intent of the Congress in enacting the 1909 Copyright Act, and it has been so construed by the 3d, 5th, 9th and 10th Circuits in the following cases: *Duchess Music Corp. v. Stern,* 458 F. 2d 1305 (9th Cir.), *cert. denied,* 409 U.S. 847 (1972); *Edward B. Marks Music Corp. v. Colorado Magnetics, Inc.,* 497 F. 2d 285, *aff'd on rehearing en banc,* 497 F. 2d 292 (10th Cir. 1974), *cert. denied,* 419 U.S. 1120 (1975); *Jondora Music Publishing Co. v. Melody Recordings, Inc.,* 506 F. 2d 392 (3d Cir. 1974, as amended 1975), *cert. denied,* 421 U.S. 1012 (1975); and *Fame Publishing Co. v. Alabama Custom Tape, Inc.,* 507 F. 2d 667 (5th Cir.), *cert. denied,* 423 U.S. 841 (1975).

Under this provision, it would be possible to obtain a compulsory license for the use of copyrighted music under section 115 if the owner of the sound recording being duplicated authorizes its duplication. This does not, however, in any way require the owner of the original sound recording to grant a license to duplicate the original sound recording. It is not intended that copyright protection for sound recordings be circumscribed by requiring the owners of sound recordings to grant a compulsory license to unauthorized duplicators or others.

The second clause of subsection (a) is intended to recognize the practical need for a limited privilege to make arrangements of music being used under a compulsory license, but without allowing the music to be perverted, distorted, or travestied. Clause (2) permits arrangements of a work "to the extent necessary to conform it to the style or manner of interpretation of the performance involved," so long as it does not "change the basic melody or fundamental character of the work." The provision also prohibits the compulsory licensee from claiming an independent copyright in his arrangement as a "derivative work" without the express consent of the copyright owner.

Procedure for obtaining compulsory license

Section 115(b)(1) requires anyone who wishes to take advantage of the compulsory licensing provisions to serve a "notice of intention to obtain a compulsory license," which is much like the "notice of intention to use" required by the present law. Under section 115, the notice must be served before any phonorecords are distributed, but service can take place "before or within 30 days after making" any phonorecords. The notice is to be served on the copyright owner, but if the owner is not identified in the Copyright Office records, "it shall be sufficient to file the notice of intention in the Copyright Office."

The Committee deleted clause (2) of section 115(b) of S. 22 as adopted by the Senate. The provision was a vestige of jukebox provisions in earlier bills, and its requirements no longer served any useful purpose.

Clause (2) [formerly clause (3)] of section 115(b) provides that "failure to serve or file the notice required by clause (1) . . . forecloses the possibility of a compulsory license and, in the absence of a negotiated license, renders the making and distribution of phonorecords actionable as acts of infringement under section 501 and fully subject to the remedies provided by sections 502 through 506." The remedies provided in section 501 are those applicable to infringements generally.

Royalty payable under compulsory license

Identification of copyright owner. — Under the present law a copyright owner is obliged to file a "notice of use" in the Copyright Office, stating that the initial recording of the copyrighted work has been made or licensed, in order to recover against an unauthorized record manufacturer. This requirement has resulted in a technical loss of rights in some cases, and serves little or no purpose where the registration and assignment records of the Copyright Office already show the facts of ownership. Section 115(c)(1) therefore drops any formal "notice of use" requirements and merely provides that, "to be entitled to receive royalties under a compulsory license, the copyright owner must be identified in the registration or other public records of the Copyright Office." On the other hand, since proper identification is an important precondition of recovery, the bill further provides that "the owner is entitled to royalties for phonorecords manufactured and distributed after being so identified, but is not entitled to recover for any phonorecords previously made and distributed."

Basis of royalty. — Under the present statute the specified royalty is payable "on each such part manufactured," regardless of how many "parts" (i.e., records) are sold. This basis for calculating the royalty has been revised in section 115(c)(2) to provide that "the royalty under a compulsory license shall be payable for every phonorecord made and distributed in accordance with the license." This basis is more compatible with the general practice in negotiated licenses today. It is unjustified to require a compulsory licensee to pay license fees on records which merely go into inventory, which may later be destroyed, and from which the record producer gains no economic benefit.

It is intended that the Register of Copyrights will prescribe regulations insuring that copyright owners will receive full and prompt payment for all phonorecords made and distributed. Section 115(c)(2) states that "a phonorecord is considered 'distributed' if the person exercising the compulsory license has voluntarily and permanently parted with its possession." For this purpose, the concept of "distribution" comprises any act by which the person exercising the compulsory license voluntarily relinquishes possession of a phonorecord (considered as a fungible unit), regardless of whether the distribution is to the public, passes title, constitutes a gift, or is sold, rented, leased, or loaned, unless it is actually returned and the transaction cancelled. Neither involuntary relinquishment, as through theft or fire, nor the destruction of unwanted records, would constitute "distribution."

The term "made" is intended to be broader than "manufactured," and to include within its scope every possible manufacturing or other process capable of reproducing a sound recording in phonorecords. The use of the phrase "made and distributed" establishes the basis upon which the royalty rate for compulsory licensing under section 115 is to be calculated, but it is in no way intended to weaken the liability of record pressers and other manufacturers and makers of phonorecords for copyright infringement where the compulsory licensing requirements have not been met. As under the present law, even if a presser, manufacturer, or other maker had no role in the distribution process, that person would be regarded as jointly and severally liable in a case where the court finds that infringement has taken place because of failure to comply with the provisions of section 115.

Under existing practices in the record industry, phonorecords are distributed to wholesalers and retailers with the privilege of returning unsold copies for credit or exchange. As a result, the number of recordings that have been "permanently" distributed will not usually be known until some time — six or seven months on the average — after the initial distribution. In recognition of this problem, it has become a well-established industry practice, under negotiated licenses, for record companies to maintain reasonable reserves of the mechanical royalties due the copyright owners, against which royalties on the returns can be offset. The Committee recognizes that this practice may be consistent with the statutory requirements for monthly compulsory license accounting reports, but recognizes the possibility that, without proper safeguards, the maintenance of such reserves could be manipulated to avoid making payments of the full amounts owing to copyright owners. Under these circumstances, the regulations prescribed by the Register of Copyrights should contain detailed provisions ensuring that the ultimate disposition of every phonorecord made under a compulsory license is accounted for, and that payment is made for every phonorecord "voluntarily and permanently" distributed. In particular, the Register should prescribe a point in time when, for accounting purposes under section 115, a phonorecord will be considered "permanently distributed," and should prescribe the situations in which a compulsory licensee is barred from maintaining reserves (e.g., situations in which the compulsory licensee has frequently failed to make payments in the past.)

Rate of royalty. — A large preponderance of the extensive testimony presented to the Committee on section 115 was devoted to the question of the amount of the statutory royalty rate. An extensive review and analysis of the testimony and arguments received on this question appear in the 1974 [1975] Senate report (S. Rep. No. 94-473) at page 91-94. [*See* pp. 401-04 *infra.*]

While upon initial review it might be assumed that the rate established in 1909 would not be reasonable at the present time, the committee believes that an increase in the mechanical royalty rate must be justified on the basis of existing economic conditions and not on the mere passage of 67 years. Following a thorough analysis of the problem, the Committee considers that an increase of the present two-cent royalty to a rate of 2¾ cents (or .6 of one cent per minute or fraction of playing time) is justified.* This rate will be subject to review by the Copyright Royalty Commission, as provided by section 801, in 1980 and at 10-year intervals thereafter.

Accounting and payment of royalties; effect of default

Clause (3) of Section 115(c) provides that royalty payments are to be made on a monthly basis, in accordance with requirements that the Register of Copyrights shall prescribe by regulation. In order to increase the protection of copyright proprietors against economic harm from companies which might refuse or fail to pay their just obligations, compulsory licensees will also be required to make a detailed cumulative annual statement of account, certified by a Certified Public Accountant.

---

* The conference committee accepted the Senate version of the "playing time" alternative, i.e., .5 of one percent per minute. Conf. Rep. at 77. For 1980 adjustments by Copyright Royalty Tribunal, see p. 411 *infra.* — Eds. Note.

A source of criticism with respect to the compulsory licensing provisions of the present statute has been the rather ineffective sanctions against default by compulsory licensees. Clause (4) of section 115(c) corrects this defect by permitting the copyright owner to serve written notice on a defaulting licensee, and by providing for termination of the compulsory license if the default is not remedied within 30 days after notice is given. Termination under this clause "renders either the making or the distribution, or both, of all phonorecords for which the royalty had not been paid, actionable as acts of infringement under section 501 and fully subject to the remedies provided by sections 502 through 506."

SENATE REPORT

S. Rep. No. 94-473, 94th Cong., 1st Sess. 91-94 (1975)

Rate of royalty. — A large preponderance of the extensive testimony presented to the committee on section 115 was devoted to the question of whether the statutory royalty rate should be left at 2 cents per composition per phonorecord or whether it should be increased. The bill provides that with respect to each work embodied in the phonorecord, the royalty shall be either 2½ cents, or ½ cents per minute of playing time or fraction thereof, whichever amount is larger. During the hearings and subsequently considerable economic data was submitted concerning the establishment of the royalty rate. An analysis of this data was prepared by Edward Knight of the Congressional Reference Service of the Library of Congress.

The following is a summary of the economic arguments presented during and after the hearings, and of the committee's analysis of them, showing the basis for the royalty rate finally adopted.

1. *The need for an increase by copyright holders.* — Although 2 cents in 1909 had the purchasing power of 12 cents in today's economy, the songwriters and publishers acknowledged the invalidity of comparing the modern music industry with its 1909 counterpart and focused instead on the economic trends of the past decade. They maintain that 2 cents at the time of the 1965 House hearings was 6.1 percent of the list price per song on a typical album whereas today it is only 2.8 percent; and that, despite an aggregate increase in mechanical royalty payments, they represented almost 6 percent of industry sales in 1965 and less than 4 percent in 1975. They point out that the 2.5 cents approved by the House represents today less than 1.5 cents in 1965 dollars and only 3.6 percent of today's price per song on a typical album (compared with 7.6 percent in 1965).

In contradiction, the record manufacturers presented statistics aimed at showing that an increase in the statutory fee above 2¢ would be unjustified and inequitable. They argued that inflationary trends since 1909 are only one factor to be considered in setting the rate, and that the adverse effects of inflation have been offset by the tremendous increase in the volume of records sold, the great decrease in record prices, and the introduction of long-playing records, tapes, cartridges and cassettes containing ten to twelve selections (with a statutory royalty for each). They asserted that copyright owners are amply compensated at the present rate; that in the last decade alone, their income from mechanical royalties in the aggregate, and per released tune, have more than doubled; and that income going to copyright owners from mechanical royalties has risen much faster than inflation. Moreover, the record manufacturers contend, copyright owners receive substantially greater financial gains from the phonorecord industry than the record companies themselves, and that the 1909 statute was designed to give copyright owners about five percent of the manufacturers' wholesale selling price, while their share today is around 7.4 percent. They further argued that copyright owners earn very substantial revenues from other sources, such as performance royalties from the broadcast of records. By contrast, the record manufacturers derive profits solely from their sale of records, the value and creative character of which are largely the result of their efforts and expenditures rather than those of the music publisher.

2. *Potential impact of increase on record industry.* — Much of the statistical data presented by the record companies at the hearings was in support of the argument that an increase in the rate would have a grave impact on the entire record industry, including manufacturers, artists, performing talent, distributors, retailers, jukebox operators, and even copyright holders. They asserted that, if the statutory rate were 3¢, the total increase in annual dollar payments to copyright owners would approximate $50 million, or 39 percent of the pre-tax profits of the entire U.S. recording industry in 1974, the second-best year the recording industry ever had. They argued that, unless record prices were to be raised considerably, the higher royalty would generate irresistible pressures tending to force out many companies, especially smaller ones, and that similar pressures would operate on wholesalers and retailers. They maintained that some 80 percent of all releases lose money (although copyright owners still receive their royalties on them), and that increasing the mechanical rate would raise the percentage of failures still higher. Ultimately, they argued, the level of activity in the industry and the number of new recordings would be seriously depressed, and strong forces would be [unleashed] to restructure the industry, impairing competition and leading to concentration of control.

In reply, the songwriters and publishers maintain that four giant record companies dominate the record industry which is largely controlled by entertainment conglomerates whose consolidated reports and intra-company transactions it is claimed conceal the true profit figures of particular divisions. They cite testimony by a top record industry executive in support of the fact that a record company's profit on the typical recording sold is far greater than that claimed in industry presentations to the Congress and far greater than that of the composer and publisher combined. Noting that record company sales continue to mount to new highs each year — increasing from 1964-1974 more than twice as much as royalty collections, despite steep price increases and a faltering economy — they see no reason why an industry which has more than doubled the price per recorded selection over the last decade should be excused from paying fair compensation to those who created the music.

3. *Potential impact of increase on consuming public.* — If the statutory rate were raised to 3¢, the record manufacturers predicted an increased price to consumers of 35¢ per $6.98 long-playing record, or a total of nearly $100 million per year. This prediction assumed that the record manufacturer could not absorb the increase in mechanical royalties, and that record marketers, in turn, would have to pass the increase on down the line to the consumer, with each distributor adding an increment to his price because of his added costs and risks. The record manufacturers also forecast that the variety of musical offerings would be restricted; that the quality of musical offerings would deteriorate; that composers, especially unknowns, would find fewer opportunities for having their works recorded; that record manufacturers would have to avoid risks on new and unusual compositions, reduce the number and length of selections, record fewer serious works, and rely more on the public domain for popular

material. A letter to the committee from the Consumer Federation of America voiced similar concerns.

In response to these predictions, the songwriters and publishers argued that the identical predictions were made by the same record industry consultant at the House hearings 10 years ago about the dangers of a 12 cent per record increase, and that since that time it is claimed the industry has increased prices by more than $3.00 without a single one of these predictions about the fate of recorded music coming true. As additional indications of the record industry's own lack of concern about increased prices, they contend that the industry refused to pass on to the consumer the savings made possible by the excise tax repeal of 1965 and raised monaural prices by $1.00 to match stereo prices in 1967. The maximum increase possible of one cent per song or ten cents per record under a new 3 cent ceiling, they add, would be an insignificant fraction of the amount by which the industry has increased prices in the last 10 years and still give the creators of the music a smaller share of the current price per recorded song than 2.5 cents would have given them a decade ago. Music consumers represented by the National Federation of Music Clubs have also supported a higher ceiling as a means of encouraging the writing of more and better music.

4. *The statutory fee as a ceiling or as an established rate.* — One of the principal arguments of the copyright owners was that, in contrast to record manufacturers whose prices are not fixed and who are not obliged to pay copyright owners any minimum amount, the authors and publishers are deprived of any right to bargain above the two-cent ceiling. They stress that the statutory rate is merely a maximum: the record manufacturer can also negotiate for less, but the copyright owner can never ask for more. The actual average royalty paid, according to a music publisher's survey, is 1.62 cents, down 34 percent in real purchasing power from the 1.51 cent average of a decade ago. The authors and publishers thus stress that an increase in the ceiling will not automatically increase all royalty rates, that their bargaining power versus the giants of the record industry will still keep most royalty rates below any new ceiling, and that increased royalties will be obtained only for those songs with sufficient appeal to enable free market forces to bolster their rate of return above the present artificially low level. Thus they seek not an automatic rate increase but room to negotiate.

On the other side, the record manufacturers argued that as a practical matter the statutory rate establishes the fee actually paid in most instances, and that for business reasons, it is impossible for individual companies to bargain for special discriminatory rates for particular compositions. They cited a survey of some 2,600 selections issued by two major record companies during the greater part of 1974, which found that some 81 percent of all copyright licenses (as distinguished from phonorecords sold) were at the two-cent rate, and that of the remaining 19 percent, the vast majority were for budget, club and premium records, or albums on which the artist had an interest or the publisher granted a block or medley discount. In other words, 99.2% of all the tunes licensed were at 2¢ or regular, stereotyped variations below the standards of 2¢. The basic position of the record manufacturers was that a one-cent increase would simply establish a higher prevailing rate rather than providing more room for negotiation. The great majority of licenses would be issued at 3¢, and budget, club and other such albums would be licensed slightly below 3¢.

Committee Conclusion

While upon initial review it might be assumed that the rate established in 1909 would not be reasonable at the present time, the committee believes that an increase in the mechanical royalty rate must be justified on the basis of existing economic conditions and not on the mere passage of 66 years.

The economic evidence presented by the record manufacturers shows that, at the two-cent rate, publisher and composer income from mechanical royalty payments — in the aggregate, and on a per tune basis — has more than doubled over the last ten years. Their statistics also show that a three-cent rate would increase mechanical royalty payments by nearly $50 million, which could add nearly $100 million a year to consumer record costs. The effects of such an increase would be felt not only by consumers, but also by working musicians, retailers, wholesalers, and juke box operators, all of whom oppose an increase.

The committee has concluded, therefore, that the advocates of a rate increase have failed to prove the justification for an increase in the rate above 2½ cents, or one-half cent per minute of playing time, whichever is greater. This represents an increase of more than 25 percent. In any event, the publishers and composers will have the opportunity to present their case to the Copyright Royalty Tribunal, an expert body qualified to review the economic evidence in detail.

QUESTIONS

1. Is the compulsory license for recordings of musical compositions subject to attack under the copyright and patent clause of the Constitution?

2. It can probably be demonstrated that the fears of economic monopoly which justified the compulsory license in 1909 were unwarranted in 1976, when the new Copyright Act was passed. Given the control normally allowed by law to the copyright owner over the commercial exploitation of his or her work, is the fact that the recording industry is accustomed to operating under the compulsory license sufficient reason to preserve it in the current law?

3. Assume that a witty recording musician (whom we shall fancifully call Spike Jones) records his version of a recently successful love ballad, which incorporates speed-ups, hiccoughs, ambulance sirens, and the like; his version becomes quite popular, and many phonorecords are sold and considerable airtime given. If Jones tenders 2-3/4 cents for each record sold, has he infringed? If so, is that a sound result? If the infringement is not saved by § 115, is there some other section or principle on which Jones might rely? (Consider later whether the radio stations which play the Jones record are liable for infringement.)

THE "HARRY FOX LICENSE"

A large number of music publishers/copyright owners have authorized an organization called the Harry Fox Agency to grant licenses for the mechanical reproduction of music. Such reproduction includes synchronization with motion pictures, and other audio-visual works, and recordings of dramatic-musical material, both of which involve a variety of contractual terms and conditions. But perhaps the greatest volume of transactions involves the recording of non-dramatic music under a document in the form of a letter from the Fox Agency, which (a) identifies the copyrighted work; (b) identifies the publisher(s) for whom the Fox office is acting as agent; (c) provides for any variation from the statutory rate; (d) sets forth any special provisions; and (e) contains substantially the following terms:

You have advised us, in our capacity as Agent for the Publisher(s) referred to in (B) supra, that you wish to obtain a compulsory license to make and to distribute phonorecords of the copyrighted work referred to in (A) supra, under the compulsory license provision of Section 115 of the Copyright Act.

Upon your doing so, you shall have all the rights which are granted to, and all the obligations which are imposed upon, users of said copyrighted work under the compulsory license provision of the Copyright Act, after phonorecords of the copyrighted work have been distributed to the public in the United States under the authority of the copyright owner by another person, except that with respect to phonorecords thereof made and distributed hereunder:

1. You shall pay royalties and account to us as Agent for and on behalf of said Publisher(s) quarterly, within forty-five days after the end of each calendar quarter, on the basis of phonorecords made and distributed;

2. For such phonorecords made and distributed, the royalty shall be the statutory rate in effect at the time the phonorecord is made, except as otherwise stated in (C) supra;

3. This compulsory license covers and is limited to one particular recording of said copyrighted work as performed by the artist and on the phonorecord number identified in (C) supra; and this compulsory license does not supersede nor in any way affect any prior agreements now in effect respecting phonorecords of said copyrighted work;

4. In the event you fail to account to us and pay royalties as herein provided for, said Publisher(s) or his Agent may give written notice to you that, unless the default is remedied within 30 days from the date of the notice, this compulsory license will be automatically terminated. Such termination shall render either the making or the distribution, or both, of all phonorecords for which royalties have not been paid, actionable as acts of infringement under, and fully subject to the remedies provided by, the Copyright Act;

5. You need not serve or file the notice of intention to obtain a compulsory license required by the Copyright Act. . . .

QUESTIONS

1. Suppose a corporate "licensee" fails to live up to the terms of this "license." Can the president of the corporation, who signed the license on behalf of the licensee, escape copyright liability on the ground that he is not liable for the corporation's contractual debts? *See Shapiro, Bernstein & Co. v. Gabor,* 266 F. Supp. 613 (S.D.N.Y. 1966).

2. Identify the differences between the "Harry Fox license" and the strict terms of old § 1(e) and the current § 115. Is the "Harry Fox license" a "compulsory license" within the meaning of Transitional and Supplementary sec. 106?

HOUSE REPORT

H.R. Rep. No. 94-1476, 94th Cong., 2d Sess. 173-75 (1976)

Chapter 8. Copyright Royalty Commission

Chapter 8 establishes a Copyright Royalty Commission for the purpose of periodically reviewing and adjusting statutory royalty rates for use of copyrighted materials pursuant to compulsory licenses provided in sections 111 (secondary transmissions by cable systems), 115 (mechanical royalties) and 116 (jukebox) of the bill. In addition, the Commission will make determinations as to reasonable terms and rates of royalty payments as provided in section 118 (public broadcasting), and to resolve disputes over the distribution of royalties paid pursuant to the statutory licenses in sections 111 and 116.

The Committee recognizes that the industries affected by the royalty rates over which the Commission has jurisdiction are very different, and it is therefore expected that any adjustment of a rate by the Commission shall be based on the economic conditions peculiar to the industries affected by that rate. Likewise, the Committee recognizes the fact that the cable television industry is a developing industry in transition, whereas the recording and jukebox industries are long-established. Therefore, the Committee has chosen periods of different lengths in which the Commission is to review the rates affecting those industries. Rates for retransmission of copyrighted works by cable television systems will be reviewed in 1980 and each subsequent fifth year. Rates established for mechanical reproduction will be reviewed in 1980, 1987, and in each subsequent 10th year. Rates for performance by jukebox will be reviewed in 1980, and in each subsequent 10th year. Rates and terms under section 118 will be reviewed in 1982 and in each subsequent fifth year. The Committee does not intend that rate changes, whether up or down, should necessarily be made as the result of such periodic reviews.

The Committee has chosen to stagger the times for review of the various rates established under the bill so as to balance the workload of the Commission. Cable and copyright owners agreed to a set of standards for the adjustment of rates which the Committee in large measure has accepted. No specific standards governing the establishment or adjustment of rates by the Commission, other than rates for cable transmissions, have been detailed in the legislation, because the Committee did not wish to limit the factors that the Commission might consider in a world of constantly changing economics and technology. However, it is anticipated that the Commission will consider the following objectives in determining a reasonable rate under sections 115 and 116:

(1) The rate should maximize the availability of diverse creative works to the public.

(2) The rate should afford the copyright owner a fair income, or if the owner is not a person, a fair profit, under existing economic conditions, in order to encourage creative activity.

(3) The rate should not jeopardize the ability of the copyright user

    (a) to earn a fair income, or if the user is not a person, a fair profit, under existing economic conditions, and

    (b) to charge the consumer a reasonable price for the product.

(4) The rate should reflect the relative roles of the copyright owner and the copyright user in the product made available to the public with respect to

relative creative contribution, technological contribution, capital investment, cost, risk, and contribution to the opening of new markets for creative expression and media for their communication.

(5) The rate should minimize any disruptive impact on the structure of the industries involved and on generally prevailing industry practices.

Similar considerations are noted in connection with Commission review of rates and terms for public broadcasting in the discussion of section 118, above.

Structure of the Copyright Royalty Commission

The Senate bill provides that, upon certifying the existence of a controversy concerning distribution of statutory royalty fees or upon periodic petition for review of statutory royalty rates by an interested party, the Register of Copyrights, is to convene a three member panel to constitute a Copyright Royalty Tribunal for the purpose of resolving the controversy or reviewing the rates.

The Senate bill provides that the Tribunal be appointed by the Register from among the membership of the American Arbitration Association or similar organization. The Tribunal is to exist within the Library of Congress.

Due to constitutional concern over the provision of the Senate bill that the Register of Copyrights, an employee of the Legislative Branch, appoint the members of the Tribunal, the Committee adopted an amendment providing for direct appointment of three individuals by the President. The name of the Tribunal was changed to the Copyright Royalty Commission.

Although under the Committee Amendment, the Commission is to be an independent authority, it is to receive administrative support from the Library of Congress.

The Commission is authorized to appoint a staff to assist it in carrying out its responsibilities. However, it is expected that the staff will consist only of sufficient clerical personnel to provide one full time secretary for each member and one or two additional employees to meet the clerical needs of the entire Commission. Members of the Commission are expected to perform all professional responsibilities themselves, except where it is necessary to employ outside experts on a consulting basis. Assistance in matters of administration, such as payroll and budgeting, will be available from the Library of Congress.

The Committee expects that the President shall appoint members of the Commission from among persons who have demonstrated professional competence in the field of copyright policy.

CONFERENCE REPORT

H.R. Rep. No. 94-1733, 94th Cong., 2d Sess. 81-82 (1976)

Senate bill

Chapter 8 of the Senate bill established a Copyright Royalty Tribunal in the Library of Congress, for the purpose of periodically reviewing and adjusting statutory royalty rates with respect to the four compulsory licenses provided by the bill, and of resolving disputes over the distribution of royalties from cable transmissions and jukebox performances. Upon certifying the existence of a controversy concerning distribution of statutory royalty fees, or upon periodic

petition for review of statutory royalty rates by an interested party, the Register
of Copyrights was to convene a three-member panel to constitute a Copyright
Royalty Tribunal to resolve the controversy or review the rates. Determinations
by the Tribunal were to be submitted to the two Houses of Congress, and were
to be final unless voted upon and rejected by one of the two Houses within a
specified period. Rate adjustments were not subject to judicial review, and the
grounds for judicial review of royalty distributions were limited to misconduct or
corruption of a Tribunal member.

House bill

The House bill amended chapter 8 to provide for a permanent three-member
Copyright Royalty Commission, which was to be an independent body but would
receive administrative support from the Library of Congress. The commissioners were to be appointed by the President for staggered five-year terms, and
the Commission's proceedings were made generally subject to the Administrative
Procedure Act. Any final determinations of the Commission would be reviewable
by the U.S. Court of Appeals on the basis of the record before the Commission.
Under sections 111, 116, and chapter 8 of the House bill, the Register of Copyrights was to perform the recording functions and do the paperwork and initial
accounting connected with the compulsory licensing procedures established for
cable transmissions and jukebox performances. However, after the Register had
deducted the costs involved in these procedures and deposited the royalties in
the U.S. Treasury, the Commission would assume all duties involved in
distributing the royalties, regardless of whether or not there were a dispute.

Conference substitute

The conference substitute conforms in general to the House bill, but with
several changes. The body established by chapter 8 is to be named the Copyright
Royalty Tribunal, and is to consist of five commissioners appointed for staggered
seven-year terms by the President with the advice and consent of the Senate. The
Tribunal is to be an independent agency in the legislative branch; a new section
defines the responsibilities of the Library of Congress to provide administrative
support to the Tribunal, and establishes specific regulatory authority governing
the procedures and responsibilities for disbursement of funds. The House
receded on its language appearing in the last sentence of section 801(b)(1)
[relevant factors for rate determinations], and the conference agreed to a substitute for that language.

EXCERPTS FROM ANNUAL REPORT OF THE COPYRIGHT ROYALTY TRIBUNAL (1979)

The Copyright Royalty Tribunal: Creation and Membership

The Copyright Royalty Tribunal (Tribunal) was created by section 801(a) of
Public Law 94-553, the General Revision of the Copyright Law of 1976, and is
composed of five commissioners appointed by the President with the advice and
consent of the Senate. The commissioners are:

Thomas C. Brennan of New Jersey
Douglas E. Coulter of New Hampshire
Mary Lou Burg of Wisconsin
Clarence L. James, Jr. of Ohio

Frances Garcia of Texas

They were sworn in on November 10, 1977. The chairmanship rotates in order of senority on December 1 of each year. In 1978 the chairman was Thomas C. Brennan; in 1979, Douglas E. Coulter.

Statutory Responsibilities

The Tribunal's statutory responsibilities are:

(a) To make determinations concerning copyright royalty rates in the areas of cable television covered by 17 U.S.C. 111.

(b) To make determinations concerning copyright royalty rates for phonorecords (17 U.S.C. 115) and for coin-operated phonorecord players (jukeboxes) (17 U.S.C. 116).

(c) To establish and later make determinations concerning royalty rates and terms for non-commercial broadcasting (17 U.S.C. 118).

(d) To distribute cable television and jukebox royalties under 17 U.S.C. 111 and 17 U.S.C. 116 deposited with the Register of Copyrights.

General Administration

The only staff of the Tribunal is a personal assistant to each commissioner. The legislative history of the Copyright Act reflects the intention that the Tribunal remain a small independent agency in which the commissioners perform all professional responsibilities themselves, except where it is necessary to employ outside experts on a consulting basis. While larger agencies might not find this practical, the direct access by the public to commissioners has been found beneficial by the Tribunal.

Summary of the First Year of Operation of the Tribunal

Compulsory License for Non-Commercial Broadcasting

The first statutory responsibility of the Tribunal under the Copyright Act was to establish rates and terms of compulsory royalty payment for non-commercial broadcasting for certain uses of published non-dramatic musical works and published pictorial, graphic, and sculptural works (17 U.S.C. 118). The proceedings to establish such rates and terms were completed, as required by the Statute, within six months of their commencement, and the final rule was made effective June 8, 1978 (43 FR 25068-73). Several rates were established, but the principal focus was on the royalty to be paid by Public Broadcasting Service (PBS) and National Public Radio (NPR) to the American Society of Composers, Authors, and Publishers (ASCAP). Voluntary licensing agreements had already been reached with the two other performing rights societies BMI and SESAC. The royalty determined by the Tribunal to be paid to ASCAP was a blanket license for the entire ASCAP repertory and was a flat dollar fee, not a formula.

Access to Phonorecord Players

The Tribunal also adopted regulations under 17 U.S.C. 116(c)(5) under which persons expected to have claims to the royalty fees for coin-operated phonorecord players (jukeboxes) might have access to those phonorecord players (43 FR 40498), made effective October 19, 1978. The purpose of this regulation was to allow those expected to have a claim access to jukeboxes so that they might determine by sampling procedures or otherwise the proportional contribution of their musical works to the compulsory licensing fees. The regulation was made as unburdensome as possible on the jukebox operators, still consistent with the purpose of the Copyright Act. Jukebox operators were required to file an initial listing of the location of their jukeboxes with the Tribunal and then submit an update of any changes annually.

Claims to Phonorecord Royalty Fees

Pursuant to 17 U.S.C. 116(c)(2) the Tribunal adopted a regulation requiring those with claims to jukebox royalty fees to file such claims with the Tribunal in January of each year and, unless there is no controversy, to file in November a statement of that portion of the royalty fees they feel entitled to. The regulation was adopted on September 12, 1978 (43 FR 40501-2).

Claims to Cable Royalty Fees

Finally, pursuant to 17 U.S.C. 111(d)(5)(A) the Tribunal adopted regulations prescribing the filing of claims to cable royalty fees. These were adopted May 31, 1978 (43 FR 24528-9), and stated that because it was impossible for claimants to have had access to the information filed by cable operators with the Copyright Office before filing with the Tribunal in July 1978, only a minimal filing would be required for the first six months of 1978. Provision was made for the Tribunal to determine later what supplemental information it would require for claims for the first half of 1978 and what more complete filings for the second half of 1978 would be required in July 1979. The regulation stipulated that for all years subsequent to 1978 claims must be filed in July of the following year.

Copyright Research Studies

The Tribunal determined that some research in areas strictly related to licensing and royalties would be appropriate and took preliminary measures to gather data on the extent of taping by audio recorders.

Agency Rules of Procedure

On October 23, 1978, the Tribunal published its proposed Agency Rules of Procedure in the Federal Register (43 FR 49318-26). They were drafted in language that was intended to be simple, concise and directed at only the purpose for which the rules would be used. They were formally adopted at a public meeting on November 9, 1978, and were published in the Federal Register on November 17, 1978 (43 FR 53719-28).

Since the submission of its 1979 Fiscal Year Report, the Tribunal has been engaged in the heaviest workload mandated by its statutory timetable. During the year 1980, royalty rates for phonorecords of non-dramatic music under § 115, cable retransmission under § 111, and jukebox performances under § 116 were all reviewed. In addition, the Tribunal embarked on its first distribution proceedings of royalties from cable and jukeboxes.

The Tribunal increased the royalty rate for phonorecords from 2¾ cents per work or ½ cent per minute (whichever is larger) to 4 cents per work or ¾ cent per minute (whichever is larger). The increase is applicable to phonorecords made and distributed on or after July 1, 1981, and is subject to annual upward adjustment, commencing December 1, 1981. The first adjustment is to be "directly proportionate to the change, if any, in the average suggested retail list price of albums between the twelve-month period ending October 31, 1980 and the twelve-month period ending October 31, 1981." 46 Fed. Reg. 892 (Jan. 5, 1981). Subsequent changes use comparable twelve-month periods.

Juke box fees were increased as follows:
(a) Commencing on January 1, 1982 — $25
(b) Commencing on January 1, 1984 — $50
(c) Effective January 1, 1987, the $50 fee will be subject to an adjustment based on the change in the cost of living between February 1, 1981 and August 1, 1986.

[46 Fed. Reg. 890 (Jan. 5, 1981).]

As to the cable rate determination, see 46 Fed. Reg. 892 (Jan. 5, 1981) and p. 452 *infra*. As to the cable royalty distribution proceedings, see 45 Fed. Reg. 50621 (July 30, 1980), 45 Fed. Reg. 63026 (Sept. 23, 1980), and p. 453 *infra*.

Since virtually all these initial Tribunal determinations are the subject of appeals pending during the summer of 1981, the student is advised to follow judicial developments in this area.

2. SOUND RECORDINGS UNDER § 114

An effort must always be made to emphasize the distinction between a recorded composition (usually musical) and the recorded performance of such composition. It is the latter — called a "sound recording" — that is the subject of a set of specialized provisions in the 1976 Act, e.g., § 402 (notice), § 407 (deposit). Before noting the specific limitations on the exclusive rights of such works, we should recall their history. See *Goldstein v. California*, 412 U.S. 546, 178 USPQ 129 (1973).

Until 1971, recorded performances were protected, if at all, by state law. See *Capitol Records, Inc. v. Mercury Records Corp.*, 221 F.2d 657, 105 USPQ 163 (2d Cir. 1955). It was such protection that was preserved by *Goldstein*. In 1971, Public Law 92-140 offered federal protection for the first time to sound recordings provided that they were "fixed" between February 15, 1972, and December 31, 1974. The latter deadline was later removed, Public Law 93-573, 88 Stat. 1873. The 1976 statute carries forward protection of these sound recordings under generally similar limitations.

Section 114 expressly limits the rights of the owner in such works to protection against recordings "that directly or indirectly recapture the actual sounds fixed in the [protected] recording." The provision does not prevent a recording "that consists entirely of an independent fixation of other sounds, even though such sounds imitate or simulate those in the copyrighted sound recording."

While imitation through an independent recording is thus permitted, capturing the fixed sounds by re-recording — even with some technical changes — can still amount to infringement. *United States v. Taxe*, 380 F. Supp. 1010, 184 USPQ 5 (C.D. Cal. 1974), *aff'd*, 540 F.2d 961, 192 USPQ 204 (9th Cir. 1976). In construing the requirement that the protected work be "fixed" after February 15, 1972 (17 U.S.C. § 1 (f)), the *Taxe* court held that where an album or a tape produced after that date contains some songs which were first recorded before 1972, the proprietor can nevertheless secure protection for the remaining songs which satisfy the statutory standard. The court also found that re-recording of the album or tape can still constitute infringement of the copyright in the sound recording under § 1(f) where superficial changes have been made by speeding up or slowing down the recording, deleting certain frequencies and tones, or adding sounds from a "moog" synthesizer. The jury was instructed that it could convict the defendants of criminal infringement of a recording copyright under such circumstances as long as "the final product [is] 'recognizable' as the same performance as recorded in the original." 380 F. Supp. at 1015, 184 USPQ at 7.

Two further characteristics of the limited right accorded to sound recordings may be noted. First, the "home recording" exemption expressed in the legislative history of § 1(f) of the 1909 Act, H.R. Rep. No. 92-487, 92d Cong., 1st Sess. 7 (1971), is not expressly found in the 1976 Act, but neither is any indication that a change in this regard was intended. One court has now found the "exemption," implied in the present law. *Universal City Studios v. Sony Corp. of America,* 430 F. Supp. 429, 444 (C.D. Cal. 1979) (appeal pending).

It is also noteworthy that these works do not enjoy a separate performance right, i.e., the right to control or be compensated for broadcast of other public performance of a genuine sound recording. The issues raised by this latter limitation have survived the 1976 Act which expressly deferred the question. Some detailed attention to this continuing controversy is warranted.

Section 114(d) provides that the Register of Copyrights, after consulting with the affected interests, "shall submit to the Congress a report setting forth recommendations as to whether this section should be amended to provide for performers and copyright owners of copyrighted material any performance rights in such material," along with specific legislative recommendations if appropriate. Extensive reports, economic as well as legal, and international as well as domestic, were prepared for the Register and published in *Performance Rights in Sound Recordings,* 95th Cong., 2d Sess. (June 1978) (House Jud. Comm. Print No. 15). On the basis of these reports as well as public hearings, the Register in March 1978 set forth her own report and recommendations to Congress pursuant to Section 114(d). The Register first explored a number of issues bearing on the question of extending performing rights to performers and copyright owners in sound recordings; her conclusions and supporting discussion are set forth immediately below. She then proposed a bill, the principal features of which are as follows:

1. Section 106(4) would be amended to extend the right of public performance to sound recordings, and the definition of "perform" in § 101 would be amended to include the making audible of sounds in a sound recording.

2. Section 114(c) would be amended to provide for a compulsory license to perform a sound recording when phonorecords of that sound recording are publicly distributed in the United States or elsewhere with the consent of the copyright owner. The person intending to perform the sound recording as compulsory licensee is to file an advance notice in the Copyright Office, is subsequently to deposit with the Register an annual statement of account and a royalty fee, and is to be liable for the usual remedies for infringement in the event of failure so to file or deposit. Compulsory-license royalties are to be payable only for performances of sound recordings fixed on or after February 15, 1972.

3. Compulsory licensees have the option to compute royalty fees on either a prorated basis (based generally upon the proportion of time or number of days

the licensee devotes to the performance of sound recordings, with royalties fixed accordingly by the Copyright Royalty Tribunal) or on a blanket basis (which the bill itself would base generally upon gross receipts from advertisers or subscribers during the accounting period). Public performances on jukeboxes and on cable television are to generate royalty payments pursuant to §§ 116 and 111, respectively.

4. The Copyright Royalty Tribunal is to divide the collected royalty payments (less governmental administrative costs) among all claimants, either pursuant to the claimants' agreement regarding the size of their respective shares (such agreement to be exempted from the antitrust laws) or if there is a dispute regarding the division of the royalties, according to the Tribunal's own determination. The distribution is to be divided between "owners of copyright" and "performers," with the latter receiving no less than fifty percent; performers on any particular sound recording are to divide the royalties for that recording "on a per capita basis, without regard to the nature, value, or length of their respective contribution." The Copyright Royalty Tribunal, when distributing royalties collected on account of compulsorily-licensed jukebox performances under § 116, is similarly to distribute one eighth of those royalties between performers and copyright owners of the sound recordings.

5. A "performer" is defined as an instrumental musician, singer, conductor, actor, narrator or other person whose performance of a literary, musical, or dramatic work is embodied in a sound recording, whether or not that person's contribution was a "work made for hire." A "copyright owner" is defined as the "author of a sound recording" or a person who has acquired the rights initially owned by such an author.

Because it will afford the student a glimpse into the issues underlying a notably unresolved matter of legislative copyright policy, we will examine in some detail the Register's analysis of the legal and economic issues surrounding this proposed grant of performing rights.

PERFORMANCE RIGHTS IN SOUND RECORDINGS, 95th Cong., 2d Sess. (1978) (House Jud. Comm. Print No. 15)

Basic Issues and Conclusions

The following is an effort to present, in outline form, the basic issues of public policy, constitutional law, economics, and Federal statutory law raised by proposals for performing rights in sound recordings, together with a bare statement of the conclusion I have reached on each of them, and a highly condensed discussion of the reasons behind each conclusion.

1. The Fundamental Public Policy Issue

Issue: Should performers, or record producers, or both, enjoy any rights under Federal law with respect to public performances of sound recordings to which they have contributed?

Conclusion: Yes.

Discussion: The Copyright Office supports the principle of copyright protection for the public performance of sound recordings. The lack of copyright protection for performers since the commercial development of phonograph records has had a drastic and destructive effect on both the performing and the recording arts. Professor Gorman's fascinating study shows that, in seeking to combat the vast technological unemployment resulting from the use of recorded rather than live performances, the labor union movement in the United States may in some ways have made the problem worse. It is too late to repair past wrongs, but this does not mean they should be allowed to continue. Congress should now do whatever it can to protect and encourage a vital artistic profession under the statute constitutionally intended for this purpose: the copyright law.

Broadcasters and other commercial users of recordings have performed them without permission or payment for generations. Users today look upon any requirement that they pay royalties as an unfair imposition in the nature of a "tax." However, any economic burden on the users of recordings for public performance is heavily outweighed, not only by the commercial benefits accruing directly from the use of copyrighted sound recordings, but also by the direct and indirect damage done to performers whenever recordings are used as a substitute for live performances. In all other areas the unauthorized use of a creative work is considered a copyright infringement if it results either in damage to the creator or in profits to the user. Sound recordings are creative works, and their unauthorized performance results in both damage and profits. To leave the creators of sound recordings without any protection or compensation for their widespread commercial use can no longer be justified.

2. Constitutional Issues

a. Issue: Are sound recordings "the writings of an author" within the meaning of the Constitution?

Conclusion: Yes.

Discussion: Arguments that sound recordings are not "writings" and that performers and record producers are not "authors" have become untenable. The courts have consistently upheld the constitutional eligibility of sound recordings for protection under the copyright law. Passage of the 1971 Sound Recording Amendment was a legislative declaration of this principle, which was reaffirmed in the Copyright Act of 1976.

b. Issue: Can sound recordings be "the writings of an author" for purposes of protection against unauthorized duplication (piracy or counterfeiting), but not for purposes of protection against unauthorized public performance?

Conclusion: No.

Discussion: Either a work is the "writing of an author" or it is not. If it is, the Constitution empowers Congress to grant it any protection that is considered justified. There is no basis, in logic or precedent, for suggesting that a work is a "writing" for some purposes and not for others.

c. Issue: Would Federal legislation to protect sound recordings against unauthorized public performance be unconstitutional: (i) if there has been no affirmative showing of a "need" on the part of the intended beneficiaries and hence no basis for asserting Congressional authority to "promote the progress of science and useful arts"; or (ii) if there has been an affirmative showing that compensation to the intended beneficiaries is "adequate" without protection of performing rights?

Conclusion: No.

Discussion: These are actually disguised economic arguments, not constitutional objections. Congressional authority to grant copyright protection has never been conditioned on any findings of need, or of the likelihood that productivity or creativity will increase. The established standard is that Congress has complete discretion to grant or withhold protection for the writings of authors, and that the courts will not look behind a Congressional enactment to determine whether or not it will actually provide incentives for creation and dissemination. It is perfectly appropriate to argue that a particular group of creators is adequately compensated through the exercise of certain rights under copyright law, and therefore Congress should not grant them additional rights.

It is not appropriate to argue that a Federal statute granting these rights could be attacked on the constitutional ground that it did not "promote the progress of science and useful arts."

d. Issue: Would the establishment of performance rights interfere with the First Amendment rights of broadcasters and other users of sound recordings?
Conclusion: No.

Discussion: The courts have been generally unreceptive to arguments that the news media have a right to use copyrighted material, beyond the limits of fair use in particular cases, under theories of freedom of the press or freedom of speech. These arguments seem much weaker where the copyrighted material is being used for entertainment purposes, where the user is benefiting commercially from the use, or where the use is subject to compulsory licensing.

3. Economic Issues

a. Issue: Do the benefits accruing to performers and record producers from the "free airplay" of sound recordings represent adequate compensation in the form of increased record sales, increased attendance at live performances, and increased popularity of individual artists?

Conclusion: No, on balance and on consideration of all performers and record producers affected.

Discussion: This is the strongest argument put forward by broadcasters and other users. There is no question that broadcasting and jukebox performances give some recordings the kind of exposure that benefits their producers and individual performers through increased sales and popularity. The benefits are hit-or-miss and, if realized, are the result of acts that are outside the legal control of the creators of the works being exploited, that are of direct commercial advantage to the user, and that may damage other creators. The opportunity for benefit through increased sales, no matter how significant it may be temporarily for some "hit records," can hardly justify the outright denial of any performing rights to any sound recordings. That denial is inconsistent with the underlying philosophy of the copyright law: that of securing the benefits of creativity to the public by the encouragement of individual effort through private gain (*Mazer v. Stein,* 347 U.S. 201 (1954)).

b. Issue: Would the imposition of performance royalties represent a financial burden on broadcasters so severe that stations would be forced to curtail or abandon certain kinds of programming (public service, classical, etc.) in favor of high-income producing programming in order to survive?

Conclusion: There is no hard economic evidence in the record to support arguments that a performance royalty would disrupt the broadcasting industry, adversely affect programming, and drive marginal stations out of business.

Discussion: This has been the single most difficult issue to assess accurately, because the arguments have consisted of polemics rather than facts. An independent economic analysis of potential financial effects on broadcasters was commissioned by the Copyright Office in an effort to provide an objective basis for evaluating the arguments and assertions on both sides of this issue. This study concludes on the basis of statistical analysis that the payment of royalties is unlikely to cause serious disruption within the broadcasting industry. There are arguments aplenty to the contrary, but there is no hard evidence to support them.

c. Issue: Would the imposition of a performance royalty be an unwarranted windfall for performers and record producers?

Conclusion: No.

Discussion: As for performers, the independent economic survey commissioned by the Copyright Office indicates that only a small proportion of performers participating in the production of recordings receive royalties from the sale of records and that, even if they do, royalties represent a very small proportion of their annual earnings. While the statistics collected with respect to record producers is [sic] less conclusive, the economic analysis concludes that the amount generated by the Danielson bill [e.g., H.R. 6063, 95th Cong., 1st Sess.] for record companies would be less than one-half of one percent of their estimated net sales.

4. Legal Issues

a. Issue: Assuming that some legal protection should be given to sound recordings against unauthorized public performance should it be given under the Federal copyright statute?

Conclusion: Yes.

Discussion: Considerations of national uniformity, equal treatment, and practical effectiveness all point to the importance of Federal protection for sound recordings and under the Constitution the copyright law provides the appropriate legal framework. Preemption of state law under the new copyright statute leaves sound recordings worse off than they were before 1978, since previously an argument could be made for common law performance rights in sound recordings.

b. Issue: What form should protection take?

Conclusion: The best approach appears to be a form of compulsory licensing, as procedurally simple as possible.

Discussion: No one is arguing for exclusive rights, and it would be unrealistic to do so. The Danielson bill represents a good starting point for the development of definitive legislation.

c. Issue: Who should be the beneficiaries of protection?

Conclusion: There are several possibilities; since performers and record producers both contribute copyrightable authorship to sound recordings they should both benefit.

Discussion: Special considerations that must be taken into account include the fact that many performers on records are "employees for hire," the unequal bargaining positions in some cases and the status of arrangers.

d. Issue: How should the rates be set?

Conclusion: Congress should establish an initial schedule, which the Copyright Royalty Tribunal would be mandated to reexamine at stated intervals.

Discussion: It would seem necessary to establish minimum statutory rates at the outset, rather than leaving the initial task to the Tribunal. Review of the statutory rates by the Copyright Royalty Tribunal should be mandatory after a period of time sufficient to permit the development of a functioning collection and distribution system.

QUESTIONS

1. Articulate as precisely as you can what elements of authorship comprise a sound recording, and how they differ from the works (literary or musical) which are inscribed in the sound recording. Who contributes any such authorship?

2. Is a sound recording a "writing" subject to protection by Congress under the copyright clause of the Constitution? Is there an "author" of a sound

recording, for purposes of the Constitution? Who is the owner of copyright in a sound recording? (This will determine such matters as whose name is placed in the notice of copyright. Review the appropriate sections of the Act.)

3. In hearings before the House Judiciary Subcommittee in 1975, representatives of tape duplicators contended that a few very large record companies control the bulk of the records distributed, and that a huge number of recorded performances, going back several decades, are completely unavailable to the public because the "majors" will neither release them, license them, nor permit their unauthorized duplication. These witnesses therefore urged that a compulsory licensing system should be created that would permit the public to have access to these old recordings and would generate royalties for the performing artists. The Register of Copyrights, in her Second Supplementary Report (Oct.-Dec. 1975), ch. VIII, p. 23, agreed "that a real problem exists with large and growing catalogs of recordings that record companies are sitting on and will neither release nor license"; she suggested that the problem might be considered by the Copyright Royalty Tribunal in connection with its survey of the recording industry to determine possible rate adjustments under § 115.

a. Do you agree that the reluctance of the major recording companies to re-release classic recordings of yesteryear justifies the invocation of a compulsory license to permit dubbing (and thus an exemption from § 114)? How should the statutory provision be drafted?

b. Does the Copyright Royalty Tribunal have the authority, as the Register suggests, to make a study or take more assertive action on this matter of a possible compulsory license?

4. What is the reason for permitting a person to duplicate exactly the sounds in a copyrighted sound recording through independent fixation, while barring the "dubbing" of those copyrighted sounds? Why should not the former method of "reproduction" be just as much an infringement under § 106(1) as is the latter?

5. What are the arguments for and against granting owners of copyright in a sound recording the exclusive right to perform that recording in public, e.g., on a radio broadcast or at a discotheque? Consider such matters as the artistic contributions of the owner of copyright in the sound recording, the economic impact on the user, the difficulties of collection and distribution of royalties, and whether any such right should be absolute or, instead, subject to a compulsory license.

6. As noted above, the legislative history of the Sound Recording Amendment of 1971 indicates a willingness to exempt from liability the "home recording" off the air or from phonorecords of musical or other works for private listening. Would such an exemption shelter a company which sells electronic supplies, including blank tapes, and which installs in its stores coin-operated "make-a-tape" machines, which can in two minutes reproduce on a blank cassette tape the sounds from a pre-recorded tape (which the company supplies to the make-a-tape customer)? *See Elektra Records Co. v. Gem Electronic Distributors, Inc.,* 360 F. Supp. 821 (E.D.N.Y. 1973).

7. With respect to the proposal to grant performing rights to sound recordings:

a. Consider whether it is appropriate to divide royalties among all performers on a per capita basis, regardless of their artistic contribution to the recorded performance.

b. Given the general tendency of the Constitution and the 1976 Copyright Act to use an "exclusive right" as a means of promoting the creation of literary and artistic works, is a strong enough case made for a compulsory license in the case of sound recordings?

c. Note that in distributing royalties from jukebox performances, the Register's bill would take one dollar from every eight dollars paid annually (before the 1980 adjustments by the Copyright Royalty Tribunal) per jukebox and distribute that dollar among performers and copyright owners of the sound recordings. Would it not be more appropriate to require that the compulsory licensee pay nine dollars per jukebox, so as not to impair royalty payments for the owners of copyright in the musical compositions?

HOUSE REPORT

H.R. Rep. No. 94-1476, 94th Cong., 2d Sess. 101, 103-05 (1976)

Section 112 of the bill concerns itself with a special problem that is not dealt with in the present statutes but is the subject of provisions in a number of foreign statutes and in the revisions of the Berne Convention since 1948. This is the problem of what are commonly called "ephemeral recordings": copies or phonorecords of a work made for purposes of later transmission by a broadcasting organization legally entitled to transmit the work. In other words, where a broadcaster has the privilege of performing or displaying a work either because he is licensed or because the performance or display is exempted under the statute, the question is whether he should be given the additional privilege of recording the performance or display to facilitate its transmission. The need for a limited exemption in these cases because of the practical exigencies of broadcasting has been generally recognized, but the scope of the exemption has been a controversial issue. . . .

Recordings for instructional transmissions

Section 112(b) represents a response to the arguments of instructional broadcasters and other educational groups for special recording privileges, although it does not go as far as these groups requested. In general, it permits a nonprofit organization that is free to transmit a performance or display of a work, under section 110(2) or under the limitations on exclusive rights in sound recordings specified by section 114(a), to make not more than thirty copies or phonorecords and to use the ephemeral recordings for transmitting purposes for not more than seven years after the initial transmission. . . .

Religious broadcasts. — Section 112(c) provides that it is not an infringement of copyright for certain nonprofit organizations to make no more than one copy for each transmitting organization of a broadcast program embodying a performance of a nondramatic musical work of a religious nature or of a sound recording of such a musical work. In order for this exception to be applicable there must be no charge for the distribution of the copies, none of the copies may be used for any performance other than a single transmission by an organization possessing a license to transmit a copyrighted work, and, other than for one copy that may be preserved for archival purposes, the remaining copies must be destroyed within one year from the date the program was first transmitted to the public. . . .

Copyright status of ephemeral recordings

A program reproduced in an ephemeral recording made under section 112 in many cases will constitute a motion picture, a sound recording, or some other kind of derivative work, and will thus be potentially copyrightable under section 103. In section 112(e) it is provided that ephemeral recordings are not to be copyrightable as derivative works except with the consent of the owners of the copyrighted material employed in them. . . .

F. PERFORMING RIGHTS

1. PRE-1976 PERFORMING RIGHTS

a. "For Profit" Performances

Performing rights came relatively late in statutory copyright development. The right was first recognized as to dramatic compositions by the amendatory Act of 1856, 11 Stat. 138, and as to musical compositions by the Act of 1897, 29 Stat. 481. Neither was limited to performances "for profit," but where the performance of music was "willful, and for profit," the act constituted a misdemeanor punishable by imprisonment "for a period not exceeding one year." Rev. Stat. § 4966.

At the turn of the twentieth century, the main source of revenue for the composer had long been by way of royalties from the sale of copies of his or her work in the form of sheet music, and sometimes these ran into large sums. Before radio, an average hit song may have sold over a million copies of sheet music. (This was reportedly reduced to 50,000 by 1940.) See Shull, *Collecting Collectively: ASCAP's Perennial Dilemma,* 7 *ASCAP Copyright Law Symposium* 35, n.2 (1956).

Little thought was given to the performing right, notwithstanding that by the Act of 1897 damages for unlicensed performance were collectible "at such sum, not less than $100 for the first and $50 for every subsequent performance, as to the court shall appear to be just." Although copyrighted music was played for years in public places throughout the country, only a few reported cases are found dealing with infringement of this right under the pre-1909 law, and the outcome was not encouraging to the composer. But soon all this was to be changed. The increasing use of popular music, so vastly stimulated by the rise of the motion picture and radio industries, and the contemporaneous decline in revenue from the sale of copies, at last awakened composers to the possibilities inherent in the performing right.

In 1909, the Copyright Act was amended to give to the owner of copyright in a musical composition the exclusive right to perform it "publicly for profit." In order to take full advantage of that new statutory right, a group of prominent popular composers — among them Victor Herbert and John Philip Sousa — in 1914 formed the American Society of Composers, Authors and Publishers, the first performing rights organization in the United States. The purpose of the organization was to serve as a clearinghouse for performing-rights licensing (thereby reducing the cost of individual licensing) and as an agency to monitor performances and police infringements. With the aid of their able and dedicated attorney, Nathan Burkan, ASCAP embarked on a litigation campaign to establish their statutory rights. First attempts were not promising; the Court of Appeals for the Second Circuit held that the term "for profit" in the 1909 Act meant a direct pecuniary charge to hear the performance, i.e., an admission fee. This view was, however, resoundingly overturned by the United States Supreme Court in a decision of major significance, *Herbert v. Shanley Co.,* 242 U.S. 591

(1917), written in characteristically insightful and pithy style by Mr. Justice Holmes.

The Shanley Company, in its restaurant on Broadway, used the services of professional singers, accompanied by an orchestra, to perform on its stage such songs as Victor Herbert's "Sweethearts," from an operetta of the same name. The Court found this kind of performance to be "for profit" in spite of the fact that no separate charge was made for the music. Justice Holmes stated:

> If the rights under the copyright are infringed only by a performance where money is taken at the door, they are very imperfectly protected.... The defendants' performances are not eleemosynary. They are part of a total for which the public pays, and the fact that the price of the whole is attributed to a particular item which those present are expected to order is not important. It is true that the music is not the sole object, but neither is the food, which probably could be got cheaper elsewhere. The object is a repast in surroundings that to people having limited powers of conversation, or disliking the rival noise, give a luxurious pleasure not to be had from eating a silent meal. If music did not pay, it would be given up. If it pays, it pays out of the public's pocket. Whether it pays or not, the purpose of employing it is profit, and that is enough.

A number of other decisions gave broad compass to the phrase "for profit." In *M. Witmark & Sons v. Pastime Amusement Co.*, 298 F.2d 479 (E.D.S.C. 1924), *aff'd*, 2 F.2d 1020 (4th Cir. 1924), a motion picture theater owner who employed an organist to render appropriate music of her own choice during movie performances was held to infringe; the court rejected the arguments that the organist was an independent contractor and that her performance did not directly generate profit for the theater owner. In a number of "dancehall" cases, such as *Dreamland Ball Room v. Shapiro, Bernstein & Co.*, 36 F.2d 354 (7th Cir. 1929), it was held that the owner of a dancehall who engaged an orchestra and undertook to make a profit was an infringer, even though the orchestra leader may have technically been an independent contractor. And in *Associated Music Publishers, Inc. v. Debs Memorial Radio Fund, Inc.*, 141 F.2d 852 (2d Cir. 1944), a nonprofit broadcasting station, operated for educational and cultural purposes and paying for only one third of its airtime by accepting commercial advertising, was held to have performed "for profit" the plaintiff's song even though it was played on a sustaining (i.e., no commercials) program.

b. "Public" Performances

It will be seen that the statutory definition of public performance in section 101 of the 1976 Act recognizes that a performance can be public even though received in separate places and/or at different times. This is consistent with the earlier determination that a radio broadcast is "public." *See, e.g., Jerome H. Remick & Co. v. American Automobile Accessories Co.*, 5 F.2d 411 (6th Cir.), *cert. denied*, 269 U.S. 556 (1925). Under the 1909 law, a number of cases raising the question of what constitutes a "public" performance centered about face-to-face situations or exhibition of a motion picture at a single location, such as in the *Wyatt* decision expressly rejected in the 1976 statute. *See* p. 423 *infra. But see Lerner v. Club Wander In, Inc.*, 174 F. Supp. 731, 122 USPQ 595 (D. Mass. 1959) (performance may be public notwithstanding right to exclude members of public who do not meet club "standards"). The question became less pressing as to motion pictures because of the ruling in *Patterson v. Century Productions, Inc.*, 93 F.2d 489, 35 USPQ 471 (2d Cir. 1937), *cert. denied*, 303 U.S. 655, 37 USPQ 844 (1938), that the flashing upon the screen of a picture results in making an enlarged copy thereof, and therefore constituted a violation of the right to copy granted in § 1(a) of the 1909 law, regardless of the public or private character of the performance.

2. THE 1976 ACT FRAMEWORK

At first blush, the 1976 Act appears to enlarge the rights of the owner of copyright in a musical composition by eliminating the requirement that an infringing performance be "for profit." However, many nonprofit performances (along with other uses) are exempt under particularized provisions. (Consider the philosophical implications of such a change in statutory design, along with its possible impact upon the conduct of litigation.) Congress was concerned with two discrete kinds of public performances: so-called "face-to-face" performances, where the listeners are present at the "place" of performance and hear the sounds without the aid of amplification devices, and "multiple performances," including the transmission of sound to distant listeners through the use of radio or television technology. Accordingly, after an exploration of a variety of general issues produced by performing right exemptions, the materials will focus on the special problems of multiple performance.

§ 106. Exclusive rights in copyrighted works

Subject to sections 107 through 118, the owner of copyright under this title has the exclusive rights to do and to authorize any of the following:

. . . .

(4) in the case of literary, musical, dramatic and choreographic works, pantomimes, and motion pictures and other audiovisual works, to perform the copyrighted work publicly;

. . . .

§ 101. Definitions

As used in this title, the following terms and their variant forms mean the following:

. . . .

To "perform" a work means to recite, render, play, dance, or act it, either directly or by means of any device or process or, in the case of a motion picture or other audiovisual work, to show its images in any sequence or to make the sounds accompanying it audible.

. . . .

To perform or display a work "publicly" means —

(1) to perform or display it at a place open to the public or at any place where a substantial number of persons outside of a normal circle of a family and its social acquaintances is gathered; or

(2) to transmit or otherwise communicate a performance or display of the work to a place specified by clause (1) or to the public, by means of any device or process, whether the members of the public capable of receiving the performance or display receive it in the same place or in separate places and at the same time or at different times.

To "transmit" a performance or display is to communicate it by any device or process whereby images or sounds are received beyond the place from which they are sent.

. . . .

HOUSE REPORT

H.R. Rep. No. 94-1476, 94th Cong., 2d Sess. 62-65 (1976)

Rights of public performance and display

Performing rights and the "for profit" limitation. — The right of public performance under section 106(4) extends to "literary, musical, dramatic, and choreographic works, pantomimes, and motion pictures and other audiovisual works and sound recordings" and, unlike the equivalent provisions now in effect, is not limited by any "for profit" requirement. The approach of the bill, as in many foreign laws, is first to state the public performance right in broad terms, and then to provide specific exemptions for educational and other nonprofit uses.

This approach is more reasonable than the outright exemption of the 1909 statute. The line between commercial and "nonprofit" organizations is increasingly difficult to draw. Many "non-profit" organizations are highly subsidized and capable of paying royalties, and the widespread public exploitation of copyrighted works by public broadcasters and other noncommercial organizations is likely to grow. In addition to these trends, it is worth noting that performances and displays are continuing to supplant markets for printed copies and that in the future a broad "not for profit" exemption could not only hurt authors but could dry up their incentive to write.

The exclusive right of public performance is expanded to include not only motion pictures, including works records on film, video tape, and video disks, but also audiovisual works such as filmstrips and sets of slides. This provision of section 106(4), which is consistent with the assimilation of motion pictures to audiovisual works throughout the bill, is also related to amendments of the definitions of "display" and "perform" discussed below. The important issue of performing rights in sound recordings is discussed in connection with section 114.

Definitions

Under the definitions of "perform," "display," "publicly," and "transmit" in section 101, the concepts of public performance and public display cover not only the initial rendition or showing, but also any further act by which that rendition or showing is transmitted or communicated to the public. Thus, for example: a singer is performing when he or she sings a song; a broadcasting network is performing when it transmits his or her performance (whether simultaneously or from records); a local broadcaster is performing when it transmits the network broadcast, a cable television system is performing when it retransmits the broadcast to its subscribers; and any individual is performing whenever he or she plays a phonorecord embodying the performance or communicates the performance by turning on a receiving set. Although any act by which the initial performance or display is transmitted, repeated, or made to recur would itself be a "performance" or "display" under the bill, it would not be actionable as an infringement unless it were done "publicly," as defined in section 101. Certain other performances and displays, in addition to those that are "private," are exempted or given qualified copyright control under sections 107 through 118.

To "perform" a work, under the definition in section 101, includes reading a literary work aloud, singing or playing music, dancing a ballet or other choreographic work, and acting out a dramatic work or pantomine. A performance may be accomplished "either directly or by means of any device or process," including all kinds of equipment for reproducing or amplifying sounds or visual images, any sort of transmitting apparatus, any type of electronic retrieval system, and any other techniques and systems not yet in use or even invented.

The definition of "perform" in relation to "a motion picture or other audio visual work" is "to show its images in any sequence or to make the sounds accompanying it audible." The showing of portions of a motion picture, filmstrip, or slide set must therefore be sequential to constitute a "performance" rather than a "display," but no particular order need be maintained. The purely aural performance of a motion picture sound track, or of the sound portions of an audiovisual work, would constitute a performance of the "motion picture or other audiovisual work"; but, where some of the sounds have been reproduced separately on phonorecords, a performance from the phonorecord would not constitute performance of the motion picture or audiovisual work.

The corresponding definition of "display" covers any showing of a "copy" of the work, "either directly or by means of a film, slide, television image, or any other device or process." Since "copies" are defined as including the material object "in which the work is first fixed," the right of public display applies to original works of art as well as to reproductions of them. With respect to motion pictures and other audiovisual works, it is a "display" (rather than a "performance") to show their "individual images nonsequentially." In addition to the direct showings of a copy of a work, "display" would include the projection of an image on a screen or other surface by any method, the transmission of an image by electronic or other means, and the showing of an image on a cathode ray tube, or similar viewing apparatus connected with any sort of information storage and retrieval system.

Under clause (1) of the definition of "publicly" in section 101, a performance or display is "public" if it takes place "at a place open to the public or at any place where a substantial number of persons outside of a normal circle of a family and its social acquaintances is gathered." One of the principal purposes of the definition was to make clear that, contrary to the decision in *Metro-Goldwyn-Mayer Distributing Corp. v. Wyatt,* 21 C.O. Bull. 203 (D. Md. 1932), performances in "semipublic" places such as clubs, lodges, factories, summer camps, and schools are "public performances" subject to copyright control. The term "a family" in this context would include an individual living alone, so that a gathering confined to the individual's social acquaintances would normally be regarded as private. Routine meetings of businesses and governmental personnel would be excluded because they do not represent the gathering of a "substantial number of persons."

Clause (2) of the definition of "publicly" in section 101 makes clear that the concepts of public performance and public display include not only performances and displays that occur initially in a public place, but also acts that transmit or otherwise communicate a performance or display of the work to the public by means of any device or process. The definition of "transmit" — to communicate a performance or display "by any device or process whereby images or sound are received beyond the place from which they are sent" — is broad enough to include all conceivable forms and combinations of wired or wireless communications media, including but by no means limited to radio and television broadcasting as we know them. Each and every method by which the images or sounds comprising a performance or display are picked up and conveyed is a "transmission," and if the transmission reaches the public in any form, the case comes within the scope of clauses (4) or (5) of section 106.

Under the bill, as under the present law, a performance made available by transmission to the public at large is "public" even though the recipients are not gathered in a single place, and even if there is no proof that any of the potential recipients was operating his receiving apparatus at the time of the transmission. The same principles apply whenever the potential recipients of the transmission represent a limited segment of the public, such as the occupants of hotel rooms or the subscribers of a cable television service. Clause (2) of the definition of "publicly" is applicable "whether the members of the public capable of receiving the performance or display receive it in the same place or in separate places and at the same time or at different times."

§ 110. Limitations on exclusive rights: Exemption of certain performances and displays

Notwithstanding the provisions of section 106, the following are not infringements of copyright:

(1) performance or display of a work by instructors or pupils in the course of face-to-face teaching activities of a nonprofit educational institution, in a classroom or similar place devoted to instruction, unless, in the case of a motion picture or other audiovisual work, the performance, or the display of individual images, is given by means of a copy that was not lawfully made under this title, and that the person responsible for the performance knew or had reason to believe was not lawfully made;

(2) performance of a nondramatic literary or musical work or display of a work, by or in the course of a transmission, if —

(A) the performance or display is a regular part of the systematic instructional activities of a governmental body or a nonprofit educational institution; and

(B) the performance or display is directly related and of material assistance to the teaching content of the transmission; and

(C) the transmission is made primarily for —

(i) reception in classrooms or similar places normally devoted to instruction, or

(ii) reception by persons to whom the transmission is directed because their disabilities or other special circumstances prevent their attendance in classrooms or similar places normally devoted to instruction, or

(iii) reception by officers or employees of governmental bodies as a part of their official duties or employment;

(3) performance of a nondramatic literary or musical work or of a dramatico-musical work of a religious nature, or display of a work, in the course of services at a place of worship or other religious assembly;

(4) performance of a nondramatic literary or musical work otherwise than in a transmission to the public, without any purpose of direct or indirect commercial advantage and without payment of any fee or other compensation for the performance to any of its performers, promoters, or organizers, if —

(A) there is no direct or indirect admission charge; or

(B) the proceeds, after deducting the reasonable costs of producing the performance, are used exclusively for educational, religious, or charitable purposes and not for private financial gain, except where the copyright owner has served notice of objection to the performance under the following conditions;

(i) the notice shall be in writing and signed by the copyright owner or such owner's duly authorized agent; and

(ii) the notice shall be served on the person responsible for the performance at least seven days before the date of the performance, and shall state the reasons for the objection; and

(iii) the notice shall comply, in form, content, and manner of service, with requirements that the Register of Copyrights shall prescribe by regulation;

. . . .

(6) performance of a nondramatic musical work by a governmental body or a nonprofit agricultural or horticultural organization, in the course of an annual agricultural or horticultural fair or exhibition conducted by such body or organization; the exemption provided by this clause shall extend to any liability for copyright infringement that would otherwise be imposed on such body or organization, under doctrines of vicarious liability or related infringement, for a performance by a concessionnaire, business establishment, or other person at such fair or exhibition, but shall not excuse any such person from liability for the performance;

(7) performance of a nondramatic musical work by a vending establishment open to the public at large without any direct or indirect admission charge, where the sole purpose of the performance is to promote the retail sale of copies or phonorecords of the work, and the performance is not transmitted beyond the place where the establishment is located and is within the immediate area where the sale is occurring;

(8) performance of a nondramatic literary work, by or in the course of a transmission specifically designed for and primarily directed to blind or other handicapped persons who are unable to read normal printed material as a result of their handicap, or deaf or other handicapped persons who are unable to hear the aural signals accompanying a transmission of visual signals, if the performance is made without any purpose of direct or indirect commercial advantage and its transmission is made through the facilities of: (i) a governmental body; or (ii) a noncommercial educational broadcast station (as defined in section 397 of title 47); or (iii) a radio subcarrier authorization (as defined in 47 CFR 73.293 — 73.295 and 73.593 — 73.595); or (iv) a cable system (as defined in section 111(f)).

(9) performance on a single occasion of a dramatic literary work published at least ten years before the date of the performance, by or in the course of a transmission specifically designed for and primarily directed to blind or other handicapped persons who are unable to read normal printed material as a result of their handicap, if the performance is made without any purpose of direct or indirect commercial advantage and its transmission is made through the facilities of a radio subcarrier authorization referred to in clause (8) (iii), *Provided,* That the provisions of this clause shall not be applicable to more than one performance of the same work by the same performers or under the auspices of the same organization.

HOUSE REPORT

H.R. Rep. No. 94-1476, 94th Cong., 2d Sess. 81-86 (1976)

Clauses (1) through (4) of section 110 deal with performances and exhibitions that are now generally exempt under the "for profit" limitation or other provisions of the copyright law, and that are specifically exempted from copyright liability under this legislation. Clauses (1) and (2) between them are intended to cover all of the various methods by which performances or displays in the course of systematic instruction take place.

Face-to-face teaching activities

Clause (1) of section 110 is generally intended to set out the conditions under which performances or displays, in the course of instructional activities other than educational broadcasting, are to be exempted from copyright control. The clause covers all types of copyrighted works, and exempts their performance or display "by instructors or pupils in the course of face-to-face teaching activities of a nonprofit educational institution," where the activities take place "in a classroom or similar place devoted to instruction."

There appears to be no need for a statutory definition of "face-to-face" teaching activities to clarify the scope of the provision. "Face-to-face teaching activities" under clause (1) embrace instructional performances and displays that are not "transmitted." The concept does not require that the teacher and students be able to see each other, although it does require their simultaneous presence in the same general place. Use of the phrase "in the course of face-to-face teaching activities" is intended to exclude broadcasting or other transmissions from an outside location into classrooms, whether radio or television and whether open or closed circuit. However, as long as the instructor and pupils are in the same building or general area, the exemption would extend to the use of devices for amplifying or reproducing sound and for projecting visual images. The "teaching activities" exempted by the clause encompass systematic instruction of a very wide variety of subjects, but they do not include performances or displays, whatever their cultural value or intellectual appeal, that are given for the recreation or entertainment of any part of their audience.

Works affected. — Since there is no limitation on the types of works covered by the exemption, teachers or students would be free to perform or display anything in class as long as the other conditions of the clause are met. They could read aloud from copyrighted text material, act out a drama, play or sing a musical work, perform a motion picture or filmstrip, or display text or pictorial material to the class by means of a projector. However, nothing in this provision is intended to sanction the unauthorized reproduction of copies or phonorecords for the purpose of classroom performance or display, and the clause contains a special exception dealing with performances from unlawfully made copies of motion pictures and other audiovisual works, to be discussed below.

Instructors or pupils. — To come within clause (1), the performance or display must be "by instructors or pupils," thus ruling out performances by actors, singers, or instrumentalists brought in from outside the school to put on a program. However, the term "instructors" would be broad enought to include guest lecturers if their instructional activities remain confined to classroom situations. In general, the term "pupils" refers to the enrolled members of a class.

Nonprofit educational institution. — Clause (1) makes clear that it applies only to the teaching activities "of a nonprofit educational institution," thus excluding from the exemption performances or displays in profit-making institutions such as dance studios and language schools.

Classroom or similar place. — The teaching activities exempted by the clause must take place "in a classroom or similar place devoted to instruction." For example, performances in an auditorium or stadium during a school assembly, graduation ceremony, class play, or sporting event, where the audience is not confined to the members of a particular class, would fall outside the scope of clause (1), although in some cases they might be exempted by clause (4) of section 110. The "similar place" referred to in clause (1) is a place which is "devoted to instruction" in the same way a classroom is; common examples would include a studio, a workshop, a gymnasium, a training field, a library, the stage of an auditorium, or the auditorium itself, if it is actually used as a classroom for systematic instructional activities.

Motion pictures and other audiovisual works. — The final provision of clause (1) deals with the special problem of performances from unlawfully-made copies of motion pictures and other audiovisual works. The exemption is lost where the copy being used for a classroom performance was "not lawfully made under this title" and the person responsible for the performance knew or had reason to suspect as much. This special exception to the exemption would not apply to performances from lawfully-made copies, even if the copies were acquired from someone who had stolen or converted them, or if the performances were in violation of an agreement. However, though the performance would be exempt under section 110(1) in such cases, the copyright owner might have a cause of action against the unauthorized distributor under section 106(3), or against the person responsible for the performance, for breach of contract.

Projection devices. — As long as there is no transmission beyond the place where the copy is located, both section 109(b) and section 110(1) would permit the classroom display of a work by means of any sort of projection device or process.

Instructional broadcasting

Works affected. — The exemption for instructional broadcasting provided by section 110(2) would apply only to "performance of a non-dramatic literary or musical work or display of a work." Thus, the copyright owner's permission would be required for the performance on educational television or radio of a dramatic work, of a dramatico-musical work such as an opera or musical comedy, or of a motion picture. Since, as already explained, audiovisual works such as filmstrips are equated with motion pictures, their sequential showing would be regarded as a performance rather than a display and would not be exempt under section 110(2). The clause is not intended to limit in any way the copyright owner's exclusive right to make dramatizations, adaptations, or other derivative works under section 106(2). Thus, for example, a performer could read a nondramatic literary work aloud under section 110(2), but the copyright owner's permission would be required for him to act it out in dramatic form.

Systematic instructional activities. — Under section 110(2) a transmission must meet three specified conditions in order to be exempted from copyright liability. The first of these, as provided by subclause (A), is that the performance or display must be "a regular part of the systematic instructional activities of a governmental body or a nonprofit educational institution." The concept of "systematic instructional activities" is intended as the general equivalent of "curriculums," but it could be broader in a case such as that of an institution using systematic teaching methods not related to specific course work. A transmission would be a regular part of these activities if it is in accordance with the pattern of teaching established by the governmental body or institution. The use of commercial facilities, such as those of a cable service, to transmit the performance or display, would not affect the exemption as long as the actual performance or display was for nonprofit purposes.

Content of transmission. — Subclause (B) requires that the performance or display be directly related and of material assistance to the teaching content of the transmission.

Intended recipients. — Subclause (C) requires that the transmission is made primarily for:

(*i*) Reception in classrooms or similar places normally devoted to instruction, or

(*ii*) Reception by persons to whom the transmission is directed because their disabilities or other special circumstances prevent their attendance in classrooms or similar places normally devoted to instruction, or

(*iii*) Reception by officers or employees of governmental bodies as a part of their official duties or employment.

In all three cases, the instructional transmission need only be made "primarily" rather than "solely" to the specified recipients to be exempt. Thus, the transmission could still be exempt even though it is capable of reception by the public at large. Conversely, it would not be regarded as made "primarily" for one of the required groups of recipients if the principal purpose behind the transmission is reception by the public at large, even if it is cast in the form of instruction and is also received in classrooms. Factors to consider in determining the "primary" purpose of a program would include its subject matter, content, and the time of its transmission.

Paragraph (i) of subclause (C) generally covers what are known as "in-school" broadcasts, whether open- or closed-circuit. The reference to "classrooms or similar places" here is intended to have the same meaning as that of the phrase as used in section 110(1). The exemption in paragraph (ii) is intended to exempt transmissions providing systematic instruction to individuals who cannot be reached in classrooms because of "their disabilities or other special circumstances." Accordingly, the exemption is confined to instructional broadcasting that is an adjunct to the actual classwork of nonprofit schools or is primarily for people who cannot be brought together in classrooms such as preschool children, displaced workers, illiterates, and shut-ins.

There has been some question as to whether or not the language in this section of the bill is intended to include instructional television college credit courses. These telecourses are aimed at undergraduate and graduate students in earnest pursuit of higher educational degrees who are unable to attend daytime classes because of daytime employment, distance from campus, or some other intervening reason. So long as these broadcasts are aimed at regularly enrolled students and conducted by recognized higher educational institutions, the committee believes that they are clearly within the language of section 110 (2)(C)(ii). Like night school and correspondence courses before them, these telecourses are fast becoming a valuable adjunct of the normal college curriculum.

The third exemption in subclause (C) is intended to permit the use of copyrighted material, in accordance with the other conditions of section 110(2), in the course of instructional transmissions for Government personnel who are receiving training "as a part of their official duties or employment."

Religious services

The exemption in clause (3) of section 110 covers performances of a nondramatic literary or musical work, and also performances "of dramatico-musical works of a religious nature"; in addition, it extends to displays of works of all kinds. The exemption applies where the performance or display is "in the course of services at a place of worship or other religious assembly." The scope of the clause does not cover the sequential showing of motion pictures and other audiovisual works.

The exemption, which to some extent has its counterpart in sections 1 and 104 of the present law, applies to dramatico-musical works "of a religious nature." The purpose here is to exempt certain performances of sacred music that might be regarded as "dramatic" in nature, such as oratorios, cantatas, musical settings of the mass, choral services, and the like. The exemption is not intended to cover performances of secular operas, musical plays, motion pictures, and the like, even if they have an underlying religious or philosophical theme and take place "in the course of [religious] services."

To be exempted under section 110(3) a performance or display must be "in the course of services," thus excluding activities at a place of worship that are for social, educational, fund raising, or entertainment purposes. Some performances of these kinds could be covered by the exemption in section 110(4), discussed next. Since the performance or display must also occur "at a place of worship or other religious assembly," the exemption would not extend to religious broadcasts or other transmissions to the public at large, even where the transmissions were sent from the place of worship. On the other hand, as long as services are being conducted before a religious gathering, the exemption would apply if they were conducted in places such as auditoriums, outdoor theaters, and the like.

Certain other nonprofit performances

In addition to the educational and religious exemptions provided by clauses (1) through (3) of section 110, clause (4) contains a general exception to the exclusive right of public performance that would cover some, though not all, of the same ground as the present "for profit" limitation.

Scope of exemption. — The exemption in clause (4) applies to the same general activities and subject matter as those covered by the "for profit" limitation today: public performances of nondramatic literary and musical works. However, the exemption would be limited to public performances given directly in the presence of an audience whether by means of living performers, the playing of phonorecords, or the operation of a receiving apparatus, and would not include a "transmission to the public." Unlike the clauses (1) through (3) and (5) of section 110, but like clauses (6) through (8), clause (4) applies only to performing rights in certain works, and does not affect the exclusive right to display a work in public.

No profit motive. — In addition to the other conditions specified by the clause, the performance must be "without any purpose of direct or indirect commercial advantage." This provision expressly adopts the principle established by the court decisions construing the "for profit" limitation: that public performances given or sponsored in connection with any commercial or profit-making enterprises are subject to the exclusive rights of the copyright owner even though the public is not charged for seeing or hearing the performance.

No payment for performance. — An important condition for this exemption is that the performance be given "without payment of any fee or other compensation for the performance to any of its performers, promoters, or organizers." The basic purpose of this requirement is to prevent the free use of copyrighted material under the guise of charity where fees or percentages are paid to performers, promoters, producers, and the like. However, the exemption would not be lost if the performers, directors, or producers of the performance, instead of being paid directly "for the performance," are paid a salary for duties encompassing the performance. Examples are performances by a school orchestra conducted by a music teacher who receives an annual salary, or by a service band whose members and conductors perform as part of their assigned duties and who receive military pay. The committee believes that performances of this type should be exempt, assuming the other conditions in clause (4) are met, and has not adopted the suggestion that the word "salary" be added to the phrase referring to the "payment of any fee or other compensation."

Admission charge. — Assuming that the performance involves no profit motive and no one responsible for its gets paid a fee, it must still meet one of two alternative conditions to be exempt. As specified in subclauses (A) and (B) of section 110(4), these conditions are: (1) that no direct or indirect admission charge is made, or (2) that the net proceeds are "used exclusively for educational, religious, or charitable purposes and not for private financial gain."

Under the second of these conditions, a performance meeting the other conditions of clause (4) would be exempt even if an admission fee is charged, provided any amounts left "after deducting the reasonable costs of producing the performance" are used solely for bona fide educational, religious, or charitable purposes. In cases arising under this second condition and as provided in subclause (B), where there is an admission charge, the copyright owner is given an opportunity to decide whether and under what conditions the copyrighted work should be performed; otherwise, owners could be compelled to make involuntary donations to the fund-raising activities of causes to which they are opposed. The subclause would thus permit copyright owners to prevent public performances of their works under section 110(4) (B) by serving notice of objection, with the reasons therefor, at least seven days in advance.

QUESTIONS

1. In the 1909 Act, public performances of copyrighted music and nondramatic literary works (specifically lectures, sermons and addresses) were not infringements provided they were not "for profit" (a term that the statute left undefined). The 1976 Act expanded the performance right by making *all* public performances prima facie infringements while exempting only specifically delineated ones. What were the reasons for the "for profit" limitation in the 1909 Act? Were there good reasons for abandoning it when drafting the 1976 Act? Indeed, so long as Congress was considering a change, why did it not choose to authorize the public performance of even dramatic works, provided they were "not for profit"?

2. In examining the detailed exemption provisions of the 1976 Act, determine the extent to which they give the copyright owner greater protection than did the 1909 Act. Are there any circumstances in which they give the copyright owner *less* protection? Are all of these changes sound? Even if the exemptions in § 110 give neither greater nor less protection than under the 1909 Act, is there any practical difference in the approach taken by the drafters of the two acts?

3. During a special church service directed at the younger generation, a performance is given of substantial excerpts (in sequence) from the rock musical "Jesus Christ Superstar." Is this an infringement of copyright?

4. The House Report, in discussing Section 110(3) states: "The exemption would not extend to religious broadcasts or other transmissions to the public at large, even where the transmissions were sent from the place of worship." Is this another example of an attempt through legislative history to limit the apparent reach of fairly clear statutory language?

5. Is a nonprofit requirement found in the religious exemption in § 110(3)? If such a requirement is implied how is it to be interpreted?

6. By providing in § 110(4)(B) for the serving by the copyright owner of a "notice of objection" to certain nonprofit public performances, does Congress contemplate that advance word of all such performances must be communicated

by the promoters or performers to the copyright owner? If not, how often will the copyright owner actually be aware of such performances? Ought the copyright owner, in order to deal with this problem, serve a "blanket" notice of objection, covering all of his musical compositions, to all institutions where there is some chance of its performance (e.g., all colleges and all secondary schools)? (Obviously, ASCAP or BMI could much more effectively serve such notices than could individual composers.) Would such a blanket notice, served in futuro, be adequate under § 110(4) to remove the exemption? See 37 CFR § 201.13.

7. If the § 110(4)(B) exemption seeks to prevent involuntary contributions to causes not supported by particular copyright owners, could atheists complain about the § 110(3) exemptions? Are there any First Amendment objections to § 110(3)?

3. MULTIPLE PERFORMANCES

An interesting sequence of judicial history developed the definition under the 1909 law of what constituted a "performance." Four Supreme Court cases dominated this history:

(1) **Buck v. Jewell-La Salle Realty Co.**, 283 U.S. 191, 9 USPQ 17 (1931). The act of a hotel proprietor of making available to its guests, by means of radio receivers and loud speakers in public and private rooms, the *unauthorized* rendition of copyrighted music by a neighboring broadcasting station was here held to constitute *performance* of the original program. The Court held further that foreknowledge of the selections to be played was immaterial, because intention to infringe is not essential under the Copyright Act, and that one who merely "tunes in" on his receiving set actually performs the work in the statutory sense of the term and therefore runs the risk of incurring a suit for infringement if he does so in public for the purpose of commercial profit. The court of appeals accordingly found on remand that the specific acts of the proprietor of the hotel constituted a "public performance for profit." 51 F.2d 726, 10 USPQ 70 (8th Cir. 1931).

If an initial broadcasting "performance" takes place under an unrestricted license from the owner of the performing rights, it is arguable that the license would implicitly also extend to its commercial reception and distribution by others. *Buck v. Debaum,* 40 F.2d 734 (S.D. Cal. 1929); *Buck v. Jewell-La Salle Realty Co.,* 283 U.S. 191, 199, n.5, 9 USPQ 17, 19 n.5. In response to a warning to this effect sounded in a *Buck* footnote, the American Society of Composers, Authors and Publishers has expressly provided that its broadcast license does not run in favor of persons picking up the broadcast, such as the LaSalle Hotel.

(2) **Fortnightly Corp. v. United Artists Television, Inc.,** 392 U.S. 390, 158 USPQ 1 (1968). The retransmission of local copyrighted television programs by community antenna television systems was held not to "perform" the programs. In a 5-to-1 decision, the Court drew a dichotomy between broadcasters and viewers and, after analysis of the functions of each, determined that a CATV system "falls on the viewer's side of the line," since it "no more than enhances the viewer's capacity to receive the broadcaster's signals." The Court treated *Buck* as "a questionable 35-year-old decision that in actual practice has not been applied outside its own factual context," 392 U.S. at 401, n.30, 158 USPQ at 6, n.30, namely, where the original broadcast had been unauthorized. *Id.,* n.18. The dissenting opinion of Mr. Justice Fortas argued that "the interpretation of the term 'perform' cannot logically turn on the question whether the material that is used is licensed or not licensed." 392 U.S. at 406, n.5, 158 USPQ at 8, n.5.

A philosophical underpinning of the majority opinion seems to have been the message in Kaplan, An Unhurried View of Copyright 57 (1967), that " 'use' is not the same thing as 'infringement', that use short of infringement is to be encouraged. . . ." *See* 392 U.S. at 393, n.8, 158 USPQ at 3, n.8.

(3) **Teleprompter Corp. v. Columbia Broadcasting System, Inc.,** 415 U.S. 394, 181 USPQ 65 (1974). The opinion in *Fortnightly* was accompanied by footnotes that warned "while we speak in this opinion generally of CATV, we necessarily do so with reference to the facts of this case," (note 25) and more specifically that "[s]ome CATV systems, about 10%, originate some of their own programs. We do not deal with such systems in this opinion" (note 6). Accordingly, it was soon argued that the *Fortnightly* case did not cover systems which originated certain programs; used microwave transmissions (rather than solely cable); included commercials in their transmissions; interconnected with other systems; and offered subscribers "distant signals," i.e., signals not ordinarily receivable by house-top antennas or both house-top and tower-mounted antennas. The Court of Appeals for the Second Circuit held in *Teleprompter* that this last characteristic did distinguish such a system from those involved in *Fortnightly,* because its "function in this regard is no longer merely to enhance the subscriber's ability to receive signals that are in the area; it is now acting to bring signals into the community that would not otherwise be receivable on an antenna, even a large community antenna erected in that area."

The Supreme Court reversed, rejecting all of the attempts to distinguish the *Fortnightly* case.

The importation of distant broadcast signals was deemed no different functionally from that of strengthening local signals blocked by buildings or topography. "The privilege of receiving the broadcast electronic signals and of converting them into the sights and sounds of the program inheres in all members of the public who have the means of doing so. The reception and rechanneling of these signals for simultaneous viewing is essentially a viewer function, irrespective of the distance between the broadcasting station and the ultimate viewer." The Court also rejected the claim that the cable system importing distant signals does more than perform a passive retransmission function and instead, by picking and choosing those distant signals to be transmitted, functions much like a local broadcaster choosing the mix of national and local programming it will broadcast. The Court stated that the local broadcaster exercises a "creative choice" among its broadcasting possibilities, while "an operator of a CATV system . . . makes a choice as to which broadcast signals to rechannel to its subscribers, and its creative function is then extinguished"; it simply then carries the signals without editing them. (The Court made no mention whatever of the *Buck* decision.) Finally, the Court rejected the plaintiff's contention that cable retransmission of distant programs should infringe because of the deleterious impact upon the economics and market structure of copyright licensing. The Court's discussion of this issue is worth setting forth in full.

When a copyright holder first licenses a copyrighted program to be shown on broadcast television, he typically cannot expect to recoup his entire investment from a single broadcast. Rather, after a program has had a "first run" on the major broadcasting networks, it is often later syndicated to affiliates and independent stations for "second run" propagation to secondary markets. The copyright holders argue that if CATV systems are allowed to import programs and rechannel them into secondary markets they will dilute the profitability of later syndications, since viewer appeal, as measured by various rating systems, diminishes with each successive showing in a given market. We are told that in order to ensure "the general benefits derived by the public from the labors of authors," *Fox Film Corp. v. Doyal,* 286 U.S. 123, 127, and " 'the incentive to further efforts for the same important objects' " *id.,* at 127-128, *citing Kendall v. Winsor,* 21 How. 322, 328, 16 L. Ed. 165, current licensing relationships must be maintained.

In the television industry, however, the commercial relations between the copyright holders and the licensees on the one hand and the viewing public on the other are such that dilution or dislocation of markets does not have the direct economic or copyright significance that this argument ascribes to it. Unlike propagators of other copyrighted material, such as those who sell books, perform live dramatic productions, or project motion pictures to live audiences, holders of copyrights for television programs or their licensees are not paid directly by those who ultimately enjoy the publication of the material—that is, the television viewers—but by advertisers who use the drawing power of the copyrighted material to promote their goods and services. Such advertisers typically pay the broadcasters a fee for each transmission of an advertisement based on an estimate of the expected number and characteristics of the viewers who will watch the program. While, as members of the general public, the viewers indirectly pay for the privilege of viewing copyrighted material through increased prices for the goods and services of the advertisers, they are not involved in a direct economic relationship with the copyright holders or their licensees.[13]

By extending the range of viewability of a broadcast program, CATV systems thus do not interfere in any traditional sense with the copyright holders' means of extracting recompense for their creativity or labor. When a broadcaster transmits a program under license from the copyright holder he has no control over the segment of the population which may view the program—the broadcaster cannot beam the program exclusively to the young or to the old, only to women or only to men—but rather he gets paid by advertisers on the basis of all viewers who watch the program. The use of CATV does not significantly alter this situation. Instead of basing advertising fees on the number of viewers within the range of direct transmission plus those who may receive "local signals" via a CATV system, broadcasters whose reception ranges have been extended by means of "distant" signal CATV rechanneling will merely have a different and larger viewer market.[14] From the point of view of the broadcasters, such market extension may mark a reallocation of the potential number of viewers each station may reach, a fact of no direct concern under the Copyright Act. From the point of view of the copyright holders, such market changes will mean that the compensation a broadcaster will be willing to pay for the use of copyrighted material will be calculated on the basis of the size of the direct broadcast market augmented by the size of the CATV market.[15]

---

[13] Some commentators have suggested that if CATV systems must pay license fees for the privilege of retransmitting copyrighted broadcast programs, the CATV subscribers will in effect be paying twice for the privilege of seeing such programs: first through increased prices for the goods and services of the advertisers who pay for the television broadcasts and a second time in the increased cost of the CATV service. Note, CATV and Copyright Liability: On a Clear Day You Can See Forever, 52 Va. L. Rev. 1505, 1515 (1966): Note, CATV and Copyright Liability, 80 Harv. L. Rev. 1514, 1522-1523 (1967). See n. 15, infra.

[14] Testimony and exhibits introduced in the District Court indicate that the major rating services cover in their compilations statistics concerning the entire number of viewers of a particular program, including those who receive the broadcast via "distant" transmission over CATV systems. The weight given such statistics by advertisers who bid for broadcast time and pay the fees which support the broadcasting industry was not, however, established. See n. 15, infra.

[15] It is contended that copyright holders will necessarily suffer a net loss from the dissemination of their copyrighted material if license-free use of "distant" signal

These shifts in current business and commercial relationships, while of significance with respect to the organization and growth of the communications industry, simply cannot be controlled by means of litigation based on copyright legislation enacted more than half a century ago, when neither broadcast television nor CATV was yet conceived. Detailed regulation of these relationships, and any ultimate resolution of the many sensitive and important problems in this field, must be left to Congress.

QUESTIONS

1. Does not the rule underlying *Fortnightly* completely destroy the doctrine of multiple performances? For example, why is it not arguable that under that rule the only person who really "performs" a copyrighted song is the band playing in the television studio, and all that the television network or station is doing is assisting the viewer to hear sounds otherwise inaudible?

2. The Court in *Fortnightly* had confidently stated that no reasonable person could claim that the viewer "performed" the dramatic and musical works being shown on television merely by turning the knob. Was that assertion compelled by the language of the 1909 Act? Is not that assertion completely repudiated by the language of the 1976 Act?

3. Is there some less foolish rationale for the Court's decision in *Fortnightly* than the broadcaster-viewer distinction (labeled "simplistic" by Justice

---

importation is permitted. It is said that importation of copyrighted material into a secondary market will result in a loss in the secondary market without increasing revenues from the extended primary market on a scale sufficient to compensate for that loss. The assumption is that local advertisers supporting "first run" programs will be unlikely to pay significantly higher fees on the basis of additional views in a "distant" market because such viewers will typically have no commercial interest in the goods and services sold by purely local advertisers. For discussion of the possible impact of CATV "distant" signal importation on advertiser markets for broadcast television, see 52 Va.L.Rev., at 1513-1516; 80 Harv.L.Rev., at 1522-1525. The Court of Appeals noted that "[n]o evidence was presented in the court below to show that regional or local advertisers would be willing to pay greater fees because the sponsored program will be exhibited in some distant market, or that national advertisers would pay more for the relatively minor increase in audience size that CATV carriage would yield for a network program," and concluded that "[i]ndeed, economics and common sense would impel one to an opposite conclusion." 476 F.2d, at 342 n. 2. Thus, no specific findings of fact were made concerning the precise impact of "distant" signal retransmission on the value of program copyrights. But such a showing would be of very little relevance to the copyright question we decide here. At issue in this case is the limited question of whether CATV transmission of "distant" signals constitutes a "performance" under the Copyright Act. While securing compensation to the holders of copyrights was an essential purpose of that Act, freezing existing economic arrangements for doing so was not. It has been suggested that the best theoretical approach to the problem might be "[a] rule which called for compensation to copyright holders only for the actual advertising time 'wasted' on local advertisers unwilling to pay for the increase in audience size brought about by the cable transmission." Note, 87 Harv.L.Rev. 665, 675 n. 32 (1974). But such a rule would entail extended factfinding and a legislative, rather than a judicial, judgment. In any event, a determination of the best alternative structure for providing compensation to copyright holders, or a prediction of the possible evolution in the relationship between advertising markets and the television medium, is beyond the competence of this Court.

Blackmun)? If, for example, the Court had utilized an "implied license" analysis covering television receivers within the range of the broadcaster's "local" signals, would not the result have been the same but the rationale somewhat more tenable? Would not such an analysis, however, have compelled a different result in the *Teleprompter* case? Do you believe such a difference would be supportable on the basis of both logic and economic analysis?

TWENTIETH CENTURY MUSIC CORP. v. AIKEN

422 U.S. 151 (1975)

Mr. Justice Stewart delivered the opinion of the Court.

The question presented by this case is whether the reception of a radio broadcast of a copyrighted musical composition can constitute copyright infringement, when the copyright owner has licensed the broadcaster to perform the composition publicly for profit.

I

The respondent George Aiken owns and operates a small fast-service food shop in downtown Pittsburgh, Pa., known as "George Aiken's Chicken." Some customers carry out the food they purchase, while others remain and eat at counters or booths. Usually the "carry-out" customers are in the restaurant for less than five minutes, and those who eat there seldom remain longer than 10 or 15 minutes.

A radio with outlets to four speakers in the ceiling receives broadcasts of music and other normal radio programming at the restaurant. Aiken usually turns on the radio each morning at the start of business. Music, news, entertainment, and commercial advertising broadcast by radio stations are thus heard by Aiken, his employees, and his customers during the hours that the establishment is open for business.

On March 11, 1972, broadcasts of two copyrighted musical compositions were received on the radio from a local station while several customers were in Aiken's establishment. Petitioner Twentieth Century Music Corp. owns the copyright on one of these songs, "The More I See You"; petitioner Mary Bourne the copyright on the other, "Me and My Shadow." Petitioners are members of the American Society of Composers, Authors and Publishers (ASCAP), an association that licenses the performing rights of its members to their copyrighted works. The station that broadcast the petitioners' songs was licensed by ASCAP to broadcast them.[1] Aiken, however, did not hold a license from ASCAP.

The petitioners sued Aiken in the United States Court for the Western District of Pennsylvania to recover for copyright infringement. Their complaint alleged

---

[1] For a discussion of ASCAP, see K-91, Inc. v. Gershwin Publishing Corp., 372 F.2d 1 (CA9).

ASCAP's license agreement with the Pittsburgh broadcasting station contained, as is customary, the following provision:

Nothing herein contained shall be construed as authorizing LICENSEE [WKJF-FM] to grant to others any right to reproduce or perform publicly for profit by any means, method or process whatsoever, any of the musical compositions licensed hereunder or as authorizing any receiver of any radio broadcast to perform publicly or reproduce the same for profit, be any means, method or process whatsoever.

that the radio reception in Aiken's restaurant of the licensed broadcasts infringed their exclusive rights to "perform" their copyrighted works in public for profit. The District Judge agreed, and granted statutory monetary awards for each infringement. 356 F. Supp. 271. The United States Court of Appeals for the Third Circuit reversed that judgment, 500 F. 2d 127, holding that the petitioners' claims against the respondent were foreclosed by this Court's decisions in *Fortnightly Corp. v. United Artists,* 392 U.S. 390, and *Teleprompter Corp. v. CBS,* 415 U. S. 394. We granted certiorari. 419 U. S. 1067.

II

The Copyright Act of 1909, 35 Stat. 1075, as amended, 17 U. S. C. § 1 et seq., gives to a copyright holder a monopoly limited to specified "exclusive" rights in his copyrighted works. As the Court explained in *Fortnightly Corp. v. United Artists, supra:*

> The Copyright Act does not give a copyright holder control over all uses of his copyrighted work. Instead, § 1 of the Act enumerates several "rights" that are made "exclusive" to the holder of the copyright. If a person, without authorization from the copyright holder, puts a copyrighted work to a use within the scope of one of these "exclusive rights," he infringes the copyright. If he puts the work to a use not enumerated in § 1, he does not infringe. 392 U. S., at 393-395.

Accordingly, if an unlicensed use of a copyrighted works does not conflict with an "exclusive" right conferred by the statute, it is no infringement of the holder's rights. No license is required by the Copyright Act, for example, to sing a copyrighted lyric in the shower.[4]

The limited scope of the copyright holder's statutory monopoly, like the limited copyright duration required by the Constitution, reflects a balance of competing claims upon the public interest: Creative work is to be encouraged and rewarded, but private motivation must ultimately serve the cause of promoting broad public availability of literature, music, and the other arts. The immediate effect of our copyright law is to secure a fair return for an "author's" creative labor. But the ultimate aim is, by this incentive, to stimulate artistic creativity for the general public good. "The sole interest of the United States and the primary object in conferring the monopoly," this Court has said, "lie in the general benefits derived by the public from the labors of authors." *Fox Film Corp. v. Doyal,* 286 U. S. 123, 127. See *Kendall v. Winsor,* 21 How. 322, 327-328; *Grant v. Raymond,* 6 Pet. 218, 241-242. When technological change has rendered its literal terms ambiguous, the Copyright Act must be construed in light of this basic purpose.

The precise statutory issue in the present case is whether Aiken infringed upon the petitioners' exclusive right, under the Copyright Act of 1909, 17 U. S. C. § 1 (e), "[t]o perform the copyrighted work publicly for profit." We may assume that the radio reception of the musical compositions in Aiken's restaurant occurred "publicly for profit." See *Herbert v. Shanley Co.,* 242 U. S. 591. The

---

[4] Cf. Wall v. Taylor, 11 Q. B. D. 102, 106-107 (1883) (Brett, M. R.):

Singing for one's own gratification without intending thereby to represent anything, or to amuse any one else, would not, I think, be either a representation or performance, according to the ordinary meaning of those terms, nor would the fact of some other person being in the room at the time of such singing make it so. . . .

dispositive question, therefore, is whether this radio reception constituted a "performance" of the copyrighted works.

When this statutory provision was enacted in 1909, its purpose was to prohibit unauthorized performances of copyrighted musical compositions in such public places as concert halls, theaters, restaurants, and cabarets. See H. R. Rep. No. 2222, 60th Cong., 2d Sess (1909). An orchestra or individual instrumentalist or singer who performs a copyrighted musical composition in such a public place without a license is thus clearly an infringer under the statute. The entrepreneur who sponsors such a public performance for profit is also an infringer—direct or contributory. See generally 1 & 2 M. Nimmer, Copyright §§ 102, 134 (1974). But it was never contemplated that the members of the audience who heard the composition would themselves also be simultaneously "performing," and thus also guilty of infringement. This much is common ground.

With the advent of commercial radio, a broadcast musical composition could be heard instantaneously by an enormous audience of distant and separate persons operating their radio receiving sets to reconvert the broadcast to audible form. Although Congress did not revise the statutory language, copyright law was quick to adapt to prevent the exploitation of protected works through the new electronic technology. In short, it was soon established in the federal courts that the broadcast of a copyrighted musical composition by a commercial radio station was a public performance of that composition for profit—and thus an infringement of the copyright if not licensed. In one of the earliest cases so holding, the Court of Appeals for the Sixth Circuit said:

> While the fact that the radio was not developed at the time the Copyright Act . . . was enacted may raise some question as to whether it properly comes within the purview of the statute, it is not by that fact alone excluded from the statute. In other words, the statute may be applied to new situations not anticipated by Congress, if, fairly construed, such situations come within its intent and meaning. . . . While statutes should not be stretched to apply to new situations not fairly within their scope, they should not be so narrowly construed as to permit their evasion because of changing habits due to new inventions and discoveries.
>
> . . . .

If, by analogy to a live performance in a concert hall or cabaret, a radio station "performs" a musical composition when it broadcasts it, the same analogy would seem to require the conclusion that those who listen to the broadcast through the use of radio receivers do not perform the composition. And that is exactly what the early federal cases held. "Certainly those who listen do not perform, and therefore do not infringe." *Jerome H. Remick & Co. v. General Electric Co., supra,* at 829. "One who manually or by human agency merely actuates electrical instrumentalities, whereby inaudible elements that are omnipresent in the air are made audible to persons who are within hearing, does not 'perform' within the meaning of the Copyright Law." *Buck v. Debaum,* 40 F. 2d 734, 735 (SD Cal. 1929).

Such was the state of the law when this Court in 1931 decided *Buck v. Jewell-LaSalle Realty Co.,* 283 U. S. 191. In that case the Court was called upon to answer the following question certified by the Court of Appeals for the Eighth Circuit: "Do the acts of a hotel proprietor, in making available to his guests, through the instrumentality of a radio receiving set and loud speakers installed in his hotel and under his control and for the entertainment of his guests, the hearing of a copyrighted musical composition which has been broadcast from a radio transmitting station, constitute a performance of such composition within the meaning of 17 USC Sec. 1 (e)?" The Court answered the certified question in the affirmative. In stating the facts of the case, however, the Court's opinion made clear that the broadcaster of the musical composition was not licensed to perform it, and at least twice in the course of its opinion the Court indicated that the answer to the certified question might have been different if the broadcast itself had been authorized by the copyright holder.[10]

We may assume for present purposes that the *Jewel-LaSalle* decision retains authoritative force in a factual situation like that in which it arose.[11] But, as the Court of Appeals in this case perceived, this Court has in two recent decisions explicitly disavowed the view that the reception of an electronic broadcast can constitute a performance, when the broadcaster himself is licensed to perform the copyrighted material that he broadcasts. *Fortnightly Corp. v. United Artists,* 392 U. S. 390; *Teleprompter Corp. v. CBS,* 415 U. S. 394.

The language of the Court's opinion in the *Fortnightly* case could hardly be more explicitly dispositive of the question now before us:

> The television broadcaster in one sense does less than the exhibitor of a motion picture or stage play; he supplies his audience not with visible images but only with electronic signals. The viewer conversely does more than a member of a theater audience; he provides the equipment to convert electronic signals into audible sound and visible images. Despite these deviations from the conventional situation contemplated by the framers of the Copyright Act, broadcasters have been judicially treated as exhibitors, and viewers as members of a theater audience. Broadcasters perform. Viewers do not perform. Thus, while both broadcaster and viewer play crucial roles in the total television process, a line is drawn between them. One is treated as active performer; the other, as passive beneficiary. 392 U. S., at 398-399 (footnotes omitted).

The *Fortnightly* and *Teleprompter* cases, to be sure, involved television, not radio, and the copyrighted materials there in issue were literary and dramatic works, not musical compositions. But, as the Court of Appeals correctly observed: "[I]f Fortnightly, with its elaborate CATV plant and Teleprompter with its even more sophisticated and extended technological and programming facilities were not 'performing,' then logic dictates that no 'performance' resulted when the [respondent] merely activated his restaurant radio." 500 F. 2d, at 137.

To hold in this case that the respondent Aiken "performed" the petitioners' copyrighted works would thus require us to overrule two very recent decisions of this Court. But such a holding would more than offend the principles of *stare decisis;* it would result in a regime of copyright law that would be both wholly unenforceable and highly inequitable.

The practical unenforceability of a ruling that all of those in Aiken's position are copyright infringers is self-evident. One has only to consider the countless business establishments in this country with radio or television sets on their premises — bars, beauty shops, cafeterias, car washes, dentists' offices, and drive-ins — to realize the total futility of any evenhanded effort on the part of copyright holders to license even a substantial percentage of them.[12]

---

[10] "[W]e have no occasion to determine under what circumstances a broadcaster will be held to be a performer *or the effect upon others of his paying a license fee."* 283 U. S., at 198 (emphasis added). See also *id.,* at 199 n. 5.

[11] The decision in *Jewell-LaSalle* might be supported by a concept akin to that of contributory infringement, even though there was no relationship between the broad-

[12] The Court of Appeals observed that ASCAP now has license agreements with some 5,150 business establishments in the whole country, 500 F. 2d 127, 129, noting that these

And a ruling that a radio listener "performs" every broadcast that he receives would be highly inequitable for two distinct reasons. First, a person in Aiken's position would have no sure way of protecting himself from liability for copyright infringement except by keeping his radio set turned off. For even if he secured a license from ASCAP, he would have no way of either foreseeing or controlling the broadcast of compositions whose copyright was held by someone else. Secondly, to hold that all in Aiken's position "performed" these musical compositions would be to authorize the sale of an untold number of licenses for what is basically a single public rendition of a copyrighted work. The exaction of such multiple tribute would go far beyond what is required for the economic protection of copyright owners,[14] and would be wholly at odds with the balanced congressional purpose behind 17 U. S. C. § 1 (e):

> The main object to be desired in expanding copyright protection accorded to music has been to give to the composer an adequate return for the value of his composition, and it has been a serious and a difficult task to combine the protection of the composer with the protection of the public, and to so frame an act that it would accomplish the double purpose of securing to the composer an adequate return for all use made of his composition and at the same time prevent the formation of oppressive monopolies, which might be founded upon the very rights granted to the composer for the purpose of protecting his interests. H. R. Rep. No. 2222, 60th Cong., 2d Sess., 7 (1909).

For the reasons stated in this opinion, the judgment of the Court of Appeals is affirmed.

It is so ordered.

Mr. Justice Blackmun, concurring in the result.

My discomfort, now decisionally outdated to be sure, with the Court's opinion and judgment is threefold:

1. My first discomfort is factual. Respondent Aiken hardly was an innocent "listener," as the Court seems to characterize him throughout its opinion and particularly *ante,* at 162. In one sense, of course, he was a listener, for as he operated his small food shop and served his customers, he heard the broadcasts himself. Perhaps his work was made more enjoyable by the soothing and entertaining effects of the music. With this aspect I would have no difficulty.

But respondent Aiken installed four loudspeakers in his small shop. This, obviously, was not done for his personal use and contentment so that he might hear the broadcast, in any corner he might be, above the noise of commercial transactions. It was done for the entertainment and edification of his customers.

---

caster and the hotel company and, therefore, technically no question of actual contributory infringement in that case. *Id.,* at 197 n. 4.

include "firms which employ on premises sources for music such as tape recorders and live entertainment." *Id.,* at 129 n. 4. As a matter of so-called "policy" or "practice," we are told, ASCAP has not even tried to exact licensing agreements from commercial establishments whose radios have only a single speaker.

[14] The petitioners have not demonstrated that they cannot receive from a broadcaster adequate royalties based upon the total size of the broadcaster's audience. On the contrary, the respondent points out that generally copyright holders can and do receive royalties in proportion to advertising revenues of licensed broadcasters, and a broadcaster's advertising revenues reflect the total number of its listeners, including those who listen to the broadcasts in public business establishments.

It was part of what Mr. Aiken offered his trade, and it added, in his estimation, to the atmosphere and attraction of his establishment. Viewed in this light, respondent is something more than a mere listener and is not so simply to be categorized.

2. My second discomfort is precedential. Forty-four years ago, in a unanimous opinion written by Mr. Justice Brandeis, this Court held that a hotel proprietor's use of a radio receiving set and loudspeakers for the entertainment of hotel guests constituted a performance within the meaning of § 1 of the Copyright Act, 17 U. S. C. § 1. *Buck v. Jewell-LaSalle Realty Co.,* 283 U. S. 191 (1931). For more than 35 years the rule in *Jewell-LaSalle* was a benchmark in copyright law and was the foundation of a significant portion of the rather elaborate licensing agreements that evolved with the developing media technology. Seven years ago the Court, by a 5-1 vote, and with three Justices not participating, held that a community antenna television (CATV) station that transmitted copyrighted works to home subscribers was not performing the works, within the meaning of § 1 of the Copyright Act. *Fortnightly Corp. v. United Artists,* 392 U. S. 390 (1968). The divided Court only briefly noted the relevance of *Jewell-LaSalle* and announced that that decision "must be understood as limited to its own facts." *Id.,* at 396-397, n. 18. I have already indicated my disagreement with the reasoning of *Fortnightly* and my conviction that it, rather than *Jewell-LaSalle,* is the case that should be limited to its facts. *Teleprompter Corp. v. CBS,* 415 U. S. 394, 415 (1974) (dissenting opinion). I was there concerned about the Court's simplistic view of television's complications, a view perhaps encouraged by the obvious inadequacies of an ancient copyright Act for today's technology. A majority of the Court, however, felt otherwise and extended the simplistic analysis rejected in *Jewell-LaSalle,* but embraced in *Fortnightly,* to even more complex arrangements in the CATV industry. *Teleprompter Corp. v. CBS, supra.*

I had hoped, secondarily, that the reasoning of *Fortnightly* and *Teleprompter* would be limited to CATV. At least in that context the two decisions had the arguably desirable effect of protecting an infant industry from a premature death. Today, however, the Court extends *Fortnightly* and *Teleprompter* into radio braodcasting, effectively overrules *Jewell-LaSalle,* and thereby abrogates more than 40 years of established business practices. I would limit the application of *Teleprompter* and *Fortnightly* to the peculiar industry that spawned them. Parenthetically, it is of interest to note that this is precisely the result that would be achieved by virtually all versions of proposed revisions of the Copyright Act. See, *e. g.,* § 101 of S. 1361, 93d Cong., 2d Sess., which sought to amend 17 U. S. C. § 110 (5). See also §§ 48 (5) and (6) of the British Copyright Act of 1956, 4 & 5 Eliz. 2, c. 74, which distinguishes between the use of a radio in a public place and "the causing of a work or other subject-matter to be transmitted to subscribers to a diffusion service."

Resolution of these difficult problems and the fashioning of a more modern statute are to be expected from the Congress. In any event, for now, the Court seems content to continue with its simplistic approach and to accompany it with a pragmatic reliance on the "practical unenforceability," of the copyright law against persons such as George Aiken.

3. My third discomfort is tactical. I cannot understand why the Court is so reluctant to do directly what it obviously is doing indirectly, namely, to overrule *Jewell-LaSalle.* Of course, in my view, that decision was correct at the time it was decided, and I would regard it as good law today under the identical statute and with identical broadcasting. But, as I have noted, the Court in *Fortnightly* limited

Jewell-LaSalle "to its own facts," and in *Teleprompter* ignored its existence completely by refusing even to cite it. This means, it seems to me, that the Court did not want to overrule it, but nevertheless did not agree with it and felt, hopefully, that perhaps it would not bother us anymore anyway. Today the Court does much the same thing again by extracting and discovering great significance in the fact that the broadcaster in *Jewell-LaSalle* was not licensed to perform the composition. I cannot join the Court's intimation — surely stretched to the breaking point — that Mr. Justice Brandeis and the unanimous Court for which he spoke would have reached a contrary conclusion in *Jewell-LaSalle* in 1931 had that broadcaster been licensed. The Court dances around *Jewell-LaSalle,* as indeed it must, for it is potent opposing precedent for the present case and stands stalwart against respondent Aiken's position. I think we should be realistic and forthright and, if *Jewell-LaSalle* is in the way, overrule it.

Although I dissented in *Teleprompter,* that case and *Fortnightly,* before it, have been decided. With the Court insisting on adhering to the rationale of those cases, the result reached by the Court of Appeals and by this Court is compelled. Accepting the precedent of those cases, I concur in the result.

MR. CHIEF JUSTICE BURGER, with whom MR. JUSTICE DOUGLAS joins, dissenting.

In *Fortnightly Corp. v. United Artists,* 392 U. S. 390, 402 (1968), Mr. Justice Fortas observed that cases such as this call "not for the judgment of Solomon but for the dexterity of Houdini." There can be no really satisfactory solution to the problem presented here, until Congress acts in response to longstanding proposals. My primary purpose in writing is not merely to express disagreement with the Court but to underscore what has repeatedly been stated by others as to the need for legislative action. Radio today is certainly a more commonplace and universally understood technological innovation than CATV, for example, yet we are, basically, in essentially the same awkward situation as in the past when confronted with these problems. We must attempt to apply a statute designed for another era to a situation in which Congress has never affirmatively manifested its view concerning the competing policy considerations involved.

Yet, the issue presented can only be resolved appropriately by the Congress; perhaps it will find the result which the Court reaches today a practical and equitable resolution, or perhaps it will find this "functional analysis" [1] too simplistic an approach, cf. *Teleprompter Corp. v. CBS,* 415 U. S. 394, 415 (1974) (Blackmun, J., dissenting), and opt for another solution.

The result reached by the Court is not compelled by the language of the statute; it is contrary to the applicable case law and, even assuming the correctness and relevance of the CATV cases, *Fortnightly, supra,* and *Teleprompter, supra,* it is not analytically dictated by those cases. In such a situation, I suggest, "the fact that the Copyright Act was written in a different day, for different factual situations, should lead us to tread cautiously here. Our major object . . . should be to do as little damage as possible to traditional copyright principles and to business relationships, until the Congress legislates and relieves the embarrassment which we and the interested parties face." *Fortnightly, supra,* at 404 (Fortas, J., dissenting).

As the Court's opinion notes, in *Buck v. Jewell-LaSalle Realty Co.,* 283 U. S. 191 (1931), answering a precisely phrased certified question, the Court construed the Copyright Act in a manner which squarely conflicts with what is

---

[1] "Broadcasters perform. Viewers do not perform." Fortnightly Corp. v. United Artists, 392 U.S. 390, 398 (1968) (footnotes omitted).

held today. Congress, despite many opportunities, has never legislatively overruled *Buck, supra.* It was not overruled in *Fortnightly* but treated "as limited to its own facts." 392 U. S., at 396-397, n. 18. Even assuming the correctness of this dubious process of limitation, see *Fortnightly, supra,* at 405 (Fortas, J., dissenting); *Teleprompter, supra,* at 415 (Blackmun, J., dissenting), *Buck* is squarely relevant here since the license at issue expressly negated any right on the part of the broadcaster to further license performances by those who commercially receive and distribute broadcast music. Moreover, even accepting, *arguendo,* the restrictive reading given to *Buck* by the Court today, and assuming the correctness of *Fortnightly* and *Teleprompter* in the CATV field, it is not at all clear that the analysis of these latter cases supports the result here.[2] Respondent was more than a "passive beneficiary." *Fortnightly, supra,* at 399. He took the transmission and used that transmission for commercial entertainment in his own profit enterprise, through a multispeaker audio system specifically designed for his business purposes.[3] In short, this case does not call for what the Court describes as "a ruling that a radio listener 'performs' every broadcast that he receives . . .". Here, respondent received the transmission and then put it to an independent commercial use. His conduct seems to me controlled by *Buck's* unequivocal holding that:

> One who hires an orchestra for a public performance for profit is not relieved from a charge of infringement merely because he does not select the particular program to be played. Similarly, when he tunes in on a broadcasting station, for his own commercial purposes, he necessarily assumes the risk that in so doing he may infringe the performing rights of another. 283 U. S., at 198-199.

See also *Herbert v. Shanley Co.,* 242 U. S. 591 (1917).

In short, as Mr. Justice Douglas observed in the *Teleprompter* case: "The Court can [reach] the result it achieves today only by 'legislating' important features of the Copyright Act out of existence." 415 U. S., at 421. In my view, we should bear in mind that "[o]ur ax, being a rule of law, must cut straight, sharp, and deep; and perhaps this is a situation that calls for the compromise of theory and for the architectural improvisation which only legislation can accomplish." *Fortnightly, supra,* at 408 (Fortas, J., dissenting).

QUESTIONS

1. In deciding whether the owner of copyright of a song has rights which have been infringed through "performance," ought it matter whether it is feasible for the copyright owner — or its licensee such as ASCAP or BMI — to police those rights, or whether it will do so evenhandedly?

2. If a piano player in a nightclub or restaurant, after being informed that ASCAP has licensed the performance of all music in its repertoire, proceeds to

---

[2] Recent congressional proposals have treated the present problem distinctly from CATV questions. See, *e. g.,* S. 1361, 93d Cong., 2d Sess. (1974). See also British Copyright Act of 1956, §§ 48 (5), (6), 4 & 5 Eliz. 2, c. 74.

[3] Indeed, in its consideration of S. 1361, the Senate Committee on the Judiciary undertook to distinguish use of "ordinary radios" from situations "where broadcasts are transmitted to substantial audiences by means of loudspeakers covering a wide area." S. Rep. No. 93-983, p. 130 (1974). The value of this distinction, without drawing a line on the number of outlets that would be exempt is at best dubious; this version leaves the obvious gap in the statute to be filled in by the courts.

play as well music in the BMI repertoire (without being aware of that fact), should the difficulty of "keeping straight" which songs are licensed by which group warrant denying performance rights to composers affiliated with BMI? Is the analysis significantly different when Mr. Aiken turns on his radio — after securing an ASCAP license — and unwittingly communicates music licensed by BMI?

3. If the economics of licensing and royalty computation were deemed immaterial in determining the reach of the performance right in the *Teleprompter* case, was it proper for the Court to make so much of them in the *Aiken* case?

4. The Court appears to suggest that singing in the shower does not infringe because it is not a "performance." Although such singing is indeed not an infringement, is that not for some other reason? (Put aside the question who would do the policing!)

5. Muzak, the music transcription service (operated by permitting the subscriber to "key in" to a private frequency on FM), filed a brief amicus curiae in support of defendant Aiken. Should Aiken's victory be applauded by Muzak? Will the Court's decision shelter Aiken's use of Muzak music in his establishment?

§ 111. Limitations on exclusive rights: Secondary transmissions

(a) Certain Secondary Transmissions Exempted. — The secondary transmission of a primary transmission embodying a performance or display of a work is not an infringement of copyright if —

> (1) the secondary transmission is not made by a cable system, and consists entirely of the relaying, by the management of a hotel, apartment house, or similar establishment, of signals transmitted by a broadcast station licensed by the Federal Communications Commission, within the local service area of such station, to the private lodgings of guests or residents of such establishment, and no direct charge is made to see or hear the secondary transmission;
> . . . .

HOUSE REPORT

H.R. Rep. No. 94-1476, 94th Cong., 2d Sess. 91-92 (1976)

General exemptions

Certain secondary transmissions are given a general exemption under clause (1) of section 111(a). The first of these applies to secondary transmissions consisting "entirely of the relaying, by the management of a hotel, apartment house, or similar establishment" . . . of a transmission to the private lodgings of guests or residents and provided "no direct charge is made to see or hear the secondary transmission."

The exemption would not apply if the secondary transmission consists of anything other than the mere relay of ordinary broadcasts. The cutting out of advertising, the running in of new commercials, or any other change in the signal relayed would subject the secondary transmitter to full liability. Moreover, the term "private lodgings" is limited to rooms used as living quarters or for private parties, and does not include dining rooms, meeting halls, theatres, ballrooms, or similar places that are outside of a normal circle of a family and its social acquaintances. No special exception is needed to make clear that the mere placing of an ordinary radio or television set in a private hotel room does not constitute an infringement.

The genesis of this exemption is clearly the *Buck* case, p. 431 *supra*. Similarly the *Aiken* case — which came down as section 110 was being shaped and reshaped — gave rise to a specific exemption, § 110(5). The differing treatment of this provision by the Senate Committee in 1975 and the House Committee in 1976 required resolution in the Conference Committee. This tortuous history merits detailed exposition.

Copyright Act of 1976: The Final Product

§ 110. Limitations on exclusive rights: Exemption of certain performances and displays

Notwithstanding the provisions of section 106, the following are not infringements of copyright:

. . . .

(5) communication of a transmission embodying a performance or display of a work by the public reception of the transmission on a single receiving apparatus of a kind commonly used in private homes, unless —

    (A) a direct charge is made to see or hear the transmission; or

    (B) the transmission thus received is further transmitted to the public . . . .

1974 Senate Version

Unlike the first four clauses of section 110, clause (5) is not to any extent a counterpart of the "for profit" limitation of the present statute. It applies to performances and displays of all types of works, and its purpose is to exempt from copyright liability anyone who merely turns on, in a public place, an ordinary radio or television receiving apparatus of a kind commonly sold to members of the public for private use. The main effect of this exemption would be to allow the use of ordinary radios and television sets for the incidental entertainment of patrons in small business or professional establishments such as taverns, lunch counters, hairdressers, dry cleaners, doctor's offices, and the like. The clause has nothing to do with cable television systems, and there is no intention to exempt performances in large commercial establishments, such as bus terminals, supermarkets, factories, or department stores, where broadcasts are transmitted to substantial audiences by means of loudspeakers covering a wide area. The exemption would also be denied in any case where the audience is charged directly to see or hear the transmission.

The basic rationale of this clause is that the secondary use of the transmission by turning on an ordinary receiver in public is so remote and minimal that no further liability should be imposed. In the vast majority of these cases no royalties are collected today, and the exemption should be made explicit in the statute. (S. Rep. No. 93-983 at 129-30 (1974).)

1975 Senate Version

While this legislation has been under consideration in the Congress, the Federal courts have considered several issues relevant to this exemption in the context of the Copyright Act of 1909. This clause has nothing to do with cable television systems and is not intended to generally exempt performances or displays in commercial establishments for the benefit of customers or employees. Thus, this exemption would not apply where broadcasts are transmitted by means of loudspeakers or similar devices in such establishments as bus terminals, supermarkets, factories and commercial offices, department and clothing stores, hotels, restaurants and quick-service food shops of the type involved in *Twentieth Century Music Corp. v. Aiken.* The exemption would also be denied in any case where the audience is charged directly to see or hear the transmission. (S. Rep. No. 94-473. See 122 Cong. Rec. S1546 (daily ed. Feb. 6, 1976).)

1976 House Version

The majority of the Supreme Court in the *Aiken* case based its decision on a narrow construction of the word "perform" in the 1909 statute. This basis for the decision is completely overturned by the present bill and its broad definition of "perform" in section 101. The Committee has adopted the language of section 110(5), with an amendment expressly denying the exemption in situations where "the performance or display is further transmitted beyond the place where the receiving apparatus is located"; in doing so, it accepts the traditional, pre-*Aiken,* interpretation of the *Jewell-LaSalle* decision, under which public communication by means other than a home receiving set, or further transmission of a broadcast to the public, is considered an infringing act.

Under the particular fact situation in the *Aiken* case, assuming a small commercial establishment and the use of a home receiver with four ordinary loudspeakers grouped within a relatively narrow circumference from the set, it is intended that the performances would be exempt under clause (5). However, the Committee considers this fact situation to represent the outer limit of the exemption, and believes that the line should be drawn at that point. Thus, the clause would exempt small commercial establishments whose proprietors merely bring onto their premises standard radio or television equipment and turn it on for their customers' enjoyment, but it would impose liability where the proprietor has a commercial "sound system" installed or converts a standard home receiving apparatus (by augmenting it with sophisticated or extensive amplification equipment) into the equivalent of a commercial sound system. Factors to consider in particular cases would include the size, physical arrangement, and noise level of the areas within the establishment where the transmissions are made audible or visible, and the extent to which the receiving apparatus is altered or augmented for the purpose of improving the aural or visual quality of the performance for individual members of the public using those areas. (H.R. Rep. No. 94-1476 at 86-87 (1976).)

1976 Conference Report

Senate bill

Section 110 of the Senate bill set forth eight specific exceptions to the exclusive rights to perform and display copyrighted works. The first four exceptions were roughly the equivalent of the "for profit" limitations on performing rights under the present law. Section 110(5) provided an exemption for public communication of a transmission received on an ordinary receiving set unless a direct charge is made or the transmission "is further transmitted to the public."

. . . .

House bill

The House bill amended the last four clauses of section 110. With respect to clause (5), it made the exemption inapplicable to cases where there is a further transmission "beyond the place where the receiving apparatus is located."

. . . .

Conference substitute

. . . .

With respect to section 110(5), the conference substitute conforms to the language in the Senate bill. It is the intent of the conferees that a small commercial establishment of the type involved in *Twentieth Century Music Corp. v. Aiken,* 422 U.S. 151 (1975), which merely augmented a home-type receiver and which was not of sufficient size to justify, as a practical matter, a subscription to a commercial background music service, would be exempt. However, where the public communication was by means of something other than a home-type receiving apparatus, or where the establishment actually makes a further transmission to the public, the exemption would not apply. (Conf. Rep. at 74-75 (1976).)

QUESTIONS

1. Does the description of Mr. Aiken's fast-food establishment by the conferees accord with the facts set forth in the Supreme Court opinion *supra?*

2. Is it relevant to consider whether an establishment *should* subscribe to a background music service in determining liability? Is it circular?

3. Each of defendant's three restaurants has a radio receiver connected to four ceiling-mounted speakers which are located in the public area of the restaurant which contains approximately 1,000 square feet. The receivers are Realistics, sold through Radio Shack. The Realistics have a power output of eleven watts. Four operating speakers are attached to each receiver. In addition, seventy-volt line transformers are attached to each speaker.

The radios are turned on when the stores open and remain on throughout all business hours playing music and any other items which are broadcast over the particular station to which the set is tuned. The receivers are installed, owned and serviced by a cigarette vending company as a part of its arrangements to provide vending machines on defendant's premises.

Does defendant's conduct constitute an infringement of plaintiff's copyrights under the Copyright Act of 1976?

4. JUKEBOX EXEMPTION — § 116

The 1909 law in its multifaceted Section 1(e) contained an express exemption from liability for unauthorized performance of music by means of coin-operated machines where there is no admission fee to the place of performance. This provision was the notorious "jukebox exemption." Originally designed to insulate the "penny parlor," it was long attacked as an illogical historical relic but withstood numerous legislative attempts at repeal. It is only against this background that one can understand the accomplishments of § 116, which might otherwise appear modest.

The section addresses itself to public performance of a nondramatic musical work "by means of a coin-operated phonorecord player." A detailed definition of such a machine, set forth in § 116(e), includes an echo of the 1909 law in its limitation to machines located "in an establishment making no direct or indirect charge" for admission. In one of the few cases construing the 1909 law exemption, the court found it inapplicable because of a $1 admission charge, even though the charge was imposed for a live band performance and not for the accused jukebox operated during band breaks. *Quackenbush Music, Ltd. v. Wood,* 381 F. Supp. 904, 184 USPQ 210 (M.D. Tenn. 1974). An earlier decision involving the exemption also construed it strictly in favor of the copyright proprietor, by holding that the machine must be actually operated by the deposit of coins and not otherwise, as by disconnecting the wires and controlling the operation of the machine without coins. *Buck v. Kelly,* 7 USPQ 164 (D. Mass. 1930).

If the machine qualifies, then § 116 accords the opportunity of a compulsory license to its "operator" (as defined in § 116(e)) in return for a total payment of $8 per box per year. The proprietor of the location is broadly exempt from liability. The operator must file an application, pay the fee, and affix the certificate received to the player. Regulations have been adopted implementing certain controversial aspects of this provision. 37 C.F.R. § 201.16.

Royalty distribution by the Copyright Royalty Tribunal, after collection by the Register of Copyrights, is generally similar to that provided for cable under § 111. Access to locations was provided to copyright owners under Tribunal regulations, which have recently been issued under the authority of § 116(c)(5). See 37 C.F.R. Part 303, 43 Fed. Reg. 53719 (Nov. 17, 1978). The jukebox industry launched a broad-gauged judicial attack on these regulations but it foundered procedurally. *Amusement and Music Operators Ass'n v. Copyright Royalty Tribunal,* CCH Copy. L. Rep. ¶25,172 (D.C. Cir. 1980) (Review of Tribunal action may be sought only in U.S. Court of Appeals).

Section 116(c)(4) includes the first statutory recognition in this country of a "performing rights society," which is exemplified in its definition by ASCAP, BMI, and SESAC. § 116(e). Moreover, an express antitrust exemption is provided to claimants in order to encourage them to agree as to the proportionate distribution or common collection of fees. § 116(c)(2). Indeed such cooperation would appear sorely needed if anything is to be economically recoverable after costs. The statutory $8 rate was subject to review by the Copyright Royalty Tribunal in 1980 and is not to be reviewed again until 1990 and every tenth year thereafter. §804(a). The 1980 review increased the rate to $25 ($50 commencing in 1984) subject to a cost of living adjustment in 1987. This has been appealed. *See* p. 411 *supra.*

QUESTIONS

1. This provision represents an expansion of the compulsory license concept beyond the traditional mechanical reproduction of music in phonorecords discussed. (Public broadcasting and cable retransmission, to be explored immediately below, are the other areas in which compulsory licenses are now utilized.) Having in mind the reasons for introducing and perpetuating the phonorecord limitation, are there similar (or indeed any) reasons justifying the jukebox provision? Does the modest amount of the rate initially fixed throw any light on this question?

2. What would you imagine the degree of compliance to be with the filing and certificate requirements of Section 116? Verify your estimate by engaging in some empirical research at your local pizza parlor. Who does the statute contemplate will monitor these statutory requirements?

5. PUBLIC BROADCASTING — § 118

A limitation on performing rights adopted late in the 1976 Act development is the compulsory license for public broadcasting. As originally introduced by Senator Mathias in 1975, the provision covered non-dramatic *literary* works as well as music and the visual arts. The Copyright Office, which had devoted two decades of effort to copyright revision, responded as follows:

> The Copyright Office considers the dangers of an unqualified compulsory license for literary works so great and the need for it so unproven, that it could not support a copyright bill containing such a provision, including the revision bill as it was reported by the Senate Judiciary Subcommittee on October 7, 1975. The loss of control by authors over the use of their work in a major mass communications medium, and the dangers of State control and loss of freedom of expression implicit in the proposed system, would probably be too high a price to pay even if public broadcasting were being severely hampered by the legal obligation to get clearances. . . .

Draft, Second Supplementary Report of the Register of Copyrights on the General Revision of the U.S. Copyright Law: 1975 Revision Bill VI-28 (1975). The Office offered the following explanation of the issues underlying this provision (*id.* VI 14-17):

> The arguments of the public broadcasters in favor of the amendment can be summarized as follows:
>
> 1. Congress, since the House of Representatives last acted on the bill in 1967, has demonstrated an "overriding concern for the financial and administrative burdens of noncommercial broadcasting," notably through the Public Broadcasting Act. Public broadcasting is financed by public support and donations; it does not permit any commercial exploitation.
>
> 2. While Congressional commitment should support some form of special consideration for noncommercial broadcasting in the copyright area, it "does not necessarily mean that noncommercial broadcasters would not be willing to make some form of payments to copyright holders in recognition of the valuable contributions that their works make in the production of programs of high quality and excellence."
>
> 3. H.R. 2223, in its present form, would face public broadcasters "with a multitude of administratively cumbersome and very costly rights 'clearance' problems that cannot help but impair the vitality of their enterprise." Administrative overhead for individual clearances would be more than any royalties, and far beyond the budgets of any public broadcaster.
>
> 4. Public broadcasting is therefore seeking a compulsory license, but one that differs from the other compulsory licensing systems in the revision bill in three respects:
>
> a) It covers only non-dramatic works, and does not apply to motion pictures and other audiovisual works. It does not cover unpublished works or dramatizations of non-dramatic works.
>
> b) Unlike the other compulsory licensing schemes, where the initial rate is set in the statute, it calls upon the Copyright Royalty Tribunal to set the initial rates after "full and detailed consideration of exactly what type and amount of royalty fees are appropriate for the various kinds of copyrighted works and public broadcasting exposure."
>
> c) It "specifically encourages substitution of mutually acceptable arrangements between copyright owners and public broadcasting for Tribunal determinations."
>
> The arguments of the representatives of the musical performing rights societies can be summarized as follows:

1. The clearinghouse arrangements under which copyrighted music is licensed for performance under the present law have worked well, and there is nothing about public broadcasting that sets it apart from all other users of music.

2. Compulsory licensing is wrong in principle. The three compulsory licenses now in the revision bill are there for historical reasons, none of which apply to public broadcasting, and are the result of carefully worked out compromises.

3. Television broadcasts require both "performing" and "synchronization" licenses. Public broadcasters recognize that they need synchronization licenses in order to duplicate their programs lawfully, since the "for profit" limitation of the present law does not apply to reproduction rights. At one time they obtained synchronization licenses, and they have been negotiating for performing licenses, that would include synchronization rights, for a decade. Although their gross revenues have grown from $100 million to $250 million, and although they are using more music than ever, they have not paid any license fees during this period.

4. Under current law, public broadcasting is liable for copyright infringments of both performance and synchronization rights: their performances are "for profit" under the decisions interpreting the 1909 Act; copyright owners have exercised forbearance in the expectation that agreement would be reached.

5. Public broadcasting has grown and changed significantly in the past decade and will continue to do so. It now competes with commercial broadcasting as a national medium, and its programming contains much of the same types of entertainment and cultural material presented by commercial broadcasters. The revenues of public broadcasting have grown significantly, and the Mathias Amendment does not take in to account its potential for future growth.

6. None of the justifications put forward in favor of the Mathias Amendment are valid: there is no problem in clearing music for broadcasting, and license fees that have been offered were all reasonable. There is no difference between commercial and public broadcasting that justifies a compulsory license. As drafted, the Amendment is ambiguous, impractical and unworkable, and Government intervention is unnecessary and unwise.

The outcome was a compulsory license with respect to performing rights in published nondramatic musical, pictorial, graphic, and sculptural works performed or displayed on "a noncommercial educational broadcast station," § 118(d), by a "public broadcasting entity," § 118(g). In addition, such entities may record and distribute programs embodying such works for broadcasts by other such stations. § 118(d)(2). (They also enjoy under § 114(b) the right to reproduce sound recordings for educational broadcasting purposes.) Provision is made for public schools and other nonprofit institutions to tape the broadcast of the specified works for nonprofit face-to-face instructional use within 7 days.

Literary works were not included in this compulsory license, but antitrust exemptions were provided to facilitate negotiations between groups. These have borne fruit in developing certain clearance procedures and suggested norms as recognized in another mandated report of the Register. See § 118(c).

The fees and other terms concerning use under § 118 are not set forth in the statute; rather the immediate task of determining them was given to the Copyright Royalty Tribunal, in the absence of voluntary negotiation. The latter is also encouraged, *inter alia,* by antitrust exemptions. § 118(b). Specific timetables are imposed by the statute, and some uncertainties initially arose from the declination of President Carter to accept the first entry in the timetable — appointment of the Tribunal itself by April 19, 1977. *See* Brylawski, *The Copy-*

right Royalty Tribunal, 24 U.C.L.A. L. Rᴇᴠ.1265, 1270 (1977). Nevertheless, the Tribunal proceeded under the remaining time strictures of the section to hold hearings and make its determination on June 8, 1978. *See* 43 Fed. Reg. 25070. This initial "rule" included a flat annual payment of $1,250,000, subject to cost-of-living increases, for ASCAP (the only major performing rights society with which voluntary agreement was not reached) and specified per-use schedules for performance of musical compositions not represented by a society, for recording of musical compositions, and for pictorial, graphic, and sculptural works.

6. CABLE TRANSMISSION — § 111

To understand the very elaborate provisions of the Copyright Act dealing with cable television, it is necessary to understand the manner in which cable TV has been regulated by the Federal Communications Commission.* The principal charge of the FCC is to regulate over-the-air radio and television broadcasting. When it was first presented with the problem of cable television (then widely known as community antenna television, or CATV) in 1959, the Commission declined to take jurisdiction; it concluded that it had no statutory jurisdiction and that cable posed no threat to broadcast television. By 1966, however, the rapid growth of cable television induced the FCC to impose a virtual freeze upon its further spread; it prohibited cable systems located in the largest 100 television markets (based on viewing population) from importing distant signals unless they underwent a lengthy evidentiary proceeding (only one of which was ever completed). A challenge to the FCC's jurisdiction to regulate cable television was rebuffed by the United States Supreme Court in 1968, in *United States v. Southwestern Cable Co.,* 392 U.S. 157 (1968). The same year, the Commission modified its policy and conditioned the right of cable systems to import distant signals upon the consent of the broadcasting station transmitting those signals; apparently no such consents were secured. After another one or two modifications in regulatory policy, the FCC finally adopted rules in 1972 which provide the basic outline for cable regulation to this day.

The major distinction to be drawn for both FCC and copyright regulation is between cable re-transmission of "local" broadcast signals (i.e., those which reach the viewers in the area where the cable system is located) and "distant" signals (i.e., those which are imported from broadcast stations at such a distance that they could not otherwise be received by viewers in the area in which the cable system is located). If a cable system is located in the "local service area" of a broadcast station (the primary transmitter) then the system *must* carry that station's programs to the cable subscribers. If a cable system is, however, re-transmitting distant signals, then it *may* do so — says the Federal Communications Commission — only under certain conditions, depending upon the size of the television market in which the cable system is located. A cable system may carry as many distant signals as are necessary to reach a "minimum complement." In the top fifty markets, a cable system may import enough distant signals to provide three network stations, three independent stations (typically UHF stations), and two additional independent stations if the market already has three independent stations. In the next fifty markets, a cable system may carry enough distant signals to provide three network stations and two independent stations. In a yet smaller market, the cable system may carry enough signals to offer three network stations and one independent station. (A system located outside of all markets may carry as many distant signals as it wishes.) Regardless of its location, a cable system may carry an unlimited number of noncommercial signals (e.g.

---

* The FCC is now in the process of changing regulations concerning syndicated exclusivity and distance-signal importation. The impact of these and other deregulatory changes on copyright cannot be accurately predicted.

originally "educational" now, public television). The purpose of these rules is to assure some range of diversity of programming (and choice of viewing time) for market audiences, but without interfering unduly with the dominant positions (and thus the income and financial stability) of the major network and independent stations.

(It suffices to say that these basic regulations are interlaced with a host of exceptions. For example, under regulations endorsing "exclusivity," a cable system may not carry a program from a distant network station if a local network station is carrying the same program at the same time. Similarly, a cable system may not carry a syndicated program for a showing during the same season.)

The purpose and structure of Section 111 of the Copyright Act can be understood with this regulatory background in mind. The copyright provisions are designed not only to advance the usual policies — providing a fair market return to the copyright owner as an incentive for creative authorship — but also to reinforce the broadcasting regulatory policies of the Federal Communications Commission.

The cable system will be entitled to re-transmit distant signals, pursuant to a compulsory license, if, basically, such re-transmission is permitted by the Federal Communications Commission. More technically, the compulsory license applies and distant signals may be imported by a cable system (provided statutory royalties are paid), if: (1) the primary transmission is by a broadcast station licensed by the FCC (or by the appropriate governmental authority in Canada or Mexico), and (2) the secondary transmission by the cable system is permitted by the FCC, and (3) the cable system complies with the requirements of Section 111(d) (requiring that the cable system register, file statements of accounts, and pay royalties). (Section 111 (c) (1)). The House Committee stated (at page 89 of H. Rep. No. 94-1476) that although the cable systems, which derive income from re-transmitting copyrighted programs, should be required to pay the creators of such programs, individual royalty negotiations with all of the copyright owners would be unduly burdensome. Accordingly, a compulsory license is to be granted for the re-transmission of over-the-air broadcast signals that the FCC permits a cable system to carry.

Section 111(d) sets forth the steps which a cable system must take in order to avail itself of the compulsory license. It must first timely register with the Copyright office, giving the name of the owner of the cable system and the names and locations of primary transmitters (i.e., broadcast stations) whose signals are "regularly carried" by the cable system. [Section 111(d)(1).] In addition, the cable system must deposit with the Register of Copyrights, twice each year, a statement of account, containing the names and locations of broadcast stations whose signals the cable system has re-transmitted in the preceding six months, the total number of subscribers to the cable system, the gross amounts paid to the cable system for the service of providing secondary transmissions (as distinguished from subscriber payments for installations or for a pay-movie channel), and logs showing the non-network programs carried by the cable system beyond the local service area of the primary transmitter. [Section 111(d)(2)(A).] Finally, the above statement of accounts must be accompanied by royalties, which are to be based upon different percentages, set forth in the statute, of the gross receipts from subscribers for the service of providing secondary transmissions.

The statutory provisions for the computation of royalties are among the lengthiest in the Act. In establishing a multiplier, to be applied to the gross receipts of the cable system, it was Congress's intention to require the payment of a royalty only for the carriage of distant broadcast signals embodying programs which are not network programs. No royalty is to be exacted for the re-transmission of local signals (*required* by the FCC), since this does not threaten the existing market for owners of copyrighted programs; the price that the copyright owner receives from the station is based on what the station can get from advertisers, and what advertisers pay is determined by the number of viewers of the program, which will take account of the persons in the "local service area," whether they receive the program off-the-air or as re-transmitted on cable. Similarly, the re-transmission of network programming, including programs from distant markets, does not injure the copyright owner, who is compensated, when he (or she or it) deals with the network, on the basis of all of the markets served by the network. However, as the House Report states (p. 90): "[T]he transmission of distant non-network programming by cable systems causes damage to the copyright owner by distributing the program in an area beyond which it has been licensed. Such re-transmission adversely affects the ability of the copyright owner to exploit the work in the distant market. It is also of direct benefit to the cable system by enhancing its ability to attract subscribers and increase revenues. For these reasons, the Committee has concluded that the copyright liability of cable television systems under the compulsory license should be limited to the re-transmission of distant non-network programming. The royalty fee is determined by a two-step computation. First, a value called a "distant signal equivalent" is assigned to all 'distant' signals. . . . Different values are assigned to independent, network, and educational stations because of the different amounts of viewing of non-network programming carried by such stations. For example, the viewing of non-network programs on network stations is considered to approximate 25 percent. These values are then combined and a scale of percentages is applied to the cumulative total."

Thus, under Section 111(d)(2),* every cable system which re-transmits primary broadcasts must pay a royalty fee (for the half-year accounting period) of 0.817 of 1 percent of its gross receipts (as above described) for the "privilege" of re-transmitting nonnetwork programs beyond the primary transmitter's local service area. This fee must be paid for that privilege whether or not it is exercised, i.e., even if the cable system re-transmits only broadcasts which originate locally. If a cable system in fact exercises the privilege, it must pay a royalty fee of 0.817 of 1 percent of its gross receipts for its first Distant Signal Equivalent, and 0.514 of 1 percent of its gross receipts for each of its second, third, and fourth Distant Signal Equivalents; and the threshold fee paid for the "privilege" of retransmitting distant signals is to be applied against these fees. (In Section 111(f) the definition of "distant signal equivalent" assigns a value of one to each independent station and a value of one-quarter to each network station and non-commercial educational station.) Thus, a station carrying three distant signals (more than most cable systems carry) will have to pay only 1.845 percent of its gross receipts as a royalty covering all of the copyrighted programs re-transmitted from those broadcast stations throughout the six-month period covered by its statement of account. The Act also provides for much reduced royalty rates for cable systems with more modest gross receipts: if half-year gross receipts are less than $107,000, there will be a royalty charge of between $20 and $535, regardless of the number of Distant Signal Equivalents; and if gross receipts are between $107,000 and $214,000, there is a sliding-scale royalty with a maximum of $1600, regardless of the number of DSEs. A very large proportion of cable systems would have to pay a half-year royalty of only $20.00!

---

* As adjusted by the Copyright Royalty Tribunal in 1980. *See* p. 411 *supra*.

The Register of Copyrights receives all of these fees from all cable systems operating under the compulsory license, deducts the administrative costs, and deposits them with the Treasury for investment in interest-bearing United States securities and for later distribution by the Copyright Royalty Tribunal. [Section 111(d) (3).] The accumulated fees are to be distributed to copyright owners whose works were included in secondary transmissions of non-network television programs beyond the local service area of the primary transmitter. [Section 111(d) (4).] No royalty fees may be claimed by or distributed to copyright owners for the re-transmission of either "local" or "network" programs. The distribution of royalties to all claimants follows the pattern of the other statutory compulsory licenses. Claimants file in July of each year with the Copyright Royalty Tribunal, and are encouraged (notwithstanding the antitrust laws) to agree among themselves regarding the division of the royalties or to designate a common agent. (This is an obvious expression of hope that an ASCAP-type clearinghouse system will arise to represent copyright owners of television programs.) If the Copyright Royalty Tribunal determines on August 1 that there is no controversy regarding distribution, it shall proceed to distribute (after deducting administrative costs). If there is a controversy among the claimants, the CRT will resolve it (but it may in the meantime distribute amounts not in controversy). [Section 111(d) (5).]

As noted above, the Tribunal has now completed its first distribution proceeding. *See* p. 410 *supra*. It was forced to grapple with conflicting theories as to what copyrighted "works" were intended by Congress to be recognized under this provision. For example, is the owner of a copyrighted cartoon character used in a television program entitled to cable royalties? Is the creativity in programming sufficient to make a broadcast day a copyrightable compilation? Answering both of these questions in the negative, the Tribunal determined that cable royalties should be divided among copyright owner claimants as follows:

Motion Picture Association of America and other program syndicators — 75%

Sports Claimants — 12%

Public Broadcasting Service — 5.25%

Music Performing Rights Societies — 4.5%

U.S. and Canadian Television Broadcasters — 3.25%

See 45 Fed. Reg. 50621 (July 30, 1980) and 45 Fed. Reg. 63026 (Sept. 23, 1980). Appeals have been filed.

Having discussed those cable re-transmissions for which there is no copyright liability at all, and those which are subject to compulsory license, it remains only to catalogue those cable re-transmissions which constitute an *infringement*. Much of these rules flow directly from what has already been discussed.

It is, for example, an infringement for a cable system to re-transmit programs when the primary transmission is not by a licensed broadcast station but is rather by a closed-circuit television broadcast to theatres, or is a background music service such as Muzak, or is a pay-cable program. [Section 111(b).] It is also an infringement for a cable system "willfully or repeatedly" to re-transmit signals which they are not permitted by the FCC to carry, or to re-transmit signals without having taken the usual steps of recording, filing accounts and paying royalties. [Section 111(c) (2).] Since the FCC rules are complicated, and it would not be unusual for a cable system to misinterpret them innocently, full copyright liability is imposed under this section only for "willful or repeated" violations of the FCC regulations; there must be "a degree of aggravated negligence which borders on willfulness" (House Report at p. 93).

A cable system is also fully liable for copyright infringement if it willfully alters (by deleting, adding, or changing) the content of any program in the primary transmission, or the advertising on that program (i.e., advertising carried either during the program, or immediately before or after). (There is a minor exception for modifying advertising in a program of market research, with the consent of all affected parties.) Such willful changes in program content or advertising, in the words of the House Report, "significantly alter the basic nature of the cable re-transmission service and makes its function similar to that of a broadcaster. Further, the placement of substitute advertising in a program by a cable system on a 'local' signal harms the advertiser and, in turn, the copyright owner, whose compensation for the work is directly related to the size of the audience that the advertiser's message is calculated to reach. On a 'distant' signal, the placement of substitute advertising harms the local broadcaster in the distant market because the cable system is then competing for local advertising dollars without having comparable program costs." (pp. 93-94).

Although Canadian and Mexican primary transmissions may be re-transmitted by cable pursuant to the compulsory license provisions, this privilege extends only within stipulated geographic limits; if the cable systems falls outside those limits, there is an infringement. [Section 111(c) (4).]

Finally, a cable system will (subject to certain limited exceptions) infringe when, rather than re-transmitting a primary transmission simultaneously, it first records the primary transmission and then transmits the recorded program at a later time. This flows from the definition of "secondary transmission" in Section 111(f). The major significance is to permit such recording by Hawaiian cable systems, since they are not capable of otherwise picking up off-the-air signals from any point on the mainland; severe restrictions are placed upon the taping and the showing of the tape (only one showing is permitted), which must be promptly destroyed, with affidavits to be filed so attesting. [Section 111(e).]

QUESTIONS

What, if any, are the copyright infringements in the following cases?

1. E exhibits a copyrighted painting, which it owns, in an art gallery, without the consent of A, the artist and owner of copyright. E exhibits the same painting on a television program.

2. H Hotel hires a three-piece band to play copyrighted music at the hotel restaurant; there is no admission charge or entertainment charge. E (exclusive) membership social club has a band playing the same music at weekend dances. (If these are infringements, how does the copyright owner find out?)

3. Lawrence Welk plays a copyrighted song in a television studio; ABC television network transmits the performance to its local television affiliates, which broadcast it; a viewer turns on the television set in a room filled with family friends.

4. H Hotel pipes the sound from the Welk television show into the hotel elevators and private guest rooms. It also plays a different rendition of that song through its Muzak system, into private guest rooms.

5. A jukebox operator places a phonorecord of C's song in a coin-operated jukebox, and the record is frequently played; the performance of the song is by P and the record is made by the R Recording Company.

6. Arthur Miller's "Death of a Salesman" is performed by students in a 12th-grade classroom.

a) Assume instead one of the performers is a professional actor, an alumnus of the school.

b) Assume instead that the student performance is in the school auditorium.

c) Assume that the student classroom performance is transmitted by closed-circuit television to all high school English classes in the school district.

7. The high school glee club opens an assembly program in the school auditorium with a copyrighted hymn. It also sings the hymn at the beginning of a school football game; tickets are sold to the game, the proceeds being devoted to uniforms and other expenses of the school's athletic teams and musical organizations.

8. The high school glee club makes a recording of the copyrighted song, and publicly distributes the recording. Jolly Roger Records "dubs" the sounds onto its own phonorecords (without any consents) and sells them to the public. A disc jockey plays the glee club record over local radio station WDJ.

7. PERFORMING RIGHTS SOCIETIES

Today public performance is the major source of revenue in the music industry, and ASCAP licenses the performance rights of its over 25,000 members to approximately 50,000 direct users—generating well over $125 million in royalties annually. Broadcast Music, Inc., a broadcaster-owned organization formed during a 1939 split from ASCAP, and SESAC (a much smaller, privately owned specialty organization) perform similar functions. "As a practical matter virtually every domestic copyrighted composition is in the repertory of either ASCAP, which has over 3 million compositions in its pool, or BMI, which has over one million. . . . Almost all broadcasters hold blanket licenses from both ASCAP and BMI." *CBS v. ASCAP,* 400 F.Supp. 737, 742 (S.D.N.Y. 1975), *rev'd,* 562 F.2d 130 (2d Cir. 1977), *rev'd,* 441 U.S. 1 (1979), *on remand,* 205 USPQ 880 (2d Cir. 1980).

Copyright holders — the composers, lyricists and publishers — become members of ASCAP or BMI by granting the non-exclusive right to license public performance of their musical compositions in a non-dramatic fashion. These rights are in turn granted to networks, local television stations, radio stations, nightclubs, hotels, and other users in blanket licensing agreements which allow the licensee full use of any licensed works. Licensing fees vary from industry to industry (although similarly situated licensees must be treated equally). The networks pay a flat fee. Local television and radio stations pay a fee based on sponsorship receipts (less certain deductions). Fees for "general establishments" depend on a number of factors: drinking prices, seating capacity, frequency of music performances, type of rendition, admission charges, etc. Hotel and motel fees take into account total entertainment expenditures; concert rates depend on admission price and seating capacity; background music users such as Muzak pay a fee based primarily on the number and character of subscribers. Users who contend that a proposed ASCAP fee is unreasonable may have a reasonable fee determined by the United States District Court for the Southern District of New York; BMI users can resort to arbitration.

Collecting the money from users, even with the variety of fee schedules, is relatively simple because of the nature of the blanket licensing which permits licensees to use any and all music in the repertoire. But the very simplicity of collecting a single fee from a blanket licensee creates difficulties in the apportioning and distributing of the collected royalties. Surveys and logging of broadcasts are conducted by the performing rights organization which then apply formulas in order to distribute royalties. Dissatisfied members or affiliates have remedies under the ASCAP and BMI consent decrees. A closer look at the history and provisions of the ASCAP decree is in order.

The increasing importance of the broadcast industry in the late 1930s heightened the importance of performance rights licensing. With ASCAP operating almost alone in the field, a growing antagonism developed between the society and the broadcast users of copyrighted musical works. Finally, angered over what they considered exorbitant licensing fees and unacceptable ASCAP practices, the broadcasters refused to negotiate with ASCAP, forming their own performance rights organization and boycotting ASCAP music. "This was the era when 'Jeanie With the Light Brown Hair' was burned in effigy on college campuses and the listening public was surfeited with Latin American rhythms." [Statement of March 13, 1958 of Victor Hansen before the House Select Comm. on Small Business, Subcomm. No. 5, Hearings, Policies of American Society of Composers, Authors, and Publishers 138-141 (March-April 1958).]

On February 25, 1941, the Antitrust Division of the Department of Justice filed a civil complaint against ASCAP, charging Sherman Act violations. When a consent agreement was signed one week later, three major ASCAP practices were significantly altered. *See* 1940-43 Trade Cases ¶ 56,104 (S.D.N.Y. 1941). First, ASCAP was prohibited from discriminating against similarly situated licensees. Previously, it had been an ASCAP practice to withhold certain music in an attempt to extract higher fees from users. Second, ASCAP could no longer acquire exclusive rights to license members' performance rights. Nonetheless, the impact of this new provision was substantially deadened by the fact that the Society could still require that all self-negotiated royalties be placed into the ASCAP pot for general distribution. Third, ASCAP was required to offer per-program licenses in addition to the blanket licenses. Other provisions relating to membership voting rights, Board elections (in an attempt to rid the Society of a self-perpetuating board) and distribution of royalties were included in the original decree.

Though a breakthrough in the normalization of ASCAP procedures, the 1941 decree was far from the solution to the problems resulting from ASCAP's predominance in the area of performance rights licensing. Old problems — license terms, continued membership restrictions, uneven royalty distribution — joined with new problems in motion picture (*see Alden-Rochelle, Inc. v. ASCAP,* 80 F. Supp. 888 (S.D.N.Y. 1948); *M. Witmark & Sons v. Jensen,* 80 F. Supp. 843 (S.D. Minn. 1948)) and television licensing brought about amendments in 1950.

The new judgment, amended on March 14, 1950 (1950-51 Trade Cases, ¶ 62,595 (S.D.N.Y. 1950)), was referred to as open door and open window to ASCAP's internal workings. Timberg, *The Antitrust Aspects of Merchandising Modern Music: The ASCAP Consent Judgment of 1950,* 19 LAW & CONTEMP. PROB. 294 (1954). Particularly important changes in the new decree included: 1) the right of composers, authors and publishers to negotiate licenses on their own without a requirement that the royalties be divided among all ASCAP members; 2) provision for a genuine economic choice between the blanket license and the per program license; 3) membership requirements were further relaxed; 4) movie theatre licensing was prohibited, i.e., the performance of music was cleared by the producer "at the source" (the result of the *Alden-Rochelle* case); 5) a procedure for determination of reasonable fees by the District Court for the Southern District of New York was established; 6) more internal governance regulations were imposed; 7) an easier and fairer process of withdrawal from the Society was made available; and 8) distribution of royalties was mandated to be based on less subjective terms than dictated in the earlier accord and was to be based primarily on a more objective survey system.

Ten years later, the decree was once again amended in a joint ASCAP-Justice Department attempt to clarify many of the earlier provisions. The survey and revenue distribution systems were rationalized. Resigning members got the right to maintain full receipts if the work remained licensed by ASCAP and the resignee had not joined another society. The new decree also established a procedure for adjudicating grievances of members, including an internal Board of Review and the right to appeal to an outside body. Finally, membership and voting right regulations were again slightly restricted. The new mechanism for determining voting rights through performance credits included a tapering of higher credit values to relieve concentration of voting power. *See generally* Garner, *United States v. ASCAP: The Licensing Provisions of the Amended Final Judgment of 1950,* 23 BULL. COPYRIGHT SOC'Y 119 (1976). For the BMI consent decree, *see* 1966 Trade Cases, ¶ 71,941 (S.D.N.Y. 1966).

Although this twenty year history of antitrust consent decrees helped calm the government, certain users subject to ASCAP and BMI licensing — particularly the broadcasters — were still not satisfied. They simply could not accept blanket licensing which exacted the same fee regardless of the level of use. A decade-long attack by a television network proved to be unsuccessful.

CBS v. ASCAP, 620 F.2d 930, 205 USPQ 880 (2d Cir. 1980), *cert. denied,* — U.S. —, 101 S. Ct. 1491, 66 L. Ed. 2d — (1981), represents the fourth round in litigation challenging ASCAP's and BMI's practice of offering only blanket licenses to a television network using copyrighted musical compositions. Under the blanket license, the licensee may use any music in the repertory of the licensor, as often as desired, for a single fee. Payment is either a flat sum or a percentage of the licensee's revenue and is therefore not related to the amount used or the particular works used. CBS claimed, *inter alia,* that the blanket license was an agreement unlawfully restraining trade in violation of § 1 of the Sherman Act and sought to have ASCAP and BMI barred from using it, or, alternatively, to require them to charge predetermined amounts each time copyrighted music is used on the air.

In the first round of this protracted litigation (*CBS v. ASCAP,* 400 F. Supp. 737, 187 USPQ 431 (S.D.N.Y. 1975)), the District Court found that CBS had not proved its allegations and dismissed the complaint. In the second round (*CBS v. ASCAP,* 562 F.2d 130, 195 USPQ 209 (2d Cir. 1977)), the Second Circuit Court of Appeals ruled that the blanket license was an illegal price-fixing device and thus a *per se* violation of § 1. The third round was argued before the Supreme Court and that Court ruled that the blanket license was not a *per se* violation of § 1, remanding the case to have the licensing practice evaluated using rule of reason analysis (*BMI v. CBS,* 441 U.S. 1, 201 USPQ 497 (1979)).

In applying rule-of-reason standards in the last round, the Second Circuit held that CBS must first establish that the practice has a restraining effect in the industry. This issue was deemed to have been left unresolved by the Supreme Court's decision.* The fact that there is no price competition among songs is not determinative on this question. However, it is crucial that there is the opportu-

---

* The Court of Appeals cited two reasons for this conclusion. First, the specific holding by the Supreme Court says only that the blanket license is not a *per se* violation of § 1. Second, at one point Justice White's opinion states that the majority is "uncertain whether the practice on its face has the effect . . . of restraining competition among the individual composers." 441 U.S. at 13, 201 USPQ at 503.

nity to obtain individual performing rights. "If the opportunity to purchase performing rights to individual songs is fully available, then it is customer preference for the blanket license, and not the license itself, that causes the lack of price competition among songs." 205 USPQ at 884. The issue then is whether direct licensing is feasible.

The Court of Appeals, after reviewing the District Court's findings, agreed that "CBS has failed to prove the factual predicate of its claim — the nonavailability of alternatives to the blanket license. . ." 400 F. Supp. at 780-81, 187 USPQ at 464. This suggests the burden of proof was being placed on CBS. *See* Hartnick, *The Network Blanket License Triumphant — The Fourth Round of the ASCAP-BMI-CBS Litigation,* 2 COMMUNICATION AND THE LAW 49 (1980).

CBS had urged four barriers to direct licensing. First, money spent to acquire performance rights from individual composers would be wasted once CBS has already paid ASCAP for performance rights to all music. But the court found that CBS could negotiate to avoid overlapping licenses. Second, CBS claimed no machinery existed to handle the numerous transactions required by direct negotiations. However, such machinery does exist for motion picture and other use of music and the necessary machinery could be modeled on that example. Therefore, the District Court had found that "the relatively modest machinery required could be developed during a reasonable planning period." *Id.* at 765, 187 USPQ at 451-452. Third, CBS argued that copyright owners would be reluctant to deal directly with it (the "disinclination" issue). But, to the contrary, the evidence developed at the trial indicated that "copyright proprietors would wait at CBS' door." *Id.* at 779, 187 USPQ at 463. Fourth, CBS feared that it would be subjected to unreasonable demands for high fees by the owners of copyright on music already recorded on the sound tracks of taped programs and feature films (the "music-in-the-can" problem). However, the District Court had found no factual basis for such fears and, in any case, the danger was not a result of the blanket license.

Pervading these assessments is the court's view that CBS in reality faces a no risk situation. "If CBS were to forego the blanket license, seek direct licenses, and then discover, . . ., that a competitive market among copyright owners was not a feasible alternative to the blanket license, it would be entitled, under the consent decree, to assure itself of continued performing rights by immediately obtaining a renewed blanket license. Indeed, Paragraph IX of the ASCAP decree permits CBS to use any music covered by a license application, without payment of a fee, subject to whatever fees are subsequently negotiated or determined to be reasonable by the court if negotiations fail." 205 USPQ at 887.

8. "GRAND" AND "SMALL" RIGHTS

The performing rights organizations license only nondramatic musical rights, the so-called "small" rights. The "grand" (dramatic) rights are licensed only by the copyright holders, who have traditionally felt capable of monitoring the more detectable dramatic performances. Little was it realized that this dramatic/non-dramatic distinction generated a definitional problem of increasing significance. Until recently there has been a dearth of litigation on this issue. A 1955 case held that a medley of songs from *The Student Prince* performed as part of a ten-scene costumed extravaganza revue was not a dramatic presentation. *April Productions, Inc. v. Strand Enterprises. Inc.,* 221 F.2d 292 (2d Cir. 1955). Rather, the performance by Ben Yost and His Royal Guardsmen was an "entr'acte" and contributed nothing to the show's overall plot.

The problem was once again confronted — this time with a different result — in a series of cases involving performances of selections from the rock opera *Jesus Christ Superstar*. In *Rice v. American Program Bureau*, 446 F.2d 685 (2d Cir. 1971), a booking agent who had secured an ASCAP license was enjoined from performing either the work in its entitrety or even excerpts accompanied by words, pantomime, dance or visual representations of the opera as a whole. In *Robert Stigwood Group, Ltd. v. Sperber*, 457 F.2d 50 (2d Cir. 1972), another performance was enjoined. Here, the performance was without costume, but almost all of the songs were presented in identical sequence to the original and performers maintained specific characters throughout the performance. The court held that the performance was dramatic even without scenery, costumes and dialogue and despite the concert setting. The court's injunctive decree, arguably overbroad, forbade:

(1) performing any song in such a way as to follow another song in the same order as in the original *Jesus Christ Superstar* opera;

(2) performing any songs from the opera accompanied by dramatic action, scenic accessory or costumes.

Nimmer, in his treatise THE LAW OF COPYRIGHT (1978), suggests three possible ways to distinguish between dramatic performances (not covered by the ASCAP license to the performer) and non-dramatic performances. One extreme, put forward by former ASCAP attorney Herman Finkelstein, defines non-dramatic performances as "renditions of a song ... without dialogue, scenery or costumes." (Finkelstein, *The Composer and the Public Interest — Regulation of Performing Right Societies*, 19 LAW & CONTEMP. PROB. 275, 283 n.32 (1954)). This, however, is both too broad and too narrow. It excludes the *Sperber* type dramatic performance and those performances which although costumed, scened and with dialogue are nonetheless non-dramatic. "A literal acceptance of this definition would mean that any nightclub, vaudeville or television performance would be dramatic if the singer is not dressed in street clothes, or if a backdrop other than a curtain is used or if the singer engages in introductory patter." (NIMMER, THE LAW OF COPYRIGHT 10.10 [E] 1978)).

At the other extreme is the *April Productions* rule, that "the performance of a noninstrumental musical composition (i.e. lyrics and music) would be dramatic only if it were accompanied by material from the dramatico-musical work of which the composition was a part." Nimmer argues the overbreadth of such a view, posing, hypothetically, that "[u]nder the rule of this case one could by simply obtaining an ASCAP license perform in a new musical play all the music from 'South Pacific' providing the 'book' for the new production is not borrowed from 'South Pacific.' " *Id.*

Nimmer suggests as more appropriate the language in the ASCAP blanket television license which defines a dramatic performance as ". . . a performance of a musical composition on a television program in which there is a definite plot depicted by action and where the performance of the musical composition is woven into and carries forward the plot and its accompanying action. The use of dialogue to establish a mere program format or the use of any non-dramatic device merely to introduce a performance of a composition shall not be deemed to make such a performance dramatic." He continues: "A performance of a musical composition is dramatic if it aids in telling a story, otherwise it is not." (Is this the same as a formulation attributed by Professor Nimmer to an entertainment executive: "Delete the proposed musical performance from the production (be it stage, motion picture, or television); if after such deletion the continuity or story line of the production is in no way impeded or obscured, then the proposed performance is non-dramatic — otherwise it is dramatic"?)

G. FAIR USE

1. LEGISLATIVE HISTORY OF § 107

Copyright statutes up through the 1909 law spoke in terms of "exclusive" rights, but these were quite early subjected to a judge-made rule of reason ultimately known as "fair use." *See Folsom v. Marsh,* 9 Fed. Cas. 342, 348, No. 4,901 (C.C.D. Mass. 1841). In 1958, a study looking toward the general revision of the 1909 copyright law framed the legislative issues to be faced with respect to this concept. *See* Latman, *Fair Use of Copyrighted Works,* 2 STUDIES ON COPYRIGHT 5, 34 (Arthur Fisher Mem. ed. 1963). As in the case of the thirty-four other general revision studies, no position was taken, but the following options were set forth:

1. Should a statutory provision concerning fair use be introduced into the U.S. law?

2. If so:

(a) Should the statute merely recognize the doctrine in general terms and leave its definition to the courts?

(b) Should the statute specify the general criteria of fair use? If so, what should be the basic criteria?

3. Should specific situations be covered? If so, what specific situations?

It will have been observed that the statute does indeed contain a number of exemptions and limitations in favor of education, religion, the handicapped, and non-profit endeavors. *See, e.g.,* §§ 110(1), (2), (3), (4), (7), (8), 118. A special library reproduction privilege provided in § 108 will be examined below. *See* VARMER, PHOTODUPLICATION OF COPYRIGHTED MATERIALS BY LIBRARIES ET AL., 2 STUDIES ON COPYRIGHT 815 (Arthur Fisher Mem. ed. 1963). These provisions clearly represent the type of "specific situations" which might have been treated entirely under the rubric of fair use as suggested in Option 3, but were instead treated by way of express exemption or limitation. *See generally* Seltzer, *Exemptions and Fair Use in Copyright: The Exclusive Rights Tensions in the 1976 Copyright Act,* 24 BULL. COPYRIGHT SOC'Y 215 (1977).

In the early stages of the revision process there had been a good deal of vacillation as to which approach to take on the fair use issue. This resulted from a familiar phenomenon in the history of copyright law and lore — shifting positions by competing interests as to whether to pin something down by way of legislative provision or test case, or to rely on agreements, trade custom or luck to vindicate a position. Thus the 1961 Register's Report recommended "a provision affirming and indicating the scope of the principle that fair use does not infringe the copyright owner's rights." The first bill, H.R. 11947, and S. 3008, 88th Cong. 2d Sess. (1964), in its attempt at "indicating the scope of the principle" (an attempt remarkably precursive of the ultimate form of § 107) succeeded in making nearly everybody unhappy. Accordingly, the 1965 bill, *e.g.,* H.R. 4347 and S. 1006, 89th Cong., 1st Sess. (1965), contained the following paradigm of terseness: "Notwithstanding the provisions of section 106, the fair use of a copyrighted work is not an infringement of copyright." This was also greeted by controversy which produced once again a longer version of the section, with illustrations of purposes qualifying for fair use and the criteria for its determination. *See* H.R. 2512, 90th Cong., 1st Sess. (1966). This was the version passed by the House in 1967, and with some last-minute refinements initiated by educators it became § 107 of the 1976 Act.

§ 107. **Limitations on exclusive rights: Fair use**

Notwithstanding the provisions of section 106, the fair use of a copyrighted work, including such use by reproduction in copies or phonorecords or by any other means specified by that section, for purposes such as criticism, comment, news reporting, teaching (including multiple copies for classroom use), scholarship, or research, is not an infringement of copyright. In determining whether the use made of a work in any particular case is a fair use the factors to be considered shall include—

(1) the purpose and character of the use, including whether such use is of a commercial nature or is for nonprofit educational purposes;

(2) the nature of the copyrighted work;

(3) the amount and substantiality of the portion used in relation to the copyrighted work as a whole; and

(4) the effect of the use upon the potential market for or value of the copyrighted work.

HOUSE REPORT

H.R. Rep. No. 94-1476, 94th Cong., 2d Sess. 65-66 (1976)

General background of the problem

The judicial doctrine of fair use, one of the most important and well-established limitations on the exclusive right of copyright owners, would be given express statutory recognition for the first time in section 107. The claim that a defendant's acts constituted a fair use rather than an infringement has been raised as a defense in innumerable copyright actions over the years, and there is ample case law recognizing the existence of the doctrine and applying it. The examples enumerated at page 24 of the Register's 1961 Report, while by no means exhaustive, give some idea of the sort of activities the courts might regard as fair use under the circumstances: "quotation of excerpts in a review or criticism for purposes of illustration or comment; quotation of short passages in a scholarly or technical work, for illustration or clarification of the author's observations; use in a parody of some of the content of the work parodied; summary of an address or article, with brief quotations, in a news report; reproduction by a library of a portion of a work to replace part of a damaged copy; reproduction by a teacher or student of a small part of a work to illustrate a lesson; reproduction of a work in legislative or judicial proceedings or reports; incidental and fortuitous reproduction, in a newsreel or broadcast, of a work located in the scene of an event being reported."

Although the courts have considered and ruled upon the fair use doctrine over and over again, no real definition of the concept has ever emerged. Indeed, since the doctrine is an equitable rule of reason, no generally applicable definition is possible, and each case raising the question must be decided on its own facts. On the other hand, the courts have evolved a set of criteria which, though in no case definitive or determinative, provide some gauge for balancing the equities. These criteria have been stated in various ways, but essentially they can all be reduced to the four standards which have been adopted in section 107: "(1) the purpose and character of the use, including whether such use is of a commercial nature or is for non-profit educational purposes; (2) the nature of the copyrighted work; (3) the amount and substantiality of the portion used in relation to the copyrighted work as a whole; and (4) the effect of the use upon the potential market for or value of the copyrighted work."

These criteria are relevant in determining whether the basic doctrine of fair use, as stated in the first sentence of section 107, applies in a particular case: "Notwithstanding the provisions of section 106, the fair use of a copyrighted work, including such use by reproduction in copies or phonorecords or by any other means specified by that section, for purposes such as criticism, comment, news reporting, teaching (including multiple copies for classroom use), scholarship, or research, is not an infringement of copyright."

The specific wording of section 107 as it now stands is the result of a process of accretion, resulting from the long controversy over the related problems of fair use and the reproduction (mostly by photocopying) of copyrighted material for educational and scholarly purposes. For example, the reference to fair use "by reproduction in copies or phonorecords or by any other means" is mainly intended to make clear that the doctrine has as much application to photocopying and taping as to older forms of use; it is not intended to give these kinds of reproduction any special status under the fair use provision or to sanction any reproduction beyond the normal and reasonable limits of fair use. Similarly, the newly-added reference to "multiple copies for classroom use" is a recognition that, under the proper circumstances of fairness, the doctrine can be applied to reproductions of multiple copies for the members of a class.

The Committee has amended the first of the criteria to be considered — "the purpose and character of the use" — to state explicitly that this factor includes a consideration of "whether such use is of a commercial nature or is for non-profit educational purposes." This amendment is not intended to be interpreted as any sort of not-for-profit limitation on educational uses of copyrighted works. It is an express recognition that, as under the present law, the commercial or non-profit character of an activity, while not conclusive with respect to fair use, can and should be weighed along with other factors in fair use decisions.

General intention behind the provision

The statement of the fair use doctrine in section 107 offers some guidance to users in determining when the principles of the doctrine apply. However, the endless variety of situations and combinations of circumstances that can rise in particular cases precludes the formulation of exact rules in the statute. The bill endorses the purpose and general scope of the judicial doctrine of fair use, but there is no disposition to freeze the doctrine in the statute, especially during a period of rapid technological change. Beyond a very broad statutory explanation of what fair use is and some of the criteria applicable to it, the courts must be free to adapt the doctrine to particular situations on a case-by-case basis. Section 107 is intended to restate the present judicial doctrine of fair use, not to change, narrow, or enlarge it in any way.

2. FAIR USE: THE TRADITIONAL UNDERSTANDING

Because the drafters of the 1976 Act intended to incorporate the doctrine of fair use as it was shaped judicially — both with regard to the general situations in which it comes into play, and the factors to be used by courts in applying it — it is essential for the student of copyright to turn to the prior case law. For example, the statutory reference to "criticism" and "comment" recalls the universal and long-held assumption of American judges that a critic or reviewer may quote liberally from the work under consideration. Related to criticism is "scholarship," another listed purpose for fair use in Section 107 and a setting in which fair use has also been important. This privilege flows from the frequent necessity of scholars to reproduce portions of earlier works. As Professor Chafee stated in his seminal article, *Reflections on the Law of Copyright,* 45 Colum. L. Rev. 503, 511 (1945): "The world goes ahead because each of us builds on the work of our predecessors. A dwarf standing on the shoulders of a giant can see farther than the giant himself."

A major case which explores the application of the fair use doctrine to scholarship is *Rosemont Enterprises, Inc. v. Random House, Inc.,* 366 F.2d 303, 150 USPQ 715 (2d Cir. 1966), *cert. denied,* 385 U.S. 1009, 152 USPQ 844 (1967). There, a Random House biography of Howard Hughes copied material from copyrighted *Look* magazine articles about Hughes; copyright in the *Look* articles had been acquired by Rosemont, an entity created by Hughes' own representatives. The court of appeals noted both that the borrowed passages were insubstantial in quantity (in proportion to both the *Look* articles and the Random House book) and that the fair use doctrine sheltered the defendant. It is worth quoting excerpts from the court's discussion of the fact that the defendant was motivated by commercial gain, of the contribution made by the defendant to the public interest, of the importance of researchers relying upon earlier works, and of the idea of fair use generally.

ROSEMONT ENTERPRISES, INC. v. RANDOM HOUSE, INC.

366 F.2d 303, 150 USPQ 715 (2d Cir. 1966), *cert. denied,*
385 U.S. 1009, 152 USPQ 844 (1967)

Moore, Circuit Judge. . . .

"Fair use" is a "privilege in others than the owner of a copyright to use the copyrighted material in a reasonable manner without his consent, notwithstanding the monopoly granted to the owner . . . ." Ball, Copyright and Literary Property 260 (1944). See generally Latman, Fair Use of Copyrighted Works, Study No. 14, prepared for the Subcommittee on Patents, Trademarks and Copyrights, Senate Comm. on the Judiciary, 86th Cong., 2d Sess. (Comm. Print 1960). The fundamental justification for the privilege lies in the constitutional purpose in granting copyright protection in the first instance, to wit, "To Promote the Progress of Science and the Useful Arts." U. S. Const. art. 1, § 8. See *Mathews Conveyor Co. v. Palmer-Bee Co.,* 135 F.2d 73 (6th Cir. 1943); Note, 56 Colum.L.Rev. 585, 595 (1956). To serve that purpose, "courts in passing upon particular claims of infringement must occasionally subordinate the copyright holder's interest in a maximum financial return to the greater public interest in the development of art, science and industry." *Berlin v. E. C. Publications Inc.,* 329 F.2d 541, 544 (2d Cir. 1964). Whether the privilege may justifiably be applied to particular materials turns initially on the nature of the materials, e. g., whether their distribution would serve the public interest in the free dissemination of information and whether their preparation requires some use of prior materials dealing with the same subject matter. Consequently, the privilege has been applied to works in the fields of science, law, medicine, history and biography. See Latman, supra at 10.

Biographies, of course, are fundamentally personal histories and it is both reasonable and customary for biographers to refer to and utilize earlier works dealing with the subject of the work and occasionally to quote directly from such works. Cf. *Harris v. Miller,* 50 U.S.P.Q. 306, 309 (S.D.N.Y.1941). This practice is permitted because of the public benefit in encouraging the development of historical and biographical works and their public distribution, e.g., so "that the world may not be deprived of improvements, or the progress of the arts be retarded." *Sayre v. Moore,* 1 East 361, 102 Eng.Rep. 138, 139 (K.B. 1801); see

West Publishing Co. v. Edward Thompson Co., 169 F. 833, 837 (E.D.N.Y.1909). Indeed, while the Hughes biography may not be a profound work, it may well provide valuable source material for future biographers (if any) of Hughes or for historians or social scientists. Contrary to the district court's view, the arts and sciences should be defined in their broadest terms, see *Sampson & Murdock Co. v. Seaver-Radford Co.,* 140 F. 539, 541 (1st Cir. 1905), particularly in view of the development of the field of social sciences.

(a) Commercial Gain

Whether an author or publisher reaps economic benefits from the sale of a biographical work, or whether its publication is motivated in part by a desire for commercial gain, or whether it is designed for the popular market, i.e., the average citizen rather than the college professor, has no bearing on whether a public benefit may be derived from such a work. Moreover, the district court in emphasizing the commercial aspects of the Hughes biography failed to recognize that "[a]ll publications presumably are operated for profit . . . ." *Koussevitzky v. Allen, Towne & Heath,* 188 Misc. 479, 483, 68 N.Y.S.2d 779, 783, aff'd, 272 App.Div. 759, 69 N.Y.S.2d 432 (1st Dept. 1947), and that "both commercial and artistic elements are involved in almost every [work] . . . ." Note, 56 Colum.L.Rev. supra at 597. . . .

(b) The Public Interest

By this preliminary injunction, the public is being deprived of an opportunity to become acquainted with the life of a person endowed with extraordinary talents who, by exercising these talents, made substantial contributions in the fields to which he chose to devote his unique abilities. . . .

"Everyone will agree that at some point the public interest in obtaining information becomes dominant over the individual's desire for privacy." *Sidis v. F-R Pub. Corp.,* supra, 113 F.2d at 809. Hughes has long been a newsworthy personality. Any biography of Hughes, of necessity, must recite the events of his life because biography in itself is largely a compilation of the past. Thus, in balancing the equities at this time in our opinion the public interest should prevail over the possible damage to the copyright owner.

(c) Independent Research

One other aspect of the district court's decision bears discussion. While recognizing that "historical fact and events in themselves are in the public domain and are not entitled to copyright protection . . .," *Lake v. Columbia Broadcasting System, Inc.,* 140 F.Supp. 707, 708-709 (S.D.Cal.1956); see *Collins v. Metro-Goldwyn Pictures Corp.,* 106 F.2d 83, 86 (2d Cir. 1939), and that "a writer may be guided by earlier copyrighted works . . .," *Benny v. Loew's, Inc.,* 239 F.2d supra, at 536; see *Oxford Book Co. v. College Entrance Book Co.,* 98 F.2d 688, 691 (2d Cir. 1938), the court asserted in sweeping language that an author is not entitled to utilize the fruits of another's labor in lieu of independent research and relying on *Toksvig v. Bruce Publishing Co.,* 181 F.2d 664 (7th Cir. 1950), stated that such activity could not be considered a fair use. Moreover, the court assigned the "apparent lack of independent research" as an additional reason for refusing to honor defendant's fair use claim. With this conclusion we disagree as a matter of law.

In *Toksvig v. Bruce Publishing Co.,* supra, the Seventh Circuit affirmed the grant of an injunction, in favor of an author who had written a careful biography of Hans Christian Andersen based on exhaustive research into Danish sources, against the publication of a subsequent biography of Andersen by an author who due to his inability to speak or read Danish had not independently examined the Danish sources and who had copied twenty-four specific passages of the first author's book. While the decision can be considered to rest on the ground that substantial and material copying was demonstrated, see Nimmer, Copyright at 133n. 576 (1964), the court went on to say that the use of plaintiff's book was not a fair use for the reason that reliance on the English translations of the Danish sources enabled the defendant to complete her book in much less time than it took plaintiff. Id. at 667. We, however, cannot subscribe to the view that an author is absolutely precluded from saving time and effort by referring to and relying upon prior published material. Cf. *Oxford Book Co. v. College Entrance Book Co.,* 98 F.2d 688 (2d Cir. 1938). It is just such wasted effort that the proscription against the copyright of ideas and facts, and to a lesser extent the privilege of fair use, are designed to prevent. See Gorman, Copyright Protection for the Collection and Representation of Facts, 76 Harv.L.Rev. 1569, 1584 (1963) (criticizing *Toksvig v. Bruce Publishing Co.,* supra). . . .

Two additional points should be made about the *Rosemont* case. First, by emphasizing such factors as the importance of the defendant's work to the public interest and the extent to which the defendant must of necessity use prior materials, the court reminds us that the four listed criteria in Section 107 are illustrative only and not exclusive. Second, in his concurring opinion (joined by another judge on the panel), Judge Lumbard adverted to the "spirit of the First Amendment" as limiting the plaintiff's use of the copyright laws for the purpose of restraining the publication of adverse biographical information. The interplay between copyright and the First Amendment will be considered at greater length at p. 473 *infra*.

An interesting counterpoint to the *Rosemont* case, involving biographical material at least as compelling, is the decision of the same court in *Meeropol v. Nizer,* 560 F.2d 1061, 195 USPQ 273 (2d Cir. 1977), *cert. denied,* 434 U.S. 1013 (1978). There the sons of Julius and Ethel Rosenberg brought an action for an injunction and damages against Louis Nizer, who in his book *The Implosion Conspiracy* used 28 copyrighted letters written by the Rosenbergs while awaiting their execution for espionage. The court of appeals reversed the summary judgment granted for the defendant, concluding that questions of fact remained surrounding the application of the fair use doctrine. The defendant relied upon the language of the *Rosemont* case regarding the limited relevance of commercial motive and also stressed the modest "effect of the use upon the potential market for or value of the copyrighted work" (a criterion borrowed by the court from the not-yet-effective Section 107). The court was not satisfied, concluding that, on remand, the fair use defense should turn upon "the purpose for which the letters were included in the book, whether the book is bought because it contains the Rosenberg letters, the necessity for verbatim copying of the letters, and the effect of the use of the copyrighted letters on their future market. . . ."

We agree that the mere fact that Nizer's book might be termed a popularized account of the Rosenberg trial lacking substantial scholarship and published for commercial gain, does not, standing alone, deprive Nizer or his publishers of the fair use defense. For a determination whether the fair use defense is applicable on the facts of this case, however, it is relevant whether or not the Rosenberg letters were used primarily for scholarly, historical reasons, or predominantly for commercial exploitation. . . .

A key issue in fair use cases is whether the defendant's work tends to diminish or prejudice the potential sale of plaintiff's work. *Marvin Worth Productions v. Superior Films Corp.,* 319 F. Supp. 1269, 1274 (S.D.N.Y. 1970); 2 M. Nimmer Copyright, § 145. The fact that the Rosenberg letters have been out of print for 20 years does not necessarily mean that they have no future market which can be injured. 2 M. Nimmer, *supra* at 649. The market for republication or for sale of motion picture rights might be affected by the infringing work. . . . The [district court] proceeded to hold that the use of the letters in *The Implosion Conspiracy* was entitled to the fair use defense because it found the use of copyrighted letters by Nizer to be unsubstantial. "The letters . . ." it held, "do not in any sense form a major part of defendants' work." *Id.* at 1213. We disagree. . . .

Defendants-appellees reprinted verbatim portions of 28 copyrighted letters, a total of 1957 words. Although these letters represent less than one percent of *The Implosion Conspiracy,* the letters were prominently featured in promotional material for the book. The fact that the letters were quoted out of chronological order, many undated, without indication of elisions or other editorial modifications is relevant to a determination of the purpose for their use and the necessity for verbatim quotations for the sake of historical accuracy.

Perhaps many of the observations made by the Court of Appeals in both *Rosemont* and *Meeropol* can be intruded into Section 107 through a broad construction of its first listed criterion: the purpose and character of the defendant's use. It will be recalled that this factor, as well as the others listed in the section, purports to restate judicial doctrine. The dichotomy between commercial use and nonprofit educational use, also stipulated in Section 107(1), calls to mind *Henry Holt & Co. v. Liggett & Meyers Tobacco Co.,* 23 F. Supp. 302 (E.D. Pa. 1938). There, an advertising use of three sentences from a scholarly work was deemed an infringement, while quantitatively greater uses for more educational purposes have apparently been tolerated. In other contexts testing the purpose of a use, "incidental" uses, such as the inclusion of song lyrics in a story or article have been deemed of a character deserving latitude. *See, e.g., Shapiro, Bernstein & Co. v. P.F. Collier & Son Co.,* 26 USPQ 40 (S.D.N.Y. 1934). Consider whether this latitude should be accorded to the following use of copyrighted lyrics in "The Talk of the Town" column of The New Yorker:

The death of Pearl White in Paris made us think of a song everybody sang when we were thirteen and "The Perils of Pauline" was being shown every week at the Nemo Theater, on Broadway and 110th Street. As nearly as we can remember it, the chorus went:

"Poor Pauline, I pity poor Pauline!
One night she's drifting out to sea,
Then they tie her to a tree
I wonder what the end will be,
This suspense is awful!
Bing! Bang! Biff! They throw her o'er the cliff,
They dynamite her in a submarine.
In the lion's den she sits with fright,
The lion goes to take a bite —
Zip, goes the fillum! — Good night!
Poor Pauline!"

There was another chorus — something about how they try to feed her up on Paris green, but

"Of course, her horse
Cries "Nay, nay, nay, Pauline!""
We forget the rest. As 1940 creeps on, it often seems to us that we have forgotten practically everything of any importance.

See Broadway Music Corp. v. F.R. Publishing Corp., 31 F. Supp. 817 (S.D.N.Y. 1940).

QUESTIONS

1. Is fair use a question of fact or of law? Is it, for example, to be decided by the jury or (after legal argument or briefing) by the court? Does fair use lend itself to some standard such as "proof by a preponderance of the evidence?"

2. How, if at all, do the factors which are utilized in determining fair use differ from those which are utilized in determining infringement? If you believe that there is little difference, does it make sense to place upon the plaintiff the burden of proving infringement while, as is commonly done, placing upon the defendant the burden of proving fair use? Consider each of the factors deemed pertinent under Section 107 to a finding of fair use, and determine whether these suggest an appropriate allocation of the burden.

3. Cannot a trial court on summary judgment properly conclude, after reading *The Implosion Conspiracy,* that: (a) no reasonable person would buy the book principally to secure the text of the Rosenberg letters? (b) the effect of the book upon the future market for the sale of rights in the letters is likely to be minimal? and (c) verbatim copying of the letters in the book was important in order to convey the truth and to establish a serious literary tone?

4. Even assuming that an author, in writing a book such as that about the Rosenbergs, may ultimately be motivated by commercial ends, ought it not be sufficient to warrant sustaining the defense of fair use that the book is a thorough recounting and interpretation of a major historical event? Is the "scholarship" standard which is defined so broadly in *Rosemont* to be applied to the defendant's work as a whole or only to the specific use made therein of the plaintiff's copyrighted work?

5. If the court is suggesting that the fair use defense might be lost when the defendant's quotation is used for promotion or sensationalism, does that not unwisely invite scrutiny of the defendant's psychological motivation?

TIME INC. v. BERNARD GEIS ASSOCIATES

293 F. Supp. 130 (S.D.N.Y. 1968)

WYATT, DISTRICT JUDGE.

This is a motion by plaintiff for summary judgment "interlocutory in character" on the issue of liability alone, as authorized by Rule 56(c) of the Federal Rules of Civil Procedure.

Time Incorporated (Time Inc.), the plaintiff, is a corporation which, among other things, publishes "Life", "Time" and "Fortune" magazines; it also publishes books; and it has "Broadcast divisions" (Hardy affidavit, p. 7), the operations of which are not explained but presumably involve radio or television broadcasting or both. The events in suit principally concern "Life" magazine, which is an activity or division of Time Inc. and is not a separate corporation. For simplicity, however, the word "Life" is hereafter often used in describing or in referring to events when the more technically correct expression would be "Time Inc.", the plaintiff.

When President Kennedy was killed in Dallas on November 22, 1963, Abraham Zapruder, a Dallas dress manufacturer, was by sheer happenstance at the scene taking home movie pictures with his camera. His film — an historic document and undoubtedly the most important photographic evidence concerning the fatal shots — was bought a few days later by Life; parts of the film were printed in several issues of the magazine. As to these issues and their contents (including, of course, the Zapruder pictures) and as to the film itself, Life has complied with all provisions of the Copyright Act (17 U.S.C. § 1 and following; the Act).

Defendant Thompson has written a book, "Six Seconds in Dallas" (the Book), which is a study of the assassination. It is a serious, thoughtful and impressive analysis of the evidence. The Book contains a number of what are called "sketches" but which are in fact copies of parts of the Zapruder film. Defendant Bernard Geis Associates (Associates), a partnership, published the Book on November 18, 1967 and defendant Random House, Inc. has been distributing the Book to the public. Defendant Bernard Geis is the only general partner of Associates.

This action was commenced on December 1, 1967. The complaint in a single count charges that certain frames of the Zapruder film were "stolen surreptitiously" from Life by Thompson and that copies of these frames appear in the Book as published. The complaint avers that the conduct of defendants is an infringement of statutory copyrights, an unfair trade practice, and unfair competition.

While the word "frame" with respect to motion picture film is generally understood, it may be advisable briefly to explain it. A motion picture consists of a series of photographs showing the objects in a scene in successive positions slightly changed. When the series is presented in rapid succession, the optical effect is of a picture in which the objects move. Each separate photograph in the series is called a "frame". Webster's Third New International Dictionary, pp. 902, 1475.

. . . .

I

The facts are almost entirely established beyond any dispute and without any dispute, except as expressly noted in the following recital.

A. Making of the Film and its Purchase by Life

On November 22, Zapruder decided to make a motion picture film of the President passing by. He had an 8 millimeter color home movie camera with a "telephoto" lens. At first he thought to take the pictures from his office in an office building at 501 Elm Street, at the corner of Elm and Houston Streets where the President's car would make a left turn from Houston into Elm Street. Then he felt he could get better pictures on the ground, so he went down with several others from his office and walked along Elm Street toward a triple underpass trying to pick the best spot for his camera. He tried several places and finally settled on a pedestal of concrete about 4 feet high on a slope; from this point he could look up Elm Street away from the underpass and see the corner where the left turn would be made, after which the President's car would come toward and pass directly in front of him on its way to the underpass; it was a "superb spot" (the Book, p. 4) for his pictures. He tried out the camera, felt that he was not steady, and then had his receptionist come up on the pedestal and steady him while he ran the camera.

The procession came into view and with the speed control at "Run" (about 18 frames per second) Zapruder started his camera, not knowing the horror it would record. When the car came close to Zapruder, there were the sudden shots and the reactions of those in the car — all caught on Zapruder's color film.

On the same day — November 22 — Zapruder had the original color film developed and three color copies made from the original film.

(There are about 480 frames in the Zapruder film, of which 140 show the immediate events of the shooting and 40 are relevant to the shots themselves. While working with the film, agents of the Secret Service or of the Federal Bureau of Investigation identified each frame with a number, beginning with "1" for the frame showing the lead motorcycles coming into view on Houston Street and continuing the numbers in sequence for the frames following; these numbers have since been used to identify the frames.)

On the same or the next day, Zapruder in his Dallas office turned over two copies of the film to the Secret Service, specifying that it was strictly for government use and not to be shown to newspapers or magazines because he expected to sell the film.

Life then negotiated with Zapruder and on November 25 by written agreement bought the original and all three copies of the film (two of which were noted as then in the possession of the Secret Service) and all rights therein, for $150,000 to be paid in yearly instalments of $25,000.

B. Use of the Film by Life and by the Warren Commission

In its next edition (cover date November 29, 1963) Life featured some 30 of the Zapruder frames, calling them a "remarkable and exclusive series". Doubtless because of time pressure, the frames were in black and white.

Life published on December 7, 1963 a special "John F. Kennedy Memorial Edition". This featured 9 enlarged Zapruder frames in color, telling how they came to be taken and how they recorded the tragic sequence "with appalling clarity".

President Johnson on November 29, 1963 appointed a Commission with Chief Justice Warren as Chairman (the Commission) to investigate the killing of President Kennedy. This Commission on September 24, 1964 submitted its lengthy report (the Warren Report) and all the evidence before it.

The Commission made extensive use of the Zapruder film, and placed great reliance on it, as evidenced in the Report (for example, pp. 97, 98-115). Six of the Zapruder frames are shown in the body of the Report (at pp. 100-103, 108, 114) and some 160 Zapruder frames are included (in volume XVIII) in the Exhibits of the Commission printed and submitted with the Report.

At the request of the Commission and on February 25, 1964, Life took the original Zapruder film to Washington and showed it to representatives of the Commission, the FBI and the Secret Service.

Life then prepared for the Commission from the original film 3 sets of 35 millimeter color transparencies of those frames desired by the Commission, except for frames 207 through 212. It appears that these frames in the original had been accidentally damaged in handling. Life could not supply copies from the original of these frames, but the two copies of the Secret Service made from the original were available and one of these was marked in evidence as Exhibit 904 (V Report 178). Life also made available to the Commission for its use in Washington the copy in Life's possession made from the original film.

There appears to be no privilege for the United States to use copyrighted material without the consent of the owner. A statute (28 U.S.C. § 1498(b)) gives a remedy in the Court of Claims for copyright infringement by the United States. Another statute (17 U.S.C. § 8) provides that publication by the government of copyrighted material does not cause any "abridgment" of the copyright and does not authorize "any use . . . of such copyright material without the consent of the copyright proprietor."

Life did in fact consent to use by the Commission of the Zapruder film and to its reproduction in the Report, provided a usual notice of copyright was given. Apparently this proviso was disregarded by the Commission.

Shortly after the submission of the Report, Life featured it in an issue (cover date, October 2, 1964) with a cover containing enlargements in color of five Zapruder frames. The text for the article on the Report was by a member of the Commission. The Zapruder film was described as "one of the most important pieces of evidence to come before the . . . Commission". Eight Zapruder frames, enlarged and in color, were printed alongside the text.

The Commission deposited in the National Archives all of its evidence and working papers; this would include at least one copy of the complete Zapruder film together with the transparencies supplied by Life. Researchers thus have access to the Zapruder film and to the Zapruder frames which were exhibits to the Commission Report. The Archivist states, however, that if anyone asks for copies of the film he or she is advised: "Life Magazine has advised us that while it will permit the film to be shown to qualified researchers, it cannot permit the reproduction of the film". The Archivist states that copies of the Zapruder frames will be furnished on request but that such copies are stamped on the back to indicate that permission to publish should be secured from Life.

The Report and its accompanying volumes of testimony were printed by the Government Printing office and so may be purchased from that office.

C. Criticism of the Report; Employment of Thompson by Life

There gradually developed a substantial volume of criticism of the Report, centered on its findings (Report, pp. 18, 22) that all the shots were fired from one place and that the person firing those shots acted alone.

Thompson was among those particularly interested in the Report; he became convinced that the Report was incomplete and he doubted its principal conclusion.

Thompson began studying the problem and was led to the evidence placed in the National Archives by the Commission. He apparently had an especial interest in the Zapruder frames and wanted to see the film and frames which Life had in the hope that these would be clearer than those in the Archives.

. . . .

[The court held the Zapruder films copyrightable, finding that the pictures "have many elements of creativity" but suggesting that any photograph could be the subject of copyright.]

IV

As already noted, the so-called "sketches" in the Book are in fact copies of the copyrighted film. That they were done in charcoal by an "artist" is of no moment. As put in Nimmer on Copyright, page 98:

It is of course, fundamental, that copyright in a work protects against unauthorized copying not only in the original medium in which the work was produced, but also in any other medium as well. Thus copyright in a photograph will preclude unauthorized copying by drawing or in any other form, as well as by photographic reproduction.

There is thus an infringement by defendants unless the use of the copyrighted material in the Book is a "fair use" outside the limits of copyright protection.

V

Whether the use by defendants of the Zapruder pictures is a "fair use" is the most difficult issue in the case. There is no reason to delay decision for a trial, however, because the facts are fully exposed without dispute and both sides agree that summary judgment is proper, each asking for such judgment. In a somewhat similar situation, summary judgment has been found proper. *Berlin v. E. C. Publications, Inc.,* 329 F.2d 541 (2d Cir. 1964).

Unlike the owner of a patent (35 U.S.C. § 154), the owner of a copyright is not given by statute (17 U.S.C. § 1) any exclusive right to use the work. The word "use" does not appear in the statute. Whatever the significance of this omission may be, the copyright owner does have the exclusive right to "print, reprint, publish, copy and vend the copyrighted work".

Despite such exclusive rights, the courts have nonetheless recognized that copying or other appropriation of a copyrighted work will not entail liability if it is reasonable or "fair". The doctrine is entirely equitable and is so flexible as virtually to defy definition. Our Court of Appeals (L. Hand, A. N. Hand, Patterson, C.J.J.) some years ago described the issue of fair use as "the most troublesome in the whole law of copyright". *Dellar v. Samuel Goldwyn, Inc.,* 104 F.2d 661 (2d Cir. 1939).

The earliest discussion of the principle was in 1841 by Mr. Justice Story at Circuit in *Folsom v. Marsh,* 9 Fed.Cas. p. 342, No. 4,901. The question arose over the copyright in certain letters of George Washington and was thus stated by Mr. Justice Story (9 Fed.Cas. at 348):

> The question, then, is, whether this is a justifiable use of the original materials, such as the law recognizes as no infringement of the copyright of the plaintiffs.

It was concluded that there was an invasion of the copyright and liability. The test of fair use was primarily the degree of injury to the plaintiff (9 Fed.Cas. at 348, 349):

> If so much is taken, that the value of the original is sensibly diminished, or the labors of the original author are substantially to an injurious extent appropriated by another, that is sufficient, in point of law, to constitute a piracy pro tanto.
>
> . . . .
>
> But if the defendants may take three hundred and nineteen letters, included in the plaintiffs' copyright, and exclusively belonging to them, there is no reason why another bookseller may not take other [sic] five hundred letters, and a third, one thousand letters, and so on, and thereby the plaintiffs' copyright be totally destroyed.

It would be idle to consider any number of the cases because each was decided on its own facts.

In this Circuit, the most recent case is *Rosemont Enterprises, Inc. v. Random House, Inc.*, 366 F.2d 303 (2d Cir. 1966). The Court took a somewhat liberal view of the fair use principle. Judge Moore emphasized the factor of "public interest in the free dissemination of information" and found that the "public benefit" to be derived from the challenged work was in no way affected by any motive of defendant for commercial gain.

. . . .

[The court proceeded to examine the earlier proposed versions of Section 107, and the pertinent commentary in the legislative reports.]

The difficult job is to apply the relevant criteria.

There is an initial reluctance to find any fair use by defendants because of the conduct of Thompson in making his copies [surreptiously after business hours] and because of the deliberate appropriation in the Book, in defiance of the copyright owner. Fair use presupposes "good faith and fair dealing". Schulman, Fair Use and the Revision of the Copyright Act, 53 Iowa L.Rev. 832 (1968). On the other hand it was not the nighttime activities of Thompson which enabled defendants to reproduce copies of Zapruder frames in the Book. They could have secured such frames from the National Archives, or they could have used the reproductions in the Warren Report or in the issues of Life itself. Moreover, while hope by a defendant for commercial gain is not a significant factor in this Circuit, there is a strong point for defendants in their offer to surrender to Life all profits of Associates from the Book as royalty payment for a license to use the copyrighted Zapruder frames. It is also a fair inference from the facts that defendants acted with the advice of counsel.

In determining the issue of fair use, the balance seems to be in favor of defendants.

There is a public interest in having the fullest information available on the murder of President Kennedy. Thompson did serious work on the subject and has a theory entitled to public consideration. While doubtless the theory could be explained with sketches of the type used at page 87 of the Book and in The Saturday Evening Post [and conceded by Life to be "fair" and permissible], the explanation actually made in the Book with copies is easier to understand. The Book is not bought because it contained the Zapruder pictures; the Book is bought because of the theory of Thompson and its explanation, supported by [the] Zapruder pictures.

There seems little, if any, injury to plaintiff, the copyright owner. There is no competition between plaintiff and defendants. Plaintiff does not sell the Zapruder pictures as such and no market for the copyrighted work appears to be affected. Defendants do not publish a magazine. There are projects for use by plaintiff of the film in the future as a motion picture or in books, but the effect of the use of certain frames in the Book on such projects is speculative. It seems more reasonable to speculate that the Book would, if anything, enhance the value of the copyrighted work; it is difficult to see any decrease in its value.

VI

Plaintiff has no cause of action under the State law for unfair competition.

. . . The motion of plaintiff is denied. The Clerk is directed to enter judgment in favor of defendants.

THE FIRST AMENDMENT, THE PUBLIC
INTEREST AND FAIR USE

The foregoing extract comprises the entire discussion of "fair use" in *Time v. Geis* except for reference to the House-passed revision bill in 1967, with its § 107 and Committee gloss substantially as set forth at pp. 461-62 *supra*. Yet this case, as a dramatic application of the *Rosemont* case, carries forward the "public interest" emphasis of that decision. The two cases may well represent a turning point in the law of fair use in this regard. For example, while purporting to apply the relevant criteria, crystallized in the then-emerging § 107, Judge Wyatt seems to have considered as the overriding consideration "a public interest in having the fullest information available on the murder of President Kennedy." This suggests the possibility of a "public interest" factor outweighing all others — a precept arguably bubbling under the surface of cases involving new technology. Moreover, the focus of public interest in these cases was public access to information. Each of these themes — public interest in general and access to information in particular — have been developed, sometimes separately and not always explicitly, in the period since 1968.

It will be recalled that *Rosemont* had involved a biography of Howard Hughes which contained some material from the sparse previously published material about the secretive tycoon, including an earlier series of magazine articles, the copyrights in which were acquired by the Hughes' corporation. It was under these compelling circumstances that the court spoke of "the public interest in the free dissemination of information" (quoted in *Time, Inc. v. Geis)*. Indeed, two of the judges in *Rosemont* would have denied the preliminary injunction simply because the very creation of the plaintiff corporation and its acquisition of the magazine copyrights were for the purpose of suppressing information about Hughes. In a concurring opinion they stated:

> The spirit of the First Amendment applies to the copyright laws at least to the extent that the courts should not tolerate any attempted interference with the public's right to be informed regarding matters of general interest when anyone seeks to use the copyright statute which was designed to protect interests of quite a different nature.

Against the background of *Rosemont*, the striking facts of *Time, Inc. v. Geis* may have been responsible for scholarly consciousness-raising with respect to the potential copyright-First Amendment conflict. *See* Sobel, *Copyright and the First Amendment: A Gathering Storm?*, 19 COPYRIGHT L. SYMP. 43 (1971) (written in 1969); Nimmer, *Copyright vs. The First Amendment,* 17 BULL. COPYRIGHT SOC'Y 255 (1970); Nimmer, *Does Copyright Abridge the First Amendment Guarantees of Free Speech and Press?,* 17 U.C.L.A. L. REV. 1180 (1970). But the question mark in the title of the Sobel article seemed supported by decisions which rejected First Amendment defenses out-of-hand. *See, e.g., Walt Disney Productions v. The Air Pirates,* 345 F. Supp. 108 (N.D. Cal. 1972); *Robert Stigwood Group Ltd. v. O'Reilly,* 346 F. Supp. 376, 383 (D. Conn. 1972); *Metro-Goldwyn-Mayer, Inc. v. Showcase Atlanta Cooperative Productions, Inc.* at p. 485 *infra; Marvin Worth Productions v. Superior Films Corp.,* 319 F. Supp. 1269 (S.D.N.Y. 1970) (*semble*). As noted in the appellate decision affirming summary judgment for the copyright owner in the *Air Pirates* case, *infra,* the idea/expression dichotomy is considered by some to avoid the conflict. *See Sid & Marty Krofft Television v. McDonald's Corp.,* 562 F.2d 1157 (9th Cir. 1977). Professor Nimmer indicates in his 1970 article a narrow limitation on the usefulness of the dichotomy in cases where verbatim reproduction (such as in depicting the My Lai massacre in the Viet Nam War or the Kennedy assassination) is virtually required to convey the idea. In some cases, verbatim reproduction, while not required to convey an idea, is required to convey the idea effectively. *See Elsmere Music, Inc. v. NBC,* 482 F. Supp. 741 (S.D.N.Y.), *aff'd,* 623 F.2d 252 (2d Cir. 1980), p. 483 *infra.* In other cases the distinction between an idea and expression will be difficult to draw. *See Nichols v. Universal Pictures Corp.,* p. 347 *supra.* In still others it will be non-existent. *Compare Herbert Rosenthal Jewelry Corp. v. Kalpakian,* p. 343 *supra* (copyright protection denied) *with Triangle Publications, Inc. v. Knight Ridder Newspapers, Inc.,* 626 F.2d 1171 (5th Cir. 1980) (dissenting opinion) (". . . when the idea and the expression are one and the same, the copyright interest should nearly always prevail over the generally incidental First Amendment concerns.")

Is the First Amendment subsumed under the doctrine of fair use or is it a separate defense? There has not yet developed a complete judicial consensus on this question. In *Italian Book Corp. v. American Broadcasting Co.,* 458 F. Supp. 65 (S.D.N.Y. 1978), a band playing a song was taped by a television crew filming a street festival in Greenwich Village; after being synchronized with a reporter's voice, the scene was shown as part of a one-minute segment on the same evening's news program. In finding this fortuitous and incidental use non-competitive and uninjurious, the court held that "the fair use doctrine, an integral part of copyright law, requires dismissal of the complaint" and that the First Amendment issue need not be reached, particularly where compensation and not prohibition was plaintiff's objective.

A similar approach was taken by the district court in *Triangle Publications, Inc. v. Knight Ridder Newspapers, Inc.,* 445 F. Supp. 875 (S.D.Fla. 1978), *aff'd,* 626 F.2d 1171 (5th Cir. 1980), where the court clearly took the view that the defenses are separate, holding that a television display of plaintiff's copyrighted magazine cover was not fair use (by emphasizing, surely unduly, the commercial nature of the use), but that nevertheless defendant's comparative advertising was protected by the First Amendment. The Court of Appeals for the Fifth Circuit affirmed, expressly on fair use grounds. (Two of the judges proceeded, in separate opinions, to address the First Amendment argument — and to reach opposite conclusions!)

An amalgamation of the two defenses is found in *Keep Thomson Governor Committee v. Citizens for Gallen Committee,* 457 F. Supp. 957 (D.N.H. 1978), a political campaign for Governor of New Hampshire which was shifted to the arena of a copyright action. Plaintiff purchased the copyright in a song "Live Free or Die" and used it in a political advertisement. Defendant copied some 15 seconds of this advertisement, with the music clearly heard in the background, and added about 45 seconds of narrative outlining defendant Gallen's criticism of the program of plaintiff's candidate. In finding fair use, the court's application of the four factors set forth in § 107 is laced with First Amendment considerations as a result of the court's acceptance of the conclusion that "[c]onflicts between interests protected by the First Amendment and the copyright laws can be resolved by application of the fair use doctrine." *See Wainwright Securities Corp. v. Wall Street Transcript Corp.,* 558 F.2d 91 (2d Cir. 1977), *cert. denied,* 434 U.S. 1014 (1978).

As indicated above, the "public interest" is not always articulated in First Amendment terms. Thus, in *Williams & Wilkins Co. v. U.S.,* 487 F.2d 1345 (Ct. Cl. 1973), *aff'd by an equally divided Court,* 420 U.S. 376 (1975), in which compensation was sought for Government photocopying of copyrighted medical journals, the court was "convinced that medicine and medical research will be injured by holding these particular practices to be an infringement." Moreover, there may well have been an unarticulated public interest in immunizing activity where "the personal, individual focus" of the library user is present. Such an interest clearly underlay the reasoning in the "Betamax" opinion, p. 495 *infra,* which emphasized that the challenged video-recording of broadcast programs was done "by individuals or families in the privacy of their own home for use in their home."

Lest one forget that fair use is a flexible, equitable, rule of reason, and is not automatically available whenever the "public interest" is invoked, we should note the words of Chief Judge Kaufman in *Iowa State Univ. Research Foundation v. ABC,* 621 F.2d 57 (2d Cir. 1980).

> The fair use doctrine is not a license for corporate theft, empowering a court to ignore a copyright whenever it determines the underlying work contains material of public importance. Indeed, we do not suppose that appellants would embrace their own defense theory if another litigant sought to apply it to the ABC evening news.

3. PARODY

In the days when the motion picture industry was expressing some concern about that upstart television (the 1950s), the comedian Jack Benny decided to dust off an old radio skit he had used. It was a fifteen-minute burlesque of the melodrama "Gaslight" with Ingrid Bergman co-starring in the radio parody of her original role. Bergman had furnished Benny's writers with a copy of the shooting script of "Gaslight" and the writers also viewed the motion picture. No objection to the radio skit had been made by Loew's, the producer of "Gaslight."

In 1952 and 1953, Benny produced another fifteen-minute burlesque of "Gaslight," but this time did so in the course of his half-hour television program. It was called "Autolight" (and co-starred Barbara Stanwyck in the leading female role). District Judge Carter set forth the following comparison of the two works (omitting a comparison of dialogue):

I. Generally

Benny TV Program	MGM's "Gaslight"
1. Locale: London	London
2. Period: 1871 when story begins.	"Early 1870's" when story begins.
3. Main setting: Gloomy old 4-story house.	Gloomy, old 4-story house.
4. Characters:	
(a) Husband "CHARLES Manningham" (played by Benny) murdered a woman *15* years ago in this very house; married present wife so that " in the guise of an English gentleman" he can pursue search for jewels of murdered woman. He is following plan of driving his wife insane. He goes out nightly, sneaks back into attic to search. Is finally captured by man from Scotland Yard.	(a) Husband "Gregory Anton" (played by CHARLES Boyer) murdered a women *10* years ago in this very house; married present wife (who inherited house) so he can pursue search for jewels of murdered woman. He is following plan of driving his wife insane. He goes out nightly, sneaks back to attic to search. Is finally caught by man from Scotland Yard.

(b) Wife, "BELLA Manningham" much in love with husband; pained that he leaves her alone night after night; worried she is losing mind; asks for his sympathy;

she is victim of husband's plan to drive her insane; learns of husband's past; asks to see husband alone before he is taken away, and taunts him then calls Inspector.

(c) *Scotland Yard Inspector*

"INSPECTOR" (Played by Noble) Has been watching house for some time; comes to call on wife when husband out; tells her of husband's past, the murder of a woman in this house years ago; in talking with wife, Inspector gets her to admit she knows it is her husband prowling in the attic who makes strange noises there at night. Upon return of husband, Inspector has hidden, but appears when husband is bullying wife; places husband under arrest; allows wife to talk with husband alone a few moments while he waits outside door, then at her call, comes back and takes husband away into custody. We feel there is affection between Inspector and wife.

(d) *Maid "ELIZABETH"*
Question by husband about picture out of place; denies touching it.

(e) *Other servant in house:*
Butler, "Jeeves."

(b) Wife, "PAULA Anton" much in love with husband; pained that he leaves her alone nightly, fears that she is losing mind; asks for husband's sympathy;
Ditto

(c) *Scotland Yard Inspector*

"Brian Cameron" (Played by Joseph Cotton)

Ditto

(d) Maid "ELISABETH"
Ditto

(e) *Other servant in house:*
Maid, "Nancy."

II. Story Points

(a) Husband pursuing a sinister, diabolical scheme to drive wife crazy.

(b) Husband murdered a woman years ago in this very house.

(c) Husband marries present wife, comes to this very house, so he can search for jewels of murdered woman, in attic.

(d) In order to search, husband leaves wife night after night, and pretends he is going elsewhere, actually coming back to own attic.

(e) Husband's method of driving wife insane, includes following —

(1) Telling her she is always forgetting things;

TV program: Wife "doesn't remember" things she does, husband tells her.

MGM script: Wife inclined to lose things and forget things, husband tells her.

(2) Puts picture(s) out of place, then accuses wife of having done this and forgotten it:

TV program: Turns 2 pictures upside down.

MGM script: Takes little picture off wall and hides it.

(3) Confines wife to her room, and he goes out night after night.

(4) Humiliates wife in front of servant(s) by calling her in to be questioned when picture found out of place.

TV program: (Maid, Elizabeth, is quizzed)

MGM script: (Maids, Elizabeth and Nancy are quizzed)

(5) Husband's searching for jewels in attic, has following effects which increase idea of wife's insanity:

(a) When he turns on gaslight in attic, lights in her room go lower; then later when he turns off gaslight in attic, her lights in her room come up higher again.

(b) His search in attic (makes queer noises) (has queer effect).

TV program: Wife complains of headaches, but when Inspector explains her husband was up in attic searching for jewels she says her headache is gone.

MGM script: Wife thinks she's hearing imaginary footsteps in attic.

(f) Husband calls in servants, after he has misplaced picture, questions them, in order to cast suspicion on his wife.

(g) Husband tells wife she is getting hysterical, and should sit down and calm herself:

(h) Husband asks why wife does these crazy things; says she is insane:

(i) Running idea that wife forgets things:

(j) Gaslights go down after husband leaves, and come up just before he returns:

(k) Wife pleads for sympathy and kindness from husband:

(*l*) Inspector from Scotland Yard, has been watching house, comes to visit wife when husband out, tells her of husband's dark past, reassures her of her sanity, captures husband.

(I) Watching house

(II) Visits wife

(III) Tells of husband's crime

(IV) Reassures wife of sanity

(V) Captures husband

(m) Husband returns, starts to bully wife again, when Inspector comes on scene.

(n) Wife asks to speak to husband alone, before Inspector takes him away; Inspector finally agrees and waits outside room within call.

TV program: Inspector ties up husband because wife asks to talk with him alone.

MGM script: Inspector already had tied husband up.

(o) Husband, tied up in chair, tries to talk wife into getting knife and cutting him loose.

TV program: Knife in desk.

MGM script: Knife in cupboard.

(p) Wife pretends she is going to release husband by cutting bonds with knife, then frightens him by implying instead she will kill him with the knife, then calls Inspector.

"The comparison leads the court to the following conclusions of fact: (1) that the locale and period of the work are the same; (2) the main setting is the same; (3) the characters are generally the same; (4) the story points are practically identical; (5) the development of the story, the treatment (except that defendants' treatment is burlesque), the incidents, the sequences of events, the points of suspense, the climax are almost identical and finally, (6) there has been a detailed borrowing of much of the dialogue with some variation in wording."

The Court posed the key issue as follows: "If this was the ordinary plagiarism case, without the defense of burlesque as a fair use, it would be crystal clear, under the controlling authorities, that there had been access, a substantial taking and therefore infringement.

"We are thus brought face to face then with the major issue in the case. Is a substantial taking of a copyrighted property permissible when the taking is by use of burlesque and rests for justification on the theory of fair use?"

After an extensive review of the doctrine of fair use, Judge Carter then answered this question in the negative. *Loew's, Inc. v. CBS, Inc.*, 131 F. Supp. 165 (S.D. Cal. 1955).

The Court of Appeals for the Ninth Circuit agreed with Judge Carter's determination that a "parodized or burlesque taking is to be treated no differently from any other appropriation. . . ." In its affirmance, the appellate court found that "there is only a single decisive point in the case. One cannot copy the substance of another's work without infringing his copyright." *Benny v. Loew's, Inc.*, 239 F.2d 532 (9th Cir. 1956).

The Supreme Court granted certiorari, but split 4-4 (Mr. Justice Douglas abstaining), 356 U.S. 43 (1958), and in accordance with tradition, issued no opinions or even an indication of how individual Justices voted.

While the *Jack Benny* case was on appeal to the Ninth Circuit, Judge Carter was confronted with another parody case — Sid Caesar's television skit "From Here to Obscurity," a burlesque of the film "From Here to Eternity." He found for defendant, because "[u]nlike Loew's, here there was a taking only sufficient to cause the viewer to recall and conjure up the original . . . a necessary element of burlesque." *Columbia Pictures Corp. v. NBC*, 137 F. Supp. 348 (S.D. Cal. 1955).

The court's summary of the two works is appended to the opinion and interested students should consult this appendix to form their own opinion on infringement (recognizing, in any event, that the summaries were produced by a court finding no infringement). The court's conclusions, among others, were:

> The writers of the burlesque "From Here To Obscurity" were familiar with the motion picture "From Here To Eternity." There are similarities between the burlesque and the motion picture. The locale is the same. There are similarities in certain of the general settings, in parts of some of the situations and in the use in both the burlesque and the picture of some of the same principal members of the cast of characters, i.e., a private, a sergeant, a dancehall girl, and the private's friend. There is also some similarity between the burlesque and the motion picture in incident, and in some of the details of the development, treatment and expression. All such similarities are the result of the intentional use of the motion picture by the writers of the burlesque in order to accomplish the purposes of a burlesque.

> Although the burlesque "From Here To Obscurity" uses material appearing in the motion picture "From Here To Eternity," the burlesque is a new, original and different literary work as compared with the motion picture; and possesses new, original and different development, treatment and expression. There is no substantial similarity between said burlesque and said motion picture as to theme, characterizations, general story line, detailed sequence of incidents, dialogue, points of suspense, sub-climax or climax.

In *Berlin v. E.C. Publications, Inc.*, 329 F.2d 541 (2d Cir.), *cert. denied*, 379 U.S. 822 (1964), "Mad Comics" furnished lyrics to be "sung to the tune of" plaintiffs' parodied songs.

> "Two examples are the following — the lyrics on the left hand side being the original lyrics, the lyrics on the right hand side being the defendants' parodies:

The last time I saw Paris	The first time I saw Maris
Her heart was warm and gay,	He'd signed up with the A's!
I heard the laughter	He slugged the ball but
of her heart	never found

in ev'ry street cafe.

The last time I saw Paris,
Her trees were dressed for spring,
And lovers walked beneath
    those trees,
and birds found songs to sing.

I dodged the same old taxicabs
that I had dodged for years;
The chorus of their squeaky horns
was music to my ears.

The last time I saw Paris
Her heart was warm and gay.
No matter how they change her
I'll remember her that way.

How big league baseball pays!

The next time I saw Maris
A Yankee he'd become!
And now endorsements earn
    for him
A most substantial sum!

He signed a contract with Gillette
To plug their razor blades!
And when he found he cut himself,
He went and plugged Band-Aids!

The last time I saw Maris
He plugged six brands of beer!
The Democrats should pay him
To plug the New Frontier!

Blue Skies
smiling at me
Nothing but Blue Skies
do I see,

Bluebirds
singing a song
Nothing but Bluebirds
all day long,

Never saw the sun
shining so bright,
Never saw things
going so right,

Noticing the days
hurrying by,
When you're in love
my! how they fly,

Blue days
all of them gone
Nothing but blue skies
from now on.

Blue Cross
Had me agree
To a new Blue Cross
Policy!

Blue Cross
Said I would be
Happy that Blue Cross
Covered me!

Then I took a fall,
Leg in a splint;
They said that I
Should read the fine print!

When a very high
Fever I ran,
They told me I
Took out the wrong plan!

That's Blue Cross!
There seems to be
Plenty for Blue Cross!
None for me!"

The district court held that the direction to the reader to sing was not equivalent to reproduction of the music. In affirming summary judgment on most of the claims, the court of appeals held that the brief phrases of lyrics taken "fell far short of the 'substantial' takings which were involved in Benny"; rather, they were only what was necessary to "recall or conjure up" the original. There was, of course, a tracking of the meter, but Judge Kaufman stated: "We doubt that even so eminent a composer as plaintiff Irving Berlin should be permitted to claim a property interest in iambic pentameter." The result in the "Mad Comics" case was a finding of no infringement. The court ruled "as a general proposition . . . parody and satire *are* deserving of substantial freedom. . . ." [Emphasis in original.] Consider whether this freedom is particularly justified by the unlikelihood that a copyright owner will satirize his or her own work. *See* p. 484 *infra.*

WALT DISNEY PRODUCTIONS v. THE AIR PIRATES

581 F.2d 751 (9th Cir. 1978)

[*See* p. 170 *supra.*]
. . . .

At least since this Court's controversial ruling in *Benny v. Loew's Inc.*, 239 F.2d 532 (9th Cir. 1956), affirmed by an equally divided Court, 356 U.S. 43, 78 S.Ct. 667, 2 L.Ed.2d 583, the standards for applying the fair use defense in parody cases, like the standards for applying fair use in other contexts, have been a source of considerable attention and dispute. See 2 *Nimmer on Copyright* § 145. As a general matter, while some commentators have urged that the fair use defense depends only on whether the infringing work fills the demand for the original (see, e. g., Note, *Piracy or Parody: Never the Twain,* 38 U.Colo.L.Rev. 550 (1966); see generally 2 *Nimmer on Copyright* § 145), this Court and others have also consistently focused on the substantiality of the taking. See, *e. g., Benny v. Loew's Inc.*, 239 F.2d 532 (9th Cir. 1956), affirmed by an equally divided Court, 356 U.S. 43, 78 S.Ct. 667, 2 L.Ed.2d 583; *Rosemont Enterprises, Inc. v. Random House, Inc.*, 366 F.2d 303 (2d Cir. 1966), certiorari denied, 385 U.S. 1009, 87 S.Ct. 714, 17 L.Ed.2d 546; 17 U.S.C. § 107(3) (codifying old law). But cf. *Williams & Wilkins Co. v. United States,* 487 F.2d 1345, 203 Ct.Cl. 74 (1973), affirmed by an equally divided Court, 420 U.S. 376, 95 S.Ct. 1344, 43 L.Ed.2d 264.

In inquiring into the substantiality of the taking, the district court read our *Benny* opinion to hold that any substantial copying by a defendant, combined with the fact that the portion copied constituted a substantial part of the defendant's work, automatically precluded the fair use defense. That such a strict reading of *Benny* was unjustified is indicated first by the fact that it would essentially make any fair use defense fruitless. If the substantiality of the taking necessary to satisfy the first half of that test is no different from the substantiality necessary to constitute an infringement, then the *Benny* test would be reduced to an absurdity, covering any infringement except those falling within the much-criticized and abandoned exception for cases in which the part copied was not a substantial part of the defendant's work. Compare *Rosemont Enterprises, Inc. v. Random House, Inc.*, 256 F.Supp. 55 (S.D.N.Y. 1966), reversed on other grounds, 366 F.2d 303 (2d Cir. 1966), certiorari denied, 385 U.S. 1009, 87 S.Ct. 714, 17 L.Ed.2d 546; see 2 *Nimmer on Copyright* § 143.2.

The language in *Benny* concerning the substantiality of copying can be given a reading much more in keeping with the context of that case and the established principles at the time of that case if the opinion is understood as setting a threshold that eliminates from the fair use defense copying that is virtually complete or almost verbatim. Accord 2 *Nimmer on Copyright* § 145. It was an established principle at the time of *Benny* that such verbatim copying precluded resort to the fair use defense. See, *e. g., Leon v. Pacific Telephone & Telegraph Co.,* 91 F.2d 484 (9th Cir. 1937). Moreover, the *Benny* facts presented a particularly appropriate instance to apply that settled principle. As the *Benny* district court found, Benny's "Autolight" tracked the parodied "Gas Light" in almost every respect: the locale and period, the setting, characters, story points, incidents, climax and much of the dialogue all were found to be identical. 131 F.Supp. 165, 171. In this context, *Benny* should not be read as taking the drastic step of virtually turning the test for fair use into the test for infringement. See *Columbia Pictures Corp. v. National Broadcasting Co.,* 137 F.Supp. 348 (S.D.Cal.

1955). To do otherwise would be to eliminate fair use as a defense except perhaps for those infringers who added an extra act at the end of their parody.

Thus *Benny* should stand only as a threshold test that eliminates near-verbatim copying. In the absence of near-verbatim copying, other courts have analyzed the substantiality of copying by a parodist by asking whether the parodist has appropriated a greater amount of the original work than is necessary to "recall or conjure up" the object of his satire. *Berlin v. E. C. Publications, Inc.,* 329 F.2d 541 (2d Cir. 1964), certiorari denied, 379 U.S. 822, 85 S.Ct. 46, 13 L.Ed.2d 33; see *Columbia Pictures Corp. v. National Broadcasting Co.,* 137 F.Supp. 348 (S.D.Cal. 1955).[13]

In order to facilitate application of either the *Benny* threshold test or the *Berlin* test, it is important to determine what are the relevant parts of each work that are compared in analyzing similarity. Plaintiff assumes in its brief that the graphic depiction, or pictorial illustration, is separately copyrightable as a component part, so that a verbatim copy of the depiction alone would satisfy the *Benny* test. Defendants proceed on the assumption that comparing their characters with plaintiff's involves a comparison not only of the physical image but also of the character's personality, pattern of speech, abilities, and other traits. Apparently this issue has not been addressed previously, and neither position is without merit. On the one hand, since an illustration in a book or catalogue can be copyrighted separately (see, *e. g., Lin-Brook Builders Hardware v. Gertler,* 352 F.2d 298 (9th Cir. 1965)), it might follow that an illustration in a comic strip is entitled to the same protection by virtue of Section 3 of the former Copyright Act. On the other hand, to a different extent than in other illustrations, a cartoon character's image is intertwined with its personality and other traits, so that the "total concept and feel" (*Roth Greeting Cards v. United Card Co.,* 429 F.2d 1106, 1110 (9th Cir. 1970)) of even the component part cannot be limited to the image itself.[14]

We need not decide which of these views is correct, or whether this copying was so substantial to satisfy the *Benny* test, because it is our view that defendants took more than is allowed even under the *Berlin* test as applied to both the conceptual and physical aspects of the characters. In evaluating how much of a taking was necessary to recall or conjure up the original, it is first important to recognize that given the widespread public recognition of the major characters involved here, such as Mickey Mouse and Donald Duck (see *e. g.,* R. 191-193), in comparison with other characters very little would have been necessary to place Mickey Mouse and his image in the minds of the readers. Second, when the medium involved is a comic book, a recognizable caricature is not difficult to

---

[13] In so construing *Benny,* we necessarily disagree with its dictum that a parody is treated no differently than any other taking. See Berlin v. E. C. Publications, Inc., 329 F.2d 541 (2d Cir. 1964), certiorari denied, 379 U.S. 822, 85 S.Ct. 46, 13 L.Ed.2d 33.

[14] While not explicitly noting these competing arguments or focusing on whether an image is a protectable component part, most of the cases dealing with cartoon characters have considered the character's personality and other traits in addition to its image. *See e.g.,* Detective Comics, Inc. v. Bruns Publications, Inc., 111 F.2d 432 (2d Cir. 1940); Warner Brothers Inc. v. Film Ventures International, 403 F.Supp. 522, 525 (C.D.Cal. 1975). See also Sid & Marty Krofft Television v. McDonald's Corp., 562 F.2d 1157, 1169 (9th Cir. 1977); 1 Nimmer on Copyright § 30; Note, The Protection Afforded Literary and Cartoon Characters Through Trademark, Unfair Competition and Copyright, 68 Harv.L.Rev. 349 (1954). In what appears to be the only two cases that have viewed a character only as an image (King Features Syndicate v. Fleischer, 299 F.2d 533 (2d Cir. 1924); Fleischer v. Freundlich, 73 F.2d 276 (2d Cir. 1936)), the alleged copying was of a doll, which could have only an image and no conceptual character traits; therefore the issue of whether the comic character's depiction included a personality was not raised.

draw, so that an alternative that involved less copying is more likely to be available than if a speech, for instance, is parodied. Also significant is the fact that the essence of this parody did not focus on how the characters looked, but rather parodied their personalities, their wholesomeness and their innocence.[15] Thus arguably defendants' copying could have been justified as necessary more easily if they had paralleled closely (with a few significant twists) Disney characters and their actions in a manner that conjured up the particular elements of the innocence of the characters that were to be satirized. While greater license may be necessary under those circumstances, here the copying of the graphic image appears to have no other purpose than to track Disney's work as a whole as closely as possible.

Defendants' assertion that they copied no more than necessary appears to be based on an affidavit, which stated that "the humorous effect of parody is best achieved when at first glance the material appears convincingly to be the original, and upon closer examination is discovered to be quite something else" (Br. 20-21). The short answer to this assertion, which would also justify substantially verbatim copying, is that when persons are parodying a copyrighted work, the constraints of the existing precedent do not permit them to take as much of a component part as they need to make the "best parody." Instead, their desire to make the "best parody" is balanced against the rights of the copyright owner in his original expressions. That balance has been struck at giving the parodist what is necessary to conjure up the original, and in the absence of a special need for accuracy (compare *Meeropol v. Nizer,* 560 F.2d 1061, 1071 (2d Cir. 1977), certiorari denied, 434 U.S. 1013, 98 S.Ct. 727, 54 L.Ed.2d 756), that standard was exceeded here. By copying the images in their entirety, defendants took more than was necessary to place firmly in the reader's mind the parodied work and those specific attributes that are to be satirized. See Netterville, *Parody, Mimicry and Humorous Commentary,* 35 So.Cal.L.Rev. 225, 238 (1962).

Because the amount of defendant's copying exceeded permissible levels, summary judgment was proper. See *Berlin v. E. C. Publications,* 329 F.2d 541 (2d Cir. 1964), certiorari denied, 379 U.S. 822, 85 S.Ct. 46, 13 L.Ed.2d 33. While other factors in the fair use calculus may not be sufficient by themselves to preclude the fair use defense, this and other courts have accepted the traditional American rule that excessive copying precludes fair use. See, *e. g., Benny v. Loew's Inc.,* 239 F.2d 532 (9th Cir. 1956), affirmed by an equally divided Court, 356 U.S. 43; *Walt Disney Productions v. Mature Pictures Corp.,* 389 F.Supp. 1397 (S.D.N.Y. 1975); see generally *Berlin v. E. C. Publications,* 329 F.2d 541 (2d Cir. 1964), certiorari denied, 379 U.S. 822.[16]

C. First Amendment Considerations

Defendants also insist that the First Amendment should bar any liability for their parody because otherwise protected criticism would be discouraged. There is of course some tension between the First Amendment and the Copyright Act,

---

[15] In making this distinction, we do not regard it as fatal, as some courts have done (see, *e. g.,* Walt Disney Productions v. Mature Pictures Corp., 389 F.Supp. 1397 (S.D.N.Y. 1975)), that the "Air Pirates" were parodying life and society in addition to parodying the Disney characters. Such an effect is almost an inherent aspect of any parody. To the extent that the Disney characters are not also an object of the parody, however, the need to conjure them up would be reduced if not eliminated.

[16] This exclusion of other factors is not a drastic step, since the level of permissible copying selected in *Benny* was set with a recognition of and as a compromise with other concerns such as the nature and character of the use.

which was enacted pursuant to the Copyright Clause of the Constitution but defendants' claim can be dismissed without a lengthy discussion that it otherwise might merit in light of our recent decision in *Sid & Marty Krofft Television v. McDonald's Corp.,* 562 F.2d 1157, 1170 (9th Cir. 1977). In that case we endorsed not only Judge Wollenberg's dismissal of defendants' First Amendment claim here, but also the accommodation that "the idea-expression line represents an acceptable definitional balance as between copyright and free speech interests." Because the defendants here could have expressed their theme without copying Disney's protected expression, *Sid & Marty Krofft* requires that their First Amendment challenge be dismissed. See also *Zacchini v. Scripps-Howard Broadcasting Co.,* 433 U.S. 562, 577 and n. 13.

. . . .

Judgment affirmed as to copyright infringement and reversed and remanded as to trademark infringement, unfair competition and trade disparagement.

QUESTIONS

1. In what respect does the *Air Pirates* opinion indicate parodies *should* be treated differently from other takings?
2. With respect to the pivotal finding on excessive taking, doesn't the court's requirement of a "caricature," rather than a "copy," of Mickey Mouse run the risk that the public will be uncertain it is Mickey being parodied?
3. Why isn't parody one of those cases referred to by the court as having "a special need for accuracy" such as the letters from Julius and Ethel Rosenberg in *Meeropol v. Nizer,* or the Zapruder films of the Kennedy assassination? *See Time, Inc. v. Geis,* p. 467 *supra.*
4. Are you as comfortable as the court is with the idea/expression dichotomy as the accommodation between the First Amendment, which protects ideas, and copyright, which protects only particular forms of expressing ideas?
5. Reconsider the discussion of the interaction between copyright policies and First Amendment policies, at p. 473 *supra.* Do the First Amendment policies which might be thought to justify wide permission to copy in preparing works of biography or history apply in comparable degree to the preparation of works of parody?

The *Benny* and *Air Pirates* tests of fair use relating to parody were applied in a case pitting New York City against biblical Sodom. See *Elsmere Music, Inc. v. NBC,* 482 F. Supp. 741 (S.D.N.Y.), *aff'd,* 623 F.2d 252 (2d Cir. 1980). The satirical late night television show "Saturday Night" decided to satirize a very successful New York City "commercial" campaign centered about a copyrighted song entitled "I Love New York." Although this song consisted of a 45-word lyric and 100 measures of music, the heart of the composition was a four note motif (the notes DCDE) sung with the words "I Love New York" and it was this motif that was sung repetitively throughout the campaign. Defendant's use of this motif four times with the words "I Love Sodom" was deemed by the district court to be "a significant (albeit less than extensive) portion" and thus "far more than merely a *de minimis* taking." This finding required a determination of whether defendant's activities constituted fair use. Defendant used the song as the highlight of a mythical campaign to improve the image of Sodom, satirizing the comparable campaign of New York City which gave rise to its song. The court applied the quantitative parody test used in the *Air Pirates* case and determined that "the repetition of the phrase sung *a capella* and lasting for only eighteen seconds cannot be said to be clearly more than was necessary to 'conjure up' the original. Nor was it so substantial a taking as to preclude this use from being a fair one."

The latter quoted sentence seems to accord with the test in the *Jack Benny* case, which recognizes a threshold beyond which fair use is precluded. In its discussion of the *de minimis* argument, the *Elsmere* court also seemed to recognize the existence of a *minimal* threshold (found to have been exceeded in this case) below which infringement is impossible even without regard to the fair use doctrine. This three-tier approach — with fair use to be considered only in the middle area between quantitatively minimal and near-verbatim taking — is useful, at least as far as traditional fair use situations are concerned. As will be seen, it is less applicable in areas of new technology in which the entire work is usually taken and yet fair use may be recognized.

There are, however, some who would argue that it is misleading to employ fair use analysis only as a second step in a two-step analysis, the first being consideration of quantity alone. Those who so argue believe that the societal policies which are commonly reserved for fair use analysis come into play, whether or not avowedly, in determining as well *where* the quantitative thresholds are properly to be placed for tier one and tier three (i.e., when it is proper to find a prima facie infringement) — as well, indeed, as whether certain components of a work are copyrightable at all. For example, one might consider whether the underlying analysis of the issue in the *Elsmere* case would be any different if the ultimate conclusion was that what the defendant copied was quantitatively *de minimis,* or that the four-note motif and the "I love" phrase which the defendant copied were noncopyrightable, instead of the conclusion that the "tier two" copying was privileged by virtue of the fair use doctrine.

In finding that the extent of use was not excessive, the "I Love New York" court approved the repetition of the motif as furthering the overall satirical effect — an objective perhaps reminiscent of the "best parody" sought by the *Air Pirates* defendants and there rejected by the court. The court also implicitly applied the fourth criterion set forth in Section 107, holding that defendant's "I Love Sodom" neither had nor could have had the effect of fulfilling the demand for the original. Such a conclusion would give rather free rein to parody as a literary form, far more so than with history or biography, since, as has been mentioned above, the parodist employs a technique which the author of the original work is disinclined to utilize in preparing and exploiting versions of that work; moreover, the parodist identifies the work which is the source of his inspiration and assumes that the audience is already familiar with that work. Finally, the *Elsmere* court grappled with the emerging question as to whether the copyrighted work (as distinguished from some independent substantive issue) must itself be the object of parody. The court held that this was not a necessary ingredient, but proceeded to find it present in the case at hand.

In its per curiam affirmance, which noted that "in today's world of often unrelieved solemnity, copyright law should be hospitable to the humor of parody," the Court of Appeals for the Second Circuit suggested expansion of the latitude available to parodies:

> A parody is entitled at least to "conjure up" the original. Even more extensive use would still be fair use, provided the parody builds upon the original, using the original as a known element of modern culture and contributing something new for humorous effect or commentary.

[Review the facts of the *Jack Benny* case, and consider whether the formulation of the Second Circuit would shelter even the Benny parody of "Gaslight."]

A stricter approach was taken in a decision finding the musical cabaret production "Scarlett Fever" to infringe the copyright in "Gone With the Wind." *Metro-Goldwyn Mayer, Inc. v. Showcase Atlanta Coop. Prods., Inc.,* 479 F. Supp. 351, 203 USPQ 822 (N.D. Ga. 1979). The court approved the following definition of parody: "A parody is a work in which the language or style of another work is closely imitated or mimicked for comic effect or ridicule." The court required "some critical comment or statement about the original work which reflects the original perspective of the parodist — thereby giving the parody social value beyond its entertainment function." Since in overall effect defendant's work failed this test, it could not qualify as a parody, and in any event the defendant was found to have taken more than needed. [Before drawing the distinction between social value and entertainment value for purposes of applying the fair use doctine, might not the court have benefitted from a re-examination of the opinion of Mr. Justice Holmes, and particularly his admonition to judges, in the *Bleistein* case, *supra* p. 22?]

The "Scarlett Fever" case also focused on the fourth criterion in Section 107 — "the effect of the use upon the potential market for or value of the copyrighted work." The court recognized that "potential" effect on the market, while inherently speculative, is what must be tested, and concluded that the defendant's satirical production was likely to harm the potential market or value of the plaintiff's renowned romantic novel because they both had the same overall function of entertaining. [Would this not effectively destroy *all* parody? What in fact *is* meant in Section 107(4) by the effect on the plaintiff's market or upon the value of his work? Does it encompass customer loss or ridicule flowing from the defendant's satirical disparagement?]

The importance of using *potential,* rather than actual, effect in applying this criterion was stressed by Professor Nimmer in *Photocopying and Record Piracy: Of Dred Scott and Alice in Wonderland,* 22 U.C.L.A. L. Rev. 1052 (1975). Simply counting lost dollars (or noting the absence of any proof of loss) is, it is suggested, an exercise relating to damages, not fair use. *Cf. Universal City Studios v. Sony Corp. of America,* 480 F. Supp. 429, 451 (C.D. Cal. 1979), p. 495 *infra.* Fair use properly addresses the question whether the use involved is of such a nature as to tend to harm. If it is, the use is not fair, even if harm has not yet befallen the plaintiff.

The proper application of the fourth criterion is particularly important in view of the frequent conclusion that it is the most significant factor. *See, e.g., Triangle Publications, Inc. v. Knight Ridder Newspapers, Inc.,* 626 F.2d 1171 (5th Cir. 1980). *But see* Hayes, *Classroom "Fair Use": A Reevaluation,* 26 Bull. Copyright Soc'y 101 (1978) (amount and substantiality of taking more frequently cited factor).

QUESTION

A copyrighted poster shows a formation of five members of the "Dallas Cowboy Cheerleaders" in costume and against a particular background. Defendant's poster shows five former members of the group with a similar formation, uniforms and background, but with their halter tops opened and their breasts exposed. Is this a parody? Is it justified by the doctrine of fair use? By the First Amendment? In connection with the last question consider the following argument:

First Amendment values ... are not the only interests of constitutional dimension in this litigation. ... The judgment of the Constitution is that free expression is enriched by protecting the creation of authors from exploitation by others, and the Copyright Act is the congressional implementation of that judgment.

See Dallas Cowboy Cheerleaders, Inc. v. Scoreboard Posters, Inc., 600 F.2d 1184 (5th Cir. 1979).

4. LOOKING TOWARD THE NEW TECHNOLOGY

NEW YORK TIMES CO. v. ROXBURY DATA INTERFACE, INC.

434 F. Supp. 217 (D.N.J. 1977)

MEANOR, DISTRICT JUDGE.

Plaintiffs, holders of certain copyrights, move under Fed.R.Civ.P. 65(a) for a preliminary injunction pursuant to § 112 of the Copyright Act of 1909, 17 U.S.C. § 112 (1970), to halt alleged infringement of their copyrights. The suit presents an interesting and seemingly novel question regarding the extent of the proprietary rights inhering in a copyright. The issue is whether a copyrighted work may be indexed by an outsider without the permission of the holders of the copyrights to the original work.

Plaintiffs publish the New York Times Index annually. As indicated by its name, the Times Index essentially correlates data which has appeared in The New York Times in a given year with citations to the pages and columns of The New York Times on which the data appears. The data is denominated by various headings in the Times Index. These headings include the names of people, places, institutions, events, and the general headings which cover broad subject matters, *e. g.,* "fires." The Times Index has been published annually, with a few hiatuses, since 1863, and covers the years from 1851 to the present.[1]

In addition to correlating data with page citations to The New York Times, the Times Index contains abstracts of certain Times articles. The Times Index is a publication of substantial size. For example, the 1972 Index consists of over 2500 small-margined pages of fine print. The external dimensions of the volume are 12 inches by 9½ inches by 3½ inches. Similarly, volume 1 of the two-volume 1933 Index contains almost 1500 pages of closely packed fine print. The external dimensions of the first volume of the 1933 Index are 10 inches by 7 inches by 2¾ inches.

In addition to their annual index, plaintiffs publish four cumulative indexes to The New York Times. The New York Times Obituaries Index, published in 1970, lists the names of persons whose obituary has appeared in The New York Times between 1858 and 1968. The New York Times Book Review Index is a cumulative index to material published in the weekly New York Times Book Review since 1896. The Book Review Index contains the names of the authors of reviewed books and of the reviewers. The New York Times Film Review Index is a cumulative index to film reviews published in The New York Times since 1913. This index contains the names of many directors, actors, screenwriters, producers and others involved in filmmaking. The New York Times Theater Review Index is a multivolume, cumulative index to theater reviews published in The New York Times since 1870. The Theater Review Index contains the names of playwrights, actors, directors, producers and others associated with the stage.

Plaintiffs also operate a computer data bank which consists of a subject index to The New York Times from 1969 to the present. Plaintiffs state that access to

---

[1] Plaintiffs subsequently have compiled and published Times Indexes for those years during which no contemporaneous Times Indexes had been compiled.

the data in the computer is obtained through certain "key words," of which approximately 350,000 are personal names. Plaintiffs sell subscriptions to the computer data bank and collect a fee based on use.

Plaintiffs allege that they hold valid copyrights on all of the annual Times Indexes and the cumulative indexes, and on the contents of the computer data bank. Plaintiffs assert that the Times Indexes are protected both as books and as compilations. *See* 17 U.S.C. §§ 5(a) & 7 (1970). Although defendants have indicated that they may challenge the validity of at least some of these copyrights, the court will assume the validity of these copyrights for the purposes of this motion.

Defendants are in the process of publishing a 22-volume personal name index to the annual New York Times Index. Two of the 22 volumes have been published, covering names beginning with the Letter "A" through "Blo." Defendants compiled their index by perusing all of the annual New York Times Indexes covering the years 1851 to 1974 and culling every personal name that appeared as a heading. The culled names appear in defendants' index in alphabetical order. After each name appears citations to pages of the New York Times Index on which the name appears. Some names are followed by the year of death, certain titles held by the person, and years of birth and death; most, if not all, of this information was taken from the Times Index. Physically, each of the first two volumes of the set is approximately ten inches long, seven inches wide, and an inch thick. Each volume is covered with brown cloth and has gold lettering on the front and binding. The title of defendants' index, as printed on the cover, reads, "PERSONAL/NAME INDEX/TO 'THE NEW YORK TIMES INDEX'/1851-1974." The title is divided into four lines, as indicated by the slashes above. The words "PERSONAL NAME INDEX" appear in letters $^3/_8$ of an inch high; "TO 'THE NEW YORK TIMES INDEX'" is written in $^3/_{16}$ inch letters; and the years appear in $^3/_{32}$ inch type. Approximately 4¾ inches below the title on the cover of all but the first volume will appear the following phrases in $^1/_8$ inch gold lettering: "AN INDEPENDENT WORK NOT PUBLISHED OR APPROVED BY THE NEW YORK TIMES." On the binding, an abbreviated title appears: PERSONAL/NAME/INDEX/1851/-/1974. The binding also contains the volume number, an indication of the names appearing in the volume, and the logotype of Roxbury Data Interface, Inc.

Defendants compiled the first volume of their index in the following manner. Defendants hired several people to peruse each volume of the Times Index for the years 1851 to 1974, and to extract every personal name beginning with the letter "A." In addition to the name itself, the employees were instructed to copy any pseudonyms, nicknames, titles, years of birth and death, and to note the page and year of the Times Index on which the name appeared. Each extract was recorded on a three by five inch card. Defendants state that because the Times Index does not always list as a separate heading certain personal names which appear under certain subject matter headings, *e. g.,* murders, defendants' employees were instructed to peruse certain subject matter headings for names beginning with the letter "A," as well as the "A" section of each Times Index. Defendants then sorted into alphabetical order the names taken from each Times Index. The resulting 120 stacks of cards then were sorted into five alphabetized stacks, which finally were sorted by the two named authors into the lists that were published. During each of these sortings, defendants made some effort to standardize variant spellings of names where no confusion would result, list separately different people with the same names, and consolidate listings of single individuals appearing under different names. The extent of these efforts is disputed and unclear; it is clear that defendants' efforts failed in a number of cases and an appropriate warning to users appears in the Introduction to the second volume. Defendants also transformed the personal names which appear in all capital letters in the Times Indexes to capital and small letters in their index. The first two volumes contain approximately 240,000 names. The complete set is expected to list over 3,000,000 names. Editorial costs for compilation of the entire set will be $213,000.00, according to defendants' projection. This projection does not include the cost of typesetting and publishing the index. Defendants plan to sell the 22 volumes at a price of $600.00 to $650.00 per set.

Plaintiffs contend that the copying of these names constitutes a prima facie case of copyright infringement, entitling plaintiffs to a preliminary injunction. Defendants point out that it would be impossible for them to publish a personal name index to the New York Times Index without copying the names from the Times Index. In order to obtain a preliminary injunction, plaintiffs must show "a strong likelihood" of prevailing on the merits. *Kontes Glass Co. v. Lab Glass, Inc.,* 373 F.2d 319, 321 (3d Cir. 1967). While the general rule in alleged infringement of creative works seems to presume irreparable harm from a copyright holder's showing of a clear probability of success on the merits, *see American Metropolitan Enterprises, Inc. v. Warner Brothers Records, Inc.,* 389 F.2d 903, 905 (2d Cir. 1968), the most recent Third Circuit opinion indicates that plaintiffs may be required to make some showing of irreparable harm. *Kontes Glass Co., supra,* at 320.

The primary function of the Times Index is the correlation of data with citations to the pages and columns of The New York Times on which the data appears. This correlation constitutes the substance of plaintiffs' copyrights. *See Kane v. Pennsylvania Broadcasting Co.,* 73 F.Supp. 307 (E.D.Pa.1947). *Cf. Affiliated Hospital Products, Inc. v. Merdel Game Mfg. Co.,* 513 F.2d 1183, 1188 (2d Cir. 1975) (copyright on rule book only protects arrangement of rules); *Benny v. Loew's Inc.,* 239 F.2d 532, 536 (9th Cir. 1956), *aff'd by an equally divided Court,* 356 U.S. 43 (1958) (copyright on screenplay protects arrangement of events); *Triangle Publications, Inc. v. Sports Eye, Inc.,* 415 F.Supp. 682, 686 (E.D.Pa.1976) (only form for expressing horse racing data is copyrightable). If defendants had copied both the personal names and the correlated citations to the pages of The New York Times from the Times Index, plaintiffs would appear to have a strong claim to infringement of their copyrights. *See, e. g., Leon v. Pacific Tel. & Tel. Co.,* 91 F.2d 484 (9th Cir. 1937); *Southwestern Bell Tel. Co. v. Nationwide Independent Directory Serv., Inc.,* 371 F.Supp. 900 (W.D.Ark.1974). Defendants, however, copied only the names appearing in the Times Index and correlated those names to citations of the multivolume New York Times Index on which the names appear.

Plaintiffs take the position that their copyrights extend beyond the correlation of data to page citations to The New York Times and encompass the effort entailed in extracting the personal names and other data from The New York Times. While plaintiffs could not copyright the personal names, they clearly could obtain a copyright on a compilation of names appearing in The New York Times. A question arises, however, whether or not millions of names scattered over more than one hundred volumes and integrated with a great mass of other data can qualify as a compilation. In addition, while it is clear to this court that each personal name and its correlated citation to The New York Times would qualify as a unit for copyright protection under 17 U.S.C. § 3 (1970), which protects component parts of copyrighted works, it is not clear that either the personal name or the citation to The New York Times, standing alone, would qualify for such protection.

Assuming without deciding that plaintiffs' copyrights on their annual indexes encompass the use of the indexed personal names, the court must consider whether or not defendants' admitted copying from plaintiffs' indexes constitutes a "fair use" of that material. The "fair use" doctrine is a judicially created limitation on the exclusive right of copyright holders to use their copyrighted materials. In determining whether a use constitutes a fair use or a copyright infringement, courts have considered four factors:

(1) the purpose and character of the use;

(2) the nature of the copyrighted work;

(3) the amount and substantiality of the portion used in relation to the copyrighted work as a whole; and

(4) the effect of the use upon the potential market for or value of the copyrighted work.

The fair use doctrine was codified in section 107 of Congress' recent general revision of the copyright law, which will become effective January 1, 1978. Section 107 of the new statute contains the four factors listed above. Although the statute is not effective until next January, the guidelines set out therein are useful since they represent a codification of the case law. H.R.Rep. No. 1476, 94th Cong., 2d Sess. 65 (1976), U.S.Code Cong. & Admin. News 1976, p. 5659. *See, e. g., Marvin Worth Products v. Superior Films Corp.*, 319 F.Supp. 1269 (S.D.N.Y.1970); Annot., 23 A.L.R.3d 139 (1969).

(1) The purpose and character of the use is at least twofold: (1) to make money for the defendants, and (2) to facilitate access by the public to information concerning certain individuals. While whether the alleged infringer seeks financial gain from its use is a factor to be considered, the fact that defendants seek to profit financially will not preclude their use from being a fair use. *Rosemont Enterprises, Inc. v. Random House, Inc.*, 366 F.2d 303, 307-08 (2d Cir. 1966), *cert. denied*, 385 U.S. 1009 (1967). It seems likely that defendants' index will serve the public interest in the dissemination of information. Without defendants' index, an individual seeking to find articles which appeared in The New York Times on a certain person whose career spanned, say, forty years, would be compelled to search through forty volumes of the Times Index. Using defendants' index, the researcher would discover immediately the pages and volumes of the Times Index on which the name of his subject appears. Armed with this information, the researcher then can proceed to a few of the forty potentially relevant volumes of the Times Index, from which he will be directed to the pages and columns of The New York Times itself. On its face, defendants' index appears to have the potential to save researchers a considerable amount of time and, thus, facilitate the public interest in the dissemination of information. Defendants have placed in the record affidavits from a librarian and a professor of library science in support of this observation.

(2) The nature of the Times Index does not require extensive comment, except to note that it is rather in the nature of a collection of facts than in the nature of a creative or imaginative work. Since the Times Index is a work more of diligence than of originality or inventiveness, defendants have greater license to use portions of the Times Index under the fair use doctrine than they would have if a creative work had been involved. *See Benny v. Loew's Inc., supra*, at 536; *Gardner v. Nizer*, 391 F.Supp. 940, 943, *modified on other grounds*, 396 F.Supp. 63 (S.D.N.Y.1975).

(3) Plaintiffs assert that defendants' index quantitatively uses approximately fifty percent of the headings in the Times Index while defendants prefer to categorize the use as constituting eight percent of the words in the Times Index.

This semantic difference refers to substantially the same quantum of use. Although the quantum of material taken from the copyrighted work must be considered, a bald quantitative approach is not determinative. While the taking of as little as three sentences has been held to constitute an infringement, *Henry Holt & Co. v. Liggett & Myers Tobacco Co.*, 23 F.Supp. 302, 303 (E.D.Pa.1938), the copying of an entire work has been held to be a fair use, *Williams & Wilkins Co. v. United States*, 487 F.2d 1345, 1348 (Ct.Cl.1973), *aff'd by an equally divided Court*, 420 U.S. 376 (1975). The inadequacy of a pure quantitative approach obviously results from the fact that the quantum of appropriated material must be interrelated with a number of other factors, such as the quality and substantiality of the appropriated material, the need to use the appropriated material in the manufacture of defendants' product, and the other factors discussed herein.

As stated above, the substance of plaintiffs' copyrights, as far as they pertain to personal names, covers the correlation of personal names with citations to the pages and columns of The New York Times. Defendants have not copied any of these correlations, but, rather, have taken only the personal names appearing in the Times Indexes; defendants, of course, also have copied the volume and page numbers of the Times Indexes where the personal names appear. Plaintiffs place much reliance on cases involving the appropriation of telephone and other directory listings. *E.g., Leon v. Pacific Tel. & Tel. Co., supra; Cincinnati & Suburban Bell Tel. Co. v. Brown*, 44 F.2d 631 (S.D.Ohio 1930); *Southern Bell Tel. & Tel. Co. v. Donnelly*, 35 F.Supp. 425 (S.D.Fla.1940); *Sammons v. Larkin*, 38 F.Supp. 649 (D.Mass.1940), *modified on other grounds*, 126 F.2d 341 (1st Cir. 1942); *American Travel & Hotel Directory Co. v. Gehrig Publishing Co.*, 4 F.2d 415 (S.D.N.Y. 1925); *Hartford Printing Co. v. Hartford Directory & Publishing Co.*, 146 F. 332, *damages awarded*, 148 F. 470 (C.C.D.Conn. 1906); *Social Register Association v. Murphy*, 129 F. 148 (C.C.D.R.I.1904). Each of these cases involved a defendant who copied both the name and the correlated data which formed the essence [2] of the plaintiff's work and then sought to publish this copied material in its entirety as a new and virtually identical or very similar directory in direct competition with the plaintiff's directory. An analogous situation might exist in the instant suit if defendants had copied the personal names and the correlated citations to The New York Times. Defendants in the instant suit neither have copied the correlated data along with the personal names nor seek to publish a virtually identical index which would be in direct competition with the Times Index. In addition, all of the cases relied on by plaintiffs involved one-volume works devoted exclusively to the listing of the copied names and in which names were arranged in an order, usually alphabetical; defendants copied not only the names and correlated data, but also, by and large,[3] the order in

---

[2] In a few of the cases relied upon by plaintiffs, *i.e.*, those involving social directories, the selection of the name itself may have assumed greater importance than it does in compilations of fact. For example, the compilation of a social directory involves the compiler's subjective judgment of who within a community possesses a social status sufficient to require listing in his directory. Each name in a social directory is a product of the compiler's judgment rather than the publication of a fact. In contrast, the compilation of a telephone directory requires the compiler only to ascertain the fact of telephone subscribership; the compiler is not required to make any significant subjective judgment. Similarly, the compilation of a personal name index does not require the compiler to make the same type of subjective judgments as to what names to include as does the compilation of a social directory.

[3] In some of the competitive telephone directory cases, the copied lists were rearranged from alphabetical to numerical order. *E.g., Leon v. Pacific Tel. & Tel. Co.*,

which the names were listed. The instant case involves well over one hundred volumes in which millions of personal names are listed among millions of other listings. Defendants did not copy a list, as defendants in the above cited cases had done. Defendants rather extracted the names from the multivolume Times Index and compiled their own alphabetical listing. While this distinction is not determinative, it must be noted. The above cited cases, therefore, do not compel a finding of a prima facie infringement of plaintiffs' copyrights in the instant case.

Under this third factor, the court also must consider the extent to which defendants' index requires the copying of the names from the Times Index. *See Marvin Worth Products v. Superior Films Corp., supra*, at 1274. For all practical purposes, defendants could not publish their personal name index without copying the names from the Times Index. Plaintiffs indicate that defendants theoretically [4] could have obtained the same information directly from The New York Times, as had the compilers of the Times Index. If defendants had copied from the Times Index both the personal names and the correlated citations to The New York Times, plaintiffs' argument would have merit because defendants would have produced an abridgment or other version of the Times Index without expending efforts equal to the compilers of the Times Index. *See, e.g.*, 17 U.S.C. § 1(b) (1970) and cases cited *supra*. Since defendants have not produced an abbreviated index to The New York Times in direct competition with the Times Index, however, plaintiffs' position is not convincing.

Plaintiffs finally argue that defendants' use cannot be a fair use because defendants have failed to exercise any independent effort aside from the effort entailed in "copying" the personal names. Plaintiffs point out that defendants' index consists only of names extracted from the Times Index, with virtually no information added by defendants. In light of the nature of the work, an index, this circumstance is not surprising. As outlined *supra*, defendants are expending substantial effort and money in culling the millions of personal names from over 100 volumes of the Times Index, alphabetizing those names, and editing the entries into their final form. This independent work is precisely the labor that an original indexer must undertake.

(4) The discussion now turns to the effect of the personal name index on the potential market for the Times Index. In the area of copyright law dealing with compilations and directories, this factor of competitive effect looms large.

> The decisions [involving directories and similar compilations] recognize or suggest that the competitive or noncompetitive character of the publication making the claimed infringing use may be of particular importance. Thus, the courts have indicated that the uses which a noncompetitor, or even one who is not in direct competition with the copyright proprietor or whose work will not injure the potential market for the copyrighted material, may make of the copyrighted directory are greater or less limited than the uses allowed to a direct competitor.

---

supra. In that case, however, plaintiff's entire telephone directory was copied and rearranged, offering precisely the same correlation of names and telephone numbers, except that defendants had inverted that correlation and deleted addresses, as appeared in plaintiff's directory.

[4] Plaintiffs also deny defendants' right to compile an index to The New York Times, presumably because defendants would be copying words from a copyrighted work and unfairly exploiting The New York Times' copyright.

Annot., 23 A.L.R.3d 139, 252 (1969), *citing Sampson & Murdock Co. v. Seaver-Radford Co.,* 140 F. 539 (1st Cir. 1905); *Sub-Contractors Register, Inc. v. McGovern's Contractors & Builders Manual, Inc.,* 69 F.Supp. 507 (S.D.N.Y.1946); *Consumers Union v. Hobart Mfg. Co.,* 189 F.Supp. 275 (S.D.N.Y. 1960); *Social Register Association v. Murphy,* 128 F. 116 (C.C.D.R.I.1904). *See Kane v. Pennsylvania Broadcasting Co., supra,* at 307.

The effect of defendants' personal name index on the market for the Times Index appears slight. Since defendants' index carries citations only to the New York Times Index, defendants' index is useless unless its user has access to the Times Index, from which he will be directed to the articles appearing in The New York Times. Despite the absolute dependence of defendants' index on the Times Index, plaintiffs allege potential and actual harm to the sales of the Times Index flowing from the publication of the personal name index. Plaintiffs appear to concede that the market for defendants' personal name index will be, for the most part, libraries which have many volumes of the Times Index. Plaintiffs point out, however, that many of the potential purchasers of defendants' index will own many volumes, but not complete sets, of the Times Index. Plaintiffs argue that libraries, given their limited funds alloted to the purchase of new books and reference materials, may choose to procure defendants' index in preference to purchasing back issues of the Times Index. The principal weakness of this argument derives from the essential difference in function of the two works. If a librarian wishes to obtain a more complete reference to The New York Times, he will purchase back issues of the Times Index. On the other hand, if the librarian wants to obtain a handy reference to the personal names appearing in the Times Index, he will purchase defendants' index. The two works clearly do not compete directly in the sense that telephone, city or social directories do. That is to say, purchase of defendants' index in no way supersedes the need for plaintiff's index; indeed, both the viability and the utility of the personal name index depends entirely on the Times Index. Defendants' index competes for library dollars with the Times Index no more directly than does an encyclopedia, a dictionary, or any other publication.[5] The publication of every new book no doubt increases competition for library dollars. This competition, however, does not amount to the direct competitive effect which would preclude defendants' use from being a fair use.

Plaintiffs also allege that their computer data bank and some of their other cumulative indexes, particularly the Obituaries Index, will suffer competitive harm from the publication of defendants' index. Plaintiffs, however, do not allege infringement of any of their copyrights on the cumulative indexes or the computer data bank; plaintiffs claim infringements only of their copyrights on the annual Times Indexes. Plaintiffs cite no authority for the proposition that potential competitive injury to noninfringed publications of the copyright holder must be taken into account in determining whether an allegedly infringing use is a fair use. The newly enacted general revision of the copyright law, as well as the case law which it codifies, instruct the court to weigh "the effect of the use upon the potential market for or value of the copyrighted work" from which the

---

[5] Only if libraries generally allotted a specified portion of their annual book-buying funds to purchase of volumes of the Times Index and decided to use a portion of that Times Index fund for the procurement of the personal name index might plaintiffs' argument have merit. Even in this situation, however, plaintiffs would have to show that funds allotted to purchase of the Times Index never have been or are likely to be in the future diverted to the purchase of other works.

material was taken. Since none of the personal names were extracted from the computer data bank or from any of the cumulative indexes, the court cannot consider the possible competitive injury to these works in determining whether defendants' use of the annual Times Index is a fair use.

Plaintiffs also argue that publication of defendant's index deprives them of the right to exploit their copyrights. Since nothing stands in the way of plaintiffs' publishing a work to rival defendants' index, plaintiffs actually are arguing that publication of defendants' index will have an adverse effect on any personal name index to the Times Index which plaintiffs may wish to publish in the future. This argument is merely a restatement of plaintiffs' argument that a copyrighted work cannot be indexed without permission of the holders of the copyright to the original work. Plaintiffs seek to analogize themselves to a writer of a play or novel and defendants to a filmmaker seeking to make a movie from the copyrighted play or novel. This analogy is not convincing. First, defendants have not copied the substance of plaintiffs' copyrights — the correlation of personal names and other data with citations to the pages of The New York Times. If defendants had published microfilm of the Times Index, defendants would have infringed plaintiffs' copyrights and plaintiffs' analogy would be well taken. Second, defendants' index is not another version of plaintiffs' index, but a work with a different function and form. Third, no creative idea of plaintiffs' has been appropriated by defendants. Finally, no list comparable to defendants' index can be found in the Times Index; the personal names are scattered over more than one hundred volumes.

Plaintiffs place much reliance on *Leon v. Pacific Tel. & Tel. Co., supra,* and dicta in *Reed v. Holliday,* 19 F. 325 (C.C.W.D.Pa. 1884). . . . In *Reed,* plaintiffs published an English language textbook. The textbook instructed readers to analyze sentences by diagraming them. Each lesson in the textbook concluded with a list of sentences to be diagramed by the reader or student. Defendant published a "Teacher's Manual" to the textbook in which all the sentences appearing in the textbook were diagramed. The court found that the sentences were a material and substantial part of plaintiffs' work, and held that plaintiffs' copyright had been infringed. The court went on in dicta, which is quoted in plaintiffs' brief, to equate the protection of a copyright to that of a patent. Whatever the stage of the development of the fair use doctrine in 1884, it is clear today that the existence of that doctrine creates the principal difference between the protection afforded by a copyright and that given by a patent. The existence of the fair use doctrine means that copyrights, unlike patents, do not confer the exclusive right to the use of the protected work. *See, e. g., Loew's Inc. v. Columbia Broadcasting System, Inc.,* 131 F.Supp. 165, 174 (S.D.Cal.1955), *aff'd sub nom. Benny v. Loew's Inc., supra.*

Plaintiffs state that they are considering publication of a personal name index. Evidence in the record indicates that one of the individual defendants, during his employment by plaintiffs, proposed creation of a personal name index in 1971. In 1973, the same defendant proposed that his corporation, Roxbury Data Interface, Inc., and plaintiffs enter into an agreement for publication of a personal name index. Both proposals were rejected on the grounds that the idea was intrinsically poor and of dubious profitability. The author of these two rejections testified by deposition that he had no information which would cause him to change his prior estimates as to the small market for a personal name index to the Times Index. There is no compelling evidence that plaintiffs will publish a personal name index. It thus appears likely that prohibition of defendants' publication not only will extend plaintiffs' copyrights expansively, but also will impede the public interest in the dissemination of information. In addition, plaintiffs, should they decide to publish a personal name index, are free to do what defendants probably cannot do — compile a personal name index based on the Times Index which can refer users directly to The New York Times, although business judgment may direct them not to publish such an index.

Plaintiffs finally argue that appearance of the words "The New York Times" in the title of defendants' index will lead to confusion as to the publisher of the personal name index and will damage the reputation of The New York Times Company. Defendants, however, clearly have a right to label their product correctly. *See Societe Comptoir v. Alexander's Dep't Stores,* 299 F.2d 33, 36 (2d Cir. 1962). Furthermore, defendants have attempted to dispel any confusion as to the publisher of the personal name index. In labeling their index, defendants have refrained from using the black letter type utilized in the masthead of The New York Times and in the titles of all the New York Times annual and cumulative indexes. In addition, all but the first volume of defendants' index will carry the following notice on their covers: "AN INDEPENDENT WORK NOT PUBLISHED OR APPROVED BY THE NEW YORK TIMES." . . .

In *Universal Athletic Sales Co. v. Salkeld,* 511 F.2d 904 (3d Cir.), *cert. denied,* 423 U.S. 863 (1975), the court stated:

> To establish a copyright infringement, the holder must first prove that the defendant has copied the protected work and, second, that there is a substantial similarity between the two works. The criterion for the latter requirement is whether an ordinary lay observer would detect a substantial similarity between the works. . . . Phrased in an alternative fashion, it must be shown that copying went so far as to constitute improper appropriation, the test being the response of the ordinary lay person.

511 F.2d at 907 (citations omitted). While defendants admittedly have copied the personal names from plaintiffs' indexes, the personal name index differs substantially from the Times Index, in form, arrangement, and function.

In fine, application of the four factors discussed above reveals:

(1) that one purpose of the personal name index is to obtain financial gain for its publishers;

(2) that the personal name index will serve the public interest in the dissemination of information;

(3) that the Times Index is a work more of diligence and fact than of creativity and imagination;

(4) that virtually all of the information appearing in the personal name index was taken from the Times Index;

(5) that defendants expended substantial time, effort and money in compiling their index to the Times Index;

(6) that defendants did not copy the correlation of the personal name index with citations to The New York Times in any case;

(7) that the very nature of the personal name index required that defendants copy the names which they were indexing;

(8) that the effect of the personal name index on the potential market for the Times Index appears slight or nonexistent.

Placing these considerations into the variable equation of fair use indicates that plaintiffs have failed to demonstrate a clear likelihood of success on the merits which would warrant the granting of their motion for a preliminary injunction. This conclusion obviates discussion both of the necessity of plaintiffs showing irreparable harm and of defendants' challenge to the validity of some or all of plaintiffs' copyrights. Plaintiffs' motion for a preliminary injunction is denied.

Counsel for defendants will submit an appropriate order with consent as to form within 10 days.

QUESTIONS

1. List from the opinion the various publications copyrighted by plaintiff and identify the copyrights sued upon. Would you, as plaintiff, have alleged infringement of some or all of the other copyrights? What obstacles might be foreseen as to each?

2. Why does the fourth factor in § 107 point so unequivocally in one direction in this case and what did the plaintiff try to do about it?

3. Do you agree that each correlated name should be protected as a copyrightable unit? How would you have decided the question whether plaintiffs' copyrights on their annual indexes encompass the use of the indexed personal names?

4. What is the difference between plaintiff's work and the Mobil Guide or Guide Michelin? Should such difference affect the scope of protection?

5. Why is the amount of defendant's independent labor relevant? Would it be in the case of a completely unauthorized translation? Is it relevant in this connection to quote Judge Learned Hand in the *Letty Lynton* case, *supra* at p. 352, that "no plagiarist can excuse the wrong by showing how much of his work he did not pirate"?

6. Assume that a cartologist explores a hitherto unexplored geographic area and that he prepares, publishes and copyrights a painstakingly detailed map of that area. Another individual refers to that map and makes an unauthorized chart which lists the distances between all points on the map, as well as altitudes and population (also shown on the map for the first time). Has copyright on the map been infringed? Does the answer rest upon an analysis of copyrightability? Of infringement? Of fair use? Is there any difference in the determining factors under these analyses?

7. Assume that a highly regarded teacher of high school physics prepares a book with text and problems which quickly becomes the best-selling work in the field. Another teacher publishes a pamphlet, advertised as a book of solutions to the problems in the copyrighted text. In the pamphlet, the problems are not copied; the solutions consist of arithmetic equations, which show how the problem should be solved (utilizing, of course, the numbers utilized in the copyrighted textbook problems), and they are accompanied where possible with diagrams (also utilizing the same numbers). Does the solutions book infringe the copyright on the problem book? *See Addison-Wesley Publishing Co. v. Brown*, 223 F. Supp. 219 (E.D.N.Y. 1963).

UNIVERSAL CITY STUDIOS, INC. v. SONY CORP. OF AMERICA

480 F. Supp. 429 (C.D. Cal. 1979)

FERGUSON, DISTRICT JUDGE.

Article I, § 8, Cl. 8 of the United States Constitution empowers Congress: "To promote the Progress of Science and useful Arts, by securing for limited Times to Authors and Inventors the exclusive Right to their respective Writings and Discoveries." The Copyright Act passed by Congress in 1909 and revised in 1976 gives authors exclusive rights over some but not all uses of their works. As the Supreme Court wrote in *Twentieth Century Music Corp. v. Aiken*, 422 U.S. 151, 156 (1974):

The limited scope of the copyright holder's statutory monopoly, like the limited copyright duration required by the Constitution, reflects a balance of competing claims upon the public interest: Creative work is to be encouraged and rewarded, but private motivation must ultimately serve the cause of promoting broad public availability of literature, music, and the other arts. (footnotes omitted.)

This case tests the scope of copyright protection for audiovisual material broadcast on public airwaves, and its resolution requires balancing of strong competing claims.

Plaintiffs, Universal City Studios, Inc. ("Universal") and Walt Disney Productions, Inc. ("Disney"), are producers and copyright owners of audiovisual material, some of which they choose to sell for telecast over public airwaves. Defendants include the manufacturer, Sony Corporation ("Sony"), and the distributor, Sony Corporation of America ("Sonam"), of the "Betamax," a videotape recorder ("VTR") which can record this telecast off-the-air and make a copy of the audiovisual material which can be viewed at another time. Other corporate defendants are certain retail stores (Carter Hawley Hale Stores, Inc.; Henry's Camera Corporation; Associated Dry Goods Corporation; and Federated Department Stores, Inc.) which sell the Betamax, and the advertising agency, Doyle Dane Bernbach, Inc. ("DDBI") which promotes it. The only individual defendant is William Griffiths who used his Betamax in his home to copy plaintiffs' broadcast material for his own home use.

Plaintiffs' main contentions are that this recording and that of other individuals infringed their copyrights and that the corporate defendants are either direct or contributory infringers or are vicariously liable for the infringement. Plaintiffs also contend that defendants have interfered with their business relations and unfairly competed with them. Finally, plaintiffs assert that the retail defendants violated copyright law when they recorded portions of plaintiffs' programs to demonstrate the Betamax to a prospective purchaser.

Plaintiffs allege that they will suffer great monetary damage if this infringement is allowed to continue. Defendants contend that home copying for home use is not an infringement and, even if it were, defendants could not be held responsible under any theory of infringement or vicarious liability. The resolution of these issues first requires a determination of whether Congress gave authors monopoly power over this use and, if so, whether the corporate defendants are in any way liable. As will be discussed, these determinations are not easily made. Protection of the public interest requires balancing the need for wide availability of audiovisual works against the need for monetary reward to authors to assure production of these works.

After three years of litigation, five weeks of trial and careful consideration of extensive briefing by both sides, this court finds:

a) Neither the Copyright Act of 1909 ("Old Act") nor the revised Act of 1976 ("New Act") gave copyright holders monopoly power over an individual's off-the-air copying in his home for private, non-commercial use. This court is not deciding whether tape duplication or copying from pay television is prohibited. Nor is this court ruling on off-the-air recording by individuals or groups for use outside the home.

b) Even if the Copyright Act did prohibit home-use copying, Sony, Sonam, DDBI and the retail stores would not be liable under any of the theories of direct or contributory infringement or vicarious liability.

c) The retail defendants have not infringed plaintiffs' copyrights.

d) Even if home-use copying were infringement and defendants were deemed liable therefor, this court could not grant the injunctive relief requested by plaintiffs.

e) None of the defendants has unfairly competed with plaintiffs or interfered with their advantageous business relations.

. . . .

Home-Use Recording

"Home-use" recording as used in this opinion is the operation of the Betamax in a private home to record a program for subsequent home viewing. The programs involved in this lawsuit are broadcast free to the public over public airwaves. The court heard extensive testimony from defendant William Griffiths and four non-defendant individuals about this activity, and the court's declaration of non-infringement is limited to this home use-situation.

It is important to note the limits of this holding. Neither pay nor cable television stations are plaintiffs in this suit and no defendant recorded the signals from either. The court is not ruling on tape swapping, organized or informal. The court is not ruling on tape duplication within the home or outside, by individuals, groups or corporations. Nor is the court ruling on off-the-air recording for use outside the home, e. g., by teachers for classrooms, corporations for employees, etc. No defendant engaged in any of these activities and the facts necessary to determine their legality are not before this court.

The ramifications of this new technology are greater than the boundaries of this lawsuit. A court reviewing the limited claims of specified parties in a particular factual setting cannot and should not undertake the role of a government commission or legislative body exploring and evaluating all the uses and consequences of the videotape recorder.

I. Infringement and Fair Use

Recordings made prior to January 1, 1978 are governed by the Old Act (1909) and those made after that date are governed by the New Act (1976). The testimony showed that Marc Wielage had recorded two broadcasts, one Universal and one Disney, after January 1, 1978. All other incidents of copying occurred prior to that date, and these included the recording of five Universal titles by defendant Griffiths; nine Universal and seven Disney by Wielage; two Universal by Soule; one Universal and six Disney by the Lowes; and two Universal by the Birds.

This court finds that this home-use recording is not an infringement under either the Old Act or the New Act. This finding rests on statutory interpretations of both the Old and the New Acts, the legislative history of the New Act, and the doctrine of fair use.

A. The Old Act

Section I of the Copyright Act, 17 U.S.C. § 1, gave the copyright owner the "exclusive right: (a) To print, reprint, publish, copy, and vend the copyrighted work; . . .." Under this broad, unqualified language, Betamax recording appears to be an infringing activity. The legislative history does not discuss home-use recording; in 1909, television and its ensuing technology was not even contemplated by Congress.

In applying the Old Act, courts created the fair use doctrine to immunize some forms of copying from the literal implications of the statute. The fair use doctrine is discussed extensively below. This court concludes that home-use copying is fair use. This conclusion is based on the doctrine as it was developed by the courts under the Old Act and left unaltered by the New Act. Therefore, this conclusion applies equally to instances of home-use recording under the Old and New Acts.

B. The New Act

Copyright holders have monopoly power only over those uses of their works that Congress has protected through legislation; their rights do not exist independent of Congressional action. The broad language of the New Act suggests that copyright holders have monopoly power over all reproductions of their works. Legislative history, however, shows that Congress did not intend this broad statement to include reproductions of sound recordings for home use. The central question here is whether Congress intended the same language to give copyright holders of audiovisual works monopoly power over off-the-air recording of their works for home use. Legislative history does not show this intent. On the occasions when the issue was discussed by Congress, all indications were that Congress did not intend to give monopoly power over this use.

. . . .

[Congress's incorporation of the 1971 "record piracy" legislation in § 106 of the 1976 Act] is significant because Congress, in passing the [1971] legislation, clearly expressed its intent not to restrain home sound recording from broadcasts, tapes or records where the recording is for private, non-commercial use. As the House Report which accompanied the 1971 Amendment stated:

Home Recording

In approving the creation of a limited copyright in sound recordings it is the intention of the Committee that this limited copyright not grant any broader rights than are accorded to other copyright proprietors under the existing title 17. Specifically, it is not the intention of the Committee to restrain the home recording, from broadcasts or from tapes or records, of recorded performances, where the home recording is for private use and with no purpose of reproducing or otherwise capitalizing commercially on it. This practice is common and unrestrained today, and the record producers and performers would be in no different position from that of the owners of copyright in recorded musical compositions over the past 20 years.

H.Rep.No. 487, 92d Cong., 1st Sess. 7, *reprinted in* [1971] U.S.Code Cong. & Admin. News, pp. 1566, 1572.

Thus, while the language of § 106 of the New Act appears to give copyright holders exclusive rights over all recordings, the Congressional intent was that home-use sound recording was not prohibited. Holders of copyrights in sound recordings were not to have any "broader rights than are accorded to other copyright proprietors." U.S.Code Cong. & Admin.News 1971, p. 1572. Defendants contend that, as with home-use sound recording, Congress did not intend to protect copyright holders from off-the-air audiovisual recording for home-use, even though the statute does not expressly so state.

The issue of home-use recording was not addressed in any subsequent House or Senate report. The reports accompanying the 1976 general revision legislation did not restate Congressional refusal to give monopoly power over home-use recording, but the language of the 1971 Amendment was incorporated into the New Act without any suggestion that legislative intent had changed.

The 1971 House Report is not the only support for a finding that the Copyright Act does not prohibit home-use recording. Home-use recording from radio and television broadcasts was discussed in committee hearings, floor debates and reports from the Office of Copyrights. Statements from all three sources are relevant to a determination of legislative intent.

In June, 1971, Subcommittee No. 3 of the House Committee on the Judiciary met in hearings on the sound recording amendment. Representative Beister of Pennsylvania engaged in the following dialogue about off-the-air recording with Ms. Barbara Ringer, then Assistant Register of Copyrights:

> *Mr. Beister.* I do not know that I can add very much to the questions which you have been asked so far.
>
> I can tell you I must have a small pirate in my own home.
>
> My son has a cassette tape recorder, and as a particular record becomes a hit, he will retrieve it onto his little set.
>
> Now, he may retrieve in addition something else onto his recording, but nonetheless, he does retrieve the basic sound, *and this legislation, of course, would not point to his activities, would it?*
>
> *Miss Ringer.* I think the answer is clearly, "No, it would not."
>
> I have spoken at a couple of seminars on *video cassettes lately, and this question is usually asked: "What about the home recorders?"*
>
> The answer I have given and will give again is that *this is something you cannot control. You simply cannot control it.*

Hearings on S. 646 before the Subcomm. No. 3 of the House Judiciary Comm., 92d Cong., 1st Sess. 22 (June 9 and 10, 1971).

Ms. Ringer proceeded to discuss the problem of unauthorized video recordings finding their way into the market. She recognized that this was a problem which Congress might face in the future but stated that it could not be met by carrying copyright enforcement into the home or by banning devices for off-the-air recording. Her testimony continued:

> But *I do not see anybody going into anyone's home and preventing this sort of thing, or forcing legislation that would engineer a piece of equipment not to allow home taping.*
>
> *Mr. Beister:* Secondly, *with respect to video cassettes,* are we approaching an additional problem, *not with respect to private use,* but with respect to public distribution after it has been retrieved over a home set?
>
> *Miss Ringer:* The answer is very definitely, "yes." (*Id.* at 22-23.)

... Treatment of home-use recording is consistent outside the legislative history, as well. Indeed, since 1955, the Copyright Office of the Library of Congress and the Register of Copyrights consistently avoided and even opposed efforts to protect copyright owners against home-use recording.

In 1961, the Office issued a report which urged that private performance of a copyrighted film or motion picture not be restrained. The Register contended that statutory damages for such infringement "would be grossly excessive" and that "private performances could rarely be discovered or controlled." The Register directly confronted the issue of home-use videotape recording:

> New technical devices will probably make it practical in the future to reproduce televised motion pictures in the home. We do not believe the private use of such a reproduction can or should be precluded by copyright.

Copyright Law Revision, Report of the Register of Copyrights (July, 1961), p. 30.

As discussed above, the Copyright Office, through Barbara Ringer, continued to advocate this view throughout the years of legislative revision. The Office was an active participant in drafting, promoting and explaining the legislation for Congress and always maintained that home-use recording is not an infringement.

This position of the Office developed in part from a concern about invasion of the individual's privacy in his home. As Ms. Ringer testified, home recording simply cannot be controlled. Nobody is going into anyone's home to prevent it. . . . Here, legislative history shows that, in balance, Congress did not find that protection of copyright holders' rights over reproduction of their works was worth the privacy and enforcement problems which restraint of home-use recording would create.

C. Fair Use

Analysis of whether home-use recording is an infringement cannot end with the statuory language and legislative history. While the Old Act was in effect, courts devised the doctrine of fair use, which creates a "privilege in others than the owner of a copyright to use the copyrighted material in a reasonable manner without his consent, notwithstanding the monopoly granted to the owner . . . ." *Rosemont Enterprises, Inc. v. Random House, Inc.,* 366 F.2d 303, 306 (2d Cir. 1966), *quoting* Ball, *Copyright and Literary Property* 260 (1966). Fair use has always been a doctrine without rigid definition. "The line which must be drawn between fair use and copyright infringement depends on an examination of the facts in each case. It cannot be determined by resort to any arbitrary rules or fixed criteria." *Meeropol v. Nizer,* 560 F.2d 1061, 1068 (2d Cir. 1977), *cert. denied,* 434 U.S. 1013 (1978) (citations omitted).

In this case, new technology has spawned a copyright question of first impression. This court finds that the legislative history of the New Act shows that Congress did not intend to restrain the home-use copying at issue here. Even if this finding were erroneous, the legislative history would be sufficient to raise doubts about the meaning of the statutory language of § 106. This language appears to give copyright holders the exclusive right to reproduce their works in copies or phonorecords. Yet legislative history shows an intent to allow home-use copying of both sound recordings and broadcasted audiovisual material.

In *Twentieth Century Music Corp. v. Aiken, supra,* 422 U.S. at 156, the Supreme Court stated that "[w]hen technological change has rendered its literal terms ambiguous, the Copyright Act must be construed in light of [its] basic purpose." (footnote omitted). The fair use doctrine is a tool for such construction.

The New Act did not change fair use. It did, however, codify the doctrine for the first time and characterize fair use as noninfringement rather than excused infringement. In doing so, both the House and the Senate emphasized that they did not intend to alter the judicial fair use doctrine. . . .

As Congress recognized, the doctrine of fair use must be flexible to deal with technological change. It is an equitable tool for balancing competing claims in copyright cases. The Copyright Act gives copyright owners control of only some uses of their works. *Fortnightly Corp. v. United Artists,* 392 U.S 390, 393-94 (1968).

. . . [The language of § 107] shows that the factors listed are neither exclusive nor required. The factors are illustrative, not definitive. As has been noted, the statute gives no guidance as to the relative weight of the factors and only generally defines the scope of each. 3 *Nimmer on Copyright* § 13.05[A].

Thus, courts are left with great discretion to consider new factors and interpret those codified in new ways. As Congress acknowledged in the House and Senate Reports on the New Act quoted *supra,* such flexibility is necessary in an era of great technological development.

This case invites application of the fair use doctrine to new technology in a new context: off-the-air videotape recording at home for noncommercial home use. While no court has previously addressed this issue, fair use doctrine cases do suggest both an approach and an answer.

The parties' briefing has focused on three cases which illustrate the treatment of fair use in a noncommercial context. Neither these cases nor any others within this court's knowledge, however, discuss copying within a private home using signals beamed over public airwaves.

The three cases addressing fair use in the noncommercial context are *Wihtol v. Crow,* 309 F.2d 777 (8th Cir. 1963); *Williams & Wilkins v. United States, supra;* and *Encyclopaedia Britannica Educational Corp. v. Crooks,* 447 F.Supp. 243 (W.D.N.Y.1978). Their facts must be reviewed.

In *Wihtol,* a church choir director incorporated the entire copyrighted hymn "My God and I" into a new arrangement which was publicly performed by both a high school and a church choir. The Eighth Circuit found the choir director directly liable for infringement and the employer church liable under the doctrine of *respondeat superior.*

In *Encyclopaedia Britannica,* the district court granted a preliminary injunction to plaintiffs, producers of educational audiovisual works, against defendants, local government officials who would tape plantiffs' works off-the-air, make copies of them and distribute them to the schools. In granting this preliminary relief, the court held that the fair use defense did not overcome plaintiffs' showing of a *prima facie* case. The court first carefully distinguished *Williams & Wilkins,* discussed *infra,* and then held:

> The scope of BOCES' activities is difficult to reconcile with its claim of fair use. This case does not involve an isolated instance of a teacher copying copyrighted material for classroom use but concerns a highly organized and systematic program for reproducing videotapes on a massive scale. BOCES has acquired videotape equipment worth one-half million dollars, uses five to eight full-time personnel to carry out its program, and makes as many as ten thousand tapes per year. For the last twelve years, these tapes have been distributed throughout Erie County to over one hundred separate schools.
>
> Considering all of these factors, I find that the plaintiffs have established a prima facie case entitling them to preliminary relief. As BOCES points out, the applicability of the defense of fair use raises numerous questions of fact which cannot be resolved without a full trial on the merits. At this stage in the proceedings, I find that the substantiality of the copying and the possible impact on the market for education films tip the balance in favor of the plaintiffs, outweighing BOCES' noncommercial, educational purpose in copying the films.

447 F.Supp. at 252.

In *Williams & Wilkins,* the Court of Claims found that copying by the National Institutes of Health ("NIH") and the National Library of Medicine ("NLM") of entire articles published in plaintiff's journals was fair use under the Old Act. The court relied on many factors "and not upon any one, or any combination less than all." 487 F.2d 1345 at 1362. While these factors included elements of the traditional four, the court exercised its discretion to consider other factors it deemed relevant to the issue of fair use in the particular factual context.

The court listed eight factors. First, the court noted that NIH and NLM are non-profit institutions and that with both the libraries and the requesters, "scientific progress, untainted by any commercial gain from the reproduction, is the hallmark of the whole enterprise of duplication." 487 F.2d at 1354. Second, the court relied on the two-part factor of "a system of limitations" imposed and enforced by the institutions and the "effectiveness of that system to confine the duplication for the personal use of scientific personnel who need the material for their work . . .." 487 F.2d at 1355. This factor, in the court's view, reduced the significance of the absolute number of copies of an article which must be made. Third, the court found it significant that photocopying had been going on ever since the Copyright Act was adopted with "apparent general acceptance" and asked "whether this marked increase in volume [through improved technology] changes a use which was generally accepted as 'fair' into one which has now become unfair." 487 F.2d at 1356. Fourth, the court was convinced that "medical science would be seriously hurt if such library photocopying were stopped." *Id.* Fifth, the court held that the "record simply does not show a serious adverse impact, either on plaintiff or on medical publishers generally, from the photocopying practices of the type of NIH and NLM." 487 F.2d at 1359. Sixth, the court was reluctant to find infringement because of the "grave uncertainty of the coverage of 'copy' in Section 1 of the 1909 Act . . ." *Id.* The court noted that "this is now preeminently a problem for Congress . . .." 487 F.2d at 1360. Seventh, the court reviewed legislative reports for revision of the 1909 Act and found it [sic] showed that photocopying can be "fair use" in proper circumstances. 487 F.2d at 1361. Finally, the eighth factor which the court found relevant to fair use was that foreign countries have statutes which allow such photocopying. *Id.*

The *Williams & Wilkins* case, affirmed by an evenly divided Supreme Court, has little precedential value. Its holding is specifically limited to its unique factual situation. Furthermore, it has been strongly criticized,[2] with the harshest criticism leveled at the Court's treatment of the harm issue (discussed *infra*). The value of the case lies in its demonstration of the relevance of the fair use doctrine when copyright protection is tested by new technology and noncommercial use.

Wihtol and *Encyclopaedia Britannica* are also of little precedential value. *Wihtol* involved public performance of the copyrighted material. *Encyclopaedia Britannica* is limited because it was an opinion granting only preliminary relief. The court was not conclusively finding infringement but rather only a *prima facie* case thereof. Even if that court had made a final determination on infringement, the case nonetheless would be more dissimilar to the situation here than similar. The most important difference is that it did not involve home-use off-the-air recording but rather "a highly organized and systematic program for reproducing videotapes on a massive scale." 447 F.Supp. at 252.

A comparison of the factual settings in the decided cases with that of the present case reveals two distinguishing factors:

(1) Home-use recording is done by individuals or families in the privacy of their own home for use in their home.

(2) The material copied has been voluntarily sold by the authors for broadcast over the public airwaves to private homes free of charge.

These distinctions narrow the issue before this court. They shape the four factors of the traditional fair use analysis and guide the court in defining appropriate expectations of the copyright holder and the public.

As discussed above, the traditional four factors in determining fair use are listed in § 107 without reference to weight or priority. Several commentators,

---

[2] *See e. g.,* 3 Nimmer on Copyright § 13.05[E].

however, have suggested that fair use cases show that the fourth factor of harm to the copyrighted work is or should be considered first when determining fair use,[3] and the issue of harm has received the most emphasis in this lawsuit. For these reasons, it is discussed first in this analysis of fair use.

1. Harm

The Court of Claims in *Williams & Wilkins* found that library photocopying was fair use because ". . . plaintiff has failed to prove its assumption of economic detriment, in the past or potentially for the future. . . . This record simply does not show a serious adverse impact, either on plaintiff or on the owner's potential market for the work." 487 F.2d at 1359. This approach by the Court of Claims has been widely criticized as inappropriate for determining fair use. One of the most forceful criticisms is from Professor Melville Nimmer, who writes that the court confused the issue of harm for purposes of damages with the harm concept in fair use. According to Nimmer, the court should have asked "not whether the particular photocopying activities of the defendant resulted in damages to the plaintiff, but rather whether wholesale photocopying of plaintiffs' journals by any and all libraries and similar institutions would decimate the plaintiffs' potential market." Nimmer, *Photocopying and Record Piracy: Of Dred Scott and Alice in Wonderland,* 22 U.C.L.A. L. Rev. 1052, 1054 (1975).

As in *Williams & Wilkins, supra,* the issue of harm is important in this lawsuit for three determinations: (1) whether the use is fair use, (2) whether an injunction is appropriate, and, (3) assuming infringement, what the damages are. Actual harm may not be essential to any of these three determinations. Without it however, the determinations are much more difficult. It has been suggested that for purposes of fair use, the question should not be what are the past effects but rather what are the probable effects. Freid, *Fair Use and the New Act, supra,* at 505 n. 39. As to the injunction issue, the question is whether any irreparable harm will occur if an injunction is not issued. As will be discussed, this prognostication of irreparable injury is particularly difficult for a court to make when no harm has occurred to date and predictions of future harm are based on personal belief and speculation. The only issue where actual harm is neither necessary nor particularly helpful is the issue of damages. Under both the Old and the New Acts, once infringement is found, statutory damages can be awarded when no actual damages have been proven.

Plaintiffs have admitted that no actual harm to their copyrights has occurred to date. Plaintiffs' experts also admitted that they knew neither the year in which the predicted harm would occur nor the number of Betamax purchases which would cause the harm. Yet they vigorously maintained throughout trial that harm to their copyrights would not only be a probable effect of Betamax usage, but an imminent effect.

The bases for this contention are discussed extensively below in the context of the injunction issue and will not be repeated here. It should be noted, however, that plaintiffs' argument is more complicated and speculative than was the plaintiff's in *Williams & Wilkins.* In *Williams & Wilkins,* the plaintiff asked the court to predict that if many readers obtained a journal article free of charge from the library, the readers would not subscribe to the journal and the plaintiff would be

---

[3] *See, e. g.,* 3 Nimmer on Copyright § 13.05[A][4]; Seltzer, Exemptions and Fair Use, *supra,* at 36; Freid, Fair Use and the New Act, 22 N.Y.L.S. Rev. 497 (1976-1977); and Comment, Betamax and Infringement of Television Copyright, 1977 Duke L.J. 1181, 1209.

injured. Here, plaintiffs ask the court to find harm based on many more assumptions. Plaintiffs first assume that a large proportion of the 75 million television households in this country will in the near future own the Betamax machine which today costs approximately $875; then they assume that a significantly large number of these Betamax owners will have both the financial ability and the desire to buy many Betamax tapes (today costing approximately $20 each) to record movies and episodes from TV series, and that they will keep these tapes for repeat viewing over many years. They further assume that a viewer will watch these Betamax playbacks at a time when he would otherwise be watching live television. Plaintiffs also assume that even if the tapes were not kept over a long period of time, Betamax owners will still injure the value of their copyrights by deleting commercials from movies and television series. Futhermore, plaintiffs assume that because the Betamax allows more persons to view the original telecast, fewer persons will be in the rerun audience. As is discussed more fully in Part IV *infra,* some of these assumptions are based on neither fact nor experience, and plaintiffs admit that they are to some extent inconsistent and illogical. They surface from a system of marketing which developed because producers and broadcasters could control the time at which the public views materials beamed to them over public airwaves. The Betamax reduces that control, and plaintiffs predict that harm will result.

Because this prediction of harm is based on so many assumptions and on a system of marketing which is rapidly changing, this court is hesitant to identify "probable effects" of home-use copying. Yet even if this factor of the fair use analysis were determined in plaintiffs' favor, it would not render the use unfair. The other three factors, and other considerations which the court finds relevant, must be balanced with the harm.

Before proceeding to a discussion of these factors, the court notes that the extent of the harm which plaintiffs ask the court to assume is probable is unclear. Harm which "imperils the existence of a publication" is more destructive of a fair use defense than is harm which would "limit profits." *See* Freid, *Fair Use and the New Act, supra,* at 509 n. 53. Plaintiffs' experts have testified that if Betamax is not enjoined, their profits will decrease, and that for some programs, they may not recoup their production costs. If this happens, plaintiffs warn, they will have to reduce the quality, or at least the production costs, of their audiovisual works. Plaintiffs have not said that they will no longer be able to produce this material. Indeed it would be difficult for these plaintiffs to so contend. Their profits have increased yearly, including the years in which VTR technology was introduced and growing. They exploit their material in many ways other than free television. Networks pay them substantial sums of money for their product before it even reaches the television viewer who copies it. Of course, plaintiffs claim that this copying indirectly reduces the revenue by affecting ratings and advertising. If this is true, plaintiffs have marketing alternatives at hand to recoup some of that predicted loss. They stand ready to make their product available in cassettes and compete with the VTR industry. They have proven resilient to change in market practices arising from other technological inventions, *e. g.,* cable television, pay television.

It is true, however, that copyright holders in the television industry have come to expect substantial financial reward. They are entitled to reap the highest profit they can within the industry. The Betamax and other technological advances will undoubtedly change the industry and introduce new considerations into plaintiffs' marketing considerations.

Copyright law, however, does not protect authors from change or new considerations in the marketing of their products. As the Supreme Court stated in *Teleprompter Corp. v. Columbia Broadcasting System, Inc.:* "While securing compensation to the holders of copyright was an essential purpose of that Act, freezing existing economic arrangements for doing so was not." 415 U.S. 394, 414 n. 15 (1974). In any event, any harm which might be possible must be weighed with other fair use factors.

2. Nature of the Material

This factor has not been discussed extensively in fair use cases. In *Rosemont Enterprises, Inc., supra,* at 307, the court asked whether the nature was such that "distribution would serve the public interest in the free dissemination of information." In *Williams & Wilkins, supra,* at 1356, the court found that the materials were necessary to the development of medical science. The Senate Report accompanying the New Act, S.Rep.No.473, *supra,* suggests that the use of a news article would be judged differently from the use of a musical composition and that reproduction of material which is usually unavailable would be more justifiable than reproduction of readily available material.

The material at the heart of this lawsuit cannot be categorized as "scientific" or "educational." This court cannot, nor would it desire to, pronounce the "New Mickey Mouse Club" episode which the court viewed at trial to be "mere entertainment," or "educational," or "informational," or "beneficial." As the Supreme Court wrote in *Stanley v. Georgia,* 394 U.S. 557, 566 (1969), "The line between the transmission of ideas and mere entertainment is much too elusive for this Court to draw, if indeed such a line can be drawn at all."

Inability to draw these lines does not leave this court without guidance on this factor, however. The most important aspect of the "nature" of the materials involved here is one that courts examining fair use in other media have not had to confront. This case involves only that copyrighted material which plaintiffs voluntarily choose to have telecast over public airwaves to individual homes free of charge. Plaintiffs are not paid for this material by the viewers. While the audience does not pay directly for the programs, however, this telecast is not a gratuity from the plaintiffs. They are paid for the program by the broadcaster at a rate sometimes below production costs and sometimes above. As the Supreme Court discussed in *Teleprompter, supra,* the payment process distinguishes the copyright owner in the television industry from most others:

> Unlike propagators of other copyrighted material, such as those who sell books, perform live dramatic productions, or project motion pictures to live audiences, holders of copyrights for television programs or their licensees are not paid directly by those who ultimately enjoy the publication of the material — that is, the television viewers — but by advertisers who use the drawing power of the copyrighted material to promote their goods and services. Such advertisers typically pay the broadcasters a fee for each transmission of an advertisement based on an estimate of the expected number and characteristics of the viewers who will watch the program. While, as members of the general public, the viewers indirectly pay for the privilege of viewing copyrighted material through increased prices for the goods and services of the advertisers, they are not involved in a direct economic relationship with the copyright holders or their licensees.

415 U.S. at 411-12 (footnote omitted).

The direct payment from broadcasters and advertisers has made the "free" offering to the public very profitable for plaintiffs. The opportunity to use the public airwaves allows plaintiffs to disseminate their works more widely than they ever could on their own.

This characteristic of the material is significant because of its interaction with the issue of harm. Because plaintiffs derive their revenues only indirectly from the alleged infringers of their work, the harm resulting from the infringement is more speculative. This has been discussed briefly above and will be addressed more extensively in Part IV.

3. Purpose of Use

Courts have traditionally applied this factor by asking whether the copyrighted material is used for criticism, research or other independent work.

. . . .

Plaintiffs contend that in this case there is no independent use. Betamax owners use the copy for the same purposes as the original. They add nothing of their own.

While this is true, application of this factor is not so limited. Section 106 [sic] of the New Act does not require this line of interpretation. Congress did not require independent use when finding home use sound recording to be fair use.

The salient characteristics of the use here are that it is noncommercial and in the home. Plaintiffs correctly point out that noncommercial use does not mean fair use. This is true, just as commercial use does not automatically bar fair use. *Meeropol v. Nizer, supra,* at 1069; *Rosemont Enterprises, Inc. v. Random House, Inc., supra,* at 307. The noncommercial nature of the use here, however, does broaden the scope of the doctrine. *Loew's Incorporated v. Columbia Broadcasting System, supra,* 131 F.Supp. at 175.

Here, the use is not only noncommercial but also private. This lawsuit concerns individuals in their homes copying material to view at a later time in their homes. At issue is not whether they can take the copy to the church or school and show it to a larger group. What this court rules on is home noncommercial use.

The purpose of this use is to increase access to the material plaintiffs choose to broadcast. This increase in access is consistent with the First Amendment policy of providing the fullest possible access to information through the public airwaves. *Columbia Broadcasting System, Inc. v. Democratic National Committee,* 412 U.S. 94, 102 (1973). This access is not just a matter of convenience, as plaintiffs have suggested. Access has been limited not simply by inconvenience but by the basic need to work. Access to the better program has also been limited by the competitive practice of counterprogramming.

Betamax owners use plaintiffs' works noncommercially and privately. This use increases the owners' access to material voluntarily broadcast to them free of charge over public airwaves. Because the use occurs within private homes, enforcement of a prohibition would be highly intrusive and practically impossible. Such intrusion is particularly unwarranted when plaintiffs themselves choose to beam their programs into these homes.

4. Substantiality

The fourth traditional fair use factor is the "substantiality" of the use. Generally, the more substantial the taking from the copyrighted work, the less likely it is that the fair use defense will be available. Like the other variables in the fair use analysis, the substantiality factor is inextricably bound with the issue of harm. Obviously, in the normal case of copying, the effect that the infringing copy has on the market for the original will depend to a large extent on whether the copy can substitute for the original. As Professor Nimmer has written:

> [I]ncorporating substantially all of a short story in what purports to be a literary criticism of the story will serve to fulfill the needs of those who wish to read the story as well as those who merely wish to study the reviewer's criticism. The same result is not as clear, but arguably pertains in the *Gaslight* case [*Benny v. Loew's, Inc., supra.* . .] That is, those who saw the Jack Benny burlesque not only enjoyed his parody, but also became rather fully familiar with the serious underlying story so that they might not thereafter wish to see the plaintiff's original work.

3 *Nimmer on Copyright* § 13.06[D].

Home use recording off-the-air usually involves copying the entire work. This fact, however, does not defeat the defense of fair use, because all factors must be taken together.[4] When considered with the nature of the material and the noncommercial private use, this taking of the whole still constitutes fair use, because there is no accompanying reduction in the market for "plaintiff's original work."

Plaintiffs contend that the fair use defense is barred in this case by the substantiality factor.

It is true that, taken out of context, dicta in *Meeropol* and *Rosemont* appear to preclude resort to a fair use defense when copying is nearly verbatim, but the context of the dicta reveals that the Second Circuit was concerned about substantiality only when it produced harm to the complaining party.

. . . .

The present proceeding is not a parody case, and, since there has been no distribution, there has been no publication. 17 U.S.C. § 101. The underlying rationale for the threshold substantiality test as discussed in the above cases is, therefore, not applicable here. The issue before this court is not what degree of copying is necessary to "recall or conjure up" the object of a satire as it was in *Air Pirates.* Nor is the issue whether "wholesale copying and publication" is one of the "many uses [of copyrighted works] which do not constitute infringement." [*Leon v. Pacific Telephone & Telegraph Co.,* 91 F.2d 484, 486 (9th Cir. 1937)]

Section 107 of the New Act states that in determining whether the use made of a work in any particular case is a fair use, the factors considered shall include the traditional four. Substantiality is simply listed as one of these factors; it is given no special position in relation to the others. In codifying the fair use doctrine, Congress recognized that there are no simple rules which can be applied as to all cases. As H.Rep.No.1476, *supra,* at 5679, stated:

---

[4] As one commentator has concluded:

> Too rigid an application of the substantiality criterion . . . would severely limit dissemination of copyrighted works by new technologies. . . . Indeed, to aid research and education, certain applications of these technologies have been statutorily recognized as fair use. [*See* 17 U.S.C. § 108(a)].

Note, Home Videorecording: Fair Use or Infringement?, 52 S.Calif.L.Rev. 573, 608 (1979) (citations omitted).

Of course, the spread of new technologies poses significant risks for copyright owners, and wholesale reproduction will, in many instances, limit the market for the original work. 3 *Nimmer on Copyright* § 13.05[E]. When that is the case, substantiality of the taking will combine with harm to preclude a fair use defense.

Indeed, since the doctrine is an equitable rule of reason, no generally applicable definition is possible, and each case raising the question must be decided on its own facts.

In the unique factual context of this case, the guidance offered in § 107 is followed: all four factors are considered, as well as other criteria relevant to balancing the equities between the parties, and no element is given preclusive effect.

. . . .

Accordingly, this court finds that the home-use copying made possible by this new technology constitutes fair use of plaintiffs' works. The use, limited to home recording and playback of audiovisual material broadcast free of charge to Betamax owners over public airwaves, is noncommercial and does not reduce the market for plaintiffs' works.

II. Recording by Retail Defendants

The central focus of this lawsuit has been home-use recording. Plaintiffs also contend, however, that retail stores infringe copyrights (1) when they record segments of plaintiffs' shows off-the-air, and (2) when they play these recordings back for the purpose of demonstrating the Betamax to potential purchasers. Specifically, plaintiffs allege that defendants Carter Hawley, Federated/Bullock's, Associated/Robinson's and Henry's Camera have infringed certain copyrights.

The facts supporting these allegations are weak. As discussed, all copying by the retail defendants was made at the request of Paul Ruid, a private investigator retained by plaintiffs' law firm. While Ruid did not request a specific program for taping or a specific length of recording, he did pose as a potential customer and request a demonstration of Betamax capabilities. At best the evidence shows that in response to this request, Broadway copied an 8-minute segment of "Adam 12" (Universal) and a 15-minute segment of a "Major Adams" (Universal) episode, and that Associated/Robinson's made two 8-minute recordings of the "Gemini Man" (Universal). It was not established at trial that Bullock's had succeeded in making any recording (Ruid never saw a playback of the alleged recording from "Captains and the Kings") and there was no testimony about recording by Henry's Camera.

The retail stores defend their actions on two grounds: (1) any infringement which may have occurred was induced and encouraged by plaintiffs, and, therefore, principles of equity bar suit on these actions; and (2) such copying is fair use.

Plaintiffs' claims against retail stores for their demonstrations are novel. There is no precedent for suing retail stores for displaying public televisions tuned to copyrighted programs, and plaintiffs do not complain here about this aspect of the retail defendants' activity.

Without deciding whether Ruid sufficiently "encouraged" activity so as to bar this suit, this court finds there has been no infringement. The retail stores' use of plaintiff Universal's product as presented in this suit is fair use.

Universal admits that no harm has resulted from the retail defendants' copying and playback of Universal products. Furthermore, Universal does not predict any future harm from the copying itself. The underlying concern is not about the copying by the stores but rather about the sales of Betamax. Universal sues the retail defendants because it believes that the stores are liable for contributory infringement by virtue of the subsequent sale of the machine. As Sidney Sheinberg, president and chief operating officer of MCA, testified, Universal would not bring the retail defendants into court to challenge the demonstration copying if there were no sales.

Demonstration copying and playback do not compete in any way with plaintiffs' products. The stores do not record and play back entire shows. The testimony does not show any librarying by the retail stores or any intent to use or profit from the copyrighted works. The only intent is to demonstrate the machine. For these reasons, the court finds that the demonstration copying of these retail defendants is fair use.

This cause of action against the retail stores is without precedent. There has been no suit to challenge photocopying to demonstrate a photocopier; playing a record to demonstrate a stereo system; or recording off a radio to demonstrate a recorder. The only damage claimed by Universal is that the demonstrations give an "imprimatur of acceptance" to copying off-the-air. As already discussed, this court finds that home-use copying is acceptable. In any event, this imprimatur is insufficient to render the retail defendants' demonstration use unfair.

Plaintiffs' claim that the sale of the machines constitutes contributory infringement is discussed below.

III. Liability of the Corporate Defendants

Even if this court were to hold that home-use copying is an infringement under the Old and New Acts and is not fair use, the court could not find defendants Sonam, Sony, DDBI and the retail stores liable for this infringement. Plaintiffs contend that these defendants are liable under any of three theories: (a) direct infringement, (b) contributory infringement and (c) vicarious liability. This court cannot find any of the corporate defendants liable on any of these theories.

A. Direct Infringement

Plaintiffs contend that Sony and Sonam are liable as direct infringers for the copying done by Betamax owners because they furnished the instrumentality for the allegedly infringing activity and they knew and expected that the major use of Betamax would be to record copyrighted material off-the-air, including motion pictures owned by Universal and Disney. To support this contention, plaintiffs cite deposition testimony from Sonam executives and DDBI memos and advertisements which plaintiffs claim show expectation and encouragement of the recording of copyrighted material. Plaintiffs emphasize that DDBI knew of this potential copyright infringement and successfully sought from Sony an indemnity agreement.

To support a finding of direct infringement from this evidence, plaintiffs cite *Kalem Co. v. Harper Brothers*, 222 U.S. 55 (1911); *Elektra Records Co. v. Gem Electronic Distributors, Inc.*, 360 F.Supp. 821 (E.D.N.Y. 1973) and *Universal Pictures Co. v. Harold Lloyd Corp.*, 162 F.2d 354 (9th Cir. 1947). While the lines between direct infringement, contributory infringement and vicarious liability are not clearly drawn, it appears from the courts' discussions of direct infringement in these three cases that plaintiffs' evidence here does not prove direct infringement. The involvement of the defendants in the infringing activity discussed in these cases was much more substantial and direct than that alleged against defendants here.

It is true that one can be found to have infringed directly even without participating in the actual infringing activity. In *Kalem*, a film producer was found liable for infringement through public exhibition of a film even though third persons had actually exhibited the film. There, however, the defendant-producer had not only advertised that the film could be used for public exhibition but had actually produced the infringing film, which contained scenes from the book "Ben Hur." The court found that public exhibition of this film infringed the book's copyright, and the film producer was held liable.

Elektra, the most recent case relied on by plaintiffs, is completely distinguishable. Not only did it not involve home use recording, but it expressly distinguished such recording. Defendants operated a store where they (1) sold blank tapes; (2) maintained on their premises a coin-operated machine ("Make-A-Tape") which could duplicate onto blank tapes from prerecorded tapes; and (3) loaned purchasers of blank tapes prerecorded copyrighted works for duplication on the Make-A-Tape machine. There was even some suggestion at trial that the defendants directly assisted in the duplication.

The court found that defendants' Make-A-Tape operation "clearly evidences their commercial exploitation . . . for profit in derogation of plaintiffs' rights of exclusive publication." 360 F.Supp. at 823 (footnote omitted).

One of the defenses in *Elektra* was that the "individual and self-service nature" of Make-A-Tape duplication made it analogous to home recording for home use. The court expressly rejected this argument:

> That exception [home recording] does not cover situations where the copying is done for the "purpose of reproducing or otherwise capitalizing commercially on it." House Report No. 92-487, U.S.Code Cong. & Admin.News, *supra* at p. 1572. The facts of record here bespeak commercial exploitation and nothing else. In lending the copyrighted sound recording to the customer without charge, in selling the less costly blank tape from which the spurious but exact copy may be made, and in providing the equipment whereby it may be speedily done at minimal cost, defendants are engaging in mass piracy on a custom basis. To view this activity as a form of "home recording" would stretch imagination to the snapping point. To refuse to protect plaintiffs' exclusive reproduction and publication rights in such circumstances would defeat the very purpose of the sound recording amendment and nullify the intent of Congress.

360 F.Supp. at 824-25.

This statement by the *Elektra* court highlights why the case has little precedential value for this decision. Defendants Sony and Sonam manufacture and market the Betamax and blank tapes. They do not, however, loan or otherwise provide the copyrighted work. Rather, copyright owners sell their works for broadcast to the public free of charge over public airwaves. The copying occurs not in a store operated and managed by the defendants but rather in a person's home, a location in which individual privacy is constitutionally protected and over which defendants have no control. Furthermore, defendants' acts of selling the Betamax and blank tapes to consumers can easily lead to noninfringing uses. In *Elektra,* the intent to infringe was clear: the prerecorded tapes were momentarily loaned to purchasers of blank tapes specifically for use in the store on the Make-A-Tape machine.

The videotape recorder, like a tape recorder, is a staple item of commerce. Its uses are varied. As Justice Holmes recognized in *Kalem,* "[i]n some cases where an ordinary article of commerce is sold nice questions may arise as to the point at which the seller becomes an accomplice in a subsequent illegal use by the buyer." 222 U.S. at 62. Nice questions do arise here. Defendants have provided the public with a machine capable of recording off-the-air. In *Kalem,* manufacturers of the film and the camera used to make the infringing dramatization of "Ben Hur" were not sued; nor was the manufacturer of the Make-A-Tape machine in *Elektra.* There is no precedent for finding the corporate defendants here liable for direct infringement.

The *Harold Lloyd* case relied on by plaintiffs primarily discusses contributory infringement, not direct infringement, and is addressed below.

B. Contributory Infringement

The Second Circuit has offered the most clear definition of contributory infringement:

[O]ne who, with knowledge of the infringing activity, induces, causes or materially contributes to the infringing conduct of another, may be held liable as a "contributory" infringer.

Gershwin Publishing Corp. v. Columbia Artists Management, Inc., 443 F.2d 1159, 1162 (2d Cir. 1971) (footnote omitted).

. . . .

This court agrees with defendants that their knowledge was insufficient to make them contributory infringers. In the contributory infringement cases cited by plaintiffs, the requisite knowledge is greater than that possessed by the corporate defendants here.

In the *Gershwin* case, *supra,* the court found a concert artists' managing company to be a contributory infringer because the management company knew that the artists were performing copyrighted works and would not secure a copyright license, and yet it helped to form and direct an artists' association and create an audience for them.

Here, no employee of Sony, Sonam or DDBI had either direct involvement with the allegedly infringing activity or direct contact with purchasers of Betamax who recorded copyrighted works off-the-air. Henry's Camera sold the Betamax to Griffiths' sons, but no testimony shows that the store or its employees knew that Griffiths would record copyrighted works.

Plaintiffs assert, however, that these defendants knew it was likely that people would use the Betamax to record copyrighted works and that this constitutes constructive knowledge. Even assuming that such probability were both accurate and sufficient to create "constructive knowledge" of the recording of copyrighted works, these defendants could not know that this was an infringing activity. Unlike the management agency which knew that the artists would not get a copyright license or the advertising agency [in the *Screen Gems* case, *infra*] whose employee knew that records were being made without paying a compulsory license fee, defendants here could not know what copyright law required. Before this lawsuit, that issue had not been determined. As discussed above, this court finds that home use recording is not an infringement. Even if this finding were incorrect, defendants could not be held responsible for knowing otherwise.

It is also doubtful that these defendants have met the other requirement for contributory infringement: inducement or material contribution to the infringing activity. Plaintiffs contend that Sony, Sonam, DDBI and Henry's Camera through advertising "induced" the infringing activities of recording copyrighted shows and librarying. As discussed above, Sony (through DDBI) and Henry's Camera did advertise the use of Betamax for recording favorite shows and compiling a library. Once again, however, there was no evidence that any of the copies made by Griffiths or the other individual witnesses in this suit were influenced or encouraged by these advertisements.

Plaintiffs' claims are unprecedented. Unlike the defendant in *Gershwin*, defendants here do not arrange for and direct the programming for the infringing activity. Unlike the defendants in [*Screen Gems-Columbia Music, Inc. v. Mark-Fi Records, Inc.*, 256 F.Supp. 399 (S.D.N.Y. 1966) and 327 F.Supp. 788 (S.D.N.Y. 1971)] defendants here do not sell or advertise the infringing work. Plaintiffs sue defendants because they manufacture, distribute, advertise and sell a product capable of a variety of uses, some of them allegedly infringing.

Selling a staple article of commerce — *e.g.*, a typewriter, a recorder, a camera, a photocopying machine — technically contributes to any infringing use subsequently made thereof, but this kind of "contribution," if deemed sufficient as a basis for liability, would expand the theory beyond precedent and arguably beyond judicial management.

In patent law, manufacturers, distributors, retailers and advertisers of staple articles of commerce suitable for substantial noninfringing use cannot be held liable as contributory infringers. *See* 35 U.S.C. § 271(c); *Aro Manufacturing Co. v. Convertible Top Co.*, 377 U.S. 476, 488-89 (1964); *Henry v. A. B. Dick Co.*, 224 U.S. 1, 48 (1912). As the Court in *Henry* noted, to hold otherwise would "block the wheels of commerce." *Id.*

Whether or not patent law has precedential value for copyright law and the Betamax is capable of "substantial" noninfringing use, the underlying rationale for the patent rule is significant. Commerce would indeed be hampered if manufacturers of staple items were held liable as contributory infringers whenever they "constructively" knew that some purchasers on some occasions would use their product for a purpose which a court later deemed, as a matter of first impression, to be an infringement.

C. Vicarious Liability

Screen Gems I, supra, and *Gershwin* discussed vicarious liability as well as contributory infringement. As the *Gershwin* court noted, the roots of vicarious liability lie in the doctrine of *respondeat superior:* an employer is liable for the actions of his agent. Vicarious liability for copyright infringements is not dependent on an employer-employee relationship. Vicarious liability can be imposed when a party has the "right and ability to supervise the infringing activity and also has a direct financial interest in such activities." *Gershwin*, 443 F.2d at 1162. *Accord, Screen Gems I*, 256 F.Supp. at 402. Here defendants have neither the right nor the ability to control Betamax purchasers' use of the machines in their homes, and any financial benefit is derived from use of the machine whether or not this use is infringing.

In *Gershwin*, the court found that while the management company had no formal power to police the artists' association, it participated pervasively in the direction of the association and its programming, and the association depended on it for direction "in matters such as this." 443 F.2d at 1163. With these facts, the court found that the management company was in a position to police the artists.

In *Shapiro, Bernstein & Co. v. H. L. Green Co.*, 316 F.2d 304 (2d Cir. 1963), the court never used the term "vicarious liability" but did discuss *respondeat superior* in the context of copyright infringement. Drawing an analogy to cases where a dance hall's management was found liable for infringing music performed by the bands it hired, the court found that a chain store owner was liable for the sale of infringing record albums by a concessionaire within its store. There the store owner retained the ultimate right of supervision over the record concession and took a proportionate share of the sale of the infringing records.

In *Chess Music, Inc. v. Sipe,* 442 F.Supp. 1184 (D. Minn.1977), a tavern owner was found vicariously liable for the infringing performances of the live bands he hired. The court held that the owner "is deemed to have acquiesced in the musicians' performance as he allowed the musicians the discretion to select the performance." 442 F.Supp. at 1185.

Plaintiffs contend that defendants have similar power to supervise home recording of copyrighted works. They suggest that defendants could develop a jamming system to prevent recording of anything copyrighted. Whether or not such jamming is technologically feasible, this "supervision" would not be within the power of these defendants. A jamming system would most likely require the cooperation of many others: broadcasters, producers and perhaps the Federal Communications Commission.

Plaintiffs also assert that defendants could remove the tuner from the Betamax and thereby make it impossible to record off-the-air. Even if defendants were required to do this, however, an outboard tuner could be purchased separately.

The most effective way for defendants to control the recording of copyrighted audiovisual work is to stop selling the Betamax. Plaintiffs, however, have cited no case in which a defendant's "power to supervise" was based on his ability to terminate the business.

The second requirement, financial benefit, may also be absent here. In *Shapiro* and *Screen Gems I* and *II,* the infringing records benefited the defendants directly; they received a share of the revenue from the sales. In *Gershwin,* the management company received a fee for its assistance in programming and arranging the artists' performances. Here, defendants do not profit from the infringing activity directly. They receive financial benefit from the sale of tapes, regardless of their subsequent use. They benefit directly from the allegedly infringing use only if they sell more because that use is available.

. . . [For a discussion of the unavailability of injunctive relief even had infringement been found, *see* p. 526 *infra.*].

VI. Summary

This lawsuit presents to the court only some of the issues raised by the videotape recorder technology. The court finds that home-use recording from free television is not a copyright infringement and that, even if it were, the corporate defendants are not liable and an injunction is not appropriate.

This litigation leaves many issues undecided. Like the court in *Williams & Wilkins, supra,* this court recognizes that the full resolution of these issues is

> preeminently a problem for Congress: . . . Obviously there is much to be said on all sides. The choices involve economic, social and policy factors which are far better sifted by a legislature. The possible intermediate solutions are also of the pragmatic kind legislatures, not courts, can and should fashion.

487 F.2d at 1360.

This court is bound by the factual context of this litigation. The facts do not show harm to plaintiffs even if infringing activity has occurred. Most of plaintiffs' predictions of harm hinge on speculation about audience viewing patterns and ratings, a measurement system which Sidney Sheinberg, MCA's president, calls a "black art" because of the significant level of imprecision involved in the calculations. Testimony at trial suggested that Betamax may require adjustments in marketing strategy, but it did not establish even a likelihood of harm. Nor did the testimony invoke concern that denial of monopoly power over home-use recording would significantly dissuade authors and producers from creating audiovisual material for television.

In so ruling, this court does not minimize plaintiffs' concerns. The new technology of videotape recording does bring uncertainty and change which, quite naturally, induce fear. History, however, shows that this fear may be misplaced. As Lewis Wasserman, Chairman of MCA, observed at trial: "[P]eople that have constantly forecast the doom of a particular industry in the entertainment industry have historically been wrong. . . . They forecast the doom of radio stations when television developed on the horizon. Radio stations are more profitable today than they have ever been." Television production by plaintiffs today is more profitable than it has ever been, and, in five weeks of trial, there was no concrete evidence to suggest that the Betamax will change the studios' financial picture.

QUESTIONS

1. Before addressing itself to the questions of infringement and fair use, the court (at p. 497 *supra*) emphasizes "the limits of this holding," noting the situations involving taping *not* before the court. One example is off-air taping for use in schools. To what extent will the *Universal v. Sony* ruling nevertheless furnish precedent for any, some, or all of these situations? What are the distinguishing features (if any) of each?

2. Does the court satisfactorily analyze each of the four "factors" for determining fair use pursuant to § 107? Does it give undue weight to any? Is the fourth factor analyzed in terms of actual or potential harm? See p. 503 *supra*.

3. Does this case simply stand for the proposition that "personal use" is fair use as is provided more explicitly in a number of foreign statutes?

4. The court purported to rule for the corporate defendants on the independent alternative grounds of no direct infringement and no secondary infringement even had there been direct infringement. To what extent did the first holding influence the second?

5. If full resolution of the issues raised in this case is "preeminently a problem for Congress," doesn't this reverse the direction taken by Congress in § 107 — to permit further judicial development of an equitable rule of reason? If not, what should the proper legislative solution be: Should there be resort to still another compulsory license? Should the suggestion of a tax be adopted? If so, should it be imposed on video-recording equipment or blank tape and how should the proceeds be distributed?

5. EDUCATIONAL AND LIBRARY PHOTOCOPYING

a. Education

One of the most controversial purposes touched upon in § 107 is "teaching." We have already examined a number of specific exemptions for educational uses sprinkled through the statute. *See, e.g.,* § 110(1), § 110(2), and § 112(b). In addition, teachers will continue to rely on the general principles of fair use as now embodied in § 107.

These partial limitations were enacted instead of the blanket exemption for teaching proposed by educational groups. H.R. Rep. No. 94-1476, *supra* at 66-67. *Cf.* S. Rep. No. 94-473, *supra* at 63-65. An impetus for this proposal was a case which demonstrated that a teacher could be held liable for arranging and minimally duplicating and performing a musical work, despite the absence of profit and a number of other circumstances seemingly favoring the defendant. *Wihtol v. Crow,* 309 F.2d 777, 135 USPQ 385 (8th Cir. 1962).

DRAFT, SECOND SUPPLEMENTARY REPORT OF THE REGISTER OF COPYRIGHTS, chapter II, pp. 2-6, 25-28, 30 (1975)

No issue arising under the general revision bill has been hashed over more thoroughly than the extent to which educators can reproduce and distribute copyrighted works outside of copyright control. The 1973 hearings on this question in the Senate, and the 1975 hearings in the House, produced some changes in position but no new arguments on the substantive issues. These arguments can be summarized very briefly as follows:

Arguments of educational organizations:

1. It is important that the doctrine of fair use be recognized in the statute, and that its applicability to reproduction for educational and scholarly purposes be made as clear as possible in the statute and report.

2. A provision on fair use alone is not sufficient to answer the needs of education, since teachers need more certainty about what they can and cannot do than the unpredictable doctrine of fair use can provide.

3. Teachers actually create a market for authors and publishers, and are not interested in the kind of mass copying that damages copyright owners.

4. Teachers must be enabled to make creative use of all of the resources available to them in the classroom to supplement textbooks and to seize the "teachable moment," by reproducing a variety of copyrighted materials, such as contemporaneous reports and analyses, isolated poems, stories, essays, etc., for purposes of emphasis, illustration, or bringing a lesson up to date.

5. The "not-for-profit" principle of present law should be applied to restricted educational copying that will not hurt the publishing industry and that will further American education, which is the paramount public interest.

6. Subjecting the use of modern teaching tools to requirements for advance clearance and payment of fees will stifle originality in teaching and inhibit the use of the teacher's imagination and ingenuity.

7. Various proposals for voluntary or compulsory licensing are too complicated and burdensome to be acceptable to teachers, who would be deterred from using valuable works by the necessity for paperwork and payments. Any blanket scheme would imply payment for all uses, even those that would be considered free under the doctrine of fair use.

Arguments of authors and publishers:

1. The doctrine of fair use should be confirmed in the statute, but by its nature it is an equitable rule of reason that must be flexible to avoid a statutory freezing of unintended results. Authors and publishers have no desire to oppress teachers or to stop minor or incidental reproduction of the sort that is undoubtedly fair use under the present law; their concern is with the potential danger of massive, unreasonable abuse.

2. Arguments that, since reproductions for educational and scholarly purposes have become increasingly easy and cheap, they should be made legal, are unreasonable and untenable.

3. The present "for profit" limitation has nothing whatever to do with copying. The argument that education should be exempt because it does not make a profit overlooks the fact that uncompensated educational uses, particularly in the textbook, reference book, and scientific publishing areas, result in direct and serious loss to copyright owners, and destroy the incentives for authorship and publication. Education is the textbook publisher's only market, and the main source of income of many authors.

4. Reproducing devices in educational establishments have proliferated tremendously, and unit costs continue to decrease. It is becoming easier and cheaper to make a copy than to buy one. Uninhibited reproduction of copyrighted material by a single educator, taken alone, might not do measurable damage to a particular author or publisher, but uninhibited reproduction of copyrighted material by all educators and educational establishments will literally destroy some important forms of authorship and publishing.

. . . .

5. Workable voluntary licensing systems that would place no unwarranted budgetary or administrative burdens on copyright owners, and that would fully recognize the doctrine of fair use, are already being worked out, and should be expanded and encouraged by all concerned.

. . . .

Upon close analysis the following seems to be a fair, if somewhat oversimplified, summary of the main positions with respect to fair use and the problem of reproduction for educational and scholarly purposes:

1. There is general agreement that, because of the importance of the problem and the lack of judicial precedent, Congress should clarify its intentions as to whether certain educational practices are or are not to be considered fair use, but without freezing the application of the doctrine or opening the door to widespread abuse.

2. There are essentially two ways of accomplishing this: 1) by a detailed interpretation of "fair use" in the legislative report; or 2) by an explicit statutory exemption.

3. Following extended discussions, the authors and publishers agreed to the present wording of section 107 and to an interpretative commentary with respect to educational uses along the lines of the 1966, 1967, and 1974 legislative reports. They have consistently and strongly opposed any explicit educational exemption.

4. Although the educators consistently favored an explicit exemption, they agreed at one point to accept the approach of a legislative interpretation of fair use on certain conditions, including the expanded wording of section 107, certain changes in the language of the commentary, and further insulation from liability for innocent infringement. After the first Commissioner's decision in favor of the copyright owner in the *Williams & Wilkins* litigation, the educators returned to their proposal for an outright exemption, which clearly remains their first choice. However, it also appears that the position of the educators is still flexible enough for them to accept the approach of a legislative interpretation of section 107, provided it is sufficiently clear and reasonable from their point of view, and provided certain changes are made elsewhere in the bill.

General comments.

The Copyright Office adheres to its position favoring the present language of section 107, coupled with a clear legislative interpretation in the Committee reports. The proposed language for an express educational exemption is much too broad, but in any event we seriously doubt whether satisfactory statutory language for this purpose could ever be achieved. . . .

Over the years, some of the educators have seemed to be arguing that, with respect to photocopying, they enjoy under the present law a "not-for-profit" limitation co-extensive with that applicable to certain performances, and that somehow this "right" is being taken away from them. This line of argument tended to produce a rather testy reaction, since plainly the only explicit "not-for-profit" limitations on the copyright owner's exclusive rights under the present law are with respect to public performances of nondramatic literary and musical works. On the other hand, although the commercial or nonprofit character of a use is not necessarily conclusive with respect to fair use, in combination with other factors it can and should weigh heavily in fair use decisions. It would certainly be appropriate to emphasize this point in the legislative commentary dealing with fair use and educational photocopying. . . .

A significant letter to Chairman Kastenmeier dated August 1, 1975 and signed jointly by Townsend Hoopes, President of the Association of American Publishers, Inc. and Sheldon Elliot Steinbach, Chairman of the Ad Hoc Committee on Copyright Law Revision, states:

> Pursuant to the suggestion made by you and several of your Subcommittee members during the hearings in June on H.R. 2223, representatives of publishers, authors, and educators have resumed their direct discussions of issues relating to the permissible limits of the photocopying of copyrighted materials for educational purposes.

The joint letter expresses the hope that an "agreed document" will emerge from the discussions "by early November, which we understand would be a date early enough to ensure full consideration by your Subcommittee." There is thus some genuine reason to hope that the interested parties will be able to provide direct assistance to the Congress in its final review of this problem in connection with the revision bill.

Conclusion

The question of educational photocopying was expressly excluded from the mandate of the National Commission on New Technological Uses of Copyrighted Works, on the assumption that, at the time when the Commission bill was drafted, the issue was essentially settled. The immediate key to a reasonable legislative solution in 1975 appears to lie in a well-drafted legislative interpretation of section 107, coupled with some possible changes in the language or interpretation of the provisions dealing with infringement actions and remedies.

Beyond this immediate legislative solution, however, there is a fact that must be faced. Right now, there are activities connected with teaching that constitute infringement, not fair use, and these are bound to increase. Everyone seems to assume that they will somehow be licensed and that royalties will somehow be paid, but as a practical matter this cannot and will not be done on an individual, item-by-item basis. We are entering an era when blanket licensing and collective payments are essential if the educator is not to be a scofflaw and the author's copyright is not to be a hollow shell. It is not going to be easy, but once the scope of fair use in this field of activity has been clarified by legislative action, immediate efforts to establish workable licensing or clearinghouse arrangements will have to begin.

The ultimate legislative response includes express mention of "teaching (including multiple copies for classroom use)" as a "purpose" potentially leading to a fair use finding. But the bulk of such response has been in a most abundant discussion in the committee reports about the subject. *See* S. Rep. No. 94-473, *supra* at 63-65. *Cf.* H.R. Rep. No. 83, 90th Cong., 1st Sess. 32-35 (1967). Indeed, the six pages devoted to this subject in the 1976 House report led its drafters to warn that "the concentrated attention given the fair use provision in the context of classroom teaching activities should not obscure its application in other areas." H.R. Rep. No. 94-1476, *supra* at 72. Fair use outside the context of education is discussed, with illustrative examples given, in S. Rep. No. 94-473, *supra* at 61-62, 65-67, and H.R. Rep. No. 94-1476, *supra* at 72-74.

The committee discussions in 1967, 1975, and 1976 culminated in *Guidelines for Classroom Copying in Not-For-Profit Educational Institutions,* H.R. Rep. No. 94-1476, *supra* at 68-71. These are reproduced in the Appendix. The House committee expressed the belief that these guidelines, agreed upon by certain interested groups, "are a reasonable interpretation of the minimum standards of fair use." *Id.* at 72. The conferees stated that they "accept as part of their understanding of fair use" the Guidelines, as corrected and amended. *See* 122 Cong. Rec. H10727 (Sept. 21, 1976), H10875 (Sept. 22, 1976). The Guidelines seem to offer for the first time what users have long sought — some numerical guide to how much can be taken. And indeed their very purpose is to fulfill "the need for greater certainty and protection for teachers." H.R. Rep. No. 94-1476, *supra* at 72. It is made quite clear that this "greater certainty" may be temporary because of changing conditions.

The Guidelines permit single copying for the teacher's own scholarly or educational use of a chapter, article, etc. Multiple copies for distribution of one copy per pupil are permitted under more stringent restrictions. They must meet tests of brevity, spontaneity, and cumulative effect, and include a notice of copyright. For example, a complete article of less than 2,500 words may be reproduced, as may "an excerpt from any prose work of not more than 1,000 words or 10% of the work, whichever is less, but in any event a minimum of 500 words." And the timing must be such "that it would be unreasonable to expect a timely reply to a request for permission." No copying of any kind may "be repeated with respect to the same item by the same teacher from term to term."

A separate set of guidelines has been developed for educational uses of music that permits temporary, emergency copying for an imminent performance and copying for each pupil of sections of the work which would not be a performable unit or in any case more than 10 percent of the whole work. Limited rights to edit or simplify and to make single recordings are also permitted under the music guidelines. H.R. Rep. No. 94-1476, *supra* at 71.

It has been assumed that the courts, which have long been struggling with difficult *ad hoc* fair use determinations, will enthusiastically reach out for guidelines such as these. Whether this is true and the extent to which the courts will adapt these Guidelines to other contexts remain to be seen.

One issue expressly left unresolved by Congress is the problem of off-the-air taping for nonprofit educational use. The House committee stated that "the fair use doctrine has some limited application in this area, but it appears that the development of detailed guidelines will require a more thorough exploration. . . ." H.R. Rep. No. 94-1476, *supra* at 71-72.

It will be recalled from the discussion in the "Betamax" opinion that at least one case has now arisen involving this activity on an unusually broad scale. In *Encyclopedia Britannica Educational Corp. v. Crooks,* 447 F. Supp. 243 (W.D.N.Y. 1978), a preliminary injunction was granted against local officials who systematically taped educational audiovisual works off-the-air, made copies of them, and distributed them to schools pursuant to a catalogue.

The exploration urged in the House Report has been undertaken by representatives of the several affected interest groups — producers of commercial television programming, educational film producers, commercial and public broadcasters, talent guilds, schools, etc. With the guidance of the Copyright Office and the House Committee a working group has been seeking solutions.

In the meantime, there has emerged a form of license being offered to schools which would permit taping and use under specified conditions for a fee.

b. Library Photocopying

The shock waves sent through the educational community by *Wihtol v. Crow,* 309 F.2d 777, 135 USPQ 385 (8th Cir. 1962), were replicated in the library community by the commencement of the *Williams & Wilkins* case. Both educators and librarians came to feel uncertain in their reliance on general fair use principles and soon proposed a specific exemption with regard to their photocopying activities. After the *Williams & Wilkins* trial decision in favor of the publisher, 172 USPQ 670 (1972), librarians sought to broaden their exemption; the ultimate result of this quest is another fairly complex provision which will now be examined.

The first matter to consider is the interrelation of the special exemption for libraries and archives in § 108 with the fair use provision in § 107. This is particularly necessary because of the matters left unresolved by *Williams & Wilkins* in the application of fair use principles to library photocopying. The statute seems to be clear in providing the § 108 exemption entirely apart from any fair use possibilities enjoyed by the library. § 108(f)(4). This has led to the library position that Section 108 "merely identifies certain copying situations which are conclusively presumed to be legal without affecting the right of fair use which continues as a general and flexible concept of law." Library Photocopying and the U.S. Copyright Law of 1976, p. vii (Special Libraries Association Pamphlet, Dec. 29, 1977). On the other hand, the author/publisher groups take the view that "Section 108 authorizes certain kinds of library photocopying that could not qualify as 'fair use.'" Photocopying by Academic, Public and Nonprofit Research Libraries 5 (Association of American Publishers, Inc., and Authors League Pamphlet, May 1978). In any event, the library exemption in § 108 does not extend to the library patron, who therefore must still rely on the § 107 formulation of fair use. § 108(f)(2).

The provisions of § 108 may be summarized as follows: (1) It defines the coverage of works negatively through partial exclusions set forth in § 108(h). The net result is that the section is most important with respect to books, periodicals, sound recordings, and television news programs (§ 108(f)(3)). (2) It sets forth general preconditions for library photocopying in § 108(a) and (g). (3) It specifies in § 108(b), (c), (d), and (e) the situations in which, under limitations and conditions over and above those in (a) and (g), works may be reproduced. (4) It covers miscellaneous matters in § 108(f) and provides in § 108(i) for a report from the Register in 1983 and at five-year intervals thereafter "setting forth the extent to which this section has achieved the intended statutory balancing of the rights of creators, and the needs of users."

To qualify, a library or archives need not be nonprofit or open to the public. It must, however, make the reproduction and distribution of material "without any purpose of direct or indirect commercial advantage" and, if not open to the public, be open at least to persons doing research in a specialized field who are not necessarily affiliated with the institution in question. The legislative interpretation of these requirements finally permitted libraries in a for-profit organization potentially to qualify, but subject to all the conditions and prohibitions of the section. H.R. Rep. No. 94-1733, *supra* at 73-74. *But cf.* Brennan, *Legislative History and Chapter 1 of S.22,* 22 N.Y.L.S. L. REV. 193, 202 (1976); S. Rep. No. 94-473, *supra* at 67. Thus, it is the reproduction and distribution which must be nonprofit, not the enterprise.

Additionally, the reproduction must contain a copyright notice. § 108(a)(3). It will be interesting to note whether a library must affirmatively add some kind of notice when it has been omitted (under the temporary umbrella of § 405, see pp. 293-95, *supra)* or whether a library need only repeat on the reproduction itself whatever notice is affixed anywhere on the copy of the work from which the reproduction is taken. The view of certain libraries thus far is even less ambitious, i.e., that this subsection merely requires a warning or "notice" that the material may be copyrighted.

The privilege is to make "no more than one copy or phonorecord of a work." § 108(a). This means no more than one *at a time,* as long as the reproduction is "isolated and unrelated" and not "the related or concerted reproduction or distribution of multiple copies or phonorecords of the same material...." § 108(g)(1). The additional limitation against "systematic reproduction or distribution," which applies to periodical articles, is discussed below.

Two of the situations in which reproduction is permitted for a library's own use have never caused any controversy. One, originally introduced into the 1967 House-passed H.R. 2512, 90th Cong., 1st Sess., provides for facsimile reproduction of unpublished works for archival preservation. § 108(b). (This privilege, as well as others provided in § 108, is subject to any contractual obligation undertaken by the library in connection with the deposit of a manuscript. § 108(f)(4).) The other permits facsimile reproduction of a published work solely for the replacement of a copy or phonorecord "that is damaged, deteriorating, lost, or stolen," but only "if the library or archives has, after a reasonable effort, determined that an unused replacement cannot be obtained at a fair price." § 108(c). *See* H.R. Rep. No. 94-1476, *supra* at 75-76. This provision, as well as others in § 108, is analyzed against the background of fundamental copyright concepts in a recent article, Seltzer, *Exemptions and Fair Use in Copyright: The "Exclusive Rights" Tensions in the New Copyright Act,* 24 BULL. COPYRIGHT SOC'Y 215, 307 (1977).

Unavailability of copies at a fair price after reasonable investigation is also the standard for the slightly more controversial "out of print" provision in § 108(c). This permits the reproduction, under such circumstances, of an entire work for a user if the library has no notice that the material will be used for other than "private study, scholarship, or research" and it prominently posts a warning to be prescribed by regulation. § 108(e). Such a regulation has already been issued. 37 C.F.R. § 201.14 (1977).

This provision was introduced in 1969 (S. 543, 91st Cong.) as librarians responded to the commencement of the *Williams & Wilkins* case. After the trial decision favorable to the publisher in 1972, efforts were redoubled to secure an exemption for journal articles even if not "out of print." The result was the special provision in § 108(d), subject to the limiting provisions in § 108(g)(2) and partially clarified by another set of guidelines. This complex structure dealing with a narrow question may be traced as follows:

A reproduction, directly or through interlibrary "loan," may be made of "no more than one article or other contribution to a copyrighted collection or periodical issue" or of a "small part of any other copyrighted work" under the same provisions as to good faith and posted warnings as in the "out of print" provision in § 108(e).

But such reproduction, as indicated above, must be "isolated and unrelated" and specifically must not be "systematic." § 108(g)(2). Examples of "systematic" copying are furnished in the Senate Report:

Senate Report No. 94-473 at 70-71 (1975)

Multiple copies and systematic reproduction

Subsection (g) provides that the rights granted by this section extend only to the "isolated and unrelated reproduction of a single copy", but this section does not authorize the related or concerted reproduction of multiple copies of the same material whether made on one occasion or over a period of time, and whether intended for aggregate use by one individual or for separate use by the individual members of a group. For example, if a college professor instructs his class to read an article from a copyrighted journal, the school library would not be permitted, under subsection (g), to reproduce copies of the article for the members of the class.

Subsection (g) also provides that section 108 does not authorize the systematic reproduction or distribution of copies or phonorecords of articles or other contributions to copyrighted collections or periodicals or of small parts of other copyrighted works whether or not multiple copies are reproduced or distributed. Systematic reproduction or distribution occurs when a library makes copies of such materials available to other libraries or to groups of users under formal or informal arrangements whose purpose or effect is to have the reproducing library serve as their source of such material. Such systematic reproduction and distribution, as distinguished from isolated and unrelated reproduction or distribution, may substitute the copies reproduced by the source library for subscriptions or reprints or other copies which the receiving libraries or users might otherwise have purchased for themselves, from the publisher or the licensed reproducing agencies.

While it is not possible to formulate specific definitions of "systematic copying", the following examples serve to illustrate some of the copying prohibited by subsection (g).

(1) A library with a collection of journals in biology informs other libraries with similar collections that it will maintain and build its own collection and will make copies of articles from these journals available to them and their patrons on request. Accordingly, the other libraries discontinue or refrain from purchasing subscriptions to these journals and fulfill their patrons' requests for articles by obtaining photocopies from the source library.

(2) A research center employing a number of scientists and technicians subscribes to one or two copies of needed periodicals. By reproducing photocopies of articles the center is able to make the material in these periodicals available to its staff in the same manner which otherwise would have required multiple subscriptions.

(3) Several branches of a library system agree that one branch will subscribe to particular journals in lieu of each branch purchasing its own subscriptions, and the one subscribing branch will reproduce copies of articles from the publication for users of the other branches.

The committee believes that section 108 provides an appropriate statutory balancing of the rights of creators, and the needs of users. However, neither a statute nor legislative history can specify precisely which library photocopying practices constitute the making of "single copies" as distinguished from "systematic reproduction". Isolated single spontaneous requests must be distinguished from "systematic reproduction". The photocopying needs of such operations as multicounty regional systems must be met. The committee therefore recommends that representatives of authors, book and periodical publishers and other owners of copyrighted material meet with the library community to formulate photocopying guidelines to assist library patrons and employees. Concerning library photocopying practices not authorized by this legislation, the committee recommends that workable clearance and licensing procedures be developed.

———————

Because librarians contended that the "systematic" disqualification thus introduced in the Senate swallowed up the whole exemption, a proviso was inserted by the House committee in § 108(g)(2) as follows:

> That nothing in this clause prevents a library or archives from participating in interlibrary arrangements that do not have, as their purpose or effect, that the library or archives receiving such copies or phonorecords for distribution does so *in such aggregate quantities as to substitute for a subscription to or purchase of such work.* (Emphasis added.)

This proviso, which addresses itself only to the interlibrary situation and not reproduction by a library directly for its patrons, was accepted in the House-passed version of S. 22.

The question whether this proviso would be accepted by the Senate conferees was eased by the clarification of its scope. This was accomplished by the development of guidelines by the interested parties under the aegis of the National Commission on New Technological Uses of Copyrighted Works (CONTU), directed solely to the definition of "such aggregate quantities . . ." in the proviso to § 108(g)(2). H.R. Rep. No. 94-1733, *supra* at 72-73. For example, the basic formula deemed to warrant subscription to a given periodical is a group of requests "within any calendar year for a total of six or more copies of an article or articles published in such periodical within five years prior to the date of the request." *Id.*

The result of this particular development is: (a) A library whose requests exceed the number set forth in the guidelines is deemed to be substituting for subscription or purchase. Accordingly it does not come within the proviso to § 108(g)(2). (b) That being the case, it may be deemed to be engaging in "systematic reproduction" within the meaning of § 108(g)(2). (c) Such activity would disqualify it from the exemption in § 108(d). Its only recourse, unless other parts of § 108 apply, is to argue that, despite the foregoing, it is still engaging in fair use within the meaning of § 107.

It is no wonder that some libraries, preferring to avoid the mine field described above, are removing themselves from photocopying activities. Some install coin-operated machines seeking to avail themselves of the provision in § 108(f)(1) that:

> Nothing in this section —
> (1) shall be construed to impose liability for copyright infringement upon a library or archives or its employees for the unsupervised use of reproducing equipment located on its premises: *Provided,* That such equipment displays a notice that the making of a copy may be subject to the copyright law. . . .

The possible liability of libraries in connection with coin-operated machines is, together with many other issues in this area, a problem not restricted to the United States. *See, e.g., University of New South Wales v. Moorhouse,* 6 Australian Law Reports 193 (1975); Catterns, *"The Americans, Baby" by Moorhouse: An Australian Story of Copyright and the New Technology,* 23 Bull. Copyright Soc'y 213 (1976).

Some libraries are utilizing the services of emerging clearinghouses, such as the Copyright Clearance Center, which collects and distributes photocopying royalties to periodical publishers who display their rates on the pages of their publications.

In any event, the library photocopying issue has not been fully resolved by either litigation or statute. The recommendations of CONTU suggest several more years of a "holding operation" while facts are assembled and views gathered by the Register with a view toward a 1983 report under § 108(i). CONTU's only recommendation for legislation in this area is the posting of a warning on the premises of commercial copiers as a condition of the potential availability of fair use. *Final Report* 119-24 (July 31, 1978).

QUESTIONS

1. Consider the following uses of a short song written for four-part chorus and copyrighted by *C*. Copyright infringement or fair use? (Something else?)

(a) *S* (a scholar), for convenience in research, secures a copy of the song in a music library and hand-copies it onto blank musical notation sheets.

(b) *S* pays ten cents per page to photocopy the song on the library photocopy machine.

(c) *S* reproduces the song on an electromagnetic computer tape by which he accumulates data for a computer analysis of melodic, harmonic and rhythmic patterns.

(d) *S* reproduces the song in his textbook on musical form, 5,000 copies of which are being used in university music courses throughout the United States.

(e) *T* (a teacher) holds up a copy of the song (which he purchased) in front of his classroom — and then circulates it among the students — in the course of a lesson in music history.

(f) *T* uses a projection machine and projects the purchased copy of the song onto a screen in front of the classroom.

(g) *T* makes 30 photocopies of the song for use in classroom instruction.

(h) *T* makes 30 photocopies of the song for use in his music mid-term examination.

(i) *D* (glee club director) purchased 20 copies of the song for a glee club performance but in spite of precautions five students lost their copies and *G*, on the eve of performance, supplied replacement copies on the photocopy machine.

(j) *D* leads the glee club in the song as background music to stage action by the college drama club, in a play designed to raise money for the school athletic program.

2. Tom Tilden is a teacher of high school English, who regularly has his students read some of the plays of Shakespeare. Last month, the copyrighted motion picture of *Hamlet* was shown on television. Tilden used his videotape machine to make a tape of the film as it was being shown on television, and last week he ran the tape through a classroom television set so that the film could be viewed by his students during the school day. Has the Copyright Act been violated? If so, what are the remedies?

H. REMEDIES

§ 501. Infringement of copyright

(a) Anyone who violates any of the exclusive rights of the copyright owner as provided by sections 106 through 118, or who imports copies or phonorecords into the United States in violation of section 602, is an infringer of the copyright.

(b) The legal or beneficial owner of an exclusive right under a copyright is entitled, subject to the requirements of sections 205(d) and 411, to institute an action for any infringement of that particular right committed while he or she is the owner of it. The court may require such owner to serve written notice of the action with a copy of the complaint upon any person shown, by the records of the Copyright Office or otherwise, to have or claim an interest in the copyright, and shall require that such notice be served upon any person whose interest is likely to be affected by a decision in the case. The court may require the joinder, and shall permit the intervention, of any person having or claiming an interest in the copyright.

(c) For any secondary transmission by a cable system that embodies a performance or a display of a work which is actionable as an act of infringement under subsection (c) of section 111, a television broadcast station holding a copyright or other license to transmit or perform the same version of that work shall, for purposes of subsection (b) of this section, be treated as a legal or beneficial owner if such secondary transmission occurs within the local service area of that television station.

(d) For any secondary transmission by a cable system that is actionable as an act of infringement pursuant to section 111(c) (3), the following shall also have standing to sue: (1) the primary transmitter whose transmission has been altered by the cable system; and (ii) any broadcast station within whose local service area the secondary transmission occurs.

HOUSE REPORT

H.R. Rep. No. 94-1476, 94th Cong., 2d Sess. 158-60 (1976)

The bill, unlike the present law, contains a general statement of what constitutes infringement of copyright. Section 501(a) identifies a copyright infringer as someone who "violates any of the exclusive rights of the copyright owner as provided by sections 106 through 118" of the bill, or who imports copies or phonorecords in violation of section 602. Under the latter section an unauthorized importation of copies or phonorecords acquired abroad is an infringement of the exclusive right of distribution under certain circumstances.

The principle of the divisibility of copyright ownership, established by section 201(d), carries with it the need in infringement actions to safeguard the rights of all copyright owners and to avoid a multiplicity of suits. Subsection (b) of section 501 enables the owner of a particular right to bring an infringement action in that owner's name alone, while at the same time insuring to the extent possible that the other owners whose rights may be affected are notified, and given a chance to join the action.

The first sentence of subsection (b) empowers the "legal or beneficial owner of an exclusive right" to bring suit for "any infringement of that particular right committed while he or she is the owner of it." A "beneficial owner" for this purpose would include, for example, an author who had parted with legal title to the copyright in exchange for percentage royalties based on sales or license fees. . . .

In addition to cases involving divisibility of ownership in the same version of a work, section 501(b) is intended to allow a court to permit or compel joinder of the owners of rights in works upon which a derivative work is based. . . .

Vicarious liability for infringing performances

The committee has considered and rejected an amendment to this section intended to exempt the proprietors of an establishment, such as a ballroom or night club, from liability for copyright infringement committed by an independent contractor, such as an orchestra leader. A well-established principle of copyright law is that a person who violates any of the exclusive rights of the copyright owner is an infringer, including persons who can be considered related or vicarious infringers. To be held a related or vicarious infringer in the case of performing rights, a defendant must either actively operate or supervise the operation of the place wherein the performances occur, or control the content of the infringing program, and expect commercial gain from the operation and either direct or indirect benefit from the infringing performance. The committee has decided that no justification exists for changing existing law, and causing a significant erosion of the public performance right.

1. INJUNCTIONS

Injunctive relief is grounded on long-established principles of equity and presumably will operate under the 1976 Act the same as under the 1909 Act. *Cf.* § 405(b) (innocent infringer misled by absence of notice may be permitted to pay reasonable license fee in lieu of being enjoined). Section 502(a) of the 1976 Act clearly provides that, except as against the Government, a court "may . . . grant temporary and final injunctions on such terms as it may deem reasonable to prevent or restrain infringement of a copyright." *Cf.* §§ 101(b) and 112 of 1909 law. Both statutes provide for nationwide service of such injunctions and certain mechanics for out-of-district enforcement. § 502(b) of 1976 law; § 113 of 1909 law.

Whenever equity has jurisdiction to grant an injunction by final decree, it has the power to grant a preliminary injunction, generally for the purpose of maintaining the status quo. Preliminary injunctions have been very important in copyright cases. The standard for granting a preliminary injunction has become a little less consistent in recent years, but two things are clear: (1) In common with other types of cases, the plaintiff is not obliged to make out such a case on the merits as would be required for a decree after trial; (2) in copyright cases, it is considerably easier to secure a preliminary injunction than in most other cases.

In a recent analysis of these questions, the U.S. District Court for the Southern District of New York stated as follows:

> "Under the general standard in effect in this [Second] Circuit it is incumbent on the party seeking the injunction to show either probable success on the merits and possible irreparable injury or serious questions going to the merits of the litigation and a balance of hardships tipping decidedly toward the moving party. See *Columbia Pictures Indus., Inc. v. American Broad. Cos., Inc.,* 501 F.2d 894, 897 (2d Cir. 1974); *Sonesta Int'l Hotels Corp. v. Wellington Associates,* 483 F.2d 247, 250 (2d Cir. 1973); *Checker Motors Corp. v. Chrysler Corp.,* 405 F.2d 319 (2d Cir.), cert. denied, 394 U.S. 999 (1969). . . ." *Selchow & Righter Co. v. Book-of-the-Month Club, Inc.,* 192 USPQ 530, 533 (S.D. N.Y. 1976).

This rule, applicable to cases in general, requires a showing of possible irreparable harm under the second prong of this test. *See Selchow & Righter Co. v. McGraw-Hill Book Co.,* 580 F.2d 25, 198 USPQ 577, 579 (2d Cir. 1978).

A long-held view has been that if the plaintiff establishes a *prima facie* case as to validity of copyright and its infringement, a temporary injunction will generally be issued. *American Code Co. v. Bensinger,* 282 Fed. 829 (2d Cir. 1922); *Houghton Mifflin Co. v. Stackpole Sons, Inc.,* 104 F.2d 306, 42 USPQ 96 (2d Cir.), *cert. denied,* 308 U.S. 597, 43 USPQ 521 (1939). Detailed proof of actual damages is not necessary if infringement appears and damages may probably follow. *Rushton v. Vitale,* 218 F.2d 434, 104 USPQ 158 (2d Cir. 1955); *Henry Holt & Co. v. Liggett & Myers Tobacco Co.,* 23 F. Supp. 302, 37 USPQ 449 (E.D. Pa. 1938). It has even been said that "[a] copyright holder in the ordinary case may be presumed to suffer irreparable harm when his right to the exclusive use of the copyrighted material is invaded." *American Metropolitan Enterprises of New York, Inc. v. Warner Bros. Records, Inc.,* 389 F.2d 903, 905, 157 USPQ 69, 70 (2d Cir. 1968). Although some district courts have found a requirement of at least a threshold showing of irreparable harm in copyright cases, *Selchow & Richter Co. v. Book-of-the-Month Club, Inc., supra,* 192 USPQ at 533, the presumption of harm in copyright cases is still apparently being recognized — although it still helps to establish some specific basis for finding injury. *See Novelty Textile Mills, Inc. v. Joan Fabrics Corp.,* 558 F.2d 1090, 195 USPQ 1 (2d Cir. 1977) [*supra* p. 338].

In addition to an injunction, other specific nonmonetary relief — such as impounding and destruction of the infringing articles — has been available to a successful plaintiff under both the 1909 and 1976 statutes. *See Duchess Music Corp. v. Stern,* 458 F.2d 1305, 173 USPQ 278 (9th Cir. 1972); *Elektra Records Co. v. Gem Electronic Distributors, Inc.,* 360 F. Supp. 821, 179 USPQ 617 (E.D.N.Y. 1973). For the mechanics to be utilized under the 1976 Act, see § 503 and the House Report at 160.

UNIVERSAL CITY STUDIOS v. SONY CORP. OF AMERICA

480 F. Supp. 429 (C.D. Cal. 1979)

. . . [The facts of the case and the court's decision on liability are set forth at p. 495 *supra.*]

V. Injunctive Relief

Plaintiffs seek injunctive relief. They ask the court to exercise its equitable powers to restrain defendants from manufacturing, distributing, selling or offering for sale Betamax or Betamax tapes; from using Betamax or Betamax tapes to copy motion pictures owned and copyrighted by plaintiffs; from advertising that Betamax and Betamax tapes may be used for the purpose of making copies of television shows, including motion pictures owned and copyrighted by plaintiffs; and from exhibiting or playing all videotape copies made by defendants of motion pictures owned and copyrighted by plaintiffs. Plaintiffs have suggested alternatively that the court require Sony to modify the Betamax to render it incapable of recording copyrighted works off the air.

An injunction is an equitable remedy. Its issuance is a matter of court discretion. As the Court recognized in *Hecht v. Bowles,* 321 U.S. 321 (1944), "We are dealing here with the requirements of equity practice with a background of several hundred years of history. . . . The historic injunctive process was designed to deter, not to punish." 321 U.S. at 329.

There are no rigid rules to instruct courts when to issue injunctions. An injunction is never a matter of absolute right. As the Supreme Court recently stated in *Tennessee Valley Authority v. Hill,* 437 U.S. 153, 193 (1978):

It is correct, of course, that a federal judge sitting as a chancellor is not mechanically obligated to grant an injunction for every violation of law. . . . As a general matter it may be said that "[s]ince all or almost all equitable remedies are discretionary, the balancing of equities and hardships is appropriate in almost any case as a guide to the chancellor's discretion." D. Dobbs, Remedies 52 (1975).

An injunction is a harsh and drastic remedy. *Kass v. Arden-Mayfair, Inc.*, 431 F.Supp. 1037 (C.D.Cal.1977). Courts have recognized:

There is no power the exercise of which is more delicate, which requires greater caution, deliberation and sound discretion, or more dangerous in a doubtful case, than the issuing of an injunction. . . . The right must be clear, the injury impending or threatened, so as to be averted only by the protecting preventive process of injunction: but that will not be awarded in doubtful cases, or new ones, not coming within well established principles for if it issues erroneously, an irreparable injury is inflicted, for which there can be no redress, it being the act of a court, not of the party who prays for it.

Detroit Newspaper Publishers Association v. Detroit Typographical Union No. 18, International Typographical Union, 471 F.2d 872, 876 (6th Cir. 1972), *quoting* 3 Barron & Holtzoff, *Federal Practice and Procedure* (Wright Ed.) § 1431.

This is a doubtful case. An injunction would deprive the public of a new technology capable of noninfringing uses (see *infra*). Furthermore, the need for an injunction is not clear.

Courts look for irreparable harm to the plaintiff before issuing injunctive relief, and here plaintiffs' fears of irreparable harm are speculative at best. Plaintiffs contend that if the court finds that copyright infringement has occurred, irreparable harm is presumed, and it becomes defendants' burden to prove that further harm will not occur in the future.

The bulk of this opinion has been addressed to this court's reasons for finding that home-use copying does not constitute infringement. Even if the court had concluded otherwise, however, it would not find an injunction appropriate.

It is true that courts have acknowledged that actual harm from copyright infringement is very difficult to prove, and, "in the ordinary case," irreparable harm is presumed when the copyright holder's "right to the exclusive use of the copyrighted material is invaded." *American Metropolitan Enterprises of New York, Inc. v. Warner Brothers Records, Inc.*, 389 F.2d 903, 905 (2d Cir. 1968). Plaintiffs claim that no court has ever refused to grant a permanent injunction in a copyright case when infringement has been proven, even when there has been no evidence of harm. Plaintiffs cite *Chappell & Co. v. Middletown Farmers Market & Auction Co.,* 334 F.2d 303 (3d Cir. 1964) (direct infringer permanently enjoined); *Big Sky Music v. Todd,* 388 F.Supp. 498 (S.D.Ga.1974) (injunction against owner and operator of nightclub for copyright infringement by live bands performing in the club); *Fisher-Price Toys, Division of Quaker Oats Co. v. My-Toy Co., Inc.,* 385 F.Supp. 218 (S.D.N.Y.1974) (direct infringer permanently enjoined); *Shapiro, Bernstein & Co., Inc. v. "Log Cabin Club Association,"* 365 F.Supp. 325, 328 (N.D.W.Va.1973) (injunction against president and manager of association for musical copyright infringements occurring in club operated by association); *Peter Pan Fabrics, Inc. v. Dixon Textile Corp.,* 188 F.Supp. 235, 238 (S.D.N.Y.1960) (direct infringer permanently enjoined); *Adviser's, Inc. v. Wiesen-Hart, Inc.,* 161 F.Supp. 831 (S.D.Ohio 1958) (direct infringer permanently enjoined) and *Gordon v. Wier,* 11 F.Supp. 117, 124 (E.D.Mich.1953), *aff'd,* 216 F.2d 508 (6th Cir. 1954) (direct infringer permanently enjoined).

This litigation, however, is not the "ordinary" copyright case where plaintiffs seek an injunction against the direct infringer or the person who controls the infringing activity. Plaintiffs here ask the court to enjoin the manufacturer, distributors, retailers and advertiser of a machine used by persons in private homes for allegedly infringing activities. There is no precedent for plaintiffs' requested injunction.

No such injunction was granted in the cases cited by plaintiffs. Indeed, this court has found no case in which the manufacturers, distributors, retailers and advertisers of the instrument enabling the infringement were sued by the copyright holders. For example, in *Williams & Wilkins Co. v. United States, supra,* and *Wihtol v. Crow, supra,* plaintiffs did not make the manufacturer or seller of photocopy machines a defendant. In *Encyclopaedia Britannica Educational Corp. v. Crooks, supra,* the infringer was a school district that videotaped copyrighted programs, but the manufacturer of the tape recorders and the tape used in the infringement was not made a defendant. In *Elektra Records Co. v. Gem Electronic Distributors, Inc., supra,* the infringer owned retail stores which installed coin-operated tape recorders (Make-A-Tape) for customer use in duplicating prerecorded copyrighted tapes. The manufacturer of the recorders used in the infringement was not made a defendant. In *Screen Gems-Columbia Music, Inc. v. Mark-Fi Records, Inc., supra,* the infringer (Mark-Fi) was a manufacturer of bootleg phonograph records, but the manufacturer of the record pressing equipment used in the infringement was not made a defendant.

As noted above, an injunction is an equitable remedy. Plaintiffs' request for an injunction against the corporate defendants is unique, and the equitable considerations are different from those found in the typical copyright case. Because the defendant's role in the asserted infringement is indirect, and because defendant's product is also used for purposes where no infringement could be alleged (*e. g.,* recording material which is not copyrighted or where permission to record is given), it is necessary to weigh the evidence of harm offered at trial. The court must consider this evidence in the context of the effect of an injunction in this case.

Plaintiffs predict a wide range of harmful effects from the various uses of Betamax. Some of these effects are immediate; others are delayed. Plaintiffs contend that each will result from one of the following uses of the Betamax machine:

1. Recording material off-the-air but never viewing the copy.

2. Time-Shifting: Recording off-the-air while not viewing the program, watching the copy within a short period of time and erasing it thereafter.

3. Librarying: Recording off-the-air and saving the tape for more than one subsequent viewing.

4. Avoiding commercials either by using the pause button while recording or by fast-forwarding while playing back.

Plaintiffs' prediction of harm from each of these uses assumes that the public will own and use a very large number of Betamax recorders. By the end of 1978, after four years of increasing sales of Betamax and several years of sales of its competitors, plaintiffs had experienced no harm. In addition to admitting that there has been no harm to date, plaintiffs admit they cannot predict at what date or level of sales the expected harms will occur. The growth of Betamax ownership will be affected by price. Today the machine costs approximately $875 with each tape costing approximately $20. The growth of ownership will also be influenced by competition from Universal's prerecorded discs and other prerecorded cassettes.

Each listed use is addressed below with plaintiffs' accompanying prediction of harm and the assumptions underlying that prediction.

A. *Recording But Never Viewing*

People may occasionally tape more material than they will watch. For example, defendant Griffiths testified that he recorded "Alpha Caper" but erased it before ever watching it.

Plaintiffs contend that even this recording merits concern as a *per se* violation of the copyright law. They do admit, however, that their copyright is not actually injured by this activity. Without this injury, this court will not issue an injunction against the corporate defendants based on this use.

B. *Time-Shifting*

At least two time-shifting situations were discussed at trial. First, a person may be at work at 4:30 p. m. and want to tape a program telecast then for his viewing later that evening. For example, Lowe testified that his son would record Mickey Mouse cartoons in the afternoon for both of them to watch that evening when Lowe returned home from work. Second, during sweep periods when counter-programming is most intense, a Betamax owner may want to record one network's program while watching another. For example, plaintiffs' witnesses testified about "Betamax Sunday," February 18, 1979. On that evening, one network broadcast "Gone With the Wind" against the other network's "One Flew Over the Cuckoo's Nest" against the other network's "Elvis." The public may well have wanted to see all three, but the networks forced a choice. Betamax increases the viewer's access from one to two programs.

Plaintiffs foresee many harms from time-shifting: (1) a decrease in the size of the live audience at the time of telecast; (2) a loss to live television or other plaintiff-sponsored entertainment at the time of viewing the copy; (3) a loss to the rerun audience; and (4) a loss to theater or film rental exhibition of the same program.

(1) Plaintiffs fear that persons "watching" the original telecast of a program will not be measured in the live audience and ratings and revenues will decrease. There was testimony at trial, however, that Nielsen Ratings has already developed the ability to measure when a Betamax in a sample home is recording the program. Thus, the Betamax owner will be measured as a part of the live audience. The later diary can augment that measurement with information about subsequent viewing.

(2) Plaintiffs predict that live television or movie audiences will decrease as more people watch Betamax tapes as an alternative. Here plaintiffs assume that people will view copies when they would otherwise be watching television or going to the movie theater. There is no factual basis for this assumption. It seems equally likely that Betamax owners will play their tapes when there is nothing on television they wish to see and no movie they want to attend. Defendants' survey does not show any negative effect of Betamax ownership on television viewing or theater attendance.

Plaintiffs rely on the concept that "viewing time is relatively inelastic," that persons will spend only so many hours watching any kind of television. Even if that is true, the time-shifting function may simply rearrange these hours. Instead of watching two hours each night of the week, the viewer may go bowling while recording his favorite Monday night program and watch it in addition to his regular two hours on Saturday.

Furthermore, this court cannot possibly enjoin fractionalization. There is no way, nor should there be, for plaintiffs to limit the availability of alternatives to television viewing. Games, books, movies — even people — all divert potential viewers from the television set. It is impossible for plaintiffs or this court to isolate the diversion of Betamax from that of these competitors.

(3) Plaintiffs fear that time-shifting will reduce audiences for telecast reruns. The underlying assumptions here are particularly difficult to accept. Plaintiffs explain that the Betamax increases access to the original televised material and that the more people there are in this original audience, the fewer people the rerun will attract. Yet current marketing practices, including the success of syndication, show just the opposite. Today, the larger the audience for the original telecast, the higher the price plaintiffs can demand from broadcasters for rerun rights. There is no survey within the knowledge of this court to show that the rerun audience is comprised of persons who have not seen the program. In any event, if ratings can reflect Betamax recording, original audiences may increase and, given current market practices, this should aid plaintiffs rather than harm them. . . .

(4) Plaintiffs suggest that theater or film rental exhibition of a program will suffer because of time-shift recording of that program. This suggestion lacks merit. By definition, time-shift recording entails viewing and erasing, so the program will no longer be on tape when the later theater run begins. Of course, plaintiffs may fear that the Betamax owners will keep the tapes long enough to satisfy all their interest in the program and will, therefore, not patronize later theater exhibitions. To the extent that this practice involves librarying, it is addressed in section V.C., *infra*. It should also be noted that there is no evidence to suggest that the public interest in later theatrical exhibitions of motion pictures will be reduced any more by Betamax recording than it already is by the television broadcast of the film.

Plaintiffs' experts admitted at several points in the trial that the time-shifting without librarying would result in "not a great deal of harm." Plaintiffs' greatest concern about time-shifting is with "a point of important philosophy that transcends even commercial judgment." They fear that with any Betamax usage, "invisible boundaries" are passed: "the copyright owner has lost control over his program."

These "nuances," "perceptions," and "points of philosophy" are understandable, though not always logical. They do not, however, justify an injunction. Harm from time-shifting is speculative and, at best, minimal.

The audience benefits from the time-shifting capability have already been discussed. It is not implausible that benefits could also accrue to plaintiffs, broadcasters, and advertisers, as the Betamax makes it possible for more persons to view their broadcasts.

C. Librarying

Plaintiffs' fear of harm goes beyond time-shifting use. They also fear that persons will not erase the tapes after one viewing but rather will build a library, *i. e.,* maintain the tapes for subsequent repeat viewing. Plaintiffs argue that persons who record and watch playbacks are removed from audiences for live television and entertainment alternatives. This contention fails for the reasons discussed above. (*See* V.B.2.) Plaintiffs also argue that a Betamax owner who has a copy will not watch the same program when rerun on television or re-released for theater exhibition.

This prediction also assumes too much. First, it assumes that a large number of Betamax owners will have both the desire and the income to maintain a library. Each tape costs approximately $20. An extensive library will be very expensive, and it has not been proven that many persons will "library" to any significant extent. Additionally, prerecorded discs of special programs or movies will compete with the Betamax recording. These prerecorded discs arguably are more desirable than off-the-air recordings. They have not been edited for television, and they have no commercials. Plaintiff Universal has already released full versions of "Animal House" and "The Sting" for $15.95 each. There was testimony at trial that Twentieth Century-Fox has already released fifty titles for software to be used on home videotape recorders.

To the extent that librarying does occur, it is not clear that movie audiences will decrease. There is no survey or other evidence showing that persons who own a copy of a movie will not attend a theater exhibition of that movie. Theater-going is usually a social event which affords persons a larger viewing screen, better sound and an unedited version of the film. Even if theater audiences did decrease, this decrease would be offset by the corresponding increase in the audience for the original telecast of movies. When this increase is anticipated and measured, revenue from the initial sale to television should be greater.

D. Avoiding Advertisements

Plaintiffs have also speculated about the reaction of advertisers to Betamax. They predict that if Betamax owners use the pause control to delete commercials or the fast forward to pass them by, advertisers will pay less to networks and networks will pay less to producers and owners. It must be remembered, however, that to omit commercials, Betamax owners must view the program, including the commercials, while recording. To avoid commercials during playback, the viewer must fast-forward and, for the most part, guess as to when the commercial has passed. For most recordings, either practice may be too tedious. As defendants' survey showed, 92% of the programs were recorded with commercials and only 25% of the owners fast-forward through them. Advertisers will have to make the same kinds of judgments they do now about whether persons viewing televised programs actually watch the advertisements which interrupt them.

E. Injunction Would Not Be An Appropriate Remedy

The possibility that some of plaintiffs' suggested harms will occur is neither sufficiently certain nor adequately threatening to warrant an injunction against the corporate defendants. Moreover, before issuing any injunction, a court must also consider the potential harm from the injunction itself. An injunction prohibiting the marketing of Betamax or requiring destruction of its off-the-air recording capability would deprive Sony of financial reward for years of investment and improvement of this technology. Even if it were deemed that home-use recording of copyrighted material constituted infringement, the Betamax could still legally be used to record noncopyrighted material or material whose owners consented to the copying. An injunction would deprive the public of the ability to use the Betamax for this noninfringing off-the-air recording.

Defendants introduced considerable testimony at trial about the potential for such copying of sports, religious, educational and other programming. This included testimony from representatives of the Offices of the Commissioners of the National Football, Basketball, Baseball and Hockey Leagues and Associations, the Executive Director of National Religious Broadcasters and various educational communications agencies. Plaintiffs attack the weight of the testimony offered and also contend that an injunction is warranted because infringing uses outweigh noninfringing uses.

Whatever the future percentage of legal versus illegal home-use recording might be, an injunction which seeks to deprive the public of the very tool or article of commerce capable of some noninfringing use would be an extremely harsh remedy, as well as one unprecedented in copyright law.

An injunction against the Betamax would be inefficient and unwise for other reasons. Its enforcement would be nearly impossible and in any event highly intrusive. The machines are in private homes. If defendants were ordered to recall these as plaintiffs request, this order would be unenforceable without extensive inquiry into the activities of Betamax owners in their homes.

As discussed above, this court finds that home-use recording of broadcast material is not an infringement, and that if it were, the corporate defendants would not be found liable for the activity. Even if the court had found otherwise, however, an injunction would not be issued. No likelihood of harm was shown at trial, and plaintiffs admitted that there had been no actual harm to date. Thus there is insufficient evidence to support a finding of harm adequate to sustain the drastic remedy of injunction. . . .

2. INDIVIDUAL AND VICARIOUS LIABILITY

It must always be remembered that copyright infringement is a tort. *Cf. Turton v. United States,* 212 F.2d 354, 101 USPQ 164 (6th Cir. 1954). Accordingly all persons participating therein are liable. In a typical case, this may include the publisher, printer, and vendor. *See American Code Co. v. Bensinger,* 282 Fed. 829 (2d Cir. 1922). But the net of liability may extend much farther — to those having a less direct involvement in the infringement as well as to individuals perpetrating the infringing acts on behalf of a corporate employer. And although absence of knowledge or intention may affect the shaping of remedies, it is not a defense. *See Latman & Tager, Liability of Innocent Infringers of Copyrights,* 2 STUDIES ON COPYRIGHT 1045 (Arthur Fisher Mem. ed. 1963).

Infringers are not merely those subject to rules of vicarious liability exemplified by the agency principle of *respondeat superior.* For reconfirmation under the 1976 Act, *see* H.R. Rep. No. 94-1476. It has been aptly stated:

> When the right and ability to supervise coalesce with an obvious and direct financial interest in the exploitation of copyrighted materials — even in the absence of actual knowledge that the copyright monopoly is being impaired [citations omitted] — the purposes of copyright law may be best effectuated by the imposition of liability upon the beneficiary of that exploitation.

Shapiro, Bernstein & Co., Inc. v. H.L. Green Co., 316 F.2d 304, 307, 137 USPQ 275, 277 (2d Cir. 1963).

In the *H.L. Green* case, the proprietor of a department store was held liable, along with its phonograph record concessionaire. This was consistent with a line of "ballroom cases," e.g., *Dreamland Ball Room, Inc. v. Shapiro, Bernstein & Co., Inc.,* 36 F.2d 354, 3 USPQ 288 (7th Cir. 1929), as well as related contexts, e.g., *Buck v. Jewell-LaSalle Realty Co.,* 283 U.S. 191, 9 USPQ 17 (1931), emphasizing that liability was not limited to intentional infringements or strict principal-agent situations.

In an effort to apply or extend this principle (often with a view toward finding more solvent defendants), plaintiffs have joined such entities as advertising agencies or radio stations on which allegedly piratical merchandise is advertised, . *Screen Gems-Columbia Music, Inc. v. Mark-Fi Records, Inc.,* 256 F. Supp. 399,

150 USPQ 523 (S.D.N.Y. 1966), as well as sponsors of allegedly infringing broad-casts. *Davis v. E.I. du Pont De Nemours & Co.*, 240 F. Supp. 612, 145 USPQ 258 (S.D.N.Y. 1965). *Cf. Rohauer v. Killiam Shows, Inc.*, 379 F. Supp. 723, 183 USPQ 592 (S.D.N.Y. 1974), *rev'd on other grounds,* 551 F.2d 484, 192 USPQ 545 (2d Cir. 1977), *cert. denied,* 431 U.S. 949, 194 USPQ 304 (1977).

In copyright cases, a corporate officer or employee personally involved in or directing the infringement is liable along with his or her corporation. *H.M. Kolbe Co., Inc. v. Shaff,* 240 F. Supp. 588, 145 USPQ 77 (S.D.N.Y. 1965), *aff'd,* 352 F.2d 285, 147 USPQ 336 (2d Cir. 1965). *Cf. Shapiro, Bernstein & Co., Inc. v. Gabor,* 266 F. Supp. 613, 152 USPQ 170 (S.D.N.Y. 1966) ("Harry Fox license" does not shield individual from tort liability where "license" not complied with).

In addition to the foregoing, a defendant may be liable for contributory infringement. While this doctrine in copyright cases is not as developed as it is in the patent law, *see* 35 U.S.C. § 271(b) and (c), it has been said that this is one area where knowledge is required, i.e., to be liable one must intentionally aid another to infringe. *See, e.g.,* 45 COLUM. L. REV. 644, 645 (1945). *Compare Harper v. Shoppell,* 26 Fed. 519 (S.D. N.Y.), *motion for new trial denied,* 28 Fed. 613 (1886), *with Kalem v. Harper Bros.,* 222 U.S. 55 (1911). The dimensions of this doctrine in copyright cases was, of course, explored in *Universal City Studios, Inc. v. Sony Corp.* at p. 495 *supra. Cf. Elektra Records Co. v. Gem Electronic Distributors, Inc.,* 360 F. Supp. 821, 179 USPQ 617 (E.D.N.Y. 1973).

3. DAMAGES

§ 504. Remedies for infringement: Damages and profits

(a) In General — Except as otherwise provided by this title, an infringer of copyright is liable for either —

(1) the copyright owner's actual damages and any additional profits of the infringer, as provided by subsection (b); or

(2) statutory damages, as provided by subsection (c).

(b) Actual Damages and Profits. — The copyright owner is entitled to recover the actual damages suffered by him or her as a result of the infringement, and any profits of the infringer that are attributable to the infringement and are not taken into account in computing the actual damages. In establishing the infringer's profits, the copyright owner is required to present proof only of the infringer's gross revenue, and the infringer is required to prove his or her deductible expenses and the elements of profit attributable to factors other than the copyrighted work.

. . . .

HOUSE REPORT

H.R. Rep. No. 94-1476, 94th Cong., 2d Sess. 161-63 (1976)

In general

A cornerstone of the remedies sections and of the bill as a whole is section 504, the provision dealing with recovery of actual damages, profits, and statutory damages. The two basic aims of this section are reciprocal and correlative: (1) to give the courts specific unambiguous directions concerning monetary awards, thus avoiding the confusion and uncertainty that have marked the present law on the subject, and, at the same time, (2) to provide the courts with reasonable latitude to adjust recovery to the circumstances of the case, thus avoiding some of the artificial or overly technical awards resulting from the language of the existing statute.

Subsection (a) lays the groundwork for the more detailed provisions of the section by establishing the liability of a copyright infringer for either "the copyright owner's actual damages and any additional profits of the infringer," or statutory damages. Recovery of actual damages and profits under section 504(b) or of statutory damages under section 504(c) is alternative and for the copyright owner to elect; as under the present law, the plaintiff in an infringement suit is not obliged to submit proof of damages and profits and may choose to rely on the provision for minimum statutory damages. However, there is nothing in section 504 to prevent a court from taking account of evidence concerning actual damages and profits in making an award of statutory damages within the range set out in subsection (c).

Actual damages and profits

In allowing the plaintiff to recover "the actual damages suffered by him or her as a result of the infringement," plus any of the infringer's profits "that are attributable to the infringement and are not taken into account in computing the actual damages," section 504(b) recognizes the different purposes served by awards of damages and profits. Damages are awarded to compensate the copyright owner for losses from the infringement, and profits are awarded to prevent the infringer from unfairly benefiting from a wrongful act. Where the defendant's profits are nothing more than a measure of the damages suffered by the copyright owner, it would be inappropriate to award damages and profits cumulatively, since in effect they amount to the same thing. However, in cases where the copyright owner has suffered damages not reflected in the infringer's profits, or where there have been profits attributable to the copyrighted work but not used as a measure of damages, subsection (b) authorizes the award of both.

The language of the subsection makes clear that only those profits "attributable to the infringement" are recoverable; where some of the defendant's profits result from the infringement and other profits are caused by different factors, it will be necessary for the court to make an apportionment. However, the burden of proof is on the defendant in these cases; in establishing profits the plaintiff need prove only "the infringer's gross revenue," and the defendant must prove not only "his or her deductible expenses" but also "the elements of profit attributable to factors other than the copyrighted work."

QUESTIONS

1. Give an example of a situation in which the plaintiff "has suffered damages not reflected in the infringer's profits."

2. Give an example of a situation in which "there have been profits attributable to the copyrighted work but not used as a measure of damages."

3. How would you go about proving damages in a copyright case? In other words, what financial harm could you show? How would you attempt to meet this proof as the defendant's attorney?

4. Suppose the defendant infringes plaintiff's copyright by embodying plaintiff's design for costume jewelry into gold jewelry. How should defendant's profits be apportioned so as to afford plaintiff an appropriate recovery? *See Sheldon v. Metro-Goldwyn Pictures Corp.,* 309 U.S. 390 (1940). In determining recoverable profits, is an allowance for overhead deductible? *See Sammons v. The Colonial Press, Inc.,* 126 F.2d 341, 348 (1st Cir. 1942). *Cf. Schnadig Corp. v. Gaines Mfg. Co.,* 620 F.2d 1166 (6th Cir. 1980).

5. Thomas Lace Company of New York and Nottingham manufactures and sells lace fabric principally for use in the ladies' lingerie field. For the 1980 spring season, Thomas received an order from Paramount Lingerie Company for an imported lace from England bearing a floral design for use in a girdle to be sold under a new Paramount trademark "THE YOUNG THING." Thomas copyrighted its design, called it "Pansy" and sold 100,000 yards to Paramount at a price of $1.25 per yard. Thomas sold "Pansy" to no one else but Paramount.

For the 1980 fall season, Paramount approached Jerome Lace Company and asked Jerome to produce a domestic lace which would have the look of the Thomas "Pansy" design. Jerome complied and Paramount proceeded to purchase 200,000 yards of the domestic Jerome lace at a price of $1.00 per yard. Paramount used the Jerome lace in its "THE YOUNG THING" line. Jerome also sold this lace only to Paramount.

When Thomas discovered that Jerome was supplying Paramount with a domestic lace, its President complained to Paramount, noting that if Paramount had told Thomas it wanted a domestic lace, Thomas could have supplied it. Thereupon Paramount placed an order with Thomas for an additional 400,000 yards of domestic lace at $1.10 per yard, but continued buying from Jerome, placing with the latter a second order for 100,000 yards.

Thomas' direct costs for its imported lace amounted to $1.05 per yard and for its domestic lace $.95 per yard. Thomas' overhead for the year amounted to $100,000. Its gross sales for the year amounted to $2,000,000.

The direct costs of Jerome for the domestic lace was $.85 per yard. Its overhead amounted to $50,000. Its gross sales were $500,000. Jerome sold 20 different patterns during the year.

What monetary relief should be awarded Thomas in the event of a finding of copyright infringement?

§ 504. Remedies for infringement: Damages and profits

. . . .

(c) Statutory Damages —

(1) Except as provided by clause (2) of this subsection, the copyright owner may elect, at any time before final judgment is rendered, to recover, instead of actual damages and profits, an award of statutory damages for all infringements involved in the action, with respect to any one work, for which any one infringer is liable individually, or for which any two or more infringers are liable jointly and severally, in a sum of not less than $250 or more than $10,000 as the court considers just. For the purposes of this subsection, all the parts of a compilation or derivative work constitute one work.

(2) In a case where the copyright owner sustains the burden of proving, and the court finds, that infringement was committed willfully, the court in its discretion may increase the award of statutory damages to a sum of not more than $50,000. In a case where the infringer sustains the burden of proving, and the court finds, that such infringer was not aware and had no reason to believe that his or her acts constituted an infringement of copyright, the court in its discretion may reduce the award of statutory damages to a sum of not less than $100. The court shall remit statutory damages in any case where an infringer believed and had reasonable grounds for believing that his or her use of the copyrighted work was a fair use under section 107, if the infringer was: (i) an employee or agent of a nonprofit educational institution, library, or archives acting within the scope of his or her employment who, or such institution, library, or archives itself, which infringed by reproducing the work in copies or phonorecords; or (ii) a public broadcasting entity which or a person who, as a regular part of the

nonprofit activities of a public broadcasting entity (as defined in subsection (g) of section 118) infringed by performing a published nondramatic literary work or by reproducing a transmission program embodying a performance of such a work.

HOUSE REPORT

H.R. Rep. No. 94-1476, 94th Cong., 2d Sess. 162-63 (1976)

Statutory damages

Subsection (c) of section 504 makes clear that the plaintiff's election to recover statutory damages may take place at any time during the trial before the court has rendered its final judgment. The remainder of clause (1) of the subsection represents a statement of the general rates applicable to awards of statutory damages. Its principal provisions may be summarized as follows:

1. As a general rule, where the plaintiff elects to recover statutory damages, the court is obliged to award between $250 and $10,000. It can exercise discretion in awarding an amount within that range but, unless one of the exceptions provided by clause (2) is applicable, it cannot make an award of less than $250 or of more than $10,000 if the copyright owner has chosen recovery under section 504(c).

2. Although, as explained below, an award of minimum statutory damages may be multiplied if separate works and separately liable infringers are involved in the suit, a single award in the $250 to $10,000 range is to be made "for all infringements involved in the action." A single infringer of a single work is liable for a single amount between $250 and $10,000, no matter how many acts of infringement are involved in the action and regardless of whether the acts were separate, isolated, or occurred in a related series.

3. Where the suit involves infringement of more than one separate and independent work, minimum statutory damages for each work must be awarded. For example, if one defendant has infringed three copyrighted works, the copyright owner is entitled to statutory damages of at least $750 and may be awarded up to $30,000. Subsection (c) (1) makes clear, however, that, although they are regarded as independent works for other purposes, "all the parts of a compilation or derivative work constitute one work" for this purpose. Moreover, although the minimum and maximum amounts are to be multiplied where multiple "works" are involved in the suit, the same is not true with respect to multiple copyrights, multiple owners, multiple exclusive rights, or multiple registrations. This point is especially important since, under a scheme of divisible copyright, it is possible to have the rights of a number of owners of separate "copyrights" in a single "work" infringed by one act of a defendant.

4. Where the infringements of one work were committed by a single infringer acting individually, a single award of statutory damages would be made. Similarly, where the work was infringed by two or more joint tortfeasors, the bill would make them jointly and severally liable for an amount in the $250 to $10,000 range. However, where separate infringements for which two or more defendants are not jointly liable are joined in the same action, separate awards of statutory damages would be appropriate.

Clause (2) of section 504(c) provides for exceptional cases in which the maximum award of statutory damages could be raised from $10,000 to $50,000, and in which the minimum recovery could be reduced from $250 to $100. The basic principle underlying this provision is that the courts should be given discretion to increase statutory damages in cases of willful infringement and to lower the minimum where the infringer is innocent. The language of the clause makes clear that in these situations the burden of proving willfulness rests on the copyright owner and that of proving innocence rests on the infringer, and that the court must make a finding of either willfulness or innocence in order to award the exceptional amounts.

The "innocent infringer" provision of section 504(c) (2) has been the subject of extensive discussion. The exception, which would allow the reduction of minimum statutory damages to $100 where the infringer "was not aware and had no reason to believe that his or her acts constituted an infringement of copyright," is sufficient to protect against unwarranted liability in cases of occasional or isolated innocent infringement, and it offers adequate insulation to users, such as broadcasters and newspaper publishers, who are particularly vulnerable to this type of infringement suit. On the other hand, by establishing a realistic floor for liability, the provision preserves its intended deterrent effect; and it would not allow an infringer to escape simply because the plaintiff failed to disprove the defendant's claim of innocence.

In addition to the general "innocent infringer" provision clause (2) deals with the special situation of teachers, librarians, archivists, and public broadcasters, and the nonprofit institutions of which they are a part. Section 504(c) (2) provides that, where such a person or institution infringes copyrighted material in the honest belief that what they were doing constituted fair use, the court is precluded from awarding any statutory damages. It is intended that, in cases involving this provision, the burden of proof with respect to the defendant's good faith should rest on the plaintiff.

QUESTIONS

1. Under what circumstances should a plaintiff elect statutory damages? At what point in the proceeding? Can the court decide to award statutory damages under the 1976 Act or is the election solely the plaintiff's?

2. Suppose a 1979 Christmas line of six plush toys infringes copyright by depicting a comic strip character in different poses. The 1980 Christmas line of the same manufacturer includes four different versions of the character. If a successful copyright infringement suit for statutory damages is brought against all these items in 1981, what is the maximum recovery?

4. COSTS AND ATTORNEY'S FEES

Both costs and attorney's fees are discretionary under § 505 of the 1976 Act, although registration may be required as a precondition for a discretionary award under § 412. See p. 303 supra.

Although an award to the "prevailing party" of "a reasonable attorney's fee as part of the costs" was discretionary under § 116 of the 1909 Act, the other elements of costs were mandatory, thus removing the latter from the operation of Rule 54(d) of the Federal Rules of Civil Procedure which permits discretion. See H.M. Kolbe Co. v. Armgus Textile Co., 315 F.2d 70, 137 USPQ 9 (2d Cir. 1963). Under both statutes, neither costs nor attorney's fees are available to or against the Government. See S. Rep. No. 94-473, supra at 145; H.R. Rep. No. 94-1476, supra at 163.

The 1976 Act continues the language "prevailing party" to describe the potential recipient of an attorney fee award. This can sometimes be a troublesome definition. See e.g., Shapiro, Bernstein & Co. v. 4636 S. Vermont Ave., Inc., 367

F.2d 236, 151 USPQ 231 (9th Cir. 1966). There is no statutory limitation to "exceptional cases" as in the patent law, 35 U.S.C. § 285, or the trademark law, 15 U.S.C. § 1117. *But cf. Ideal Toy Corp. v. J-Cey Doll Co.,* 290 F.2d 710, 129 USPQ 241 (2d Cir. 1961); *Rose v. Bourne,* 176 F. Supp. 605, 123 USPQ 29 (S.D.N.Y. 1959), *aff'd,* 279 F.2d 79, 125 USPQ 509 (2d Cir.), *cert. denied,* 364 U.S. 880, 127 USPQ 555 (1960) (penalty element important in fee awards and should not be made in bona fide dispute; $7,500 awarded).

In any event, it now seems acknowledged that a different standard is applied in determining whether to make an award to a successful plaintiff or a successful defendant. Although the former seems to enjoy something like an automatic surcharge, the latter may often have to show bad faith in the commencement or prosecution of the action. *See Davis v. E.I. du Pont de Nemours & Co.,* 257 F. Supp. 729, 732, 151 USPQ 36, 39 (S.D.N.Y. 1966).

In making the award, the court gives consideration to the importance of the questions involved, the amount of pecuniary damages, the value of the professional services rendered, and the success achieved. *Universal Film Co. v. Copperman,* 218 Fed. 577, 581, 582 n.1 (2d Cir. 1914). For a more elaborate statement of the elements to be considered, *see In re Osofsky,* 50 F.2d 925, 927 (S.D.N.Y. 1931). The amount awarded — to the successful party and not to the attorney — is often less than the amount of fees actually paid. Thus in the *du Pont* case, *supra,* 2,000 partner hours in arduous litigation yielded only $15,000. Cf. *Peter Pan Fabrics, Inc. v. Jobela Fabrics, Inc.,* 139 USPQ 368 (S.D.N.Y. 1963), *rev'd on other grounds,* 329 F.2d 194, 140 USPQ 631 (2d Cir. 1964) (150 partner hours/$2,250).

FEDERAL PREEMPTION OF STATE LAW

A. RIGHTS OUTSIDE COPYRIGHT

The intricacies of copyright explored in the preceding pages should not obscure the fact that we have been dealing with a narrow area of law. We need not dwell on the seamlessness of law or the obvious interfacing of copyright with contracts, tax, federal procedure, etc. We should note, however, the frequency with which a claimed interference with rights related to intellectual property cannot be fully articulated in terms of an infringement of copyright. Among the variety of legal theories potentially applicable, certain torts characteristically appear. It is our intention to furnish a glimpse into three of them — "passing off," misappropriation, and the right of publicity. Each of them is a field unto itself and is frequently explored in detail in advanced torts courses. Nothing more is attempted here than to suggest the contours of these torts through representative cases. We will then be in a position to study the extent to which state rights and remedies may be preempted by federal copyright.

The student has already been introduced to the tort commonly known as "passing off," particularly as it relates to the copying of the titles of literary works or the names of characters. *See* pp. 50-52, *supra*. A person is said to violate the law when he so promotes his goods or services as to create a likelihood that consumers will believe them to be (or be associated with) the goods or services of another. The purpose of the tort rule is to protect the reputation or goodwill of that other person and to protect the consuming public against confusion or deception. The application of the "passing off" theory to literary-property cases is rather straightforward.

It has been held, for example, that when a successful play entitled "The Gold Diggers" was made into a successful motion picture entitled "Gold Diggers of Broadway," it was unlawful for another to market a motion picture entitled "Gold Diggers of Paris" (at least without a conspicuous disclaimer that the picture was not based on the play or the earlier motion picture). *Warner Bros. Pictures, Inc. v. Majestic Pictures Corp.*, 70 F.2d 310 (2d Cir. 1934). It has also been unlawful to draw popular comic-strip characters, using their names, in comic-strip settings unauthorized by the creator of the characters; the court concluded that "the figures and names have been so connected with the [artist] as their originator or author that the use by another of new cartoons exploiting the characters . . . would be unfair to the public and to the plaintiff." *Fisher v. Star Co.*, 231 N.Y. 414, 132 N.E. 133, *cert. denied*, 257 U.S. 654 (1921) ("Mutt and Jeff").

In the two other state torts of pertinence to copyright, treated immediately below, the gist of the tort is something other than the "likelihood of confusion" which is essential to the tort of "passing off." In some instances, however, it is not easy to draw a sharp analytical line (witness the discussion of "deception" in the opinions in the *International News Service* case), but it may be necessary to draw such lines when it comes to determining whether a particular rule of state tort law survives preemption by virtue of the federal Copyright Act.

1. MISAPPROPRIATION

INTERNATIONAL NEWS SERVICE v. ASSOCIATED PRESS

248 U.S. 215 (1918)

MR. JUSTICE PITNEY delivered the opinion of the court.

The parties are competitors in the gathering and distribution of news and its publication for profit in newspapers throughout the United States. The Associated Press, which was complainant in the District Court, is a cooperative organization, incorporated under the Membership Corporations Law of the State of New York, its members being individuals who are either proprietors or representatives of about 950 daily newspapers published in all parts of the United States. That a corporation may be organized under that act for the purpose of gathering news for the use and benefit of its members and for publication in newspapers owned or represented by them, is recognized by an amendment enacted in 1901 (Laws N.Y. 1901, c. 436). Complainant gathers in all parts of the world, by means of various instrumentalities of its own, by exchange with its members, and by other appropriate means, news and intelligence of current and recent events of interest to newspaper readers and distributes it daily to its members for publication in their newspapers. The cost of the service, amounting approximately to $3,500,000 per annum, is assessed upon the members and becomes a part of their costs of operation, to be recouped, presumably with profit, through the publication of their several newspapers. Under complainant's by-laws each member agrees upon assuming membership that news received through complainant's service is received exclusively for publication in a particular newspaper, language, and place specified in the certificate of membership, that no other use of it shall be permitted, and that no member shall furnish or permit anyone in his employ or connected with his newspaper to furnish any of complainant's news in advance of publication to any person not a member. And each member is required to gather the local news of his district and supply it to the Associated Press and to no one else.

Defendant is a corporation organized under the laws of the State of New Jersey, whose business is the gathering and selling of news to its customers and clients, consisting of newspapers published throughout the United States, under contracts by which they pay certain amounts at stated times for defendant's service. It has wide-spread news-gathering agencies; the cost of its operations amounts, it is said, to more than $2,000,000 per annum; and it serves about 400 newspapers located in the various cities of the United States and abroad, a few of which are represented, also, in the membership of the Associated Press.

The parties are in the keenest competition between themselves in the distribution of news throughout the United States; and so, as a rule, are the newspapers that they serve, in their several districts. . . .

The bill was filed to restrain the pirating of complainant's news by defendant in three ways: First, by bribing employees of newspapers published by complainant's members to furnish Associated Press news to defendant before publication, for transmission by telegraph and telephone to defendant's clients for publication by them; Second, by inducing Associated Press members to violate its by-laws and permit defendant to obtain news before publication; and Third, by copying news from bulletin boards and from early editions of complainant's newspapers and selling this, either bodily or after rewriting it, to defendant's customers.

The District Court, upon consideration of the bill and answer, with voluminous affidavits on both sides, granted a preliminary injunction under the first and second heads; but refused at that stage to restrain the systematic practice admittedly pursued by defendant, of taking news bodily from the bulletin boards and early editions of complainant's newspapers and selling it as its own. The court expressed itself as satisfied that this practice amounted to unfair trade, but as the legal question was one of first impression it considered that the allowance of an injunction should await the outcome of an appeal. 240 Fed. Rep. 983, 996. Both parties having appealed, the Circuit Court of Appeals sustained the injunction order so far as it went, and upon complainant's appeal modified it and remanded the cause with directions to issue an injunction also against any bodily taking of the words or substance of complainant's news until its commercial value as news had passed away. 245 Fed. Rep. 244, 253. The present writ of certiorari was then allowed. 245 U.S. 644.

The only matter that has been argued before us is whether defendant may lawfully be restrained from appropriating news taken from bulletins issued by complainant or any of its members, or from newspapers published by them, for the purpose of selling it to defendant's clients. Complainant asserts that defendant's admitted course of conduct in this regard both violates complainant's property right in the news and constitutes unfair competition in business. And notwithstanding the case has proceeded only to the stage of a preliminary injunction, we have deemed it proper to consider the underlying questions, since they go to the very merits of the action and are presented upon facts that are not in dispute. As presented in argument, these questions are: 1. Whether there is any property in news; 2. Whether, if there be property in news collected for the purpose of being published, it survives the instant of its publication in the first newspaper to which it is communicated by the news-gatherer; and 3. Whether defendant's admitted course of conduct in appropriating for commercial use matter taken from bulletins or early editions of Associated Press publications constitutes unfair competition in trade.

The federal jurisdiction was invoked because of diversity of citizenship, not upon the ground that the suit arose under the copyright or other laws of the United States. Complainant's news matter is not copyrighted. It is said that it could not, in practice, be copyrighted, because of the large number of dispatches that are sent daily; and, according to complainant's contention, news is not within the operation of the copyright act. Defendant, while apparently conceding this, nevertheless invokes the analogies of the law of literary property and copyright, insisting as its principal contention that, assuming complainant has a right of property in its news, it can be maintained (unless the copyright act be complied with) only by being kept secret and confidential, and that upon the publication with complainant's consent of uncopyrighted news by any of complainant's members in a newspaper or upon a bulletin board, the right of property is lost, and the subsequent use of the news by the public, or by defendant for any purpose whatever becomes lawful. . . .

In considering the general question of property in news matter, it is necessary to recognize its dual character, distinguishing between the substance of the information and the particular form or collocation of words in which the writer has communicated it.

No doubt news articles often possess a literary quality, and are the subject of literary property at the common law; nor do we question that such an article, as a literary production, is the subject of copyright by the terms of the act as it now stands. . . .

But the news element — the information respecting current events contained in the literary production — is not the creation of the writer, but is a report of matters that ordinarily are *publici juris;* it is the history of the day. It is not to be supposed that the framers of the Constitution, when they empowered Congress "to promote the progress of science and useful arts, by securing for limited times to authors and inventors the exclusive right to their respective writings and discoveries" (Const., Art I, § 8, par. 8), intended to confer upon one who might happen to be the first to report a historic event the exclusive right for any period to spread the knowledge of it.

We need spend no time, however, upon the general question of property in news matter at common law, or the application of the copyright act, since it seems to us the case must turn upon the question of unfair competition in business. And, in our opinion, this does not depend upon any general right of property analogous to the common-law right of the proprietor of an unpublished work to prevent its publication without his consent; nor is it foreclosed by showing that the benefits of the copyright act have been waived. We are dealing here not with restrictions upon publication but with the very facilities and processes of publication. The peculiar value of news is in the spreading of it while it is fresh; and it is evident that a valuable property interest in the news, as news, cannot be maintained by keeping it secret. Besides, except for matters improperly disclosed, or published in breach of trust or confidence, or in violation of law, none of which is involved in this branch of the case, the news of current events may be regarded as common property. What we are concerned with is the business of making it known to the world, in which both parties to the present suit are engaged. That business consists in maintaining a prompt, sure, steady, and reliable service designed to place the daily events of the world at the breakfast table of the millions at a price that, while of trifling moment to each reader, is sufficient in the aggregate to afford compensation for the cost of gathering and distributing it, with the added profit so necessary as an incentive to effective action in the commercial world. The service thus performed for newspaper readers is not only innocent but extremely useful in itself, and indubitably constitutes a legitimate business. The parties are competitors in this field; and, on fundamental principles, applicable here as elsewhere, when the rights or privileges of the one are liable to conflict with those of the other, each party is under a duty so to conduct its own business as not unnecessarily or unfairly to injure that of the other. *Hitchman Coal & Coke Co. v. Mitchell,* 245 U. S. 229, 254.

Obviously, the question of what is unfair competition in business must be determined with particular reference to the character and circumstances of the business. The question here is not so much the rights of either party as against the public but their rights as between themselves. See *Morison v. Moat,* 9 Hare, 241, 258. And although we may and do assume that neither party has any remaining property interest as against the public in uncopyrighted news matter after the moment of its first publication, it by no means follows that there is no remaining property interest in it as between themselves. For, to both of them alike, news matter, however little susceptible of ownership or dominion in the absolute sense, is stock in trade, to be gathered at the cost of enterprise, organization, skill, labor, and money, and to be distributed and sold to those who will pay money for it, as for any other merchandise. Regarding the news, therefore, as but the material out of which both parties are seeking to make profits at the same time and in the same field, we hardly can fail to recognize that for this purpose, and as between them, it must be regarded as *quasi* property, irrespective of the rights of either as against the public. . . .

The question, whether one who has gathered general information or news at pains and expense for the purpose of subsequent publication through the press has such an interest in its publication as may be protected from interference, has been raised many times, although never, perhaps, in the precise form in which it is now presented. . . .

Not only do the acquisition and transmission of news require elaborate organization and a large expenditure of money, skill, and efforts; not only has it an exchange value to the gatherer, dependent chiefly upon its novelty and freshness, the regularity of the service, its reputed reliability and thoroughness, and its adaptability to the public needs; but also, as is evident, the news has an exchange value to one who can misappropriate it.

The peculiar features of the case arise from the fact that, while novelty and freshness form so important an element in the success of the business, the very processes of distribution and publication necessarily occupy a good deal of time. Complainant's service, as well as defendant's, is a daily service to daily newspapers; most of the foreign news reaches this country at the Atlantic seaboard, principally at the City of New York, and because of this, and of time differentials due to the earth's rotation, the distribution of news matter throughout the country is principally from east to west; and, since in speed the telegraph and telephone easily outstrip the rotation of the earth, it is a simple matter for defendant to take complainant's news from bulletins or early editions of complainant's members in the eastern cities and at the mere cost of telegraphic transmission cause it to be published in western papers issued at least as early as those served by complainant. Besides this, and irrespective of time differentials, irregularities in telegraphic transmission on different lines, and the normal consumption of time in printing and distributing the newspaper, result in permitting pirated news to be placed in the hands of defendant's readers sometimes simultaneously with the service of competing Associated Press papers, occasionally even earlier.

Defendant insists that when, with the sanction and approval of complainant, and as the result of the use of its news for the very purpose for which it is distributed, a portion of complainant's members communicate it to the general public by posting it upon bulletin boards so that all may read, or by issuing it to newspapers and distributing it indiscriminately, complainant no longer has the right to control the use to be made of it; that when it thus reaches the light of day it becomes the common possession of all to whom it is accessible; and that any purchaser of a newspaper has the right to communicate the intelligence which it contains to anybody and for any purpose, even for the purpose of selling it for profit to newspapers published for profit in competition with complainant's members.

The fault in the reasoning lies in applying as a test the right of the complainant as against the public, instead of considering the rights of complainant and defendant, competitors in business, as between themselves. The right of the purchaser of a single newspaper to spread knowledge of its contents gratuitously, for any legitimate purpose not unreasonably interfering with complainant's right to make merchandise of it, may be admitted; but to transmit that news for commercial use, in competition with complainant — which is what defendant has done and seeks to justify — is a very different matter. In doing this defendant, by its very act, admits that it is taking material that has been acquired by complainant as the result of organization and the expenditure of labor, skill, and money, and which is salable by complainant for money, and that defendant in appropriating it and selling it as its own is endeavoring to reap where it has not sown, and by disposing of it to newspapers that are competitors of complainant's members is appropriating to itself the harvest of those who have sown. Stripped of all disguises, the process amounts to an unauthorized interference with the normal operation of complainant's legitimate business precisely at the point where the profit is to be reaped, in order to divert a material portion of the profit from those who have earned it to those who have not; with special advantage to defendant in the competition because of the fact that it is not burdened with any part of the expense of gathering the news. The transaction speaks for itself, and a court of equity ought not to hesitate long in characterizing it as unfair competition in business. . . .

The contention that the news is abandoned to the public for all purposes when published in the first newspaper is untenable. Abandonment is a question of intent, and the entire organization of the Associated Press negatives such a purpose. . . . [P]ublication by each member must be deemed not by any means an abandonment of the news to the world for any and all purposes, but a publication for limited purposes; for the benefit of the readers of the bulletin or the newspaper as such; not for the purpose of making merchandise of it as news, with the result of depriving complainant's other members of their reasonable opportunity to obtain just returns for their expenditures.

It is to be observed that the view we adopt does not result in giving to complainant the right to monopolize either the gathering or the distribution of the news, or, without complying with the copyright act, to prevent the reproduction of its news articles; but only postpones participation by complainant's competitor in the processes of distribution and reproduction of news that it has not gathered, and only to the extent necessary to prevent that competitor from reaping the fruits of complainant's efforts and expenditure, to the partial exclusion of complainant, and in violation of the principle that underlies the maxim *sic utere tuo,* etc.

It is said that the elements of unfair competition are lacking because there is no attempt by defendant to palm off its goods as those of the complainant, characteristic of the most familiar, if not the most typical, cases of unfair competition. *Howe Scale Co. v. Wyckoff, Seamans & Benedict,* 198 U. S. 118, 140. But we cannot concede that the right to equitable relief is confined to that class of cases. In the present case the fraud upon complainant's rights is more direct and obvious. Regarding news matter as the mere material from which these two competing parties are endeavoring to make money, and treating it, therefore, as *quasi* property for the purposes of their business because they are both selling it as such, defendant's conduct differs from the ordinary case of unfair competition in trade principally in this that, instead of selling its own goods as those of complainant, it substitutes misappropriation in the place of misrepresentation, and sells complainant's goods as its own.

Besides the misappropriation, there are elements of imitation, of false pretense, in defendant's practices. The device of rewriting complainant's news articles, frequently resorted to, carries its own comment. The habitual failure to give credit to complainant for that which is taken is significant. Indeed, the entire system of appropriating complainant's news and transmitting it as a commercial product to defendant's clients and patrons amounts to a false representation to them and to their newspaper readers that the news transmitted is the result of defendant's own investigation in the field. But these elements, although accentuating the wrong, are not the essence of it. It is something more than the advantage of celebrity of which complainant is being deprived. . . .

There is some criticism of the injunction that was directed by the District Court upon the going down of the mandate from the Circuit Court of Appeals. In brief, it restrains any taking or gainfully using of the complainant's news, either bodily or in substance, from bulletins issued by the complainant or any of its members, or from editions of their newspapers, *"until its commercial value as news to the complainant and all of its members has passed away."* The part complained of is the clause we have italicized; but if this be indefinite, it is no more so than the criticism. Perhaps it would be better that the terms of the injunction be made specific, and so framed as to confine the restraint to an extent consistent with the reasonable protection of complainant's newspapers, each in its own area and for a specified time after its publication, against the competitive use of pirated news by defendant's customers. But the case presents practical difficulties; and we have not the materials, either in the way of a definite suggestion of amendment, or in the way of proofs, upon which to frame a specific injunction; hence, while not expressing approval of the form adopted by the District Court, we decline to modify it at this preliminary stage of the case, and will leave that court to deal with the matter upon appropriate application made to it for the purpose.

The decree of the Circuit Court of Appeals will be

Affirmed.

MR. JUSTICE CLARKE took no part in the consideration or decision of this case.

MR. JUSTICE HOLMES:

When an uncopyrighted combination of words is published there is no general right to forbid other people repeating them — in other words there is no property in the combination or in the thoughts or facts that the words express. Property, a creation of law, does not arise from value, although exchangeable — a matter of fact. Many exchangeable values may be destroyed intentionally without compensation. Property depends upon exclusion by law from interference, and a person is not excluded from using any combination of words merely because someone has used it before, even if it took labor and genius to make it. If a given person is to be prohibited from making the use of words that his neighbors are free to make some other ground must be found. One such ground is vaguely expressed in the phrase unfair trade. This means that the words are repeated by a competitor in business in such a way as to convey a misrepresentation that materially injures the person who first used them, by appropriating credit of some kind which the first user has earned. The ordinary case is a representation by device, appearance, or other indirection that the defendant's goods come from the plaintiff. But the only reason why it is actionable to make such a representation is that it tends to give the defendant an advantage in his competition with the plaintiff and that it is thought undesirable that an advantage should be gained in that way. Apart from that the defendant may use such unpatented devices and uncopyrighted combinations of words as he likes. The ordinary case, I say, is palming off the defendant's product as the plaintiff's, but the same evil may follow from the opposite falsehood — from saying, whether in words or by implication, that the plaintiff's product is the defendant's, and that, it seems to me, is what has happened here.

Fresh news is got only by enterprise and expense. To produce such news as it is produced by the defendant represents by implication that it has been acquired by the defendant's enterprise and at its expense. When it comes from one of the great news-collecting agencies like the Associated Press, the source generally is indicated, plainly importing that credit; and that such a representation is implied may be inferred with some confidence from the unwillingness of the defendant to give the credit and tell the truth. If the plaintiff produces the news at the same time that the defendant does, the defendant's presentation impliedly denies to the plaintiff the credit of collecting the facts and assumes that credit to the defendant. If the plaintiff is later in western cities it naturally will be supposed to have obtained its information from the defendant. The falsehood is a little more subtle, the injury a little more indirect, than in ordinary cases of unfair trade, but I think that the principle that condemns the one condemns the other. It is a question of how strong an infusion of fraud is necessary to turn a flavor into a poison. The dose seems to me strong enough here to need a remedy from the law. But as, in my view, the only ground of complaint that can be recognized without legislation is the implied misstatement, it can be corrected by stating the truth; and a suitable acknowledgment of the source is all that the plaintiff can require. I think that within the limits recognized by the decision of the Court the defendant should be enjoined from publishing news obtained from the Associated Press for   hours after publication by the plaintiff unless it gives express credit to the Associated Press; the number of hours and the form of acknowledgment to be settled by the District Court.

Mr. Justice McKenna concurs in this opinion.

Mr. Justice Brandeis dissenting. . . .

[T]he fact that a product of the mind has cost its producer money and labor, and has a value for which others are willing to pay, is not sufficient to ensure to it this legal attribute of property. The general rule of law is, that the noblest of human productions — knowledge, truths ascertained, conceptions, and ideas — become, after voluntary communication to others, free as the air to common use. Upon these incorporeal productions the attribute of property is continued after such communication only in certain classes of cases where public policy has seemed to demand it. These exceptions are confined to productions which, in some degree, involve creation, invention, or discovery. But by no means all such are endowed with this attribute of property. The creations which are recognized as property by the common law are literary, dramatic, musical, and other artistic creations; and these have also protection under the copyright statutes. The inventions and discoveries upon which this attribute of property is conferred only by statute, are the few comprised within the patent law. There are also many other cases in which courts interfere to prevent curtailment of plaintiff's enjoyment of incorporeal productions; and in which the right to relief is often called a property right, but is such only in a special sense. In those cases, the plaintiff has no absolute right to the protection of his production; he has merely the qualified right to be protected as against the defendant's acts, because of the special relation in which the latter stands or the wrongful method or means employed in acquiring the knowledge or the manner in which it is used. Protection of this character is afforded where the suit is based upon breach of contract or of trust or upon unfair competition.

The knowledge for which protection is sought in the case at bar is not of a kind upon which the law has heretofore conferred the attributes of property; nor is the manner of its acquisition or use nor the purpose to which it is applied, such as has heretofore been recognized as entitling a plaintiff to relief.

First: Plaintiff's principal reliance was upon the "ticker" cases; but they do not support its contention. The leading cases on this subject rest the grant of relief, not upon the existence of a general property right in news, but upon the breach of a contract or trust concerning the use of news communicated; and that element is lacking here. . . .

If the news involved in the case at bar had been posted in violation of any agreement between the Associated Press and its members, questions similar to those in the "ticker" cases might have arisen. But the plaintiff does not contend that the posting was wrongful or that any papers were wrongfully issued by its subscribers. On the contrary it is conceded that both the bulletins and the papers were issued in accordance with the regulations of the plaintiff. Under such circumstances, for a reader of the papers purchased in the open market, or a reader of the bulletins publicly posted, to procure and use gainfully, information therein contained, does not involve inducing anyone to commit a breach either of contract or of trust, or committing or in any way abetting a breach of confidence.

Second: Plaintiff also relied upon the cases which hold that the common-law right of the producer to prohibit copying is not lost by the private circulation of a literary composition, the delivery of a lecture, the exhibition of a painting, or the performance of a dramatic or musical composition. These cases rest upon the ground that the common law recognizes such productions as property which, despite restricted communication, continues until there is a dedication to the public under the copyright statutes or otherwise. But they are inapplicable for two reasons. (1) At common law, as under the copyright acts, intellectual productions are entitled to such protection only if there is underneath something evincing the mind of a creator or originator, however modest the requirement. The mere record of isolated happenings, whether in words or by photographs not involving artistic skill, are denied such protection. (2) At common law, as under the copyright acts, the element in intellectual productions which secures such protection is not the knowledge, truths, ideas, or emotions which the composition expresses, but the form or sequence in which they are expressed; that is, "some new collocation of visible or audible points, — of lines, colors, sounds, or words." See *White-Smith Music Co. v. Apollo Co.,* 209 U. S. 1, 19; *Kalem Co. v. Harper Brothers,* 222 U. S. 55, 63. An author's theories, suggestions, and speculations, or the systems, plans, methods, and arrangements of an originator, derive no such protection from the statutory copyright of the book in which they are set forth; and they are likewise denied such protection at common law.

. . . .

Third: If news be treated as possessing the characteristics not of a trade secret, but of literary property, then the earliest issue of a paper of general circulation or the earliest public posting of a bulletin which embodies such news would, under the established rules governing literary property, operate as a publication, and all property in the news would then cease. Resisting this conclusion, plaintiff relied upon the cases which hold that uncopyrighted intellectual and artistic property survives private circulation or a restricted publication; and it contended that in each issue of each paper, a restriction is to be implied that the news shall not be used gainfully in competition with the Associated Press or any of its members. There is no basis for such an implication. But it is also well settled that where the publication is in fact a general one, even express words of restriction upon use are inoperative. In other words, a general publication is effective to dedicate literary property to the public, regardless of the actual intent of its owner. In the cases dealing with lectures, dramatic and musical performances, and art exhibitions, upon which plaintiff relied, there was no general publication in print comparable to the issue of daily newspapers or the unrestricted public posting of bulletins. The principles governing those cases differ more or less in application, if not in theory, from the principles governing the issue of printed copies; and in so far as they do differ, they have no application to the case at bar.

Fourth: Plaintiff further contended that defendant's practice constitutes unfair competition, because there is "appropriation without cost to itself of values created by" the plaintiff; and it is upon this ground that the decision of this court appears to be based. To appropriate and use for profit, knowledge and ideas produced   by   other   men,   without   making   compensation   or   even acknowledgment, may be inconsistent with a finer sense of propriety; but, with the exceptions indicated above, the law has heretofore sanctioned the practice. Thus it was held that one may ordinarily make and sell anything in any form, may copy with exactness that which another has produced, or may otherwise use his ideas without his consent and without the payment of compensation, and yet not inflict a legal injury; and that ordinarily one is at perfect liberty to find out, if he can by lawful means, trade secrets of another, however valuable, and then use the knowledge so acquired gainfully, although it cost the original owner much in effort and in money to collect or produce.

Such taking and gainful use of a product of another which, for reasons of public policy, the law has refused to endow with the attributes of property, does not become unlawful because the product happens to have been taken from a rival and is used in competition with him. The unfairness in competition which hitherto has been recognized by the law as a basis for relief, lay in the manner or means of conducting the business; and the manner or means held legally unfair, involves either fraud or force or the doing of acts otherwise prohibited by law. In the "passing off" cases (the typical and most common case of unfair competition), the wrong consists in fraudulently representing by word or act that defendant's goods are those of plaintiff. See *Hanover Milling Co. v. Metcalf,* 240 U. S. 403, 412-413. In the other cases, the diversion of trade was effected through physical or moral coercion, or by inducing breaches of contract or of trust or by enticing away employees. In some others, called cases of simulated competition, relief was granted because defendant's purpose was unlawful; namely, not competition but deliberate and wanton destruction of plaintiff's business.

That competition is not unfair in a legal sense, merely because the profits gained are unearned, even if made at the expense of a rival, is shown by many cases besides those referred to above. He who follows the pioneer into a new market, or who engages in the manufacture of an article newly introduced by another, seeks profits due largely to the labor and expense of the first adventurer; but the law sanctions, indeed encourages, the pursuit. He who makes a city known through his product, must submit to sharing the resultant trade with others who, perhaps for that reason, locate there later. *Canal Co. v. Clark,* 13 Wall. 311; *Elgin National Watch Co. v. Illinois Watch Co.,* 179 U. S. 665, 673. He who has made his name a guaranty of quality, protests in vain when another with the same name engages, perhaps for that reason, in the same lines of business; provided, precaution is taken to prevent the public from being deceived into the belief that what he is selling was made by his competitor. One bearing a name made famous by another is permitted to enjoy the unearned benefit which necessarily flows from such use, even though the use proves harmful to him who gave the name value. *Brown Chemical Co. v. Meyer,* 139 U. S. 540, 544; *Howe Scale Co. v. Wyckoff, Seamans & Benedict,* 198 U. S. 118; *Donnell v. Herring-Hall-Marvin Safe Co.,* 208 U. S. 267; *Waterman Co. v. Modern Pen Co.,* 235 U. S. 88. See *Saxlehner v. Wagner,* 216 U. S. 375.

The means by which the International News Service obtains news gathered by the Associated Press is also clearly unobjectionable. It is taken from papers bought in the open market or from bulletins publicly posted. No breach of contract such as the court considered to exist in *Hitchman Coal & Coke Co. v. Mitchell,* 245 U. S. 229, 254; or of trust such as was present in *Morison v. Moat,* 9 Hare, 241; and neither fraud nor force, is involved. The manner of use is likewise unobjectionable. No reference is made by word or by act to the Associated Press, either in transmitting the news to subscribers or by them in publishing it in their papers. Neither the International News Service nor its subscribers is gaining or seeking to gain in its business a benefit from the reputation of the Associated Press. They are merely using its product without making compensation. See *Bamforth v. Douglass Post Card & Machine Co.,* 158 Fed. Rep. 355; *Tribune Co. of Chicago v. Associated Press,* 116 Fed. Rep. 126. That, they have a legal right to do; because the product is not property, and they do not stand in any relation to the Associated Press, either of contract or of trust, which otherwise precludes such use. The argument is not advanced by characterizing such taking and use a misappropriation.

It is also suggested, that the fact that defendant does not refer to the Associated Press as the source of the news may furnish a basis for the relief. But the defendant and its subscribers, unlike members of the Associated Press, were under no contractual obligation to disclose the source of the news; and there is no rule of law requiring acknowledgment to be made where uncopyrighted matter is reproduced. The International News Service is said to mislead its subscribers into believing that the news transmitted was originally gathered by it and that they in turn mislead their readers. There is, in fact, no representation by either of any kind. Sources of information are sometimes given because required by contract; sometimes because naming the source gives authority to an otherwise incredible statement; and sometimes the source is named because the agency does not wish to take the responsibility itself of giving currency to the news. But no representation can properly be implied from omission to mention the source of information except that the International News Service is transmitting news which it believes to be credible.

Nor is the use made by the International News Service of the information taken from papers or bulletins of Associated Press members legally objectionable by reason of the purpose for which it was employed. The acts here complained of were not done for the purpose of injuring the business of the Associated Press. Their purpose was not even to divert its trade, or to put it at a disadvantage by lessening defendant's necessary expenses. The purpose was merely to supply subscribers of the International News Service promptly with all available news. . . . There is in defendant's purpose nothing on which to base a claim for relief.

Fifth: The great development of agencies now furnishing country-wide distribution of news, the vastness of our territory, and improvements in the means of transmitting intelligence, have made it possible for a news agency or newspapers to obtain, without paying compensation, the fruit of another's efforts and to use news so obtained gainfully in competition with the original collector. The injustice of such action is obvious. But to give relief against it would involve more than the application of existing rules of law to new facts. It would require the making of a new rule in analogy to existing ones. The unwritten law possesses capacity for growth; and has often satisfied new demands for justice by invoking analogies or by expanding a rule or principle. This process has been in the main wisely applied and should not be discontinued. Where the problem is relatively simple, as it is apt to be when private interests only are involved, it generally proves adequate. But with the increasing complexity of society, the public interest tends to become omnipresent; and the problems presented by new demands for justice cease to be simple. Then the creation or recognition by courts of a new private right may work serious injury to the general public, unless the boundaries of the right are definitely established and wisely guarded. In order to reconcile the new private right with the public interest, it may be necessary to prescribe limitations and rules for its enjoyment; and also to provide administrative machinery for enforcing the rules. It is largely for this reason that, in the effort to meet the many new demands for justice incident to a rapidly changing civilization, resort to legislation has latterly been had with increasing frequency. . . .

A legislature, urged to enact a law by which one news agency or newspaper may prevent appropriation of the fruits of its labors by another, would consider such facts and possibilities and others which appropriate enquiry might disclose. Legislators might conclude that it was impossible to put an end to the obvious injustice involved in such appropriation of news, without opening the door to other evils, greater than that sought to be remedied. Such appears to have been the opinion of our Senate which reported unfavorably a bill to give news a few hours' protection; and which ratified, on February 15, 1911, the convention adopted at the Fourth International American Conference; and such was evidently the view also of the signatories to the International Copyright Union of November 13, 1908; as both these conventions expressly exclude news from copyright protection. . . .

Courts are ill-equipped to make the investigations which should precede a determination of the limitations which should be set upon any property right in news or of the circumstances under which news gathered by a private agency should be deemed affected with a public interest. Courts would be powerless to prescribe the detailed regulations essential to full enjoyment of the rights conferred or to introduce the machinery required for enforcement of such regulations. Considerations such as these should lead us to decline to establish a new rule of law in the effort to redress a newly-disclosed wrong, although the propriety of some remedy appears to be clear.

METROPOLITAN OPERA ASSOCIATION v. WAGNER-NICHOLS RECORDER CORP.

199 Misc. 787, 101 N.Y.S.2d 483 (Sup. Ct. 1950), *aff'd*, 279 App. Div. 632, 107 N.Y.S.2d 795 (1st Dep't 1951)

GREENBERG, JUSTICE.

The plaintiffs Metropolitan Opera Association, Inc. (hereinafter referred to as "Metropolitan Opera"), and American Broadcasting Company, Inc. (hereinafter referred to as "American Broadcasting"), and the intervening plaintiff, Columbia Records, Inc. (hereinafter referred to as "Columbia Records"), move for a preliminary injunction to restrain the defendants from recording, advertising, selling or distributing musical performances of Metropolitan Opera broadcast over the air, and from using the name "Metropolitan Opera" or any similar name which is calculated to mislead the public into believing that the records sold by the defendants are records of performances made or sold under the control or supervision or with the consent of the plaintiffs.

The defendants, by cross-motion, seek [a] dismissal of the complaints on the ground that they fail to state facts sufficient to constitute a cause of action and are insufficient as matter of law. . . .

The complaints of the plaintiffs allege in substance:

Metropolitan Opera is an educational membership corporation. Over a period of sixty years it has, by care, skill and great expenditure, maintained a position of pre-eminence in the field of music and grand opera. By reason of this skill and pre-eminence it has created a national and worldwide audience and thereby a large market for radio broadcasts and phonograph recordings of its performances. Metropolitan Opera has sold the exclusive right to broadcast its performances and the exclusive right to record its performances, as set forth below, and uses the proceeds to defray part of its operating expenses.

It has sold the exclusive right to make and sell phonograph records of its operatic performances and to use the names "Metropolitan Opera Orchestra," "Metropolitan Opera Chorus" and any other names identified with Metropolitan in connection with these phonograph records to Columbia Records, which has acquired a reputation and good will of great value. This contract is for a five-year period ending December 31, 1951. The exclusive nature of these rights is of the essence of the contract. In payment for these exclusive rights Metropolitan Opera receives royalties on records sold, with a guaranteed minimum of $125,000 during the five-year term of the contract. Columbia Records is required to pay the entire cost of each performance of an opera which it records. Metropolitan Opera has reserved to itself the right to approve all phonograph records of its performances before they may be offered for sale to the public.

Pursuant to this contract Metropolitan Opera's performances of three operas have been recorded and are now being offered for sale and sold. Columbia Records has incurred very substantial expenses in making these recordings and in preparing for the recording of additional operas, and it has extensively advertised the records and its exclusive right to record Metropolitan Opera performances.

Metropolitan Opera has sold the exclusive right to broadcast its opera performances during the 1949-50 season to American Broadcasting, for which Metropolitan Opera receives $100,000. Under this contract American Broadcasting is prohibited from making recordings of such performances except for certain limited purposes related to broadcasting. Negotiations for a similar contract for the 1950-51 and 1951-52 opera seasons are in progress. Under the contract for the 1949-50 season, American Broadcasting broadcast Metropolitan Opera performances of eighteen operas between November 26, 1949, and March 25, 1950.

Since November 26, 1949, the defendants have recorded these broadcast performances of Metropolitan Opera and have used their master recordings to make phonograph records of Metropolitan Opera performances. The defendants have advertised and sold these records as records of broadcast Metropolitan Opera performances. By reason of this publicity and the reputation of Metropolitan Opera, these records have aroused wide interest. Since the defendants, unlike Columbia Records, pay no part of the cost of the performance of the operas and are held to no standard of artistic or technical excellence, they incur only the very small cost of recording these performances "off the air." The quality of their recordings is inferior to that of Columbia Records and is so low that Metropolitan Opera would not have approved the sale and release of such records to the general public. By reason of their negligible costs, defendants are able in competition with Columbia Records to sell their records at considerably less than those of the latter, with a consequent loss of revenue to Columbia Records and Metropolitan Opera. . . .

The defendants urge that the complaints fail to state a cause of action in that they do not allege the defendants are "palming off" their recordings as those of plaintiffs, or that plaintiffs are in competition with the defendants. They further urge that plaintiffs have no property right in the broadcast performances and that the defendants are therefore free to record these performances and sell their recordings.

The defendants' cross-motion attacking the complaints must necessarily be considered first.

In passing upon the question of the sufficiency of a complaint alleging unfair competition it is helpful to bear in mind the origin and evolution of this branch of law. It originated in the conscience, justice and equity of common-law judges. It developed within the framework of a society dedicated to freest competition, to deal with business malpractices offensive to the ethics of that society. The theoretic basis is obscure, but the birth and growth of this branch of law is clear. It is an outstanding example of the law's capacity for growth in response to the ethical as well as the economic needs of society. As a result of this background the legal concept of unfair competition has evolved as a broad and flexible doctrine with a capacity for further growth to meet changing conditions. There is no complete list of the activities which constitute unfair competition (Nims, Unfair Competition and Trademarks, 4th ed., 1947, Chaps. I and II; Handler, Unfair Competition, 21 Iowa L. Rev., p. 175; Schechter, The Rational Basis of Trademark Protection, 40 Harv.L.Rev. 813).

The statement of a suffcent cause of action in unfair competition, in the last analysis, is therefore dependent more upon the facts set forth and less upon technical requirements than in most causes of action. This may best be illustrated by a consideration of the objections raised by the defendants.

The defendants contend that no cause of action is stated due to the absence of an allegation of "palming off." One of the inferences which may fairly be drawn from the allegations of the complaint and the prayers for relief is that the activities of the defendants appropriate and trade on the name and reputation of Metropolitan Opera and tend to mislead the public into believing the recordings are made with the co-operation of Metropolitan Opera and under its supervision. However, even in the absence of such an inference the failure to allege "palming off" would not be a fatal defect. The early cases of unfair competition in which relief was granted were cases involving "palming off" — that is, 'the fraudulent representation of the goods of the seller as those of another. The early decisions condemning this practice were based on the two wrongs inflicted thereby: (1) The deceit and fraud on the public; and (2) the misappropriation to one person of the benefit of a name, reputation or business good will belonging to another. *Taylor v. Carpenter,* 3 Fed.Cas. page 742, No. 13,784, 3 Story 458, D. Mass. 1844; *Howard v. Henriques,* 5 N.Y. Super. Ct. 725, 1851.

With the passage of those simple and halcyon days when the chief business malpractice was "palming off" and with the development of more complex business relationships and, unfortunately, malpractices, many courts, including the courts of this state, extended the doctrine of unfair competition beyond the cases of "palming off." The extension resulted in the granting of relief in cases where there was no fraud on the public, but only a misappropriation for the commercial advantage of one person of a benefit or "property right" belonging to another. . . .

The significance and limits of [*International News Serv. v. Associated Press*] have been widely discussed. That it extended the doctrine of unfair competition to cases based on misappropriation of property has been accepted by the leading authorities. Chief Justice Hughes in *A. L. A. Schechter Poultry Corporation, et al. v. United States,* 295 U.S. 495, at page 531, stated: ". . . 'Unfair competition,' as known to the common law, is a limited concept. Primarily, and strictly, it relates to the palming off of one's goods as those of a rival trader. . . . In recent years, its scope has been extended. It has been held to apply to misappropriation as well as misrepresentation, to the selling of another's goods as one's own — to misappropriation of what equitably belongs to a competitor. *International News Service v. Associated Press,* 248 U.S. 215, 241, 242."

The doctrine of extending unfair competition beyond cases of "palming off" has similarly been recognized and applied by the courts of this state. . . .

The defendants also raise the objection that the complaint does not include an allegation that the parties are actual competitors. This objection is rendered untenable by the intervention of Columbia Records. However, again, the existence of actual competition between the parties is no longer a prerequisite. . . .

The modern view as to the law of unfair competition does not rest solely on the ground of direct competitive injury, but on the broader principle that property rights of commercial value are to be and will be protected from any form of unfair invasion or infringement and from any form of commercial immorality, and a court of equity will penetrate and restrain every guise resorted to by the wrongdoer. The courts have thus recognized that in the complex pattern of modern business relationships, persons in theoretically non-competitive fields may, by unethical business practices, inflict as severe and reprehensible injuries upon others as can direct competitors. That defendants' piratical conduct and practices have injured and will continue to injure plaintiff admits of no serious challenge, and possible money damages furnishes no adequate remedy. That such practices constitute unfair competition both with Metropolitan Opera and Columbia Records is made abundantly clear by the record. Plaintiff Metropolitan Opera derives income from the performance of its operatic productions in the presence of an audience, from the broadcasting of those productions over the radio, and from the licensing to Columbia Records of the exclusive privilege of making and selling records of its own performances. Columbia Records derives income from the sale of the records which it makes pursuant to the license granted to it by Metropolitan Opera. Without any payment to Metropolitan Opera for the benefit of its extremely expensive performances, and without any cost comparable to that incurred by Columbia Records in making its records, defendants offer to the public recordings of Metropolitan Opera's broadcast performances. This constitutes unfair competition. *International News Service v. Associated Press,* 248 U.S. 215.

The New York courts have applied the rule in the International News Service case in such a wide variety of circumstances as to leave no doubt of their recognition that the effort to profit from the labor, skill, expenditures, name and reputation of others which appears in this case constitutes unfair competition which will be enjoined. . . .

The defendants raise the further objection that the complaints fail to state a cause of action in that they set forth no property rights of the plaintiffs. Clearly, some property rights in the plaintiffs and interference with and misappropriation of them by defendants are necessary to a cause of action. However, "property rights," as has often been pointed out, are rights which are recognized and protected by the courts by excluding others therefrom. The designation is therefore more in the nature of a legal conclusion than a description.

The rights which the plaintiffs allege in their complaint are:

(1) The right of Metropolitan Opera to exclusive use, directly or indirectly, of the name and reputation which it has developed over a sixty-year period.

(2) The exclusive right of Metropolitan Opera to the productions which it creates by the use of its skill, artists, money and the organization it has developed.

(3) As a corollary of the latter the exclusive right to license the use of its performances and productions commercially in radio broadcasts, recordings and in other forms upon such terms as are agreed upon as to payments and the maintenance of artistic and technical standards in accord with the reputation of the Metropolitan Opera.

(4) The rights of plaintiffs Columbia Records and American Broadcasting being their exclusive recording and broadcasting rights derived from their agreements with Metropolitan Opera for which they have paid and in which they have invested substantial sums of money, time and skill.

The question presented is thus whether these rights are rights which the courts have recognized and protected and should recognize and protect as "property rights."

The Court of Appeals in *Fisher v. Star Company,* 231 N.Y. 414, 132 N.E. 133, 19 A.L.R. 937, quoted with approval the broad definition of property rights laid down by the Supreme Court of the United States in the *International News Service* case, supra, 231 N.Y. at page 429, 132 N.E. at page 137, 19 A.L.R. 937: " '... The rule that a court of equity concerns itself only in the protection of property rights treats any civil right of a pecuniary nature as a property right. ... And the right to acquire property by honest labor or the conduct of a lawful business is as much entitled to protection as the right to guard property already acquired. ... It is this right that furnishes the basis of the jurisdiction in the ordinary case of unfair competition.' "

The right to the exclusive use of one's own name and reputation has long been recognized by the courts, as evidenced by the early protection of trade marks and trade names, and the "palming off" cases, *Maison Prunier v. Prunier's Restaurant & Cafe, Inc.,* supra.

The law has also, as Justice Brandeis points out in his dissent in the *International News Service* case, supra, protected the creative element in intellectual productions — that is, the form or sequence of expression, the new combination of colors, sounds or words presented by the production. The production of an opera by an opera company of great skill, involving as it does, the engaging and development of singers, orchestra, the training of a large chorus and the blending of the whole by expert direction into a finished interpretative production would appear to involve such a creative element as the law will recognize and protect against appropriation by others.

The performance of the opera in the opera house and the broadcast of the opera performance over the network of American Broadcasting under an exclusive broadcasting contract with Metropolitan Opera did not abandon the plaintiffs' rights to this performance. At common law the public performance of a play, exhibition of a picture or sale of a copy of the film for public presentation did not constitute an abandonment of nor deprive the owner of his common-law rights. *Palmer v. DeWitt,* 47 N.Y. 532; *Ferris v. Frohman,* 223 U.S. 424; *American Tobacco Co. v. Werckmeister,* 207 U.S. 284; *Universal Film Mfg. Co. v. Copperman,* 2 Cir., 218 F. 577. In the *International News Service* case, supra, the court in discussing this question of publication and abandonment stated 248 U.S. at pages 240-241: "The contention that the news is abandoned to the public for all purposes when published in the first newspaper is untenable. Abandonment is a question of intent, and the entire organization of the Associated Press negatives such a purpose. The cost of the service would be prohibitive if the reward were to be so limited. ... Their [by-laws] effect is that publication by each member must be deemed not by any means an abandonment of the news to the world for any and all purposes, but a publication for limited purposes; for the benefit of the readers of the bulletin or the newspaper as such; not for the purpose of making merchandise of it as news, with the result of depriving complainant's other members of their reasonable opportunity to obtain just returns for their expenditures."

In the light of these cases the performance of operas by Metropolitan Opera and their broadcast over the network of American Broadcasting cannot be deemed a general publication or abandonment so as to divest Metropolitan Opera of all of its rights to the broadcast performances. The care with which the Metropolitan Opera made its limited grants, granting exclusive right to a single network and restricting the latter's right to record and granting exclusive rights to record to Columbia Records, again reserving the right to approve all records before their release, shows clearly no intent to abandon but, on the contrary, an attempt to retain effective control over the broadcasting and recording of its performances. The fact that performances to-day can take place over the radio as well as in the theatre and thereby reach a wider audience does not change the principle involved. The publication in this case is certainly no wider nor more unlimited than the publication of news in Associated Press member newspapers and bulletins which was held by the Supreme Court of the United States to constitute limited publication.

Rights of a similar nature have been repeatedly recognized and upheld by the courts. As has been stated before, the doctrine is a broad and flexible one. It has allowed the courts to keep pace with constantly changing technological and economic aspects so as to reach just and realistic results.

In *Fisher v. Star Company,* supra, the Court of Appeals, after quoting the broad definition of a property right by the Supreme Court of the United States, upheld the exclusive right of a cartoonist to the use of cartoon characters he had created in the newspapers. The court enjoined the defendants from using "Mutt and Jeff" in connection with cartoons not drawn by the plaintiff. The reasoning of the court is of interest. It stated 231 N.Y. at page 433, 132 N.E. at page 139, 19 A.L.R. 937: "If appellant's employees can so imitate the work of the respondent that the admirers of 'Mutt and Jeff' will purchase the papers containing the imitations of the respondent's work, it may result in the public tiring of the 'Mutt and Jeff' cartoons by reason of inferior imitations or otherwise, and in any case in financial damage to the respondent and an unfair appropriation of his skill and the celebrity acquired by him in originating, producing and maintaining the characters and figures so as to continue the demand for further cartoons in which they appear." The reasoning is also applicable to the instant case.

In *Rudolph Mayer Pictures, Inc. v. Pathe News, Inc.,* [235 App. Div. 774, 255 N.Y.S. 1016], the court protected the exclusive right which plaintiff had obtained from the Dodger Athletic Club, lessee of Ebbets Field, to take and sell motion pictures of the Sharkey-Walker contest. The court affirmed without opinion a preliminary injunction enjoining the defendants from distributing pictures it had taken of the boxing match. The court in its later decision in *Madison Square Garden Corporation v. Universal Pictures, Inc.,* supra, referring to this case, stated 255 App.Div. at page 465, 7 N.Y.S.2d at page 851: ". . . Defendants argued that plaintiffs had no property right which could be protected; that the right to take photographs of a boxing match was not a form of property known to the law, and that defendants' acts did not constitute unfair competition. In overruling these contentions, we necessarily held that the defendants had violated a property right and should be enjoined."

There is no reason apparent to this court why the rights of a nonprofit organization sponsoring one of the arts should receive less protection than those of the sponsor of sporting events. The law at least regards both these diverse facets of human endeavor with impartial and approving judgment. The fostering and encouragement of fine performances of grand opera, and their preservation and dissemination to wide audiences by radio and recordings are in the public interest. The Metropolitan Opera, over a period of sixty years, has developed one of the finest, if not the finest, opera companies available to Americans. Through the media of recordings and broadcasts, an avenue of culture has been opened to vast numbers of Americans who have been able to enjoy the fruits of this great enterprise. To many, it is the only available source of grand opera. To refuse to the groups who expend time, effort, money and great skill in producing these artistic performances the protection of giving them a "property right" in the resulting artistic creation would be contrary to existing law, inequitable, and repugnant to the public interest. To hold that the broadcasts of these performances, making them available to a wider audience of Americans, deprives the Metropolitan Opera of all of its rights in this production and abandons the production to anyone to appropriate and exploit commercially, would indeed discourage the broadcasting of such operas and penalize not only the Metropolitan Opera but the public which now benefits from these broadcasts. Equity will not bear witness to such a travesty of justice; it will not countenance a state of moral and intellectual impotency. Equity will consider the interests of all parties coming within the arena of the dispute and admeasure the conflict in the scales of conscience and on the premise of honest commercial intercourse.

The complaints can also be sustained as stating a cause of action for unjustifiable interference with contractual rights of the plaintiffs. With full knowledge of the contract by which Metropolitan Opera has granted to Columbia Records the exclusive privilege of recording Metropolitan operas, the defendants have assumed the exercise of that privilege. Their action not only constitutes an attempt to secure the very benefit which the contract grants to Columbia Records, but also an interference with contractual relations which will be enjoined by a court of equity. . . .

Defendants' cross-motion is therefore denied.

We come next to the original motion: The motion by the plaintiffs for a preliminary injunction. . . . Unless the defendants are enjoined before the season starts, Metropolitan Opera is likely to lose the major part of its royalties from the sale of the authorized records, and Columbia Records will similarly suffer a serious loss.

The continuance of defendants' activities during this coming season is also likely to cause to the Metropolitan Opera an irreparable harm far beyond even the damage to the present contracts for its broadcasting and recording rights. The release and sale of recordings of Metropolitan Opera performances unapproved as to quality and unlimited as to amount, yet clearly designated or known to be performances of Metropolitan Opera, may injure the reputation Metropolitan Opera has built up by so much travail and may seriously damage or glut the market for its works. . . .

The conclusion here reached is not an onslaught on the currents of competition; it does not impose shackles on the arteries of enterprise. It simply quarantines business conduct which is abhorrent to good conscience and the most elementary principles of law and equity.

The preliminary injunction is granted. Bond is fixed in the sum of $2,500. Settle order.

In **Pottstown Daily News Pub. Co. v. Pottstown Broadcasting Co.,** 411 Pa. 383, 192 A.2d 657 (1963), the publisher of the "Pottstown Mercury," a newspaper, instituted an action in equity against the owner of WPAZ, a radio station, to enjoin the latter "from any further appropriation of the plaintiff's local news without its permission or authorization." The gist of the complaint was that the plaintiff's newspaper

and the radio station both "disseminate news to the same general area and sell advertising within the same area"; that the News Company expends considerable money to operate its newspaper and particularly "to develop its sources of local news, train personnel, and to accurately and concisely compose local news items", such specialized treatment of local news being the principal factor in its circulation and sale of advertising copy; that the News Company "has copyrighted such local news items", notice of such copyright being carried on the masthead of the newspaper; that the Broadcasting Company, "without license, permission or authority", uses the local news gathered by the personnel of the News Company and published in its newspaper, for its own daily broadcast of news "in violation of the right that the [News Company] has obtained by copyrighting *and also* violates the property rights of the [News Company] in the aforesaid news items." (Emphasis supplied.)

In upholding the legal sufficiency of a claim of unfair competition, the court stated:

In this day and age no court can fail to take note of the fact that newspapers, radio and television stations compete with each other for advertising which has become a giant in our economy. In fact, the presentation of news and entertainment has become almost a subsidiary function of newspapers, radio and television stations. Advertising is the life-blood of newspapers, radio and television and the presentation of news by all three media is a service designed to attract advertisers.

Taking into consideration the circumstances and the character of the businesses of the respective parties, as averred, the News Company has a commercial package of news items to service its advertising business upon which to base a cause of action in tort against a competitor allegedly converting the news items to its own uses in pursuit of advertising. The distinction we draw is fine; for the purpose of an action of unfair competition the specialized treatment of news items as a service the newspaper provides for advertisers gives to the News Company a limited property right which the law will guard and protect against wrongful invasion by a competitor whereas, for the purpose of an action for the infringement of copyright, the specialized treatment of the news is protected because "the law seeks to encourage creative minds" (*Morse v. Fields,* D.C., 127 F.Supp. 63).

Competition in business is jealously protected by the law and the law abhors that which tends to diminish or stifle competition. While a competitor may, subject to the patent, copyright and trademark laws, imitate his rival's business practices, processes and methods, yet the protection which the law affords to competition does not and should not countenance the usurpation of a competitor's investment and toil. In the case at bar, if the News Company can establish by proof that the Broadcasting Company has, without authority, used the local news items gathered through the specialized methods and by the trained personnel of the News Company, such unauthorized use constitutes a violation of a property right.

In **New York World's Fair 1964-1965 Corp. v. Colourpicture Publishers, Inc.,** 21 A.D.2d 896, 142 USPQ 237 (2d Dept. 1964), the court, in a 3-2 memorandum opinion, found that "a photograph of a unique building, structure or object situated within the World's Fair grounds, to which an admission fee is charged, is a photograph of a show in which plaintiff has a property right. Therefore, defendants may not photograph that building, structure or object without the plaintiff's permission." An exclusive license to depict such buildings, etc., had been granted by plaintiff to a third party but the dissenters found that "the precise scope or nature of the rights sought to be licensed cannot be determined."

The dissenters in the World's Fair case may, among other things, have been uncomfortable with the uncertain "nature and scope" of unfair competition in general. As to its "nature," note the plaintiffs' theory in the following case.

Columbia Broadcasting System, Inc. v. Documentaries Unlimited, Inc., 42 Misc. 2d 723, 248 N.Y.S.2d 809 (Sup. Ct. 1964). Plaintiffs Columbia Broadcasting System, Inc. and a news broadcaster on one of its radio stations, Allan Jackson, brought an action (styled as an action for infringement of common law copyright) against the defendant phonograph record producer, which had recorded "off the air" Jackson's news announcement concerning the assassination of President Kennedy and had incorporated it (one minute in length) in a 43-minute phonograph record entitled "JFK, the Man, the President." Jackson had read from United Press International and Associated Press releases and had interpolated sentences and phrases of his own. In rendering summary judgment for the plaintiffs, the court stated:

> It is clear also that Jackson did not merely repeat the news releases handed to him but added to them matter of his own composition. The significant element, however, is that his voice and style of talking, which in his profession is the foundation and source of employment and income, were appropriated by defendant without his consent. A broadcaster's voice and style of talking is, to all intents and purposes, his personality, a form of art expression, and his distinctive and valuable property. It comes with ill grace from defendant, which selected Jackson's broadcast from all the broadcasted announcements made on every radio station on that dramatic and tragic occasion, to now assert that it has no literary or artistic values and does not rise to the dignity of a property right. Obviously, there must have been some special feature in Jackson's manner, voice and/or content which appealed to defendant and, presumably, would in their estimation have appeal for the general public.
>
> There is no question as to defendant's right to incorporate the news as released publicly and to have it read, together with any matter added by defendant, by any person with his consent; but that is entirely different from what was here done. This is a clear case of appropriation for commercial profit of another's property right. The extent and relative value of that appropriation is a matter for proof at an assessment.

A number of other courts have found liability for the bodily appropriation of a performer's voice and style, but have distinguished cases in which the defendant has merely imitated that voice and style. (The latter situation is exemplified in the following case.) Is this a tenable distinction?

SINATRA v. GOODYEAR TIRE & RUBBER CO.

435 F.2d 711 (9th Cir. 1970)

TRASK, CIRCUIT JUDGE. This is an appeal brought by Nancy Sinatra from a summary judgment entered against her in favor of appellees, on her complaint against Goodyear Tire and Rubber Company based upon unfair competition, on the ground that there was no genuine issue as to a material fact. The district court's jurisdiction was founded on diversity of citizenship. 28 U.S.C. § 1332. This court has jurisdiction under 28 U.S.C. § 1291.

Plaintiff-appellant is a professional entertainer. She had made a recording of a song entitled "These Boots Are Made For Walkin'" which had become popular. The music, lyrics and arrangement of this composition had been copyrighted with Criterion Music as the copyright proprietor.

The defendants Goodyear Tire and Rubber Company, a corporation, and Young and Rubicam, Inc., an advertising agency, conceived the idea of coining the phrase "wide boots" as a descriptive term for tires manufactured by defendant Goodyear. As part of a widespread advertising campaign based upon this "wide boots" theme, the defendants produced and exhibited six radio and television commercials centered around a musical background using the music and revised lyrics from "These Boots Are Made For Walkin'" in combination with the voice of a female singer who was not shown on the screen or identified by name. In the four television commercials, two had a group of female voices singing the song and two had a single female voice. All four had a male voice narrating the commercial with four girls dressed in high boots and "mod" clothes appearing briefly with rolling tires. Each of the two radio commercials had a single female voice singing the song and a male narrator giving the commercial.

The complaint alleges that the song has been so popularized by the plaintiff that her name is identified with it; that she is best known by her connection with the song; that said song and the arrangement used by defendants "has acquired a secondary meaning"; that the defendants selected a singer whose voice and style was deliberately intended to imitate the voice and style of the plaintiff; and that the physical appearance and dress of the girls who appeared in fleeting views on the television commercials utilized the mannerisms and dress of the plaintiff. All of this, the complaint alleges, was intentionally accomplished for the purpose of deceiving the public into believing that the plaintiff was a participant in the commercials.

Plaintiff Sinatra further alleged that the defendant Young and Rubicam had previously contacted her agent in an effort to employ her on behalf of Goodyear but no contract was concluded.

She thereupon prayed for general and punitive damages, an accounting of all sales of Goodyear tires during the period the commercials were used and a reasonable royalty therefrom, together with a permanent injunction restraining defendants from further use of all of the commercials.

The defendants filed a motion to dismiss and a motion for summary judgment supported by affidavit and exhibits consisting of the film and tapes in question. The plaintiff filed her counteraffidavit and that of her agent.

Upon these papers the district court found:

> "The performances of 'These Boots Are Made for Walkin'' on each of said two radio commercials and four television commercials are anonymous; that is, there is no audio or visual representation, holding out, or inference that any of the commercials embody the performance or voice of any particular individual or individuals."

The Court thus concluded in part:

> "Defendants did not pass-off; that is, they did not mislead the public into thinking their commercials were the product of plaintiff or anyone else. Imitation alone does not give rise to a cause of action; there is, therefore, no genuine issue of fact and defendants are entitled to Summary Judgment."

On appeal, Sinatra asserts that her complaint alleged the essential elements of the tort of passing-off and raised genuine issues as to material facts so that the district court erred in granting summary judgment. We disagree and affirm.

At the outset it must be remembered that this is not a copyright infringement case.[2] The copyright proprietor was Criterion Music. Criterion owned the copyright on the music, the lyrics and the arrangements of "These Boots Are Made For Walkin'." On March 3, 1967, and before the production of the commercials complained about, Criterion entered into a written agreement with Young and Rubicam on behalf of the defendant Goodyear for a license to use the composition, "including any arrangements thereof owned or controlled by you, music and/or lyrics. . . ." Complete rights were given for television and radio and for commercial use for advertising purposes on behalf of Goodyear. The written agreement with all of its provisions, warranties and representations was accepted and approved by Lee Hazelwood, designated as the author.

Neither is it a case where an actual tape or other recording of the voice of the plaintiff has been replayed. It is not falsely stated to be a Nancy Sinatra rendition. The defendant candidly admitted for purposes of the motion for summary judgment and the district court assumed that the vocal rendition was an imitation of plaintiff's recorded performance of this particular song. . . .

Under the laws of California unfair competition is defined by code. As thus defined, unfair competition shall mean and include "unlawful, unfair or fraudulent business practices and unfair, untrue or misleading advertising. . . ."

An examination of the cases decided under the statute immediately disclosed an obvious distinction on the facts between this case and the great mass of unfair competition cases. There is no competition between Nancy Sinatra and Goodyear Tire Company. Appellant is not in the tire business and Goodyear is not selling phonograph records. There is no passing-off by the defendant of the plaintiff's products as its own either by simulation of name, slogan, device or other unfair trade practice.

No real assistance is therefore obtained from the California statute or cases decided under it. Neither counsel has relied upon the statute or the ordinary cases construing it. We turn then to an examination of the general authorities cited by Sinatra to determine if a cause of action exists.

Dean Prosser defines the tort of "passing-off" as involving the basic idea of competing for custom in the trade. Thus it is:

> "The making of some false representation to the public or to third persons, likely to induce them to believe that the goods or services of another are those of the plaintiff. . . . The test laid down in such cases has been whether the resemblance is so great as to deceive the ordinary customer acting with the

---

[2] The complaint did not allege copyright infringement. Defendants acquired a license to use the copyrighted music, lyrics and arrangement of "These Boots Are Made For Walkin'" from Criterion Music, the copyright proprietor, on March 3, 1967. Rather, plaintiff alleges the intentional "passing-off" of the voice and mannerisms of others as her own for commercial exploitation.

caution usually exercised in such transactions, so that he may mistake one for the other." Prosser, *Law of Torts* 982-83 (1964).

Here we have a claim of an incidental or secondary passing-off. Appellant seeks to bring her case within the orbit of the traditional pattern of unfair competition by asserting that because some people would read her voice into the commercial the defendant has increased its sale of tires "by many millions of dollars."

Counsel has called attention to, and we have discovered, four cases which directly bear on appellant's claim. They are: *Davis v. Trans World Airlines*, 297 F.Supp. 1145 (C.D.Cal.1969); *Lahr v. Adell Chemical Co.*, 300 F.2d 256 (1st Cir.1962); *Sim v. H. J. Heinz Co., Ltd.*, [1958] 1 W.L.R. 313 (C.A.1959); and *Gardella v. Log Cabin Products, Inc.*, 89 F.2d 891 (2d Cir.1937).

Gardella was the *Aunt Jemima* case. In it the defendants used a singer and an actor in an advertising campaign for Aunt Jemima Pancake Flour and Log Cabin Syrup over a radio station. They were presented under the name of "Aunt Jemima", a name which, with a picture of the character, had been registered as a trademark since 1890. The plaintiff was a stage and radio performer who had used the name in many performances and in recordings. Although plaintiff obtained a recovery in damages in the district court, it was reversed because it was improperly based in part upon a claim under the state's Civil Rights law. The claim based upon unfair competition was sent back to be established, if at all, upon standards set out in the court's opinion. The court pointed out that although the name "Aunt Jemima" was used by both performers, the use of the name for the fictitious character was protected by the trademark registration and the only duty of the defendants was one of identification to prevent confusion with the theatrical Aunt Jemima who was the plaintiff and who had an established reputation and earning power as a performer. Absent confusion or deception, the court stated, imitation alone was not sufficient to sustain the claim. The court further suggested that so long as the pancake Aunt Jemima advertised her own products, imitation would not be deception. 89 F.2d at 897.

In *Sim, supra,* the Heinz Company developed an advertising program using speech from a cartoon figure. Alastair Sim, a well known actor, alleged that the advertiser employed another actor, Ron Moody, to make the vocal comments. Moody had in the past simulated the voice of Sim and the complaint was that he did so on these television commercials. The application for an injunction was denied on appeal. Lord Justice Hodson expressing some doubt said:

"I would only add this. This is, on any view of the matter, a novel form of action of passing off. The plaintiff contends that his voice as an actor is part of his stock-in-trade and therefore is something which he is entitled to protect as part of his goods. No doubt that is an arguable case, but there are various questions to be determined in this action, which has not yet been tried, including the question whether this voice can in truth be regarded as a property and whether, in the circumstances of this case there could be said to be anything in the nature of unfair trade competition in a common field, where in the one case you have an actor who uses his voice in the performance of his particular occupation and, on the other hand, another actor who, in some way or other, uses his voice to imitate a voice on television for advertising purposes." 1 W.L.R. at 319.

Lahr v. Adell Chemical Co., supra, was also a television commercial in which a cartoon duck was used to speak with a voice alleged to be the simulated voice of Bert Lahr, a successful professional entertainer. The complaint alleged three causes of action, for unfair competition, for invasion of privacy, and for defamation. An order dismissing the complaint for failure to state a claim was reversed on the basis of a claim of unfair competition. The court on appeal pointed out that the plaintiff had achieved stardom:

> "[I]n substantial measure because his 'style of vocal comic delivery which, by reason of its distinctive and original combination of pitch, inflection, accent and comic sounds,' has caused him to become 'widely known and readily recognized . . . as a unique and extraordinary comic character.'" 300 F.2d at 257.

The court held that the imposter was "stealing his thunder" and that on the face of the allegations the plaintiff was entitled to have his complaint go to trial. It was clear however that a cause of action for damage to reputation was not stated.

> "If every time one can allege, 'Your (anonymous) commercial sounded like me, but not so good,' and contend the public believed, in spite of the variance, . . . that his abilities had declined, the consequences would be too great to contemplate." 300 F.2d at 259.

It appears that *Lahr* was decided on the basis of a singular uniqueness of quality of voice that made his situation not just a difference of degree but a difference in kind.

> "We may agree with defendant that plaintiff has not shown any 'property' interest entitled to copyright protection. And we might hesitate to say that *an ordinary singer whose voice, deliberately or otherwise*, sounded sufficiently like another to cause confusion was not free to do so. Plaintiff here alleges a peculiar style and type of performance, unique in a far broader sense." 300 F.2d at 259 (emphasis supplied).

. . . In *Lahr* and *Sim* the defendants were not dealing in materials in which the defendants had a copyright. Or, to elaborate, in *Lahr* and *Sim* the plaintiffs claimed a "secondary meaning" in pure sound, their individual vocal characteristics. The protection sought was not for the combination of sound together with copyrighted lyrics, melody and arrangement, as here. In this case appellant's complaint is not that her sound is uniquely personal; it is that the sound in connection with the music, lyrics and arrangement, which made her the subject of popular identification, ought to be protected. But as to these latter copyrightable items she had no rights. Presumably, she was required to obtain permission of the copyright owner to sing "Boots", and to make an arrangement of the song to suit her own tastes and talents. Had she desired to exclude all others from use of the song so that her "secondary meaning" with the song could not be imitated she could have purchased those rights from the copyright proprietor. One wonders whether her voice, and theatrical style, would have been identifiable if another song had been presented, and not "her song", which unfortunately for her was owned by others and licensed to the defendants.[12] But that case is not before us now.

---

[12] The tapes and the movies introduced as exhibits were viewed and heard by this court. To the untrained ear the sound of the voice carried no recognition, and no confusion of source. It was of professional quality but there was no readily identifiable accent (Maurice Chevalier), range, quality, (Lahr or Andy Devine), or pitch which would distinguish it to the ordinary listener from many others or identify it with any particular person. Although the actresses who appeared fleetingly and did not sing, wore boots, such props for this particular song carried no more originality than a snow scene for a rendition of "White Christmas."

Davis v. Trans World Airlines, supra, involved a television commercial where the airline used the music, lyrics and arrangement of a popular song "Up, Up and Away" to which it had acquired the rights from the copyright proprietor. Plaintiffs, a nationally known singing group called "The Fifth Dimension," had made a well known recording of the same song. The singing in the commercial was anonymous, as here. The district court held on the motion for summary judgment that there had been no passing-off and that imitation alone did not give rise to a cause of action. In any event, *Davis* does not aid Sinatra for the court there denied recovery upon similar facts and a similar, if not identical, legal theory to that urged by Sinatra.

The judgment of the district court is affirmed.

2. RIGHT OF PUBLICITY

HAELAN LABORATORIES, INC. v. TOPPS CHEWING GUM, INC.

202 F.2d 866 (2d Cir.), *cert. denied,*
346 U.S. 816 (1953)

FRANK, CIRCUIT JUDGE.

After a trial without a jury, the trial judge dismissed the complaint on the merits.[1] The plaintiff maintains that defendant invaded plaintiff's exclusive right to use the photographs of leading baseball-players. Probably because the trial judge ruled against plaintiff's legal contentions, some of the facts were not too clearly found.

1. So far as we can now tell, there were instances of the following kind:

(a). The plaintiff, engaged in selling chewing-gum, made a contract with a ball-player providing that plaintiff for a stated term should have the exclusive right to use the ball-player's photograph in connection with the sales of plaintiff's gum; the ball-player agreed not to grant any other gum manufacturer a similar right during such term; the contract gave plaintiff an option to extend the term for a designated period.

(b). Defendant, a rival chewing-gum manufacturer, knowing of plaintiff's contract, deliberately induced the ball-player to authorize defendant, by a contract with defendant, to use the player's photograph in connection with the sales of defendant's gum either during the original or extended term of plaintiff's contract, and defendant did so use the photograph.

Defendant argues that, even if such facts are proved, they show no actionable wrong, for this reason: The contract with plaintiff was no more than a release by the ball-player to plaintiff of the liability which, absent the release, plaintiff would have incurred in using the ball-player's photograph, because such a use, without his consent, would be an invasion of his right of privacy under Section 50 and Section 51 of the New York Civil Rights Law; this statutory right of privacy is personal, not assignable; therefore, plaintiff's contract vested in plaintiff no "property" right or other legal interest which defendant's conduct invaded.

Both parties agree, and so do we, that, on the facts here, New York "law" governs. And we shall assume, for the moment, that, under the New York

---

[1] Plaintiff abandoned its appeal from the dismissal of that part of the complaint asserting unfair competition and trademark infringement. Defendant has abandoned its cross-appeal from the dismissal of its counterclaim.

decisions, defendant correctly asserts that any such contract between plaintiff and a ball-player, in so far as it merely authorized plaintiff to use the player's photograph, created nothing but a release of liability. On that basis, were there no more to the contract, plaintiff would have no actionable claim against defendant. But defendant's argument neglects the fact that, in the contract, the ball-player also promised not to give similar releases to others. If defendant, knowing of the contract, deliberately induced the ball-player to break that promise, defendant behaved tortiously.[2] See, e. g., *Hornstein v. Podwitz,* 254 N.Y. 443, 173 N.E. 674, 84 A.L.R. 1; 6 Corbin, Contracts (1951) Sec. 1470.

2. The foregoing covers the situations where defendant, by itself or through its agent, induced breaches. But . . . we have a different problem; . . . in instances — alleged in one paragraph of the complaint and to which the trial judge in his opinion also (although not altogether clearly) refers — where defendant, "with knowledge of plaintiff's exclusive rights," used a photograph of a ball-player without his consent during the term of his contract with plaintiff.[3]

With regard to such situations, we must consider defendant's contention that none of plaintiff's contracts created more than a release of liability, because a man has no legal interest in the publication of his picture other than his right of privacy, i. e., a personal and non-assignable right not to have his feelings hurt by such a publication.

A majority of this court rejects this contention. We think that, in addition to and independent of that right of privacy (which in New York derives from statute), a man has a right in the publicity value of his photograph, i. e., the right to grant the exclusive privilege of publishing his picture, and that such a grant may validly be made "in gross," i. e., without an accompanying transfer of a business or of anything else. Whether it be labelled a "property" right is immaterial; for here, as often elsewhere, the tag "property" simply symbolizes the fact that courts enforce a claim which has pecuniary worth.

This right might be called a "right of publicity." For it is common knowledge that many prominent persons (especially actors and ball-players), far from having their feelings bruised through public exposure of their likenesses, would feel sorely deprived if they no longer received money for authorizing advertisements, popularizing their countenances, displayed in newspapers, magazines, busses, trains and subways. This right of publicity would usually yield them no money unless it could be made the subject of an exclusive grant which barred any other advertiser from using their pictures.

. . . .

Plaintiff, in its capacity as exclusive grantee of a player's "right of publicity," has a valid claim against defendant if defendant used that player's photograph during the term of plaintiff's grant and with knowledge of it. It is no defense to such a claim that defendant is the assignee of a subsequent contract between that player and Russell, purporting to make a grant to Russell or its assignees. For the prior grant to plaintiff renders that subsequent grant invalid during the period of the grant (including an exercised option) to plaintiff, but not thereafter.

3. We must remand to the trial court for a determination (on the basis of the present record and of further evidence introduced by either party) of these facts: (1) the date and contents of each of plaintiff's contracts, and whether plaintiff

---

[2] Defendant is also liable if he thus induced any player to breach his contract to renew.

[3] On the remand, the judge should make findings on this subject, on the basis of the evidence now in the record and such additional evidence as the parties may introduce.

exercised its option to renew; (2) defendant's or Players' conduct with respect to each such contract.

Of course, if defendant made a contract with a ball-player which was not executed — or which did not authorize defendant to use the player's photograph — until the expiration of the original or extended term of plaintiff's contract with that player, or which did not induce a breach of the agreement to renew, then defendant did no legal wrong to plaintiff. The same is true of instances where neither defendant nor Players induced a breach of plaintiff's contract, and defendant did not use the player's photograph until after the expiration of such original or extended or option term.

If, upon further exploration of the facts, the trial court, in the light of our opinion, concludes that defendant is liable, it will, of course, ascertain damages and decide what equitable relief is justified.

Reversed and remanded.

The *Haelan* decision did not create the "right of publicity," but it did give a name and some separate identity to one branch of what had been a developing "right of privacy." Dean Prosser was able to identify "four distinct kinds of invasion of four different interests of the plaintiff, which are tied together by the common name ["right of privacy"], but otherwise have almost nothing in common except that each represents an interference with the right of the plaintiff 'to be let alone.'" He stated the four branches of the tort as: (1) intrusion upon the plaintiff's physical solitude or seclusion; (2) public disclosure of private facts; (3) false light in the public eye; and (4) appropriation of plaintiff's name or likeness for defendant's benefit. W. PROSSER, TORTS 804-09 (4th ed. 1971). To protect his interest with respect to the first three branches of the "right of privacy," the injured party attempts to minimize the intrusion or publication of the damaging matter; but the individual asserting a right of publicity does not necessarily object to the commercial exploitation so long as it redounds to his own financial benefit (as in the *Haelan* case).

An issue that has arisen in a number of recent cases is whether the "right of publicity" may be inherited and enforced after the death of the "celebrity." In *Price v. Hal Roach Studios, Inc.,* 400 F. Supp. 836 (S.D.N.Y. 1975), it was held that the right commercially to exploit the names and likenesses of the famed comedians Laurel and Hardy could be transferred upon and enforced after their deaths. That view was temporarily endorsed by the Court of Appeals for the Second Circuit, in *Factors Etc., Inc. v. Pro Arts, Inc.,* 579 F.2d 215 (2d Cir. 1978), *cert. denied,* 440 U.S. 908 (1979), in a case involving the unauthorized sale of a poster of Elvis Presley after his death; but the court later abandoned this position, — F.2d — (2d Cir. 1981), in deference to that adopted by the Court of Appeals for the Sixth Circuit in the following case.

Memphis Development Foundation v. Factors Etc., Inc., 616 F.2d 956 (6th Cir.), *cert. denied,* — U.S. — (1980). The plaintiff in this action for declaratory judgment was a Tennessee nonprofit corporation, which prepared plans to erect a large bronze statue of Elvis Presley in downtown Memphis and to send an eight-inch pewter replica of the statue to any member of the public contributing

$25 or more. The defendant was Factors Etc., Inc., which had taken a transfer from Boxcar Enterprises (to whom Presley had made a transfer in his lifetime) of the right to exploit the name and likeness of Elvis Presley after his death. When Factors claimed that the Foundation was in effect selling the statuettes for $25 apiece and appropriating the exclusive right to reap commercial value from the name and likeness of Presley, the Foundation sought a declaratory judgment and Factors counterclaimed for damages and an injunction against further distribution of the replicas. The District Court issued a preliminary injunction allowing the Foundation to build the Presley memorial but prohibiting it from manufacturing or distributing the statuette.

The court of appeals reversed. It acknowledged that several courts and writers had treated the right of publicity as property which may be passed on to heirs or assigns, in part because of the inducement this might provide creatively to exploit one's name, image or likeness during one's lifetime. But it disagreed, concluding that the basic motivations for fame and stardom "are the desire to achieve success or excellence in a chosen field, the desire to contribute to the happiness or improvement of one's fellows and the desire to receive the psychic and financial rewards of achievement.... The desire to exploit fame for the commercial advantage of one's heirs is by contrast a weak principle of motivation. It seems apparent that making the right of publicity inheritable would not significantly inspire the creative endeavors of individuals in our society." The court then enumerated other reasons for rejecting the inheritability of the right of publicity:

On the other hand, there are strong reasons for declining to recognize the inheritability of the right. A whole set of practical problems of judicial line-drawing would arise should the courts recognize such an inheritable right. How long would the "property" interest last? In perpetuity? For a term of years? Is the right of publicity taxable? At what point does the right collide with the right of free expression guaranteed by the first amendment? Does the right apply to elected officials and military heroes whose fame was gained on the public payroll, as well as to movie stars, singers and athletes? Does the right cover posters or engraved likenesses of, for example, Farah Fawcett Majors or Mahatma Gandhi, kitchen utensils ("Revere Ware"), insurance ("John Hancock"), electric utilities ("Edison"), a football stadium ("RFK"), a pastry ("Napoleon"), or the innumerable urban subdivisions and apartment complexes named after famous people? Our legal system normally does not pass on to heirs other similar personal attributes even though the attributes may be shared during life by others or have some commercial value. Titles, offices and reputation are not inheritable. Neither are trust or distrust and friendship or enmity descendible. An employment contract during life does not create the right for heirs to take over the job. Fame falls in the same category as reputation; it is an attribute from which others may benefit but may not own.

The law of defamation, designed to protect against the destruction of reputation including the loss of earning capacity associated with it, provides an analogy. There is no right of action for defamation after death. See Restatement (Second) of Torts § 560 (rev. ed. 1977). The two interests that support the inheritability of the right of publicity, namely, the "effort and creativity" and the "hopes and expectations" of the decedent, would also support an action for libel or slander for destruction of name and reputation after death. Neither of these reasons, however, is sufficient to overcome the common law policy terminating the action for defamation upon death.

Fame often is fortuitous and fleeting. It always depends on the participation of the public in the creation of an image. It usually depends on the communication of information about the famous person by the media. The intangible and shifting nature of fame and celebrity status, the presence of widespread public and press participation in its creation, the unusual psychic rewards and income that often flow from it during life and the fact that it may be created by bad as well as good conduct combine to create serious reservations about making fame the permanent right of a few individuals to the exclusion of the general public. Heretofore, the law has always thought that leaving a good name to one's children is sufficient reward in itself for the individual, whether famous or not. Commercialization of this virtue after death in the hands of heirs is contrary to our legal tradition and somehow seems contrary to the moral presuppositions of our culture.

There is no indication that changing the traditional common law rule against allowing heirs the exclusive control of the commercial use of their ancestor's name will increase the efficiency or productivity of our economic system. It does not seem reasonable to expect that such a change would enlarge the stock or quality of the goods, services, artistic creativity, information, invention or entertainment available. Nor will it enhance the fairness of our political and economic system. It seems fairer and more efficient for the commercial, aesthetic, and political use of the name, memory and image of the famous to be open to all rather than to be monopolized by a few. An equal distribution of the opportunity to use the name of the dead seems preferable. The memory, name and pictures of famous individuals should be regarded as a common asset to be shared, an economic opportunity available in the free market system.

QUESTIONS

1. To what extent does the court's reasoning in the *Memphis Development* case suggest that there should be no cause of action at all for violation of the right of publicity? *Should* there be such a right? Does any court possess the analytical and policy "tools" necessary to determine whether to create such a right? (Compare the warnings of Justice Brandeis in the *International News Service* case.)

2. Had the court in the *Memphis* case reached a contrary decision, would it have afforded a basis for a successful claim by Factors to prevent the several young men performing around the country as Elvis impersonators from continuing to do so?

3. Could Nancy Sinatra have successfully framed her claim against the Goodyear Company as one for breach of her right of publicity?

4. Bela Lugosi is remembered for his portrayal of Count Dracula in the famous Universal motion picture of the 1930s. His contract with Universal contained a standard provision authorizing the company to display photographs of him in his Dracula make-up and garb for purposes of advertising the exhibition of the film. Some years after Lugosi's death, Universal commenced a successful merchandising campaign centered around the sale of Dracula tee-shirts, towels, dolls, ashtrays, and the like, all bearing the Dracula-Lugosi countenance. Lugosi's son and only heir has commenced an action against Universal for an injunction and an accounting of profits. Should he prevail?

B. THE SUPREMACY CLAUSE

The Supremacy Clause of the U.S. Constitution is found in the second paragraph of Article VI as follows:

This Constitution, and the Laws of the United States which shall be made in Pursuance thereof; and all Treaties made, or which shall be made, under the

Authority of the United States, shall be the supreme Law of the Land; and the Judges in every State shall be bound thereby, any Thing in the Constitution or Laws of any State to the contrary notwithstanding.

QUESTIONS

1. Note the potentially preemptive effect of: (a) the U.S. Constitution itself and (b) constitutional federal laws, and (c) treaties. Identify, within each of these sources, provisions dealing with patents and copyrights which might preempt state law on the same subject. Why were trademarks omitted from the previous question?

2. Does the supremacy clause operate to preempt federal laws?

3. Are state laws ever nullified when they are not expressly "contrary" to federal law?

C. THE CASE LAW ON PREEMPTION

SEARS, ROEBUCK & CO. v. STIFFEL CO.

376 U.S. 225 (1964)

MR. JUSTICE BLACK delivered the opinion of the Court.

The question in this case is whether a State's unfair competition law can, consistently with the federal patent laws, impose liability for or prohibit the copying of an article which is protected by neither a federal patent nor a copyright. The respondent, Stiffel Company, secured design and mechanical patents on a "pole lamp" — a vertical tube having lamp fixtures along the outside, the tube being made so that it will stand upright between the floor and ceiling of a room. Pole lamps proved a decided commercial success, and soon after Stiffel brought them on the market Sears, Roebuck & Company put on the market a substantially identical lamp, which it sold more cheaply, Sears' retail price being about the same as Stiffel's wholesale price. Stiffel then brought this action against Sears in the United States District Court for the Northern District of Illinois, claiming in its first count that by copying its design Sears had infringed Stiffel's patents and in its second count that by selling copies of Stiffel's lamp Sears had caused confusion in the trade as to the source of the lamps and had thereby engaged in unfair competition under Illinois law. There was evidence that identifying tags were not attached to the Sears lamps although labels appeared on the cartons in which they were delivered to customers, that customers had asked Stiffel whether its lamps differed from Sears', and that in two cases customers who had bought Stiffel lamps had complained to Stiffel on learning that Sears was selling substantially identical lamps at a much lower price.

The District Court, after holding the patents invalid for want of invention, went on to find as a fact that Sears' lamp was "a substantially exact copy" of Stiffel's and that the two lamps were so much alike, both in appearance and in functional details, "that confusion between them is likely, and some confusion has already occurred." On these findings the court held Sears guilty of unfair competition, enjoined Sears "from unfairly competing with [Stiffel] by selling or attempting to sell pole lamps identical to or confusingly similar to" Stiffel's lamp, and ordered an accounting to fix profits and damages resulting from Sears' "unfair competition."

The Court of Appeals affirmed.[1] 313 F.2d 115. That court held that, to make out a case of unfair competition under Illinois law, there was no need to show that Sears had been "palming off" its lamps as Stiffel lamps; Stiffel had only to prove that there was a "likelihood of confusion as to the source of the products" — that the two articles were sufficiently identical that customers could not tell who had made a particular one. Impressed by the "remarkable sameness of appearance" of the lamps, the Court of Appeals upheld the trial court's findings of likelihood of confusion and some actual confusion, findings which the appellate court construed to mean confusion "as to the source of the lamps." The Court of Appeals thought this enough under Illinois law to sustain the trial court's holding of unfair competition, and thus held Sears liable under Illinois law for doing no more than copying and marketing an unpatented article.[2] We granted certiorari to consider whether this use of a State's law of unfair competition is compatible with the federal patent law. 374 U. S. 826.

Before the Constitution was adopted, some States had granted patents either by special act or by general statute, but when the Constitution was adopted provision for a federal patent law was made one of the enumerated powers of Congress because, as Madison put it in *The Federalist* No. 43, the States "cannot separately make effectual provision" for either patents or copyrights. That constitutional provision is Art. I, § 8, cl. 8, which empowers Congress "To promote the Progress of Science and useful Arts, by securing for limited Times to Authors and Inventors the exclusive Right to their respective Writings and

---

[1] No review is sought here of the ruling affirming the District Court's holding that the patent is invalid.

[2] 313 F. 2d, at 118 and nn. 6, 7. At least one Illinois case has held in an exhaustive opinion that unfair competition under the law of Illinois is not proved unless the defendant is shown to have "palmed off" the article which he sells as that of another seller; the court there said that "[t]he courts in this State do not treat the 'palming off' doctrine as merely the designation of a typical class of cases of unfair competition, but they announce it as the rule of law itself — the test by which it is determined whether a given state of facts constitutes unfair competition as a matter of law. ... The 'palming off' rule is expressed in a positive, concrete form which will not admit of 'broadening' or 'widening' by any proper judicial process." Stevens-Davis Co. v. Mather & Co., 230 Ill. App. 45, 65-66 (1923). In spite of this the Court of Appeals in its opinions both in this case and in Day-Brite Lighting, Inc. v. Compco Corp., 311 F. 2d 26, rev'd [*infra*], relied upon one of its previous decisions in a trade-name case, Independant Nail & Packing Co. v. Stronghold Screw Products, 205 F. 2d 921 (C. A. 7th Cir. 1953), which concluded that as to use of trade names the *Stevens-Davis* rule had been overruled by two subsequent Illinois decisions. Those two cases, however, discussed only misleading use of trade names, not copying of articles of trade. One prohibited the use of a name so similar to that of another seller as to deceive or confuse customers, even though the defendant company did not sell the same products as the plaintiff and so in one sense could not be said to have palmed off its goods as those of a competitor, since the plaintiff was not a competitor. Lady Esther, Ltd. v. Lady Esther Corset Shoppe, Inc., 317 Ill. App. 451, 46 N.E.2d 165 (1943). The other Illinois case on which the Court of Appeals relied was a mandamus action which held that under an Illinois statute a corporation was properly denied registration in the State when its name was "deceptively similar" to that of a corporation already registered. Investors Syndicate of America, Inc. v. Hughes, 378 Ill. 413, 38 N. E. 2d 754 (1941). The Court of Appeals, by holding that because Illinois forbids misleading use of trade names it also forbids as unfair competition the mere copying of an article of trade without any palming off, thus appears to have extended greatly the scope of the Illinois law of unfair competition beyond the limits indicated in the Illinois cases and beyond any previous decisions of the Seventh Circuit itself. Because of our disposition of these cases we need not decide whether it was correct in doing so.

Discoveries." Pursuant to this constitutional authority, Congress in 1790 enacted the first federal patent and copyright law, 1 Stat. 109, and ever since that time has fixed the conditions upon which patents and copyrights shall be granted, see 17 U.S.C. §§ 1-216; 35 U. S. C. §§ 1-293. These laws, like other laws of the United States enacted pursuant to constitutional authority, are the supreme law of the land. See *Sperry v. Florida,* 373 U. S. 379 (1963). When state law touches upon the area of these federal statutes, it is "familiar doctrine" that the federal policy "may not be set at naught, or its benefits denied" by the state law. *Sola Elec. Co. v. Jefferson Elec. Co.,* 317 U. S. 173, 176 (1942). This is true, of course, even if the state law is enacted in the exercise of otherwise undoubted state power.

The grant of a patent is the grant of a statutory monopoly; [5] indeed, the grant of patents in England was an explicit exception to the statute of James I prohibiting monopolies.[6] Patents are not given as favors, as was the case of monopolies given by the Tudor monarchs, see *The Case of Monopolies (Darcy v. Allein),* 11 Co. Rep. 84 b., 77 Eng. Rep. 1260 (K. B. 1602), but are meant to encourage invention by rewarding the inventor with the right, limited to a term of years fixed by the patent, to exclude others from the use of his invention. During that period of time no one may make, use, or sell the patented product without the patentee's authority. 35 U. S. C. § 271. But in rewarding useful invention, the "rights and welfare of the community must be fairly dealt with and effectually guarded." *Kendall v. Winsor,* 21 How. 322, 329 (1859). To that end the prerequisites to obtaining a patent are strictly observed, and when the patent has issued the limitations on its exercise are equally strictly enforced. To begin with, a genuine "invention" or "discovery" must be demonstrated "lest in the constant demand for new appliances the heavy hand of tribute be laid on each slight technological advance in an art." *Cuno Engineering Corp. v. Automatic Devices Corp.,* 314 U. S. 84, 92 (1941); see *Great Atlantic & Pacific Tea Co. v. Supermarket Equipment Corp.,* 340 U. S. 147, 152-153 (1950); *Atlantic Works v. Brady,* 107 U. S. 192, 199-200 (1883). Once the patent issues, it is strictly construed, *United States v. Masonite Corp.,* 316 U. S. 265, 280 (1942), it cannot be used to secure any monopoly beyond that contained in the patent, *Morton Salt Co. v. G. S. Suppiger Co.,* 314 U. S. 488, 492 (1942), the patentee's control over the product when it leaves his hands is sharply limited, see *United States v. Univis Lens Co.,* 316 U. S. 241, 250-252 (1942), and the patent monopoly may not be used in disregard of the antitrust laws, see *International Business Machines Corp. v. United States,* 298 U. S. 131 (1936); *United Shoe Machinery Corp. v. United States,* 258 U. S. 451, 463-464 (1922). Finally, and especially relevant here, when the patent expires the monopoly created by its expires, too, and the right to make the article — including the right to make it in precisely the shape it carried when patented — passes to the public. *Kellogg Co. v. National Biscuit Co.,* 305 U. S. 111, 120-122 (1938); *Singer Mfg. Co. v. June Mfg. Co.,* 163 U. S. 169, 185 (1896).

---

[5] Patent rights exist only by virtue of statute. Wheaton v. Peters, 8 Pet. 591, 658 (1834).

[6] The Statute of Monopolies, 21 Jac. I, c. 3 (1623), declared all monopolies "contrary to the Laws of this Realm" and "utterly void and of none Effect." Section VI, however, excepted patents of 14 years to "the true and first Inventor and Inventors" of "new Manufactures" so long as they were "not contrary to the Law, nor mischievous to the State, by raising Prices of Commodities at home, or Hurt of Trade, or generally inconvenient. ..." Much American patent law derives from English patent law. See Pennock v. Dialogue, 2 Pet. 1, 18 (1829).

uniformity

Thus the patent system is one in which uniform federal standards are carefully used to promote invention while at the same time preserving free competition.[7] Obviously a State could not, consistently with the Supremacy Clause of the Constitution, extend the life of a patent beyond its expiration date or give a patent on an article which lacked the level of invention required for federal patents. To do either would run counter to the policy of Congress of granting patents only to true inventions and then only for a limited time. Just as a State cannot encroach upon the federal patent laws directly, it cannot, under some other law, such as that forbidding unfair competition, give protection of a kind that clashes with the objectives of the federal patent laws.

In the present case the "pole lamp" sold by Stiffel has been held not to be entitled to the protection of either a mechanical or a design patent. An unpatentable article, like an article on which the patent has expired, is in the public domain and may be made and sold by whoever chooses to do so. What Sears did was to copy Stiffel's design and to sell lamps almost identical to those sold by Stiffel. This it had every right to do under the federal patent laws. That Stiffel originated the pole lamp and made it popular is immaterial. "Sharing in the goodwill of an article unprotected by patent or trade-mark is the exercise of a right possessed by all — and in the free exercise of which the consuming public is deeply interested." *Kellogg Co. v. National Biscuit Co., supra,* 305 U. S., at 122. To allow a State by use of its law of unfair competition to prevent the copying of an article which represents too slight an advance to be patented would be to permit the State to block off from the public something which federal law has said belongs to the public. The result would be that while federal law grants only 14 or 17 years' protection to genuine inventions, see 35 U. S. C. §§ 154, 173, States could allow perpetual protection to articles too lacking in novelty to merit any patent at all under federal constitutional standards. This would be too great an encroachment on the federal patent system to be tolerated.

Sears has been held liable here for unfair competition because of a finding of likelihood of confusion based only on the fact that Sears' lamp was copied from Stiffel's unpatented lamp and that consequently the two looked exactly alike. Of course there could be "confusion" as to who had manufactured these nearly identical articles. But mere inability of the public to tell two identical articles apart is not enough to support an injunction against copying or an award of damages for copying that which the federal patent laws permit to be copied. Doubtless a State may, in appropriate circumstances, require that goods, whether patented or unpatented, be labeled or that other precautionary steps be taken to prevent customers from being misled as to the source, just as it may protect businesses in the use of their trademarks, labels, or distinctive dress in the packaging of goods so as to prevent others, by imitating such markings, from misleading purchasers as to the source of the goods.[9] But because of the federal patent laws a State may not, when the article is unpatented and uncopyrighted, prohibit the copying of the article itself or award damages for such copying. Cf. *G. Ricordi & Co. v. Haendler,* 194 F. 2d 914, 916 (C. A. 2d Cir. 1952). The judgment below

---

[7] The purpose of Congress to have national uniformity in patent and copyright laws can be inferred from such statutes as that which vests exclusive jurisdiction to hear patent and copyright cases in federal courts, 28 U. S. C. § 1338 (a), and that section of the Copyright Act which expressly saves state protection of unpublished writings but does not include published writings, 17 U. S. C. § 2.

[9] It seems apparent that Illinois has not seen fit to impose liability on sellers who do not label their goods. Neither the discussions in the opinions below nor the briefs before us cite any Illinois statute or decision requiring labeling.

did both and in so doing gave Stiffel the equivalent of a patent monopoly on its unpatented lamp. That was error, and Sears is entitled to a judgment in its favor.

Reversed.

COMPCO CORP. v. DAY-BRITE LIGHTING, INC.

376 U.S. 234 (1964)

MR. JUSTICE BLACK delivered the opinion of the Court.

As in *Sears, Roebuck & Co. v. Stiffel Co.,* [*supra*], the question here is whether the use of a state unfair competition law to give relief against the copying of an unpatented industrial design conflicts with the federal patent laws. Both Compco and Day-Brite are manufacturers of fluorescent lighting fixtures of a kind widely used in offices and stores. Day-Brite in 1955 secured from the Patent Office a design patent on a reflector having cross-ribs claimed to give both strength and attractiveness to the fixture. Day-Brite also sought, but was refused, a mechanical patent on the same device. After Day-Brite had begun selling its fixture, Compco's predecessor began making and selling fixtures very similar to Day-Brite's. This action was then brought by Day-Brite. One count alleged that Compco had infringed Day-Brite's design patent; a second count charged that the public and the trade had come to associate this particular design with Day-Brite, that Compco had copied Day-Brite's distinctive design so as to confuse and deceive purchasers into thinking Compco's fixtures were actually Day-Brite's, and that by doing this Compco had unfairly competed with Day-Brite. The complaint prayed for both an accounting and an injunction.

The District Court held the design patent invalid; but as to the second count, while the court did not find that Compco had engaged in any deceptive or fraudulent practices, it did hold that Compco had been guilty of unfair competition under Illinois law. The court found that the overall appearance of Compco's fixture was "the same, to the eye of the ordinary observer, as the overall appearance" of Day-Brite's reflector, which embodied the design of the invalidated patent; that the appearance of Day-Brite's design had "the capacity, to identify [Day-Brite] in the trade and does in fact so identify [it] to the trade"; that the concurrent sale of the two products was "likely to cause confusion in the trade"; and that "[a]ctual confusion has occurred." On these findings the court adjudged Compco guilty of unfair competition in the sale of its fixtures, ordered Compco to account to Day-Brite for damages, and enjoined Compco "from unfairly competing with plaintiff by the sale or attempted sale of reflectors identical to, or confusingly similar to" those made by Day-Brite. The Court of Appeals held there was substantial evidence in the record to support the District Court's finding of likely confusion and that this finding was sufficient to support a holding of unfair competition under Illinois law.[2] 311 F. 2d 26. Although the District Court had not made such a finding, the appellate court observed that "several choices of ribbing were apparently available to meet the functional needs of the product," yet Compco "chose precisely the same design used by the plaintiff and followed it so closely as to make confusion likely." 311 F. 2d, at 30. A design which identifies its maker to the trade, the Court of Appeals held, is a "protectable" right under Illinois law, even though the design is unpatentable.[3] We granted certiorari. 374 U. S. 825.

---

[2] The Court of Appeals also affirmed the holding that the design patent was invalid. No review of this ruling is sought here.

[3] As stated in *Sears, Roebuck & Co. v. Stiffel Co.,* [*supra*], we do not here decide whether the Court of Appeals was correct in its statement of Illinois law.

To support its findings of likelihood of confusion and actual confusion, the trial court was able to refer to only one circumstance in the record. A plant manager who had installed some of Compco's fixtures later asked Day-Brite to service the fixtures, thinking they had been made by Day-Brite. There was no testimony given by a purchaser or by anyone else that any customer had ever been misled, deceived, or "confused," that is, that anyone had ever bought a Compco fixture thinking it was a Day-Brite fixture. All the record shows, as to the one instance cited by the trial court, is that both Compco and Day-Brite fixtures had been installed in the same plant, that three years later some repairs were needed, and that the manager viewing the Compco fixtures — hung at least 15 feet above the floor and arranged end to end in a continuous line so that identifying marks were hidden — thought they were Day-Brite fixtures and asked Day-Brite to service them. Not only is this incident suggestive only of confusion *after* a purchase had been made, but also there is considerable evidence of the care taken by Compco to prevent customer confusion, including clearly labeling both the fixtures and the containers in which they were shipped and not selling through manufacturers' representatives who handled competing lines.

Notwithstanding the thinness of the evidence to support findings of likely and actual confusion among purchasers, we do not find it necessary in this case to determine whether there is "clear error" in these findings. They, like those in *Sears, Roebuck & Co. v. Stiffel Co., supra,* were based wholly on the fact that selling an article which is an exact copy of another unpatented article is likely to produce and did in this case produce confusion as to the source of the article. Even accepting the findings, we hold that the order for an accounting for damages and the injunction are in conflict with the federal patent laws. Today we have held in *Sears, Roebuck & Co. v. Stiffel Co., supra,* that when an article is unprotected by a patent or a copyright, state law may not forbid others to copy that article. To forbid copying would interfere with the federal policy, found in Art. I, § 8, cl. 8, of the Constitution and in the implementing federal statutes, of allowing free access to copy whatever the federal patent and copyright laws leave in the public domain. Here Day-Brite's fixture has been held not to be entitled to a design or mechanical patent. Under the federal patent laws it is, therefore, in the public domain and can be copied in every detail by whoever pleases. It is true that the trial court found that the configuration of Day-Brite's fixture identified Day-Brite to the trade because the arrangement of the ribbing had, like a trademark, acquired a "secondary meaning" by which that particular design was associated with Day-Brite. But if the design is not entitled to a design patent or other federal statutory protection, then it can be copied at will.

As we have said in *Sears,* while the federal patent laws prevent a State from prohibiting the copying and selling of unpatented articles, they do not stand in the way of state law, statutory or decisional, which requires those who make and sell copies to take precautions to identify their products as their own. A State of course has power to impose liability upon those who, knowing that the public is relying upon an original manufacturer's reputation for quality and integrity, deceive the public by palming off their copies as the original. That an article copied from an unpatented article could be made in some other way, that the design is "nonfunctional" and not essential to the use of either article, that the configuration of the article copied may have a "secondary meaning" which identifies the maker to the trade, or that there may be "confusion" among purchasers as to which article is which or as to who is the maker, may be relevant evidence in applying a State's law requiring such precautions as labeling; however, and regardless of the copier's motives, neither these facts nor any others can furnish a basis for imposing liability for or prohibiting the actual acts of copying and selling. Cf. *Kellogg Co. v. National Biscuit Co.,* 305 U. S. 111, 120 (1938). And of course a State cannot hold a copier accountable in damages for failure to label or otherwise to identify his goods unless his failure is in violation of valid state statutory or decisional law requiring the copier to label or take other precautions to prevent confusion of customers as to the source of the goods.[5]

Since the judgment below forbids the sale of a copy of an unpatented article and orders an accounting for damages for such copying, it cannot stand.

Reversed.

Mr. Justice Harlan, concurring in the result.[*]

In one respect I would give the States more leeway in unfair competition "copying" cases than the Court's opinions would allow. If copying is found, other than by an inference arising from the mere act of copying, to have been undertaken with the dominant purpose and effect of palming off one's goods as those of another or of confusing customers as to the source of such goods, I see no reason why the State may not impose reasonable restrictions on the future "copying" itself. Vindication of the paramount federal interest at stake does not require a State to tolerate such specifically oriented predatory business practices. Apart from this, I am in accord with the opinions of the Court, and concur in both judgments since neither case presents the point on which I find myself in disagreement.

QUESTIONS

1. Is the conflict articulated in *Sears* and *Compco* "constitutional" or "statutory," i.e., was state unfair competition law found to conflict with the patent and copyright clause of the U.S. Constitution or with the federal patent law? What is the obvious consequence of this distinction?

2. Would the *Sears-Compco* rule apply to subject matter outside the constitutional power of Congress? Within such power but outside the scope of subject matter covered by the patent statute? How does this latter category differ from the subject matter actually involved in *Sears* and *Compco*?

3. What evidence is there as to whether the sweep of these cases reaches copyright? As a matter of policy should copyright be distinguished? Of what relevance is the 1976 Act's extension of statutory copyright to unpublished works?

4. Would a state law complementing federal protection, e.g., adding a remedy unavailable in the federal act for a valid patent, be permitted?

---

[5] As we pointed out in *Sears, Roebuck & Co. v. Stiffel Co., [supra]*, n. 9, there is no showing that Illinois has any such law.

[*] This opinion applies also to No. 108, *Sears, Roebuck & Co., v. Stiffel Co., [supra.]*

5. What are examples of "other precautionary steps," over and above labeling, permitted the states and under what circumstances?

6. The rule fashioned by the Supreme Court in the *International News Service* case was part of the "federal common law" which was applied in diversity-of-citizenship cases and which was, of course, overturned in *Erie R.R. v. Tompkins,* 304 U.S. 64 (1938). Could a *state* court today adopt such a doctrine of "misappropriation," consistent with the *Sears* and *Compco* decisions?

GOLDSTEIN v. CALIFORNIA

412 U.S. 546 (1973)

MR. CHIEF JUSTICE BURGER delivered the opinion of the Court.

We granted certiorari to review petitioners' conviction under a California statute making it a criminal offense to "pirate" recordings produced by others.*

In 1971, an information was filed by the State of California, charging petitioners in 140 counts with violating § 653h of the California Penal Code. The information charged that, between April 1970 and March 1971, petitioners had copied several musical performances from commercially sold recordings without the permission of the owner of the master record or tape.[1] Petitioners moved to dismiss the complaint on the grounds that § 653h was in conflict with Art. I, § 8, cl. 8, of the Constitution, the "Copyright Clause," and the federal statutes enacted thereunder. Upon denial of their motion, petitioners entered pleas of *nolo contendere* to 10 of the 140 counts; the remaining counts were dismissed. On appeal, the Appellate Department of the California Superior Court sustained the validity of the statute. After exhausting other state appellate remedies, petitioners sought review in this Court.

---

* The conduct for which the petitioners were criminally charged took place in 1970 and 1971. The student will recall that at that time the 1909 Copyright Act had not yet been amended to bar the unauthorized duplication of sound recordings. — Eds.

[1] In pertinent part, the California statute provides:

"(a) Every person is guilty of a misdemeanor who:
(1) Knowingly and willfully transfers or causes to be transferred any sounds recorded on a phonograph record, . . . tape, . . . or other article on which sounds are recorded, with intent to sell or cause to be sold, . . . such article on which such sounds are so transferred, without the consent of the owner.
"(2) . . . .
" . . . .
"(b) As used in this section, "person" means any individual, partnership, corporation or association; and "owner" means the person who owns the master phonograph record, . . . master tape, . . . or other device used for reproducing recorded sounds on phonograph records, . . . tapes, . . . or other articles on which sound is recorded, and from which the transferred recorded sounds are directly or indirectly derived."

Specifically, each count of the information alleged that, in regard to a particular recording, petitioners had, "at and in the City of Los Angeles, in the County of Los Angeles, State of California . . . wilfully, unlawfully and knowingly transferred and caused to be transferred sounds recorded on a tape with the intent to sell and cause to be sold, such tape on which such sounds [were] so transferred . . . ."

I

Petitioners were engaged in what has commonly been called "record piracy" or "tape piracy" — the unauthorized duplication of recordings of performances by major musical artists. Petitioners would purchase from a retail distributor a single tape or phonograph recording of the popular performances they wished to duplicate. The original recordings were produced and marketed by recording companies with which petitioners had no contractual relationship. At petitioners' plant, the recording was reproduced on blank tapes, which could in turn be used to replay the music on a tape player. The tape was then wound on a cartridge. A label was attached, stating the title of the recorded performance — the same title as had appeared on the original recording, and the name of the performing artists.[4] After final packaging, the tapes were distributed to retail outlets for sale to the public, in competition with those petitioners had copied.

Petitioners made no payments to the artists whose performances they reproduced and sold, or to the various trust funds established for their benefit; no payments were made to the producer, technicians, or other staff personnel responsible for producing the original recording and paying the large expenses incurred in production.[5] No payments were made for the use of the artists' names or the album title.

The challenged California statute forbids petitioners to transfer any performance fixed on a tape or record onto other records or tapes with the intention of selling the duplicates, unless they have first received permission from those who, under state law, are the owners of the master recording. Although the protection afforded to each master recording is substantial, lasting for an unlimited time, the scope of the proscribed activities is narrow. No limitation is placed on the use of the music, lyrics, or arrangement employed in making the master recording. Petitioners are not precluded from hiring their own musicians and artists and recording an exact imitation of the performance embodied on the master recording. Petitioners are even free to hire the same artists who made the initial recording in order to duplicate the performance. In essence, the statute thus provides copyright protection solely for the specific expressions which compose the master record or tape.

Petitioners' attack on the constitutionality of § 653h has many facets. First, they contend that the statute establishes a state copyright of unlimited duration, and thus conflicts with Art. I, § 8, cl. 8, of the Constitution. Second, petitioners claim that the state statute interferes with the implementation of federal policies inherent in the federal copyright statutes. 17 U. S. C. § 1 *et seq.* According to petitioners, it was the intention of Congress, as interpreted by this Court in *Sears,*

---

[4] An additional label was attached to each cartridge by petitioners stating that no relationship existed between petitioners and the producer of the original recording or the individuals whose performances had been recorded. Consequently, no claim is made that petitioners misrepresented the source of the original recordings or the manufacturer of the tapes.

[5] The costs of producing a single original longplaying record of a musical performance may exceed $50,000 or $100,000. *Tape Industries Assn. of America v. Younger,* [316 F. Supp. 340 (C.D. Cal. 1970)], at 344; Hearings on S. 646 and H. R. 6927 before Subcommittee No. 3 of the House Committee on the Judiciary, 92d Cong., 1st Sess., 27-28 (1971). For the performance recorded on this record, petitioners would pay only the retail cost of a single longplaying record or a single tape.

Roebuck & Co. v. Stiffel Co., 376 U. S. 225 (1964), and *Compco Corp. v. Day-Brite Lighting,* 376 U. S. 234 (1964), to establish a uniform law throughout the United States to protect original writings. As part of the federal scheme, it is urged that Congress intended to allow individuals to copy any work which was not protected by a federal copyright. Since § 653h effectively prohibits the copying of works which are not entitled to federal protection, petitioners contend that it conflicts directly with congressional policy and must fall under the Supremacy Clause of the Constitution. Finally, petitioners argue that 17 U. S. C. § 2, which allows States to protect unpublished writings,[6] does not authorize the challenged state provision; since the records which petitioners copied had previously been released to the public, petitioners contend that they had, under federal law, been published.

We note at the outset that the federal copyright statutes to which petitioners refer were amended by Congress while their case was pending in the state courts. In 1971, Pub. L. 92-140, 85 Stat. 391, 17 U. S. C. §§ 1 (f), 5 (n), 19, 20, 26, 101 (e), was passed to allow federal copyright protection of recordings. However, § 3 of the amendment specifically provides that such protection is to be available only to sound recordings "fixed, published, and copyrighted" on and after February 15, 1972, and before January 1, 1975, and that nothing in Title 17, as amended is to "be applied retroactively or [to] be construed as affecting in any way any rights with respect to sound recordings fixed before" February 15, 1972. The recordings which petitioners copied were all "fixed" prior to February 15, 1972. Since, according to the language of § 3 of the amendment, Congress did not intend to alter the legal relationships which govern these recordings, the amendments have no application in petitioners' case.

II

Petitioners' first argument rests on the premise that the state statute under which they were convicted lies beyond the powers which the States reserved in our federal system. If this is correct, petitioners must prevail, since the States cannot exercise a sovereign power which, under the Constitution, they have relinquished to the Federal Government for its exclusive exercise.

A

. . . .

Article I, § 8, cl. 8, of the Constitution gives to Congress the power —

> To promote the Progress of Science and useful Arts, by securing for limited Times to Authors and Inventors the exclusive Right to their respective Writings and Discoveries . . . .

The clause thus describes both the objective which Congress may seek and the means to achieve it. The objective is to promote the progress of science and the arts. As employed, the terms "to promote" are synonymous with the words "to stimulate," "to encourage," or "to induce." To accomplish its purpose, Congress

---

[6] Title 17 U. S. C. § 2 provides: "Nothing in this title shall be construed to annul or limit the right of the author or proprietor of an unpublished work, at common law or in equity, to prevent the copying, publication, or use of such unpublished work without his consent, and to obtain damages therefor."

may grant to authors the exclusive right to the fruits of their respective works. An author who possesses an unlimited copyright may preclude others from copying his creation for commercial purposes without permission. In other words, to encourage people to devote themselves to intellectual and artistic creation, Congress may guarantee to authors and inventors a reward in the form of control over the sale or commercial use of copies of their works.

The objective of the Copyright Clause was clearly to facilitate the granting of rights national in scope. While the debates on the clause at the Constitutional Convention were extremely limited, its purpose was described by James Madison in the Federalist:

> The utility of this power will scarcely be questioned. The copyright of authors has been solemnly adjudged, in Great Britain, to be a right of common law. The right to useful inventions seems with equal reason to belong to the inventors. The public good fully coincides in both cases with the claims of individuals. The States cannot separately make effectual provision for either of the cases, and most of them have anticipated the decision of this point, by laws passed at the instance of Congress.[11]

The difficulty noted by Madison relates to the burden placed on an author or inventor who wishes to achieve protection in all States when no federal system of protection is available. To do so, a separate application is required to each state government; the right which in turn may be granted has effect only within the granting State's borders.[12] The national system which Madison supported eliminates the need for multiple applications and the expense and difficulty involved. In effect, it allows Congress to provide a reward greater in scope than any particular State may grant to promote progress in those fields which Congress determines are worthy of national action.

Although the Copyright Clause thus recognizes the potential benefits of a national system, it does not indicate that all writings are of national interest or that state legislation is, in all cases, unnecessary or precluded. The patents granted by the States in the 18th century show, to the contrary, a willingness on the part of the States to promote those portions of science and the arts which were of local importance. Whatever the diversity of people's backgrounds, origins, and interests, and whatever the variety of business and industry in the 13 Colonies, the range of diversity is obviously far greater today in a country of 210 million people in 50 States. In view of that enormous diversity, it is unlikely that all citizens in all parts of the country place the same importance on works relating to all subjects. Since the subject matter to which the Copyright Clause is addressed may thus be of purely local importance and not worthy of national attention or protection, we cannot discern such an unyielding national interest as to require an inference that state power to grant copyrights has been relinquished to *exclusive* federal control.

---

[11] The Federalist No. 43, p. 309 (B. Wright ed. 1961).

[12] Numerous examples may be found in our early history of the difficulties which the creators of items of national import had in securing protection of their creations in all States. For example, Noah Webster, in his effort to obtain protection for his book, A Grammatical Institute of the English Language, brought his claim before the legislatures of at least six States, and perhaps as many as 12. See B. Bugbee, The Genesis of American Patent and Copyright Law 108-110, 120-124 Wash., D. C., 1967); H. R. Rep. No. 2222, 60th Cong., 2d Sess., 2 (1909). Similar difficulties were experienced by John Fitch and other inventors who desired to protect their efforts to perfect a steamboat. See Federico, State Patents, 13 J. Pat. Off. Soc. 166, 170-176 (1931).

The question to which we next turn is whether, in actual operation, the exercise of the power to grant copyrights by some States will prejudice the interests of other States. As we have noted, a copyright granted by a particular State has effect only within its boundaries. If one State grants such protection, the interests of States which do not are not prejudiced since their citizens remain free to copy within their borders those works which may be protected elsewhere. The interests of a State which grants copyright protection may, however, be adversely affected by other States that do not; individuals who wish to purchase a copy of a work protected in their own State will be able to buy unauthorized copies in other States where no protection exists. However, this conflict is neither so inevitable nor so severe as to compel the conclusion, that state power has been relinquished to the exclusive jurisdiction of the Congress. Obviously when some States do not grant copyright protection — and most do not — that circumstance reduces the economic value of a state copyright, but it will hardly render the copyright worthless. The situation is no different from that which may arise in regard to other state monopolies, such as a state lottery, or a food concession in a limited enclosure like a state park; in each case, citizens may escape the effect of one State's monopoly by making purchases in another area or another State. Similarly, in the case of state copyrights, except as to individuals willing to travel across state lines in order to purchase records or other writings protected in their own State, each State's copyrights will still serve to induce new artistic creations within that State — the very objective of the grant of protection. We do not see here the type of prejudicial conflicts which would arise, for example, if each State exercised a sovereign power to impose imposts and tariffs; nor can we discern a need for uniformity such as that which may apply to the regulation of interstate shipments.

Similarly, it is difficult to see how the concurrent exercise of the power to grant copyrights by Congress and the States will necessarily and inevitably lead to difficulty. At any time Congress determines that a particular category of "writing" is worthy of national protection and the incidental expenses of federal administration, federal copyright protection may be authorized. Where the need for free and unrestricted distribution of a writing is thought to be required by the national interest, the Copyright Clause and the Commerce Clause would allow Congress to eschew all protection. In such cases, a conflict would develop if a State attempted to protect that which Congress intended to be free from restraint or to free that which Congress had protected. However, where Congress determines that neither federal protection nor freedom from restraint is required by the national interest, it is at liberty to stay its hand entirely.[16] Since state protection would not then conflict with federal action, total relinquishment of the State's power to grant copyright protection cannot be inferred.

As we have seen, the language of the Constitution neither explicitly precludes the States from granting copyrights nor grants such authority exclusively to the Federal Government. The subject matter to which the Copyright Clause is addressed may at times be of purely local concern. No conflict will necessarily arise from a lack of uniform state regulation, nor will the interest of one State be significantly prejudiced by the actions of another. No reason exists why Congress must take affirmative action either to authorize protection of all categories of writings or to free them from all restraint. We therefore conclude

---

[16] For example, Congress has allowed writings which may eventually be the subject of a federal copyright, to be protected under state law prior to publication. 17 U. S. C. § 2.

that, under the Constitution, the States have not relinquished all power to grant to authors "the exclusive Right to their respective Writings."

B

Petitioners base an additional argument on the language of the Constitution. The California statute forbids individuals to appropriate recordings at any time after release. From this, petitioners argue that the State has created a copyright of *unlimited* duration, in violation of that portion of Art. I, § 8, cl. 8, which provides that copyrights may only be granted "for limited Times." Read literally, the text of Art. I does not support petitioners' position. Section 8 enumerates those powers which have been granted *to Congress;* whatever limitations have been appended to such powers can only be understood as a limit on congressional, and not state, action. Moreover, it is not clear that the dangers to which this limitation was addressed apply with equal force to both the Federal Government and the States. When Congress grants an exclusive right or monopoly, its effects are pervasive; no citizen or State may escape its reach. As we have noted, however, the exclusive right granted by a State is confined to its borders. Consequently, even when the right is unlimited in duration, any tendency to inhibit further progress in science or the arts is narrowly circumscribed. The challenged statute cannot be voided for lack of a durational limitation.

III

Our conclusion that California did not surrender its power to issue copyrights does not end the inquiry. We must proceed to determine whether the challenged state statute is void under the Supremacy Clause. No simple formula can capture the complexities of this determination; the conflicts which may develop between state and federal action are as varied as the fields to which congressional action may apply. "Our primary function is to determine whether, under the circumstances of this particular case, [the state] law stands as an obstacle to the accomplishment and execution of the full purposes and objectives of Congress." *Hines v. Davidowitz,* 312 U. S. 52, 67 (1941). We turn, then, to federal copyright law to determine what objectives Congress intended to fulfill.

By Art. I, § 8, cl. 8, of the Constitution, the States granted to Congress the power to protect the "Writings" of "Authors." These terms have not been construed in their narrow literal sense but, rather, with the reach necessary to reflect the broad scope of constitutional principles. While an "author" may be viewed as an individual who writes an original composition, the term, in its constitutional sense, has been construed to mean an "originator," "he to whom anything owes its origin." *Burrow-Giles Lithographic Co. v. Sarony,* 111 U. S. 53, 58 (1884). Similarly, although the word "writings" might be limited to script or printed material, it may be interpreted to include any physical rendering of the fruits of creative intellectual or aesthetic labor. *Ibid.; Trade-Mark Cases,* 100 U. S. 82, 94 (1879). Thus, recordings of artistic performances may be within the reach of Clause 8.

While the area in which Congress *may* act is broad, the enabling provision of Clause 8 does not require that Congress act in regard to all categories of materials which meet the constitutional definitions. Rather, whether any specific category of "Writings" is to be brought within the purview of the federal statutory scheme is left to the discretion of the Congress. The history of federal copyright statutes indicates that the congressional determination to consider specific classes of writings is dependent, not only on the character of the writing, but also on the commercial importance of the product to the national economy. As our technology has expanded the means available for creative activity and has provided economical means for reproducing manifestations of such activity, new areas of federal protection have been initiated.[17]

Petitioners contend that the actions taken by Congress in establishing federal copyright protection preclude the States from granting similar protection to recordings of musical performances. According to petitioners, Congress addressed the question of whether recordings of performances should be granted protection in 1909; Congress determined that any individual who was entitled to a copyright on an original musical composition should have the right to control to a limited extent the use of that composition on recordings, but that the record itself, and the performance which it was capable of reproducing were not worthy of such protection.[18]

---

[17] The first congressional copyright statute, passed in 1790, governed only maps, charts, and books. Act of May 31, 1790, c. 15, 1 Stat. 124. In 1802, the Act was amended in order to grant protection to any person "who shall invent and design, engrave, etch or work . . . any historical or other print or prints . . . ." Act of Apr. 29, 1802, c. 36, 2 Stat. 171. Protection was extended to musical compositions when the copyright laws were revised in 1831. Act of Feb. 3, 1831, c. 16, 4 Stat. 436. In 1865, at the time when Mathew Brady's pictures of the Civil War were attaining fame, photographs and photographic negatives were expressly added to the list of protected works. Act of Mar. 3, 1865, c. 126, 13 Stat. 540. Again in 1870, the list was augmented to cover paintings, drawings, chromos, statuettes, statuary, and models or designs of fine art. Act of July 8, 1870, c. 230, 16 Stat. 198.

In 1909, Congress agreed to a major consolidation and amendment of all federal copyright statutes. A list of 11 categories of protected works was provided. The relevant sections of the Act are discussed in the text of our opinion. The House Report on the proposed bill specifically noted that amendment was required because "the reproduction of various things which are the subject of copyright has enormously increased," and that the President has specifically recommended revision, among other reasons, because the prior laws "omit[ted] provision for many articles which, under modern reproductive processes, are entitled to protection." H. R. Rep. No. 2222, supra, n. 12, at 1 (quoting Samuel J. Elder and President Theodore Roosevelt).

Since 1909, two additional amendments have been added. In 1912, the list of categories in § 5 was expanded specifically to include motion pictures. The House Report on the amendment noted:

"The occasion for this proposed amendment is the fact that the production of motion-picture photoplays and motion pictures other than photoplays has become a business of vast proportions. The money invested therein is so great and the property rights so valuable that the committee is of the opinion that the copyright law ought to be so amended as to give to them distinct and definite recognition and protection." H. R. Rep. No. 756, 62d Cong., 2d Sess., 1 (1912).

Finally, in 1971, § 5 was amended to include "sound recordings." Congress was spurred to action by the growth of record piracy, which was, in turn, due partly to technological advances. See Hearings on S. 646 and H. R. 6927, supra, n. 5, at 4-5, 11 (1971). It must be remembered that the "record piracy" charged against petitioners related to recordings fixed by the original producer prior to Feb. 15, 1972, the effective date of the 1971 Act.

[18] 17 U. S. C. § 1 (e).

. . . .

Petitioners' argument does not rest entirely on the belief that Congress intended specifically to exempt recordings of performances from state control. Assuming that no such intention may be found, they argue that Congress so occupied the field of copyright protection as to pre-empt all comparable state action. *Rice v. Santa Fe Elevator Corp.*, 331 U. S. 218 (1947). This assertion is based on the language of 17 U. S. C. §§ 4 and 5, and on this Court's opinions in *Sears, Roebuck & Co. v. Stiffel Co.*, 376 U. S. 225 (1964), and *Compco Corp. v. Day-Brite Lighting*, 376 U. S. 234 (1964).

Section 4 of the federal copyright laws provides:

> The works for which copyright may be secured under this title shall include all the writings of an author. 17 U.S.C. § 4.
>
> . . . .
>
> The above specifications shall not be held to limit the subject matter of copyright as defined in section 4 of this title . . . . 17 U.S.C. § 5.

Since § 4 employs the constitutional term "writings," it may be argued that Congress intended to exercise its authority over all works to which the constitutional provision might apply. However, in the more than 60 years which have elapsed since enactment of this provision, neither the Copyright Office, the courts, nor the Congress has so interpreted it. The Register of Copyrights, who is charged with administration of the statute, has consistently ruled that "claims to exclusive rights in mechanical recordings . . . or in the performances they reproduce" are not entitled to protection under § 4. 37 CFR § 202.8 (b) (1972). With one early exception, Amercian courts have agreed with this interpretation; and in 1971, prior to passage of the statute which extended federal protection to recordings fixed on or after February 15, 1972, Congress acknowledged the validity of that interpretation. Both the House and Senate Reports on the proposed legislation recognized that recordings qualified as "writings" within the meaning of the Constitution, but had not previously been protected under the federal copyright statute. H. R. Rep. No. 92-487, pp. 2,5 (1971); S. Rep. No. 92-72, p. 4 (1971). In light of this consistent interpretation by the courts, the agency empowered to administer the copyright statutes, and Congress itself, we cannot agree that §§ 4 and 5 have the broad scope petitioners claim.

Sears and *Compco*, on which petitioners rely, do not support their position. In those cases, the question was whether a State could, under principles of a state unfair competition law, preclude the copying of mechanical configurations which did not possess the qualities required for the granting of a federal design or mechanical patent. The Court stated:

> [T]he patent system is one in which uniform federal standards are carefully used to promote invention while at the same time preserving free competition. Obviously a State could not, consistently with the Supremacy Clause of the Constitution, extend the life of a patent beyond its expiration date or give a patent on an article which lacked the level of invention required for federal patents. To do either would run counter to the policy of Congress of granting patents only to true inventions, and then only for a limited time. Just as a State cannot encroach upon the federal patent laws directly, it cannot, under some other law, such as that forbidding unfair competition, give protection of a kind that clashes with the objectives of the federal patent laws. *Sears, Roebuck & Co. v. Stiffel Co.*, 376 U. S., at 230-231 (footnotes omitted).

In regard to mechanical configurations, Congress had balanced the need to encourage innovation and originality of invention against the need to insure competition in the sale of identical or substantially identical products. The standards established for granting federal patent protection to machines thus indicated not only which articles in this particular category Congress wished to protect, but which configurations it wished to remain free. The application of state law in these cases to prevent the copying of articles which did not meet the requirements for federal protection disturbed the careful balance which Congress had drawn and thereby necessarily gave way under the Supremacy Clause of the Constitution. No comparable conflict between state law and federal law arises in the case of recordings of musical performances. In regard to this category of "Writings," Congress has drawn no balance; rather, it has left the area unattended, and no reason exists why the State should not be free to act.[28]

IV

More than 50 years ago, Mr. Justice Brandeis observed in dissent in *International News Service v. Associated Press:*

The general rule of law is, that the noblest of human productions — knowledge, truths ascertained, conceptions, and ideas — become, after voluntary communication to others, free as the air to common use. 248 U.S. 215, 250 (1918).

But there is no fixed, immutable line to tell us which "human productions" are private property and which are so general as to become "free as the air." In earlier times, a performing artist's work was largely restricted to the stage; once performed, it remained "recorded" only in the memory of those who had seen or heard it. Today, we can record that performance in precise detail and reproduce it again and again with utmost fidelity. The California statutory scheme evidences a legislative policy to prohibit "tape piracy" and "record piracy," conduct that may adversely affect the continued production of new recordings, a large industry in California. Accordingly, the State has, by statute, given to recordings the attributes of property. No restraint has been placed on the use of an idea or concept; rather, petitioners and other individuals remain free to record the same compositions in precisely the same manner and with the same personnel as appeared on the original recording.

In sum, we have shown that § 653h does not conflict with the federal copyright statute enacted by Congress in 1909. Similarly, no conflict exists between the federal copyright statute passed in 1971 and the present application of § 653h, since California charged petitioners only with copying recordings fixed prior to February 15, 1972. Finally, we have concluded that our decisions in *Sears* and *Compco,* which we reaffirm today, have no application in the present case, since Congress has indicated neither that it wishes to protect, nor to free from protection, recordings of musical performances fixed prior to February 15, 1972.

We conclude that the State of California has exercised a power which it retained under the Constitution, and that the challenged statute, as applied in

---

[28] Petitioners place great stress on their belief that the records or tapes which they copied had been "published." We have no need to determine whether, *under state law,* these recordings had been published or what legal consequences such publication might have. *For purposes of federal law,* "publication" serves only as a term of art which defines the legal relationships which Congress has adopted under the federal copyright statutes. As to categories of writings which Congress has not brought within the scope of the federal statute, the term has no application.

this case, does not intrude into an area which Congress has, up to now, pre-empted. Until and unless Congress takes further action with respect to recordings fixed prior to Feburary 15, 1972, the California statute may be enforced against acts of piracy such as those which occurred in the present case.

Affirmed.

MR. JUSTICE DOUGLAS, with whom MR. JUSTICE BRENNAN and MR. JUSTICE BLACKMUN concur, dissenting.

. . . .

Cases like *Sears* were surcharged with "unfair competition" and the present one with "pirated recordings." But free access to products on the market is the consumer interest protected by the failure of Congress to extend patents or copyrights into various areas. The drive for monopoly protection is strong as is evident from a reading of the committee reports on the 1971 Act. Yet, Congress took but a short step, setting up a trial period to consider the new monopoly approach. It was told that state laws, such as we have in this case, were being challenged on the ground that the Federal Constitution had pre-empted the field, even in [the] absence of a provision for making it possible to obtain a copyright for sound recordings. But the House Committee made only the following comment:

> While the committee expresses no opinion concerning this legal question, it is clear that the extension of copyright protection to sound recordings would resolve many of the problems which have arisen in connection with the efforts to combat piracy in State courts.

The Department of Justice in commenting on the proposals that resulted in the 1971 Act told the House:

> We believe that extending copyright to reproduction of sound recordings is the soundest, and in our interpretation of *Sears* and *Compco,* the only way in which sound recordings should be protected. Copyright protection is narrowly defined and limited in duration, whereas state remedies, whose validity is still in doubt, frequently create broad and unwarranted perpetual monopolies. Moreover, there is an immediate and urgent need for this protection.

The need for uniformity was stated by Judge Learned Hand in a dissent in *Capitol Records, Inc. v. Mercury Records Corp.,* 221 F. 2d 657. That case involved the duplication of uncopyrighted sound recordings, the court holding that state law prevailed where there was no federal copyright provision. Judge Hand emphasized in his dissent that "uniformity" was one of the principal purposes of the Patent and Copyright Clause and that uniformity could be obtained only by pre-emption. He said:

> If, for example in the case at bar, the defendant is forbidden to make and sell these records in New York, that will not prevent it from making and selling them in any other state which may regard the plaintiff's sales as a "publication"; and it will be practically impossible to prevent their importation into New York. That is exactly the kind of evil at which the clause is directed. *Id.,* at 667.

I would reverse the judgment below.

MR. JUSTICE MARSHALL, with whom MR. JUSTICE BRENNAN and MR. JUSTICE BLACKMUN join, dissenting.

The argument of the Court, as I understand it, is this: Art. I, § 8, cl. 8, of the Constitution gives Congress the power "[t]o promote the Progress of Science and useful Arts, by securing for limited Times to Authors and Inventors the exclusive Right to their respective Writings and Discoveries." The Framers recognized that individual States might have peculiarly local interests that Congress might not consider worthy of attention. Thus, the constitutional provision does not, of its own force, bar States from promoting those local interests. However, as the Court noted in *Sears, Roebuck & Co. v. Stiffel Co.,* 376 U. S. 225 (1964), with respect to every particular item within general classes enumerated in the relevant statutes, Congress had balanced the need to promote invention against the desire to preserve free competition, and had concluded that it was in the national interest to preserve competition as to every item that could not be patented. That is, the fact that some item could not be patented demonstrated that, in the judgment of Congress, it was best to let competition in the production of that item go unrestricted. The situation with regard to copyrights is said to be similar. There Congress enumerated certain classes of works for which a copyright may be secured. 17 U. S. C. § 5. Its silence as to other classes does not reflect a considered judgment about the relative importance of competition and promotion of "Science and useful Arts." Thus, the Court says, the States remain free to protect as they will "writings" not in the enumerated classes, until Congress acts. Since sound recordings fixed prior to February 15, 1972, were not enumerated by Congress as subject to copyrighting,[1] the States may protect such recordings.

With respect, I cannot accept the final step of this argument. In my view, Congress has demonstrated its desire to exercise the full grant of constitutional power. Title 17 U. S. C. § 4, states: "The works for which copyright may be secured under this title shall include *all the writings of an author*" (emphasis added). The use of the constitutional terms "writings" and "author" rather strongly suggests that Congress intended to follow the constitutional grant. It could exercise the power given it by the Constitution in two ways: either by protecting all writings, or by protecting all writings within designated classes and leaving open to competition all writings in other classes. Section 5 shows that the latter course was chosen, for it enumerates various classes of works that may be registered.[2] Ordinarily, the failure to enumerate "sound recordings" in § 5 would not be taken as an expression of Congress' desire to let free competition reign in the reproduction of such recordings, for, because of the realities of the legislative process, it is generally difficult to infer from a failure to act any affirmative conclusions. Cf. *Cleveland v. United States,* 329 U. S. 14, 22 (1946) (Rutledge, J., concurring). But in *Sears* and its companion case, *Compco Corp. v. Day-Brite Lighting,* 376 U. S. 234 (1964), the Court determined that with respect to patents and copyrights, the ordinary practice was not to prevail. In view of the importance of not imposing unnecessary restraints on competition, the Court adopted in those cases a rule of construction that, unless the failure to provide patent or copyright protection for some class of works could clearly be shown to reflect a judgment that state regulation was permitted, the silence

---

[1] Sound recordings fixed after that date may be copyrighted. Pub. L. 92-140, 85 Stat. 391, 17 U. S. C. § 5 (n) (1970 ed., Supp. I).

[2] From the language of § 4 and the proviso of § 5, it could be rather strongly argued that Congress had intended to afford protection to every writing. I agree with the Court, however, that the consistent administrative interpretation of those sections, in conjunction with the practical difficulty of applying to novel cases certain statutory requirements, like that requiring placement of the notice of copyright on every copy, 17 U. S. C. § 10, precludes such an argument.

of Congress would be taken to reflect a judgment that free competition should prevail. I do not find in *Sears* and *Compco* a limitation on that rule of construction to general classes that Congress has enumerated although, of course, on the facts of those cases only items in such classes were involved; rather, the broadest language was used in those cases.[3] Nor can I find in the course of legislation sufficient evidence to convince me that Congress determined to permit state regulation of the reproduction of sound recordings. For, whenever technological advances made extension of copyright protection seem wise, Congress has acted promptly. See *ante*, n. 17.[4] This seems to me to reflect the same judgment that the Court found in *Sears* and *Compco:* Congress has decided that free competition should be the general rule, until it is convinced that the failure to provide copyright or patent protection is hindering "the Progress of Science and useful Arts."

The business of record piracy is not an attractive one; persons in the business capitalize on the talents of others without needing to assess independently the prospect of public acceptance of a performance. But the same might be said of persons who copy "mechanical configurations." Such people do provide low-cost reproductions that may well benefit the public. In light of the presumption of *Sears* and *Compco* that congressional silence betokens a determination that the benefits of competition outweigh the impediments placed on creativity by the lack of copyright protection, and in the absence of a congressional determination that the opposite is true, we should not let our distaste for "pirates" interfere with our interpretation of the copyright laws. I would therefore hold that, as to sound recordings fixed before February 15, 1972, the States may not enforce laws limiting reproduction.

QUESTIONS

1. Contrast the approach to preemption reflected in *Goldstein* on the one hand and *Sears-Compco* on the other. Did the Court in *Goldstein* satisfactorily distinguish *Sears* and *Compco*? Articulate the basis of the distinction. Was the Court saying, simply, that the *Sears-Compco* philosophy applies only to potentially patentable subject matter and not to potentially copyrightable subject matter? Is this a tenable distinction? (Note that the Court, earlier in its opinion,

---

[3] It bears noting that in Sears, Roebuck & Co. v. Stiffel Co., 376 U. S. 225 (1964), the Court repeatedly referred to the patent and copyright statutes as if the same rules of interpretation applied to both. See *e. g., id.,* at 228, 231 n. 7: Compco Corp. v. Day-Brite Lighting, 376 U. S. 234, 237 (1964).

[4] Between 1909 and 1951, Congress' attention was repeatedly drawn to problems of copyrighting sound recordings. Many bills to provide copyright protection for such recordings were introduced, but none were enacted. See Ringer, The Unauthorized Duplication of Sound Recordings, Studies Prepared for the Subcommittee on Patents, Trademarks, and Copyrights of the Senate Committee on the Judiciary, 86th Cong., 2d Sess., 21-37 (Comm. Print 1961). Respondent argues that Congress failed to enact these bills primarily out of uncertainty about the relationship between federal law and international copyright conventions, and was comforted in the knowledge that protection was available under state law. See Brief for Respondent 28-32. However, it is enough that Congress was aware of the problem, and could have acted, as it did when other technological innovations presented new problems, rather expeditiously. The problems that Congress confronted in 1971 did not spring up in 1970, but had existed, and Congress had not acted, for many years before.

adverts to state patent laws of the eighteenth century. Would there be any scope for validity of such laws today, after *Goldstein*?)

2. Consider carefully the Court's statement that "the subject matter to which the Copyright Clause is addressed may thus be of purely local importance and not worthy of national attention or protection." On behalf of the Court — writing in an age of communications satellites, television, computers and telephone-transmissible photocopies — what constitutionally copyrightable subject matter would you give as examples? What is peculiarly "local" about an Elvis Presley recording as compared, for example, to a map of Washington Square (which the Founding Fathers promptly brought within the scope of the first Copyright Act in 1790)? How did the Court determine that sound recordings had been "left . . . unattended" by Congress?

3. In *CBS v. DeCosta*, 377 F.2d 315 (1st Cir.) *cert. denied*, 389 U.S. 1007 (1967), defendants appealed from a jury award of $150,000 for their misappropriation in the television series "Have Gun Will Travel" of the character of Paladin created by DeCosta. The Court of Appeals for the First Circuit reversed, finding that photographs, fully conveying the appearance of DeCosta's Paladin, were distributed, apparently without copyright notice, together with great quantities of cards bearing his chess symbol, name and slogan. These were deemed "unquestionably 'writings' within the meaning of the copyright clause, and arguably copyrightable under the statute." The pivot of the reversal was the *Sears-Compco* doctrine, refined by the Court as follows:

> Thus, if a "writing" is within the scope of the constitutional clause, and Congress has not protected it, whether deliberately or by unexplained omission, it can be freely copied.

How is this interpretation affected by *Goldstein?* The answer is provided by a later chapter in this controversy.

DeCOSTA v. COLUMBIA BROADCASTING SYSTEM, INC.

520 F.2d 499 (1st Cir. 1975)

COFFIN, CHIEF JUDGE.

. . . .

The claim below, in the remaining counts two and three of the complaint, asserted a wilful and intentional infringement of plaintiff's common law trademark and/or service mark and unfair competition. The plaintiff sought both injunctive and monetary relief, including an accounting for all profits made by defendants in broadcasting "Have Gun Will Travel". The first count [common law misappropriation] had been tried before a jury. When this court reversed the result obtained in that trial, the case was returned to the district court where the parties entered into a stipulation that counts two and three be determined by the district judge on the basis of the trial transcript, including all exhibits, together with a stipulation of additional testimony. 383 F.Supp. 326, 327.

. . . .

Picking our way through the cluster of issues in several related but different fields of the law, we start where we left off, at *DeCosta I*. We there gave what has since been characterized as an expansive reading to *Sears* and *Compco*. See, e. g., Comment, *Copyright Pre-emption and Character Values; The Paladin Case as an Extension of Sears and Compco*, 66 Mich.L.Rev. 1018 (1967-1968). We held that "if a 'writing' is within the scope of the constitutional clause, and Congress has not protected it, whether deliberately or by unexplained omission, it can be freely copied." 377 F.2d at 319. Since the cards — including the photograph — "were unquestionably 'writings' within the meaning of the copyright clause, and arguably were copyrightable under the statute", *id.* at 321, we concluded that plaintiff could [not] prevent others from copying them.[22]

We now know, after *Goldstein v. California,* 412 U.S. 546, 560 (1973), that "under the Constitution, the States have not relinquished all power to grant to authors 'the exclusive Right to their respective Writings'." In *Kewanee Oil Co. v. Bicron Corp.,* 416 U.S. 470, 478-479 (1974), this holding was summarized: "at least in the case of writings, the States were not prohibited from encouraging and protecting the efforts of those within their borders by appropriate legislation." Were we to take this literally, we would see no reason to look on *Goldstein* as relevant to this case; plaintiff relies on a common law service mark as subsumed also by a federal statute, 15 U.S.C. § 1125 (part of the Lanham Act), but not state legislation. Nevertheless, since the countervailing state law found sufficient in *Kewanee* was common law, not statutory law, we do not read its capsule of *Goldstein* literally.

We face a dilemma. *Goldstein* tells us that we were, in our interpretation of the preemptive reach of the Copyright Clause, over-inclusive. And yet, what we decided in *DeCosta I* has settled, for this case, the issue of misappropriation. Had *Sears* and *Compco* remained unglossed, we might well rule that *DeCosta I* had predetermined our decision on the second and third causes of action. For if defendants could not be prohibited from copying the cards, which gave the defendants all that they took from plaintiff and incorporated in their series, would not any sanction, whether based on service mark infringement or unfair competition, denigrate their license? We do not, however, rest on any such implications of *De Costa I,* realizing that we do not have a tabula rasa to write upon.

A starting point, of course, is the explicit domain left open in *Sears,* that a state "may protect businesses in the use of their trademarks, labels, or distinctive dress in the packaging of goods so as to prevent others, by imitating such markings, from misleading purchasers as to the source of such goods." 376 U.S. 225, 232. . . . [The court rendered judgment for the defendants, holding that the plaintiff was not engaged in a "business" and that there was no evidence of likelihood that television viewers would be led by confusion to believe that the character depicted on "Have Gun Will Travel" was Mr. DeCosta. "Absent the ultimate fact of confusion, we cannot find a basis for liability for common law service mark infringement or unfair competition."]

KEWANEE OIL CO. v. BICRON CORP.

416 U.S. 470 (1974)

Mr. Chief Justice Burger delivered the opinion of the Court.

We granted certiorari to resolve a question on which there is a conflict in the courts of appeals: whether state trade secret protection is pre-empted by operation of the federal patent law. In the instant case the Court of Appeals for the

---

[22] To the extent that a "character" was "ineffable", incapable of "concrete describable manifestation of intellectual creation", and therefore ineligible for copyright protection, we thought it also ineligible for any protection, state or federal. Pre-*Goldstein,* this supposition had respectable support. *See* Nimmer, The Law of Copyright, Vol. 1, § 30, p. 137, n. 595.

Sixth Circuit held that there was pre-emption. The Courts of Appeals for the Second, Fourth, Fifth, and Ninth Circuits have reached the opposite conclusion.

I

Harshaw Chemical Co., an unincorporated division of petitioner, is a leading manufacturer of a type of synthetic crystal which is useful in the detection of ionizing radiation. In 1949 Harshaw commenced research into the growth of this type crystal and was able to produce one less than two inches in diameter. By 1966, as the result of expenditures in excess of $1 million, Harshaw was able to grow a 17-inch crystal, something no one else had done previously. Harshaw had developed many processes, procedures, and manufacturing techniques in the purification of raw materials and the growth and encapsulation of the crystals which enabled it to accomplish this feat. Some of these processes Harshaw considers to be trade secrets.

The individual respondents are former employees of Harshaw who formed or later joined respondent Bicron. While at Harshaw the individual respondents executed, as a condition of employment, at least one agreement each, requiring them not to disclose confidential information or trade secrets obtained as employees of Harshaw. Bicron was formed in August 1969 to compete with Harshaw in the production of the crystals, and by April 1970, had grown a 17-inch crystal.

Petitioner brought this diversity action in United States District Court for the Northern District of Ohio seeking injunctive relief and damages for the misappropriation of trade secrets. The District Court, applying Ohio trade secret law, granted a permanent injunction against the disclosure or use by respondents of 20 of the 40 claimed trade secrets until such time as the trade secrets had been released to the public, had otherwise generally become available to the public, or had been obtained by respondents from sources having the legal right to convey the information.

The Court of Appeals for the Sixth Circuit held that the findings of fact by the District Court were not clearly erroneous, and that it was evident from the record that the individual respondents appropriated to the benefit of Bicron secret information on processes obtained while they were employees at Harshaw. Further, the Court of Appeals held that the District Court properly applied Ohio law relating to trade secrets. Nevertheless, the Court of Appeals reversed the District Court, finding Ohio's trade secret law to be in conflict with the patent laws of the United States. The Court of Appeals reasoned that Ohio could not grant monopoly protection to processes and manufacturing techniques that were appropriate subjects for consideration under 35 U. S. C. § 101 for a federal patent but which had been in commercial use for over one year and so were no longer eligible for patent protection under 35 U. S. C. § 102 (b).

We hold that Ohio's law of trade secrets is not pre-empted by the patent laws of the United States, and, accordingly, we reverse.

II

Ohio has adopted the widely relied-upon definition of a trade secret found at Restatement of Torts § 757, comment *b* (1939). *B. F. Goodrich Co. v. Wohlgemuth,* 117 Ohio App. 493, 498, 192 N. E. 2d 99, 104 (1963); *W. R. Grace & Co. v. Hargadine,* 392 F. 2d 9, 14 (CA6 1968). According to the Restatement,

[a] trade secret may consist of any formula, pattern, device or compilation of information which is used in one's business, and which gives him an opportunity to obtain an advantage over competitors who do not know or use it. It may be a formula for a chemical compound, a process of manufacturing, treating or preserving materials, a pattern for a machine or other device, or a list of customers.

. . . .

The protection accorded the trade secret holder is against the disclosure or unauthorized use of the trade secret by those to whom the secret has been confided under the express or implied restriction of nondisclosure or nonuse. The law also protects the holder of a trade secret against disclosure or use when the knowledge is gained, not by the owner's volition, but by some "improper means," Restatement of Torts § 757 (a), which may include theft, wiretapping, or even aerial reconnaissance. A trade secret law, however, does not offer protection against discovery by fair and honest means, such as by independent invention, accidental disclosure, or by so-called reverse engineering, that is by starting with the known product and working backward to divine the process which aided in its development or manufacture.

Novelty, in the patent law sense, is not required for a trade secret, *W. R. Grace & Co. v. Hargadine*, 392 F. 2d. at 14. "Quite clearly discovery is something less than invention." *A. O. Smith Corp. v. Petroleum Iron Works Co.*, 73 F. 2d 531, 538 (CA6 1934), modified to increase scope of injunction, 74 F. 2d 934 (1935). However, some novelty will be required if merely because that which does not possess novelty is usually known; secrecy, in the context of trade secrets, thus implies at least minimal novelty.

The subject matter of a patent is limited to a "process, machine, manufacture, or composition of matter, or . . . improvement thereof," 35 U. S. C. § 101, which fulfills the three conditions of novelty and utility as articulated and defined in 35 U. S. C. §§ 101 and 102, and nonobviousness, as set out in 35 U. S. C. § 103. If an invention meets the rigorous statutory tests for the issuance of a patent, the patent is granted, for a period of 17 years, giving what has been described as the "right of exclusion." R. Ellis, Patent Assignments and Licenses § 4, p. 7 (2d ed. 1943). This protection goes not only to copying the subject matter, which is forbidden under the Copyright Act, 17 U. S. C. § 1 *et seq.*, but also to independent creation.

III

The first issue we deal with is whether the States are forbidden to act at all in the area of protection of the kinds of intellectual property which may make up the subject matter of trade secrets.

Article I, § 8, cl. 8, of the Constitution grants to the Congress the power

[t]o promote the Progress of Science and useful Arts, by securing for limited Times to Authors and Inventors the exclusive Right to their respective Writings and Discoveries . . . .

In the 1972 Term, in *Goldstein v. California*, 412 U. S. 546 (1973), we held that the cl. 8 grant of power to Congress was not exclusive and that, at least in the case of writings, the States were not prohibited from encouraging and protecting the efforts of those within their borders by appropriate legislation. The States could, therefore, protect against the unauthorized rerecording for sale of performances fixed on records or tapes, even though those performances qualified as "writings" in the constitutional sense and Congress was empowered to legislate regarding such performances and could pre-empt the area if it chose to do so. This determination was premised on the great diversity of interests in our Nation — the essentially non-uniform character of the appreciation of intellectual achievements in the various States. Evidence for this came from patents granted by the States in the 18th century. 412 U. S., at 557.

Just as the States may exercise regulatory power over writings so may the States regulate with respect to discoveries. States may hold diverse viewpoints in protecting intellectual property relating to invention as they do in protecting the intellectual property relating to the subject matter of copyright. The only limitation on the States is that in regulating the area of patents and copyrights they do not conflict with the operation of the laws in this area passed by Congress, and it is to that more difficult question we now turn.

IV

The question of whether the trade secret law of Ohio is void under the Supremacy Clause involves a consideration of whether that law "stands as an obstacle to the accomplishment and execution of the full purposes and objectives of Congress." *Hines v. Davidowitz,* 312 U. S. 52, 67 (1941). See *Florida Avocado Growers v. Paul,* 373 U. S. 132, 141 (1963). We stated in *Sears, Roebuck & Co. v. Stiffel Co.,* 376 U. S. 225, 229 (1964), that when state law touches upon the area of federal statutes enacted pursuant to constitutional authority, "it is 'familiar doctrine' that the federal policy 'may not be set at naught, or its benefits denied' by the state law. *Sola Elec. Co. v. Jefferson Elec. Co.,* 317 U. S. 173, 176 (1942). This is true, of course, even if the state law is enacted in the exercise of otherwise undoubted state power."

The laws which the Court of Appeals in this case held to be in conflict with the Ohio law of trade secrets were the patent laws passed by the Congress in the unchallenged exercise of its clear power under Art. I, § 8, cl. 8, of the Constitution. The patent law does not explicitly endorse or forbid the operation of trade secret law. However, as we have noted, if the scheme of protection developed by Ohio respecting trade secrets "clashes with the objectives of the federal patent laws," *Sears, Roebuck & Co. v. Stiffel Co., supra,* at 231, then the state law must fall. To determine whether the Ohio law "clashes" with the federal law it is helpful to examine the objectives of both the patent and trade secret laws.

The stated objective of the Constitution in granting the power to Congress to legislate in the area of intellectual property is to "promote the Progress of Science and useful Arts." The patent laws promote this progress by offering a right of exclusion for a limited period as an incentive to inventors to risk the often enormous costs in terms of time, research, and development. The productive effort thereby fostered will have a positive effect on society through the introduction of new products and processes of manufacture into the economy, and the emanations by way of increased employment and better lives for our citizens. In return for the right of exclusion — this "reward for inventions," *Universal Oil Co. v. Globe Co.,* 322 U. S. 471, 484 (1944) — the patent laws impose upon the inventor a requirement of disclosure. To insure adequate and full disclosure so that upon the expiration of the 17-year period "the knowledge of the invention enures to the people, who are thus enabled without restriction to practice it and profit by its use," *United States v. Dubilier Condenser Corp.,* 289 U. S. 178, 187 (1933), the patent laws require that the patent application shall include a full and clear description of the invention and "of the manner and process of making and using it" so that any person skilled in the art may make and use the invention. 35 U. S. C. § 112. When a patent is granted and the information contained in it is circulated to the general public and those especially skilled in the trade, such additions to the general store of knowledge are of such importance to the public weal that the Federal Government is willing to pay the high price of 17 years of exclusive use for its disclosure, which disclosure, it is assumed, will stimulate ideas and the eventual development of further significant advances in the art. The Court has also articulated another policy of the patent law: that which is in the public domain cannot be removed therefrom by action of the States.

> [F]ederal law requires that all ideas in general circulation be dedicated to the common good unless they are protected by a valid patent. *Lear, Inc. v. Adkins,* 395 U. S., at 668.

See also *Goldstein v. California,* 412 U. S., at 570-571; *Sears, Roebuck & Co. v. Stiffel Co., supra; Compco Corp. v. Day-Brite Lighting, Inc.,* 376 U. S. 234, 237-238 (1964); *International News Service v. Associated Press,* 248 U. S. 215, 250 (1918) (Brandeis, J., dissenting).

The maintenance of standards of commercial ethics and the encouragement of invention are the broadly stated policies behind trade secret law. "The necessity of good faith and honest, fair dealing, is the very life and spirit of the commercial world." *National Tube Co. v. Eastern Tube Co.,* 3 Ohio C. C. R. (n. s.), at 462. In *A. O. Smith Corp. v. Petroleum Iron Works Co.,* 73 F. 2d, at 539, the Court emphasized that even though a discovery may not be patentable, that does not

> destroy the value of the discovery to one who makes it, or advantage the competitor who by unfair means, or as the beneficiary of a broken faith, obtains the desired knowledge without himself paying the price in labor, money, or machines expended by the discoverer.
>
> . . . .

Having now in mind the objectives of both the patent and trade secret law, we turn to an examination of the interaction of these systems of protection of intellectual property — one established by the Congress and the other by a State — to determine whether and under what circumstances the latter might constitute "too great an encroachment on the federal patent system to be tolerated." *Sears, Roebuck & Co. v. Stiffel Co.,* 376 U. S., at 232.

As we noted earlier, trade secret law protects items which would not be proper subjects for consideration for patent protection under 35 U. S. C. § 101. As in the case of the recordings in *Goldstein v. California,* Congress, with respect to nonpatentable subject matter, "has drawn no balance; rather, it has left the area unattended, and no reason exists why the State should not be free to act." *Goldstein v. California, supra,* at 570 (footnote omitted).

Since no patent is available for a discovery, however useful, novel, and nonobvious, unless it falls within one of the express categories of patentable subject matter of 35 U. S. C. § 101, the holder of such a discovery would have no reason to apply for a patent whether trade secret protection existed or not. Abolition of trade secret protection would, therefore, not result in increased disclosure to the public of discoveries in the area of nonpatentable subject matter. Also, it is hard to see how the public would be benefited by disclosure of customer lists or advertising campaigns; in fact, keeping such items secret encourages businesses to initiate new and individualized plans of operation, and constructive competition results. This, in turn, leads to a greater variety of business methods than would otherwise be the case if privately developed marketing and other data were passed illicitly among firms involved in the same enterprise.

Congress has spoken in the area of those discoveries which fall within one of the categories of patentable subject matter of 35 U. S. C. § 101 and which are, therefore, of a nature that would be subject to consideration for a patent. Processes, machines, manufactures, compositions of matter, and improvements thereof, which meet the tests of utility, novelty, and nonobviousness are entitled to be patented, but those which do not, are not. The question remains whether those items which are proper subjects for consideration for a patent may also have available the alternative protection accorded by trade secret law.

Certainly the patent policy of encouraging invention is not disturbed by the existence of another form of incentive to invention. In this respect the two systems are not and never would be in conflict. Similarly, the policy that matter once in the public domain must remain in the public domain is not incompatible with the existence of trade secret protection. By definition a trade secret has not been placed in the public domain.[13]

The more difficult objective of the patent law to reconcile with trade secret law is that of disclosure, the *quid pro quo* of the right to exclude. *Universal Oil Co. v. Globe Co.,* 322 U. S., at 484. We are helped in this stage of the analysis by Judge Henry Friendly's opinion in *Painton & Co. v. Bourns, Inc.,* 442 F. 2d 216 (CA2 1971). There the Court of Appeals thought it useful, in determining whether inventors will refrain because of the existence of trade secret law from applying for patents, thereby depriving the public from learning of the invention, to distinguish between three categories of trade secrets:

(1) the trade secret believed by its owner to constitute a validly patentable invention; (2) the trade secret known to its owner not to be so patentable; and (3) the trade secret whose valid patentability is considered dubious. *Id.,* at 224.

[If trade secret protection were denied to subject matter known not to be patentable, no disclosure would follow, since the patent alternative would not be available and since rejected and abandoned patent applications are not open to public inspection; moreover, business resources would be unproductively devoted to guaranteeing that employees and licensees would not disclose, scientific and technological research could become fragmented, and industrial espionage would be condoned. "Instead, then, of licensing others to use his invention and making the most efficient use of existing manufacturing and marketing structures within the industry, the trade secret holder would tend either to limit his utilization of the invention, thereby depriving the public of the maximum benefit of its use, or engage in the time-consuming and economically wasteful enterprise of constructing duplicative manufacturing and marketing mechanisms for the exploitation of the invention." When subject matter is arguably patentable, there are some who will be deterred from applying for patent protection because of the risk and costs of invalidity, whether or not trade secret protection is available; others will clearly seek the patent route, even if trade secret protection is available, because the rewards of a patent are so far superior. The abolition of protection for trade secrets will induce many with "close" patent claims to apply for a patent, and this may result in the issuance of patents for "the chaff as well as the wheat" and delay society's use of inventions ultimately rejected by the Patent Office; in either case, patent policy will be

---

[13] An invention may be placed "in public use or on sale" within the meaning of 35 U. S. C. § 102(b) without losing its secret character. Painton & Co. v. Bourns, Inc., 442 F. 2d, at 224, n. 6; Metallizing Engineering Co. v. Kenyon Bearing & Auto Parts Co., 153 F. 2d 516, 520 (CA2), cert. denied, 328 U. S. 840 (1946).

frustrated. As for subject matter which the inventor believes to be clearly patentable, the advantages of the patent over trade secret protection (e.g., against reverse engineering) are so strong that "the possibility that an inventor who believes his invention meets the standards of patentability will sit back, rely on trade secret law, and after one year of use forfeit any right to patent protection . . . is remote indeed." Thus, in the first two categories, trade secret protection reinforces patent policy, and in the third category it does not frustrate it.]

. . . Neither complete nor partial pre-emption of state trade secret law is justified.

Our conclusion that patent law does not pre-empt trade secret law is in accord with prior cases of this Court. . . . Trade secret law and patent law have co-existed in this country for over one hundred years. Each has its particular role to play, and the operation of one does not take away from the need for the other. Trade secret law encourages the development and exploitation of those items of lesser or different invention than might be accorded protection under the patent laws, but which items still have an important part to play in the technological and scientific advancement of the Nation. Trade secret law promotes the sharing of knowledge, and the efficient operation of industry; it permits the individual inventor to reap the rewards of his labor by contracting with a company large enough to develop and exploit it. Congress, by its silence over these many years, has seen the wisdom of allowing the States to enforce trade secret protection. Until Congress takes affirmative action to the contrary, States should be free to grant protection to trade secrets.

Since we hold that Ohio trade secret law is not pre-empted by the federal patent law, the judgment of the Court of Appeals for the Sixth Circuit is reversed, and the case is remanded to the Court of Appeals with directions to reinstate the judgment of the District Court.

It is so ordered.

MR. JUSTICE POWELL took no part in the decision of this case.

MR. JUSTICE MARSHALL, concurring in the result.

Unlike the Court, I do not believe that the possibility that an inventor with a patentable invention will rely on state trade secret law rather than apply for a patent is "remote indeed." State trade secret law provides substantial protection to the inventor who intends to use or sell the invention himself rather than license it to others, protection which in its unlimited duration is clearly superior to the 17-year monopoly afforded by the patent laws. I have no doubt that the existence of trade secret protection provides in some instances a substantial disincentive to entrance into the patent system, and thus deprives society of the benefits of public disclosure of the invention which it is the policy of the patent laws to encourage. This case may well be such an instance.

But my view of sound policy in this area does not dispose of this case. Rather, the question presented in this case is whether Congress, in enacting the patent laws, intended merely to offer inventors a limited monopoly in exchange for disclosure of their invention, or instead to exert pressure on inventors to enter into this exchange by withdrawing any alternative possibility of legal protection for their inventions. I am persuaded that the former is the case. State trade secret laws and the federal patent laws have co-existed for many, many years. During this time, Congress has repeatedly demonstrated its full awareness of the existence of the trade secret system, without any indication of disapproval. Indeed, Congress has in a number of instances given explicit federal protection to trade secret information provided to federal agencies. See, *e. g.,* 5 U. S. C. § 552(b)(4); 18 U. S. C. § 1905; see generally Appendix to Brief for Petitioner. Because of this, I conclude that there is "neither such actual conflict between the two schemes of regulation that both cannot stand in the same area, nor evidence of a congressional design to preempt the field." *Florida Avocado Growers v. Paul,* 373 U. S. 132, 141 (1963). I therefore concur in the result reached by the majority of the Court.

MR. JUSTICE DOUGLAS, with whom MR. JUSTICE BRENNAN concurs, dissenting.

Today's decision is at war with the philosophy of *Sears, Roebuck & Co. v. Stiffel Co.,* 376 U. S. 225, and *Compco Corp. v. Day-Brite Lighting, Inc.,* 376 U. S. 234. Those cases involved patents — one of a pole lamp and one of fluorescent lighting fixtures each of which was declared invalid. The lower courts held, however, that though the patents were invalid the sale of identical or confusingly similar products to the products of the patentees violated state unfair competition laws. We held that when an article is unprotected by a patent, state law may not forbid others to copy it, because every article not covered by a valid patent is in the public domain. Congress in the patent laws decided that where no patent existed, free competition should prevail; that where a patent is rightfully issued, the right to exclude others should obtain for no longer than 17 years, and that the States may not "under some other law, such as that forbidding unfair competition, give protection of a kind that clashes with the objectives of the federal patent laws," 376 U. S., at 231.

The product involved in this suit, sodium iodide synthetic crystals, was a product that could be patented but was not.

. . . .

The conflict with the patent laws is obvious. The decision of Congress to adopt a patent system was based on the idea that there will be much more innovation if discoveries are disclosed and patented than there will be when everyone works in secret. Society thus fosters a free exchange of technological information at the cost of a limited 17-year monopoly.

A trade secret,[3] unlike a patent, has no property dimension. That was the view of the Court of Appeals, 478 F. 2d 1074, 1081; and its decision is supported by what Mr. Justice Holmes said in *Du Pont Powder Co. v. Masland,* 244 U. S. 100, 102:

> The word property as applied to trade-marks and trade secrets is an unanalyzed expression of certain secondary consequences of the primary fact that the law makes some rudimentary requirements of good faith. Whether the plaintiffs have any valuable secret or not the defendant knows the facts, whatever they are, through a special confidence that he accepted. The property may be denied but the confidence cannot be. Therefore the starting point for the present matter is not property or due process of law, but that the defendant stood in confidential relations with the plaintiffs, or one of them. These have given place to hostility, and the first thing to be made sure of is that the defendant shall not fraudulently abuse the trust reposed in him. It is the usual incident of confidential relations. If there is any disadvantage in the fact that he knew the plaintiffs' secrets he must take the burden with the good.[4]

---

[3] Trade secrets often are unpatentable. In that event there is no federal policy which is contravened when an injunction to bar disclosure of a trade secret is issued. Moreover, insofar as foreign patents are involved our federal patent policy is obviously irrelevant. S. Oppenheim, Unfair Trade Practices 264-265 (2d ed. 1965). As respects further contrasts between patents and trade secrets see Milgrim, Trade Secret Protection and Licensing, 4 Pat. L. Rev. 375 (1972).

[4] As to Goldstein v. California, 412 U. S. 546, the ruling of Mr. Justice Bradley concerning the distinction between patents and copyright is relevant:

A suit to redress theft of a trade secret is grounded in tort damages for breach of a contract — a historic remedy, *Cataphote Corp. v. Hudson,* 422 F. 2d 1290. Damages for breach of a confidential relation are not pre-empted by this patent law, but an injunction against use is pre-empted because the patent law states the only monopoly over trade secrets that is enforceable by specific performance; and that monopoly exacts as a price full disclosure. A trade secret can be protected only by being kept secret. Damages for breach of a contract are one thing; an injunction barring disclosure does service for the protection accorded valid patents and is therefore pre-empted.

From the findings of fact of the lower courts, the process involved in this litigation was unique, such a great discovery as to make its patentability a virtual certainty. Yet the Court's opinion reflects a vigorous activist anti-patent philosophy. My objection is not because it is activist. This is a problem that involves no neutral principle. The Constitution in Art. I, § 8, cl. 8, expresses the activist policy which Congress has enforced by statutes. It is that constitutional policy which we should enforce, not our individual notions of the public good.

I would affirm the judgment below.

QUESTIONS

1. How does the Court's approach in *Kewanee* differ, if it does at all, from its approach in *Goldstein?*

2. Is not the *Kewanee* Court in effect upholding the power of the states to enact laws promoting a patent-like monopoly conditioned upon the maintenance of secrecy by the discoverer or inventor? Considering the Court's language in *Goldstein,* especially that at the end of Part III of its opinion, at pp. 582-83 *supra,* is it not startling to find the *Kewanee* Court relying on *Goldstein* rather than ignoring or distinguishing it?

3. The *Kewanee* Court states more than once that state enforcement and promotion of business secrecy will foster constructive competition. What exactly does the Court mean? Is the Court not ignoring the extent to which such secrecy constitutes an inhibition upon competition, improvement in methods, cheaper production, and the like? And is not the latter assumption the one upon which Congress operates in its patent laws?

4. The Court buttresses its conclusion that state trade-secret law is not preempted by observing: "Certainly the patent policy of encouraging invention is not disturbed by the existence of another form of incentive to invention." Would the Court's logic justify a state's granting a patent monopoly of ten additional years, after a seventeen-year federal patent had expired? Would the Court's logic justify a state's making it a crime to infringe a patent granted by the United States Patent Office? If you would find these forms of state protection unpalatable under the federal patent scheme, how is state trade-secret protection different?

The difference between the two things, letters-patent and copyright, may be illustrated by reference to the subjects just enumerated. Take the case of medicines. Certain mixtures are found to be of great value in the healing art. If the discoverer writes and publishes a book on the subject (as regular physicians generally do), he gains no exclusive right to the manufacture and sale of the medicine; he gives that to the public. If he desires to acquire such exclusive right, he must obtain a patent for the mixture as a new art, manufacture, or composition of matter. He may copyright his book, if he pleases; but that only secures to him the exclusive right of printing and publishing his book. So of all other inventions or discoveries. Baker v. Selden, 101 U. S. 99, 102-103.

5. Does the Court strengthen its position when, near the end, it points out the policies underlying trade secret law — promotion of the sharing of knowledge, promotion of efficient business operations, providing a reward to the inventor through contracting with others for development and sale — policies which appear to be congruent with those underlying the patent laws? Could a federal law which regulates inventions coexist with a state law which, in the laudatory language of the Court, "encourages the development and exploitation of those items of lesser or different invention than might be accorded protection under the patent laws"?

6. Justice Douglas appears to argue, in his footnote 4, that preemption of state law is more essential to promote the objectives of the Constitution and Congress with respect to patent than it is with regard to copyright. It is apparently on this basis that he would distinguish the *Goldstein* case. Are you persuaded? How does this approach compare to that taken by Justice Douglas in his dissent from the denial of certiorari in *Lee v. Runge*, p. 35 *supra*?

Is not the entire dissent undermined by the concession in the first two sentences of footnote 3? If not, what do you make of these statements?

7. Do you agree with the view that *Kewanee* is "at war with the philosophy" of *Sears* and *Compco*? Might not the *Sears, Compco, Goldstein*, and *Kewanee* cases all be harmonized by distinguishing between subject matter which is not patentable or copyrightable at all *and* subject matter which is patentable or copyrightable but which fails to meet the constitutional or statutory standards for protection, such as originality, novelty, non-obviousness, etc.?

ZACCHINI v. SCRIPPS-HOWARD BROADCASTING CO.

433 U.S. 562 (1977)

MR. JUSTICE WHITE delivered the opinion of the Court.

Petitioner, Hugo Zacchini, is an entertainer. He performs a "human cannonball" act in which he is shot from a cannon into a net some 200 feet away. Each performance occupies some 15 seconds. In August and September 1972, petitioner was engaged to perform his act on a regular basis at the Geauga County Fair in Burton, Ohio. He performed in a fenced area, surrounded by grandstands, at the fair grounds. Members of the public attending the fair were not charged a separate admission fee to observe his act.

On August 30, a freelance reporter for Scripps-Howard Broadcasting Co., the operator of a television broadcasting station and respondent in this case, attended the fair. He carried a small movie camera. Petitioner noticed the reporter and asked him not to film the performance. The reporter did not do so on that day; but on the instructions of the producer of respondent's daily newscast, he returned the following day and videotaped the entire act. This film clip, approximately 15 seconds in length, was shown on the 11 o'clock news program that night, together with favorable commentary.[1]

---

[1] The script of the commentary accompanying the film clip read as follows:

This ... now ... is the story of a *true spectator* sport ... the sport of human cannonballing ... in fact, the great *Zacchini* is about the only human cannonball around, these days ... just happens that, *where* he is, is the Great Geauga County Fair, in Burton ... and believe me, although it's not a *long* act, it's a thriller ... and you really need to see it *in person* ... to appreciate it.... (Emphasis in original.) App. 12.

Petitioner then brought this action for damages, alleging that he is "engaged in the entertainment business," that the act he performs is one "invented by his father and ... performed only by his family for the last fifty years," that respondent "showed and commercialized the film of his act without his consent," and that such conduct was an "unlawful appropriation of plaintiff's professional property." App. 4-5. Respondent answered and moved for summary judgment, which was granted by the trial court.

The Court of Appeals of Ohio reversed. The majority held that petitioner's complaint stated a cause of action for conversion and for infringement of a common-law copyright, and one judge concurred in the judgment on the ground that the complaint stated a cause of action for appropriation of petitioner's "right of publicity" in the film of his act. All three judges agreed that the First Amendment did not privilege the press to show the entire performance on a news program without compensating petitioner for any financial injury he could prove at trial.

Like the concurring judge in the Court of Appeals, the Supreme Court of Ohio rested petitioner's cause of action under state law on his "right to [the] publicity value of his performance." 47 Ohio St. 2d 224, 351 N. E. 2d 454, 455 (1976). The opinion syllabus, to which we are to look for the rule of law used to decide the case, declared first that one may not use for his own benefit the name or likeness of another, whether or not the use or benefit is a commercial one, and second that respondent would be liable for the appropriation, over petitioner's objection and in the absence of license or privilege, of petitioner's right to the publicity value of his performance. *Ibid.* The court nevertheless gave judgment for respondent because, in the words of the syllabus:

A TV station has a privilege to report in its newscasts matters of legitimate public interest which would otherwise be protected by an individual's right of publicity, unless the actual intent of the TV station was to appropriate the benefit of the publicity for some non-privileged private use, or unless the actual intent was to injure the individual. *Ibid.*

We granted certiorari, 429 U. S. 1037 (1977), to consider an issue unresolved by this Court: whether the First and Fourteenth Amendments immunized respondent from damages for its alleged infringement of petitioner's state-law "right of publicity." Pet. for Cert. 2. Insofar as the Ohio Supreme Court held that the First and Fourteenth Amendments of the United States Constitution required judgment for respondent, we reverse the judgment of that court.

. . . .

II

The Ohio Supreme Court held that respondent is constitutionally privileged to include in its newscasts matters of public interest that would otherwise be protected by the right of publicity, absent an intent to injure or to appropriate for some nonprivileged purpose. If under this standard respondent had merely reported that petitioner was performing at the fair and described or commented on his act, with or without showing his picture on television, we would have a very different case. But petitioner is not contending that his appearance at the fair and his performance could not be reported by the press as newsworthy items. His complaint is that respondent filmed his entire act and displayed that film on television for the public to see and enjoy. This, he claimed, was an appropriation of his professional property. The Ohio Supreme Court agreed that petitioner had "a right of publicity" that gave him "personal control over commercial display and exploitation of his personality and the exercise of his talents." This right of "exclusive control over the publicity given to his performances" was said to be such a "valuable part of the benefit which may be attained by his talents and efforts" that it was entitled to legal protection. It was also observed, or at least expressly assumed, that petitioner had not abandoned his rights by performing under the circumstances present at the Geauga County Fair Grounds.

The Ohio Supreme Court nevertheless held that the challenged invasion was privileged, saying that the press "must be accorded broad latitude in its choice of how much it presents of each story or incident, and of the emphasis to be given to such presentation. No fixed standard which would bar the press from reporting or depicting either an entire occurrence or an entire discrete part of a public performance can be formulated which would not unduly restrict the 'breathing room' in reporting which freedom of the press requires." 47 Ohio St. 2d, at 235, 351 N. E. 2d, at 461. Under this view, respondent was thus constitutionally free to film and display petitioner's entire act.[5]

The Ohio Supreme Court relied heavily on *Time, Inc. v. Hill*, 385 U. S. 374 (1967), but that case does not mandate a media privilege to televise a performer's entire act without his consent. Involved in *Time, Inc. v. Hill* was a claim under the New York "Right of Privacy" statute [6] that Life Magazine, in the course of reviewing a new play, had connected the play with a long-past incident involving petitioner and his family and had falsely described their experience and conduct at that time. The complaint sought damages for humiliation and suffering flowing from these nondefamatory falsehoods that allegedly invaded Hill's privacy. The Court held, however, that the opening of a new play linked to an actual incident was a matter of public interest and that Hill could not recover without showing that the Life report was knowingly false or was published with reckless disregard for the truth — the same rigorous standard that had been applied in *New York Times Co. v. Sullivan*, 376 U. S. 254 (1964).

Time, Inc. v. Hill, which was hotly contested and decided by a divided Court, involved an entirely different tort from the "right of publicity" recognized by the Ohio Supreme Court. As the opinion reveals in *Time, Inc. v. Hill,* the Court was steeped in the literature of privacy law and was aware of the developing distinctions and nuances in this branch of the law. The Court, for example, cited W. Prosser, Law of Torts 831-832 (3d ed. 1964), and the same author's well-known

---

[5] The court's explication was as follows:

The proper standard must necessarily be whether the matters reported were of public interest, and if so, the press will be liable for appropriation of a performer's right of publicity only if its actual intent was not to report the performance, but, rather, to appropriate the performance for some other private use, or if the actual intent was to injure the performer. It might also be the case that the press would be liable if it recklessly disregarded contract rights existing between the plaintiff and a third person to present the performance to the public, but that question is not presented here. 47 Ohio St. 2d, at 235, 351 N. E. 2d, at 461.

[6] Section 51 of the New York Civil Rights Law (McKinney 1976) provides an action for injunction and damages for invasion of the "right of privacy" granted by § 50:

A person, firm or corporation that uses for advertising purposes, or for the purposes of trade, the name, portrait or picture of any living person without having first obtained the written consent of such person, or if a minor of his or her parent or guardian, is guilty of a misdemeanor.

article, Privacy, 48 Calif. L. Rev. 383 (1960), both of which divided privacy into four distinct branches.[7] The Court was aware that it was adjudicating a "false light" privacy case involving a matter of public interest, not a case involving "intrusion," 385 U.S., at 384-385, n. 9, "appropriation" of a name or likeness for the purposes of trade, *id.,* at 381, or "private details" about a non-newsworthy person or event, *id.,* at 383 n. 7. It is also abundantly clear that *Time, Inc. v. Hill* did not involve a performer, a person with a name having commercial value, or any claim to a "right of publicity." This discrete kind of "appropriation" case was plainly identified in the literature cited by the Court [8] and had been adjudicated in the reported cases.[9]

The differences between these two torts are important. First, the State's interests in providing a cause of action in each instance are different. "The interest protected" in permitting recovery for placing the plaintiff in a false light "is clearly that of reputation, with the same overtones of mental distress as in defamation." Prosser, *supra,* 48 Calif. L. Rev., at 400. By contrast, the State's interest in permitting a "right of publicity" is in protecting the proprietary interest of the

---

[7] "The law of privacy comprises four distinct kinds of invasion of four different interests of the plaintiff, which are tied together by the common name, but otherwise have almost nothing in common except that each represents an interference with the right of the plaintiff . . . 'to be let alone.' " Prosser, Privacy, 48 Calif. L. Rev., at 389. Thus, according to Prosser, some courts had recognized a cause of action for "intrusion" upon the plaintiff's seclusion or solitude; public disclosure of "private facts" about the plaintiff's personal life; publicity that places the plaintiff in a "false light" in the public eye; and "appropriation" of the plaintiff's name or likeness for commercial purposes. One may be liable for "appropriation" if he "pirate[s] the plaintiff's identity for some advantage of his own." *Id.,* at 403.

[8] See, for example, W. Prosser, Law of Torts 842 (3d ed. 1964); Bloustein, Privacy as an Aspect of Human Dignity: An Answer to Dean Prosser, 39 N. Y. U. L. Rev. 962, 986-991 (1964); Kalven, Privacy in Tort Law — Were Warren and Brandeis Wrong?, 31 Law & Contemp. Prob. 326, 331 (1966).

[9] *E.g.,* Ettore v. Philco Television Broadcasting Corp., 229 F. 2d 481 (CA3), cert. denied, 351 U. S. 926 (1956); Sharkey v. National Broadcasting Co., 93 F. Supp. 986 (SDNY 1950); Pittsburgh Athletic Co. v. KQV Broadcasting Co., 24 F. Supp. 490 (WD Pa. 1938); Twentieth Century Sporting Club, Inc. v. Transradio Press Service, 165 Misc. 71, 300 N. Y. S. 159 (1937); Hogan v. A. S. Barnes & Co., 114 U. S. P. Q. 314 (Pa. Ct. C. P. 1957); Myers v. U. S. Camera Publishing Corp., 9 Misc. 2d 765, 167 N. Y. S. 2d 771 (1957). The cases prior to 1961 are helpfully reviewed in Gordon, Right of Property in Name, Likeness, Personality and History, 55 Nw. U.L. Rev. 553 (1960).

Ettore v. Philco Television Broadcasting Corp., supra, involved a challenge to television exhibition of a film made of a prize fight that had occurred some time ago. Judge Biggs, writing for the Court of Appeals, said:

There are, speaking very generally, two polar types of cases. One arises when some accidental occurrence rends the veil of obscurity surrounding an average person and makes him, arguably, newsworthy. The other type involves the appropriation of the performance or production of a professional performer or entrepreneur. Between the two extremes are many gradations, most involving strictly commercial exploitation of some aspect of an individual's personality, such as his name or picture. 229 F.2d, at 486.
. . . The fact is that, if a performer performs for hire, a curtailment, without consideration, of his right to control his performance is a wrong to him. Such a wrong vitally affects his livelihood, precisely as a trade libel, for example, affects the earnings of a corporation. If the artistry of the performance be used as a criterion, every judge perforce must turn himself into a literary, theatrical or sports critic. *Id.,* at 490.

individual in his act in part to encourage such entertainment.[10] As we later note, the State's interest is closely analogous to the goals of patent and copyright law, focusing on the right of the individual to reap the reward of his endeavors and having little to do with protecting feelings or reputation. Second, the two torts differ in the degree to which they intrude on dissemination of information to the public. In "false light" cases the only way to protect the interests involved is to attempt to minimize publication of the damaging matter, while in "right of publicity" cases the only question is who gets to do the publishing. An entertainer such as petitioner usually has no objection to the widespread publication of his act as long as he gets the commercial benefit of such publication. Indeed, in the present case petitioner did not seek to enjoin the broadcast of his act; he simply sought compensation for the broadcast in the form of damages.

Nor does it appear that our later cases, such as *Rosenbloom v. Metromedia, Inc.,* 403 U.S. 29 (1971); *Gertz v. Robert Welch, Inc.,* 418 U.S. 323 (1974); and *Time, Inc. v. Firestone,* 424 U. S. 448 (1976), require or furnish substantial support for the Ohio court's privilege ruling. These cases, like *New York Times,* emphasize the protection extended to the press by the First Amendment in defamation cases, particularly when suit is brought by a public official or a public figure. None of them involve an alleged appropriation by the press of a right of publicity existing under state law.

Moreover, *Time, Inc. v. Hill, New York Times, Metromedia, Gertz,* and *Firestone* all involved the reporting of events; in none of them was there an attempt to broadcast or publish an entire act for which the performer ordinarily gets paid. It is evident, and there is no claim here to the contrary, that petitioner's state-law right of publicity would not serve to prevent respondent from reporting the newsworthy facts about petitioner's act. Wherever the line in particular situations is to be drawn between media reports that are protected and those that are not, we are quite sure that the First and Fourteenth Amendments do not immunize the media when they broadcast a performer's entire act without his consent. The Constitution no more prevents a State from requiring respondent to compensate petitioner for broadcasting his act on television than it would privilege respondent to film and broadcast a copyrighted dramatic work without liability to the copyright owner, Copyrights Act, 17 U.S.C. App. § 101 *et seq.* (1976 ed.); cf. *Kalem Co. v. Harper Bros.,* 222 U.S. 55 (1911); *Manners v. Morosco,* 252 U.S. 317 (1920), or to film and broadcast a prize fight, *Ettore v. Philco Television Broadcasting Corp.,* 229 F. 2d 481 (CA3), cert. denied, 351 U. S. 926 (1956); or a baseball game, *Pittsburgh Athletic Co. v. KQV Broadcasting Co.,* 24 F. Supp. 490 (WD Pa. 1938), where the promoters or the participants had other plans for publicizing the event. There are ample reasons for reaching this conclusion.

The broadcast of a film of petitioner's entire act poses a substantial threat to the economic value of that performance. As the Ohio court recognized, this act is the product of petitioner's own talents and energy, the end result of much time, effort, and expense. Much of its economic value lies in the "right of exclusive control over the publicity given to his performance"; if the public can see the

---

[10] The Ohio Supreme Court expressed the view "that plaintiff's claim is one for invasion of the right of privacy by appropriation, and should be considered as such." 47 Ohio St. 2d, at 226, 351 N. E. 2d, at 456. It should be noted, however, that the case before us is more limited than the broad category of lawsuits that may arise under the heading of "appropriation." Petitioner does not merely assert that some general use, such as advertising, was made of his name or likeness; he relies on the much narrower claim that respondent televised an entire act that he ordinarily gets paid to perform.

act free on television, it will be less willing to pay to see it at the fair.[12] The effect of a public broadcast of the performance is similar to preventing petitioner from charging an admission fee. "The rationale for [protecting the right of publicity] is the straight-forward one of preventing unjust enrichment by the theft of good will. No social purpose is served by having the defendant get free some aspect of the plaintiff that would have market value and for which he would normally pay." Kalven, Privacy in Tort Law — Were Warren and Brandeis Wrong?, 31 Law & Contemp. Prob. 326, 331 (1966). Moreover, the broadcast of petitioner's entire performance, unlike the unauthorized use of another's name for purposes of trade or the incidental use of a name or picture by the press, goes to the heart of petitioner's ability to earn a living as an entertainer. Thus, in this case, Ohio has recognized what may be the strongest case for a "right of publicity" — involving, not the appropriation of an entertainer's reputation to enhance the attractiveness of a commercial product, but the appropriation of the very activity by which the entertainer acquired his reputation in the first place.

Of course, Ohio's decision to protect petitioner's right of publicity here rests on more than a desire to compensate the performer for the time and effort invested in his act; the protection provides an economic incentive for him to make the investment required to produce a performance of interest to the public. This same consideration underlies the patent and copyright laws long enforced by this Court. As the Court stated in *Mazer v. Stein,* 347 U.S. 201, 219 (1954):

> The economic philosophy behind the clause empowering Congress to grant patents and copyrights is the conviction that encouragement of individual effort by personal gain is the best way to advance public welfare through the talents of authors and inventors in "Science and useful Arts." Sacrificial days devoted to such creative activities deserve rewards commensurate with the services rendered.

These laws perhaps regard the "reward to the owner [as] a secondary consideration," *United States v. Paramount Pictures,* 334 U. S. 131, 158 (1948), but they were "intended definitely to grant valuable, enforceable rights" in order to afford greater encouragement to the production of works of benefit to the public. *Washingtonian Publishing Co. v. Pearson,* 306 U. S. 30, 36 (1939). The Constitution does not prevent Ohio from making a similar choice here in deciding to protect the entertainer's incentive in order to encourage the production of this type of work. Cf. *Goldstein v. California,* 412 U. S. 546 (1973); *Kewanee Oil Co. v. Bicron Corp.,* 416 U. S. 470 (1974).

There is no doubt that entertainment, as well as news, enjoys First Amendment protection. It is also true that entertainment itself can be important news. *Time, Inc. v. Hill.* But it is important to note that neither the public nor respondent will be deprived of the benefit of petitioner's performance as long as his commercial stake in his act is appropriately recognized. Petitioner does not seek to enjoin the broadcast of his performance; he simply wants to be paid for it. Nor do we think that a state-law damages remedy against respondent would represent a species of liability without fault contrary to the letter or spirit of *Gertz v. Robert Welch, Inc.,* 418 U. S. 323 (1974). Respondent knew that petitioner objected to televising his act but nevertheless displayed the entire film.

---

[12] It is possible, of course, that respondent's news broadcast increased the value of petitioner's performance by stimulating the public's interest in seeing the act live. In these circumstances, petitioner would not be able to prove damages and thus would not recover. But petitioner has alleged that the broadcast injured him to the extent of $25,000, App. 5, and we think the State should be allowed to authorize compensation of this injury if proved.

We conclude that although the State of Ohio may as a matter of its own law privilege the press in the circumstances of this case, the First and Fourteenth Amendments do not require it to do so.

Reversed.

MR. JUSTICE POWELL, with whom MR. JUSTICE BRENNAN and MR. JUSTICE MARSHALL join, dissenting.

Disclaiming any attempt to do more than decide the narrow case before us, the Court reverses the decision of the Supreme Court of Ohio based on repeated incantation of a single formula: "a performer's entire act." The holding today is summed up in one sentence:

> Wherever the line in particular situations is to be drawn between media reports that are protected and those that are not, we are quite sure that the First and Fourteenth Amendments do not immunize the media when they broadcast a performer's entire act without his consent. *Ante,* at 574-575.

I doubt that this formula provides a standard clear enough even for resolution of this case.[1] In any event, I am not persuaded that the Court's opinion is appropriately sensitive to the First Amendment values at stake, and I therefore dissent.

Although the Court would draw no distinction, *ante,* at 575, I do not view respondent's action as comparable to unauthorized commercial broadcasts of sporting events, theatrical performances, and the like where the broadcaster keeps the profits. There is no suggestion here that respondent made any such use of the film. Instead, it simply reported on what petitioner concedes to be a newsworthy event, in a way hardly surprising for a television station — by means of film coverage. The report was part of an ordinary daily news program, consuming a total of 15 seconds. It is a routine example of the press' fulfilling the informing function so vital to our system.

The Court's holding that the station's ordinary news report may give rise to substantial liability [2] has disturbing implications, for the decision could lead to a degree of media self-censorship. Cf. *Smith v. California,* 361 U. S. 147, 150-154 (1959). Hereafter, whenever a television news editor is unsure whether certain film footage received from a camera crew might be held to portray an "entire

---

[1] Although the record is not explicit, it is unlikely that the "act" commenced abruptly with the explosion that launched petitioner on his way, ending with the landing in the net a few seconds later. One may assume that the actual firing was preceded by some fanfare, possibly stretching over several minutes, to heighten the audience's anticipation: introduction of the performer, description of the uniqueness and danger, last-minute checking of the apparatus, and entry into the cannon, all accompanied by suitably ominous commentary from the master of ceremonies. If this is found to be the case on remand, then respondent could not be said to have appropriated the "entire act" in its 15-second newsclip — and the Court's opinion then would afford no guidance for resolution of the case. Moreover, in future cases involving different performances, similar difficulties in determining just what constitutes the "entire act" are inevitable.

[2] At some points the Court seems to acknowledge that the reason for recognizing a cause of action asserting a "right of publicity" is to prevent unjust enrichment. See, *e.g., ante,* at 576. But the remainder of the opinion inconsistently accepts a measure of damages based not on the defendant's enhanced profits but on harm to the plaintiff regardless of any gain to the defendant. See, *e.g., ante,* at 575 n. 12. Indeed, in this case there is no suggestion that respondent television station gained financially by showing petitioner's flight (although it no doubt received its normal advertising revenue for the news program

act," [3] he may decline coverage — even of clearly newsworthy events — or confine the broadcast to watered-down verbal reporting, perhaps with an occasional still picture. The public is then the loser. This is hardly the kind of news reportage that the First Amendment is meant to foster. See generally *Miami Herald Publishing Co. v. Tornillo,* 418 U. S. 241, 257-258 (1974); *Time, Inc. v. Hill,* 385 U. S. 374, 389 (1967); *New York Times Co. v. Sullivan,* 376 U. S. 254, 270-272, 279 (1964).

In my view the First Amendment commands a different analytical starting point from the one selected by the Court. Rather than begin with a quantitative analysis of the performer's behavior — is this or is this not his entire act? — we should direct initial attention to the actions of the news media: what use did the station make of the film footage? When a film is used, as here, for a routine portion of a regular news program, I would hold that the First Amendment protects the station from a "right of publicity" or "appropriation" suit, absent a strong showing by the plaintiff that the news broadcast was a subterfuge or cover for private or commercial exploitation.[4]

I emphasize that this is a "reappropriation" suit, rather than one of the other varieties of "right of privacy" tort suits identified by Dean Prosser in his classic article. Prosser, Privacy, 48 Calif. L. Rev. 383 (1960). In those other causes of action the competing interests are considerably different. The plaintiff generally seeks to avoid any sort of public exposure, and the existence of constitutional privilege is therefore less likely to turn on whether the publication occurred in a news broadcast or in some other fashion. In a suit like the one before us, however, the plaintiff does not complain about the fact of exposure to the public, but rather about its timing or manner. He welcomes some publicity, but seeks to retain control over means and manner as a way to maximize for himself the monetary benefits that flow from such publication. But having made the matter public — having chosen, in essence, to make it newsworthy — he cannot, consistent with the First Amendment, complain of routine news reportage. Cf. *Gertz v. Robert Welch, Inc.,* 418 U. S. 323, 339-348, 351-352 (1974) (clarifying the different liability standards appropriate in defamation suits, depending on whether or not the plaintiff is a public figure).

Since the film clip here was undeniably treated as news and since there is no claim that the use was subterfuge, respondent's actions were constitutionally privileged. I would affirm.

— revenue it would have received no matter which news items appeared). Nevertheless, in the unlikely event that petitioner can prove that his income was somehow reduced as a result of the broadcast, respondent will apparently have to compensate him for the difference.

[3] Such doubts are especially likely to arise when the editor receives film footage of an event at a local fair, a circus, a sports competition of limited duration (*e.g.,* the winning effort in a ski-jump competition), or a dramatic production made up of short skits, to offer only a few examples.

[4] This case requires no detailed specification of the standards for identifying a subterfuge, since there is no claim here that respondent's news use was anything but bona fide. Cf. 47 Ohio St. 2d 224, 351 N. E. 2d 454, 455 (the standards suggested by the Supreme Court of Ohio, quoted *ante,* at 565). I would point out, however, that selling time during a news broadcast to advertisers in the customary fashion does not make for "commercial exploitation" in the sense intended here. See W. Prosser, Law of Torts 806-807 (4th ed. 1971). Cf. New York Times Co. v. Sullivan, 376 U. S. 254, 266 (1964).

Mr. Justice Stevens, dissenting. . . .

The Ohio Supreme Court held that respondent's telecast of the "human cannonball" was a privileged invasion of petitioner's common-law "right of publicity" because respondent's actual intent was neither (a) to appropriate the benefit of the publicity for a private use, nor (b) to petitioner.

QUESTIONS

1. How does the Court treat the vexing questions of preemption that created the tortuous path from *Sears* and *Compco* to split decisions in *Goldstein* and *Kewanee?* If you have difficulty finding the Court's treatment of these matters, consider the extent to which its analysis of the proper scope of the First Amendment is akin to the kind of analysis one might undertake on the issue of preemption through the copyright law.

2. The Court refers on several occasions to the similarity of goals between the state right of publicity and the federal patent and copyright laws. What is properly to be inferred from this similarity, when considering the question of preemption of state law? Indeed, had the Ohio courts in the *Zacchini* case upheld his cause of action against the broadcasting company on the theory that it had made an unauthorized copy of a performance which he had developed through time, effort, and ingenuity, so that there was an "infringement of common law copyright" in that performance, would not the case for preemption have been compelling? Of what relevance to these questions was the format or medium of Zacchini's act as taped by the defendant?

3. Although the Court notes that Mr. Zacchini was seeking monetary damages only, and was not through an injunction seeking to interfere with the public's deriving information about his performance, is there anything in the Court's opinion which would justify withholding an injunction had Mr. Zacchini requested one? (Compare Mr. Justice Douglas's similar concession in his dissent in *Kewanee,* at p. 596 *supra.*) Is the distinction not merely politic, rather than being rationally supportable?

4. Starting from the assumption that state law could prevent the unauthorized televising on a news program of an entire nine-inning professional baseball game, for example the last game of the World Series, does it follow that the news coverage of the "entire" act of Mr. Zacchini must also be deemed tortious? Are there *any* circumstances in which First Amendment considerations would dictate a permission to televise the entire Zacchini performance? What, for example, if Mr. Zacchini, a local figure of some note, missed the target, and was severely injured?

D. THE SAGA OF SECTION 301

The preceding cases dealing with the preemption of state law show the Supreme Court attempting to divine the intention of Congress concerning the continuing vitality of state tort and trade-secret law — when Congress has not made its intention explicitly manifest. One would think that problems of federal preemption would be dispelled if Congress were specifically to address the matter in its legislation. Congress in fact did so in § 301 of the 1976 Act. In the words of the House Report (at p. 130), the preemption principles set forth in § 301 are "intended to be stated in the clearest and most unequivocal language possible, so as to foreclose any conceivable misinterpretation of its unqualified intention that Congress shall act preemptively, and to avoid the development of any vague borderline areas between State and Federal protection." In exploring the following materials, the student should consider whether this congressional objective has been achieved.

Section 301(a) reads as follows:

> On and after January 1, 1978, all legal or equitable rights that are equivalent to any of the exclusive rights within the general scope of copyright as specified by section 106 in works of authorship that are fixed in a tangible medium of expression and come within the subject matter of copyright as specified by sections 102 and 103, whether created before or after that date and whether published or unpublished, are governed exclusively by this title. Thereafter, no person is entitled to any such right or equivalent right in any such work under the common law or statutes of any State.

Without doubt, there is no more significant (and probably no more troublesome) question underlying the Act than the preemptive effect of this provision. Basically, this question is: How much of the common law (or state statutory law), particularly that of unfair competition, is left standing or is permitted to develop by the new copyright law?

In the analysis of this perhaps unanswerable question, several things at least are clear:

(1) The statute covers, as it must, only works "fixed in a tangible medium of expression." This is clearly intended to be most comprehensive and to cover not only things such as sound recordings, computer-readable material, and other known forms of fixation but also works fixed by any method "later developed." Moreover, it has already been seen that the limitation of preemption to "subject matter of copyright as specified by sections 102 and 103" still covers a very broad area of material. Nevertheless oral works (such as improvised speeches), live jazz performances, and live demonstrations or displays by cathode rays are frequently never fixed in a tangible medium of expression. (As already noted, live broadcasts simultaneously taped are considered "fixed" under § 101. *See* p. 67 *supra.*) Accordingly, copying and other copyright-type uses of such material are not regulated by the federal statute, and state regulation thereof is not preempted. This result is confirmed by § 301(b), which presents something of a mirror image of § 301(a) and expressly saves state rights and remedies "with respect to . . . subject matter that does not come within the subject matter of copyright as specified by sections 102 and 103, including *works of authorship not fixed in any tangible medium of expression.*" (Emphasis added.)

(2) Rights or remedies under other federal statutes are expressly saved from preemption by § 301(d). The patent statute, Title 35, U.S.C., is an example of such other (non-preempted) federal statute; and so too is a more recent statutory source of copyright implications, the Federal Communications Act, 47 U.S.C. § 151 *et seq. See, e.g.,* § 111 of the Copyright Act. *Cf. Home Box Office, Inc. v. Federal Communications Commission,* 567 F.2d 9 (D.C. Cir. 1977). Perhaps the most intriguing statutory exception is offered by the Lanham Act, 15 U.S.C. § 1051 *et seq.,* not only in its provision for trademark registration of shapes which might otherwise be copyrightable, *see, e.g., In re International Playtex Corp.,* 153 USPQ 377 (T.T.A.B. 1967); *In re Mogen David Wine Corp.,* 328 F.2d 925, 140 USPQ 575 (C.C.P.A. 1964), 372 F.2d 539, 152 USPQ 593 (C.C.P.A. 1967), but also in its more open-ended "false representation" provision, § 43(a), 15 U.S.C. § 1125(a). *See Maternally Yours, Inc. v. Your Maternity Shop, Inc.,* 234 F.2d 538, 110 USPQ 462 (2d Cir. 1956) (concurring opinion). *Cf. Gilliam v.*

American Broadcasting Co., 538 F.2d 14, 192 USPQ 1 (2d Cir. 1976). *See* p. 370 *infra.*

(3) Section 301 expressly obliterates "publication" as the dividing line between federal protection under the statute and common law protection (the new dividing line being "creation," i.e., "fixation"). Works are protected under the statute "whether published or unpublished" and indeed whether created before or after January 1, 1978. This means, at the very least, the abolition of common law literary property, often called "common law copyright," covering the copying of manuscripts, letters, diaries, private presentations, and other unpublished material fixed in a tangible medium of expression.

We turn now to aspects of § 301 that are not so clear. The requirements for preemption under this section include not only a "subject matter" test discussed above but also an "equivalent rights" test. Section 301(a) preempts only rights *equivalent* to any of the exclusive rights of copyright as specified by Section 106; accordingly subsection 301(b)(3) expressly saves rights with respect to "activities violating legal or equitable rights that are *not* equivalent to any of the exclusive rights within the general scope of copyright as specified by section 106." (Emphasis added). It is clear that this is becoming the area in which the most controversy will arise, in part because of the legislative history.

Earlier versions of § 301(b)(3) contained examples of non-preempted claims. Thus, the 1963 preliminary draft expressly saved state remedies for "breaches of trust, invasions of privacy," and "deceptive trade practices including passing off and false representation." Copyright Law Revision, Part 3, Preliminary Draft for Revised U.S. Copyright Law and Discussions and Comments on the Draft 18 (House Judiciary Committee Print 1964). But committee reports accompanying these bills stated that "where the cause of action involves the form of 'unfair competition' commonly referred to as misappropriation, which is nothing more than copyright protection under another name, section 301 is intended to have preemptive effect." E.g., H.R. Rep. No. 83, 90th Cong., 1st Sess. 100 (1967).

The language enumerating examples of non-preempted rights was gradually expanded, most notably in 1975. In that year companion bills (S. 22 and H.R. 2223, 94th Cong. 1st Sess.), as introduced, contained as examples:

breaches of contract, breaches of trust, invasion of privacy, defamation, and deceptive trade practices such as passing off and false representation.

The Department of Commerce urged expansion of this group of examples and particularly wished some, but not all, forms of misappropriation to be saved. Thus, in an appearance before the House subcommittee, the Assistant Commissioner of Patents testified as follows.

TESTIMONY OF RENE D. TEGTMEYER, ASSISTANT COMMISSIONER OF PATENTS, DEPARTMENT OF COMMERCE

Mr. Tegtmeyer. Mr. Chairman, I appreciate this opportunity to appear before your subcommittee to express the views of the Department of Commerce and its support for H.R. 2223 with certain modifications which I shall explain. . . .

Turning to the question of preemption, we agree with the preemption of State copyright laws pursuant to section 301(a), and with the principle embodied in that section that there should be a single, Federal system for copyright. However, the language of subsection (b)(3) of section 301 should, in our view, be modified to make it clear that the phrase "all rights in the nature of copyright" will not be construed to preempt parts of the State law of unfair competition which are now codified in statute or established by Federal and State court decisions applying the common law.

Section 301(b)(3) is intended to exempt State unfair competition law from the preemptive effect of section 301(a). Among the rights and remedies not preempted are those arising from the violation of rights "not equivalent to any exclusive rights within the general scope of copyright." These "not equivalent" rights are said by the bill to include "breaches of contract, breaches of trust, invasion of privacy, defamation, and deceptive trade practices such as passing off and false representation." The problem we have is that this listing is incomplete, and the language is more limited than that which would describe the present scope of established State unfair competition law.

As a solution, we propose a more comprehensive and inclusive listing of unfair competition torts in subsection (b)(3). The proposed amendment:

(3) Activities violating rights that are not equivalent to any of the exclusive rights within the general scope of copyright as specified by section 108, including breaches of contract, breaches of trust, invasion of privacy, defamation, and acts, trade practices, or courses of conduct which cause or are likely to cause confusion, mistake or deception, or which are likely to result in passing off, false or misleading representations, disparagement, wrongful disclosure or misappropriation of a trade secret or confidential information, or activities which otherwise constitute unfair competition by misrepresentation or misappropriation.

In our opinion, this proposed amendment would more accurately state the range of unfair competition torts which are now regulated by the States, so that the examples listed will not be limiting.

It should be noted that the phrase "unfair competition by ... misappropriation" is included in our amendment. Obviously, the "misappropriation" of all of the words of a literary work would be in the nature of copyright, and State laws in this area should be preempted. However, we do not believe that the entire body of State unfair competition law based upon the landmark Supreme Court decision in *International News Service v. Associated Press* (248 U.S. 215 (1918)) should be preempted. While some State decisions relying on the *INS* case may be held inapplicable under section 301(a), we believe that such a remedy should continue to be available for the type of conduct prescribed in the *INS* case.

Mr. Kastenmeier. Do you not understand those who have thus far designed the copyright bill to specifically exclude State unfair competition laws for a reason?

Mr. Tegtmeyer. I mentioned in the testimony that we agree with the preemption of the State laws as to copyright-type protection but feel that the bill should not upset the present protection that is available under State statutes and the common law of unfair competition. We specially mentioned the *International News* case in this connection. That case represents an example of one area which we particularly feel should not be preempted by the copyright law because the copyright law does not provide the same nature of protection that the *International News* case decision does.

That is, the content of the news was protected in that case as opposed to the wording or manner of expression of the news.

Mr. Kastenmeier. On that point, have you conferred with the Copyright Office or any other Federal agencies? Do you find them in agreement with your position?

Mr. Tegtmeyer. We have been in contact with some other Federal agencies and in contact with the Copyright Office, as well. We have not found agreement with our position on all points.

Mr. Kastenmeier. Thank you. I yield to the gentleman from Illinois, Mr. Railsback.

Mr. Railsback. Mr. Tegtmeyer, I find myself in somewhat of a dilemma; who actually speaks for the administration?

There seem to be disagreements with virtually everybody. We have the Department of State disagreeing with everybody except on the manufacturing clause and now we have the Department of Commerce that takes a different view. Does anyone purport to speak for the administration?

Mr. Tegtmeyer. Our testimony only purports to speak for the Department of Commerce.

Congressional recognition of this position came first on the Senate side. In reporting out S. 22 on November 20, 1975, the Senate Judiciary Committee added as examples of non-preempted claims in § 301(b)(3) trespass, conversion, and "rights against misappropriation not equivalent" to any exclusive rights within the general scope of copyright as specified by § 106. The Committee noted:

> "Misappropriation" is not necessarily synonymous with copyright infringement, and thus a cause of action labeled as "misappropriation" is not preempted if it is in fact based neither on a right within the general scope of copyright as specified by section 106 nor on a right equivalent thereto.

(Senate Report at 116.) Although this proposed expansion of saved claims did not seem to go as far as the Department of Commerce had suggested, it was much too far for another federal agency, the Department of Justice. After an unsuccessful attempt to convince the Senate to reject its Committee's recommendation, Justice sent a letter to Chairman Kastenmeier of the House Judiciary Subcommittee on Courts, Civil Liberties and the Administration of Justice, extracts of which follow:

LETTER OF DEPARTMENT OF JUSTICE TO CHAIRMAN KASTENMEIER (July 27, 1976)

Section 301 would provide that the federal Copyright Act would preempt all state regulation of rights in the nature of copyright protection. However, certain exceptions to complete preemption would be made by subsection (b) of section 301. The Senate-passed bill made two significant additions to the exceptions, both of which are opposed by this Department. These additions seemingly allow ... protection under the theory of misappropriation. . . .

A. Misappropriation

Paragraph (3) of section 301(b) would exempt from preemption, state common law or statutory rights that are not equivalent to the exclusive rights granted by the Copyright Act. The Copyright Act would grant rights such as the exclusive right to make copies of the copyrighted work (Section 106). In addition to the rights that paragraph (3) previously specifically listed as non-equivalent rights (e.g., breach of contract and breach of trust) the committee has now added "rights against misappropriation not equivalent to any of such exclusive rights. . . ." The committee report accompanying the bill asserts that there is a need for this provision because "state law should" be able to permit the misappropriation theory to apply. S. Rep. 94-473, 94th Cong., 1st Sess. 116 (1975) (hereinafter, "Senate Report").

This Department is concerned that inclusion of the above quoted phrase in section 301 would sanction use of the highly anticompetitive "misappropriation" theory, and may defeat the underlying purpose of the preemption section.

1. The Misappropriation Doctrine Is Anticompetitive

This Department strongly opposes allowance of monopolies based on the theory of "misappropriation." This term is not defined in the proposed Act, but the concept apparently stems from the much-criticized decision of the Supreme Court in *International News Service v. Associated Press*, 248 U.S. 215 (1918) (hereinafter, the "INS" case). In *INS*, the Supreme Court held that the defendant news service committed an unlawful act of unfair competition by copying the plaintiff's uncopyrighted published news stories from east coast newspapers and wiring them [to their] west coast subscribing newspapers. The Court found that even though the plaintiff would have had no rights against the public, who were entitled or privileged to copy the articles, nonetheless the defendant had "misappropriated" the published work done by the plaintiff and was therefore liable to the plaintiff. The Court's theory was that the defendant's conduct was unlawful because it sought to "reap where it has not sown" (248 U.S. at 239). This unjust enrichment theory could be used broadly to prohibit the copying of uncopyrighted published materials, the manufacture by others of unpatented goods, the use by a doctor of a surgical technique developed by another doctor, or the use of an advertising technique which another has developed at his own expense. The effect of the theory is boundless — it is potentially applicable each time a person engages in conduct that imitates some work that was developed at another's expense.

The courts generally have declined to follow the suggestion in the *INS* case that the traditional unfair competition doctrine be expanded to cover so-called "misappropriation." See, e.g., *G. Ricordi & Co. v. Haendler,* 194 F.2d 914, 916 (2d Cir. 1952); *National Comics Pub., Inc. v. Fawcett Pub., Inc.,* 191 F.2d 594, 603 (2d Cir. 1951); *RCA Mfg. Co. v. Whiteman,* 114 F.2d 86, 90 (2d Cir.), cert. denied, 311 U.S. 712 (1940); *Cheney Bros. v. Doris Silk Corp.,* 35 F.2d 279, 280 (2d Cir. 1929), cert. denied, 281 U.S. 728 (1930). Indeed, District Judge Wyzanski once stated his belief that the Supreme Court would follow the Brandeis dissent in *INS* and overrule *INS* if given the opportunity. *Triangle Pub., Inc. v. New England Newspaper Pub. Co.,* 46 F. Supp. 198, 204 (D. Mass. 1942). This view is supported by the recent *Sears* and *Compco* decisions, in which the Supreme Court reversed decisions from a court of appeals that prohibited copying of unpatented products, without even attempting to distinguish *INS*. See also *Columbia Broadcasting System, Inc. v. DeCosta*, 377 F.2d 315, 318 (1st Cir.), cert. denied, 389 U.S. 1007 (1967), in which the court found both that *INS* was no longer authoritative, since it occurred before *Erie R.R. Co. v. Tompkins,* 304 U.S. 64 (1938), and that it was overruled by *Sears* and *Compco*.

The New York State courts, in a series of cases beginning with appropriation of news and artistic productions, retrieved the "misappropriation" theory of *INS* innocuous desuetude and gradually extended the doctrine into the area of unfair competition in the sale of ordinary merchandise. The *INS* doctrine has also been codified in the New York General Business Law (§ 368-d). The bulk of authority elsewhere in the United States, however, is against the recognition of "misappropriation" as an independent basis for recovery in imitation cases *(West Point Mfg. Co. v. Detroit Stamping Co.,* 222 F.2d 581, 598-99 (6th Cir. 1955) (misappropriation is "contrary to the great weight of authority")).

This Department supports the position taken in the foregoing majority line of cases, and opposes any attempt to limit nondeceptive copying of uncopyrighted or unpatented subject matter by the general public. We believe that sound policy reasons underlie the weight of authority that opposes the *INS* "misappropriation" doctrine.

The "misappropriation" theory is vague and uncertain. The "misappropriation" provision of section 301 does not indicate what it is that is not to be appropriated. It may extend beyond an appropriation of the forms or styles of ordinary merchandise to include an appropriation of mere ideas, or technology or other know-how long in the public domain. Neither the *INS* case, other cases, nor proposed paragraph (3) adequately defines the conduct prohibited, or establishes any standard for distinguishing improper, as opposed to proper, copying.

The "misappropriation" doctrine may be used contrary to copyright and antitrust policies to sustain perpetual monopolies over printed matter, and contrary to patent and antitrust policies to sustain perpetual monopolies over alleged inventions which do not qualify for patent protection. In the *Sears* and *Compco* cases, noted above, the Supreme Court set aside such grants and held the states to be without power to block off from the public the nondeceptive copying of an unpatentable article. The Court held this [on] the ground that such grants contravene the federal patent statutes and constitutional provisions.

Furthermore, imitation is the life-blood of competition. Mere commercial copying is neither unlawful, nor immoral; instead it is often a commercial and economic necessity. Copying very often supports and promotes competition — it spurs further invention and innovation, permits newcomers to enter markets, and generally, by bringing forward functionally equivalent products and services, is a necessary condition for the competitive forces of the marketplace acting to lower prices, satisfy consumer demand, and allocate production optimally.

2. Preemption Would Be Nullified

Paragraph (3), as noted above, lists causes of action, such as for breach of contract, that are specifically identified in the introductory phrase as giving "rights that are not equivalent to any of the exclusive rights" that would be granted by section 106 of the proposed Copyright Act. These are causes of action different in nature from that for copyright infringement (see Senate Report, p. 115). Apparently what is meant is that, for example, one may sue to enjoin reproduction of an uncopyrighted book if there is a contract between the parties prohibiting the defendant from reproducing it. Thus, reproducing the literary expression itself may be prohibited under a cause of action for breach of contract.

Similarly, paragraph (3) exempts from preemption "rights against misappropriation not equivalent to any of such rights" specified in section 106. This apparently would permit states to prohibit the reproduction of the literary expression itself under a "misappropriation" theory. "Misappropriation" would stand in the place of breach of contract as a cause of action in the book example above. Any copying of copyrightable subject matter that has not been federally protected could be prohibited under the amorphous theory of "misappropriation."

The Senate Report states (p. 116) that reproduction of "the literary expression" itself should be preempted and should not be able to be prohibited under the "misappropriation" theory; yet that is what inclusion of the term "misappropriation" in paragraph (3) would prohibit. The preemption sought by the omnibus Copyright Act revision bill would be nullified by paragraph (3).

While "misappropriation" is almost certain to nullify preemption, any of the causes of action listed in paragraph (3) following the phrase "as specified by section 106" may be construed to have the same effect. For example, a court could construe the copying of an uncopyrighted published book to be an invasion of the author's right to privacy, i.e., the right to keep the control of the publication of his book privately to himself. In order to more clearly delineate [for] the courts the area to be preempted, we recommend striking the specific causes of action listed in paragraph (3) so as to amend that paragraph [not] to preempt only: "(3) activities violating legal or equitable rights that are not equivalent to any of the exclusive rights within the general scope of copyright as specified by section 106;."

3. Recommendation

For the reasons discussed, this Department recommends that section 301(b)(3) be amended as suggested above.

The letter was unsuccessful in convincing the House subcommittee or its parent Judiciary Committee to change § 301(b)(3). The Committee Report (of September 3, 1976) on the section follows (pp. 129-33):

SECTION 301. FEDERAL PREEMPTION OF RIGHTS EQUIVALENT TO COPYRIGHT

Single Federal System

Section 301, one of the bedrock provisions of the bill, would accomplish a fundamental and significant change in the present law. Instead of a dual system of "common law copyright" for unpublished works and statutory copyright for published works, which has been the system in effect in the United States since the first copyright statute in 1790, the bill adopts a single system of Federal statutory copyright from creation. Under section 301 a work would obtain statutory protection as soon as it is "created" or, as that term is defined in section 101, when it is "fixed in a copy or phonorecord for the first time." Common law copyright protection for works coming within the scope of the statute would be abrogated, and the concept of publication would lose its all-embracing importance as a dividing line between common law and statutory protection and between both of these forms of legal protection and the public domain.

By substituting a single Federal system for the present anachronistic, uncertain, impractical, and highly complicated dual system, the bill would greatly improve the operation of the copyright law and would be much more effective in carrying out the basic constitutional aims of uniformity and the promotion of writing and scholarship. The main arguments in favor of a single Federal system can be summarized as follows:

1. One of the fundamental purposes behind the copyright clause of the Constitution, as shown in Madison's comments in The Federalist, was to promote national uniformity and to avoid the practical difficulties of determining and enforcing an author's rights under the differing laws and in the separate courts of the various States. Today, when the methods for dissemination of an author's work are incomparably broader and faster than they were in 1789, national uniformity in copyright protection is even more essential than it was then to carry out the constitutional intent.

2. "Publication," perhaps the most important single concept under the present law, also represents its most serious defect. Although at one time, when works were disseminated almost exclusively through printed copies, "publication" could serve as a practical dividing line between common law and statutory protection, this is no longer true. With the development of the 20th-century communications revolution, the concept of publication has become increasingly artificial and obscure. To cope with the legal consequences of an established concept that has lost much of its meaning and justification, the courts have given "publication" a number of diverse interpretations, some of them radically different. Not unexpectedly, the results in individual cases have become unpredictable and often unfair. A single Federal system would help to clear up this chaotic situation.

3. Enactment of section 301 would also implement the "limited times" provision of the Constitution, which has become distorted under the traditional concept of "publication." Common law protection in "unpublished" works is now perpetual, no matter how widely they may be disseminated by means other than "publication"; the bill would place a time limit on the duration of exclusive rights in them. The provision would also aid scholarship and the dissemination of historical materials by making unpublished, undisseminated manuscripts available for publication after a reasonable period.

4. Adoption of a uniform national copyright system would greatly improve international dealings in copyrighted material. No other country has anything like our present dual system. In an era when copyrighted works can be disseminated instantaneously to every country on the globe, the need for effective international copyright relations, and the concomitant need for national uniformity, assume ever greater importance.

Under section 301, the statute would apply to all works created after its effective date, whether or not they are ever published or disseminated. With respect to works created before the effective date of the statute and still under common law protection, section 303 of the statute would provide protection from that date on, and would guarantee a minimum period of statutory copyright.

Preemption of State law

The intention of section 301 is to preempt and abolish any rights under the common law or statutes of a State that are equivalent to copyright and that extend to works coming within the scope of the Federal copyright law. The declaration of this principle in section 301 is intended to be stated in the clearest and most unequivocal language possible, so as to foreclose any conceivable misinterpretation of its unqualified intention that Congress shall act preemptively, and to avoid the development of any vague borderline areas between State and Federal protection.

Under section 301(a) all "legal or equitable rights that are equivalent to any of the exclusive rights within the general scope of copyright as specified by section 106 are governed exclusively by the Federal copyright statute if the works involved are "works of authorship that are fixed in a tangible medium of expression and come within the subject matter of copyright as specified by sections 102 and 103." All corresponding State laws, whether common law or statutory, are preempted and abrogated. Regardless of when the work was created and whether it is published or unpublished, disseminated or undisseminated, in the public domain or copyrighted under the Federal statute, the States cannot offer it protection equivalent to copyright. Section 1338 of title 28, United States Code, also makes clear that any action involving rights under the Federal copyright law would come within the exclusive jurisdiction of the Federal courts. The preemptive effect of section 301 is limited to State laws: as stated expressly in subsection (d) of section 301, there is no intention to deal with the question of whether Congress can or should offer the equivalent of copyright protection under some constitutional provision other than the patent-copyright clause of article 1, section 8.

As long as a work fits within one of the general subject matter categories of sections 102 and 103, the bill prevents the States from protecting it even if it fails to achieve Federal statutory copyright because it is too minimal or lacking in originality to qualify, or because it has fallen into the public domain. On the other hand, section 301(b) explicitly preserves common law copyright protection for one important class of works: works that have not been "fixed in any tangible medium of expression." Examples would include choreography that has never been filmed or notated, an extemporaneous speech, "original works of authorship" communicated solely through conversations or live broadcasts, and a dramatic sketch or musical composition improvised or developed from memory and without being recorded or written down. As mentioned above in connection with section 102, unfixed works are not included in the specified "subject matter of copyright." They are therefore not affected by the preemption of section 301, and would continue to be subject to protection under State statute or common law until fixed in tangible form.

The preemption of rights under State law is complete with respect to any work coming within the scope of the bill, even though the scope of exclusive rights given the work under the bill is narrower than the scope of common law rights in the work might have been.

Representatives of printers, while not opposed to the principle of section 301, expressed concern about its potential impact on protection of preliminary advertising copy and layouts prepared by printers. They argued that this material is frequently "pirated" by competitors, and that it would be a substantial burden if, in order to obtain full protection, the printer would have to make registrations and bear the expense and bother of suing in Federal rather than State courts. On the other hand, these practical problems are essentially procedural rather than substantive, and the proposal for a special exemption to preserve common law rights equivalent to copyright in unpublished advertising material cannot be justified. Moreover, subsection (b), discussed below, will preserve other legal grounds on which the printers can protect themselves against "pirates" under State laws.

In a general way subsection (b) of section 301 represents the obverse of subsection (a). It sets out in broad terms and without necessarily being exhaustive, some of the principal areas of protection that preemption would not prevent the States from protecting. Its purpose is to make clear, consistent with the 1964 Supreme Court decisions in *Sears Roebuck & Co. v. Stiffel Co.,* 376 U.S. 225, and *Compco Corp. v. Day-Brite Lighting, Inc.,* 376 U.S. 234, that preemption does not extend to causes of action, or subject matter outside the scope of the revised Federal copyright statute.

The numbered clauses of subsection (b) list three general areas left unaffected by the preemption: (1) subject matter that does not come within the subject matter of copyright; (2) causes of action arising under State law before the effective date of the statute; and (3) violations of rights that are not equivalent to any of the exclusive rights under copyright.

The examples in clause (3), while not exhaustive, are intended to illustrate rights and remedies that are different in nature from the rights comprised in a copyright and that may continue to be protected under State common law or statute. The evolving common law rights of "privacy," "publicity," and trade secrets, and the general laws of defamation and fraud, would remain unaffected as long as the causes of action contain elements, such as an invasion of personal rights or a breach of trust or confidentiality, that are different in kind from copyright infringement. Nothing in the bill derogates from the rights of parties to contract with each other and to sue for breaches of contract; however, to the extent that the unfair competition concept known as "interference with contract relations" is merely the equivalent of copyright protection, it would be preempted.

The last example listed in clause (3) — "deceptive trade practices such as passing off and false representation" — represents an effort to distinguish between those causes of action known as "unfair competition" that the copyright statute is not intended to preempt and those that it is. Section 301 is not intended to preempt common law protection in cases involving activities such as false labeling, fraudulent representation, and passing off even where the subject matter involved comes within the scope of the copyright statute.

"Misappropriation" is not necessarily synonymous with copyright infringement, and thus a cause of action labeled as "misappropriation" is not preempted if it is in fact based neither on a right within the general scope of copyright as specified by section 106 nor on a right equivalent thereto. For example, state law should have the flexibility to afford a remedy (under traditional principles of equity) against a consistent pattern of unauthorized appropriation by a competitor of the facts (i.e., not the literary expression) constituting "hot" news, whether in the traditional mold of *International News Service v. Associated Press*, 248 U.S. 215 (1918), or in the newer form of data updates from scientific, business, or financial data bases. Likewise, a person having no trust or other relationship with the proprietor of a computerized data base should not be immunized from sanctions against electronically or cryptographically breaching the proprietor's security arrangements and accessing the proprietor's data. The unauthorized data access which should be remediable might also be achieved by the intentional interception of data transmissions by wire, microwave or laser transmissions, or by the common unintentional means of "crossed" telephone lines occasioned by errors in switching.

The proprietor of data displayed on the cathode ray tube of a computer terminal should be afforded protection against unauthorized printouts by third parties (with or without improper access), even if the data are not copyrightable. For example, the data may not be copyrighted because they are not fixed in a tangible medium of expression (i.e., the data are not displayed for a period [of] not more than transitory duration).

Nothing contained in section 301 precludes the owner of a material embodiment of a copy or a phonorecord from enforcing a claim of conversion against one who takes possession of the copy or phonorecord without consent.

A unique and difficult problem is presented with respect to the status of sound recordings fixed before February 12, 1972, the effective date of the amendment bringing recordings fixed after that date under Federal copyright protection. In its testimony during the 1975 hearings, the Department of Justice pointed out that, under section 301 as then written:

> This language could be read as abrogating the anti-piracy laws now existing in 29 states relating to pre-February 15, 1972, sound recordings on the grounds that these statutes proscribe activities violating rights "equivalent to . . . the exclusive rights within the general scope of copyright. . . ." Certainly such a result cannot have been intended for it would likely effect the immediate resurgence of piracy of pre-February 15, 1972, sound recordings.

The Department recommended that section 301(b) be amended to exclude sound recordings fixed prior to February 15, 1972 from the effect of the preemption.

The Senate adopted this suggestion when it passed S. 22. The result of the Senate amendment would be to leave pre-1972 sound recordings as entitled to perpetual protection under State law, while post-1972 recordings would eventually fall into the public domain as provided in the bill.

The Committee recognizes that, under recent court decisions, pre-1972 recordings are protected by State statute or common law, and that [they] should not all be thrown into the public domain instantly upon the coming into effect of the new law. However, it cannot agree that they should in effect be accorded perpetual protection, as under the Senate amendment, and it has therefore revised clause (4) to establish a future date for the pre-emption to take effect. The date chosen is February 15, 2047, which is 75 years from the effective date of the statute extending Federal protection to recordings.

Subsection (c) makes clear that nothing contained in Title 17 annuls or limits any rights or remedies under any other Federal statute.

This was not, however, to be the end of the story. When the bill came up for debate on the House floor on Sept. 22, 1976, the following occurred:

> *Mr. Seiberling.* Mr. Chairman, I offer an amendment.
> The Clerk read as follows:
> [strike out the words "including rights against misappropriation not equivalent to any of such exclusive rights, breaches of contracts, breaches of trust, trespass, conversion, invasion of privacy, defamation, and deceptive trade practices such as passing off and false representation]
>
> . . . .
> *Mr. Seiberling.* Mr. Chairman, my amendment is intended to save the "federal preemption" of State law section, which is section 301 of the bill, from being inadvertently nullified because of the inclusion of certain examples in the exemptions from preemption.
> This amendment would simply strike the examples listed in section 301(b)(3).
> The amendment is strongly supported by the Justice Department, which believes that it would be a serious mistake to cite as an exemption from preemption the doctrine of "misappropriation." The doctrine was created by the Supreme Court in 1922 and it has generally been ignored by the Supreme Court itself and by the lower courts ever since.
> Inclusion of a reference to the misappropriation doctrine in this bill, however, could easily be construed by the courts as authorizing the States to pass

misappropriation laws. We should not approve such enabling legislation, because a misappropriation law could be so broad as to render the preemption section meaningless . . . .

Mr. Railsback: Mr. Chairman, may I ask the gentlemen from Ohio, for the purpose of clarifying the amendment that by striking the word "misappropriation" the gentleman in no way is attempting to change the existing state of the law, that is as it may exist in certain States that have recognized the right of recovery relating to "misappropriation": is that correct?

Mr. Seiberling: That is correct. All I am trying to do is prevent the citing of them as examples in a statute. We are, in effect, adopting a rather amorphous body of State law and codifying it, in effect. Rather I am trying to have this bill leave the State law alone and make it clear we are merely dealing with copyright laws, laws applicable to copyrights.

Mr. Railsback: Mr. Chairman, I personally have no objection to the gentleman's amendment in view of that clarification and I know of no objections from this side.

. . . .

Mr. Kastenmeier: Mr. Chairman, I too have examined the gentleman's amendment and was familiar with the position of the Department of Justice. Unfortunately, the Justice Department did not make its position known to the committee until the last day of markup.

Mr. Seiberling: I understand.

Mr. Kastenmeier: However, Mr. Chairman, I think that the amendment the gentleman is offering is consistent with the position of the Justice Department and accept it on this side as well. 122 Cong. Rec. H-10910 (daily ed. Sept. 22, 1976).

The question posed by this debate is whether the scope of § 301(b)(3) has been changed by the deletion of the examples of non-preempted claims. One might argue that the history of this clause reflects the addition of examples to insure non-preemption. On the other hand, the floor debate can be cited to show that the new copyright law does not attempt "to change the existing state of the law, that is as it may exist in certain states that have recognized the right of recovery relating to 'misappropriation.' " Yet the amendment was described by Chairman Kastenmeier as "consistent with the position of the Justice Department" which clearly wanted to preempt misappropriation.

The Conference report merely reported the House deletion of examples and the acquiescence of the Senate conferees, without illuminating this question.

QUESTIONS

1. Where does this tortuous legislative history leave a state claim for misappropriation? For the other torts expressly saved in earlier versions of § 301(b)?

2. Defendant wrote a book on the cloning of humans. He had earlier obtained an unpublished nine-page abstract of plaintiff's doctoral thesis on research involving genetic transplantation on rabbits. Plaintiff objected to defendant's appropriation of plaintiff's ideas and experimental techniques disclosed in his abstract. He sued for common law misappropriation of these ideas. Is this claim preempted? Does § 102(b) help or hurt plaintiff? *See Bromhall v. Rorvik,* 478 F. Supp. 361 (E.D. Pa. 1979).

3. The *Nation* magazine without authority publishes excerpts from a manuscript of former President Ford's book *A Time to Heal* shortly before excerpts are to be published in *Time* magazine and *Reader's Digest* and the book is to be published by Harper & Row. As a result, Time, Inc. cancels its publication

plans and its agreement with the copyright owners. Can the latter sue the *Nation* for conversion and/or interference with contract rights? *See Harper & Row, Publishers, Inc. v. Nation Associates, Inc.,* 501 F. Supp. 848 (S.D.N.Y. 1980).

4. Which, if any, of the following state statutes are preempted by § 301:

(a) N.Y. Gen. Bus. Law §224 which provides:

Whenever a work of fine art is sold or otherwise transferred by or on behalf of the artist who created it, or his heirs or personal representatives, the right of reproduction thereof is reserved to the grantor until it passes into the public domain by act or operation of law unless such right is sooner expressly transferred by an instrument, note or memorandum in writing signed by the owner of the rights conveyed or his duly authorized agent. Nothing herein contained, however, shall be construed to prohibit the fair use of such work of art. Added L. 1966, c. 668, §2, eff. Sept. 1, 1966.

(b) A provision of the penal law which makes it a misdemeanor ti distribute commercially a phonograph record, disc, tape or other article embodying an illegally recorded performance without the consent of the owner of such recorded performance.

(c) A proposed state statute protecting designs of useful articles (or of typeface).

(d) A proposed state statute protecting characters.

Index